The SAGE
Handbook of

Political
Communication

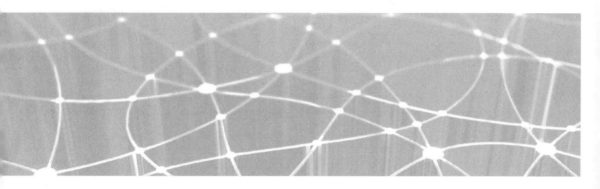

The SAGE
Handbook of
Political
Communication

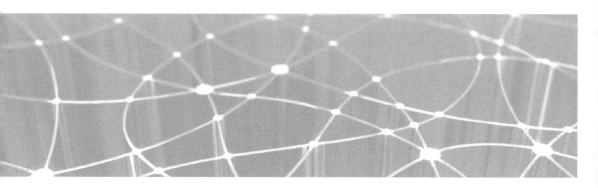

Edited by
Holli A. Semetko and
Margaret Scammell

Los Angeles | London | New Delhi
Singapore | Washington DC

SAGE Publications Ltd
1 Oliver's Yard
55 City Road
London EC1Y 1SP

SAGE Publications Inc.
2455 Teller Road
Thousand Oaks, California 91320

SAGE Publications India Pvt Ltd
B 1/I 1 Mohan Cooperative Industrial Area
Mathura Road
New Delhi 110 044

SAGE Publications Asia-Pacific Pte Ltd
33 Pekin Street #02-01
Far East Square
Singapore 048763

Library of Congress Control Number: 2011937949

British Library Cataloguing in Publication data

A catalogue record for this book is available from the British Library

ISBN 978-1-84787-439-9
ISBN 978-1-4462-0101-5 (pbk)

Typeset by Cenveo Publisher Services
Printed in India at Replika Press Pvt Ltd
Printed on paper from sustainable resources

Contents

Notes on Contributors

Kees Aarts is Professor of Political Science in the School of Management and Governance and Scientific Director of the Institute for Innovation and Governance Studies (IGS) at the University of Twente. His research focuses on democracy, elections and electoral behavior, in the Netherlands as well as in an international comparative perspective.

Sean Aday is an Associate Professor of Media and Public Affairs and International Affairs at George Washington University, where he is also director of the Institute for Public Diplomacy and Global Communication and of the Global Communication MA program. His work focuses on the intersection of the press, politics and public opinion, especially in relation to war and foreign policy, and he has been involved in media and government capacity training projects globally, including in Iraq and Afghanistan.

Scott L. Althaus is an Associate Professor of Political Science and Communication at the University of Illinois Urbana-Champaign. His research examines the communication processes by which ordinary citizens and government officials exchange politically relevant information, as well as the impact of strategic communication efforts on news discourse and public opinion. He is the author of *Collective Preferences in Democratic Politics* (Cambridge University Press, 2003), which addresses the uses of opinion surveys for political representation. He is currently working on books about the dynamics of public support for war and the role of strategic communication in shaping news coverage about war.

Susan A. Banducci is Professor of Political Science at the University of Exeter. She is currently coordinating a training network in electoral democracy that involves 18 researchers from 9 countries. Her research focuses on campaigns, elections and media and has appeared in *The Journal of Politics*, *British Journal of Political Science*, *Electoral Studies*, *Journal of European Public Policy* and *Information Polity*.

Kevin G. Barnhurst is Professor, Department of Communication, University of Illinois at Chicago. For the International Communication Association (ICA), he was the founding chair of Visual Communication Studies. His books include *Media Queered: Visibility and its Discontents* (Lang, 2007), an edited collection; *The Form of News, A History* (Guilford, 2001), with John Nerone, the ICA Outstanding Book of 2003 and recipient of the MEA Suzanne Langer Award (2002) and AEJMC Covert Award for media history (2001); and *Seeing the Newspaper* (St Martin's, 1994), winner of a Mellett citation for media criticism and named an *In These Times* magazine best book. His more than 100 publications include scholarly work in English, Italian and Spanish.

Vanessa B. Beasley is an Associate Professor of Communication Studies at Vanderbilt University. She is the author of *You, the People: American National Identity in Presidential Rhetoric* (Texas A&M University Press) and editor of *Who Belongs in America: Presidents, Rhetoric and Immigration* (Texas A&M University Press). Her research has also been published in *Quarterly Journal of Speech*, *Rhetoric & Public Affairs*, *Political Communication*, *Communication Monographs* and elsewhere. The recipient of numerous teaching awards, Beasley teaches courses in mass media and politics, presidential rhetoric, rhetorical criticism and the history of public address in the USA.

W. Lance Bennett is Professor of Political Science and Ruddick C. Lawrence Professor of Communication at University of Washington in Seattle. He is also Director of the Center for Communication & Civic Engagement (www.engagedcitizen.org). He has authored numerous books and articles on ways in which mediated communication affects the qualities and processes of civic engagement and political participation. He is editor of *Civic Life Online: Learning How Digital Media Can Engage Youth* (MIT Press, 2008).

Bruce Bimber is Professor of Political Science and (by affiliation) Communication at the University of California, where he is also Founder and Director Emeritus of the Center for Information Technology and Society. He studies political communication, especially the role of digital media in political behavior and collective action. He is the author of *Information and American Democracy* (Cambridge University Press, 2003), *Campaigning Online* (with Richard Davis, Oxford University Press, 2003) and *The Politics of Expertise in Congress* (SUNY Press, 1996). His most recent book is *Collective Action in Organizations* (with Andrew Flanagin and Cynthia Stohl, Cambridge University Press, 2012). He is a Fellow of the American Association for the Advancement of Science.

Jay G. Blumler is an Emeritus Professor of Public Communication at the University of Leeds, where he directed its Centre for Television Research from 1963 to his retirement in 1989, and Emeritus Professor of Journalism at the University of Maryland, where he taught and researched throughout the 1980s. His first publication in the field was a booklet on Television and Citizenship (with John Madge, 1966). Other major works include: *Television in Politics: Its Uses and Influence* (with Denis McQuail, 1968), *The Uses of Mass Communications: Current Perspectives on Gratifications Research* (with Elihu Katz, 1974), *The Crisis of Public Communication* (with Michael Gurevitch, 1995), 'The Third Age of Political Communication: Influences and Features' (with Dennis Kavanagh, 1999) and *The Internet and Democratic Citizenship: Theory, Practice and Policy* (with Stephen Coleman, 2009).

María José Canel is Professor of Political Communication at the University Complutense of Madrid, Spain. She is also Vice Chair of the Political Communication Section (IAMCR) and of the European Communication Research and Education Association (ECREA) and Founding President of ACOP Asociación de Comunicación Política. She has published nationally and internationally on government communication and related matters: *Morality Tales: Political Scandals in Britain and Spain in the 1990s* (co-authored with K. Sanders, Hampton Press, 2006); *Comunicación de las instituciones públicas* [*Communicating Public Institutions*] (Tecnos, 2007). She has also published in *Local Government Studies, Journal of Political Communication, European Journal of Communication* and *Journalism: Theory, Practice and Criticism.*

Sam Cherribi is Senior Lecturer in Sociology at the Emory University and has served two terms in the Dutch parliament. His previous book, *In the House of War: Dutch Islam Observed* was published by Oxford University Press in 2010. His new book is titled *Bullets of Truth: How Al Jazeera is Becoming the New Arab State* (Forthcoming). The book exposes how Al Jazeera, the flagship media network of the Arab world, has been shaping world politics and society leading up to and in the wake of the Arab Spring uprisings.

Dennis Chong holds the John D. and Catherine T. MacArthur Chair in Political Science at Northwestern University. He is the editor of the Cambridge University Press book series, *Cambridge Studies in Public Opinion and Political Psychology*. He has written books and articles on a wide range of subjects in the behavioral sciences including collective action, rationality, ideology, political tolerance and public opinion. He is currently completing a book on the framing of political communications.

Stephen Coleman is Professor of Political Communication at the Institute of Communications Studies at the University of Leeds. His two most recently published books are: *The Internet and Democratic Citizenship: Theory, Practice and Policy* (with Jay G. Blumler, Cambridge University Press, 2009); *The Media and the Public: 'Them' and 'Us' in Media Discourse* (with Karen Ross, Wiley-Blackwell, 2010) and *Connecting Democracy: Online Consultation and the Flow of Political Communication* (co-edited with Peter Shane, Cambridge, MA: MIT Press). His next book, to be published by Cambridge University Press, is a cultural study of voting.

Ann N. Crigler is Professor of Political Science at the University of Southern California. She is co-author, editor or co-editor of *Common Knowledge: News and the Construction of Political Meaning*

(University of Chicago Press, 1992), *Crosstalk: Citizens, Candidates and the Media in a Presidential Campaign* (University of Chicago Press, 1996), which won the 2003 Doris Graber Best Book Award given by the American Political Science Association's Political Communication Division, *The Psychology of Political Communication* (University of Michigan Press, 1996) and *Rethinking the Vote: The Politics and Prospects of American Election Reform* (Oxford University Press, 2004) as well as numerous articles and essays on political communication, elections, emotions and political behavior. Her most recent book is a co-edited volume, *The Affect Effect: Dynamics of Emotion in Political Thinking and Behavior* (University of Chicago Press, 2007).

Richard Davis is Professor of Political Science at Brigham Young University. He is the author of *Typing Politics: The Role of Blogs in American Politics* (Oxford University Press, 2009), *The Web of Politics* (Oxford University Press, 1999) and *Politics Online: Blogs, Chatrooms, and Discussion Groups in American Democracy* (Routledge, 2005). He is co-editor of *Making a Difference: A Comparative View of the Role of the Internet in Election Politics* (with Stephen Ward, Diana Owen and David Taras, Lexington, 2008). He also is co-author of *Campaigning Online* (with Bruce Bimber, Oxford University Press, 2003) and *New Media and American Politics* (with Diana Owen, Oxford University Press, 1998).

Michael X. Delli Carpini is Dean of the University of Pennsylvania's Annenberg School for Communication. He is author or co-author of *Stability and Change in American Politics: The Coming of Age of the Generation of the 1960s* (New York University Press, 1986), *What Americans Know about Politics and Why It Matters* (Yale University Press, 1996), which won the 2008 American Association of Public Opinion Researchers Book Award, *A New Engagement? Political Participation, Civic Life and the Changing American Citizen* (Oxford University Press, 2006), *Talking Together: Public Deliberation and Political Participation in America* (University of Chicago Press, 2009) and *After Broadcast News: Media Regimes, Democracy, and the New Information Environment* (Cambridge University Press, 2011), as well as numerous articles, essays and edited volumes on political communications, public opinion, political knowledge and political socialization.

Claes H. de Vreese is Professor and Chair of Political Communication and Scientific Director of The Amsterdam School of Communication Research at the Department of Communication Science at the University of Amsterdam. He is the founding Director of the Center for Politics and Communication (www.polcomm.org) and Ajunct Professor of Political Science and Journalism at the University of Southern Denmark. He is also the Editor-in-Chief of the *International Journal of Public Opinion Research* (IJPOR). His research interests include comparative journalism research, the effects of news, public opinion and European integration, effects of information and campaigning on elections, referendums and direct democracy.

James N. Druckman holds the Payson S. Wild Chair in Political Science and is a faculty fellow at the Institute for Policy Research at Northwestern University. He is an editor of the University of Chicago Press book series, *Chicago Studies in American Politics* and the journal *Public Opinion Quarterly*. His work focuses on preference formation and communication. He is currently completing a book on the framing of political communications.

Robert M. Entman is J.B. and M.C. Shapiro Professor of Media and Public Affairs and Professor of International Affairs at The George Washington University. Author most recently of *Projections of Power: Framing News, Public Opinion and US Foreign Policy* (Chicago University Press, 2004), he is working on *Framing Failure* with George Washington colleagues Sean Aday and Steven Livingston. His other books include *The Black Image in the White Mind: Media and Race in America* (with Andrew Rojecki, University of Chicago, 2000), which won Harvard's Goldsmith Book Prize, the Lane Award from the American Political Science Association and other awards.

William P. Eveland, Jr is a Social & Behavioral Sciences Joan N. Huber Faculty Fellow and Professor of Communication and Political Science at the Ohio State University. His current research examines the role of political discussion in creating informed and active citizens. He has also published on the role of traditional news media and new communication technologies in political learning and participation. He has been recipient of the International Communication Association's Young Scholar Award (2003) and the Association for Education in Journalism & Mass Communication's Krieghbaum Under-40 Award (2007).

Joanna Everitt is a Professor of Political Science at the University of New Brunswick in Saint John. She specializes in Canadian politics, gender and politics and political behavior. She is the co-author of *Advocacy Groups: The Canadian Democratic Audit* (with Lisa Young, University of British Columbia Press, 2004) and the co-editor of *Citizen Politics: Research and Theory in Canadian Political Behavior* (Oxford University Press, 2002). Her work has also appeared in dozens of articles in journals and edited collections.

Fred Fletcher is University Professor Emeritus, Communication Studies and Political Science at York University. He was founding Director of the Joint Graduate Program in Communication and Culture (at York and Ryerson Universities), 1998–2006 and has served as President of the Canadian Communication Association and of the Canadian Media Research Consortium. He is co-author of *Canada Online! The Internet, Media and Emerging Technologies* (2008), *Report Card on the Canadian News Media* (2004) and its sequel, *Canadian Audiences and the Future of News* (2008) and *Fairness in the Media: A Study of Perceptions of Fairness in Political Coverage* (2008). He is editor and co-author of a comparative volume, *Media, Elections and Democracy* (1991). Dr Fletcher's paper, 'The Future of News in the Digital Era', was published in *Australian Policy Online* in July 2007.

Deen G. Freelon is a PhD student in the Department of Communication at the University of Washington in Seattle. His research interests address the ways in which digital communication technologies influence political communication practices (and vice versa) at the individual, national and international levels.

Kim L. Fridkin is a professor of Political Science at Arizona State University. She has contributed articles to the *American Political Science Review*, *American Journal of Politics* and the *Journal of Politics*. She is the co-author of *No-Holds Barred: Negative Campaigning in U.S. Senate Campaigns* (Prentice Hall, 2004), co-author of *The Spectacle of U.S. Senate Campaigns* (Princeton University Press, 1999) and author of *The Political Consequences of Being a Woman* (Columbia University Press, 1996). Professor Fridkin's current research interests are negative campaigning, women and politics and senate elections.

Christine Garlough is an Assistant Professor of Rhetoric, Department of Communication Arts at the University of Wisconsin-Madison. Her interests revolve around the areas of rhetorical theory, feminist theory and critical social theory. Her work with grassroots feminist groups in India and diasporic South Asian communities in the USA has focused on the use of performance to make rhetorical claims about issues of social justice and human rights. This research, combining ethnographic fieldwork and rhetorical analysis, has been published in outlets such as *Quarterly Journal of Speech*, *Journal of American Folklore* and *Women's Studies in Communication*.

Rachel K. Gibson is Professor of Political Science in the Institute for Social Change, University of Manchester and directs the cross-disciplinary Democracy, Citizens and Elections Research Network (DCERN) based in the School of Social Sciences (www.dcern.org.uk). She has published widely in international journals and edited several books on parties and citizens use of the Internet including *The Internet and Politics: Citizens, Voters and Activists* (with Sarah Oates and Diana Owen, Routledge, 2005), *Electronic Democracy: Political Organisations, Mobilisation and Participation Online* (with Andrea Römmele and Stephen Ward, Routledge, 2004) and *Political Parties and the Internet: Net Gain?* (with Stephen J. Ward and Paul Nixon, Routledge, 2003).

Elisabeth Gidengil is the Hiram Mills Professor of Political Science and Director of the Centre for the Study of Democratic Citizenship at McGill University in Montreal. Her research interests include voting behavior and public opinion, media and politics, political engagement and biopolitics. She is the co-editor of *Gender and Social Capital* (with Brenda O'Neill, Routledge, 2004) and is the author of numerous book chapters and journal articles.

Ian Glenn is currently Professor of Media Studies and Director of the Centre for Media Studies at the University of Cape Town. Recent publications have included a critical edition of the early French naturalist and social commentator François Le Vaillant, a study of the South African broadcast policy situation co-authored with Jane Duncan, and articles on ANC rhetoric.

Doris A. Graber is Professor of Political Science at the University of Illinois at Chicago where she teaches political communication, political psychology and public opinion courses. She has published 15 books, many in multiple editions, including the award-winning *Processing Politics: Learning from Television in the Internet Age*; *Mass Media and American Politics*, her most recent publication is *On Media and Making Sense of Politics* (2010). She has served as president of political science, political psychology and public opinion organizations and is founding editor of *Political Communication* and book review editor of *Political Psychology*.

Daniel C. Hallin is Professor and Chair of the Department of Communication at the University of California San Diego. His research concerns political communication and the role of the news media in democratic politics. He has written on the media and war, including Vietnam, Central America and the Gulf War. He has also written on television coverage of elections, demonstrating the shrinking 'sound bite' and offering an interpretation of its meaning for political journalism. His new research focuses on comparative analysis of the news media's role in the public sphere, concentrating on Europe and Latin America.

Gregory G. Holyk is a survey consultant for the Chicago Council on Global Affairs. He teaches American politics, political communication and public opinion. His published works include *United States Public Support for the United Nations* (forthcoming) and *What Explains Torture Coverage During Wartime? A Search for Realistic Answers* in *Terrorism and Torture: An Interdisciplinary Perspective* (with Doris Graber, 2008). He received a PhD in political science from the University of Illinois at Chicago.

Muzammil M. Hussain is a graduate student at the University of Washington in Seattle, and researcher at the Center for Communication and Civic Engagement, working on the Civic Learning Online and Information Technology and Political Islam projects. His research focuses on digital media and civic information systems in advanced democracies, and ICT uses by civic activists in developing societies.

Myiah J. Hutchens is a PhD candidate in the School of Communication at the Ohio State University. She studies the role of mass and interpersonal communication in knowledge acquisition with a special focus on the socialization process. Her research has been published in journals such as *Political Communication*, *Journal of Communication* and *Communication Methods and Measures*.

Ronald Inglehart is Professor of Political Science and Program Director at the Institute for Social Research at the University of Michigan; he is also affiliated with the Higher School of Economics, St Petersburg, Russia. His research deals with changing belief systems and their impact on social and political change. He helped found the Euro-Barometer surveys and directs the World Values Surveys. Related books include *Modernization and Postmodernization: Cultural, Economic and Political Change in 43 Societies* (1997), *Rising Tide* (with Pippa Norris, 2003) and *Modernization, Cultural Change and Democracy* (with Christian Welzel, 2004).

Shanto Iyengar holds the Chandler Chair in Communication at Stanford University where he is also Professor of Political Science and Director of the Political Communication Laboratory. He is the author and co-author of several books, including *News That Matters* (with Don Kinder), *Is Anyone Responsible? Explorations in Political Psychology* (co-edited with William McGuire), *Going Negative* (with Stephen Ansolabehere), *Do the Media Govern* (co-edited with Richard Reeves) and *Media Politics: A Citizen's Guide*. Iyengar serves as editor of the journal *Political Communication*. Since 2006, he has contributed a regular research column for Washingtonpost.com.

Marion R. Just is the William R. Kenan, Jr. Professor in the Department of Political Science at Wellesley College and an Associate at the Joan Shorenstein Center on Press, Politics and Public Policy at Harvard's Kennedy School of Government. Her research focuses on elections, politics and the media. She is a co-author of *We Interrupt This Broadcast: ... How to Improve Local News and Win Ratings*, *Crosstalk: Citizens, Candidates and the Media in a Presidential Campaign* and *Common Knowledge: News and the Construction of Political Meaning*. She is a co-editor of *Framing Terrorism: The News Media, the Government and the Public* and *Rethinking the Vote: Politics and Prospects of Election Reform*.

Patrick J. Kenney is the Director of the School of Politics and Global Studies at Arizona State University. Professor Kenney has authored and co-authored articles in the *American Political Science Review*, *American Journal of Political Science*, *Political Behavior* and the *Journal of Politics*. He has co-authored two books with Kim Fridkin, *The Spectacle of U.S. Senate Campaigns* (Princeton University Press, 1999) and *No-Holds Barred: Negativity in U.S. Senate Campaigns* (Prentice Hall, 2004). His research areas are in campaigns, elections and voting behavior.

Andrew Kerner is an Assistant Professor of Political Science at the University of Michigan. His research focuses on the politics of corporate finance, with a particular focus on foreign direct investment, corporate governance and the impacts of pension reform. His recent publications include 'Why Should I Believe You: The Costs and Consequences of Bilateral Investment Treaties' and 'The International and Domestic Determinants of Insider Trading Laws' (with Jeffrey Kucik) in *International Studies Quarterly*.

Eun-mee Kim is an Associate Professor of Communication at Seoul National University in Seoul, where she teaches broadcasting and telecommunication media, social implications of media technology and cultural industries among other things. Her research interest covers the use of digital media, emergence of participatory culture, and their various cultural and social implications, especially how ideas are created, disseminated and shared through media and networks.

Joohan Kim is Professor at the Department of Communication at Yonsei University in Seoul. His current research interests include measuring communication effects through neuroscientific methods such as fMRI and EEG. Kim has published numerous books and articles in scholarly journals, including *Journal of Communication, Political Communication, Communication Theory, Journalism and Mass Communication Quarterly, Psychological Reports, Computers and Human Behavior, Human Studies* and *Semiotica*.

Min Gyu Kim is a doctoral student at the Department of Communication at Yonsei University in Seoul. He specializes in advanced statistical analyses and co-authored *Writing Scholarly Papers Using Structural Equation Modeling*, a well-known statistics textbook among social scientists. Min Gyu Kim has published numerous journal articles.

Sophie Lecheler is an Assistant Professor in Political Communication at the Amsterdam School of Communication Research at the University of Amsterdam. Her research interests include political framing theory, news processing, experimental research and political journalism. Lecheler has published articles in several journals, including the *Journal of Communication, Communication Research, Journalism and Mass Communication Quarterly and European Political Science Review*.

Jae Kook Lee is Assistant Professor of School of Journalism at Indiana University. His main research interests are political communication and public opinion in the new media environment. His research has been published in scholarly journals, including *Journalism & Mass Communication Quarterly and Journalism: Theory, Practice, and Criticism*.

Nam-Jin Lee is a PhD candidate, School of Journalism and Mass Communication at the University of Wisconsin-Madison. His recent publications include co-authored chapters 'Communication and Education' and 'Framing and Agenda Setting' (with D. Shah, D. McLeod and M. Gotlieb); and co-authored articles 'Communication Competence as a Foundation for Civic Competence' (with D. Shah and J. McLeod) in *Political Communication* and 'Framing Policy Debates' (with D. McLeod and D. Shah) in *Communication Research*.

Steven Livingston is Professor of Media and Public Affairs and International Affairs at The George Washington University in Washington, DC. Livingston has written scores of research publications appearing in academic journals and books. His most recent book, *When the Press Fails: Political Power and the News Media from Iraq to Katrina* (W. Lance Bennett and Regina Lawrence, co-authors), was published in 2007. In 2008–09, Livingston has made three trips to Iraq and one to Afghanistan to conduct research on a new book co-authored with Robert Entman and Sean Aday entitled *Framing Failure*.

Paolo Mancini is Professor at the Dipartimento Istituzioni e Società, Facoltà di Scienze Politiche, Università di Perugia in Italy. Mancini's interests focus on the relationship between news media and politics observed in a comparative dimension. Mancini's major publications include: *Politics, Media and Modern Democracy* (with David Swanson, Praeger, 1996), *Manuale di comunicazione politica* (Laterza, 1996), *Il sistema fragile* (Carocci, 2000). In 2004 with Dan Hallin he published *Comparing Media Systems: Three Models of Media and Politics* (Cambridge University Press), for which they won the 2005

Goldsmith Book Award from Harvard University, the 2005 Diamond Anniversary Book Award of the National Communication Association and the 2006 outstanding Book Award of the International Communication Association.

Robert Mattes is Professor of Political Studies and Director of the Democracy in Africa Research Unit at the University of Cape Town. He is also Senior Adviser to, and a co-founder of Afrobarometer, a groundbreaking regular survey of public opinion in 20 African countries. He has also helped to launch and run other major research projects such as the South African National Election Study and the African Legislatures Project. His research has focused on the development of democratic attitudes and practices in South Africa and across sub-Saharan Africa. He is the co-author (with Michael Bratton and E. Gyimah-Boadi) of *Public Opinion, Democracy and Markets In Africa* (Cambridge University Press, 2005) and has authored or co-authored numerous articles.

Jack M. McLeod is Maier-Bascom Professor Emeritus, School of Journalism and Mass Communication at the University of Wisconsin-Madison. He recently co-authored chapters: 'Communication and Education: Creating Competence for Socialization into Public Life (with D. Shah, D. Hess and N. Lee) and 'Levels of Analysis' and 'Political Communication Effects' (with D. McLeod and G. Kosicki). He co-edited (with D. Shah) the special issue on communication and political socialization for *Political Communication*.

Alyssa C. Morey is a PhD student in the School of Communication at the Ohio State University. Her interests include the study of social and political discussion networks, psychological precursors to approach or avoid political discussion and disagreement and the role of political discussion in generating normative democratic outcomes. She has also done research on psychophysiological reactions to emotional political advertising, the effects of different forms of political satire in entertainment media and political tolerance.

Pippa Norris is the McGuire Lecturer in Comparative Politics at the John F. Kennedy School of Government at Harvard University and ARC Laureate Fellow and Professor of Government and International Relations at the University of Sydney. She has also served as Director of the Democratic Governance Group at United Nations Development Programme in New York. Her research compares political institutions and behavior in many countries worldwide. In 2011 she was awarded the Johan Skytte prize in political science (with Ronald Inglehart), the ARC Laureate, a honorary doctorate by Edinburgh University and a special recognition award by the PSA UK. She has published almost 40 books, including most recently *Does Democratic Governance Work: The Impact of Regimes on Prosperity, Welfare and Peace* (Cambridge University Press, 2012), *Democratic Deficits* (Cambridge University Press, 2011), *Cosmopolitan Communications: National Diversity in a Globalized World* (with Ronald Inglehart, Cambridge University Press, 2009) and *Public Sentinel: The News Media and Governance Reform* (World Bank, 2010).

Sarah Oates is Professor of Political Communication at the University of Glasgow, Scotland, where she founded the MSc program in political communication. She studies the role of information in supporting or subverting democracy and has written extensively on the post-Soviet media. She served as an expert media analyst in election observance missions in Russia and Kazakhstan for the European Institute for the Media. She is the author of *Introduction to Media and Politics* (Sage, 2008) and *Television, Democracy and Elections in Russia* (Routledge, 2006). Her newest co-authored publication, *Terrorism, Elections, and Democracy* (Palgrave Macmillan, 2010), compares the role of terrorist threat in election campaigns in the USA, UK and Russia. She is currently at work on a monograph about the political limits of the Internet in the post-Soviet sphere for the Digital Politics series at Oxford University Press. In August 2012, she will become Professor at the Philip Merrill College of Journalism at the University of Maryland.

Diana Owen is an Associate Professor of Political Science and Director of American Studies at Georgetown University. She is among the founders of Georgetown's graduate program in Communication, Culture and Technology. Her publications include *Media Messages in American Presidential Elections* (Greenwood Press, 1991), *New Media and American Politics* (with Richard Davis, Oxford University Press, 1998), *The Internet and Politics: Citizens, Activists, and Voters* (co-editor, Routledge, 2006), *Making a Difference: The Internet and Elections in Comparative Perspective* (co-editor, Lexington, 2008) and *American Government and Politics in the Information Age* (with David L. Paletz and Timothy E.

Cook, FlatWorld Knowledge Press, 2011). She has published numerous articles and book chapters on political communication, American government, political socialization and civic engagement, elections and voting behavior and mass political behavior.

Mark Allen Peterson is an Associate Professor of Anthropology and International Studies at Miami University. He has conducted fieldwork in Egypt, India and the USA. He is the author of *Anthropology and Mass Communication: Myth and Media in the New Millennium* (Berghahn, 2003) and co-author of *International Studies: An Interdisciplinary Approach to Global Issues* (Westview, 2008). He has published articles in *Anthropology Today, Anthropological Quarterly, Childhood, Contemporary Islam, New Review of Hypermedia and Multimedia* and *Social Anthropology* as well as chapters in the books *At War With Words* (Walter de Gruyter, 2003), *Media Anthropology* (Sage, 2005), *Folklore/Cinema* (Utah State University Press, 2007) and *The Anthropology of News and Journalism* (Indiana University Press, 2010).

Kelly Quinn is a PhD candidate and instructor in the Department of Communication at the University of Illinois at Chicago. She holds an MSLIS in Library Science from Dominican University and an MBA from Northwestern University, both in Illinois. Her research examines how adults create and maintain social relationships through their technology practices. She has presented her work to the Association of Internet Researchers, the National Communication Association and the Midwest Association of Public Opinion Research.

Stephen D. Reese is Jesse H. Jones Professor of Journalism and Associate Dean for Academic Affairs in the College of Communication at the University of Texas. His research has been published in numerous book chapters and articles and he is co-author, along with Pamela Shoemaker, of *Mediating the Message: Theories of Influence on Mass Media Content*. He edited *Framing Public Life: Perspectives on Media and Our Understanding of the Social World* and, more recently, was section editor for "Media Production and Content" in the ICA *Encyclopedia of Communication*.

June Woong Rhee is Professor at the Department of Communication at Seoul National University. He has published articles on media effects studies in *Journal of Communication, Communication Research* and *Political Communication*. His recent interest includes public spheres, public communication, citizenship and public service media. He was an adviser to the Korea Broadcasting System on election forecasting and newsroom development. He received his PhD from the Annenberg School for Communication, University of Pennsylvania.

Piers Robinson is a senior lecturer in International Politics, University of Manchester. He researches the relationship between communications, media and world politics. His book *The CNN Effect: The Myth of News, Foreign Policy and Intervention* (Routledge, 2002) analyzed the relationship between news media, US foreign policy and humanitarian crises. Recent research involves analysis of British news media coverage of the 2003 Iraq invasion and the research monograph from this work is entitled *Pockets of Resistance: British News Media, War and Theory in the 2003 Invasion of Iraq* (Manchester University Press, 2010). He is co-editor of the journal *Critical Studies on Terrorism* (Routledge) and has published articles in leading journals including the *Journal of Communication, Journal of Peace Research* and the *Review of International Studies*.

Karen Sanders is Head of the Department of Advertising and Institutional Communication at CEU San Pablo University in Madrid, where she holds a chair, and Visiting Professor at the IESE Business School at the University of Navarra. She was a founding member of the Department of Journalism Studies at the University of Sheffield in the UK in 1995 where she directed the MA Political Communication program until 2006. She has published widely in the fields of communication ethics and political communication. Her latest book is *Communicating Politics in the 21st Century* (Palgrave Macmillan, 2009). She was a founding member of the Institute of Communication Ethics in 2002 and of the Association of Political Communication in 2008.

Margaret Scammell is a Lecturer in Media and Communications at the London School of Economics. Her research interests are in political communications, especially political campaigning, Americanization and globalization of campaigning, media and elections, governments and news management, political marketing, political journalism and the appropriate role of media in democratic countries. She is the co-author of *On Message: Communicating the Campaign* (Sage, 1999) and *Media, Journalism and Democracy* (Ashgate Dartmouth, 2000) and has published numerous journal articles.

Holli A. Semetko is Vice Provost for International Affairs, Director of The Halle Institute for Global Learning and Professor of Political Science at Emory University. She was formerly professor and chair of audience and public opinion research at the University of Amsterdam, and founding chair of the board for the Amsterdam School of Communications Research where she continues to serve as an honorary professor. She is also an honorary professor at the University of Twente. Her current research focuses on media and public opinion in international relations, comparative politics and in election campaigns around the world.

John Street is a Professor of Politics at the University of East Anglia. He is author of several books, including *Politics and Popular Culture* (Polity, 1997), *Mass Media, Politics and Democracy* (Palgrave, 2001 and 2011) and *Music and Politics* (Polity, 2011). He has written extensively on the relationship between politics and popular culture and has just completed – with colleagues at the University of East Anglia – two Economic and Social Research Council projects, one on the use of music in political action, and the other on the political use of popular culture by first-time voters in the UK.

Richard Tait is Professor of Journalism and Director, Centre for Journalism, Cardiff University. He was Editor of BBC Newsnight and the 1987 BBC General Election Results Programme; Editor of Channel 4 News from 1987 to 1995 and Editor-in-Chief of Independent Television News (ITN) from 1995 to 2002. He was a member of the Independent Review into Government Communications (2004) and the Hansard Society Commission on the Communication of Parliamentary Democracy (2006).

Hubert Tworzecki is an Associate Professor of Political Science at Emory University. His research interests include: voting behavior, party systems and voter alignments in new democracies of Eastern and Central Europe; the comparative study of citizenship and nationhood and political communications and media effects on attitudes and behavior. He is the author of *Parties and Politics in Post-1989 Poland* (Westview Press, 1996) and *Learning to Choose: Electoral Politics in East-Central Europe* (Stanford University Press, 2002).

Lynn Vavreck is an Associate Professor of Political Science at the University of California in Los Angeles. In addition to UCLA, Dr Vavreck has worked at the White House, Dartmouth College and Princeton University. She is the author of two books, *The Message Matters: The Economy and Presidential Campaigns* and *Campaign Reform: Insights and Evidence* (co-edited with Larry Bartels) and numerous journal articles. In 2008, she was co-principal investigator (with Simon Jackman) of the Cooperative Campaign Analysis Project, a six-wave 20,000-person panel study.

Debra Spitulnik Vidali is an Associate Professor in the Department of Anthropology at Emory University. She directs the Re-Generation Initiative on media and civic engagement. Dr Vidali has published widely on the complex media and language landscapes of contemporary Africa and the USA, particularly as they relate to public spheres and popular culture. Past and current research includes: media and democracy in Africa and in the USA; talk radio and oral traditions in Africa; ethnography of media audiences in Zambia and in the USA; the nation-building functions of Zambian radio and US newscasting; the politics of alternative media in Africa and young adults' engagements and disengagements with media and politics in the USA.

Rens Vliegenthart is an Assistant Professor in Political Communication in the Department of Communication Science and at the Amsterdam School of Communication Research (ASCoR), University of Amsterdam. His research focuses on media-politics dynamics, with a special interest in the role of non-institutional actors, such as social movements. Furthermore, he has an interest in methods for comparative research in political communication and the application of time series analysis in that area.

Silvio Waisbord is Professor in the School of Media and Public Affairs at The George Washington University. He is the editor of the *International Journal of Press/Politics*. He is the author and co-editor of several books, including the forthcoming *Reinventing Professionalism: News and Journalism in Global Perspective* (Polity).

Stefaan Walgrave is Professor in Political Science at the University of Antwerp, Belgium and head of the Media, Movements, and Politics research group (M²P). His research focuses mainly on media and politics and on social movements and political protest. In political communication, his main research is political agenda-setting by the mass media. Regarding social movements and protest, his research tackles the determinants and features of protest participation by individuals. He is the co-editor of *The World Says No to War: Demonstrations against the War on Iraq* with Dieter Rucht (University of Minnesota Press, 2010) and the author of numerous journal articles.

Stephen Ward is a senior lecturer in Politics at the European Studies Research Institute, University of Salford in the UK. His research interests focus on e-democracy and, in particular, political campaigning, elections, parties and political participation online. Among his publications are: *Making a Difference: A Comparative View of the Role of the Internet in Election Politics* (co-edited with Richard Davis, Diana Owen and David Taras Rowman Littlefield, Lexington Books, 2008), *Electronic Democracy: Political Organisations, Mobilisation and Participation Online* (co-edited with Rachel Gibson and Andrea Römmele, Routledge, 2004) and *Political Parties and the Internet: Net Gain?* (co-edited with Rachel Gibson and Paul Nixon, Routledge, 2003).

Chris Wells is a PhD candidate at the University of Washington in Seattle, where he is a graduate adviser at the Center for Communication and Civic Engagement. His research focuses on political communication, civic engagement, voter knowledge and the flow of political information through digital networks.

Jisuk Woo is Professor at the Graduate School of Public Administration at Seoul National University. Her research focuses on the role of communication and media in policy processes, and the Internet law and policy including copyright, privacy and Internet governance. Woo has published a book, *Copyright Law and Computer Programs: The Role of Communication in Legal Structure* (Garland Publishing, 2000) and numerous articles in scholarly journals, including the *Political Communication, New Media and Society, Critical Studies in Mass Communication* and *Visual Communication Quarterly*.

Mary Lynn Young is an Associate Professor and past Director of the University of British Columbia Graduate School of Journalism in Vancouver. Dr Young's research interests include gender and the media, newsroom sociology, media credibility, media economics and content analysis. She has worked as an editor, national business columnist and senior crime reporter at major daily newspapers in Canada and the USA. She has published several articles in academic journals, including the *American Review of Canadian Studies* and the *Canadian Journal of Communication*.

Xian Zhou is Professor of Cultural Studies at Nanjing University, China, where he is also Director of Institute for Advanced Studies in Humanities and Social Sciences, and has been associate vice president of Nanjing University. His books, published in Chinese, include *The Turn of Visual Culture* (2008), *Cultural Representations and Cultural Studies* (2007) and *Critique of Aesthetic Modernity* (2005), and he has contributed to numerous journals and collections in China. He is co-editor of *Cultural Studies in China* and particularly interested in media culture and critical theory.

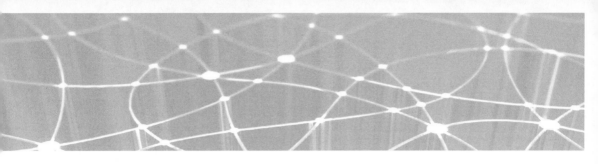

Introduction: The Expanding Field of Political Communication in the Era of Continuous Connectivity

Holli A. Semetko and Margaret Scammell

In less than the working lifetime of most individuals, in just a few decades, political communication as practiced and as a field of scholarly investigation has been transformed by a new era of continuous connectivity. The transformation began with broadcasting in the last decades of the 20th century, when advances in cable and satellite technology brought forth more choices for information and entertainment from around the world than ever before. New global 24/7 news channels, such as Al-Jazeera, built new transnational audiences. By the turn of the 21st century, with the explosive growth of the Internet and the widespread use of mobile phones and texting, the information environment had transformed into a global and local marketplace rich with opportunity.

In the first decade of the 21st century, many stories became world news because citizens were empowered by new social media such as Facebook and Twitter or their local variants. Even in closed societies where access to information is routinely controlled and denied by authorities, connectivity means that many local protests and crackdowns can become global news. Today, individuals, organizations, campaigns and social movements, and governments around the world are all affected by the opportunities and issues presented by the new media environment (Bennett, 2003; Graber 2003).

Although everything appears to have been profoundly changed by the new norm of ubiquitous wireless connectivity, the questions and concerns that lie at the heart of the interdisciplinary field of political communication remain the same. Questions about access and control, choice and contents, and impacts on learning, opinions and behavior have been addressed in a number of national and international contexts (examples include Cappella and Jamieson, 1997; Diebert et al., 2008, 2010, 2011; Graber 2001; Mutz, 2007; Prior, 2005). Today's scholars and practitioners are as just driven by an interest in understanding the mechanisms of power and influence as their predecessors.

Precisely these issues were at the heart of the phone hacking scandal in the UK in early 2011 that rocked the empire of the world's most powerful media magnate, Rupert Murdoch. The scandal raised internationally resonant and profoundly important ethical questions for journalists, criminal investigators, politicians and governments about their work and relationships. Professor Richard Tait, Director of the Center for Journalism at the Cardiff School of Journalism, Media and Cultural Studies, whose experience includes serving as a BBC governor and trustee, and an editor, producer and editor-in-chief at ITN, Channel 4 news, and BBC television, provides the latest insights on the implications of this scandal for journalism and politics and the field of political communication research in this volume.

The SAGE Handbook of Political Communication is a timely resource for students, scholars and practitioners around the world. Leading experts from more than a dozen countries have contributed to this volume. The volume stands apart from most handbooks in which summaries of the literature are the main focus. The 40 chapters in this volume go beyond that to advance innovative arguments about timely issues and present new data, and many offer new approaches and methods for doing political communication research.

In what follows, we discuss the expanding field of political communication, beginning with its' multidisciplinary past and present. Over the past decade there has been the beginning of convergence across theories and approaches that marks the development of the field. We discuss what the future holds for this vibrant and growing field before outlining the contents of the five sections of the Handbook.

A MULTIDISCIPLINARY PAST AND PRESENT

The roots of the field of political communication are deep and multi-disciplinary. The comments of a number of leading scholars acknowledge the historic influence of an array of disciplines in the arts and social sciences (see The Future of Political Communication Research, 2005; Graber, 2003; Bennett and Iyengar 2008). Indeed, in universities around the world today, many different academic departments, schools and programs provide the institutional bases for what we would describe as research and teaching in political communication including: communication, journalism and media studies, political science and history, international relations, public and international affairs, cultural studies, sociology, psychology, anthropology, marketing, advertising, public relations and economics. Generations of graduates from these programs have gone on to become practitioners and many have become scholars.

Innovative political communication research can be found in a wide array of journals. Around the world a large number of journals include articles with a political communication focus, such as the *Asian Journal of Communication*, *Communication Research*, the *European Journal of Political Research*, the *European Journal of Communication*, *Journal of Communication*, *Media Culture & Society*, and the *Journal of Political Marketing* among others. There are two longstanding and widely recognized dedicated journals in this interdisciplinary field – *Political Communication* and *International Journal of Press*

Politics – and the editorship of the former is shared between representatives of the political communication sections of the International Communication Association (ICA) and the American Political Science Association (APSA). The University of Southern California's (USC) E-Governance Lab at the School of Policy, Planning and Development also home to the *Journal of E-Government* that focuses on e-governance and how state and local governments can improve their use of information technology and enhance the delivery of public services and information. Another example of a new journal that provides a dedicated channel for research on political communication is the online *Journal of Information Technology & Politics* launched in 2009. These last two journals are connected with the APSA's Information, Technology and Politics (ITP) organized section. There is also the *International Journal of Communication*, an open-source, online journal launched in 2006 at USC's Annenberg School, edited by Manuel Castells and Larry Gross, which has published more than 40 political communication related articles in its first four years. Judging from this brief overview, we can expect that political communication research will continue grow in a wide range of publication outlets.

Political communication research also appears to be well and thriving in many of the traditional discipline-based journals in political science and economics. Our review of a number of journals archived in JSTOR in political science and economics, for example, found that 194 articles focusing directly on political communication topics were published between 2000 and 2009. The number of articles increased over time, with 43% of the 194 articles published between 2000 and 2004 and 57% published between 2005 and 2009. This review included: *American Economics Review*, *American Journal of Political Science*, *American Political Science Review*, *British Journal of Political Science*, *Journal of Economic Perspectives*, *Journal of Political Economy*, *Journal of Politics*, *Political Behavior* and *The Quarterly Journal of Economics*.

Most political scientists and communication scholars do not read academic journals in economics and would be surprised to learn that research on political communication can be found in these outlets. *The Quarterly Journal of Economics*, for example, published several articles that directly address compelling political communication research questions, based on an analysis of keywords and abstracts, as the following article titles suggest: 'Radio's Impact on Public Spending' (2004), 'A Measure of Media Bias' (2005), 'Television and Voter Turnout' (2006) and 'The Fox News Effect: Media Bias and Voting' (2007). *The American Economics Review* published six articles relevant to political com-munication in this time period on such topics as the market for news, the randomness of social networks, and *The New York Times* and the market for local newspapers.

The expansion of the field is evidenced by the growth of publications in these various outlets in the social sciences. The structure of the academic disciplines and their often similarly named top journals has no doubt limited general awareness of some of these findings that help us to recognize the growth of political communication research in the first decade of the twenty-first century. Many scholars in political communication based in departments of political science or communica-tions may not even be aware of some of the pio-neering work published by economists in economics journals, yet some of this work directly addresses major questions facing scholars in the field of political communication around the world. One such question, for example, is whether media bias effects voting.

Most will recall that it was only after a highly charged debate and contested 2000 US presiden-tial election result that President George W. Bush entered what became the first of two terms in office. News around the world on Election Day in November 2000 reported on the problems with US voting booths and the fact that some citizens were prevented from voting in battleground states, such as Ohio and Florida. The hotly disputed first-term presidency began only after a 5–4 Supreme Court vote and a highly charged public debate. Much innovative research has been published on the 2000 US election by scholars in political science and communication around the world, but it was research published in *The Quarterly Journal of Economics* that established how the Republicans' path to the presidency began four years earlier in October 1996 when the conserva-tive Fox News Channel was rolled out in the cable systems of 20% of US towns. Drawing on presi-dential and congressional voting data from more than 9000 towns where Fox News was introduced between 1996 and 2000, economists Stefano Dellavigna and Ethan Kaplan (2009: 1187) estab-lish significant effects on the vote and conclude that Fox News 'convinced 3 to 28 percent of its viewers to vote Republican, depending on the audience measure'. Xinshu Zhao's (2008) careful analysis of the vote revealed that the 2000 US presidential election result was invalid and his study on the plight of elections in democracies around the world became a best-selling book in China.

In this new information era, research in the tra-ditional disciplines of political science, sociology, journalism, psychology and anthropology, each of which has contributed in different ways to the development of the field called political

communication, has been impacted dramatically as scholars seek new ways to conceptualize the expanding field, adapt old methodologies and create new ones. Our research on publications in just some of the social science journals shows that research in the field is growing. The multidiscipli-nary roots of the field remain visible in a number of journals that we describe as dedicated to politi-cal communication research. In addition, we find that fundamental research questions in the field are being addressed in publications from other disciplines such as economics.

As the substantive research in the field is expanding across more disciplines, over the past decade there also has been the beginning of con-vergence across of theories and approaches that marks the development of the field. This conver-gence gives primacy to the perspective of the citi-zen as a consumer and producer of contents, and draws upon research in marketing, branding, public relations, public affairs and public diplomacy.

Citizens as Content Consumers and Creators: Branding, Public Relations and Public Diplomacy

As the mass media systems moved from a 'one to many' model to a 'many to many' model, the field of political communication shifted from a mass media model to what Margaret Scammell (2007: 611) has called 'a consumer model of political communication'. The concept of the brand sub-sumes all, she argues. Branding has moved from products to politicians, with the same methods and practices in politics that are common in mar-keting and public relations. Scammell's (2007) case study of the branding of Prime Minister Tony Blair in the UK 2005 general election is an early example of what observers of global political mar-keting find are growing similarities in the market-ing practices of political parties around the world (Lees-Marshment et al., 2009).

Research and theory concerning elections and campaign effects, marketing, public relations, public affairs and public diplomacy all can be described as falling within concept of a process that Jesper Strömbäck and Spiro Kiousis (2011) call 'political public relations'. Their definition of the process clearly falls under the umbrella of political communication: 'Political public rela-tions is the management process by which an organization or individual actor for political pur-poses, through purposeful communication and action, seeks to influence and to establish, build, and maintain beneficial relationships and reputations with its key publics to help support its mission and achieve its goals'. In addition to the usual work of political parties, governments and politicians, this process also describes public affairs and public diplomacy activities that involve state as well as non-state actors ranging from artists and producers of culture to non-governmental organizations.

The field of political communication incorporates the new public diplomacy that involves corporate and non-state actors, grassroots and transnational organizations and citizens whose activities, though not controlled by the state, may nevertheless foster knowledge building, learning and, potentially, impacts on opinions and behavior.

THE FUTURE: INNOVATION

Today's scholars aim to identify new approaches and methods for studying the process of political communication under media hyper conditions, alongside flourishing activity among citizens as consumers and creators of content. Entertainment and the arts are more visible and varied than ever before in this new information age. Individual content creators upload hundreds of thousands of new videos daily to sites such as YouTube. In 2009, just four years after its launch, YouTube was seen by more than 1 billion viewers each day. Facebook, founded in 2004, had more than 500 million users in early 2010.

Individuals and organizations are also more vulnerable than ever before because of the security issues that go along with reliance on technology and social networks. Cyber attacks are a daily cost for companies in doing business while governments aim to find ways to prevent cyber war. Cyber attacks are a coordinated form of millions of requests, known as distributed-denial-of-service or DDOS attacks, to overload and shut down servers. These have been common practice in war and conflict between nations recent years, such as the cyber attacks on the Georgian government's servers just prior to Russia's 2008 invasion of the country.

The familiar phrase 'the only constant is change', has a special meaning for scholars and practitioners in the field of political communication. Failure to innovate is not an option. Under these rapidly changing conditions, scholars and practitioners have to constantly reassess their research priorities.

ORGANIZATION OF THE HANDBOOK

Evidence of the transformational impact of the Internet in societies around the world can be found throughout this volume. The Handbook is organized into five parts.

Part I discusses the developments in technology and the media that have broadened the terrain for political communications especially over the past decade. Trends in the media industry, entertainment media and popular culture are discussed, as well as the still unfolding impact of the Internet on citizens, journalism and the news business, political parties and campaigning, and government approaches to communications. As normative conclusions are often part of political communication research, Part I concludes with an innovative agenda that sets forth standards for normative evaluations of media and citizen performance.

Part II addresses how individuals and groups are engaging with one another, learning and communicating in the new media environment, and discusses potential future scenarios. The first four chapters each take different perspectives on traditional media, new media and social media to discuss the transformational impacts on civil society and civic learning. The last four chapters focus on specific sites for studying citizens and civic engagement including women as political communicators, negative campaigning and its impacts, commercialization and public service broadcasting in the European context, and the value of social networks.

Part III focuses on the latest developments in research designs and methods for studying political communication in the varying contexts of traditional, old and new media. New perspectives on how to measure effects and content are presented in this section, drawing on new data provided by the chapter authors.

Part IV concerns the conceptual importance of power in political communication research. The chapters in this section draw upon various contexts including foreign policy, war and combat, political rhetoric, everyday conversations and social media.

Part V focuses on the various geographic contexts for political communication practice and research. From China and Korea to Latin America, from Russia and the new EU states to transnational Al-Jazeera, the local, national, regional and transnational contexts are discussed in the chapters in this final section. In the penultimate chapter in the volume, Paolo Mancini and Daniel Hallin offer their comments on comparative political communication research. In the last chapter of this section, which is also the last chapter in the volume, leading broadcaster and professor of journalism Richard Tait discusses the impact of the Britain's phone hacking scandal and the implications for the future of journalism.

REFERENCES

Bennett, W. L. (2003) *News: The Politics of Illusion*. New York: Longman.

Cappella, J. N. and Jamieson, K. H. (1997) *Spiral of Cynicism*. New York: Oxford University Press.

Deibert, R. J., Palfrey, J. G., Rohozinski, R. and Zittrain, J. (2008) *Access Denied: The Practice and Policy of Global Internet Filtering*. Cambridge, MA: MIT Press.

Deibert, R. J., Palfrey, J. G., Rohozinski, R. and Zittrain, J. (2010) *Access Controlled: The Shaping of Power, Rights and Rule in Cyberspace*. Cambridge, MA: MIT Press.

Deibert, R. J., Palfrey, J. G., Rohozinski, R. and Zittrain, J. (2011) *Access Contested: Security, Identity and Resistance in Asian Cyberspace*. Cambridge, MA: MIT Press.

De Vreese, C. H. and Semetko, H. A. (2006) *Political Campaigning in Referendums*. London: Routledge.

Dellavigna, S. and Kaplan E. (2009) 'The Fox News Effect: Media Bias and Voting', *The Quarterly Journal of Economics*, 122(3): 1187–234.

Graber, D. A. (2001) *Processing Politics: Learning from Television in the Internet Age*. Chicago, IL: University of Chicago Press.

Graber, D. A. (2003) *The Power of Communication: Managing Information in Public Organizations*. Washington, DC: CQ Press.

Graber, D. A. (2005) 'Political Communication Faces the 21st Century', *Journal of Communication*, September: 479–507.

Lees-Marshment, J., Rudd C. and Stromback J. (eds) (2009) *Global Political Marketing*. London: Taylor and Francis.

Mutz, D. C. (2007) 'Effects of "In-Your-Face" Television Discourse on Perceptions of a Legitimate Opposition', *American Political Science Review*, 101(4): 621–35.

The Future of Political Communication Research: Where We've Been, Where We're Going (2005) Roundtable discussion at the annual meeting of the American Political Science Association in Washington, DC, 1–4 September 2005. Includes comments from Gladys Engle Lang, Kurt Lang, Kathleen Hall Jamieson, Thomas Patterson, Roderick Hart, Elihu Katz, Doris Graber, W. Lance Bennett, Donald Shaw, Shanto Iyengar, and Q&A discussion. See http://www.politicalcommunication.org/history.html

Prior, M. (2005) 'News vs. Entertainment: How Increasing Media Choice Widens Gaps in Political Knowledge and Turnout', *American Journal of Political Science*, 49(3): 577–92.

Scammell, M. (2007) 'Political Brands and Consumer Citizens: The Rebranding of Tony Blair', *The Annals of the American Academy of Political and Social Science*, 611(1): 176–92

Strombeck, J. and Kiousis, S. (eds) (2011) Political Public Relations: Principles and Applications. In Strömbäck, Jesper & Kiousis, Spiro (Eds.), *Political public relations. principles and applications*. (pp. 1–32). London: Routledge.

Zhao, X. (2008) *Xuanju de Kunjing – Minzhu Zhidu ji Xianzheng Gaige Pipan* [*Plight of Elections – A Critique of the World's Election Systems and Constitutional Reforms*], revised and expanded edition. Chengdu: Sichuan People's Publishing House.

PART I

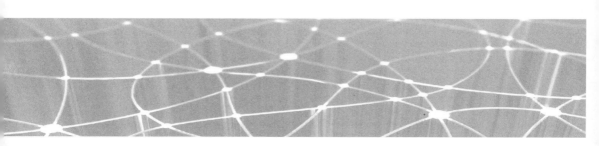

1

Entertainment Media and the Political Engagement of Citizens

Michael X. Delli Carpini

In 2004 *Star Academy*, the reality television show in which up to 20 contestants from throughout the Arab world live together 'on-air' for four months, showcase their musical talents in a weekly concert, and are gradually eliminated by way of audience voting through phone calls and text messaging, 'captured the largest audience in pan-Arab television history, reaching up to 80 per cent of viewers in some countries' (Kraidy, 2009: 2). Despite, or more accurately because of the popularity of this and similar programs, 'Arab reality TV is so controversial that it has triggered street riots, contributed to high-level political resignations, compelled clerics to issue hostile *fatwas,* and fanned transnational media wars' (Kraidy, 2009: 3).

Similar (though only rarely as dramatic) examples of 'entertainment' media generating public, media and/or elite political debate and controversy can be found throughout the world, ranging from the long-standing tradition of 'telenovelas', which are most closely associated with Latin American countries but which can be found in various forms in countries such as Germany, Indonesia, Russia, Portugal, the Philippines, Egypt, India, Kenya, Tanzania, Canada and the USA; to the popularity of 'massive, multiplayer online games' in countries such as Korea; to the effective mix of sports and politics used by Italian Prime Minister Silvio Berlusconi; to the global riots, protests and public debates that followed the publication of controversial cartoons of the

prophet Mohammed in the Danish newspaper *Jyllands-Posten.*

While the sociopolitical impact of entertainment media is often subtle and/or unintended (for example, as with many online games such as *World of Warcraft*, movies such as *Slumdog Millionaire* or television shows such as the original version of the Peruvian telenovela, *Simplemente Maria*), increasingly the potential power of entertainment media has not been lost on those interested in influencing the opinions, attitudes and behaviors of citizens. These more conscious efforts to influence various publics through entertainment media include both government and non-governmental organization sponsorship of 'pro-social' programming (Singhal and Rogers, 1999), as well the use of entertainment media to reach voters/constituents by elected officials and candidates for office.

For example, when Ross Perot announced his third-party candidacy for the US president in February of 1992 on the *Larry King Live* cable television talk show it created something of a firestorm within the journalistic profession. Prior to this watershed moment such pronouncements (in modern times) had only occurred through the traditional format of a press conference, announced well in advance, at which the mainstream news media could question the candidate about his (or rarely her) qualifications for office. Perot's decision was viewed by many as further evidence that he was not a 'serious' candidate.

Sixteen years later the appearance of candidates – as well as elected and appointed officials – on non-news media has become commonplace, as much a requirement of the rituals of campaigning and governing as the long-standing Sunday morning news shows. Indeed, in comparison to new gatekeepers such as Jon Stewart, Stephen Colbert, Bill Maher, Jay Leno, David Letterman or Matt Drudge, Larry King's journalistic credentials now look rather mainstream. Adding to this changed media environment has been the apparent increase in the amount of overtly political content of prime-time entertainment television (for example, *Family Guy*, *24* or *The West Wing*), docudramas (for example, *The Reagans* or *The Path To 9–11*), fictional and non-fictional films (*The Day After Tomorrow*, *Fahrenheit 911*, *Sicko*, *United 93*, *World Trade Center* or *An Inconvenient Truth*) and the numerous blogs, websites and social networking sites that blend culture, politics, satire and/or opinion (for example, The Drudge Report, YouTube, Facebook or Meetup.org). So, too, has the more visible role played by celebrities (from Toby Keith to Al Franken to The Dixie Chicks) in political discourse, the proliferation of cable news networks' opinionated talk and interview shows (for example, *The Sean Hannity Show, Countdown with Keith Olbermann, The O'Reilly Factor* or *The Rachel Maddow Show*), and the 'softening' of the content of traditional network news (for example, both the choice of Katie Couric to anchor the *CBS Evening News*, and the format and content changes that accompanied her hiring). By 2008, 'entertainment' media in its various forms were arguably as much a factor in politics as more traditional sources of news (consider Tina Fey's satirical caricature of Sarah Palin on *Saturday Night Live* and the way this portrayal intersected with more mainstream news coverage and commentary, or Jon Stewart's biting critiques of the lack of independent investigative reporting about the financial sector prior to the economic meltdown in 2009).

That the line between news and entertainment has blurred over the last few decades is now something of a truism. There remains, however, more significant disagreement regarding the extent of this change (since examples of the kinds mentioned above can be found in earlier years) and, more centrally, regarding what, if any, influence these changes are having on the political attitudes and actions of citizens. It is this second topic – the impact of potentially politically relevant entertainment media on citizens and how we attempt to study it – that is the focus of this chapter. More specifically I provide an overview, synthesis and critique of the small but growing body of quantitative research designed to gauge the effects of entertainment media on the political attitudes,

opinions, knowledge and participation of the public. To do this, I first discuss examples of research that attempts to gauge the impact of entertainment media on the democratic engagement of citizens, grouping this research into three categories based on their underlying theories and assumptions. I then turn to a discussion of the collective strengths and weaknesses of this body of research. Finally, I conclude by making some tentative suggestions for how research in this area might be fruitfully expanded.

In doing this, I should note that I am giving short shrift to a much larger body of media scholarship that has long studied entertainment media, either in its own right (for example, film studies, cinema studies, even the study of print fiction) or as a social force (for example, 'entertainment-education' research on children and media, racial, gender and class stereotyping or health-related behaviors; or content, rhetorical and discourse analyses of the political and social messages imbedded in entertainment genres). I also focus mainly, though not exclusively, on research conducted within the USA, in large part because of the longer tradition of using quantitative analyses to study the influence of media on citizens' political opinions, attitudes and behaviors. I believe however, that the research discussed below is collectively both of relevance to and could benefit from these other research traditions.

HOW DOES ENTERTAINMENT MEDIA AFFECT DEMOCRATIC ENGAGEMENT?

Until recently and with few exceptions, quantitative studies of the effects of media on the political attitudes, opinions, knowledge and behavior of citizens have treated entertainment as irrelevant. For example, the *Handbook of Political Communication Research* (Kaid, 2004) devoted no more than a few lines to the topic of entertainment. As entertainment media has become a more legitimate topic of study (because of the increased presence of politically relevant content in these genres, because of a new-found realization of this content's potential import and/or because of the increasing dominance of entertainment over news consumption) quantitative political communication scholars have struggled to integrate these genres into existing theories and findings. Broadly speaking, these extant efforts can be broken down into three loosely chronological though overlapping and competing views: (1) those that see entertainment media as particularly effective genres for reinforcing deep-seated, semi-conscious and hegemonic values; (2) those that see such media as at best a distraction from politics and at worst a cause of disengagement and (3) those that see entertainment media as an alternative venue for many of the same processes of learning and opinion formation that occur through traditional news and public affairs genres.

Entertainment Media as Cultivator of Sociopolitical Worldviews

Some of the earliest quantitative research on the political influence of entertainment media saw their major impact as a source of deep seated, often erroneous attitudes about the state of the world in which citizens live. Most notable in this research tradition is the work of George Gerbner and his various colleagues collectively known as 'cultivation analysis' (Gerbner et al., 1978, 1980, 1982, 1984, 1986, 2002; see also Morgan et al., 2009). Cultivation analysis posited and provided evidence that the content of mainstream media (especially entertainment media) was largely homogeneous, that it presented a view of the world that was often at odds with reality, and that the social and political perspectives of heavy users of the media were influenced by this content. As such, it cultivated worldviews that in turn could influence more proximate opinions about political issues and public figures of the day. Implicit (though less well addressed) in this approach was that the biases contained in mainstream entertainment media were not random, but rather reflected the dominant, even hegemonic social, economic and political agendas of those in positions of power.

Despite its continued reference, cultivation theory and research was and remains something of an outlier in communication research, due in part to its polyglot nature. On the one hand, its acceptance of the sociopolitical power of entertainment and of the subtle, long-term, collective and hegemonic implications of consuming such media connect it (implicitly or explicitly) to a variety of more developed traditions within critical media studies that raise concerns over 'mass culture' (Adorno, 1941; 1963/1975; Horkheimer and Adorno, 1947/2002), 'cultural imperialism' (Schiller, 1976; Tunstall, 1977), 'media concentration' (Bagdikian, 1983) and 'mass propaganda' (Lasswell, 1927). On the other hand, its focus on how citizens' attitudes and opinions were shaped by mediated messages, and its use of survey research and quantitative analyses, connect it with more mainstream media effects research.

While demonstrating suggestive relationships between heavy television use and a variety of political and social attitudes (see also, Besley, 2006, 2008), cultivation analysis was and remains

'ghettoized' from both its mainstream and critical roots. Regarding the former, the effort to use quantitative methods arguably better suited to uncovering specific, short-term effects to test theories that were based on more collective, long-term processes proved problematic, suffering from several familiar methodological shortcomings: less than optimal measures of media exposure (largely self-reports in response to fairly broad survey questions about media use), limited data (largely one-time, cross-sectional surveys) and simplistic statistical methods (largely correlation analyses with controls for possible confounding effects). As a result, it has been difficult to draw convincing conclusions regarding causality. Regarding the latter, while the notion of a largely hegemonic worldview might have been an accurate description of the media environment of the 1970s and 1980s, this is less clearly the case in the more complex and diverse mediated world of the 21st century. In addition, the growing popularity of audience response analysis and the realization that citizens are not simply empty vessels, but rather can take an active role in constructing meaning from the media they consumed, further challenged the theory underlying cultivation research.

Entertainment Media as a Distraction or a Source of Disengagement

As audiences for traditional news and public affairs media have declined over the last few decades (Pew Research Center for the People and the Press, 2008; Project for Excellence in Journalism, 2009) several scholars have coupled this trend with the parallel decline in many indicators of democratic engagement to argue that entertainment media acts at best as a distraction from politics and at worst as a source of political disengagement. One of the strongest proponents of this view is Robert Putnam (1995a,b, 2000), who argues that time devoted to entertainment media use, especially among younger generations, is the major source of decline in 'social capital'.

While acknowledging that it can have its 'dark side', Putnam persuasively argues and documents that the presence of social capital – broadly a connectedness of citizens to others in their community – results in a wide range of individual and collective benefits including better education, safer and more productive neighborhoods, economic prosperity, healthier, happier children and adults and a more vibrant, participatory democracy (Putnam, 2000: 287–363).

The relationship between social capital and democratic engagement is twofold. On the one hand, the concept of social capital includes within it many forms of civic and political engagement, including membership in civic organizations, attending public meetings, talking about political issues, volunteering and participating in elections. On the other hand, high levels of general community involvement and social interaction (which are also components of social capital) are likely to increase more explicitly civic and political engagement and so strengthen the quality and effectiveness of democracy.

Putnam's argument and evidence regarding the positive benefits of social capital have been generally well received. More controversial, however, has been his research documenting the erosion of social capital over the past three decades and his theories regarding the sources of this decline. Of particular relevance to this chapter is his indictment of entertainment television as a major source of decreasing social capital in general and democratic engagement in particular (Putman, 1995a, 2000). Putnam's evidence on the decline in newspaper readership, the penetration of television into the American household, the growth in the number of hours people spend watching television and of having the television on even when not watching and the dominance of television over other forms of more social leisure activity (Putnam, 2000: 216–28) is compelling and supported by other data and research (Bogart, 1989; Bowden and Offer, 1994; Comstock, 1989; Kubey and Csikszentmihalyi, 1990; US Census Bureau, 2009) and various surveys conducted by the Pew Research Center for the People and the Press.

His hypothesized relationship between the rise of television and the decline in social capital has been a matter of dispute, however (Norris, 1996, 1999). Putnam argues that this impact, which is especially prevalent among younger generations, results from a combination of television's usurpation of time that could (and in the past was) otherwise used for more civic-minded activities, the psychological effects of television that inhibit social participation, and the specific content of television that undermines civic motivations (2000: 237).

One way to understand the link between entertainment media use and social capital is through the concept of 'social trust'. Social trust (also known as 'interpersonal trust') is a dispositional orientation toward others in one's community. High social trust indicates feelings of connectedness to and faith in fellow citizens, or more simply, 'a "standing decision" to give most people – even those whom one does not know from direct experience – the benefit of the doubt' (Rahn and Transue, 1998: 545). People scoring high on measures of social trust are significantly more likely to interact with fellow citizens informally,

as well as through membership in community groups, working with them to solve a local problem, or volunteering (Borgida et al., 1997; Brehm and Rahn, 1997; Rahn and Transue, 1998; Uslaner, 1995). In short, social trust is an individual-level, psychological measure of the more behavioral and collective concept of social capital.

Research indicates that the level of social trust in the USA has declined significantly over the past 30 years, paralleling other indicators of declining social capital (Brehm and Rahn, 1997; Putnam, 2000). This decline is especially noticeable among younger adults. Much as with arguments regarding the decline in overall social capital, entertainment television and to a lesser extent new media such as the Internet, have been singled out as a major cause of the decline in social trust. As noted by Shah et al., this argument is based in part on aggregate trends in increasing television and Internet use and declining newspaper readership, as well as 'time displacement' and 'mean world' theories of television:

> Time spent with television is thought to privatize leisure time at the expense of civic activities and to foster beliefs that the world is as threatening as the social reality of the 'airwaves' (Brehm and Rahn, 1997; Gerbner, Gross, Morgan, and Signorielli, 1980; Morgan and Shanahan, 1997). Likewise, epidemiological research has connected amount of television viewing with lower levels of physical and mental health (Sidney et al., 1996). These studies, albeit crude in their operationalization of media variables, lend support to the view that media use is related to changes in life contentment, social trust, and civic participation. (2001: 143)

This argument has been extended to the Internet. Research by Nie and Erbring (2000) suggests that time spent online comes at the direct expense of more social activities, leading heavy Internet users to become physically and psychologically disconnected from their social environment. And Kraut et al. conclude from their research that '[l]ike watching television, using a home computer and the Internet generally implies physical inactivity and limited face-to-face social interaction' (1998: 1019). More recent research has challenged these findings, however. For example, Hampton, et al. (2011) found that users of social network sites reported higher levels of social trust (as well as other indicators of 'social capital') than non-users.

Additional research generally supports (while also complicating) the argument that entertainment media use decreases social capital and trust. In one of the more comprehensive efforts to explore this relationship, Shah et al. (2001) distinguish among overall television use, the use of television for 'hard news', overall newspaper use, the use of newspapers for 'hard news', overall Internet use and the use of the Internet for 'social recreation', 'product consumption', 'financial management' and 'information exchange'. They find that when controlling for demographic characteristics, using newspapers for hard news and using the Internet for information exchange (measured as 'exploring an interest or hobby', 'searching for school or educational purposes' or 'sending an email') had a significant positive effect on social trust for the general population. They also find differences by age, however. For the 'Civic Generation' (pre baby-boomers) only using newspapers for hard news produced a significant positive effect on social trust. For baby boomers, only using the Internet for information exchange produced a significant positive effect. And for Generation Xers, use of the Internet for social recreation produced a significant *negative* effect on social trust, while using the Internet for information exchange produced a significant positive effect. And Williams (2006) found a decline in social capital (including bridging social capital) among online game players, though he also found some evidence for an increase in a diffuse sense of community among players themselves.

Research on the negative civic and political consequences of entertainment media has extended beyond social trust and general indicators of community involvement to other key components of democratic citizenship such as political attitudes, opinions, efficacy, knowledge and participation (Baumgartner and Morris, 2006; Besley, 2006; Bonfadelli, 2002; Couldry and Markham, 2007; Hess, 2006; Hooghe, 2002; Johnson and Kaye, 2003; Kaye and Johnson, 2002; Keum et al., 2004; Kim and Han, 2005; Kim and Vishak, 2008; Morgan and Shanahan, 1992; Prior, 2005, 2007; Scheufele and Nisbet, 2002; Sweetser and Kaid, 2008). Though some studies have been equivocal (Baumgartner, 2007; Moy and Scheufele, 2000; Nabi et al., 2007; Pasek et al., 2006), the general, albeit still tentative conclusion emerging from this line of research is that 'informational and communicative uses of the media may prove beneficial to the health of society, whereas recreational and entertainment uses may erode public involvement' (Shah et al., 2001: 144), a conclusion consistent with that of Putnam. It also suggests that while this relationship results in part from simple time displacement away from other, more interpersonal and community-oriented activities, it also results from the availability of greater nonnews choices that exacerbate existing differences between politically interested and less interested citizens; from the physiological effects of passive media experiences; from the particular ways in which humor and other forms of entertainment are attended to and processed and from the actual content of the entertainment media consumed.

Entertainment Media as an Alternative Source of Political Engagement

A third and somewhat more recent strand of quantitative research on the political effects of entertainment media partially challenges the more pessimistic conclusions of cultivation, distraction and disengagement scholars. This growing body of research argues – and finds – that just as traditional news media can vary in their form, content, audiences and thus effects on political attitudes and actions, so too can entertainment media. The results of this research suggest that under the right conditions and for the right people, politically relevant entertainment media can affect citizens' attitudes, opinions, knowledge and behavior in much the same way as traditional news and public affairs broadcasting has been found to do.

For example, Baum (2002, 2003a,b) finds that 'soft news' sources such as daytime and evening talk shows and infotainment news can increase awareness about major public issues among citizens who are unmotivated to learn about these issues through traditional news venues. Baum (2005) and Baum and Jamison (2006) find that watching candidate appearances on soft news talk shows such as *Oprah* increases the likelihood that such viewers (if they are generally not very politically motivated to begin with) will vote for a candidate whose stances most closely reflect the preferences of the viewer/voter him or herself. The premise of this line of research is straightforward: a large and growing number of citizens eschew traditional news, but do attend to soft news outlets, often for their entertainment value. However, such shows increasingly include politically relevant information, and do so in easily digestible forms. As a result, viewers are coincidently exposed to this information and benefit to some degree from it. In short, these studies suggest that entertainment media can serve as an alternative source of political information, especially for those who do not attend to more traditional news sources. This conclusion is partially disputed by Prior (2003), however, who finds no evidence of increased political knowledge among viewers of these kinds of entertainment shows. And Brewer and Cao (2006), while generally supporting Baum's research, find that watching presidential candidates on late-night talk shows correlates with greater political knowledge, but watching them on morning talk shows showed no relationship with knowledge and watching them on news magazine talk shows produced mixed results.

Attending to entertainment can also affect viewers' political opinions. For example, Glynn et al. (2007), drawing partly on agenda-setting theory and partly on cultivation analysis, find that exposure to daytime talk shows such as *Oprah* increases support for government intervention into the social issues being discussed, even moderating the effects of political ideology on these issues. Jackson and Darrow (2005) and Jackson (2007) find that young adults are more likely to support issue positions that are endorsed by well-known celebrities. Jamieson and Cappella (2008) find that conservative talk radio shows act as a kind of 'echo chamber' reinforcing and increasing the conservative views of their listeners and increasing the negative images they hold of political opponents. Talk radio can also increase listeners' likelihood of holding and expressing a political opinion even if the opinion is unpopular, and increase the likelihood that listeners will participate in politics (Lee, 2007). Similar effects on opinion expression and participation have been found for both late-night television comedy and daytime television talk shows, though the effects of the former are especially pronounced for more politically sophisticated viewers (Moy et al., 2005a).

Another body of research focuses more exclusively on the political influence of humor and satire. To date, this research is mixed on whether comedy and satire enhances, detracts from or is unrelated to democratic engagement, and under what conditions it does so. Research by Baumgartner and Morris (2006) suggests that levels of self-efficacy mediate the potential positive effects of watching programs such as *The Daily Show*. Hollander (2005) finds that watching late night satirical talk shows and political comedy can increase recognition of political figures and topics, but not recall of them. Young (2004) finds partial evidence that citizens' ratings of candidate traits (for example, honesty or intelligence), when mediated by partisan dispositions and prior levels of political knowledge, can be influenced by the way these traits are caricatured by late night talk show hosts. Cao (2008) finds that watching political comedy is associated with greater political knowledge for younger and more educated viewers, but less political knowledge for older or less educated ones. And Moy et al. (2005b) find that voters' evaluations of presidential candidates are shaped by these candidates' appearance on late night comedy shows.

Some of the research on humor and satire focuses on its interactions with traditional news use. Diddi and LaRose (2006) find that college students are largely 'news grazers' whose specific combination of traditional news, cable news, satire and the Internet ultimately depends on a combination of learned habits and sought after gratifications. And Young and Tisinger (2006) find that watching *The Daily Show* complements and reinforces rather than substitutes for traditional news consumption. However, while these findings seem positive, Holbert et al. (2007), using an experimental design, cautions that the order in which one watches entertainment news (*The Daily Show*) and traditional news (*CNN*) affects the gratification one gets out of the second genre watched (for example, the political gratification from traditional news is decreased for viewers with low political efficacy if they first watch satirical news).

One of the few areas within the quantitative study of entertainment and politics that has a longer (if still spotty) history has been the genre of dramas and docudramas. Adams et al. (1985), using a quasi-experimental field experiment, found that watching the Hollywood movie *The Right Stuff* (about the original US astronauts) produced increased positive feelings about the presidential candidacy of former astronaut John Glenn. Carlson (1985) found that watching prime time law enforcement dramas eroded support for civil and criminal rights among viewers. Lenart and McGraw (1989), using a panel survey, found that watching the docudrama, *Amerika* (in which the USA is taken over by the Soviet Union) increased support for conservative policies toward the Soviet Union (see also Lasorsa, 1989).

More recently, Holbert et al. (2003) using a pre-test, post-test experimental design found that watching *The West Wing* led both to an increased belief in the importance of a president being 'engaging', and improved ratings of both George W. Bush and Bill Clinton, suggesting the positive feelings held for the fictional president on *The West Wing* carried over to the current and former president through priming. Holbert et al. (2003) found that watching primetime dramas that presented more progressive views of women increased support for greater gender equality, while watching shows with more traditional gender roles did the opposite. Holbrook and Hill (2005), using both surveys and experimental designs, found that watching crime dramas increased concerns about crime in the real world, and through priming subsequently affected ratings of the president. And Holbert and Hansen (2006) found that watching Michael Moore's *Fahrenheit 9–11* primed opinions about George W. Bush, but only when mediated through citizens' levels of partisanship, affective ambivalence and need for closure.

Taken as a whole, the quantitative research on the political influence of soft news, talk shows, humor, satire and drama discussed above, while far from definitive, takes us several steps beyond the 'cultivation' and 'distraction' hypotheses.

First, it focuses more explicitly on genres (and even specific films or shows) that have political content rather than treating 'media use' or 'entertainment' as a single category. Second, it is more sophisticated (though still limited) in the kinds of effects one might hypothesize, often by drawing on extant theories used in the study of news (for example, priming), but on occasion beginning to develop theories that acknowledge the potential unique contributions of specific genres (for example, the value of narrative as a tool for learning, or the ability of humor to bypass more central information processing). Third, it more subtly parses the negative and positive consequences of entertainment media as a source of political information, acknowledging that either or both is possible. Fourth, it uses more nuanced (though still often problematic) measures of both media exposure and of democratic engagement. Fifth, it uses more varied and sophisticated (though still sometimes limited) methods, including panel designs, field experiments and laboratory experiments. And sixth, it takes into account the conditional aspects of influence, allowing for differential effects across different genres and among different types of audiences/citizens.

STRENGTHS, WEAKNESSES AND SUGGESTIONS FOR FUTURE RESEARCH

While never completely ignored, the political influence of entertainment media has been under-theorized and under-studied by quantitative researchers interested in the public engagement of citizens. These shortcomings are beginning to be remedied, with a growing body of research addressing this issue. To date this body of research has produced suggestive, though still inconclusive and sometimes contradictory results.

Perhaps the single most important conclusion to be drawn from this research is the simple fact that entertainment media appears to matter to individuals' political attitudes, opinions, knowledge and behavior. Among the more specific conclusions one might draw are the following, though further research on even these findings is still needed:

- Entertainment media use *writ large* is correlated with lower levels of many of the aspects of 'democratic engagement' discussed above and described in more detail below. This is especially true when entertainment media use comes at the expense of the use of news and public affairs media.

- When the entertainment media environment presents a consistent picture of the world across mediums and genres, this picture is correlated with the ways audiences view the real world, regardless of the accuracy of the mediated version.
- Consumption of various entertainment genres (humor, drama, talk), and various media (television, film, games, the Internet) with explicitly political content is correlated with political attitudes, opinions, awareness, behaviors and (less consistently) knowledge in a way consonant with the specific information and frames contained in the media presentations.
- Beyond these very broad patterns, it is clear that the influence of politically relevant entertainment media varies significantly depending upon the form and content of the medium, genre and even specific 'event' (for example, the specific broadcast, website, song) being attended to.
- Similarly, the influence of politically relevant entertainment media varies depending upon on a host of demographic (for example, age), attitudinal (for example, political efficacy) and behavioral (for example, news media use) characteristics.

To be sure, while these 'conclusions' offer enough promise to warrant further study, they are tentative and limited: for example, we cannot even say with any confidence whether and under what conditions entertainment media as a source of political information is more beneficial for political sophisticates or for the politically disengaged. If we are to better understand the role of entertainment media in politics, a number of shortcomings – many of them generic to the quantitative analysis of political communication, but some specific to the topic of politically relevant entertainment media – need to be addressed. Among these areas for development are the following.

Effect on What? Expanding the Range of Citizen Attributes We Study

While there is no simple or universally agreed upon list of the necessary, let alone sufficient, attributes of engaged citizenship most theory and research would include: (1) adherence to democratic norms and values (for example, internal and external efficacy or agency, political and social trust, political interest, civic duty, political tolerance); (2) having a set of empirically grounded attitudes and beliefs about the nature of the political and social world (for example, one's ideological orientation, partisanship, views on the relative importance of equality versus freedom, general notions about fundamental issues such as race, gender or class); (3) holding stable, consistent and informed opinions on major public issues of the day (for example, assessments of the performance of the party or president in power, support for or opposition to a specific policy or piece of legislation) and (4) engaging in behaviors designed to directly or indirectly influence the quality of public life for oneself and others (for example, volunteering to work at a local soup kitchen, voting, participating in a demonstration).[1] Underlying all of these elements is the assumption that citizens also have the skills (for example, reasoning, critical thinking, argumentation, oral and written communication) and resources (for example, knowledge, time, money) necessary to develop informed values, attitudes and opinions, connect them together, and translate them into effective action.[2]

Over half a century of quantitative research has produced a reasonably coherent set of findings regarding the conditions under which the consumption of news and public affairs media are likely to nurture these various attributes of engaged citizenship, and when they are likely to foster cynicism, apathy, ignorance or disengagement (see Delli Carpini [2004] for a review of this literature). As the media environments within which citizens obtain, exchange, increasingly create and use politically relevant information change and expand, the study of media influence must change and expand as well.

At a minimum this means a more comprehensive consideration of the influence of politically relevant entertainment media on *all* the 'standard' attributes of democratic citizenship discussed briefly above. As this chapter makes clear, a good deal of progress has been made in this regard. But more research on more of these attributes is needed so that collectively we can produce a set of findings that at least parallel extant research on the effects of more traditional news and public affairs media use.

More ambitiously, however, we need to consider whether this new information environment requires us to rethink or expand what we mean by engaged citizenship. For example, does participation in 'massive multiplayer online games' constitute a form of civic engagement in its own right? A new pathway to such engagement? Does the mixture of information and critique or of fact and fiction that characterize *The Colbert Report* or *The Daily Show* require reconceptualizing what we mean by 'cynicism', 'skepticism' or even 'knowledge'? Are the civic skills necessary for consuming politically relevant entertainment media different from those needed for watching the evening news? Is discussing a social or political issue in a celebrity chat room

the equivalent of face-to-face conversation or deliberation?

Effect of What? Expanding our Notions of Politically Relevant Entertainment Media

Understandably, most quantitative research on the political impact of entertainment media has focused largely on content that has similarities to what we find in more traditional news media (for example, direct mentions of contemporary political institutions, processes, issues or people). In limiting ourselves in this way, however, we may be missing some of the most powerful effects of entertainment. Underlying more proximate political attitudes, opinions and behaviors are a myriad of social and cultural attitudes, beliefs, opinions and behaviors that form the building blocks for their more explicitly political offspring. It is in the formation of these fundamental building blocks where entertainment media may play its greatest role. If this is the case, the kinds of media we deem 'politically relevant' must expand dramatically. An episode of *The Simpsons* that reinforces or challenges gender stereotypes may be as politically relevant as one that explicitly lampoons campaign advertising. *American Idol's* mix of 'expert' and 'public' opinion or *Survivor's* representation of community, competition and 'democracy' may be as or more politically influential than a docudrama about the *9–11* terrorist attacks. Playing an online game such as *Worlds of Warcraft* may have as much or more political significance as playing an explicitly politically motivated game such as *Pork Invaders*.

Of particular relevance regarding the 'what' of the study of entertainment media's political effects is theory and research falling under the rubric of 'entertainment-education' (Singhal and Rogers, 1999). This tradition, global in scope, focuses largely on conscious efforts to bring about social change through the structure and content of carefully designed entertainment genres (for example, telenovelas) intended to affect the attitudes, opinions and behaviors of the public or some segment of it. While these efforts focus largely on what might, at first blush, appear 'apolitical' (for example, health-related behaviors, attitudes about gender, race or class relations, literacy) they have clear, if sometimes unintended or unforeseen, political implications.

Of course expanding our notions of both politically relevant attitudes, beliefs and behaviors, and of politically relevant media runs the risk of losing any coherent sense of what we mean by 'political'; a slippery slope that much of the more qualitative, post-modern research on entertainment media has arguably found itself caught on. And developing creative quantitative methods to study these media and their effects is a daunting issue. Nonetheless, the complexity of the task is in and of itself not enough to argue against attempting it, lest we confirm the criticism that quantitative media effects research simplifies and reduces political reality to the point of missing the forest for the trees. In this area there is much to be gained from returning to some of the tenets of cultivation theory as well as turning to the theories that inform cultural studies approaches to the media – and much to be taught from these exchanges as well.

Effects of What, When and on Who? Exploring the Moderators and Mediators Entertainment Media Effects

Due in part to the diversity of their form and content, and in part to their diverse, complex and shifting audience structures, talking about the effects of 'entertainment media' writ large is ultimately a losing proposition. While much progress has been made in beginning to parse the effects of entertainment media, much more work needs to be done. What is clear from the research reviewed earlier is that the effects of entertainment media are highly contingent and contextual. But we are still a good way from answering even basic questions regarding these complex relationships. Under what conditions is entertainment media more likely to benefit political sophisticates or political novices? Under what conditions are they likely to encourage or dissuade political engagement? For whom is visual, aural or textual media most or least beneficial? Are their age differences in the political impact of various media and are these differences generational or life cycle? How does class, gender or race interact with the form and substance of entertainment media to produce political effects? How and for whom do interactive media produce political effects? Do the motivations for seeking out certain kinds of entertainment media affect their political influence? How does the overall mix of one's media diet affect its short- and long-term impact? If we are to provide valid and reliable answers to these and other questions we need to consider, in better theorized and more subtle ways than we have to date, the interaction of medium, genre and content with the psychological, political and demographic characteristics of audiences/users.

Of particular relevance here is the need for both a stronger exchange among researchers whose research focuses on different parts of the globe, and more comparative and/or non-US-based quantitative studies of the political effects of entertainment media. Such an exchange and research agenda would greatly expand our understanding of the conditions under which entertainment media does or does not influence political attitudes and actions, as well as the types of entertainment media that are most likely to do so.

Expanding Research on the Applicability of Existing Theories to Entertainment Media

As noted above, much of the existing research on politically relevant entertainment implicitly or explicitly substitutes this form of media for more traditional news to explore its ability to inform citizens and influence their political attitudes, opinions and behaviors through agenda-setting, framing and priming, persuasion, learning, etc. This approach is worthwhile and should be more systematically and consciously developed. Can entertainment media influence the public's political agenda? Do entertainment media frame issues in ways that prime citizens' evaluations of issues and public figures? Can citizens obtain relevant political information from entertainment media? Can entertainment media influence political opinions and behaviors through persuasive messages?

The studies reviewed earlier in this paper provide at least suggestive evidence that this may be the case, but more research is needed: research that is more explicit in elaborating why and how one might expect these theories to translate from news to entertainment (for example, why should we expect citizens to treat entertainment in the same way they do public affairs and news?); that is more specific and subtle in delineating the political content of entertainment media (for example, what political facts are included, or what frames or arguments are presented, both in individual programs and more collectively in the larger media environment?); that is better able to measure exposure to the relevant entertainment (for example, that ask about or observe exposure to both specific films, programs, etc., as well as to politically relevant media more broadly); that is designed to disentangle cause and effect (for example through laboratory experiments, natural experiments and/or panel studies) and so forth. In short, quantitative research on entertainment media needs to be at least as sophisticated in its methods, data and analytic techniques as studies of more mainstream news media have become.

Theorizing and Testing What Is Unique about Entertainment Media

Were we to 'simply' match the range, sophistication and findings of extant research on the influence of traditional news media, we would have made great strides in understanding the role of politically relevant entertainment media in the democratic process. However, a more ambitious research agenda would go beyond this by considering what distinguishes entertainment from non-entertainment and how these differences might enhance or limit the former's political influence.

Holbert (2005) provides a useful typology for thinking about the potential political relevance of various entertainment genres, categorizing them along two dimensions – the extent to which the politics contained in them is explicit (for example, when a candidate appears on a talk show) or implicit (for example, when a scene in a drama or comedy more subtly relates to sociopolitical issues), and the extent to which politics is the primary (for example, *The Daily Show* or *The West Wing*) or the secondary (for example, a talk show like *Oprah* that occasionally addresses politics directly) topic of the genre. But even this approach misses much of what may be distinctive both across entertainment genres and between entertainment and non-entertainment genres.

The work of Young (2004, 2008) on humor is an important step in the right direction, in particular her efforts to distinguish – theoretically and empirically – the potential effects of different kinds of humor. Similarly, characteristics of entertainment such as narrative dramatic structures, serials, the blending of fact and fiction, the use of music and images, identification with characters and hosts, the quality and content of discourse, etc., all seem ripe for producing theories about the potential political influence of entertainment media that would differ from those postulated about news and public affairs programming. And more sophisticated theorizing about the different ways that citizens choose, attend to and process entertainment (as opposed to news and public affairs) media and how these differences might affect their political influence is needed. Uses and gratifications theory as well as elaboration likelihood models (ELM) are promising starts in this direction, but only starts. Here again theory and research from the 'Entertainment-Education' tradition, which in many ways is more fully developed than what is typically found in political communication studies, offers a potentially fruitful avenue. Equally promising may be building on theory and research from the cultural studies, discourse and audience analyses, ethnography, and critical studies traditions, adapting them as appropriate to more explicitly political and quantitative research.

Developing a More Integrative Theory of Political Communication Influence

Ultimately, if we are interested in understanding how the current media environment influences citizens, we may need to move beyond the very genre distinctions upon which much current research is based. Ideally we would instead consider the attributes or dimensions of media that arguably are most relevant to democratic engagement, and assess the political relevance of media of all kinds against these attributes or dimensions. While definitively identifying these attributes or dimensions is beyond the scope of this chapter, undoubtedly they would include aspects of both the form and content of mediated messages, and would center collectively on the democratic utility of the mediated message in question (that is, its potential for enhancing or detracting from a democratically engaged citizenry). If done correctly, such an approach would find various mediated messages congregating in ways that are different from our more traditional categorizations such as 'news versus entertainment', 'comedy versus drama' or 'print versus image' and 'television versus Internet'.

Such an approach, if possible, would go a long way toward developing more comprehensive, integrative theories of the influence of politically relevant media, theories that better reflect the hybridized nature of the media environment in which we increasingly live. It would also help in addressing what may be the two biggest challenges facing the quantitative study of the influence of the media: gauging exposure to politically relevant messages and assessing the long-term effects of such exposure.

NOTES

1 Often a distinction is made between political, civic and civil behavior. *Political* behavior is generally defined as activities intended directly or indirectly to affect the selection of elected representatives and/or the development, implementation or enforcement of public policy through government (for example voting, working for a political party, contacting an elected official, holding an appointed or elected office). *Civic* behavior refers to participation – as an individual or a member of a group – intended to directly address public concerns through methods that are outside of elections and government (for

example, volunteering to work in a soup kitchen or homeless shelter, or forming a neighborhood watch association to address the problem of crime). Finally, *civil* behavior is participation in the institutions and organizations of civil society that, while not directly aimed at directly or indirectly solving public problems, help build the social capital of a community (for example, coaching a Little League team, organizing a church-run social event).

2 Effective democratic citizenship also requires institutional and systemic structures and processes – democracy is not simply a matter of individual will and choice. Given the focus of this chapter, however, my emphasis is on individual requisites and attributes.

REFERENCES

Adams, W. C., Salzman, A., Vantine, W., Suelter, L., Baker, A., Bonvouloir, L., Brenner, B., Ely, M., Feldman, J. and Ziegel, R. (1985) 'The Power of The Right Stuff: A Quasi-Experimental Field Test of the Docudrama Hypothesis', *Public Opinion Quarterly*, 49(3): 300–39.

Adorno, T. (1941) 'On Popular Music', *Studies in Philosophy and Social Sciences*, 9(1): 17–48.

Adorno, T. (1963/1975) 'Culture Industry Reconsidered', *New German Critique*, 6: 12–19.

Bagdikian, B. (1983) *The Media Monopoly*. Boston, MA: Beacon Press.

Baumgartner, J. C. (2007) 'Humor on the Next Frontier: Youth, Online Political Humor, and the JibJab Effect', *Social Science Computer Review*, 25(3): 319–38.

Baumgartner, J. C. and Morris, J. S. (2006) 'The Daily Show Effect: Candidate Evaluations, Efficacy, and American Youth', *American Politics Research*, 34(3): 341–67.

Baum, M. (2002) 'Sex, Lies and War: How Soft News Brings Foreign Policy to the Inattentive Public', *American Political Science Review*, 96(1): 91–109.

Baum, M. (2003a) 'Soft News and Political Knowledge: Evidence of Absence or Absence of Evidence', *Political Communication*, 20(2): 173–90.

Baum, M. (2003b) *Soft News Goes to War: Public Opinion and American Foreign Policy in the New Media Age*. Princeton, NJ: Princeton University Press.

Baum, M. (2005) 'Talking the Vote: Why Presidential Candidates Hit the Talk Show Circuit', *American Journal of Political Science*, 49(2): 213–34.

Baum, M. and Jamison, A. S. (2006) 'The Oprah Effect: How Soft News Helps Inattentive Citizens Vote Consistently', *Journal of Politics*, 68(4): 946–59.

Besley, J. C. (2006) 'The Role of Entertainment Television and Its Interactions with Individual Values in Explaining Political Participation', *Harvard International Journal of Press-Politics*, 11(2): 41–63.

Besley, J. C. (2008) 'Media Use and Human Values', *Journalism & Mass Communication Quarterly*, 85(2): 311–30.

Bogart, L. (1989) *Press and Public*. Hillsdale, NJ: Lawrence Erlbaum Associates.

Bonfadelli, H. (2002) 'The Internet and Knowledge Gaps: A Theoretical and Empirical Investigation', *European Journal of Communication*, 17(1): 65–84.

Borgida, E., Sullivan, J., Haney, B., Burgess, D., Rahn, W., Snyder, M. and Transue, J. (1997) 'A Selected Review of Trends and Influences of Civic Participation', research paper of the Center for the Study of Political Psychology. Minneapolis.

Bowden, S. and Offer, A. (1994) 'Household Appliances and the Use of Time: United States and Britain Since the 1920s', *Economic History Review*, 47(4): 725–48.

Brehm, J. and Rahn, W. (1997) 'Individual-Level Evidence for the Causes and Consequences of Social Capital', *American Journal of Political Science*, 41(3): 999–1023.

Brewer, P. R. and Cao, X. (2006) 'Candidate Appearances on Soft News Shows and Public Knowledge About Primary Campaigns', *Journal of Broadcasting & Electronic Media*, 50(1): 18–35.

Cao, X. (2008) 'Political Comedy Shows and Knowledge About Primary Campaigns: The Moderating Effects of Age and Education', *Mass Communication & Society*, 11(1): 43–61.

Carlson, J. M. (1985) *Prime Time Law Enforcement: Crime Show Viewing and Attitudes Toward the Criminal Justice System*. New York: Praeger.

Comstock, G. (1989) *Evolution of American Television*. Newark Park, CA: Sage.

Couldry, N. and Markham, T. (2007) 'Celebrity Culture and Public Connection: Bridge or Chasm', *International Journal of Cultural Studies*, 10(4): 403–21.

Delli Carpini, M. X. (2004) 'Mediating Democratic Engagement: The Impact of Communication on Citizens' Involvement in Political and Civic Life', in L. L. Kaid (ed.), *Handbook of Political Communication*. Mahwah, NJ: Lawrence Erlbaum Associates. pp. 395–434.

Diddi, A. and LaRose, R. (2006) 'Getting Hooked on News: Uses and Gratifications and the Formation of News Habits Among College Students in an Internet Environment', *Journal of Broadcasting & Electronic Media*, 50(2): 193–210.

Gerbner, G., Gross, L., Morgan, M., Signorielli, N. and Shanahan, J. (2002) 'Growing Up with Television: Cultivation Processes', in J. Bryant and D. Zillmann (eds.), *Media Effects: Advances in Theory and Research*. Mahwah, NJ: Lawrence Erlbaum Associates. pp. 43–67.

Gerbner, G., Gross, L., Jackson-Beeck, M., Jeffries-Fox, S. and Signorielli, N. (1978) 'Cultural Indicators: Violence Profile No. 9', *Journal of Communication*, 28(3): 178–93.

Gerbner, G., Gross, L., Morgan, M. and Signorielli, N. (1982) 'Charting the Mainstream: Television's Contribution to Political Orientations', *Journal of Communication*, 32(2): 100–27.

Gerbner, G., Gross, L., Morgan, M., and Signorielli, N. (1984) 'Political Correlates of Television Viewing', *Public Opinion Quarterly*, 48(1): 283–300.

Gerbner, G., Gross, L., Morgan, M. and Signorielli, N. (1986) 'Living With Television: The Dynamics of the Cultivation

Process', in J. Bryant and D. Zillmann (eds.), *Perspectives on Media Effects.* Hillsdale, NJ: Lawrence Erlbaum Associates. pp. 17–40.

Gerbner, G., Gross, L., Morgan, M., and Signorielli, N. (1980) 'The "Mainstreaming" of America: Violence Profile No. 11', *Journal of Communication*, 30(3): 10–29.

Glynn, C. J., Huge, M., Reineke, J. B., Hardy, B. W. and Shanahan, J. (2007) 'When Oprah Intervenes: Political Correlates of Daytime Talk Show Viewing', *Journal of Broadcasting & Electronic Media*, 51(2): 228–44.

Hampton, K. N., Goulet, L. S., Rainie, L. and Purcell, K. (2011) *Social Networking Sites and Our Lives: How People's Trust, Personal Relationships, and Civic and Political Involvement are Connected to Their Use of Social Networking Sites and Other Technologies.* Washington, DC: Pew Research Center's Internet and American Life Project.

Hess, V. K. (2006) 'Political Apathy Among Young Adults: The Influence of Late-Night Comedy in the 200 Election'. PhD dissertation, University of Washington.

Holbert, R. L. (2005) 'A Typology for the Study of Entertainment Television and Politics', *American Behavioral Scientist*, 49(3): 436–53.

Holbert, R. L., Lambe, J. L., Dudo, A. D. and Carlton, K. A. (2007) 'Primacy Effects of The Daily Show and National TV News Viewing: Young Viewers, Political Gratifications, and Internal Political Self-Efficacy', *Journal of Broadcasting & Electronic Media,* 51(1): 20–38.

Holbert, R. L., Pillion, O., Tschida, D., Armfield, G., Kinder, K., Cherry, K., and Daulton, A. (2003) 'The West Wing as Endorsement of the U. S. Presidency: Expanding the Bounds of Priming in Political Communication', *Journal of Communication*, 53(3): 427–43.

Holbert, R. L., Shah, D. V. and Kwak, N. (2003) 'Political Implications of Prime-Time Drama and Sitcom Use: Genres of Representation and Opinions Concerning Women's Rights', *Journal of Communication*, 53(1): 45–60.

Holbert, R. L. and Hansen, G. J. (2006) 'Fahrenheit 9–11, Need for Closure and the Priming of Affective Ambivalence: An Assessment of Intra-Affective Structures by Party Identification', *Human Communication Research*, 32(2): 109–29.

Holbrook, R. A. and Hill, T. G. (2005) 'Agenda Setting and Priming in Prime Time Television: Crime Dramas as Political Cues', *Political Communication*, 22(3): 277–95.

Hollander, B. A. (2005) 'Late Night Learning: Do Entertainment Programs Increase Political Campaign Knowledge for Young Viewers', *Journal of Broadcasting and Electronic Media*, 49(4): 402–15.

Hooghe, M. (2002) 'Watching Television and Civic Engagement: Disentangling the Effects of Time, Programs, and Stations', *Harvard International Journal of Press/Politics*, 7(2): 84–104.

Horkheimer, M. and Adorno, T. W. (1947/2002) *Dialectic of Enlightenment: Philosophical Fragments*, in G. S. Noerr (ed.) and E. Jephcott (trans.). Stanford, CA: Stanford University Press.

Jackson, D. J. (2007) 'Selling Politics: The Impact of Celebrities' Political Beliefs on Young Americans', *Journal of Political Marketing*, 6(4): 67–83.

Jackson, D. J. and Darrow, T. I. A. (2005) 'The Influence of Celebrity Endorsements on Young Adults' Political Opinions', *Harvard International Journal of Press Politics*, 10(2): 80–98.

Jamieson, K. H. and Cappella, J. N. (2008) *Echo Chamber: Rush Limbaugh and the Conservative Media Establishment.* New York: Oxford University Press.

Johnson, T. J. and Kaye, B. K. (2003) 'Around the World Wide Web in 80 Ways: How Motives for Going Online are Linked to Internet Activities Among Politically Interested Internet Users', *Social Science Computer Review*, 21(3): 304–25.

Kaye, B. K. and Johnson, T. J. (2002) 'Online and in the Know: Uses and Gratifications of the Web for Political Information', *Journal of Broadcasting and Electronic Media*, 46(1): 54–71.

Kim, S. and Han, M. (2005) 'Media Use and Participatory Democracy in South Korea', *Mass Communication & Society*, 8(2): 133–53.

Kim, Y. M. and Vishak, J. (2008) 'Just Laugh You Don't Need to Remember: The Effects of Entertainment Media on Political Information Acquisition and Information Processing in Political Judgment', *Journal of Communication*, 58(2): 338–60.

Kaid, L. L. (ed.) (2004) *Handbook of Political Communication Research.* Mahwah, NJ: Lawrence Erlbaum Associates.

Keum, H., Devanathan, S., Deshpande, S., Nelson, M. R. and Shah, D. V. (2004) 'The Citizen-Consumer: Media Effects at the Intersection of Consumer and Civic Culture', *Political Communication*, 21(3): 369–91.

Kraidy, M. (2009) *Reality Television and Arab Politics: Contention in Public Life.* New York: Cambridge University Press.

Kraut, R. E., Kiesler, S., Mukhopadhyay, T., Scherlis, W., and Patterson, M. (1998) 'Social Impact of the Internet: What Does It Mean', *Communications of the ACM*, 41(12): 21–22.

Kubey, R. and Csikszentmihalyi, M. (1990) *Television and the Quality of Life: How Viewing Shapes Everyday Experience.* Hillsdale, NJ: Lawrence Erlbaum Associates.

Lasorsa, D. L. (1989) 'Real and Perceived Effects of Amerika', *Journalism Quarterly*, 66(2): 373–78.

Lasswell, H. D (1927) *Propaganda Technique in the World War.* London: Kegan Paul, Trench, Trubner & Co., Ltd.

Lee, F. L. (2007) 'Talk Radio Listening, Opinion Expression and Political Discussion in a Democratizing Society', *Asian Journal of Communication*, 17(1): 78–96.

Lenart, S. and McGraw, K. M. (1989) 'America Watches Amerika: Television Docudramas and Political Attitudes', *Journal of Politics*, 51(3): 697–713.

Morgan, M., Shanahan, J. and Signorielli, N. (2009) 'Growing Up With Television: Cultivation Processes', in J. Brant and M. B. Oliver (eds.), *Media Effects: Advances in Theory and Research.* New York: Routledge. pp. 34–49.

Morgan, M. and Shanahan, J. (1992) 'Television Viewing and Voting 1972–1989', *Electoral Studies*, 11(1): 3–20.

Morgan, M. and Shanahan, J. (1997) 'Two Decades of Cultivation Research: An Appraisal and Meta-analysis', in B.R. Burleson (ed.), *Communication Yearbook 20.* Thousand Oaks, CA: Sage. pp. 1–45.

Moy, P. and Scheufele, D. A. (2000) 'Media Effects on Political and Social Trust', *Journalism and Mass Communication Quarterly*, 77(4): 744–59.

Moy, P., Xenos, M. A. and Hess, V. K. (2005a) 'Communication and Citizenship: Mapping the Political Effects of Infotainment', *Mass Communication & Society*, 8(2): 111–31.

Moy, P., Xenos, M. A. and Hess, V. K. (2005b) 'Priming Effects of Late-Night Comedy', *International Journal of Public Opinion Research*, 18(2): 198–210.

Nabi, R., Moyer-Guse, E. and Byrne, S. (2007) 'All Joking Aside: A Serious Investigation into the Persuasive Effect of Funny Social Issue Messages', *Communication Monographs*, 74(1): 29–54.

Nie, N. and Erbring, L. (2000) 'Internet and Society: A Preliminary Report', Stanford Institute for the Quantitative Study of Society. Stanford University.

Norris, P. (1996) 'Does Television Erode Social Capital: A Reply to Putnam', *PS: Political Science and Politics*, 29(3): 474–79.

Norris, P. (1999) 'The Impact of Television on Civic Malaise', in P. Norris, J. Curtice, D. Sanders, M. Scammell and H. Semetko (eds.), *On Message: Communicating the Campaign*. Thousand Oaks, CA: Sage.

Pasek, J., Kenski, K., Romer, D. and Jamieson, K. H. (2006) 'America's Youth and Community Engagement: How Use of the Mass Media is Related to Civic Activity and Political Awareness in 14 to 22 Year Olds', *Communication Research*, 33(3): 115–35.

Pew Research Center for the People and the Press (2008) 'Key News Audiences Now Blend Online and Traditional Sources Audience Segments in a Changing News Environment', http://people-press.org/report/444/news-media

Prior, M. (2003) 'Any Good News in Soft News? The Impact of Soft News Preference on Political Knowledge', *Political Communication*, 20(2): 149–71.

Prior, M. (2005) 'News Versus Entertainment: How Increasing Media Choice Widens the Gap in Political Knowledge and Turnout', *American Journal of Political Science*, 49(3): 577–92.

Prior, M. (2007) *Post-Broadcast Democracy: How Media Choice Increases Inequality in Political Involvement and Polarizes Elections*. New York: Cambridge University Press.

Project for Excellence in Journalism (2009) 'State of the News Media: An Annual Report on American Journalism', http://www.stateofthenewsmedia.com/2009/index.htm

Putnam, R. (1995a) 'Bowling Alone: America's Declining Social Capital', *The Journal of Democracy*, 6(1): 65–78.

Putnam, R. (1995b) 'Tuning in, Tuning Out: The Strange Disappearance of Social Capital in America', *PS: Political Science and Politics*, 28(4): 664–83.

Putnam, R. (2000) *Bowling Alone*. New York: Simon and Schuster.

Rahn, W. and Transue, J. (1998) 'Social Trust and Value Change: The Decline of Social Capital in American Youth, 1976–1995', *Political Psychology*, 19(3): 545–65.

Scheufele, D. A. and Nisbet, M. C. (2002) 'Being a Citizen Online: New Opportunities and Dead Ends', *Harvard International Journal of Press/Politics*, 7(3): 55–75.

Schiller, H. (1976) *Communication and Cultural Domination*. White Plains, NY: International Arts and Sciences Press.

Shah, D. V., Kwak, N. and Holbert, R. L. (2001) '"Connecting" and "Disconnecting" with Civic Life: Patterns of Internet Use and the Production of Social Capital', *Political Communication*, 18(2): 141–62.

Sidney, S., Sternfeld, B., Haskell, W. L., Jacobs, D. R., Chesney, M. A. and Hulley, S. B. (1996) 'Television Viewing and Cardiovascular Risk Factors in Young Adults: The CARDIA study', *Annals of Epidemiology*, 6(2): 154–59.

Singhal, A. and Rogers, E. (1999) *Entertainment-Education: A Communication Strategy for Social Change*. Mahwah, NJ: Lawrence Erlbaum Associates.

Sweetser, K. D. and Kaid, L. L. (2008) 'Stealth Soapboxes: Political Information Efficacy, Cynicism and Uses of Celebrity Weblogs among Readers', *New Media & Society*, 10(1): 67–91.

Tunstall, J. (1977) *The Media Are American*. New York: Columbia University Press.

US Census Bureau (2009) Statistical Abstract of the United States (128th edn). http://www.census.gov/statab

Uslaner, E. (1995) 'Faith, Hope and Charity: Social Capital, Trust and Collective Action', paper presented at the annual meeting of the American Political Science Association. Chicago, IL.

Williams, D. (2006) 'Groups and Goblins: The Social and Civic Impact of an Online Game', *Journal of Broadcasting and Electronic Media*, 50(4): 651–70.

Young, D. G. (2004) 'Late Night Comedy in Election 2000: Its Influence on Candidate Trait Ratings and the Moderating Effects of Political Knowledge and Partisanship', *Journal of Broadcasting and Electronic Media*, 48(1): 1–22.

Young, D. G. (2008) 'The Privileged Role of the Late-Night Joke: Exploring Humor's Role in Disrupting Argument Scrutiny', *Media Psychology*, 11(1): 119–42.

Young, D. G. and Tisinger, R. M. (2006) 'Dispelling Late-Night Myths: News Consumption among Late-Night Comedy Viewers and the Predictors of Exposure to Various Late-Night Shows', *The Harvard International Journal of Press/Politics*, 11(3): 113–34.

2

Do Cosmopolitan Communications Threaten Traditional Moral Values?

Pippa Norris and Ronald Inglehart

Most societies have experienced a flood of information from diverse channels originating far beyond local communities and national borders. Ideas and images are transmitted from society to society through terrestrial, cable and satellite television and radio stations, feature films, DVDs and video games, books, newspapers and magazines, advertising bill-boards, the music industry and the audiovisual arts, the digital world of the Internet, websites, Tivo, streaming YouTube videos, iPod players, podcasts, wikis and blogs, as well as through interpersonal connections via mobile cellular and fixed line telephony, social networking websites (like MySpace, Facebook and Twitter), emails, VoIP (Skype) and instant text messaging. The world has come to our front door.

These profound changes are widely observed. But the consequences – especially the impact of the penetration of the mass media into geographically isolated cultures, which were previously stranded at the periphery of modern communication grids – are far from clear. What happens to communities living in distant rural villages in Bhutan, as well as far-flung districts and remote provinces in Burkina Faso, Burma and Afghanistan, once the world connects directly to these places and people living in these places learn more about the world? In particular, will this process generate cultural convergence around modern social values and is national diversity threatened?

Multiple studies have documented the growth of cosmopolitan communications, in which technological, structural and economic developments have expanded the pace and density of cross-border information flows. Despite extensive speculation and debate, little has been established about the consequences of this development on national cultures. This chapter focuses on one of the most important ways that cosmopolitan communications may potentially affect citizens, through reshaping traditional moral values, such as those concerning sexuality, religiosity and marriage, in conservative national cultures. Part I outlines the theoretical debate surrounding these issues and reviews the previous empirical literature. Part II outlines the components of moral values and how these can be compared cross-nationally using individual-level data from the most recent wave of the World Values Survey conducted in 2005–7. The comparative research design examines the impact of regular use of a variety of news sources, including newspapers, radio/television news and the Internet, in pooled models containing data from over 50 nations. The impact of news media exposure is compared in Part III using multilevel models. The conclusion summarizes the major findings, considers certain important qualifications and considers their implications.

THEORIES OF COSMOPOLITAN COMMUNICATIONS

Debate about the supposed peril arising from 'cultural imperialism', 'Coca-colonization' or 'McDonalization' has raged for almost half a century. Nor is this a dated remnant of the Cold War era; new protectionist cultural policies have been implemented during the last few years, including by UNESCO and the European Union. Yet the basic assumptions underlying the assumed threat of cultural imperialism on national cultures need to be challenges and reframed. We theorize that the expansion of information flowing primarily from the global North to South will have the greatest impact on modernizing values in cosmopolitan societies characterized by integration into world markets, freedom of the press and widespread access to the media. Parochial societies lacking these conditions are less likely to be affected by these developments. Moreover within countries, many poorer sectors continue to lack the resources and skills necessary to access modern communication technologies. Important social psychological barriers further limit the capacity of the media to alter enduring values and attitudes. By neglecting the role of these sequential firewalls, the risks to national cultural diversity have commonly been exaggerated. These conditions are not simply confined to the most hermetically sealed and rigidly controlled autocracies, such as Burma and North Korea, or to isolated villages and provincial communities off the mass communications grid in Tibet, Bhutan and Mali; instead these barriers are ubiquitous in many parts of the world.

The Influence of the Mass Media on Social Values

Theories of powerful media effects assume that a wide range of social values and behavioral practices are learnt from the ideas and images typically carried in popular television entertainment, glossy magazines, websites, music videos, consumer advertising, feature films and news reports. In particular, cultivation theories developed by Gerbner and his colleagues treat the mass media as one of the standard agencies of socialization, rivaling the role of parents and the family, peer-groups, teachers and religious authorities, and social norms operating within the local community and national culture (Gerbner et al., 1994). Socialization is a multidimensional process involving the acquisition of knowledge, attitudes and values. In particular, cultivation theory emphasizes that frequency of exposure to the mass media, especially television viewing, leads toward the internalization of the messages. Through this process, the media are thought capable of shaping moral values, including attitudes toward the family, marriage and divorce, orientations toward sex roles, support for gender equality and tolerance of sexual diversity as well as shaping broader religious values, beliefs and practices. Regular exposure to messages conveyed by mass communications is believed to have a cumulative effect upon moral values and behavior, with a particularly influential role upon impressionable young children and adolescents during their formative years as they transition to adulthood (Buerkel-Rothfuss and Mayes, 1981).

There are several reasons why sexual socialization, in particular, may be influenced by mass communications, affecting everything learnt about sexuality from the biology of reproduction and the risks of sexual behavior to attitudes toward love, romantic relationships and marriage. First, sexuality is pervasive throughout the Western media (Strasburger and Donnerstein, 1999). From prime-time television sitcoms and dramas to feature films and magazines, for example, the media present countless verbal and visual examples of how dating, intimacy, sex, love, marriage, divorce and romantic relationships are handled. Content analysis studies have shown that the explicit depiction of sexuality has become more common in popular American television entertainment over the years. For example, a longitudinal analysis of US broadcast and cable channels from 1997 to 2002 documented that talk about sex was shown more often than sexual behavior, though both types of contents increased significantly during the period under review; for example, the percentage of shows portraying sexual intercourse doubled from 7 to 14% (Kunkel et al., 2007).

Content analysis of mainstream magazines has also documented increasingly graphic sexual images and messages; for example, the discussion of intimate relationships makes the largest category of topics covered in women's magazines, and references to sexual issues rose in recent decades (Duffy and Gotcher, 1996; Scott, 1986). Hollywood feature films are also commonly sexualized; one study of the 50 top-grossing films of 1996 indicated that almost two-thirds contained at least one sex scene (Bufkin and Eschholz, 2000). Images in music videos also reflect these patterns; up to three-quarters of all music videos are estimated to contain implicit sexual imagery (Baxter et al., 1985). Sexuality is pervasive in mass advertising, whether through images of explicit beauty products or else used as a mechanism to sell everything from cars to consumer durables, and this type of content has also been found to have grown over time (Reichert et al., 1999).

Yet the proportion and explicitness of sexually graphic contents available in the traditional mainstream media pales in comparison to the contents of online pornography on adult websites, which studies suggest are widely accessed by young people in the USA (Carroll et al., 2008; Wolak et al., 2007). It is difficult to determine the extent of sex on the Internet with any degree of reliability nevertheless estimates suggest that the pornography industry generated worldwide revenues of US$97 billion in 2006, with an estimated 4.2 million pornographic websites (representing 12% of all websites), attracting on average 75 million unique visitors per month (Ropelato, 2008). Sexualized contents in popular entertainment are therefore pervasive in the contemporary mass media. This material is also widely consumed, especially among the adolescent population; surveys suggest that young people in the USA spend more time engaged with the mass media than they typically spend either in school or interacting with their parents (Hofferth and Sandberg, 2001).

In addition to sexual socialization, mass communications may also affect the acquisition of many other broader moral, ethical and religious values. Investigative journalists report extensively about financial and sexual scandals, in their watchdog role, such as headlining stories of corruption and bribery in public life (Lull and Hinerman, 1998; Thompson, 2000). This coverage may shape public perceptions about standards in public life, such as attitudes toward transparency and probity, as well as trust in political institutions and leaders. The news headlines also report stories about many contemporary issues surrounding the politics of sex and gender, such as controversial debates surrounding abortion and contraception, euthanasia, stem cell research, sexually transmitted diseases and HIV/AIDS, women's equality and the women's movement, homosexual rights, gay marriage and the role of gays in the military (Castañeda and Campbell, 2006; Norris, 1997). Again this coverage may be expected to influence public opinion, such as liberal attitudes of tolerance toward homosexuality, abortion and divorce, as well as attitudes toward the appropriate division of sex roles for women and men in the home, workplace and public sphere, and attitudes toward gender equality (Norris, 1997; Poindexter et al., 2007). A growing body of literature has also documented how the mass media also commonly touch many broader aspects of religiosity, in the USA and elsewhere (de Vries and Weber, 2001; Hoover, 2006; Hoover and Clark, 2002; Meyer and Moors, 2005). This process occurs through explicit use of mass communications by religious groups and authorities, such as proselytizing radio and television broadcasts, printed publications, cassette tapes,

television talk shows, Internet social networking websites, soap operas and documentary films. It also happens through the mainstream media's implicit framing of wider issues of religion and spirituality, for example, in the values conveyed through routine news reports about science and technology, the depiction of religious minorities or coverage of international affairs (Badaracco, 2004). Mass communications can thereby potentially shape the strength of religious values, identities and beliefs in society.

The belief that moral values and social norms are shaped by media messages is not simply theoretical; instead these assumptions underpin many of the fears about the impact of Western/US television on developing societies, encouraging government agencies to implement policies of cultural protectionism. Societies often limit the importation of certain types of cultural products which are defined to provide an offense to public decency, such as laws against trafficking in child pornography (Akdeniz, 2008; Barendt 2005). Many countries have official rating systems classifying the contents of movies, designed to inform parents and to protect young people. Even in relatively liberal countries with a strong tradition of free speech, such as the UK and USA, broadcaster self-censorship, government regulation, viewer councils and sometimes pressures from commercial sponsors also limit certain types of television programming being shown if they are deemed to offend standards of 'decency' and 'good taste', for example, in terms of language and offensive speech, violence or obscenity (Arthurs, 2004; Bauder, 2007; Silverman, 2007). Many nations also attempt to ban pornography, including Iran, Syria, Bahrain, Egypt, UAE, Kuwait, Malaysia, Indonesia, Singapore, Kenya, India, Cuba and China. The most conservative countries exercise the strictest limits on foreign imports, for example, the Saudi state uses filters to prevent Internet contents 'which breaches public decency' or 'which infringes the sanctity of Islam', and breaches of these standards are also subject to criminal law (Diebert et al., 2008).

Despite the pervasiveness of moral and social values in the media, systematic evidence establishing the relative impact of these messages on public opinion is far from conclusive. For example, much social psychological research about the acquisition of sexual attitudes and values has been based upon experimental studies conducted among the US student population, although it is not clear how far it is possible to generalize from this particular group to other peoples and places. A comprehensive meta-analysis reviewing the empirical literature on this topic in the USA suggests that, compared with the thousands of studies about the influence of violence in the media, far less is known with any certainty about the impact of mass communications on the process of sexual socialization and the acquisition of broader moral values (Ward, 2003). The literature review concluded that social science has failed to establish a direct connection between the total amount of television viewing and subsequent patterns of sexual behavior and experiences. The use of more specific programming genres, such as viewing music videos or soaps, has reported slightly stronger but still limited results on sexual attitudes, expectations and behaviors. The direct link between use of the media and any subsequent moral attitudes is difficult to establish through experimental or correlational research techniques, and it is even more problematic to trace the indirect consequences for behavior.

Moreover, rather than assuming a simple 'hypodermic needle' effect from frequency of viewing to the absorption of messages, as cultivation theories presuppose, research needs to take account of two-way interaction effects which arise from the selection of which materials to consume (soap operas or documentaries? Reality TV or news?), and also the ways that media messages interact with existing predispositions, cultural standards and direct personal experiences (Steele and Browne, 1995). For example, religious predispositions and moral values affect media choices, such as listening to conservative talk radio stations or tuning into religious television broadcasts, as well as possibly being reinforced by this exposure (German, 2007).

Most mass communications and social psychological research has focused on examining the media content and the audience effects of the media in the USA and Europe, yet the cross-national evidence about developing societies remains scarce. If social, sexual and moral values are indeed shaped by mass communications, then these effects should be most clearly evident where Western media, reflecting relatively liberal orientations, penetrate the most traditional conservative cultures. This chapter therefore scrutinizes the effects of media use on a wide range of social values, and examines whether any effects arising from this process are especially powerful in societies that are most open to cosmopolitan information flows.

RESEARCH DESIGN, CONCEPTS AND MEASURES

To estimate the effects of media exposure on a wide range of social and moral values, we first need to establish suitable evidence and measures.

We first need to classify the extent to which societies are open to information flows across national borders.

The idea of *cosmopolitan communications* is conceptualized here to represent the degree of information flowing across national borders, including the extent to which people interact today within a single global community, or whether these networks remain more localized and parochial (Hannerz, 1990; Vertovec and Cohen, 2002). The term 'cosmopolitan' and 'parochial' is employed here descriptively without implying any normative judgment about either type of society. Cosmopolitan communications is understood as openness toward ideas and information derived from divergent cultures, deepening awareness of other places and peoples, including their languages, habits and customs. Greater understanding and broader knowledge about other countries is generally viewed as desirable, but it can also be seen as reflecting a superficial smattering of familiarity with world cultures, and the loss of identity. There are also some recognized advantages to being deeply immersed within dense communication networks rooted within one particular local community. In practice, all contemporary societies reflect a mix of local and global information sources, and there are important variations among social sectors within countries. But there is also a recognizable continuum stretching from the most isolated and parochial societies at the periphery of communication networks, at one extreme, exemplified by rural and illiterate groups living in Myanmar (Burma), North Korea, Syria and Rwanda, to the other extreme, consisting of highly educated groups in Switzerland, Luxembourg and Sweden, that are densely interconnected with information flows from the rest of the world.

The idea of cosmopolitan communications is operationalized in terms of three closely related aspects. *External barriers* include the degree to which national borders are open or closed, whether imports of cultural goods and services are limited by tariffs, taxes or domestic subsidies, and the extent to which there are restrictions on the movement of people through international travel, tourism and labor mobility. To compare the extent to which countries are integrated into international networks, we draw upon the KOF Globalization Index. This provides comprehensive annual indicators of the degree of economic, social and political globalization in 120 countries around the world since the early 1970s (Dreher et al., 2008).

Internal barriers arise from limits on media freedom within societies that also restrict the flow of news and information, including through the legal framework governing freedom of expression and information (such as penalties for press offences); patterns of intimidation affecting journalists and the news media (such as imprisonment, deportation or harassment of reporters) and the nature of state intervention in the media (such as state monopolies of broadcasting, political control over news and the use of official censorship). The most isolationist regimes seek to control domestic public opinion through rigid censorship of any channels of external information, controlling state broadcasting and limiting access to foreign news. To measure the free flow of news and information internally within each society, we draw upon annual estimates of media freedom developed by Freedom House.[1]

Finally, *economic underdevelopment* is also an important barrier to information; poorer nations generally lack modern communication infrastructures, such as an efficient telecommunication sector and a well-developed, multi-channel broadcasting service, and large sectors of the population in these countries often do not have the resources or skills to access media technologies. To compare national levels of media access, we monitor differences in economic development, measured by per capita GDP in purchasing power parity. Economic development is closely correlated with patterns of media access. In combination, these three factors are combined to develop the Cosmopolitanism Index, which is operationalized, tested for reliability and then applied to compare and classify societies. Figure 2.1 presents the global rankings in 2005, from the most cosmopolitan to the most parochial societies worldwide.

Moral Values

To examine moral values, principle components factor analysis with varimax rotation was used to examine the underlying attitudinal dimensions of 21 items included in the fifth wave of the World Values Survey. The items are listed in Table 2.1 and the results show the five attitudinal dimensions that emerged. The first concerns sexual and moral values, utilizing where respondents placed themselves on 10-point scales ranging from 'never justified' to 'always justifiable' concerning a series of items about abortion, divorce, homosexuality, prostitution, euthanasia and suicide. The second dimension used a similar set of items to monitor attitudes toward ethical standards in public life, including the justifiability of cheating on taxes, avoiding paying a fare on public transport, falsely claiming government benefits and accepting a bribe. The third dimension concerned religious values (the importance of God, the importance of religion), religious practices (including whether the person took some moments of prayer or meditation, and the

frequency of attendance at religious services) and whether people identified as religious. In previous research, these items emerged as some of the most important aspects of religiosity, applicable in many different types of societies and faiths, and they have been widely used as standard measures in the literature on the sociology of religion (Norris and Inglehart, 2004). The fourth concerned attitudes toward gender equality, in work, politics and education. These items have also been used before to tap orientations toward sex roles for women and men in many different cultures (Inglehart and Norris, 2003). Finally, three items formed the final dimension concerning attitudes toward family and marriage. Since the responses in each of these dimensions were highly intercorrelated, these items were combined and the resulting scales were standardized to 100-point scales for ease of comparison.

ANALYSIS AND RESULTS

We can start by comparing the mean distribution of responses on these scales for low, moderate and high news media users living in both parochial and cosmopolitan societies, without any prior controls. Analysis of variance (ANOVA) was used to assess the significance and strength of the difference among groups. As shown in Table 2.2, there were moderately strong and significant differences for those living in parochial and cosmopolitan societies for all the value scales except for those concerning family values, where there was no significant difference. Moreover these values also varied in a fairly consistent pattern among types of media users. As shown in Figure 2.2, illustrating the variations for the battery of items concerning sexual and moral values, such as whether homosexuality, abortion and divorce are justifiable, the heaviest news media users proved the most liberal toward these values in both types of society, but the gap by media use was largest (17 percentage points) within cosmopolitan nations. This mirrors the pattern found in terms of religiosity, as illustrated in Figure 2.3, where here media users proved usually the most secular, and again the largest gap (19 points) lay within cosmopolitan societies. Similar results can be seen for responses toward gender equality in Figure 2.4, with media users in cosmopolitan societies the most egalitarian in their perceptions of the appropriate roles for men and women in education, the workforce and politics as well as expressing liberal family values. Again, similar patterns are evident in disapproval of low ethical standards, such as cheating on taxes, falsely claiming government benefits or accepting bribery,

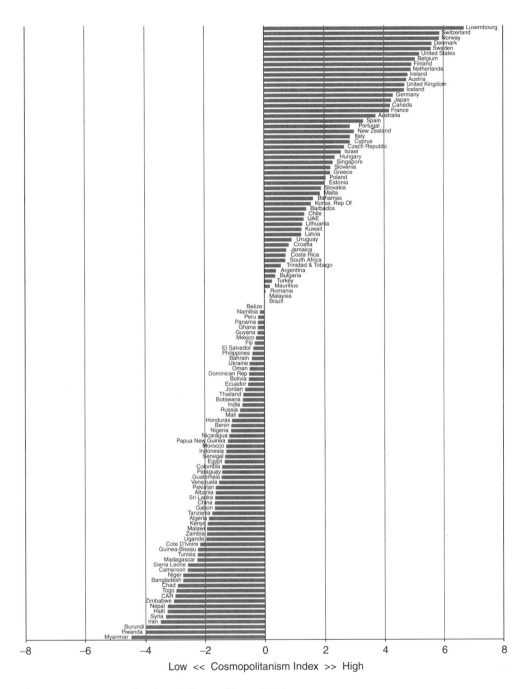

Figure 2.1 Cosmopolitanism Index rankings, 2005
Note: The Cosmopolitanism Index is conceptualized as the permeability of societies to information flows and it is constructed according to levels of globalization, media freedom and economic development, with all indices standardized. See text for details.

Table 2.1 Dimensions of social and moral values

	Liberal sexual and moral values	Tolerate low ethical standards in public life	Religious values and practices	Egalitarian gender equality values	Liberal family values
Justifiable: abortion	0.806				
Justifiable: divorce	0.782				
Justifiable: homosexuality	0.767				
Justifiable: prostitution	0.735				
Justifiable: euthanasia	0.704				
Justifiable: suicide	0.625				
Justifiable: cheating on taxes		0.818			
Justifiable: avoiding a fare on public transport		0.803			
Justifiable: claiming government benefits		0.783			
Justifiable: someone accepting a bribe		0.769			
Importance of God			0.819		
Religious identity			0.782		
Takes moments of prayer, meditation…			0.770		
Religion important in life			0.752		
Often attend religious services			0.682		
Men make better business executives than women do (disagree)				0.865	
Men make better political leaders than women (disagree)				0.828	
University more important for a boy than a girl (disagree)				0.779	
Woman as a single parent (approve)					0.741
Family important in life (disagree)					0.588
Marriage is an out-dated institution (agree)					0.488
Proportion of variance	*17.8*	*13.2*	*14.9*	*10.7*	*5.8*

Notes: Factor analysis extraction method: principal component analysis. Rotation method: varimax with Kaiser normalization. Coefficients of 0.40 or less were dropped from the analysis. See Appendix A for the specific items and the construction of the scales.
Source: World Values Survey 2005–7.

although heavier media users in cosmopolitan standards reject these practices by only a modest margin over lower media users.

Nevertheless, multilevel regression analysis is needed to see whether these initial observations are confirmed after controlling for the social characteristics of media users. Table 2.3 presents the results of separate models run for each value scale, including the individual level demographic characteristics and socioeconomic resources, plus news media use, as well as the national-level Cosmopolitan Index, and the cross-level interaction effect combining using the media with living in a more cosmopolitan society. The individual-level results largely confirm the observations suggested from comparing the descriptive means; even after controlling for education, age and income, individual use of the news media was significantly linked to more tolerant and liberal orientations toward sexual and moral values, to disapproval of unethical standards in public life, to more secular orientations, to supporting gender equality and to liberal family values. The strength of the coefficients for media use varied across the different value scales, but in all cases the results proved statistically significant. As previous studies have commonly reported, younger people and the better educated also proved consistently more liberal toward sexual and moral values, family values and gender equality, less tolerant of low ethical standards in public life, and more secular in their values and practices.

At the national level, living in a more cosmopolitan society was also significantly linked to

Table 2.2   Values by type of society and media use

Type of society	Media use 3-pt categorized	Liberal sexual and moral values	Tolerate low ethical standards in public life	Religious values and practices	Egalitarian gender equality values	Liberal family values
Parochial	Low	27	25	86	66	67
	Moderate	33	28	81	70	70
	High	34	26	80	70	70
	Total	**31**	**27**	**83**	**68**	**69**
Cosmopolitan	Low	32	25	79	64	63
	Moderate	43	22	65	73	69
	High	49	21	60	78	72
	Total	**43**	**22**	**66**	**73**	**69**
Total	Low	29	25	84	65	66
	Moderate	38	25	75	71	69
	High	43	23	69	75	71
	Total	**37**	**25**	**76**	**70**	**69**
Strength of association		0.269***	0.116***	0.327***	0.110***	0.003

Note: The mean position of categories of media users on the 100-point value scales by type of society, no controls. See Table 8.1 for the items used in the construction of the scales. ANOVA was used to assess the strength of association (eta) and the statistical significance of the difference between types of society. ***$p = 0.001$.
Source: World Values Survey 2005–7.

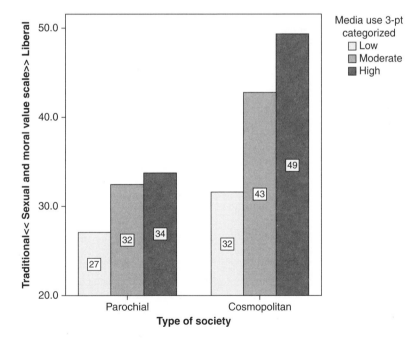

Figure 2.2   Social and moral values by media use and type of society
Note: The mean position of categories of media users on the 100-point value scales by type of society, no controls. See Table 8.1 for the items used in the construction of the scales.
Source: World Values Survey 2005–7.

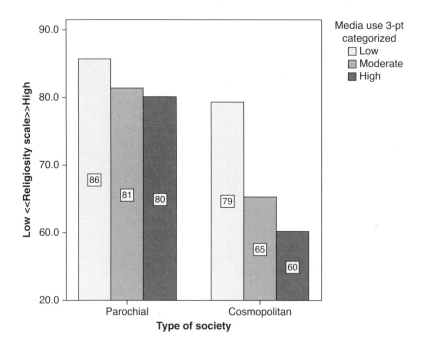

Figure 2.3   Religiosity by media use and type of society
Note: The mean position of categories of media users on the 100-point value scales by type
of society, no controls. See Table 8.1 for the items used in the construction of the scales.
Source: World Values Survey 2005–7.

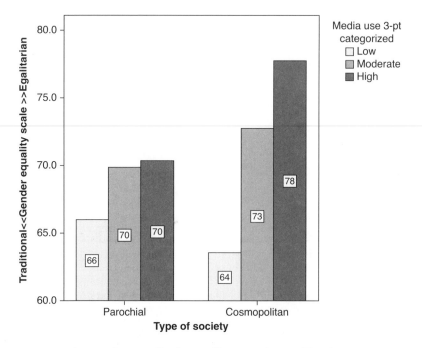

Figure 2.4   Support for gender equality by media use and type of society
Note: The mean position of categories of media users on the 100-point value scales by type
of society, no controls. See Table 8.1 for the items used in the construction of the scales.
Source: World Values Survey 2005–7.

Table 2.3   Multilevel regression models explaining social values

	Liberal sexual and moral values	Tolerate low ethical standards in public life	Religious values and practices	Egalitarian gender equality values	Liberal family values
Demographic characteristics					
Age (years)	**−2.17*****	**−2.34*****	**3.46*****	**−0.951*****	**−1.52*****
	(0.099)	(0.083)	(0.113)	(0.081)	(0.075)
Gender (male = 1)	0.064	**0.725*****	**−3.05*****	**−3.60*****	**−0.679*****
	(0.090)	(0.075)	(0.103)	(0.074)	(0.068)
Socioeconomic resources					
Household income 10-pt scale	**1.25*****	**0.481*****	**−0.507*****	**0.351*****	**0.721*****
	(0.107)	(0.090)	(0.124)	(0.088)	(0.082)
Education 9-pt scale	**1.66*****	**−0.850*****	**−0.495*****	**2.283*****	**0.291*****
	(0.115)	(0.097)	(0.134)	(0.094)	(0.088)
Media use					
News media use scale	**0.936*****	**−0.443*****	**-0.277***	**0.867*****	**0.780*****
	(0.112)	(0.094)	(0.131)	(0.092)	(0.086)
Cosmopolitanism index	**8.84*****	−1.40	**−9.39****	**4.64*****	1.70
(globalization + development + freedom)	(1.47)	(1.77)	(2.42)	(1.14)	(1.18)
Cosmopolitanism* media use scale	**0.569*****	−0.055	0.158	**−0.190***	0.021
	(0.109)	(0.092)	(0.123)	(0.090)	(0.085)
Constant (intercept)	38.5	25.4	72.8	71.0	69.4
Schwartz BIC	380,457	379,100	319,932	387,905	328,937
No. respondents	43,088	44,565	35,826	45,755	40,198
No. nations	37	37	30	38	33

Note: All independent variables were standardized using mean centering (z-scores). Models present the results of the REML multilevel regression models (for details, see Appendix C) including the beta coefficient (the standard error below in paren-thesis) and the significance. The 100-point scales are constructed from the items listed in Table 8.1. The 100-point media use scale combined use of newspapers, radio/television news, the Internet, books and magazines. $*p = 0.05$; $**p = 0.01$; $***p = 0.001$. See Appendix A for details about the measurement, coding and construction of all variables. Significant coefficients are highlighted in **bold**.
Source: World Values Survey 2005–7.

Table 2.4   Multilevel regression models explaining liberal sexual and moral values

	Cosmopolitanism index	Globalization index	Economic development	Media Freedom	Media access
Demographic characteristics					
Age (years)	−2.17***	−2.17***	−2.17***	−2.17***	−2.17***
	(0.099)	(0.099)	(0.099)	(0.099)	(0.099)
Gender (male = 1)	0.064	0.064	0.064	0.064	0.064
	(0.090)	(0.090)	(0.090)	(0.090)	(0.090)
Socioeconomic resources					
Household income 10-pt scale	1.25***	1.25***	1.25***	1.25***	1.25***
	(0.107)	(0.107)	(0.107)	(0.107)	(0.107)
Education 9-pt scale	1.66***	1.66***	1.66***	1.66***	1.66***
	(0.115)	(0.115)	(0.115)	(0.115)	(0.115)
Media use					
News media use scale	0.936***	0.936***	0.936***	0.936***	0.936***
	(0.112)	(0.112)	(0.112)	(0.112)	(0.112)
Cosmopolitanism index (globalization + development + freedom)	8.84***				
	(1.47)				
Globalization index		10.01***			
		(1.61)			
Economic development			9.14***		
			(1.52)		
Media freedom				10.64***	
				(1.60)	
Societal-level media access					6.65***
					(1.64)
Cosmopolitanism* media use	0.569***	0.579***	0.547***	0.583***	0.649***
	(0.109)	(0.109)	(0.123)	(0.109)	(0.085)
Constant (intercept)	38.5	33.4	38.0	37.0	
Schwartz BIC	380,457	380,455	380,457	380,453	380,457
No. respondents	43,088	43,088	43,088	43,088	43,088
No. nations	37	37	37	37	37

Note: All independent variables were standardized using mean centering (z-scores). Models present the results of the REML multilevel regression models (for details, see Appendix C) including the beta coefficient (the standard error below in parenthesis) and the significance. The 100-point scales are constructed from the items listed in Table 8.1. The 100-point media use scale combined use of newspapers, radio/television news, the Internet, books and magazines. $*p = 0.05$; $**p = 0.01$; $***p = 0.001$. See Appendix A for details about the measurement, coding and construction of all variables. Significant coefficients are highlighted in **bold**.
Source: World Values Survey 2005–7.

more liberal sexual and moral values, to support for gender equality and to more secular values and practices. Previous studies have reported that more affluent post-industrial societies are usually both more egalitarian in their beliefs about the most appropriate roles for women and men, as well as typically less religious than developing societies, with a few notable exceptions (Norris and Inglehart, 2004). In terms of cross-level interaction effects, use of the media in cosmopolitan societies was also significantly linked to stronger liberal sexual and moral values but, unexpectedly, the interactive relationship also proved less egalitarian, not more, toward equality between women and men.

To explore whether the national-level relationships were driven mainly by levels of economic development, or by broader characteristics of more open media systems, models were re-run for the sexual and moral value scale specifying, alternatively, national-levels of globalization, economic development, media freedom and societal-level media use. The results in Table 2.4 show that each of these national-level contextual variables proved strong and significant. The results could not simply be reduced to levels of per capita GDP, however, since both the Globalization Index and the Media Freedom Index proved slightly stronger predictors of social values. Obviously, the correlations which exist among these societal-level variables makes it difficult to disentangle this further, as economic development is closely linked to patterns of media access, levels of integration into global markets and levels of media freedom. But the analysis suggests that any comprehensive explanation should take account of more than the simple impact of economic development alone.

CONCLUSION AND DISCUSSION

Theories of cultural imperialism posit that sexualized messages conveyed by the global mass media will threaten traditional moral values, such as those concerning sexuality and marriage, in more conservative societies. Strong accounts of media effects, including the cultivation theory developed by Gerbner et al. (1994), claim that the frequency of exposure to the mass media, especially habitually watching many hours of television, leads toward the gradual internalization of the messages that are being communicated. Through the long-term process of lifetime socialization, the media are thought capable of influencing many moral standards, especially through the presentation of powerful ideas and images of sexuality, love, the family and marriage, the roles of women

and men and the broader treatment of religion and spirituality. Concern about the potential threat to traditional cultures arising from the values typically contained in Western media, such as the explicit treatment of sexuality contained in movies and entertainment television, have led toward protectionist measures by regulatory agencies. In the most extreme cases, this has led some states toward banning or censoring the contents, and even in democracies with a long tradition protecting freedom of expression, this concern has encouraged policies restricting access to certain types of media contents, designed to protect children and adolescents. But the media are only one agency of socialization and deep-rooted moral values and behavioral norms are acquired through many other sources, such as the influence arising from parents and the family, as well as other role models and experience of growing up in the local community. In highly conservative societies, these agencies may outweigh the images and ideas conveyed by imported cultural products, so that the meaning of more liberal or secular messages can be reinterpreted, or simply rejected, by the audience.

The survey evidence presented in this chapter suggests a consistent relationship linking patterns of media use with moral values; even after introducing controls, those who are most heavily engaged in using the mass media are usually more liberal toward sexual and moral values less tolerant of unethical standards of public life, less religious, more liberal in family values and more egalitarian toward the roles of women and men. At the same time, these relationships are strongest in the more cosmopolitan societies, which are most open to information flows across national borders, while having only limited correlation in the more parochial societies. The strongest interaction concerns sexual and moral values, where greater media use within cosmopolitan societies was associated with more liberal and tolerant orientations towards issues such as homosexuality, divorce and abortion.

Nevertheless, the evidence we have considered, while comparing a comprehensive range of social values using multilevel models in many more societies than previous research, remains limited in certain regards. Most importantly, the cross-national comparisons cannot conclusively establish the direction of causality implied in this relationship; it may be that exposure to the mass media generates more liberal and less traditional value orientations, but self-selection bias is also likely to operate in what people are predisposed to watch or read. As the 'uses and gratification' theory suggests, people actively choose how to spend their leisure time and how the media can best meet their prior interests and needs, such as for information, entertainment, escape or social interaction (Blumler and Katz, 1974). In reality, we believe that a two-way mutually reciprocal interactive process is probably at work here, where prior motivation determines information exposure and then, in turn, media use reinforces cultural values. Without experimental studies, or panel survey data interviewing the same respondents over time, however, it remains impossible to determine how this process works and to prove this hunch. In addition, to establish a more watertight case, further research is required to provide more specific information about particular genres and contents of the mass media which people in the survey regularly accessed, including analyzing cross-cultural variations in the moral and social values typically reflected in television, newspapers, websites and magazines in different countries. We need to know what people are typically watching or reading in far more detail – and over a long-term period to establish cumulative effects. These challenges remain for future research to address.

Nevertheless, the survey evidence analyzed here established the general or diffuse pattern linked with using a wide range of media sources in a diverse range of societies worldwide. Consistently with our overall argument, more liberal and egalitarian moral and social values are associated with exposure to the news media. In this regard, use of mass communications is analogous to the impact of education and age, reinforcing modern values and more tolerant attitudes. These patterns are also found in the more parochial societies, but the strength of these correlations remains more limited. In these places, the combined effects of the lack of economic development, lack of integration into global communication markets and networks, lack of media freedom and lack of media access all limit the degree of cultural change arising from cross-border information flows.

NOTES

1   For more methodological details and results, see Freedom House (2007) *Global Press Freedom 2007*, www.freedomhouse.org. The IREX *Media Sustainability Index* provides another set of indicators (http://www.irex.org/resources/index.asp). The Media Sustainability Index benchmarks the conditions for independent media in a more limited range of countries across Europe, Eurasia, the Middle East, and North Africa. Unfortunately, the IREX index does not contain sufficient number of cases worldwide to provide a further cross-check for this study.

REFERENCES

Akdeniz, Y. (2008) *Internet Child Pornography and the Law: National and International Responses.* Burlington, VT: Ashgate.

Arthurs, J. (2004) *Television and Sexuality: Regulation and the Politics of Taste.* Buckingham: Open University Press.

Badaracco, C. H. (ed.) (2004) *Quoting God: How Media Shape Ideas about Religion and Culture.* Texas: Baylor University Press.

Barendt, E. M. (2005) *Freedom of speech.* 2nd edn. New York: Oxford University Press.

Bauder, J. (ed.) (2007) *Censorship.* Detroit: Greenhaven Press.

Baxter, R. L., De Riemer, C. Landini, A., Leslie, L. and Singletary, M. W. (1985) 'A Content Analysis of Music Videos', *Journal of Broadcasting and Electronic Media*, 29(3): 333–40.

Blumler, J. and Katz, E. (1974) *The Uses of Mass Communication.* Thousand Oaks, CA: Sage.

Buerkel-Rothfuss, N. L. and Mayes, S. (1981) 'Soap Opera Viewing: The Cultivation Effect', *Journal of Communication*, 31(3): 108–15.

Bufkin, J. and Eschholz, S. (2000) 'Images of Sex and Rape: A Content Analysis of Popular Film', *Violence Against Women*, 6(12): 1317–44.

Carroll, J. S., Padilla-Walker, L. M. and Nelson, L. J. (2008) 'Generation XXX – Pornography Acceptance and Use Among Emerging Adults', *Journal of Adolescent Research*, 23(1): 6–30.

Castañeda, L. and Campbell, S. B. (eds.) (2006) *News and Sexuality: Media Portraits of Diversity.* Thousand Oaks, CA: Sage.

de Vries, H. and Weber, S. (eds.) (2001) *Religion and Media.* Stanford, CA: Stanford University Press.

Diebert, R., Palfrey, J., Rohozinski, R. and Zittrain, J. (2008) *Access Denied.* Cambridge, MA: MIT Press.

Dreher, A., Gaston, N. and Martens, P. (2008) *Measuring Globalisation: Gauging Its Consequences.* New York: Springer, http://globalization.kof.ethz.ch/

Duffy, M. and Gotcher, J. M. (1996) 'Crucial Advice on How to Get the Guy: The Rhetorical Vision of Power and Seduction in the Teen Magazine', *Journal of Communication Inquiry*, 20: 32–48.

Gerbner, G., Gross, L., Morgan, M. and Signorielli, N. (1994) 'Growing Up with Television: The Cultivation Perspective', in J. Bryant and D. Zillman (eds.), *Media effects: Advances in Theory and Research.* Hillsdale, NJ: Lawrence Erlbaum Associates, pp. 17–41.

German, M. (2007) *The Paper and the Pew: How Religion Shapes Media Choice.* Lanham, MD: University Press of America.

Hannerz, U. (1990) 'Cosmopolitans and Locals in World Culture', in M. Featherstone (ed.), *Global Culture: Nationalism, Globalization and Modernity.* London: Sage. pp. 237–52.

Hofferth, S. L. and Sandberg, J. F. (2001) 'How American Children Spend their Time', *Journal of Marriage and the Family*, 63(2): 295–308.

Hoover, S. M. (2006) *Religion in the Media Age*. New York: Routledge.

Hoover, S. M. and Clark, L. S. (2002) *Practicing Religion in the Age of the Media*. New York: Columbia University Press.

Inglehart, R. and Norris, P. (2003) *Rising Tide: Gender Equality and Cultural Change Around the World*. Cambridge: Cambridge University Press.

Kunkel, D., Farrar, K. M., Eyal, K., Biely, E., Donnerstein E. and Rideout, V. (2007) 'Sexual Socialization Messages on Entertainment Television: Comparing Content Trends 1997–2002', *Media Psychology*, 9(3): 595–622.

Lull, J. and Hinerman, S. (eds.) (1998) *Media Scandals*. New York: Columbia University Press.

Meyer, B. and Moors, A. (2005) *Religion, Media, and the Public Sphere*. Bloomington, IN: University of Indiana Press.

Norris, P. (ed.) (1997) *Women, Media, and Politics*. New York: Oxford University Press.

Norris, P. and Inglehart, R. (2004) *Sacred and Secular: Religion and Politics Worldwide*. Cambridge: Cambridge University Press.

Poindexter, P., Meraz, S. and Weiss, A. S. (2007) *Women, Men, and News: Divided and Disconnected in the News Media Landscape*. Hillsdale, NJ: Lawrence Erlbaum Associates.

Reichert, R., Lambiase, J., Morgan, S., Carstarphen, M. and Zavoina, S. (1999) 'Cheesecake and Beefcake: No Matter How You Slice It, Sexual Explicitness in Advertising Continues to Increase', *Journalism and Mass Communication Quarterly*, 76(1): 7–20.

Ropelato, J. (2008) 'Internet Pornography Statistics', http://internet-filter-review.toptenreviews.com/internet-pornography-statistics.html#anchor4

Scott, J. E. (1986) 'An Updated Longitudinal Content Analysis of Sex References in Mass Circulation Magazines', *Journal of Sex Research*, 22(3): 385–92.

Silverman, D. S. (2007) *You Can't Air That: Four Cases of Controversy and Censorship in American Television Programming*. Syracuse, NY: University of Syracuse Press.

Steele, J. and Browne, J. D. (1995) 'Adolescent Room Culture: Studying Media in the Context of Everyday Life', *Journal of Youth and Adolescence*, 24(5): 551–76.

Strasburger, V. C. and Donnerstein, E. (1999) 'Children, Adolescents, and the Media: Issues and Solutions', *Pediatrics*, 103(1): 129–39.

Thompson, J. B. (2000) *Political Scandal: Power and Visibility in the Media Age*. Oxford: Polity Press.

Vertovec, S. and Cohen, R. (eds.) (2002) *Conceiving Cosmopolitanism: Theory, Context and Practice*. Oxford: Oxford University Press.

Ward, L. M. (2003) 'Understanding the Role of Entertainment Media in the Sexual Socialization of American Youth: A Review of Empirical Research', *Developmental Review*, 23(3): 347–88.

Wolak, J., Mitchell, K. and Finkelhor, D. (2007) 'Unwanted and Wanted Exposure to Online Pornography in a National Sample of Youth Internet Users', *Pediatrics*, 119(2): 247–57.

3

Political Communication in a Changing Media Environment

Fred Fletcher and Mary Lynn Young

The central social processes of political communication are particularly susceptible to changes in the media environment. At each stage of their development, the modern news media have altered the nature of the public sphere. From the printing press and the emergence of daily newspapers, news services, electronic media and the subsequent dominance of television, and now digital media, each new form of communication has changed the nature of the public discourse that supports modern liberal democracies. In this chapter, we examine the implications of recent trends in global and national media systems for political communication, with particular attention to how they play out in different national contexts.

The comparative study of political communication requires close attention to the role of journalism and the media, however funded and delivered, in the development and functioning of the various forms of liberal democracy (Hallin and Mancini, 2004). The newspaper has often been seen as an essential element in promoting not only electoral democracy and responsive governance but also the development of a deliberative public sphere (see, for example, Starr, 2004; Thompson, 1995). Even those who are committed to a deeper form of democracy regard journalism as 'arguably the most important form of public knowledge in contemporary society' (Hackett and Zhao, 1998: 1). Henry Milner has demonstrated that newspaper reading is related to political knowledge and civic engagement in North America and Europe (Milner, 2007). The decline of the daily newspaper is thus a cause for concern.

While traditional sources of political journalism in established democracies are facing major challenges, many theorists of emerging democracies believe that a free and independent media is essential to post-conflict governance, fair elections and promotion of civil society (LaMay, 2004). Because the USA, though often the source of media innovations, is frequently exceptional – with a weak public media sector, for example – it is important to view developments in global terms.

The media's public sector functions generally include a number of elements that support political communication, such as providing channels for persuasive messages from political parties and civil society advocacy groups, governance-related messages from state institutions informing citizens of services and rights, policy-related information that promotes engagement in public life through deliberation, debate, advocacy and conversations about 'problem solving' (Schudson, 1997), as well as investigative journalism and political commentary. Journalism, public communication about public matters and scrutiny of those holding social power, is in this view crucial to democracy.

When we examine the future of the media in the digital age, it is journalism itself, not a particular genre or delivery system, which should be the focus. As McQuail et al. put it, there is 'sufficient evidence to justify the view that the health of democratic politics depends on the general quality of journalism and the effective working of the press as an institution of public life' (2008: 268). Accepting this viewpoint should not, of course, deflect attention from the limitations of both state-controlled and commercial media and the potential of new and alternative media to increase diversity and challenge established perspectives.

To begin our review of the relationship between democracy and journalism in the global media system, we examine the economics of the media. Economic and democratic elements are inextricably linked and closely related to contemporary challenges to effective journalism and the tension between private interests and public service. It is important to consider the extent to which the challenges to the business models of the mainstream media in the industrial democracies play out globally and what alternative models can contribute to the development of democratic public spheres.

MEDIA ECONOMICS AND ITS RELATIONSHIP TO CITIZENSHIP

For most of its recent history, political communication research globally has devoted a great deal of attention to the relationship between the news media and various sources of power. Much has been written on the relative autonomy of journalism, whether publicly or privately funded, from governments, economic elites and other powerful institutions (like the church or the military). There has also been concern about concentration of media ownership, the commercialization of news services and the impact of the profit motive on the independence of news organizations and on quality journalism (McChesney, 2008). Proponents of deeper forms of democracy have rejoiced in the new opportunities afforded by the Internet, but few imagined the severe erosion in North America and parts of Europe of the daily newspaper, long the backbone of newsgathering systems, both locally and internationally. Political economists worried more about the effects of corporate ownership on democracy than the viability of the enterprises involved.

Increased instability because of global competition, loss of advertising and the uncertain market for 'serious' journalism has forced some newspaper closures in North America and 'rationalization' of the industry in Europe. Broadcasters too are concerned about shifts in audiences and advertising. European media organizations have in many respects taken the lead in consolidating newsrooms, forming news partnerships, while North American media have tried to converge with limited success, shrinking their newsrooms, journalism ambitions and staff (World Editors Forum, 2008). These experiments, multi-media newsrooms, outsourcing of editorial functions, among others, almost all involve fewer journalists and less attention to politics. Nevertheless, privately owned media continue to play an important role in democratic discourse (Bennett and Lawrence, 2008).

The modest but increasing movement of advertising and audiences from newspapers and television broadcasters to the Internet has produced an outpouring of worried commentary not only from business analysts and journalists, but also among media and democracy theorists, some of whom are predicting dire consequences for democracy, including: (1) a reduction in effective scrutiny of government, especially at the local level, and a consequent increase in corruption (Starr, 2009); (2) erosion of both interest in and capacity to undertake serious investigative journalism; (3) the threat to the communication of shared values and the vocabulary of precedents necessary for effective democratic participation/ deliberation, as a result of the growing personalization of communication; (4) an increase in state power over a weakened private media system (McQuail et al., 2008: 172–5; Neuman, 2008: 17–18). Historically, the democratic functions of the news media have been linked to ownership patterns and structures (McChesney, 2008), editorial investment in journalism content (Lacy and Martin, 2004; Lacy and Simon, 1994) and the nature and extent of media competition, which is linked to diversity of voice and opinion (Coulson and Lacy, 1996).

The 20th century business model for the media was based on the role of the press as an intermediary, connecting content, consumers and advertisers. The media flourished for much of the century because they benefited from the existence of a limited number of players, a result of high capital costs, and the limited spectrum available to broadcasters. These limits – and the barriers placed on media flows by public policy that favored domestic content – created zones of 'protectable scarcity' that made media operations highly profitable. These zones have become highly permeable as a result of globalizing delivery systems such as satellite transmission and the Internet (Canadian Media Research Consortium [CMRC], 2009). Even more important, perhaps, is the advent of menu-driven, customizable content delivery and the content sharing applications that have become a major feature of the online world. These developments are unbundling media content. Whether in their roles as consumers or citizens, people with Internet access no longer need to sit through a television newscast or look through a newspaper to get the information they want.

In industrialized democracies, these developments are creating concern not only for the economic viability of the journalistic enterprise but also for the community-building capacity of the new forms that are emerging. The decline in newspaper circulation has gone furthest in North America, with total daily newspaper circulation at barely 40% of households in the USA and Canada (CMRC, 2009). The reduction in newspaper readership – offset somewhat by online readership – has not been as sharp in Europe and, as we will see, circulation is still growing in many parts of the global south. For example, according to the World Association of Newspapers (2008) World Press Trends the five countries with the highest number of paid-for daily newspapers were India (2337 titles), the USA (1422), China (984), Brazil (555) and Russia (510).

The largest growth in the number of paid-for daily newspaper titles globally over the period 2003–7 occurred in Africa and Asia, both up 19%. The number of paid-for daily newspapers during that same period declined in North America (down 1.06%), as did circulation (down 6.39%). Paid-for daily circulation also rose in both Asia (17%) and South America (16%). Nevertheless, newspapers share of the global advertising market declined from 36% in 1995 to 29% in 2006, with the forecast for 2010 at 25%. Not surprisingly, Internet advertising as a proportion of overall advertising is rising globally.

Some analysts view the apparent erosion of the predominance of mainstream media as an opportunity for serious debate about alternatives such as increased government financial support and encouragement for not-for-profit and non-commercial journalism (Nichols and McChesney, 2010). The political economy critique of the established media, for example, has long viewed the media as an impediment to democratic discourse. This perspective is based on research that indicates that: (1) a limited number of major corporations control the media in most democratic countries; (2) commercial imperatives restrict the capacity of profit-oriented media to challenge the social and political status quo; (3) coverage and commentary in the mainstream media offer only limited diversity of opinion (McChesney, 2008).

This analysis focuses on structural and systemic constraints and pays less attention to the agency available to individual journalists. From a democratic perspective, these analysts see more potential in public broadcasting and alternative media (Skinner et al., 2005: 291–303), both of which seem more willing to challenge conventional wisdom and add diversity to public discourse. Prescriptions include increased support for public and alternative media and the argument that quality journalism should be seen as a 'merit good', having social value similar to public education and public libraries (Rotstein, 1988) and as an essential resource for citizenship. The Internet provides an opportunity for a wide range of journalistic options but, as will be seen, there remain problems of access.

GLOBAL MEDIA OWNERSHIP

Beginning in the 1980s, a global media system emerged, challenging domestically owned media systems. According to McChesney and Schiller (2003), media systems leading up to the 1980s were largely national with at least limited public-service functions. By the end of the 20th century, however, a new transnational media system had emerged, with a few major corporations dominating global media flows. Political economists identified approximately 100 major firms, often interconnected in various ways, which controlled the production and distribution of popular culture. In the larger Latin American countries (Mexico, Brazil, Argentina, Venezuela), a single corporation achieved dominant status in the national and regional media markets. These corporations are dominant in news and popular culture and tend to have ties with transnational corporations and the governing elite (McChesney and Schiller, 2003; Sinclair, 2002). With respect to news, the big three Western news services – Reuters, Agence France-Presse (AFP) and the Associated Press (AP) – and the major international broadcasters had disproportionate influence in shaping the news agenda.

The first decade of the 21st century saw even greater changes in the global media environment. Satellite-enabled broadcasting continued to extend its reach, bringing CNN and BBC World to the industrial democracies and the middle classes in most countries. More recently, the Internet brought new forms of news, information and networking to the same populations. At the same time, economic growth and deregulation stimulated rapid expansion of domestic media, especially broadcasting, in many countries in the global south.

These developments in the world's media systems were accompanied by some important changes in global news flows. Although there is a growing interest in international news, fueled in part by diaspora communities in many countries, the Western media have been cutting foreign correspondents. These cuts reflect increasing costs and the growing level of risk faced by foreign reporters (Sreberny and Paterson, 2004: 3–27). Nevertheless, the big three Western news agencies, along with CNN and the BBC, still dominate the news flow and perpetuate basic patterns of coverage: conflict, crisis, focus on 'elite' nations and episodic coverage of the global south (Harcup and O'Neill, 2001).

In the long run, however, the growth of 'contra flows' may be more important. Taking advantage of satellite access, regional services reporting in local languages have grown significantly in the last decade but to date have had only minimal influence on global flows (Thussu, 2007). Their presence, however, has created a competitive situation in which international services – such as Rupert Murdoch's Star-TV – have moved toward hybrid content, featuring languages and the specific interests and cultural sensitivities of target audiences (Chadha and Kavoori, 2000). In his analysis, Straubhaar (2008) concluded that news cannot be detached from national and cultural specificities.

In this new context, the extent of Western dominance may be disputed. Tunstall argues that the majority of total world audience time is spent with domestically produced media and that this share has been increasing as local and regional services have come online and governments invested in media 'as an expression of national culture' (2008: 321). The extent to which more recent developments, including Internet downloading sites and hybrid media forms and content, reinforce or undermine cultural dominance remains an open question. We need to look not only at the programming that audiences pay attention to and download, but also what they post and how they interpret what they consume (Mahtani, 2008).

The biggest impact, perhaps, has come from the increasingly global reach of Al Jazeera. Like a number of more local Arab services, Al Jazeera was founded in response to CNN to provide an Arab perspective on regional and world events and to influence pan-Arab public. Al Jazeera began full service from Qatar in Arabic in 1996 and from its inception stood out among Arab networks for its professionalism (in western terms) and its independence from the state. Its unusual access to Arab dissidents and Al-Qaeda made it an important resource for western news services as well as a counterweight to them in the Middle East. According to Straubhaar (2008: 19), 'Al Jazeera beats CNN so completely in the Arab World' because of 'the cultural specificity or proximity of its news approach, framed within a more specific set of commonly held values and traditions'.

The network became a major player in the global news flow with the advent of its English service in 2006, unlike some other regional services (Wu, 2009). With an international news staff drawn from more than 40 countries, under the direction of Western-trained professionals like Tony Burman, the former head of news at the Canadian Broadcasting Corporation, Al Jazeera offers a highly professional international news service that is now available in more than 130 countries by satellite and cable. Its reporters have access to many parts of the world where there is little coverage by other services. Its presence has arguably influenced other global broadcasters that aspire to reach international audiences to provide more nuanced coverage of world issues (Sakr, 2007).

This review underscores the fact that there are contradictory global political and cultural processes restructuring the media environment: (1) new transnational players, such as Al Jazeera, which are challenging historic news flows and the global north's cultural dominance and (2) the 'gradual deterritorialization' of the public sphere with national media separated from their state environments, with new internal and external sources affecting the formation of public opinion (Hjarvard, 2001: 36). For some analytic purposes, audiences can be divided into a cosmopolitan segment that has access to global news, mostly in English, and an often fragmented regional/local segment that prefers local media.

Comparative research focusing on issues of ownership and cultural imperialism is beginning to stimulate new theoretical perspectives. For example, Zhao's (2000) work on China suggests that state ownership or party control of media can coexist with commercialization and create some journalism innovations at the margins, such as regional newspapers. Elsewhere in Asia, Bannerjee (2002) argues that new satellite technology and cable television along with some market liberalization has destabilized broadcasting monopolies with emerging regional carriers taking advantage of the opening and strengthening local television production and programming. 'The spread and migration of Asian populations during and after the colonial period have constituted strong diasporic populations in many of these countries' (Bannerjee, 2002: 532). As a result there are now several 'geolinguistic markets' in Asia served by regional production centers, as there are in the Spanish-speaking world, and increasingly connected to diaspora communities elsewhere. These developments, according to Bannerjee are 'not a death knell for American domination of the global media landscape' (2002: 533) but rather represent new hybrid forms of news and public affairs programming that reflect elements of both the traditionally dominant western forms and local cultural and political concerns.

Arab countries in the Middle East have seen new forms of liberal commercial television media and/or government-funded broadcast outlets promote 'more professional and pluralistic approaches to news' (Ayish, 2002: 150). In China, the 'regulated marketization' of the press has 'helped to liberate the press from the state' (Zhao, 2000: 21). Yet both Ayish and Zhao are quick to point out the limitations of current media systems, such that for Ayish: 'no matter how professional and independent television is, it cannot replace true political transformations that would ensure participatory governance' (2002: 151).

Some of the most interesting research on emerging democracies in the global south indicates that the media play an important role not only in establishing a healthy public sphere but also in promoting economic and social development. As the GDP increases and the middle class grows, advertising for the domestic market becomes more important, spurring growth in advertising-supported media, which in turn can add diversity to the media environment (van der Wurff et al., 2008). It is not surprising that countries recently experiencing significant economic growth concurrent with market liberalization, such as India, have seen increases in the number of mass communications products. In India, with its long history of relative press freedom, newspaper circulation and television audiences have been growing rapidly (Tharoor, 2009; Thussu, 2005). Unlike industrial democracies, the appetite for news, both print and electronic, appears to be growing.

An active press, with a degree of press freedom, appears to be a necessary condition for democratic development (Inglehart and Norris, 2008: 5). Although the causal relationship is not always clear, the indications that an active media has played an important role can be found in case studies of the former Soviet states (Becker, 2004; McFaul, 2005), Asia (Romano and Bromley, 2005) and Africa (Hyden et al., 2002). The international media also play a role in democratization by drawing attention to human rights issues and through what Rawnsley (2005: 171) calls a demonstration effect, which was particularly important in Eastern Europe. While the media are important for democratization and global coverage can boost the morale of activists and increase their public support, on the ground work by pro-democracy groups is the critical element in promoting democracy (Rawnsley, 2005: 169–71).

The best evidence available suggests that, as Sachs puts it, 'freedom of the press is a crucial element of democratization and itself a catalyst of democratic transition' (2007: 31). Based on an analysis of measures of press freedom in 1993 and degree of democracy in 2003, Sachs (2007) concludes that a free press predicts a democratic future, but only if there is already a degree of liberalization, an opening for pluralistic political discourse. In general, the literature suggests that when state control of information is weakened and media liberalization has begun to take hold, the proliferation of information options reinforces democracy and good governance. Alternatives to state-controlled media take on the watchdog function of journalism, exposing corruption and human rights violations and create a forum for diverse voices to participate in public debate and promote government responsiveness (Inglehart and Norris 2008: 5–6).

India, which has long had a democratic political culture, has experienced a significant growth in media options since the late 1990s. For more than a century, newspapers in India have fostered diversity, public debate, early warning of public unrest and acted as a watchdog on government power, but with a framework that 'supported the role of the state as an instrument of modernity' (Thussu, 2005: 56). Deregulation and economic growth contributed to a substantial increase in private media, both local and transnational. Since the 1990s, broadcasting in India has 'grown from a state-controlled monopoly to a multiplicity of private television channels in what used to be one of the world's most protected broadcasting environments' (Thussu, 2005: 55). Combined with the expansion and consolidation of the mainly western-based transnational media corporations, India's media landscape has been transformed. The national television news sector has created eight large network news operations, mainly in Hindi but English is also well represented. 'The deregulation of the Indian newscape has created, that is crucially enlarged, a democratic and journalistic space for debate, accountability and critical investigation almost non-existent on television prior to 1996' (Wildermuth, 2001: 170).

In assessing the democratic nature of India's expanded public sphere, Thussu notes both the benefits and limitations of market-based media pluralism. 'There is no doubt that market-led broadcasting has created a more open and wider public sphere in India' (Thussu, 2005: 64), but its focus is on the urban middle class. Although the audience for Indian television has expanded rapidly through cable and satellite penetration, the total audience of about 400 million still falls short of a majority of the population (Thussu, 2005: 59). As noted above, newspaper circulation has been growing rapidly, but still reaches fewer citizens than television. Content analysis demonstrates a strong urban bias in the news, from which 'the rural poor are remarkably absent' (Thussu, 2005: 65). Although India TV, launched in 2004, has pledged to fill this gap, it is clear that market-based media pluralism does not engage the majority of the Indian population.

In the case of China, with no history of democracy, state control over the media remains strong, employing a battery of direct (censorship) and indirect (licensing) methods of control. Nevertheless, the proliferation of commercial media has increased diversity and, on some levels scrutiny of government abuses, but only in a limited way. However, as noted above, there are some cracks in state control and, if our interpretation of the literature is correct, these cracks will widen as civil society becomes more powerful and journalists continue to push the envelope (Zhao, 2005).

PUBLIC BROADCASTERS IN THE 21ST CENTURY

The history of broadcasting in specific countries produced distinctive configurations of ownership and delivery. In Europe, public service television accounts for two-thirds of the income of all broadcasters, whereas in the USA the figure is only 4% (Picard, 2008: 201). Raboy (2003) has identified three main types of media ownership systems globally: 'public service core systems', 'private enterprise core systems' and 'state core systems'. Examples of the first type include the UK (BBC), Canada (CBC) and Australia (ABC). The 'state core systems' include the 'residual systems of countries which have not yet broken with the tradition of a single, monolithic national broadcaster, as well as 'emergent' systems which, 'although built around a state-owned and controlled broadcaster, are opening up to alternative commercial and community voices, such as one finds in parts of Asia and Africa where democratization is on the agenda' (Raboy, 2003: 45). According to Raboy (2003: 45), they also include former Soviet-bloc countries, which he describes as 'transitional', insofar 'as they seem to be inclined toward the existing dominant models'. The USA is one of the few examples of a private enterprise core system.

New market complexity, marked by audience fragmentation and increased competition for advertising revenue, along with deregulation in most industrial democracies, threatens the future of public broadcasters and, indeed, national private networks. European public service broadcasters (PSBs) that once approached 100% shares now have ratings in the 20–40% range (Picard, 2002). In North America, the audience shares of all the established broadcasters have declined, including in Canada both the private broadcasters and the Canadian Broadcasting Corporation (CBC) (CMRC, 2009). However, in Canada, the mere presence of CBC still seems to have an effect on political communication with Canadians in general exhibiting a high level of confidence in the CBC, and CBC radio in particular (CMRC, 2009). And the audience share for news and public affairs programming declined only slightly between 2004 and 2008, from 16.5 to 15.1% in English and from 24.3 to 21.8% in French. CBC Radio 1 continues to reach a substantial proportion of the audience for news and public affairs (Canadian Radio-Television and Telecommunications Commission, 2009).

With the commercial broadcasters challenged by fragmented audiences and uncertain advertising revenues, public broadcasting is arguably more important than ever for a healthy public sphere.

Public broadcasters contribute directly to informing the public and also have a positive impact on the quality of journalism of competing for-profit media (Cushion and Lewis, 2009). However, public broadcasting also must deal with declining revenues and, in many countries, an increasing reliance on advertising and other forms of commercial revenue (Picard, 2002). In Asia, Bannerjee suggests the tradition has been for public service broadcasters to operate on 'shoe-string budgets' (2002: 531). The nationalistic appeal of public broadcasters is also weakening in the face of global news flows (Raboy, 2003: 46). In order to continue to reach audiences, public broadcasters must define their niche and engage their audiences in more meaningful ways (Picard, 2002).

THE CASE OF ELECTIONS

In part because election campaigns are high-stakes events – contests for power and influence – and election campaigns are public, electoral communication is an important and revealing aspect of political discourse. Even when elections do not meet the highest standards of freedom and fairness, the nature of the discourse reveals a great deal about the role of media, the nature of the communications system and the key elements of specific national democratic cultures. The effects of globalization, the economic crisis of established media and the growth of the Internet are all being felt in the conduct of election campaigns. There is a good deal of comparative research on electoral communication (Esser and Pfestch, 2004; Lees-Marshment and Lilleker, 2005), but the rapidly changing media environment requires rethinking of both theory and practice.

The consensus of current research on election campaigns is that political messages, including news coverage, have an important influence on public agendas and vote decisions. However, increased voter volatility and the growing complexity of the information environment make specifying these influences difficult. Recent Canadian research, covering several countries, indicates that issues agendas have significant influence on voting (Blais et al., 2004); voters who decide closer to the end of the electoral process respond to actual events and coverage (Fournier et al., 2004); social networks are an important part of the vote decision for some segments of the electorate (Gidengil et al., 2007). The fact that women in several countries are less supportive of neo-liberal policies than men can be explained in part by different levels of political knowledge and by 'socially communicated cues' that prime different bases for assessment (Gidengil et al., 2007: 151). These findings suggest that social networking online may become increasingly important for citizens who are not heavily involved with conventional political frames in the mainstream media.

In the industrial democracies, the diminishing reach of the traditional media is forcing political parties and candidates to seek other means to reach the electorate. Television is still dominant but the increasing availability of digitized delivery systems is making campaign strategists take notice. The mass media campaign, which has only recently become a major part of election campaigns in countries such as India and Indonesia (Bakht, 2009), is being supplemented with digital messaging. In recent elections in Australia, Canada and the USA, television news and advertising were still the most important sources of information for voters, but the Internet played an increasing role (Barney, 2009; Macnamara, 2008; Smith and Chen, 2009). In India, the dominant medium remains the newspaper, while in Indonesia it is television (Bakht, 2009). In many countries, including both established and emerging democracies, mobile devices are being targeted with computerized phone messages and texts (Rawnsley, 2005: 200n7). The media mix is increasingly complex.

Since the 1960s, US presidential campaigns have been a major source of innovation in campaign techniques. The use of polling, targeted television spots, stealth campaigns, push polls and many other approaches to campaigning originated in the USA and were adapted for use in other political systems. Indeed, American political consultants, a profession that reached its full flower in the USA, have fanned out across the world to offer advice to parties and candidates. The International Association of Political Consultants, founded in 1968, boasts more than 100 members in countries on all continents (www.ipac.org; Plasser, 2002). The US presidential campaign of 2008 featured a major advance in the use of social media to engage party supporters and recruit volunteers. The social media campaign, conducted by an army of web-savvy volunteers (and some paid professionals) went considerably beyond previous uses of the Internet to raise funds and communicate with party workers. However, only 10% of Internet users obtained political information from social networking sites and only 5% posted their own posted their own views (Barney, 2009: 94). In the Canadian election, which took place not long after, only 7% of Canadians (and 15% of those under 35) identified the Internet as their primary source of information about the Federal election (calculated from Canadian Election Study, 2008).

To date, it appears that the Internet is used by voters mainly to supplement information in the traditional media. In 2008, 40% of Americans went online to get campaign news or information, more than one in three watched campaign-related videos online and almost as many used the Internet to access primary campaign materials, like speeches and platforms (Barney, 2009). For the most part, the Internet has not yet begun to play a significant role in promoting civic engagement or online deliberative democracy, though this role seems likely to grow. Under the right circumstances, it can provide an important alternative to media that are not open to oppositional perspectives. For example, in Canada, there have been a number of Facebook campaigns presenting alternative viewpoints on the political agenda. In 2010, a Facebook protest reflected citizen anger that the Canadian Parliament was prorogued twice in 2009 – the second suspension during a particularly critical political period – effectively closing down parliamentary scrutiny of government actions (Martin, 2010). Within a few days, the number of subscribers to the protest page was approaching 200,000. In the USA, the reach and ideological diversity of political blogs has grown rapidly. Though not yet close to rivaling the audiences the websites of major news organizations, niche sites nevertheless influence key audiences and the mainstream media themselves (Project for Excellence in Journalism, 2009). Most major news organizations in Europe and North America pay close attention to the blogosphere and have established journalist blogs in the hope of engaging younger audiences. In doing so, they have provided new forms of reporting and commentary but have moved only tentatively toward integrating the conversational and social nature of the Internet into their operations (Hermida, 2009).

Political parties outside the USA have also made increased use of the Internet but in party-centered systems – that is, most parliamentary systems – the online campaign has so far been largely a convenient supplement to more conventional campaign methods. For example, email has reduced reliance on direct mail for fundraising and mobilization. Social media have been used not so much to engage voters as to circulate party propaganda. Television remains the major campaign channel and party Internet sites are used mainly as another delivery system for campaign spots, speeches, platforms, etc. (Small, 2009; Smith and Chen, 2009). Yuen-Ok Lee's (2009) study of Korean elections concludes that Internet use in election campaigns is heavily influenced by contextual factors, including the media system and the regulatory regime.

For the most part, political strategists have been reluctant to give up message control to meet social media norms. The result has been, as one Canadian Internet analysis put it, that political party websites have been 'virtual banners' rather than places for engaging conversations about public concerns, policy proposals and future directions for the country (Hillwatch, 2006). The assessment of Jackson and Lilleker of the situation in the UK applies to other established democracies: 'Political parties still seek to a significant extent to control the communication process and to inform rather than interact' (2009: 247, see also Kalnes, 2009; Macnamara, 2008; Small, 2009; Smith and Chen, 2009). In addition, getting citizens to political party websites is a challenge in an era of information overload (Smith and Chen, 2009; Zamaria and Fletcher, 2008: 229).

The news media have not fared much better in promoting engagement. Although most news organization websites provide the opportunity for the posting of public comments in response to news reports and commentaries, few provide the opportunity for the kind of interactivity that younger citizens tend to value. Boulianne (2009: 205) concludes on the basis of an extensive literature survey that the use of online news seems to promote civic engagement. The proliferation of moderated public forms and, for short messages, the use of Twitter provides some elements of interactivity but participants are still a minority, even of those under 30 years of age (Hermida, 2010; Zamaria and Fletcher, 2008: 164–6, 280).

In most of the emerging democracies, Internet use is still not widespread outside of the urban middle class. Only radio comes close to reaching a majority of citizens in many countries and it is often state-controlled and not available for campaigning, at least for opposition parties. (On a per capita basis, radio receivers are available to twice as many people as television sets worldwide. See www.nationmaster.com.) But the Internet is expanding its reach and as recent events in Iran and other Middle Eastern countries demonstrate, it is an effective tool for mobilizing support, especially among younger citizens. Although the Internet and cell phone networks are not entirely beyond state control, activist groups have become skilled at evading attempts at censorship and, as a result, the World Wide Web has made a significant contribution to social and political change in the 21st century. Citizen journalists using digital media have broadened the reach of pro-democracy movements in the Middle East (dubbed the Arab Spring) in an unprecedented collaboration with traditional journalism.

In more general terms, the emergence of online outlets for citizen journalism has a notable effect on election campaign discourse and political journalism. The impact of blogs and other forms political expression online, including the various forms of citizen journalism, on American politics has been well documented, as has the flow of information from repressive regimes (Inglehart and Norris, 2008). Not surprisingly, various forms of online journalism have added significantly to electoral discourse in other jurisdictions as well, adding different perspectives and even additional expertise to the mix (Bruns, 2008). Advocacy groups have also made good use of the Internet to participate more fully in public debate (Rawnsley, 2005: 178).

DEFIANT PUBLICS AND DIGITAL DIVIDES

The Internet and mobile communications technologies have, like most major innovations, destabilized established systems and opened up new opportunities. Political communications systems – and the theories that seek to explain them – are no exception. The Internet has not only drawn audiences and advertisers from established news media, it has also created new expectations of how news should be presented and delivered. Younger audiences, in particular, want news to be accessible, brief, searchable, available on mobile devices and interactive, with opportunities to share information and engage with it in an ongoing conversation (CMRC, 2009; Fletcher, 2007). To survive, established news organizations will have to accommodate these expectations while maintaining the loyalties or older audiences that want longer form reports with context and interpretation. While mainstream news organizations, online as well as offline, continue to be regarded as more trustworthy than the Internet, segments of the public in many countries are losing trust in the traditional media and looking elsewhere for commentary and interpretation (see, for example, Globescan, 2006).

According to Daniel Drache (2008), the Internet has enabled 'defiant publics' to challenge hegemonic ideas and regimes and reshape public discourse. Drache cites the growth of international NGOs, the proliferation of micro-activists in many countries and, in particular, the emergence of a direct challenge to the media from advocacy group posts and non-partisan sites that offer alternatives to the mainstream (2008: 6, 9, 17, 99, 104). It is clear that new media provide important opportunities for new forms of activism and challenges to both democratic and authoritarian regimes. The circulation of information and damaging videos using cell phones and other mobile devices has clearly made authoritarian control over political communication more difficult. The goal of a public sphere – or public spheres – 'where politics is done by citizens rather than for citizens' (Drache, 2008: 125) has clearly been advanced by the new communication technologies. Certainly, the Internet has been a major benefit to activists, especially in countries with limited freedom of expression.

However, as Drache himself observes 'to be a social actor today, one needs to be patched into the worldwide digital communications network' (2008: 167). If access to news and information is a necessary condition for the effective function of democracy and the process of democratization, then the persistence of access divisions remains of critical importance. While Drache (2008: 105) optimistically estimates that 60% of the world's population has access to some form of electronic communication, from radios to cell phones, there is no doubt that such access is unevenly divided. On average, for example, less than 1 in 10 people living in Africa have access to an Internet connection or cell phone, compared to well over two in three in Europe and North America (www.world-internetstats.com.) The rapid expansion of connectivity will, it seems likely, reduce the access gap but as broadband expands and applications proliferate, the digital divide between information rich and information poor, whether measured in terms of countries, regions or individuals is almost certain to persist. The focus of commercial development of the media and the Internet is on the urban middle class.

In short, the new opportunities for information-sharing and activist communication are an important supplement to the established media, but from a democratic discourse perspective, as far as can be foreseen, they are not a substitute. News consumption on the Internet appears to be even more selective and personalized than through traditional media. This raises concerns about the erosion of community and shared understandings, especially given the persistence of digital divides, with younger, better educated, more affluent urban dwellers more likely to have the social capital necessary to access the political content online. The gender gap in Internet access persists in the global south. In Europe and North America, women have almost equal access to the Internet but are less likely than men to be active online or to visit political sites (Zamaria and Fletcher, 2008). Even among those with access to the Internet, research has not shown a strong causal relationship between Internet use and political engagement (Boulianne, 2009). Indeed, Darren Barney asks the crucial question: 'Does the information abundance afforded by emerging technologies motivate significant numbers of everyday citizens to engage in forms of political judgment and action that exceed routine complicity with the depoliticizing spectacle of politics as usual?' (2009: 95).

FUTURE DIRECTIONS: MORE QUESTIONS THAN ANSWERS

In this brief survey, we have examined the economic crisis of the established news media, the importance of established media in emerging democracies and the increasing importance of the Internet.

First, we note that scholars of political communication are concerned about: (1) the economic crisis of the established news media resulting from fragmented audiences and revenue streams, raising concerns about the future of the democratic role of a pluralist press; (2) the erosion of investigative journalism and resulting weakened scrutiny of those with economic and political power; (3) the possible decline of a media-fed public sphere. 'Fears have … been expressed that a society shaped by the highly fragmented and complex networks fostered by the Internet will lack any common political agenda, shared knowledge, or meeting points' (McQuail et al., 2008: 275). There is ample evidence that as commercialized media look for ways to attract new audiences while cutting costs, there is a movement away from 'serving public functions' that is 'breeding discontent among social observers and citizens' (Picard, 2007). There is evidence that socially concerned and politically active citizens are turning away from large-scale media, leading to increased fragmentation of the public sphere. This kind of fragmentation has democratic theorists worried that deliberative democracy will become increasingly difficult as shared perceptions erode and news organizations abandon traditional public sector functions (McManus, 1994; Picard, 2007).

Perhaps the most important issues related to the political economy of the established media involve finding ways to pay for serious committed journalism globally. What happens if such journalism cannot find a paying audience? Will public institutions, such as universities and non-profit investigative groups, take up the slack? Can serious journalism be considered a 'merit good' that public funds can provide? Will the new pluralism of the Internet help to inhibit state control of public-funded journalism? In the USA, where there has been a significant turning away from standard-brand politics, there is evidence that political attention goes up when the media ring alarm bells (Althaus, 2008: 180). If traditional newsrooms disappear, will the bells be loud enough?

Second, we have seen that established media are continuing to flourish in many emerging democracies. Whereas there is concern about citizens turning away from mainstream media in the older democracies, in countries with growing levels of economic growth and education, the demand for newspapers and television services is also growing, along with the Internet and mobile devices. While the pluralism brought by deregulation and a flourishing commercial sector is seen as beneficial for the democratizing process, there is also concern about the segmentation of audiences and the persistence, or even growth, of the divide between the information-rich and the information-poor.

The emergence of a globally connected, often English-speaking middle-class, along with local elites who use indigenous-language media and the remaining segments of society that remain outside the communication loop raises new concerns about fault lines in the political process. Indeed, the torrent of information may inhibit access to relevant information for citizens. According to Raboy, policies promoting more democratic communication systems should seek to ensure 'that this cornucopia of information is meaningfully accessible to citizens and not only packaged as marketable commodities or targeted to elites' (2003: 49–50). There is also a generation gap emerging in most of the world's political systems that requires further study, since information filtering strategies may differ across generations.

Third, there is the question of the role of the Internet. Is the online world becoming so 'virtual' that, as Barney (2009: 100–1) suggests, conversation will be seen as a substitute for action? Or is the 'defiant public' the vanguard of a new global citizenship that will deepen democratic practice in the established democracies and promote democratization in others, as Drache hopes? 'Democratic politics runs the risk that the majority will be cut off from the will or the capacity to participate in an informed way in political life' (McQuail et al., 2008: 275). More generally, will access to news from around the globe online promote a 'global village' of mutual understanding or simply perpetuate historical enmities domestically and in diasporas in many countries?

Media in transitional democracies in particular need further research on two fronts: the impact of competition from transnational media players and the ownership structure and funding model needed to generate quality political reporting (LaMay, 2004). For example, LaMay (2004) cautions that the kinds of news media that find a market in developing democracies often do not have the ability (for a variety of reasons that include inexperience and low professional standards) to engage in political discourse that will further the development of democratic institutions.

Finally, there is consensus among media economists that media, and news media in particular, face an uncertain future, especially in the industrial democracies – and that political reporting is a costly but important enterprise. In conditions of instability, news organizations rarely have the resources to resist commercial and political pressure. Yet there are also some intriguing trends that suggest the media imperialism argument is being challenged as important contra flows develop globally. In this new media landscape, how is national/international political communication defined? Do political communications researchers have the theoretical tools to handle the challenges? Developing frameworks for classifying media systems is notoriously difficult (Inglehart and Norris, 2008: 10–11), but comparative research is essential for identifying key variables in the media-democracy relationship (Hallin and Mancini, 2004). As we have tried to demonstrate, effective comparative research should examine not only how political actors use various media but also the political economy of media in national and global context (Esser and Pfetsch, 2004).

ACKNOWLEDGMENT

This chapter benefited from the research assistance of Matthew Greaves and Darryl Korell and from helpful suggestions from Minelle Mahtani, University of Toronto, who kindly read the manuscript in draft form.

REFERENCES

Althaus, S. (2008) 'Free Falls, High Dives, and the Future of Democratic Accountability', in D. Graber, D. McQuail and P. Norris (eds.), *The Politics of News: The News of Politics.* 2nd edn. Washington, DC: CQ Press. pp. 161–89.

Ayish, M. I. (2002) 'Political Communication on Arab World Television: Evolving Patterns', *Political Communication,* 19(2): 137–54.

Bakht, A. (2009) 'Political Parties Raise Game in Media', 9 April, http://www.cei.asia/searcharticle/2009_04/Political-parties-raise-game-in-media/35242 (accessed 15 August 2010).

Bannerjee, I. (2002) 'The Locals Strike Back: Media Globalization and Localization in the New Asian Television Landscape', *International Communication Gazette,* 64(6): 517–35.

Barney, D. (2009) 'Politics and Emerging Media: The Revenge of Publicity', *Global Media Journal—Canadian Edition,* 1(1): 89–106.

Becker, J. (2004) 'Lessons from Russia: A Neo-Authoritarian Media System', *European Journal of Communication,* 19(2): 139–63.

Bennett, W. L. and Lawrence, R. G. (2008) 'Press Freedom and Democratic Accountability in a Time of War, Commercialism and the Internet', in D. Graber, D. McQuail and P. Norris (eds.), *The Politics of News: The News of Politics*. 2nd edn. Washington, DC: CQ Press. pp. 247–67.

Blais, A., Turgeon, M., Gidengil, E., Nevitte, N. and Nadeau, R. (2004) 'Which Matters Most: Comparing the Effects of Issues and the Economy in American, British and Canadian Elections', *British Journal of Political Science*, 34(3): 555–63.

Boulianne, S. (2009) 'Does Internet Use Affect Engagement: A Meta-Analysis of Research', *Political Communication*, 26(2): 193–211.

Bruns, A. (2008) 'Citizen Journalism in the 2007 Australian Election', *eJournalist: A Refereed Media Journal*, 8(1): 75–89.

Canadian Election Study (2008) 'Post-election Survey Data Set', http://www.ces-eec.mcgill.ca

Canadian Media Research Consortium (CMRC) (2009) 'The State of the Media in Canada', http://www.cmrcccrm.ca

Canadian Radio-Television and Telecommunications Commission (2009) 'Communication Monitoring Report 2009', http://www.crtc.gc.ca

Chadha, K. and Kavoori, A. (2000). 'Media Imperialism Revisited: Some Findings from the Asian Case', *Media, Culture and Society* 22(4): 415–432.

Coulson, D. and Lacy, S. (1996). 'Journalists' Perceptions of How Newspaper and Broadcast News Competition Affects Newspaper Content', *Journalism and Mass Communication Quarterly*, 73(2): 354–63.

Cushion, S. and Lewis, J. (2009) 'Towards a Foxification of 24-hour News Channels in Britain: An Analysis of Market-Driven and Publicly Funded News Coverage', *Journalism*, 10(2): 131–53.

Drache, D. (2008) *Defiant Publics: The Unprecedented Reach of the Global Citizen*. Cambridge: Polity Press.

Esser F. and Pfetsch, B. (2004) *Comparing Political Communication: Theories, Cases, and Challenges*. New York: Cambridge University Press.

Fletcher, F. (2007) 'The Future of News in the Digital Era', *Australian Policy Online*, July, http://www.apo.org.au

Fournier, P., Nadeau, R., Blais, A., Gidengil, E. and Nevitte, N. (2004) 'Time-of-Voting Decision and Susceptibility to Campaign Effects', *Electoral Studies*, 23(4): 661–81.

Gidengil, E., Harell, A. and Erickson, B. (2007) 'Network Diversity and Vote Choice: Women's Social Ties and Left Voting in Canada', *Politics and Gender*, 3(2): 151–77.

GlobeScan. (2006) 'Trust in the Media'. BBC / Reuters Media Center Poll. 3 May, http://www.globescan.com/news_archives/bbcreut.html

Hackett, R. and Zhao, Y. (1998) *Sustaining Democracy: Journalism and the Politics of Objectivity*. Toronto: Garamond Press.

Hallin, D. and Mancini, P. (2004) *Comparing Media Systems: Three Models of Media and Politics*. New York: Cambridge University Press.

Harcup, T. and O'Neill, D. (2001) 'What is News: Galtung and Ruge Revisited', *Journalism Studies*, 2(2): 261–80.

Hermida, A. (2010) 'Twittering the News: The Emergence of Ambient Journalism', *Journalism Practice*, 4(3): 297–308.

Hermida, A. (2009) 'The Blogging BBC', *Journalism Practice*, 3(3): 1–17.

Hillwatch E-Services (2006) 'Still Virtually Lawn Signs: Benchmarking Canadian Political Websites During the 2006 Campaign', http://www.hillwatch.com/ (accessed 22 November 2010).

Hjarvard, S. (ed.) (2001) *News in a Globalized Society*. Goteborg, Sweden: Nordicom.

Hyden, G., Leslie, M. and Ogundimu, F. F. (eds.) (2002) *Media and Democracy in Africa*. New Brunswick, NJ: Transaction Publishers.

Inglehart, R. and Norris, P. (2008) 'Silencing Dissent: Restrictive Media Environments and Regime Support', paper presented at the annual meeting of the MPSA Annual National Conference. Chicago, IL, 2–5 April.

Jackson, N. A. and Lilleker, D. G. (2009) 'Building an Architecture of Participation: Political Parties and Web 2.0 in Britain', *Journal of Information Technology & Politics*, 6(3–4): 232–50.

Kalnes, O. (2009) 'Norwegian Parties and Web 2.0', *Journal of Information Technology & Politics*, 6(3–4): 251–66.

Lacy, S. and Martin, H. (2004) 'Competition, Circulation and Advertising', *Newspaper Research Journal*, 25(1), 18–39.

Lacy, S. and Simon, T. F. (1993). *The Economics and Regulation of United States Newspapers*. Norwood, NJ: Ablex Publishing.

LaMay, C. (2004) 'Review Essay', in T. Carrothers (ed.), *Critical Mission: Essays on Democratic Promotion*, http://www.icnl.org/knowledge/ijnl/vol6iss4/special_1.htm (accessed November 2010).

Lee, Y-O. (2009) 'Internet Elections 2.0: Culture, Institutions, and Technology in the Korean Presidential Elections of 2002 and 2007', *Journal of Information Technology & Politics*, 6(3–4): 312–25.

Lees-Marshment, J. and Lilleker, D. G. (2005) *Political Marketing: A Comparative Perspective*. New York: Manchester University Press.

Mahtani, M. (2008) 'Racializing the Audience: Immigrant Perceptions of Mainstream Canadian English Language TV News', *Canadian Journal of Communication*, 33(4): 639–61.

Martin, L. (2010) 'A Snowballing Protest Shows Democracy Matters to Canadians', *The Globe and Mail*, 13 January, http://www.theglobeandmail.com/news/opinions/a-snowballing-protest-shows-democracy-matters-to-canadians/article1430272/ (accessed 15 January 2010).

McChesney, R. W. (2008) *The Political Economy of Media: Enduring Issues, Emerging Dilemmas*. New York: Monthly Review Press.

McChesney, R. W. and Schiller, D. (2003) 'The Political Economy of International Communications', paper prepared for the UNRISD Programme on Information Technologies and Social Development as part of UNRISD background work for the World Summit on the Information Society, June.

McFaul, M. (2005) 'Transitions from Post-Communism', *Journal of Democracy*, 16(3): 5–19.

McQuail, D., Graber, D. and Norris, P. (2008) 'Conclusion: Journalism and Democracy: Contemporary Challenges', in D. Graber, D. McQuail and P. Norris (eds.), *The Politics of*

News: The News of Politics. 2nd edn. Washington, DC: CQ Press. pp. 268–77.

McManus, J. (1994) *Market-Driven Journalism: Let the Citizen Beware.* Thousand Oaks, CA: Sage.

Macnamara, J. (2008) 'E-Electioneering: Use of New Media in the 2007 Australian Election', research report, Australian Centre for Public Communication. University of Technology, Sydney.

Milner, H. (2007) 'Political Knowledge and Participation among Young Canadians and Americans', IRPP working papers. November.

Neuman, W. R. (2008) 'Globalization and the New Media', in D. Graber, D. McQuail and P. Norris (eds.), *The Politics of News: The News of Politics.* 2nd edn. Washington, DC: CQ Press. pp. 230–46.

Nichols, J. and McChesney, R. (2010) 'How to Save Journalism', *The Nation,* 7 January, http://www.thenation.com (accessed 15 January 2010).

Picard, R. G. (2008) 'The Economics of Plurality: Europe and the USA Compared', in T. Gardam and D. Levy (eds.), *The Price of Plurality: Choice, Diversity, and Broadcasting Institutions in the Digital Age.* Oxford: Reuters Institute for the Study of Journalism, University of Oxford. pp. 197–205.

Picard, R. G. (2007) 'The Challenges of Public Functions and Commercialized Media', in D. A. Graber, D. McQuail and P. Norris (eds.), *The Politics of News: The News of Politics.* Washington, DC: Congressional Quarterly Press. pp. 211–29.

Picard, R. G. (2002) 'Research Note: Assessing Audience Performance of Public Service Broadcasters', *European Journal of Communication,* 17(2): 227–35.

Plasser, F. (2002) *Political Campaigning a World-wide Analysis of Campaign Professionals and Their Practices.* Westport, CT: Praeger.

Project for Excellence in Journalism (2009) 'The State of the News Media 2009', http://www.journalism.org (accessed 10 January 2010).

Raboy, M. (2003) 'Rethinking Broadcasting Policy in a Global Media Environment', in G. Ferrell Lowe and T. Hujanen (eds.), *Broadcasting & Convergence: New Articulations of the Public Service Remit.* Goteborg, Sweden: Nordicom. pp. 41–56.

Rawnsley, G. D. (2005) *Political Communication and Democracy.* New York: Palgrave Macmillan.

Romano, A. and Bromley, M. (eds.) (2005) *Journalism and Democracy in Asia.* New York: Routledge.

Rotstein, A. (1988) 'The Use and Misuse of Economics in Cultural Policy', in R. Lorimer and D.C. Wilson (eds.), *Communication Canada: Issues in Broadcasting and New Technologies.* Toronto: Kagan and Woo. pp. 140–56.

Sachs, N. (2007) 'Freedom of the Press, Democracy and Democratization', paper presented at the annual meeting of the MPSA Annual National Conference. Chicago, IL, 2–5 April.

Sakr, N. (2007) 'Challenger or Lackey: The Politics of News on Al Jazeera', in D. K. Thussu (ed.), *Media on the Move: Global Flow and Contra-Flow.* New York: Routledge. pp. 116–32.

Schudson, M. (1997) 'Why Conversation is not the Soul of Democracy?', *Critical Studies in Mass Communication,* 14(4): 297–309.

Sinclair, J. (2002) 'Mexico, Brazil and the Latin World', in J. Sinclair, E. Jacka and S. Cunningham (eds.), *New Patterns in Global Television.* New York: Oxford University Press. pp. 33–62.

Skinner, D., Compton, J. and Gasher, M. (2005) *Converging Media, Diverging Politics: A Political Economy of News Media in the United States and Canada.* Toronto: Lexinton Books.

Small, T. A. (2009) 'Regulating Canadian Elections in the Digital Age: Approaches and Concerns', *Election Law Journal,* 8(3): 189–205.

Smith, P. and Chen, P. J. (2009) 'A Canadian E-lection 2008? Online Media and Political Competition', paper presented at the annual meeting of the CPSA. Ottawa. 27–29 May.

Sreberny, A. and Paterson, C. (eds.) (2004) *International News in the 21st Century.* Eastleigh: John Libbey.

Starr, P. (2004) *The Creation of the Media: Political Origins of Modern Communication.* New York: Basic Books.

Starr, P. (2009) 'Goodbye to the Age of Newspapers (Hello to a New Era of Corruption)', *The New Republic,* 4 March: 29–35.

Straubhaar, J. D. (2008) 'Global, Hybrid or Multiple? Cultural Identities in the Age of Satellite TV and the Internet', *Nordicom Review,* 2: 11–30.

Tharoor, K. (2009) 'India's Media Explosion', *Foreign Policy,* July, http://www.foreignpolicy.com/articles/2009/07/20/indias_media_ex

Thompson, J. B. (1995) *The Media and Modernity: A Social Theory of the Media.* Stanford, CA: Stanford University Press.

Thussu, D. K. (2005) 'Media Plurality or Democratic Deficit: Private TV and the Public Sphere in India', in A. Romano and M. Bromley (eds.), *Journalism and Democracy in Asia.* New York: Routledge. pp. 55–65.

Thussu, D. K. (2007) 'Mapping Global Media Flow and Contra-Flow', in D. K. Thussu (ed.), *Media on the Move: Global Flow and Contra-Flow.* New York: Routledge. pp. 11–32.

Tunstall, J. (2008) *The Media Were American: US Mass Media in Decline.* New York: Oxford University Press.

van der Wurff, R., Bakker, P. and Picard, R. (2008) 'Economic Growth and Advertising Expenditures in Different Media and Different Countries', *Journal of Media Economics,* 21(1): 28–52.

Wildermuth, N. (2001) 'Global Going Local: Fighting for the Indian TV Audience', in S. Hjarvard (ed.), *News in a Globalized Society.* Goteborg, Sweden: Nordicom. pp. 207–257.

World Editors Forum (2008) 'Trends in the Newsroom', http://www.wan-press.org/wef

World Association of Newspapers (2008) *World Press Trends Report.* London: ZenithOptimedia.

Wu, S. (2009). 'Can East Asia Produce its Own Al Jazeera? Assessing the Potential of Channel New Asia as a Global Media Contra-flow'. Unpublished MA Thesis. Simon Fraser University.

Zamaria, C. and Fletcher, F. (2008) *Canada Online: The Internet, Media and Emerging Technologies: Uses, Attitudes, Trends and International Comparisons.* Toronto: Canadian Internet Project.

Zhao, Y. (2000) 'From Commercialization to Conglomeration: The Transformation of the Chinese Press Within the Orbit of the Party State', *Journal of Communication,* 50(2): 3–26.

Zhao, Y. (2005) 'Neoliberal Strategies, Socialist Legacies: Communication and State Transformation in China', in A. Romano and M. Bromley (eds.), *Journalism and Democracy in Asia.* New York: Routledge. pp. 23–50.

4

Blogging and the Future of News

Richard Davis

In 2005, the Liberal Party of Canada was rocked by allegations that it had used government funds to support advertising firms. A judge presiding over the hearings issued a gag order on Canadian media to prevent any reporting on the ongoing investigation. However, Ed Morrissey, a blogger in Minneapolis, began covering the hearings through an unidentified source. While Canadian media were unable to report on the most interesting news story in Canada, a blog from the USA was providing the news. For a brief time, Morrissey's blog became one of the most-read news sources for Canadians. Morrissey called his action in trumping the Canadian news media 'a historic moment for blogs' (Davis, 2009: 54).

This incident demonstrates that bloggers have come to occupy a position in newsgathering that has affected, and will yet affect, how journalists gather and report the news. This is true across the globe. A prominent New Zealand columnist argued that bloggers had become potentially the most powerful opinion makers in New Zealand (Ralston, 2007). A BBC News reporter argued that UK political parties were 'falling over themselves to woo this new breed of political blogger' (Wheeler, 2007). While in China, bloggers have become important in setting the media's agenda and shaping public opinion (Hassid, 2011).

At the same time, journalism has influenced how political blogging operates. Bloggers are affected by audience expectations about the nature of news, such as a standard of reliability in information dissemination. These expectations have been acquired through traditional journalism.

The thesis of this chapter is that journalists and bloggers have formed a relationship based not just on conflict and competition, but also on co-dependency. They are developing a symbiotic relationship that will shape how political blogging develops and how journalism is carried out in the future. This chapter first discusses how traditional journalism has created an identity crisis for political bloggers. Then, we review the ways blogs have affected journalism, such as accelerating reporting, interacting with the public, reshaping the media's watchdog role, revising journalistic standards and even altering the way journalists write. Next, we address how journalism has influenced how political blogs function, such as defining blogger norms and providing a governing model for the political blogosphere's information gathering and reporting processes. Finally, we analyze how these interactions have produced a symbiotic relationship that defines how journalists and bloggers approach each other and how they will do so in the future.

ARE BLOGGERS JOURNALISTS?

What are bloggers? Political bloggers may seem like journalists. They disseminate news to a regular audience, particularly information their readers may not get elsewhere. Their audiences come to rely on them for accurate information. Like traditional media, they have an editorial function that includes extensive commentary on current events. Some bloggers even resemble traditional journalism in their pursuit of investigative research (Loyalka, 2005; Perlmutter, 2008; Starr, 2005).

Yet, in other ways they are different. Unlike traditional journalism, blogging features interactivity. Newspapers have long included the opportunity for a small sample of readers to express their views through letters to the editor, but anyone can comment on most blogs and see their views appear on the same site as the blogger. Bloggers have been called participatory journalists because blogging is a form of journalism featuring interactivity and participation over mere spectating (Pole, 2009). Blogs also have been termed 'black market journalism' because their product is outside of the journalism system dominated by large media conglomerates (Wall, 2005: 157–8). One journalist-blogger in the UK warned that blogging and journalism cannot be equated because journalism 'usually requires research and some care in its execution' (Poirier, 2006).

Other bloggers views themselves primarily as commentators, not journalists. John Hinderaker of *Powerline* said that he is not a journalist or even a part-time journalist (Hinderaker, 2006). Eugene Volokh (*Volokh Conspiracy*) admitted he was 'an amateur pundit, which is to say someone whose hobby it is to opine on various matters that are in the news (Drezner and Farrell, 2004: 20). Still others admit that they are no substitute for journalists and do not claim to be. *Instapundit*'s Glenn Reynolds urged his readers not to rely solely or primarily on his blog for news. 'What you get here – as with any blog – is my idiosyncratic selection of things that interest me, as I have time to note them, with my own idiosyncratic comments' (Drezner and Farrell, 2004: 20).

Others see themselves primarily as activists. Progressive bloggers have used the blogosphere to mobilize the political left (Kerbel, 2009). The best known progressive activist blogger is Markos Moulitsas, founder of *Daily Kos*. Moulitsas' paramount goal has been to help the Democratic Party win elections. He consults with candidates, raises money for them and generally engages in partisan activity (Klam, 2004). He is not a journalist and has admitted that, if he were, he would be 'breaking half the canon of journalistic ethics (Smolkin, 2004). Nor is activism the province solely of the left. Prominent conservative bloggers such as Patrick Hynes work for Republican candidates, and blogs such as *Red State* and *ConfirmThem* have been active in mobilizing support or opposition to judicial appointments, depending on whether they were conservative.

Still other bloggers see themselves as journalists and commentators and even activists – all at the same time (Marshall, 2006; Moulitsas, 2006). According to Moulitsas, blogging has blended historical roles: 'Traditionally it was easier for people to find the niche ... you were either an activist or you were a writer or you were a pundit ... We're all of the above' (Marshall, 2006). These bloggers do not view a fundamental conflict between reporting on the news and commenting on it at the same time, as well as attempting to change public policy. In the same post, a blogger can offer news, add commentary and urge action on the part of the audience and policymakers. For example, *Daily Kos'* logo is 'News-Community-Action'. One journalist has summed up blogging as having 'all the liberties of a traditional journalist but few of the obligations' (Skube, 2007).

Bloggers emphasize the differences between their approach to journalism and what has been accepted as the standard journalistic approach. Traditional journalists value detachment from the story, an emphasis on description, neutrality in presenting conflicts within the story, the unidirectional nature of the communication and the importance of structure. But bloggers' emphasize the importance of personal subjectivity, the honesty of opinion expression, a role for the audience in the communication process and the absence of cohesion and organization (Wall, 2005).

However, the journalistic style proposed by bloggers is not new. Over time, traditional media has experienced the same angst over the nature of journalism. During the 1700s, printers of broadsheets agonized over their preferred role as commercial printers and their expected role of foot soldier – either in defense of the crown or in the service of a revolution. In the USA, the same debate erupted during the framing of the US Constitution as newspaper publishers sought to return to their old commercial role but were pressed into service as advocates or opponents of the proposed constitution (Rubin, 1981). Debate over journalists' role has continued since the 19th century as some elements in journalism have sought a more independent press from the clutches of partisan organizations and leaders, while others prefer the press as a mouthpiece for party principles.

However, only in the 20th century did the practice of interweaving opinion and news begin to give way to a new standard of professionalism and objectivity (Schudson, 1980). Yet, even that change seemed artificial. While the newspapers of the 18th and 19th centuries in the USA were proudly partisan and erected no barriers between news and commentary, even those of the 20th century and early 21st century have contained both editorial opinion and news reporting. The assumption held in journalism was that by putting editorial opinion and news on separate pages, the impression would be left in the minds of readers that news stories were not affected by the editorial position of the paper. By the end of the 20th century, explicit news analysis and commentary began to creep out of the editorial pages and onto the rest of the news section of the paper. Journalists also appeared to have freer rein in expressing opinions in the body of a news story, particularly a feature story.

Hence, the role of the traditional media is hardly settled in the US, and is certainly questioned in other nations as well. Journalists themselves still debate the role of journalism. Each new trend in journalism – new journalism, adversarial journalism, advocacy journalism, civic journalism – has led to a reanalysis of what journalism means. The latest – public or citizen journalism – still roils journalism (Corrigan, 2003; Merritt, 1998).

Blogs are the latest iteration of that ongoing debate. For example, the blogosphere has altered somewhat the role of the journalists as gatekeepers. Readers now have access to original documents and other sources that blogs link them to. They also have news that journalists do not include because news professionals consider that information as not meeting the definition of newsworthiness.

Yet, journalists still perceive themselves as performing the function of helping the average reader make sense of the surfeit of information before them. Not only does that role come in the form of filtering out what may not be important for the reader, listener or viewer, but also placing that news in context for the reader (Singer, 1997: 72–89). For the vast majority of readers who are not interested in searching the Internet for supplemental information on a daily basis, that journalistic function is critical.

If traditional journalism, with its lengthy history, continues to deliberate its role, it should be no surprise that the political blogosphere – with a life span barely out of the single digits – would do so as well. Moreover, it is important to remember that the roots of the blogosphere suggest no such role for it as a medium of political news and information. While the blogosphere may be viewed today by many as an alternative political information source, and therefore in competition with the traditional media in their coverage of public policy and politics, it is important to remember that blogs did not start that way. It is easy to forget that early blogs were personal journals featuring individual expression, primarily by teenagers. Any political role was tangential at best. In fact, that description is still true of a blogosphere that is populated primarily by personal journals unread by all but a handful of other people.

But as a few of those blogs turned to national politics and attracted media circulation-size audiences, they morphed from introspective diaries to political news sources. As this transformation progressed, these blogs also disseminated news stories about political events, many of which were not covered (or perhaps under-covered) by the traditional media. These new information sources still featured personal expressions by their authors (in the tradition of early blogs and the blogosphere generally), which was a radical departure from objective journalism. As these blogs changed from personal diaries to political news and information gatherers and disseminators, some bloggers envisioned themselves not as anonymous writers to family and friends but as the future of journalism. They predicted a new generation of media consumers who would eschew the traditional media forms of supposed objectivity and gravitate to the partisan and far more interesting blog sources.

CHANGING JOURNALISM

That 'eschewing' of traditional media has not yet occurred. However, the presence of the blogosphere has had an impact on traditional journalists. The blogosphere has affected how journalists do their job and how they relate to their respective audiences. This section discusses several effects the blogosphere has had on journalism and newsgathering. The first such effect we discuss is the very definition of a journalist.

Defining Journalists

Not only do bloggers question what their role is, but the emergence of bloggers has challenged the notion of what a journalist is. The issue is hardly abstract. One example of how practical the question becomes is the issue of press credentialing. Does the definition of a journalist broaden when bloggers are granted the same access to press space in the White House Press Room, the Congressional press galleries, a courtroom or a political convention? Does not that access legitimate bloggers as journalists similar to the status accorded traditional news reporters?

The question also arises when bloggers go where journalists are not allowed. In a famous instance, a blogger covering the Obama campaign was able to sit in on a fundraising event that was closed to the press. She then blogged about the event and related that the candidate had remarked that Pennsylvania voters, who would be voting in the upcoming presidential primary, were 'bitter' and that they 'cling to guns and religion'. The blog post of Obama's remark, which was made at a fundraiser, spread from the blogosphere to traditional media (Fowler, 11 April 2008). Was this individual a journalist? If she had worn press credentials, she would not have been invited to the event. Yet, her record of the event, including an audiotape, circulated as widely as a journalist's would have. Was not she then a journalist?

The question of whether the definition of a journalist should be stretched to include bloggers is one that news professionals are still wrestling with. However, the issue may be fading as increasing numbers of traditional journalists supplement their regular news coverage or columns with blogging or even turn to blogging as news organizations downsize, blurring the line between journalists and bloggers.

Accelerating Reporting

Another effect from the blogosphere is pressure to accelerate the speed of the newsgathering and reporting process. One example involved the US presidential candidate John Edwards during the 2008 campaign. Shortly before a scheduled campaign press conference, CNN, MSNBC, CBS and NBC began broadcasting stories that Edwards' wife, Elizabeth, would announce that her breast cancer was no longer in remission and that her husband would suspend his presidential campaign. The story that Edwards would stop campaigning for the presidency spread across the Internet, as well. The Edwards campaign denied the story, but that denial failed to halt the spread of the story.

The source for the news media accounts was a reporter for the political blog *Politico.com*. The reporter repeated the rumour after hearing it from only one source. The reporter justified his use of only one source, saying that blogs 'share information in real time' (Kurtz, March 23, 2007). But other media picked it up as if it was reliable. If they had not, they would have been scooped.

Obviously, speed has always been a critical facet of the news business. In the days before radio, newspapers printed several editions throughout the day in order to deliver the latest news (Emery, 1984: 238; Mott, 1962: 446–58). The advent of 24-hour television news channels in the 1980s challenged the major network news divisions to broadcast news more frequently and expand the broadcast hole devoted to news. In the mid-1990s, the Internet offered a new venue for constant news transmission, which required a steady dose of news content by media websites. Journalists now were driven by a deadline pressure imposed on them by their own news organization's embrace of new technology.

The latest source of pressure is the blogosphere. As a medium that is defined by time – the inclusion of a date and time with nearly all posts – and is capable of instantaneous updating, the blogosphere offers a near-constant content feed.

In terms of news, then, blogs can broadcast a story far more rapidly than traditional journalists.

One reason bloggers can act so quickly is the absence of journalistic routine or structure. Bloggers need not take the time journalists do to produce a news media story. Editors decide whether to cover the event and then send a journalist out to report on it. The reporter takes the time to attend the event and then write the story, including collecting contextual information and material from sources. Then there is an editing process where the story goes through layers of editors before being approved for publication. Then, in the case of print journalism, time is needed to physically publish the newspaper. News for the website skips the production stage, but still must go through the rest of the cycle. For television, the process usually is more complex due to the constraints of film crew allocation and placement, as well as production requirements.

By contrast, a blogger can post to his or her website in minutes. There is no prior assignment, no need to physically attend the event, no organizational layers, no production time. In less time than a journalist can cover a story, blog posts can go through various iterations and become old news.

This advantage can provide blogs with an important niche in delivering breaking news. In an era of 24-hour news cycles and audience expectation of near instantaneous delivery of news of an event as it occurs, traditional news media organizations face enormous pressures to be fast and first in delivering the latest news. Blogs can match, and often exceed, the traditional media's ability to inform an audience quickly.

The speed of the blogosphere presents a challenge to the media accustomed to being the first to report a story to the audience. Have the traditional media, then, lost their ability to be the first to publicize a story? If so, much like newspapers' adjustment to radio, will they have to find a niche of more in-depth reporting or more informed news reporting to replace their lost position of first out with the story?

The media's demise may be exaggerated, to paraphrase Mark Twain. The blogosphere's jump on news stories is likely to be rare because blogs lack the surveillance and newsgathering capabilities of traditional media. The kind of story that blogs can scoop the news media on would be those that news media organizations have but do not use, probably because they discount their newsworthiness. Or it could be a story that emanates from a source in the blogosphere. This could be information coming from some individual or group with unique access to that material, and would prefer to pass it through the blogosphere rather than media. Although either scenario is possible, the odds of such scooping on a regular basis are low.

There is another impact on journalism related to speed beyond the opportunity to scoop others. It is the ability to frame a story in a certain way that constitutes the 'first impression' for the news audience. Drezner and Farrell have called this a 'first-mover advantage in socially constructing interpretive frames for understanding current events' (2004: 4). One could argue that the Harriet Miers' US Supreme Court nomination in 2005 is an example of that 'first-mover advantage'. Blogs disseminated negative information about Miers faster than the White House could initiate its own image-making effort. The White House could never alter the first impressions the blogosphere gave of Miers as unfit to be a Supreme Court justice and incapable of playing the conservative warrior role the right expected a Bush Supreme Court nominee to fulfill.

The blogosphere's ability to frame is contingent on one major condition – the presence of a fairly universally accepted frame. Without that, there is no frame but only conflicting messages. Since the blogosphere is divided sharply on ideological lines, such frame consensus is difficult to achieve. In the case of Miers, the frame of Miers' shortcomings was accepted across both liberal and conservative blogs and acquired such consensus.

Changing Professional Standards

Related to speed is the absence of professional standards by bloggers that may spill over into journalistic norms. While journalists are trained to follow certain norms and codes of professional ethics in the construction of a story, bloggers have no such guidelines. Bloggers are not bound by ethic codes or professional norms to adhere to journalistic standards of reporting. A blogger need not get confirmation of a tip or check the authority of the source. Some may choose to do so in order to maintain their own credibility, but the blogosphere does not impose that expectation in the way professional journalism does for traditional journalists.

Bloggers even brag about their failure to check rumors they broadcast. While blogging as 'Wonkette', the US political blogger Ana Marie Cox saw herself as competing against gossip journalists in print media. But she said the best known print gossip columnist in Washington could not compete with her because 'he reports, that's the problem. He, like, checks facts' (Society of Professional Journalists, 2004).

Of course, such freedom also undermines the blogosphere's credibility. The Edwards story above is one example. Another occurred on election night of the 2004 US presidential campaign. The broadcast networks were reporting election results from state to state, but the blogosphere was distributing exit poll results that supposedly showed that Democratic candidate John Kerry was ahead in key swing states. Early exit poll numbers, which are incomplete, had been leaked and blogs were reporting that John Kerry would be president (Smolkin, 2005: 44). Bloggers admit that blogs can be 'raw emotion and that there are times when blogging would be better if it were tempered with more deliberation' (Marshall, 2006).

The competition from bloggers as a separate news source places new pressures on traditional journalists who are used to playing by a certain set of rules. Yet, those same rules are eschewed by their new competitor. While one operates under journalistic rules of obtaining confirmation, which typically takes time, the other competitor, the blogosphere, is able to ignore such norms. As a result, the blogosphere can lead journalists to cast aside their journalistic training in the rush to be first – or even merely to retain a measure of relevance in a fast-moving Internet environment.

Usurping the Watchdog Role

Journalists have long viewed themselves as media watchdogs who reveal politicians' mistakes and government errors. But bloggers challenge that watchdog role. They argue that traditional journalists have become too comfortable in their relationship with politicians and other elites. Bloggers claim they, not traditional journalists, are the real watchdogs today. They contend the blogosphere can be more critical of political insiders than are journalists because, unlike journalists, they enjoy a healthy distance from politicians. Journalists are unable to engage in the kind of investigative journalism they used to do because of their proximity to politicians, the bloggers say.

The bloggers' point speaks to the inherent ethical dilemma of a permanent press corps; namely, how does a reporter stay close enough to sources to get information but not so close as to become partial toward those sources (Robertson, 2002). The treatment of journalists by governmental bodies adds to the problem. Journalists who cover government sit in government-provided press rooms and typically gain ready access to a variety of government sources. Moreover, some prominent journalists have become establishment figures in their own right. Nationally syndicated columnists, television news presenters, political talk show hosts – all have become fixtures in Washington and coveted figures at dinners, parties and other social events.

Bloggers, however, are still the relative upstarts. There is still an outsider quality to their content and their approach to politics. Only a very few so far have acquired some status among national political figures. Most still operate on the fringe in terms of social status and political respectability. In several countries, including the UK, Germany and Canada, bloggers have been subject to legal action on claims of libel. In others, such as Malaysia, Saudi Arabia and India, some bloggers have been shut down by the government while others have been arrested.

That does not mean bloggers will remain on the fringe. Increasingly, bloggers are being granted inside access by various political leaders. For example, in July 2009, President Obama held a separate conference call for bloggers, a tactic similarly used by other politicians such as the US Senate Majority Leader Harry Reid and former Republican presidential candidate John McCain (Geraghty, 2008). Moreover, many bloggers are anxious to get on the 'inside' in order to have exclusive information, as their journalist counterparts do. The distinction between the 'insider' traditional press corps and the 'outsider' bloggers likely will fade.

Pitting Elites Against Non-elites

In addition to a general competition with traditional media, blogs also are affecting intra-media competition between two levels of journalism – elites (prestige newspapers, newsmagazines, networks, etc.) and non-elites. Traditionally, there is a unidirectional relationship where elite press – particularly through wire services and syndicates – becomes the source of content for non-elite publications. Non-elite journalists pick up cues from national media and then add a local angle. Less often will the relationship move in the other direction where elite media gather stories from non-elite press and include them in their content.

However, blogs are providing an opportunity for non-elite press to affect elite news content. Non-elite journalists use blogs to attract the attention of the elite press to a story. By pitching the story to an A-list (or prominent) blog, which is an easier information source to reach than the elite press, the story may reach a national audience, and perhaps be picked up by elite journalists who read the blog (Marshall, 2006). Although blog sources primarily are drawn from the elite press as well, blogs have a wider array of sources they use, including non-elite press (Vaina, 2007). This trend may help non-elite press affect the news agenda as their content moves indirectly to elite media.

Competing for a Niche Political Audience

Another impact on journalism is new competition for a niche audience. Traditional media have faced increasing competitive pressures from new information sources. Twenty-four-hour news channels and Internet news sites offer the most politically interested the opportunity for new information sources that satisfy their seemingly insatiable demands for political news. The political blogosphere is the latest entrant in that race for the eyeballs of political junkies.

However, the contest begins with the traditional media competing under a handicap of audience expectations. News media organizations provide news across a broad spectrum of topics – politics, sports, entertainment, weather, etc. Even within political news, news media rarely devote their broadcasts primarily to one topic. The audience anticipates stories on varying topics because they expect to be informed about a range of news occurring that day.

Bloggers, conversely, do not have the same obligation to report the news of the day. Any particular blog can, and will, ignore the vast majority of stories the news media cover and home in on one or two topics, if they wish. Blogs can specialize, and politics is the specialty of political blogs. This distinction in roles can be seen in an incident involving then US Senate Majority Leader Trent Lott in 2002. Lott made a comment at a birthday party for Senator Strom Thurmond that his state of Mississippi had voted for Thurmond in 1948 and 'if the rest of the country had followed our lead we wouldn't have had all these problems over all these years, either' (Bloom, 2003: 2). Political blogs picked up the story and repeated it over several days. Traditional news media also began to pick up the story, but not to the extent bloggers did. Bloggers could devote their space to the controversy because they had no obligation to cover general news. News media organizations were expected to cover other news occurring at the same time, which included, among other things, the resignation of the secretary of the treasury and a close US Senate election in Louisiana (Bloom, 2003).

De-bureaucratizing Writing

With its roots in personal journals, the blogosphere still values individualistic writing characterized by the absence of editing by another individual. In their comparison with news media, bloggers point to the absence of a news hierarchy as a distinct advantage in the quality of writing. They argue they do a better job of writing because they do not have the bureaucracy of traditional news media that 'turns even the best prose limp, lifeless, sterile, and homogenized' (Lasica, 2001).

In response to the blogosphere's perceived freshness as a medium in contrast with a bureaucratic news organization approach, individual journalists have started their own blogs, sometimes separate from organizations. Also, news media organizations have created blogs in order to capture interest in blogs among their readers and meet the imperatives of a new medium.

The style is much more real time, informal and opinion-laced – much like the blogosphere generally. One editor for *The New York Times'* website explained the role of the newspaper's blog as a vehicle for 'insights that might not rise to a full article but are worthy of reporting' (Lawson-Borders and Kirk, 2005: 549).

News organization blogs also offer more space for news. Newspapers can disseminate news that will not fit in the print edition (Strupp, 2006). This is especially true of short pieces – news notes that do not justify article-length treatment. Due to the looser space restrictions, stories or short 'news notes' can go into a blog when they would not meet the threshold for the print edition.

Ideally, blogs would be an opportunity for news media to spend more time on substantive issues. For example, during an electoral campaign a newspaper could add depth to stories about issues and candidates instead of focusing on the horse-race that dominates media coverage (Lawson-Borders and Kirk, 2005). But blog content is more likely to be shorter versions of what already appears, or perhaps even more 'inside gossip' than extensive policy discussion.

The blogosphere is creating new dilemmas for news professionals on their own websites. One is the transparency of the newsgathering process. Journalistic blogs potentially make the newsgathering process public since reporters can post story pieces online as they gather news. They need not wait to distribute a final product in the form of a printed newspaper article or a television news story. One reporter-blogger said he will inform his readers of what he is working on and what information he has even before he writes the story. It illuminates the news process and even invites reader reaction in the formation of the story (Lasica, 2001).

Blogs also raise the question of the role of editing. Should journalists' blogs be edited? Is it a violation of the norms of the blogosphere that an individual's writing is edited by someone else? Or are those norms changeable as the blogosphere acquires new members who seek to adapt the medium to their uses?

Editing is fundamental to the journalistic process, but antithetical to the original blog culture.

This dilemma is exemplified in the case of a reporter for a California newspaper who wanted to post a strongly critical statement about a gubernatorial candidate, but was forced to run copy through the editor first. Bloggers complained about the news organization's decision to edit the journalist and the newspaper eventually overturned its decision (Weintraub, 2003: 58–9). But then some of the reporter's colleagues complained, in turn, about the new double standard of editing – print stories get edited but blog posts do not (Smolkin, 2004). The approach to editing varies. For example, *The New York Times* blog is edited (Smolkin, 2004). Many others are not.

Including the Public

Blogging has presented another dilemma for traditional media – how to handle the potential for increased public involvement in the presentation of news. Bloggers challenge media claims that the news presentation must be dominated by trained professionals. They bristle at the assumption that the news media product is more legitimate because it is written and edited by trained professional journalists.

While traditional journalists have developed an aura of professionalism via journalistic education, professional societies and codes of ethics, bloggers have none of those. Many are amateurs in the process of news gathering and reporting. Not surprisingly, some journalists have disparaged the amateurism of blogging. One reporter said the power of blogs was 'like C-SPAN in the hands of a 19 year-old' (Hindman, 2008: 111).

Despite this kind of criticism of bloggers, news media organizations are responding to the technological capability and the demand for public involvement emanating from the Internet and the blogosphere. They are opening up the news presentation, particularly online, to more voices than those offered by news professionals. One example is the creation of newspaper blogs with their accompanying comment capability. Many major media publications – including elite newspapers, network news divisions and national newsmagazines – have started their own blogs (Strupp, 2006: 62). These blogs are dominated by the news professionals, but they include a comment function that offer readers, non-professionals, an opportunity to participate in the news presentation provided to online readers.

Blogs have set an example of transparency. Blogs suggest to traditional media that reporting can be open and transparent with an emphasis on public development of information (Lasica, 2003). Bloggers sometimes even actively encourage readers to provide information to them. Josh Marshall of *Talking Points Memo* has urged readers to do research for him and communicate their findings back to his audience (Perlmutter, 2008).

News organizations, in turn, have made the newsgathering process more transparent. With 24-hour news cycles and immediate deadlines, journalists offer less than complete stories, which then are updated. But they also use their own blogs to discuss the news reporting process and the evolution of stories rather than keep those secret from readers. Actually, blogs are not the only forces moving journalism in this direction. Home video, Internet-based reporting and the 24-hour news cycle also play a part.

One drawback to the increased interaction with readers through newspaper blogs is the potential for journalists to confuse the blog posters with the broad readership. News professionals may become obsessed with those who read their blogs and make comments rather than a broader audience that does not do so. Reporters may begin to tailor the news presentation in response to those who are vocal, without understanding whether those who express themselves online may represent a distinct minority. Such responses even may lead journalists to question their own news judgment. For example, one journalist blogger asserted that 'my readers know more than I do' (Lasica, 2001).

Freeing Journalists

Blogging began as a public personal expression, much like writing a personal diary and then handing it out to perfect strangers. One survey of bloggers found that the most common reason people blogged was to 'document their personal experiences and share them with others. And the most common topic of blog writing was 'my life and experiences' (Lenhart and Fox, 2006). That style carries over into political blogs. A-list political bloggers take personal thoughts and broadcast them to hundreds of thousands of people.

Through most of the 20th century, the professional norms of journalism were diametrically opposite to this personalized approach in news writing. As a vehement reaction to the partisan press of an earlier age, journalists were required to hide their true feelings behind the mask of objectivity. It was important that the reader be unaware of personal views the reporter held about the subject. Professional norms discouraged personal expression.

Over the past several decades, the pre-eminence of objectivity has been eroded by successive challenges from the 'new journalism' movement, advocacy journalism and public journalism. Moreover, public opinion about the news media has become more critical of journalists' assertions

that they maintain objectivity. Most Americans today perceive at least a fair amount of political bias in the news they get (Pew Research Center, 2007, 2008).

Blogs come as the most recent addition to the anti-objectivity trends of the past half century. But blogs are different from these previous movements because they come from outside of journalism. They offer journalists an alternative method of writing that combines the elements of previous movements such as critical analysis and advocacy journalism – but also emphasizes the human nature of the reporter over the model of the journalist as an interchangeable professional. One blogger explained that blogs 'tend to be impressionistic, telegraphic, raw, honest, individualistic, highly opinionated and passionate, often striking an emotional chord' (Lasica, 2001).

By adopting blog writing, journalists increasingly are abandoning the constraints of objective journalism. When blogging, they are more likely to express personal views, make unsubstantiated assertions and abandon the reliance on sources to make points. The blog world's norms are beginning to carry over into, and reshape, the norms of journalism. Journalists can act more like other bloggers and less like objective journalists when they write on newspaper blogs.

This liberation, however, leads to the question of how far it will extend into journalism. Will the blog writing style become the style incorporated outside the blogosphere, that is, in journalists' traditional formats of news presentation? The answer probably is no. Objective journalism took some time to establish itself as the paradigm for news presentation. Moreover, audience expectations are still relevant. The vast majority of the traditional audience still expects, and wants, a press that is free of a particular point of view (Pew Research Center, 2008).

What does that mean for individual journalists? This creates a tension within individual journalists who both blog and continue to work as daily reporters covering beats. Perhaps blogging can be viewed as a release – the liberation discussed above. For a brief time in their daily routine, they can break out of their set patterns and express personal opinions and, frankly, be themselves. But will that eventually affect their traditional writing?

And maybe an even more important question is whether journalists will be trusted as neutral descriptors of events once their personal views about those same events are expressed on blogs. Does the 'liberation' undermine journalists' credibility? The question is particularly important given the decline in credibility already experienced by the press (Pew Research Center, 2005). Will blog expression – as attractive as it may be as a release – harm journalists' ability to perform their main function as newsgatherers and reporters.

SHAPING BLOGS

Bloggers suggest they are changing journalism, or reforming it. Yet, the effects are hardly one way; journalism is shaping the evolution of blogging as well. As a practice in its infancy, blogging does not have its own traditions. Hence, the development of blogging can be heavily influenced by other forces with a more entrenched history than this embryonic medium.

Indeed, the most powerful source of influence over blogs is likely to be journalism. Journalism shares the same objectives as blogging – both seek to disseminate news and information to a particular audience. And the integration of journalists into blogging, as has been discussed previously, increases the opportunities for influence on this yet-undeveloped activity. That integration is more pronounced by the fact that blogging has emerged at the same time newsrooms are downsizing. Journalists who still want to practice their craft find blogs attractive as an alternative to unemployment or abandoning the profession.

Providing a Governing Model

The current approach to news writing has a long historical tradition. The evolution from the partisan editor to the reporter as the author of news still heavily influences the current journalistic model. Journalism based on accuracy, rapid delivery and descriptiveness has become the governing model for reporting of news. Even the mixing of analysis and commentary within reporting is not a combination blogs invented. Teddy White, who covered the US presidential elections as a reporter/analyst rather than just a standard reporter, created a new style of journalism that preceded bloggers by 40 years (Lawson-Borders and Kirk, 2005). That model then becomes one for bloggers to emulate.

Regardless of the antipathy toward traditional journalism or 'big media' on the part of many bloggers, the model of news reporting established by journalism is more likely to be emulated by political bloggers than it is to be discarded. One reason is that the blogosphere has no other model to follow that so closely resembles what they do. Moreover, their audiences have come to expect bloggers to accept much of the journalistic model. Readers accustomed to professional standards of journalism do not easily abandon those expectations in the face of a new medium. They anticipate

the blog will match reader expectations of content in accuracy, speed and freshness.

A-list blogs also increasingly are adopting the organizational style of traditional media. Individual blogs are being replaced by organizational blogs run by a staff. *The Huffington Post* is an example. Increasingly, an organization will emerge with structural layers. Editors will determine content that appears on the blog. Writers will be part of an organizational structure rather than wholly autonomous individuals.

Establishing Blogger Standards

More specifically, journalism is affecting bloggers' approaches to their tasks. Bloggers are being held to standards of professionalism that journalists created. Bloggers are expected to be accurate. Sourcing needs to be used, and those sources must be reliable. Bloggers are beginning to realize the impact their information has on a community of readers and the affect their content has on perceptions of legitimacy.

However, the blogosphere is divided over whether to accept these standards. Some bloggers want to be treated as journalists. Others prefer a different model – one that bloggers themselves will create on their own. One blogger worried that 'if you try to put the rules of mainstream journalism onto blogs, you end up sucking the life out of them' (Smolkin, 2004). But the very existence of a debate is the result of journalism's standards being employed as a yardstick for judging bloggers.

The bloggers who likely will gain the greatest audience and have the most impact both in and out of the blogosphere will be those who adhere to standards of journalism. Those bloggers who want to be like journalists have even created an organization – the Media Bloggers Association. The association seeks credentialing for journalists, equal access to sources, coverage under shield laws and the same respect accorded journalists. The association, and others that likely will follow, essentially will create a two-tiered blogging world. One part of that world will be bloggers who subscribe to a code of ethics and become journalist-like. The other will be everyone else – bloggers who wish to retain blogging's peculiarity. That division will become the equivalent of the difference between the evolution of large corporate-based newspapers and the single person, small town newspaper run on a shoe-string budget. It is important to remember that the latter model eventually disappeared. The 'wild west' atmosphere of the blog – the libertarian dream of no external constraints – is fast evaporating for those blogs who seek to be treated seriously as mainstream players.

A SYMBIOTIC RELATIONSHIP

Bloggers often describe their relationship with journalists as a competitive one. Some bloggers have suggested that the blogosphere even will replace traditional media. They envisioned a future where traditional media no longer serve a useful function. According to some bloggers, as blogs bypassed traditional media filters and news consumers got their own direct information, there would no longer be a need for traditional news media sources (Lasica, 2002).

For their part, journalists often criticize bloggers as wannabe journalists who lack the professionalism requisite for the title. Or journalists may respond with silence suggesting the blogosphere is not worthy of reply. They may pretend political blogs do not exist or acknowledge their existence but insist they have no relationship with journalism.

Certainly, competitive elements exist in the relationship. They compete because they are alike in many ways. They both gather and disseminate news. Bloggers want to be first with the story, as do journalists. Bloggers and journalists tussle over the media's agenda. Bloggers want media coverage to reflect bloggers' priorities. Journalists, however, naturally seek to maintain control over that agenda.

They compete because they overlap in the nature of their content. Both deal with straight news reporting and commentary. A-list political blogs often report current events as well as comment on them. The degree to which they do so varies significantly. For example, *The Huffington Post* features hard news coverage with lengthy late-breaking wire service stories while others such as *Eschaton* typically ignore the latest breaking news. Similarly, traditional media have included commentary and analysis in the news presentation. Newspapers editorialize on their editorial pages and allow others – both columnists and readers – to express opinion on the same pages. And broadcast news programs have included commentary at times in segregated segments either during the news hour or at other times.

Since the rise of objective journalism, that commentary usually has been relegated to separate sections in order to convey the impression of the distinctiveness of opinion as opposed to news reporting. (That has frayed in recent years as newspapers have included analysis, although not necessarily strict commentary, which is placed adjacent to news stories on the same topic.) Hence, a significant difference with bloggers is that when they do report current news, they do so usually through a mixture of both news and opinion.

The overlap between the two media, therefore, is hardly complete. That is common sense. If blogs had duplicated journalism, there would have been no appeal. Instead they offer a component of news that is underplayed in news reporting by journalists. Blogs emphasize commentary with some hard news, while news organizations offer hard news with some commentary.

That is why competition is too narrow an explanation of the relationship between journalists and bloggers. What has developed as well is a symbiotic relationship. Blogs have become integrated into the news reporting process. Journalists pay attention to them. They read blogs and occasionally they even use blogs as news sources. They sometimes use blogs for story ideas (Davis, 2009).

Journalists and bloggers benefit from the relationship in the sense that they rely on one another to provide a facet of news each has difficulty offering. For journalists, opinion and commentary occupies an uneasy place in the journalistic profession. Bloggers, on the other hand, have no difficulty with commentary. In fact, they revel in it. Their problem is an inability to match the news media's surveillance capability. Therefore, bloggers, like everyone else, primarily must rely on the news media for news. For national political bloggers, that means particular dependence on national media such as *The New York Times*, *The Washington Post* and *CNN*. They read online news sources every day, and even several times daily, and use them as springboards for blog posts.

Although critical of traditional media, some bloggers admit their dependence on traditional media. Markos Moulitsas said the media are allies with bloggers: 'I don't want to do the reporting … I need the media to do its job and provide the raw data, the raw information that then we can use to decide what's the best course for our country …' (Marshall, 2006). And John Hinderaker, a conservative blogger, has articulated the respective roles:

> I don't think that the press has a special role in constitutional terms. I think they have a special role in our economy, and that is as primary news gatherers and news disseminators. We bloggers and others in the field of commentary can do anything that journalists can do. Sometimes we do it better; sometimes maybe we don't do it as well. But we can do it. But we don't have staffs of full-time reporters and budgets to send reporters to far-off parts of the world and so on. Somebody needs to carry out that primary news-gathering and news-reporting function. (Hinderaker, 2006)

Bloggers heavily rely on news media for news. Blog posts are replete with references to traditional media stories. It is no surprise that bloggers themselves admit that the traditional media constitute a vital source of information for them.

Markos Moulitsas confessed he gets his news mostly from newspapers (Marshall, 2006).

In fact, the very legitimacy of blogs has been enhanced by the presence of journalists among bloggers. Blogs by former or even current journalists legitimated blogs for journalists. When traditional journalists began examining blogs to determine whether they were worth their time to read, they realized some of the blog content consisted of writing by former colleagues and well-known peers. This established a level of trust in the new medium that was not shared previously by discussion groups or chat rooms. The incorporation of traditional journalists in the blogosphere has continued to attract journalist readers. As a result, the blogosphere now includes a journalistic audience that reports on blogs for a non-blog reading audience and offers the potential of magnifying the influence of the blogosphere far beyond its own borders (Drezner and Farrell, 2004).

One aspect of this symbiotic relationship is the implicit division of labor between these two entities. The division reflects the weaknesses of both; that is, journalists' eschewing of commentary and the blogs' inability to collect hard news on their own. When bloggers argue that their contribution is a substantial part of the consumer's news package, they are acknowledging this division of labor. Notice above that Moulitsas called the news product 'raw data'. The implication is that without the blogs the information provided by the news media is incomplete. It lacks the analysis – the interpretative frame – that blogs provide. Without blogs, the reader gets only descriptive information without an understanding of meaning and context.

The bloggers' contribution, however, in this symbiotic relationship may be to say what journalists cannot. For example, a journalist reporting a story about the absence of weapons of mass destruction in Iraq after the Bush administration went to war on that premise might want to add personally that the president either lied to the public or was incompetent in seeking the truth. The blogger can, and does, assert that.

Another value added is to broadcast a perspective on the news emanating from outside traditional journalism. Reaction to news now is often filtered through journalists interviewing journalists. Journalists can be accused of being too insular when they turn to each other for reaction to events. But theoretically bloggers allow journalists to see reaction that is largely outside the journalistic community. Since most bloggers spend little time in news rooms or briefing rooms or press galleries, their reaction becomes another perspective – one that may be seen as the public's reaction or at least a response by people who are more like the public than journalists are.

(Significantly, that assumption is flawed because some of the influential bloggers are affiliated with traditional media or, at one time themselves were journalists. Even those who were not journalists look far more like elites than they do the general public [Davis, 2009; Hindman, 2008].) As well, the act of gauging that reaction also is a profoundly subjective one. The two broad camps of the blogosphere – liberal and conservative – allow journalists potentially to pick and choose which blogs they seek to use in order to frame the story. The blogger potentially becomes another source for the journalist using sources to say what the journalist cannot.

Additionally, the blog analysis appears faster than editorials. Newspaper editorials currently appear once a day in the morning while blog commentary can be nearly instantaneous. For example, within minutes of any major news story, blogs are commenting on it. For journalists on a 24-hour cycle with constant deadlines, the blogs offer reaction much faster than other news sources. Of course, the instant analysis can lead to questions about whether the reaction is thoughtful and reasoned. That is not the real question for bloggers. In fact, one might argue that the more emotional the reaction, the more newsworthy the blog post.

The symbiosis goes beyond straight news versus commentary. It is also in breadth versus depth of reporting. News media possess the capability to conduct surveillance across a broad array of events. With news bureaus in various parts of the country and the globe, national news organizations are capable of drawing event-driven stories into the press, typically in short segments. Television news stories are one example, but so are newspaper stories that have become shorter over time. Blogs, by contrast, lack that capability and are not likely to ever possess it. Bloggers need journalists to perform that news gathering role they lack the resources to carry out.

Bloggers can perform a complementary function of burrowing down more deeply into details of more specific events at a level that general interest media rarely reach. Wilson Lowrey suggested bloggers 'produce content based on stories that have been abandoned by traditional journalism organizations' (2006: 12). The capability to do so does not mean they actually do so. *Instapundit*, for example, is a blog consisting of numerous brief posts rarely going beyond brief discussion, or even bare mention, of issues or events. Others, however, such as Michelle Malkin and *Daily Kos*, feature lengthy posts with extensive exposition of a particular topic. But some blogs do acquire an information niche that makes them valuable to journalists. These blogs offer specialized information that is difficult for journalists to collect elsewhere. These specialty blogs can be valuable news sources for knowledge that journalists themselves do not possess (Drezner and Farrell, 2004).

All of this description of a mutually beneficial relationship with repeated interaction may ring hollow to many journalists, and perhaps even bloggers. And they may be correct. The existence of a symbiotic relationship in a general sense does not mean every individual journalist or blogger is part of that relationship. Indeed, there are journalists who do not use blogs or pay attention to them. As individuals, they do not participate in the relationship, although they may still be affected by its existence. And there are political bloggers who rely on the media for news to varying extents, some doing so very little.

Again, the existence of a symbiotic relationship does not mean journalists and bloggers do not compete at times as well. The competition may well be an important component of the symbiosis. It helps establish the independence of the two entities, thus preventing absorption. And that independence is particularly emphasized by bloggers.

Journalists and bloggers have formed a symbiotic relationship which may well last for some time. Ironically, it is a relationship that exists despite the expressed hostility on the part of many bloggers and the public disdain or seeming neglect on the part of journalists. Bloggers have forced journalists to be more accessible, interactive, more willing to include the public in newsmaking, and even prone to view newsgathering as a more transparent process. Journalists, in turn, have become a model for bloggers who want credibility as news outlets by establishing ethical standards, stressing accuracy, and acknowledging the consequences of writing first and thinking second. As long as journalists see bloggers as potential news sources, and bloggers rely on the traditional media for news, their work will be intertwined, not distinct.

REFERENCES

Bloom, J. D. (2003) 'The Blogosphere: How a Once-Humble Medium Came to drive Elite Media Discourse and Influence Public Policy and Elections', paper presented at the 2nd annual pre-APSA Conference on Political Communication. Philadelphia, PA.

Corrigan, D. H. (2003) *The Public Journalism Movement in America: Evangelists in the Newsroom.* Westport, CT: Praeger.

Davis, R. (2009) *Typing Politics: The Role of Blogs in American Politics.* New York: Oxford University Press.

Drezner, D. W. and Farrell, H. (2004) 'The Power and Politics of Blogs', paper presented at the annual meeting of the American Political Science Association. Chicago, IL.

Emery, E. (1984) *The Press and America: An Interpretive History of the Mass Media.* 5th edn. Englewood Cliffs, NJ: Prentice-Hall Inc.

Fowler, M. (2008) 'Obama: No Surprise That Hard-Pressed Pennsylvanians Turn Bitter' Huffington Post, 11 April. http://www.huffingtonpost.com/mayhill-fowler/obama-no-surprise-that-ha_b_96188.html (accessed 11 April 2008).

Geraghty, J. (2008) 'Highlights of John McCain's Latest Conference Call With Bloggers', http://campaignspot.nationalreview.com/post/?q=MzExZDFiNTg1MjAyYmUwYWRkMDQ4YTRlZjg4ZDdlNGM= (accessed 30 July 2009).

Glasser, T. L. (ed.) (1999) *The Idea of Public Journalism.* New York: Guilford Press.

Grant, S. (2007) *We're All Journalists Now: The Transformation of the Press and the Reshaping of the Law in the Internet Age.* New York: Free Press.

Hassid, J. (2011) 'Safety Valve or Pressure Cooker? Evaluating the Role of Internet Discourse in Chinese Political Life, paper presented at the annual meeting of the American Political Science Association. Seattle, WA.

Hinderaker, J. (2006) 'FRONTLINE: News War: Interviews John Hinderaker', http://www.pbs.org/wgbh/pages/frontline/newswar/interviews/hinderaker.html (accessed 30 July 2009).

Hindman, M. (2008) *The Myth of Digital Democracy.* Princeton, NJ: Princeton University Press.

Kerbel, M. (2009) *Netroots: Online Progressives and the Transformation of American Politics.* Boulder, CO: Paradigm Publishers.

Klam, M. (2004) 'Fear and Laptops on the Campaign Trail', *The New York Times Magazine,* http://www.nytimes.com/2004/09/26/magazine/26BLOGS.html?ex=1253937600&en=6ace5dcb675bf750&ei=5088&partner=rssnyt (accessed 3 August 2009).

Kurtz, H. (2007) 'Politico Rushes to Crack the Story and Ends Up With Egg on Its Face', 23 March *The Washington Post.* http://www.washingtonpost.com/wp-dyn/content/article/2007/03/22/AR2007032202180.html (accessed 30 November 2011)

Lasica, J. D. (2001) 'Weblogs: A New Source of News', http://www.ojr.org/ojr/workplace/1017958782.php (accessed 30 July 2009).

Lasica, J. D. (2002) 'Blogging as a Form of Journalism', http://www.ojr.org/ojr/lasica/1019166956.php (accessed 31 July 2009).

Lasica, J. D. (2003) 'Blogs and Journalism Need Each Other', *Nieman Reports,* Fall: 71. http://www.nieman.harvard.edu/reportsitem.aspx?id=101042 (accessed 3 August 2009).

Lawson-Borders, G. and Kirk, R. (2005) 'Blogs in Campaign Communication', *American Behavioral Scientist,* 49(4): 548–59.

Lenhart, A. and Fox, S. (2006) 'Bloggers: A Portrait of the Internet's New Storytellers', http://www.pewinternet.org/Reports/2006/Bloggers.aspx?r=1 (accessed 30 July 2009).

Lowrey, W. (2006) 'Mapping the Journalism-Blogging Relationship', *Journalism,* 7(4): 477–500.

Loyalka, M. D. (2005) 'Blog Alert: Battalion of Citizen Investigative Reporters Cannot be Ignored by Mainstream Media', *The IRE Journal*, 28(4): 19–20.

Marshall, J. (2006) 'FRONTLINE: News War: Interviews Josh Marshall', http://www.pbs.org/wgbh/pages/frontline/news-war/interviews/marshall.html (accessed 30 July 2009).

Merritt, D. (1998) *Public Journalism and Public Life: Why Telling the News is Not Enough*. Mahwah, NJ: Lawrence Erlbaum Associates.

Mott, F. L. (1962) *American Journalism: A History: 1690–1960*. New York: MacMillan Co.

Moulitsas, M. (2006) 'FRONTLINE: New War: Interviews Markos Moulitsas', http://www.pbs.org/wgbh/pages/frontline/newswar/interviews/moulitsas.html (accessed 31 July 2009).

Perlmutter, D. (2008) *Blogwars: The New Political Battleground*. New York: Oxford University Press.

Pew Research Center for The People & The Press (2005) 'Public More Critical of Press, But Goodwill Persists', http://people-press.org/reports/pdf/248.pdf (accessed 30 July 2009).

Pew Research Center for The People & The Press (2007) 'Internet News Audience Highly Critical of News Organizations', http://peoplepress.org/reports/pdf/348.pdf (accessed 30 July 2009).

Pew Research Center for The People & The Press (2008) 'Internet's Broader Role in Campaign 2008: Social Networking and Online Videos Take Off', http://people-press.org/reports/pdf/384.pdf (accessed 30 July 2009).

Pole, A. (2009). *Blogging the Political: Politics and Participation in a Networked Society*. New York: Routledge.

Poirier, A. (2006) 'Blogging is Not Journalism', *Guardian*, 21 March, http://www.guardian.co.uk/commentisfree/2006/mar/21/blogisnotjournalism

Ralston, B. (2007). 'Public Opinion on Key Turns Rabid', *New Zealand Herald*, 7 Oct. http://www.nzherald.co.nz/politics/news/article.cfm?c_id=280&objectid=10468322 (accessed 30 November 2011).

Robertson, L. (2002) 'Romancing the Source', *American Journalism Review*, 47(2), http://www.ajr.org/Article.asp?id=2520 (accessed 3 August 2009).

Rubin, R. (1981) *Press, Party, and Presidency*. New York: WW. Norton.

Schudson, M. (1980) *Discovering the News*. New York: Basic Books.

Singer, J. B. (1997) 'Still Guarding the Gate? The Newspaper Journalist's Role in an On-line World', *Convergence*, 3(1): 72–89.

Skube, M. (2007). 'Blogs: All the Noise That Fits' *Los Angeles Times*, 19 August. http://articles.latimes.com/2007/aug/19/opinion/op-skube19 (accessed 30 November 2011).

Smolkin, R. (2004) 'The Expanding Blogosphere', *American Journalism Review*, 66: 38–43, http://www.ajr.org/Article.asp?id=3682 (accessed 30 July 2009).

Smolkin, R. (2005) 'Lessons Learned', *American Journalism Review*, 69: 44, http://www.ajr.org/article.asp?id=3783 (accessed 3 August 2009).

Society of Professional Journalists, Columbia University Graduate School of Journalism (2004) *Wonkette in the Flesh: An Evening with Ana Marie Cox*. Columbia School of Journalism.

Starr, A. (2005) 'Open-Source Reporting', *The New York Times Magazine*, http://www.nytimes.com/2005/12/11/magazine/11ideas_section3–3.html?ex=1291957200&en=80b42abda110a1b3&ei=5088&partner=rssnyt&emc=rss (accessed 3 August 2009).

Strupp, J. (2006) 'Voting for the Web', *Editor & Publisher*, October: 62.

Vaina, D. (2007) 'Newspapers and Blogs: Closer Than We Think?', *Online Journalism Review* http://www.ojr.org/ojr/stories/070423_vaina/ (accessed 30 July 2009).

Wall, M. (2005) '"Blogs of War": Weblogs as News', *Journalism*, 6(2): 157–8.

Weintraub, D. (2003) 'Scuttlebutt and Speculation Fill a Political Weblog', *Nieman Reports*, Winter: 58–9, http://www.nieman.harvard.edu/reportsitem.aspx?id=100923 (accessed 3 August 2009).

Wheeler, B. (2006) 'Battle of the Conference Blogs', BBC News. 15 September. http://news.bbc.co.uk/2/hi/uk_news/politics/5343334.stm. (accessed 30 November 2011).

5

Political Organizations and Campaigning Online

Rachel K. Gibson and Stephen Ward

In recent years, academic interest in political campaigning has increased significantly, particularly with regard to understanding its importance in elections and effects on voter turnout and choices (Farrell and Schmitt-Beck, 2003; Holbrook, 1996; Norris et al., 1999). Attention has also focused on the changing nature of the campaign itself and the new tools and techniques that are being used to communicate with voters. Key questions posed by scholars have focused on whether we have moved into a new more hi-tech and professionalized era in which the style and management of campaigns is being fundamentally transformed (Blumler and Kavanagh, 1999; Farrell and Webb, 2000; Johnson, 2007; Norris, 2000; Strachan, 2003; Swanson and Mancini, 1996). While these areas of study have sought to incorporate the effect of the new information and communication technologies (ICTs), the very recent arrival of these tools on the political scene and their rapidly changing functionalities has meant that a comprehensive understanding of their implications for political organizations' campaign practice has not as yet been fully developed.

This chapter seeks to address this gap in the literature by first locating online technologies within the longer trajectory of campaign change and charting their adoption across political systems worldwide. We then turn to look at how online campaigning is affecting parties' in the wider electoral context, specifically in terms of levels of inter-party competition and mobilization of voters. Are certain types of organization benefiting more from switching to digital forms of campaigning? In a final step, we extend the analytical lens to examine the implications of

new media campaigns for organizations' internal structures and grassroots support base. How far is online electioneering promoting the decentralization of campaign management and more democratic input from members and supporters? We conclude by reflecting on extent to which the new media is transforming the manner and effectiveness of political campaigning as well as possibly the organizations undertaking these new practices.

POLITICAL ORGANIZATIONS, CAMPAIGN CHANGE AND NEW ICTs

The study of political campaigns has increased markedly over the past two decades. The work of Bowler and Farrell (1992) and Butler and Ranney (1992), in particular, signalled the start of more intensive period of comparative analysis of campaigns, particularly those taking place in national elections. This growth in interest, however, was predicated on the earlier work of party scholars such as Kircheimer (1966), Epstein (1967), Rose (1967) and then later Panebianco (1988) who had charted the rise of the electoral-professional party and the growing centrality of voter mobilization efforts within party organizations and operations. In addition, the voting literature had moved beyond individual sociological and psychological explanations of voter behaviour to encompass more proximate and contextual factors such as issues, economic performance and candidate image. Campaign messages and intensity were also seen as increasingly influential for interpreting voter turnout and choices (Aarts and Semetko, 2003; Alvarez, 1997; Cho, 2005; Conover and Feldman, 1989; Denver et al., 2003; de Vreese et al., 2006; Fisher and Denver, 2008; Gerber and Green, 2000; Hetherington, 1996; Just et al., 1996; Luntz, 1988; Peter et al., 2004; Schmitt-Beck, 2003; Semetko et al., 1991).

A primary focus of this emerging campaigns literature has been the new hi-tech tools and 'marketing' techniques that parties and candidates are using in their efforts to communicate with voters (Butler and Collins, 1994; Henneberg, 2002; Lees-Marshment, 2001; Newman, 1999; Norris, 2000; Plasser, 2000; Swanson and Wring, 1997). Initiatives have typically included the hiring of specialist media and PR consultants to ensure a sophisticated televisual appeal for the parties' message and its leaders, the conducting of extensive public opinion research through focus groups and surveys and the development of large private databases for direct mailing and telemarketing. Given the geographic origins of many of these techniques in the USA, the term 'Americanization' became popular shorthand to describe the changes taking place (Butler and Ranney, 1992; Farrell and Webb, 2000; Gurevitch, 1999; Kavanagh, 1995; Negrine and Papathanassopoulos, 1996; Scammell, 1999). Other scholars opted for less context specific terminology, preferring to see the new practices as part of a wider process of societal 'modernization' (Plasser and Plasser, 2002) or even as part of a 'postmodern' era (Norris, 2000). Overall, these developments were seen as reaching something of an apotheosis in the slick and highly managed victories of Clinton's 'war room' in 1992, and Berlusconi's Forza Italia in 1994, Schroeder's SPD in the German federal election of 1998 and of course the New Labour machine in the UK in 1997 (Green and Smith, 2003; Mancini, 1999; Wring, 2005).

While these trends toward a more professionalized mode of electoral management have continued into the post-2000 era, work in the area has also pointed to the growth of more localized and direct forms of campaign communication that target specific groups of key voters (Farrell, 2006; Fisher and Denver, 2008). The continuing breakdown of traditional class divides and the changing demographic and economic structure of post-industrial society has meant an increasing pluralization of political interests and blurring of partisan loyalties. Political parties along with other organizations and institutions of the state increasingly need to undertake more continuous, direct and interactive dialogue with voters to understand their changing preferences and align their own policy profiles (Farrell, 2006; Gibson and Römmele, 2009; Wlezien, 2010). The UK

Minister Douglas Alexander who oversaw the Labour Party's re-election effort in 2001 neatly summarized these developments in an interview when he noted that the days of the 'centralized election campaign' were over. Marketing techniques that regarded the electorate 'as an homogenized mass' were no longer viable he argued. Instead, parties need to find 'new ways to communicate directly' with voters in the future.[1]

The role of the new ICTs within this process of change and transformation of the political campaigns landscape has been presented so far as one that supports and extends this move toward a more niche-driven and nuanced style of voter communication. Digital channels such as websites, email and SMS are seen largely as building on and expanding the voter targeting efforts embodied in activities such as direct mail and telemarketing (Farrell, 2006). Attention to, and discussion of, the interactive potential and participatory element that new media bring to campaigns has been more limited however. While this is largely due to the more static nature of web applications available in the earlier so-called web 1.0 era, the introduction of new user-driven web tools, such as blogs, video sharing channels and social networking sites, clearly add significant new possibilities for two-way and even multi-way conversation between parties and voters. Thus, as well as accelerating trends toward a more niched and modularized style of campaign communication and away from the nationalized 'one-size-fits-all' campaign logic of the television age, new ICTs may be opening up even more radical possibilities for a new more 'bottom-up' and participatory element within campaigns which may see some significant shifts in their management and wider societal impact.

ONLINE CAMPAIGNING WORLDWIDE

The first section of the chapter was designed to locate new ICTs within the broader changes taking place to political organizations' campaign style. It was argued that they are generally seen as promoting a narrower more direct mode of communication with voters but that they can also foster new and more participatory opportunities to involve citizens in the election. In this section, we profile the body of empirical work that has grown up over the past decade tracking the use of new ICTs in political campaigns worldwide and assess far the findings support the idea that such changes are underway?

Although it is still relatively early days to be drawing conclusions about Internet-induced change in the campaign arena or indeed any other sphere of contemporary political life, a substantial body of empirical evidence now exists on this topic that does permit some meaningful insight to be drawn into these questions. The first point to note is that this evidence appears to be somewhat divided. Studies outside of the USA, and particularly those prior to the arrival of web 2.0 technologies, appear to provide little support for the notion that a significant change in campaign communication is taking place as a result of the new ICTs, especially in terms of any moves toward a more interactive approach. Repeated studies across a number of contexts have presented parties and candidates as highly cautious and conservative in their new media campaigns. Rather than exploiting the unique participatory potential of the technology the focus has been on reproducing information produced for offline distribution to a broad audience (Bimber and Davis, 2003; Davis, 1998; Gibson et al., 2003a,b; Gibson and Ward, 1998; Margolis and Resnick, 2000; Newell, 2001; Roper, 1999; Strandberg, 2006, 2009; Ward et al., 2008; Ward and Gibson, 1998). Such timidity has resulted in their election websites typically being dismissed as 'shovelware' or 'cyberbrochures' (Foot and Schneider, 2006; Kamarck, 2002). That said, it is not too surprising that political elites viewed the possibilities of such interactivity with some suspicion (Coleman, 2001; Stromer-Galley, 2000). Permitting open comment and discussion on the site risked highlighting internal dissent and voter criticism of the party. Coming so soon after the television era where message management and strict central control over the campaign agenda ruled the day, it is little wonder that party operatives found a swift transition to this new world of weaker regulation difficult.

Alongside this picture of inertia and 'no change', more recent strands of the literature have reported findings which are considerably more supportive of the idea that a new more 'bottom-up' form of campaigning may be emerging as the array of new web 2.0 tools spreads (Gueorguieva, 2007; Trammell et al., 2006). This is particularly the case in the context of the two recent US presidential election contests. The online campaigns of Democrat candidates' Howard Dean and Barack Obama are seen as having dramatically raised the bar in the levels of voter interactivity and participation they inspired. Starting with Dean's *Blog for America* and continuing through to the customized 'MyBo' site of the Obama team, the opportunities these campaigns provided to ordinary supporters to get involved and actively contribute through blogging, raising funds and canvassing via SMS for the candidates (Greengard, 2009; Haynes and Pitts, 2009; Norquay, 2008). One specific initiative of the Obama campaign, the 'Call Friends' iPhone application, proves perhaps

particularly worthy of note in this regard. Designed by volunteers it allowed users to download an application that converted their mobile phone into a mini-campaign tool. Listed contacts became targets for automatically generated messages reminding them to vote and to do so for Obama.

Ultimately, these new tools helped create a sense of involvement and even ownership of the campaign which was captured in the 'Yes We Can!' slogan promoted by the Obama team. Joe Trippi, the e-campaign manager for Dean talked at length in his book about the way in which the technology was expressly deployed to break down the 'us and them' mentality that had dominated previous presidential campaigning 'war rooms' and to establish a new grass or netroots supporter-led model (Trippi, 2005). Perhaps in these recent but very prominent examples of online campaigning, therefore, we are seeing the flowering of the more interactive localized and grassroots style of campaigning that the technologies in theory at least appear to promote. It is also worthwhile to note that so far these 'success stories' appear to be limited to the individual candidate-centred model of campaigns rather than those driven by strong party organizations. Thus, the extent to which campaigns in the more party-centric regions of the world can emulate this more individualized participatory approach remains an open question.

ONLINE CAMPAIGNING AND PARTY COMPETITION

In addition to helping us understand the extent to which a new style of campaigning is taking hold across political organizations, international studies of online campaigns have also focused on a further set of interesting and important questions relating to electoral competition. The first of these pertains to how far the rise of new technologies might increase the competitiveness of minor parties and candidates and make elections more open, unpredictable and volatile. The equalization hypothesis (Corrado and Firestone, 1996; Morris, 2000; Selnow, 1998) contends that the relatively low cost of online campaigns and lack of centrally produced and edited news sources increases opportunities for outsider groups to communicate their message to a wider range of voters. The idea that the Internet could erode the dominance of mainstream actors has gained support with the success of mavericks such as Reform Party candidate Jesse Ventura in the Minnesota Gubernatorial elections of 1998 and Roh Moo-Hyun in the 2002 South Korean presidential election.

Despite these individual success stories, however, the wider academic literature – particularly that focusing on systems with strong parties – has proved more supportive of the normalization thesis, with the major players emerging as dominant forces within cyberspace (Bimber and Davis, 2003; Gibson et al., 2003c; Margolis and Resnick, 2000; Norris, 2000; Resnick, 1999; Ward et al., 2008). Repeated studies of party websites across Europe, Australia and North America has demonstrated that major parties and candidates operated more sophisticated e-campaigns and used a wider range of web tools than did their minor party counterparts (Conway and Dorner, 2004; Farmer and Fender, 2005; Gibson and Ward, 1998, Gibson et al., 2003a,b; Margolis and Resnick, 2000; Newell, 2001; Strandberg, 2006, 2009). Furthermore, the visibility of mainstream parties (in terms of links in to their websites, position on search engines and advertising of websites through mainstream media), was generally considerably higher (Davis, 1999; Gibson et al., 2003a; Hindman et al., 2003; Hindman, 2008; Vincente-Merino, 2009). Smaller and fringe parties/candidates on the other hand tended to lack the capacity (staff and financial resources) to fully exploit the benefits of e-campaigning (Gibson et al., 2003c).

Within this general perception of a continuation in major parties' power and electoral dominance in the Internet age, identification of some underlying subtle changes to inter-party relations have also been argued for and are worthy of note here (Anstead and Chadwick, 2009; Cunha et al., 2003; Ward, 2005). In particular, it has been noted that while a well-run Internet campaign alone is not enough to guarantee success, the reduction in start-up costs it makes possible are significant, allowing a wider range of parties and candidates to survive than would otherwise be the case (Bimber, 1998; Dalton and Wattenberg, 2000). In part, this is because the new media electoral arena does offer slightly more equal coverage than the traditional media. Indeed, in some systems it might be continuing a trend of increasing the number of candidates competing at elections (Ghillebaert, 2009). Second, web tools enable some smaller parties and organizations (particularly those on the far right), to create a multiplier effect, that is, to appear larger than they are in reality through a professionalized online presence (Copsey, 2003; Gerstenfeld et al., 2003; March, 2005). Third, empirical studies across a number of countries have repeatedly highlighted that some minor party families, most notably the Green Party and the far right, were heavy users of technology and ran reasonably competitive online campaigns (Gibson and Ward, 2003; Sudulich, 2009; Ward, 2005). Some far-right organizations,

partly because of their semi-covert nature, have used the net extensively for both recruitment and networking (Caiani and Wagemann, 2009; Copsey, 2003; Whine, 2000). Indeed, these parties are now heavily dependent on the technology for their day-to-day operation and existence.

Overall then, while online campaigning has not dramatically upped levels of electoral competition its effects on inter-party relations are not entirely negligible. Clearly, the web can assist certain less well-known candidates and parties to raise their visibility with the electorate and build a stronger rapport with their activists. The barriers presented by electoral systems and representation thresholds and the difficulties in securing mass media exposure all still remain as obstacles to minor actors' success however. So it may be the case that while the Internet makes it easier for fringe parties to survive, it does not provide any guarantees that they can thrive.

ONLINE CAMPAIGNING AND THE ELECTORATE

Studies of Internet campaigns have also spent an increasing amount of time assessing its effects on voter behaviour. In broad terms, this work has tended to concentrate on who is using web sources for political information, what sources are being used and the effects (if any) that such sources have on politically relevant attitudes and activities. Studies from the US Pew Internet and American Life project have delivered a rich history of evidence to indicate that voters' awareness and attention to web campaign efforts has grown over time particularly within the 2008 election cycle (Rainie 2007; Rainie et al., 2005; Smith and Rainie, 2008). While in 1996, only 4% of the Internet-using population was reported as to have accessed some type of election-related material online, by 2008 this stood at 55% (Kohut et al., 2000; Smith, 2009).

Outside the USA, the numbers accessing campaign material or who have engaged in some type of online political activity are generally lower. In the 2007 French presidential elections, an event where the two main candidates waged high profile online campaigns, around one in five Internet users were reported to have accessed election sites (Vaccari, 2008; Vedel and Michalska, 2007). Parliamentary elections elsewhere in Australia and Denmark (2007) and the UK (2005) also appear to have attracted minority audiences, with studies reporting between 15 and 20% of voters as having accessed some election news and information online (Gibson and McAllister, 2006; Lusoli and Ward, 2005; Viborg-Andersen and Medaglia, 2008).

In terms of the extent to which Internet campaigns are actually affecting voter behaviour on election-day much of the analysis has centred on the mobilization versus reinforcement debate. The key question posed here is how to what extent the Internet can bring new people into the political process or whether it instead simply serves as a means for 'preaching to the converted' and already active. Less attention has been given to the next stage of the voting process, that is, vote choice and the extent to which the online campaign actually influences the support a candidate or party receives. On the first question, the consensus of most studies, especially the early ones, was that the Internet had limited impact (Bimber, 2001; Bimber and Davis, 2003; Davis, 1999; Norris, 2001, 2003). Audiences were found to be very small and their appeal confined largely to an elite of educated and informed individuals who were often well developed political identities who were often party supporters, members and activists. However, as use of the medium has spread and the range of politically relevant activities widened beyond basic use, more consistent findings of mobilization have emerged (Anduiza et al., 2008; De Zuniga et al., 2009; Gibson et al., 2005; Jensen et al., 2006; Krueger, 2002; Lupia and Philpot 2005; Mossberger et al., 2007; Moy et al., 2005; Quintelier and Vissers, 2008; Stanley and Weare, 2004). Certainly, the meteoric rise (and equally spectacular fall) of Howard Dean as a candidate for the Democratic presidential nomination in 2004 was seen to underscore the potential of the web as a voter recruitment device (Hindman, 2005; Trippi, 2005). Survey work by Williams et al. (2004) on attendees at the offline 'meetups' arranged through the online site revealed that a great number of those attending were political novices and professed little prior interest in politics.

In terms of the second question of whether web campaigns actually influence vote choice, the evidence is rather limited although increasingly positive. Detailed survey work by Bimber and Davis (2003) on the 2000 election cycle found little evidence that candidates' e-campaigns were able to convert undecided voters to their cause. However, earlier work using aggregate vote shares across candidates for the US Congress in 1996 had concluded a significantly higher vote total for those who campaigned online (D'Alessio, 1997). As the literature exploring this question has developed further, positive findings about the potential for voter conversion through web campaigning has been uncovered. In particular, work by Gibson and McAllister (2006, 2008) on Australian e-campaigns and Sudulich and Wall

(2010) on Irish online electioneering have reported a strong and consistent association between candidate vote shares and their having run an e-campaign controlling for a wide range of individual and organizational resources and contextual factors.

Although questions about causal direction are yet to be fully resolved a range of explanations for how these positive effects may be occurring have been developed and empirically explored. In brief, from a psychological perspective it has been contended that being online exposes citizens to more information which in turn increases their interest in politics and possibly the development of new cognitive resources (beyond the traditional socio-economic) that produce higher rates of participation, particularly among younger populations (Krueger, 2002; Lupia and Philpot, 2005; Mossberger et al., 2007). From a more rational actor perspective, it is also likely that the Internet significantly lowers costs for voters by promoting faster and easier access to information about the candidates and parties as well as the voting/registration process itself, thereby increasing turnout. However, as some scholars have pointed out the greater volume of information available in the online environment could also increase the complexity of decision making and so may have a differential impact on voters, possibly reducing participation rates among the less cognitively able (Prior, 2007).

One particularly intriguing explanation that has emerged from recent work within the UK and Belgium is the possibility of an indirect or a two-step mobilization effect whereby campaign sites activate the activists who then go mobilize others in their offline networks (Norris and Curtice, 2008; Vissers, 2009). Here the lesson for parties and candidates would seem to be that web outreach efforts are best conceived of as resources for a committed base of activists/supporters to go on and spread the word rather than to reach the wider electorate directly. The effect, as Vissers (2009) has neatly summarized it, is campaigners 'preaching through', rather than to, the converted.

While for the candidates the verdict at the ballot box undoubtedly remains the most important measure of any web campaign effects, from an academic perspective these studies suggest the need for a broadening of conceptual and empirical models of electoral outcomes and campaign effects. The use of web 2.0 tools by campaigns and voters now mean that the most significant and widespread changes in voters' outlooks and activities may be taking place well in advance of election day. The socially embedded and 'always on' nature of new campaign technologies, such as Facebook and Twitter, mean that the 'reach' of the campaign message may far exceed that taking place in the officially sponsored 'old' media channels and engage a new body of potential participants in a much more personalized manner. The receipt or sending of political jokes via email or mobile phone, reading or posting to a blog or advertising support for a candidate or political cause on one's social networking profile constitute small but potentially meaningful new political acts that may energize the previously inactive (Shifman et al., 2007). Such developments may then require an expansion of traditional political science approaches and models for understanding voter behaviour.

ORGANIZATIONAL CHANGE AND ONLINE CAMPAIGNING – DECENTRALIZATION?

New ICTs are also seen to hold quite radical implications for how organizations manage or run campaigns. Such shifts were alluded to in the first section of the chapter when it was suggested that Internet-based communication was helping to challenge the centralized model of campaigning developed during the television era. However, much of this discussion centred on changes in the content and mode of voter communication rather the implications for parties' internal structures. In this final section of the chapter, we explore this contention more fully by introducing the work that has examined the effects of new media campaigns for political organizations' internal structure. In particular, we look at the impact of new media campaigns on two sets of party relationships: those between election candidates and the party and, more widely, in terms of power relations between party leaders and activists and members.

Party–Candidate Relationship

The plurality of viewpoints permitted and even promoted by the Internet means that campaigns are now potentially more fragmented and open to a wider range of alternative and even dissenting voices than ever before. From personal websites to blogs, social networking profiles and online video, the new media provide a wider platform and more extensive tools for candidates to personalize and develop their campaigns individually, especially within constituency-based electoral systems. The potential that this provides for challenging the authoritative voice of the party HQ is evident. With minimal resources candidates can now highlight their own policy standpoints, voting records and provide voters with more information about themselves than was previously possible. While such trends may be less manifest in candidate-centred systems, such as the USA where an individualized approach to campaigning is the norm, elsewhere in countries where parties are traditionally strong, the impact could be more marked and long lasting (Anstead and Chadwick, 2009).

Empirical exploration of these trends has been relatively limited with most of the in-depth study of Internet campaigns having concentrated on the national level. It is possible, however, to draw together a growing body of literature on local Internet campaigns that shed some light on this question of campaign diversification and candidate independence. At a very basic level, studies of the spread and uptake of online campaigning at the sub-national level make clear that the use of the Internet as a medium of challenge and dissent has been quite limited to date. Beyond the USA, it is clear that the spread of the online campaign below the national level has been slow and rather sporadic (Carlson, 2006; Carlson and Djupsund, 2001; Gibson and Römmele, 2005; Gibson and Ward, 2003; Gibson et al., 2008a,b; Sudulich and Wall, 2010; Ward, 2005; Ward and Gibson, 2003; Ward et al., 2008). While institutional factors such as the frequency of elections, the need for private fund-raising and the level of existing party control over branch activities have prompted some of this inertia, cultural biases and scepticism toward online campaigning in getting the message across to voters and the importance placed on traditional campaign techniques of canvassing and leafleting have also played a role in determining the rapidity of uptake (Ward et al., 2008).

Of more direct relevance to questions about organizational diversification and decentralization in the Internet campaign era are those studies that have looked at the content of candidate web campaigns. Here the messages are rather contradictory. In general, a picture of conformity, conservatism and standardization appears to emerge with not many sites appearing to deviate from a set menu of features covering party history, leader profiles, current issues/campaigns, media and press resources.[2] While much of this is not necessarily enforced by diktat, studies of the UK, Australia and Canada where party discipline and control is seen as strong have reported a standardization and control of candidates online output by central party office through production of website templates (Gibson et al., 2008b; Smith and Chen, 2009; van Onselen and van Onselen, 2008; Ward, 2005). Such measures, while providing much needed assistance to resource-strapped local organizations, also help to prevent candidates going off message and generating unwanted opportunities for the traditional news media to highlight inconsistencies in the party message. The use of templates and standardized web tools also helps to convey a degree of professionalization and broad technological awareness across the party that may be important with certain key constituencies such as younger voters or urban professionals. Thus, rather paradoxically, while the Internet may be intensifying trends toward more localized campaigns and a more interactive and personalized dialogue with voters, it may also be providing an impetus for stronger central support and guidance as more of the less tech-savvy representatives and branches of the party seek to develop, manage and co-ordinate e-campaigns.

Power Relations: Internal Democracy and Online Campaigns

Aside from the specific candidate–party relationship, there has been increasing speculation about how online campaigning may be generating a broader change in the organizational culture of parties by enhancing their levels of internal democracy. Much has been made of the general democratizing influence of new technologies and their ability to help organizations resist the iron law of oligarchy in favour of more flexible, grassroots decentralized modes of behaviour (Bimber, 1998; Lofgren and Smith, 2003; Margetts, 2006; Pickerill, 2003). The creation of Intranets, internal discussion fora and email lists clearly have the capacity to make organizational elites more accountable to ordinary members. The greater volume and speed of information flows offered via computer mediated communication combined with its interactivity and decentralization into people's homes means members/supporters can have more frequent and direct access to elites to communicate their opinion on policy and organizational matters. In turn, individual members and informal groups within the party organization can also more effectively communicate with one another and network independently without the need to move through official channels or headquarters.

Empirical research into these trends has been sparse with most studies tending to follow the normalization logic to contend that online tools largely work to support an existing organizational culture rather than transform it (Römmele, 2003; Sudulich, 2009; Vincente-Merino, 2009). Those organizations with a pre-existing commitment to decentralized structures and grassroots networking, such as Green parties or protest and new social movements, are generally found to make more participatory use of the technology (Conway and Dorner, 2004; Gibson and Ward, 2003; Norris, 2003; Vincente-Merino, 2009). More hierarchically structured entities (that is, the mainstream political parties) have tended to adopt an experimental approach, running a series of 'one-off' consultations in which individuals are given opportunities to comment and 'have their say' but without this having an obvious and decisive impact on party leaders or policies.[3] This pattern of reinforcement of existing power relations is also observed in the data from party membership surveys conducted in the UK and Scandinavia during 2000–01. Here the research found that joiners tended to be more passive than their offline counterparts and those members making most active uses of the technologies were more likely to be already heavily involved in party affairs (Lusoli and Ward, 2004; Pedersen and Saglie, 2005; Ward et al., 2002).

The recent growth in the use of the new web 2.0 tools and the manner in which they were deployed by Obama in the 2008 US presidential election campaign has revived hopes for the technology's internal democratizing effects (Kalnes, 2009). The devolution of campaign activities into the hands of ordinary supporters that occurred during Obama's bid for office has been seen as effectively rewriting the rule book on how to manage and run a successful bid for political office.[4] Powered by the new media, campaigns can now offer interested amateurs the chance to become part of the team so they can independently canvass and fund raise on behalf of the candidate and perhaps even more crucially, work with and organize other volunteers (Christiansen and Roberts, 2009; Stromer-Galley, 2009). These new methods of involvement clearly come at something of a price for the party and the candidate, however, in terms of maintaining a clear message and keeping track of the activities and events organized in their name. After decades of professionally building and controlling a political brand, elites may find it difficult to accept this 'shared' model of responsibility. Furthermore, some have questioned the extent to which the Obama campaign in fact released a new decentralized grassroots model.[5] Closer scrutiny of the small dollar donations which powered Obama's campaign has shown for instance that while he did receive a much larger number of small contributions than had previous presidential candidates these were often from the same people and so cumulated as mid-range donations across the period. Also a substantial component of the final haul of dollars did come from large donations.[6] Whether the reality quite lived up to the hype, therefore, is something for the future literature in this area to fully examine.

CONCLUSION

This chapter has surveyed political organizations' and particularly political parties' use of new media for campaign purposes. We have looked specifically at how far this process of adoption is affecting change both within and across parties, as well as their relationship with voters and style of campaign communication. Overall, the review has produced little support for the idea that the incorporation of new ICTs is leading to radical and widespread change across these domains. The arrival of websites and email are seen largely to have accelerated ongoing trends toward a more targeted and direct style of voter communication. Opportunities to facilitate a more participatory campaign experience for voters through newer applications such as blogs, social networking profiles and online video do not appear to have been widely taken up. Furthermore, while it does appear that some smaller organizations can attain greater visibility for their message in the online environment compared to the world of the mainstream media, in general the major parties retain their position of dominance in the quality and extent of their presence. One area where more significant change does appear to be underway, however, is in the internal side of party operation where a more grassroots led approach to campaign management and message creation has been detected, at least within the USA. In the UK, the evidence points toward the emergence of a new networked model of campaigning comprising official and quasi-official groups and individuals working together in traditional and newer viral and virtual ways to mobilize voters. Whether this will continue beyond the most recent election cycle and expand beyond America is of course an important and as yet unanswered question.

Explaining the reticence of political organizations to fully exploit the campaign potential of the new ICTs is beyond the scope of this chapter. However, we would offer the following points to consider. First, extensive and systematic study of online campaigning in the new web 2.0 era is limited. Subsequent work may start to reveal a more radical picture of change as a better understanding develops of how these newer user-driven tools are being used. Second, the chapter has shown that for the most part candidates' and parties' online election efforts do not command a majority audience, although among the minority of voters that do pay attention, signs of mobilization have been detected. Thus, significant investment of time and resources in developing a 'state-of-the-art' Internet campaign would be seen by most managers as a risky strategy. No doubt as the generation of 'digital natives' (those younger citizens who have been socialized into Internet technologies since birth [Palfrey and Gasser, 2008]), come to political maturity a stronger commitment to e-campaigning will emerge.

Certainly, it is clear that the Internet is becoming an increasingly important medium for younger members of the electorate at a time when use of other media is in decline. Finally, it is also important to remember that context matters and that new ICTs do not exist in a vacuum. The way the technologies are deployed is inevitably shaped and constrained by the wider institutional, electoral environment and organizational cultures. The presidentialized and personalized model of government found in the USA combined with its weaker parties and freer rules on donation and expenditure creates an environment that is more conducive to rapid innovation and the type of supporter-led model of operations outlined above.

Thus, despite the opportunities that the Internet presents to open up current campaign practices and organization to a wider range of citizen input we expect the professionals to continue to play an important management and agenda-setting role. This is not to say that no changes are foreseen in the medium to longer term. Widening adoption of broadband and further well-publicized instances of the success of Obama-style networked campaigns will no doubt embolden parties and candidates to more seriously engage with the possibilities that the technology presents. Should such enthusiasm take hold then looking to the future we can speculate on a number of key changes to the campaigns landscape. In particular, we may see increasing moves toward a blurring of activist, member and supporter roles as the boundaries of the campaign and the wider organization become more porous. Ultimately, the notion of a campaign as a fixed event during which official activists attempt to mobilize a rather unwilling electorate may itself be replaced by a more fluid concept, whereby campaigning becomes a socially embedded and continuous phenomenon relying primarily on a changing configuration of individuals and groups, drip-feeding campaign news and information to family, neighbours and workplace contacts through their increasingly inter-connected online lives. Thus, rather than a top-down command and control logic driving the campaign, the key skills for parties and candidates to develop will be those of facilitating, supporting and targeting the efforts of more informal and unofficial frontline networks.

NOTES

1 'Politics must change or die, says minister', by Patrick Wintour. Available at: http://www.guardian.co.uk/uk/2002/feb/08/politics.labour (accessed on 30 December 2008).

2   It should be noted here that some scholars have noted increasing traces of individualization and personalization by candidates through their online role and a willingness to distance themselves from the party (Zittel, 2009).

3   For example, in the run-up to the 2005 election the Labour Party initiated the 'Big Conversation' consisting of both offline and online consultation. The exercise was supposedly designed to allow the public a voice in shaping the direction of both government and party policy in the form of the party manifesto. The online and text components were aimed at opening up the debate beyond party members to a more general wider audience. The exercise was widely derided as merely another exercise in Labour spin. Critics noted that the online element seemed to resemble more of a survey rather than any discussion, conversation or dialogue. Although no topic was apparently off-limits, the main debates were organized around 13 questions framed by the party. Nor was the consultation process necessarily transparent. It was not clear what would happen to comments or suggestions, etc. There were allegations that critical comments and emails were censored or edited and that some of the contributors to the website had been handpicked by the party. While others saw the 'Big Conversation' as a cynical exercise in political marketing with the main effort to gather email addresses (Lilleker and Negrine, 2006).

4   See 'Lessons from the Barack Obama Social Media Campaign' by J. A. Vargas. Available at: <http://www.scribd.com/doc/15679573/Lessons-from-the-Barack-Obama-Social-Media-Campaign> (accessed on 31 August 2009); 'The First 21st Century Campaign' by R. Brownstein. 19 April 2008. National Journal Available at: <http://www.national-journal.com/njmagazine/cs_20080416_3324.phpl> (accessed on 31 August 2009); 'How Obama's Internet Campaign Changed Politics' by Claire Cain Miller New York Times. 7 November 2008. Available at: http://bits.blogs.nytimes.com/2008/11/07/how-obamas-Internet-campaign-changed-politics/ (accessed 1 September 2009).

5   See articles 'How good was Obama's campaign?' and 'The other US election myth: Obama's fundraising base' by Mark Pack, former UK Liberal Democrat Party web campaign manager for counterviews on the democratizing impact of the Obama campaign. Available at: <http://www.mattwardman.com/blog/2008/12/01/the-other-us-election-myth-obama%E2%80%99s-fundraising-base-gearbox-by-mark-pack/> and <http://www.mattwardman.com/blog/2009/06/15/how-good-was-obama%E2%80%99s-campaign-gearbox-by-mark-pack/> (accessed 1 September 2009).

6   See Report from the Campaign Finance institute 'REALITY CHECK: Obama Received About the Same Percentage from Small Donors in 2008 as Bush in 2004'. 24 November 2008. Available at: <http://www.cfinst.org/pr/prRelease.aspx?ReleaseID=216> (accessed on 1 September 2009).

REFERENCES

Aarts, C. and Semetko, H. A. (2003) 'The Divided Electorate: Media Use and Political Involvement', *Journal of Politics*, 65(3): 759–84.

Alvarez, R. M. (1997) *Information and Elections*. Ann Arbor, MI: University of Michigan Press.

Anduiza E., Gallego, A., Cantijoch, M. and San Martin, J. (2008) 'Online Resources, Political Participation and Equality', paper presented at the Annual Meeting of the American Political Science Association. Boston, 28–31 August.

Anstead, N. and Chadwick, A. (2009) 'Parties, Election Campaigning, and The Internet: Toward a Comparative Institutional Approach', in A. Chadwick and P. Howard (eds.), *Handbook of Internet Politics*. London: Routledge. pp. 56–71.

Bimber, B. (1998) 'The Internet and Political Transformation: Populism, Community and Accelerated Pluralism', *Polity*, 31(1): 133–60.

Bimber, B. (2001) 'Information and Political Engagement in America', *Political Research Quarterly*, 54(1): 53–68.

Bimber, B. and Davis, R. (2003) *Campaigning Online: The Internet and US Elections*. Oxford: Oxford University Press.

Blumler, J. G. and Kavanagh, D. (1999) 'The Third Age in Political Communication: Influences and Features', *Political Communication*, 16(3): 209–30.

Bowler, S. and Farrell, D. (eds.) (1992) *Electoral Strategies and Political Marketing*. London: Macmillan.

Butler, P. and Collins, N. (1994) 'Political Marketing: Structure and Process', *European Journal of Marketing*, 28(1): 19–34.

Butler, D. and Ranney, A. (eds.) (1992) *Electioneering: A Comparative Study of Continuity and Change*. Oxford: Oxford University Press.

Brownstein, R. (2008). 'The First 21st-Century Campaign', 19 April, http://www.nationaljournal.com/njmagazine/cs_20080416_3324.php?related=true&story1=nj_20080712_6713&story2=nj_20080705_6449&story3=nj_20080628_6029 (accessed 15 July 2008).

Carlson, T. and Djupsund, C. (2001) 'Old Wine in New Bottles? The 1999 Finnish Election Campaign on the Internet', *Harvard International Journal of Press Politics*, 6(1): 68–87.

Carlson, T. (2006) '"It's a Man's World"? Male and Female Election Campaigning on the Internet', *Journal of Political Marketing*, 6(1): 41–67.

Caiani, M. and Wagemann, C. (2009) 'Online Networks of the Italian and German Extreme Right: An Explorative Study with Social Network Analysis', *Information, Communication and Society*, 12(1): 66–109.

Cho, J. H. (2005) 'Media, Interpersonal Discussion, and Electoral Choice', *Communication Research*, 32(3): 295–322.

Christiansen, K. and Roberts, M. (2009) 'Respect, Empower and Include: The New Model Army', in N. Anstead and W. Straw (eds.), *The Change We Need: What Britain Can Learn from Obama's Victory*. London: The Fabian Society. pp. 41–8.

Coleman, S. (2001) 'Online Campaigning', *Parliamentary Affairs*, 54(4): 679–88.

Conover, P. J. and Feldman, S. (1989) 'Candidate Perception in an Ambiguous World: Campaigns, Cues and Inference Processes', *American Journal of Political Science*, 33(4): 912–40.

Conway, M. and Dorner, D. G. (2004) 'An Evaluation of New Zealand Political Party Websites', *Information Research*, 9(4): 1–24.

Copsey, N. (2003) 'Extremism on the Net: The Far Right and The Value of The Internet', in R. Gibson, P. Nixon and S. Ward (eds.), *Net Gain? Political Parties and the Internet*. London, Routledge. pp. 218–33.

Corrado, A. and Firestone, C. (1996) *Elections in Cyberspace: Toward a New Era in American Politics*. Washington, DC: Aspen Institute.

Cunha, C., Martin, I., Newell, J. and Ramiro, L. (2003) 'Southern European Parties and Party Systems, and the New ICTs', in R. Gibson, P. Nixon and S. Ward (eds.), *Net Gain? Political Parties and the Internet*. London: Routledge. pp. 70–97.

Dalton, R. and Wattenberg, M. (eds.) (2000) *Parties Without Partisans: Political Change in Advanced Industrial Democracies*. Oxford: Oxford University Press.

Davis, R. (1998) The *Web of Politics. The Internet's Impact on the American Political System*. Oxford: Oxford University Press.

D'Alessio, D. W. (1997) 'Use of the Web in the 1996 US Election', *Electoral Studies*, 16(4): 489–501.

Denver, D., Hands, G., Fisher, J. and MacAllister, I. (2003) 'Constituency Campaigning in Britain 1992–2001', *Party Politics*, 9(4): 541–59.

DeVreese, C. H. and Semetko, H. A. (2004) 'News Matters: Influences on the Vote in the Danish 2000 Euro Referendum Campaign', *European Journal of Political Research*, 43(5): 699–722.

de Vreese, C. H., Banducci, S., Semetko, H. A. and Boomgaarden, H. (2006) 'The News Coverage of the 2004 European Parliamentary Election Campaign in 25 Countries', *European Union Politics*, 7(4): 477–504.

De Zuniga, H. G., Puig-I-Abril, E. and Rojas, H. (2009) 'Weblogs, Traditional Sources Online and Political Participation: An Assessment of how the Internet is Changing the Political Environment', *New Media and Society*, 11(4): 553–74.

Epstein, L. (1967) *Political Parties in Western Democracies*. London: Pall Mall Press.

Farmer, R. and Fender, R. (2005) 'E-Parties: Democratic and Republican State Parties in 2000', *Party Politics*, 11(1): 47–58.

Farrell, D. (2006) 'Political Parties in a Changing Campaign Environment', in R. Katz and W. Crotty (eds.), *A Handbook of Party Politics*. London: Sage. pp. 122–33.

Farrell, D. and Schmitt-Beck, R. (eds.) (2003) *Do Political Campaigns Matter?* London: Routledge.

Farrell, D. and Webb, P. (2000) 'Political Parties as Campaign Organizations', in R. Dalton and M. Wattenberg (eds.), *Parties without Partisans*. Oxford: Oxford University Press. pp. 102–28.

Fisher, J. and Denver, D. (2008) 'From Foot-Slogging to Call Centres and Direct Mail: A Framework for Analysing the Development of District-Level Campaigning', *European Journal of Political Communication*, 47(6): 794–826.

Foot, K. and Schneider, S. (2006) *Web Campaigning*. Cambridge, MA: MIT Press.

Gerber, A. and Green, D. P. (2000) 'The Effects of Personal Canvassing, Telephone Calls, and Direct Mail on Voter Turnout: A Field Experiment', *American Political Science Review*, 94(3): 653–64.

Gerstenfeld, P. B., Grant, D. R. and Chiang, P. C. (2003) 'Hate Online: A Content Analysis of Extremist Internet Sites', *Analyses of Social Issues and Public Policy*, 3(1): 29–44.

Ghillebaert, C. (2009) 'The Virtual Tribute of Would-Be Candidates to Democracy. Has the Internet Become the Best or the Last Resort of Candidates for Presidency in France?', paper presented at ECPR workshop 'Parliaments, Parties and Politicians in Cyberspace'. Lisbon, 14–19 April.

Gibson, R. K. and McAllister, I. (2006) 'Does Cybercampaigning Win Votes? Online Political Communication in the 2004 Australian Election', *Journal of Elections, Public Opinion and Parties*, 16(3): 243–64.

Gibson, R. K. and McAllister, I. (2008) 'Do Online Election Campaigns Win Votes? The 2007 Australian YouTube Election', paper presented at the Annual Meeting of the American Political Science Association. Boston, 28–31 August.

Gibson, R. K. and Römmele, A. (2005) '"Down Periscope": The Search for High-Tech Campaigning at the Local Level in The 2002 German Federal Election', *Journal of E-Government*, 2(3): 85–109.

Gibson, R. K. and Römmele, A. (2009) 'Measuring the Professionalization of Political Campaigning', *Party Politics*, 15(3): 265–93.

Gibson, R. K. and Ward, S. J. (1998) 'UK Political Parties and the Internet: Politics as Usual in the New Media?', *Harvard International Journal of Press/Politics*, 3(3): 14–38.

Gibson, R. and Ward, S. (2003) 'Letting the Daylight in? Australian Parties' use of the World Wide Web at the State and Territory Level', in R. Gibson, P. Nixon and S. Ward (eds.), *Net Gain? Political Parties and the Internet*. London: Routledge. pp. 139–60.

Gibson, R. K., Margolis, M., Resnick, D. and Ward, S. J. (2003a) 'Election Campaigning on the WWW in the US and UK: A Comparative Analysis', *Party Politics*, 9(1): 47–76.

Gibson, R. K., Römmele A. and Ward, S. J. (2003b) 'German Parties and Internet Campaigning in the 2002 Federal Election', *German Politics*, 12(1): 79–104.

Gibson, R., Nixon, P. and Ward, S. (eds.) (2003c) *Net Gain? Political Parties and the Internet*. London: Routledge.

Gibson, R. K., Lusoli, W. and Ward, S. J. (2005) 'Online Participation in the UK: Testing a Contextualised Model of Internet Effects', *British Journal of Politics and International Relations*, 7(4): 561–83.

Gibson, R. K., Lusoli, W. and Ward, S. (2008a) 'Italian Elections Online: 10 years on', in J. Newell (ed.), *The Italian General Election 2006: Romano Prodi's Victory.* Manchester: MUP. pp. 177–201.

Gibson, R. K., Lusoli, W. and Ward, S. J. (2008b) 'Nationalizing and Normalizing the Local? A Comparative Analysis of Online Candidate Campaigning in Australia and Britain', *Journal of Information Technology and Politics,* 4(4): 15–30.

Green, D. P. and Smith, J. K. (2003) 'Professionalization of Campaigns and the Secret History of Collective Action Problems', *Journal of Theoretical Politics,* 15(3): 321–39.

Greengard, S. (2009) 'The First Internet President', *Communications of the ACM,* 52(2): 16–18.

Gueorguieva, V. (2007) 'Voters, MySpace and YouTube: The Impact of Alternative Communication Channels on the 2006 Election Cycle and Beyond', *Social Science Computer Review,* 26(3): 288–300.

Gurevitch, M. (1999) 'Whither the Future? Some Afterthoughts', *Political Communication,* 16(3): 281–84.

Haynes, A. A. and Pitts, B. (2009) 'Making an Impression: New Media in the 2008 Presidential Nomination Campaigns', *PS: Political Science & Politics,* 42(1): 53–8.

Henneberg, S. C. M. (2002) 'Understanding Political Marketing', in N. O'Shaughnessy and S. Henneberg (eds.), *The Idea of Political Marketing.* Westport, CT: Praeger. pp. 93–170.

Hetherington, M. J. (1996) 'The Media's Role in Forming Voters' National Economic Evaluations in 1992', *American Journal of Political Science,* 40(2): 372–95.

Hindman, M. (2005) 'The Real Lessons of Howard Dean: Reflections on the First Digital Campaign', *Perspectives on Politics,* 3(1): 121–28.

Hindman, M. (2008) *The Myth of Digital Democracy.* Princeton, NJ: Princeton University Press.

Hindman, M., Tsioutsiouliklis, K. and Johnson, J. A. (2003) 'Googlearchy? How a Few Heavily Linked Sites Dominate Politics on the Web', paper presented at the Annual Meetings of the Midwest Political Science Association. Chicago, IL, 4 April.

Holbrook, T. (1996) *Do Campaigns Matter?* Thousand Oaks, CA: Sage.

Jensen, M. J. Danziger, J. and Venkatesh, A. (2006) 'Civil Society and Cyber Society: The Role of the Internet in Community Associations and Democratic Politics', *The Information Society,* 23(1): 39–50.

Johnson, D. (2007) *No Place for Amateurs: The Professionalization of Modern Campaigns.* London: Routledge.

Just, M., Crigler, A., Alger, D. and Cook, T. (1996) *Crosstalk: Citizens, Candidates, and the Media in a Presidential Campaign.* Chicago, IL: University of Chicago Press.

Kalnes, O. (2009) 'Web 2.0 in the Norwegian 2007 and 2009 Campaigns', paper presented at ECPR General Conference. Potsdam, Germany, 10–12 September.

Kamarck, E. C. (2002) 'Political Campaigning on the Internet: Business as Usual?', in E. C. Kamarck and J. S. Nye (eds.), *Governance.com: Democracy in the Information Age.* Washington, DC: Brookings Institute.

Kavanagh, D. (1995) *Election Campaigning: The New Marketing of Politics.* Oxford: Blackwell.

Kircheimer, O. (1966) 'The Transformation of Western European Party Systems', in J. La Palombara and M. Weiner (eds.), *Political Parties and Political Development.* Princeton, NJ: Princeton University Press. pp. 177–200.

Kohut, A., Doherty, C. P. K., Flemming, G., Dimmock, M., Samanaranyake, N. and Rainie, L. (2000) 'Youth Vote Influenced By Online Information Internet Election News Audience Seeks Convenience, Familiar Names', http://www.pewInternet.org/~/media//Files/Reports/2000/PRC_Politics_Report.pdf.pdf (accessed 5 December 2011).

Krueger, B. S. (2002) 'Assessing the Potential of Internet Political Participation in the United States', *American Politics Research,* 34(6): 759–76.

Lees-Marshment, J. (2001) 'The Marriage of Politics and Marketing', *Political Studies,* 49(4): 692–713.

Lilleker, D. and Negrine, R. (2006) 'Mapping a Market-Orientation: Can We Only Detect Political Marketing Through the Lens of Hindsight?', in B. Newman and P. Davies (eds.), *Winning Elections with Political Marketing.* Hawarth Press. pp. 33–58.

Lofgren, K. and Smith, C. (2003) 'Political Parties and Democracy in the Information Age', in R. Gibson, P. Nixon and S. Ward (eds.), *Net Gain? Political Parties and the Internet.* London: Routledge. pp. 39–52.

Luntz, Frank. I. (1988) *Candidates Consultants and Campaigns.* New York: Basil Blackwell.

Lupia, A. and Philpot, T. S. (2005) 'Views From Inside the Net: How Websites Affect Young Adults' Political Interest', *Journal of Politics,* 67(4): 1122–42.

Lusoli, W. and Ward, S. J. (2004) 'Digital Rank and File: Activists Perceptions and Use of the Internet', *British Journal of Politics and International Relations,* 7(4): 453–70.

Lusoli, W. and Ward, S. (2005) 'Logging On or Switching Off? The Public and the Internet at the 2005 General Election', in S. Coleman and S. Ward (eds.), *Spinning the Web: Online Campaigning during the 2005 General Election.* London: Hansard Society. pp. 13–21.

Mancini, P. (1999) 'New Frontiers in Political Professionalism', *Political Communication,* 16(3): 231–45.

March, L. (2005) 'Virtual Parties in a Virtual World: Russian Parties and the Political Internet', in S. Oates, D. Owen. and R. K. Gibson (eds.), *The Internet and Politics: Citizens, Activists and Voters.* London: Routledge. pp. 136–62.

Margetts, H. (2006) 'The Cyber Party', in R. Katz and W. Crotty (eds.), *Handbook of Party Politics.* London: Sage. pp. 528–35.

Margolis, M. and Resnick, D. (2000) *Politics as Usual? The Cyberspace Revolution.* London: Sage.

Morris, D. (2000) *Vote.com.* Los Angeles: Renaissance.

Mossberger, K., Tolbert, C. and McNeil R. (2007) *Digital Citizenship: The Internet, Society and Participation.* Cambridge, MA: MIT Press.

Moy, P., Manosevitch, E., Stamm, K. and Dunsmore, K. (2005) 'Linking Dimensions of Internet Use and Civic Engagement', *Journalism and Mass Communication Quarterly,* 82(3): 571–86.

Negrine, R. and Papathanassopoulos, S. (1996) 'The "Americanization" of Political Communication: A Critique', *The Harvard International Journal of Press/Politics*, 1(2): 45–62.

Newell, J. L. (2001) 'Italian Political Parties on the Web', *The Harvard International Journal of Press/Politics*, 6(4): 60–87.

Newman, B. I. (ed.) (1999) *Handbook of Political Marketing*. Thousand Oaks, CA: Sage.

Norquay, G. (2008) 'Organizing without an Organization: The Obama Networking Revolution', *Policy Options*, October: 58–61.

Norris, P. (2000) *A Virtuous Circle*. New York: Cambridge University Press.

Norris, P. (2001) *The Digital Divide*. Cambridge: Cambridge University Press.

Norris, P. (2003) 'Preaching to the Converted? Pluralism, Participation and Party Websites', *Party Politics*, 9(1): 21–46.

Norris, P. and Curtice, J. (2008) 'Getting the Message Out: A Two-Step Model of the Role of the Internet in Campaign Communication Flows During the 2005 British General Election', *The Journal of Information Technology and Politics*, 4(4): 3–13.

Norris, P., Curtice, J., Semetko, H. A. and Scammell, M. (1999) *On Message: Communicating the Campaign*. London: Sage.

Palfrey, J. and Gasser, U. (2008) *Born Digital: Understanding the First Generation of Digital Natives*. Cambridge, MA: Basic Books.

Panebianco, A. (1988) *Political Parties: Organization and Power*. Cambridge: Cambridge University Press.

Pedersen, K. and Saglie, J. (2005) 'New Technology in Ageing Parties: Internet Use in Danish and Norwegian Parties', *Party Politics*, 11(3): 359–77.

Peter, J., Lauf, E. and Semetko, H. A. (2004) 'Television Coverage of the 1999 European Parliamentary Elections', *Political Communication*, 21(4): 415–33.

Pickerill, J. (2003) *Cyberprotest: Environmental Activism Online*. Manchester: Manchester University Press.

Plasser, F. (2000) 'American Campaign Techniques Worldwide', *The Harvard International Journal of Press/Politics*, 5(4): 33–54.

Plasser, F. and Plasser, G. (2002) *Global Political Campaigning. A Worldwide Analysis of Campaign Professionals and their Practices*. Westport, CT: Praeger.

Prior, M. (2007) *Post Broadcast Democracy: How Media Choice Increases Inequality in Political Involvement and Polarizes Elections*. New York: Cambridge University Press.

Quintelier, E. and Vissers, S. (2008) 'The Effect of Internet Use on Political Participation', *Social Science Computer Review*, 26(4): 411–27.

Rainie, L. (2007) 'E-Citizen planet', paper presented at the Personal Democracy Forum Conference. New York City, NY, 18 May 2007.

Rainie, L., Cornfield, M. and Horrigan, J. (2005) 'The Internet and Campaign 2004', http://www.pewinternet.org/Reports/2005/The-Internet-and-Campaign-2004.aspx (accessed 26 June 2006).

Resnick, D. (1999) 'Politics on the Internet: The Normalization of Cyberspace', in C. Toulouse and T. Luke (eds.), *The Politics of Cyberspace*. London: Routledge. pp. 48–68.

Römmele, A. (2003) 'Political Parties and New ICTs', Party Politics, 9(1): 7–20.

Roper, J. (1999) 'New Zealand Political Parties Online: The World Wide Web as a Tool for Democratization or Political Marketing', in C. Toulouse and T. Luke (eds.), *The Politics of Cyberspace*. London: Routledge. pp. 69–83.

Rose, R. (1967) *Influencing Voters: A Study of Campaign Rationality*. London: Faber and Faber.

Scammell, M. (1999) 'Political Marketing: Lessons for Political Science', *Political Studies*, 47(4): 718–39.

Schmitt-Beck, R. (2003) 'Mass Communication, Personal Communication and Vote Choice: The Filter-Hypothesis of Media Influence in Comparative Perspective', *British Journal of Political Science*, 33(2): 233–59.

Selnow, G. (1998) *Electronic Whistle-stops: The Impact Of The Internet On American Politics*. Westport, CT: Praeger.

Semetko, H. A., Blumler, J. G., Gurevitch, M. and Weaver, D. H. (1991) *The Formation of Campaign Agendas: A Comparative Analysis of Party and Media Roles in Recent American and British Elections*. Hillsdale, NJ: Lawrence Erlbaum Associates.

Shifman, L., Coleman, S. and Ward, S. J. (2007) 'Only Joking? Online Humour and the 2005 UK General Election', *Information, Communication and Society*, 10(4): 465–87.

Smith, A. (2009) 'The Internet's Role in Campaign 2008', http://www.pewinternet.org/Reports/2009/6–The-Internets-Role-in-Campaign-2008.aspx

Smith, A. and Rainie, L. (2008) 'The Internet and the 2008 Election', http://www.pewinternet.org/Reports/2008/The-Internet-and-the-2008-Election.aspx

Smith, J. P. and Chen, P. J. (2009) 'A Canadian E-lection 2008? Online Media and Political Competition', paper presented at the annual meetings of the Canadian Political Science Association. Ottawa, 27–29 May.

Stanley, J. W. and Weare, C. (2004) 'The Effects of Internet Use on Political Participation', *Administration and Society*, 36(5): 503–27.

Strachan, C. J. (2003) *High-Tech Grass Roots. The Professionalization of Local Elections*. Lanham: Rowman & Littlefield Publishers.

Strandberg, K. (2006) *Parties, Candidates and Citizens On-Line – Studies of Politics on the Internet*. Turku: Åbo Akademi University Press.

Strandberg, K. (2009) 'Online Campaigning: An Opening for the Outsiders? An Analysis of Finnish Parliamentary Candidates' Websites in the 2003 Election Campaign', *New Media and Society*, 11(5): 835–54.

Stromer-Galley, J. (2000) 'On-line Interaction and Why Candidates Avoid it', *Journal of Communication*, 50(4): 111–32.

Stromer-Galley, J. (2009) 'The Web 2.0 Election', in N. Anstead and W. Straw (eds.), *The Change We Need: What Britain Can Learn from Obama's Victory*. London: The Fabian Society. pp. 49–58.

Sudulich, L. (2009) 'Do Ethos, Ideology, Country and Electoral Strength Make a Difference in Cyberspace? Testing An Explanatory Model Of Parties Websites', paper presented at ECPR Joint Research Workshops. Lisbon, 14–19 April.

Sudulich, M. L. and Wall, M. (2010) 'Every Little Helps Cyber Campaigning in the 2007 Irish General Election', *Journal of Information Technology and Politics*, 7(4): 340–55.

Swanson, D. L. and Mancini, P. (eds.) (1996) *Politics, Media and Modern Democracy: An International Study of Innovations in Electoral Campaigning and their Consequences.* Westport, CT: Praeger.

Trammell, K. D., Williams, A. P., Postelnicu, M. and Landreville, K. D. (2006) 'Evolution of Online Campaigning: Increasing Interactivity in Candidate Websites and Blogs Through Text and Technical Features', *Mass Communication and Society*, 9(1): 21–44.

Trippi, J. (2005) *The Revolution Will Not Be Televized: Democracy, the Internet, and the Overthrow of Everything.* New York: Regan Books.

Vaccari, C. (2008) 'Surfing to the Élysée: The Internet in the 2007 French Elections', *French Politics*, 6(1): 1–22.

van Onselen, A and van Onselen, P. (2008) 'On Message or out of Touch? Secure Web Sites and Political Campaigning in Australia', *Australian Journal of Political Science*, 43(1): 43–58.

Vedel, T. and Michalska, K. (2007) 'Political Participation and the Internet: Evidence from the 2007 French Presidential Election', paper presented at the International Conference on e-Government. Montreal, Canada.

Viborg-Andersen, K. and Medaglia, R. (2008) 'Politics as Usual? The Use of Facebook in Parliamentary Election Campaigning', paper presented at the Politics: Web 2.0 International Conference. Royal Holloway University, London.

Vincente-Merino, R. (2009) *Parties Online: A Comparative Analysis of European Party Websites.* PhD dissertation, University of Hull.

Vissers, S. (2009) 'From Preaching to the Converted to Preaching Through the Converted', paper presented at ECPR Joint Research Workshops. Lisbon, 14–19 April.

Ward, S. J., Lusoli, W. and Gibson, R. K. (2002) 'Virtually Participating: A Survey of Party Members Online', *Information Polity*, 7(4): 199–215.

Ward, S. (2005) 'The Internet and 2005 Election: Virtually Irrelevant?' in A. Geddes and J. Tonge (eds.), *The Nation Decides: The 2005 General Election.* Basingstoke: Palgrave Macmillan. pp. 188–206.

Ward, S. and Gibson, R. K. (1998) 'The First Internet Election? UK Political Parties and Campaigning in Cyberspace', in I. Crewe, B. Gosschalk and J. Bartle (eds.), *Political Communications: How Labour Won the 1997 General Election.* Ilford: Frank Cass. pp. 93–112.

Ward, S. J. and Gibson, R. K. (2003) 'Online and On Message? Candidate Websites in the 2001 General Election', *British Journal of Politics and International Relations*, 5(2): 188–205.

Ward, S., Gibson, R. K. and Lusoli, W. (2008) 'Not Quite Normal? Parties and the 2005 UK Online Election Campaign', in S. Ward, R. Davis, D. Owen and D. Taras (eds.), *Making a Difference? Internet Campaigning in Comparative Perspective.* Lanham, MD: Lexington Books. pp. 133–60.

Whine, M. (2000) 'The Use of the Internet by Far Right Extremists', in T. Douglas (ed.), *Cybercrime: Law, Security and Privacy in the Information Age.* London: Routledge. pp. 234–50.

Williams, C., Weinberg, B. and Gordon, J. (2004) 'When Online and Offline Politics "Meetup": An Examination of the Phenomenon, Presidential Campaign and its Citizen Activists', paper presented at the Annual Meeting of the American Political Science Association. Chicago, IL.

Wlezien, C. (2010) 'Election Campaigns', in L. LeDuc, R. Niemi and P. Norris (eds.), *Comparing Democracies III.* Thousand Oaks, CA: Sage.

Wring, D. (1997) 'Reconciling Marketing with Political Science: Theories of Political Marketing', *Journal of Marketing Management*, 13(7): 651–63.

Wring, D. (2005) *The Politics of Marketing the Labour Party.* Basingstoke: Palgrave Macmillan.

Zittel, T. (2009) 'Lost in Technology? Political Parties and Online Campaigning in Germany's Mixed Member Electoral System', *Journal of Information Technology and Politics*, 6(3/4): 298–311.

6

Popular Culture and Political Communication

John Street

The campaign to elect Barack Obama as the 44th President of the USA was seen as distinctive in many ways, not least, of course, in its outcome. But one of its other distinctions lay in its sophisticated and extensive use of popular culture. This was not just a serious political campaign. There were times when it resembled a rock tour, others when it was pure show business, scripted by Hollywood and choreographed by MTV. This was a campaign that made use of Facebook and other social networking sites, of YouTube and late night talk shows. It had its own soundtrack in will.i.am's pop video version of an Obama speech, in which a host of film, sports and music stars made fleeting appearances. And then there was the Inauguration concert itself in January 2009, when the Capitol echoed to the sounds and speeches of Bruce Springsteen, Tom Hanks, Stevie Wonder, Beyoncé, Garth Brooks, Shakira, Denzel Washington and many others. If all this was not sufficient evidence of the intimacy of popular culture and political communication, we need only remind ourselves that President Obama's campaign and election victory were eerily foreshadowed by the final series of the television drama *The West Wing*.

But if the Obama presidency represents a classic illustration of the intimacy between popular culture and political communication, it certainly does not represent the first such case. While a Handbook of this kind, were it to have been published 20 years ago, might not have thought to include a chapter on 'popular culture and political communication', it would have been perfectly possible to have written such a piece then – or indeed several decades earlier. The elections of

John F. Kennedy or of Ronald Reagan were both – in their different ways – examples of the close proximity of political communication to popular culture. Indeed, many election campaigns – spread across time and location – have sought to harness popular culture to political communication, albeit without the technical sophistication of the postmodern era, to borrow Pippa Norris's (1996) classification of changing forms of media-driven electoral communication. Equally, accounts of political communication in authoritarian regimes, whether in Nazi Germany, Stalin's Soviet Union, Franco's Spain or Mussolini's Italy, would reference the manifold ways in which popular culture was used to convey propaganda and to maintain political order. My suggestion in this chapter is that popular culture has always been a part of political communication, and that less has changed than conventional wisdom would suggest and less has taken a turn for the worse than the doomsayers would have us believe (Franklin, 2003; Hart, 1999; Postman, 1987). What has changed is our approach to understanding and analyzing political communication and its debt to popular culture. Or rather, we have reverted to an account that would resonate with our forebears in the ancient world, where politics and aesthetics (Ankersmit, 1996) and politics as performance (Corner, 2003) were as familiar conjunctions then as they are now.

My purpose in this chapter, though, is not to trace in detail the history of the relationship between popular culture and political communication, nor is it to engage at length with the rather tired debate about the effect of popular culture on political communication. Typically, this latter has been couched in term of some notion of 'dumbing down', driven by the thought that modern forms of political communication have borrowed the language and conventions of popular culture, and in so doing have opted to simplify the message, emptying it of detail and subtlety, and appealing to the lowest common denominator. This is the warning that we see expressed in films such as Robert Redford's *The Candidate* (1971), or in books like Neil Postman's *Amusing Ourselves to Death* (1987). The problems with these debates are twofold. They tend to appeal to some notional past in which political communication was qualitatively 'better' than it is now. Such claims are immensely difficult to sustain – 'better' in terms of what? measured against what criteria? Furthermore, these normative judgments themselves rest upon empirical claims about the effects of given forms of communication. We lack any sustained research into the effects of popular cultural communication on political engagement and discourse (although this state of affairs is beginning to change). And just as we need to be wary of critics, so we need to be watchful of allies. It may well be that 'infotainment' (Brants, 1998; McQuail et al., 2005), the cross-breeding of media's informational and entertainment roles, does indeed enhance political engagement and does represent a new form of political communication. But again, we need to be aware of the continuities with the past and the limits to our current knowledge about its impact on the present. In short, while the combination of popular and political communication is important and deserves our attention, its importance may lie less in its novelty and more in its continuity.

Nonetheless, as we start to reflect on the links between popular culture and political communication, we cannot overlook the fact that there are some who argue that this link, however longstanding it may be, threatens the very existence of democracy. Robert Putnam's hugely influential *Bowling Alone* (2000) has posited that popular culture's political role has been confined to the negative effect of disengaging citizens. Entertainment television, in particular, stands accused not just of stealing time from citizens who might otherwise engage in collective public acts, but of breeding attitudes which undermine the practice of civic engagement. But even here the picture is less clear-cut and less worrying than it seems. While there is considerable evidence for Putnam's 'time stealing' thesis (Hooghe, 2002), it is not universally supported (Moy et al., 1999). Nor does the evidence support unambiguously the thought that popular culture breeds sentiments that work against democratic participation (Besley, 2006; Hooghe, 2002).

It might seem that, in moving from the use of popular culture in political communication to the effects of popular culture on political participation, we have strayed a long way from the ostensible subject of this chapter. However, the relationship between popular culture and political communication can only be understood, I want to suggest, through this wider perspective, and future work in the field needs to acknowledge this. However, in order to make this case, it is important that we begin by focusing on the more conventional, narrower definition of the topic. It is worth noting here, that in talking about popular culture, attention is primarily upon mass forms of commercially produced popular culture – entertainment television, music and film. This focus leaves largely untouched the broader definitions of popular culture, identified by Raymond Williams (1985) and others, that would include anthropological accounts of the phenomenon. My concern here is with how mass-produced popular culture, whose primary aim is to entertain, has become part of the routines of political communication. And my argument is that, in studying political communication, we not only need to be alive to the changing formats and technologies in which it occurs, but also to the variety of genres and forms in which it exists. Political communication does not just take place when citizens encounter news and current affairs; it happens too when they are being entertained.

USES OF POPULAR CULTURE FOR POLITICAL COMMUNICATION

The relationship of popular culture to political communication typically begins by focusing on the interests and ambitions of political actors, most notably candidates and parties in elections and governments in power. These actors are motivated by the desire to win power and then to retain it. Their use of popular culture is determined instrumentally by the extent to which it enables them to achieve their specific political goals. Although it makes a difference in some respects as to whether we are talking about dictatorships or democracies, the disposition is similar: how can popular culture be used to secure popular, political support?

Popular culture, as I have defined it, is marked by its ability to attract and entertain large numbers of people. There are few, if any, barrier to accessing it, and relatively little formal demand made of those who wish to enjoy it. Indeed, it is this very power to attract and engage which is elicited in political communication. Hence, the Nazis' use of film in works like *The Triumph of the Will* is but one example of how a form of mass culture was used to convey a particular message (Steinweis, 1993). In the same way, Soviet Russia, particularly under Stalin, placed forms of popular culture in the service of communist propaganda (Ross, 2007; Starr, 1983). In democratic states, too, film and popular music were part of the propaganda of war (Carruthers, 1998) and of election campaigns (Davies and Wells, 2002). Campaign songs have been a key feature of the American election since the early 20th century, if not before. In the UK, increasing concern has been devoted to the choice of music to play at party conferences or in election broadcasts (Harris, 2003). Such issues are themselves the product of thinking about how music can be used to 'brand' a party. The language of advertising underwrites the way in which electoral politics is communicated. And the same concern that is shown in selecting music is also deployed in seeking endorsees from among the celebrity supporters or the television formats which may be used to reach specific audience or deliver specific messages. The rationale behind these uses of popular culture derive from assumptions about the effects of popular culture (Adorno and Horkheimer, 1979; Marcuse, 1964) and about the logic of political communication in a fragmented society (Downs, 1957; Swanson and Mancini, 1996), and the way that these have been codified within political marketing (Lilleker and Lees-Marshment, 2005; Savigny, 2008).

The political uses of popular culture are not confined to parties and candidates at election time. They also form part of the maintenance of power. This is evident, for example, in the changing character of government communication, in which the advertisement has assumed ever greater importance. In the UK, the government's advertising budget has risen significantly, until the government has become the advertisers' leading client. The rise in spending has also been accompanied by a brasher style of communication, in which the conventions of advertising have been more willingly embraced. This has, in turn, prompted debates about whether such advertising remains true to its constitutional responsibility of informing the public or providing propaganda on behalf of the government (Rosenbaum, 1997; Scammell, 1995). Accompanying the rise of the glossy advertisement has been the ever greater use of celebrities to communicate government policy. In the UK, substantial sums of government money have been used to underwrite the cost of hiring celebrities to promote policy. In 2009, the *Daily Telegraph* reported that £90,000 had been spent on hiring television actors, pop stars and fashion models to front a health awareness campaign (Swaine, 2009). Later in the year, it was announced that the same government department had appointed the

ex-judge of a television talent competition to become a 'dance champion', again as part of a national health campaign (Baldwin and Lister, 2009).

The instrumental use of popular culture for political communication does not end with governments and those who aspire to join or run them. Non-governmental actors are also major users of popular culture to communicate their political message. The stars of music and film feature prominently on the websites of organizations like Amnesty, Oxfam and Greenpeace. They are recruited through the now extensive teams of artist or celebrity liaison workers that exist within NGOs, following a model of celebrity ambassadors that the UN has used since its earliest days. Major music festivals such as Glastonbury are used by Oxfam (among others) to bring attention to their cause. Rock stars such as Bruce Springsteen, Sting and Peter Gabriel have led major rock tours on behalf of Amnesty. And perhaps most famously of all, there have been events such as Live Aid and Live8, in which Bob Geldof and his colleagues have organized international political movements on the back of vast pop music concerts (Denselow, 1989; Lahusen, 1996; Street et al., 2008).

There are, as we have seen, many examples of the use of popular culture as a tool of political communication. Not only does such use have an extensive political history, but it also crosses political ideologies and systems, and embraces many forms of political organization. We tend to treat such examples as the product of intentional decisions to exploit the possibilities which popular culture seems to offer. While such strategic thinking may account for significant aspects of the phenomenon, it does not exhaust the account that might be given.

EXPLAINING THE USE OF POPULAR CULTURE FOR POLITICAL COMMUNICATION

The instrumental political uses of popular culture can be explained in a variety of ways. It has an imitative dimension, in the sense that it represents a fashion or trend in political communications. This process of imitation is achieved, in part, by mere observation, but more systematically through the exchange of personnel (Kavanagh, 1995). But as is evident, imitation alone provides only a partial explanation. It does not provide an account of why the first mover made their particular move, nor why any imitator chooses to imitate this or that form of communication, amidst the infinite array of possible models. The answer to such questions has to lie in wider changes.

David Swanson and Paolo Mancini (1996) provide a persuasive account of the developing use of popular culture in the story they tell of political communication under conditions of modernization. For them the key lies in the collapse of traditional institutions of political communication: the extended family, the political party, the trade union, the church and so on. One of the effects of modernization is to diminish the impact and role of such institutions, and to forge a more individualized society in which the mass media becomes the core means of communication. The effect of this is that the citizen becomes part of a crowd, rather than a community, and becomes part of a mass audience for mass media. A similar story, albeit told from different political perspectives, is recounted by the Frankfurt School (for example, Adorno and Horkheimer, 1979) or by the Austrian economist Joseph Schumpeter (1976). From all these different perspectives, the mass media assume ever greater importance, and as that mass media incorporates many different forms of communication (including popular entertainment), these too assume ever larger significance as sources of information and influence.

This narrative is given a further twist by those who argue that mass media shape all forms of communication according to their 'logic'. Writers such as Jacques Ellul (1973), Joshua Meyrowitz (1985) and Thomas Meyer (2002) all suggest that the conventions and norms of media come to determine the nature of political communication. The speech delivered to large audiences in grand halls is replaced by the intimate fireside chat. To the extent that this is the logic of popular entertainment, so political communication comes increasingly to imitate the forms and style of popular culture. Political advertising draws more and more on the conventions of commercial advertising, itself indebted to the devices of Hollywood or the pop video.

Such changes themselves depend on skills capable of delivering the new style of political communication. Hence, the increasing attention that has been paid to the professionalization of political communication in its transformation (Negrine, 2008; Saunders, 2009; Stanyer, 2007). Communication is seen as a specialist task that requires specialized knowledge and expertise. These latter capacities are increasingly associated with advertising and marketing. The underlying logic here is of a model of political communication that draws on the insights of rational actor theory and its application to politics by writers such as Anthony Downs (1957) and by the founders of marketing such as Edward Bernays. The rational voter has only limited time, resources or incentives to delve into the details of competing party promises and records. They need a shortcut to judgment, and parties offer these in the form of a brand. These in turn are conveyed through images and gestures, the tools of the world of popular culture. Parties and politicians increasingly turn to the advertising and marketing professionals to create their brand, and these latter recruit Hollywood film directors and pop video makers to craft their forms of political communication.

This rationalist account of the rise of popular culture in political communication has a romanticist parallel. The historian Frank Ankersmit (1996) argues that all forms of representative politics are exercises in aesthetics. The very act of representing entails not the representative mirroring or imitating those he or she claims to represent, but rather in creating, through gestures and words, an image of that which he/she claims to represent. Just as a painting, with its daubes of paint, does not reproduce the original landscape or the artist's model, so the representative does not reproduce his/her constituency. They re-imagine it – they 're-present' it. To this extent, representative politics is a competition between rival artists, and political communication becomes a cultural process in which style is crucial (Pels, 2003).

A final set of perspectives which helps account for the ways in which popular culture becomes part of political communication can be attributed to those who evoke or subscribe to the notion of 'post-democracy'. Where the previous perspectives focus on the logic of political communication, here the focus is on the practice of political institutions. Writers such as Danilo Zolo (1992) and Colin Crouch (2004) argue that the institutions of mass democracy are no longer capable of delivering the promises of representation and accountability that are their defining features. Instead of being located in the practices of elections and parliaments, power is increasingly held by unelected, global elites. So, the argument runs, as the formal legitimating mechanisms become increasingly attenuated, legitimacy is mythologized in the 'spectacle' of mass participation and accountability. These spectacles are performed with the aid of mass media and in the language and style of entertainment. The electoral process becomes an extension of the voters' 'participation' in game shows and talent shows. Modern mass societies enact the 'spectacle' of democracy, and citizens, rather than being active participants, become spectators. Politics becomes a branch of show business (and the Hollywood superstar Arnold Schwarzenegger becomes the Governor of California).

To summarize the discussion in this section: we have considered a number of the general perspectives and arguments which help account for the interplay of political communication and popular culture. We have moved from macro-level theories, which see the connection being forged in large-scale social and political transformations, to meso-level accounts which focus on the 'logic' of the medium of communication and on the professionalization of the communicators. We have also considered the arguments of those who locate the change in the nature of political communication itself, whether from the perspective of the individual rational actor, or from the nature of representation itself.

What all these different approaches have in common is the suggestion that popular culture serves some specific, prior political need. Popular culture provides an answer to a particular political problem or performs a particular function. The focus is primarily on the political dimension of the relationship. It is time now to turn to the other dimension: how is it that popular culture communicates politically? Political communication is not, after all, the exclusive province of political actors. Part of the logic of political uses of popular culture is that it – popular culture – is able to register political thoughts and attitudes. The question is how? How do movies and music, film stars and rock performers, communicate politically? To answer this question, we will turn, not to the literature of political communication, but rather to that of cultural studies. It is here that we find discussion of the way politics is contained within, and communicated by, popular culture.

POPULAR CULTURE AS POLITICAL COMMUNICATION

The use of popular culture to communicate politics depends on an account of how it is that a media form that is designed primarily to entertain – to occupy those pages of newspapers or those parts of the broadcasting schedule *not* given over to news and current affairs – can be seen to communicate political ideas and values. The thought that entertainment is political is a familiar one. It is a staple of Marxist-influenced writers before and after Antonio Gramsci (1971), but is also present on the political right (Bloom, 1987). But while there is considerable agreement that popular culture is rarely 'just entertainment', there is considerable divergence when attention turns to the question of where exactly the politics in popular culture resides. In fact, popular culture engages with politics in a wide variety of ways. In what follows, some of the key variants are described.

Representing the Political

This is the most familiar and traditional way of linking political communication to popular culture. It is a perspective in which popular culture becomes an extension of news and current affairs. The focus is upon the many examples of popular culture which deal with *explicitly* political topics. So we have such instances as the US drama series *The West Wing* or the UK comedy series *Yes, Prime Minister* or *The Thick of It*, or Hollywood films such as *JFK, The Candidate* or *The American President*. We have, too, a long-established tradition of protest song in popular music (Denselow, 1989; Denisoff and Peterson, 1972). In these many different examples, political communication and popular culture are linked simply by virtue of their subject matter.

However, this superficial connection hides a deeper significance for the way popular culture communicates politics. Liesbet van Zoonen (2005), for example, has dawn attention to the contrasting narratives which are used to tell the story of politics in popular culture's representation of it. She identifies four such narratives: quest, conspiracy, bureaucracy and soap opera. Each represents politics in a different way. The quest offers the thought that politics sets a series of challenges which, if successfully negotiated, will result in triumph. In the quest narrative, politics is about the struggle of individuals and teams. The conspiracy narrative represents politics as a system run by hidden forces that are unaccountable to anyone and motivated by malign interests. The bureaucracy narrative again presents politics as a system, but this time as a system without an intentional operator. And finally, the soap opera narrative returns us to the action of individuals, but in this instance without the identifiable goal of the quest. Instead, politics consists of the endless interplay of those individuals; there is little identifiable 'progress', but a constant reversion to the status quo, as new problems and conflicts emerge and are (re)solved. van Zoonen's reading of the narratives of popular culture's representations of politics is a variant on other such accounts of the treatment of politics in popular culture, whether in comedy (Wagg, 1998), film (Neve, 1992) or music (Street, 1997).

Revealing the Political

Analyses of popular culture that take politics as their subject matter shade into another example of the way popular culture and political communication are linked. The focus is once again upon the text, but this time the political is 'revealed', rather than directly represented. The politics is read into the text, or the text is seen as consciously or not acting as a metaphor for present political concerns or anxieties. Douglas Kellner (1995) uses the term 'transcoding' to capture the process. Rather than simply translating a particular set of political values or views into cultural form (in the way that we translate words in one language to those in another), the politics is converted from one code – the experience of 'real life' global politics – to that of the medium involved (that is, Hollywood action films). So it is that Kellner reads the Rambo movies as expressing the US frustration at the loss of the Vietnam war, or the film *Independence Day* is read in terms of other US anxieties, or the plot of the television series *Heroes* is seen as replaying the experience of 9/11. Popular culture, from this perspective, communicates politics as ideology. It establishes forms of 'common sense' or 'normality' that are themselves politically partial and implicated in an ongoing political struggle.

Politically Positioning the Audience

The two approaches that we have so far considered connect popular culture to political communication through a reading of the text. Their question is: what does this or that film or television program communicate about contemporary politics? How is politics portrayed; what sort of values are associated with it? There is a variant on this approach, which draws on both examples we have considered so far. It explicitly links the text to the audience, and asks how works of popular culture construct – in the business of communicating – a relationship between an audience and political power. The language used here involves talking about how reality is 'framed' and how the audience are 'positioned', and it owes much to the work in mainstream political communication by Shanto Iyengar (1991) and others.

Elements of this approach are contained in van Zoonen's (2005) account of the different narratives which popular culture offers in representing politics. For example, she suggests that the quest narrative invites audiences to think of politics as a heroic enterprise, whereas the bureaucratic narrative encourages fatalism. The contrasting narratives establish different relationships to the political realm. In a similar way, Robert Putnam (2000: 242) attributes the decline in social capital in the USA in part to a fatalist individualism that he sees as prevalent within certain forms of entertainment television.

These examples of the way representations of politics position audiences in relation to power and political engagement connect to a yet wider form of political engagement. Here, the attention is upon how popular culture serves to create communities of interest. This idea is well captured in

Benedict Anderson's (1983) famous phrase 'the imagined community', or in the more critical perspective suggested by Eric Hobsbawm and Terrence Ranger's notion (1992) of the 'invented tradition'. What lies behind both these is the thought that collective identities can be forged through cultural representations. There is, as a result, a wealth of research into the way that cultural forms help to generate and construct a collective identity. Examples of this are to be found in studies of racial representations in music (Rose, 1994) and in entertainment television (Gray, 1995), or of women's identity in soap operas (Gerharty, 1991), literary fiction (Radway, 1991) and magazines (McRobbie, 1991). There is a further set of examples where music, for instance, is seen to be used to forge oppositional political identities in dictatorships (Urban, 2004) and in democracies (Fischlin and Heble, 2003). Each of these examples is illustrative of the way in which popular culture communicates and constructs political identities.

Dramatizing Political Morality

The final element in this story of popular culture's capacity to communicate politically is to be found in its ability to energize politics. This connects to the previous theme, in the sense that it links to popular culture's contribution to collective action. However, rather than establishing or creating a common feature among a group of people, this time the concern is with how popular culture is able to inspire enthusiasm or indignation in people. As Jane Bennett (2001) has argued, ethical commitments have to be 'energized' if they are to be the basis of political action. One source of this energy, according to Bennett, is popular culture. A similar train of argument can be detected in Ron Eyerman and Andrew Jamison's (1991) work on social movements. They suggest that popular music and musicians are key to animating forms of collective action, not just by conveying knowledge, but in providing leadership and inspiration. Vestiges of their argument are to be found in other claims about the importance of culture generally in the account we give of political thought and action (the so-called 'cultural turn'), and of the increasing clamour to incorporate an account of emotion in politics (Goodwin et al., 2001).

This brief survey has been designed to illustrate the various ways in which popular culture is seen to communicate political attitudes and values. These attitudes or values may or may not derive from the deliberate intentions of the cultural actor. They remain, nonetheless, an important source of political communication, and as such fall within the remit of all who are interested in the study of it. Which brings us to the final section of this chapter. We have, so far, considered the deliberate political uses of popular culture, and how popular culture is deemed to communicate politically. It is time now to bring these dimensions together and to consider the implications for our understanding of political communication and for our research into it.

IMPLICATIONS FOR THE STUDY OF POLITICAL COMMUNICATIONS

One of the lessons that might be learnt from studying the relationship between popular culture and political communication is that these two do not represent discrete realms, but are closely – even inseparably – entwined. Political communication is a form of popular culture; and popular culture communicates political ideas and values. Put another way, the formal distinctions that separate news and current affairs from entertainment are just that: formal distinctions, and as such are hard to establish and maintain in practice.

Liesbet van Zoonen makes the claim for this merging of the realms in her discussion of the continuity between the fan of popular culture and the political citizen. This is revealed in the similarity she detects in the relationship of fan to star and of citizen to representative. She writes of how popular culture can help forge 'the emotional constitution of electorates that involves the development and maintenance of affective bonds between voters, candidates, and parties' (2005: 66). While popular culture is limited in its capacity to convey information or enable rational deliberation, van Zoonen argues, it can and does contribute to the affective dimension of politics.

Popular culture's continuity with formal political communication is also evoked by John Corner and others (Corner and Pels, 2003). Corner makes the case for viewing politicians as performers, and politics, at least in key respects, as a performance. Corner's (2003) claim points to the way in which political communication is not simply a matter of uttering words and sentences, but of how physically they are conveyed in intonation and gesture, and how what is communicated is not confined to the words and sentences uttered, but to the appearance of the speaker, and beyond that their image, which includes more than appearance. Connecting politics to performance, and by implication to style, links it to popular culture through the metaphor of drama, to the range of roles that can be adopted and the meanings that are associated with them. These associations are made explicit in the instance of the celebrity politician.

This phenomenon, which is receiving increasing attention (Corner and Pels, 2003; Marshall, 1997 and 2006; West and Orman, 2003), serves as a focal point for the coalescence of popular culture and political communication.

The celebrity politician comes in many guises, but for this discussion we consider two basic types. The first is the conventional politician who adopts the devices, platforms and stars of popular culture in order to promote their representative claims. The second is the star of popular culture – the actor, musician or sports person – who uses their fame to claim representation of political causes or interests (see Street, 2004, for a fuller exposition of this distinction). Each type uses popular culture, albeit in slightly different ways, to communicate with their audience or constituency. Both forms of celebrity politician have been subject to criticism for this – either because, as a conventional politician, they are seen to have trivialized or diminished the quality of political communication, or because, in the case of the star with political aspirations, their claims to expertise or to representativeness are suspect. Their expertise is in entertainment, not in international economics, and they are not subject to any system of formal election and accountability; they are just popular in the market place (West and Orman, 2003).

Such criticisms, while quite plausible or valid, do nothing to eliminate the fact of the celebrity politician, and hence the need for scholars of political communication to engage with it. This engagement can take two forms – the normative and the empirical analysis. So far, we have seen more of the former than the latter, to the extent that criticism of the celebrity politician has been met with counter-claims from those who wish to argue that the celebrity politician represents a valid alternative form of political representation (Nash, 2009; Saward, 2006). Rather less attention has been given to the empirical analysis of the celebrity politician, but such work can provide useful insights into the interplay of popular culture and political communication. There are two key elements to such research. The first concerns the conditions of celebrity politics – when and how the celebrity politician comes to legitimate their representative claims. The second concerns the effects of such claims – are citizens moved and changed by celebrity politics?

Taking first the question of how the celebrity politician comes to adopt certain forms of communication or to be allied with certain causes, it is important to note that this was not the product of some automatic or natural process. While the benefit of hindsight might suggest an inevitability to the coalition of, say, soul musicians and the civil rights movement in the 1960s, this was not the case.

There is a complex historical narrative to be unravelled. In the same way, events like Live Aid are contingent upon a vast array of factors. Christian Lahusen (1996) points to the range of forms of capital – social, cultural and financial – that are necessary in order to create a communicative event of the size and scale of Live Aid and other such coalitions of popular culture and political campaign. And what is true for such events is also true for the individual celebrity politician, seeking out new forms of political communication in the sites and styles of popular culture (Harris, 2003).

The second dimension to the analysis of the celebrity politician is the question of their effect. Do they make a difference, and if so, of what kind? This is relatively unchartered territory, including, as it does, both elite and mass behaviour. With regard to the former, events live Live8 would seem to provide *prima facie* evidence of the capacity of celebrity politicians to influence elite behaviour. The G8 leaders appeared to change policy on developing world debt in the aftermath of Live8, and Geldof claimed the campaign as a success. However, there is much dispute about the relationship of cause and effect, not least because of arguments about whose interests were, in fact, served by the change of policy. Critics took the view that Live8 had ill-served the interests of those it sought to aid, and that the outcome was much less of a success than was being claimed (Sireau and Davis, 2007). Such arguments were compounded by questions about whether the changes in policy were made, not because of the mass array of stars and their fans, but because of the existing agendas of the G8 leaders (Hague et al., 2008).

Research into the mass effects of celebrity politics is also at a formative stage. Experimental evidence (Jackson and Darrow, 2005) suggests that a measurable 'celebrity effect' can be achieved. Campaigns endorsed by a celebrity can benefit from their support, but this depends on the celebrity – not all celebrities are equally credible or persuasive. Real world tests of such effects are less assured in their results. Some do suggest that there may be a discernible endorsement effect (Garthwaite and Moore, 2008), while others are more sceptical (Couldry and Markham, 2007). A team of researchers at the University of Michigan-Dearborn have offered qualified evidence for the power of celebrities to advance political advocacy, rather than – as has been supposed – to 'make the news' (Thrall et al., 2008). The limited state of research into celebrity politics will change, particularly as the phenomenon itself grows. In doing so, we will be able to move beyond the rather stark debate that divides those who welcome, and those who condemn, such developments. Instead, we will be able to assess more accurately and evaluate more analytically the impact of celebrity politics, and the particular aspect of the relationship of popular culture and political communication that it represents.

CONCLUSION

While research into the conditions and effects of the celebrity politician remains limited, it continues to be an important field in which to investigate the relationship of political communication and popular culture. Underlying such research is a set of assumptions which stretch beyond this particular case. These assumptions are both cultural and political in that they draw upon ideas about what is entailed in political communication and what disciplines and literature are appropriate to unravelling its mysteries. To the extent that political communication is understood as a performance, then the insights and ideas garnered from disciplines and fields in which performance is central have much to offer.

At the same time, reflecting on the relationship of popular culture to political communication draws our attention to the multifarious ways in which popular culture – defined here in terms of its desire to entertain rather than inform – conveys political attitudes and values. Attempts to limit formally the field of political communication tend to exclude the contribution of popular culture, to the detriment of our comprehension of political discourse in the modern world. In analysing the way in which politics is communicated through popular culture we are drawn into questions about how these performances affect those who hear or see them. And paradoxically perhaps, as we see the ever closer links between the realms of popular culture and political communication, we see the continuity between our past and our present, when politics as performance was viewed as a necessary assumption rather than an aberration.

However, while the focus on popular culture and political communication leads to a conclusion which suggests that less has changed than we might have imagined, it does not invite complacency. It argues, in fact, for the need for research and analysis that is different from that which has gone before. It does not mean simply treating political communication as popular culture, or vice versa. Rather it means an increasing sensitivity to the performative dimension of politics and an extension of the range of media forms that are included within 'political communication'.

REFERENCES

Adorno, T. and Horkheimer, M. (1979) 'The Culture Industry: Enlightenment as Mass Deception', in *Dialectic of Enlightenment*. London: Verso. pp. 120–67.

Anderson, B. (1983) *Imagined Communities*. London: Verso.

Ankersmit, F. (1996) *Aesthetic Politics*. Stanford, CA: Stanford University Press.

Baldwin, T. and Lister, S. (2009) 'Dumped ballroom judge given task of putting UK on its feet', *The Times*, 13 August, http://www.thetimes.co.uk

Bennett, J. (2001) *The Enchantment of Modern Life*. Princeton, NJ: Princeton University Press.

Besley, J. (2006) 'The Role of Entertainment Television and its Interaction with Individual Values in Explaining Political Participation', *Harvard International Journal of Press/Politics*, 11(2): 41–63.

Bloom, A. (1987) *The Closing of the American Mind*. New York: Simon and Schuster.

Brants, K. (1998) 'Who's afraid of infotainment?', *European Journal of Communication*, 13(3): 313–35.

Carruthers, S. (1998) '*The Manchurian Candidate* (1962) and the Cold War Brainwashing Scare', *Historical Journal of Film, Radio and Television*, 18(1): 75–94.

Corner, J. (2003) 'Mediated Persona and Political Culture', in J. Corner and D. Pels (eds.), *Media and the Restyling of Politics*. London: Sage. pp. 67–84.

Corner, J. and Pels, D. (eds.) (2003) *Media and the Restyling of Politics*. London: Sage.

Couldry, N. and Markham, T. (2007) 'Celebrity Culture and Public Connection: Bridge or Chasm?', *International Journal of Cultural Studies*, 10(4): 403–21.

Crouch, C. (2004) *Post-Democracy*. Cambridge: Polity Press.

Davies, P. and Wells, P. (eds.) (2002) *American Film and Politics from Reagan to Bush*. Manchester: Manchester University Press.

Desinsoff, S. and Peterson, R. (eds.) (1972) *The Sounds of Social Change*. New York: Rand McNally.

Denselow, R. (1989) *When the Music's Over*. London: Faber & Faber.

Downs, A. (1957) *An Economic Theory of Democracy*. New York: Harper & Row.

Ellul, J. (1973) *The Political Illusion*. New York: Vintage

Eyerman, R. and Jamison, A. (1991) *Social Movements: A Cognitive Approach*. London: Polity Press.

Fischlin, D. and Heble, A. (eds.) (2003) *Rebel Musics: Human Rights, Resistant Sounds, and the Politics of Music Making*. Montreal: Black Rose Books.

Franklin, B. (2003) *Packaging Politics: Political Communication in Britain's Media Democracy*. 2nd edn. London: Edward Arnold.

Garthwaite, C. and Moore, T. (2008) 'The Role of Celebrity Endorsements in Politics: Oprah, Obama, and the 2008 Democratic Primary', http://econ-server.umd.edu/~garthwaite/celebrityendorsements_garthwaitemoore.pdf

Gerharty, C. (1991) *Women and Soap Opera*. Cambridge: Polity Press.

Goodwin, J., Jasper, J. and Polletta, F. (eds.) (2001) *Passionate Politics: Emotions and Social Movements*. Chicago, IL: University of Chicago Press.

Gramsci, A. (1971) *Selections from the Prison Notebooks*. ed. and trans. Q. Hoare and G. Nowell-Smith. London: Lawrence and Wishart.

Gray, H. (1995) *Watching Race: Television and the Struggle for 'Blackness'*. Minneapolis, MN: University of Minnesota Press.

Hague, S., Street, J. and Savigny, S. (2008) 'The Voice of the People? Musicians as Actors', *Cultural Politics*, 4(1): 5–24.

Harris, J. (2003) *The Last Party: Britpop, Blair and the Demise of English Rock*. London: Fourth Estate.

Hart, R. (1999) *Seducing America: How Television Charms the Modern Voter*. New York: Oxford University Press.

Hobsbawm, E. and Ranger, T. (eds.) (1992) *The Invention of Tradition*. Cambridge: Cambridge University Press.

Hooghe, M. (2002) 'Watching Television and Civic Engagement', *Harvard International Journal of Press/Politics*, 7(2): 84–104.

Iyengar, S. (1991) *Is Anyone Responsible? How Television Frames Political Issues*. Chicago, IL: Chicago University Press.

Jackson, D. and Darrow, T. (2005) 'The Influence of Celebrity Endorsements on Young Adults' Political Opinions', *Harvard International Journal of Press/Politics*, 10(3): 80–98.

Kavanagh, D. (1995) *Election Campaigning: The New Marketing of Politics*. Oxford: Blackwells.

Kellner, D. (1995) *Media Culture*. London: Routledge.

Lahusen, C. (1996) *The Rhetoric of Moral Protest: Public Campaigns, Celebrity Endorsement and Political Mobilization*. Berlin: Walter de Gruyter.

Lilleker, D. and Lees-Marshment, J. (2005) *Political Marketing: A Comparative Approach*. Manchester: Manchester University Press.

Marcuse, H. (1964) *One-Dimensional Man: Studies in the Ideology of Advanced Industrial Society*. London: Routledge & Kegan Paul.

Marshall, P. D. (1997) *Celebrity and Power: Fame in Contemporary Culture*. Minneapolis, MN: University of Minnesota Press.

Marshall, P. D. (ed.) (2006) *The Celebrity Culture Reader*. New York: Routledge.

McQuail, D., Golding, G. and De Bens, E. (eds.) (2005) *Communication Theory and Research*. London: Sage.

McRobbie (1991) *Feminism and Popular Culture*. Basingstoke: Palgrave Macmillan.

Meyer, T. (2002) *Media Democracy*. Cambridge: Polity Press.

Meyrowitz, J. (1985) *No Sense of Place: The Effect of Electronic Media on Social Behaviour*. New York: Oxford University Press.

Moy, P., Scheufele, D. and Holbert, R. L. (1999) 'Television Use and Social Capital: Testing Putnam's Time Displacement Hypothesis', *Mass Communication and Society*, 2(1): 27–45.

Nash, K. (2009) *The Cultural Politics of Human Rights: Comparing the US and UK*. Cambridge: Cambridge University Press.

Negrine, R. (2008) *The Transformation of Political Communication: Continuities and Changes in Media and Politics.* Basingstoke: Palgrave Macmillan.

Neve, B. (1992) *Film and Politics in America: A Social Tradition.* London: Routledge.

Norris, P. (1996) *Electoral Change since 1945.* Oxford: Blackwell.

Pels, D. (2003) 'Aesthetic Representation and Political Style: Re-Balancing Identity and Difference in Media Democracy', in J. Corner and D. Pels (eds.), *Media and the Restyling of Politics.* London: Sage. pp. 41–66.

Postman, N. (1987) *Amusing Ourselves to Death.* London: Methuen.

Putnam, R. (2000) *Bowling Alone: The Collapse and Revival of American Community.* London: Simon and Schuster.

Radway, J. (1991) *Reading the Romance: Women, Patriarchy and Popular Literature.* Chapel Hill: University of North Carolina Press.

Rose, T. (1994) *Black Noise: Rap Music and Black Culture in Contemporary America.* Hanover: Wesleyan University Press.

Rosenbaum, M. (1997) *From Soapbox to Soundbite.* London: Macmillan.

Ross, A. (2007) *The Rest is Noise: Listening to the Twentieth Century.* New York: Farrar, Strauss and Giroux.

Saunders, K. (2009) *Communicating Politics in the Twenty-First Century.* Basingstoke: Palgrave Macmillan.

Savigny, H. (2008) *The Problem of Political Marketing.* New York: Continuum.

Saward, M. (2006) 'The Representative Claim', *Contemporary Political Theory*, 5(3): 297–318.

Scammell, M. (1995) *Designer Politics: How Elections are Won.* London: Macmillan.

Schumpeter, J. (1976) *Capitalism, Socialism and Democracy.* London: George Allen.

Sireau, N. and Davis, A. (2007) 'Interest Groups and Mediated Mobilization: Communication in the Make Poverty History Campaign', in A. Davis (ed.), *The Mediation of Power: A Critical Introduction.* London: Routledge. pp. 131–50.

Starr, F. (1983) *Red & Hot: The Fate of Jazz in the Soviet Union.* New York: Oxford University Press.

Stanyer, J. (2007) *Modern Political Communications: Mediated Politics in Uncertain Times.* Cambridge: Polity Press.

Steinweis, A. (1993) *Art, Ideology and Economics in Nazi Germany.* Chapel Hill, NC: University of North Carolina Press.

Street, J. (1997) *Politics and Popular Culture.* Cambridge: Polity Press.

Street, J. (2004) 'Celebrity Politicians: Popular Culture and Political Representation', *British Journal of Politics and International Relations*, 6(4): 435–52.

Street, J., Hague, S. and Savigny, H. (2008) 'Playing to the Crowd: The Role of Music and Musicians in Political Participation', *British Journal of Politics & International Relations*, 10(2): 269–85.

Swaine, J. (2009) 'Celebrities aid £90,000 by Government to Front Public Health Campaigns', *Daily Telegraph*, 11 January, http://www.telegraph.co.uk

Swanson, D. and Mancini, P. (eds.) (1996) *Politics, Media, and Modern Democracy.* New York: Praeger.

Thrall, T. A., Lollio-Fakhreddine, J., Berent, J. J., Donnelyy, L., Herrin, W., Paquett, Z., Wenglinski, R. and Wyatt, A. (2008) 'StarPower: Celebrity Advocacy and the Evolution of the Public Sphere', *Harvard International Journal of Press/Politics*, 13(4): 362–85.

Urban, M. (2004) *Russia Gets the Blues: Music, Culture, and Community in Unsettled Times.* Ithaca, NY: Cornell University Press.

van Zoonen, L. (2004) 'Imagining the Fan Democracy', *European Journal of Communication*, 19(1): 39–52.

van Zoonen, L. (2005) *Entertaining the Citizen: When Politics and Popular Culture Converge.* Lanham, MD: Rowman & Littlefield.

Wagg, S. (ed.) (1998) *Because I Tell a Joke or Two: Comedy, Politics and Social Difference.* London: Routledge.

West, D. and Orman, J. (2003) *Celebrity Politics.* Upper Saddle River, NJ: Prentice Hall.

Williams, R. (1985) *Keywords: A Vocabulary of Culture and Society.* New York: Oxford University Press.

Zolo, D. (1992) *Democracy and Complexity.* Cambridge: Polity Press.

7

Government Communication: An Emerging Field in Political Communication Research

María José Canel and Karen Sanders

In February 2009, the US Congress passed a US$787 billion stimulus package designed to put the country on the road to economic recovery. Thereafter, managing 'the stimulus story' became, as *Time* magazine reported, 'a full-time White House preoccupation' (Scherer, 2009: 31). Obama and his team understood that without a concerted effort to communicate the plan, it would almost certainly fail in the court of public opinion.

The quality of government matters for human well-being. Governing necessarily involves constant exchanges of information and communication about policies, ideas and decisions between governors and the governed. Despite its key importance for 21st-century politics, the study of government communication is an under-researched area of political communication studies, finding itself in a kind of theoretical no-man's land between political communication, public relations and organizational communication research.

This chapter examines three related issues. First, it examines what we mean by government communication. This task poses a number of challenges not least that of settling what kinds of institutions count as *governmental* in the diverse settings of democratic politics.[1] Second, the article draws together the distinctive contributions to the study of government communication found in the political communication literature. Third, the chapter argues that perspectives developed by public relations and organizational communication studies may have much to offer political communication scholars studying government communication. Finally, we suggest a number of issues that could form part of a research agenda for government communication (see Sanders, 2011).

DEFINING GOVERNMENT COMMUNICATION

In defining government communication we adopt two complementary epistemological strategies. The first might be termed an *a priori* approach: it relies on an analysis of characteristics of communication in diverse institutional settings that, though based on empirically known facts (a form of *a posteriori* knowledge), is true by virtue of the meanings we ascribe to social and political institutions. The second strategy can be termed *a posteriori*: it examines the empirical research carried out to date by scholars together with the broad thematic and theoretical approaches offered by political communication to map what the academy understands as constituting the subject matter and methods for the study of government communication. The *a priori* approach runs the risk of imposing historically and culturally conditioned meanings on our area of study and the second runs up against the limits of the research itself. However, we consider them necessary starting points to identify the strengths and the weaknesses of political communication's contribution to understanding government communication.

The term 'government communication' is often used to refer solely to top-level executive communication. But it can also be used to refer to institutions established by government to do its work at national, regional and local levels. Our tentative, broadly framed definition of government communication attempts to capture this multilayered reality Government communication 'refers to the aims, role and practice of communication implemented by *executive* politicians and officials of public institutions in the service of a political rationale, and that are themselves constituted on the basis of the people's indirect or direct consent and are charged to enact their will' (Canel and Sanders, 2011). This definition includes prime ministerial or presidential communication as well as mayoral or local and regional government communication; but it is contrasted with the deliberative communication legislatures use to decide public policy through determining the law, and with the judiciary whose function is to make judgments in relation to disputes about the application of the law. Other kinds of public sector institutions such as the UK's National Health Service or continental Europe's state universities would also be excluded. These institutions clearly have an executive function in that they seek to execute politically defined public policies but their primary end is the *provision* or *delivery* of public goods such as health and education. The definition also embraces a range of political regimes that evince varying degrees of recognition of political rights and civil liberties following the Freedom House set of indicators showing governments to be democratic (free), consolidating democracies (partly free) and non-democratic (not free) (Freedom House, 2009).

Government necessarily implies the principle of *publicness* in two senses: first, there is always a public institutional setting even in the most authoritarian regimes; second, again regardless of the political realities, it is almost always claimed that government is constituted on the basis of the people's direct or indirect consent and charged to enact their will (Puddington, 2009). Of course, government communication is not always public: heads of state or government make private phone calls to their peers; secret back channels are used for delicate issues; government leaders may have closed meetings with party members and ministers may privately brief journalists. However, government's institutional setting is public, directed to external audiences and played out partly in the space of appearance with important implications for the operational conditions for communication (Fisher and Horsley, 2007: 378).

Graber (2003: 6–18) distinguishes public from private organizations along three key dimensions (see also Fisher and Horsley, 2007: 378–79; Garnett, 1992; Rainey et al., 1976). First, the *environment* of public sector institutions is typically less open to market competition with less incentive to reduce costs, less concern with consumer preferences and more subject to legal and formal constraints affecting managers' choices of procedures and operational areas than in the private sector.

Second, *organization–environment transactions* in public organizations are more subject to sanctions and controls and to significant public scrutiny in line with public interest expectations including fair and accountable action. The context of intense public and media scrutiny is linked to the organizational orientation to the public good and often finds regulatory expression in freedom of information legislation and/or commitments to transparency and openness. Ultimately, public organizations are usually required to have a high degree of accountability to political and public constituencies. On the one hand, as Graber (2003: 11) has noted, this can lead to cautious operating styles as managers seek to avoid bad publicity. On the other, it can ensure a flow of information that enhances the quality of civic life.

Finally, in relation to *internal structures and processes*, public sector organizations tend to be more complex than their private sector counterparts. There is more diversity and uncertainty about objectives and decision-making criteria and a greater possibility that goals will clash. They tend to have less decision-making autonomy and flexibility; less flexibility in establishing performance incentives; more application of formal regulations and more political roles for top managers. Public organizational communication and, in particular, government communication, operates in a political environment. This often leads to short-termism. Political considerations, events and culture structure resources, personnel and goals. Heads of communication in government ministries, agencies and institutions may be appointed on the basis of partisan rather than professional criteria.

In sum, public and more specifically government communication wrestles with considerable complexity in terms of goals, needs, audiences, definition and resources. The multilayered and organizationally diverse nature of government communication is a key factor in the complexity of understanding its needs, goals and resources. In relation to the issue of goals, for example, government communication often has to juggle what appear to be conflicting objectives set by political masters. Many scholars, especially, as we shall see, those working in the political communication tradition, consider communication goals related to persuasion to be particularly problematic. In relation to publics, government communication again must operate on a multilayered level, taking into account a very diverse group of stakeholders including other politicians, service users, minority groups, regulatory bodies, etc.

Graber's analysis is helpful but we must be careful about extrapolating it to settings outside the liberal democratic model that underpins it. A number of countries have developed complex government communication systems but without the concomitant implementation of civil liberties and political freedoms found in many electoral democracies (Freedom House, 2009). In other words, our approach to the study of government communication has to take into account the regime variety that does in fact exist in the world including divergences in media ecologies and political systems.

THE POLITICAL COMMUNICATION PERSPECTIVE

Scholars working in the political communication tradition have mostly centered on the USA and taken executive, and more particularly, presidential communication as their point of departure.[2] However, in order to understand the broader sweep of political communication's thinking about government communication, it is worth examining the conceptual and methodological perspectives it has contributed to this area of research.

In his review of political communication research, Swanson noted the breadth of its portfolio but concluded that its central focus is on 'the role of communication in political processes and institutions associated with electoral campaigning and governing' (2000: 190). These core issues prompt a concern with understanding media effects and normative themes related to the quality and health of democratic discourse and institutions examined from multidisciplinary perspectives. An early 21st-century review of political communication research identified five key sites and methodological perspectives (Lin, 2004; also see Graber, 2005) namely:

- rhetorical analysis of political discourse;
- propaganda studies;
- voting studies;
- mass media effects;
- interplay of influence between government, press and public opinion.

These themes and methodological approaches in fact crisscross each other. The interplay of influence between government, press and public opinion can be approached from the perspective of rhetorical analysis or propaganda studies. Therefore, in using Lin's description to examine further political communication's contribution to the study of government communication, one must be careful to point out that thematic concerns often overlap and multiple methodological approaches apply. Broadly speaking, the following five main thematic concerns can be discerned: (1) chief executive communication; (2) the development of the permanent campaign; and, linked to this; (3) that of government advertising and publicity; (4) the structure and organization of government communication and (5) the development of news management strategies.

Chief Executive Communication and Rhetorical Studies

This is perhaps the area that has received most significant attention from the US scholars, beginning with Neustadt's (1960) classic study *Presidential Power* and continuing with work by Denton and Hahn (1986), Tulis (1987), Smith and Smith (1994) and Denton and Holloway (1996). Studies of presidential rhetoric and its shaping of political reality (Zarefsky, 2004) and its influence (or not) on its audience (Edwards, 2003) have produced a rich vein of work from diverse disciplinary perspectives using methodological approaches from the humanities and social sciences. Cox (2001) also examines presidential rhetoric but within the framework of a consideration of communication strategy.

Chief executive communication has also been explored in a number of other national contexts including Argentina (de Masi, 2001), Australia (Young, 2007) and the UK (Franklin, 2004; Seymour Ure, 2003). Chief executive communication strategies in relation to political scandal and to terrorism have been examined in work examining Spain and the UK (Canel and Sanders, 2006, 2009). References to chief executive communication can also be found in more generalist literature (for example, McNair, 2007; Oates, 2008; Stanyer, 2007).

The Permanent Campaign, Political Advertising, Public Diplomacy and Propaganda Studies

The development of strategic government communication was identified some time back by Blumenthal (1980). The techniques of election campaigns – gathering intelligence, targeting audiences, promoting messages, rapid rebuttal – become part of the machinery of government as the ubiquity, speed and quantity of contemporary media result in governments making substantial institutional and personal investments in communication, employing communication specialists to advise on strategy and carry out communication functions.

The development of the permanent campaign has been closely followed by political communication scholars who have frequently adopted a critical approach based on a tradition arising out of propaganda studies (for example, McChesney, 2008). In this analysis, the structural relationship between the media and state power is unmasked as one that 'manufactures consent' (Herman and Chomsky, 1988), producing a bystander public bereft of real power.

Scholars from a number of political communication traditions have noted what they consider to be the troubling implications of a 'third age of political communication' (Blumler and Kavanagh, 1999; Ornstein and Mann, 2000), where campaigning, that seeks to win not engage, becomes the settled style and substance of government. The health and quality of democracy and citizenship are at the heart of the concerns explored in a number of studies (for example, Patterson, 1994, 2003), particularly at times of crisis when events and issues such as war, terrorism and the environment become of vital public interest (Norris et al., 2003). The development of the permanent campaign brings the practice of public relations squarely into the frame together with its methods and tools (see Strömbäck and Kiousis, 2011).

Political advertising has also been a major research focus of political communication scholars but principally in the field of election campaign advertising (Kaid and Holtz-Bacha, 2006). Government advertising in general and the area of government social marketing communication in particular (health campaigns; environmental change; driving behavior, etc.) has generated a considerable body of research but mainly by scholars working within distinct communication traditions from political communication (Rice and Atkin, 2001).

Finally, as governments increasingly see the attractions of 'soft power' (Nye, 2004) to achieve foreign policy objectives, the area of public diplomacy is one which has become a greater focus of interest. 'Public diplomacy' can be understood as the diffuse set of actions undertaken to influence favorably public attitudes in ways that will support foreign policy goals in political, military or economic affairs. As yet, there is no substantial body of research in the area, although analysts such as Leonard et al. (2005) are contributing to the development of an approach that focuses on 'mutuality', on long-term trust-building rather than short-term image-building.

Structure and Organization of Government Communication

The logistical and operational issues of how governments organize their communication have been a significant area of research and debate examining too the relationship between government and its citizens, although thus far work has centered mainly on the organizational chart, roles, functions and decision-making processes of White House communication (Kumar, 2003a,b, 2007; Kumar and Sullivan, 2003).

The examination of government communication practices associated with the development of electronic technology has generated a significant

literature on issues associated with e-democracy and e-government examining, for example, the potential to unharness the democratic energies of the people (for example, Axford and Huggins, 2001; Chadwick, 2006; Izurieta et al., 2003; Saco, 2002). This growing area of research reflects a common theme in political communication studies namely, the development of media technologies and practices and their impact on political practices and institutions and, more especially, the quality of democratic life.

News Media Relations and Effects Research

Government communication takes place in a mediated environment and it is perhaps unsurprising that one of the most significant areas of scholarship in political communication in relation to government communication is the news media/government nexus. The media are a key factor in the environment in which governments operate. Research has focused on such areas as source relationships to explain the ebb and flow of power between politicians and journalists. Generally speaking, politicians seek control, journalists seek novelty and revelation. Conflict is frequently the order of the day and, as scholars such as Patterson (1994) have shown, conflict itself is sought by journalists as the *leifmotif* of politics. In the view of some scholars 'the indexing hypothesis – selecting content patterns that are cued by the positions of decisive actors in a political conflict – still explains most routine political reporting' (Bennett, 2004: 292). Other scholars have looked to the model of 'primary definition' to explain the dynamics of source – reporter relationship (Gitlin, 1980; Hall, 1982; Herman and Chomsky, 1988). Here sources are identified as the forces who hold the balance of power, using their institutional muscle as well as logistical and ideological resources to ensure that certain stories are told and others not. Source power has also been explored in agenda setting and agenda building studies of the media, a major area of political communication research initiated by McCombs and Shaw's pioneering study that examined the relationship between public and media agendas (McCombs and Shaw, 1972; see also Weaver et al., 2004). This tradition of research has been particularly notable in the analysis of election campaigns (for example, Semetko et al., 1991). Election campaigns are, of course, one of the principal subjects of political communication studies and the role of news media in priming – the activation of certain associations in our memory that leads us to privilege some criteria and terms in assessing candidates over others – and framing news stories, with their potential and real audience effects, has been a significant area of work (for example, Reese et al., 2003; Bennett and Iyengar, 2010).

Finally, a major area of study, and one that reflects an interest that runs through much of the work outlined above, examines the development of the news media as a political actor in contemporary politics and how even, in Cook's words, 'news media today are not merely part of politics: they are part of government' (2005: 3).

More recent work (see, for example, Dahlgren, 2009; Brants and Voltmer, 2011) examines the changing media environment and its implications for politicians' performance and presentation as well as citizens' interactions and civic culture.

Theoretical Contributions from Political Communication

This review of work carried out from the political communication perspective suggests that systematic research developing a critical analysis of baseline issues for the field or for modeling government communication to lay the foundations for comparative study going beyond the mainly descriptive has yet to be carried out. However, much useful work has been done and the political communication tradition provides at least two valuable theoretical standpoints from which to orient future government communication research.

Perhaps unsurprisingly, given political communication's home disciplines among others of political science and rhetoric, the emphasis on the exploration of and sensitivity to institutional and social contexts, on the one hand, and the attention to normative concerns on the other, are key theoretical concerns of political communication and provide us with helpful indicators for government communication research designs of the future.

Drawing on Blumler and Kavanagh's (1999) analysis of the arrival of a third age for political communication, Swanson (2000: 192) points to the trend to examine communication's institutional and social contexts. He suggests that this is a useful corrective to social science research that either adopts a fragmented approach to the study of communication or applies overly ethnocentric models to explore complex communication phenomena. Hallin and Mancini (2004) have been particularly prominent in developing models to compare media and political systems that are sensitive to political, cultural and historical contexts. Their work is valuable in its potential to extend the boundaries and improve the rigor of comparative

research notwithstanding the challenges of this endeavor (Norris, 2009).

A second distinctive contribution from political communication scholars is a normative concern with how communication 'performs its civic functions at the center of social and political life, and also to point the way toward shaping communication to better serve democratic processes' (Swanson, 2000: 200). Of course, normative concerns are not unique to political communication. However, in this field there is, we would argue, a distinct feature: research conclusions have tended to emphasize 'the crisis of communication for citizenship' (Bucy and D'Angelo, 1999: 329), mitigated to some degree by more recent work on the democratic potential of digital technology (Chadwick, 2006; Davis, 2010). This has the positive consequence of pointing research to notions of purpose and performance but it may be too that it has contributed to a kind of intellectual pessimism about the possibility of creating the conditions for civic conversation in contemporary media democracies (Sanders, 2009: 229–33).

PERSPECTIVES FROM PUBLIC RELATIONS AND ORGANIZATIONAL COMMUNICATION RESEARCH

We want to suggest now that political communication scholars might find some grounds for intellectual optimism by exploring work being carried out in the cognate fields of organizational communication and public relations. As far as specific work on government communication is concerned, a review of the relevant literature suggests that, as for political communication, the subject is under-researched. However, there are two areas in which research in the field can offer pointers for those working in the political communication tradition.

First, we can identify converging themes with those being explored by political communication scholars. These include the issues of media relations, issue management (Bowen, 2005; Jaques, 2006), the development of professional profiles and competences (Gregory, 2006); crisis communication (Coombs and Holladay, 2010) and public diplomacy (Signitzer and Wamser, 2006). To take issue management, for example, in the public relations literature this refers to the work undertaken by companies to identify emerging political, social and economic trends and plan communication in accordance with the potential threats and opportunities they pose. Political communication scholars are also keen to explore the requirement for and implication of communication strategies in relation to public policies (Cox, 2001) and may be able to draw upon some of the insights of the work being carried out in cognate fields.

Second, public relations and organizational communication scholars can offer a fresh conceptual approach to issues common to researchers working in the field of government communication. We have identified three themes where they appear to offer new perspectives, namely, governments' relationship with the public; how governments and publics can evaluate performance through the concept of reputation and finally, how communication is core to organizational performance and thus intrinsic to any consideration of relationship and reputation quality. We will next examine briefly each of these issues.

Symmetrical Relationships and Mutuality

Broadly speaking, a revision of the public relations literature (Botan and Hazleton, 2006; Botan and Taylor, 2004; Heath, 2010; Vasquez and Taylor, 2001) shows that the underlying research perspective is centered on the construction of relationships between organizations and publics. The public is not seen as an impartial and passive spectator of organizations' communication, an approach that is not so clearly present in perspectives from the field of political communication. The field of public relations has evolved from a more business-oriented field to a more socially oriented one, keen to put the public back into research.

In their revision of the state of the art, Botan and Taylor (2004: 651) assert a similar view, charting the evolution of research from what they consider the functional perspective to what they call the 'co-creation' perspective. While the former sees publics and communication as tools or means to achieve organizational ends, the latter considers the public to be partners in the creation of meaning and communication. This perspective places an implicit value on relationships, going beyond the achievement of an organizational goal and instead placing the emphasis on advancing mutual understanding.

These authors locate here Grunig's symmetrical/excellence model of public relations, with its claim that it fosters ethical public relations practices (Grunig and Grunig, 1992; Grunig and Hunt, 1984). This model is the major framework that has guided public relations scholarship for the past 30 years (Botan and Hazleton, 2006: 6). Mutual benefit, mutual understanding, win–win mixed motivated communication, etc. are concepts used to denominate purposes of organizational public relations. They have inspired analysis of government communication (Fisher and Horsley, 2007; Gregory, 2006) as well as debate about

their providing the basis for a model of government communication, although Grunig in work with Jaatinen (1999) acknowledges that his model would have to be adapted to the peculiar conditions of government communication.

The interest of this approach is that, in centering the analysis on the establishment of relationships, the understanding of the 'public' is fundamentally altered. Government communication is conceived as the cultivation of long-term relationships oriented to mutual understanding rather than being modeled on short-term, vote-winning approaches to communication.

The Concept of Government Reputation

The idea that organizations' success depends on how they are viewed by key stakeholders has led both academic and communication practitioners to suggest frameworks and models that prescribe steps toward the 'strategic' use of communication. Consequently, concepts such as 'corporate identity' and 'corporate reputation' have gained purchase. The management of intangibles and, more particularly, of reputation has increasingly become the guiding philosophy of communication departments (Cornelissen et al., 2006).

One of the most important issues in the study of the notion of an organization's reputation is whether reputation is purely perceptual or purely experiential (through the company's activities and services or products provided). Two concepts are key to pinning down that of reputation: first, that of 'identity' defined essentially as consisting in what an organization presents of itself in terms of behavior, communication and symbolism as well as visual, non-material aspects of the institution; the second is that of 'image' understood as the mental structure of the organization that publics form as the result of the processing of information related to the organization. Whereas identity is what the organization *is* (including the organizational behavior, its products and services), corporate image is stakeholders' perceptions of it. For some authors, reputation is more closely related to the notion of 'image' and therefore, perceptual (stakeholders' net image of a company) (Fombrum, 1996) and for others, it is more closely related to the notion of identity as the result of corporation behavior (Villafañé, 2004: 31–2). In this latter sense, reputation is associated with the behavior of an organization. For this reason, reputation can not only be measured but also verified by hard facts and reality checks.

There is, as far as we are aware, no research examining government communication or communication in the public sector from the perspective of corporate communication. Although many studies have centered on government leaders' popularity or public perceptions of public policies, no work has been done so far on what is the meaning of public leaders' reputation (and the correspondingly important question of the difference between public policies perceived and public policies performed); nor has work been carried out on how to build the reputation of government institutions and their leaders. Political communication research has also centered more on issues of image so that one can find discussions such as those of Waterman et al. (1999) that suggest that 'the image-is-everything presidency' is sufficient. In this sense, research perspectives that emphasize the significance of reputation helpfully shift the focus to the reality of political outcomes and the truth of who and what a leader is.

Communication as the Core Process of All Organizations

The central idea that inspires the field of organizational communication is that communication is fundamental to the study of organizations. This approach is applied in the only handbook in the field examining public administration communication (Garnett and Kouzmin, 1997). In addition to this study, Graber's (2003) work offers one of the few systemic and comprehensive analyses of communication in the public sector. It too is theoretically grounded in the field of organizational communication. Although open to dynamic approaches, applying different methodologies and perspectives, she uses analyses of systems-wide communication flows and applies it to analyze the structure of the communications networks within public agencies. Although she considers that positivist theories will remain dominant in the study of organizational communication, she also argues that they can usefully be complemented by humanistic approaches. Since, as Graber suggests, quoting Viteritti, 'meaningful communication between government and the people is not merely a management practicality. It is a political, albeit moral, obligation that originates from the basic covenant that exists between the government and the people' (2003: 226).

FUTURE RESEARCH DIRECTIONS FOR GOVERNMENT COMMUNICATION

Examining the subject of government communication from a range of research traditions in the field of communication studies suggests a number of issues that are ripe for development. Here we suggest five.

The Question of Professionalization

Originally framed as an Americanization hypothesis within the political communication literature, the adoption and development of a set of practices and attitudes collectively known as 'professionalization' were considered by political communication scholars as driven by developments in the US political communication (for example, Negrine, 2008). Scholars are now more likely to ascribe these developments to 'modernization', the view that professionalization results from processes of social differentiation and changes in media systems and technology (Holtz-Bacha, 2004). Within political communication, the professionalization thesis could be summarized as follows: political actors have been forced to adopt and develop complex communication practices in order to deal with the huge demands of the contemporary news environment. This professionalization has, however, been detrimental to policymaking, to the substance of politics with consequences such as the de-politicization of politics and the loss of ideological identity; image and communication skills become key; political consultants become more important than politicians; politics becomes a strategic game or talk show, a type of politics that stimulates stereotypes and clichés undermining citizens' trust in political institutions (Canel, 2006 and Sanders, 2009 for an overview of all these trends).

From the political communication perspective, 'professionalization' has often been cast in a negative role (Hamelink, 2007). Of course, not all researchers in this tradition take this view (for example, McNair, 2007; Negrine, 2008). However, there may be something to learn from public relations' scholars and, in particular, the work of Grunig (2001), who suggests that attempting to achieve mutual understanding, even when engaged in asymmetrical communication in the 'win–win' zone of communication, is in fact the really professional way to communicate. In other words, it may be that Leonard's (2005) notion of mutuality, in which mutual understanding is the goal and where both persuasion and information are considered appropriate, can be considered to be the truly 'professional' way to communicate. But how would this apply in different political environments? Could standards and indicators of professional government communication be developed for countries as diverse as China, Norway and Mexico?

A number of researchers have sought to operationalize indicators of professionalism in government communication in specific national contexts. Gregory (2006) provides a framework for British government communicators designed to drive up performance and improve the consistency of the communications function across government. The framework suggests that effective research, planning, implementation, evaluation and management processes provide the platform for effective communication activity that should be underpinned by the acquisition of the appropriate skills and competences. A Dutch research team (Vos, 2006; see also Vos and Westerhoudt, 2008), inspired by the quality management literature, have designed an instrument to assess government communication in relation to issues such as required competences, the priority given to communication, transparency and accessibility. Sanders et al. have examined the professionalization of central government communication in Germany, Spain and the UK applying a framework developed using indicators derived from the sociology of work and from the strategic planning and quality literature (Sanders et al., 2011). These studies provide pointers for ways in which researchers can explore in measurable terms what is meant by professionalization in government communication.

Information and Persuasion

The issue of professionalization is linked to that of the debates surrounding the relationship between the informational and persuasive goals of government communication (for example, Negrine, 2008). In the case of the USA, this debate adopts the form of the distinction between two units, the House of Communications (whose role is strategy) and the Press Office (whose role is to be an information conduit) (Kumar, 2001a,b). While the first unit plans in advance, the second one is responsible for day-to-day operations: it implements the strategy. The separate offices have different functions but 'when they mix, the audiences for both can be confused about what is persuasion and what is information' (Kumar, 2001a: 614).

In the UK, debates about government use of 'spin' – presentation of policy – dominated the media during Alastair Campbell's years as Tony Blair's communication chief. The criticism can be summarized as follows: New Labour displaced attention from the *substance* of politics to its *presentation*, blurring fact and opinion (Ingham, 2003; Seymour Ure, 2003) and jeopardized the British Whitehall model of non-partisan government communication (Sanders, 2009: 78–80).

These examples raise questions for future research such as where does the line lie between the role a government has in giving information and in persuading? Does persuasion necessarily clash with information? Is persuasion less professional? Could not it be the case that professional persuasion allows people to be better informed on public policies? Is an emphasis on explanation the most persuasive form of communication in an information-rich environment? Can these issues be conceptualized in a similar way in the distinct political and cultural environments of, for instance, Singapore, Brazil and Sweden? Answering these questions means thinking about how trust can be built in the relations between the governors and the governed and how concepts such as 'government reputation' and 'mutuality' may help in this enterprise.

Evaluating Government Communication

Developing a framework for the evaluation of government communication is also a key task for researchers. A review of studies (Canel, 2007: 201–9) suggests key areas of study including the organizational chart, that acts as the formal representation of the place communication occupies in the decision-making processes; the role of the leader; the tasks carried out by those engaged in communication; public feedback mechanisms, arguing that these provide useful indicators of the degree to which communication is carried out as a strategic function.

Evaluating citizens' perceptions of government actions and, related to this, being clearer about the reasons governments have for monitoring public opinion are also key areas for future work. Some of the literature on presidential communication and public perceptions of political leaders considers constant presidential polling of public opinion as a negative result of the permanent campaign where a sophisticated and routinized 'public opinion apparatus' is developed to measure public approval, shifting the emphasis from polling the public's policy preferences to polling its non-policy evaluations related to leaders' personal image and appeal (Jacobs and Burns, 2004).

However, an alternative view is that evaluating public perceptions allows an 'important connection between the citizenry, presidential promises, accountability and presidential performance, measured according to public opinion polls as well as policy results' (Rimmerman, 1991: 234; see also Jacobs and Burns, 2004) to be established. Thus, examining public perceptions of government may be considered a helpful input into policy development. Once again concepts such as 'reputation' and 'mutuality' may help us to focus research toward examining not only image but also verifiable facts about government performance that allow us to develop more robust indicators of the match between perception and experience of government.

Studying Government Communication Comparatively

Comparative research in political communication has looked at issues such as media effects, media content, political advertising and, of course, election campaigns. However, there are, as far as we are aware, no general comparative studies of government communication. Such studies can provide helpful insights into the role of culture, structure and agency in political communication as well as providing baseline empirical data for theoretical development and hypothesis building. They can be useful for clarifying concepts and for discovering the scope of their application, making us more aware of the dangers of overgeneralization and ethnocentrism. Case studies are a useful starting point for generating basic data as seen, for example, in Semetko's (2009) four-country study (Kenya, Mexico, the Russian Federation and Turkey) of election campaigns and news media partisan balance. Her work highlights differences and similarities within the distinct components and characteristics of these countries' media and political systems that point to shared challenges and possible strategies for improving governance capacity in them. Case study research can be usefully complemented by the large-scale data sets (for example, those available from Freedom House, Transparency International, Eurostat, etc.) that help provide quantitative evidence for broader patterns and relationships. Norris' (2009) critical review of comparative political communication studies points to the need for such mixed methods research designs and the overall requirement for the use of more rigorously defined concepts in order to generate meaningfully comparative data. These are challenging tasks but, we suggest, necessary ones for the development of government communication research.

FINAL THOUGHTS

The subject of government communication is at the intersection of diverse methodological and disciplinary approaches. Political communication scholars have examined specific features of government communication such as presidential rhetoric, communication strategies and media relations, attending to political and social contexts

and normative issues such as the relationship between communication and democracy. While there are relatively few studies in the field of public relations and organizational communication dealing specifically with government communication, we would argue that some of their conceptual analyses could be fruitfully applied to the exploration of government communication. Concepts such as 'symmetrical communication', 'mutuality' and 'reputation' would be useful tools in exploring some of the research issues already identified. Subjects such as issue management, corporate social responsibility or evaluation of relations with organizational stakeholders – examining transparency (Fairbanks et al., 2007), accountability and the generation of trust, for example – enriches political communication's discussion of common key concerns.

The challenge involves exploring the insights for the understanding of strategic communication offered by diverse theoretical approaches (Coger, 2006). In her review of the role of communication in public organizations, Graber (2003: 13–4) suggests that the study of organizational communication lacks an overarching theory, both in relation to the level of analysis (should it be a macro- or micro-level?) and to the theoretical and the ideological lenses through which organizational communication should be viewed. Graber suggests, however, that, like other areas of the social sciences, the study of organizational communication benefits more from multiple theoretical perspectives and a rich array of research strategies. We agree and believe that similar considerations apply to the study of government communication.

To conclude, we suggest that government communication presents an inviting field for future research and given its significance is too important a challenge to ignore.

NOTES

1 The phrase 'democratic politics' can be put to a number of uses that in some examples are so far removed from what one might consider 'democratic' as to empty the term of any commonly recognized reference. We cannot hope to resolve these definitional and ideological challenges here but note their importance for the issues being considered. In their discussion of the characteristics of Habermas' normative theory of the public sphere, Norris and Odugbemie acknowledge that 'no single country or place serves as a perfect example of the democratic public sphere' (2009: 12). Nevertheless, those features that characterize the fully functioning democratic public sphere – civil liberties and political rights protected by an established constitutional and legal

order, pluralistic and accessible information sources and a flourishing civil society – provide, they suggest, the necessary conditions for healthy democratic governance. We agree.

2   Our review of the literature shows there is a limited amount of work outside the USA, something we hope to remedy in part with the future publication of a broadly drawn range of case studies of government communication (see Sanders, K. and Canel, M. J. (in press) (eds.) *Government Communication. Cases and Challenges*. London: Bloomsbury).

REFERENCES

Axford, B. and Huggins, R. (eds.) (2001) *New Media and Politics*. London: Sage.

Bennett, W. L. (2004) 'Gatekeeping and Press-Government Relations: A Multigated Model of News Construction', in L. L. Kaid (ed.), *Handbook of Political Communication Research*. Mahwah, NJ: Lawrence Erlbaum Associates. pp. 283–314.

Bennett, L. and Iyengar, S. (2010) 'The Shifting Foundations of Political Communication: Responding to a Defense of the Media Effects Paradigm', *Journal of Communication*, 60(1): 35–39.

Blumenthal, S. (1980) *The Permanent Campaign*. New York: Simon and Schuster.

Blumler, J. G. and Kavanagh, D. (1999) 'The Third Age of Political Communication: Influences and Features', *Political Communication*, 16(3): 209–30.

Botan, C. and Hazleton, V. (2006) 'Public Relations in a New Age', in C. Botan and V. Hazleton (eds.), *Public Relations Theory II*. Mahwah, NJ: Lawrence Erlbaum Associates. pp. 1–18.

Botan, C. and Taylor, M. (2004) 'Public Relations State of the Field', *Journal of Communication*, 54(4): 645–61.

Bowen, S. A. (2005) 'A Practical Model for Ethical Decision Making in Issues Management and Public Relations', *Journal of Public Relations Research*, 17(3): 191–216.

Brants, K. and Voltmer, K. (eds.) (2011) *Political Communication in Postmodern Democracy: Challenging the Primacy of Politics*. London: Palgrave Macmillan.

Bucy, E. and D'Angelo, P. (1999) 'The Crisis of Political Communication: Normative Critiques and Democratic Processes', *Communication Yearbook*, 22: 301–40.

Canel, M. J. (2006) *Comunicación política* [*Political Communication*]. Madrid: Tecnos.

Canel, M. J. (2007) *Comunicación de las instituciones públicas* [*Communication for Public Institutions*]. Madrid: Tecnos.

Canel, M. J. and Sanders, K. (2006) *Morality Tales. Political Scandals and Journalism in Britain and Spain in the 1990s*. Cresskill, NJ: Hampton Press.

Canel, M. J. and Sanders, K. (2009) 'Crisis Communication and Terrorist Attacks: Framing a Response to the 2004 Madrid Bombings and 2005 London Bombings', in T. Combs (ed.), *Handbook of Crisis Communication*. Oxford: Blackwell. pp. 449–66.

Canel, M. J. and Sanders, K. (2011) 'Government Communication', *International Encyclopedia of Communication Online*, Wiley Blackwell.

Chadwick, A. (2006) *Internet Politics: States, Citizens and New Communication Technologies*. Oxford: Oxford University Press.

Coger, K. K. (2006) 'Public Relations Research at the Crossroads', *Journal of Public Relations Research*, 18(2): 177–90.

Cook, T. (2005) *Governing with the News. The News Media as a Political Institution*. 2nd edn. Chicago, IL: University of Chicago Press.

Coombs, T. and Holladay, S. J. (eds.), (2010) *Handbook of Crisis Communication*. Oxford: Blackwell.

Cornelissen, J., van Bekkum, T. and van Ruler, B. (2006) 'Corporate Communications: A Practice-Based Theoretical Conceptualization', *Corporate Reputation Review*, 9(2): 114–33.

Cox, H. L. (2001) *Governing from Center Stage. White House Communication Strategies During the Age of Television Politics*. Cresskill, NJ: Hampton Press.

Dahlgren, P. (2009) *Media and Political Engagement: Citizens, Communication, and Democracy*. Cambridge: Cambridge University Press.

Davis, A. (2010) *Political Communication and Social Theory*. London: Routledge.

De Masi, O. A. (2001) *Comunicación gubernamental* [*Govermental Communication*]. Barcelona: Paidos.

Denton, R. E. and Hahn, D. (1986) *Presidential Communication: Description and Analysis*. New York: Praeger.

Denton, R. E. and Holloway, R. L. (1996) 'Clinton and the Town Hall Meetings: Mediated Conversation and the Risk of Being "In Touch"', in R. E. Denton and R. L. Holloway (eds.), *The Clinton Presidency. Images, Issues and Communication Strategies*. Westport, CT: Praeger. pp. 17–41.

Edwards III, G. C. (2003) *On Deaf Ears: The Limits of the Bully Pulpit*. New Haven, CT: Yale University Press.

Fairbanks, J., Plowman, K. and Rawlins, B. (2007) 'Transparency in Government Communication', *Journal of Public Affairs*, 7(1): 23–37.

Fisher, B. and Horsley, J. S. (2007) 'The Government Communication Decision Wheel: Toward a Public Relations Model for the Public Sector', *Journal of Public Relations Research*, 19(4): 377–93.

Fombrum, C. J. (1996) *Reputation. Realizing Value from the Corporate Image*. Boston, MA: Harvard Business School Press.

Franklin, B. (2004) *Packaging Politics: Political Communications in Britain's Media Democracy*. London: Edward Arnold.

Freedom House (2009) 'Combined Average Ratings: Independent Countries 2009', http://www.freedomhouse.org/template.cfm?page=475&year=2009 (accessed 1 October 2009).

Garnett, J. L. and Kouzmin, A. (1997) *Handbook of Administrative Communication*. New York: Marcel Dekker.

Garnett, J. L. (1992) *Communicating for Results in Government. A Strategic Approach for Public Managers*. San Francisco, CA: Jossey-Bass Publishers.

Gitlin, T. (1980) *The Whole World is Watching: Mass Media and the Making and Unmaking of the New Left*. Berkeley, CA: University of California Press.

Graber, D. (2003) *The Power of Communication. Managing Information in Public Organizations*. Washington, DC: CQ Press.

Graber, D. (2005) 'Political Communication Faces the 21st Century', *Journal of Communication*, 55(3): 479–507.

Gregory, A. (2006) 'A Development Framework for Government Communicators', *Journal of Communication Management*, 10(2): 197–210.

Grunig, J. E. (2001) 'Two Way Symmetrical Public Relations: Past, Present and Future', in R. L. Heath and G. Vasquez (eds.), *Handbook of Public Relations*. Thousands Oaks, CA: Sage. pp. 11–30.

Grunig, J. E. and Grunig, L. (1992) 'Models of Public Relations and Communication', in J. Grunig (ed.), *Excellence in Public Relations and Communication Management*. Hillsdale, NJ: Lawrence Erlbaum Associates. pp. 285–326.

Grunig, J. E. and Hunt, T. (1984) *Managing Public Relations*. New York: Holt, Rinehart and Winston.

Grunig, J. E. and Jaatinen, M. (1999) 'Strategic, Symmetrical Public Relations in Government. From Pluralism to Societal Corporatism', *Journal of Communication Management*, 3(3): 218–34.

Hall, S. (1982) 'The Rediscovery of Ideology: Return of the Repressed in Media Studies', in M. Gurevitch, T. Bennett, J. Curran and J. Woollacott (eds.), *Culture, Society, Media*. London: Methuen. pp. 56–90.

Hallin, D. C. and Mancini, P. (2004) *Comparing Media Systems. Three Models of Media and Politics*. Cambridge: Cambridge University Press.

Hamelink, C. (2007) 'The Professionalization of Political Communication: Democracy at Stake?', in R. Negrine, P. Mancini, C. Holtz-Bacha and S. Papathassopoulos (eds.), *The Professionalization of Political Communication*. Bristol: Intellect. pp. 179–88.

Heath, R. (ed.) (2010) *The Sage Handbook of Public Relations*. Sage (2nd edition).

Herman, E. and Chomsky, N. (1988) *Manufacturing Consent*. New York: Pantheon Books.

Holtz-Bacha, C. (2004) 'Political Campaign Communication: Conditional Convergence of Modern Media Elections', in F. Esser and B. Pfetsch (eds.), *Comparing Political Communication*. Cambridge: Cambridge University Press. pp. 213–30.

Ingham, B. (2003) *The Wages of Spin*. London: John Murray.

Izurieta, R., Perina, R. M. and Arterton, C. (eds.) (2003) *Estrategias de comunicación para gobiernos* [*Communication Strategies for Governments*]. Buenos Aires: La Crujía.

Jacobs, L. and Burns, M. (2004) 'The Second Face of the Public Presidency: Presidential Polling and the Shift from Policy to Personality Polling', *Presidential Studies Quarterly*, 34(3): 536–51.

Jaques, T. (2006) 'Issue Management: Process Versus Progress', *Journal of Public Affairs*, 6(1): 69–74.

Kaid, L. L. and Holtz-Bacha, C. (eds.) (2006) *The SAGE Handbook of Political Advertizing*. Thousand Oaks, CA: Sage.

Kumar, M. J. (2007) *Managing the President's Message. The White House Communications Operations*. Baltimore, MD: John Hopkins University Press.

Kumar, M. J. (2003a) 'The Contemporary Presidency: Communications Operations in the White House of President George W. Bush: Making News on His Terms', *Presidential Studies Quarterly*, 33(2): 366–93.

Kumar, M. J. (2003b) 'The pressures of White House Work Life: Naked in a Glass House', in M. J. Kumar and T. Sullivan (eds.), *The White House World. Transitions, Organization and Office Operations*. College Station, TX: A&M University Press. pp. 94–107.

Kumar, M. J. (2001a) 'The Office of Communications', *Presidential Studies Quarterly*, 31(4): 609–34.

Kumar, M. J. (2001b) 'The Office of the Press Secretary', *Presidential Studies Quarterly*, 31(2): 296–322.

Kumar, M. J. and Sullivan, T. (eds.) (2003) *The White House World. Transitions, Organization, and Office Operations*. College Station, TX: Texas A&M University Press.

Leonard, M., Small, A. with Rose, M. (2005) *British Public Diplomacy in the 'Age of Schisms'*. London: The Foreign Policy Centre.

Lin, Y. (2004) 'Fragmentation of the Structure of Political Communication Research: Diversification or Isolation?', in L. L. Kaid (ed.), *Handbook of Political Communication Research*. Mahwah, NJ: Lawrence Erlbaum Associates. pp. 69–108.

McChesney, R. (2008) *The Political Economy of Media: Enduring Issues, Emerging Dilemmas*. New York: Monthly Review Press.

McCombs, M. and Shaw, D. (1972/1996) 'The Agenda-Setting Function of Mass Media', in O. Boyd-Barrett and C. Newbold (eds.), *Approaches to Media: A Reader*. London: Arnold. pp. 153–63.

McNair, B. (2007) *An Introduction to Political Communication*. 4th edn. London: Routledge.

Negrine, R. (2008) *The Transformation of Political Communication*. Basingstoke: Palgrave Macmillan.

Neustadt, R. (1960) *Presidential Power. The Politics of Leadership with Reflections on Johnson and Nixon*. Cambridge, MA: Harvard University Press.

Norris, P. (2009) 'Comparative Political Communications: Common Frameworks or Babelian Confusion?', *Government and Opposition*, 44(3): 321–40.

Norris, P., Kern, M. and Just, M. R. (eds.) (2003) *Framing Terrorism. The News Media, the Government and the Public*. New York/London: Routledge.

Norris, P. and Odugbemie, S. (2009) 'Evaluating Media Performance', in P. Norris (ed.), *The Public Sentinel: News Media and Governance Reform*. Washington, DC: The World Bank. pp. 3–30.

Nye, J. (2004) 'The Benefits of Soft Power', http://hbswk.hbs.edu/archive/4290.html (accessed 9 July 2007).

Oates, S. (2008) *Introduction to Media and Politics*. London: Sage.

Ornstein, N. J. and Mann, T. (eds.) (2000) *The Permanent Campaign and Its Future*. Washington, DC: The American Enterprise Institute for Public Policy Research.

Patterson, T. (1994) *Out of Order*. New York: Vintage Books.

Patterson, T. (2003) *The Vanishing Voter: Public Involvement in an Age of Uncertainty.* New York: Vintage Books.

Puddington, A. (2009) 'Freedom in the World 2009: Setbacks and Resilience', http://www.freedomhouse.org/template.cfm?page=130&year=2009 (accessed 1 October 2009).

Rainey, H. G., Backoff, R. W. and Levine, C. H. (1976) 'Comparing Public and Private Organizations', *Public Administration Review*, 36(2): 233–444.

Reese, S. D., Gandy, O. and Grant, A. E. (eds.) (2003) *Framing Public Life. Perspectives on Media and Our Understanding of the Social World.* Mahwah, NJ: Lawrence Erlbaum Associates.

Rice, R. and Atkin, C. (eds.) (2001) *Public Communication Campaigns.* 3rd edn. Thousand Oaks, CA: Sage.

Rimmerman, C. A. (1991) 'The "Post-Modern" Presidency. A New Presidential epoch? A Review Essay', *The Western Political Quarterly*, 44(1): 221–38.

Saco, D. (2002) *Cybering Democracy.* Minnesota, MN: University of Minnesota Press.

Sanders, K. (2009) *Communicating Politics in the 21st Century.* Basingstoke: Palgrave Macmillan.

Sanders, K. (2011) 'Political Public Relations and Government Communication', in J. Strömbäck and S. Kiousis (eds.), *Political Public Relations: Principles and Applications.* London/New York: Routledge. pp. 177–192.

Sanders, K., Canel, M. J. and Holtz-Bacha, C. (2011) 'Communicating Governments: A Three Country Comparison of How Governments Communicate with Citizens', *The International Journal of Press and Politics*, 16(4): 523–47.

Scherer, M. (2009) 'What Happened to the Stimulus?', *Time*, 31 July: 28–31.

Semetko, H. A. (2009) 'Election Campaigns: Partisan Balance, and the News Media', in P. Norris (ed.), *The Public Sentinel. News Media and Governance Reform.* Washington, DC: The World Bank. pp. 163–92.

Semetko, H. A., Blumler, J. G., Gurevitch, M. and Weaver, D. (1991) *The Formation of Campaign Agendas: A Comparative Analysis of Party and Media Roles in Recent American and British Elections.* Hillsdale, NJ: Lawrence Erlbaum Associates.

Seymour Ure, C. (2003) *Prime Ministers and the Media. Issues of Power and Control.* Oxford: Blackwell.

Signitzer, B. and Wamser, C. (2006) 'Public Diplomacy. A Specific Governmental Public Relations Function', in C. Botan and V. Hazleton (eds.), *Public Relations Theory II.* Mahwah, NJ: Lawrence Erlbaum Associates. pp. 435–64.

Smith, C. A. and Smith, K. (1994) *The White House Speaks: Presidential Leadership as Persuasion.* Westport, CT: Praeger.

Stanyer, J. (2007) *Modern Political Communication. Mediated Politics in Uncertain Times.* Cambridge: Polity Press.

Strömbäck, J. and Kiousis, S. (eds.) (2011) *Political Public Relations: Principles and Applications.* London/New York: Routledge.

Swanson, D. (2000) 'Political Communication Research and the Mutations of Democracy', *Communication Yearbook*, 23: 189–205.

Tulis, J. (1987) *The Rhetorical Presidency.* Princeton, NJ: Princeton University Press.

Vasquez, G. M. and Taylor, M. (2001) 'Public Relations: An Emerging Social Science Enters the New Millennium', *Communication Yearbook*, 24: 319–42.

Villafañé, J. (2004) *La buena reputación. Claves del valor intangible de las empresas* [*Good Reputation. Keys to Intangible Value for Corporations*]. Madrid: Pirámide.

Vos, M. (2006) 'Setting the Research Agenda for Governmental Communication', *Journal of Communication Management*, 10(3): 250–58.

Vos, M. and Westerhoudt, E. (2008) 'Trends in government communication in the Netherlands', *Journal of Communication Management*, 12(1): 18–29.

Waterman, R., St Clair, G. and Wright, R. (1999) *The Image-Is-Everything Presidency: Dilemmas in American Leadership.* Boulder, CO: Westview Press.

Weaver, D., McCombs, M. and Shaw, D. (2004) 'Agenda-setting Research Issues, Attributes, and Influences', in L. L. Kaid (ed.), *Handbook of Political Communication Research.* Mahwah, NJ: Lawrence Erlbaum Associates. pp. 257–82.

Young, S. (ed.) (2007) *Government Communication in Australia.* Cambridge: Cambridge University Press.

Zarefsky, D. (2004) 'Presidential Rhetoric and the Power of Definition', *Presidential Studies Quarterly*, 14(3): 607–19.

8

What's Good and Bad in Political Communication Research? Normative Standards for Evaluating Media and Citizen Performance

Scott L. Althaus

Normative concerns about what is good or bad in news coverage have been a common feature of political communication scholarship since the discipline's roots. They remain a familiar part of contemporary research. For example, one of the reasons for studying the characteristics of news coverage about public affairs is that we want to know whether this news coverage is fulfilling or failing the informational needs of democratic systems. But when normative concerns show up in political communication research, they often take the form of assertions rather than assessments. Normative assertions are evaluative claims that fail to mention the evaluative standards used to reach conclusions. Normative assertions about media performance often appear as throwaway lines in an empirical study's concluding discussion or as preparatory throat-clearing before an empirical study is introduced.

It is no wonder that the typical scholarly response to such offhanded claims is a shrug of the shoulders. Assertions about what is good or bad in news coverage can be seen as harmless diversions that authors may indulge so long as they remain superfluous to the main points. Like the

semicolon or the human appendix, one suspects that the typical normative assertion in political communication research is probably useless, and can therefore be tolerated so long as it does no harm.

This chapter is about something different and more helpful for advancing the horizons of political communication research: normative assessment. Whereas a normative assertion advances a particular evaluative claim about an empirical finding without clarifying the basis of evaluation, a normative assessment aims to identify multiple evaluative claims that *could be made* about an empirical finding while also identifying the standards underlying those value judgments. This chapter details how normative assessments relevant for political communication research can be made and defended. But because normative assessments are less commonly seen in the political communication literature than normative assertions, the value of appraising the normative implications of our research may be less than obvious. A brief discussion on this point is therefore in order before describing the types of normative assessment that can be applied to empirical research findings and illustrating some benefits that closer attention to normative standards can bring to empirical research.

NORMATIVE ASSESSMENT IN EMPIRICAL RESEARCH

Normative claims are prescriptive rather than descriptive. They address how things ought to be rather than how things are. By moving beyond description to question whether 'how things are' is good news or bad news for the practice of democratic politics, normative analysis can offend the sensibilities of empirical political communication scholars. Social-scientific research aims to understand what is, and until the 'is' gets figured out, speculation about what ought to be can seem at best premature, and at worst potentially damaging to the aim of conducting value-neutral empirical research. However, these important concerns come into play only when normative claims are used to advance arguments about what 'ought' to be. This is just one application of normative analysis, and probably the least useful for enriching empirical research. In contrast, this chapter concerns a different application of normative analysis.

Normative assessment aims to identify and acknowledge theoretical assumptions taking the form of value judgments that provide a rationale for empirical research or that provide a contextual foundation for empirical analysis. These value judgments are ever-present in empirical research. As Diana Mutz notes, 'empirical research findings are interesting and/or important precisely because they tell us something about some consequence that is positively or negatively valued' (2008: 523). That is, claims about the importance or relevance of empirical findings to matters of public concern necessarily rest on normative value judgments. The problem is that these value judgments usually remain hidden in empirical research, and may even go unrecognized by the scholars who implicitly make them.

Normative assessment can be useful in empirical research by clarifying which value judgments are supporting claims about the importance or theoretical relevance of empirical findings. The point is not to contend that one state of the world is somehow 'better' than another in an absolute sense, but rather to evaluate when and why a pattern of findings might be more important for some social problems than others, or might align more readily with some theoretical concerns than others. Normative assessment makes no claim about how the empirical world ought to be. It focuses instead on clarifying how empirical findings may hold implications for different schools of thought that themselves make claims about how the world ought to be.

Making normative assessments more explicit in empirical research is important because empirical research is never entirely value-neutral. The relevance of empirical findings can be determined only when the researcher clarifies why those findings are important, and judgments of importance are almost always predicated on some type of normative claim. Bringing these usually hidden claims to light is a particularly useful reason for making normative assessment a more routine component of empirical research: it clarifies the standards being used to make judgments about why a finding is important and what its broader theoretical implications might be.

The importance of normative assessment for political communication research has long been understood within the field. Among the leading figures in early political communication research, Paul Lazarsfeld (1957) famously advocated for the relevance of political philosophy to empirical research on mass politics. His argument advanced three main benefits of joining normative to empirical analysis: that the analytical precision of modern empirical research could lead to new appreciation of how philosophical arguments might be relevant to mass politics, that new hypotheses and conceptual refinements valuable for empirical analysis could emerge from a fresh look at 'classic' normative arguments, and that the joining of normative and empirical analysis could advance theoretical insights within political philosophy.

These benefits remain as important today as they were in Lazarsfeld's era, and political communication scholarship stands to realize some particular gains from making normative assessments of empirical findings. Explicit attention to the criteria for drawing normative judgments could clarify a broader range of communication phenomena relevant for empirical study, beyond the typical focus on the content of mainstream news and the attentiveness of audiences to that mainstream news flow. Clarifying the normative dimensions of empirical findings would also define a wider horizon of normative starting points for making sense of research findings. For example, while much attention has been given to the 'problem' of increasing market segmentation that leads to declining audiences for traditional news products (for example, Katz, 1996; Prior, 2007), the same tendency can be seen as a 'solution' for democratic communication from a different normative vantage point (this point will be taken up at length later in this chapter). In addition, explicitly identifying the normative first principles undergirding an evaluative judgment helps to anchor empirical findings more clearly in larger conversations about the nature of democratic communication that are taking place beyond the ranks of political communication scholars (Althaus, 2006). Clarifying the relevance of empirical research to the concerns of political philosophy can help orient non-specialists to the reasons why our empirical findings might be important to a broader range of scholars. Most importantly, normative assessment can help empirical political communication researchers avoid unrealistic expectations for media and citizen performance that arise from lack of reflective engagement with normative theories of democratic politics.

Normative assessment is therefore more like appraisal than argument. It clarifies the relevance of empirical findings for core debates in political philosophy rather than engaging directly in any kind of philosophical debate. Normative assessment detours around arguments about how to improve the quality of political communication. It sidesteps claims that one model of democracy or of the news is somehow better than another. Normative assessment aims merely to identify the core assumptions underlying statements of value that scholars use to assess the relevance or importance of their empirical findings. Such statements of value become judgments rather than assertions only when they are properly located and understood within larger theoretical frameworks. Normative assessment aims to do this by clarifying the implications that empirical findings have for normative theories about the ends and means of democratic politics.

HIDDEN VALUE JUDGMENTS IN EMPIRICAL RESEARCH

Although normative assessments are routinely conducted in empirical political communication scholarship, they are rarely noticed because they are usually hidden in arguments that take the form of enthymemes rather than syllogisms. Aristotle's *Rhetoric* observes that most arguments made in everyday language borrow from the logical structure of formal syllogisms – if Premise *X*, and also Premise *Y*, then Conclusion *Z* – except that one of the premises is left unstated. A syllogism with a missing premise is called an enthymeme, and an enthymeme can be persuasive only when the unstated premise is supplied by the audience.

Most arguments in everyday life and even in formal scholarship take the form of enthymemes. Enthymematic arguments most commonly appear as a conclusion supported by a reason. If the conclusion seems sensibly drawn from the reason, it is because we are supplying an additional premise

to complete the formal syllogism. In many cases, this unstated premise is a value judgment that explains why the stated reason is valid for drawing the conclusion. And because this form of argumentation is so familiar, we often fail to notice that the value judgment is even part of the argument.

A good example of this sort of enthymematic reasoning comes from Thomas Patterson's (1993) *Out of Order*, which contrasts the different types of information supplied by campaign news coverage when elections are framed as a game between two players rather than as two competing visions for governing the country. Patterson's argument about the historical importance of shifting from policy-oriented news to strategy-oriented news in American election coverage is clear and concise:

> The voters ... bring a governing schema to the campaign. Their chief concerns are what government has done before the election, what it will do after the election, and how this will affect them. The game schema, however, asks them to concentrate on who is winning, and why. The result is a breakdown in the type of communication that should occur during the course of the election. (1993: 88)

In this passage, Patterson argues that because game-framed news coverage has increasingly supplanted policy-framed news coverage, the electoral communication system in the USA is no longer serving the needs of citizens. The conclusion ('the American electoral communication system is broken') is smartly drawn from the stated reason ('because game-framed election coverage has driven out policy-framed coverage'). But this argument also rests on an unstated premise, that voting decisions are supposed to be made from policy considerations. Only if this unstated premise also holds does it follow that the communication system is broken because game-framed election news has become the norm. But where does this unstated value judgment come from, and what normative argument can justify its application to this case? We do not know, for it is left as an unexamined part of the theoretical framework undergirding Patterson's argument.

There is nothing odd about this kind of omission. To the contrary, political communication studies make routine use of enthymematic reasoning, and with good effect. However, this kind of argument only persuades when the unstated value judgment already resonates with its audience. Such an argument can therefore only convince those who need no persuading. More importantly, enthymematic reasoning closes off lines of scholarly inquiry by directing attention away from unstated value judgments that are themselves contested and worthy of study. And because these unstated value judgments are therefore implicitly asserted rather than explicitly defined, the normative underpinnings of empirical research findings often go unnoticed and therefore unrecognized. Making them an explicit part of the scholarly conversation would do much to clarify what is really at stake in our research, because often disagreements about the importance or relevance of empirical findings are, at a deeper level, disagreements over the normative standards implicitly used to frame those empirical findings.

Normative assessment is therefore not some kind of new or unusual type of scholarly initiative. It has long been a standard part of empirical research, but conventional use of enthymematic reasoning has relegated it to an unstated backdrop of shared value judgments that implicitly justify the importance or relevance of empirical findings. A more valuable type of normative assessment would be more explicit, clarifying when and how value judgments are being applied to empirical findings, and would run deeper, clarifying the standards against which value judgments are drawn rather than merely asserting the relevance of a value.

FOUR LEVELS OF NORMATIVE ASSESSMENT

In reflecting on the different contributions that normative assessment can make to empirical research, it is useful to think of these contributions as representing different levels of clarity and rigor in the process of articulating or justifying the normative relevance of empirical findings. Four such levels of normative assessment are summarized in Table 8.1, with each row representing a progressively deeper level of clarity and rigor in orienting a study's empirical findings to normative benchmarks.

First-level Normative Assessment

The first level of normative assessment occurs whenever enthymematic reasoning produces an implicit assertion of a finding's relevance or importance to a normative question. It is probably the most common type of normative assessment in empirical political communication research, and shows up as an argument that a particular finding is good or bad (or welcome, or troubling) for this or that reason. In this first level of normative assessment, the relationship of a conclusion to a reason is moderated by a value judgment that is itself merely asserted without clarifying either its origin or its validity for the argument being made. First-level normative assessment takes the form of attaching some sort of normative label to an empirical finding, often to assert the finding's importance or relevance to a current controversy or set of longstanding concerns.

This level of normative assessment is the least satisfying of the four because it tells us only what the evaluative claim is. Missing is any mention of the criteria on which the claim of relevance or

Table 8.1 Levels of normative assessment in empirical research

Level of normative assessment	Type of normative claim	Form of normative claim	Value for empirical research
First level: Attaching a normative label to a finding	Assertion about the relevance or importance of a finding	'Finding A is troubling because of Reason X'	Expresses the author's evaluative stance
Second level: Identifying criterion values	Judgment about whether a finding lacks or possesses a criterion value	'Finding A is troubling because it lacks Quality X'	Provides a rationale for the author's evaluative stance
Third level: Defining standards for applying or interpreting criterion values	Judgment about the level of a criterion value that a finding lacks or possesses	'Finding A is troubling because it has less than Y amount of Quality X'	Clarifies how the rationale for the author's evaluative stance could be applied to other cases
Fourth level: Ordering competing values and standards within system theories or comparative frameworks	Judgment about which criterion values are appropriate for evaluating a finding	'Finding A is troubling from the standpoint of Theory Z, because Theory Z requires Y amount of Quality X'	Positions the author's evaluative stance within larger theoretical debates

importance is based, or any reason why the claim is a valid one. Nonetheless, even this level of normative assessment is valuable for empirical research because it expresses the author's evaluative stance: by revealing an author's claim about the potential importance of an empirical finding, this first level of normative assessment invites further consideration of the criteria used to evaluate the finding's potential relevance to normative questions.

Second-level Normative Assessment

The second level of normative assessment goes beyond implicit assertion to identify values that can serve as criteria for drawing normative judgments about empirical findings. These 'criterion values' can take many forms. They are sometimes presented as desirable activities or outcomes such as including non-official viewpoints when constructing the news (for example, Sigal, 1973) or presenting news stories in a broader context to give them a larger meaning (for example, Bennett, 2008). Sometimes they take the form of abstract values – such as freedom, liberty or order – whose realization is posited as the ultimate goal or purpose for democratic communication (for example, McQuail, 1992). Sometimes criterion values are defined explicitly (for example, Blasi, 1977; Coleman and Blumler, 2009; Gurevitch and Blumler, 1990; Mutz, 2006; van Cuilenburg and McQuail, 2003), but often they are the unstated premises implied by enthymematic reasoning. Occasionally, one finds elaborate theoretical frameworks developed to support normative ideals for media performance developed from a single core value (for example, Commission on the Freedom of the Press, 1947; Meiklejohn, 1960) or multiple core values that are all posited to be normatively equivalent in status (for example, the importance of freedom, equality and order in McQuail [1992]). But such efforts to provide explicit theoretical foundations for value identification remain exceptional.

Normative assessment at this second level is more commonly seen in implicit forms that define criterion values indirectly through positional critiques or idealized contrasts. Positional critiques describe a finding as having too much or too little of a particular characteristic. News coverage is said to be too accepting of the government's preferred framing of a foreign policy crisis, or overly critical during the campaign season, or insufficiently issue-oriented when reporting on the parties and candidates. Yet such positional claims invoke a criterion value without usually providing clear standards for how the value should be applied when drawing a normative judgment.

The news is said to be too critical, or too passive, or too soft, without ever spelling out what 'good' news coverage is supposed to look like. Because evaluations are made without supplying a clear metric of judgment, positional critiques offer limited traction on the slippery slope of evaluating media and citizen performance.

Idealized contrasts have similar strengths and limitations as positional critiques. Idealized contrasts identify criterion values by comparing an empirical finding against an ideal state of the world. Unlike positional critiques, which apply a judgment to what is, this second approach emphasizes what ought to be. But like positional critiques, such claims about media performance tend to be asserted in passing and without considering rival perspectives. Idealized contrasts might begin as an offhanded remark like 'classical democratic theory requires an informed citizenry' (as claimed, among others, by Lippmann [1922]), and proceed to draw an unfavorable inference about the media's ability to deliver the information that these ideal citizens are posited to require. This claim about the importance of informed citizens in classical democratic theory happens to be false (for example, Althaus, 2003, 2006; Pateman, 1970). However, if false claims are widely seen as valid within a community of scholars, as in this case, they stand little chance of being rooted out.

In whatever form, normative assessment at this second level goes beyond that from the first level by identifying a criterion value to support the normative claim being advanced. The result is a nominal judgment, where an empirical finding is said to either lack or possess the criterion value being invoked. The normative rationale for the author's evaluative stance is made clear by highlighting a criterion value, and for this reason the second level of normative assessment represents a significant theoretical step forward from the first level, which merely asserted a normative claim. But the second level of normative assessment involves assertion of a different sort, for it assumes the appropriateness of an evaluative criterion without developing a clear metric for determining how the criterion value should be applied or interpreted. If the news is insufficiently critical of government perspectives, how critical is critical enough? Without clear standards for applying a criterion value to an empirical finding, it will be difficult for other scholars to extend an author's evaluative stance to other cases.

Third-level Normative Assessment

The third level of normative assessment defines standards for applying criterion values to empirical findings. By defining such standards, normative assessment at the third level aims to draw judgments about the degree to which an empirical finding possesses a criterion value. As with the second level of normative assessment, criterion values at the third level can appear as positional critiques, idealized contrasts or as explicit definitions. Instead of the nominal judgment supplied by the second level of normative assessment, the third level offers an ordinal or interval measure of the amount of a criterion value that is revealed in an empirical finding. The level of conceptual clarity required to produce such a measure yields two benefits for empirical research. By translating abstract criterion values into operational forms, normative assessment at the third level clarifies the empirical relevance of these criterion values, which otherwise might appear so hopelessly abstract as to have little practical worth for empirical research. The other important benefit is that operational measures of criterion values, once defined, can be applied to other cases by different researchers. This puts normative assessment within the range of a larger community of scholars and allows for further empirical refinement of normative concepts.

Despite these several improvements over second-level appraisals, normative assessment at the third level is more commonly seen in media economics and communication policy than in political communication research. One reason is that political communication research rarely evaluates media compliance with licensing criteria or other regulatory frameworks, which are often derived from criterion values. Such analysis is more common outside political communication, where the need to develop clear standards for assessing such things as degree of market diversity and concentration of media ownership requires operationalizing abstract criterion values into measurable forms. Regulatory compliance is sometimes studied within political communication, and third-level normative assessment often accompanies such efforts. A good example is Westerståhl's (1983) effort to define measurable criteria for the journalistic norm of objectivity that could be used to assess compliance with Swedish broadcast regulations. Another is McQuail's (2003) nuanced theoretical framework for defining media responsibilities and evaluating media accountability from various normative perspectives.

Third-level normative assessment occasionally occurs as an unintended byproduct of rigorous hypothesis testing. One example comes from efforts by American scholars to measure the degree of political bias in news coverage, in which bias is understood comparatively as any substantial difference between media outlets in numbers of positive and negative stories, or in the overall amount of coverage devoted to one candidate over another, or in the evaluative tone of news coverage given to a particular topic (for example, D'Alessio and Allen, 2000; Gilens and Hertzman, 2000; Hofstetter, 1976). These studies often define bias in negative terms as the absence of evenhandedness rather than in positive terms as the presence of particular content characteristics. In this way, the criterion values in these studies sometimes take the form of arbitrary benchmarks (for example, relative parity in measured content characteristics) that have the primary virtue of being easy to test rather than being deeply resonant in normative theory. But as this example illustrates, normative assessment at even the third level can proceed without explicit normative theorizing or even clearly defined criterion values.

Defining clear standards for applying criterion values to empirical findings provides a deeper form of normative anchoring than merely identifying abstract criterion values. But normative assessment at the third level shares an important shortcoming with first- and second-level assessment that limits its usefulness for empirical research. The various criterion values that are implicitly assumed in first-level assessment, identified in second-level assessment, and operationalized in third-level assessment can seem perfectly reasonable and appealing as standards for media or citizen performance when studied in isolation from other criterion values. Yet when taken together, it quickly becomes clear that satisfying one criterion value must often come at the expense of satisfying another (for example, Gurevitch and Blumler, 1990). For example, increasing the amount of 'serious' news coverage of public affairs could, after a point, start driving some audience segments away from the news altogether. The value of providing a broad and sober perspective on events of the day would then be conflicting with the value of sustaining a broad audience for public affairs programming (cf. Mutz, 2006). Conflicts of this sort among criterion values can only be resolved by somehow prioritizing their respective claims on media or citizen performance. This in turn requires broader normative frameworks to supply compelling rationales for ordering criterion values in particular ways, clarifying their functions and forms with respect to other criterion values, and determining which institutions or actors are responsible for carrying out various roles that might be associated with different criterion values.

Fourth-level Normative Assessment

The fourth level of normative assessment draws upon larger theoretical frameworks to clarify not only which criterion values are relevant for evaluating particular empirical relationships but also how different criterion values are related to one another and how conflicts between criterion values can be resolved. To achieve this degree of conceptual clarity, theoretical anchoring points suitable for fourth-level normative assessment will often fall into two groups: comparative frameworks and system theories. Comparative frameworks develop evaluative criteria from empirical analysis that can be used to resolve tensions between competing criterion values. Some comparative frameworks derive this insight by contrasting the forms and functions of media or political institutions as they currently exist in different political units (for example, Ferree et al., 2002; Kleinsteuber, 2004; Pfetsch, 2004; Wirth and Kolb, 2004). Other comparative frameworks order the priority of different evaluative standards by analyzing the historical evolution of media institutions (for example, Åsard and Bennett, 1997; Blumler and Kavanagh, 1999; Cook, 2005; Høyer and Pöttker, 2005; Schudson, 1998b), or political institutions (for example, Bimber, 2003; Dewey, 1927; Habermas, 1989; Manin, 1997) to assess how – and how well – those institutions function in the present relative to the past. It is probably unusual for historical or comparative studies to actually engage in fourth-level normative assessment (notable exceptions include Delli Carpini and Keeter, 1996; Hallin and Mancini, 2004; Schudson, 1998a). But by drawing points of comparison between the past and the present or among similar entities at a single point in time, historical and comparative research furnishes important points of contrast that could be used to anchor normative assessments of media or citizen performance.

In contrast to the empirical comparisons afforded by comparative frameworks from past to present or across equivalent units, system theories posit abstract theoretical models of what 'good' democratic decision-making, participation or communication looks like (for example, Christians et al. 2009; Teorell, 2006). For example, Benjamin Barber's (1984) concept of 'strong democracy' provides a clear system of criterion values that can be used to evaluate the quality of democratic deliberation and citizen involvement in democratic politics. In contrast, Robert Dahl's (1956, 1989) concept of polyarchy represents a rival system theory that provides a different ordering of criterion values from that supplied by Barber. The competing perspectives advanced by Barber and Dahl provide contrasting claims that can be usefully applied to assess the meaning and relevance of empirical findings about political communication processes.

Many system theories are specific enough to define a division of political labor among various actors or institutions. These actors or institutions may be given special roles or functions within a holistic framework that prescribes particular ends and means for democratic politics (for example, Christiano, 1996; Habermas, 1996a, 2006; more generally, see Held, 2006; Price and Neijens, 1997; Teorell, 2006). Because clarifying the tasks or roles that a particular actor or institution is responsible for completing often suggests a clear basis for evaluating how well those tasks or roles are being accomplished (Kuklinski and Quirk, 2001; Lupia, 2006), system theories that supply this level of detail are particularly valuable for fourth-level normative assessment.

System theories hold at least three practical advantages over comparative frameworks for fourth-level normative assessment. First, since system theories present abstract normative arguments rather than specific empirical comparisons, they can be more flexible and adaptive than comparative frameworks for fourth-level normative assessment. Because comparative frameworks are ideally used for evaluating apples against apples, using them in normative assessment usually requires empirical findings that have fallen from apple trees. In contrast, system theories often can be used to assess pomegranates as easily as apples because the basis of comparison derives from reason rather than observation. The normative standards required for making value judgments are therefore more easily derived from systems theories than from comparative frameworks. Second, proper interpretation of historical precedents or comparable cases often requires immersion in a large and constantly updating body of contextual knowledge. System theories, in contrast, can often be applied to assess empirical findings at such a high level of generality that the opportunity costs of keeping current with relevant literatures remains fairly low after an initial investment to gain familiarity with salient and longstanding debates in normative democratic theory. Third, system theories tend to provide broader evaluative horizons than comparative frameworks. Rather than comparing the present to the past or to other cases in the present, system theories can be used to compare the present to the future, and the future can be anything. This flexibility entails an obvious risk: the set of possible things that might someday be is infinitely larger than the set of actual things that have once been, and the practical value of speculative assessment probably goes down as the ceiling for speculative thinking goes up. But this risk of increasing irrelevance should be weighed against the countervailing risk of neglecting Hume's guillotine.

In his *Treatise of Human Nature*, David Hume argued against deriving normative theory from empirical observation. Hume's argument high-lighted what became known as the 'is-ought' problem: the risk of deriving illegitimate norma-tive arguments about what 'ought to be' from empirical observations about what 'is'. The is-ought problem finds a solution in Hume's guillo-tine: if normative theory ought to originate in reason alone, then normative claims should be cleanly separated from any genesis in empirical observation. Although the importance of the is-ought problem to normative theory is contested, the practical wisdom of Hume's guillotine can be seen in what may be the most well-known attempt in political communication research to derive normative theory from empirical observation: Siebert, Peterson and Schramm's (1956) classic *Four Theories of the Press*. Their effort seemed useful for a while, but its descriptive typology of press systems proved incomplete and increasingly time-bound as the years wore on (Christians et al., 2009; Nerone, 1995). The main problem seems to be that the effort to synthesize a small number of normative typologies out of existing press systems sprung forward without a deeper grounding in normative democratic theory and without a suffi-cient appreciation of how its normative claims were reifying the empirical contours of a particu-lar historical moment. As a result, the theoretical typology introduced by *Four Theories* is no longer widely used by political communication scholars, nor is it clearly applicable to the differentiated media system of the 21st century. This is the prac-tical risk of neglecting Hume's guillotine: the most likely consequence of deriving normative standards from empirical observation is a shallow theoretical framework with a short shelf-life. Avoiding this outcome requires the use of com-parative frameworks that are informed by larger normative debates in democratic theory (for exam-ple, Hallin and Mancini, 2004; Norris, 2000).

Normative assessment at the fourth level provides a powerful tool for clarifying the rele-vance of empirical findings for larger concerns in democratic politics, particularly when assessment proceeds from system theories. System theories allow the analyst to identify and operationalize criterion values for evaluating empirical findings by locating those criterion values within larger theoretical frameworks that define an entire system of roles and expectations for different actors and institutions along with the first principles that can order relevant criterion values when they conflict with one another. In this way, fourth-level norma-tive assessment can identify evaluative criteria for normative judgments that are usually hidden in first-level assessment while avoiding many of the limitations common to second- and third-level assessment. And when well-known system theories are used in fourth-level normative

assessment, the importance of empirical findings to different normative perspectives can be effi-ciently conveyed with a minimum of explanation.

Several notable examples of fourth-level nor-mative assessment can now be found in the political communication literature (for example, Baker, 2002; Dahlgren, 2009; Delli Carpini et al., 2004; Ettema, 2007; Hallin and Mancini, 2004; Mendelberg, 2002; Norris, 2000; Sunstein, 2001), but this type of normative assessment is still rarely seen in empirical studies. To illustrate the ease with which fourth-level normative assessment can be conducted, as well as the value to empirical scholarship for doing so, the rest of this chapter presents a fourth-level assessment of two current normative concerns in the political communica-tion literature: the decline of social responsibility journalism and the increasing levels of audience segmentation across media properties.

FOURTH-LEVEL NORMATIVE ASSESSMENT IN PRACTICE

Different theories of democracy envision different roles for citizens to play, with some limiting citi-zen involvement to participating in occasional elections and others expecting citizens to deliber-ate actively and frequently about important mat-ters of public policy (Baker, 2002; Habermas, 1996b; Held, 2006). Contrary to popular myth, few theories of democracy require anything like a highly informed citizenry as a precondition for popular rule (for example, Althaus, 2003, 2006; Pateman, 1970). But the efficiency and quality of representation is likely to be enhanced under all theories of democracy as citizens become better informed about the actions of their elected representatives and the important public issues of the day (Althaus, 2003; Delli Carpini and Keeter, 1996).

Against this backdrop, two important concerns have begun to occupy the attention of political communication researchers in recent years: the threats to the future of social responsibility jour-nalism brought about by increased economic competition accompanying newer forms of public affairs content like 'soft news' outlets, blogs and social media (for example, Blumler and Kavanagh, 1999; Downie and Schudson, 2009; Gurevitch et al., 2009), and the increasing segmentation of news audiences into smaller groups of likeminded persons, caused in part by the increasing availabil-ity of non-news entertainment programming (for example, Katz, 1996; Prior, 2007; Webster, 2005). Both developments appear to threaten traditional scholarly expectations of what 'good' democratic communication should look like. Yet the normative basis on which such a conclusion might be sustained remains unclear. Under what conditions does decreasing social responsibility journalism and increasing audience segmentation become a problem for democratic communication? Are there other normative perspectives that suggest different conclusions about the potential importance of these trends?

Assessing the normative relevance of these trends from the standpoint of three alternative models of political accountability – those posited by the democratic theories of republicanism, pluralism and elitism – provides a useful context for clarifying the conditions under which these trends can be seen as a hindrance or a help to 'good' democratic communication. The discussion that follows draws heavily from Part II of Edwin Baker's (2002) *Media, Markets, and Democracy*, as Baker has so ably contrasted the communication requirements of republican, pluralist and elite models of democracy, as well as the forms of

'complex democracy' envisioned by theorists such as Jürgen Habermas (1996a) and Thomas Christiano (1996). 'Complex democracy' is a hybrid of republicanism and pluralism and so is ignored in the present discussion for the sake of clarifying major lines of difference among the three traditional alternatives. The typology offered by Baker, whose main lines of argument are summarized in Table 8.2, is a stylized rendering of multiple strands of democratic theory representing broad traditions within political philosophy (see, for instance, the use of similar typologies in Habermas, 1996b; Held, 2006; Teorell, 2006).

Republicanism can be thought of as rule by deliberated consensus, a system designed to help citizens discover their common interests by communicating with one another across lines of difference. Different models of republicanism place different responsibilities on citizens, but all tend to lean heavily on citizens to articulate, defend and advance their interests in search of the best solution for the whole. In extreme forms

Table 8.2 Three theories of democracy, three models of political accountability

Theory of democracy	Role of citizens beyond voting	Assumes that citizens	What should ultimately prevail	Primary role of the news media	'Best fit' media system
Republicanism: rule by deliberated consensus	Follow public affairs and deliberate collectively	Discover their common interests	The best argument	• Promote civic virtue in citizens • Expose corruption/ lapses in virtue • Create a common forum for informed, objective and inclusive debate	Social responsibility journalism; low audience segmentation
Pluralism: rule by interest groups	Form groups and bargain collectively	Advance their particular interests	The strongest pressure (under fair rules)	• Tell groups when their interests are at stake • Mobilize groups to promote their interests • Make officials aware of what groups want	Advocacy journalism; high audience segmentation
Elitism: rule by experts	Remain loyal to the political system	Cannot identify their interests	The least corrupt and least inept leaders	• Expose public corruption and incompetence • Promote the legitimacy of the system	Either market-driven or social responsibility journalism; degree of audience segmentation may be irrelevant

Source: Adapted from chapters 6, 7 and 8 of C. Edwin Baker's (2002) *Media, Markets,* and *Democracy.* New York: Cambridge University Press.

of republicanism, such as those advanced by Rousseau and carried forward in the communitarian tradition, citizens might be expected to legislate for themselves, political representation by elected officials might be minimal or absent, and collective choices might be decided primarily by the force of the better argument.

Pluralism is rule by competing groups, where likeminded citizens join together to advance their particular interests by bringing collective pressure to bear on governing institutions. Institutions serve to regulate the processes by which political decisions are reached, so that no group is unfairly advantaged in the competition for scarce resources. Although pluralism is sometimes equated with liberalism, pluralism is one form of liberalism and is of more recent vintage than liberal theory, which traces back to 18th century thinkers such as Madison and Locke and forward through John Stuart Mill to contemporaries such as Dahl (1989) and Rawls (1971). Within liberal theories, ensuring a fair political procedure for collective decision making becomes the most proximate way of producing good collective decisions. Instead of judging the quality of the outcome, pluralism therefore emphasizes the quality of the process. This typically implies that the strongest pressure operating under fair rules should prevail.

Elitism is a minimalist model of democracy with the fewest expectations for ordinary citizens. A premise often shared by elite models is that the world has become so complicated and politics so obtuse that ordinary citizens have lost the capacity to identify their political interests and solve their political problems. Although it may sound distasteful, this premise is shared not only by elitism but also by a wide range of contemporary theories of democracy, as demonstrated in the exchange between Walter Lippmann and John Dewey from the 1920s (Dewey, 1927; Lippmann, 1922, 1925). Both Lippmann (embracing an elite form of liberalism) and Dewey (advancing classic republican ideals within a liberal institutional framework) shared the premise that the complex structure of modern society made it difficult for ordinary citizens to judge their political interests. Their exchange hinged on whether this problem was potentially remediable. Within elite theories such as those advanced by Schumpeter (1974 [1942]) and Weber (Ciepley, 1999; Held, 2006), competition among teams of experts or charismatic leaders produces political decisions. As this competition ensues, citizens play the critical role of umpire by removing from office those leaders or teams of experts judged least desirable or competent.

Limited levels of citizen vigilance threaten democratic accountability most directly when democracy is conceived along republican lines, less so when it is conceived along pluralist lines, and least in elite models of democracy. Baker (2002: 148–53) offers an important theoretical contribution for political communication research by outlining the ideal media systems implied by each of these models of democracy. He notes that republicanism works best when it is served by information media that promote civic virtue in citizens, expose lapses in virtue among political leaders, and create a common forum for objective, informed and inclusive debate. This republican ideal for political accountability, exemplified in the trustee or social responsibility model of political journalism (Commission on the Freedom of the Press, 1947; Siebert et al., 1956), is precisely what many political communication scholars seem to expect of the contemporary media environment.

However, the ideal media systems for pluralism and elitism would have quite different characteristics. Pluralism's ideal media system, according to Baker, would be tasked with providing the necessary conditions for sustaining a multiplicity of groups and helping those groups promote their particular interests. News media would serve pluralism best by telling groups when their interests were at stake, mobilizing groups to promote those interests and making officials aware of what groups want. This view of journalism's role harkens back to Tocqueville's (1969 [1835]) vision of the newspaper as a former and sustainer of group-based civic engagement. A group-based version of democracy risks being poorly served by a news system that delivers an objective, factual account of public affairs designed to appeal to the widest possible audience. Instead, the ideal news system for pluralist democracy would be narrowly targeted to specific groups. The goal is not that each group would have its views represented within every channel of communication, but that each group would have its *own* channels of communication to keep it abreast of developments affecting its welfare, help it form persuasive arguments in support of its interests, and allow it to convey those interests to political leaders. This idea is similar to the subaltern counterpublic system envisioned by political theorist Nancy Fraser (1992), in which a large number of group-specific public spheres provide communicative resources for groups to debate effectively in the main public sphere. In other words, the ideal media system for pluralism would be founded on advocacy journalism so that groups could be served with rhetorical ammunition along with factual information (for example, Lasch, 1990).

Baker suggests that the ideal media system for elite democracy would enable yet a third version of political accountability. According to Baker, elite democracy works best when the news media do mainly two things: promote the legitimacy of the expert-driven political system and expose instances of corruption or incompetence among political leaders. Promoting the legitimacy of the system helps to insulate expert leaders from the destabilizing attacks of demagogues, who might threaten to mobilize a normally quiescent mass public against that public's own interests (which, in this view, are understood best by experts). Exposing corruption or incompetence helps to maximize the efficiency of an elite-driven political system by providing a market mechanism for exposing rent-seeking behavior, punishing inept officials and holding leaders responsible for bad choices. It is notable that elitism requires nothing like a socially responsible news media to do this job: a market-driven, infotaining, Chicken Little news system built around fulminating party hacks and scandal-mongering slime-slingers could probably meet all the requirements for political accountability in an elite democracy so long as it offered no fundamental challenge to the legitimacy of the political order. Social responsibility journalism might provide a useful service for elitism, but elite democracies probably could function without it. An advocacy-based news system, conversely, could be downright threatening: it would tend to serve as a destabilizing presence by mobilizing groups of citizens around their perceived interests in ways that could undermine the smooth operation of an expert-driven democratic order.

These three theories of democracy outlined by Baker differ not only in terms of ideal media systems for maintaining political accountability, but also in how those models of accountability are undermined or enhanced by the growing levels of market segmentation in news systems around the world. Market segmentation is the division of one large potential audience into several smaller actual audiences, each exposed to different media. Increased levels of market segmentation tend to produce more specialized and customized content, all the better to satisfy varied consumer preferences for information delivery and form. Higher levels of segmentation also tend to produce specialized information flows to different audiences, which could reduce the chances that a population would hear about major issues of public concern at roughly the same time or in the same way. At the extreme, high levels of audience segmentation could insulate audiences from news of politics altogether, polarize attitudes about public problems, and shield incumbent politicians from being held accountable through the electoral process (for example, Katz, 1996; Prior, 2007; Sunstein, 2001).

Baker points out that higher levels of audience segmentation are anathema to the deliberative and broadly inclusive form of political accountability envisioned by republicanism. A gradually fragmenting media system, growing audience segmentation and lack of sustained popular attention to public affairs bode poorly for the republican ideal of an ever-engaged citizenry served by a small number of socially responsible news organizations. But the same developments have little consequence for the more limited forms of political accountability required for elite democracy. Quite the contrary, market-driven news that caters to popular preferences rather than challenging them nicely serves the needs of elite democracy. Baker suggests that the increasing segmentation of the news audience may matter little to the forms of accountability that hold elite democracy in check. Elitism has no important role prescribed for collective deliberation by the citizenry, requiring only that citizens exercise an occasional form of popular sovereignty limited to the ballot box.

There is an interesting twist when it comes to accountability mechanisms for pluralist democracy. The same developments that spell bad news for republican forms of democracy and indifferent news for elitism make for potentially good news when it comes to pluralism and its distinctive version of group-based political accountability. Baker argues that higher levels of audience segmentation serve the needs of pluralist democracy by increasing market incentives for news outlets to diversify into specialty products catering to the needs of distinctive groups. The growing prominence of partisan news outlets on cable television and the World Wide Web is a welcome development for the accountability mechanisms supporting pluralist conceptions of democracy. Historically, advocacy journalism has been the norm in democratic societies rather than the exception. And although the growth of sensationalizing and partisan news outlets is taken in some corners as a sign of how far news standards have fallen (for example, Patterson, 1993; Schudson, 1998b), even in the USA the standard medium for public affairs news from colonial times until well after World War I was either a partisan newspaper or a sensationalistic outlet catering to 'lowbrow' tastes, tracing its lineage from the penny press of the 1830s through the yellow press of the early 19th century (for example, Hamilton, 2004; Schudson, 1978, 1998a; Schudson and Tifft, 2005). From the standpoint of pluralist theories of democracy, the slow demise of social responsibility journalism in the USA over the past 30 years can be seen not as a cause for alarm but rather a return to a more vibrant and typical accountability system that had served the needs of democracy long before the rise of objective journalism in the early 20th century. That noted, any erosion of the overall audience for news may be a cause for concern even for pluralism.

In short, Baker argues that different theories of democracy propose different models of accountability and are served best by different kinds of media systems. His analysis reminds us that the meaning of changes in the forms of political journalism and the segmentation of news audiences depends on one's theoretical vantage point. Recent developments may be cause for concern when our preferred model of democracy traces back to republicanism, or its newer hybrids proposed by Habermas and others. But those developments could potentially better suit the needs of pluralist democracy than the 'common carrier' news system that had been in place in many countries for the latter half of the 20th century. These same developments have an uncertain relevance for elite theories of democracy.

Baker's argument makes clear that common concerns articulated in political communication-research about increasing market segmentation and declining standards for 'quality' journalism appear to be premised on a republican conception of democracy. Curiously, this narrow theoretical orientation to republicanism also happens to guide much empirical research on public opinion (Althaus, 2006). Yet few scholars articulating such concerns would probably endorse the theoretical assumptions and institutional structures that republican models of democracy entail. Republican theories, particularly those in the deliberative tradition, are controversial among political philosophers for having extremely high – many would say unrealistic – expectations for citizen involvement in politics. Many republican theories, following the lead of Rousseau, reject the idea of political representation and posit that self-government necessarily entails direct government by the people without political intermediaries such as elected officials. Few political communication scholars would probably find much wisdom in such a system. Moreover, although political communication research often contrasts 'good' policy-oriented news coverage against 'bad' news coverage emphasizing the personality and character of individual politicians (for example, Capella and Jamieson, 1997; Mughan, 2000; Sabato et al., 2000), republican theories of democracy are deeply concerned about the moral virtue of politicians, since the aims and outcomes of citizen deliberation could easily be misused by self-serving leaders (for example, Held, 2006; Thucydides, 1960). During periods in which republican ideals for democracy reigned supreme in the USA, news coverage of character issues and personal failings was the norm while news coverage of policy was the exception (Schudson, 1998a). This suggests that character coverage addressing the private lives of public officials is at least as important as policy coverage

of political issues within republican theories of democracy, despite expectations to the contrary among political communication scholars.

By revealing the theoretical origins of common expectations about what makes for 'good' political communication, normative assessment at the fourth level identifies the conditions required to claim that an empirical finding is important or relevant to a larger set of concerns. This helps to confirm that the claim is being made accurately, and that other implications entailed by the claim are taken into account. By drawing attention to theoretical 'blind spots' within empirical research, normative assessment at the fourth level also highlights unfamiliar normative perspectives that might warrant further consideration. Viewing the erosion of social responsibility journalism and the growing segmentation of news audiences from the perspective of Baker's (2002) normative assessment raises questions rarely asked in political communication research about the merits of advocacy journalism, pluralist models of democracy and today's highly segmented media systems relative to social responsibility journalism, republican models and the less-segmented media systems of the past. Some might even find these perspectives to offer more compelling and nuanced frameworks for democratic communication than those grounded in the conventional esteem for social responsibility journalism and, by extension, republican theories of democracy.

In short, normative assessment at the fourth level not only leads scholars to check whether their empirical findings hold different implications when viewed from different normative perspectives, but also helps to temper unrealistic expectations for media and citizen performance that are sometimes advanced within empirical scholarship. Criterion values for news coverage or citizen involvement are sometimes invoked or admired without recognizing that they conflict with other desirable criterion values. Democracy is, among other things, a process for legitimizing the difficult tradeoffs that must be made among all of the worthy goals that might be put before the people. Yet because such tradeoffs are often neglected by empirical researchers, the normative expectations in which empirical findings are couched often entail hidden consequences. Rephrasing a second-level claim like 'The news is insufficiently critical' into a third-level question like 'How critical is critical enough' invites greater empirical specificity, but only by addressing fourth-level concerns like 'What is the purpose of critical news' does it become clear where the important tradeoffs lie. And only at that level does it become clear that the real contention is often not over how adversarial the news should be, but rather which model of democracy should the news be organized around. From Baker's analysis, we can infer that the news should probably be most critical of government claims in an advocacy press system, since pluralism places greater emphasis on mobilizing the likeminded around their narrow interests than on enlightening the citizenry as a whole regarding its common interests. If proponents of a 'less-passive' news system have something in mind other than advocacy journalism in the service of pluralistic mobilization, fourth-level normative assessment can clarify the end goal that critical news is supposed to be serving as well as the larger theoretical framework in which that goal is posited as an important aim.

CONCLUSION

Political communication research often asserts that empirical findings are important or relevant for democratic politics without identifying the value judgments that support these assertions. One consequence is that although empirical studies often make normative claims, empirical scholars may fail to recognize those claims as normative because the value judgments are lurking in the background as unstated premises. Empirical scholars therefore routinely advance normative arguments about the importance or relevance of their findings to the larger world without being aware that they are doing so. Because these normative arguments are often disconnected from their theoretical origins, inconsistencies among normative claims become hard to spot and the demands of competing claims become difficult to resolve.

The goal of normative assessment is to address these problems by locating, disclosing and refining the normative assumptions already being used by empirical researchers to explain the importance of their findings for the practice of democratic politics. Instead of leaving matters by concluding that the news is somehow too critical – or not critical enough – normative assessment invites us to consider what the news is supposed to do or be from different theoretical perspectives. The purpose of normative assessment within empirical research is never to assert one's preferred version of reality. It is rather to clarify the chain of assumptions that lead from first principles to claims about media and citizen performance. Normative assessment aims to supply the missing 'backstory' that is required to evaluate a claim that the media ought to be something other than what it is, or seems to be.

Inattention to the normative origins of value judgments in political communication research can give rise to peculiar types of theoretical dissociation. On the one hand, some criterion values drawn from republican theory are often emphasized and celebrated in the literature (for example, the importance of including multiple perspectives in public deliberation, an emphasis on 'serious' analysis of public affairs) while other important criterion values (for example, scrutinizing the moral health of politicians) are misrecognized and incorrectly assumed to interfere with 'good' democratic communication even though republican theory considers them essential. On the other hand, it often goes unrecognized that common concerns in empirical political communication research about apparent problems such as increasing market segmentation and the decline of social responsibility journalism are mainly 'problems' for a particular school of thought within normative democratic theory. Only after other schools of thought are recognized and brought into the conversation does it become apparent that the bad news for republicanism might be good news for pluralism and a matter of indifference for elitism.

Making the value judgments that underlie empirical analysis a more explicit part of the scholarly conversation would provide several benefits for empirical research in political communication. Besides clarifying how claims of relevance or importance are based on value judgments that are themselves context-dependent, making normative assessment a more common part of empirical analysis would strengthen areas of theoretical weakness in empirical scholarship. Broadening the theoretical perspectives common to political communication scholarship is also likely to open up new areas of empirical research, as new hypotheses and research questions arise from a broader consideration of what democratic theorists have to say about democratic communication.

The need to draw from broader currents of normative thinking about 'good' communication is especially apparent today. Many prevailing assumptions about what's good and bad in political communication seem closely tied to a top-down, mass-audience, mainstream news system that no longer exists. The rapid emergence of the complex and extremely porous information exchange system now in place throughout the world demands new ways of thinking about what communication is supposed to do for democracies, how that communication is supposed to take place, and who is supposed to be communicating. This systemic transition now underway in the structure of democratic communication raises theoretical problems that parallel those confronting political communication researchers in the early days of the field. Around the time of World War II, the new modes of empirical inquiry being applied to mass communication scholarship were giving rise to theoretical drift that threatened to consign much scholarship to idle speculation. The warning served by Paul Lazarsfeld and Robert Merton regarding the need to properly ground normative claims about media and citizen performance within larger theoretical frameworks remains as apt today as it was more than half a century ago:

> Unless we locate these patterns in historical and sociological terms, we may find ourselves confusedly engaged in condemning without understanding, in criticism which is sound but largely irrelevant. (1948: 109)

APPENDIX: RECOMMENDED READINGS THAT REVIEW SYSTEM THEORIES USEFUL FOR FOURTH-LEVEL NORMATIVE ASSESSMENT

Baker, E. C. (2002) *Media, Markets, and Democracy.* New York: Cambridge University Press.

Christians, C. G., Glasser, T. L., McQuail, D., Nordenstreng, K. and White, R. A. (2009) *Normative Theories of the Media: Journalism in Democratic Societies.* Urbana, IL: University of Illinois Press.

Habermas, J. (1996) 'Three normative models of democracy', in S. Benhabib (ed.), *Democracy and Difference: Contesting the Boundaries of the Political.* Princeton, NJ: Princeton University Press.

Held, D. (2006) *Models of Democracy.* 3rd edn. Cambridge: Polity Press.

Lijphart, A. (1999) *Patterns of Democracy: Government Forms and Performance in Thirty-six Countries.* New Haven, CT: Yale University Press.

Manin, B. (1997) *The Principles of Representative Government.* New York: Cambridge University Press.

Minar, D. (1960) 'Public opinion in the perspective of political theory', *Western Political Quarterly,* 13(1): 31–44.

Price, V. and Neijens, P. (1997) 'Opinion Quality in Public Opinion Research', *International Journal of Public Opinion Research,* 9(4): 336–60.

Teorell, J. (2006) 'Political Participation and Three Theories of Democracy: A Research Inventory and Agenda', *European Journal of Political Research,* 45(5): 787–810.

Thompson, D. F. (1970) *The Democratic Citizen: Social Science and Democratic Theory in the Twentieth Century.* New York: Cambridge University Press.

REFERENCES

Althaus, S. L. (2003) *Collective Preferences in Democratic Politics: Opinion Surveys and the Will of the People.* New York: Cambridge University Press.

Althaus, S. L. (2006) 'False Starts, Dead Ends, And New Opportunities in Public Opinion Research', *Critical Review,* 18(1–3): 75–104.

Åsard, E. and Bennett, W. L. (1997) *Democracy and the Marketplace of Ideas: Communication and Government in the United States and Sweden.* New York: Cambridge University Press.

Baker, C. E. (2002) *Media, Markets, And Democracy.* New York: Cambridge University Press.

Barber, B. (1984) *Strong Democracy.* Berkeley, CA: University of California Press.

Bennett, W. L. (2008) *News: The Politics of Illusion.* 8th edn. White Plains, NY: Longman.

Bimber, B. (2003) *Information and American Democracy: Technology in the Evolution of Political Power.* New York: Cambridge University Press.

Blasi, V. (1977) 'The Checking Value in First Amendment Theory', *American Bar Foundation Research Journal,* 2(3): 521–649.

Blumler, J. G. and Kavanagh, D. (1999) 'The Third Age of Political Communication: Influences and Features', *Political Communication,* 16(3): 209–30.

Capella, J. N. and Jamieson, K. H. (1997) *The Spiral of Cynicism: The Press and the Public Good.* New York: Oxford University Press.

Christiano, T. (1996) *The Rule of the Many: Fundamental Issues in Democratic Theory.* Boulder, CO: Westview Press.

Christians, C. G., Glasser, T. L., McQuail, D., Nordenstreng, K. and White, R. A. (2009) *Normative Theories of the Media: Journalism in Democratic Societies.* Urbana, IL: University of Illinois Press.

Ciepley, D. (1999) 'Democracy Despite Voter Ignorance: A Weberian Reply to Somin and Friedman', *Critical Review,* 13(1–2): 191–227.

Coleman, S. and Blumler, J. G. (2009) *The Internet and Democratic Citizenship: Theory, Practice and Policy.* New York: Cambridge University Press.

Commission on the Freedom of the Press (1947) *A Free and Responsible Press.* Chicago, IL: University of Chicago Press.

Cook, T. E. (2005) *Governing With the News: The News Media as a Political Institution.* 2nd edn. Chicago, IL: University of Chicago Press.

D'Alessio, D. and Allen, M. (2000) 'Media Bias in Presidential Elections: A Meta-Analysis', *The Journal of Communication,* 50(4): 133–56.

Dahl, R. A. (1956) *A Preface to Democratic Theory.* Chicago, IL: University of Chicago Press.

Dahl, R. A. (1989) *Democracy and Its Critics.* New Haven, CT: Yale University Press.

Dahlgren, P. (2009) *Media and Political Engagement: Citizens, Communication, And Democracy.* New York: Cambridge University Press.

Delli Carpini, M. X., Cook, F. L. and Jacobs, L. R. (2004) 'Public Deliberation, Discursive Participation, And Citizen Engagement: A Review of the Empirical Literature', *Annual Review of Political Science,* 7: 315–44.

Delli Carpini, M. X. and Keeter, S. (1996) *What Americans Know About Politics and Why It Matters.* New Haven, CT: Yale University Press.

Dewey, J. (1927) *The Public and Its Problems*. New York: H. Holt and Company.

Downie, L. and Schudson, M. (2009) *The Reconstruction of American Journalism*. New York: Columbia School of Journalism.

Ettema, J. S. (2007) 'Journalism as Reason-Giving: Deliberative Democracy, Institutional Accountability, and the News Media's Mission', *Political Communication*, 24(2): 143–60.

Ferree, M. M., Gamson, W. A. and Gerhards, J. (2002) *Shaping Abortion Discourse: Democracy and the Public Sphere in Germany and the United States*. New York: Cambridge University Press.

Fraser, N. (1992) 'Rethinking the Public Sphere: A Contribution to the Critique of Actually Existing Democracy', in C. Calhoun (ed.), *Habermas and the Public Sphere*. Cambridge, MA: MIT Press. pp. 109–42.

Gilens, M. and Hertzman, C. (2000) 'Corporate Ownership and News Bias: Newspaper Coverage of the 1996 Telecommunications Act', *The Journal of Politics*, 62(2): 369–86.

Gurevitch, M. and Blumler, J. G. (1990) 'Political Communication Systems and Democratic Values', in J. Lichtenberg (ed.), *Democracy and the Mass Media*. New York: Cambridge University Press. pp. 269–89.

Gurevitch, M., Coleman, S. and Blumler, J. G. (2009) 'Political Communication—Old and New Media Relationships', *The ANNALS of the American Academy of Political and Social Science*, 625(1): 164–81.

Habermas, J. (1989) *The Structural Transformation of the Public Sphere: An Inquiry Into a Category of Bourgeois Society*. Translated by T. Burger and F. Lawrence. Cambridge, MA: MIT Press.

Habermas, J. (1996a) *Between Facts and Norms: Contributions to a Discourse Theory of Law and Democracy*. Translated by W. Rehg. Cambridge, MA: MIT Press.

Habermas, J. (1996b) 'Three Normative Models of Democracy', in S. Benhabib (ed.), *Democracy and Difference: Contesting the Boundaries of the Political*. Princeton, NJ: Princeton University Press. pp. 21–30.

Habermas, J. (2006) 'Political Communication in Media Society: Does Democracy Still Enjoy an Epistemic Dimension? The Impact of Normative Theory on Empirical Research', *Communication Theory*, 16(4): 411–26.

Hallin, D. C. and Mancini, P. (2004) *Comparing Media Systems: Three Models of Media and Politics*. New York: Cambridge University Press.

Hamilton, J. T. (2004) *All the News That's Fit to Sell: How the Market Transforms Information Into News*. Princeton, NJ: Princeton University Press.

Held, D. (2006) *Models of Democracy*. 3rd edn. Cambridge: Polity Press.

Hofstetter, C. R. (1976) *Bias in the News: Network Television Coverage of the 1972 Election Campaign*. Columbus, OH: Ohio State University Press.

Høyer, S. and Pöttker, H. (eds.) (2005) *Diffusion of the News Paradigm 1850–2000*. Göteborg: Nordicom.

Katz, E. (1996) 'And Deliver Us from Segmentation', *Annals of the American Academy of Political and Social Science*, 546(July): 22–33.

Kleinsteuber, H. J. (2004) 'Comparing Mass Communication Systems: Media Formats, Media Contents, And Media Processes', in F. Esser and B. Pfetsch (eds.), *Comparing Political Communication: Theories, Cases, and Challenges*. New York: Cambridge University Press. pp. 64–86.

Kuklinski, J. H. and Quirk, P. J. (2001) 'Conceptual Foundations of Citizen Competence', *Political Behavior*, 23(3): 285–311.

Lasch, C. (1990) 'Journalism, Publicity, And the Lost Art of Argument', *Gannett Center Journal*, 4(2): 1–11.

Lazarsfeld, P. F. (1957) 'Public Opinion and the Classical Tradition', *Public Opinion Quarterly*, 21(1): 39–53.

Lazarsfeld, P. F. and Merton, R. K. (1948) 'Mass Communication, Popular Taste and Organized Social Action', in L. Bryson (ed.), *The Communication of Ideas, A Series of Addresses*. New York: Harper and Brothers. pp. 95–118.

Lippmann, W. (1922) *Public Opinion*. New York: Free Press.

Lippmann, W. (1925) *The Phantom Public*. New York: MacMillan.

Lupia, A. (2006) 'How Elitism Undermines the Study of Voter Competence', *Critical Review*, 18(1): 217–32.

Manin, B. (1997) *The Principles of Representative Government*. New York: Cambridge University Press.

McQuail, D. (1992) *Media Performance: Mass Communication and the Public Interest*. Newbury Park, CA: Sage.

McQuail, D. (2003) *Media Accountability and Freedom of Publication*. New York: Oxford University Press.

Meiklejohn, A. (1960) *Political Freedom: The Constitutional Powers of the People*. New York: Harper and Brothers.

Mendelberg, T. (2002) 'The Deliberative Citizen: Theory and Evidence', *Political Decision Making, Deliberation, and Participation*, 6: 151–93.

Mughan, A. (2000) *Media and the Presidentialization of Parliamentary Elections*. New York: Palgrave Macmillan.

Mutz, D. C. (2006) *Hearing the Other Side: Deliberative Versus Participatory Democracy*. New York: Cambridge University Press.

Mutz, D. C. (2008) 'Is Deliberative Democracy a Falsifiable Theory?', *Annual Review of Political Science*, 11(1): 521–38.

Nerone, J. C. (ed.) (1995) *Last Rights: Revisiting Four Theories of the Press*. Urbana, IL: University of Illinois Press.

Norris, P. (2000) *A Virtuous Circle: Political Communications in Postindustrial Societies*. New York: Cambridge University Press.

Pateman, C. (1970) *Participation and Democratic Theory*. London: Cambridge University Press.

Patterson, T. (1993) *Out of Order*. New York: Knopf.

Pfetsch, B. (2004) 'From Political Culture to Political Communications Culture: A Theoretical Approach to Comparative Analysis', in F. Esser and B. Pfetsch (eds.), *Comparing Political Communication: Theories, Cases, And Challenges*. New York: Cambridge University Press. pp. 344–66.

Price, V. and Peter N. (1997) 'Opinion Quality in Public Opinion Research', *International Journal of Public Opinion Research*, 9(4): 336–60.

Prior, M. (2007) *Post-Broadcast Democracy: How Media Choice Increases Inequality in Political Involvement and Polarizes Elections*. New York: Cambridge University Press.

Rawls, J. A. (1971) *A Theory of Justice*. Cambridge, MA: Belknap Press.

Sabato, L. J., Stencel, M. and Lichter, S. R. (2000) *Peepshow: Media and Politics in an Age of Scandal*. Lanham, MD: Rowman & Littlefield Publishers.

Schudson, M. (1978) *Discovering the News: A Social History of American Newspapers*. New York: Basic Books.

Schudson, M. (1998a) *The Good Citizen: A History of American Civic Life*. New York: Free Press.

Schudson, M. (1998b) 'The Public Journalism Movement and Its Problems', in D. A. Graber, D. McQuail and P. Norris (eds.), *The Politics of News: The News of Politics*. Washington, DC: CQ Press. pp. 132–49.

Schudson, M. and Tifft, S. E. (2005) 'American Journalism in Historical Perspective', in K. H. Jamieson and G. Overholser (eds.), *Institutions of American Democracy: The Press*. New York: Oxford University Press. pp. 17–47.

Schumpeter, J. (1976) *Capitalism, Socialism, and Democracy*. 1st edn. New York: Harper & Row.

Siebert, F. S., Peterson, T. and Schramm, W. (1956) *Four Theories of the Press: The Authoritarian, Libertarian, Social Responsibility and Soviet Communist Concepts of What the Press Should Be and Do*. Urbana, IL: University of Illinois Press.

Sigal, L. (1973) *Reporters and Officials: The Organization and Politics of Newsmaking*. Lexington, MA: D.C. Heath and Co.

Sunstein, C. (2001) *Republic.com*. Princeton, NJ: Princeton University Press.

Teorell, J. (2006) 'Political Participation and Three Theories of Democracy: A Research Inventory and Agenda', *European Journal of Political Research*, 45(5): 787–810.

Thucydides (1960) *The History of the Peloponnesian War*. Translated by R. Crawley, R. Feetham and R. Livingstone. New York: Oxford University Press.

Tocqueville, A. (1969/1835) *Democracy in America*. G. Lawrence (trans.), J. P. Mayer (ed.). New York: HarperPerennial. (1st edn, 1835.)

van Cuilenburg, J. and McQuail, D. (2003) 'Media Policy Paradigm Shifts: Towards a New Communications Policy Paradigm', *European Journal of Communication*, 18(2):181–207.

Webster, J. G. (2005) 'Beneath the Veneer of Fragmentation: Television Audience Polarization in a Multichannel World', *Journal of Communication*, 55(2): 366–82.

Westerståhl, J. (1983) 'Objective News Reporting: General Premises', *Communication Research*, 10(3): 403–24.

Wirth, W. and Kolb, S. (2004) 'Designs and Methods of Comparative Political Communication Research', in F. Esser and B. Pfetsch (eds.), *Comparing Political Communication: Theories, Cases, and Challenges*. New York: Cambridge University Press. pp. 87–114.

PART II

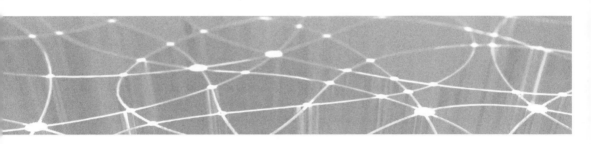

9

Digital Media and Citizenship

Bruce Bimber

INTRODUCTION

In less than two decades, digital media have become a routine part of private and public life, from the ways that friendships are made and products purchased to the ways that leaders are elected to office. Spanning the intersection of digitally enabled private and public lives is the domain of citizenship, where personal interests and concerns are made public, where political learning occurs, political expression and affiliation play out, and where opportunities for public engagement and collective action are created and remade.

These and other aspects of citizenship are undoubtedly in flux at this time in history. Many observers note that citizens in advanced democracies are participating less in ways that are traditionally 'political' and oriented toward institutions of the state, but are engaging more in ways that are civic and oriented away from institutions (Bennett, 2008; Dalton, 2008; Inglehart, 1997; Zukin et al., 2006). Though the origins of this shift extend back several decades, digital media have become implicated in them, in some cases accelerating and ramifying older trends (Bimber, 2003). Partly because digital media are so intertwined with generational change, and partly for other reasons, new technologies appear to be affecting when and how people participate as well as the character of people's orientations toward public affairs.

In this chapter, I survey some of the changing landscape of digital media and citizenship. To do this, I describe five topics of research in political communication that bear directly on questions of the citizen. In choosing these five from a larger set of possibilities, I employed several criteria. I wanted important topics that are actively under investigation today and that hold some promise for new insights in the medium-term to long-term future of research. I also wanted topics both 'old' and 'recent' within the rather short scope of the history of digital media. With one exception, I chose topics directly connected to such broader concerns in political science and communication as public opinion or participation. This meant excluding interesting topics that are more specific to digital media, such as privacy or access to technology – important concerns, but beyond the scope of this chapter. I also include as a topic the changing character of digital media itself, which is of central relevance to theoretical problems and to measurement and empirical issues.

The first two topics are: (1) the effects of digital media on political participation rates and (2) digital media and exposure to political difference. These are first-generation topics of scholarship in that they emerged during the Web 1.0 period, which ended roughly with the bursting of the US technology stock bubble in 2001–02 and the business retraction associated with it. Both remain actively under investigation by scholars, and in many ways the questions associated with them have grown more compelling over time, rather than less. I then turn to three topics more appropriately associated with the Web 2.0 period or social media era, which denotes the marked technological shift toward social media that accompanied the recovery of the technology sector in the mid-2000s. These are: (3) differentiation in media itself; (4) the changing character of political participation and engagement and (5) changing opportunities for collective action.

CITIZENSHIP ISSUES FROM THE FIRST GENERATION OF DIGITAL MEDIA

Use of digital media has been implicated with issues of citizenship for a considerable time. Roughly a decade before the web emerged, the existence of The Well and other online groups suggested to some observers that meaningful community could rest entirely upon human interaction through computer systems (Rheingold, 1993). This claim generated a debate that still echoes (Castronova, 2005; Feenberg and Barney, 2004). By the mid-1990s, with the commercialization of the web, ideas about digital media and citizenship grew far grander. A central theme espoused by advocates of new technology was the elite-challenging character of digital media, with its apparent capacity to decentralize institutional arrangements of all kinds, reduce the influence of intermediaries and empower individuals acting alone or collaboratively. This theme was visible in the writings of 'digerati' such as Negroponte (1995), social theorists such as Castells (1996) and journalists such as Friedman (2005) – the latter a decade later. As Turner (2006) observes, this was a remarkable set of expectations to be attached to technologies that had emerged from Cold War era industrial institutions. As we will see later, however, these themes reflected larger shifts underway across advanced democracies that de-emphasized citizens' sense of obligation to institutions and their processes.

Also in the mid-1990s, other implications of digital media for citizenship became clear as well. Serious academic and social concerns with inequality and the 'digital divide' date to this time. In the USA, a 1995 Commerce Department report entitled 'Falling Through the Net' (US Department of Commerce, 1995) legitimated concerns about inequality in access to technology exacerbating traditional inequalities of other kinds. Within a few years, the global dimensions of the digital divide were clearer (Norris, 2001), and also a new branch of discussion about digital media, citizenship and power was focusing on the response of authoritarian regimes to digital media (Kalathil and Boas, 2003).

In democratic states, starting first in the USA, candidates for office began experiments with digital media in the mid-1990s, and by 2000 they had developed reasonably elaborate efforts to mobilize or persuade citizens, though exactly what the consequences of the technologies would be were not at all clear then (Bimber and Davis, 2003; Howard, 2006). By the late 1990s, similar efforts were underway by interest groups, parties, and other political organizations in Europe and the USA (Gibson et al., 2004), and questions about the effects of these new technologies extended to matters of political participation and public opinion.

By the late 1990s and early 2000s, the agenda of research about digital media was covering a broad range of citizenship issues, from equality and community to power and mobilization. At present, few of those grand questions about citizenship and digital media have been answered, though a good many mid-level questions are much clearer now, such as whether social capital can be built online – it can (Shah et al., 2001). Many of large questions about the changing character of citizenship will have to await the passage of time and further development of digital media. Two issues that emerged in this first generation of digital media continue to be of interest at present among researchers, and in both cases reasonable promise exists for new insights in the foreseeable future. These involve democratic participation rates, and exposure to political difference.

Participation Rates

Questions about participation effects emerged early in the literature on digital media and participation. The Internet became widely diffused into politics in the USA in the late 1990s, and somewhat later in other advanced democracies, at a time when concerns with declining voter participation were quite strong. It was not unreasonable to wonder whether a new media era might affect participation rates, just as the birth of newspapers help launch voting participation in the USA in the early 19th century, and the rise of broadcasting in the 20th century appeared to contribute to a turn away from voting (Bimber, 2003). Against many hopeful speculations (Abramson et al., 1988), a handful of scholars argued that the Internet does not or is not likely to support increased rates of participation, largely because the new tools are likely to be differentially adopted by those already likely to participate (Hill and Hughes, 1998; Margolis and Resnick, 2000; Putnam, 2000). Opposing this view were a range of arguments about decreasing costs and increasing opportunities for engagement (Bimber, 2003). Differing expectations over this and related questions have been characterized as 'optimistic' and 'pessimistic' perspectives (Xenos and Moy, 2007), and as a debate between 'mobilization' and 'reinforcement' (Cantijoch, 2009; Krueger, 2002).

By the mid-2000s, a considerable body of studies had been reported showing some positive relationship between Internet use and rates of various forms of participation, mainly in the USA. At the same time, few studies actually reported null findings. While this latter fact may simply reflect journal editors' selection bias against null studies, a lot of literature has now reported a variety of positive effects from use of digital media on various aspects of participation (Boulianne, 2009). In the USA, findings come variously from the National Election Studies, Pew surveys and some custom surveys. This variety of studies and data sources creates a considerable presumption that some positive association exists. As Xenos and Moy write, 'the moving target of technology use patterns has at least slowed down to a point where tests of competing theoretical expectations may be more fruitfully conducted' (2007: 713).

Prior (2007) finds positive main effects from Internet access on turnout in some years, and a positive main effect on political knowledge in 2000. Bimber (2003, 1999) finds small effects of Internet use on campaign donations, attending a political and communication with government. Mossberger et al. (2008) find positive effects from Internet use on political discussion, political knowledge and political interest, with particular effects among younger citizens. Mossberger et al. (2008) also find positive effects from use of chat rooms and political use of email on turnout. Xenos and Moy (2007) find that Internet use has a direct effect on information acquisition and use – that is, political knowledge or opinionation, independent of political interest, and that Internet use interacts with interest for a positive effect on civic participation, political participation and political talk. Jennings and Zeitner (2003) use the 1982 and 1997 waves of the University of Michigan long-term socialization data to test for consequences of Internet adoption among their panelists, finding a positive association between political involvement and political Internet use. Wojcieszak (2009) finds participation in extremist online discussion groups is associated with participation, controlling for ideology, news and general political discussion. Excellent reviews of the participation literature are available (Boulianne, 2009; Mossberger et al., 2008; Xenos and Moy, 2007).

Currently, scholars are attempting to account for how political interest moderates the association between participation and use of digital media, and to address endogenity problems. For example, Prior's (2007) work suggests that despite a positive main effect of Internet use on participation, for people with a high orientation toward entertainment in their media use Internet use decreases participation. In the Xenos and Moy (2007) model predicting civic and political participation, an interaction term for seeing political information online and interest is larger than the online information term alone, suggesting that Internet effects are indirect. Shah et al. (2001) find that Internet use can either increase or decrease social capital, depending on the orientation of users. Anduiza et al. (2009) also emphasize the

importance of cognitive abilities and motivation in understanding the relationship of use of digital media to political knowledge. Their work using a Spanish sample shows Internet use is associated with more political knowledge, after controlling for education, interest, political discussion and use of various media. They also find counter-intuitive interactions between Internet use, interest and education. Boulianne (2011) addresses the problem of endogeneity with simultaneous equation modeling on panel data, and finds that while political interest drives use of television news, the relationship from news use to political interest is stronger than the other direction for both online and print news. Bimber and Copeland (2011) show that the association between participation and digital media varies greatly from year to year, casting doubt on the generalizability of single cross-sectional studies. The state of empirical findings on this topic might be summarized as follows. (1) Digital media use has become a routine part of many people's political practice in developed nations, especially the USA. (2) A very modest, positive association between participation rates and digital media use has repeatedly been shown by a variety of scholars using a variety of data sets, but it does not appear in all studies or for all kinds of participation or in all years. (3) The importance of the relationship has been difficult to assess, as has the direction of causality.

In theoretical terms, there are at least three explanations at play for why an association exists between use of digital media and political participation. The instrumental interpretation is focused on information and choice. Digital media make available to interested citizens an effectively unlimited number of alternatives for learning about politics, and enormous choice about which political interests to pursue and how. Digital media also create opportunities for action. They reduce costs associated with political participation, and change the calculus of participation favorably.

The second explanation involves mobilization efforts. Because digital media have created a denser, tighter system of political communication, citizens are better able to communicate mobilizing messages horizontally among themselves through social media, and political elites are able to tailor mobilizing messages with great specificity to specific groups, and to produce essentially continuous streams of communication. Use of digital media therefore affects participation by increasing exposure to effective mobilizing messages rather than – or in addition to – changing the calculus of free-riding.

A third reason for the association between digital media use and political participation involves the contextual character of media use in political action, and it in effect reverses the implied direction of causation. In this view, digital media serve as a tool of action for those who have decided to act. That is, media are part of the context in which engaged citizens pursue their interests: political behavior leads to use of the media, rather than the other way around. This possibility has generally been viewed in the empirical literature as an obstacle to statistical inference due to endogeneity. Theoretically, however, it is quite helpful to consider two-way causation as part of the larger picture of digital media in politics. As Bimber, Flanagin and Stohl (2012) argue, digital media change the context in which people act, having become a routine part of political participation for those who are politically interested. This is an important part of the story of digital media and participation, rather than an obstacle to interpretation.

Exposure to Political Difference

The second classic problem in the study of digital media and citizenship promising insights in the foreseeable future involves exposure to political difference. The revolution in media in the 1990s presented citizens opportunities to exercise a great deal more choice and control over their exposure to media (Bimber and Davis, 2003; Mutz and Martin, 2001; Stroud, 2007). Partly as a result, the literature on selective exposure underwent something of a renaissance starting in the mid-2000s (Garrett, 2009; Iyengar and Hahn, 2009; Mutz and Mondak, 2006; Slater, 2007; Stroud, 2007, 2008; Taber and Lodge, 2006; Wojcieszak and Mutz, 2009). This interest in effects of digital media coincided with interest on the part of public opinion scholars and others with political polarization in the USA.

Where digital media are concerned, Sunstein's (2001) application of Negroponte's concept of the 'Daily Me' to describe highly self-regulated exposure to the public sphere helped crystallize a debate. Sunstein's speculation that digital media would lead to massive selective exposure effects and political fragmentation served for several years as one of two major critiques of citizenship in the digital era, with the other involving political inequality and the digital divide. The hold of Sunstein's polemic on the academic debate weakened by the late 2000s, as empirical work was reported making clear that citizens were not utilizing fully the capacities of new media environments to wall themselves off from politically challenging messages.

Selective exposure effects based on political ideology or partisanship are indeed readily demonstrable in the lab (Garrett, 2009; Iyengar and Hahn, 2009), as well as in surveys (Mutz and Hahn, 2009; Mutz and

Martin, 2001; Stroud, 2008, 2007). Despite the doubts of some scholars (Kinder, 2003), and a history of mixed results in the scholarship of the 1960s and, it is now relatively clear that an impetus toward selective exposure to media exists. It is also clear that a number of factors affect this relationship. For instance, selective exposure effects may be stronger for hard news than soft, and may exhibit an interaction between interest and ideology (Iyengar and Hahn, 2009), as well as varying in magnitude across campaign cycles (Stroud, 2008).

Most importantly for the debate about digital media and selective exposure is the fact that the strength of selective exposure varies across communication environments. Stroud (2008) compares selective exposure across newspaper, talk radio, cable news and the Internet, and finds stronger effects for the Internet, especially compared to newspapers. This finding is generally consistent with Mutz and Martin (2001), who find a curvilinear relationship in exposure to difference in interpersonal contexts such as work and voluntary associations, where Independents are more likely than strong partisans on either the left or right to be exposed to political difference. For exposure to political difference in mass media, however, where choice is lower, Mutz and Martin (2001) find a linear relationship between partisan identification and exposure to difference. Mutz and Mondak (2006) elaborate on the effects of varying social contexts on exposure to political disagreement, especially on the extent to which workplaces provide a high level of such exposure compared to other environments for interpersonal discussion.

It is reasonable theoretically to expect relatively strong selective exposure effects in those digital media environments with higher levels of choice, compared to traditional media. Such expectations find empirical support in recent work. However, just as common as findings that selective exposure effects exist are also findings that at least some exposure to political difference occurs as well in most contexts. The presence of countervailing forces to selective exposure, including exposure to political difference, has been theorized by Slater (2007) using a simple systems-theoretical argument. Since selective exposure alone leads to opinion reinforcement, which in turn leads to greater selective exposure in a positive feedback loop, then the presence of relatively stable levels of political ideology implies the presence of some combination of ceiling effects, countervailing influences such as socialization, or exposure to political difference.

Several studies provide estimates for levels of exposure to political difference. Iyengar and Hahn (2009) show in an experimental setting that

Democrats chose (conservative) Fox News stories at about one-third the rate of Republicans, while Republican selection of CNN/NPR, the liberal option in their design, occurred at about half the rate of Democrats. These findings represent non-trivial levels of cross-over exposure. Stroud (2008) produces similar estimates from survey research. She finds that Democrats consume conservative media between a third and half as frequently as did Republicans, while Republicans consume a liberal media outlet at something more than half the rate of Democrats. Stroud concludes that while an unmistakable influence of partisan predisposition and ideology on choice of media exists, 'partisan selective exposure is not so pervasive that people have completely surrounded themselves with likeminded media outlets' (2009: 359) .

Garrett (2009) reaches a similar conclusion, distinguishing between reinforcement-seeking and challenge-avoiding media choices. He finds that challenge-avoidance is weaker than generally believed, despite the strength of reinforcement-seeking behavior. This effect is especially relevant to the rich and sometimes inadvertent nature of digital media. Garrett also finds that experimental subjects who did encounter opinion-challenging news spent more time looking at it than in the case of opinion-reinforcing news. Similarly, in a panel study of audiences for the film *Fahrenheit 9/11*, which attacked George W. Bush's handling of the 2001 terrorist attacks, Stroud (2007) finds that Democratic political orientation predicted exposure to the film, but that Republican orientation was not a significant predictor either negatively or positively.

At present it is relatively clear that selective exposure effects, while real, are incomplete. While from the existence of patterns of selective exposure to the claim that digital media will contribute to polarization of the public sphere it is unwarranted to leap, it is true that selective exposure is greater in environments of greater choice, and much of what digital media offers is in fact greater choice.

The future challenge to researchers is therefore to understand what the sum of people's media experiences is with respect to exposure to political difference. In many ways digital media recapitulate most preceding media (print, radio, television, film), as well as some interpersonal communication environments (correspondence, discussion, voluntary associations). For this reason, we should not expect a single effect of digital media toward more selective exposure or greater opinion polarization, but a variety of effects across different contexts (Bimber, 2008) and also across varying individual characteristics, such as political interest, knowledge. A much richer understanding of the totality of the media environment linked with more nuanced models that account for individual-level variation is needed.

Issues from the Second Generation of Digital Media

The adoption of social media tools by citizens starting around 2004 did not settle questions about political participation rates, exposure to political difference and other issues from the first generation of digital media, but brought to light new challenges for the study of political communication. The new generation of media that became available were oriented toward horizontal communication organized around networks, and provided tools for citizens themselves to create and contribute in ways that broke down boundaries between social, creative and political domains. It also changed the epistemology of the Internet, creating new concepts such as 'social search', in which information is searched and ordered as a function of each individual searcher's social network rather than on objective ranking criteria.

Changing Digital Media

The profusion of digital media tools up to and especially after the mid-2000s has a number of implications for theory and research methods. Originally, scholars typically conceptualized and measured use of digital media in simple terms, such as use of 'the Internet', 'email', 'the web' 'going online' or in the case of the ANES starting in 1996, whether people have 'seen election information on the Internet/web'.

These approaches no longer capture the diversity of political uses of digital media. During the 2008 presidential campaign, substantial numbers of citizens engaged with the campaigns or learned about them using digital media that confound such simple concepts. The Barack Obama campaign sent text messages to citizens' cell phones, posted short videos on YouTube, employed virtual billboard advertising inside video game environments, and used both commercial social networking sites such as Facebook and a proprietary custom social networking site. It also undertook an organized effort to promote writing about the candidate by bloggers, as well as email and traditional web tools. In addition to these campaign-driven efforts, of course citizens had available a full array of news websites, blogs, discussion forums and the like.

Some sense of the magnitude of citizen attention to politics through these means is available. An April 2008 survey by Pew, during the primary season, showed that among Democrats over 60%

of Obama supporters and 40% of Clinton supporters watched political video online. This figure amounts to roughly three times the number who signed petitions, forwarded email or contributed money (Smith, 2009). The same study found that more than 25% of Obama supporters and more than 15% of McCain supporters reported having obtained campaign information from a social networking site. Other data suggest that by election day, roughly three million people had become 'supporters' of Obama or McCain on Facebook (TechPresident, 2008). The media metrics firm Nielsen (2008) reported that the Obama campaign's single text message announcing its Vice Presidential choice reached 2.9 million people.

New video forms are now especially important. Among the most widely viewed videos of the 2008 campaign season were 'Obama Girl' and 'Yes We Can', neither of which was produced by a campaign organization, interest group, political party, independent '527' group or news organization. This fact, along with the attention citizens paid directly to campaign videos, such as Obama's March 2008 'race speech' in Philadelphia, suggests that the historically shrinking, superficial news 'sound bite' may not be dead, but certainly it is now challenged by opportunities citizens have to watch original political video for a matter of minutes, not seconds.

Old approaches to measuring political use of digital media are inadequate to characterizing this political communication environment. Traditional measures, such as those in the ANES time series, typically rest implicitly on either an audience-based or interpersonal conception of communication, in which citizens either sought out and consumed messages produced and framed by a small class of elites (public officials, interest groups, news organizations, activists), communicated with others they know, or sent messages to political institutions and other elites. Digital media have expanded the repertoire of political acts, opening up new demands for scholars theoretically and empirically. The act of producing political messages (for example, on YouTube, Flickr, Wikipedia or blogs) to be distributed to medium-scale or even large audiences differs fundamentally from 'going online' and 'seeing political information'.

Political messages embedded in the social context of Facebook or Twitter differ theoretically than those produced by elites, because social network theories are just as important as framing theory in understanding them – likely more so. When news media make choices about whether to cover a speech or how much attention to devote to it, theories of gatekeeping or agenda-setting can help us make sense; when citizens decide to watch a YouTube video of that speech, the theoretical

problems shift. The theoretical implications of text messages sent by political figures that are able to reach citizens literally anywhere and anytime are yet to be worked out, as is the meaning of citizens choosing to follow a public official on Twitter.

In the face of these challenges, some studies have recently been reported with findings from more nuanced and subtle approaches to measuring how people use digital media. For example, in a survey of Spanish and American citizens, Jensen (2009) finds evidence that Web 2.0-style online environments may work against the Web 1.0 tendency of the most interested and informed citizens making greatest use of traditional digital media. Differentiating among digital media forms suggests that new social media tools may be implicated in younger and newer participants' engagement in politics. Cantijoch (2009) differentiates voluntary searches of political information online from proclivity to involuntary exposure to political information, such as can happen by receipt of email, browsing the web without a political purpose in mind, or being exposed to political messages in other environments, such as a chat room or social networking site. She finds voluntary exposure to political information online is not related to participation in protest-oriented politics, while proclivity to involuntary exposure is. Hindman (2008) similarly argues that advertent and inadvertent uses of digital media have different implications with respect to exposure to political difference, and Krueger (2009) finds different effects from solicited and unsolicited email. Gil de Zúñiga et al. (2011) show that social media use moderates the relationship between traditional Internet use and acts of political consumerism. Despite these advances, much more insight is needed into the varying implications for citizenship of uses of digital video, social networking sites, and text messaging, and how these may be different from implications of more traditional uses of the web or email.

One question sometimes raised by the profusion of these tools is whether any in particular technology constitutes the center or core of digital media. Is there a central medium around which others can be seen as revolving? Traditionally, there were two answers to this question: 'email' and the 'web'. Neither of these answers is any longer satisfactory. Currently, the answer might be 'social media', however this term encompasses quite a range of tools, from Facebook and Twitter to YouTube and Wikipedia, each of which has many distinctive functions. Rather than attempting to differentiate the effects of each digital media tool now employed by citizens, some researchers have suggested focusing instead on mid-level conceptualization of general features of the media environment. The advantages of not tying research to specific tools in such a rapidly changing technical environment are clear. For example, many digital media tools contribute toward more porous and permeable boundaries between the public and private spheres, between news, campaigning and political talk, and between organizational boundaries (Bimber et al., 2005; Brundidge, 2009). This should lead to more inadvertency in people's exposure to political messages, and more fluid and rapid collective action, regardless of the specific digital media tool in question. Another consequence of many digital media tools is the increased presence of network effects in the spread of messages and in public attention. This leads to preferential growth effects and other non-linearities (Barabasi, 2002), including highly unequal distributions of influence (Hindman, 2008). Another important mid-level concept is choice, since much of what digital media accomplish is to expand citizens' choices (Prior, 2007; Sunstein, 2001). It is likely that future advances in research will come from both more fine-grained measurement of what precisely it is that people do with digital media in political ways, and from better conceptualization of the major categories of tools and clusters of technological affordances that matter across time.

Changing Character of Engagement

Digital media tools may not be all that is changing. As we saw above, questions about whether digital media will affect participation have often focused on traditional civic acts that have been of concern to scholars for several decades – voting participation, correspondence with elected officials, volunteering time for a campaign, donating money and the like. Scholarly concern with the rate of these civic acts reflects a common view in political science and other disciplines that democracies are facing a crisis of participation, especially in the USA, due to declining participation rates, declining social capital, a turn away from news, especially by younger citizens, and declining trust in government (Macedo, 2005; Patterson, 2002; Putnam, 2000).

An alternative view interprets changes in participation not simply as a decline in the unique set of behaviors central to good citizenship but instead as a shift between approaches to citizenship, in the context of expanding repertoires of political action available to people. This trend has been described in various ways. In the most general terms, declining traditional participation is sometimes usefully interpreted in terms of a shift toward post-material, lifestyle politics that involves less interest in elite- and institution-driven participation, and a rising

preference among citizens of advanced democracies for citizen-directed advocacy, challenges to elites or interest in civic matters not tied directly to the national policymaking apparatus (Bennett, 1998; Dalton et al., 2004; Inglehart, 1997).

A number of scholars have suggested specific rubrics for differentiating approaches to citizenship. Zukin et al. (2006) differentiate 'political' participation aimed at the state, such as voting or working for a candidate, and 'civic' engagement aimed at solving social problems or helping others. They argue that civic engagement rates are actually quite healthy. Dalton (2008) differentiates older duty-based citizenship norms from engagement-based norms. He shows duty-based citizenship to involve a cluster of values involving compliance with authority, and the duty to vote, obey laws and serve on juries or in the military – duties oriented toward the institutions of the state and their processes. Engagement-based citizenship norms entail, among other things, contributions to groups and communities, the exercise of political values in the marketplace, and an orientation toward helping out those who are worse off. Declining rates of traditional participation, he argues, reflect the consequences of generational change, in which older citizens holding duty-based values are replaced with younger citizens holding engagement-based values. Bennett (2008), writing about young citizens, differentiates the engaged and disengaged paradigms for interpreting participation rates, arguing that younger citizens find unappealing and often inauthentic the messages and appeals to participation that come from traditional organizers and institutions. Younger citizens are motivated, he argues, more by personal expression and the opportunity to produce and project publicly their own identities. As Inglehart argues, '[t]he confusion over whether participation is rising or falling arises from the fact that we are dealing with two distinct processes: elite-directed participation is eroding, but more autonomous and active forms of participation are rising' (1997: 311). A central component of this view is long-term changes in values and norms associated with generational replacement, as the 'materialist' generations that experienced the deprivations of the Great Depression and World War II were replaced by younger generations with differing values than their predecessors and different orientations toward institutions, other citizens, self-expression and political identity.

Scholars advocating this position tend to fault the traditional view in political science about declining citizenship for failing to recognize the importance of generational change and especially the distinction between elite-directed and self-directed forms of participation (Dalton, 2008; Inglehart, 1997). The problem is not only conceptual but empirical. Many surveys, especially the ANES in the USA, are election-centric, emphasizing tradition institution-oriented participation. A successful example of broadening measurement and conceptualization involves political consumerism. Stolle et al. (2005) show political consumerism to be a meaningful and measurable component of citizen's portfolio of participation, and find that political consumerism is correlated with mistrust of institutions but trust in other citizens, as well as with political efficacy.

Digital media emerged from the corporate and academic labs at a time in history perfectly suited to accelerate these generational changes stemming back decades. Engagement-oriented citizen norms situate younger people perfectly to exploit many of the affordances of digital media. The new media facilitate political acts that are expressive, in which citizens can give voice to their civic concerns on their own terms, rather than the terms of parties or interest groups (Zukin et al., 2006). They can so do by becoming a supporter or 'friend' of a politician on a social networking site, following a public figure or activist on Twitter, or writing politically relevant 'tweets' themselves. Digital media also facilitate advocacy on citizens' own terms, such as forwarding political emails to friends, or using text messages, Twitter or social networking to call attention to an issue or organize a political event. It should come as no surprise that the flexible, decentralized technologies of new media would be taken up in these political ways by generations of citizens whom Inglehart characterized in the 1990s as averse to elite-directed politics and attracted to more active and autonomous ways of being political.

Dalton (2008) specifically shows that duty-based norms of participation, which are associated with electoral politics, are negatively correlated with Internet activism, as well as protest. Reinforcing the argument of Bennett (2008) and others, Foot and Schneider (2006) show that many approaches to digital media use by candidates and campaign organizations in 2004 in the USA did not appeal to younger citizens, who found them inauthentic or over-managed.

Another characteristic of digital media that facilitates expression of the newer sets of values and orientations toward civic life involves boundaries between private and public lives. A key feature of post-material citizenship in which elite-centric and institution-centric participation is less important involves the blurring of boundaries between the private realm of daily life and the public realm of politics (Bennett, 1998; Stolle et al., 2005). Here too the digital media of the 2000s have been developed and adapted in ways that express these values. Observers of digital media characterize it as blurring boundaries between organizations, between states, between communities and between individuals' public and private lives (Bimber et al., 2005; Brundidge, 2009).

Diminished boundaries between private and public spheres, as well as the continuous and ubiquitous character of connectedness via technology are sometimes described as the 'live' nature of social media. This live character is apparent in politics, as political communication occurs around the clock, without regard for the citizen's location, and often on time scales that are effectively spontaneous or instantaneous. In live politics, the citizen may be political on his or her own time schedule, rather than synchronized to the agendas of news organizations, public officials or organizers. The live character of citizenship through digital media is now increasingly expressed in terms of politics being personal. 'All politics is personal' updates the old aphorism popularized by Speaker Tip O'Neill about all politics being local. In fact, politics may always have been personal in the sense that people have always been motivated more by the concerns of their personal lives than by abstract policy debates conducted in Washington or on the pages of *The New York Times*. But before the rise of digital media, opportunities for acting out personal politics were more limited to the local, and opportunities for expressing these at the national scale largely defined by elites and formal organizations. Digital media may help make clear that to a large degree politics is and always has been highly personal. As Bennett and Segerberg (2011) argue, this personal character of people's conception of politics is manifest in the new shape of collective actions, such as the Indignados movement in Spain, the continuing protests against G-20 meetings, and more recently the Occupy Wall Street movement that began in 2011.

One can think about digital media and the changing character of participation in terms of two broad cultural trends coming together. The first is the generation-based shift described by Inglehart (1997), Dalton (2008), Bennett (1998) and others away from traditional institution-centric, duty-based forms of citizenship toward broader, more personal, more civic-oriented norms of engagement. The second trend is the cultural movement associated with digital media. Since the days of The Well, when new technology was associated with libertarian and countercultural ideals, certain evolving set of values and cultural norms has been associated with aspects of technology. By the time of the emergence of social media, many people building new tools saw themselves not only as technologists but as advocates of cultural change. The values associated with this culture involved openness, collaboration, sharing and informality. They entail an aversion to the proprietary, the formal, the bureaucratic and the institutional. Strands of these norms are visible in the free culture movement and open source movements, as well as the independent media movement, and in technology industry-based events such as the Burning Man festival (Turner, 2009). Advocates of these new ideals, such as Doc Searls in the Linux World, Craig Newmark of Craigslist or Jimmy Wales of Wikipedia, are not political activists, and would not necessarily identify themselves as being concerned with citizenship norms. However theirs and many others' concern with changing socio-economic culture through technology has led to digital media tools that are in many ways a perfect fit for the new generations of citizens with post-political, post-institutional norms.

The challenges to future scholarship here are considerable. Ramifying, ubiquitous digital media endow citizens with greater choice and also with diminished boundaries; media connect people to the state but also facilitate civically rich lives oriented away from institutions; media facilitate the action of interest groups and also permit citizens to act autonomously in self-organized ways. As a number of scholars have observed, it is possible for a citizen to lead a broadly civic life that is rich in civic engagement but who scores low on classic measures of institution-oriented participation, especially campaign-centric measures such as displaying a campaign button, campaign sticker, or sign, donating money to a campaign or voting (Dalton, 2008; Zukin, et al., 2006). Identifying and measuring political actions in this context, as well as making arguments about cause and effect, is a substantially more difficult problem than measuring voting and party membership (Stolle et al., 2005).

Shape of Collective Action

The fifth area of scholarship on digital media and citizenship deals with organization-level questions associated with collective action. Around the time that the web commercialized and political actors began using it in the mid-1990s, a debate developed about how use of new media might alter the structure of political opportunities for citizens and the shape of collectivities. A prominent position in this debate was the view that digital media would promote unmediated communication between citizens and government, contributing to a trend in politics away from traditional intermediaries such as parties, interest groups and civic associations (Corrado and Firestone, 1996; Grossman, 1995). A different line of argument held that citizens' use of digital media would be likely to accelerate the formation

and action of political intermediaries, with the result being a richer and more well-developed set of linkage organizations that operate more fluidly, temporarily and in response to specific mobilizing events rather than long-term membership commitments (Bimber, 1998, 2003; Firestone, 1995).

The classic collective action rubric involved three elements. An underlying set of needs, desires and interests on the part of publics lies chiefly latent; organizations accumulate and expend resources, formulate strategies, frame messages and act to mobilize those latent needs, desires and interests; the result is action and the expression of demands toward political targets. However, this classic rubric is challenged continuously in the age of digital media where organizations do not play the crucial role traditionally assumed. This has been true of the Indignados in Spain, the G-20 protests, the Tunisian and Egyptian revolutions, anti-government protests in Moldova, Ukraine, Belarus and elsewhere, the Occupy movement, and many other cases large and small. Some of the key characteristics of these actions are: cases lacking central, identifiable leaders calling people to action; cases in which action emerges first and organization is subsequently built or developed as established groups join emergent actions; cases in which activists, informal groups, and formal organizations work together in network structures.

Research on collective action and digital media is currently addressing these problems. It focuses on the growth of new forms of association of all kinds, some of which, like Twitter protest groups, are ephemeral, and some of which, such as MoveOn or the Tea Party have become institutionalized. Digital media have opened the door to a period of organizational fecundity that, in the USA, surpasses even the Progressive Era, when many key structures of the interest group system and party system were laid (Bimber et al., 2009). Another related observation is that the availability of digital media is leading to a period of 'organizational hybridity' in which collective action organizations are expanding their repertoires of action (Chadwick, 2007). Because single groups now often engage citizens in multiple ways, it is increasingly untenable to classify organizations using old categories such as 'interest group', 'social movement organization', 'community group' or 'civic association' with respect to functions such as the generation of social capital, the development of social identity, representation of interests or mobilization of citizens into action (Bimber et al., 2012).

New theory focuses on several features of the new shape of collective action. One claim is that the crucial linkage between citizens' needs and desires on the one hand and collective action on the other is not organization, but organizing; organizing under conditions of high information costs, limited opportunities for communication, and strong, difficult-to-cross public–private boundaries typically requires formal organization. Where opposite conditions obtain, organizing can occur without organization (Bimber et al., 2005). The key insight in this argument is that the costs of organization have now become a variable rather than a given (Earl and Kimport, 2011). Bennett and Segerberg (2011) describe a spectrum of collective action organizing, with classic organization-centric action at one end, and self-organized, emergent, spontaneous organizing at the other. They are interested in the central location on this spectrum as the locus of collective action in digital media era. In this central location, which they call the 'logic of connective action', organizations do not command or mobilize in the traditional way, but take a step back, enabling loose networks of people to express themselves on their own terms.

In this emerging view of collective action, the citizen is not an individual with a bundle of interests and concerns, making decisions to join or free ride when asked by elites to engage in collective actions, or making discrete decisions about annual membership in groups. In this new view, the citizen is embedded in social networks and a complex organizational environment, with the capacity for continuous communication, and with the capacity to shift readily from social concerns to political ones, as well as shifting among political concerns. The same citizen is exposed to a rich variety of formal and informal organizations, and may understand herself to 'belong' to none of them while being open to interaction or participation in any of them. How to understand what citizens do in this context is the chief challenge ahead for the study of collective action and digital media.

CONCLUSION

This discussion has focused on one feature of public opinion (exposure to political difference), a traditional behavioral question (participation rates), a cultural and generational issue (the meaning and norms of citizenship), an organizational problem (the structure of collective action) and on the changing character of digital media itself. These do not comprise the totality of citizenship in the age of digital media (see Jorba and Bimber, 2012), but they cover important parts of the terrain. Scholarship on these topics reveals the intertwined nature of cultural change, technological innovation and citizens' relationship to political structures around them. It is clear that the uses to

which people put digital media open up citizen politics to potentially greater scale, and also to more personal and individual terms in which choice and agency are crucial. These uses also serve in some ways to amplify trends underway for many years, and to accelerate the pace of politics, especially in the domain of collective action. Whether these changes are coming at the cost of sustained citizen attention to hard problems and broad exposure to political ideas is an open question. If citizen politics is not to lose its coherence and its relevance to institutional politics, it may be precisely because of the interplay between traditional, well-resourced organizations and news sources that sustain agendas and relationships to policymakers, and the informal, personal networks and media that make politics relevant and timely to citizens on their own changing terms. Digital media are therefore implicated in the increased volatility and complexity of the social context for politics, as well as in citizens' and organizations' responses to that changing context. The changes underway appear to be a long way from over.

ACKNOWLEDGMENT

The author wishes to thank several people for timely and insightful intellectual exchanges that helped shape parts of this chapter, and whose work is cited here. These are Andrew Flanagin and Cynthia Stohl, at the University of California, Santa Barbara, and the participants and organizers of the 2009 international workshop: 'Citizen Politics—Are the New Media Reshaping Political Engagement?', especially Eva Anduiza and Laia Jorba of the Universitat Autónoma de Barcelona.

REFERENCES

Abramson, J., Arterton, F. and Orren, G. (1998) *The Electronic Commonwealth*. Cambridge, MA: Harvard University Press.

Anduiza, E., Gallego, A. and Jorba, L. (2009) 'The Political Knowledge Gap in the New Media Environment: Evidence from Spain', paper prepared for delivery at the International Seminar Citizen Politics: Are the New Media Reshaping Political Engagement? Barcelona, 28–30 May.

Barabasi, A. L. (2002) *Linked: The New Science of Networks*. New York: Perseus Books.

Bennett, W. L. (2008) 'Changing Citizenship in the Digital Age', in W. L. Bennett (ed.), *Civic Life Online: Learning How Digital Media Can Engage Youth*. Cambridge, MA: MIT Press. pp. 1–24.

Bennett, W. L. (1998) 'The Uncivic Culture: Communication, Identity, And the Rise of Lifestyle Politics', *PS: Political Science and Politics,* 31(4): 740–61.

Bennett, W. L., Breunig, C. and Givens, T. (2008) 'Communication and Political Mobilization: Digital Media and the Organization of Anti-Iraq War Demonstrations in the US', *Political Communication,* 25(3): 269–89.

Bennett, W. L. and Segerberg, A. (2011). 'The Logic of Connective Action: Digital Media and the Personalization of Contentious Politics', paper presented at the 6th General Conference of the European Consortium for Political Research, Reykjavik, Iceland. 25–27 August.

Bimber, B. (1998) 'The Internet and Political Transformation: Populism, Community, and Accelerated Pluralism', *Polity,* 31(1): 133–60.

Bimber, B. (1999) 'The Internet and Citizen Communication With Government: Does the Medium Matter?', *Political Communication,* 16(4): 409–28.

Bimber, B. (2003) *Information and American Democracy: Technology in the Evolution of Political Power.* New York: Cambridge University Press.

Bimber, B. (2008) 'The Internet and Political Fragmentation', in P. Nardulli (ed.), *Domestic Perspectives on Contemporary Democracy.* Urbana, IL: University of Illinois Press. pp. 155–70.

Bimber, B. and Copeland, L. (2011). 'Digital Media and Political Participation Over Time in the US', paper presented at the 6th General Conference of the European Consortium for Political Research, Reykjavik, Iceland. 25–27 August.

Bimber, B. and Davis, R. (2003) *Campaigning Online: The Internet in US Elections.* New York: Oxford University Press.

Bimber, B., Flanagin, A. and Stohl, C. (2005) 'Reconceptualizing Collective Action in the Contemporary Media Environment', *Communication Theory,* 15(4): 365–88.

Bimber, B., Stohl, C. and Flanagin, A. (2009) 'Technological Change and the Shifting Nature of Political Organization', in A. Chadwick and P. Howard (eds.), *Routledge Handbook of Internet Politics.* New York: Routledge. pp. 72–85.

Bimber, B., Flanagin, A. and Stohl, C. (2012) *Collective Action in Organizations: Interacting and Engaging in an Era of Technological Change.* New York: Cambridge University Press.

Boulianne, S. (2009) Does Internet Use Affect Engagement? A Meta-Analysis of Research. *Political Communication,* 26: 193–211.

Boulianne, S. (2011). Using Panel Data to Examine Reciprocal Effects Between News Media and Political Interest. *Political Communication,* 28: 147–62.

Brundidge, J. (2009) 'Political Discussion and News Use in the Contemporary Public Sphere: The "Accessibility" and "Traversability" of the Internet', paper presented at the annual meeting of the International Communication Association. Chicago.

Cantijoch, M. (2009) 'Reinforcement and Mobilization: The Influence of the Internet on Different Types of Political Participation', paper prepared for delivery at 'Citizen Politics: Are Media Reshaping Political Engagement?' conference, Barcelona, 28–30 May.

Castells, M. (1996) *The Rise of the Network Society, The Information Age: Economy, Society and Culture, Vol. I.* Cambridge, MA: Blackwell.

Castronova, E. (2005) *Synthetic Worlds: The Business and Culture of Online Games.* Chicago, IL: University of Chicago Press.

Chadwick, A. (2007) 'Digital Network Repertoires and Organizational Hybridity', *Political Communication,* 24(3): 283–301.

Corrado, A. and Firestone, C. (eds.) (1996) *Elections in Cyberspace: Toward a New Era in American Politics.* Washington, DC: Aspen Institute.

Dalton, R. (2008) *The Good Citizen: How a Younger Generation Is Reshaping American Politics.* Washington, DC: CQ Press.

Dalton, R., Scarrow, S. and Cain, B. (2004) 'Advanced Democracies and the New Politics', *Journal of Democracy,* 15(1): 124–38.

Earl, J. and Schussman, A. (2003) 'The New Site of Activism: On-line Organizations, Movement Entrepreneurs, and the Changing Location of Social Movement Decision-making', in P. Coy (ed.), *Consensus Decision Making, Northern Ireland and Indigenous Movements.* New York: JAI Press. pp. 155–87.

Feenberg, A. and Barney, D. (eds.) (2004) *Community in the Digital Age: Philosophy and Practice.* Lanham, MD: Rowman and Littlefield.

Firestone, C. (1995) 'The New Intermediaries', in D. Bollier (ed.), *The Future of Community and Personal Identity in the Coming Electronic Culture.* Washington, DC: Aspen Institute. pp. 39–43.

Foot, K. and Schneider, S. (2006) *Web Campaigning.* Cambridge, MA: MIT Press.

Friedman, T. (2005) *The World Is Flat: A Brief History of the Twenty-First Century.* New York: Farrar, Straus and Giroux.

Garrett, R. K. (2009) 'Echo Chambers Online? Politically Motivated Reinforcement Seeking', *Journal of Computer-Mediated Communication,* 14(2): 265–85.

Gibson, R. K., Römmele, A. and Ward, S. (eds.) (2004) *Electronic Democracy: Political Organizations, Mobilization and Participation Online.* London: Routledge.

Gil de Zúñiga, H., Copeland, L. and Bimber, B. (2011). 'Political Consumerism and Political Communication: The Social Media Connection', paper presented at the 36th Annual Conference of the Midwest Association for Public Opinion Research, Chicago, Nov. 2011.

Grossman, L. (1995) *The Electronic Republic: Reshaping Democracy in the Information Age.* New York: Viking.

Hill, K. and Hughes, J. (1997) 'Computer Mediated Political Communication: The USENET And Political Communities', *Political Communication,* 14(1): 3–27.

Hindman, M. (2008) *The Myth of Digital Democracy.* Princeton, NJ: Princeton University Press.

Howard, P. (2006) *New Media Campaigns and the Managed Citizen.* New York: Cambridge University Press.

Hill, K. A. and Hughes, J. E. (1997) 'Computer Mediated Political Communication: The USENET and Political Communities', *Political Communication,* 14: 3–27.

Inglehart, R. (1997) *Modernization and Postmodernization: Cultural, Economic, and Political Change in 43 Societies.* Princeton, NJ: Princeton University Press.

Iyengar, S. and Hahn K. S. (2009) 'Red Media, Blue Media: Evidence of Ideological Selectivity in Media Use', *Journal of Communication*, 59(1): 19–39.

Jennings, M. and Zeitner, V. (2003) 'Internet Use and Civic Engagement: A Longitudinal Analysis', *Public Opinion Quarterly*, 67(3): 311–34.

Jensen, M. (2009) 'Political Participation, Alienation, And the Internet in the United States and Spain', paper prepared for delivery at 'Citizen Politics: Are Media Reshaping Political Engagement?' conference, Barcelona, 28–30 May.

Jorba, L. and Bimber, B. (2012) 'The Impact of Digital Media on Citizenship from a Global Perspective,' in E. Anduiza, M. Jensen, and L. Jorba (eds.), *Digital Media and Political Engagement Worldwide: A Comparative Study.* New York, NY: Cambridge University Press.

Kalathil, S. and Boas, T. (2003) *Open Networks, Closed Regimes: The Impact of the Internet on Authoritarian Rule.* Washington, DC: Carnegie Endowment for International Peace.

Kinder, D. (2003) 'Communication and Politics in the Age of Information', in D. O. Sears, L. Huddy and R. Jervis (eds.), *Oxford Handbook of Political Psychology.* New York: Oxford University Press. pp. 357–93.

Krueger, B. (2002) 'Assessing the Potential of Internet Political Participation in the United States: A Resource Approach', *American Politics Quarterly*, 30(5): 476–98.

Krueger, B. (2009) 'Opt in Or Tune Out: Online Mobilization and Political Participation', paper prepared for delivery at the International Seminar Citizen Politics: Are the New Media Reshaping Political Engagement? Barcelona, 28–30 May.

Macedo, S. (2005) *Democracy At Risk: How Political Choices Undermine Citizen Participation, and What We Can Do About It.* Washington, DC: Brookings Institution.

Margolis, M. and Resnick, D. (2000) *Politics as Usual: The Cyberspace 'Revolution'.* Thousand Oaks, CA: Sage.

Mossberger, K., Tolbert, C. J. and McNeal, R. S. (2008) *Digital Citizenship: The Internet, Society, and Participation.* Cambridge, MA: MIT Press.

Mutz, D. C. and Martin, P. S. (2001) 'Facilitating Communication Across Lines of Political Difference: The Role of Mass Media', *American Political Science Review*, 95(1): 97–114.

Mutz, D. C. and Mondak, J. J. (2006) 'The Workplace as a Context for Cross-Cutting Political Discourse', *Journal of Politics,* 68(1): 140–55.

Negroponte, N. (1995) *Being Digital.* New York: Vintage.

Nielsen (2008) 'Obama's V.P. Text Message Reaches 2.9 Million', 26 August, http://blog.nielsen.com/nielsenwire/?s=obama+2.9 (accessed 23 June 2009).

Norris, P. (2001) *Digital Divide: Civic Engagement, Information Poverty, and the Internet Worldwide.* New York: Cambridge University Press.

Patterson, T. (2002) *The Vanishing Voter: Public Involvement in An Age of Uncertainty.* New York: Knopf.

Putnam, R. (2000) *Bowling Alone: The Collapse and Revival of American Community.* New York: Simon and Schuster.

Prior, M. (2007) *Post-Broadcast Democracy: How Media Choice Increases Inequality in Political Involvement and Polarizes Elections.* New York: Cambridge University Press.

Rheingold, H. (1993) *The Virtual Community: Homesteading on the Electronic Frontier.* New York: Harper Perennial.

Shah, D. V., Kwak, N. and Holbert, R. L. (2001) '"Connecting" And "Disconnecting" With Civic Life: Patterns of Internet Use and the Production of Social Capital', *Political Communication*, 18(2): 141–62.

Slater, M. (2007) 'Reinforcing Spirals: The Mutual Influence of Media Selectivity and Media Effects and Their Impact on Individual Behavior and Social Identity', *Communication Theory*, 17(3): 281–303.

Smith, A. (2009) The Internet's Role in Campaign 2008. Washington, DC: Pew Internet & American Life Project. http://www.pewinternet.org/Reports/2009/6–The-Internets-Role-in-Campaign-2008.aspx (accessed 30 November, 2011).

Stolle, D., Hooghe, M. and Micheletti, M. (2005) 'Politics in the Supermarket: Political Consumerism as a Form of Political Participation', *International Political Science Review*, 26(3): 245–69.

Stroud, N. J. (2007) 'Media Effects, Selective Exposure, and Fahrenheit 9/11', *Political Communication*, 24(4): 415–32.

Stroud, N. J. (2008) 'Media Use and Political Predispositions: Revisiting the Concept of Selective Exposure', *Political Behavior*, 30(3): 341–66.

Sunstein, C. (2001) *Republic.com.* Princeton, NJ: Princeton University Press.

Taber, C. S. and Lodge, M. (2006) 'Motivated Skepticism in the Evaluation of Political Beliefs', *American Journal of Political Science*, 50(3): 755–69.

TechPresident (2008) 'Facebook Supporters 2008', http://techpresident.com/scrape_plot/facebook/2008 (accessed 23 June 2009).

Turner, F. (2006) *From Counterculture to Cyberculture: Steward Brand, The Whole Earth Network, And the Rise of Digital Utopianism.* Chicago, IL: University of Chicago Press.

Turner, F. (2009) 'Burning Man At Google: A Cultural Infrastructure for New Media Production', *New Media and Society*, 11(1–2): 73–94.

US Department of Commerce (1995) 'Falling Through the Net: A Survey of the 'Have Nots' In Rural and Urban America', National Telecommunications and Information Administration, Washington, DC.

Wojcieszak, M. (2009) 'Carrying Online Participation Offline: Mobilization by Radical Online Groups and Politically Dissimilar Offline Ties', *Journal of Communication*, 59(3): 564–586.

Wojcieszak, M. and Mutz, D. (2009) 'Online Groups and Political Discourse: Do Online Discussion Spaces Facilitate Exposure to Political Disagreement?', *Journal of Communication*, 59(1): 40–56.

Xenos, M. and Moy, P. (2007) Direct and Differential Effects of the Internet on Political and Civic Engagement. *Journal of Communication,* 57, 704–18.

Zukin, C., Keeter, S., Andolina, M., Jenkins, K. and Delli Carpini, M. X. (2006) *A New Engagement? Political Participation, Civic Life, and the Changing American Citizen.* New York, NY: Oxford University Press.

10

Digital Media and Youth Engagement

W. Lance Bennett, Deen G. Freelon,
Muzammil M. Hussain and Chris Wells[1]

The story of communication and civic engagement that has developed over the past century of political communication scholarship goes something like this. Civic engagement begins with attention to information that arouses interest in various forms of public life, ranging from community involvement, to concern about issues, to taking political action. The information that stimulates engagement may be communicated through issue framing in the news, candidate position-taking in election campaigns, or social movements demanding inclusion in such processes. The symbolic qualities of communication interact with properties of the social environment in which it is received to produce various effects: arousing or killing interest and attention, enabling or inhibiting public opinion formation, and facilitating or undermining political action.

In recent years, a new story about the nature of citizenship and engagement has begun to take shape. The plot is centered on how young citizens use digital media. This emerging story of political communication and civic engagement involves changes in societies and communication technologies, and resulting changes in the nature of citizenship and political organization. In modern democratic societies that matured in the mid-to-late 20th century, political communication tended to be organized institutionally around authorities using mass media channels to cue individual identifications with values embodied by parties, unions, churches, branches of government, movements and the press (Blumler and Kavanagh, 1999; Lippmann, 1922; Zaller, 1992). Citizens of

this era engaged with these public institutions out of a sense of duty or obligation (Bennett, 1998, 2008; Dalton, 2008; Schudson, 1998). Over the past several decades, these foundations of the civic engagement process have begun to change rapidly. Early adopters of emerging civic styles tend to be younger citizens who have come of age in changing societies that have been described by various theorists as late modern (Giddens, 1991) or post-bureaucratic (Bimber, 2003). As mass social membership organizations and authoritative institutions decline in this late modern era, publics display less interest in seeking common information (Putnam, 2000). At the same time, individuals become more likely to join fluid networks organized by social technologies (Benkler, 2006). Among the resulting changes is that information sourced from elite gatekeepers (the core of the news) is becoming less credible, while compelling public communication based on different gatekeeping rules (for example, crowd sourcing) and media formats (citizen produced multi-media content) flows horizontally over digitally mediated networks.

Underlying these changes in political communication are fundamental shifts in the norms and practices of citizenship itself. As identifications with institutions, conventional leaders and civil society organizations grow weaker, affiliations with personally motivating issues and causes produce new self-actualizing citizen motivation and action repertoires (Bennett, 2008; Inglehart, 1997). These new generations of *actualizing citizens* often form loose networks for communication and action in a variety of political contexts using social technologies (Bennett, 2008; Bennett and Wells, 2009; Bennett et al., 2009). These communication networks may result in large-scale collective action that can be channeled into conventional forms such as election campaigns or interest activism if the organizations coordinating such actions can redefine themselves around more loosely tied, entrepreneurial relationships with individuals (Bimber et al., 2005; Bimber, Chapter 9 in this Handbook).

Efforts to understand the relationship between communication and engagement in such times of change have produced considerable differences among scholars. Some continue to use fading modern-era civic norms to evaluate youth civic practices, often with a resulting focus on the problems with youth disengagement such as (pre-2004) declines in voting, and continuing deficits in political knowledge and news consumption (for a review, see Bennett, 2008; Bennett and Wells, 2009). Meanwhile, others recognize that the foundations of citizenship, communication and political organization are changing, and that new patterns of engagement may be emerging (Bennett, 2008; Bimber, Chapter 9 in this Handbook). The result is that there are two conflicting and not easily reconciled paradigms of communication and civic engagement. One civic paradigm is anchored in norms and practices of *dutiful citizenship* (DC) centered around the sense of responsibility to serve one's community, become informed and channel preferences to government through parties and interest organizations. The emerging civic paradigm involves the emerging practices of *actualizing citizenship* (AC), which emphasizes new repertoires of political action based on personal expression through social networks often using digital media (Bennett, 2008; Bennett et al., 2009).

If we step back and look at the communication processes that are in play in these two civic worlds, we also see coming clashes over some of the core assumptions about political communication itself. Many core models in the field are rooted in a fading era of mass media and media effects based on strategic delivery of messages to large audiences. Research reveals growing audience fragmentation and proliferation of information channels, resulting in various difficulties (for example, soaring costs and diminishing effects) associated with large-scale information targeting. One important trend here, among others, is the growing tendency for individuals to seek self-affirming information. Scholars of political communication may need to pursue new and creative approaches to theorizing and studying 'media effects' in this changing civic communication environment (Bennett and Iyengar, 2008;

Chaffee and Metzger, 2001; Gurevitch et al., 2009).

This chapter offers an overview of what we see as the emerging foundations of civic engagement in this changing era of citizenship and politics. In particular, we contend that the image of a citizenry whose interaction with traditional public information involves passive consumption of top-down mass communication content no longer holds for most people under 30. This chapter examines an emerging era of citizenship defined by: (1) new sources, channels and formats for civic information; (2) changing patterns of public expression and (3) new communication-centered structures for the organization of action. The trends apply, with some variation, across many post-industrial democracies.

Thinking about shifting patterns of citizenship, communication and civic engagement requires some conceptual shorthand, such as the simple distinction between DC and AC. Typologies risk over-generalizing about the memberships of their categories as though they were a uniform group. We do not wish to imply that all young citizens are civic actualizers who are adept with digital tools. This is far from the case. Nor do we imply that all older citizens hold a dutiful conception of citizenship, or that they are exclusively mass media users (although they dominate the graying and declining news audiences and they vote at higher rates). The two civic types are undoubtedly mixed, both within demographic groups and within individuals. However, younger citizens tend to adopt more actualizing civic and communication styles than their elders. The second danger of drawing too-clean distinctions is that there is a tendency to assume that all young people are 'digital natives', easily tackling any task involving information technology. This is not the case (Hargittai and Walejko, 2008). Livingstone (2008) has noted that even young people deeply embedded in social networking sites may be unaware of basic options and functionalities within those environments.

With reference to the importance of these changes in citizenship styles, we explore three shifts in the dimensions of civic engagement related to communication We first consider the topic of *becoming informed* by looking at the shift from mass distribution of information to multiplying sources and channels, often selected through personal preferences, recommendation algorithms and friend networks. We next address changes in public expression by looking at *participatory media and shared content production*. Citizens not only consume information differently, but in the process, they also participate in its production. Here we develop an understanding of the important shift from top-down framing of issues and cueing of publics to more bottom-up personal involvement in the production of public information and the shaping of opinion discourse. Finally, we examine *social media and the organization of political action* by looking at the mobilizing potential of social media through the lens of how young people are connecting to politics – of various sorts – through emerging information technologies. This leads us to consider ways in which communication processes themselves constitute forms of political organization and action that involve networks not just as information channels but also as political structures.

BECOMING INFORMED: THE DECLINE OF NEWS AND THE PROLIFERATION OF OTHER INFORMATION SOURCES AND FORMS

The cohort differences between teens and young adults, and older Americans in regard to news consumption are pronounced. While 35% of older Americans read a newspaper every day, only 16% between 18- and 30-year-olds, and less than 10% of those 12- to 17-year-olds do (Patterson, 2007). For national and local television, as well as radio news, the trends spiral downward similarly, indicating that each successive generation finds less meaning and use for traditional news (Patterson, 2007). Perhaps not surprisingly, these trends are also accompanied by declining trust and credibility in news. The perceived accuracy of the press is now at an all-time low, with only 18% believing that the press deals fairly with all sides, and 29% thinking journalists get the facts straight (Kohut, 2009). In fact, nearly one-half of 19- to 39-year-olds would not miss their local paper if it disappeared (Kohut and Remez, 2009). The story unfortunately is also much the same in other Western democratic nations, such as the UK, where a recent review finds that 18- to 24-year-olds tend to 'reject the news; find it boring/depressing; don't have time, and generally [are] uninterested in the news …' (Currah, 2009).

If audiences, especially the young, increasingly reject news, where do they turn for political information? Like adults, teens and young adults do get their news primarily from television, but younger Americans also increasingly turn to the Internet and their immediate social networks (Patterson, 2007). In 2010, 44% of Americans reported receiving news through internet or mobile sources (Pew, 2010). The long tail of the online news supply is dominated by a mix of conventional organizations (for example, CNN), algorithm-driven aggregators (for example, Google News) and local paper websites tailing off into blogs and

listserves (Dutta-Bergman, 2004; Horrigan, 2006). In 2008, the Internet bypassed newspapers for the general public as the second-most important source of national and international news, and for young people, the Internet has nearly eclipsed television as well (Kohut and Remez, 2008). However, the problems of trust and credibility also persist online, with majorities finding online news no more informative, reliable or trustworthy than its offline equivalent (Ahlers, 2006; see also Melican and Dixon, 2008). One cautious point of optimism is that although audiences may be turning away from news, it is hard not to 'bump' into news in the information-saturated mediascape (Tewksbury et al., 2001), which happened to 50% of Internet users during the 2004 presidential elections (Rainie et al., 2005). The flip side of this finding is that for young people, the majority who report consuming news online tend to bump into it accidentally on their way to other places, whereas most older online consumers actively seek it out (Patterson, 2007). This suggests that at best, online news is no more useful for young citizens than its conventional media versions. If the news itself is in free fall, are there other information sources that young citizens may be using?

Changing Civic Information Formats

Political satire and late night comedy programming are increasingly attractive to younger Americans, rivaling their consumption of mainstream news. Fully 21% of those aged between 18 and 30 learned about candidates via *Saturday Night Live* and *The Daily Show* in 2004 (Pew, 2004), programs with more than 40% of viewers in the 18- to 29-year-old demographic (Pew, 2008). Beyond thousands of political jokes told annually by late night comedians (Niven et al., 2003), the quantity of substantive information in *The Daily Show* with Jon Stewart and broadcast network news was, by some measures, equal (Fox et al., 2007). Moreover, comedy programming like *The Daily Show* seems to improve recognition and recall in young voters (Hollander, 2005), and political comedy audiences are among the highest consumers of traditional news (Young and Tisinger, 2006). However, satirical content such as *The Colbert Report* may fly over the heads of some young people, and may lower trust in government and media (Baumgartner and Morris, 2008). Whether such trust levels are well-founded is an interesting question, but the clear implication is that political comedy offers perspective lacking in conventional news, and may actually shore up flagging news consumption among younger citizens. An interesting research question involves the importance of access to this program content online via YouTube, the Comedy Central site and via links from email, blogs and other sites.

Another area of interaction between news and alternative information formats is blogging, where majorities of those engaged routinely consume high levels of news (Lenhart and Fox, 2006). Scholars are still sorting out the relationships between blogging and journalism, the dynamics of which are clearly in play and changing rapidly (Carlson, 2007; Kenix, 2009; Lowrey, 2006; Messner and Distaso, 2008; Reese et al., 2007; Wall, 2005). What is clear, however, is that blogging is less a younger person's medium than political comedy (de Zúñiga et al., 2007). Indeed, where political comedy makes news somewhat palatable for young people, blogging is less effective.

Whether it is put in perspective by comedy or blogs, it seems that the news itself is increasingly at odds with a participatory media culture that enables direct access to information that bypasses journalistic gatekeepers. During the 2008 presidential elections, 23% of Americans got campaign information directly from candidate emails, 35% from campaign videos and 39% accessed primary documents and materials, such as position papers and speech transcripts (Smith and Rainie, 2008). Candidates and political elites have long used the Internet to communicate directly with constituents in the USA (D'Alessio, 2000; Stromer-Galley, 2000) and in other Western democracies (Jackson and Lilleker, 2007; Lusoli and Ward, 2005). An important and growing format for direct consumption is online video, with 60% of Internet users having viewed such videos. The figure for all categories of direct video consumption among 18- to 29-year-olds is 90% (Madden, 2007, 2009). In light of these trends, it is not surprising that election campaigns are changing their media strategies. In 2008, for example, the Obama campaign posted over 1800 video clips on YouTube, generating over one billion minutes of total viewership by election day (Delany, 2009).

These trends are clearly related to different ways of using communication technologies. More than half of 18- to 24-year-olds are actively engaged by Web 2.0 social technologies compared to just 8% of older Americans. However, interactivity alone does not seem to lead to increased news consumption. A study of young Finns found that interactive features did not increase engagement with content (Hujanen and Pietkainen, 2004). By contrast, providing political action options along with information may well increase online civic information use (Chung, 2008; Livingstone, 2003; Vromen, 2007).

These shifting forms and uses of information have been termed a new (digital) media culture by Dueze (2006) and Jenkins (2006a,b; Jenkins

et al., 2006), among others. This mediated civic culture is primarily defined by the characteristics of: participation (that is, becoming active agents in processes of meaning-making), remediation (adopting, modifying, manipulating and reforming ways of understanding reality) and bricolage (assembling and sharing individualized versions of reality). In this context, past information forms such as news appear less relevant to younger AC citizens who see themselves playing a more active role in selecting, engaging, organizing and acting with civic information. Indeed, it is hard to separate the consumption of information from its production and sharing in networked publics.

PUBLIC EXPRESSION: PARTICIPATORY MEDIA AND SHARED CONTENT PRODUCTION

The emergence of participatory media, such as blogs, online forums, streaming video and social network sites (SNSs), allow for an impressive range of content production by non-technical endusers. These communication technologies have been used for making friends, coping with grief, and creating direct information flows about 9/11 and various natural disasters. For our purposes, they are interesting because they enable direct and often large-scale content creation and distribution by non-elite citizens, particularly younger demographics. Not only do these technologies lower communication costs and other barriers (Davis, 1999; DiMaggio et al., 2001), but they enable public discourses to be initiated by formerly excluded media populations (Bennett, 2008; Jenkins et al., 2006; Kann et al., 2007). Although there is a great deal of research still needed on the qualities and effects of this participatory communication experience, we are beginning to see some general patterns.

Research on User-generated Civic Content

A 2009 survey found that of the 83% of 18- to 24-year-olds who possess an SNS profile, two-thirds had used it for at least one of the following political activities: discovering who their friends are voting for, posting political content, seeking candidate information, starting or joining a political group, and 'friending' political candidates (Smith, 2009; see also Raynes-Goldie and Walker, 2008; Smith and Rainie, 2008). By contrast, young people continue to engage in the fewest offline political activities, defined as direct inter-actions with government, the mainstream media or civil society (Smith et al., 2009).

One possible inference here is that expression trumps political action among young citizens. However, little research has thus far addressed this important question. One study that examined SNS user artifacts was a content analysis of African-American-focused SNS *Blackplanet* (Byrne, 2007), which found that although the site hosted an abundance of civic discussion, it rarely led to offline civic action. One possible explanation here comes from our studies of a sample of 90 youth engagement websites in the USA grouped into four types: online-only (which have no brick-and-mortar counterpart, for example Youthnoise and TakingITGlobal); government/candidate (self-explanatory, for example Barack Obama.com and College Republicans); community/service (which emphasize youth development and leadership, for example the YMCA and Key Club) and interest/activist (which take stands on live political issues, for example the *NRA* and the *Sierra Club*). We found that those sites emphasizing *actualizing* citizen styles offered the highest levels of opinion expression opportunities, but were similar to *dutiful* citizen sites in terms of heavily managing action opportunities (Civic Learning Online project, 2009). There seems to be a disconnection in these online civic communities between ena-bling expression, yet managing action, a point we will return to in the next section.

Studies of the quality of online youth expres-sion have generated a similarly ambiguous spec-trum of findings. Feezel et al. (2009) analyzed user-generated posts to political group pages on Facebook, and found them to be high in opinion but low in new information and thoughtful discus-sion. By contrast, the results of Kushin and Kitchener's (2009) analysis of comments to a Facebook group on the issue of state-sanctioned torture portray a largely flame-free discursive environment in which cross-cutting debate flour-ished. In a link analysis of comments on the *Facebook* pages of candidates in the 2008 US presidential elections, Robertson et al. (2009a) observed that user-contributed hyperlinks served various political functions, including opinion expression, evidence provision, argument rebuttal, encouragement of political engagement and candidate ridicule.

The state of research into user-generated online video is similarly embryonic. Early studies looked mainly at electoral content (Carlson and Strandberg, 2008) and youth civic engagement effects (McKinney and Rinn, 2009). The 2009 conference 'YouTube and the 2008 Election Cycle in the United States' (forthcoming as a special issue of the *Journal of Information Technology*

and Politics) began to set a research agenda in this area. Some papers explored YouTube as a top-down communication channel used by electoral candidates (Klotz, 2009; Williams and Gulati, 2009), while others examined participatory con-tent sharing such as viral videos (Boynton, 2009; Wallsten, 2009) and election-related user-generated content (Ricke, 2009; Robertson, 2009b). However, both Boynton (2009) and Wallsten (2009) operationalize virality as cumulative views over time, thus leaving unexamined the defining element of viral transmission: person-to-person sharing. Conversely, Ricke (2009) and Robertson (2009b) addressed user-expression surrounding online video, with the former concluding that the CNN/YouTube debates were highly inclusive of youth and minority citizens, and the latter noting that Facebook users posted YouTube links to the candidates' Facebook walls (comment sections) in order to debate, support and ridicule both the candidates and each other.

In addition to SNSs and online video, web sites explicitly intended to foster youth political and civic engagement have also attracted empirical attention (Bachen et al., 2008; Civic Learning Online, 2009; Gerodimos, 2008; Livingstone, 2007; Montgomery et al., 2004; Raynes-Goldie and Walker, 2008). As noted above, we studied the relationship between the type of citizenship tar-geted by various US online youth engagement sites and the kinds of activities going on in those sites. One of our studies looked at the activity patterns associated with different affordances for user expression. We found an abundance of user-contributed content in each of the participatory features we investigated (discussion forums and user-created groups, blogs and take action fea-tures). We also found that sites appealing to AC civic styles had far higher participation volumes than predominantly DC sites (Civic Learning Online, 2009). As noted above, however, this volume of expressive activity occurs in the context of fairly common limitations placed on the ena-bling of user-organized actions in these same environments. This tension between using social technologies to promote expression and at the same time limit more autonomous activism runs through the emerging literature on digital media and political action as indicated in the next section.

SOCIAL MEDIA AND THE ORGANIZATION OF POLITICAL ACTION

Beyond information consumption and production, how do social technologies affect the quality of civic action? In an effort to cast a broad net, we consider research in three diverse areas of: electoral campaigns; traditional civil society organizations and emerging political and quasi-political action in online gaming and networking environments.

Electoral Engagement

The American presidential election of 2008 was a watershed in the use of digital communication, exemplifying some of the important changes occurring in how young people relate to and participate in electoral processes. Those changes have significant implications for the way that political communication scholars understand the relationship between young citizens, candidates and the ever more complex media environment.

Perhaps the most striking opportunity seized by various candidates, and particularly by Barack Obama in 2008, was the development of digitally mediated relationships with constituents. This was facilitated both by his campaign's presence on mainstream SNSs – already heavily populated by potential supporters only a click away from friendship or supporter status – and by the creation of my.barackobama.com, an in-house networking environment with all the functionalities of a typical SNS, but all focused on helping Obama become elected. Within the established networking platforms Obama's support was robust throughout the campaign, and by election day he had some 840,000 MySpace friends, contrasted with McCain's 218,000, and almost 2.5 million Facebook supporters, compared with McCain's 623,000 (Techpresident, 2008). Across 15 different networking platforms the Obama campaign networked some 5 million online supporters (Delaney, 2009).

The opportunity to create such an active and to some extent personalized relationship with candidates is clearly attractive to young citizens (Xenos and Foot, 2008). Not only did Obama win 2-to-1 among young citizens, but his supporters were also more likely than McCain's to sign up for election alerts and volunteer activities online, give money online, share multimedia messages and send texts about the campaign to friends (Smith 2009: 9, 78). In this light, the election of 2008 should mark a starting point for political communication scholars to begin re-evaluating the possibilities of candidate-supporter relationships. Understanding the nature of changes in campaign communication strategies is also an important item on the research agenda (Gurevitch et al., 2009).

It is likely that participatory media have raised citizen expectations about interacting with and contributing to campaigns, what Xenos and Foot (2008) describe as 'coproductive interactivity' in campaign media environments. They suggest that this is both appealing to young citizens and rather terrifying for campaigns (Xenos and Foot, 2008). While such coproduction may create tensions inside campaigns and ultimately with supporters, a good deal of online participation by supporters occurs beyond the control of campaigns. Indeed, Obama benefited tremendously from unsolicited coproductive messages from supporters across the web. Independent videos such as 'I've got a crush on Obama' (by web comedy troupe Barely Political) and 'Yes We Can' (from pop star will.i.am) both received more online views than anything produced within the official campaign media environment. Similarly, the 'Dear Mr. Obama' video from a returning Iraq veteran was viewed and shared far more than any official McCain campaign video. While suggesting that externally created campaign media can boost participation, these often powerful supporter networks can also challenge the need of campaigns to shape their own media environments (Gueorguieva, 2008; Sifry, 2007).

In addition to changing the structure of candidate–supporter relationships, online engagement may introduce new dynamics into the polarization and fragmentation noted by observers of conventional media (Prior, 2007). While some have argued that these problems are reproduced online (Sunstein, 2001), growing research results suggest more sanguine possibilities. In his study of the 2006 Netherlands General Elections, Utz (2009) found that social networking sites were more likely to expose politically uninterested citizens to candidates' pages than traditional websites. More generally, studies on interactivity have shown beneficial effects on citizens' sense of efficacy and knowledge of candidate issue stances (Tedesco, 2007; Warnick et al., 2005).

Civil Society and Government

In the classic formulations of civil society (for example, Putnam, 2000; Skocpol and Fiorina, 1999), citizens make sense of the political world and their role in it through their activity in community and interest groups. As noted earlier, many scholars whom we have associated with the dutiful citizenship paradigm have expressed concerns about threats to conventional citizenship and participation due to the decline of these group memberships. However, other scholars are theorizing how bases for individual participation (that we associate with actualizing citizenship) are shifting away from long-standing institutional organizations to digitally mediated networked relationships (for example, Bennett, 2008; Bimber et al., 2005; see also Bimber, Chapter 9 in this Handbook; Vliegenthart and Walgrave, Chapter 30 in this Handbook).

Beyond these paradigm differences about the nature and forms of engagement, research on civil society is also important for understanding places and processes where citizens develop their civic skill repertoires, which include: communication and knowledge development, political organizing and understanding how to act in civic contexts. Among the most obvious places where such socialization might occur are the schools. Yet formal civic education has appeared increasingly problematic, in part because adults who create curriculum may fail to understand the transition from DC to AC citizenship, and thus continue to promote civic standards that young people find to be out of touch with their lived political experience (Bennett et al., 2009; Syvertsen et al., 2007). It is also clear that school environments fail to develop some of the basic digital media skills that may be helpful for participation in online politics (Hargittai and Walejko, 2008; Livingstone et al., 2005; Rheingold, 2008).

Research on how online communities constitute virtual civil society experiences for young citizens suggests that these environments have been less than successful in anticipating the changes in youth citizen identities and participation preferences. In a qualitative study of several prominent youth civic engagement environments in the UK, Coleman (2008) introduced a framework of *managed* and *autonomous* online communication experiences. Managed sites tended to carefully structure users' opportunities for interacting with the site, and limit their opportunities for defining the contours of that interaction; in contrast, more autonomous sites offered users considerable latitude to decide what topics they wanted to communicate about, and what form that communication would take, thus offering an experience more in line with young citizens' expectations of a Web 2.0 experience. Disappointingly, Coleman saw websites from government and traditional civil society organizations overwhelmingly offering managed experiences, while youth-built sites tended to be poorly resourced, and perhaps too starkly opposed to conventional engagement. There were few signs of more balanced civic options.

Similar patterns have been found in various studies in different nations. In a pioneering US study, Montgomery and colleagues (2004) found that most sites were not taking advantage of interactive features, a state of affairs reconfirmed later by Bachen et al. (2008), who also noted the lack of active civic pedagogical techniques offered. Looking at youth mobilization sites from the UK, Gerodimos (2008) similarly found low levels of the kinds of interactive connections to political processes likely to motivate young citizens to action. His conclusion was that there was an overemphasis among youth web site producers on '*participationism* (that is, participation for participation's sake)' and too little awareness of the kinds of experiences that would productively lead young citizens to engagement and efficacy (Gerodimos, 2008: 983). These findings appear again in a study of youth engagement sites in seven European nations, suggesting that developers of youth sites tend to be promoting a model of engagement that is out of step with the civic and media preferences of young citizens (European Commission, 2007).

As introduced earlier, our work in this area has used the Dutiful-Actualizing citizenship framework to explore how the adoption of implicit citizenship models shapes the engagement opportunities offered by youth civic websites. Perhaps not surprisingly, we found that traditional civil society organizations such as government, parties, interest groups and community youth organizations displayed a high level of commitment to the dutiful citizen model, to the exclusion of more Actualizing socialization possibilities in different areas of civic skills development (learning, expression, organizing and action). Sites existing only in online form – with no formal ties to an offline organization – performed somewhat better by offering actualizing experiences with peer sharing of information and opportunities for user-generated expression, but when it came to opportunities to create groups and share action ideas they also tended to manage participation rather than enabling much user-generated political networking and action planning. (For a description of methods and findings, along with the few notable exceptions to these patterns, see Bennett et al., 2009.)

These rather discouraging findings call for improved conceptualization of the possibilities and elements of youth engagement through civic sites. The area seems to be dominated by an outdated style of citizenship (Bennett et al., 2008) and a hobbling degree of misunderstanding on the part of sites' producers about their intended audience (Livingstone, 2007). We need to develop a better understanding of why civic organizations have been so slow to embrace networked and interactive tools (Gerodimos, 20008), and there is a need for more research on what effects different online civic environments have on which youth (Raynes-Goldie and Walker, 2008).

Emergent Forms of Political Action

Beyond the conventional sites of political action, there are other online environments that offer fertile ground for the young people engaging in contentious action of a various forms. These range from collective action taking place in multi-player games (Jenkins, 2006a), to fan communities organizing to protest the corporate treatment of music stars and other cultural objects. Jenkins et al. (2006) see such 'participatory cultures' as defining elements of digitally networked society, and young citizens' participation in them as fundamental to their citizenship. Such young citizens are willing to jockey for opportunities to create and modify – not only consume – culture, and in cases where that inclination has been in conflict with owners of cultural products' we have seen organizing that looks remarkably political.

Earl and colleagues argue for the political significance of such cultural contestation (Earl and Kimport, 2009; Earl and Schussmann, 2008). They document the rise of online petition tools for conveying fans' appeals to corporations such as Sony BMG and Disney to change their practices – such as by modifying concert tour schedules or allowing copyright exceptions (Earl and Schussman, 2008: 71). In the context of young people's lives and the producer–consumer relationships of the digital age, they argue 'that it is useful to expand notions of civic engagement to include cultural contestation that attempts to redefine the relationship between corporations and consumers of their products' (Earl and Schussman, 2008: 74). The tools and networking strategies employed by those young activists are not substantially different from the new modes of 'conventional' collective action being theorized elsewhere (Bimber et al., 2005; see also Bimber, Chapter 9, and Vliegenthart and Walgrave, Chapter 30, in this Handbook).

Games involve other areas of civic life online that warrant more study. Although the civic virtue of online games may seem dubious for those operating with the DC paradigm, Jenkins (2006a,b; Jenkins, et al., 2006) has argued for the civic importance of various forms of collective action within game environments such as World of Warcraft and the Sims Online. His description of gamers' affiliations with guilds, and their ensuing sense of personal responsibility to the welfare of the group – some staying up all night out of a sense of obligation to other group members (Jenkins, 2006b) – sound intriguingly like the kinds of civic experiences attributed to offline community involvement. In at least one example, a young person took that personal responsibility to the next level, waging an in-game political campaign to become mayor of the Sims Online town (Jenkins et al., 2006).

Others point to forms of virtual organizing in online communities in which users have banded together to resist policies proposed by website owners and administrators. Benkler (2006: 75) cites an example from the world of Second Life in which aggrieved participants staged a protest that would have been obviously political in any real world context – stacking tea crates around the Washington Monument to protest proposed 'tax' increases. Similar protests have taken place in World of Warcraft (Zackheim, 2005), Facebook and Myspace (Boyd, 2007). These quasi-civic experiences are occurring in the heart of the youth Internet experience: video games, which 97% of 12- to 17-year-olds report playing (Lenhart et al., 2008). What relevance gaming experiences have for more conventional political engagement is a critical question for empirical research. A pioneering study of the relation between games and civic orientations showed that playing games that encourage cooperation, address social issues, and involve playing with others, along with participation in online forums about games, are all predictive of higher civic outcomes (Kahne et al., 2008).

This discussion indicates that political communication scholars would also do well to consider the broadly changing contexts in which young citizens experience politics. Although by many of the conventional DC standards noted earlier, young citizens may seem disengaged. Yet, by emerging AC criteria such as peer knowledge sharing, participatory content creation, and inventing alternative forms of political action, they may be doing just fine – and even changing the practical definitions of citizen engagement in the process.

CONCLUSION

This chapter opened with references to the profound changes in civic engagement brought about a century ago by the rise of strong civic institutions, a national press system, and the norms of dutiful citizenship as described by Lippmann (1922) and Dewey (1927), among others. It remains to be seen whether the changes associated with the decline of this last civic era and the rise of a participatory digital media culture will be as fundamental as that earlier transformation of citizenship and engagement. Nonetheless, we believe that the evidence and research reviewed above makes a strong case for the significance of current shifts in patterns of citizenship and communication. Not surprisingly, these currents of change have triggered a number of normative concerns that need to become better integrated with empirical research.

Normative Concerns: Selective Exposure, Information Overload and Digital Literacy

The emergence of a participatory media culture and the growth of new civic information practices have raised a number of key normative concerns for scholars. Perhaps the issue receiving the most attention is the possibility of attitude-reinforcing selective exposure and political fragmentation (Bennett and Iyengar, 2008; Garrett, 2009; Graf and Aday, 2008; Sunstein, 2001; Bimber, Chapter 9 in this Handbook). Even subtle shifts in selective exposure can be significant, as online use of *The New York Times* compared to its paper version led to different public agendas due to audience selectivity (Althaus and Tewksbury, 2002). Moreover, the online news audience generally consumes less public affairs content when given greater choice (Tewksbury, 2003). Recent investigations have also raised concerns about news recommendation engines (for example, favoriting/rating and reading/sharing systems) and their consequences for audience attention (Knobloch-Westerwick et al., 2005; Thorson, 2008).

Although evidence for selective exposure does exist, the normative implications are not always so clear. For example, many citizens sought alternative sources online that better fulfilled their standards for credibility during the early Iraq War years, but that is perhaps a good thing considering the lack of critical national press coverage at the time (Bennett et al., 2007; Best et al., 2005; Choi et al., 2006). Moreover, individual level selectivity is also not the only cause of selective exposure, as specialized content from news outlets is increasingly aimed at attracting selected demographics (Tewksbury, 2005).

Another area of normative concern is the possibility of information overload (Bawden and Robinson, 2009; Nordenson, 2008), and the lack of adequate skills to navigate the ever more cluttered mediascape (Chiang et al., 2009). Compounding the skill question is evidence of stratified engagement with participatory media based on socioeconomic status, age and gender (Hargittai and Hinnant, 2008; Hargittai and Walejko, 2008). More optimistically, it has been demonstrated that socialization and education can help overcome the socioeconomic divide (Howard and Massanari, 2007), prompting scholarly calls for increased investment in digital literacy assessments (Hargittai, 2009) and digital skills development (Jenkins et al., 2006; Rheingold, 2008).

A Research Agenda for Socially Networked Publics

Based on the rapidly growing scholarship noted above, several directions for future research can already be identified. The first of these might be called *the politics of apolitical spaces* – the emergence of political activity in online environments, from SNSs to games, which are not explicitly dedicated to politics. We need to learn more about why young people find these environments so attractive so that key elements can be transferred to more explicitly civic spaces. Research also needs to compare the nature of engagement in these spaces with more explicit political activity. One early study here suggests that apolitical spaces may host significantly more cross-cutting discussion than sites officially devoted to political news and commentary (Wojcieszak and Mutz, 2009). A related issue in need of more investigation is that of *public versus private voice* (Rheingold, 2008; Zukin et al., 2006) – the question of what audiences are being addressed by expression in different digital contexts. The greater the amount of youth political activity taking place in SNSs, the more important it becomes to ascertain whether youth are speaking to broad publics or only within closed friend networks. We may have to curb our enthusiasm about SNS political expression somewhat if research begins to indicate that young people are willing to discuss politics informally with people they know, but not with strangers they might disagree with. More research is also needed to *compare online and offline civic activity*. Numerous studies have classified various forms of conventional offline civic and political activity (Verba et al., 1995; Zukin et al., 2006). Yet, few studies of online engagement offer guidelines for differentiating and comparing activities such as discovering which candidate their friends intended to vote for, starting/joining online political groups, and posting political content in SNSs (Smith, 2009; Smith and Rainie, 2008). Finally, we need to pay more attention to *the qualities of the political content generated online*. To what extent do we find rational–critical argument, evidence-free rants, calls to action, pointers to useful offsite content (Robertson et al., 2009a) and how do we evaluate these characteristics?

While there is clearly a good deal of research potential ahead, we already see evidence of an emerging era of citizenship in which young citizens are taking advantage of opportunities to personally shape their information, expression and action environments. Civic institutions – from schools teaching civic education to political parties trying to mobilize voters – operate at their own peril if they continue to reflect only the older DC civic paradigm and fail to recognize and credibly communicate with emerging AC civic styles. The goal here is not to abandon one model of citizenship and communication for the other, but to find ways to balance them in everyday communication and action repertoires. And as young citizens persist in changing the way we communicate and act, the norms and structures connecting them to the political process will ultimately change as well. Recognizing and understanding these changes present exciting challenges for theory and research.

NOTE

1 The authors are listed alphabetically and contributed equally to the chapter. We acknowledge the support of the John D. and Catherine T. MacArthur Foundation program on Digital Media and Learning.

REFERENCES

Ahlers, D. (2006) 'News Consumption and the New Electronic Media', *Harvard International Journal of Press/Politics*, 11(1): 29–52.

Althaus, S. L. and Tewksbury, D. (2002) 'Agenda Setting and the "New" News: Patterns of Issue Importance Among Readers of the Paper and Online Versions of The New York Times', *Communication Research*, 29(2): 180–207.

Bachen, C., Raphael, C., Lynn, K. M., McKee, K. and Philippi, J. (2008) 'Civic Engagement, Pedagogy and Information Technology on Web Sites for Youth', *Political Communication*, 25(3): 290–310.

Baumgartner, J. C. and Morris, J. S. (2008) 'One "Nation," Under Stephen? The Effects of The Colbert Report on American Youth', *Journal of Broadcast and Electronic Media*, 52(4), 622–43.

Bawden, D. and Robinson, L. (2009) 'The Dark Side of Information: Overload, Anxiety and Other Paradoxes and Pathologies', *Journal of Information Science*, 35(2): 180–91.

Benkler, Y. (2006) *The Wealth of Networks: How Social Production Transforms Markets and Freedom*. New Haven, CT: Yale University Press.

Bennett, W. L. (1998) 'The Uncivic Culture: Communication, Identity and the Rise of Lifestyle Politics', *PS: Political Science and Politics*, 31(4): 740–61.

Bennett, W. L. (2008) 'Changing Citizenship in the Digital Age', in W. L. Bennett (ed.), *Civic Life Online: Learning How Digital Media Can Engage Youth*. Cambridge, MA: MIT Press. pp. 1–24.

Bennett, W. L. and Iyengar, S. (2008) 'A New Era of Minimal Effects? The Changing Foundations of Political Communication', *Journal of Communication*, 58(4): 707–31.

Bennett, W. L., Lawrence, R. and Livingston, S. (2007) *When the Press Fails: Political Power and the News Media from Iraq to Katrina*. Chicago, IL: University of Chicago Press.

Bennett, W. L. and Wells, C. (2009) 'Civic Engagement: Bridging Differences to Build a Field of Civic Learning', *International Journal of Learning and Media*, 1(3): 1–10.

Bennett, W. L., Wells, C. and Freelon, D. G. (2009) 'Communicating Citizenship Online: Models of Civic Learning in the Youth Web Sphere', report from the Civic Learning Online Project, center for communication and civic engagement. University of Washington, Seattle.

Bennett, W. L., Wells, C. and Rank, A. (2009) 'Young Citizens and Civic Learning: Two Paradigms of Citizenship in the Digital Age', *Citizenship Studies*, 13(2): 105–20.

Best, S., Chmielewski, B. and Krueger, B. (2005) 'Selective Exposure to Online Foreign News During the Conflict with Iraq', *Harvard International Journal of Press/Politics*, 10(4): 52–70.

Bimber, B. (2003) *Information and American Democracy: Technology in the Evolution of Political Power*. New York: Cambridge University Press.

Bimber, B., Flanagin, A. J. and Stohl, C. (2005) 'Reconceptualizing Collective Action in the Contemporary Media Environment', *Communication Theory*, 15(4): 365–88.

Blumler, J. G. and Kavanagh, D. (1999) 'The Third Age of Political Communication: Influences and Features', *Political Communication*, 16(3): 209–30.

Boyd, D. M. (2007) 'MySpace, MyPublic, MyVoice: Political Engagement in Social Network Sites', paper presented at the International Communication Association. San Francisco, May. http://www.allacademic.com/meta/p170000_index.html (accessed 1 November 2009).

Boynton, G. R. (2009) 'Going Viral: The Dynamics of Attention', paper presented at the Youtube and the 2008 Election Cycle in the United States conference, Amherst, MA. http://youtubeandthe2008election.jitp2.net/paperhome/bboynton (accessed 23 October 2009).

Byrne, D. N. (2007) 'Public Discourse, Community Concerns and Civic Engagement: Exploring Black Social Networking Traditions on BlackPlanet.com', *Journal of Computer-Mediated Communication*, 13(1): 319–40.

Carlson, M. (2007) 'Blogs and Journalistic Authority: The Role of Blogs in US Election Day 2004 Coverage', *Journalism Studies*, 8(2): 264–79.

Carlson, T. and Strandberg, K. (2008) 'Riding the Web 2.0 Wave: Candidates on YouTube in the 2007 Finnish National Elections', *Journal of Information Technology and Politics*, 5(2): 159–74.

Chaffee, S. and Metzger, M. (2001) 'The End of Mass Communication', *Mass Communications and Society*, 4(4): 365–79.

Choi, J. H., Watt, J. H. and Lynch, M. (2006) 'Perceptions of News Credibility About the War in Iraq: Why War Opponents Perceived the Internet as the Most Credible Medium', *Journal of Computer-Mediated Communication*, 12(1): 209–29.

Chiang, I. P., Huang, C. Y. and Huang, C. W. (2009) 'Characterizing Web Users' Degree of Web 2.0-ness', *Journal of the American Society for Information Sciences and Technology*, 60(7): 1349–57.

Chung, D. S. (2008) 'Interactive Features of Online Newspapers: Identifying Patterns and Predicting Use of Engaged Readers', *Journal of Computer-Mediated Communication*, 13(3): 658–79.

Civic Learning Online Project (2009), www.engagedyouth.org (accessed 20 November 2009).

Coleman, S. (2008) 'Doing IT for Themselves: Management Versus Autonomy in Youth E-citizenship', in W. L. Bennett (ed.), *Civic Life Online: Learning How Digital Media Can Engage Youth*. Cambridge, MA: MIT Press. pp. 189–206.

Currah, A. (2009) 'What's Happening to Our News: An Investigation into the Likely Impact of the Digital Revolution on the Economics of News Publishing in the UK', *Reuters Institute for the Study of Journalism*, http://reutersinstitute. politics.ox.ac.uk/publications/risj.html (accessed 10 October 2009).

D'Alessio, D. (2000) 'Adoption of the World Wide Web by American Political Candidates, 1996–1998', *Journal of Broadcast and Electronic Media*, 44(4): 456–568.

Dalton, R. (2008) *The Good Citizen: How a Younger Generation is Reshaping American Politics*. Washington, DC: CQ Press.

Davis, R. (1999) *The Web of Politics: The Internet's Impact on the American Political System*. New York: Oxford University Press.

Delany, C. (2009) 'Learning from Obama: Lessons for Online Communicators in 2009 and Beyond', http://www.epoli-tics.com/learning-from-obama/ (accessed 29 October 2009).

Dewey, J. (1927) *The Public and Its Problems*. New York: Holt.

Deuze, M. (2006) 'Participation, Remediation, Bricolage: Considering Principal Components of a Digital Culture', *The Information Society*, 22(2): 63–75.

DiMaggio, P., Hargittai, E., Neuman, W. R. and Robinson, J. P. (2001) 'Social Implications of the Internet', *Annual Review of Sociology*, 27(1): 307–36.

Dutta-Bergman, M. J. (2004) 'Complementarity in Consumption of News Types Across Traditional and New Media', *Journal of Broadcast and Electronic Media*, 48(1): 41–60.

Earl, J. and Kimport, K. (2009) 'Movement Societies and Digital Protest: Fan Activism and Other Nonpolitical Protest Online', *Sociological Theory*, 27(3): 220–43.

Earl, J. and Schussman, A. (2008) 'Contesting Cultural Control: Youth Culture and Online Petitioning', in W. L. Bennett (ed.), *Civic Life Online: Learning How Digital Media Can Engage Youth*. Cambridge, MA: MIT Press. pp. 71–95.

European Commission (2007) 'Young People, the Internet and Civic Participation', *European Commission Sixth Framework Program*, Report D6. http://www.civicweb.eu/content/blogcategory/3/7/ (accessed 29 December 2008).

Feezell, J. T., Conroy, M. and Guerrero, M. (2009) 'Facebook is Fostering Political Engagement: A Study of Online Social Networking Groups and Offline Participation', *SSRN eLibrary*, http://papers.ssrn.com/Sol3/papers.cfm?abstract_id=1451456

Fox, J. R., Koloen, G. and Sahin, V. (2007) 'No Joke: A Comparison of Substance in The Daily Show with Jon Stewart and Broadcast Network Television Coverage of the 2004 Presidential Election Campaign', *Journal of Broadcast and Electronic Media*, 51(2): 213–27.

Garrett, R. K. (2009) 'Echo Chambers Online?: Politically Motivated Selective Exposure Among Internet News Users', *Journal of Computer-Mediated Communication*, 14(2): 265–85.

Gerodimos, R. (2008) 'Mobilizing Young Citizens in the U.K.: A Content Analysis of Youth and Issue Websites', *Information Communication and Society*, 11(7): 964–88.

Graf, J. and Aday, S. (2008) 'Selective Attention to Online Political Information', *Journal of Broadcast and Electronic Media*, 52(1): 86–100.

Giddens, A. (1991) *Modernity and self-identity: Self and Society in the Late Modern Age*. Stanford, CA: Stanford University Press.

Gueorguieva, V. (2008) 'Voters, MySpace and YouTube: The Impact of Alternative Communication Channels on the 2006 Election Cycle and Beyond', *Social Science Computer Review*, 26(3): 288–300.

Gurevitch, M., Coleman, S. and Blumler, J. G. (2009) 'Political Communication: Old and New Media Relationships', *Annals of the American Academy of Political and Social Science*, 625: 164–81.

Hargittai, E. (2009) 'An Update on Survey Measures of Web-Oriented Digital Literacy', *Social Science Computer Review*, 27(1): 130–37.

Hargittai, E. and Hinnant, A. (2008) 'Digital Inequality: Differences in Young Adults' Use of the Internet', *Communication Research*, 35(5): 602–21.

Hargittai, E. and Walejko, G. (2008) 'The Participation Divide: Content Creation and Sharing in the Digital Age', *Information Communication and Society*, 11(2): 239–56.

Hollander, B. A. (2005) 'Late-Night Learning: Do Entertainment Programs Increase Political Campaign Knowledge for Young Viewers?', *Journal of Broadcast and Electronic Media*, 49(4): 402–15.

Horrigan, J. (2006) 'Online News: For Many Home Broadband Users, the Internet is a Primary News Source', *Pew Internet and American Life Project*, http://www.pewinternet.org/Data-Tools/Get-The-Latest-Statistics.aspx (accessed 10 October 2009).

Howard, P. N. and Massanari, A. (2007) 'Learning to Search and Searching to Learn: Income, Education and Experience Online', *Journal of Computer-Mediated Communication*, 12(3): 846–65.

Hujanen, J. and Pietikainen, S. (2004) 'Interactive Uses of Journalism: Crossing Between Technological Potential and Young People's News-Using Practices', *New Media and Society*, 6(3): 383–402.

Inglehart, R. (1997) *Modernization and Postmodernization: Cultural, Economic and Political Change in 43 Societies.* Princeton, NJ: Princeton University Press.

Jackson, N. A. and Lilleker, D. G. (2007) 'Seeking Unmediated Political Information in a Mediated Environment: The Uses and Gratifications of Political Parties' E-newsletters', *Information, Communication and Society*, 10(2): 242–64.

Jenkins, H. (2006a) *Convergence Culture: Where Old and New Media Collide.* New York: New York University Press.

Jenkins, H. (2006b) '"Random Acts of Journalism": Defining Civic Media', *Confessions of an Aca/Fan*, 25 September, http://www.henryjenkins.org/2006/09/civic_media_in_the_digital_age.html (accesssed 28 October 2009).

Jenkins, H. with Clinton, K., Purushotma, R., Robison, A. and Weigel, M. (2006) 'Confronting the Challenges of Participatory Culture: Media Education for the 21st Century', http://www.newmedialiteracies.org/files/working/NMLWhitePaper.pdf (accessed 29 January 2009).

Kahne, J., Middaugh, E. and Evans, C. (2008). 'The Civic Potential of Video Games', Civic Engagement Research Group, Mills College, http://www.civicsurvey.org/White_paper_link_text.pdf (accessed 2 November 2009).

Kann, M. E., Berry, J., Gant, C. and Zager, P. (2007) 'The Internet and Youth Political Participation', *First Monday*, 12(8).

Kenix, L. J. (2009) 'Blogs as Alternative', *Journal of Computer-Mediated Communication*, 14(4): 790–22.

Klotz, R. J. (2009) 'The Sidetracked 2008 YouTube Senate Campaign', paper presented at the Youtube and the 2008 Election Cycle in the United States conference. Amherst, MA. http://youtubeandthe2008election.jitp2.net/paperhome/rklotz.

Knobloch-Westerwick, S., Sharma, N., Hansen, D. L. and Alter, S. (2005) 'Impact of Popularity Indications on Readers' Selective Exposure to Online News', *Journal of Broadcast and Electronic Media*, 49(3): 296–313.

Kohut, A. (2009) 'Public Evaluations of the News Media: 1985–2009 – Press Accuracy Rating Hits Two Decade Low', *Pew Research Center for The People and The Press*, http://people-press.org/reports/ (accessed 10 October 2009).

Kohut, A. and Remez, M. (2009) 'Limbaugh Flap Draws More Coverage than Interest – Many Would Shrug if Their Local Newspaper Closed', http://people-press.org/reports/ (accessed 10 October 2009).

Kohut, A. and Remez, M. (2008) 'Biggest Stories of 2008: Economy Tops Campaign – Internet Overtakes Newspapers as News Outlet', http://people-press.org/reports/ (accessed 10 October 2009).

Kushin, M. J. and Kitchener, K. (2009) 'Getting Political on Social Network Sites: Exploring Online Political Discourse on Facebook', paper presented at the Annual Convention of the Western States Communication Association. Mesa, AZ. http://papers.ssrn.com/sol3/papers.cfm?abstract_id=1300565 (accessed 24 October 2009).

Lenhart, A. and Fox, S. (2006) 'Bloggers: A Portrait of the Internet's New Storytellers', http://www.pewinternet.org/Data-Tools/Get-The-Latest-Statistics.aspx (accessed 10 October 2009).

Lenhart, A., Kahne, J., Middaugh, E., Macgill, A., Evans, C. and Vitak, J. (2008) 'Teens, Video Games and Civics', http://www.pewinternet.org/Reports/2008/Teens-Video-Games-and-Civics.aspx (accessed 2 November 2009).

Lippmann, W. (1922) *Public Opinion.* Harcourt, Brace and Company, Inc.

Livingstone, S. (2003) 'Children's Use of the Internet: Reflections on the Emerging Research Agenda', *New Media and Society*, 5(2): 147–66.

Livingstone, S. (2007) 'The Challenge of Engaging Youth Online: Contrasting Producers' and Teenagers' Interpretations of Websites', *European journal of communication*, 22(2): 165–84.

Livingstone, S. (2008) 'Taking Risky Opportunities in Youthful Content Creation: Teenagers' Use of Social Networking Sites for Intimacy, Privacy and Self-Expression', *New Media and Society*, 10(3): 393–411.

Livingstone, S., Bober, M. and Helsper, E. (2005) 'Active Participation or Just More Information?', *Information, Communication and Society*, 8(3): 287–314.

Lowrey, W. (2006) 'Mapping the Journalism–Blogging Relationship', *Journalism: Theory, Practice and Criticism*, 7(4): 477–500.

Lusoli, W. and Ward, J. (2005) 'Politics Makes Strange Bedfellows': The Internet and the 2004 European Parliament Election in Britain', *Harvard International Journal of Press/Politics*, 10(4): 71–97.

Madden, M. (2009) 'The Audience for Online Video-Sharing Sites Shoots Up', http://www.pewinternet.org/Data-Tools/Get-The-Latest-Statistics.aspx (accessed 10 October 2009).

Madden, M. (2007) 'Online Video', http://www.pewinternet.org/Data-Tools/Get-The-Latest-Statistics.aspx (accessed 10 October 2009).

Melican, D. B. and Dixon, T. L. (2008) 'News on the Net: Credibility, Selective Exposure and Racial Prejudice', *Communication Research*, 35(2): 1511–68.

Messner, M. and Distaso, M. W. (2008) 'The Source Cycle: How Traditional Media and Weblogs Use Each Other as Sources', *Journalism Studies*, 9(3): 447–63.

McKinney, M. S. and Rill, L. A. (2009) 'Not Your Parents' Presidential Debates: Examining the Effects of the CNN/YouTube Debates on Young Citizens' Civic Engagement', *Communication Studies*, 60(4): 392–406.

Montgomery, K., Gottlieb-Robles, B. and Larson, G. O. (2004) '*Youth as E-citizens: Engaging the Digital Generation.* Washington, DC: Center for Social Media, American University.

Niven, D., Lichter, S. R. and Amundson, D. (2003) 'The Political Content of Late Night Comedy', *Harvard International Journal of Press/Politics*, 8(3): 1181–33.

Nordenson, B. (2008) 'Overload! Journalism's Battle for Relevance in an Age of Too Much Information', *Columbia Journalism Review*, November/December, http://www.cjr.org/feature/overload_1.php (accessed 20 October 2009).

Patterson, T. (2007) 'Young People and News', *Joan Shorestein Center on the Press, Politics and Public Policy*, http://www.hks.harvard.edu/presspol/publications/reports.html (accessed 10 October 2009).

Pew (2004) 'Cable and Internet Loom Large in Fragmented Political News Universe', *Pew Research Center for The People and The Press,* http://people-press.org/reports/ (accessed 10 October 2009).

Pew (2008) 'Key News Audiences Now Blend Online and Traditional News Sources', *Pew Research Center for The People and The Press,* http://people-press.org/reports/ (accessed 10 October 2009).

Pew (2010) 'Americans Spending More Time Following News', Pew Research Center for The People and The Press, http://www.people-press.org/2010/09/12/americans-spending-more-time-following-the-news/ (accessed 15 January 2012).

Prior, M. (2007) *Post-Broadcast Democracy: How Media Choice Increases Inequality in Political Involvement and Polarizes Elections.* New York: Cambridge University Press.

Putnam, R. (2000) *Bowling Alone: The Collapse and Revival of American Community.* New York: Simon and Schuster.

Rainie, L., Cornfield, M. and Horrigan, J. (2005) 'The Internet and Campaign 2004', http://www.pewinternet.org/Data-Tools/Get-The-Latest-Statistics.aspx (accessed 10 October 2009).

Raynes-Goldie, K. and Walker, L. (2008) 'Our Space: Online Civic Engagement Tools for Youth', in W. L. Bennett (ed.), *Civic Life Online: Learning How Digital Media Can Engage Youth.* Boston, MA: MIT Press. pp. 161–88.

Reese, S. D., Rutigliano, L., Hyun, K. and Jeong, J. (2007) 'Mapping the Blogosphere: Professional and Citizen-Based Media in the Global News Arena', *Journalism: Theory, Practice and Criticism,* 8(3): 235–62.

Rheingold, H. (2008) 'Using Participatory Media and Public Voice to Encourage Civic Engagement', in W. L. Bennett (ed.), *Civic Life Online: Learning How Digital Media Can Engage Youth.* Boston, MA: MIT Press. pp. 97–118.

Ricke, L. C. (2009) 'A New Opportunity for Democratic Engagement: The CNN-YouTube Presidential Candidate Debates', paper presented at the Youtube and the 2008 Election Cycle in the United States conference, Amherst. MA. http://youtubeandthe2008election.jitp2.net/ paperhome/lricke (accessed 23 October 2009).

Robertson, S. P., Vatrapu, R. K. and Medina, R. (2009a) 'The Social Life of Social Networks: Facebook Linkage Patterns in the 2008 US Presidential Election', in *Proceedings of the 10th Annual International Conference on Digital Government Research: Social Networks: Making Connections between Citizens, Data and Government.* pp. 6–15.

Robertson, S. P., Vatrapu, R. K. and Medina, R. (2009b) 'YouTube and Facebook: Online Video 'Friends' Social Networking', paper presented at the Youtube and the 2008 Election Cycle in the United States conference. Amherst, MA. http://youtubeandthe2008election.jitp2.net/ paperhome/scottrob (accessed 23 October 2009).

Schudson, M. (1998) *The Good Citizen: A History of American Civic Life.* New York: Free Press.

Sifry, M. L. (2007) 'The Battle to Control Obama's Myspace', *techPresident* 1 May, http://techpresident.com/blog-entry/ battle-control-obamas-myspace (accessed 29 October 2009).

Skocpol, T. and Fiorina, M. P. (eds.) (1999) *Civic Engagement in American Democracy.* Washington, DC: Brookings Institute Press.

Smith, A. (2009) 'The Internet's Role in Campaign 2008', http://www.civicsurvey.org/White_paper_link_text.pdf (accessed 2 November 2009).

Smith, A. and Rainie, L. (2008) 'The Internet and the 2008 election', http://www.pewinternet.org/Reports/2008/ The-internet-and-the-2008-Election.aspx (accessed 5 April 2009).

Smith, A., Schlozman, K. L., Verba, S. and Brady, H. (2009) 'The Internet and Civic Engagement', http://www.pewinternet.org/Reports/2009/15–The-internet-and-Civic-Engagement.aspx (accessed 10 October 2009).

Stromer-Galley, J. (2000) 'On-line Interaction and Why Candidates Avoid it', *Journal of Communication,* 50(4): 1111–32.

Sunstein, C. (2001) *Republic.com.* Princeton, NJ: Princeton University Press.

Syvertsen, A. K., Flanagan, C. A. and Stout, M. D. (2007) 'Best Practices in Civic Education: Changes in Students' Civic Outcomes', *CIRCLE Working Papers.* Center for Information and Research on Civic Learning and Engagement (CIRCLE), http://www.eric.ed.gov/ERICWebPortal/content-delivery/servlet/ERICServlet?accno=ED498893 (accessed 1 November 2009).

techPresident (2008) Archived Data, http://techpresident.com/ scrape_plot/archives (accessed 23 October 2009).

Tedesco, J. C. (2007) 'Examining Internet Interactivity Effects on Young Adult Political Information Efficacy', *American Behavioral Scientist,* 50(9): 1183–94.

Tewksbury, D. (2003) 'What do Americans Really Want to Know? Tracking the Behavior of News Readers on the Internet', *Journal of Communication,* 53(4): 694–710.

Tewksbury, D. (2005) 'The Seeds of Audience Fragmentation: Specialization in the Use of Online News Sites', *Journal of Broadcast and Electronic Media,* 49(3): 332–48.

Tewksbury, D., Weaver, A. J. and Maddex, B. D. (2001) 'Accidentally Informed: Incidental News Exposure on the World Wide Web', *Journalism and Mass Communication Quarterly,* 78(3): 533–54.

Thorson, E. (2008) 'Changing Patterns of News Consumption and Participation: News Recommendation Engines', *Information, Communication and Society,* 11(4): 473–89.

Utz, S. (2009) 'The (Potential) Benefits of Campaigning via Social Network Sites', *Journal of Computer-Mediated Communication,* 14(2): 221–43.

Verba, S., Schlozman, K. L. and Brady, H. E. (1995) *Voice and Equality: Civic Voluntarism in American Politics.* Cambridge, MA: Harvard University Press.

Vromen, A. (2007) 'Australian Young People's Participatory Practices and Internet Use', *Information, Communication and Society,* 10(1): 48–68.

Wall, M. (2005) '"Blogs of War": Weblogs as News', *Journalism: Theory, Practice and Criticism,* 6(2): 153–72.

Wallsten, K. (2009). '"Yes We Can": How Online Viewership, Blog Discussion, Campaign Statements and Mainstream Media Coverage Produced a Viral Video Phenomenon', paper presented at the Youtube and the 2008 Election Cycle in the United States conference. Amherst, MA. http://youtubeandthe2008election.jitp2.net/paperhome/kwallsten (accessed 23 October 2009).

Warnick, B., Xenos, M., Endres, D. and Gastil, J. (2005) 'Effects of Campaign-to-User and Text-Based Interactivity in Political Candidate Campaign Web Sites', *Journal of Computer-Mediated Communication*, 10(3), http://apps.isiknowledge.com.offcampus.lib.washington.edu/full_record.do?product=WOS&colname=WOS&search_mode=RelatedRecords&qid=6&SID=4Bk39H7aDe4kBFeb2eC&page=1&doc=1&cacheurlFromRightClick=no (accessed 1 November 2009).

Williams, C. and Gulati, J. (2009) 'Congressional use of YouTube in 2008: Its Frequency and Rationale', paper presented at the Youtube and the 2008 Election Cycle in the United States conference. Amherst, MA. http://youtubeandthe2008election.jitp2.net/paperhome/cwilliams

Wojcieszak, M. E. and Mutz, D. C. (2009) 'Online Groups and Political Discourse: Do Online Discussion Spaces Facilitate Exposure to Political Disagreement?', *Journal of Communication*, 59(1): 40–56.

Xenos, M. and Foot, K. A. (2008) 'Not Your Father's Internet: The Generation Gap in Online Politics', in W. L. Bennett (ed.), *Civic Life Online: Learning How Digital Media Can Engage Youth*. Cambridge, MA: MIT Press. pp. 51–70.

Young, D. G. and Tisinger, R. M. (2006) 'Dispelling Late-Night Myths: News Consumption Among Late-Night Comedy Viewers and the Predictors of Exposure to Various Late-Night Shows', *Harvard International Journal of Press/Politics*, 11(3): 113–34.

Zackheim, B. (2005) 'World of Warcraft Causes Riots in the Streets', 1 February, http://www.joystiq.com/2005/02/01/world-of-warcraft-causes-riots-in-the-streets/ (accessed 2 November 2009).

Zaller, J. (1992) *The Nature and Origins of Mass Opinion*. Cambridge: Cambridge University Press.

Zukin, C., Keeter, S., Andolina, M., Jenkins, K. and Delli Carpini, M. X. (2006) *A New Engagement? Political Participation, Civic Life, and the Changing American Citizen*. New York: Oxford University Press.

de Zúñiga. H., Veenstra, A., Vraga, E., Wang, M., DeShano, C., Perlmutter, D. and Shah, D. (2007) 'Online and Offline Activism: Communication Mediation and Political Messaging Among Blog Readers', paper presented at the annual convention of the Association for Education in Journalism and Mass Communication. Washington, DC, 9–12 August.

11

The Internet and Citizenship: Democratic Opportunity or More of the Same?

Stephen Coleman and Jay G. Blumler

Democracy, at its best, should be noisy: brimming with pluralistic sources of information competing to tell their stories; with parties, campaigns and advocates filling the public sphere with their calls for attention; with diverse values and preferences exposed to public reason in an inclusive sphere of deliberative debate; and with a new generation of future citizens setting out their stalls and practising new ways of making a difference.

Democracy as it is now, at least in the USA and the UK, is certainly noisy. Too much of it is a shrill, raucous, cacophonous babble that fills the air, and increasingly the airwaves. It is noise that dissipates into the frustrating vacuity of the angry headline, the denunciating mob and the resignation of cynical apathy. Consider the US healthcare reform 'debate' in which, according to Jim Fishkin (2009: WK9) writing in *The New York Times*, 'lawmakers are finding their town hall meetings disrupted by hecklers, many echoing anti-healthcare reform messages from talk radio and cable television'. Paul Krugman's (2009) account of 'recent town halls, where angry protesters – some of them, with no apparent sense of irony, shouting 'This is America!' – have been drowning out, and in some cases threatening, members of Congress trying to talk about health reform' paints a picture of democracy as an eerie echo chamber filled with noise, but little sense.

Consider also the UK media's response to the MPs' expenses scandal that rocked British politics in 2009: Peter Oborne (2009: 15), writing in the *Daily Mail* told his readers that 'Nobody can say any longer that our politicians are motivated by honesty, duty or patriotism. Almost to a man and woman they have been exposed as cheats and crooks whose primary motivation is lining their own pockets rather than serving Britain'; while a record 3.8 million viewers tuned in for the BBC *Question Time* programme (14 May 2009) in which politicians were jeered at by a studio audience who referred to them as being no different from benefits cheats, 'mealy mouthed' and 'all the same'. In both of these situations, basic norms of democracy, requiring an informed, balanced, meaningful and consequential consideration of an important public issue, were recklessly ignored. The prospect of calm civic reflection was abandoned in favour of a carnival of unrestrained virulence.

All of this has had troubling consequences for the practice of citizenship. First, when all politics is made to seem either fraudulent or futile, the most likely public response is to disengage. There is a clear relationship between falling voter turnout in most countries and a generalized sense of political inefficacy. Second, even when citizens do feel motivated to engage with public affairs, there is a growing gap between the long-term character of socio-political problems and the short-term pressures that tend to dominate the political agenda. This leads too often to a public discourse framed by the pragmatic priorities of immediacy, with both politicians and journalists strategizing in ways that ignore durable consequences. Third, as the political communication system has come to be characterized by intensified competition for public attention, media messages have tended to become increasingly consumed by sensationalism (in the case of mainstream, offline journalism) and extremism (in the case of online blogging and debate). None of this looks good for the prospects of a public sphere in which the exercise of public reason nurtures a democracy of agonistic civility.

But perhaps that is not the point of citizenship. Maybe neither democracy, as a system of self-government, nor the media, as vehicles for the circulation of ideas, need any longer pay lip service to the civic norms that we are lamenting. In this chapter, we begin by addressing the contestability of the terms of democratic citizenship and then proceed to ask whether digital media offer opportunities for the cultivation of new and appealing forms of democratic space. We conclude by setting out a policy for a more deliberative democracy and seek to show how this would benefit governments, the media and citizens.

THE CONTESTED TERMS OF CITIZENSHIP

We propose to outline four conceptions of citizenship, which, although not mutually exclusive, each set out different priorities for politicians, journalists and citizens.

A first of these – the self-styled realistic model – tends to place minimal responsibilities upon citizens, believing them to be too busy and insufficiently attentive to be able to do more than observe political affairs from a distance and vote occasionally for whichever leader or party seems to be most worthy of their support. As Schumpeter (1976) put it, 'Democracy means only that the people have the opportunity of accepting or refusing the men who are to rule them'. In removing the demos from its classical role as occupants of a permanently influential public domain, these theorists have emphasized a more relaxed, monitorial function for the citizenry. As Schudson (2000: 3) has put it, monitorial citizens should be informed enough and alert enough to identify danger to their personal good and danger to the public good. When such danger appears on the horizon, they should have the resources – in trusted relationships, in political

parties and elected officials, in relationships to interest groups and other trustees of their concerns, in knowledge of and access to the courts as well as the electoral system, and in relevant information sources to jump into the political fray and make a lot of noise.

The role of the media, therefore, is to serve as sophisticated fire alarms, with journalists ever-ready to alert citizens to personal and public dangers and point them towards trustworthy institutions capable of addressing their concerns. The role of politicians in this model of citizenship is to be responsive to the surveillant anxieties of those they represent. As a conception of citizenship-lite, this has the virtue of not raising expectations about anyone's contribution to democracy; it seems to assume that democratic norms can be realized while most of us are busy doing something else.

But there are three problems that Schudson's model does not address. First, it renders citizens' monitorial awareness predominantly dependent upon the issues and problems that are defined by the media's news values, with all the biases, distortions and selectivity involved therein. Second, monitorial citizenship is based upon an assumption that public institutions are working well. Citizens are to go to them if they feel in danger, but what if these institutions – parties, legislatures, courts, the electoral system – are themselves part of the danger? What, in other words, if the grounds of public disquiet are the failings of representative bodies to represent public interests, preferences and values and of judicial bodies to behave in accordance with public judgments of fairness? (Lack of public confidence in the British Parliament's capacity to put its own house in order is a case in point.) Monitorial citizenship could operate effectively in situations where danger is singular or accidental, but what about if it is structural or endemic? Third, the only part of Schudson's remedy that goes beyond an appeal to institutions refers to the possibility of jumping into the political fray and making a lot of noise. But that begs the questions: What sort of noise? With what expectation of consequences? And, anyway, who can shout loudest and make their noise heard? If, as we have suggested, much current political noise recedes into redundancy, what sort of citizenship would it cultivate, leading to a 'spiral of noisiness' and ever more audacious ways of getting heard? And what would stop monitorial citizens from deciding on the next occasion that jumping into the noisy fray would be a waste of their time?

A second conception of citizenship is rooted in metaphors of the marketplace. The individual citizen, it is said, is a free agent, out to maximize personal gain. Libertarian theorists (Berger and

Neuhaus, 1977; Saunders, 1993) paint this as a precondition of liberty; rational choice theorists (Aldrich, 1993; Mueller, 2003) are less sanguine, arguing that citizens are simply trapped within the systemic logic of a collective action dilemma that dooms them to seek low information costs and opportunities to freeload on the civic energies of others. The role of the media here is a utilitarian one: provide citizens with what they need to get what they want and abandon all claims to be promoting social harmony, civility or progress. For politicians, the task is to understand and accept the rules of the game; as in business, the shrewdest player will go furthest. Democracy is thereby played out in a sort of marketplace of ideas in which a combination of acute strategy and broad appeal raises some interests to the top of the political agenda, while dismissing others to the margins. A fundamental problem with this model is that relegation to the periphery tends to face the same groups over and over again: those who are poorest, weakest, least educated, confident and organized tend not to have the resources available to make their mark as marketized citizens. Lacking the means of making an impact upon the mass-media debate, the marginalized are most likely to resort to disengaged sullenness or repertoires of action that circumvent the hegemonic agenda. Faced with an issue such as the US healthcare debate, the outcome of which will in all probability affect them more than anyone else, marginalized citizens are less likely to be the noisy people exchanging banal slogans at public meetings, than those who are spoken about and for by others, as if they were civically disenfranchised. A crucial weakness of this model is that it is at odds with the inescapably collective character of the main challenges faced by most democracies today.

The limitations of the above two models from the perspective of normative democratic theory have given rise to a third conception of citizenship which emphasizes the value of participatory practices. Since the 1960s, an acknowledgement on the part of governments and policy experts that they cannot be expected to know everything, especially in relation to the life of communities, has prompted a range of initiatives designed to promote active citizenship. From public consultations, neighbourhood councils and citizens' juries to organized volunteering on local projects and attempts to bring civil-society organizations into the policy process, the ideal of participatory democracy has been regarded as the only alternative to political alienation. This has called for new civic skills, taught in schools through the citizenship/civics curriculum and increasingly been promoted by national and local policies intended to 'engage the disengaged'. The media have played a major part in all of this, opening themselves up to public interaction through call-ins, studio discussions, outreach events, phone-votes and emails from audience members. Indeed, the urge to create an 'interactive' relationship with audiences, decades prior to the rise of online media, signalled a change in the mission of journalism from one of addressing to one of conversing (Coleman and Ross, 2010). Politicians have been deeply affected by these more open communicative relationships, which have rendered them more visible, reachable and vulnerable than ever before. The rhetoric of media participation is replete with democratic claims, sometimes justifiable insofar as media interactivity does open up politics to citizens and citizens to one another. However, there are serious limitations. A populist vein runs through many of these participatory exercises, casting the media as ever-mobile ring-leaders, ready to stoke up emotions around the latest reason for public anger. Used in such formats, active citizens can be reduced to one-line, vox pop caricatures, thrown into situations in which the image of the brawling mob displaces public discussion and left feeling more excluded from meaningful debate than if they had been totally ignored. And moments of collective action can be reduced to a 'hit and run' character: occurring almost by chance and passing fleetingly. Furthermore, even when, as sometimes happens, media attempts to involve the public do lead to new ideas, revealed experiences and a sense that something needs to be done, there is a lack of any formal connection to institutions that can follow them up. Citizens experience the frustration of seeming to be talking to themselves and often give up, leaving the field even clearer for ranters who are not particularly bothered about constructive outcomes. All of this has led to a tragic paradox: there exist more opportunities than ever before for citizens wishing to have their say, via the media or to local or national government, but there is a more pervasive sense of disappointment than ever before that citizens are outside the citadels of power and that those within do not know how to listen to them.

The failings of participatory democracy in its populist form have given rise to a renewed interest in the democratic norm of deliberation. The idea of nurturing informed, thoughtful citizens, whose exposure to one another's experiences and arguments might equip them to perform a role as intelligent participants in their own governance, goes beyond the traditional boundaries of liberal democracy, positing the idea of democracy as a forum in which issues and policy proposals are debated and discussed on their merits rather than a game in which the attainment and retention of power is the principal goal (Calhoun, 1999; Dahlgren, 2005; Habermas, 1989). In some versions, this view appears decidedly utopian, out of reach for real-world people, media and politicians, liable therefore to confinement in academic treatises or elaborate experiments. In other words, deliberative democrats' lofty insistence upon the force of the strongest argument always having to prevail under procedurally rationalist conditions, is probably too demanding to become a cornerstone of feasible politics.

A *more* deliberative democracy, however, is not an unattainable ideal. Pragmatically framed policies to make the media a more discursive space, representative institutions more open to public input and dialogue, and citizenship more efficacious in its direct linkage to policy formation and decision-making are likely to be the most effective antidotes to the democratic din we began by discussing. But the more one rehearses the terms of this more deliberative, multi-perspectival, efficacious conception of citizenship, the more clearly its absence becomes apparent. With very few exceptions, the mass media, which are so good at delivering entertainment and basic information, seem to have given up any practical hope of serving as a critically discursive forum. In frustration, a number of political communication scholars have turned to the rise of the Internet as a promising space for enlightened civic discourse.

THE VULNERABLE POTENTIAL OF THE INTERNET

The widespread perception that in politics these days, the Internet seems on a roll, while citizenship is on a slide leads us to ask whether the former could be harnessed to reverse the latter and, if so, how. We do so by first, considering the potential and limitations of the Internet as a democratic space; then, exploring these characteristics in the context of online initiatives that have embodied the priorities of the four conceptions of citizenship outlined above and finally, reflecting on how the Internet might help to engender a more deliberative democracy: one in which politicians, the media and citizens could all be released from the systemic defects of the current political communication system.

We begin by exploring the democratic potential of the Internet, which we describe as *vulnerable potential* because it will only be realized through imaginative policy interventions designed to shape and nurture its democratic affordances. Six features of online communication are suggestive of this democratic potential.

First, unlike broadcasting, which has provoked long-running debates about how far, when and over what programmes its audiences may be regarded as active or passive (Ang, 1991; Katz, 1996; Livingstone, 1998, 2004, 2005; Wood, 2007), the Internet is unquestionably a medium of predominantly active users. Typically, one decides which web site to visit and then, through a sequence of follow-up decisions, one may click on other pages or pursue other links of interest, ponder the material received and possibly even talk about it with others. Admittedly, the extent and depth of such activity should not be exaggerated or idealized. Empirical studies of web site usage report far more exposure to main than subsequent pages (Dutton et al., 1999). But if the Internet tends to encourage a more active disposition to communications than the mainstream media, then some of this should transfer over to people's reception through it of news, public affairs and politics (Coleman et al., 2008; Thurman, 2008).

Second, the Internet's discursive role diverges from that of older media, insofar as it is possible to involve large numbers of users themselves in a more full expression and exchange of experiences and opinions on a given topic. It can be a medium for engaging more widely in, and not just presenting and following, civic dialogue. Whereas broadcasting works within tight time limits and essentially *shows* its audiences *other* people discussing political issues, over the Internet content receivers can easily become content producers (Coleman and Ross, 2010; Deuze, 2006; Hermida and Thurman, 2008).

Third, by making it easier for individuals to find and follow what concerns them personally, and by lowering the cost of obtaining information, the influence of social status on political involvement is reduced. Citizens and groups with few resources can undertake acts of communication and monitoring that previously were the domain mainly of resource-rich organizations and individuals who were most likely to be sufficiently motivated to participate (Bimber, 2000). The online parliamentary consultations conducted in the UK, involving groups such as survivors of domestic violence, flood victims and targets of hate speech, have shown how new voices can be brought into the policy debate (Coleman, 2004; Moe, 2008).

Fourth, online communication allows people to overcome some of the most traditionally intractable coordination problems standing in the way of collective action. Citizens can discuss ideas, experiences and strategies with one another over a period of hours, days, weeks or months in an asynchronous fashion. This allows time for reflective debate and space to develop evidence and argumentation. Compare this with a three-hour meeting or a two-day consultation conference, in which each witness is allocated a limited slot in which to have his or her say. Participation can be open to all, regardless of geographical spread. Thus, communities of interest and passion can form locally, regionally, nationally and globally, with citizens able to make connections that would probably not have happened otherwise (Bruns, 2006; Cleaver, 1998; Downing, 2003; Goggin and Newell, 2003; Graham and Khosravi, 2002; Haas, 2005; Kahn and Kellner, 2004; Kalathil and Boas, 2006; Pickard, 2006; Semetko and Krasnoboka, 2003; Skelton and Valentine, 2003; Soon and Kluver, 2007; Tarrow, 2005; Wheeler, 2005; Zittrain et al., 2003).

Fifth, while online civic engagement often starts out by being narrowly focused on a local issue, it tends often to develop into a broader network, involving both online and offline connections between a range of people who would not have otherwise met and discovered what they shared (Bennett et al., 2008; Fenton, 2008).

Sixth, citizens who engage in online discussions can encounter new ideas and sources of information and new ways of thinking about issues (Barabas, 2004; Iyengar et al., 2005; Janssen and Kies, 2005; Min, 2007; Monnoyer-Smith, 2006; Price and Cappella, 2002; Shane, 2004), although the extent to which this takes place at present remains an empirical question.

Thus far, however, there is a broad academic consensus that the Internet's civic potential has been greater than its use. Six main barriers to the realization of democratic ends can be identified.

First, experimentation thus far has been fragmented, small-scale and of disparate value. Examples of successful practice are still limited to relatively small numbers within a few countries. No structure exists to facilitate learning and exchange across the different efforts; to maintain continuity of activity; to identify and institutionalize best practice and to create a more substantial and valued space for civic deliberation.

Second, much online discourse is characterized by a tilt away from informed argument and extended rationalism. While diverse forms and styles of online communication are an attractive reflection of new opportunities for people to speak not only for, but as themselves, unless narratives of personal experience and expressions of affective sensibility are somehow harnessed to strategies of policy formation and decision making, they risk becoming marginalized. There is a real danger that online forums become a new version of the echo-chamber, phone-in show, easily derided and ignored by elites.

Third, much of what passes as political discussion online reflects a failure to appreciate that policy problems almost always involve trade-offs. The Internet is good for letting people say what

they would like to see happen and what they do not like, but has thus far developed few constructive mechanisms for helping people to determine effective solutions in the face of scarce resources. For example, e-petitions, in which citizens can call for government to fund particular projects or advance new laws are all very well as ways of promoting grassroots agendas, but useless as a means of deciding who gets what, when and how. Politics entails competitive decisions about the allocation of values. How can such decisions be made if each demand, protest or debate occupies its own cyber-silo, with no capacity to engage or compromise with other equally forceful demands? The consequence of this is the intensification of demand-driven politics and personal-interest-centred citizenship that is already a depressing feature of mainstream media debate.

Fourth, online communication offers political leaders the enticing prospect of 'disintermediation', that is, addressing target audiences without the critical intervention of the media. But most information (and all politically valuable information) is far from being raw and objective. The interpretive role of public-service media, as well as their professional role as non-partisan regulators of communication, is often needed to ensure that public discussion is not controlled by the very political elites (be they politicians, bureaucrats or well-resourced corporations), which produce much public information and may wish to influence the agenda for and direction of public debate. For online discussion to be democratic, it must be structured in a manifestly fair fashion (Wright and Street, 2007).

Fifth, representative government needs to hear from not only a large number of citizens, but from a range that reflects the broadest possible spectrum of social actors. The evidence so far has been that higher-status citizens are the most likely to participate in online debates, thereby reinforcing communicative inequalities, knowledge gaps and patterns of political exclusion (Bonfadelli, 2002; Boulianne, 2009; Jääskeläinen and Savolailen, 2003; Price et al., 2006; Prior, 2007).

Sixth, if the Internet is to play any serious role in the reinvigoration of democratic citizenship, those who engage in forms of online discussion need to be able to feel that there is a visibly consequential relationship between public inputs and political outcomes. Thus far, online communication has tended to be most energetic, productive and satisfying across horizontal lines of interaction. As a space of citizen-to-citizen, many-to-many networking, the Internet has certainly opened up new opportunities for collective sociability and discussion. However, vertical interactivity, between citizens and governments, parliaments, local councils or global bodies tends to be underdeveloped, blighted by institutional blockages or one-way streets. Where political institutions do interact with citizens online, such initiatives are usually top-down, with elites setting the rules, framing agendas, designing spaces that reflect their own terms of engagement and, above all, feeling free to ignore inconvenient public input. So, while on the horizontal level peer-to-peer practices have adapted creatively to the informal, acephalous, non-proprietorial, unbounded logic of the network, much vertical online communication seems to replicate the worst aspects of the established political communication system, with politicians running blogs that look like old-fashioned newsletters, parties producing YouTube content that looks like television election broadcasts, newspapers publishing the same old stories online and citizens as disheartened as ever by the serial failures of politicians to engage with them dialogically.

These tensions between manifest democratic affordances of the Internet and empirically observable limitations have led us to refer to the Internet as possessing a *vulnerable democratic potential* (Blumler and Coleman, 2001; Blumler and Gurevitch, 2002; Coleman and Blumler, 2009). A key determinant of this vulnerability is the contested definition of democratic citizenship. Given the normative differences between the four conceptions of citizenship we have outlined above, it is hardly surprising that under-theorized attempts to promote 'digital citizenship' or 'e-democracy' are likely to become trapped within whichever civic model they happen to have embraced. In the next section, we turn to the consequences of these divergent applications of e-citizenship.

FOUR MODELS OF E-CITIZENSHIP

Just as television producers must first imagine their audiences and then devise ways of addressing them, those initiating projects intended to allow Internet users to become better informed, more talkative and politically efficacious inevitably start out with a conception of citizenship in their own minds which informs both the design and the evaluation of their projects. Thus, framed by theoretical assumptions, online civic behaviour is configured and constrained. Following on from the typology set out above, we shall consider four illustrations of how conceptual foundations generate specific architectures and modes of e-citizenship.

The BBC's Democracy Live site (http://news. bbc.co.uk/democracylive/) sets out to bring together 'live and on-demand video coverage of proceedings in our national political institutions and the European Parliament'. BBC publicity for the site states that:

> By its very nature, the business of politics can be lengthy. Can you/would you watch an entire six-hour long debate from the House of Commons? Possibly. But you'd need to be a battle-hardened political observer or someone with a very keen interest in the subject to do so.
>
> Democracy Live gives you the ability to search for a specific word or words spoken in the proceedings and the results will give you links to the points in the video where they were spoken. The ability to home in on the passages which are of direct interest and relevance to you is at the heart of Democracy Live's purpose. (Coyle, 2009)

It is undoubtedly an ambitious project, allowing users to follow a particular elected representative, search for themes using word tags and access guides to how the UK's various representative institutions work. What is conspicuously missing here is an opportunity to interact with the content by making comments, challenging dubious or false information, submitting evidence to committees of inquiry or appealing to others (within a particular constituency or community, for instance) to take action. In short, the site is purely monitorial. It provides the kind of 'relevant information' source that Schudson thinks citizens need, but no way of 'jump[ing] into the political fray and mak[ing] a lot of noise' (2000: 16), as he says citizens ought to do when things go wrong. The site's implicit message about democratic citizenship – and, to some extent, about the BBC's online role within it – is that democracy is something to be witnessed and absorbed rather than enacted through co-production. Compared with the BBC's earlier i-can project (discussed in Coleman and Blumler, 2009), Democracy Live offers much more content, but far fewer opportunities for meaningful agency.

The aim for MySociety's Pledge Bank site (http://www.pledgebank.com/) is 'to help get people past the barrier of not wanting to act alone' (http://www.mysociety.org/moin.cgi/PledgeBank/ WhatItDoes). The site producers offer an example of how they expect Pledge Bank to contribute to more effective citizenship:

> Your child comes home from school with a small flyer given to them by their teacher. It reads: 'I will help organize the school summer fair, but ONLY IF 10 parents will help too. Go to www.pledgebank. com/school if you would like to make the same pledge I have.'
>
> When the parent types the address into their web browser, they are taken to a page where within 10 seconds they can put their name to the pledge.

What happens next depends on the parents. Imagine that 12 parents sign up. In this case all signatories are sent an email congratulating them, asking them to fulfill their pledge, and offering them a simple way of discussing the plan. And if fewer than 10 people sign up, everyone is emailed and told 'Better luck next time.'

At the time of writing, the (few) pledges on the site include 'I will refuse to fill out the 2011 UK census unless there is a Cornish ethnicity tick box, but only if 1,000 other people will do the same' (signed by 602 people), 'I will do all my shopping in Boscombe for the next 9 weeks, but only if 10 other people will join me' (signed by 16 people) and 'I will sign up to a council garden waste collection for about £50 a year, but only if 500 other local people will do the same' (signed by 20). Appealing to the lone citizen, in constant battle against freeriders and collective apathy – the banes of rational choice theory – Pledge Bank serves as a sort of civic stock exchange. But can citizenship be nurtured in the same way as profits from stocks and shares are realized? Is civic action really just a matter of investing in momentum? If it is, then Pledge Bank does not appear to be an ideal tool for generating it: few of the existing pledges are close to reaching their intended quotas; if this were the stock exchange, world markets would cease to trade. But we would argue that the Pledge Bank model of *homo economicus,* acting as a sovereign artificer and hoping to overcome the seemingly intractable problems of collective rationality, appeals to an etiolated notion of democratic citizenship in which each individual must re-invent collective action each time they are confronted by a social problem. Going back to the example of the school summer fair, one wonders why the school itself is not organizing this or why there is not a parent–teacher association that can take on this responsibility or whether the 'Better luck next time' message is the most appropriate response to parents who cannot find the time or money to provide a summer treat for their children. In short, this model of e-citizenship appears to ignore social structure and resource inequalities. The real market, in which some are able to purchase outcomes while others, however needy or industrious, find it materially impossible to make the differences they want to achieve by voluntarism alone, undermines its marketplace model for the allocation of civic energies.

Examples of populist e-participation abound. As a site for virtual rallies in which the megaphone sloganizing of the past is replaced by the concerted circulation of clichés, prejudices and dogma, the Internet can sometimes appear to be a vast collection of soapboxes from which the many are free to shout, while few choose to listen.

Democratic politics is about more than position-taking; its function is to arrive at legitimate, fair and consequential resolutions. In the UK, the Number 10 e-petitions site (http://petitions.number10.gov.uk/), established in November 2006, attracted around 6 million email signatures to approximately 30,000 petitions. These ranged from an e-petition calling upon the prime minister to scrap road pricing, which attracted over a million signatures, and another calling for a 'mega-mosque' not to be built in East London (even though there had been no planning permission sought for such a building), which attracted over one-quarter of a million signatures, to a vast number of less popular petitions that have amounted to little more than online graffiti. Half of all submitted e-petitions were rejected by the prime minister's office on the grounds that they were offensive or that they duplicated existing petitions. The only option available to the public in this mode of e-participation is to submit or sign a petition. There is no space for proposals to be debated or amended. The force of numbers rather than argument prevails. For most e-petitioners, the efficacy of their action was extremely limited: they received a duplicated email from 10 Downing Street telling them what the government was planning to do, usually regardless of their advice.

Despite criticisms of the Number 10 e-petitions as being largely symbolic and populist, the British government elected in 2010 introduced an expanded system, whereby e-petitions receiving over 100,000 signatures are eligible for debate in Parliament. Without the public being invited to deliberate on such changes to legislation, however, this has the ring of a populist gimmick, reinforcing the cacophonous image of online political expression.

Spaces of online public deliberation are far less common or high-profile. They are often experimental and short-lived or under-resourced and therefore under-publicized. Nonetheless, Dahlberg offers the optimistic observation that:

> many spaces of discourse exist online that may be seen as extending the public sphere. Besides the many insular virtual communities and individualistic political websites, there are numerous forums of informal public interaction on Usenet groups, e-mail lists, web boards and chat groups where participants enter into rational–critical debate. (2001: 620)

Dahlberg's best example of such a space is Minnesota E-Democracy's Mn-Politics Discuss site, which is 'an online forum where political claims relating to the concerns of those living in Minnesota are put forward with reasons and critically assessed by others' (2001: 625). Indeed, the apparent success of this initiative led the UK government to fund a number of experimental local online forums based upon the Minnesota model. Aiming 'to provide a vibrant online space where citizens, elected officials and community leaders – with diverse ideas and backgrounds – can discuss the important local issues … in a civil and respectful manner' (E-Democracy.Org, 2008), it is clear from a cursory look at the UK Local Issue Forums, based in Brighton and Hove (http://forums.e-democracy.org/groups/bh/messages/topics.html?start=20&end=40) and Newham (http://forums.e-democracy.org/groups/newham-issues/messages/topics.html) that they are being used by very few people; that elected officials are not participating and that several of the comments constitute partisan position-taking rather than deliberative debate. In the Brighton and Hove forum, the most popular discussion thread in recent months has attracted 16 comments from 8 people and in the Newham forum 21 comments from 4 people. This is not to disparage the efforts that have been made to structure and promote these initiatives, but to acknowledge that, even these relatively well organized and publicized online spaces, have failed to convince citizens and elected representatives 'with diverse ideas and backgrounds' that this kind of civic engagement is worthwhile. A key reason for this is their disconnection from the constitutional processes of government. Like the Number 10 e-petitions, which invite mass expression without explaining *how* inputs will feed into the policy process, the Local Issues Forums encourage a rather more structured form of public debate, but set no criteria for its effectiveness. Political efficacy is a key driver of civic engagement, both offline and online – and repeated experience of inconsequential discussion is bound to militate against further participation, at least for most people (Coleman et al., 2008; Finkel, 1985; Theiss-Morse and Hibbing, 2005; Verba et al., 1987).

To summarize these examples, we have suggested that each is based upon a particular conception of citizenship and its limits. The BBC's Democracy Live provides a wealth of information that citizens need, but then leaves 'the monitorial citizen' stranded, without any means of engaging in a dialogue with his or her representative. MySociety's Pledge Bank appeals to the lone citizen, seeking to overcome rational-choice challenges, but seems to reflect a notion of democratic citizenship that ignores structures of solidarity and the politics of inequality. The Number 10 e-petitions offer citizens a direct path to the machinery of the state, but the project fails to re-engineer the political machine so that it might somehow utilize this input. The Local Issues Forums provide a space for public deliberation

of locally relevant issues, but seems not to be able to take the conversation beyond this space, thereby undermining political efficacy. One might argue that by having all of these different models of e-citizenship, there is scope for them to serve collectively the many dimensions of democratic citizenship. But this is not the case, for none of these online spaces meet a most important criterion of democratic effectiveness: the capacity to make a difference through the public expression and debate of arguments. For all of their separate strengths and energies, these examples lead us to conclude that, despite its vulnerable potential as a democratic space, the Internet still has much to accomplish if it is to contribute in any meaningful way to the reinvigoration of citizenship. How might that happen?

A POLICY FOR A MORE DELIBERATIVE DEMOCRACY

Creating a more deliberative democracy entails harnessing the diverse range of ways that public experience can be brought to bear on decision making at every level: local, regional, national and transnational. It entails actively bringing citizens in to the processes of policy formation and decision making with a view to learning from their experience and expertise. It entails encouraging story-telling as well as position-stating, debate as well as agenda-setting, the voices of the confident as well as the encouraged contributions of those accustomed to being unheard. In short, it entails a radical commitment to a more participative, discursive and evidence-based approach to governing.

There is very little likelihood of this happening through piecemeal experimentation of the kind that we have described above. It calls for a bold imaginative act of public policy designed to move away from a political communication system in which citizens are suspicious spectators, journalists periodically cry 'Gotcha!' and politicians strive to craft catchy messages that will appeal to editors, reporters and hopefully voters. And towards a democracy that is more mutually interactive; that promotes more authentic conversation between representatives and represented; that creates room for substantive public deliberation that can help to shape and evaluate policy: an online civic commons. Establishing a trusted public space in which the dispersed energies, self-articulations and aspirations of citizens can be rehearsed in public within a process of ongoing feedback to the various levels and centres of governance will depend upon three elements of policy being in place: the creation of a trusted aegis; the generation of efficient pathways, both vertical and horizontal, through which messages can circulate and a plan to ensure that public inputs are not dismissed or distorted as policy outputs are produced.

Aegis

Neither governments nor commercial bodies can be relied upon to run an online civic commons. They have too many interests at stake. Neither incorporated within existing constellations of power nor detached from them, the power of an online civic commons would inhere in its invulnerability to the claims and tactics of vested interests seeking to buy out, shut up, drown out or override the voices of the public. An independent public agency, designed to forge fresh links between communication and politics and to connect the voice of the people more meaningfully to the daily activities of democratic institutions would need to be set up. It would be publicly funded, but would have to be entirely independent from government. Its task would be to elicit, gather and coordinate citizens' deliberations upon and reactions to problems faced and proposals issued by public bodies (ranging from local councils to parliaments and government departments), which would then be expected to react formally to whatever emerges from the public discussion.

Unlike the standalone projects considered above, an online civic commons would work most effectively by helping diverse social networks to be fully open and accountable to one another. In connecting local experience, habits, knowledge and common sense to official structures of political representation, while responding sensitively to asymmetries of social power between and within networks, a civic commons could contribute towards the realization of the most challenging aspect of citizenship: the creation of 'a space of appearance' (Arendt, 1958: 198) in which strangers are brought together as mutually dependent members of a public.

Pathways

Castells (1989:146) refers to the Internet as 'a space of flows'. An online civic commons might be regarded as a space of political flows, providing structured pathways for the circulation of messages vertically – from citizens to representatives and vice versa – and horizontally – from citizens to citizens. Unlike the random pathways of social media, the policy intention here would be to ensure that all paths lead at some point to spaces of shared discourse. While such structured discourse should not aspire to satisfy all of the lofty norms set by the philosophical advocates of deliberative democracy, great effort should be made to ensure that debates are well-informed; unpopular arguments and marginalized voices are not excluded; standards of civility are upheld; all voices, regardless of education or background, are given an equal opportunity to set agendas and influence policy; power-holders are prompted to engage fully and patterns of debate are made as transparent and meaningful as possible. The latter might be achieved through techniques of argument visualization, which could help to reduce data to intelligible proportions (Atkinson et al., 2006; Donath, 2002; Mancini and Buckingham-Shum, 2006; Renton and Macintosh, 2007; Sack, 2000).

Outputs

The key failing of much e-citizenship so far, as exemplified by the projects considered above, has been an absence of outcomes. Too often citizens are invited to 'have their say', only to discover that the expressive act was the beginning and the end of their political role. Apart from people who like debating for the sake of it, few of us are likely to continue for long giving input to a process that is wholly disconnected from outcomes. If an online civic commons is to provide a space for revitalized citizenship, it has to be constitutionally connected in ways that clearly demonstrate how civic input is being evaluated, refuted (where necessary) and acted upon (where appropriate). From the outset, the terms of civic engagement need to be elucidated. In a representative democracy, citizens elect politicians to make decisions. A civic commons would not work if the public expected to displace their elected representatives; neither would it work if politicians or unelected officials treated public input dismissively, disdainfully or cynically. This is why the terms of citizenship are more important to the potential for online democracy than the modes of technology that are adopted. Only if the vulnerable potential of the Internet to create a more interactive, inclusive and networked public debate is coupled with a conception of citizenship that embraces the consequential political effects of these affordances can a relationship between new, digital media and the reinvigoration of citizenship be reasonably predicted.

CONCLUSION

Critics of the position we have set out might argue that it is overly idealistic about ordinary people's readiness for involvement in public affairs. But dismissal out of hand of people's appetite for such engagement is surely a recipe for manipulation by political leaders, on the one hand, and trivialization of the political agenda by journalists, on the other. The public response to this trend (already well underway) would be further disengagement from the traditional political sphere and mass migration to communicative spaces in which its own ideas and beliefs are taken seriously – as it were, horizontally, but not yet vertically. Such a chasm between mass public discourse and institutional representation can only lead to a steady corrosion of the democratic contract.

In fact, the political communication system stands to gain at all points from the expansion of online democratic space. Politicians and governments could establish more direct relationships with citizens. Journalists could enter into an expanded political sphere, beyond the controlled zones of press releases, staged events and nebulous rumour. And citizens, freed from their current dependence upon headlines and soundbites, can experience what happens when their views and values are exposed to public reason and have to make sense within the complexity of real-world governance.

If the kind of agency we are proposing were to be created, it would need to become a champion for citizenship, something that our political system has hitherto lacked. It couldn't be (mustn't be) preachy. It couldn't be (mustn't be) pushy. If it is to stand any chance of success, it must embrace fully the open-ended networks, the porous thematic boundaries and the versatile playfulness that characterize Web 2.0. While a civic commons agency would not need to invent public talk or civic energy, one of its principal roles would be to nurture forms and habits of active citizenship by experimenting with new ways of expressing, hearing and learning from public voice.

There has been a recent upsurge in normative thinking among scholars about political communication and citizenship (Bennett, 2007; Corner and Pels, 2006; Couldry and Langer, 2005; van Zoonen, 2004), but so far it does not seem to have had a policy pay-off. Our proposal for an online civic commons constitutes an attempt to create clear linkage between norms and policy. In taking up the challenge of reinvigorating public discussion it would at least stand a chance of unleashing and fruitfully realizing those better civic selves that are so heavily suppressed in how we have been 'doing' political communication in recent years.

REFERENCES

Aldrich, J. (1993) 'Rational choice and Turnout', *American Journal of Political Science*, 37(1): 246–78.

Ang, I. (1991) *Desperately Seeking the Audience*. London: Routledge.

Arendt, H. (1958) *The Human Condition*. New York: Rowman & Littlefield.

Atkinson, K., Bench-Capon, T. and Modgil, S. (2006) 'Argumentation for Decision Support', *Lecture Notes in Computer Science*, 4080: 822–31.

Barabas (2004) 'Virtual Deliberation: Knowledge From Online Interaction Versus Ordinary Discussion', in P. Shane (ed.), *Democracy Online: The Prospects for Political Renewal Through the Internet*. New York: Routledge. pp. 239–52.

Bennett, W. L., Breunig, C. and Givens, T. (2008) 'Communication and Political Mobilization: Digital Media and the Organization of Anti-War Demonstrations in the US', *Political Communication*, 25(3): 269–89.

Bennett, W. L. (2007) 'Civic Life Online: Learning How Digital Media Can Engage Youth', in W. L Bennett (ed.), *Changing Citizenship in the Digital Age*. Cambridge, MA: MIT Press. pp. 1–24.

Berger, P. L. and Neuhaus, R. J. (1977). *To Empower People: The Role of Mediating Structures in Public Policy*. Washington, DC: American Enterprise Institute for Public Policy Research.

Bimber, B. (2000) 'The Study of Information Technology and Civic Engagement', *Political Communication*, 17(4): 329–33.

Blumler, J. G. and Coleman, S. (2001) *Realizing Democracy Online: A Civic Commons in Cyberspace*. London: Institute of Public Policy Research.

Blumler, J. G. and Gurevitch, M. (2002) 'The New Media and Our Political Communication Discontents: Democratizing Cyberspace', *Information, Communication & Society*, 4(1): 1–13.

Bonfadelli, H. (2002) 'The Internet and Knowledge Gaps: A Theoretical and Empirical Investigation', *European Journal of Communication*, 17(1): 65–84.

Boulianne, S. (2009) 'Does Internet Use Affect Engagement? A Meta-Analysis of Research', *Political Communication*, 26(2): 193–211.

Bruns, A. (2006) *Gatewatching: Collaborative Online News Production*. New York: Lang.

Calhoun, C. J. (ed.) (1999) *Habermas and the Public Sphere*. Cambridge, MA: MIT Press.

Castells, M. (1989) *The Informational City*. Cambridge, MA: Blackwell.

Cleaver, H. (1998) 'The Zapatista Effect: The Internet and the Rise of an Alternative Political Fabric', *Journal of International Affairs*, 26(2): 621–40.

Coleman, S. and Ross, K. (2010) *The Media and the Public: 'Them' and 'Us' in Media Discourse*. New York: Wiley-Blackwell.

Coleman, S. and Blumler, J. G. (2009) *The Internet and Democratic Citizenship: Theory, Practice, Policy*. New York: Cambridge University Press.

Coleman, S., Morrison, D. and Svennevig, M. (2008) 'New Media and Political Efficacy', *International Journal of Communication*, 2: 771–91.

Coleman, S. (2004) 'Connecting Parliament to the Public via the Internet', *Information, Communication & Society*, 7(1): 1–22.

Corner, J. and Pels, D. (2006) *Media and the Restyling of Politics: Consumerism, Celebrity and Cynicism.* London: Sage.

Couldry, N. and Langer, A. (2005) 'Media Consumption and Public Connection: Toward a Typology of the Dispersed Citizen', *Communication Review,* 8(2): 237–57.

Coyle, M. (2009) 'Democracy Live', 2 November, http://www.bbc.co.uk/blogs/aboutthebbc/2009/11/democracy-live.shtml

Dahlberg, L. (2001) 'Computer-Mediated Communication and The Public Sphere: A Critical Analysis', *Journal of Computer Mediated Communication,* 7(1).

Dahlgren, P. (2005) 'The Internet, Public Spheres, and Political Communication: Dispersion and Deliberation', *Political Communication,* 22(5): 147–62.

Deuze, M. (2006) 'Participation, Remediation, Bricolage: Considering Principal Components of a Digital Culture', *Information Society,* 22(2): 63–75.

Donath, J. (2002) 'A Semantic Approach to Visualizing Conversations', *Communications of the ACM,* 45(4): 45–9.

Downing, J. (2003) 'The Independent Media Center Movement and the Anarchist Socialist Tradition', in N. Couldry and J. Curran (eds.), *Contesting Media Power: Alternative Media in a Networked World.* New York: Rowman & Littlefield. pp. 243–258.

Dutton, W., Elberse, A. and Hale, M. (1999) 'A Case Study of a Netizen's Guide to Elections', *Communications of the ACM,* 42(12): 48–54.

Fenton, N. (2008) 'Mediating Solidarity', *Global Media and Communication,* 4(1): 37–57.

Finkel, S. (1985) 'Reciprocal Effects of Participation and Political Efficacy: A Panel Analysis', *American Journal of Political Science,* 29(4): 891–913.

Fishkin, J. (2009) 'Town Halls by Invitation', *The New York Times,* 16 August: 9.

Goggin, G. and Newell, C. (2003) *Digital Disability: The Social Construction of Disability in New Media.* New York: Rowman & Littlefield.

Graham, M. and Khosravi, S. (2002) 'Reordering Public and Private in Iranian Cyberspace: Identity, Politics, and Mobilization', *Identities: Global Studies in Power and Culture,* 9(2): 219–46.

Haas, T. (2005) 'From "Public Journalism" to the "Public's Journalism"' Rhetoric and Reality in the Discourse on Weblogs', *Journalism Studies,* 6(3): 387–96.

Habermas, J. (1989) *The Structural Transformation of the Public Sphere: An Enquiry into a Category of Bourgeois Society.* Cambridge: Polity Press.

Hermida, A. and Thurman, N. (2008) 'A Clash of Cultures: The Integration of User-Generated Content Within Professional Journalistic Frameworks at British Newspaper Websites', *Journalism Practice,* 2(3): 343–56.

Iyengar, S., Luskin, R. and Fishkin, J. (2005) 'Facilitating Informed Public Opinion: Evidence from Face-to-face and Online Deliberative Polls', unpublished paper. http://pcl.stanford.edu/common/docs/research/iyengar/2003/facilitating.pdf

Jääskeläinen, P. and Savolainen, R. (2003) 'Competency in Network Use as a Resource for Citizenship: Implications for the Digital Divide', *Information Research,* 8(3).

Janssen, J. and Kies, R. (2005) 'Online Forums and Deliberative Democracy', *Acta Politica,* 40(3): 317–35.

Kahn and Kellner (2004) 'New Media and Internet Activism: From the "Battle of Seattle" to Blogging', *New Media & Society,* 6(1): 87–95.

Kalathil, S, and Boas, T. (2006) *Open Networks, Closed Regimes: The Impact of the Internet on Authoritarian Rule.* New York: Carnegie Endowment for International Peace.

Katz, E. (1996) 'Viewers' Work', in J. Hay, L. Grossberg and E. Wartella (eds.), *The Audience and its Landscape.* Boulder, CO: Westview. pp. 9–22.

Krugman, P. (2009) 'The Town Hall Mob', *The New York Times,* 7 August: 19.

Livingstone, S. (1998) *Making Sense of Television: The Psychology of Audience Interpretation.* London: Routledge.

Livingstone, S. (2004) 'Media Literacy and the Challenge of New Information and Communication Technologies', *Communication Review,* 7(1): 3–14.

Livingstone, S. (2005) 'On the Relation Between Audiences and Publics', in S. Livingstone (ed.), *Audiences and Publics: When Cultural Engagement Matters for the Public Sphere.* Bristol: Intellect Books. pp. 17–42.

Mancini, C. and Buckingham-Shum, S. (2006) 'Modelling Discourse in Contested Domains: A Semiotic and Cognitive Framework', *International Journal of Human-Computer Studies,* 64(11): 1154–71.

Min, S. J. (2007) 'Online vs. Face-to-Face Deliberation: Effects on Civic Engagement', *Journal of Computer-Mediated Communication,* 12(4).

Moe, H. (2008) 'Dissemination and Dialogue in the Public Sphere: A Case for Public Service Media Online', *Media, Culture & Society,* 30(3): 319–36.

Monnoyer-Smith, L. (2006) 'Citizens' Deliberation on the Internet: An Exploratory Study', *International Journal of Electronic Government Research,* 2(3): 58–74.

Mueller, D. (2003) *Public Choice III.* Cambridge: Cambridge University Press.

Oborne, P. (2009) 'Make Them Pay the Money Back, Sack the Spivs Who Let Them Get Away with it and Put the Thieves on Trial', *Daily Mail,* 9 May.

Pickard, V. (2006) 'United Yet Autonomous: Indymedia and the Struggle to Sustain a Radical Democratic Network', *Media, Culture & Society,* 28(3): 315–36.

Price, V. and Cappella, J. (2002) 'Online Deliberation and its Influence: The Electronic Dialogue Project in Campaign 2000', *IT & Society,* 1(1): 303–29.

Price, V., Nir, L. and Cappella, J. (2006) 'Normative and Informational Influences on Online Political Discussion', *Communication Theory,* 16(1): 47–64.

Prior, M. (2007) *Post-Broadcast Democracy: How Media Choice Increases Inequality in Political Involvement and Polarizes Elections.* New York: Cambridge University Press.

Renton A. and Macintosh, A. (2007) 'Computer Supported Argument Maps as a Policy Memory', *The Information Society,* 23(2): 125–33.

Sack, W. (2000) 'Conversation Map: An Interface for Very-Large-Scale Conversations', *Journal of Management Information Systems,* 17(3): 73–92.

Saunders, P. (1993) 'Citizenship in a Liberal Society', in B. Turner (ed.), *Citizenship and Social Theory*. London: Sage.

Schudson, M. (2000) 'Good Citizens and Bad History: Today's Political Ideals in Historical Perspective', *Communication Review*, 4(2): 1–19.

Schumpeter, J. (1976) *Capitalism, Socialism, and Democracy*. 5th edn. London: Allen and Unwin.

Semetko, H. A. and Krasnoboka, N. (2003) 'The Political Role of the Internet in Societies in Transition: Russia and Ukraine Compared', *Party Politics*, 9(1): 77–104.

Shane, P. (ed.) (2004) *Democracy Online: The Prospects for Political Renewal through the Internet*. New York: Routledge.

Skelton, T. and Valentine, G. (2003) 'Political Participation, Political Action and Political Identities: Young Deaf People's Perspectives', *Space & Polity*, 7(2): 117–34.

Soon, C. and Kluver, R. (2007) 'The Internet and Online Political Communities in Singapore', *Asian Journal of Communication*, 17(3): 246–65.

Tarrow, S. (2005) *The New Transnational Activism*. Cambridge: Cambridge University Press.

Theiss-Morse, E. and Hibbing, J. (2005), 'Citizenship and Civic Engagement', *Annual Review of Political Science*, 8: 227–49.

Thurman, N. (2008) 'Forums for Citizen Journalists? Adoption of User Generated Content Initiatives by Online News Media', *New Media & Society*, 10(1): 139–57.

Verba, S., Nie, N. and Kim, J. (1987) *Participation and Political Equality: A Seven-Nation Comparison*. Chicago, IL: University of Chicago Press.

Watt, N. (2009) 'Tory Plans to Reform Parliament Would Give Voters Chance to Alter Bills', *Guardian*, 4 October, http://www.guardian.co.uk/politics/2009/oct/04/conservative-hague-parliament-voters-bills

Wheeler, D. (2005) *The Internet in the Middle East: Global Expectations and Local Imaginations in Kuwait*. Albany, NY: State University of New York Press.

Wood, H. (2007) 'The Mediated Conversational Floor: An Interactive Approach to Audience Reception Analysis', *Media, Culture & Society*, 29(1): 75–104.

Wright, S. and Street, J. (2007) 'Democracy, Deliberation and Design: The Case of Online Discussion Forums', *New Media & Society*, 9(5): 849–69.

Zittrain, J. and Edelman, B. (2003) 'Internet Filtering in China', *Internet Computing IEEE*, 7(2): 70–7.

van Zoonen, L. (2004) 'Imagining the Fan Democracy', *European Journal of Communication*, 19(1): 39–52.

recreational activities. Therefore, when citizens do pay attention to politics, they generally concentrate on information relevant to their personal interests.

The inability to answer current politics questions does not necessarily mean that people do not know the answers. Even when we attend to information, process it, and store it in LTM, there are many cognitive roadblocks to successful retrieval of that information at a later date. Because political information is often boring for average citizens because they cannot relate it to their everyday lives, they may process it at a very superficial level. That then reduces the likelihood of locating it in memory and retrieving it. Much of the political information offered by the news media pertains to names, facts, and numbers about various political issues. Names and numbers are exactly the kinds of data that fade from memory quickly because they contribute relatively little to an understanding of various situations. The important thing is that although details fade fast from memory, the meanings derived from those details remain. People also use various cognitive tactics to deal with the vast amount of information they remember over time. We now turn to this topic.

Schemas

Schemas are the information packages that people assemble as they face similar situations repeatedly. These conceptual packages guide us through everyday life so that we can respond almost automatically to each recurring scenario without requiring much thought or attention. A schema is a:

> cognitive structure consisting of organized knowledge about situations and individuals that has been abstracted from prior experiences ... [M]ost schemata contain conceptions of general patterns along with a limited repertoire of examples to illustrate these patterns ... Schemata include information about the main features of situations or individuals and about the relationships among these features. They also include information about the expected sequences of occurrences or behaviors under various contingencies ... [People] may have ready-made evaluations and feelings about all aspects of these scenarios, and they make inferences based on these scenarios. (Graber, 1993: 28–9)

For example, over repeated exposures, people develop schemas about walking on city streets. They learn that drivers will stop at stop signs and this knowledge allows pedestrians to cross streets safely, expecting that most drivers will follow

precedent. Pedestrians do not have to go to the trouble of repeatedly rethinking the problem of safe passage across traffic. Their schemas – stored understandings derived from the past memories – help in future decision making and obviate the need for constant re-learning and re-developing reactions to similar situations.

The fact that schemas provide organization to our memories and serve as filters or windows through which we perceive and react to new information is both beneficial and harmful. Schemas save much valuable time and cognitive effort. But they also lead to rigidities because they reinforce prior beliefs and inhibit new thinking. As predicted by personal gratification and cognitive dissonance theories, we are more likely to pay attention to and process information that matches an already-existing schema because it is a pleasant psychological experience to process information with which we agree and a troubling experience to discover that others disagree with us. At a basic level, humans seek to avoid unpleasant experiences. Our schemas also make congruent information easier to process, store and accurately retrieve (Graber, 1993; Popkin, 1994; Rosenberg, 1988). We are less likely to incorporate new and contrary information into our schemas (Granberg and Brown, 1989; Marcus, 1988; Rahn et al., 1994). The problem of cognitive rigidity that may accompany schema building is particularly serious if schemas contain wrong information including distorted stereotypes.

Cognitive Shortcuts

We have explained how low motivation and limited attention resources reduce the amount of detailed information that people pick up about politics and store in their memories. The fact that people nonetheless have many well-developed political schemas indicates that they certainly accumulate a great deal of useful political information over their life time on topics with which they have some experience (Lupia and McCubbins, 1998; Mondak, 1995; Popkin, 1994; Sniderman et al., 1991). Another very useful cognitive shortcut mentioned earlier is concentrating on message meanings rather than attempting to remember all message details. We store only general impressions, global assessments, or brief summaries of encounters and add them to already existing schemas (Krosnick, 1990; Lau and Redlawsk, 2001; Ottati and Wyer, 1990). We create new schemas sparingly.

To ease the burden of processing political information, people regularly avoid burdensome tasks such as comparing policy options. The many complex plans proposed for healthcare reform are an example. Instead of attempting to formulate their own choices, most people adopt the judgments of advocates whom they trust and whose knowledge they respect. Citizens' judgments about a potential advisor's trustworthiness and integrity are often based on quick visual assessments of facial expressions or body language. Televised close-ups of candidates, for example, usually permit reasonably accurate estimations of competence, integrity, and vigor (Grabe and Bucy, 2009; Graber, 1996; Masters, 2001; Tetlock, 1999; Todorov et al., 2005). Party identification provides another simple, yet very effective heuristic cue to guide citizens to support candidates that are likely to represent their views (Popkin, 1994). People also use trusted personal friends and public figures as guides for their own political judgments. Friends who share political values and pay close attention to the mass media can provide important information and opinions during informal conversations. Given the complexity of current political issues, the odds are great that experts' opinions are more likely to be on target than the views of average citizens. Most citizens therefore benefit from opting for guidance.

The extensive use of these shortcuts, and the motivations which underlie their use, agree with Downs' (1957) model of rational political behavior and Simon's (1957) model of bounded rationality. According to these theories, it is not rational for citizens to spend significant resources on learning about politics, given the small political roles that average people in representative democracies actually play, compared to citizens who lived in earlier direct democracies.

Emotions

New research from the frontiers of political psychology has demonstrated the integral role of emotions in political learning. Crigler and Just (Chapter 17 in this Handbook) provide a broader, more detailed account of the role of emotions in politics. Here it is sufficient to concentrate on the impact of emotions on knowledge acquisition and on processing visual political information. Early research in political psychology concluded that emotions harm political reasoning. Presumably, they led to poor quality, irrational political decisions. Emotional political messages allegedly were disseminated to misinform and mislead the public, often for crass political gain. Disdain for emotional elements in decision making, coupled with a focus on rational choice as the epitome of political decision making, then led to a devaluation of audiovisual information because pictures arouse emotions (Marcus et al., 2000; Somit and Peterson, 1998).

By now, these negative judgments about the impact of emotions have been thoroughly discredited. Newer research shows that visuals that generate emotions are more likely to be noted, encoded and embedded in LTM than their purely verbal counterparts. In short, modern research demonstrates that emotions facilitate political information processing, political decision making and political participation. Emotional encoding does not hamper reasoning, it enhances it (Damasio, 1994; LeDoux, 1996; Marcus et al., 2000; Sniderman et al., 1991). Marcus and colleagues have been at the forefront in this research effort.

Research in psychobiology has shown that emotional reactions to visual images are processed incredibly quickly. Emotional brain centers are activated before higher brain areas in the cerebral cortex and help guide attention and processing of significant information (Barry, 2005; Damasio, 1994; Davidson and Irwin, 1999; Grabe and Bucy, 2009; LeDoux, 1996; Marcus et al., 2000; Marcus, 2002). As always, the brain stores general impressions rather than detailed information. General impressions are supplemented by 'gut' reasoning, which refers to the sometimes vague but often strong intuitive feelings that people have about the merits of people and situations. Decisions based on gut reasoning tend to be right more often than decisions based on abstract reasoning (Wilson et al., 1989).

AUDIOVISUAL AND VERBAL LEARNING

Underlying Assumptions

To understand the contribution of visuals to political learning, we must first address the debate over the efficacy of learning through various media formats. This essentially boils down to a comparison of political learning through television or through newspapers. Adherents to the fact-mastery school and other critics claim that audiovisual presentation of politics turns it into a spectacle that encourages citizens to become passive, disinterested observers, who neglect their civic duties. Television deters viewers from logical thinking about politics, while encouraging them to make political decisions based on emotional reactions to irrelevant personality characteristics of political leaders. Indeed, early research seemed to show that television discouraged political learning (Becker and Whitney, 1980; Gunter, 1987). By contrast, newspapers are praised for their ability to inform the public and enhance public debate and, therefore, enhance democracy (Habermas, 1989; McLuhan, 1994; Postman, 1986; Putnam, 2000; Schudson, 1998). When television's critics content-analyze televised news, they focus almost exclusively on the verbal content rather than adding the visual content that is such an important part of audiovisual information presentation.

Misgivings about the contributions of audiovisuals to political learning are understandable, given the difference in end goals between the fact-mastery school and the behavioral school. Television is, indeed, inferior to newspapers in terms of providing a broad array of diverse factual details and abstract information. For example, if the subject is global warming, words are superior in discussing the chemistry of the atmosphere and the future economic consequences of environmental regulations. But graphic audiovisuals showing a shrinking glacier and a shuttered charcoal factory are far more likely to make the problem come alive for ordinary citizens. Television excels in providing a holistic overall impression and a 'feel' for specific political situations.

New research in cognitive psychology, biology and political psychology exonerates television news and visual learning in general from their reputations as inferior mediums for conveying political information. New studies show that television news viewing is positively related to understanding politics (Chaffee and Frank, 1996; Chaffee et al., 1994; Kleinnijenhuis, 1991; Norris, 2000; Sotirovic and McLeod, 2004; Weaver and Drew, 2006). Despite the ambiguities inherent in visual images, people generally understand and agree upon the meanings conveyed by television pictures (Messaris, 1994; Philo, 1990; Sullivan and Masters, 1993).

Why are audiovisual media a good source for learning about politics? The primary answers are that audiovisuals are better able to convey the complex interactions of real situations and can do so quickly and relatively painlessly. The reality of what is involved in torturing prisoners is grasped instantaneously and seared into memory when one sees the pictures of the Abu Ghraib abuses. Verbal descriptions cannot convey this reality instantly, if ever. Political leaders understand this difference in impact and therefore often prohibit showing arousing pictures of human misfortunes while allowing publication of verbal descriptions. News media, too, understand the unique power of visuals and refrain from showing human disasters even when they are willing and eager to verbally describe gruesome happenings in detail. Television brings viewers as close as possible to actually experiencing events first-hand.

Biological Factors

Biologically, the visual system takes precedence over the language areas of the brain. Vision develops in infants very rapidly and is by far the dominant mode of perception in infancy. Once verbal capacities develop, children still rely heavily on visual cues and vision remains the dominant form of learning (Barry, 2005). A substantial portion (roughly one-fifth) of the total area of the cerebral cortex is dedicated to the visual cortex and over 90% of the information that reaches the brain is visual (Gangwer, 2009). Over thirty million neurons are activated by the presentation of a single picture of a house or a face (Levy et al., 2004).

The brain's easier handling of visual information is also reflected in processing speed. The brain processes visual information roughly sixty thousand times faster than text (Gazzaniga, 1992; Newell, 1990). The reason is that human brains process all picture details simultaneously whereas words, either spoken or written, must be processed serially (Messaris, 1994; Messaris and Abraham, 2001; Paivio, 1971; Van der Molen and Van der Voort, 2000).

Language also requires learning a vocabulary; it is not an innate skill like seeing (although Chomsky has demonstrated that humans are innately predisposed to acquire language and will do so automatically with exposure). People can extract the gist of a visual scene in less than one-tenth of a second. These automatic gut level visual processes are, at a very basic level, an adaptation to the evolutionary need to quickly process fight or flight visual information. Verbal information can automatically produce visual information and often does. The physiology of 'seeing it in the mind's eye' closely resembles seeing things in actuality. However, the pictures are less accurate than actual visual images presented by television (Gyselinck and Tardieu, 1999). Print news elicits imagined mental pictures; audiovisual news depicts the real thing.

Audiovisuals ease two major information processing problems: (1) failure to embed information in LTM and (2) inability to retrieve it (Berry and Brosius, 1991; Brosius, 1993; Crigler et al., 1994; Woodall, 1986). When messages include audiovisuals rich in relevant information, the chances are enhanced that at least a few will be stored and that they can later be retrieved from memory. Visual information is head-and-shoulders above verbal information in accuracy of recall (Bucy and Newhagen, 1999). Television visuals allow close scrutiny of faces, which plays an incredibly important part in assessing the character of humans, forming impressions and making judgments, especially when it comes to politics. In fact, face recognition has been so important in human evolution that the brain has developed specific neurons for face recognition (O'Toole, 2005).

Given these factors, audiovisual information formats are ideal because they suit human physiology best and they require least effort to gain understanding about political situations. However, audiovisuals also have drawbacks such as perpetuating stereotypes and reinforcing existing schemas. Print formats are ideal means for conveying abstract ideas and detailed facts, but one may question whether or not this is the kind of information that citizens want and need to carry out the duties of citizenship.

User-friendliness

Beyond biological advantages there are practical considerations that make television an attractive medium for learning about politics. Television is the public's most popular and trusted form of news. People deem it the easiest, quickest and most pleasant way to keep politically informed (Grabe and Kamhawi, 2004; Grabe et al., 2009). Television makes politics dramatic, entertaining, and exciting for the general public. Arousing interest in political news has been a major hurdle because other aspects of life have been more important for average citizens. Television, through its entertaining and arousing visuals, helps to overcome low levels of motivation for political learning.

The ease of decoding televised political messages aids people who are poorly educated and lack reading skills. That is important because illiteracy rates (including functional illiteracy) in the USA and many other countries are quite high. That means that newspapers, which are generally written at advanced reading levels, and textual information on the Internet are inaccessible to people with low reading skills. Television allows them to learn about politics and participate in political life (Grabe and Kamhawi, 2004).

In sum, the information that we have presented clearly shows that audiovisual information is an effective tool for conveying the kind of information that citizens find useful for learning about politics and participating in civic life. Moreover, the assumptions that guide the behavioral school are in tune with human physiology and human inclinations to use cognitive resources sparingly. Social scientists' ability to accurately measure political message processing is expanding thanks to functional magnetic resonance imaging (fMRI) technology that permits researchers to measure brain activity in real time during exposure to audiovisual political stimuli. Although this research is still in its infancy, it holds tremendous promise for further uncovering how political messages are processed, and how they affect learning, knowledge storage and attitudes.

ENVIRONMENTAL INFLUENCES

Armed with knowledge about the cognitive processes that structure political learning, we are now ready to discuss environmental influences that also shape political learning significantly. A crucial question concerns the nature of the sources from which citizens draw the information that underlies their political judgments. These sources include long-term, individual-level influences such as previous personal or vicarious experiences, socioeconomic background, education, family background, party identification and political ideology. There are also social influences on political learning such as general societal norms, the norms of particular social groups and awareness of public opinion trends. On balance, news media probably have the most profound impact. Journalists' gatekeeping, framing and story-telling skills affect the amount, type and quality of political information available.

The news media also play a critical role in determining how political events are visually presented. Camera angles, backgrounds, and capturing particular facial expressions, such as a smile or a frown, affect perceptions of candidates and public officials. The use of visual imagery 'unavoidably alters the spatial and temporal dimensions of reality, creating mediated versions of people, places, and events that are fundamentally different from unmediated experience' (Graber, 2001: 86; also see Griffin, 1992; Philo, 1990). Journalists construct news by seamlessly stringing together pieces of events that did not occur in such an order, thereby making news inherently 'unrealistic' even though it records actual events. Some camera angles can make people and events look more imposing than they are, and others can detract from their appearance. Visual distortions may lead to inaccurate perceptions. Worries about using pictures to deceive the public are most acute in the case of campaign advertising especially because of the ample evidence that shows that people who rely heavily on television shape their views accordingly (Gerbner et al., 1982). The least informed are the most vulnerable to these distortions because they do not have a wealth of stored information to allow them to judge the accuracy of television portrayals.

An Example of Audiovisual Politicking: Election Campaigns[3]

Political learning is extremely important during election campaigns. Candidates spend huge amounts of money, time and effort during campaigns to be seen and heard and the mass media cover their efforts extensively. Although the media's chances of influencing voting behavior are reduced thanks to political predispositions such as family background, education, and party identification, research demonstrates that audiovisual media coverage is crucial for election outcomes. Broadcasts shape political attitudes during campaigns and affect the voting decisions (Bucy, 2003; Drew and Weaver, 2006; Lanzetta et al., 1985; Masters, 2001; Masters and Sullivan, 1993; Todorov et al., 2005). According to Grabe and Bucy, 'the nonverbal communication that news visuals convey forms the basis of political impressions and evaluations as well as more elaborate decisional processes up to and including vote choice' (2009: 266).

How does this happen? Human beings learn to judge other humans through interpreting cues displayed in their faces and body language. The skills of reading faces and body language are honed over a life time. That explains why views of candidates' faces allow voters to make judgments about their trustworthiness, intentions, sincerity and emotions (Bucy and Bradley, 2004; Bucy and Newhagen, 1999). The ample visuals provided in television campaign coverage enable quick, reasonably accurate judgments of the candidates' character and traits.

Politicians and their aides are keenly aware of the importance of presenting their candidate in a visually appealing manner. That explains why podiums are adjusted during televised debates so that neither candidate looks taller than the other. John F. Kennedy's election victory over Richard Nixon has often been attributed to the fact that Kennedy's mannerisms and behavior were more visually appealing during the debates. Voters who watched the debates on television thought Kennedy had won, while those who listened on the radio thought Nixon won.

FUTURE DIRECTIONS

Audiovisual Learning Under the Microscope

The importance of audiovisual messages on television and the Internet is bound to increase in the 21st century because many print media and their audiences are shriveling and most people get the lion's share of their political information from television and the Internet (Gitlin, 2002; Stephens, 1998). New generations of citizens are growing up in a visually saturated environment, making it important to devote more research to the study of the political impact of these changed settings. We must bury the lingering myth of the inferiority of

audiovisuals for conveying political messages and concentrate on exploring their effects under various conditions, tracking their strengths and weaknesses and the diverse modes of delivery.

Research resources are likely to be shifted from studies of verbal political information toward studying visual materials, employing far more complicated methodologies than are currently in wide use. Social scientists will focus on understanding how meanings are conveyed audiovisually, how potential audiences can be attracted to political content and how audiovisual information contributes to political knowledge (Graber, 1986, 2001; Masters, 2001). Grabe and Bucy's (2009) exhaustive research of the use of visuals during elections is a good example of the directions that future research will take. Future research must also explore which facts citizens need to master to perform their civic duties adequately and which have no practical uses for monitorial citizens. Currently, we lack clear, research-based answers that delineate the changing nature of citizenship in the 21st century (Dalton, 2008; Mossberger et al., 2008). Such research is sorely needed.

The Rise of Amateur Journalism

The Internet has irrevocably changed the game of politics, including the presentation of the news (see Bimber, Chapter 9, in this Handbook for more details). It has given people more control over the flow of information that they disseminate and receive. Search engines make it easy to look for information on specific topics of interest, reach trusted sources and access single news articles or videos without having to search through a whole newspaper or watch a whole news show on television. Blogs, microblogs, email, and social networking websites allow average citizens to send and receive their preferred information independent of the news packages assembled by major news enterprises. Ordinary citizens can be their own information gatekeepers and amateur reporters can frame and publicize information they consider important. Citizens can manage their excursions into journalism through their own web pages on the Internet. Wireless technologies allow them access to political information whenever and wherever they want it. The opportunities for personalizing news should increase the likelihood that people will access political information and learn from it. Future research will tell us whether or not that is actually true and how, if at all, it changes politics.

Thanks to new technologies, news now features more varied visuals because many people use their portable devices to take pictures of ongoing situations. Recording events live has become easy because of the proliferation of cell phones equipped with cameras, and because of light-weight, hand-held video cameras. The use of Internet webcams is also changing the nature of political exchanges because people can see each other during interactions. That allows them to use facial cues and body language cues to assess the situation with a much greater sense of assurance that they have sufficient information for sound decisions.

Polarization Issues

In the past, national unity and the need for toler-ance and acceptance of political compromises have benefited from a news supply that reflected a moderately partisan or non-partisan stance. When news media began to mushroom in the 21st cen-tury, with cable television in the lead, that muted tone changed, partly in response to heightened competition for audiences that media need to obtain lucrative advertising. To arouse the atten-tion of disinterested publics, the political dialog sharpened and became much more partisan. Correspondingly, the public also became more polarized in their political views. Observers wor-ried that democratic governance might be imper-iled. Increased partisanship among news channels might mean that there is no widely shared infor-mation stream able to generate a common societal knowledge base. Audiences might be pleased by news that mirrored their own points of view, but this slanted approach is apt to disconnect them from fellow citizens with different interests. News focused on audience preferences and interests might also lead to a narrowing of the news agenda and, in the effort to address the widest possible audience, it could lead to pandering to low-brow tastes. But, are these changes, including polariza-tion, really a serious threat to democratic govern-ance? Do they have the feared consequences? What, if anything, needs to be done to restore civility to the public dialog? These important, pressing questions will, in the future, require media scholars' careful consideration.

Another significant change in political news is the shift toward more talk and commentary. An army of pundits delivers opinions about political situations, in competition with more traditional, objective, balanced news reports. The punditry format focuses more on verbal discussion of com-plex political issues rather than showing diverse pictures that illustrate the political scene. The consequences of this change need to be examined. Among others, they raise the question whether political pundits will increasingly serve as valua-ble shortcuts on which citizens rely to form their own opinions.

News in a Softer Style

The news style has also veered toward 'infotain-ment', privileging 'soft' human interest stories over 'hard' political event reporting, with possible substantial effects for interest, attention, learning, and storing of political knowledge. Comedy Central's *The Daily Show*, for example, provides current political news in a funny, satirical format. The producers repeatedly warn that the shows are unreliable representations of real-world news. Still, a growing number of young, well-educated adults watch such shows as sources of current political information and commentary. Whether viewers of these political comedy shows actually learn any new information is questionable because enjoyment of the humor requires a solid base of knowledge about the current political climate. People lacking such information are unlikely to turn to such shows.

By contrast, the knowledge base needed for learning about politics from television dramas is much narrower. Many of the dramas featured on nighttime television base their story lines on current political events. For example, *Grey's Anatomy* exposes viewers to the American health-care system and *Crime Scene Investigation* (CSI) covers criminal justice issues. Research is just beginning to explore how much or little people learn about current political issues from these shows and how this information influences their views about public policies in these realms (Graber, 2010).

Digital Divide and the Knowledge Gap

Casting news into softer formats may alleviate the chronic problem of disparities in political sophis-tication and participation between the economi-cally and educationally privileged portions of the population and their less-blessed fellow citizens. Those with higher incomes, education, and status are more likely to have the time and means to become knowledgeable about politics including citizenship obligations. They also find political information more useful and interesting. Because they develop a broader array of political schemas, additional political learning is relatively effortless for them. Poorly educated citizens, by contrast, tend to have much narrower political schema bases, and therefore find it more difficult to relate to and absorb the flood tides of political informa-tion. They learn less so that the knowledge gap between the poor and rich widens steadily.

However, changes in the definition and meas-urement of 'political knowledge' may reveal that the gap in usable political knowledge is far smaller than the gap in recollection of factual details. From a real-life perspective, that is good news, indeed. Increased computer literacy, starting in elementary school and greater availability of technologies that give access to the Internet will also further the spread of political understanding. American youngsters raised in the 21st century know a great deal more about their world than their 19th century counterparts. The Internet, particularly its audiovisual offerings, may be an ideal tool for decreasing the knowledge gap (Drew and Weaver, 2006; Prior, 2007). Offering political insights in new, more easily consumed, formats gives hope of creating better informed publics and more democratic societies.

To make best use of the new technologies, research is urgently needed to investigate what effects the very substantial changes in news presentation have on political learning and knowledge acquisition. Do the 'new' media singly, or in combination, provide the information that citizens need to understand the political scene and to monitor it effectively? Do new media enterprises alert citizens when situations arise that require citizen involvement? Or do they trivialize politics, produce polarization and encourage citizens to be political spectators who dodge their citizenship duties, leaving them in the care of tiny, unrepresentative attentive publics and interest groups?

From a broader perspective, can the market forces that are evolving in the 21st century produce a media scene that assures the survival of a free press that can adequately serve citizens' political information needs? Can privately controlled news media that must earn profits supply the right kinds of news, at the right time, packaged in formats that attract widespread attention and allow citizens to monitor the performance of their chosen representatives? The answers are still uncertain but, given the state of current knowledge, it is clear that audiovisuals will continue to play a vital part in keeping the public civically informed and engaged.

NOTES

1 Several points in the chapter connect closely with topics covered in other chapters in this volume. For instance, knowledge and visual learning are closely related to Bennett et al.'s chapter (10, in this Handbook) and Kevin G. Barnhurst and Kelly Quinn's chapter on visual communication (Chapter 22, in this Handbook). When topics overlap, we will refer the reader to the appropriate chapter for a more detailed discussion.

2 More on this in the third section that compares audiovisual learning with purely verbal reading and listening.

3 The following chapters in this volume cover campaigning and political advertising in much more detail: Gibson and Ward (Chapter 5) on political organizations and campaigning online and Fridkin and Kenny (Chapter 14) on the impact of negative campaigning. Therefore, we will only briefly address these issues here as an example of the importance of visuals.

REFERENCES

Althaus, S. L. (2003) *Collective Preferences in Democratic Politics: Opinion Surveys and the Will of the People.* New York: Cambridge University Press.

Bartels, L. M. (1996) 'Uninformed Votes: Information Effects in Presidential Elections', *American Journal of Political Science*, 40(1): 194–230.

Barry, A. M. (2005) 'Perception Theory', in K. L. Smith, S. Moriarty, G. Barbatsis and K. Kenny (eds.), *Handbook of Visual Communication: Theory, Methods, and Media.* Mahwah, NJ: Lawrence Erlbaum Associates. pp. 45–62.

Becker, L. B. and Whitney, C. D. (1980) 'Effects of Media Dependencies: Audience Assessment of Government', *Communication Research*, 7(1): 95–120.

Berry, C. and Brosius, H. B. (1991) 'Multiple Effects of Visual Format on TV News Learning', *Applied Cognitive Psychology*, 5(6): 519–28.

Brosius, H. B. (1993) 'The Effects of Emotional Pictures in Television News', *Communications Research*, 20(1): 105–24.

Bucy, E. P. (2003) 'Emotion, Presidential Communication, and Traumatic News: Processing the World Trade Center Attacks', *The Harvard International Journal of Press/Politics*, 8(4): 76–96.

Bucy, E. P. and Bradley, S. D. (2004) 'Presidential Expressions and Viewer Emotion: Counterempathic Responses to Televised Leader Displays', *Social Science Information*, 43(1): 59–94.

Bucy, E. P. and Newhagen, J. E. (1999) 'The Emotional Appropriateness Heuristic: Processing Televised Presidential Reactions to the NEWS', *Journal of Communication*, 49(4): 59–79.

Chaffee, S. H. and Frank, S. (1996) 'How Americans Get Political Information: Print Versus Broadcast News', *Annals of the American Academy of Political and Social Science*, 546(1): 48–58.

Chaffee, S. H., Zhao, X. and Leshner, G. (1994) 'Political Knowledge and the Campaign Media of 1992', *Communication Research*, 21(3): 305–24.

Crigler, A. N., Just, M. R. and Neuman, W. R. (1994) 'Interpreting Visual Versus Audio Messages in Television News', *Journal of Communication*, 44(4): 132–49.

Conover, P. J. and Feldman, S. (1984) 'How People Organize the Political World: A Schematic Model', *American Journal of Political Science*, 28(1): 95–126.

Damasio, A. R. (1994) *Descartes Error: Emotion, Reason, and the Human Brain.* New York: Grossett/Putnam.

Dalton, R. J. (2008) *The Good Citizen: How a Younger Generation is Reshaping American Politics*. Washington, DC: CQ Press.

Davidson, R. J. and Irwin, W. (1999) 'The Functional Neuroanatomy of Emotion and Affective Style', *Trends in Cognitive Sciences*, 3(1): 11–21.

Delli Carpini, M. X. and Keeter, S. (1996) *What Americans Know About Politics And Why it Matters*. New Haven, CT: Yale University Press.

Downs, A. (1957) *An Economic Theory of Democracy*. New York: Harper and Row.

Drew, D. and Weaver, D. H. (2006) 'Voter Learning in the 2004 Presidential Election: Did the Media Matter?', *Journalism and Mass Communication Quarterly*, 83(1): 25–42.

Gamson, W. A. (1992) *Talking Politics*. New York: Cambridge University Press.

Gangwer, T. (2009) *Visual Impact, Visual Teaching: Using Images to Strengthen Learning*. Thousand Oaks, CA: Corwin Press.

Gazzaniga, M. S. (1992) *Nature's Mind: The Biological Roots of Thinking, Emotions, Sexuality, Language and Intelligence*. Harmondsworth: Penguin.

Gerbner, G., Gross, L., Morgan, M. and Signorielli, N. (1982) 'Charting the Mainstream: Television's Contributions to Political Orientations', *Journal of Communication*, 32(2): 100–27.

Gitlin, T. (2002) *Media Unlimited: How the Torrent of Images and Sounds Overwhelm our Lives*. New York: Metropolitan Books.

Glynn, I. (1999) *An Anatomy of Thought: The Origin and Machinery of the Mind*. New York: Oxford University Press.

Goleman, D. (1995) *Emotional Intelligence*. New York: Bantam Books.

Grabe, M. E. and Bucy, E. P. (2009) *Image Bite Politics: News and the Visual Framing of Elections*. New York: Oxford University Press.

Grabe, M. E. and Kamhawi, R. (2004) 'Cognitive Access to New and Traditional Media: Evidence from Different Strata of the Social Order', in E. P. Bucy and J. E. Newhagen (eds.), *Media Access: Social and Psychological Dimensions of New Technology Use*. Mahwah, NJ: Lawrence Erlbaum Associates. pp. 27–46.

Grabe, M. E., Kamhawi, R. and Yegiyan, N. (2009) 'Informing Citizens: How People with Different Levels of Education Process Television, Newspapers, and Web News', *Journal of Broadcasting and Electronic Media*, 9(1): 90–111.

Graber, D. A. (1986) 'Mass Media and Political Images in Elections', *Research in Micropolitics*, 1(1): 127–60.

Graber, D. A. (1990) 'Seeing is Remembering: How Visuals Contribute to Learning from Television News', *Journal of Communication*, 40(3): 134–55.

Graber, D. A. (1993) *Processing the News: How People Tame the Information Tide*. Lanham, MD: University Press of America.

Graber, D. A. (1996) 'Say It with Pictures', *Annals of the American Academy of Political and Social Science*, 546(1): 85–96.

Graber, D. A. (2001) *Processing Politics: Learning from Television in the Internet Age*. Chicago, IL: University of Chicago Press.

Graber, D. A. (2010) *On Media and Making Sense of Politics*. Boulder, CO: Paradigm Publishers.

Granberg, D. and Brown, T. A. (1989) 'On Affect and Cognition in Politics', *Social Psychology Quarterly*, 52(3): 171–82.

Griffin, M. (1992) 'Looking at TV News: Strategies for Research', *Communication*, 13(2): 121–41.

Gunter, B. (1987) *Poor Reception: Misunderstanding and Forgetting Broadcast News*. Hillsdale, NJ: Lawrence Erlbaum Associates.

Gyselinck, V. and Tardieu, H. (1999) 'The Role of Illustrations in Text Comprehension: What, When, for Whom, and Why?', in H. van Oostendorp and S. R. Goldman (eds.), *The Construction of Mental Representations During Reading*. Mahwah, NJ: Lawrence Erlbaum Associates. pp. 195–218.

Habermas, J. (1989) *The Structural Transformation of the Public Sphere: An Inquiry into a Category of Bourgeois Society*. Thomas Burger (trans.). Cambridge, MA: MIT Press.

Kleinnijenhuis, J. (1991) 'Newspaper Complexity and the Knowledge Gap', *European Journal of Communication*, 6(4): 499–522.

Krosnick, J. (1990) 'Americans Perceptions of Presidential Candidates: A Test of the Projection Hypothesis', *Journal of Social Issues*, 46(2): 159–82.

Lang, A. (1995) 'Defining Audio/Video Redundancy from a Limited-Capacity Information Processing Perspective', *Communication Research*, 22(1): 86–115.

Lanzetta, J. T., Sullivan, D. G., Masters, R. D. and McHugo, G. J. (1985) 'Emotional and Cognitive Responses to Televised Images of Political Leaders', in S. Kraus and R. M. Perloff (eds.), *Mass Media and Political Thought: An Information-Processing Approach*. Beverly Hills, CA: Sage. pp. 85–116.

Lau, R. R. and Redlawsk, D. P. (2001) 'Advantages and Disadvantages of Cognitive Heuristics in Political Decision Making', *American Journal of Political Science*, 45(4): 951–71.

LeDoux, J. E. (1996) *The Emotional Brain: The Mysterious Underpinnings of Emotional Life*. New York: Simon and Schuster.

Levy, I., Hasson, U. and Malach, R. (2004) 'One Picture is Worth at Least a Million Neurons', *Current Biology*, 14(11): 996–1001.

Lupia, A. and McCubbins, M. D. (1998) *The Democratic Dilemma: Can Citizens Learn What They Need to Know?* New York: Cambridge University Press.

Marcus, G. E. (1988) 'The Structure of Emotional Response: 1984 Presidential Candidates', *American Political Science Review*, 82(3): 737–61.

Marcus, G. E. (2002) *The Sentimental Citizen: Emotion in Democratic Politics*. University Park, PA: Pennsylvania State University Press.

Marcus, G. E. W., Neuman, R. and MacKuen, M. (2000) *Affective Intelligence and Political Judgment*. Chicago, IL: University of Chicago Press.

Masters, R. D. (2001) 'Cognitive Neuroscience, Emotion, and Leadership', in J. H. Kuklinski (ed.), *Citizens and Politics: Perspectives from Political Psychology*. New York: Cambridge University Press. pp. 68–102.

Masters, R. D. and Sullivan, D. G. (1993) 'Nonverbal Behavior and Leadership: Emotion and Cognition in Political

Information Processing', in S. Iyengar and W. J. McGuire (eds.), *Explorations in Political Psychology*. Durham, NC: Duke University Press. pp. 150–82.

McLuhan, M. (1994) *Understanding Media: The Extensions of Man*. Cambridge, MA: MIT Press.

McGraw, K. M. and Pinney, N. (1990) 'The Effects of General and Domain-Specific Expertise on Political Memory and Judgment', *Social Cognition*, 8(1): 9–30.

Messaris, P. (1994) *Visual Literacy: Image, Mind, and Reality*. Boulder, CO: Westview Press.

Messaris, P. and Abraham, L. (2001) 'The Role of Images in Framing News Stories', in S. D. Reese, O. H. Gandy Jr. and A. E. Grant (eds.), *Framing Public Life: Perspectives on Media and our Understanding of the Social World*. Hillside, NJ: Lawrence Erlbaum Associates. pp. 215–26.

Mondak, J. J. (1995) *Nothing to Read: Newspapers and Elections in a Social Experiment*. Ann Arbor, MI: University of Michigan Press.

Mossberger, K., Tolbert, C. J. and McNeal, R. S. (2008) *Digital Citizenship: The Internet, Society, and Participation*. Cambridge, MA: MIT Press.

Neuman, W. R., Just, M. R. and Crigler, A. N. (1992) *Common Knowledge: News and the Construction of Political Meaning*. Chicago, IL: University of Chicago Press.

Newhagen, J. E. and Reeves, B. (1992) 'The Evening's Bad News: Effects of Compelling Negative Television News Images on Memory', *Journal of Communication*, 42(2): 25–41.

Newell, A. (1990) *Unified Theories of Cognition*. Cambridge, MA: Harvard University Press.

Norris, P. (2000) *A Virtuous Circle: Political Communications in Postindustrial Societies*. Cambridge: Cambridge University Press.

O'Toole, A. J. (2005) 'Psychological and Neural Perspectives on Human Face Recognition', in S. Z. Li and A. K. Jain (eds.), *Handbook of Face Recognition*. New York: Springer. pp. 349–70.

Ottati, V. C. and Wyer, R. S. Jr. (1990) 'The Cognitive Mediators of Political Choice: Toward a Comprehensive Model of Political Information Processing', in J. A. Ferejohn and J. H. Kuklinski (eds.), *Information and Democratic Processes*. Urbana, IL: University of Illinois Press. pp. 186–216.

Paivio, A. (1971) *Imagery and Verbal Process*. New York: Hold, Rinehart, and Winston.

Philo, G. (1990) *Seeing and Believing: The Influence of Television*. London: Routledge.

Popkin, S. L. (1994) *The Reasoning Voter: Communication and Persuasion in Presidential Campaigns*. 2nd edn. Chicago, IL: University of Chicago Press.

Postman, N. (1986) *Amusing Ourselves to Death: Public Discourse in the Age of Show Business*. New York: Penguin Books.

Prior, M. (2007) *Post-Broadcast Democracy: How Media Choice Increases Inequality in Political Involvement and Polarizes Elections*. New York: Cambridge University Press.

Putnam, R. (2000) *Bowling Alone: The Collapse and Revival of American Community*. New York: Simon and Schuster.

Rahn, W. M., Aldrich, J. H. and Borgida, E. (1994) 'Individual and Contextual Variations in Political Candidate Appraisal', *American Political Science Review*, 88(1): 193–99.

Robinson, J. P. and Levy, M. R. (1986) *The Main Source: Learning from Television News*. Beverly Hills, CA: Sage.

Rosenberg, S. W. (1988) *Reason, Ideology, and Politics*. Princeton, NJ: Princeton University Press.

Schudson, M. (1998) *The Good Citizen: A History of American Civic Life*. New York: Free Press.

Simon, H. (1957) *Models of Man, Social and Rational: Mathematical Essays on Rational Human Behavior in a Social Setting*. New York: Wiley.

Smith, E. R. A. N. (1989) *The Unchanging American Voter*. Berkeley, CA: University of California Press.

Sniderman, P. M., Brody, R. A. and Tetlock, P. E. (eds.) (1991) *Reasoning and Choice: Explorations in Political Psychology*. Cambridge: Cambridge University Press.

Somit, A. and Peterson, S. A. (1998) 'Biopolitics After Three Decades: A Balance Sheet', *British Journal of Political Science*, 28(3): 559–71.

Sotirovic, M. and McLeod, J. M. (2004) 'Knowledge as Understanding: The Information Processing Approach to Political Learning', in L. L. Kaid (ed.), *Handbook of Political Communication Research*. Mahwah, NJ: Lawrence Erlbaum Associates. pp. 357–94.

Stephens, M. (1998) *The Rise of the Image, the Fall of the Word*. New York: Oxford University Press.

Sullivan, D. G. and Masters, R. D. (1993) 'Nonverbal Behavior, Emotions, and Democratic Leadership', in G. E. Marcus and R. L. Hanson (eds.), *Reconsidering the Democratic Public*. University Park, PA: Pennsylvania State University Press. pp. 307–32.

Tetlock, P. E. (1999) 'Theory Driven Reasoning About Plausible Pasts and Probable Futures in World Politics: Are We Prisoners of Our Own Preconceptions?', *American Journal of Political Science*, 43(2): 335–66.

Todorov, A., Mandisodza, A. N., Goren, A. and Hall, C. C. (2005) 'Inferences of Competence from Faces Predict Election Outcomes', *Science*, 308(5728): 1623–26.

Van der Molen, J. H. W. and Van der Voort, T. H. A. (2000) 'Children's and Adults Recall of Television and Print News in Children's and Adult News Formats', *Communication Research*, 27(2): 132–60.

Weaver, D. H. and Drew, D. (2006) 'Voter Learning in the 2004 Presidential Election: Did the Media Matter?', *Journalism and Mass Communication Quarterly*, 83(1): 25–42.

Wilson, T. D., Dunn, D. S., Kraft, D. and Lisle, D. J. (1989) 'Introspection, Attitude Change, and Attitude-Behavior Consistency: The Disruptive Effects of Explaining Why We Feel the Way We Do', *Advances in Experimental Social Psychology*, 22: 287–343.

Woodall, W. G. (1986) 'Information-Processing Theory and Television News', in J. P. Robinson and M. R. Levy (eds.), *The Main Source: Learning from Television News*. Beverly Hills, CA: Sage. pp. 133–58.

Zaller, J. (1992) *The Nature and Origins of Mass Opinion*. Cambridge: Cambridge University Press.

13

Women as Political Communicators: Candidates and Campaigns

Susan A. Banducci with Elisabeth Gidengil and Joanna Everitt

INTRODUCTION

Though not usually assumed to matter in electoral politics, gender could be considered one of the primary cleavages in contemporary politics. Although some gender differentiation in participation and partisan preferences have been noted, gender is not viewed as a major cleavage by scholars. The extent to which gender has been mobilized in campaign communication varies by cultural and campaign context. Given that women make up over one-half of the electorate in most countries, the lack of visibility of women in political news signals that politics still is largely construed as a man's world. Issues such as gender mainstreaming, gender and information technology and gender and development have emerged on the global political agenda. Furthermore, the high profile candidacies and campaigns of party leaders such as Angela Merkel and Hilary Clinton have brought attention again to the plight of women running for national political offices. These global trends have coincided with a re-emerging academic interest in explaining and understanding whether, how and why women are marginalized in politics. Throughout this chapter, I suggest that further understanding of women as political communicators is needed from a cross-national perspective that can account for how the political context shapes both how women communicate in the political environment, how the media cover women in politics and how this influences women in the electorate.

To what extent do women face exclusion in media and politics? Women's progress in the electoral arena has been remarkable over the last 25 years. Women have achieved major success as party leaders and prime ministers, as candidates for high national political office and as legislative candidates. The increase in the number of women party leaders and candidates has meant that women are also serving in elected office in greater numbers. However, despite these advances, there are still noticeable gaps in the representation of women and women's issues in the national and supra-national arena. According to the Inter-Parliamentary Union (IPU) statistics, women around the globe still lag far behind men in terms of holding elected office and hold, globally, less than 20% of the seats in lower houses.

At the mass level, a number of studies have found that women are generally less interested (Jennings and Niemi, 1981; Verba et al., 1995) and less knowledgeable than men about politics (Delli Carpini and Keeter, 1996). While these studies have been focused on the USA, similar differences have also been found in Europe (Christy, 1987; Inglehart, 1981). There is renewed interest in examining these global trends in women's political engagement and, in particular, how these trends are related to women's elected representation and political communication systems.

In this chapter, I have three objectives related to emerging debates in the area of gender and political communication. Given that there is not space to summarize all of the relevant research over the past decade or so, I have chosen to focus on three areas that show promising developments for understanding the changing role of women in the political realm. First, I review the literature on gender stereotypes of political candidates. The stereotyping of female candidates can be considered to be at the root (or at least demonstrate the psychological dimension) explaining the marginalized role of women in politics. These stereotypes are reinforced through the news media covered therefore it is necessary to understand their dynamics before moving on to further analysis of the news coverage of women in politics. Second, I will summarize the literature on media coverage of female candidates and introduce some comparative data that reflects what the common understanding of the bias against female candidates in the news. Finally, I consider how news coverage and the visibility of women candidates can influence the political engagement of women in the electorate. Given that the news media play a central role in contemporary election campaigns (Scammel and Semetko, 2000), it seems reasonable to take the campaign context as a point for examining the role of women in the media.

GENDER STEREOTYPES: WOMEN AND POLITICAL ROLES

The media have a crucial and increasing role in shaping the image of politicians. The IPU in its report on women politicians and the media write that 'The media tend to treat women politicians as women and objects rather than as political protagonists, something they rarely do for male politicians' (IPU, 2007; web report). The media often use gendered stereotypes in their portrayal of women politicians. There is a well developed scholarly literature on the role that gender stereotypes play in voters' assessments of political candidates. Many of these studies show that voters attribute very different traits and issue competencies to male and female candidates. However, there is disagreement within this body of research about the extent of these stereotypes and their consequences for political candidates, particularly women candidates. Experimental studies tend to conclude that gender stereotypes are often applied to female candidates and can adversely affect them (Huddy and Terkildson, 1993a,b; Rosenwasser and Dean, 1989). This is because those traits that matter to voter choice are more likely to be associated with male candidates. On the other hand, studies based on aggregate data or survey data tend to conclude that real female candidates are not disadvantaged in the electoral arena (Everitt et al., 2009).

Previous experimental studies have found that voters attribute different personality traits and issue competencies to hypothetical candidates who are identical in every respect but their sex (Huddy and Terkildsen, 1993a,b; Rosenwasser and Dean, 1989; Rosenwasser and Seale, 1988). The results indicate that male candidates are perceived as tough, aggressive and assertive, while their female counterparts are described as warm, people-oriented, gentle, kind, passive, caring and sensitive. Female candidates are also stereotyped as being more moral, hardworking and honest than their male counterparts (Huddy and Terkildsen, 1993a,b; Rosenwasser and Dean, 1989). Although most of these studies have been conducted in the USA, similar results have been found across a wide number of countries (Williams and Best, 1990).

Matland and King (2002) present the most comprehensive review of the experiments to date. They conclude that experimental research 'show there are general categories of public policies (such as "nurturing" and "compassion" issues) in which female candidates are deemed better ... "[e]ducation," "helping the poor," and "supporting the arts" are all issues that voters seem to believe female candidates are better at handling' (Matland and King, 2002: 126). However, they note that on 'issues that male candidate are superior at handling, the experimental results are ambiguous' (Matland and King, 2002: 126). Huddy and Terkildsen in an earlier review of similar literature found that '[T]here are pervasive and remarkably uniform differences in the personality traits ascribed to men and women' (1993a: 121). However, they point to disagreement over stereotypes over 'male' issues such as the economy. In regard to experiments about candidate traits, Matland and King conclude that 'these experiments show that male traits are generally seen as more desirable and are associated with being a more effective legislator. What these studies fail to do, however, is prove that male candidates automatically have higher levels of these male traits' (2002: 126).

In an unpublished meta-analysis, Banducci et al. (2003) provide a more nuanced interpretation of the implications of gender stereotyping. Analyzing over 30 studies, they show that the studies clearly demonstrate the pervasiveness of these stereotypes in the assessments of female candidates, but are not convinced that they hurt women to the degree that some of the experimental literature suggests. In a quantitative assessment of the results of past gender stereotyping studies they verify the fact that female candidates are regularly subjected to 'feminine' stereotypes. However, it is also clear that 'masculine' stereotypes are not applied uniquely to male candidates except in campaigns for the highest political offices.

There are several reasons that may account for why female stereotypes are more pervasive than male stereotypes. First, politics has traditionally been considered a man's world and continues to be portrayed as such by the media coverage given to election campaigns and candidate debates (Gidengil and Everitt, 1999). Therefore, stereotypes may be based on occupation rather than gender. Carlson and Boring (1981) demonstrated this finding that indices measuring the difference between hypothetical candidates' masculinity and femininity scores were in a masculine direction for both male and female candidates. They conclude that this reflects the extent to which politics is still viewed as a masculine enterprise.

Second, this assessment of political candidates may also reflect broader changes in the degree to which gender role stereotyping occurs within a society in which women are assuming new social roles. This may have led to a decrease in the differences between women and men on these qualities. Interestingly, over this same period men have also increasingly indicated that they possessed more of these 'masculine' traits, however, the increase among men has not occurred to the same degree as among women.

Leeper (1991) has argued that the paucity of women in high elected office reinforces the stereotype that politics is a man's game and draws attention to the unique 'feminine character' of a female candidate. As a result, female candidates face the conflicting stereotypes of 'politician' and 'woman'. Indeed, conclusions drawn from stereotype studies suggest that individuals portrayed in counter-stereotypic ways are less likely to be judged by general stereotypes (for example, Sigelman et al., 1995) but may be judged by *subtypes* (Fiske and Neuberg, 1990). Thus, *female candidate* may be a subtype of *political candidates*. As a politician they are assumed to have the 'masculine' qualifications necessary for a life in politics, while as women they are perceived to have additional 'feminine' qualities not possessed by typical male candidates. Other studies that have examined stereotypes in countries that have had women as prime ministers or as leaders of national political parties have found little evidence of such gender-based stereotyping (Everitt et al., 2009). Clearly, there is a need to examine how these gender stereotypes are transmitted via news media.

Individual studies found that gender stereotyping tended to occur on issues where there was no information given for the candidates. This meant that feminine traits/strengths had to be inferred by respondents (Kahn, 1992; Leeper, 1991; Sapiro, 1981). There tends to be a reduction in the use of stereotypes as information increases (Banducci et al., 2003). This clearly suggests that people are more likely to use gender stereotypes to fill in the blanks in their knowledge about a candidate. Information then is a powerful antidote to application of gender stereotypes. Given that most citizens get their information about politics from the news media, the role of the media in covering female candidates is instrumental in influencing how citizens think about women candidates. We next turn to this issue.

MEDIA COVERAGE OF WOMEN CANDIDATES

Not surprisingly, the way media covers gender politics and women candidates has long been a matter of contention. The research reported in this chapter suggests that media coverage of women in politics reinforces rather than challenges the dominant culture, thereby contributing toward women's marginalization in public life. Much of the research on media coverage of women in politics has focused on whether women candidates and elected officials are as visible in the media as their male counterparts. In its report on women, politics and the media, the IPU conclude that the media focus on male politicians and they are less open to the achievements and concerns of female politicians. The scholarly research on this topic does suggest that media coverage of female candidates and politicians does tend to be biased. Early studies found that women candidates receive less coverage and what coverage they do receive focuses on their viability rather than issue position though this difference is more pronounced in higher offices (Kahn, 1994; Kahn and Goldenberg, 1991).

While the number of women seeking and gaining office has increased, there is still some difference in coverage. In an analysis of media coverage of women candidates between 1992 and 2000 in the USA, Jalalzai (2006, see also Smith, 1997) found that newspaper coverage of candidates has become increasingly gender-balanced and that some aspects of the coverage favor women. While much of this work has focused on the USA, studies outside the USA have found significant bias in coverage of female candidates (see, for example, Gidengil and Everitt [2003] on female party leaders in Canada).

In the most recent comparative analysis of media coverage of male and female candidates,

Kittilson and Fridkin (2008) examine media coverage of candidates in the campaign news in three countries (Canada, the USA and Australia). They find few differences in terms of the balance given to the coverage of male and female candidates. Reflecting contemporary studies from the USA, they see that women and men candidates receive comparable coverage. However, when focusing on the nature of the coverage, they find that the candidates are often portrayed in terms of longstanding stereotypes.

Given the lack of comparative data on the visibility of women candidates in the media, I present some original data collected during the 2004 European Parliamentary Election campaign. This is a unique data set in that it gives a picture of women's visibility in the news across 25 countries. Whereas these elections to the European Parliament (EP) tend to be considered less important than national elections, they still provide a useful political arena to look at women's representation in the news in a comparable election across a number of countries. To measure the visibility of women candidates during the campaign, we rely on data from the 2004 European Election Media Content Study. With the addition of 10 new member states in 2004, there are (at least) 25 different media (some countries have strong regional media systems based on language) across which news coverage will vary. The visibility of women candidates in the campaign coverage is based on an EU wide content analysis of the news media coverage leading up to the 2004 EP elections. This analysis of the coverage used the same coding rules in each country and is thus comparable across countries (for more information see de Vreese et al. [2005, 2006]).[1] Both television news and newspapers were coded in each country.[2] With two television news outlets and three newspapers per country, the sample consists of 48 television networks (in Belgium two French and two Flemish stations were included) and 75 newspapers. For newspapers, three weeks prior to the election are covered and for television the two weeks prior to the election are covered. The entire news program of each station was analyzed. The front page and one random chosen inside page of the newspaper were analyzed. Our unit of coding and of analysis is the individual news story.

The key measure used here is the visibility of the women candidates in the news media. For the indicator based on actors, one main actor and up to 20 actors were coded in each newspaper and television story. To be considered an actor, the person or entity must have been mentioned by name and quoted directly once or indirectly twice. As with the story topics, actors were coded in several steps. Two indicators for female candidate visibility are constructed. First, we calculated the

percent of all MEP (member of the European Parliament) candidates appearing in news stories that were women. While this may give an overall picture of women's visibility, previous studies have indicated that the viability of women candidates (Atkeson, 2003) and whether news stories focus on the uniqueness of women as candidates (Campbell and Wolbrecht, 2006) are the more salient aspects of female candidacies. Therefore, a measure that better reflects the viability of the female candidates where the gender of the candidate might be a feature of the news story is constructed. The measure is the percentage of candidates that appear as the main actor in a news story that are women.

Figure 13.1 shows the relationship between the proportion of women candidates in each country and their visibility in the news preceding the 2004 European election. The diagonal line represents a relationship where there is exact correspondence between the proportion of women candidates and their visibility in the news – where there is no bias in news coverage. Countries below this line have lower then expected visibility of women candidates while countries above the line show higher than expected media coverage. Austria is an extreme example that shows bias against women candidates. Over 60% of the candidates were women but they received only 20% of the media coverage of MEP candidates. Three parties in Austria have adopted gender quotas for candidates, which may account for their high proportion of candidates but this is not reflected in media coverage. Countries close to the line show a close relationship between media coverage and the number of candidates. For example, Malta has a low number of women candidates and low visibility as well. The regression line indicates that there is not a strong linear relationship between the proportion of women candidates and their coverage in the news.

In Figure 13.2, the relationship between the percentage of women candidates as main actors in news stories is plotted with the proportion of women candidates. The relationship is even weaker here and in, in fact, there is a negative relationship. In general, the media in the same countries that have bias against women candidates overall also show bias against them as the main actors in stories. Interestingly, it appears that in countries such as Austria and France where women have higher representation than average in the EP and, comparatively high representation in the national parliament, there is little attention paid to women candidates. However, in countries such as Slovakia, Ireland and Hungary where women's representation in the EP is much higher than in the national parliament, there is comparatively a close correspondence (or over-representation in

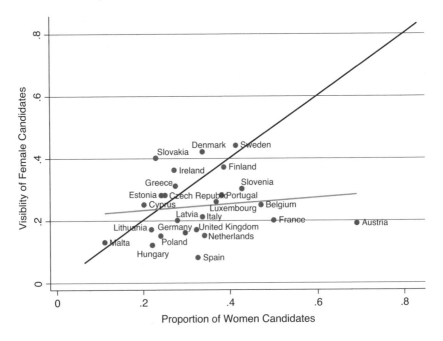

Figure 13.1   Bias in news coverage of women candidates: 2004 European Parliamentary Election news coverage
Source: 2004 European Election Media Study.

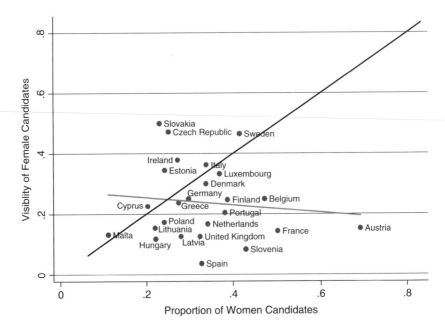

Figure 13.2   Bias in news coverage of women candidates: main actors only
Source: 2004 European Election Media Study.

the case of Slovakia) of women in the news and their candidacies. Perhaps when parties have a history of running more women, we see a drop in the coverage that focuses on the novelty of women in politics, or stories about women running as women. In the next section, I focus on the implications of this bias in coverage for the political engagement of women in the electorate.

Note the difference between the two figures is the calculation of variable on the y-axis. In Figure 13.1, visibility of women candidates is based on all actors in news stories (number of female candidates as a proportion of all candidates in news stories).

COMMUNICATING EMPOWERMENT: WHEN POLITICS IS NOT A MAN'S GAME

Differential resources and a lower level of psychological involvement in politics helps to explain some of the sex differences in political activity, but there is no clear answer to why women are less interested in politics than men. These differences remain even after controlling for socialization, resources and institutional explanations (Burns et al., 2001). In order to examine this remaining gap, some scholars have turned to the political and, more specifically, the electoral context for an explanation. Elections have the potential to cue gender relevance when women's issues are debated in a campaign or when women run for political office (Sapiro and Conover, 1997). While men and women are likely to employ similar campaign strategies, women are more likely to campaign on social issues (Dabelko and Herrnson, 1997).

Women may also be more likely to be mobilized when women run for political office. Burns et al. (2001) contend that the lack of women in politics sends a strong message that 'politics is a man's game'. They find that women are more likely to be aware of female candidates and are more likely to be interested in the campaign when women compete. They estimate that the presence of even a single female contesting or occupying a state-wide public office is enough to close the gender gap in political interest and political knowledge by more than half; moreover if women were represented equally in politics, the disparity in political engagement would be wiped out (Burns et al., 2001: 354–5). Other studies provide further evidence that the presence of women makes a difference. Hansen (1997) finds that the presence of a female Senate candidate on the ballot is associated with an increase in women's attempt to persuade others to vote. Campbell and Wolbrecht (2006) find that the visibility of women

politicians in the news inspires political engagement among adolescent girls. Similarly, Atkeson (2003) finds that women were more likely to discuss politics and have higher levels of efficacy when women ran for statewide office in competitive races.

Other studies, however, have failed to find any substantive impact. Dolan (2006) examines the increased presence of women candidates in the USA over a 14-year period and finds little support that their symbolic presence translates into an increase in political attitudes and behaviors. Similarly, Burns et al. (2001: 350) fail to find any relationship between women on the ballot and party mobilization. Koch (1997) also fails to find any impact of candidate sex on political interest.

The mixed results from these studies may result from their focus on electoral campaigns. While there may be a 'novelty factor', such effects may fade as more women run for political office. In addition, many female candidates in the USA are running as challengers in low visibility elections with little chance of winning given the nature of the incumbency advantage. Research on losers shows they are more likely to be dissatisfied with the political system and that repeated losses may result in lower turnout and trust (Anderson et al., 2005: 68–9). While campaigns have the potential to influence political attitudes and mobilize voters, there are also symbolic as well as policy consequences that are assumed to follow from the election of women. Women feel better about government when more women are included in positions of power (Mansbridge, 1999). When women are better represented on municipal legislative bodies, women are likely to be more trusting of [local] government (Ulbig, 2005). They are also likely to feel better about their representatives in Congress when they are women (Lawless, 2004).

Greater numbers of women in office alone may not be sufficient to stimulate greater engagement among women. Visibility appears crucial to maximizing the effects of women in elected office on political activity and attitudes. Visibility is a sign of an important office or election, and officeholders with the potential to shape the political agenda. In a study of women in the USA, Atkeson (2003) finds women candidates must be competitive and visible to impact women's engagement in the election. In races with competitive female candidates for statewide office, women were more internally efficacious, more likely to discuss politics, try to persuade others and comment on parties, and less likely to give 'don't know' responses in surveys.

Similarly, Campbell and Wolbrecht (2006) stress that women politician's visibility is key to reducing gender differences in political engagement – both over time and in a cross-section of the American states. Campbell and Wolbrecht examine the role model effect among women in elected office by drawing on surveys of adolescents. When women politicians are more visible in print and broadcast news media coverage, adolescent girls are more likely to indicate that they plan to become politically active. Notably, although women's entrance into Congress largely proceeded in a linear fashion, girls' political engagement jumped after two particular elections: the 1984 campaign of Geraldine Ferraro for Vice-President, and the 1992 'Year of the Woman'. Campbell and Wolbrecht theorize that these spikes in engagement are the consequences of an unusually high degree of media attention to the uniqueness of women's campaigns in national elections.

Importantly, most of these studies do not account for the visibility in the media of women in politics, which was found to be crucial in one study based in the USA. Given the importance of campaign context and women's visibility to previous studies, it is imperative to include these measures in comparative research. The divergence in findings may be reconciled by considering the conditions under which women in office have greater symbolic effects. In most of the previous studies (with the exception of Campbell and Wolbrecht, 2006), the presence of a woman candidates or the proportion of women in elected office have been used to indicate the potential for a role model effect on women's political engagement. However, one of the mechanisms by which this effect would work is through the visibility of these women candidates or officials. In other words, it must be brought to the attention of women voters that women are contesting the election or hold office. Because most citizens' experience of campaigns, elections and politics is mediated by television and newspapers, the presence of women candidates in these outlets would be crucial for their presence in campaigns or office to have an effect. Therefore, it is important to examine whether and how women candidates and politicians are covered in the press.

CONCLUSION

Despite considerable gains, women remain a minority voice in politics. As the data from the IPU indicates, in most countries women are still underrepresented in national parliament and other representative institutions. The above review suggests this has an impact on women's engagement in politics. Furthermore, the lack of women in elected office is further exacerbated by bias in the media coverage of female candidates for political office. While previous research indicates that voters hold gender-based stereotypes of women and men candidates for elected office, the degree to which candidate actions contribute to these views is less well known. To some extent, the noted bias in news coverage reflects gender stereotypes about women candidates. However, the extent to which these gender stereotypes hurt female candidates can be overstated. In fact, in some cases the stereotypes may benefit women candidates.

ACKNOWLEDGMENT

Elisabeth Gidengil and Joanna Everitt contributed to the section on gender stereotypes. This work was reported in Banducci, Gidengil and Everitt (2003).

NOTES

1   The study was funded by research grants from the Dutch Science Foundation (VENI and VIDI grants), The Halle Foundation and The Claus M. Halle Institute for Global Learning at Emory University, and the University of Amsterdam, to the principal investigators, Professor Susan A. Banducci (University of Exeter), Professor Claes H. de Vreese (Universiteit van Amsterdam) and Professor Holli A. Semetko (Emory University).

2   In total, we covered all 25 countries (except television news in Cyprus for technical reasons and Luxembourg for linguistic reasons).

REFERENCES

Anderson, C. J., Blais, A., Bowler, S., Donovan, T. and Listhaug, O. (2005) *Losers Consent: Elections and Democratic Legitimacy.* Oxford: Oxford University Press.

Atkeson, L. R. (2003) 'Not All Cues Are Created Equal: The Conditional Impact of Female Candidates on Political Engagement', *Journal of Politics*, 65(4): 1040–61.

Banducci, S. A., Everitt, J. and Gidengil, E. (2003) 'Gender Stereotypes of Political Candidates: A Meta-Analysis', paper presented at the annual meeting of the International Society of Political Psychology. Berlin, Germany, 16–19 July.

Burns, N, Schlozman, K. L. and Verba, S. (2001) *The Private Roots of Public Action: Gender, Equality, and Political Participation.* Cambridge, MA: Harvard University Press.

Campbell, D. E. and Wolbrecht, C. (2006) 'See Jane Run: Women Politicians as Role Models for Adolescents', *Journal of Politics*, 68(2): 233–47.

Carlson, J. W. and Boring, M. K. (1981) 'Androgyny and Politics: The Effects of Winning and Losing on Candidate Image', *International Political Science Review*, 4(2): 481–91.

Christy, C. (1987) *Sex Difference in Political Participation: Process of Change in Fourteen Nations.* New York: Praeger.

Dabelko, K. C. and Herrnson, P. S. (1997) 'Women's and Men's Campaigns for the U. S. House of Representatives', *Political Research Quarterly*, 50(1): 121–35.

Delli Carpini, M. X. and Keeter, S. (1996) *What Americans Know about Politics and Why it Matters.* New Haven, CT: Yale University Press.

de Vreese, C. H., Banducci, S. A., Semetko, S. and Boomgaarden, H. (2005) '"Off-line": European Parliamentary Elections on Television News in the Enlarged Europe', *Information Polity*, 10(3/4): 177–88.

de Vreese, C. H., Banducci, S. A., Semetko, S. and Boomgaarden, H. (2006) 'The News Coverage of the 2004 Parliamentary Election Campaign in 25 Countries', *European Union Politics*, 7(4): 477–506.

Dolan, K. (2006) 'Symbolic Mobilization? The Impact of Candidate Sex in American Elections', *American Politics Research*, 34(6): 687–704.

Everitt, J., Gidengil, E. and Banducci, S. A. (2009) 'Gender and Perceptions of Leader Traits: Evidence from the 1993 Canadian and 1999 New Zealand Elections', in S. Bashevkin (ed.), *Opening Doors Wider: Women's Political Engagement in Canada.* Vancouver: UBC Press. pp. 167–93.

Fiske, S. T. and Neuberg, S. L. (1990) 'A Continuum of Impression Formation, from Category-Based to Individuating Processes: Influences of Information and Motivation on Attention and Interpretation', in M. P. Zanna (ed.), *Advances in Experimental Social Psychology*, Vol. 23. San Diego, CA: Academic Press. pp. 1–74.

Gidengil, E. and Everitt, J. (1999) 'Metaphors and Misrepresentation: Gendered Mediation in News Coverage of the 1993 Canadian Leaders Debates', *Harvard International Journal of Press/Politics*, 4(1): 48–65.

Gidengil, E. and Everitt, J. (2003) 'Conventional Coverage/Unconventional Politicians: Gender and Media Coverage of Canadian Leaders Debates, 1993, 1997, 2000', *Canadian Journal of Political Science*, 36(3): 559–77.

Hansen, S. B. (1997) 'Talking about Politics: Gender and Contextual Effects in Political Proselytizing', *Journal of Politics*, 59(1): 73–103.

Huddy, L. and Terkildson, N. (1993a) 'Gender Stereotypes and the Perception of Male and Female Candidates', *American Journal of Political Science*, 37(1): 119–47.

Huddy, L. and Terkildson, N. (1993b) 'The Consequences of Gender Stereotypes for Women Candidates at Different Levels and Types of Office', *Political Research Quarterly*, 46(3): 503–25.

Inglehart, M. L. (1981) 'Political Interest in West European Women: A Historical and Empirical Political Analysis', *Comparative Political Studies*, 14(3): 299–326.

Inter-Parliamentary Union (1997) Women Politicians in the Media. http://www.ipu.org/wmn-e/media.htm.

Jalalzai, F. (2006) 'Women Candidates and the Media: 1992–2000 Elections', *Politics & Policy*, 34(3): 606–33.

Jennings, M. K. and Niemi, R. (1981) *Generations and Politics: A Panel Study of Young Adults and Their Parents.* Princeton, NJ: Princeton University Press.

Kahn, K. F. (1992) 'Does Being Male Help: An Investigation of Gender and Media Effects in US Senate Races', *Journal of Politics*, 54(2): 497–517.

Kahn, K. F. (1994) 'Does Gender Make a Difference? An Experimental Examination of Sex Stereotypes and Press Patterns in Statewide Campaigns', *American Journal of Political Science*, 38(1): 162–95.

Kahn, K. F. and Goldenberg, E. N. (1991) 'Women Candidates in the News: An Examination of Gender Differences in US Senate Campaign Coverage', *Public Opinion Quarterly*, 55(2): 180–90.

Kittilson, M. C. and Fridkin, K. L. (2008) 'Gender, Candidate Portrayals and Election Campaigns: A Comparative Perspective', *Politics & Gender*, 4(3): 371–392.

Koch, J. (1997) 'Candidate Gender and Women's Psychological Engagement in Politics', *American Politics Research*, 25(1): 118–33.

Lawless, J. L. (2004) 'Politics of Presence? Congress women and Symbolic Representation', *Political Research Quarterly*, 57(1): 81–99.

Leeper, M. S. (1991) 'The Impact of Prejudice on Female Candidates: An Experimental Look at Voter Inference', *American Politics Quarterly*, 19(2): 248–61.

Mansbridge, J. (1999) 'Should Blacks Represent Blacks and Women Represent Women? A Contingent "Yes"', *Journal of Politics*, 61(3): 628–57.

Matland, R. E. and King, D. C. (2002) 'Women as Candidates in Congressional Elections', in C. S. Rosenthal (ed.), *Women Transforming Congress.* Norman, OK: University of Oklahoma Press. pp. 119–45.

Rosenwasser, S. and Dean, N. (1989) 'Gender Role and Political Office: Effects of Perceived Masculinity/Femininity of Candidate and Political Office', *Psychology of Women Quarterly*, 13(1): 77–85.

Rosenwasser, S. J. and Seale, J. (1988) 'Attitudes Toward a Hypothetical Male or Female Presidential Candidate: A Research Note', *Political Psychology*, 9(4): 591–8.

Sapiro, V. and Conover, P. (1997) 'The Variable Gender Basis of Electoral Politics: Gender and Context in the 1992 US Election', *British Journal of Political Science*, 27(4): 497–523.

Sapiro, V. (1981) 'If US Senator Baker Were a Woman: An Experimental Study of Candidate Images', *Political Psychology*, 3(1/2): 61–83.

Scammel, M. and Semetko, H. A. (2000) *Media, Journalism and Democracy.* London: Ashgate Publishing.

Sigelman, C. K., Sigelman, L., Walkosz, B. J. and Nitz, M. (1995) 'Black Candidates, White Voters: Understanding

Racial Bias in Political Perceptions', *American Journal of Political Science*, 39(1): 243–65.

Smith, K. B. (1997) 'When All's Fair: Signs of Parity in Media Coverage of Female Candidates', *Political Communication*, 14(1): 71–82.

Ulbig, S. G. (2005) 'Political Realities and Political Trust: Descriptive Representation in Municipal Government',

paper presented at the 2005 Annual Meeting of the Southwestern Political Science Association.

Verba, S., Schlozman, K. L. and Brady, H. (1995) *Voice and Equality: Civic Volunteerism in American Politics*. Cambridge, MA: Harvard University Press.

Williams, J. E. and Best, D. L. (1990) *Measuring Sex Stereotypes: A Thirty-Nation Study*. Beverly Hills, CA: Sage.

14

The Impact of Negative Campaigning on Citizens' Actions and Attitudes

Kim L. Fridkin and Patrick J. Kenney

Cindy McCain, wife of Republican presidential candidate, John McCain, lashed out at Barack Obama during the 2008 campaign, telling a Tennessee newspaper the Illinois senator has waged the 'dirtiest campaign in American history' (Mooney, 2008). A mere two years earlier, a reporter described the 2006 midterm as 'dirtiest political season in American history' (Usborne, 2006). And, in 2004, the Republican National Committee Chairman Ed Gillespie attacked Democrats for planning what he called 'the dirtiest campaign in modern presidential politics' in the George W. Bush versus John Kerry presidential contest (USA Today, 2004).

While reporters, political pundits and politicians often decry the increasing negativity of election campaigns, negative campaigning is as old as the Republic. In 1800, when President John Adams was being challenged by Thomas Jefferson, Jefferson's camp accused President Adams of having a 'hideous hermaphroditical character, which has neither the force nor firmness of neither a man, nor the gentleness and sensibility of a woman'. Adams' supporters responded by calling Vice President Jefferson 'a mean-spirited, low-lived fellow, the son of a half-breed Indian squaw, sired by a Virginia mulatto father' (Swint, 2006: 183–4).

Plenty of negative campaigns followed the Jefferson and Adams contest. In Abraham Lincoln's first bid for election in 1860, he was

described as a 'fool, an idiot, [and] an ape' (Swint, 2006: 194). In his reelection bid in 1864, he was called a 'filthy storyteller, a despot, a liar, a thief, a braggart, a buffoon, a perjurer, a swindler, a tyrant, and a butcher' (Boller, 2004: 116).

A few years later in 1872, a heated campaign for president featuring President Ulysses S. Grant and Horace Greeley generated a great deal of mudslinging. This campaign featured dueling political cartoons from *Harper's Weekly* and *Frank Leslie's Illustrated Newspaper* where Greeley was depicted as a traitor, a flake and a nearsighted 'pumpkin-headed' clown, while Grant was described as a dictator and a drunk (Swint, 2006: 178).

Negative campaigning, then, is nothing new in American politics. However, scholars disagree about whether negative campaigning has increased in recent years. Geer (2006) examines televised political advertisements produced by major party presidential candidates from 1960 to 2004 and finds a steady growth in the percentage of negative appeals in the television ads. However, Geer does not know the frequency of airing for each of the political advertisements since such data were unavailable prior to 1996.

Lau and Pomper (2004) look at newspaper reports of senate candidates criticizing each other from 1988 to 2002 and report no growth in negativity. Similarly, Buell and Sigelman (2008) analyze statements made by major party candidates and their running mates in presidential campaigns from 1960 to 2000 as reported in *The New York Times* and find no increase in the propensity for presidential and vice presidential candidates to attack each other.

While we lack reliable and comparable data to know definitively whether the rate, volume and intensity of negative campaigning have increased over the last 25, 50 or 200 years, we do know the amount of negative advertising disseminated over the last decade has been substantial. In 2008, more than US$2.5 billion were spent on political advertising, compared to US$1.7 billion in 2004 (Atkinson, 2009). Given the enormous amount of spending in 2008 and extrapolating from the 2000 and 2004 campaigns, we can estimate that about half of these advertisements were exclusively negative, containing no positive references about either candidate (Franz et al., 2008; Kahn and Kenney, 2004).

Virtually everyone agrees that the amount of negative campaigning in contemporary campaigns is extensive. And, it is not limited to the USA. At the time of this writing, there are negative campaigns under way in Japan, Indonesia and Germany (Euroelections, 2009; Sakamaki and Nishijima, 2009; Simamora, 2009).[1] In addition, negative campaigning was evident in the 2007 Mexican national elections and in Canada's 2008 federal elections. To be sure, American political strategists do not have a monopoly on disseminating negative messages to millions of citizens via television, radio or the Internet. Given current levels of negative campaigning worldwide, a careful investigation of the impact of negative advertising on citizens' attitudes and actions is warranted. Scholars interested in voting behavior, campaigns and elections, and political communications have begun to explore how negative campaigning affects citizens. This chapter focuses on the findings from the US case because of the wide array of literature available on the subject.[2] However, in the conclusion we will offer ideas for future research, including possible comparative studies of negative campaigning. In this essay, we present, synthesize and summarize what we know about the importance of negative campaigning in the US elections.

WHY STUDY NEGATIVE CAMPAIGNING?

A fundamental element of representative democracies is that candidates and parties are free to make direct appeals to voters during campaigns. The messages presented by candidates leading up to elections are a cornerstone of healthy and functioning democracies. Campaigns are one of the few moments in large-scale democracies when competing candidates make mass appeals to wide segments of the population. During this time period, politicians present themselves and their records to citizens (Fenno, 1978; Pitkin, 1967). Campaign messages are used by candidates to describe their personal appeals, to justify their actions in office, to defend their policy positions, to outline plans for the future and to catalog reasons why their opponents should not be elected. These messages undergird the legitimacy that comes with winning elections. The victors, for the most part, make governing decisions that resonate broadly with the contours of their campaign messages and promises.

The central importance of campaign messages to functioning democracies is undisputed. What is less clear, however, is how these messages affect the beliefs and behaviors of citizens. One of the most dramatic aspects of candidates' messages is the extraordinary variance in the content and tone of their messages (for example, Franz et al., 2008; Geer, 2006; Kahn and Kenney, 1999; West, 2005). Some messages are upbeat, with uplifting music, and filled with positive images of candidates (for example, the candidate surrounded by children under American flags blowing in the breeze). Other messages are extremely negative, containing *ad hominem* attacks on candidates, peppered with dark images, threatening music and shrill and harsh language.

The amount of negative advertising over the last 40 years has coincided with some disturbing trends in American politics. During this same period, turnout has steadily decreased in national elections, leveling off at approximately 50% of the voting age population in presidential elections, citizens' trust in the US political system has declined, and we have witnessed a sharp uptick in the polarization of parties and candidates. In recent years, public angst over the harshness of televised campaigns has generated a considerable amount of commentary about how campaign messages, especially negative messages, affect the quality and health of electoral politics in the USA. Lau and Rovner (2009) document a dramatic increase in the number of stories published about negative advertising in *The New York Times*, *The Washington Post*, the *Christian Science Monitor* and the *Associated Press* newswire from 1980 to 2004. Lau and Rovner report that the number of stories was more than five times greater in 2004, compared to 1980.

Similarly, scholarly interest in negative campaigning has increased dramatically in recent years. For example, looking at the three premier journals in political science (*American Political Science Review, American Journal of Political Science* and *Journal of Politics*), not one article was published examining negative political advertising from 1900 to 1987. In the next 10-year period (1988–98), six articles appeared in these journals. And, in the most recent period (1999–2009), 12 articles were published in these three outlets. More generally, Lau and Rovner (2009) reported more than 110 books, chapters, dissertations and articles addressing negative political advertisements that have now been published, with the first article by a political scientist appearing in 1990.

This flurry of activity has produced a compelling set of questions for social scientists that center on how the content and tone of negative campaign messages influence citizens during elections. At the very least, four crucial questions emerge with direct implications for the quality of our representative democracy. First, do people learn from negative messages? Second, can negative campaign commercials influence to whom citizens give their support on Election Day? Third, do negative messages motivate or discourage citizens from participating in elections? Finally, can campaign messages affect citizens' attitudes about the very nature of the democratic system?

THEORY

There are strong theoretical reasons to expect negative communications will sharply alter the actions and attitudes of citizens. However, there are also compelling theoretical reasons to expect that negative campaign communications will have little or no effect on voters' attitudes and decisions. We begin by discussing why we expect negative campaigning to be effective. The underlying foundation for this line of thinking is that negative information, especially compared to positive information, is more memorable. Negative information is unique, making it more likely to be noticed, and more likely to be processed (Kanouse and Hanson, 1972; Lau, 1982, 1985; McGraw and Steenbergen, 1997; Richey et al., 1982). Lau (1982) explains that most people, most of the time, live in a positive world. In general, people are satisfied with their families, their neighborhoods and their jobs. Against this positive backdrop, negative information stands out and, therefore, it is more credible and more informative.

Negative information may be more memorable because it resonates with citizens' motivations to avoid costs rather than to achieve gains when making decisions (Kanouse and Hanson, 1972; Lau, 1982; McGraw and Steenbergen, 1997). More times than not, negative information carries with it harbingers of events or situations that people want to avoid. Social psychologists have demonstrated that people avoid costs across numerous situations, including placing simple bets, ethical risk taking and dealing with 'life dilemma' situations (Kahneman and Tversky, 1979; Kanouse and Hanson, 1972, Lau, 1982, 1985). It is not surprising, then, that social psychologists have shown that negative information attracts people's attention more readily than positive information and negative information has a stronger influence on people's attitudes than positive information (Hamilton and Zanna, 1974; Johnson-Cartee and Copeland, 1989; Lau, 1985).

Scholars examining elections have also shown that negative political messages carry information identifying events or situations voters should avoid during a campaign (for example, Basil et al., 1991; Brians and Wattenberg, 1996; Kahn and Geer, 1994; Wattenberg and Brians, 1999). Candidates intentionally identify, discuss and debate the risks associated with electing their opponents (for example, my opponent will raise taxes, my opponent will send the US citizens to war and my opponent will socialize medicine).

Researchers have examined whether people are more likely to remember negative political messages compared to positive political messages.

The majority of studies examining the relationship between the tone of advertisements and people's recollections of information in the commercials demonstrate that negative messages are more likely to be remembered, compared to positive advertisements (Brader, 2005; Chang, 2001, Geer and Geer, 2003; Lang, 1991; Lau and Redlawsk, 2005; Merritt, 1984; Newhagen and Reeves, 1991; Roberts, 1995; Shapiro and Reiger, 1992).[3]

In addition to being more memorable, negative messages may be effective because they are so pervasive in presidential (Franz et al., 2008; Freedman et al., 2004; Geer, 2006; Krasno and Green, 2008) and competitive congressional and senatorial elections (Kahn and Kenney, 2004; Jacobson, 2009). In the final days of competitive campaigns, especially in the battleground states during presidential elections, the campaign messages are often exclusively negative (Teinowitz, 2008). Given the preponderance of negative advertisements produced and disseminated by the candidates and the political parties on television, on the radio and online, the information costs for obtaining such messages for voters is approaching zero. Citizens are exposed to negative messages constantly as they carry out their daily routines; while they watch the news, pay their bills or drive their kids to soccer practices.

Given negative information is attention grabbing, accessible and filled with warnings and risks associated with voting for certain candidates, it makes sense to expect negative messages to shape the beliefs and behaviors of potential voters.

However, there are also compelling reasons to expect negative advertising to be ineffective during campaigns. There is a plethora of evidence suggesting that many Americans do not pay close attention to political messages, negative or otherwise (for example, Zaller, 1992). And, when people do pay attention to campaign rhetoric, they are not easily persuaded (for example, Kinder, 2003). Furthermore, the ineffectiveness of negative campaigning is entirely consistent with the cottage industry of scholarship demonstrating that the outcomes of presidential elections can be predicted before the onset of the fall campaign (for example, Campbell, 2008). All told, the conclusion that negative campaigning is ineffective is consistent with theories and evidence emanating from the voting and public opinion literature.

Given the competing theoretical expectations regarding the effectiveness of negative campaigns, it is important to review the empirical findings that have begun to accumulate over the last couple of decades. We will focus on four ways negative campaigning may influence elections. First, negative advertisements may influence what people know about the candidates targeted in the negative messages. Second, negative messages may influence how people evaluate the candidates targeted in the negative commercials as well as the candidates sponsoring the negative commercials. Third, negative messages may influence people's likelihood of participating in elections. And, finally, negative campaigning may influence people's views of the political system.

EMPIRICAL FINDINGS

Citizens' Memory and Learning

Do people learn from negative commercials? We know that negative commercials are better remembered than positive commercials. But, does the better memory for negative commercials produce higher levels of knowledge about the candidates featured in these advertisements? A review of the existing literature suggests that negative advertisements often produce greater information gains than positive commercials (for example, Brians and Wattenberg, 1996; Geer and Geer, 2003; Kahn and Kenney, 2000; Kahn and Kenney, 2004; Martin, 1999; Newhagen and Reeves, 1991; Niven, 2005; Niven, 2006). These studies, relying on both survey and experimental methods, indicate that people learn more from negative commercials, along a variety of dimensions, including policy matters and personality.

However, not all studies find that negative messages produce greater information gains.

For example, Wanta et al. (1999) find that the tone of advertisements is unrelated to citizens' levels of knowledge (Wanta et al., 1999). And, three sets of researchers have found that positive advertisements produce higher information gains than negative advertisements (Basil et al., 1991; Hitchon and Chang, 1995; Kaid et al., 1992). In each of these three studies, researchers relied on experiments to test for the relationship between the tone of the advertisements and the amount of knowledge gain.

Kahn and Kenney (2000, 2004), relying on survey data and content analysis of political advertisements, examine the relationship between the tone of commercials and knowledge gain in 97 US Senate races contested between 1988 and 1992. Kahn and Kenney find that negative commercials are more often associated with knowledge gains, compared to positive commercials. And, negative advertising is particularly important for challengers. As campaigns become more negative, Kahn and Kenney (2000, 2004) find that citizens are more likely to recall and recognize the challengers' names and they are more likely to correctly place challengers on the left–right ideological scale. In contrast, the tone of campaign commercials is less influential for incumbents. For sitting senators, the negativity of the campaign commercials does not influence people's knowledge of their candidacies.

The tone of political commercials also influences people's familiarity with the messages of campaigns. As the proportion of commercials becomes more negative, Kahn and Kenney (2000, 2004) find that people are increasingly likely to mention 'negativity' as a main theme of the campaign. Similarly, people are more likely to correctly identify the candidates' campaign themes when they witness races with numerous negative advertisements.

The literature examining the relationship between the tone of political commercials and people's knowledge about political campaigns is not voluminous. While we cannot make a definitive conclusion regarding the educative impact of negative commercials, the findings are suggestive. In particular, the majority of studies, relying on diverse methodologies, suggest that negative commercials are more likely than positive commercials to increase people's understanding about the competing candidates.

Citizens' Attitudes about Candidates and Vote Choice

The main reason that candidates air negative advertisements is to depress evaluations of their opponents. The negative information disseminated in campaign messages can alter impressions in several ways. First, negative messages may activate citizens' partisan attachment, reminding party loyalists of their long-standing affinities for the candidate of their own party (Finkel and Geer, 1998). The negative information may be based on party labels, policy predispositions or emotional appeals (Brader, 2005). Second, the negative information delivered in political advertisements may represent new information that helps citizens form initial impressions of the candidates (Kahn and Kenney, 2000; Valentino et al., 2004). Finally, the negative information may provide citizens with counterfactual information, pushing them to re-evaluate their earlier assessments of the candidates (Huber and Arceneaux, 2007; Johnston et al., 2004).

Scholars have spent considerable time and resources attempting to determine whether negative messages influence voters' views of politicians. Lau et al. (1999), in their original meta-analysis of the negative campaigning literature, reviewed 31 different studies examining the impact of negative advertisements on people's evaluations of candidates and concluded that there is 'simply no evidence that negative political advertisements are any more effective than positive ads' (Lau et al., 1999: 857).

However, more recent research supports the utility of negative messages (Franz et al., 2008; Freedman and Goldstein, 1999; Goldstein and Freedman, 2000; Lau and Pomper, 2002). Furthermore, Lau et al. (2007), in their latest meta-analysis, revised their view regarding the impact of negative advertising on people's evaluations of targeted candidates. In particular, the authors explain that two-thirds of the studies reviewed report the expected decline in affect for the target. Overall, the authors conclude by saying, 'the picture is mixed, with the bulk of the evidence pointing to a modest tendency for negative campaigns to undermine positive affect for the candidates they target' (Lau et al., 2007: 1182).

Researchers, relying on experiments, surveys and aggregate analysis, have shown that negative advertisements can depress impressions of the targeted candidate and sometimes decrease people's likelihood of voting for the candidate targeted in the negative commercial (for example, Jasperson and Fan, 2002; Kahn and Geer, 1994; Roddy and Garramone, 1988).

However, when examining the impact of negative advertisements, it is essential to examine both the intended and unintended consequences of negative advertising. The intended consequence of negative advertising is that people exposed to negative advertisements will develop more negative impressions of the candidate targeted in the negative commercial. In addition, an unintended consequence of negative advertising is the 'boomerang' or 'backlash effect' where people develop more negative impressions of the candidate sponsoring the negative advertisements. Several researchers have documented 'backlash effects' of negative advertising with experimental (for example, Garramone, 1984; Hill, 1989), aggregate (Jasperson and Fan, 2002; Lau and Pomper, 2002) and survey data (Kahn and Kenney, 2004; Lau and Pomper, 2002).[4]

When comparing the 'net effect' of negative advertising (for example, the direct effect of negative advertising minus the backlash effect of negative advertising), researchers have suggested that challengers may be more likely to benefit from negative advertising, compared to incumbents. For example, Kahn and Kenney (2004) find that negative advertising by sitting senators is more likely to depress evaluations of their own candidacies than lower evaluations of their challengers. In comparison, when challengers rely on negative advertising, these advertisements significantly and negatively influence impressions of senators without creating a backlash effect.

Researchers have been careful to differentiate between different types of negative messages. In particular, content analyses of negative advertisements demonstrate that negative messages vary along several dimensions, including (1) the substance of message, (2) the target of message and (3) the emotional content of messages (Brader, 2005; Franz et al., 2008; Geer; 2006; Kahn and Kenney, 1999). These different dimensions of negativity can alter the impact of negative campaigning on evaluations of the candidates.

Some studies have made distinctions between negative messages focusing on the candidate's personality and negative messages focusing on a candidate's policy positions (for example, Brooks and Geer, 2007; Finkel and Geer, 1998; Geer, 2006; Lau and Pomper, 2001, 2004; Min, 2004; Roddy and Garramone, 1988; Thorson et al., 1991). For example, Roddy and Garramone (1988) use an experiment to expose subjects to either a negative personality trait commercial or a negative issue commercial. The authors create the commercials featuring fictional candidates running for a congressional office. In the issue attack message, the targeted candidate's position on crime and the environment are targeted and the advertisement claims that the 'candidate's record as state senator shows that he was lenient toward criminals and against environmental protection' (Roddy and Garramone, 1988: 420). In the trait attack, the candidate is accused of being 'indecisive and inconsistent' while missing votes as a state senator. The advertisement also implies the candidate made an unethical trip to Hawaii (Roddy and

Garramone, 1988: 420). The authors show that the negative issue advertisement is somewhat more effective than the negative trait advertisements at lowering evaluations of the targeted candidate.

In addition to varying the issue or trait content of negative advertisements, scholars have begun to assess the importance of the 'relevance' of negative messages. In particular, Fridkin and Kenney (2008) argue that voters want to know how a politician is likely to influence their daily lives. For example, negative information about an incumbent's failure to provide for his or her constituents is likely to be viewed as important. In contrast, citizens are less interested in negative information that is only tangentially related to governing performance such as a candidate's behavior in college or the candidate's past marital problems. Fridkin and Kenney (2008) rely on an experiment embedded in a survey to assess whether the variation in the relevance of negative messages influences the effectiveness of the negative message. The authors find that irrelevant messages are much less effective than relevant messages at depressing impressions of the targeted candidate.

Negative messages not only vary in their content, they also vary in terms of the target of the negative messages. In particular, a number of studies have made a distinction between comparative and attack advertisements. Findings from experimental studies suggest that comparative advertisements are more effective at depressing evaluations of the target, without negatively influencing evaluations of the sponsor (for example, Pinkleton, 1997; Roddy and Garramone, 1988). Pinkelton explains that comparative commercials may be more effective than attack advertisement because 'comparative advertising is a less malicious form of political advertising' (1997: 20).

In addition, negative advertisements can vary in their emotional cues. Brader (2005, 2006), following the lead of Marcus et al. (2000), examine the role of affect in political campaigns. In particular, Brader examines how different emotional cues in political messages influence voters' attitudes toward competing candidates. Brader designed a series of experiments where he exposed participants to political commercials, using music and video cues to elicit either enthusiasm or fear. Brader shows that different cueing mechanisms alter participants' views of candidates. With regard to negative advertising, Brader findings indicate that subjects exposed to fear cues are more likely to actively process incoming information and, therefore, are more likely to be persuaded.

Finally, some research suggests that not all people are equally affected by negative campaigning (Ansolabehere and Iyengar, 1996; Kahn and Kenney, 2004). In a recent study, Fridkin and Kenney (2009) argue that some citizens have an easier time tolerating negative political messages, while others dislike public criticism and grow weary of such messages as campaigns progress. Relying on survey and contextual data in 21 US Senate contests in 2006, Fridkin and Kenney find voters' sensitivity to negative messages affect the impact that negative messages have on people's attitudes toward political candidates. In particular, they find people who do not like uncivil and irrelevant negative discourse are more responsive to the variation in the content and tone of negative commercials. In contrast, for people with higher tolerance toward negativity, the variance in the relevance and civility of messages has little influence on their evaluations of candidates running for office.

In summary, a variety of studies relying on a diversity of methods (for example, surveys, cross-sectional analysis, aggregate analysis, experiments) have looked at whether negative messages are affective at lowering citizens' evaluations of targeted candidates. The weight of the evidence suggests that negative messages depress citizens' assessments of the targeted candidates. However, the effectiveness of negative advertising depends on a series of factors, including the content of the advertisement (for example, issues versus traits, relevant versus irrelevant messages), the target of the advertisements (for example, comparative versus attack advertisement), the emotional content of the advertisements and characteristics of the people exposed to the advertisements (for example, the individual's tolerance toward negative campaigning). Finally, research clearly shows that negative advertisements are not risk-free. Several scholars have identified a backlash effect where people often develop more negative impressions of the candidate disseminating the negative messages.

While negative advertising may be effective in depressing evaluations of the candidate targeted in the negative commercials, negative campaigning can have unintended consequences. In the next section, we review research examining the relationship between negative advertising and participation in elections.

Citizens' Likelihood of Going to the Polls

The most frequently examined and most controversial question related to negative campaigning is: Do negative messages alter citizens' likelihood of going to the polls? If negative attacks are especially vicious and pervasive, citizens may become fed up with the mudslinging and decide to stay home on Election Day. Harsh attacks that last the length of a long campaign may spill past assessments of the candidates and alter citizens' views of the political system (Ansolabehere et al., 1994). Citizens may begin to readjust their attitudes toward politics more generally, becoming less trustful of government, less politically efficacious and less interested in politics. All of these attitudes have been linked to levels of turnout in various ways (for example, Verba et al., 1995).

The first scholars to look at the relationship between negative advertising and turnout were Ansolabehere et al. (1994) in an *American Political Science Review* article, 'Does Attack Advertising Demobilize the Electorate'. This article was followed by Ansolabehere and Iyengar's (1996) book, *Going Negative: How Political Advertisements Shrink and Polarize the Electorate*. In these research projects, the authors employ an impressive multi-methodological research design. The researchers conduct a series of experiments where they vary subjects' exposure to candidate commercials and they conduct an aggregate analysis examining the relationship between the tone of senate campaigns and turnout in these races in 1992. Both the aggregate analysis and the experimental research show that negative information decreases turnout. Furthermore, the experimental results suggest that negative advertising adversely affects people's attitudes toward the political system. They conclude, '... the 1992 Senate elections manifested the enormity of the public's discontent with attack advertising. The negative campaigns run by most Senate candidates in 1992 led over 6 million people to stay home and another 1 million voters to skip the Senate election' (1996: 112).

These dramatic findings caught the attention of scholars. In the decade and a half since these findings were published, a flood of studies have looked at the relationship between negative campaigning and turnout. And, the vast majority of these studies cast doubt on the strength and direction of Ansolabehere and Iyengar's original findings. Subsequent research has demonstrated that negative information either has no effect on levels of turnout or that negative advertising may actually stimulate turnout. Finkel and Geer (1998) examine presidential elections from 1960 to 1992 with contextual data and survey data and find virtually no relationship between negative messages and turnout. In a more recent study, Krasno and Green (2008) analyze voting rates in media markets and show that the volume of negative advertising purchased by the presidential campaigns during the final weeks of the 2000 election has negligible effects on voter turnout.[5]

A far larger number of studies have found a positive relationship between negative information

and the likelihood of voting. Freedman and Goldstein (1999), Goldstein and Freedman (2002) and Freedman et al. (2004) have carefully measured citizens' exposure to negative information. In this research, the scholars rely on CMAG (Campaign Media Analysis Group) data that monitors political advertising in the country's top 75 media markets. These data detail which political advertisements are aired, how often they are aired and where they are aired. The scholars combine these data with survey data indicating how often individual respondents watch television and find that exposure to negative rhetoric is related to higher turnout in the 1996 and 2000 presidential election as well as in the 1997 Virginia gubernatorial campaign.[6]

Lau and Pomper (2001, 2004) examine the US Senate races from 1988 to 1998 with both aggregate and individual level data and discover a positive relationship between increasing negativity and higher levels of turnout. Geer and Lau (2006) use a similar design and examine presidential elections from 1980 to 2000. Like Lau and Pomper (2001), they document a positive relationship between negative campaigning and turnout. Clinton and Lapinski (2004) and Hillygus (2005), using divergent research designs focusing on the 2000 presidential election, find turnout escalate with increases in negativity. Hillygus (2005) identifies very strong effects, while Clinton and Lapinski (2004) document more modest effects.

Jackson and Carsey (2007) and Kahn and Kenney (1999) examine the relationship between negative advertising and turnout in the US Senate campaigns, 1998 and 1992, respectively. By looking at the 'off-year', these researchers are eliminating the confounding effects of the presidential campaign. Jackson and Carsey merge media market-level measures of television campaign advertising (CMAG data) in the 1998 US Senate elections with individual-level survey data (the 1998 National Election Study, the 1998 Current Population Survey) and find exposure to negative campaigning produces a strong mobilization effect.

Kahn and Kenney (1999, 2004), relying on contextual data and survey data (the 1990 NES Senate Election Study) find evidence for both a stimulating and depressive effect of negative information on turnout. Kahn and Kenney find that the mobilizing or demobilizing effect of negative campaigning depends on the content and tone of the negative messages. Mudslinging (for example, harsh rhetoric on topics irrelevant to governing) decreases turnout. In contrast, when negative campaign information focuses on relevant topics and is presented in a civil manner, turnout increases. Lau and Pomper (2001) find a curvilinear relationship between negative information and turnout in the US Senate elections, suggesting that negative information stimulates turnout until negative campaigning becomes very intense. Turnout appears to decline at these very high levels of negativity.

Researchers have examined different campaigns (for example, presidential, senatorial), with different types of data (survey, aggregate, experimental), in different years (across time, presidential years, off-years) and with different measures of negativity (for example, political advertisements, news coverage, elite opinions). The majority of these studies show that negative campaigning enhances turnout, with some researchers documenting no relationship between negative advertisements and participation.[7]

In summary, we can draw some conclusions from this impressive and growing literature. First, negative information, in general, probably does not decrease turnout in a significant manner. It is possible, however, that turnout may decline when negative campaigning is so vitriolic that people lose interest in the campaign and choose to stay home. However, in most races, most of the time, the tenor and content of negative campaigning do not escalate into mudslinging (Geer, 2006; Kahn and Kenney, 2004). Second, negative campaigning appears to stimulate turnout. There is aggregate and individual level data, across different years and different types of elections, to support this claim. Third, additional research is necessary to identify the conditions when negative campaigning can mobilize (or demobilize) voters. Future studies will also help us identify the size of the mobilization (or demobilization) effect.

Citizens' Views of the Political System

Some researchers have suggested that negative advertising may lead to declines in support for the political system. In particular, increases in the amount of negative campaigning may lead to decreases in political efficacy, political trust and political interest. Evidence regarding the relationship between tone of political advertising and support for the political system are equivocal. For example, Ansolabehere et al. (1994) find that experimental subjects who view negative advertisements report somewhat lower levels of political efficacy than subjects who view positive political advertisements. Similarly, Finkel and Geer (1998), utilizing a systematic content analysis of presidential campaign advertising from 1960 to 1992 as well as NES survey data, find that campaigns with more negative advertising are associated with respondents reporting lower levels of political efficacy.

However, other researchers fail to find a negative relationship between the negativity of campaigns and people's feelings of political efficacy (for example, Brooks and Geer, 2007; Goldstein and Freedman, 2002; Pinkleton et al., 2002; Wattenberg and Brians, 1999). Wattenberg and Brians (1999), for instance, rely on NES survey data and find that people who recall seeing negative advertisements do not have lower levels of political efficacy, compared to other respondents. Similarly, Goldstein and Freedman (2002), relying on a much more sophisticated measure of advertising exposure than previous survey research, find no relationship between people's exposure to political advertising and their level of political efficacy. And, Pinkleton et al. (2002), using an experimental design, fail to find a relationship between exposure to negative advertisements and lower levels of political efficacy.

Fewer studies have examined the relationship between negative advertising and political trust. Lau et al. (2007), in their recent review of negative advertising research, identify 11 studies examining the relationship between exposure to negative campaigning and levels of political trust. The majority of these studies demonstrate that people who are exposed to negative advertising in an experimental setting (Brader, 2005; Brooks and Geer, 2007) or report exposure to negative advertising in a survey study (Globetti and Hetherington, 2000, Leshner and Thorson, 2000; Wanta et al., 1999) are more likely to report lower levels of political trust, compared to people exposed to positive advertisements (or report exposure to positive advertisements). However, the size of the relationship in most of these studies is modest. Furthermore, both Geer (2006) and Lau and Pomper (2004) report no relationship between negative advertising and levels of political trust. And, Martinez and Delegal (1990), utilizing a classical experiment as well as a survey of a local community, report trust in government actually *increases* after exposure to negative advertisements.

Finally, some researchers, relying almost exclusively on survey data, have examined whether campaigns rich in negative advertising generate higher levels of political interest, compared to campaigns with more positive advertising. While the number of studies examining this question is small, scholars have reported that negative advertising appears to enhance political interest (for example, Bartels, 2000; Patterson and Shea, 2001; Pinkleton and Garramone, 1992). For example, Patterson and Shea (2001), utilizing local newspaper editors to assess the tone of congressional elections, examine respondents' interest in local congressional campaigns. They find a modest positive relationship between the negative campaigning and people's level of interest in the campaign. And, Brooks and Geer (2007), employing a survey-based experiment, find somewhat higher levels of interest among people who are exposed to uncivil negative advertisements, compared to civil negative advertisements or positive advertisements.

Overall, the existing research investigating the relationship between negative advertising and political trust, political efficacy and political interest has yielded inconsistent results. Examining the relationship between negative advertising and political interest, efficacy and trust is challenging from a methodological standpoint. Experimental designs may not be optimal for assessing the effect that negative advertisements have on people's attitudes toward the political system. Typically, a person's level of trust in government or feelings of political efficacy are relatively stable (Miller and Shanks, 1996) and may not be altered by an experimental stimulus presented in a one-shot research study.[8] Similarly, even if an experimental dose of a negative advertising stimulus affects subjects' levels of political interest, trust or efficacy, it is unlikely that the impact of the stimulus will have long-lasting effects. And, most of the experiments reviewed here do not include repeated measures of the dependent variables (political trust, political efficacy and political interest) after subjects leave the experimental setting.

Surveys, however, also have limitations when assessing the impact of negative advertising on people's level of political trust, political interest or political efficacy. In particular, it is more difficult to identify causal relationship with surveys, compared to experiments. Most survey studies do not have precise measures regarding respondents' exposure to specific political advertisements. Therefore, it is difficult to identify the causal connection between different types of advertisements and people's level of efficacy, trust and interest. And, relying on recall of political commercials in a survey study may be problematic because certain types of individuals (for example, people with low levels of political trust) may be more likely to recall negative commercials, compared to positive commercials.[9]

In summary, it is important for scholars to examine trends in citizens' attitudes about government, such as interest in politics, trust in government and efficacy of governmental responsiveness. These attitudes are related to citizens' feelings concerning the legitimacy of democratic institutions. It is reasonable to expect that excessive negative rhetoric among political elites and candidates may influence citizens' views about politics. However, at this point, the evidence is ambiguous. More research, relying on complementary research designs, is needed to explore how negative campaigning alters citizens' attitudes toward government.

CONCLUSION

How negative campaigning affects the beliefs and behaviors of citizens and, ultimately, the outcome of elections is a topic that has captured the interests of politicians, pundits, journalists and scholars. In this essay, we have reviewed and interpreted the existing literature. Our review suggests that negative advertising can be effective, under certain circumstances. However, negative campaigning does involve certain risks. For example, people sometimes develop more negative impressions of the candidate airing negative advertisements. And, negative campaigning may produce more negative views of the political system. In extreme circumstances, negative campaigns may lead voters to stay home on Election Day.

In conclusion, we would like to identify questions ripe for future examination. We encourage researchers to explore the variance in the dimensions of negative campaigning. To begin, the medium disseminating the political messages may be significant (for example, Internet, television, radio). The 2008 presidential election was a watershed campaign in terms of campaigning on the Internet. Do negative messages presented online influence citizens differently than negative messages coming across digital televisions? And, does the mode of presentation of negative messages online matter (for example, as a commercial, as an email, as a tweet)?

In addition, it is important to examine the timing of the negative messages (for example, early versus late in the campaign). Are negative messages more important at the start of a general election campaign or are these messages more powerful at the end of the campaign cycle? In addition, it is time for researchers to explore negative campaigning in primary elections, especially presidential primaries where multiple candidates are attacking each other. Do early attacks, four to six months in advance of the Iowa caucus, resonate differently with partisans than attacks in the late spring of the presidential election year when only two candidates remain in the hunt for the nomination?

Third, researchers should examine how counterattacking messages influence the effectiveness of negative campaigning. In competitive campaigns, quality candidates with resources do not stand idly by when being attacked by their opponent. They battle back. Research should examine whether negative campaigning is more or less effective when opponents counter-attack. And, does it matter who started the attack advertising? Does it make a difference about how candidates counter-attack and on what topic? Do the presence, persistence and severity of counter-attacks influence the impact of negative commercials?

Fourth, it is important to examine how often a negative message is delivered. Since campaigns are longitudinal in nature, campaigns vary dramatically in how often candidates attack each other. Researchers should explore questions like: how many attacks are necessary to lower evaluations? Will the frequency of attack advertising lead to diminishing returns and a backlash against the attacking candidate?

Fifth, there has been virtually no attention to an examination of negative campaigning from a comparative perspective. Negative campaigning is not unique to the USA, especially across the last decade. By comparing nations, researchers can examine how variance across institutional (for example, parliamentary versus presidential systems, single member versus multi-member districts, plurality versus majority voting) and political variables (for example, party-center campaigns versus candidate-centered campaigns, length of campaigns) influence the effectiveness of negative campaigning. For example, does the effectiveness of a negative message vary when the target is a party rather than an individual? And, are presidential candidates more susceptible to negative messages than prime ministers running on a party platform?

Finally, does the impact of negative campaigning vary with the gender, race and ethnicity of candidates? We know that negative campaigning is more effective for challengers, compared to incumbents. Are negative advertisements disseminated by women or minority men more or less effective than negative commercials delivered by Anglo men? Does the gender, race or ethnicity of the targeted candidate matter? Some preliminary evidence suggests that when a male candidate is disseminating negative messages, the negative message is more effective against a male target, than a female target (Fridkin et al., 2009). However, we know little about how the race, gender and ethnicity of the attacking and targeted candidate interact to influence the impact of negative messages.

Exploring how negative campaigning influences voters is an important question in any representative democracy. Research examining the importance of negative campaigning is still in its infancy and additional research is necessary and important. In pursuing research on negative campaigning, we encourage researchers to rely on divergent designs as well as newly emerging research methodologies. With additional work, we will improve our understanding of how, when and why negative messages are consequential.

NOTES

1   Sakamaki, Sachiko and Momoko Nishijima (10 August 2009). Negative Campaigning Hits Japan as LDP Cartoon Attacks Hatoyama. http://www. bloomberg.com/apps/news. Simamora, Adianto P. (11 August 2009). Negative Campaigning Rife Among Rivals. http://www.thejakartapost.com/news. EurActive (10 August 2009). Negative EU Campaign Rocks German Coalition. http://www.euractiv.com/en/eu-elections/negative.

2   For a few notable exceptions, see Banducci and Karp (2003), Desposato (2007), Hansen and Pederson (2008) and Sigelman and Shiraev (2002).

3   A few researchers, mainly relying on experiments with a small number of subjects, show that positive advertisements are remembered better than negative commercials (for example, Basil et al., 1991; Hitchon and Chang, 1995; Kaid et al., 1992; Thorson et al., 1991).

4   A few researchers have shown that negative advertising does not depress impressions of the targeted candidate and may actually produce more positive views of the candidate attacked in the negative commercial (for example, Haddock and Zanna, 1997; Hill, 1989).

5   Wattenberg and Brians (1999), relying on recall data in 1992 and 1996, find that people who recall seeing negative advertisements are more likely to report voting in 1992. In 1996, the authors report no significant relationship between whether respondents recall seeing a negative commercial and their reported turnout.

6   See also Franz et al. (2008) for similar findings for the 2004 presidential election.

7   Ansolabehere and his colleagues (Ansolabehere and Iyengar, 1996; Ansolabehere et al., 1994) almost stand alone in identifying a demobilizing effect of negative campaigning. Several scholars have questioned the validity of Ansolabehere's aggregate analysis demonstrating that increases in negative campaigning leads to a drop in turnout (for example, Brooks, 2006; Wattenberg and Brians, 1999). For example, Brooks (2006) attempted to replicate Ansolabehere et al.'s aggregate analysis with changes in the measurement of the dependent variable and found virtually no relationship between turnout and negative campaigns.

8   In comparison, a person's interest in politics may be more likely to be affected by a short-term stimulus.

9   While experiments are superior to surveys at identifying causal relationships, the experimental set-

ting is artificial and may exaggerate the impact of negative commercials on people's political attitudes. That is, experiments have higher 'internal validity' than surveys, but lower 'external validity' (Campbell and Stanley, 1963).

REFERENCES

Atkinson, C. (2009) '2008 Political Ads Worth $2.5 Billion to $2.7 Billion', http://www.broadcastingcable.com (accessed 28 July 2009).

Ansolabehere, S. and Iyengar, S. (1996) *Going Negative: How Political Advertisements Shrink and Polarize the Electorate*. New York: Free Press.

Ansolabehere, S., Iyengar, S., Simon, A. and Valentino, N. (1994) 'Does Attack Advertising Demobilize the Electorate?', *The American Political Science Review*, 88(4): 829–38.

Banducci, S. A. and Karp, J. A. (2003) 'How Elections Change the Way Citizens View the Political System: Campaigns, Media Effects and Electoral Outcomes in Comparative Perspective', *British Journal of Political Science*, 33(3): 443–67.

Bartels, L. M. (2000) 'Campaign Quality: Standards for Evaluation, Benchmarks for Reform', in L. M. Bartels and L. Vavreck (eds.), *Campaign Reform: Insights and Evidence*. Ann Arbor, MI: University of Michigan Press. pp. 1–61.

Basil, M., Schooler, C. and Reeves, B. (1991) 'Positive and Negative Political Advertising: Effectiveness of Ads and Perceptions of Candidates', in F. Biocca (ed.), *Television and Political Advertising*, Vol. 1. Hillsdale, NJ: Lawrence Erlbaum Associates. pp. 245–62.

Boller, P. F. (2004) *Presidential Campaigns: From George Washington to George W. Bush*. New York: Oxford University Press.

Brader, T. (2005) 'Striking a Responsive Chord: How Political Ads Motivate and Persuade Voters by Appealing to Emotions', *American Journal of Political Science*, 49(2): 388–405.

Brader, T. (2006) *Campaigning for the Hearts and Minds*. Chicago, IL: University of Chicago Press.

Brians, C. L. and Wattenberg, M. P. (1996) 'Campaign Issue Knowledge and Salience: Comparing Reception from TV Commercials, TV News, and Newspapers', *American Journal of Political Science*, 40(1): 172–93.

Brooks, D. J. (2006) 'The Resilient Voter: Moving Toward Closure in the Debate over Negative Campaigning and Turnout', *The Journal of Politics*, 68(3): 684–96.

Brooks, D. J. and Geer, J. G. (2007) 'Beyond Negativity: The Effects of Incivility on the Electorate', *American Journal of Political Science*, 51(1): 1–16.

Buell, E. H., Jr. and Sigelman, L. (2008) *Attack Politics: Negativity in Presidential Campaigns Since 1960*. Lawrence, KS: University Press of Kansas.

Campbell, D. and Stanley, J. (1963) *Experimental and Quasi-Experimental Designs for Research*. Boston, MA: Houghton Mifflin.

Campbell, J. E. (2008) 'Symposium: Forecasting the 2008 Elections', *PS: Political Science and Politics*, 41(4): 679–732.

Chang, C. (2001) 'The Impacts of Emotion Elicited by Print Political Advertising on Candidate Evaluation', *Media Psychology*, 3(2): 91–118.

Clinton, J. D. and Lapinski, J. S. (2004) ''Targeted' Advertising and Voter Turnout: An Experimental Study of the 2000 Presidential Election', *The Journal of Politics*, 66(1): 69–96.

Desposato, S. (2007) 'Going Negative in Comparative Perspective: Electoral Rules and Campaign Strategies', working paper. University of Arizona.

EurActiv. (2009) 'Negative EU Campaign Rocks German Coalition', 26 May, http://www.euractiv.com/en/eu-elections/negative (accessed 10 August 2009).

Fenno, R. F. (1978) *Home Style: House Members in Their Districts*. New York: Harper Collins Publishers.

Finkel, S. and Geer, J. G. (1998) 'Spot Check: Casting Doubt on the Demobilizing Effect of Attack Advertising', *American Journal of Political Science*, 42(2): 573–95.

Franz, M. M., Freedman, P., Goldstein, K. and Ridout, T. N. (2008) 'Understanding the Effect of Political Advertising on Voter Turnout: A Response to Krasno and Green', *The Journal of Politics*, 70(1): 262–8.

Freedman, P. and Goldstein, K. (1999) 'Measuring Media Exposure and the Effects of Negative Campaign Ads', *American Journal of Political Science*, 43(4): 1189–1208.

Freedman, P., Franz, M. M. and Goldstein, K. (2004) 'Campaign Advertising and Democratic Citizenship', *American Journal of Political Science*, 48(4): 723–41.

Fridkin, K. L. and Kenney, P. J. (2008) 'The Dimensions of Negative Messages', *American Politics Research*, 36(5): 694–723.

Fridkin, K. L. and Kenney, P. J. (2009) 'The 'Not-So-Minimal' Effects of Negative Advertising: Exploring the Impact of Negative Messages on Evaluations of US Senate Candidates', paper presented at the Midwest Political Science Association Meeting. Chicago, IL.

Fridkin, K. L., Kenney, P. J. and Woodall, G. (2009) 'Bad for Men, Better for Women: The Impact of Stereotypes during Negative Campaigns', *Political Behavior*, 31(1): 53–72.

Geer, J. G. (2006) *In Defense of Negativity: Attack Ads in Presidential Campaigns*. Chicago, IL: University of Chicago Press.

Geer, J. G. and Geer, J. H. (2003) 'Remembering Attack Ads: An Experimental Investigation of Radio', *Political Behavior*, 25(1): 69–95.

Geer, J. G. and Lau, R. R. (2006) 'Filling in the Blanks: A New Method for Estimating Campaign Effects', *British Journal of Political Science*, 36(2): 269–90.

Globetti, S. and Hetherington, M. J. (2000) 'The Negative Implications of Anti-Government Campaign Rhetoric', presented at the annual meeting of the Midwest Political Science Association.

Goldstein, K. and Freedman, P. (2000) 'New Evidence for New Arguments: Money and Advertising in the 1996 Senate Elections', *Journal of Politics*, 62(4): 1087–1108.

Goldstein, K. and Freedman, P. (2002) 'Lessons Learned: Campaign Advertising in the 2000 Elections', *Political Communication*, 19(1): 5–28.

Hamilton, D. L. and Zanna, M. P. (1974) 'Context Effects in Impression Formation: Changes in Connotative Meaning', *Journal of Personality and Social Psychology*, 29(5): 649–54.

Hansen, K. M. and Pedersen, R. T. (2008) 'Negative Campaigning in a Multiparty System', *Scandinavian Political Studies*, 31(4): 408–22.

Hill, R. P. (1989) 'An Exploration of Voter Responses to Political Advertisements', *Journal of Advertising*, 18(4): 14–22.

Hillygus, S. (2005) 'Campaign Effects and the Dynamics of Turnout Intention in Election 2000', *Journal of Politics*, 67(1): 50–68.

Hitchon, J. C. and Chang, C. (1995) 'Effects of Gender Schematic Processing on the Reception of Political Commercials for Men and Women Candidates', *Communication Research*, 22(4): 430–58.

Huber, G. A. and Arceneaux, K. (2007) 'Identifying the Persuasive Effects of Presidential Advertising', *American Journal of Political Science*, 51(4): 961–81.

Jackson, R. and Carsey, T. (2007) 'US Senate Campaigns, Negative Advertising, and Voter Mobilization in the 1998 Midterm Election', *Electoral Studies*, 26(1): 180–95.

Jacobson, G. C. (2009) *The Politics of Congressional Elections.* 7th edn. New York: Longman Press.

Jasperson, A. E. and Fan, D. P. (2002) 'An Aggregate Examination of the Backlash Effect in Political Advertising: The Case of the 1996 US Senate Race in Minnesota', *Journal of Advertising*, 31(1): 1–12.

Johnson-Cartee, K. S. and Copeland, G. A. (1991) *Negative Political Advertising: Coming of Age.* Hillsdale, NJ: Lawrence Erlbaum Associates.

Johnston, R., Hagen, M. and Jamieson, K. H. (2004) *The 2000 Presidential Election and the Foundations of Party Politics.* New York: Cambridge University Press.

Kahn, K. F. and Geer, J. G. (1994) 'Creating Impressions: An Experimental Investigation of the Effectiveness of Television Advertising', *Political Behavior*, 16(1): 93–115.

Kahn, K. F. and Kenney, P. J. (1999) *The Spectacle of US Senate Campaigns.* Princeton, NJ: Princeton University Press.

Kahn, K. F. and Kenney, P. J. (2000) 'How Negative Campaigning Enhances Knowledge of Senate Elections', in J. A. Thurber, C. J. Nelson and D. A. Dulio (eds.), *Crowded Airwaves: Campaign Advertising in Elections.* Washington, DC: Brookings Institution Press. pp. 65–95.

Kahn, K. F. and Kenney, P. J. (2004) *No Holds Barred: Negativity in US Senate Campaigns.* Upper Saddle River, NJ: Pearson Prentice Hall.

Kahneman, D. and Tversky, A. (1979) 'Prospect Theory: An Analysis of Decision Under Risk', *Econometrica*, 47(2): 263–91.

Kaid, L., Chanslor, M. and Hovind, M (1992) 'The Influence of Program and Commercial Type on Political Advertising

Effectiveness', *Journal of Broadcasting and Electronic Media*, 36(3): 303–20.

Kanouse, D. E. and Hanson, L. R. Jr. (1972) 'Negativity in Evaluations', in E. E. Jones, D. E. Kanouse, H. H. Kelley, R. E. Nisbett, and S. Valins (eds.), *Attribution: Perceiving the Causes of Behavior.* Morristown, NJ: General Learning. pp. 47–62.

Kinder, D. R. (2003) 'Communication and Politics in the Age of Information', in D. O. Sears, L. Huddy and R. Jervis (eds.), *Oxford Handbook of Political Psychology.* New York: Oxford University Press. pp. 357–93.

Krasno, J. S. and Green, D. P. (2008) 'Do Televized Presidential Ads Increase Voter Turnout? Evidence from a Natural Experiment', *The Journal of Politics*, 70(1): 245–61.

Lang, A. (1991) 'Emotion, Formal Features, and Memory for Televized Political Advertisements', in F. Biocca (ed.), *Television and Political Advertising.* Vol. 1. Hillsdale, NJ: Lawrence Erlbaum Associates. pp. 221–43.

Lau, R. (1982) 'Negativity in Person Perception', *Political Behavior*, 4(4): 353–77.

Lau, R. (1985) 'Two Explanations for Negativity Effects in Political Behavior', *American Journal of Political Science*, 29(1): 353–77.

Lau, R. and Pomper, G. M. (2001) 'Effects of Negative Campaigning on Turnout in US Senate Elections, 1988–1998', *The Journal of Politics*, 63(3): 804–19.

Lau, R. and Pomper, G. M. (2002) 'Effectiveness of Negative Campaigning in US Senate Elections', *American Journal of Political Science*, 46(1): 47–66.

Lau, R. and Pomper, G. M. (2004) *Negative Campaigning: An analysis of US Senate Elections.* Lanham, MD: Roman & Littlefield, Publishers, Inc.

Lau, R. and Redlawsk, D. (2005) 'Effects of Positive and Negative Political Advertisements on Information Processing', unpublished manuscript. Rutgers University.

Lau, R. and Rovner, I. B. (2009) 'Negative Campaigning', *Annual Review of Political Science*, 12: 285–306.

Lau, R., Sigelman, L., Heldman, C. and Babbitt, P. (1999) 'The Effects of Negative Political Advertisements: A Meta-Analytic Assessment', *American Political Science Review*, 93(4): 851–76.

Lau, R., Sigelman, L. and Rovner, I. B. (2007) 'The Effects of Negative Political Campaigns: A Meta-Analytic Reassessment', *The Journal of Politics*, 69(4): 1176–1209.

Leshner, G. and Thorson, E. (2000) 'Overreporting Voting: Campaign Media Public Mood, and the Vote', *Political Communication*, 17(3): 263–78.

Marcus, G., Newman, W. R. and MacKuen, M. (2000) *Affective Intelligence and Political Judgment.* Chicago, IL: University of Chicago Press.

Martin, P. S. (1999) 'The Underwhelmed Citizen: A Theory of Media Influence on Conditional Political Participation', paper presented at the annual meeting of the American Political Science Association. Atlanta.

Martinez, M. D. and Delegal, T. (1990) 'The Irrelevance of Negative Campaigns to Political Trust: Experimental and Survey Results', *Political Communication and Persuasion*, 7(1): 25–40.

McGraw, K. M. and Steenbergen, M. (1997) 'Pictures in the Head: Memory Representation of Political Candidates', in M. Lodge and K. M. McGraw (eds.), *Political Judgment: Structure and Process*. Ann Arbor, MI: The University of Michigan Press. pp. 15–42.

Merritt, S. (1984) 'Negative Political Advertising: Some Empirical Findings', *Journal of Advertising*, 13: 27–38.

Miller, W. E. and Shanks, J. M. (1996) *The New American Voter*. Cambridge, MA: Harvard University Press.

Min, Y. (2004) 'News Coverage of Negative Political Campaigns: An Experiment of Negative Campaign Effects on Turnout and Candidate Preference', *The International Journal of Press/Politics*, 9(4): 95–111.

Mooney, A. (2008) 'Cindy McCain lashes out at media "viciousness"', 21 October, http://politicalticker.blogs.cnn.com/category/cindy-mccain/ (accessed 6 March 2009).

Newhagen, J. E. and Reeves, B. (1991) 'Emotion and Memory Responses for Negative Political Advertising: A Study of Television Commercials Used in the 1988 Presidential Election', in F. Biocca (ed.), *Television and Political Advertising*. Vol. 1. Hillsdale, NJ: Lawrence Erlbaum Associates. pp. 197–220.

Niven, D. (2005) 'Issue-Related Learning in a Gubernatorial Campaign: A Panel Study', unpublished manuscript. Florida Atlantic University.

Niven, D. (2006) 'A Field Experiment on the Effects of Negative Campaign Mail on Voter Turnout in a Municipal Election', *Political Research Quarterly*, 59(2): 203–10.

Patterson, K. D. and Shea, D. (2001) 'Local Norms and Neutral Observers: Rethinking the Effects of Negative Campaigning', presented at the annual meeting of the American Political Science Association. San Francisco.

Pinkleton, B. (1997) 'The Effects of Negative Comparative Political Advertising on Candidate Evaluations and Advertising Evaluations: An Exploration', *Journal of Advertising*, 26: 19–29.

Pinkleton, B. and Garramone, G. M. (1992) 'A Survey of Responses to Negative Political Advertising: Voter Cognition, Affect, and Behavior', *Proceedings of the 1992 Conference of the American Academy of Advertising*, 127–33.

Pinkleton, B, Um, N. H. and Austin, E. W. (2002) 'An Exploration of the Effects of Negative Political Advertising on Political Decision Making', *Journal of Advertising*, 31: 13–25

Pitkin, H. F. (1967) *The Concept of Representation*. Berkeley, CA: University of California Press.

Richey, M. H., Bono, F. S., Lewis, H. V. and Richey, H. W. (1982) 'Selectivity of Negative Bias in Impression Formation', *Journal of Social Psychology*, 116(1): 107–18.

Roberts, M. S. (1995) 'Political Advertising: Strategies for Influence', in K. E. Kendall (ed.), *Presidential Campaign Discourse: Strategic Communication Problems*. Albany, NY: SUNY Press. pp. 179–99.

Roddy, B. L. and Garramone, G. M. (1988) 'Appeals and Strategies of Negative Political Advertising',

Journal of Broadcasting and Electronic Media, 32(4): 415–27.

Sakamaki, S. and Nishijima, M. (2009) 'Negative Campaigning Hits Japan as LDP Cartoon Attacks Hatoyama', 22 July, http://www.bloomberg.com/apps/news (accessed August 10 2009).

Sigelman, L. and Shiraev, E. (2002) 'The Rational Attacker in Russia? Negative Campaigning in Russian Presidential Elections', *The Journal of Politics*, 64(1): 45–62.

Simamora, A. P. (2009) 'Negative Campaigning Rife Among Rivals', 22 May, http://www.thejakartapost.com/news. (accessed 10 August 2009).

Shapiro, M. A. and Rieger, R. H. (1992) 'Comparing Positive and Negative Political Advertising on Radio', *Journalism Quarterly*, 69(1): 135–45.

Swint, K. C. (2005) *Mudslingers: The Top 25 Negative Political Campaigns of All Time, Countdown from No. 25 to No. 1*. Westport, CT: Praeger.

Teinowitz, I. (2008) 'Political Ads Hit $1 Billon Mark; Spending, Negativity up in Battle for Senate; Boon for Spot TV', *Advertising Age*, 4 November.

Thorson, E., Christ, W. G. and Caywood, C. (1991) 'Selling Candidates Like Tubes of Toothpaste: Is the Comparison Apt?', in F. Biocca (ed.), *Television and Political Advertising*. Vol. 1. Hillsdale, NJ: Lawrence Erlbaum Associates. pp. 145–72.

USA Today (2004) 'GOP Chief: Democrats Plan 'Dirtiest Campaign' in Modern History', 12 April, http://www.usatoday.com/news/politicselections/nation/president/2004–02–12-gillespie_x.htm (accessed 6 March 2009).

Usborne, D. (2006) 'Is this the Dirtiest Election Ever? Republicans Fear Landslide Defeat', 30 October, http://www.independent.co.uk/news/world/americas/is-this-the-dirtiest-election-ever-republicans-fear-landslide-defeat-422166.html (accessed 6 March 2009).

Valentino, N. A., Hutchings, V. L. and Williams, D. (2004) 'The Impact of Political Advertising on Knowledge, Internet Information Seeking, and Candidate Preference', *Journal of Communication*, 54(2): 337–54.

Verba, S., Schlozman, K. and Brady, H. (1995) *Voice and Equality: Civic Voluntarism in American Politics*. Cambridge, MA: Harvard University Press.

Wanta, W., Lemert, J. B. and Lee, T. (1999) 'Consequences of Negative Political Advertising Exposure', in T. J. Johnson, C. E. Hays and S. P. Hays (eds.), *Engaging the Public: How Government and the Media Can Reinvigorate American Democracy*. Colorado: Roman & Littlefield. pp. 97–109.

Wattenberg, M. and Brians, C. (1999) 'Negative Campaign Advertising: Demobilizer or Mobilizer?', *American Political Science Review*, 93(4): 877–90.

West, D. M. (2005) *Air Wars: Television Advertising in Election Campaigns, 1952–2004*. Washington, DC: CQ Press.

Zaller, J. (1992) *The Nature and Origins of Mass Opinion*. Cambridge: Cambridge University Press.

15

Changes in European Public Service Broadcasting: Potential Consequences for Political Knowledge, Attitudes and Behavior

Kees Aarts and Holli A. Semetko

Research on the impact of television on political attitudes and behavior has at various times praised and criticized the medium. Television has been praised as a 'cognitive mobilizer' with its initial expansion as a mass medium that increased the public's access to political information (Dalton, 2004: 20–1). Because of the powerful visuals, television can be especially important for political learning (Graber, 1988, 2001). Others have argued that the increased volume of political information has done more to give viewers opportunities to turn away from political information entirely, and these studies were based on the US context (Entman, 1983; Prior, 2007). Research in the US context has pointed to negative relationships between political attitudes and television exposure: the negative, game-oriented nature of campaign news tends to have negative consequences for public perceptions of politics and politicians (Patterson, 1993, 2002). The erosion of social capital – social networks, norms and trust – was attributed to the increasing amount of time that Americans spend watching television (Putnam, 1995). Yet there are also important notable studies that point to the positive consequences for political attitudes and behaviors – from television

viewing in elections generally (Norris, 1996, 2000), from entertainment television (Baum, 2005; Baum and Jamison, 2006), and even from exposure to negative campaigning (Kahn and Kenney, 1999).

Europe, in contrast to the USA, has had a strong tradition of public service broadcasting. With the exception of the UK, in which there has been controlled competition between public service and commercial channels since the 1950s, public service broadcasting channels dominated national media landscapes in most of western Europe until the late 1980s and early 1990s when cable and satellite brought many more options to European viewers. Unlike central Europe after 1989 in which a plethora of commercial broadcasters emerged almost overnight, in most western European countries commercialization has developed over many years.

The value of public service broadcasting is exemplified by research that has found that exposure to commercial channels in Europe is negatively associated with political attitudes. Civic and political attitudes are affected differently by different types of television news programs (commercial versus public service) and this has been established in Britain (Newton, 1999), Belgium (Hooghe, 2002), the Netherlands (Aarts and Semetko, 2003) and other EU member states (Holtz-Bacha and Norris, 2001). These studies stem primarily from media systems characterized by a once dominant and still strong public service broadcasting ethos that was affected by commercial broadcasting in the 1990s.

As European media systems have moved toward a more liberal market model over the past two decades, homogenization emerged as one response of public broadcasting to their commercial rivals. When operating budgets of public broadcasting corporations are partly or entirely dependent on advertising income or ratings, as is the case in many countries, then pressure is felt from 'the market' of viewers and advertisers (European Audiovisual Observatory, 2002). Hallin and Mancini go further to argue that commercialization leads to a homogenization of media contents and a 'global set of media practices' (2004: 277). They discuss how commercialization has shifted the linkages of the Mediterranean and the North/Central European media systems from politics to commerce. Journalists, they argue, are increasingly focusing on information and entertainment that can be sold on the market to advertisers or in other ways. Programs such as *Big Brother* or *Who Wants to Be a Millionaire* are just two examples of how a formula developed in one country is sold, adapted and broadcast in many countries.

This shift in the political communication systems has various consequences. Since their position in the mediated communication process has been eroded, traditional political parties and related organizations have lost some of their influence to the media. Uncommon political events such as crises and scandals get relatively more prominent positioning in the media than routine political activities and accomplishments (Thompson, 2000). As the media select which scandals and issues to report, this also contributes to a growing influence of the media on European political communications (Semetko et al., 2000).

Although these basic changes in the balance of power in political communication are evident in the literature, the consequences for citizens' political knowledge and attitudes are far from clear. At first sight it could be that the consequences of commercialization for politics in Europe are negative, with the changes in the focus and contents of news diminishing the level of political discussion and information. Yet, shifting the perspective of political news from the elite to the ordinary citizen may also enhance political discussion and information, precisely because the news is popularized.

COMMERCIALIZATION: WITH WHAT EFFECT?

What are the effects, if any, of commercialization of broadcasting on political knowledge, attitudes and behavior? Previous studies drawing on data collected in Europe are limited in the sense that they rely on (repeated) cross-sectional data. When studying the impact of commercialization of broadcasting, cross-sectional data have two important shortcomings. First, they severely limit the internal validity of the results of analyses (the extent to which relationships can be regarded as truly causal). Second, they do not take the dynamic character of commercialization into account.

We are interested in the consequences of commercialization for political knowledge, interest, discussion and attitudes, such as efficacy, trust and cynicism. We make use of an unusual panel study to assess the dynamics of the relationships between the commercialization of broadcasting and citizens' political knowledge, attitudes and behavior. The panel survey data were collected over a four-year period of rapid development in one national media system that exemplifies trends in the EU.

Our data were collected in the 1998–2002 panel study of the Dutch Parliamentary Election Study (DPES). With the panel data, we are able to observe changes in the news and information preferences, and in political behavior and attitudes, among the same respondents at two time points separated by a period of four years. During this time frame, there were growing efforts by the commercial channels to attract new viewers.

The DPES is a multi-mode survey project, and the 1998–2002-panel component combines data from face-to-face interviews with results from drop-off questionnaires.[1] The 1998 study started with pre-election face-to-face interviews with a 50% response rate (net $N = 2101$). Post-election face-to-face interviews were conducted with 86% of this group (1814), and 66% (1199) of the post-election respondents filled out and sent in the drop-off questionnaire. In 1999, the respondents of the 1998 post-election survey were approached with a telephone/mail survey focusing in electoral turnout, in which 56% (1009) took part. In 2002, the same group was approached once more, with a 38% (689) response rate in the face-to-face interviews, and 35% ($N = 637$) completing a drop-off questionnaire. Most of our analyses are based on approximately 456 respondents who provided valid responses to the questions of interest in both panel waves. Although several weight variables are available, we did not weight the data. The main reasons are that the available weighting models correct only for the 1998 respondents, and that we are more interested in structures, change and relationships than in descriptives.

News Audiences

The frequency of news viewing was directly assessed in the surveys. Respondents were asked to indicate how often per week they watch the television programs that are broadcast at least five times per week. For the purposes of our analysis the news programs were assigned to two types: public television news and commercial television news. For assessing the exposure to public and commercial television news, the *number* of television news programs a respondent reports viewing regularly is not very relevant. Instead, we are interested in the *intensity* with which he or she turns to this particular type of news program. Therefore, for purposes of analysis, we recorded the highest intensity of news use per type.[2]

For each respondent, the intensity of using public and commercial television news programs was thus established both in 1998 and in 2002. The frequency distributions for the respondents in the panel study (N = 456) are depicted in Figures 15.1(a) and 15.1(b).

The respondents as a group are more intensively exposed to public television news programs than to commercial television news in both 1998 and 2002, as can be seen in Figures 15.1(a) and 15.1(b). This can to a large extent be attributed to the daily 8.00 pm NOS news, the most popular news program on Dutch television. More than 50% of the respondents watch public television news at least five days per week, with a slight increase in the period 1998–2002. In contrast, a very small percentage of the respondents never watch public television news.

The major news program on Dutch commercial television is the 7.30 pm RTL4 news. Another widely viewed news and current affairs program that was started after the 1998 election study data had been collected, is the late night show *Barend en Van Dorp* (RTL4). Although the intensity with which the respondents view commercial television news is much lower than for public television news, Figure 15.1(b) shows a clear increase in the intensity of commercial television use from 1998 to 2002.[3] The group of respondents who watch commercial television news programs more than four times per week increases from 21 to 31%; together with those who watch commercial television news three or four times per week, the group increased from 38% in 1998 to 59% in 2002. Viewing commercial news programs has definitely become more popular over the four-year period.

The frequency distributions depicted in Figures 15.1(a) and 15.1(b) provide information about the intensity of exposure to public and commercial television separately. They do not reveal to what extent news viewing on public and commercial channels is correlated. Are those who intensively watch public television news completely different people than those who intensively watch commercial television news? A profile of news audience groups, or types of viewers, is needed to address this question. Tables 15.1 and 15.2 provide these news audience profiles, in 1998 and 2002, respectively, as a typology. We collapsed each of the intensity measures reported in Figures 15.1(a) and 15.1(b) into two categories: less than three times per week and at least three times per week.

A comparison of the typologies in Tables 15.1 and 15.2 reveals some interesting facts about the development of news audiences. First, the group of respondents who do not watch either type of television news intensively has slightly decreased between 1998 and 2002.

Second, the relative size of the other three news audience groups shows that in 1998, almost one-half of the respondents intensively watched public television news but not commercial television news. This group has shrunk to a third of the respondents in 2002. At the same time, the group who views both public and commercial news programs intensively has increased from 25 to 46%. These changes over time imply that the relatively sharp distinction between public and commercial television audiences in 1998 considerably softened in four years.

Table 15.3 depicts these changes at the individual level. We can now see that a large number (39%) of those who only watched commercial television news intensively in 1998, have taken up viewing public television news with a great intensity as well by 2002. Similarly, 39% of the staunch public television news viewers of 1998 intensively watch commercial television news as well by 2002. These figures indirectly testify to the related developments of commercialization and homogenization discussed above.

Summing up, we have constructed a typology of television news audiences on the basis of the intensity with which people watch television news programs on commercial and public channels. The typology has been applied to our panel respondents in 1998 and 2002, and the comparison reveals a clear development toward a mixture of both public and commercial television news use. Although the evidence is indirect (we have not researched the contents of the news programs), this development of news use is completely in line with the expectation that the early phase of commercialization of media systems goes hand-in-hand with a homogenization of the supply of news programs.

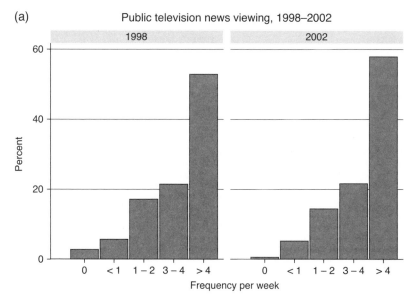

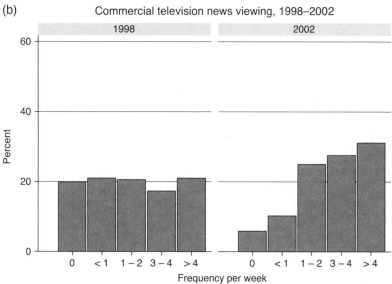

Figure 15.1   (a) Public and (b) commercial television news viewing

Demographic Characteristics of News Audiences

Before we turn to addressing the relationship between type of television news exposure and political attitudes, we discuss the relationship with demographic characteristics. Commercial television probably attracts audiences that differ from public television audiences on demographic

characteristics, such as gender, age and education, which are also important for political attitudes. Since we want to avoid attributing effects to television news use that in reality result from audience characteristics we first look at the major demographic variables.

For demographic control variables we selected gender, age (in years) and the highest completed education (in 10 categories), which were all

Table 15.1 Typology of television news viewers, 1998

		Public TV news	
		Less than 3 times per week	At least 3 times per week
Commercial TV news	Less than 3 times per week	12.3%	49.3%
	At least 3 times per week	13.4%	25.0%

Note: Entries denote percentage of all respondents in the analysis; $N = 456$.

Table 15.2 Typology of television news viewers, 2002

		Public TV news	
		Less than 3 times per week	At least 3 times per week
Commercial TV news	Less than 3 times per week	8.1%	33.1%
	At least 3 times per week	12.3%	46.5%

Note: Entries denote percentage of all respondents in the analysis; $N = 456$.

Table 15.3 Individual change in television news viewing, 1998–2002

		Type of viewer, 1998				
		Not intensively	Intensively commercial	Intensively public	Intensively both	Total
Type of viewer, 2002	Not intensively	39.3	6.6	3.6	2.6	8.1
	Intensively commercial	12.5	49.2	2.7	11.4	12.3
	Intensively public	21.4	4.9	54.7	11.4	33.1
	Intensively both	26.8	39.3	39.1	74.6	46.5
	Total	100.0% (56)	100.0% (61)	100.1% (225)	100.0% (114)	100.0% (456)

measured in the 1998 wave of the panel study. We expect that in general women in the Netherlands more often watch commercial television programs, which include relatively many soaps and light amusement shows, than men and these programs may feed into new programs. Since older people may have acquired strong viewing habits, we expect them to prefer public television over commercial channels. Those with higher levels of education probably view public television news relatively often because of its presumed greater information content. At the same time, women, younger people and those with lower levels of education also tend to have lower scores on a number of political attitudes such as interest, efficacy and trust as measured by Dutch national election studies.

The variables age and education are presented in Table 15.4 in dichotomous format (with approximately 50% of the respondents in each category). In 1998 and in 2002, women tend to view commercial news programs more intensively than men. Young persons more often intensively watch commercial news programs only. Older persons in 1998 belong more often to the 'intensively public' and 'intensively both' categories, but in 2002 they are only clearly overrepresented in the 'intensively both' group. Apparently, the increased size of the latter group in 2002 is at least partly the result of older people who have started watching commercial news programs in the 1998–2002 period under study. Finally, in 1998 the more highly educated tend to be somewhat overrepresented among those who do not intensively watch news programs at all (perhaps some of them prefer newspapers). The less well educated more often watch commercial news intensively, in both years. In 2002, we find that those with higher education are clearly overrepresented among those who watch public television news, but this group has clearly decreased in size since 1998 (see Tables 15.1 and 15.2). It appears that especially those with lower levels of education have started watching commercial news since 2002.

Table 15.4 Television news viewing and background characteristics

1998		Gender		Age		Education		Political knowledge	
		Male	Female	≤ 43	>43	Low	High	Low	High
Type of viewer	Not intensively	10.6%	13.7%	14.4%	10.3%	9.2%	15.4%	19.1%	6.2%
	Intensively commercial	9.1	16.9	17.1	9.8	17.5	9.2	22.8	5.0
	Intensively public	54.8	44.8	46.4	52.1	47.8	50.9	32.1	64.7
	Intensively both	25.5	24.6	22.1	27.8	25.4	24.6	26.0	24.1
	n =	(208)	(248)	(222)	(234)	(228)	(228)	(215)	(241)
2002		Gender		Age		Education		Political knowledge	
		Male	Female	≤ 43	>43	Low	High	Low	High
Type of viewer	Not intensively	7.2%	8.9%	11.3%	5.1%	6.6%	9.6%	13.0%	3.7%
	Intensively commercial	7.7	16.1	14.9	9.8	15.4	9.2	20.9	4.6
	Intensively public	35.6	31.0	33.8	32.5	26.3	39.9	21.9	43.2
	Intensively both	49.5	44.0	40.1	52.6	51.8	41.2	44.2	48.5
	n =	(208)	(248)	(222)	(234)	(228)	(228)	(215)	(241)

What is the relationship between political knowledge and viewing preferences? In 1998, the more knowledgeable tend to watch public television news much more often than the less knowledgeable. By 2002, although the percentage of people who exclusively watch public television news has decreased as people tend to combine news resources more often watching both public and commercial news programs intensively, the basic relationship remains the same. Those with little or no knowledge in 1998 were more inclined to be watching commercial news relatively more intensively or no news at all, compared to the high knowledge group. That relationship changed somewhat by 2002, it weakened but did not disappear. Those in the low knowledge group in 2002 also watch both commercial and public news programs, but the proportion is significantly less than those in the high knowledge group.

In summary, not all our expectations regarding the relationship with demographic characteristics are borne out by the data, mainly because the news audience groups are themselves in a state of flux. But women, younger respondents and those with lower levels of education are overrepresented among intensive viewers of commercial television news.

Political Communication and Attitudes of News Audiences

We analyzed six indicators of political communication and attitudes. For one of these, political discussion, we have only one measurement in the first, 1998, wave of the panel study. This variable refers to whether, when there is a discussion about domestic political problems, the respondent would not be interested and not listen, or would listen with interest, or would join the conversation. The other five indicators have been measured in both the 1998 and the 2002 waves of the panel. They are: subjective political interest; external efficacy; internal efficacy; political cynicism and trust in institutions. The wordings of the scale items are in the Appendix.

For these 11 dependent variables (six in 1998, five in 2002) univariate analyses of variance have been conducted. The explanatory factors are the news audience groups in 1998 and 2002, respectively, defined in Tables 15.1 and 15.2. The three demographic control variables discussed above – gender, age and education – were included in the model as (continuous) covariates.[4]

The results are summarized in Table 15.5. The table provides the (estimated) mean values of each of the dependent variables for the four news audience groups, at the mean value of the three covariates. These figures show to what extent the different news audience groups are also different on the political variables. The extent to which the dependent variables (political communication and attitudes) can be explained by the news audience groups and the demographic covariates is indicated by the eta^2 – coefficient of the model. The partial eta^2 of the type of viewer indicates which part of the explained variance is attributed to the variation in the type of viewer (the news audience groups). The statistical significance of both the model as a whole and of the main factor has been tested.[5]

In almost all analyses of variance reported in Table 15.5, the type of viewer (the news audience group respondents belong to) does make a difference for the scores on the political variables, when controlled for gender, age and education. The effect is relatively strong for joining political discussions (measured only in 1998) and subjective interest (measured in both panel waves). The news audience group one belongs to is also important for the internal efficacy score of respondent, which indicates how confident one is about one's own role in politics. Controlling for gender, age and education, the news audience group membership is less important, though still statistically significant, for political cynicism and trust in institutions. In the case of external efficacy, type of viewer reaches statistical significance only in 1998.

Substantively more interesting in Table 15.5 are the estimated means of the dependent variables when holding the controls constant at their mean values. For example, for joining a political discussion we see that the highest score (that is, the

highest probability that a respondent joins a political discussion or at least listens with interest, when holding gender, age and education constant) is found for respondents who intensively watch public television news *or* both public and commercial news (1.54). Those who do not watch television news intensively at all have the lowest mean on this variable (1.17). The viewers of news programs on commercial television have a mean score on joining a political discussion that is in between these two.

The pattern for the other dependent variables is more or less similar, with small variations. Invariably, respondents who intensively watch public television news programs alone, or in combination with commercial television news programs, have on the average higher scores on subjective interest, external and internal political efficacy, and trust in institutions, and lower scores on political cynicism. These findings control for gender, age and education. The lowest average scores (highest for cynicism) are found among those respondents who do not watch television news intensively at all or those who watch commercial television news intensively. Those who do

Table 15.5 Political discussion and attitudes, and television news viewing

1998		Joining discussion (0–2)	Subjective political interest (0–2)	External efficacy (0–5)	Internal efficacy (0–3)	Political cynicism (0–3)	Trust in institutions (0–10)
Estimated mean for type of viewer[a]	Not intensively	1.17	0.67	2.84	1.20	1.46	4.32
	Intensively commercial	1.42	0.86	2.55	1.20	1.85	4.15
	Intensively public	1.54	1.03	3.13	1.61	1.46	5.10
	Intensively both	1.54	0.98	3.06	1.37	1.61	4.49
	Eta² model	0.08**	0.13**	0.11**	0.23**	0.10**	0.05**
	Partial eta² type of viewer	0.04**	0.05**	0.02*	0.04**	0.03*	0.02*
2002							
Estimated mean for type of viewer[a]	Not intensively	–	0.77	2.47	1.01	1.81	2.73
	Intensively commercial	–	0.91	2.55	1.26	1.92	3.50
	Intensively public	–	1.07	2.85	1.37	1.55	4.01
	Intensively both	–	1.09	2.70	1.53	1.68	4.02
	Eta² model	–	0.12**	0.10**	0.18**	0.11**	0.07**
	Partial eta² type of viewer	–	0.04**	0.01	0.03**	0.02*	0.02*

Notes: [a]At the mean values of the covariates, gender, age and education. *F-statistic significant at 0.05; **F-statistic significant at 0.01.

not watch television news intensively at all have the lowest scores (highest on cynicism) on the measures of joining a discussion, subjective interest, internal efficacy and trust (the latter only in 2002). Those who watch commercial television news intensively have the lowest scores on measures of external efficacy, cynicism and trust in 1998. We should add, however, that in general the differences in scores on the dependent variables for different types of viewers, although statistically significant, are not particularly large, neither in 1998 nor in 2002. But the differences are persistent over a four-year period.

To sum up, we have shown that there are relationships between the news audience groups and an array of political communication and attitude variables. These relationships all point in the same direction: intensive viewers of public television news programs tend to score higher on political discussion, interest, efficacy and trust – and lower on political cynicism. These relationships are relatively stable over time: basically, they did not change over the period 1998–2002.

Dynamics of Political Attitudes

What are the relationships between news audience group membership, on the one hand, and political knowledge and change in political attitudes, on the other? We now turn to discussing the dynamics of political attitudes in the context of political knowledge and the type of television news use. We collapsed the 1998 audience group categories from four to two groups: high and low. Those who watch public news or both public and commercial news intensively are in the high use group, and the rest are in the low use group. Political knowledge in 1998 was also dichotomized (values 0–6 as low; 7–12 as high).

Each of the five dependent variables is displayed in Table 15.6, with the change scores on each measure computed at the individual level. For changes in the measures of external and internal efficacy which both declined over the four-year period, on average, knowledge is more important than type of public television news use to understanding that change. The highly knowledgeable became less efficacious over the four-year period. Looking at trust in institutions which also has declined on average and among all subgroups over the four-year period, it is clear that type of public news use is more important for changes in trust over the four-year period than is political knowledge. Cynicism increased generally over the four-year period among all groups, with the highest increase among those with high knowledge and low public television use.

Subjective political interest increased over the four-year period, and these changes are mainly to be found among those in the low public television news use group.

CONCLUSION

In most European broadcasting systems, commercialization is relatively recent phenomenon. These media systems provide insight into the correlates and consequences of commercialization because they are still in the midst of a twofold process of homogenization – *of the system* toward a more liberal model, and *within the system* between public and commercial broadcasting. The latter type of homogenization shows a great deal of variation across countries. In some countries, public and commercial channels, while to some extent competing for the same scarce funds, maintain their own ground with unique programming. In other countries, the public and commercial channels compete with each other by producing more similar programming. The Netherlands is an example of a country in which public broadcasting has chosen the latter strategy.

A time frame of four years is in all likelihood long enough to find some echoes of the commercialization of broadcasting in survey data. In the 1998–2002 time period in the Netherlands, both commercial channels and public channels were employing various strategies to obtain a better market positions among audiences and advertisers.

Several general findings emerge from the panel study. First, exposure to television programs, including the entire range of entertainment and information available, in the Netherlands in 1998 is structured according to a clear public-commercial divide. This means that viewing programs on commercial channels tends to be a different activity – by different viewers – than viewing programs on public channels. This structure of television use is quite stable over the time period studied.

Turning to exposure to television news programs in particular, we found that the percentage of intensive viewers of both public and commercial news almost doubled over the four-year period. Respondents who in 1998 focus almost exclusively on public television news programs, by 2002 watched commercial television news as well. This development of news use is in line with the expectation that with commercialization, the supply of news programs is homogenized.

We have shown that the type of news audience group people belong to (no intensive news viewer at all; intensive viewer of public news; intensive

Table 15.6 Public television news, political knowledge and change in political attitudes

External efficacy		Political knowledge	
		Low	High
Public TV news use	Low	−0.16	−0.41
	High	−0.28	−0.33
Internal efficacy		Political knowledge	
		Low	High
Public TV news use	Low	0.13	−0.15
	High	0.05	−0.14
Trust in institutions		Political knowledge	
		Low	High
Public TV news use	Low	−0.66	−0.67
	High	−0.91	−0.97
Cynicism		Political knowledge	
		Low	High
Public TV news use	Low	0.04	0.26
	High	0.15	0.12
Subjective political interest		Political knowledge	
		Low	High
Public TV news use	Low	0.16	0.19
	High	0.02	0.07

Note: Change scores computed at individual level, subtracting 1998 score from 2002 score.

viewer of commercial news; intensive viewer of both public and commercial news) is significantly related to indicators of political communication and political attitudes such as interest, internal efficacy, cynicism and trust, controlling for demographic characteristics such as gender, age and education. These relationships can all be interpreted in the same way: intensive viewers of public television news programs tend to score higher on political discussion, interest, efficacy and trust – and lower on political cynicism. The relationships do not change much over the four-year period.

The combination of persistent relationships together with a change in the relative size of news audience groups could also have affected the overall mean scores of the respondents on the political variables. But this is unlikely, since the major change in relative group size was from those who watch public television news intensively to the group who intensively watch both public and commercial news – and these groups do not differ greatly on the dependent variables.

This brings us to the question of causality. Can these findings only be interpreted as relationships with no direction specified, or do they also point toward a *causal* relationship between exposure to

commercial television news and political discussion and attitudes? Obviously, the causality cannot be proven. It is at the outset very likely that causal effects occur in both directions: from political communication and attitudes toward differing use of the two types of television news programs, and the other way around. Past research has approached the causality issue from different perspectives, for example by eliminating potential rival explanations for the disappearance of social capital (Putnam, 1995), or by applying simultaneous equation models (Aarts and Semetko, 2003). Here, we have controlled for some demographic characteristics that contribute to composition effects in the various news audience groups: age, gender and education. We avoided discussing the causal nature of the relationships found. But we have provided indications that the relationship between television news viewing and political communication and attitudes is not merely an effect of the composition of audiences.

Our analysis has focused on changes in the relationships between types of television news use and political attitudes in a media system in a state of transition. The four-year period is long enough to show changes in public attitudes. A period of this length is also not an option for experimental research (which is better suited to addressing causality). By focusing on the case of the Dutch media system and its public, our analysis has brought out some of the dynamic consequences of the commercialization of broadcasting for mass political attitudes. It seems clear that these consequences occur, even when it is very difficult to disentangle the precise causal order.

Comparative research will determine the extent to which our results can be generalized to other countries in the EU and beyond. The DPES design provides a useful model for obtaining information on the structure of audiences in changing national media systems, and one that has already been the basis for building upon election studies in other countries.

ACKNOWLEDGMENT

This research benefited from a grant by the Dutch Organization for Scientific Research NWO (# 400–04–706).

NOTES

1   Data and documentation can be obtained at www.dpes.nl or through the major data archives.

2   If, for example, a respondent indicated in 1998 that he watched the following three commercial news programs, *RTL4 Journaal* almost every day (coded '5'), *RTL5 Journaal* three or four times per week (coded '4') and *Actienieuws* never (coded '1'), then his assigned score on the variable 'Commercial TV news' is '5'. What counts here is a daily exposure to commercial TV news, not the additional occasional exposure to similar programs.

3   This development may be related to the increase in the news value of the 2002 election when compared with 1998: the 2002 election marked the rise of the new party LPF and the murder of its founder and leader, Pim Fortuyn, just days before the 2002 election.

4   Age and education were included with their original codings, that is, age in years and education in 10 categories.

5   The latter test merely shows whether the type of viewer contributes to the explanation of the dependent variables when controlling for the demographic covariates – it can not be used to interpret the significance of differences between the estimated means. We also performed tests for the equality of variances of the dependent variables in each of the news audience groups. None of these tests pointed toward unequal variances.

APPENDIX: QUESTION WORDINGS

Political Knowledge

Count of the number of correct answers to questions about the name, party and political function of four national politicians shown on photographs: Jacques Wallage, Thom de Graaf, Annemarie Jorritsma, Piet Bukman.

Joining Discussion

'When there is a discussion in a group about such problems in our country, do you generally join the conversation, do you listen with interest, do you not listen or are you not interested?' (coded 0: does not listen/not interested; 1: listens with interest; 2: joins conversation)

Subjective Political Interest

'Are you very interested in political topics, fairly interested or not interested?' (coded -1: not interested at all; 0: fairly interested; 1: very interested)

External Efficacy Score

Count of the number of 'not true' answers to the following questions:

- Members of parliament do not care about the opinions of people like me
- Political parties are only interested in my vote and not in my opinions
- People like me have absolutely no influence on governmental policy
- So many people vote in elections that my vote does not matter
- Usually our representatives in the Second Chamber quickly lose contact with the people in the country

Internal Efficacy Score

Count of the number of 'positive' responses to the following questions:

- I am well qualified to play an active role in politics ((fully) agree)
- I have a good understanding of the important political problems in our country ((fully) agree)
- Sometimes politics seems so complicated that people like me cannot really understand what is going on ((fully) disagree)

Political Cynicism Score

Count of the number of '(fully) agree' responses to the following questions:

- Although they know better, politicians promise more than they can deliver
- Ministers and junior-ministers are primarily concerned about their personal interests
- One is more likely to become a member of parliament because of one's political friends than because of one's abilities

Trust in Institutions

Count of answers 'very much' and 'fairly much' on the question:

Would you tell me for each of the following Dutch institutions whether you have very much, fairly much, not so much confidence or no confidence at all in them?

Institutions presented: Churches, Army, Judges, Press, Police, Second Chamber, Civil Servants, Big corporations, European Union, NATO.

REFERENCES

Aarts, K. and Semetko, H. A. (2003) 'The Divided Electorate: Effects of Media Use on Political Involvement', *Journal of Politics*, 65(3): 759–84.

Baum, M. A. (2005) 'Talking the Vote: What Happens When Presidential Candidates Hit the Talk Show Circuit', *American Journal of Political Science*, 49(2): 213–34.

Baum, M. A. and Jamison, A. S. (2006) 'The Oprah Effect: How Soft News Helps Inattentive Citizens Vote Consistently', *Journal of Politics*, 68(4): 946–59.

Dalton, R. J. (2004) *Democratic Challenges, Democratic Choices: The Erosion of Political Support in Advanced Industrial Democracies.* Oxford: Oxford University Press.

Entman, R. M. (1983) *Democracy without Citizens: Media and the Decay of American Politics.* New York: Oxford University Press.

European Audiovisual Observatory (2002). *The Economy of the European Audiovisual Sector Yearbook 2002.* Strasbourg: Council of Europe.

Graber, D. A. (1988) *Processing the News: How People Tame the Information Tide.* 2nd edn. New York: Longman.

Graber, D. A. (2001) *Processing Politics: Learning from Television in the Internet Age.* Chicago, IL: University of Chicago Press.

Hallin, D. C. and Mancini, P. (2004) *Comparing Media Systems: Three Models of Media and Politics.* Cambridge: Cambridge University Press.

Holtz-Bacha, C. and Norris, P. (2001). '"To Entertain, Inform and Educate": Still the Role of Public Television in the 1990s?', *Political Communication*, 18(2): 123–40.

Hooghe, M. (2002) 'Watching Television and Civic Disengagement: Disentangling the Effects of Time, Programs, and Stations', *Press/Politics*, 7(2): 84–104.

Kahn, K. F. and Kenney, P. J. (1999) 'Do Negative Campaigns Mobilize or Suppress Turnout? Clarifying the Relationship between Negativity and Participation', *American Political Science Review*, 93(4): 877–90.

Newton, K. (1999) 'Mass Media Effects: Mobilization or Media Malaise?', *British Journal of Political Science*, 29(4): 577–99.

Norris, P. (1996) 'Does Television Erode Social Capital? A Reply to Putnam', *PS: Political Science and Politics*, 29(3): 474–80.

Norris, P. (2000) *A Virtuous Circle: Political Communications in Postindustrial Societies.* New York: Cambridge University Press.

Patterson, T. (1993) *Out of Order.* New York: A. Knopf.

Patterson, T. (2002) *The Vanishing Voter: Public Involvement in an Age of Uncertainty.* New York: A. Knopf.

Prior, M. (2007) *Post-Broadcast Democracy: How Media Choice Increases Inequality in Political Involvement and Polarizes Elections.* New York: Cambridge University Press.

Putnam, R. D. (1995) 'Tuning in, Tuning out: The Strange Disappearance of Social Capital in America', *PS: Political Science and Politics*, 28(4): 664–83.

Semetko, H. A., de Vreese, C. H. and Peter, J. (2000) 'Europeanised Politics—Europeanised Media? European Integration and Political Communication', *West European Politics*, 23(4): 121–141.

Thompson, J. B. (2000) *Political Scandal: Power and Visibility in the Media Age.* Cambridge, UK: Polity Press.

16

Social Networks, Public Discussion and Civic Engagement: A Socialization Perspective

Jack M. McLeod and Nam-Jin Lee

Our primary objective is to examine key variables of social network structure and processes used in contemporary political communication research, their antecedents and effects. Network effects on civic engagement and the perspective of political socialization research serve as a framework for our analyses. First, however, it is important to provide context for understanding present controversies by briefly reviewing the past to explain why the development of public discussion from philosophical argument into a central concept of political communication was delayed and fragmentary.

EARLY CONTROVERSIES REGARDING PUBLIC DISCUSSION

The idea that public discussion of political issues is an essential feature of democracy has been given widespread abstract support since autocratic rule began giving way to government based on consent of the governed more than three centuries ago. In more specific terms, however, there have been recurring controversies over what democracy requires in terms of who should constitute the participants, what matters are appropriate for discussion, what benefits and negative consequences ensue from public discussion and how public opinion formed from discussion should affect the policies enacted by their representatives. Until the 20th century, these controversies were based on normative theories of democracy resting on either optimistic or pessimistic assumptions regarding abstract questions ranging from the prerequisites of societies to the inherent qualities of human nature. Direct focus on the processes and effects of public discussion was rare. An exception was the eloquent if overly optimistic proposal in 1861 by John Stuart Mill in *On Liberty*:

> There must be discussion to show how experience is to be interpreted. Wrong opinions and practices gradually yield to fact and argument, but the facts and arguments, to produce any effect on the mind, must be brought before it. Very few facts tell their own story, without comments to bring out their meaning ... He who knows only his own side of the case, knows little of that ... The fatal tendency of mankind to leave off thinking about a thing when it is no longer doubtful is the cause of their errors. (Mill, 1861/1951: ch. 2)

Although this is a philosophical argument without evidence, parts of Mill's proposal could be translated into hypotheses for testing by modern social scientific methods: that discussion is influential on the memory of past experiences; that discussion with others who hold differing points of view is essential to changing one's mind; that simply knowing facts is inadequate for constructing meaning; that without knowing diverse points of view a person does not fully understand one's own position and that failure to continue to reflect on previous decisions will make errors more likely.

Similarly, optimistic views about the benefits of public discussion were evident in the commentaries of John Dewey (1927) critical of Walter Lippmann's pessimistic elitist assessment of the limited role citizens were capable of playing in the political process. Lippmann (1922) asserted that the public lacked *omnicompetent* citizens knowledgeable in the many technical areas relevant to an increasingly complex society. Ordinary citizens, limited by time and attention span and guided by 'the pictures in their heads', were relegated to the task of voting. Between the citizens and their elected officials, Lippmann placed specialized *experts,* such as statisticians, accountants, engineers and the like, who were capable of *sublimating* their own interests in the service of providing disinterested information to public officials, who would then make political decisions. Dewey used Lippmann as a foil to justify his own views that success in modern democracy requires sustaining the local face-to-face community and transforming the 'great society' into a great community. Discussion among citizens was important to translate the specialized knowledge of experts into practical knowledge useful to the participants. It provided meaning to knowledge and thereby made common knowledge and problem solutions emergent products of social processes. According to Dewey, discussion also led citizens to look beyond their own self-interests to work for the common good.

EMPIRICAL ROOTS OF POLITICAL DISCUSSION RESEARCH

Empirical evidence examining political discussion effects on voting decisions first appeared in the renowned Columbia University studies of two presidential campaigns, 1940 in Erie county, Ohio, and 1948 in Elmira, New York (Berleson et al., 1954; Lazarsfeld et al., 1948). A third Columbia study in 1945 examined public affairs and consumer decisions in Decatur, Illinois (Katz and Lazarsfeld, 1955). All three studies claimed persuasive influences of discussion networks within small, homogeneous communities in the pre-television era. The authors admitted these were not analyses of whole communities but rather were attempts to establish generalizations independent of time and space (see Berelson et al., 1954: 4). Media (newspapers and radio) and personal networks were pitted as *competing* independent sources of influence to test an individualistic mass society theory of direct and powerful media influence. Personal networks were declared as more influential. Opinion leaders in these networks used media as a resource, but no direct influence was accorded to media. Later evaluation and modern statistical methods revealed severe conceptual and methodological weaknesses (McLeod and Blumler, 1987: 286–8), but the evidence demonstrated personal influence within homogeneous social networks nonetheless. The Columbia research represented a highly innovative methodological breakthrough in panel design analysis. It also advanced the case for communication in social networks as important *social* phenomena in contrast to the highly *individualized* research that dominated the social science of that era.

There is a question, however, of why with such promising beginnings there was almost a 20-year gap between publication of the *Personal Influence* study in 1955 and two events putatively signaling the formal birth of the political communication field – the formation of the Political Communication division of the International Communication Association in 1973 and publication of *Political Communication: Issues and Strategies for Research* edited by Steven Chaffee in 1975. Several factors account for the delay. First, after the 1948 election, foundation funding and scholarly attention to voting research shifted from the Columbia studies' focus on communication networks to the University of Michigan using national samples emphasizing individuals' political attachments with little attention to sociological influences. Second, conclusions about minimal media effects limited by a host of necessary conditions (for example, Klapper, 1960) gave little incentive to develop new research in political communication. Third, by 1955 Paul Lazarsfeld had abandoned further communication research to work on key methodological issues in sociology. Bernard Berelson had left Columbia in 1951 and further discouraged communication research by declaring that knowledge about communication effects was complete (Berelson, 1959). Elihu Katz, alone among the set of Columbia authors, continued to study communication and went on to a distinguished research career. These circumstances left little opportunity to clarify or expand the conclusions of the Columbia voting studies. Though deserving for their innovations, they became communication classics unchallenged for decades because they were the 'only wheels in town'.

Termination of a communication focus of the US voting research and the limited effects conclusions had unanticipated consequences for the development of American communication research through the 1960s. In the first half of *Personal Influence* (1955), Katz provided a theorized context to the Decatur study that contradicted the competitive relationship of media use and interpersonal discussion conclusions of the Columbia studies. In its place, he proposed a model of interdependent interaction between media, conversation, opinion and action. His attempt to 'keep media in' was unfortunately ignored by most inside and outside the communication field. In addition, the Decatur data presented in the second half of *Personal Influence* had been gathered a decade prior to Katz's theorizing and lacked appropriate measures of the network processes corresponding to the primary/small group literature concepts reviewed in the first half of the book.

Political communication research on media effects had little visibility until Steven Chaffee and other 'young Turk' scholars emerged from the post-1950s communication doctoral programs. Recognizing that media effects are always limited in various ways but sometimes much more than minimal, they set out to develop better ways of measuring media use (for example, by combining exposure and attention to news content) and to look beyond persuasion to other more likely effects of media such as knowledge gain, agenda-setting and other cognitive effects (for example, Becker et al., 1975; McCombs and Shaw, 1972) and specified various types of conditional effects of media (McLeod and Reeves, 1980). Much of the new media effects research was published in outlets founded in the 1970s, including *Communication Research*. As a result of broadening the boundaries of political communication research, stronger and more varied media effects were found that became part of a new surge of research from the mid-1970s on.

Most important for this chapter, however, is that the new scholars also rejected the idea of a competitive relationship between media and interpersonal communication (Chaffee, 1982). It must be noted, however, that only the *process* aspects of interpersonal communication (for example, frequency of discussion) tended to be represented in this new research wave. Discussion frequency was found to be closely tied to attentive use of public affairs content and often showed positive effects on political knowledge and participation. Attention to the *structural* dimensions

of discussion *networks* and their effects would await the next wave of political research of the 1990s.

CONCEPTIONS OF SOCIAL NETWORKS AND POLITICAL DISCUSSION

The concept of social networks as a basic social unit came most directly from Georg Simmel (1908/1971), a turn of the century German sociologist. He theorized that *formal* characteristics of networks, *size* and *connections* between members, would determine the probabilities of *interactions* among its members. *Form* was the key source of influence, rather than *content* in terms of values or norms of the group, or qualities of its members. His exemplar network relations were loosely connected rather than having the closely knit affective ties typical of *groups*. Simmel's emphasis on form set him apart from the majority of sociologists from his day to this who assume that the attributes of *individual* actors in groups or networks matter most.

Social networks appeared in various guises after World War II in kinship, community network and industrial relation studies and in experimental studies of the influence of network configurations and structures (for example, Bavelas, 1950), and coding systems for recording interaction in small groups (for example, Bales, 1950). During the 1970s broader and more integrative approaches were developed by Harrison White and his students at Harvard including Mark Granovetter, Barry Wellman, Charles Tilly and Stanley Milgram. They shared a reaction against the abstract structural-functionalism of Talcott Parsons that dominated the sociology at that time with its focus on symbols, norms and cultural values. Social network analysis emerged in communication at Michigan State where Everett Rogers changed his focus from straightforward diffusion of innovation to the complexities of social networks in developing nations.

Common terminology gradually emerged that defined social networks as a social structure comprised of *nodes* (individuals or organizations) which are *connected* by one or more specific types of *interdependence* (for example, friendship, liking, disliking, problem discussion). Social networks are dynamic in that the key process is *communication* between members, a natural link to the study of communication. Research from diverse fields demonstrates the relevance of social network communication on many *levels of analysis*: *global* among nations, within and between *organizations* and *communities, and groups.* In simplest form, social networks can be represented as a map of the connections (ties) between all members (nodes) in the network. Network maps can describe *structural* characteristics: *size, centralization, density, homogeneity* and types of emergent *norms*. Other terms describe the position of the individual node within the network: *centrality, closeness* and *connectedness*. The frequency rather than the content of communication is used to represent the *process* aspects of networks. Analyses are conducted on either *whole networks* with the complete set of all relationships among members or *personal networks* with the specific relationship ties of a single member. Individuals may be members of several different networks depending on their basis of interdependence.

The growing prominence of social networks was signaled by an extensive battery of network structure and process items included in the 1985 General Social Survey (GSS). The growing body of knowledge about network analysis diffused unevenly through the various sub-fields of communication research. Social networks soon became a central enduring concern for *organizational* communication scholars. Network analytic involvement with relationships rather than individual attributes made it an attractive focus for many in *interpersonal* and in *health communication* research. In contrast, *political communication* researchers paid little attention to the structural characteristics of social networks. Later they discovered to their dismay that the 1985 GSS data file contained no political items to study the influences of the elaborate set of social network measures (for example, McLeod et al., 1999).

RECONNECTION OF PUBLIC DISCUSSION TO POLITICAL COMMUNICATION RESEARCH

The 1980s were productive years for the political communication field. The rapid growth of television in political campaigns led to gradual improvements in media use measures in biennial National Election Study surveys (NES, now ANES), a dominant data source for the US elections. Growing interest in communication among political scientists was further indicated by the fact that political communication was among the first sections formed when the American Political Science Association (APSA) went to an organized section format in 1985. Interests shared by political scientists and communication researchers were signaled in 1991 when the political communication section of APSA and its respective division in ICA agreed to co-sponsor the journal *Political Communication*.

It took more than interdisciplinary cooperation to bring public discussion back into the study of political communication. The stability of the small communities of the 1940s Columbia studies described by Berelson (1952) as functionally integrated and stabilized by a balance of pluralistic homogenous networks seemed ill-fitting to the instability of American society 40 years later. Years of social protest action by citizens for civil rights and against the Vietnam War seemed to call for models of *social change* rather than the Columbia model of *social control* via opinion leaders using personal influence to protect network followers from media influence. Examination of social network structures and their dynamic processes was needed.

Social network analysis concepts were introduced into political communication by the programmatic research of Robert Huckfeldt in the 1980s that has continued to examine how citizens' interactions with others in their social networks shape political behavior (Huckfeldt, 2009). The research proceeds from the long-standing finding that individuals within micro-social organizations tend to share political preferences, a phenomenon resulting from individuals' desires to associate with others like themselves to avoid disagreement (Huckfeldt and Mendez, 2008). Because agreement shapes communication processes that avoid disagreement, little new information will enter the network and both political learning and democratic deliberation will be curtailed. Evidence showed that political heterogeneity necessary for disagreement was not rare in that less than half the two-party voters identified all their discussion partners as holding their same vote preference, and that more than one-third named a discussant who supported the opposing party's candidate (Huckfeldt et al., 2004).

Huckfeldt makes a strong case for studying interdependent political processes in social networks systems:

Politics involves, at its essence, a large set of interdependent processes – communication, persuasion, mobilization and counter-mobilization, disagreement, conflict and polarization, delegation, compromise, and cooperation. None of these occur through the actions of independent atomized individuals: all occur as a function of one or more actors interacting with other actors – both friend and foe'. Further, '...: the form and function of interdependence is inherently *density dependent* – that particular patterns of interdependence are contingent on the particular composition of the actor's social context ... The substantive and empirical point of reference concerns the communication of information *among ordinary citizens,* the consequence of these information flows for patterns of persuasion among actors, the formation and survival of opinions and preferences among actors, and the resulting choices they make'. (2009: 921)

The diverse political talk rather optimistically portrayed by Huckfeldt and his associates was challenged by Mutz (2002b, 2006) using different measures of cross-cutting (politically heterogeneous) network composition. Mutz found that, when exposed to cross-cutting talk, the relatively small proportion of citizens are entrenched in heterogeneous networks are less likely to vote and participate, and more likely to delay their voting decisions. Cross-cutting exposure deterred the more confrontational forms of participation but not more benign activities. The costs of cross-cutting talk may be partly offset by other more beneficial outcomes for political tolerance. Mutz (2002a) found that exposure to dissonant views was associated with awareness of the rationales for opposing views but not for ones own position. Exposure to consonant views failed to influence awareness for either own or others' views. Further, exposure to dissonant views had no *direct* effect on political tolerance, but had an *indirect* effect through its stimulation of learning oppositional rationales. Mutz concludes that the opposing negative and positive effects of heterogeneity imply that America may face an uncomfortable choice between a participatory but highly polarized democracy and a tolerant but largely passive polity.

BROADENING CONCEPTIONS OF POLITICAL COMMUNICATION AND DEMOCRACY

In the previous section, networks were purely *political* in being judged homogeneous or heterogeneous based on the respondents' party or candidate preferences being the same or different from those of their discussion partners. The context was most often election campaigns and the criteria were voting or other campaign activities. Disturbing claims of a 40-year decline in various forms of participation in American civic life broadened the scope of political communication (Putnam, 2000). Putnam's evidence went beyond political trends to show erosion of civic life in the marked decline since the 1960s in encounters with others in the community, informal socializing, membership in local associations, active

involvement in local organizations and participation in league bowling – the inspiration for his title *Bowling Alone*. Increased levels in some forms of volunteering were however found among older citizens (Shah et al., 2008).

Putnam links the declining trends in aggregate participation to individual behavior through the concept of *social capital,* the *norms of reciprocity* or mutual obligations associated with social networks. Trust in other people, his key indicator of social capital, slipped 20% from 1960 to 1999. Among the most important ways in which social capital varies are *bonding* and *bridging* (Putnam, 2000: 22). Bonding networks based on similarity and exclusivity are inward-looking and stimulate specific reciprocity and mobilizing solidarity. Bridging networks, in contrast, outward looking and encompassing people across diverse social structural cleavages, are advantageous in having easier linkages to external assets and for information diffusion. Bonding and bridging correspond to the concepts of network homogeneity and heterogeneity discussed earlier. Separation of bonding and bridging networks suggests that some individuals may be members of both types of networks. Thus, it is important to conceptualize homogeneity and heterogeneity as dimensions of networks and to create separate indices for each rather than conflating the two in a single zero-sum index.

Understanding of civic engagement has been enhanced greatly in recent years by separate lines of research on the influences of social network discussion and attentive use of the news media. However, those studying social networks seldom have dealt with news media use in any meaningful way. Putnam confined his concern to thinking that time spent with television would displace time available for participation. The evidence for displacement is weak and reverse causation is likely – those staying home rather than going out to participate may turn to television for diversion. Attentive use of the news, both print and online, deserves a place in models of civic engagement along with the structure and processes of social networks.

Public concern was further raised by studies casting doubt about whether citizens' levels of political knowledge were sufficient to make informed judgments about public issues. Despite a threefold increase in the proportion of Americans who have attended college, factual knowledge of politics increased only marginally from the 1960s to the mid-1990s, and decreased after education controls (Delli Carpini and Keeter, 1996). However, political knowledge reversed the trend and showed increases in the 2004 and 2008 US election campaigns (Sotirovic and McLeod, 2008). Scholars use strong arguments and some evidence as reasons for pessimism or optimism about what political talk of average citizens can add to democracy.

Controversy surrounds the amount as well as the quality of the political talk of ordinary citizens. It is clear that political junkies are only a small segment of the public. Conover et al. (2002), using survey and focus group methods, found low levels of political talk, substantial status inequalities and avoidance of argumentation within discussions. Focus group members typically gave neither reasons nor justification for the own preferences and were unlikely to listen to reasons for different perspectives.

Michael Schudson (1997) stood among the pessimists against those who like Benjamin Barber (1984) claimed 'at the heart of democracy is talk'. Sociable talk in ordinary political conversation, according to Schudson, has little to do with democracy. To be effective, political conversation should have a purpose: solving problems, defending public policies or protecting one's own interests. Democratic talk is not spontaneous but rule governed and it is this type of formal problem-solving conversation that is at the heart of democracy.

More optimistic assessments of citizens' talk are plentiful. Gamson (1992) demonstrated that average people, although deficient in factual knowledge, are capable of sophisticated, coherent conversations about public issues. They use strategies to weave cognitive devices and available cultural resources together to constitute public discourse. Wyatt et al. (2000) also demonstrated that political conversation conducted in private has political consequences. Talking about politics has positive effects for both citizens and democratic processes by improving the quality of public opinion and encouraging public action.

Various field experimental programs have demonstrated the deliberative potential of talk. A 1994 Kids Voting USA project successfully raised the civic engagement of adolescents and their parents in large part by stimulating issue discussion among peers and between them and their parents (Chaffee et al., 1995). The most celebrated experiment was the 1996 National Issues Convention that brought more than 450 randomly selected strangers to Austin, Texas, to spend three days in discussions of various public issues. Small group discussions alternated with full assemblies where participants asked questions of experts and political candidates. Substantial attitude formation and change resulted that was largely mediated by information gain on the issues (Fishkin and Luskin, 1999). Talk in monitored deliberative sessions of the National Issue Forums enhanced political sophistication (Gastil and Dillard, 1999). The external validity question becomes how to extend these small-scale but expensive, carefully planned and controlled experiments into practical applications with entire populations.

Experimental explorations of the potential of public discussion for changing attitudes and civic engagement are indicative of the current emphasis on social change that is distinctly different from the role of social networks in fostering social control in the early Columbia voting research. Research of the last 15 years also links discussion networks to their communities, organizational and neighborhood contexts by examining the bridging role of weak ties that link a network to the rest of the community. The broader scope of effects, together with greater attention to cognitive and communicative mediators, make it possible to move beyond the earlier form of what Barber called the 'thin democracy' that aggregated individuals' predefined preferences and reduced talk to 'the hedonistic speech of bargaining' (1984: 184).

The broadening conceptions of political communication in the recent wave of research is particularly important given the changing modes of access to information and to social networks, largely arising from a rapid transition to digital media technologies. Newspaper circulation has been declining for the past three decades, particularly sharply since the 1990s. Network news viewership has also fallen rapidly in recent years and more concentrated on the older demographics. News and commentaries are increasingly generated by online news sources such as political blogs, and accessed through online searches and social media, bypassing traditional channels of news distribution. Typically, information generated and distributed online tends to be more opinionated, less journalistic, and also subject to misinformation and distortion. Opinions and commentary, rather than neutral reporting typical in more traditional news sources, may be more mobilizing, especially among young people (Shah et al., 2009).

Beyond being another information source, new digital media – especially, networked digital media, such as texting, instant messaging, blogs and social networking websites – have emerged as daily communication tools for social communication, discussion and expression. Research suggests that people mainly use new network technologies to maintain or solidify their existing social ties; nonetheless, the rise of social media such as Facebook and Twitter provides users with expanded capacities for social connectivity that goes beyond the immediate circle of their local communities. While substantial evidence suggests that use of digital media for information access and expression promotes civic and political engagement (Shah et al., 2009), many have raised concerns that the unlimited choices available in online regarding information and social networks might create and reinforce 'information cocoons' or 'echo chambers', in which people interact only with those who share their interests or perspectives (Sunstein, 2007).

SOCIALIZATION PERSPECTIVES ON SOCIAL NETWORK STRUCTURE AND PROCESSES

Early political communication research reflected a commonly cited definition: 'The process by which persons learn to adopt the norms, values, attitudes, and behaviors accepted and practiced by the ongoing (political) system' (Sigel, 1965: 1). The agencies of socialization – family, schools and later the media – allegedly acted as conduits in transmitting 'facts' to the young neophyte citizens that mature citizens already knew and practiced. Youth thereby moved steadily and irreversibly toward positive political maturity. The model generated a flood of research that lasted only a decade, drying up as a result of weak findings and the realities of rising instability and social protest in the 1970s youth generation. Political socialization research virtually disappeared for 20 years, the same quiescent interval described earlier for social network research, only starting and ending 10 years later.

Movement away from the stability biases of earlier models of social control to more dynamic models proved to be the salvation of both social network and political socialization research. The changes that started from the mid-1990s paralleled those in human development, political psychology and education (Flanagan and Sherrod, 1998). What aspects of the socialization model changed? First, the earlier conception of the young child as a passive recipient of influence was refocused as an adolescent under certain conditions actively seeking personal identity through information, interaction in peer networks and experiences that may involve engagement with social issues. Their civic potential is seen as by no means fixed and changes occur well into adulthood. Second, societies are no longer seen as unified wholes but rather as arenas where many forces with differing interests are contending. Earlier criteria of successful socialization that emphasized party affiliation and unquestioning trust in government are now more problematic. Finally, the original focus on political outcomes was broadened to include processes vital to active citizenship in civil society. The processes of discussion and deliberation – thoughtful information processing, listening to diverse points of view and working out compromises – are no less important than adoption of attitudes supportive of the political system.

Contemporary perspectives assume that to understand social phenomena it is essential to identify their origins as well as their effects. Models of civic socialization locate adolescence and young adulthood as key periods of development but also assume political and civic learning continue throughout the life course. We further assume that social network structure and processes may differ at various stages of the life course and that changes in their levels and effects may occur independently of one another. Ability to concentrate on the most recent cohorts who may represent the vanguard of change is an additional advantage of this approach.

These assumptions led us to conduct primary analyses of social network variables available in archived data sets within each of six age categories from age 18 across the life course. We added use of traditional news media and Internet use to our analyses because of their close connection to network processes shown in political communication research (McLeod et al., 2009). This strategy obviously limited us to recent sample surveys with very large sample sizes sufficient to produce reliable estimates in each age category. Because our research questions involved trends over time, we were fortunate to find two very large cross-section data sets gathered during a period of record Internet adoption: the 2000 and 2006 Social Capital Benchmark Studies ($N = 13,606, 12,079$) (Putnam, 2000) and the 2002 and 2006 Civic and Political Health of the Nation (CPHN) Studies ($N = 3,246, 2,232$) (Keeter et al., 2002; Lopez et al., 2006; Zukin et al., 2006). A third study, the 2000 American National Election Study ($N = 971$) was used for analyses of communication effects in a presidential campaign.

We pose four questions regarding social networks concerning their levels of use and trends, influences on their structure and processes, their effects on participation and gaps in use based on educational attainment. For each question, we examine age-specific results along with those for the total sample. We focus most on younger citizens 18–35 in comparing them to older cohorts. Space limits prevent presentation of tables and detailed analyses, however, are available from the authors (jmmcleod@wisc.edu, leen@cofc.edu).

What Implications Do Current Age-related Patterns and Trends of Network Structure and Processes Have for the Future of Civic Engagement?

Research cited earlier suggests that larger and more heterogeneous networks promote civic engagement. Network size, the number of friends interacting with socially, is marginally lower in younger (age 18–35) than in older adults. Network heterogeneity, the socio-demographic diversity of these friends, slowly but steadily increases up to age 60 (Benchmark). The CPHN data contain no measures of network structure. Networks remained unchanged in size from 2000 to 2006, but they became significantly more heterogeneous particularly among older cohorts (Benchmark). Overall, network *structural* characteristics and trends are only slightly disadvantageous to younger citizens in their potential for participation.

Young adults dominate in two measures of network *processes*, frequency of socializing and online discussion, double that of older citizens (Benchmark). Comparisons of six-year change show a clear trend with online discussion growth matching the decline in face-to-face socializing. These content-free measures do not translate into civically relevant discussion however. Talk about public affairs and about politics both reveal life course patterns the mirror opposite those of socializing. Young adults discuss public issues only half as often as do of older adults (CPHN, 2006). Comparisons of 2006 with 2002 show a decline for both forms of issue talk for younger adults in contrast to an increase among the oldest adults.

Age discrepancies larger than those for issue talk were found in newspaper and television news use (CPHN, 2006). Further, the decline in traditional news media use was greater over four years among younger adults. A majority still read newspapers and watch news, but they no longer do so on a daily basis. Some hope was raised by evidence indicating that young adults spend the more Internet time than do their elders (Benchmark). That hope was dashed, however, by finding that their use of Internet *news* failed to reach even the low levels of their traditional news media use (CPHN). Though young adults increased their Internet news use over the previous four years, older adults showed even greater gains. Overall, the levels and trends in network processes and news use fail to show that the transition to the Internet will *automatically* compensate for a loss in face-to-face discussion and traditional news use.

What Are the Influences Shaping Levels of Social Network Structure and Processes?

What is known about the origins of social network characteristics is largely confined to adult social status factors that we cannot change in the short run. As a result, we turned to our study of adolescents where networks are more likely to be in a formative stage (Shah et al., 2009). Parents' social characteristics (for example, education, income, marital status) had remarkably little influence on adolescents' friendship network size or frequency of discussion. Adolescents' participation in classroom deliberative activities, in contrast, had strong effects on several network variables: network size; network tolerance for disagreement and political discussion outside the classroom. Parental emphasis on concept-oriented family communication (child developing and expressing independent opinions) was related to tolerance for disagreement in the adolescent's networks and discussion with others outside the family. Various network structural variables and traditional and online news use had substantial influence on political discussion.

Education, income, political interest and religious membership are associated with the size and heterogeneity of adult social networks (Benchmark). Holding of post-material values (for example, freedom to express ideas) has a strong connection to network heterogeneity (Sotirovic and McLeod, 2001). Heterogeneity and network size have strong effects on public affairs media use and reflective processing of news, both of which stimulate the amount of political talk.

What Are the Effects of Network Structure and Processes on Civic and Political Participation?

We have merely assumed to this point that network size and heterogeneity and issue discussion are important to civic engagement. The importance of discussion *processes* for participation is well documented (McLeod et al., 2009). Effects of network *structures* have been investigated less frequently. To correct this oversight, we examined civic and political participation separately using two data sets: the Benchmark 2006 and ANES 2000 study that includes the crucial network structural measures lacking in CPHN data. We ran separate hierarchical regression analyses divided by age (young 18–35, older 36–65) in each data set.

After controlling first for 10 demographic and social variables, additional blocks were entered sequentially: network structural, and finally network processes plus media use.

Several conclusions can be drawn from our results. First, both size and heterogeneity as network structural characteristics and most media use measures have substantial influence on both civic and political participation. Network structure contributes as much to participation as does discussion with others in-person or online. Much of the effects of network size are mediated through stimulation of news use and discussion. Second, the effects of network heterogeneity are far greater when measured by socio-demographic diversity (Benchmark) than when measured by political diversity (ANES). Socio-demographic heterogeneity has the strongest positive influence on both forms of participation among the 19 predictor variables in the Benchmark data. In the ANES data, political heterogeneity has a generally positive influence among younger adults, but only as an indirect effect through communication processes. Third, patterns of participation effects tend to be similar among younger and older adults; however, network size, socializing and online discussion tend to have stronger impact among younger adults. The pattern of equal *potency* of effects is in sharp contrast to the disparities in *dosage* in levels of use between generations noted earlier in our first research question.

Do Educational Gaps in Social Networks and Media Use Contribute to a Democracy Divide?

Assessments of civic engagement have generally concentrated on the *overall* strength of various influences on participation and other criteria of engagement. An equally important but less often studied evaluative standard involves *equality* among sub-groups of the population in terms of levels and effects of variables influencing civic engagement. This normative standard raises the question of the extent to which political systems are able to limit or reduce inequalities in the processes and beneficial outcomes of democracy among its major cleavages such as race and ethnicity, socioeconomic status and gender. Here we examine participation gaps based on educational attainment, divided according to whether the person has or has not attended college. We chose education because it has been shown the strongest influence on participation. We paid particular attention to younger cohorts most likely to reveal the effects of the new social media. Issues of inequality in online media have most often been viewed as the 'digital divide' based on limited online *access* of lower status groups. We recast this problem as a *democracy divide* and focus on patterns of content and information processing of both media use and discussion that constitute *communication competence* (McLeod et al., 2010; Shah et al., 2009).

We found substantial educational gaps for both network size and heterogeneity. Those with college experience have larger and more diverse friendship networks (Benchmark). Gaps are largest in the 18–21 age category, reflecting the social opportunities of college life unavailable to non-college young adults. Gaps in network size gradually diminish after age 35 in contrast to the growing disparities in heterogeneity among older adults. Significant educational gaps in frequency of socializing are confined to young adults under 35. Gaps in online discussion are apparent only among young adults 22–25 (Benchmark). Political talk gaps are much larger than those for public affairs talk (CPHN). For both types of talk, ages 26–35 reveal *gaps* twice as large as any other category.

Gaps in newspaper use are substantial with the largest concentrated among older adults (Benchmark, CPHN). College-educated citizens tend to remain readers while the non-college youth have largely abandoned newspapers. Television news use is the exception among communication variables with a *negative* gap, meaning that people who have not been to college are more likely to watch national news than college attendees (CPHN). Internet *time* reveals a substantial gap (Benchmark), but the gap is twice as large for reading online *news content* (CPHN). Across all age categories, Internet news gaps are double than those for newspapers. The large young adult gap, coupled with their relatively low levels of Internet news use, raise doubts that the Internet will soon become a substitute for the traditional news media unless strategies are developed to successfully motivate and train non-college youth to seek civic and political information online.

The very large gaps in civic participation, equal to those found for Internet news use (Benchmark, CPHN) illustrate the difficult task faced by reformers who seek to alleviate inequalities in citizenship. Gaps in political participation are somewhat less than those in civic participation but the challenges are no less formidable.

CONCLUSION: SOCIAL NETWORKS IN POLITICAL COMMUNICATION RESEARCH

We presented evidence that the structural features and discussion processes in social networks exert substantial influence on participation in public life. More specifically, citizens with larger and more demographically heterogeneous social networks and those who discuss public affairs and politics more frequently in their networks are more likely than others to be civically and politically active. Structural size and diversity of networks have direct activation effects but they also have indirect effects on participation by stimulating news media use and political discussion. News media use and discussion processes act as important interdependent mediators directing and shaping the influences of social status and the structural features of networks. This has been developed into a communication mediation model (Cho et al., 2009).

Limitations of our evidence must be acknowledged. The lack of a longer-term panel design leaves maturational and cohort effects confounded in our analyses of change. Key network and media concepts were missing in many studies and their measurement was often weak in the data sets used. We recommend for future research that network *size* be restricted to others whom the person interacts with for a particular purpose: for discussing *important matters*, *local issues* or *politics*, pertinent to the research topic. *Heterogeneity* is more fruitfully examined outside the immediate family and measured in terms of socio-demographic characteristics rather than by political affiliation. Network *homogeneity* has important effects in its own right. An individual can have separate like and unlike discussion partners for different purposes. *Discussion frequency* requires estimates of the frequency of specific types of talk rather than simply frequency of encounter.

Days-per-week frequency media measures are weaker than content-specific measures within traditional and online media (McLeod et al., 2009). Media use should include attention and information-processing as well as exposure items for optimal measurement. Examination of network effects should not be limited to conceptually 'distant' outcomes such as participation; equally important are cognitive processes that further mediate and help us understand the influence of networks and other antecedent variables. Finally, we regret that the evidence presented, necessarily confined to the USA, prevents vital comparisons across space and time that could lead to more general theoretical conclusions.

Enthusiasm for the positive contributions of news media to democratic participation must be tempered by the recent collapse of traditional news media audiences and raise doubts as to the ability of the new online social media to compensate for their losses. The changes toward online media are apt to widen rather narrow gaps in information and participation. The gap problem goes beyond restricted *access* to the Internet (the *digital divide*) among the lesser educated to add more basic concerns as to *how* the new media are used. Given the findings reported earlier that parent–child communication patterns and deliberative activities in school are the strongest predictors of social network structure, news media use and peer discussion that lead to participation

among adolescents, our suggestions for teaching *communication competence* seem quite appropriate (McLeod et al., 2010).

The consequences of the rapid change to social media for social networks are not yet clear. The new media have potentially powerful effects for the benefit or to the detriment of participatory democracy. What is clear is that the quality of discourse in civil society is under threat. In the wake of a weakened journalistic practice that provided a check on false information and rumor, partisan specialists have rushed in with disinformation, planned shout-out disruptions of public meetings and planting of rumors. The capabilities of the Internet to contact and unite geographically dispersed like-minded people, may result in the formation of homogeneous social networks that willingly disregard standards of evidence to accept and spread false information and rumors. Citizens who lack adequate education are particularly vulnerable targets for disinformation and recruitment into polarized networks. New strategies are needed to teach adolescents communication competence skills that will help them cope with problems in their adult lives as well as becoming active participants in public life.

REFERENCES

Bales, R. F. (1950) *Interaction Process Analysis*. Cambridge, MA: Addison-Wesley.

Barber, B. (1984) *Strong Democracy*. Berkeley, CA: University of California Press.

Bavelas, A. (1950) 'Communication Patterns in Task-Oriented Groups', *Journal of the Acoustical Society of America*, 22(6): 725–30.

Becker, L. B., McCombs, M. E. and McLeod, J. M. (1975) 'The Development of Political Cognitions', in S. Chaffee (ed.), *Political Communication*. Beverly Hills, CA: Sage. pp. 21–64.

Berelson, B. R. (1952) 'Democratic Theory and Public Opinion', *Public Opinion Quarterly*, 16(3): 313–330.

Berleson, B. R. (1959) 'The State of Communication Research', *Public Opinion Quarterly*, 23(1): 1–6.

Berelson, B. R., Lazarsfeld, P. F. and McPhee, W. N. (1954) *Voting: A Study of Opinion Formation in a Presidential Campaign*. Chicago, IL: University of Chicago Press.

Chaffee, S. H. (1975) *Political Communication: Issues and Strategies for Research*. Beverly Hills, CA: Sage.

Chaffee, S. H. (1982) 'Mass Media and Interpersonal Channels: Competitive, Convergent, or Complementary?', in G. Gumpert and R. Cathcart (eds.), *Inter/Media: Interpersonal Communication in a Media World*. 2nd edn. New York: Oxford University Press. pp. 57–77.

Chaffee, S. H., Pan, Z. and McLeod, J. M. (1995) 'Effects of Kids Voting San Jose: A Quasi-Experimental Evaluation', a final report to the Policy Study Center, Program in media and democracy, Annenberg School for Communication. University of Pennsylvania.

Cho, J., Shah, D. V., McLeod, J. M., McLeod, D. M., Scholl, R. M. and Gotlieb, M. R. (2009) 'Campaigns, Reflection, and Deliberation: Advancing an O-S-O-R Model of Communication Effects', *Communication Theory*, 19(1): 66–88.

Conover, P. J., Searing, D. D. and Crewe, I. M. (2002) 'The Deliberative Potential of Political Discussion', *British Journal of Political Science*, 32(1): 21–62.

Delli Carpini, M. X. and Keeter, S. (1996) *What Americans Know About Politics and why it Matters*. New Haven, CT: Yale University Press.

Dewey, J. (1927) *The Public and its Problems*. New York: Holt.

Fishkin, J. S. and Luskin, R. C. (1999) 'Bringing Deliberation to the Democratic Dialogue', in M. McCombs and A. Reynolds (eds.), *The Poll With a Human Face: The National Issues Convention Experiment in Political Communication*. Mahwah, NJ: Lawrence Erlbaum Associates. pp. 3–38.

Flanagan, C. A. and Sherrod, L. R. (1998) 'Youth Political Development: An introduction', *Journal of Social Issues*, 54(3): 447–56.

Gamson, W. A. (1992) *Talking Politics*. Cambridge: Cambridge University Press.

Gastil, J. and Dillard, J. P. (1999) 'Increasing Political Sophistication Through Public Deliberation', *Political Communication*, 16(1): 3–24.

Huckfeldt, R. (2009) 'Interdependence, Density Dependence, and Networks in Politics', *American Political Research*, 37(5): 921–50.

Huckfeldt, R. and Mendez, J. M. (2008) 'Moths, Flames, and Political Engagement: Managing Disagreement Within Communication Networks', *Journal of Politics*, 70(1): 83–96.

Huckfeldt, R., Mendez, J. M. and Osborn, T. (2004) 'Disagreement, Ambivalence, and Engagement: The Political Consequences of Heterogeneous Networks', *Political Psychology*, 25(1): 65–95.

Katz, E. and Lazarsfeld, P. F. (1955) *Personal Influence*. New York: Free Press.

Keeter, S., Zukin, C., Andolina, M. and Jenkins, K. (2002). *Civic and Public Health of the Nation: A Generational Portrait*. Center for Information and Research on Civic Learning and Engagement (CIRCLE).

Klapper, J. (1960) *The Effects of Mass Communication*. New York: Free Press.

Lazarsfeld, P. F., Berelson, B. R. and Gaudet, H. (1948) *The People's Choice*. 2nd edn. New York: Columbia University Press.

Lippmann, W. (1922) *Public Opinion*. New York: Harcourt-Brace.

Lopez, M. H., Levine, P., Both, D., Kiesa, A., Kirby, E. and Marcelo, K. (2006) *Civic and Public Health of the Nation: A Generational Portrait*. Center for Information and Research on Civic Learning and Engagement (CIRCLE).

McCombs, M. E. and Shaw, D. L. (1972) 'The Agenda-Setting Function of Mass Media', *Public Opinion Quarterly*, 36(2): 176–87.

McLeod, D. M., Kosicki, G. M. and McLeod, J. M. (2009) 'Political Communication Effects', in J. Bryant and M. B. Oliver (eds.), *Media Effects: Advances in Theory and Research*. 3rd edn. New York and London: Routledge. pp. 228–51.

McLeod, J. M. and Blumler, J. G. (1987) 'The Macrosocial Level of Communication Science', in C. Berger and S. Chaffee (eds.), *Handbook of Communication Science*. Newbury Park, CA: Sage. pp. 271–322.

McLeod, J. M. and Reeves, B. (1980) 'On the Nature of Mass Media Effects', in S. B. Withey and R. P. Ables (eds.), *Television and Social Behavior: Beyond Violence and Children*. Hillsdale, NJ: Lawrence Erlbaum Associates. pp. 17–54.

McLeod, J. M., Scheufele, D. A., Moy, P., Horowitz, E., Holbert, R. L., Zhang, W., Zubric, S. and Zubric, J. (1999) 'Understanding Deliberation: The Effects of Discussion Networks on Participation in a Public Forum', *Communication Research*, 26(6): 743–74.

McLeod, J. M., Shah, D. V., Hess, D. E. and Lee, N.-J. (2010) 'Communication and Education: Creating Competence for Socialization into Public Life', in L. Sherrod, C. Flanagan, and J. Torney-Purta (eds.), *Handbook of Research on Civic Engagement in Youth*. New York: Wiley. pp. 363–91.

Mill, J. S. (1861/1951) 'On Liberty', in *Three Essays*. Oxford: Oxford University Press. pp. 5–141.

Mutz, D. C. (2002a) 'Cross-Cutting Social Networks: Testing Democratic Theory in Practice', *American Political Science Review*, 96(1): 111–26.

Mutz, D. C. (2002b) 'The Consequences of Cross-Cutting Networks for Political Participation', *American Journal of Political Science*, 46(4): 838–55.

Mutz, D. C. (2006) *Hearing the Other Side: Deliberative Versus Participatory Democracy*. New York: Cambridge University Press.

Putnam, R. D. (2000) *Bowling Alone: The Collapse and Revival of American Community*. New York: Simon & Schuster.

Schudson, M. (1997) 'Why Conversation is not the Soul of Democracy', *Critical Studies in Mass Communication*, 14(4): 297–309.

Shah, D. V., McLeod, J. M. and Lee, N.-J. (2009) 'Communication Competence as a Foundation for Civic Competence: Processes of Socialization into Citizenship', *Political Communication*, 26(1): 102–17.

Shah, D. V., Rojas, H. and Cho, J. (2008) 'Media and Civic Participation: On Understanding and Misunderstanding Communication Effects', in J. Bryant and M. B. Oliver (eds.), *Media Effects: Advances in Theory and Research*. Mahwah, NJ: Lawrence Erlbaum Associates. pp. 207–27.

Sigel, R. S. (1965) 'Assumptions About the Learning of Political Values', *The Annals of the American Academy of Political and Social Science*, 361(1): 1–9.

Simmel, G. (1908/1971) *On Individuality and Social Forms*. Chicago, IL: University of Chicago Press.

Sotirovic, M. and McLeod, J. M. (2001) 'Values, Communication Behavior and Political Participation', *Political Communication*, 18(3): 273–300.

Sotirovic, M. and McLeod, J. M. (2008) 'US Media Coverage: Persistence of Tradition', in J. Stromback and L. Kaid (eds.), *The Handbook of Election News Coverage Around the World*. New York and London: Routledge. pp. 21–40.

Sunstein, C. R. (2007) *Republic.com 2.0*. Princeton, NJ: Princeton University Press.

Wyatt, R. O., Katz, E. and Kim, J. (2000) 'Bridging the Spheres: Political and Personal Conversation in Public and Private Spaces', *Journal of Communication*, 50(1): 71–92.

Zukin, C., Keeter, S., Andolina, M., Jenkins, K. and Delli Carpini, M. X. (2006) *A New Engagement? Political Participation, Civic Life, and the changing American Citizen*. New York: Oxford University Press.

PART III

17

Measuring Affect, Emotion and Mood in Political Communication

Ann N. Crigler and Marion R. Just

On 9 November 1989, waves of East Berliners climbed over the Wall separating East and West Berlin. Audiences around the world shared the tumultuous excitement as crowds of Berliners celebrated the reunion of families, friends and neighbors. The political decision of the GDR to stem weeks of demonstrations by piercing the Berlin Wall transported participants emotionally as well as physically. Many political transitions carry tremendous emotional freight. The first time that black South Africans went to the polls was a monumental and joyous occasion. Assassinations of heads of state convey different emotions of grief and fear. Political messages in everyday life also carry significant emotional meaning. Raising the national flag or listening to Tchaikovsky's *1812 Overture* infuse political messages with emotion. The feelings aroused by even mundane political events demonstrate how essential emotions are to the construction of political meaning and to the political effects of media. Communicating emotion is ubiquitous in political life. Individuals and groups talk emotionally about politics in everyday conversation; politicians deliver uplifting speeches; political consultants create frightening ads and stage patriotic events; journalists report these ads, speeches and events; pundits rant and rave; comedians tell political jokes and pictures capture poignant political moments. Each of these forms of communicating about politics is inherently social and emotional. In some cases, such as political advertisements

and speeches the goal is to evoke emotion in the audience. Whether or not emotional stimuli perform as intended or result in behaviors consonant with those messages is crucial to our understanding of political communication effects.

In spite of the potential importance of research on emotion, the topic has not been central to the study of political communication. One of the reasons for the lack of attention is that emotions are difficult to define and even harder to measure. The purpose of this chapter is to review how affect, emotions and mood have been defined and measured in social science research and how these concepts can usefully be incorporated into future analysis of political communication. We begin by defining the research terms and clarifying underlying theoretical assumptions about emotions. Next, we describe different methods used to analyze affect, emotions and mood in political communication. We review scholarly articles in six political science and psychology journals published since 1992 to show how emotion has been studied. We conclude by offering recommendations and avenues for future research on emotion in political communication.

We anchor our discussion in a model of communication based on Harold Lasswell's paradigm of politics – 'Who says what to whom with what effect?' (Lasswell, 1958). Emotions are essential to the process of communication and are conveyed through different messages and channels. Evoking emotion is a powerful tool of rhetoric employed by the sources of messages. Without emotion, it is impossible to convey political messages, form preferences, express the intensity of opinions or even to make political arguments. Citizens as message receivers, use emotional cues to judge candidates, help make sense of complex issues and debates and make electoral choices. Emotions are vital to communication and the construction of political meaning.

WHAT ARE AFFECT, EMOTION AND MOOD?

To understand the role of emotion in political communication research, it is important to define the terms. Affect, emotion and mood have all been used in the study of political communication. These terms are used in various ways depending on the scholar's underlying theoretical framework. Among the ancient philosophers, Plato used the term 'spirit' to describe the non-cognitive aspect of the personality, particularly in the sense of being 'spirited' (Plato, 2000: 136). Aristotle argued that emotions are 'all those feelings that so change men as to affect their judgments' (Aristotle, 1954: 91). For Aristotle, emotions oppose rationality or reason (Aristotle, 1954). Descartes expanded on the dualism between reason and emotion (Damasio, 1994; Descartes, 1996; Marcus, 2002; Neblo, 2007). In the 18th century, the term passion was widely used for emotional states including socially experienced political emotions (Madison, 1987). In the 19th century, both Charles Darwin (1965) and William James (1983) focused on the experience and expression of emotion. James argued that the feeling of 'bodily changes as they occur IS the emotion' (2003: 67). Twentieth-century, social scientists often used the term affect to describe an emotional state, which contributes to the current confusion and lack of precision of these terms.

In this chapter, we define affect, emotion and mood distinctly, but with fuzzy borders between these terms. Affect is the experience of feeling emotions and is often measured in valenced or evaluative (positive/negative or approach/avoidance) terms (Clore et al., 1994). Affect is set apart from rationality or cognition as it focuses on the feeling state and the conscious experience of emotion (Damasio, 1999; Frijda, 1993; Panksepp, 2000; Solomon, 2004). In communication, research we often ask people how they feel about a candidate, a debate or an election result (Belt et al., 2005; Crigler et al., 2006).

Mood refers to a diffuse affective state experienced by individuals or groups. Whereas people can often identify the object or source of an emotion, they experience moods in a more general way. Moods can come and go, but tend to be more long lasting than emotions (Colman, 2003). In political communication, mood is especially important to understanding the context in which communication occurs. For example, information may be perceived differently by people who are feeling hopeful or worried about a political outcome (Rahn et al., 1996).

If affect is the realized feeling of emotion and mood is a diffuse affective state, what is emotion? Emotions are states or traits of individuals or groups, which typically contain multiple components – perceptual, cognitive or evaluative, expressive, physiological and behavioral (Panksepp, 2000; Planalp, 1999). Emotion states are relatively short-term responses to stimuli. In some political communication research, participants' immediate reactions are evaluated by elapsed time between the stimulus and a keyboard stroke (Lau, 1995; Lau and Redlawsk, 2006; Redlawsk et al., 2007). Emotion traits, in contrast, are longer lasting and are associated with personality, as the emotive expression of personality. As such they tend to be associated with individuals and help to describe basic attributes of the individual's character (Mayer, 2001). For example, optimistic people and pessimistic people may evaluate information differently (Zullow and Seligman, 1990). In this chapter, we will focus primarily on emotion rather than affect or mood, because that is the scholarly area where most of the political communication research takes place. Scholars measure emotion utilizing various underlying theoretical models that differ in their degrees of precision. The most commonly used models are: valenced, dimensional or circumplex, and discrete.

Valence models differentiate emotions into two groups, typically, positive versus negative. This categorization simplifies analysis and strengthens the replicability of measurements. The valence approach was used in early public opinion survey research and is still widely used to describe political advertising (for example, Ansolabehere and Iyengar, 1995; Freedman and Goldstein, 1999; Johnston and Kaid, 2002; Lau and Pomper, 2004; Lau et al., 1999; Richards, 2004; Wattenberg and Brians, 1999). Researchers would ask survey questions about discrete emotions, but found that grouping the discrete emotions by valence better captured the emotions and improved the predictive power of the model (for example, Abelson et al., 1982). More recently, some researchers (Huddy et al., 2007; Marcus et al., 2000; Neuman et al., 2007a) argue that the valence model confounds two types of negative emotions – fear and anger. Importantly, the emotions of fear and anger map differently on the dimension of approach-avoidance (Huddy et al., 2007).

Dimensional models describe emotions on at least two dimensions, for example, one axis may be valence (positive/negative) and the other may be arousal (approach/avoidance) (for a longer discussion see Neuman et al., 2007b: ch. 1). Such a model of emotions would distinguish, for example, fear, which is a negative emotion, from anger, which is also negative; but fear engenders avoidance while anger may stimulate approach. Circumplex models also structure emotions along two dimensions (Gray, 1987; Marcus, 1988; Marcus et al., 2000; Russell, 1980). One axis of the circumplex model may be approach-avoidance as in a valence model, but discrete emotions are arranged in a circular fashion, with more intense emotions more central and less intense emotions more peripheral. The circumplex model is the basis for the theory of affective intelligence (Marcus et al., 2000; Neuman et al., 2007b).

A discrete emotion model identifies a large range of specific emotions, either in a simple list, or a structured list. The underlying theory of discrete models is that each emotion is unique in its experience, expression and associated behavior (Anderson and Guerrero, 1998; Lazarus, 1991; Lerner and Keltner, 2000; Smith and Ellsworth, 1985; Smith and Lazarus, 1993). Discrete emotions are often used in survey questions and are analyzed in a variety of political communications (Abelson et al., 1982; Brader, 2006; Conover and Feldman, 1986; Kinder, 1994; Sullivan and Masters, 1988). Some authors argue that there are only a small number of discrete primary emotions, which are combined to form more complex emotions. One of the challenges of utilizing the discrete model of emotions is that it may be difficult in practice to differentiate nuanced emotional messages, such as worry and fear. These models of emotion are critical to research on emotion by providing the tools and categories of analysis.

Whether political communication scholars model emotions as valenced, dimensional or discrete, the focus is on conscious rather than preconscious emotions. Political communication research tends to concentrate on what people say about their emotions or how they express emotions verbally. Many of the objects of political communication research are either complex emotions or states that are highly evocative of emotion such as cynicism, trust, patriotism and racism[*] (for example, Capella and Jamieson, 1997; Hutchings et al., 2006). These concepts tend to be socially and culturally based.[1] Linguistic analysis, because it is language based, studies many of the same complex or discrete emotionally evocative concepts as communications research.[2] Since political communication is language dependent, it appears that models of discrete emotions would be particularly useful for analysis. Discrete emotions can capture specific emotions that map onto the various aspects of emotion, such as intention or appraisal.

COMPONENTIAL MODEL OF EMOTION

Research on emotion distinguishes not only the types of emotion – for example, valenced or discrete – but also the components of the experience of an emotion. The most commonly used components in emotion research are: intentional, perceptual, physiological, appraisal, expressive and behavioral. Not all researchers refer to the same components, but these six aspects predominate in the philosophical and psychological literature (for example, Planalp, 1999). These components of emotions can be observed in the flow of communication. Table 17.1 shows the relationship between the various components of emotion and the Lasswell (1958) and Shannon-Weaver (1949) models of political communication.

Perception

The perceptual component involves the recognition of emotion in what is being encountered or communicated. Individuals can perceive emotions without consciousness and may perceive emotions through any of the senses. So, for example, parents may have an unconscious and immediate reaction to a crying baby. Some scholars argue that such a reaction has a basis in evolution as a protective mechanism for the infant. Perception of emotion can come through more than one channel. Surprise can be conveyed and perceived in sight, sound, touch, smell or taste, and sometimes by combinations of those channels. Perception also depends on the context in which the communication occurs.

Hamilton Jordan, a political advisor, told the story of watching a Nixon ad on television in a bar. The ad showed Hubert Humphrey laughing, juxtaposed against a series of serious problems such as the war in Vietnam and riots in cities. Jordan was aghast at the implication that Humphrey did not take these problems as he should. He asked one of his companions at the bar what he thought about Humphrey after watching the ad. The fellow said he liked a man who could remain upbeat in the face of adversity. Jordan took away from this experience first the fact that the perception of the emotion in a message may depend on the recipient.[3] This story also illustrated

Table 17.1 Measurements of affect, emotion and mood in political communication

Lasswell model of politics	Who	'Says' what	To whom
Shannon-Weaver transmission model of communication	*Source*: Individual or Group	*Message*	*Receiver*: Individual or group
Relevant components of affect, emotion and mood in models	Intention Appraisal Behavioral	Expressive	Perception Appraisal Physiological/ Neurological Behavioral
Methods of studying components of affect, emotion and mood	Historiography Interview Ethnography	*Content analysis*: Verbal Facial Voice Visual Sound Music Color Symbol *Discourse analysis*	Survey Interview Focus group Ethnography Experiment Physiological/ Neurological measures

the difference between the emotional intention of the source and the emotional perceptions of different receivers. It is possible for the recipient to interpret the message in ways entirely different from the purpose of the sender, constructing an entirely different meaning of the message. Sometimes perception can be measured against the apparent intention of the message originator. This is usually inferred rather than demonstrated because it requires knowledge of the emotions of the source as well as the message and receiver.

Physiological/neurological

Physiological/neurological measures of emotion involve changes in arousal level that occur in the body. These may be quite apparent in common exchange (for example, a sweaty hand or a blush) or they may require closer observation (for example, an increased heart beat or activity in different regions of the brain). Neurological measures can only be observed by intrusive procedures such as fMRI, PET scans, EEG or comparisons of patients with different brain lesions. Neuroscientists have identified the particular regions of the brain engaged in the processing of emotions. Using techniques such as fMRI, scientists can observe participants engaged in particular activities and measure the blood flow to these areas (Cacioppo et al., 2003; Spezio and Adolphs, 2007; Westen, 2007). For example, some political consultants have used fMRI's to see if the emotional centers of the brain are engaged by their political ads and use that information to fine-tune their messages (Tierney, 2004).

Appraisal

The interpretation of the message is located in the appraisal component of an emotion. Many of the emotions involved in political communication concern evaluation and judgment. Political communication is central to various kinds of decision-making, such as assessing a candidate, taking sides on an issue, or choosing to participate. In appraisal theory, people make judgments about a situation with regard to their goals. They may make this appraisal in a split second, as for example, when people observed the second plane crashing into the World Trade Center on 9/11. Or, the appraisal may take longer if it relies on a range of past experiences. For example, candidates make promises to which voters respond positively or negatively depending on their previous political experiences and preferences. In addition, the emotional appraisal may take longer if the situation is novel or complex, calling up no previous experience or conflicting experiences.

Expressive

The expressive aspect of emotion lies in the content domains (Planalp, 1999: 11). Expressions of emotions in content may be verbal or non-verbal. Words, settings, landmarks, crowds, faces, images, color, symbols, music and sounds all convey emotional messages (Brader, 2006; Graber, 1987; 2001; Kern, 1989). Political advertisements strategically utilize all of these expressions of emotion to construct persuasive messages. Political rhetoric also relies on the verbal expression of emotion.

American Presidents Ronald Reagan and George W. Bush rallied the public against foreign enemies using terms such as 'the evil empire' or 'the axis of evil'. Other presidents have expressed emotions in phrases such as 'proud to be an American' and 'a man from Hope'. Political figures also use non-verbal devices in speeches and political events. Adolph Hitler utilized architecture, crowds, music and military symbolism to stage rallies conveying the power of the Nazi movement. Leaders of democracies have also used these non-verbal emotional expressions. In American politics, the flag is a ubiquitous emotional image. Barack Obama's acceptance speech at the Democratic national convention was staged in front of a white portico with American flags by each mullioned window, suggesting the White House. George W. Bush wearing military garb landed a plane on an aircraft carrier bearing a red, white and blue banner declaring 'mission accomplished'.

Behavioral

The behavioral component of emotion entails the increasing or decreasing desire to take action (Planalp's 'action tendencies') and the kinds of action that follow different emotions. Different discrete emotions are associated with various proclivities to act. For example, if we consider intergroup emotions theory (Huddy and Mason, 2008; Mackie et al., 2004; Smith et al., 2007), we would predict very different behaviors on the part of strong group identifiers versus weak group identifiers and for those whose candidate was the attacker or the opponent. After watching a vicious attack ad, supporters of the opponent may feel angry or outraged if they feel that their group is in a relatively strong position. They may yell at the television screen or channel their anger toward helping their maligned candidate by volunteering or making a contribution to her campaign. For example, after a particularly incendiary speech by Patrick Buchanan on the first day of the 1992 Republican convention, the Democratic Party experienced a sharp increase in political donations. If, however, the supporters believe that their group is in a weak position, they may become sad or deflated, feeling that their candidate does not stand a chance against the attacker and is likely to lose. In contrast, supporters of the attacker may feel enthusiastic that their candidate scored a point against the disliked opponent. Their enthusiasm may encourage their participation and they may make sure to go vote. Independents (those who do not feel a strong affiliation to either partisan group) are apt to have a very different emotional reaction. They may be disgusted by the continuous negativity of the campaign and turn off politics altogether (Ansolabehere and Iyengar, 1995).

The various emotional appraisals of the ad produce significantly different behavioral reactions.

The behavior component of emotion is closely related to the expressive component. Non-verbal, behavioral emotional reactions can be observed in message receivers. These include such behaviors as facial expressions, sounds, gesticulations, laughter, tears, body language or physical attacks. Groups may express emotion activity by waving, cheering, chanting, singing, ululating, marching, lying down in the street or smashing shop windows. For example, after the alleged fraud in the 2009 Iranian presidential election, emotional cell phone messages brought protesters into the street.[4] YouTube videos of police brutality during the protests in Iran resulted in makeshift or electronic memorials around the world.

APPLYING THE COMPONENTS OF EMOTION TO THE LASSWELL MODEL OF POLITICAL COMMUNICATION

In Table 17.1, we set out the various components of emotion along the dimensions of the Lasswell model of communication – 'who says what to whom, with what effect'. The table associates each element of the model with the relevant components of emotion and the methods used to study those components in that dimension. The table shows that relatively few different methods have been used to study the emotions of the sources, messages and recipients of communication.

Sources

Emotion components related to the source – Lasswell's 'who' – include intention, appraisal and behavior. The intentions of message senders, particularly in political settings, do not always match the perceptions of the receivers. A leader's intention to reassure citizens about a situation may be challenged by citizens' own observations. In the case of American presidential candidate John McCain, his remarks in fall of 2008 that 'the fundamentals of the economy are strong' did not match citizen perceptions grounded in news that banks and brokerage houses had gone belly up.

Research methods relating to the message sender or source tend to be more qualitative than quantitative. Studies of the speeches of famous leaders rely often on historiographic research or interviews focused around questions about intent of the sender. Scholars have questioned how Lincoln composed the Gettysburg address or scrutinized William Henry Harrison's first public address (Friedenberg, 2002). Journalists and scholars have mined the views of presidential speech writers or other important political activists. Scholars have employed ethnography to understand the campaign process, as in Teddy White's close observation of *The Making of the President 1960* (1961), or Timothy Crouse's *The Boys on the Bus* (1972) or Richard Fenno's (1978) book *Home Style: US House Members in their Districts.* Scholars embedded in newsrooms, such as Herbert Gans (1979), Edward J. Epstein (1972) and John McManus (1994) have employed ethnography to understand the behavior of journalists.

Appraisal and behavioral components of source emotions are illustrated in many leadership studies. For example, John F. Kennedy's grief over the loss of his premature infant son led him to advocate for programs funding medical research on neonates (McDermott, 2008). Analysis of the Reagan presidency shows that the president was moved by the hostage crises in Lebanon to engage in behavior that became the Iran-Contra Affair even though President Reagan denied this motivation in his public statements (Johnston, 1987).[5]

Messages

The messages conveyed by sources characterize the expressive component of emotions. These expressions are analyzed primarily by content or discourse analysis. Content analysis of messages includes all manner of identifying and counting aspects of communication, primarily the incidence of words and pictures, but analysis of tone and symbols are also common. The study of political advertising can involve analysis of facial expressions, tone of voice, visual backgrounds, sounds, music, colors and symbols (Brader, 2005, 2006; Kaid, 2004; Kern, 1989). Discourse analysis is a kind of content analysis that documents the messages exchanged in the interactions of speakers.

Receivers

Given the variability in the reception of messages (the 'effects' side of the media effects literature), the bulk of scholarly research focuses on the receiver or audience. The components of emotions relevant to the receiver(s) include perception, appraisal, physiological/neurological, expressive and behavioral measures. The appraisal component refers to the evaluation of the source and the message in relation to the receiver's values, identities and goals. The appraisal component helps to explain why members of one party in the US Congress stand and applaud elements of the president's State of the Union speech while others sit on their hands. Appraisal may be directed at issues

such as taxes or same sex marriage, or to persons, such as Barack Obama.

Receivers experience emotion both physiologically and neurologically. The physiological experience of emotions refers to a variety of responses including heightened facial color (for example, embarrassment may cause people to blush), increased heart rate or temperature and changes in galvanic skin response. The lie detector, for example, is based on the premise that the subject's physiological responses change in response to different questions. From personal observation we know that people may express their emotions in a variety of obvious ways – such as laughing, crying or frowning. Behavioral emotional reactions include swooning, jumping up and down or even punching someone. Politics can stimulate a variety of emotional expressions and behavior including cheering or booing a candidate, expressing surprise at a political announcement, or feeling frightened by political advertisements.

Recipients' emotional reaction to messages is the area of communication with the greatest scholarly effort and most diverse methods. Surveys are the surprising tool of choice for study of political communication, surprising because surveys are blunt and limited in what they can measure. Survey questions necessarily limit the kind of emotions that can be studied to those that are easily identified verbally by self-report. The apparent reason for the reliance on surveys is that they are the standard methodology for the study of public opinion, the most closely allied area for the study of emotions in political communication.

If close-ended self-reports in surveys are over-specified, open-ended survey responses are not much more help to researchers. Scholars have limited tools available for analyzing the emotional content of verbatim answers. In order to escape the limitations of survey instruments, researchers have turned to in-depth interviews and focus groups that allow more free-wheeling expression of emotion (Just et al., 1996; Kern and Just, 1995).

Some researchers have adapted the use of psychiatric interview techniques in order to draw out subjects' emotions (McCracken, 1988). The problem with these methods is the methodologic opposite of surveys – the material is so diffuse and unique to the individual that both inter-coder reliability and generalizability to a larger population may be fraught.

The same concerns about interview analysis occur with focus groups, with the added dimension of social interaction. Ethnographic methods can be used to assist the analysis of both interviews and focus groups. Computer software programs (such as Ethnograph [2009]) are available to help researchers create data sets from interviews or focus groups. Even with computer aids, this form of analysis is highly labor intensive especially compared with the quick results from surveys. Some researchers have also used videos of focus groups to record the non-verbal responses of groups of individuals watching emotional stimuli, such as political advertisements. Subjects are noted pushing away from the table when troubling content is shown or shifting closer in an intense listening position when they are thoroughly engaged with the material. Focus groups as a research tool have been widely used by practitioners as 'quick and dirty' – and completely unrepresentative – group interviews. The advantage of focus groups for political consultants is that they are easy to arrange in a short space of time and cost far less than a survey or experiment. Perhaps because of the misuse of focus groups by commercial entities, scholars have not widely embraced the focus group method. In order to strengthen the results, some researchers have successfully used a repeated number of focus groups on the same topic (for example, Delli Carpini and Williams, 1994; Gamson, 1992; Jamieson, 1992; Just et al., 1996).

Experiments of all kinds permit researchers to record subjects' responses to situations, verbal or audio-visual messages, either by observation or self-report. New methods of experimentation involve fMRI as a means of identifying subjects' neurological responses to stimuli (Schreiber, 2007; Westen, 2007). The chief complaint about experimental methodologies is their generalizability to larger populations. The combined method of experiments embedded in surveys is a technique that helps to resolve this concern. Survey-experiments have been adopted by scholars both in psychology and political communication (Grant and Rudolph, 2003; Miller, 2006; Neely, 2006; Small et al., 2006). Internet sampling has made it feasible to introduce audio-visual stimuli as well as experimental wording into large-scale surveys. The National Science Foundation funded an effort to stimulate experimental survey techniques through TESS (Time-shared Experiments in the Social Sciences) (Loftis and Lupia, 2008).

Table 17.1 shows the possible components for the study of emotions and the relevant methodologies associated with the componential model of communication. Our content analysis of the literature demonstrates that of all of the potential methods, in practice the most common methodologies for measuring emotions are surveys and experiments.

CONTENT ANALYSIS OF THE LITERATURE

To analyze how emotions have been studied in the cognate disciplines of political communication, we reviewed all articles published from 1992 to 2008 in *The Journal of Communication, Political Communication, Political Psychology*, the *American Political Science Review*, the *American Journal of Political Science* and the *American Sociological Review*. We also examined the *Journal of Personality and Social Psychology* from 2005 to 2008 in order to compare political and communication research trends to those of psychology, where the study of emotion in general resides.

We identified the articles that focused on emotion, affect or mood and politics, broadly defined. Initially, we searched electronically for all articles in these journals that used the terms emotion, affect or mood AND politics. This global approach did not sufficiently capture all of the articles. There were several problems with this blunt tool: first, 'affect' has too many meanings to be employed as a search term for emotion. Second, articles that focused on specific discrete emotions but not emotion as a term were missed. Third, articles that examined particular aspects of politics but not politics as a term were also overlooked. While it was more time consuming, we resorted to hand coding of articles based on the analysis of the tables of contents of each journal, a review of abstracts and then review of articles, in order to obtain more complete and accurate results. The data include articles that focused on emotion, affect or mood, as well as those that focused on discrete emotions, such as anger, fear or hope. In addition to articles about politics, we included articles that dealt with political subjects such as political parties, campaigns, elections, government and political issues (for example, Middle East). The analysis yielded two sets of articles. The first set includes all articles in the selected journals that focused on emotion, whether or not the article's main focus was politics. The second list consists exclusively of articles that focus on emotions and included politics as a central idea. All articles (across both sets) were coded for the following variables: mention of affect/ emotion/mood, which methods and theories of emotion were used, whether the article was empirical in nature and if emotions were considered as individual or group attributes. Intra-coder reliability tests were conducted on a sample of 20% of the politics and emotions articles. Pearson correlations were high and ranged from 0.875 to 1.0.

FINDINGS

Analysis of the journals indicates that the study of emotion, affect and mood is primarily concentrated in psychology (see Table 17.2). Even though the *Journal of Personality and Social Psychology*

Table 17.2   Emotions and politics articles by journal

	All journals	All journals (political list)
AJPS	13 (8.9%)	12 (18.5%)
APSR	7 (4.8%)	7 (10.8%)
ASR	3 (2.1%)	2 (3.1%)
JOC	14 (9.6%)	7 (10.8%)
POL COMM	10 (6.8%)	8 (12.3%)
POL PSYCH	31 (21.2%)	26 (40%)
JPSP	68 (46.6%)	3 (4.6%)

(*JPSP*) was only coded from 2005 to 2008, it contained 68 articles compared to 78 articles for the political journals for the years 1992–2008 combined.

When we narrow the search to include only articles that focus on politics and emotions, however, the strictly psychology journal, *JPSP*, drops to only three articles for the four years of 2005–08 (4.6% of all articles on politics and emotion). By comparison, *Political Psychology* (*PolPsy*), which lies at the intersection of politics and psychology, has the greatest number of articles that focus on politics and emotion (26 articles, 40% of all articles on politics and emotion). The remainder of our analyses includes only the

smaller set of articles that focus not only on emotions, but emotions and politics, omitting the *Journal of Personality and Social Psychology*.

The data show that scholarly attention to the study of emotions and politics is sparse across these leading journals. In 16 years, the 6 journals included 62 articles on politics and emotion, averaging approximately two-thirds of an article per journal per year. The number of articles on politics and emotions has varied over time, peaking in 2007 with 8 articles. Trends are difficult to detect because there are many years in which no emotion and politics articles are published in these journals, but the overall trend is drifting upward (see Figure 17.1).

Although political philosophers and others clearly differentiate between emotion and affect, the analysis of the journals suggests that these terms are hardly ever differentiated. Over 30% (19) of the articles that focused on emotion and politics used the terms affect and emotion interchangeably. Across all six journals, *Political Psychology* had the most instances, over 63% (12 articles), of interchanging the terms emotion and affect. In fact, only one article provided distinct definitions for affect versus emotion. An equal number of articles (19) referenced neither affect nor emotion, but dealt with specific discrete emotions such as anger, fear or hope, or with other political constructs (see Table 17.3).

When measuring emotions, authors clearly relied on discrete or valence measures rather than circumplex measures of emotion (see Table 17.4). References to discrete emotions dominated the literature with 45.2% (28) of the articles. Valence measures were used in approximately 11% (7) of the articles followed by a combination of discrete and valence measures in 8% (5) of the articles.

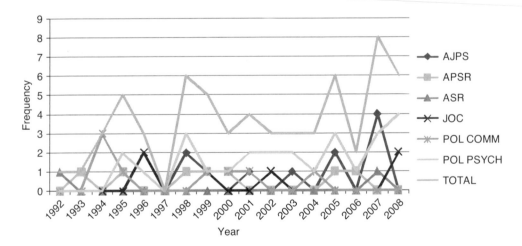

Figure 17.1   Number of journal articles by year per journal

Table 17.3   Number of articles using affect and/or emotion by journal

	Affect only	Emotion only	Affect/emotion interchangeable	Affect/emotion separate	Discrete emotion/ political construct
AJPS	3	1	2	0	6
APSR	1	0	1	0	5
ASR	0	0	0	1	1
JOC	0	3	3	0	1
POL COMM	1	6	1	0	0
POL PSYCH	3	4	12	0	6
Totals	8	14	19	1	19

Table 17.4   Articles using emotion models by journal

	Discrete	Valence	Circumplex	Discrete and valence	D/K
AJPS	6	0	0	1	5
APSR	5	0	1	0	1
ASR	1	1	0	0	0
JOC	2	1	0	1	2
POL COMM	2	2	1	0	3
POL PSYCH	12	3	0	3	8
Totals	28	7	2	5	19

These patterns are fairly consistent across all of the journals we examined.

An examination of the discrete emotions reveals that research has focused on negative emotions, particularly anger, anxiety, fear and to a lesser extent, guilt (see Table 17.5). For all politics and emotion articles, anger was found in 6.5% (4 articles), anxiety in 14.5% (9 articles), fear in 12.3% (8 articles) and guilt in 4.8% (3 articles). Hope (6.5%, 4 articles) and empathy (3.2%, 2 articles) were the most frequently studied 'positive' emotions, although neither is considered a purely positive emotion. Trust, which is more of a positive political construct than an emotion per se, was the most frequently studied, appearing in 22.6% (14 articles) of the articles.

In studying emotions and politics, survey and experimental methods dominated the research in these journals. Surveys were used in 33.8% (22) of the articles. Experiments were the next most frequently used method, found in 24.6% (16) of the sample. An additional 12.3% (8) of the articles employed a combination of survey and experimental methods (see Table 17.6). In contrast, methods used in studying emotions in the psychology journal, *JPSP*, were experiments 39%, survey 17.6% and 27.8% for experiments embedded in surveys. In other words, psychological research has relied far more on experimental methods than has political communication research.

FUTURE RESEARCH AND RECOMMENDATIONS

Emotions should be an important area for political communication research. The various components of emotions occur in all aspects of the communication process. Senders express emotions in their messages, the messages carry emotions and receivers feel emotions on the receipt of messages. All of these areas, including the whole cycle of sender, message and receiver are fruitful areas of research.

The paucity of literature on emotion in political communication is one of the main findings of our

Table 17.5   Number of articles studying discrete emotions[a]

	Anger	Anxiety	Fear	Guilt	Sadness	Empathy	Hope	Trust
AJPS	0	2	2	0	0	1	1	3
APSR	0	0	1	0	0	0	0	4
ASR	0	0	0	0	0	0	0	1
JOC	0	1	0	1	0	0	0	1
POL COMM	0	0	1	0	0	0	1	0
POL PSYCH	4	6	2	2	2	1	2	5
Totals	4	9	6	3	2	2	4	14

Note: [a]Trust is not usually considered an emotion, but is included here because of its frequency and relation to emotions and politics. The discrete emotions enthusiasm and patriotism were only coded in one article and have not been included in Table 17.5.

Table 17.6   Methodology by journal

	Experiment	Survey	Experiment and survey	Content analysis	Qualitative/ discussion
AJPS	1	7	2	0	0
APSR	1	2	0	0	2
ASR	0	0	0	0	1
JOC	4	1	0	0	1
POL COMM	1	1	0	3	2
POL PSYCH	8	11	4	0	2
Totals	15	21	7	3	8

review of the scholarship. It is possible that political science journals and scholars have resisted the study of emotions because they perceive it as a new name for older concepts, such as attitudes (of the message recipients) or evaluation of traits (of candidates). In order to justify using emotions in political communication research scholars may have to engage in the hard work of distinguishing the concept of emotion from these older or competing explanatory models.

In addition, scholars interested in pursuing emotion research have come up against the difficulties of measurement in a process that is very interactive, interpretive and nuanced. It is hard to separate the different ways in which emotions are communicated, that is, the intention of the source or the content versus the interpretation of the receiver. Furthermore, the study of emotions in cross-cultural contexts comes up against the embedding of emotion in culture.

Political communication researchers have focused on the recipient and, to a lesser extent, on the content of communication. Recipients' emotions have been studied from a range of methodological perspectives, although for the most part we

have relied on self-reports involving conscious or verbal expression (that is, affect). We need to expand our research to consider preconscious emotions that can now be measured in a variety of physiological and neurological ways, such as EEGs or fMRIs. We also have to put more emphasis on non-verbal responses of message receivers, including actions, such as clapping, cheering and laughing. These are important to the study of crowd behavior and group emotions.

In reviewing the literature on messages, there are few positive findings that involve the measurement of emotions in messages. We are going to have to dig deeper in this area, since messages usually do not explicitly convey emotions, certainly not in words (Graber, 2001). Coders find more of the emotional impact in overall narratives, visuals, colors and especially music. More qualitative schemes, such as gestalt coding, may hold the key to discovering the emotions we know to be embedded in messages (Graber, 2001).

New research has emerged on emotions related to the source, especially intentionality, and particularly that aspect of intentionality that conveys to an audience that the speaker intends a particular meaning. Scholars are exploring the various emotional states of receivers and intergroup emotions to explain the differential emotional response to messages. It would be fruitful if studies could follow the whole process of emotional exchange from the source to the message and on to the receiver. Further study should be undertaken on the social context of communication and discourse, especially in a cross-cultural context. In order to do this, we require multiple methods to understand the components of emotion and the construction of messages and meaning.

NOTES

1   In contrast, much of the psychological literature is built around a small number of presumed universal primary emotions (Ekman, 2003; Izard, 1971, 1977; Plutchik, 1980; Parrott, 2001) derived from the study of facial expressions and biology.

2   For example, Anna Wierzbicka (1999) finds that psychologists confound the concepts of disgust and revulsion as one emotion, but she finds these concepts lexically different across cultures. For emotions to be truly universal, she argues, emotions have to be independent of language.

3   Personal communication to the author.

4   Iran, however was not the first so-called 'twitter revolution'. That title was given to the uprising in Moldova in 2009 (Garber, 2009).

5   'The notes were written by Alton G. Keel Jr., the deputy national security adviser at the time, who was present at the 10 November 1986, meeting, which President Reagan also attended… The meeting took place as the Administration was seeking to secure the release of additional American hostages held in Lebanon…The notes suggest that the primary motivation of Mr. Reagan and other senior Administration officials was to continue, despite the disclosure of the sales, to gain the freedom of the American captives' (David Johnston, 'Notes Indicate Reagan Helped Hide Iran Data', *The New York Times*, 26 July 1987).

REFERENCES

Abelson, R. P., Kinder, D. R., Peters, M. D. and Fiske, S. T. (1982) 'Affective and Semantic Components in Political Person Perception', *Journal of Personality and Social Psychology*, 42(4): 619–30.

Anderson, P. A. and Guerrero, L. K. (1998) 'Principles of Communication and Emotion in Social Interaction', in P. A. Anderson and L. K. Guerrero (eds.), *Handbook of Communication and Emotion: Research, Theory, Applications, and Contexts*. New York: Academic Press. pp. 49–89.

Ansolabehere, S. and Iyengar, S. (1995) *Going Negative: How Campaign Advertising Shrinks and Polarizes the Electorate*. New York: Free Press.

Aristotle. (1954) *Rhetoric and Politics*. New York: The Modern Library, Random House.

Belt, T., Just, M. R. and Crigler, A. N. (2005) 'Accentuating the Positive in US Presidential Elections', paper presented at the annual meeting of the American Political Science Association. Washington, DC.

Brader, T. (2005) 'Striking a Responsive Chord: How Political Ads Motivate and Persuade Voters by Appealing to Emotions', *American Journal of Political Science*, 49(2): 388–405.

Brader, T. (2006) *Campaigning for Hearts and Minds: How Emotional Appeals in Political Ads Work*. Chicago, IL: University of Chicago Press.

Cacioppo, J. T. and Visser, P. S. (2003) 'Political Psychology and Social Neuroscience: Strange Bedfellows or Comrades in Arms?', *Political Psychology*, 24(4): 647–56.

Cacioppo, J. T., Berntson, G. G., Lorig, T. S., Norris, C. J., Rickett, E. and Nusbaum, H. (2003) 'Just Because You're Imaging the Brain Doesn't Mean You Can Stop Using Your Head: A Primer and Set of First Principles', *Journal of Personality and Social Psychology*, 85(4): 650–61.

Capella, J. and Jamieson, K. H. (1997) *The Spiral of Cynicism: The Press and the Public Good*. New York: Oxford University Press.

Clore, G. L., Schwarz, N. and Conway, M. (1994) 'Affective Causes and Consequences of Social Information Processing', in R. S. Wyer and T. K. Srull (eds.), *Handbook of Social Cognition*. Vol. 1. Hillsdale, NJ: Lawrence Erlbaum Associates. pp. 323–417.

Colman, A. M. (2003) *Oxford Dictionary of Psychology*. New York: Oxford University Press.

Conover, P. J. and Feldman, S. (1986) 'Emotional Reactions to the Economy: I'm Mad as Hell and I'm Not Going to Take it Anymore', *American Journal of Political Science*, 30(1): 50–78.

Crigler, A. N., Just, M. R. and Belt, T. (2006) 'The Three Faces of Negative Campaigning: The Democratic Implications of Attack Ads, Cynical News and Fear Arousing Messages', in D. P. Redlawsk (ed.), *Feeling Politics: Emotions in Political Information Processing*. New York: Palgrave Macmillan. pp. 135–63.

Crouse, T. (1972) *The Boys on the Bus*. New York: Ballantine Books.

Damasio, A. (1994) *Descartes' Error: Emotion, Reason, and the Human Brain*. New York: Avon Books.

Damasio, A. (1999) *The Feeling of What Happens: Body, Emotion and the Making of Consciousness*. London: Vintage.

Darwin, C. (1965) *The Expression of the Emotions in Man and Animals*. Introduction by Konrad Lorenz. Chicago, IL: University of Chicago Press.

Delli Carpini, M. X. and Williams, B. A. (1994) 'Methods, Metaphors, and Media Research: The Uses of Television in

Political Conversation', *Communication Research*, 21(6): 782–812.

Descartes, R. (1996) *Discourse on Method and Meditations on First Philosophy*. David Weisman (ed.). New Haven, CT: Yale University Press.

Ekman, P. (2003) *Emotions Revealed: Recognizing Faces and Feelings to Improve Communication and Emotional Life*. New York: Owl Books.

Epstein, E. J. (1972) *News from Nowhere: Television and the News*. New York: Vintage.

Ethnograph (2009) http://www.qualisresearch.com (accessed 1 July 2009).

Fenno, R. F. Jr. (1978) *Home Style: House Members in Their Districts*. Boston, MA: Little Brown.

Freedman, P. and Goldstein, K. (1999) 'Measuring Media Exposure and the Effects of Negative Campaign Ads', *American Journal of Political Science*, 43(4): 1189–208.

Friedenberg, R. V. (2002) *Notable Speeches in Contemporary Presidential Campaigns*. Westport, CT: Praeger.

Frijda, N. (1993) 'Moods, Emotion Episodes and Emotions', in M. Lewis and J. M. Haviland (eds.), *Handbook of Emotion*. New York: Guilford Press. pp. 381–401.

Gamson, W. A. (1992) *Talking Politics*. New York: Cambridge University Press.

Gans, H. (1979) *Deciding What's News*. New York: Pantheon.

Garber, M. (2009) 'Remember Moldova', *Columbia Journalism Review*, 16 June, http://www.cjr.org/behind_the_news/remember_moldova.php (accessed 26 June 2009).

Graber, D. (1987) 'Kind Words and Harsh Pictures: How Television Presents the Candidates', in K. L. Schlozman (ed.), *Elections in America*. Boston, MA: Allen & Unwin. pp. 115–41.

Graber, D. (2001) *Processing Politics: Learning from Television in the Internet Age*. Chicago, IL: University of Chicago Press.

Grant, T. J. and Rudolph, T. J. (2003) 'Value Conflict, Group Affect, and the Issue of Campaign Finance', *American Journal of Political Science*, 47(3): 453–69.

Gray, J. A. (1987) 'Perspectives on Anxiety and Impulsivity: A Commentary', *Journal of Research in Personality*, 21(4): 493–509.

Huddy, L. and Mason, L. (2008) 'Heated Campaign Politics: An Intergroup Conflict Model of Partisan Emotions', paper presented at the annual meeting of the American Political Science Association. Boston.

Huddy, L., Feldman, S. and Cassese, E. (2007) 'On the Distinct Political Effects of Anxiety and Anger', in W. R. Neuman, G. E. Marcus, A. N. Crigler and M. MacKuen (eds.), *The Affect Effect: Dynamics of Emotion in Political Thinking and Behavior*. Chicago, IL: University of Chicago Press. pp. 202–31.

Hutchings, V. L., Valentino, N. A., Philpot, T. S. and White, I. K. (2006) 'Racial Cues in Campaign News: The Effects of Candidate Issue Distance on Emotional Responses, Political Attentiveness, and Vote Choice', in D. Redlawsk (ed.), *Feeling Politics*. New York: Palgrave Macmillan. pp. 165–86.

Izard, C. (1971) *The Face of Emotion*. New York: Appleton-Century-Crofts.

Izard, C. E. (1977) *Human Emotions*. New York: Plenum Press.

James, W. (1983) *The Principles of Psychology*. Cambridge, MA: Harvard University Press.

James, W. (2003) 'What Is an Emotion?', in R. C. Solomon (ed.), *What Is an Emotion? Classic and Contemporary Readings*. 2nd edn. New York: Oxford University Press. pp. 65–76.

Jamieson, K. H. (1992) *Dirty Politics: Deception, Distraction, and Democracy*. New York: Oxford University Press.

Johnston, A. and Kaid, L. L. (2002) 'Image Ads and Issue Ads in US Presidential Advertising: Using Videostyle to Explore Stylistic Differences in Televised Political Ads from 1952 to 2000', *Journal of Communication*, 52(2): 281–327.

Johnston, D. (1987) 'Notes Indicate Reagan Helped Hide Iran Data', *The New York Times*, 26 July, http://www.nytimes.com/1987/07/26/world/notes-indicate-reagan-helped-hide-iran-data.html?scp=9&sq=Reagan%20hostages%20Iran%20missiles&st=cse (accessed 6 July 2009).

Just, M. R., Crigler, A. N., Alger, D., Kern, M. and West, D. (1996) *Crosstalk: Citizens, Candidates and the Media in a Presidential Campaign*. Chicago, IL: University of Chicago Press.

Kaid, L. L. (2004) 'Political Advertising', in L. L. Kaid (ed.), *Handbook of Political Communication Research*. Mahwah, NJ: Lawrence Erlbaum Associates. pp. 155–202.

Kern, M. (1989) *30-Second Politics: Political Advertising in the Eighties*. New York: Praeger.

Kern, M. and Just, M. R. (1995) 'The Focus Group Method, Political Advertising, Campaign News, and the Construction of Candidate Images', *Political Communication*, 12(2): 127–45.

Kinder, D. R. (1994) 'Reason and Emotion in American Political Life', in R. C. Schank and E. Langer (eds.), *Beliefs, Reasoning and Decision Making*. Hillsdale, NJ: Lawrence Erlbaum Associates.

Lasswell, H. D. (1958) *Politics: Who Gets What, When, How?* New York: Meridian Books.

Lau, R. R. (1995) 'Information Search During an Election Campaign: Introducing a Process Tracing Methodology for Political Scientists', in M. Lodge and K. McGraw (eds.), *Political Judgment: Structure and Process*. Ann Arbor, MI: University of Michigan Press. pp. 179–206.

Lau, R. and Pomper, G. (2004) *Negative Campaigning: An Analysis of US Senate Elections*. M. D. Lanham (ed.). New York: Rowman and Littlefield.

Lau, R. R. and Redlawsk, D. P. (2006) *How Voters Decide: Information Processing in a Political Campaign*. New York: Cambridge University Press.

Lau, R. R., Sigelman, L., Heldman, C. and Babbitt, P. (1999) 'The Effects of Negative Political Advertisements: A Meta-Analytic Assessment', *American Political Science Review*, 93(4): 851–75.

Lazarus, R. (1991) *Emotion and Adaptation*. New York: Oxford University Press.

Lerner, J. S. and Keltner, D. (2000) 'Beyond Valence: Toward a Model of Emotion-Specific Influences of Judgment and Choice', *Cognition and Emotion*, 14(4): 473–93.

Loftis, K. V. and Lupia, A. (2008) 'Using the Internet to Create Research Opportunities: The New Virtual Communities of

TESS and the American National Election Studies', *PS: Political Science and Politics*, 41(3): 547–50.

Mackie, D. M., Silver, L. A. and Smith, E. R. (2004) 'Emotion as an Intergroup Phenomenon', in L. Z. Tiedens and C. W. Leach (eds.), *The Social Life of Emotions*. New York: Cambridge University Press. pp. 227–45.

Madison, J. (1987) *The Federalist Papers*. Reprint. New York: Penguin Classics.

Marcus, G. E. (1988) 'The Structure of Emotional Response: 1984 Presidential Candidates', *American Political Science Review*, 82(3): 737–61.

Marcus, G. E. (2002) *The Sentimental Citizen: Emotion in Democratic Politics*. University Park, PA: Pennsylvania State University Press.

Marcus, G. E., Neuman, W. R. and MacKuen, M. (2000) *Affective Intelligence and Political Judgment*. Chicago, IL: University of Chicago Press.

Mayer, J. (2001) 'Emotion, Intelligence and Emotional Intelligence', in J. Forgas (ed.), *Affect and Social Cognition*. Mahwah, NJ: Lawrence Erlbaum Associates. pp. 410–43.

McDermott, R. (2008) *Presidential Leadership, Illness, and Decision Making*. New York: Cambridge University Press.

McCracken, G. D. (1988) *The Long Interview*. Newbury Park, CA: Sage.

McManus, J. (1994) *Market-Driven Journalism: Let the Citizen Beware?* Thousand Oaks, CA: Sage.

Miller, J. M. (2006) 'Examining the Mediators of Agenda Setting: A New Experimental Paradigm Reveals the Role of Emotions', *Political Psychology*, 28(6): 689–717.

Neblo, M. A. (2007) 'Philosophical Psychology with Political Intent', in W. R. Neuman, G. E. Marcus, A. N. Crigler and M. MacKuen (eds.), *The Affect Effect: Dynamics of Emotion in Political Thinking and Behavior*. Chicago, IL: University of Chicago Press. pp. 25–48.

Neely, F. (2006) 'Party Identification in Emotional and Political Context: A Replication', *Political Psychology*, 26(6): 667–88.

Neuman, W. R., Marcus, G. E., Crigler, A. N. and MacKuen, M. (eds.) (2007a) *The Affect Effect: Dynamics of Emotion in Political Thinking and Behavior*. Chicago, IL: University of Chicago Press.

Neuman, W. R., Marcus, G. E., Crigler, A. N. and MacKuen, M. (2007b) 'Theorizing Affect's Effects', in W. R. Neuman, G. E. Marcus, A. N. Crigler and M. MacKuen (eds.), *The Affect Effect: Dynamics of Emotion in Political Thinking and Behavior*. Chicago, IL: University of Chicago Press. pp. 1–20.

Panksepp, J. (2000) 'Affective Consciousness and the Instinctual Motor System: The Neural Sources of Sadness and Joy', in R. Ellis and N. Newton (eds.), *The Caldron of Consciousness: Motivation, Affect and Self-organization, Advances in Consciousness Research*. Amsterdam: John Benjamins Pub. Co. pp. 27–54.

Parrott, W. (2001) *Emotions in Social Psychology*. Philadelphia, PA: Psychology Press.

Planalp, S. (1999) *Communicating Emotion: Social, Moral, and Cultural Processes*. New York: Cambridge University Press.

Plato (2000) *The Republic*. G. R. F. Ferrari (ed.). Translated by Tom Griffith. New York: Cambridge University Press.

Plutchik, R. (1980) 'A General Psychoevolutionary Theory of Emotion', in R. Plutchik and H. Kellerman (eds.), *Emotion: Theory, Research, and Experience, Vol. 1, Theories of Emotion*. New York: Academic Press. pp 3–33.

Rahn, W. M., Kroeger, B. and Kite, C. M. (1996) 'A Framework for the Study of Public Mood', *Political Psychology*, 17(1): 29–58.

Redlawsk, D. P., Civettini, A. J. W. and Lau, R. R. (2007) 'Affective Intelligence and Voting: Information Processing and Learning in a Campaign', in W. R. Neuman, G. E. Marcus, A. N. Crigler and M. MacKuen (eds.), *The Affect Effect: Dynamics of Emotion in Political Thinking and Behavior*. Chicago, IL: University of Chicago Press. pp. 152–80.

Richards, B. (2004) 'The Emotional Deficit in Political Communication', *Political Communication*, 21(3): 339–52.

Russell, J. A. (1980) 'A Circumplex Model of Affect', *Journal of Personality and Social Psychology*, 39(6): 1161–78.

Schreiber, D. (2007) 'Political Cognition as Social Cognition: Are We All Political Sophisticates?', in W. R. Neuman, G. E. Marcus, A. N. Crigler and M. MacKuen (eds.), *The Affect Effect: Dynamics of Emotion in Political Thinking and Behavior*. Chicago, IL: University of Chicago Press. pp. 48–70.

Shannon, C. E. and Weaver, W. (1949) *The Mathematical Theory of Communication*. Urbana, IL: University of Illinois.

Small, D. A., Lerner J. S. and Fischoff, B. (2006) 'Emotion Priming and Attributions for Terrorism: Americans' Reactions in a National Field Experiment', *Political Psychology*, 27(2): 289–98.

Smith, C. A. and Ellsworth, P. C. (1985) 'Patterns of Cognitive Appraisal in Emotion', *Journal of Personality and Social Psychology*, 48(4): 813–38.

Smith, C. A. and Lazarus, R. S. (1993) 'Appraisal Components, Core Relational Themes, and the Emotions', *Cognition and Emotion*, 7(3–4): 233–69.

Smith, E. R., Seger, C. R. and Mackie, D. M. (2007) 'Can Emotions be Truly Group Level? Evidence Regarding Four Conceptual Criteria', *Journal of Personality and Social Psychology*, 93(3): 431–46.

Solomon, R. (2004) 'Emotions, Thoughts, and Feelings: Emotions as Engagements with the World', in R. C. Solomon (ed.), *Thinking about Feeling*. New York: Oxford University Press. pp. 76–90.

Spezio, M. L. and Adolphs, R. (2007) 'Emotional Processing and Political Judgment: Toward Integrating Political Psychology and Decision Neuroscience', in W. R. Neuman, G. E. Marcus, A. N. Crigler and M. MacKuen (eds.), *The Affect Effect: Dynamics of Emotion in Political Thinking and Behavior*. Chicago, IL: University of Chicago Press. pp. 71–95.

Sullivan, D. G. and Masters, R. D. (1988) 'Happy Warriors: Leaders' Facial Displays, Viewers' Emotions and Political Support', *American Journal of Political Science*, 32(2): 345–68.

Tierney, J. (2004) 'Using M.R.I.'s to See Politics on the Brain', *The New York Times*, 20 April, https://www.msu.edu/course/aec/810/clippings/MRI%20politics-brain.htm (accessed 26 June 2009).

Wattenberg, M. P. and Brians, C. L. (1999) 'Negative Campaign Advertising: Demobilizer or Mobilizer?', *American Political Science Review*, 93(4): 891–99.

Westen, D. (2007) *The Political Brain: The Role of Emotion in Deciding the Fate of the Nation.* New York: Public Affairs.

White, T. (1961) *The Making of the President, 1960.* New York: Atheneum Publishers.

Wierzbicka, A. (1999) *Emotions Across Languages and Cultures: Diversity and Universals.* Cambridge: Cambridge University Press.

Zullow, H. M. and Seligman, M. E. P. (1990) 'Pessimistic Rumination PredictDefeat of Presidential Candidates, 1900 to 1984', *Psychological Inquiry*, 1(1): 52–61.

18

Online Panels and the Future of Political Communication Research

Shanto Iyengar* and Lynn Vavreck

A major objective of political communication research is to assess the effects of different forms of media programming on the voting public. In the 1970s and 1980s, 'media effects' researchers concentrated on television news because that was where most Americans got their news (see Iyengar and Kinder, 1987). As new media and alternative forms of news programming gained audience share, researchers have expanded their focus accordingly.

Despite the profound changes in the media environment and related changes in the content of campaign communications, the fundamental challenges facing media effects researchers remain constant. The most basic is the challenge of obtaining accurate and precise measures of exposure to media messages. Self-reports on media exposure – long the preferred measure – are likely to yield highly exaggerated and hence inaccurate estimates of media effects. Researchers must also deal with the thorny issue of endogeneity (or two-way causation) between exposure to media programming and political predispositions, which makes it difficult to disentangle the causal effects of messages on the opinions and actions of the audience and vice versa.

Problems of imprecise measurement and weak causal inference have proven intractable in observational research such as surveys. In recent years, political communication researchers have increasingly turned to experimental methods that substitute actual exposure to media messages for self-reported exposure, and which neutralize the issue of endogeneity by assigning individuals to particular audiences on a random basis. The combination of manipulational control and random assignment yields unequivocal causal evidence. Can the results of experimental research be generalized to the real world? The standard argument against experimentation is that the findings are of questionable generalizability because of the artificiality of the experimental setting and the unrepresentativeness of the subject pool. We demonstrate, however, that this conventional wisdom no longer applies, at least to experiments administered online. The revolution in information technology enables researchers to overcome the two prime limitations of experimental research. As people become more adept with technology and spend increasing amounts of time with web-based media, experiments administered online become highly realistic for the simple reason that they mirror individuals' actual media experiences. Further, the development of relatively low cost, but probability-based techniques for sampling from nationwide opt-in Internet panels has enhanced both the power and generalizability of web experiments. Thus, technology has not only transformed the way in which candidates and voters communicate with each other, but has also redefined the methodology of political communication research.

THE CHALLENGES FACING OBSERVATIONAL RESEARCH

In March of 2008 – in the midst of one of the most heated presidential primary campaigns in history – Howard Kurtz, the media columnist for *The Washington Post*, asserted that *Saturday Night Live* (SNL) had changed the course of the 2008 presidential election. SNL writers had taken full advantage of the campaign using newsworthy and amusing moments from the candidates' activities (for example, Sarah Palin's appearance on the CBS Evening News) as fodder for their skits and impersonations. Whether it was Amy Poehler spoofing Hillary Clinton or Tina Fey playing Sarah Palin, the show's real-time ratings soared. Moreover, according to Integrated Media Measurement Incorporated (IMMI), twice as many people watched recordings of the campaign sketches – either on a digital video device or on YouTube and other websites – than watched the live broadcast (Welsh, 2008). More interestingly, in the week after the Vice Presidential debate in St Louis, IMMI reported that only half the people who saw an SNL skit on the debate watched debate itself. This disparity in audience size suggests that for many people, the SNL re-enactment was their *only* exposure to the debate.

At the very least, the evidence suggests that there was considerable public exposure to the SNL treatment of the presidential campaign. With so many people watching, Kurtz may have had a point: perhaps the SNL audience's impressions of the candidates were shaped by the programming they encountered on SNL. But can we test Kurtz's assertion more systematically?

To properly isolate the impact of SNL on public opinion, any study design must meet two requirements. First, there must be data on actual exposure to SNL content. Second, the researcher must be in a position to assess the effects of exposure to SNL on candidate preference or vote choice independent of the effects of vote choice on the decision to watch SNL. As described below, relatively few observational studies meet both these requirements.

Measurement

Exposure is a necessary condition for media influence. How can we reliably differentiate people who saw the SNL skits from those who did not? Traditionally, political communication researchers have relied upon survey respondents' self-reports to measure exposure. For instance, respondents might be asked how many times they watched SNL during the past month. Unfortunately, there is considerable evidence that self-reports of media exposure lead to profound biases in our estimates of media effectiveness, exaggerating the impact by as much as 600% (Ansolabehere and Iyengar, 1994; Price and Zaller, 1993; Vavreck, 2007).

To illustrate the problem, we present data from Vavreck's 2002 experimental study of advertising and turnout. Vavreck randomly assigned half of her sample to receive advertising treatments, including a non-partisan get-out-the-vote ad aimed at stimulating turnout in the 2002 midterm elections. The control group saw nothing. Each respondent's registration and turnout record was located after the election from official statewide databases. In Table 18.1, we re-analyze these data to demonstrate the differences in estimates of the treatment effect on actual turnout or self-reported turnout depending on whether we use self-reported or actual exposure to the treatment ad. The true effect of the ad (the effect of actual exposure on actual turnout) is to increase turnout by less than 1 point. But, when we rely on whether people say they recalled seeing an advertisement encouraging them to vote in the election, the effectiveness of the ad on their reported turnout goes up by a factor of 8.

In 'The Exaggerated Effects of Advertising on Turnout: The Dangers of Self-Reports', Vavreck (2007) shows that it is not just forgetfulness among people who were assigned to the ad that makes this difference.[1] In fact, false recall among the people in the control group who could not

Table 18.1   The effects of ads on turnout using self-reports and actual treatment

	Definitely did not see ad/self-reported turnout	Definitely saw ad/ self-reported turnout	Actual control/ validated turnout	Actual treatment/ validated turnout
Did not vote	70.56	63.24	69.80	68.89
Voted[a]	29.44	36.76	30.20	31.11
Total	100 (394)	100 (612)	100 (202)	100 (225)
	Difference = 7.32		Difference = 0.9	

Note: [a]Dependent variable (voted or not) is self-report for columns one and two. The results in columns three and four use validated vote from the files of the Secretary of State.

have seen the ad contributes more to the inflation of the treatment effect in the self-report analysis.

In order to understand how exposure to political communication affects people, we need to know who, in fact, is exposed. Survey researchers have long argued that better questions will reduce the margin of error in self-reports (Althaus and Kim, 2008; Prior, 2009), but as described below, technological advances may make survey questions entirely unnecessary.

In 2006, Jackman, Lewis and Vavreck worked with IMMI, a media measurement company based in San Mateo, California, to track the production of and exposure to campaign advertisements in the New York media market during the 2006 US Senate races in New York and New Jersey.[2] In New Jersey, the campaign was somewhat competitive between Thomas Kean, Jr, and Robert Menendez (the incumbent); in New York the race was entirely one-sided between incumbent Hillary Clinton and challenger John Spencer.[3]

IMMI has leveraged advances in mobile phone technology and Internet-based research panels to track advertising exposure through cellular phones equipped with proprietary software. In exchange for a new mobile phone and highly subsidized phone service, panelists are required to make the new phone their primary mobile device, keep the battery charged and carry the phone with them at all times. Once turned on, phones begin to digitally encode ambient audio on a regular basis (10 seconds of every 30 seconds throughout the entire day). These recordings are reduced to digital 'fingerprints', which are uploaded continuously to the IMMI servers. The phones do not record audio, nor can the digital fingerprint be 'played' at any point in time. The sole purpose of the digital code is to serve as a target that will be matched against a universe of other digital codes that were aired on all media that day in that market. In order to identify the audio fingerprints being sent by the phones, IMMI also tracks all media broadcast in the target market and maintains client-provided content files, such as commercials, promos, movies and songs. By automatically comparing the uploaded audio fingerprints captured by the phones with audio fingerprints stored on the IMMI servers, IMMI identifies all the media any given panelist is exposed to on a daily basis.

This kind of continuous data collection is new to political science and communication studies – the resulting collection is not a static file but instead a data stream that has to be captured and reduced to something useful to researchers. As data from sensing devices such as the IMMI phone become more widely available, we will have to develop new measurement strategies and methods aimed at managing and analyzing these large streams of real-time observations.

The IMMI data, coupled with survey data on any given panelist's background, allow a researcher to investigate who is exposed to advertising, who is affected by exposure, and what determines both of these things. Obviously, continuous tracking of advertising exposure is a major improvement over self-reports that measure exposure over vaguely defined periods of time.

Since the technology measures exposure to all forms of media programming, it is possible to study the effectiveness of political ads or political shows such as SNL, conditional on a whole host of other factors about the media environment, such as the amount of news programming the person was exposed to or the content of the entertainment programming encountered on any particular day. In Figure 18.1, we present data from Jackman et al.'s (2006) analysis of the 411 IMMI panelists who reside in the New York media

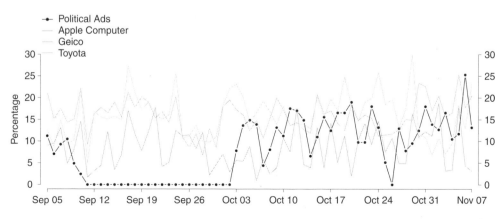

Figure 18.1   Percentage of 411 IMMI panelists viewing at least one ad per day, by selected advertisers, New York DMA

market. The figure demonstrates the relative prominence of political advertising compared to other forms of advertising. Although we tend to think of political advertising as being ubiquitous during campaigns, the data show that in fact, it is not until the last week of the campaign that political ads outnumber ads from Toyota, Geico and Apple – at least in terms of the ads people actually see.

The IMMI data can also be examined by advertiser and day part to show when and where advertisers air their ads. Jackman et al. were thus able to map the different advertising strategies of the candidates over the course of the campaign. Figure 18.2 presents these data for the New Jersey race between Keane and Menendez. Hollow dots represent the airing of an ad, while solid dots indicate that at least one IMMI panelist saw that ad at that time. Clearly, the two campaigns achieved very different levels of exposure to their advertising. Keane had 1614 unique ad buys that were seen 2770 times by 225 unique panelists. Menendez, however, had only 585 buys seen 495 times by 121 people.

What is especially interesting about the data in Figure 18.2 is that volume of advertising is *negatively* correlated with the election outcome. Keane lost the election to Menendez, who ran many fewer ads, exposed only half as many unique people, and whose ads were seen with only one-sixth the frequency of the Keane ads. These data provide a telling illustration of a recurring problem that confronts political campaign research – candidates' choices about when and how much to advertise are endogenous to the outcome we care about, namely, vote choice. In New Jersey, Keane was forced to out-advertise Menendez because he knew he was behind in the polls and had to reach a lot of voters in order to catch up. His advantage in advertising was affected by the state of public opinion rather than the other way around.

Political communication research of the future will increasingly feature technology like that developed by IMMI. As we learn more about developing and managing research panels made up of people who are frequently online or on their mobile phones, we will find ourselves awash in behavioral data about the particular media content to which people are exposed on a given day, which represents quite a dramatic contrast from self-reported media exposure.

Endogeneity and Power

The New Jersey Senate advertising above illustrated one particular version of the problem of endogeneity or reciprocal causation. The problem occurs at two levels. As seen above, candidate behavior is affected by their beliefs about the state of the race. This makes it difficult to tease out the effects of the candidates' advertising on voters' preferences. To make matters worse, the decisions that people make about what particular media programming to watch or listen to are also endogenous to their political preferences. To take an obvious example, Republicans are much more likely than Democrats to watch Fox News. Given SNL's constant lampooning of Sarah Palin, we might expect an equally significant partisan divide in the SNL audience during the 2008 campaign. On both the supply and demand side, therefore, the political communication equation is fraught with endogeneity concerns.

To return to Howard Kurtz's assertion about the transforming role of SNL, evidence from the 2007 wave of a 2007–08 panel study shows that people who report watching political satire shows like SNL are 30% more likely to be interested in politics than those who do not watch these shows – and this is before the campaign heats up (Jackman and Vavreck, 2008). In fact, among people who report exposure to programs like SNL in 2007, more than 66% report being very interested in politics and current affairs – well before these shows began to caricature the candidates. Fans of political satire are also significantly more likely to read political blogs on the Internet and email friends, coworkers and family members about politics. They are more likely to be young, white and male; to identify as Democrats or independents, and to describe themselves as more liberal than conservative (Jackman and Vavreck, 2008). Although this pattern suggests that interest in politics and a preference for Obama motivates attention to SNL political skits, not vice versa, Jackman and Vavreck's data also show that watching SNL in 2007 increased people's chances of voting for Obama in the general election.

These data make it clear why it is so difficult to test Kurtz's assertion with observational data. There is something about a person that makes them more likely to watch shows like SNL, but which also makes her more likely to vote for Obama. Unless we can measure that thing, it will always look like watching the show is driving vote choice or vice versa. The problem is that we rarely know what critical concepts we are not measuring when we write survey questions – and even if we did know, our ability to measure these concepts is crude at best.

So, to know whether Kurtz had it right, we need to know who saw the SNL skits and when they saw them. We need to acquire lots of information about these people so we can account for how their individual characteristics affected whether they viewed the show, and we also need to know their political attitudes and vote intentions – and

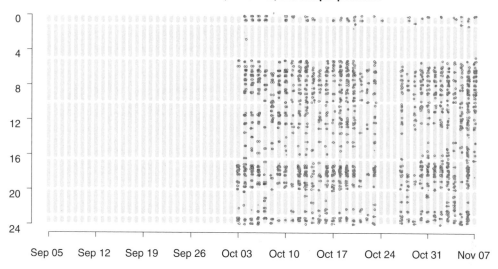

Kean: 1614 runs, 2770 hits, 225 unique panelists

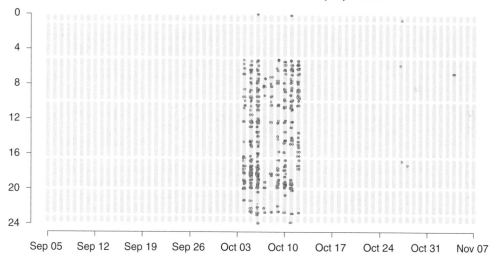

Menendez: 585 runs, 495 hits, 121 unique panelists

Figure 18.2   New Jersey Senate race advertising profiles, 2006

ultimately whether they voted in the election and for whom. And, we need to know this about tens of thousands of people over several repeated weeks of the campaign so we can eventually uncover what is likely to be a very small effect of SNL on turnout or vote choice. To answer this question we need better measures than we currently have, a research design that gets around the endogeneity issue, and access to larger samples than we typically have to isolate potentially small, but important campaign effects.

On both issues described above – measurement of exposure and endogeneity – observational work is clearly lacking. Survey data are typically based on self-reports and limited to one point in time. Lacking both a precise indicator of just who is in the audience at any given moment and the ability to separate cause from effect, observational methods give us very little leverage over questions of media effectiveness. The more promising solution lies in experimental methodology. However, before moving to experimentation, it is important to point out that there is one area of survey research in which we have made great strides recently and will continue to make progress in the years to come – and that is in the development of online surveys.

The large-scale diffusion of the Internet has made survey research more affordable – roughly two orders of magnitude less expensive than face-to-face interviewing. For the same amount of money, we could interview 1000 people in person or 86,000 people online.[4] With the significantly lowered per respondent cost, it becomes possible to track opinion over long periods of time for a set of impaneled people, or track people every day for a few weeks at a time. The substantial increase in sample size and the ability to track the same survey respondents over prolonged periods of time help observational researchers gain traction on the endogeneity problems described above.

THE BENEFITS OF EXPERIMENTATION

An alternative approach to the question posed by Howard Kurtz is to administer a randomized experiment in which we expose half the subjects to a few SNL sketches and then determine their voting preferences. The principal advantage of the experiment over the survey – and the focus of the discussion that follows – is the researcher's ability to isolate and test the effects of specific components of political messages. Consider the case of political campaigns. At the aggregate level, campaigns encompass a concatenation of messages, channels and sources, all of which may influence the audience, often in inconsistent directions. The researcher's task is to identify specific causal factors and delineate the range of their relevant attributes. Even at the relatively narrow level of campaign advertisements, for instance, there are virtually an infinite number of potential causal factors, both verbal and visual. What was it about the infamous 'Willie Horton' advertisement that is thought to have moved so many American voters away from Michael Dukakis during the 1988 presidential campaign? Was it, as widely alleged, that Horton was black? Or was it the violent and brutal nature of his described behavior, the fact that he was a convict, the race of his victim or something else entirely? Experiments make it possible to isolate the explanation, whether it be verbally based or in the form of audio-visual cues.

Of course, experiments not only shed light on treatment effects but also enable researchers to test more elaborate hypotheses concerning the interaction of message factors with individual difference variables. Not all individuals are equally susceptible to incoming messages. Perhaps Democrats

with a weak party affiliation and strong sense of racial prejudice were especially likely to sour on Governor Dukakis in the aftermath of exposure to the Horton advertisement.

In summary, the fundamental advantage of the experimental approach is the ability to isolate causal variables, which become the basis for experimental manipulations. In the next section, we describe manipulations designed to isolate the effects of racial cues in television news coverage of crime, and the physical similarity of candidates to voters.

Racial Cues in Local News Coverage of Crime

As any regular viewer of television knows, crime is a frequent topic in broadcast news. In response to market pressures, television stations have adopted a formulaic approach to covering crime, an approach designed to maximize audience interest. This 'crime script' suggests that crime is invariably violent and those who perpetrate crime are disproportionately non-white. Because the crime script is encountered so frequently, it has attained the status of common knowledge. Just as we know full well what happens when one walks into a restaurant or airport, we also know – or at least think we know – what happens when a crime occurs (Gilliam and Iyengar, 2000).

In a series of experiments, Gilliam and others documented the effects of both the racial and violence elements of the crime script on audience attitudes (Gilliam and Iyengar, 2000; Gilliam et al., 1996, 2002). For illustrative purposes, we focus here on the racial element. In essence, these studies were designed to manipulate the race/ethnicity of the principal suspect depicted in a news report while maintaining all other visual characteristics. The original stimulus consisted of a typical local news report, which included a close-up still 'mug shot' of the suspect. The picture was digitized, then 'painted' to alter the perpetrator's skin color, and re-inserted into the news report. As shown in Figure 18.3, beginning with two different perpetrators (a white male and a black male), the researchers produced altered versions of each individual in which their race was reversed, but all other features remained identical. Participants who watched the news report in which the suspect was thought to be non-white expressed greater support for 'punitive' policies, for example, imposition of 'three strikes and you're out' remedies, treatment of juveniles as adults, and support for the death penalty. Given the precision of the manipulation, these differences in the responses of the subjects exposed to the white or black perpetrators could only be attributed to the perpetrator's race.

Figure 18.3   Race of suspect manipulation

FACIAL SIMILARITY AS A POLITICAL CUE

A consistent finding in the political science literature is that voters support candidates who most
resemble themselves on questions of ideology,
policy or partisanship. But what about physical
resemblance: Are voters also attracted to candidates who look like them?

Several lines of research suggest that physical
similarity in general, and facial similarity in particular, is relevant for political choice. In particular, evolutionary psychologists argue that physical
similarity is a kinship cue and humans are motivated to treat their kin preferentially (for instance,
Burnstein et al., 1994).

In order to isolate the effects of facial similarity
on voting preferences, researchers obtained digital
photographs of 172 registered voters selected at
random from a national Internet panel (for details
on the methodology, see Bailenson et al., 2009).
Participants were asked to provide their photographs approximately three weeks in advance of
the 2004 presidential election. One week before
the election, these same participants were asked to
participate in an online survey of political attitudes that included a variety of questions about
the presidential candidates (President George W.
Bush and Senator John Kerry). The computer
screens on which these candidate questions

appeared also included photographs of the two
candidates displayed side by side. Within this
split-panel presentation, participants had their
own face either morphed with Bush or Kerry at a
ratio of 60% of the candidate and 40% of the participant.[5] Figure 18.4 shows two of the morphs
used in this study.

The results of the face morphing study revealed
a significant interaction between facial similarity
and strength of the participant's party affiliation.
Among strong partisans, the similarity manipulation had no effect; these voters were already convinced of their vote choice. But weak partisans
and independents – whose voting preferences
were not as entrenched – moved in the direction of
the more similar candidate (Bailenson et al.,
2009). Thus, the evidence suggests that non-verbal
cues can influence voting, even in the most visible
and contested of political campaigns.[6]

IMPROVED MEASURES OF AUDIENCE RESPONSE

The ability to launch experiments online has further strengthened the ability of political communication researchers to draw causal inferences

subject   "George Bush"   60:40 Blend

subject   "John Kerry"   60:40 Blend

Figure 18.4   Facial similarity manipulation

by providing more precisely calibrated indicators of audience reactions to media messages. Online experiments permit observation of information seeking behavior as well as user reactions to visual, verbal and audio-visual stimuli such as the material encountered in campaign advertisements.

Behavioral Indicators of Selective Exposure

Researchers have long assumed that people possess an innate preference for attitude-consistent messages or sources of information. According to this 'selective exposure' hypothesis, voters seek to avoid information that clashes with their pre-existing beliefs (for example, Festinger, 1957) and instead put themselves in the path of information they expect to agree with. In the words of Lazarsfeld et al:

In recent years there has been a good deal of talk by men of good will about the desirability and necessity of guaranteeing the free exchange of ideas in the market place of public opinion. Such talk has centered upon the problem of keeping

free the channels of expression and communication. Now we find that the consumers of ideas, if they have made a decision on the issue, themselves erect high tariff walls against alien notions. (1948: 89)

Given the practical difficulties of delivering large quantities of information, the typical study on selective exposure provides participants with only a limited range of choice. Indeed, Cotton observed that the selective exposure literature had failed to address 'how people actively seek and avoid information on their own' in naturalistic settings (1985: 29). However, digital technology now makes it possible to deliver voluminous quantities of information in a compact and easy to navigate format.

In a study of selective exposure during the 2000 presidential campaign, researchers provided a representative sample of registered voters with a multimedia CD containing extensive information about candidates Bush and Gore – including text of all of their stump speeches delivered between 1 July and 7 October, a full set of televised ads, and the texts of the Democratic and Republican Party platforms. The CD also included the soundtrack and transcripts of the candidates' nomination acceptance speeches as well as the first televised debate. All told, the information amounted to over 600 pages of text and two hours of multimedia (Iyengar et al., 2008).

The campaign CD was delivered to a representative sample of American adult Internet users two weeks before election day. Participants were informed in advance that their use of the CD would be examined by the researchers (and they were asked not to share the CD with members of their family or friends). As the user navigated through the CD offerings, a built-in tracking feature recorded every visited page (in the order of visit), the number of total times the CD was accessed, and the length of each browsing session in a log file on the user's hard drive. Upon completing a post-election questionnaire, participants were given instructions for finding and uploading their log-files (600 people were invited to participate in the study; of these, 226 actually used the CD for a response rate of 38%.) From these files, we were able to monitor the degree to which CD users gravitated to information provided by the candidate they preferred. The findings revealed only partial evidence of selective exposure based on partisanship; Republicans (and conservatives) showed a preference for information concerning Bush, but Democrats (and liberals) proved more even-handed in their information-seeking behavior.

The tendency for partisans on the right to show greater avoidance of attitude-discrepant information is attributable to both dispositional and contextual factors. In comparison with liberals, conservatives may have a more intense sense of group identity, thus heightening their need to avoid dissonance. On the other hand, the greater selectivity among Republicans may reflect habituation over time. Since the launch of the Fox News network in 1986, Republicans have enjoyed easy access to television news with a pro-Republican tilt. The tendency to avoid attitude-discrepant information encouraged by Fox News may have promoted similar information-seeking behaviors in a non-news context.

Continuous Tracking of Viewers' Reactions to Campaign Ads

Campaign advertising is the major source of information for voters in non-presidential elections. Understanding voters' reactions to ads is thus fundamental to understanding the effectiveness of campaigns. Most researchers who investigate the effectiveness of ad campaigns typically rely on verbal measures to gauge the influence of ads. Viewers might be asked if they agreed or disagreed with the ad in question, or if the ad elicited positive or negative feelings concerning the sponsoring candidate. These measures ask respondents to provide a post hoc summary or 'averaged' assessment of their reaction to the content and imagery of ads.

With the diffusion of online technology, it is possible to monitor viewer response to advertising on a continuous basis, over the entire playing of the ad (Iyengar et al., 2007). Rather than asking for a summary assessment *after* viewers have watched the ad, researchers can use an online 'dial' (or sliding scale) procedure that synchronizes viewers' self-reported feelings concerning the soundtrack and visual imagery they encounter at any given moment *during* the playing of the ad.

Ad dial methodology was implemented online in a study of the 2006 US Senate elections in six battleground states. A sample of approximately 1900 registered voters with Internet access was selected at random from a nationwide online panel. Participants were instructed (and given a practice task) on how to move a slider located immediately below the video in accordance with their feelings about the content of the ad. The specific instruction was: 'If what you see or hear makes you feel good, or you agree with the speaker, indicate this by moving the slider toward the green end. If, however, your reaction is negative, and you dislike what you see or hear, then move the slider to the red zone'.

Special software recorded the position of the slider once a second by evenly dividing the range of dial positions into 100 intervals, with zero indicating the left or negative end of the dial, and 100 the right or positive end. Thus, as the ad played, we could monitor voters' reactions in real time from beginning to end. At the start of each ad, the slider was positioned at the neutral or '50' position, and this was the first dial value recorded for each ad view. Figure 18.5 displays a screen shot from one of the Tennessee conditions featuring the race between Republican Bob Corker and Democrat Harold Ford Jr, with relatively positive and negative positions of the dial.

The results from this study indicated that most ads polarize partisan viewers; over the course of the ad, Democrats and Republicans inevitably move in opposite directions (see Figure 18.6). This pattern is consistent with prior research showing that exposure to campaign ads strengthens viewers' partisan predispositions (Ansolabehere and Iyengar, 1996). While partisans responded rapidly to the content of advertising, Independents were typically unmoved, remaining lukewarm over the entire playing of the ad.

A further finding from this study was that the rate of polarization proved variable across

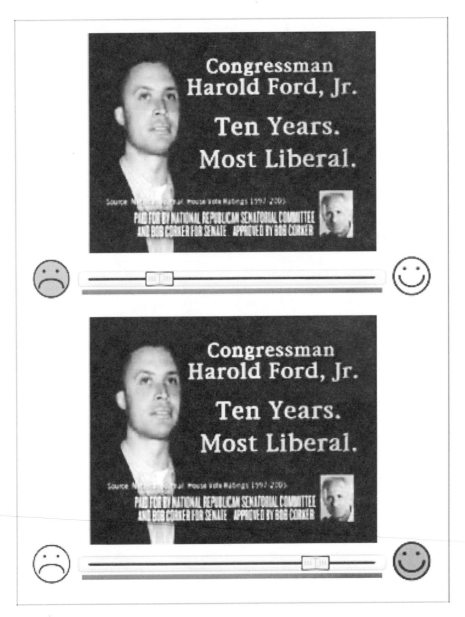

Figure 18.5   Screen shots from online dials
Note: As the ad played, participants could move the slider to indicate their feelings about the content of the ad, with the position of the dial recorded once a second.

the partisanship of the sponsoring candidate. Democrats consistently converged (arrived at their stable end point) faster in response to Democratic ads than did Republicans in response to Republican ads. In effect, Democratic ads resonated more powerfully with Democrats than Republican ads did with Republicans. Perhaps this effect was due to the partisan

appeal of the ads' messages. Democratic ads, which tended to highlight the state of the war in Iraq and the fallout from the Abramoff ethics scandal linking the Republican candidate with President Bush, mobilized the Democratic base more effectively than generic Republican appeals on national security, immigration and taxes.

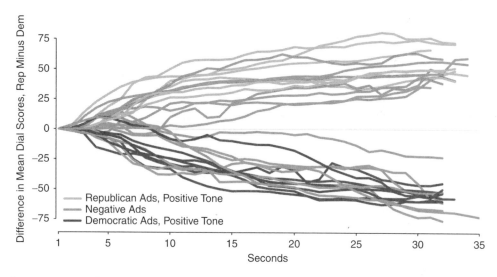

Figure 18.6   Partisan polarization in dial score

THE CHALLENGE FACING EXPERIMENTAL RESEARCH

The problem of limited generalizability, long the Achilles Heel of experimental design, occurs at three different levels: the realism of the experimental setting, the representativeness of the participant pool and the discrepancy between experimental control and self-selected exposure to media presentations.

Mundane Realism

Because of the need for tight control over exposure to the stimulus, the laboratory setting in which the experiment occurs is often quite dissimilar from the setting in which subjects ordinarily experience the 'target' phenomenon. The inherently artificial properties of lab experiments have led researchers to turn to designs in which the procedures and settings more closely reflect ordinary life.

One approach to increased realism is the use of interventions with which subjects are familiar. The Ansolabehere/Iyengar campaign advertising experiments, conducted in the Los Angeles area in the early 1990s, were realistic in the sense that they occurred during ongoing campaigns characterized by heavy levels of televised advertising (Ansolabehere and Iyengar, 1996). The presence of political advertisements in a local newscast (the vehicle used to convey the manipulation) was hardly unusual or unexpected since candidates advertise most heavily during news programs.

The advertisements featured real candidates – Democrats and Republicans, liberals and conservatives, males and females, incumbents and challengers – as the sponsors. The material that made up the experimental stimuli were selected either from actual advertisements used by the candidates during the campaign, or were produced to emulate typical campaign advertisements. In the case of the latter, the researchers spliced together footage from actual advertisements or news reports, editing the treatment ads to be representative of the genre. (The need for experimental control made it necessary for the treatment ads to differ from actual political ads in several important attributes including the absence of music and the appearance of the sponsoring candidate.)

Realism also depends upon the physical setting in which the experiment is administered. Asking subjects to report to a location on a university campus may suit the researcher but may make the experience of watching television for the participant equivalent to visiting the doctor. A more realistic strategy is to provide subjects with a milieu that closely matches the setting of their living room or den. To that end, the Ansolabehere/Iyengar experimental 'laboratory' was designed to resemble, as closely as possible, the natural 'habitat' of the television viewer. Comfortable couches and chairs were arranged in front of a television set, with houseplants and wall hangings placed around the room. Respondents also had access to refreshments and reading material (newspapers and magazines) during the viewing sessions. In many cases, a family member or friend took part in the experiment at the same time, so that subjects did not find themselves sitting next to a stranger while viewing the target advertisements.

A further step toward realism concerns the power of the manipulation (also referred to as experimental realism). Of course, the researcher would like for the manipulation to have an effect. At the same time, it is important that the required task or stimulus not overwhelm the subject (as in the Milgram obedience studies, where the task of administering an electric shock to a fellow participant proved overpowering and ethically suspect). In the case of the campaign advertising experiments, the researchers resolved the experimental realism versus mundane realism tradeoff by embedding the manipulation in a commercial break of a local newscast. For each condition, the treatment ad appeared with other non-political ads, and because subjects were led to believe that the study was about 'selective perception of news', they had no incentive to pay particular attention to ads. Overall, the manipulation was relatively modest, amounting to 30 seconds of a 15-minute recording.

In general, there is a significant tradeoff between experimental realism and manipulational control. In the advertising studies described above, the fact that subjects were exposed to the treatments in the company of others meant that their level of familiarity with fellow subjects was subject to unknown variation. And producing experimental ads that more closely emulated actual ads (for example, by including a soundtrack and featuring the sponsoring candidate) would have necessarily introduced a series of confounding variables associated with the appearance and voice of the sponsor. Despite these tradeoffs, however, it is still possible to achieve a high degree of experimental control with stimuli that closely resemble the 'naturally occurring' phenomenon of interest.

Sampling Bias

The most widely cited limitation of experiments concerns the composition of the subject pool (Sears, 1986). Typically, laboratory experiments are administered upon 'captive' populations – college students who must serve as guinea pigs in order to gain course credit. College sophomores may be a convenient subject population for academic researchers, but they are hardly comparable to 'real people'.

In conventional experimental research, it is possible to broaden the participant pool but at considerable cost/effort. Locating experimental facilities at public locations and enticing a quasi-representative sample to participate proves both cost- and labor-intensive. Typical costs include rental fees for an experimental facility in a public area (such as a shopping mall), recruitment of participants and training and compensation of research staff to administer the experiments. In the crime news experiments conducted in Los Angeles in the summer and fall of 1999, the total cost per subject amounted to approximately US$45. Fortunately, as we have already noted in the case of survey research, technology has both enlarged the pool of potential participants and reduced the per capita cost of administering an experimental study.

Today, traditional experimental methods can be rigorously and far more efficiently administered using an online platform. Utilizing the Internet as the experimental 'site' provides several advantages over conventional locales, including the ability to reach diverse populations without geographic limitations. The technology is sufficiently user friendly that most web users can now 'self-administer' experimental manipulations. Compared with conventional shopping mall studies, therefore, the costs of online experiments are minimal. Moreover, with the development of Internet research panels, it is now possible to use more rigorous sampling methods to select participants for experimental research.[7] In this sense, online experiments now emulate surveys in the sense of drawing representative samples from some national population.

Sampling from Online Research Panels

Even though online experiments administered on purely opt-in samples may provide more generalizability than the typical 'college sophomore' sample, the self-selected online participant pool is significantly biased in several important respects. The 'digital divide' is still large enough to create significant differences in socioeconomic status between participants and non-participants in online research. Online experiments that attract participants from particular media websites (such as Washingtonpost.com) are also biased in important respects (such as political ideology). Fortunately, it is now possible to overcome issues of sampling bias (assuming the researcher has access to some minimal level of funding) by administering online experiments to representative samples. In this sense, the lack of generalizability associated with experimental designs can be largely overcome.

Two market research firms have pioneered the use of web-based experiments with fully representative samples. Not surprisingly, both firms are located in the heart of Silicon Valley. The first is Knowledge Networks (KN) based in Menlo Park, and the second is Polimetrix (recently purchased by the UK polling company of YouGov) based in Palo Alto (PMX).

KN has overcome the problem of selection bias inherent to online surveys, which reach only that proportion of the population that is both online and inclined to participate in research studies, by recruiting a nationwide panel through standard probability sampling methods. At its inception, KN invited over 100,000 people living in randomly selected households to join their panel. The final panel included over 150,000 Americans between the ages of 16 and 85 to whom KN provided free access to the Internet via WebTV. In exchange, panel members agreed to participate (on a regular basis) in research studies being conducted by the firm. Today, the panel is smaller and the recruitment methods have changed, but panelists still take surveys online, either on a KN installed WebTV or on their own computers. Thus, in theory, KN delivers samples that meet the highest standards of probabilistic sampling. In practice, because the opt-in rate at initial invitation is quite low, and because those who do opt-in have an obligation to participate, KN has artificially high with-in panel response rates (Dennis et al., 2004). Still, at the heart of the panel-building process is a probabilistic methodology. KN typically delivers data from this panel that come with post-stratification weights to correct for biases in non-response just as a researcher would do who engaged in a traditional probabilistic sampling routine.

The KN method, because it starts with the probabilistic base, is expensive. To avoid the costs of paying for people's Internet usage, the PMX panel (called *PollingPoint*) is made up entirely of people who already have access to the Internet. Further, PMX does not invite panelists to join *PollingPoint* unsolicited, but instead recruits people into the panel after they have completed one PMX online survey by choice.[8] Because this method of recruitment is low-cost, PMX is able to be constantly recruiting panelists, which means that the *PollingPoint* panel is quite large – well over 1 million people. The size of this pool allows researchers at PMX to use a novel 'matching' approach to turn the purely opt-in pool into representative samples.

To extract a representative sample from this pool of self-selected panelists, PMX engages in a two-step process called sample matching. First, PMX constructs a sampling frame from the American Community Study (ACS) with additional data from the Current Population Survey voter supplement and the Pew Religious Life study. From this frame, PMX draws a stratified random sample of people similar in size to the sample they want to produce from their opt-in panel. This is called the target sample.

The next step is to search within the *PollingPoint* panel for respondents who most closely match the individuals in the target sample. On average, two–three matches are drawn for every person in the target sample and all of these people are invited to complete a client's survey. From this set of completed interviews, the final matched-sample is drawn taking the panelists who most closely match the target individuals. This method literally substitutes members of the PMX panel for individuals in a randomly drawn target sample from a corresponding frame.[9] Rivers (2006) describes the conditions under which the matched sample approximates a true random sample.

Although this sampling method is new to communication and political science, non-random sampling of various sorts has been around for decades. The PMX matched-samples have achieved impressive rates of predictive validity, thus bolstering the claims that matched samples emulate random samples on the criterion of representativeness. In the 2005 California special election, PMX accurately predicted the public's acceptance or rejection of all seven propositions (a record matched by only one other conventional polling organization), with an average error rate comparable to what would be expected given random sampling (Rivers, 2009). In 2006 and 2008, PMX correctly predicted senate and gubernatorial elections with minimal bias (Vavreck and Rivers, 2008).

Whether one is more comfortable with the KN approach to sampling that has its roots in a probabilistic method, or the PMX approach, which uses matching and weighting to remove selection biases, the truth of the matter is that the Internet is here to stay. No matter how hard researchers hold on to random sampling methods like RDD or area probability sampling, the future of communication research is online. The fact that many people now get their news, communicate with friends and watch entertainment on their computers only underscores the need for us to make the transition to online research methodologies.

CONCLUSION

The standard comparison of experiments and surveys favors the former on the grounds of precise causal inference and the latter on the grounds of greater generalizability. As we have suggested, however, traditional experimental methods can now be effectively and rigorously replicated using online strategies which have the advantage of reaching a participant pool that is more far-flung and diverse than the pool relied on by conventional experimentalists. The development of online research panels makes it possible to administer experiments on broad cross-sections of the American population. As technology diffuses still further, the generalizability gap between experimental and survey methods will continue to close.

Although information technology has clearly advanced the conduct of experimental research, there are challenges ahead. The most notable concerns the increasingly self-selected nature of media audiences. Since there is a much wider range of media choices than ever before, providing greater variability of available information, people uninterested in politics can avoid news programming altogether while political junkies can exercise discretionary or selective exposure to political information. Thus, random assignment is no longer an entirely appropriate strategy for assigning individuals to audiences (Gaines and Kuklinski, 2008). In other words, as we force subjects in experiments to comply with our treatments, we are assuming that the decision about whether to experience the treatment in the real world is unrelated to the size of the treatment's effect. If the decision about whether to watch an advertisement or read a news story conditions the effect of the treatment, not even new technology can save us from making mistaken inferences about effects.[10]

This increasing degree of endogeneity between the composition of particular media audiences and their political predispositions (and the potentially conditioning effect) has important consequences for the design of experimental research. Two recent projects highlight the importance of clever designs and the use of new technology to explain the role of political communication. Vavreck and Green (2009) take the endogeneity seriously by administering a large-scale field experiment testing the effects of non-partisan get-out-the-vote (GOTV) advertisements. They made and ran ads on popular networks in randomly assigned local cable systems during a real election. By using publicly available voter registration files that link voters to zip codes and thus cable systems, Green and Vavreck (2008) are able to demonstrate that running GOTV ads one week before a presidential election in primetime increases turnout on the target group by roughly 3 points. They are careful to call this effect the 'intent to treat' (ITT) effect, since they do not know exactly who in their treatment zip codes actually saw the ads. The ITT effect may be different from the 'treatment on the treated' (TOT) effect if not everyone who lives in the treated zip codes saw the ads – and surely this is the case. By moving the advertising experiment out of the lab and even off the Internet, Vavreck and Green are able to allow people in the treatment zip codes to 'select' in to being treated by whatever mechanisms they actually use in a real campaign when real campaign ads come on the television.

Similarly, Iyengar and Jackman (2003) randomly assigned young voters in California to receive a CD featuring the candidates contesting the 2002 gubernatorial election. Iyengar and Jackman found that actual (validated) turnout among the voters in the treatment group who used the CD was 10 percentage points higher than among young voters in the control group (who did not receive the CD). Like Vavreck and Green (2009), Iyengar and Jackman allowed people in the treatment condition to decide, on their own terms, whether they would engage with the treatment. Iyengar and Jackman speculated, however, that the large 10-point effect – the treatment on the treated effect – could be attributed not only to the treatment, but also to the ex-ante level of political interest among participants who chose to use the CD. When exposure to the experimental treatment is based on choice and the determinants of the choice also condition the effect of the treatment, it becomes necessary to estimate the average treatment effect after adjusting for self-selection.

Put more clearly, comparing treatment respondents who used the CD to the entire control group was not the right comparison – even though subjects were assigned randomly. To demonstrate this, the researchers identified a comparison set of 'interested' subjects in the control group who are the closest matches to those interested people in the treatment group who actually used the CD. In the CD experiment, 78% of those assigned to the treatment group ignored the CD, due to general disinterest in the subject matter, insufficient time, or other such factors. Those who did accept the treatment were drawn disproportionately from the ranks of the politically engaged. Thus, actual engagement with the treatment was in fact non-random and correlated with key outcome variables of interest.

Fortunately, in recent years there has been considerable progress in estimating treatment effects in non-randomized experimental or observational settings (Heckman et al., 1998; Imbens, 2004). The general idea is straightforward: although respondents have self-selected into a particular treatment or experimental condition, after the researcher controls for factors that predispose assignees to accept or refuse treatment, the outcomes of interest and treatment are no longer confounded. Given the availability of variables (covariates) known to motivate participation, the researcher can overcome the failure of random assignment and recover an unbiased estimate of the treatment effect. In particular, it is possible to carry out *matched comparisons* of treated and control participants (matching on the covariates); averaging over these matched comparisons generally produces an unbiased estimate of the causal effect of treatment (see Rosenbaum and Rubin, 1983). When the authors of the CD study used propensity score matching to generate a matched control group for their interested treatment group subjects, their estimate of the effects of the CD on turnout was reduced by more than one-half.

In summary, the use of digital technology in experimental research represents a double-edged sword. Although researchers are in a position to administer precisely controlled manipulations to an increasingly large and heterogeneous subject pool, thus increasing both statistical power and generalizability, they face a radically altered media environment in which exposure to political content is increasingly driven by choice (see Bennett and Iyengar, 2008). As a result, assignment to media treatments in the real world will inevitably depend on the participant's political preferences and estimating the effects of these treatments will require the use of more powerful statistical tools – or different experimental designs.

NOTES

*   Iyengar's contribution to this chapter was supported by the National Research Foundation of Korea Grant funded by the Korean Government (NRF-2010-330-B00028).

1   In the Ansolabehere and Iyengar experiments on campaign advertising (which spanned the 1990, 1992 and 1994 election cycles), over 50% of the participants who were exposed to a political advertisement were unable, *some 30 minutes later*, to recall having seen the advertisement (Ansolabehere and Iyengar, 1994).

2   Candidates running for office in New Jersey are forced to advertise on New York City television stations because the broadcasts reach significant areas of New Jersey.

3   The biggest spender in the New York media market was Clinton, whose overall spending was reported at US$35,364,218.00. Spending for Tom Kean, Jr, was US$18,463,780.00; and, Menendez spending was more modest at US$14,364,495.00. John Spencer did not advertise in this DMA at all, but reports overall campaign spending of US$5,660,688.00.

4   This calculation is based on face-to-face interview costs of US$1300 for two waves totaling 70 minutes and Internet interview costs of US$15.00 for two waves totaling 20 minutes. This works out to US$18.75 per minute in person and US$0.75 per minute online. These are roughly the respective costs of the 2008 American National Election Study and the 2008 Cooperative Campaign Analysis Project.

5   We settled on the 60:40 ratio after a pretest study indicated that this level of blending was insufficient for participants to detect traces of themselves in the morph, but sufficient to move evaluations of the target candidate.

6   Facial similarity is necessarily confounded with familiarity – people are familiar with their own faces. There is considerable evidence (Zajonc, 2001) that people prefer familiar to unfamiliar stimuli. An alternative interpretation of these results, accordingly is that participants were more inclined to support the more familiar-looking candidate.

7   A challenge to online research is the ability to contact people via the Internet. Unlike phone numbers, there is no collection of email addresses from which researchers can randomly draw. Moreover, anti-spam laws make it difficult for researchers to contact people via email without their express permission to do so in advance of the contact. As a consequence, Internet research companies have to build and maintain panels of people who agree to take surveys online for them. Once people agree to receive emails from an online research company, they become members of that company's panel. Most companies maintain very large panels and reward the panelists for completing surveys. Panel management is an important job at any online research firm, and requires creativity and diligence. The goal is to make the survey experience enjoyable for people, not tedious or bothersome. This requires limiting the length of surveys as well as managing the content to make sure questions are not too long or repetitive and the content is not offensive in some way.

8   In order to do this, PMX writes short, fun surveys about a variety of topics (entertainment, sports, pop-culture and politics, among others) and buys online advertising on related web sites that link to the short survey. Respondents share their opinions about everything from gay marriage to favorite recipes and then they are asked to join the *PollingPoint* Panel.

9   Because no match is perfect, the samples may still miss on some combinations of characteristics, thus PMX provides post-stratification weights. The matched cases are weighted to the sampling frame using propensity scores.

10   This, however, is one of the advantages of field experiments, particularly on advertising, since compliance with the treatment is not forced and researchers can calculate the intent-to-treat effects separately from the treatment-on-the-treated effects.

REFERENCES

Althaus, S. L. and Kim, Y. (2008) 'Priming Effects in Complex Information Environments: Reassessing the Impact of News Discourse on Presidential Approval', *Journal of Politics*, 68(4): 960–76.

Ansolabehere, S. and Iyengar, S. (1994) 'Messages Forgotten: Mis-reporting in Surveys and the Bias Toward Minimal Effects', unpublished paper. Department of Political Science, UCLA.

Ansolabehere, S. and Iyengar, S. (1996) *Going Negative.* New York: Free Press.

Bailenson, J., Iyengar, S., Yee, N. and Collins, N. (2009) 'Facial Similarity between Candidates and Voters Causes Influence', *Public Opinion Quarterly*, 72(5): 935–61.

Burnstein, E., Crandall, C. and Kitayama, S. (1994) 'Some Neo-Darwinian Decision Rules for Altruism: Weighing Cues for Inclusive Fitness as a Function of the Biological Importance of the Decision', *Journal of Personality and Social Psychology*, 67(5): 773–89.

Bennett, W. L. and Iyengar, S. (2008) 'A New Era of Minimal Effects? The Changing Foundations of Political Communication', *Journal of Communication*, 58(4): 707–31.

Cotton, J. (1985) 'Cognitive Dissonance in Selective Exposure', in D. Zillman and J. Bryant (eds.), *Selective Exposure to Communication*. Hillsdale, NJ: Lawrence Erlbaum Associates. pp. 11–34.

Dennis, J., Li, R. and Chatt, C. (2004) 'Benchmarking Knowledge Networks' Web-Enabled Panel Survey of Selected GSS Questions Against GSS In-Person Interviews', Knowledge Networks Report.

Festinger, L. (1957) *A Theory of Cognitive Dissonance.* Evanston, IL: Row, Peterson.

Gaines, B. and Kuklinski, J. (2008) 'A Case for Including Self-Selection alongside Randomization in the Assignment of Experimental Treatments', paper presented at 2008 Midwest Political Science Association Meeting. Chicago, IL.

Gilliam, F. Jr and Iyengar, S. (2000) 'Prime Suspects: The Influence of Local Television News on the Viewing Public', *American Journal of Political Science*, 44(3): 560–73.

Gilliam, F. Jr, Valentino, N. and Beckman, M. (2002) 'Where You Live and What You Watch: The Impact of Racial Proximity and Local Television News on Attitudes About Race and Crime', *Political Research Quarterly*, 55(4): 755–80.

Gilliam, F. Jr, Iyengar, S., Simon, A. and Wright, O. (1996) 'Crime in Black and White: The Violent, Scary World of Local News', *Harvard International Journal of Press/Politics*, 1(3): 6–23.

Green, D. and Vavreck, L. (2008) 'Analysis of Cluster-randomized Experiments: A Comparison of Alternative Estimation Strategies', *Political Analysis*, 16(2): 138–52.

Heckman, J., Ichimura, H. and Todd, P. (1998) 'Matching as an Econometric Evaluation Estimator', *Review of Economic Studies*, 65(2): 261–94.

Imbens, G. (2004) 'Nonparametric Estimation of Average Treatment Effects under Exogeneity: A Review', *Review of Economics and Statistics*, 86(1): 4–29.

Iyengar S. and Kinder, D. (1987) *News That Matters: Television and American Opinion*. Chicago, IL: University of Chicago Press.

Iyengar, S., Hahn, K., Krosnick, J. and Walker, J. (2008) 'Selective Exposure to Campaign Communication: The Role of Anticipated Agreement and Issue Public Membership', *Journal of Politics*, 70(1): 186–200.

Iyengar, S. and Jackman, S. (2003) 'Technology and Politics: Incentives for Youth Participation', presented at the International Conference on Civic Education Research.

Iyengar, S., Jackman, S. and Hahn, K. (2007) 'Polarization in Less than 30 Seconds: Continuous Monitoring of Voter Response to Campaign Advertising', presented at the Annual Meeting of the American Political Science Association.

Jackman, S. and Vavreck, L. (2008) *The Cooperative Campaign Analysis Project*. Palo Alto and Los Angeles, CA.

Jackman, S., Lewis, J. and Vavreck, L. (2006) 'Digital Fingerprints: Tracking Ad Exposure in Senate Elections', working paper. UCLA.

Lazarsfeld, P., Berelson, B. and Gaudet, H. (1948) *The People's Choice: How the Voter Makes up his Mind in a Presidential Campaign*. 2nd edn. New York: Columbia University Press.

Price, V. and Zaller, J. (1993) 'Who Gets the News? Alternative Measures of News Reception and Their Implications for Research', *Public Opinion Quarterly*, 57(2): 133–64.

Prior, M. (2007). *Post-Broadcast Democracy: How Media Choice Increases Inequality in Political Involvement and Polarizes Elections*. New York: Cambridge University Press.

Prior, M. (2009). 'Improving media effects research through better measures of news exposure', *Journal of Politics*, 73(1): 893–908.

Rivers, D. (2006) 'Sample Matching: Representative Sampling from Internet Panels', http://www.polimetrix.com/documents/Polimetrix_Whitepaper_Sample Matching.pdf

Rivers, D. (2009) 'Scientific Sampling for Online Research', http://www.polimetrix.com/documents/Polimetrix_Sampling.pdf

Rosenbaum, P. and Rubin, D. (1983) 'The Central Role of the Propensity Score in Observational Studies for Causal Effects', *Biometrika*, 70(1): 41–55.

Sears, D. (1986) 'College Sophomores in the Laboratory: Influences of a Narrow Data Base on the Social Psychology View of Human Nature', *Journal of Personality and Social Psychology*, 51(3): 515–30.

Vavreck, L. (2007) 'The Exaggerated Effects of Advertising on Turnout: The Dangers of Self-Reports', *Quarterly Journal of Political Science*, 2(4): 325–43.

Vavreck, L. and Green, D. P. (2009) 'Rocking the Vote: A Randomized Field Test of Advertising Effectiveness', working paper. UCLA.

Vavreck, L. and Rivers, D. (2008) 'The 2006 Cooperative Congressional Election Study', *Journal of Elections, Public Opinion, and Parties*, 18(4): 355–66.

Welsh, A. (2008) 'SNL's Palin Sketches Turn TV Upside Down: Draw Huge After-Air Audience', integrated Media Measurement Incorporated (IMMI) working paper.

Zajonc, R. (2001) 'Mere Exposure: A Gateway to the Subliminal', *Current Directions in Psychological Science*, 10(6): 224–28.

19

Social Networks and Political Knowledge

William P. Eveland, Jr, Myiah J. Hutchens
and Alyssa C. Morey

Beginning in the mid- to late-1990s, disciplines such as communication and political science witnessed an increase in studies examining social or political networks far beyond the rate of such research in prior decades. Huckfeldt and Sprague's (1995) *Citizens, Politics and Social Communication*, Putnam's (2000) popularization of the concept of social capital and the broad 'deliberative turn' in democratic theory (for example, Chambers, 2003), among other research, prompted scholars to pay greater attention to how social discussion generally, or political discussion in particular, could be important for normatively desirable political outcomes. This is part of a larger trend across both the social and physical sciences that places an increasing emphasis on social and technological networks and their impacts on numerous aspects of society (Barabási, 2003).

Of course, research before this period had not completely neglected the role of communication networks for politics. Many scholars point to the early work of Lazarsfeld and his colleagues (Katz and Lazarsfeld, 1955; Lazarsfeld et al., 1944) as the modern genesis of such an approach. And, although political communication research subsequently turned away from the network approach in favor of the Michigan School approach (Knoke, 1990; Zuckerman, 2005), there have been repeated calls for a return to the study of social networks in politics over the past 30 years (for example, Eulau and Siegel, 1981; Knoke, 1990; Straits, 1991; Weatherford, 1982; Zuckerman, 2005). It would seem that, by the second decade of the 21st century, political communication scholars have

heeded the call to understand the role of social networks in politics, and this research is now proceeding at a solid pace.

In this chapter, we first distinguish various types of social network studies and data. Second, we review the literature linking political discussion and discussion networks with *political knowledge*. Unfortunately, we must set aside research connecting political networks and other important political outcomes such as vote choice (for example, Beck et al., 2002) and participation (for example, McClurg, 2006) for another day. We then make a theoretical and empirical case for conducting further research using a special form of social network data – sociometric or whole network data. We discuss how existing concepts in the literature may be extended to this form of data, and then explain how other sociometric concepts can be used to extend our understanding of the role of social networks in producing political knowledge.

WHAT DO WE MEAN BY SOCIAL NETWORK STUDIES?

Use of the terms 'social network' or 'discussion network' is becoming more frequent among political communication scholars. This begs the question of what, exactly, distinguishes a social network study from the standard sample survey study? Some clear empirical distinctions can be applied that roughly parallel different 'degrees' or 'levels' of social network data (Marsden, 2005; Wasserman and Faust, 1994). One might think of these levels as moving from less to more exhaustively capturing a complete 'social network' in the actual data, or moving further away from a typical sample survey.[1] More generally, however, social networks are social structures connecting individuals through communication. Thus, social networks are, from our perspective, fundamentally communicative in both their structure as well as the process through which they produce effects.

Summary Network Data

The first or lowest level of network data includes studies that gather data from the perspective of the survey respondents (egos), do not distinguish individual network members (alters), and ask for convenient summary measures across alters (for example, Eveland and Hively, 2009; Kwak et al., 2005; Moy and Gastil, 2006). For instance, a study might ask survey respondents to indicate the overall frequency with which they discuss politics (independent of with whom), and then ask with how many different individuals they discuss politics to tap network size. These studies may also ask questions about discussion frequency or network size within social or political categories (for example, Roch et al., 2000; Scheufele et al., 2004) – for instance, among Democrats versus Republicans, men versus women or family versus friends – in order to capture discussion across various characteristics of network members. The distinction at this level of network data is that there is no effort to gather information about *specific* discussion partners, their attributes or their ties with one another. Some might reasonably argue that these are not social network data at all according to more traditional definitions of social network data (for example, Wasserman and Faust, 1994). Nonetheless, political communication scholars often use terms such as 'social networks' or 'discussion networks' when using data of this kind.

Egocentric Network Data

At the second level of network data, respondents are asked to identify a limited number (for example, four to six) of specific members of their social networks through a 'name generator'. Then, communication ties with these network members (for example, how often the ego discusses politics with each alter) are assessed individually (for example, Eveland, 2004; Mutz, 2002; Nir, 2005; Richey, 2009). Often survey respondents are asked to provide additional information about their network alters, such as their demographic characteristics,

party affiliation, level of political knowledge and so forth, through 'name interpreters'. Information about the relationships among the alters in a given survey respondent's network is missing at this level of network data. That is, we know something about the ties between the respondent (A) and his network alters (B and C) who were not included in the sample (for example, A ↔ B, A ↔ C), but we know nothing about the ties among his alters (for example, B ↔ C). We also do not have direct reports from the alters regarding their personal characteristics, beliefs and opinions and so must rely on the perceptions of the survey respondent.

Egocentric Network with Cognitive Social Structures Data

Building upon egocentric network data, cognitive social structures (CSS) assess the relationships among network alters based on the perception of the survey respondent (for example, B ↔ C based on the perception of A). The social structure or network ties are measured not from the perspectives of these network alters themselves (that is, reports from B or C), but instead from the perspective of a third-party informant – the ego. Missing from this level of social network data is a direct report of ties among alters from one or more of the parties to the specific tie, as well as other information about network alters directly from that alter (for example, actual report of party affiliation, direct assessment of political knowledge).

Egocentric Network with Snowball Sample Data

Snowball sample data also build upon egocentric data. Snowball sample data are collected directly from the social network alters (our friends B and C), whom the initial survey respondent identifies. Then data on the characteristics of network alters are gathered directly from these alters (see for example, Huckfeldt and Sprague, 1995). The alters are also likely to be asked about their ties with other individuals reported as part of the network identified by the ego. Sometimes this snowball procedure is continued (interviewing the alters of B and C) until no new network members are identified (see for example, Sandström and Carlsson, 2008). However, snowball and other egocentric approaches cannot identify isolates (individuals within the network who do not have communication ties to other network members) who do not happen to be selected in the original sample, nor can they identify components of the network of which an original respondent is not a member.

Sociometric or 'Whole Network' Data

Sociometric data are the 'gold standard' for capturing social networks (Johnson and Orbach, 2002). For sociometric data, a social network is typically defined by a researcher using some existing (and sometimes relatively arbitrary) boundary specifications. For instance, researchers may use a list of employees in a small business, students in a given school, members of a volunteer organization, participants in an online discussion forum or any other group with a clear boundary and a complete list of members. Researchers attempt to gather data directly from each member of the network, including characteristics of the members and their communication ties to all other members of the group.[2] Thus, sociometric data – ignoring for the moment survey non-response that affects all types of self-report data – include individual-level data from all members of a predefined network and each network member's ties to all other network members, all collected directly from each member. In this way, researchers can see beyond the direct ties to a survey respondent (egocentric data) and among the members of the network to which the ego is tied (CSS and snowball data), to the larger network structure. Isolated individuals and distinct components in the network can be identified through this technique as well. And, sociometric data can be restructured to provide information on what would amount to egocentric and snowball data (Marsden, 2002). CSS data also can be gathered as part of a sociometric study (for example, Johnson and Orbach, 2002).

Publicly Available Social Network Data

In the domain of political communication and political networks research in the USA, the inclusion of network data in large public data sets is limited. Although many national sample surveys employ summary network measures, only a few go beyond this. For instance, the General Social Survey has repeatedly gathered egocentric network data using name generators, although explicit measures of frequency of political discussion with individual alters was only obtained in 1987. In that year, there was no cap on the number of names mentioned, but name interpreter information was only gathered for the first three alters. The American National Election Study (ANES) gathered egocentric network data in 2000 with a cap of four alters for the name generator and interpreter questions. In 2006, ANES gathered up to 10

names using the name generator, collecting name interpreter and CSS data for only the first three alters.

Beyond these large, publicly funded national data sets, some scholars have made their private data publicly available (for example, Huckfeldt and Sprague's South Bend and Indianapolis-St Louis studies, the Comparative National Election Project [CNEP; Richardson and Beck, 2007] and the National Annenberg Election Study). But, compared to data including simple summary network measures and political communication data more broadly, the availability of 'higher level' social network data relevant to political communication scholars is quite limited. This could constrain expansion of work in this domain unless individual scholars begin to gather their own network data, or broader collaborative efforts to gather such data obtain significant government or foundation funding.

WHAT WE KNOW ABOUT SOCIAL NETWORKS AND POLITICAL KNOWLEDGE

Most of what we know about the relationship between social networks and political knowledge is based on summary network data and egocentric network data. Key concepts employed in this literature include political discussion frequency (that is, some measure of how often a respondent talks about politics), measures of cognitive effort related to political discussion (for example, discussion elaboration, integrative discussion, discussion attention), network size (that is, the number of individuals with whom a respondent talks about politics) and the extent to which political discussion takes place among similar or dissimilar others (for example, disagreement, heterogeneity, diversity). In terms of outcome measures, most research employs measures of factual political knowledge (for example, candidate issue stances, awareness of politically relevant current events or public figures) or indicators of awareness of arguments on various sides of political issues.

Eveland (2004) offered several theoretical reasons why political discussion should cause individuals to be more politically knowledgeable. First, through a process of information dissemination – that is, the two-step flow (Lazarsfeld et al., 1944) – information held by one individual could be transferred to another in the same way that political information flows through mass media (exposure explanation). Second, the anticipation of discussing politics could lead individuals to more thoroughly process information from the news media (anticipatory elaboration explanation). Third, the act of discussion could generate elaborations within the individual, or could be conveyed or prompted by the discussion partner, leading to greater knowledge (discussion-generated elaboration explanation). Pingree (2007) offered a detailed model of the latter two explanations.

Supporting the exposure explanation, data consistently reveal that the frequency of political discussion is related to various indicators of political knowledge (Cho et al., 2009; Delli Carpini and Keeter, 1996; Eveland and Hively, 2009; Eveland and Thomson, 2006; Holbert et al., 2002; Kwak et al., 2005). This finding appears to be more than simply correlational; panel data suggest that the stronger path is from discussion to knowledge rather than the reverse (Eveland et al., 2005). There is also support for the anticipatory elaboration and discussion-generated elaboration explanations. Those who devote more cognitive effort to thinking about their conversations and news use and making mental connections in advance of, during, and after their discussions are more likely to have higher levels of political knowledge (Cho et al., 2009; Eveland, 2004; Eveland and Thomson, 2006; Kwak et al., 2005).

There is also some evidence that individuals with larger political networks tend to be more politically informed than those with smaller networks (Kwak et al., 2005). However, this finding may result from people with larger networks talking more frequently than those with smaller networks, because significant relationships between network size and knowledge tend not to be sustained in the presence of controls for discussion frequency (for example, Eveland and Hively, 2009; Mutz, 2002). However, it does appear that network size can influence *structural* aspects of political knowledge (that is, perceived connections between different political issues and objects) even after frequency controls (Eveland and Hively, 2009).

Findings regarding the influence of various dyadic characteristics, such as political agreement, disagreement or the strength of the relationship, are more mixed. In the political communication literature, strong ties are sometimes operationalized as ties with one's spouse and family.[3] In these cases, there is some evidence that learning is greater when discussion is with weak rather than strong ties (Roch et al., 2000), based on the logic that weak ties provide access to a different subset of information than is held by the ego and those close to the ego (Granovetter, 1973).

A similar logic can be used to predict a relationship between discussion with politically dissimilar others and political knowledge. The evidence suggests that exposure to political disagreement facilitates awareness of rationales for views different from one's own (Mutz, 2002; Mutz and Mondak, 2006). Exposure to disagreement also seems to be positively related to structural knowledge (Eveland and Hively, 2009). However, exposure to political disagreement does not appear to be positively related to knowledge of more general political facts (Eveland and Hively, 2009), at least once overall discussion frequency is taken into account.

EXPANDING TO FULL SOCIOMETRIC DATA

Based primarily on summary and egocentric network data, our understanding of the nature and implications of political discussion has expanded rapidly during the past 15 years. And, there is more to learn using these data. However, compared to the almost wholly untapped potential of sociometric data, summary and egocentric network data may offer diminishing returns for the expansion of our understanding of political knowledge and discussion networks. A sociometric approach not only offers more precise measures of discussion networks compared to an egocentric or summary approach, but there are whole concepts that simply cannot be measured using anything less than sociometric data. Some of these concepts have the potential to move our understanding of the role of discussion networks for political knowledge, and normative democratic outcomes more generally, far beyond its current state. Although summary and egocentric data need not be abandoned, political communication scholars should make a concerted effort to expand into full sociometric data collection to maintain the fast-paced and valuable expansion of social network research that we have seen in the past decade.

NEW OR REVISED CONCEPTS FROM A SOCIOMETRIC SOCIAL NETWORK PERSPECTIVE

As with all data gathering and analysis approaches, the use of sociometric network data has advantages and disadvantages. Below, we offer some specific opportunities to rethink or expand upon research on social networks employing summary or egocentric data, with a particular emphasis on political knowledge and the diffusion of ideas and information. These examples are merely scratching the surface, and surely do not represent the full extent to which sociometric data may be employed in political communication scholarship.

In the discussion below, we illustrate some sociometric social network concepts numerically and graphically using actual data gathered by the authors after the presidential election in Autumn 2008. That study gathered full sociometric social network data from a probability sample ($N = 25$ groups, group response rate = 57%) of formal student activity groups from a large Midwestern research university. These groups varied in size from 13 to 34 members and included fraternal groups, sports groups, social groups, charitable groups and academic groups. Response rates within each group were at least 50%, and some were a full 100% (mean individual response rate = 84%, $N = 514$ individuals). For each member of these groups (limited only by response rate within the group), we have data on ego's candidate choice in the 2008 presidential election, ego's reported frequency of political discussion with each other group member (that is, their alters) and ego's assessment of the candidate choice and level of political knowledge for each alter. Moreover, we have individual-level data about political interest, knowledge, participation, news media use and some personality variables.

For illustrative purposes, here we emphasize a single group among the 25 from which we have data. This group has 34 formal members; 31 of these members responded to our survey, for a response rate of 91%. When available, we substituted information from network alters for missing data from the three non-respondents for analyses reported here. This group is classified by the university as a 'community service/service learning' group. The group leader reported in the leader survey that this group is 'slightly political' ('2' on a 4-point scale from 'not at all political' to 'very political'). Thus, politics was not an emphasis of this group, but political communication was taking place among many group members.

To help illustrate social network concepts, we have produced two figures using these data. Individuals (or 'nodes') are represented by squares/circles/circles-within-squares (depending on their 2008 vote choice) and labeled with numbers to protect anonymity. The shading of the nodes represents the reported vote choice of respondents – Obama, McCain or undecided. 'Ties' are represented via lines connecting the individuals. Figure 19.1 represents political discussion ties (dichotomized and made symmetrical), whereas Figure 19.2 represents general discussion ties. 'Isolates' (i.e., those who have no ties) are suppressed in these figures. Additional information regarding these figures will be addressed as they come up below.

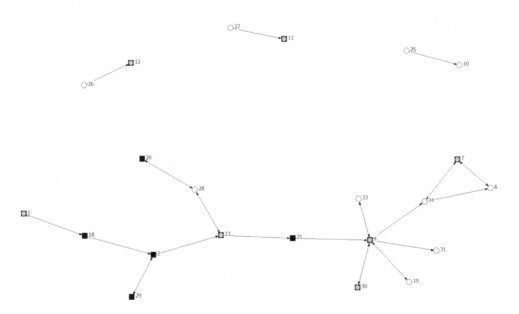

Figure 19.1   Political discussion network (symmetrical and dichotomized)
Note: Black squares = McCain voter or leaner; white circles = Obama voter or leaner; circle in square = non-leaning third-party voters and non-voters. Isolates (those who did not talk to any other group member about politics) suppressed.

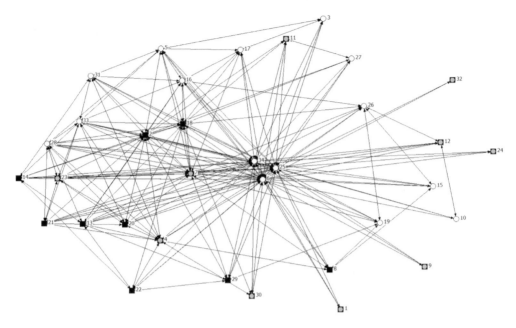

Figure 19.2   General discussion network (symmetrical and dichotomized)
Note: Black squares = McCain voter or leaner; white circles = Obama voter or leaner; circle in square = non-leaning third-party voters and non-voters.

Egonetwork Size or 'Degree Centrality'

One of the more common summary and egocentric measures employed in the political communication literature is network size. Using summary data, respondents are typically asked how many political discussion partners they have had, often bounded by a specific time frame. Using egocentric network data gathered via a name generator, network size is measured as the number of discussion partners identified by the ego. There are implications of network measurement technique not only for estimates of network size, but also for the relationship between network size and some outcome measures. There appear to be strengths and weaknesses in each approach (Eveland et al., 2009).

Using sociometric network data, egonetwork size is tapped by a concept called 'degree centrality'. When ties are measured dichotomously (discussion versus no discussion), degree centrality refers to the number of connections or paths linked to a given person or node in the network. In Figure 19.1, political network size is the number of lines connecting a given node. For instance, Node 4 has a political network size of 6, whereas Node 2 has a political network size of 3.

Typically, political communication scholars consider political discussion a reciprocal variable – if I talk to you, you must talk to me – and so this communication relationship or 'tie' is non-directional. However, in a sociometric study, both individuals in a potential dyad provide reports of discussion. The assumption would be that two individuals reporting on the same tie would provide the same response, and so missing data from unit or item non-response for one individual is often replaced with the value from his/her alter – something not possible in traditional sample survey research. However, this assumption of agreement is often not met.[4]

Having two reports on a single relationship in a sociometric study is equivalent to having two coders for the same unit in a content analysis project. Although disagreement in a content analysis raises questions about the quality of a coding scheme, and thus the data themselves, such disagreement in a natural setting can also provide the opportunity to address some interesting theoretical questions about political discussion and the measurement of political discussion in sample surveys. Using sociometric data we can ascertain individual and relational variables that might explain inconsistent reports within dyads as well as individual tendencies to over- or under-report political discussions across possible dyads.

Rather than asking both ego and alter about the same non-directional relationship, one might find it more useful to rephrase the political discussion question to be explicitly directional, such as 'From whom do you seek political information or advice?' In this case, it is clear that A can seek advice from B without the reverse being true. The number of individuals from which one person sought political advice (or claimed to talk with) would be termed 'outdegree', whereas the number of people who sought out the ego for political advice (or claimed to talk to ego) would be 'indegree'. This notion of ties being directional versus non-directional is relevant for some other measures as well.

Unlike egocentric discussant generator data, sociometric degree centrality or egonetwork size is constrained only by the actual size of the potential network (for example, membership in the student activity group). For comparison across networks of different sizes, these concepts may be normalized to the size of the 'potential' network by dividing the actual number of ties by the total number of possible connections in the network. Moreover, evidence suggests that discussant generators tend to underestimate network size for various reasons. First, most studies impose caps on network size. Second, name generators rely on free recall whereas sociometric data often require only recognition, making the latter an easier cognitive task to report fully and accurately. Marsden notes that single name generators tend 'to elicit small networks of "core ties"' (2005: 12). Name generators are also susceptible to interviewer effects, with different network sizes obtained by different interviewers (Marsden, 2003). Thus, there is not only a clear similarity in concepts between the sociometric and other forms of network data, but also increased potential of sociometric data. In the context of diffusion of information and innovation, Granovetter has argued:

> Though most diffusion studies find that personal contacts are crucial, many undertake no sociometric investigation. When sociometric techniques are used, they tend to discourage the naming of those weakly tied to the respondent by sharply limiting the numbers of choices allowed. Hence, the proposed importance of weak ties in diffusion is not measured. (1973: 1366)

Thus, one advantage of the sociometric technique is that it is more likely to capture the weak ties that may be central to learning new and innovative information (see also Weimann, 1982). This alone is an important argument for the inclusion of sociometric data in future studies.

Discussion Frequency or 'Valued Degree'

Many studies using summary or egocentric data employ an overall discussion frequency measure,

typically bounded by some time frame (for example, a week). Egocentric data allow a summation or average of discussion frequency across the named discussion partners. As we have already demonstrated with our review of the literature, political discussion frequency is an important predictor of political knowledge.

Using sociometric network data, we must return to the concept of degree. To tap egonetwork size as described above, degree is based on a dichotomous conceptualization of a communication tie (present or absent). When these communication ties are reconsidered as a frequency of communication on whatever metric (for example, days in the past week) valued degree becomes a summation of the frequency of discussion across discussion partners akin to the egocentric approach to measuring frequency.[5] Of course, such summing can lead to a value greater than the maximum number of days per week. Although this is problematic for interpretation, we would argue that it more precisely taps the frequency of discussion than a single summary of the number of days per week of discussion. Valued degree comes closer to tapping the actual quantity of conversations taking place than does a simple days per week summary measure. As a potentially more precise measure of the frequency of political discussion, valued degree should function as a better predictor of political knowledge. Again, this measure of degree can be considered non-directional as when using summary or egocentric data. However, it can also be viewed as directional with reference to indegree and outdegree as described above.

Egonetwork Density and Network Density

As we have noted above, egocentric network data gathered using a snowball approach offer data not only about the ego's discussions, but also direct information about discussions (either presence/ absence or along some frequency continuum) among the ego's alters. Similarly, CSS data provide estimates of such discussions from the perception of the ego. So, such data can estimate an egocentric measure of network density (egonetwork density), or the interconnectedness of alters who talk to the ego. However, few studies in political communication have had sufficient data to examine meaningful variations in egonetwork density due to (1) the lack of CSS or snowball data and (2) the very small network sizes when such data are present due to low caps on name generators and name interpreters.

Sociometric data offer the ability to examine egocentric network density, and variation in egonetwork density should be greater because of the larger egonetwork sizes using sociometric data. In Figure 19.1, consider the density of Node 4's egonetwork. None of Node 4's discussion partners (34, 33, 31, 19, 30 and 21) discuss politics with one another – only with Node 4. Node 4's egonetwork density is thus zero. Now consider Node 6. Node 6's political discussion partners (7, 34) also discuss politics with one another, so Node 6's egonetwork density is 1.00 (maximal).

Additionally, sociometric data allow assessment of the density of the larger network (that is, group, organization, community), rather than the ego's particular network. For instance, the overall density of the dichotomized *political* discussion network in Figure 19.1 is very low (0.0339) because there are very few political discussion links among members of this group.[6] By contrast, the density of the *general discussion* network of the same group (as represented in Figure 19.2) is much greater at 0.3440. We could also calculate network density based on the valued relationships (that is, frequency of discussion).

Density can have important implications for the diffusion of political information and opinion through networks. Dense networks are highly efficient (Sandström and Carlsson, 2008), allowing incoming information to flow quickly and thoroughly because the information has many pathways along which to spread. However, the information in such networks (that is, across different alters) is likely to be heavily redundant (Granovetter, 1973), suggesting that most information conveyed in such networks is not 'new' and so cannot contribute to knowledge gain.

Components

Some networks can be broken down into multiple components, which are defined as subsets of the network in which individuals are directly or indirectly connected to each other but are disconnected from the rest of the network. Imagine, for instance, a town that was geographically composed of three islands. Residents on each island live and interact with one another as part of a community. However, the lack of bridges to travel between the islands prevents individuals on any one island from communicating with individuals on any of the other islands. If the network were the town, each island would be a component of the network. Components cannot be identified in egocentric network data; sociometric data are required.

Identifying components in a network can be very useful in understanding political communication. In the example above, a physical barrier would seem to have created the components.

But, in political communication we might be more interested in how psychological, sociological or political barriers could produce or be reflected in components. For instance, what if Democrats in a network communicated only with other Democrats, but not Republicans or Independents? And, similarly, what if Republicans were only connected to other Republicans? In this case, we would have three components in the network, and partisanship would define those components. Other important variables that might define political network components could be race, gender, religious denomination or socioeconomic status.

In Figure 19.2 (the general discussion network), there is only one component (containing at least two individuals). With only one component, any individual in the network could theoretically get information to any other individual through some direct or indirect path of varying length. By contrast, in Figure 19.1 (the political discussion network) there are four components containing at least two individuals. Three of these four components are in fact composed of only two individuals; the fourth includes all other members of the network who are not isolates.

Political information cannot escape a component because there are no paths allowing that information to travel outside of the component; the information can only spread within the component. When components are small, this could severely curtail political information dissemination. Thus, the presence of multiple components in a network is an inhibitor of broad diffusion of political information within the network.

Betweenness Centrality

The concept of betweenness centrality refers to the frequency with which an ego is in the structural position to serve as a connecting point along the shortest path between two individuals who are not directly connected to one another. For instance, an individual could be 'between' a given Democrat and Republican who did not talk to one another directly. An individual who tended to be in such a position often in a network – that is, frequently being part of the shortest path between individuals who don't directly interact – would be high in betweenness. Individuals high in betweenness can play a central role in networks because they are part of a path between many others through which political information may or may not flow. Moreover, they hold the power to make the decision about whether that information flow will happen or not. Thus, individuals high in betweenness are powerful individuals in the network. In Figure 19.1, Nodes 4, 23 and 21 (in that order) are highest in betweenness, whereas Nodes 28 and 18 are considerably lower in betweenness. Nodes such as 1, 31 and 20 all score zero in betweenness.

A related concept is a *cutpoint*. Whereas the betweenness of a node identifies the frequency with which it serves as an inbetween across various relationships in a network, a cutpoint is a dichotomous measure identifying a node that, if removed, would cause a network to break into separate components. Cutpoints are the glue that hold otherwise separate components of a network together. Individuals high in betweenness are important in the flow of information and ideas, but cutpoints are in fact essential because in their absence information flow through the broader network is impossible. In Figure 19.1, there are seven nodes that serve as cutpoints (2, 4, 18, 21, 23, 28 and 34). We will return to the concept of cutpoints when we discuss network homophily.

Network Betweenness Centralization

A macro or network analog of the node concept of betweenness centrality is network betweenness centralization. Centralization is a measure of whole networks and thus is not measureable via egocentric approaches. Centralization is the extent to which a given network is interconnected through a small set of inbetweens; that is, a high centralization score suggests that there are a few highly central individuals and a larger number of much less central individuals in the network (that is, high variance in betweenness across individuals). Thus, whereas betweenness is a characteristic of an individual based on his or her position in the network, centralization is a concept describing inequality of node betweenness in the network as a whole.

Figure 19.1 shows a network relatively low in centralization (12.81%), whereas Figure 19.2 shows a network relatively high in centralization (17.87%), although in absolute terms both are low in centralization. As with network density, measures of network centralization are useful in making comparisons across different networks or across different types of ties (for example, general discussion versus political discussion) within a given network. A highly centralized network will require information to flow through only a few individuals (the network 'hubs') to spread throughout the network, and these individuals thus have a high level of power over information flow. A less centralized network is more egalitarian in terms of information flow, and information flow has many possible routes. In the theoretically most centralized 'wheel' network – in which everyone is tied to one individual, but to no one else – information can diffuse through the whole network only if that information is held by or shared with the one, highly central individual.

Egonetwork Homophily and Network Homophily

One of the more commonly studied concepts in political discussion research is the extent to which individuals are exposed to those with whom they disagree (for example, Huckfeldt et al., 2004; Mutz, 2006). One of the reasons these scholars have focused on this concept is that it assumes that information and ideas held by dissimilar others are useful for developing fully informed opinions and for understanding the rationales for alternative viewpoints.

The most common data used to assess exposure to disagreement are egocentric network data based on name generators. However, sociometric data allows us to address not only the egocentric homophily or similarity of the network (typically providing a larger network than in egocentric studies), but also the extent to which a broader network is divided into components on the basis of some political variable such as candidate vote choice. For example, for each individual in a network we can assess the percentage of those with whom they have ties who are similar versus dissimilar on some attribute such as candidate selection.

Homophily can also be assessed as an overall network property in order to make comparisons across networks. For instance, we can compare the extent to which the proportion of general discussion ties versus political discussion ties vary among those to whom one agrees and those with whom one disagrees in terms of candidate selection. We use the E-I index, which ranges from -1.0 to $+1.0$, where -1.0 means all ties are to individuals within one's group (homophily) and 1.0 means all ties are to individuals outside one's group, with 0 representing a perfect balance of ties inside and outside one's group. When we consider groups defined by a candidate preference, the overall homophily of the general discussion network in Figure 19.2 is only slightly biased in favor of more ties among likes than dislikes (E-I Index $= -0.1545$). This means these individuals only slightly favor those who share their political views for *general* discussion. However, the *political* discussion network in Figure 19.1 reveals a considerably stronger bias toward homogeneity in discussion partners (E-I index $= -0.6000$). Clearly, despite not being a particularly political group, this group as a whole shows a clear preference for homophilous political discussion. With recoding such a measure could also be used to tap network diversity (Eveland and Hively, 2009; Reagans and McEvily, 2003; Sandström and Carlsson, 2008) because values of zero indicate the most diverse (that is, evenly split) discussion networks and greater deviation from zero (either positively or negatively) indicate decreasing levels of diversity.

SOME LIMITATIONS AND CAUTIONS REGARDING SOCIAL NETWORK DATA

Our advocacy of a move within the subfield of political communication to full sociometric data must be tempered with an acknowledgement of potential pitfalls. First, sociometric data are very difficult to gather. There are problems with sample survey unit non-response that have led to declining telephone survey response rates in recent decades, and this problem is likely to plague sociometric data as well. And, gathering full sociometric data from any but the most modest-sized groups can be quite time-consuming and therefore arduous for survey respondents. The number of questions about network members, and additional non-network variables, must be adjusted based on the size of the networks being studied to maintain a reasonable respondent burden because each new question about a network tie must be asked of all network members. Obtaining only three pieces of information – frequency of overall discussion, frequency of political discussion and length of relationship – in a network with 31 individuals requires 90 survey questions! However, it is possible that having an 'in' with formal groups or organizations could facilitate individual-level survey response once group leaders were recruited, and the personalization of the surveys with names of network members might increase motivation to complete the survey, and to do so accurately.

The initial defining of and sampling of groups also may be difficult. Sociometric approaches assume clear boundaries for groups, which can be difficult to obtain in the absence of access to information such as formal membership lists. Obtaining access to such lists and the endorsement of group leaders is different, and possibly more difficult, than securing individual respondent consent to a telephone interview. If nothing else, moving toward sociometric data will require that political communication researchers develop new sensitivities and new skills in study design and data collection.

Another issue pertains to generalizability. Researchers are unlikely to have a population of all networks (even of a given size or type) and thus sampling of networks or groups is normally based on convenience. This makes generalizability of results across networks difficult; therefore, many studies are presented as case studies rather than attempts to statistically generalize to a broader population of networks.

Another realistic limitation of working with sociometric data is the need to learn about a diverse array of new data analysis approaches. Network analysis is conducted with specialized software programs, for which the statistics are still being actively developed and learning is ongoing. Significance tests are typically based on bootstrapping approaches since normal parametric statistical techniques are not appropriate. This statistical and software hurdle, along with others already discussed, may limit the expansion of research using sociometric data.

CONCLUSION

There has been a clear trend during the past decade toward a reconsideration of the value of studying social networks to understand important democratic outcomes such as civic engagement, political participation and political knowledge. We have briefly reviewed the empirical research addressing the link between social networks and political knowledge. We place our emphasis, however, on understanding where we might go from here. One option is to more fully exploit sociometric-based social network data to build upon the base of concepts currently studied in the literature. This approach would allow both a more detailed consideration of individual-level measures that are comparable to but perhaps more precise or thorough than those in the current literature, as well as a consideration of more macro measures describing the social or political networks themselves.

Moving forward on some of the suggestions in this chapter will require some alteration in data collection priorities. In some cases, generalizability may have to be sacrificed in favor of depth of understanding and detail. In some ways, this would be an extension of trends that have already begun with studies like the South Bend study of Huckfeldt and Sprague (1995). There are strengths and weaknesses of any study design, but we advocate greater effort to expand our data toward sociometric measurement. We believe there is a strong argument for social network analysis opening new doors to understanding the role that our social and political contacts play in conveying political information. Of course, such a claim cannot be evaluated until we put forth the effort to collect and analyze this type of data.

NOTES

1 The terminology we use below for various forms of social network data is drawn from the broader literature on social network analysis. When terms for a given type of data are inconsistent in the literature, we select the most compelling or popular term available.

2 Some studies of very large groups attempt to sample members from within these groups, although such studies are not to be found within the political communication literature.

3 Conceptually, tie strength is somewhat more complex and measurement approaches vary. Granovetter defines the strength of a tie as 'a (probably linear) combination of the amount of time, the emotional intensity, the intimacy (mutual confiding) and the reciprocal services which characterize the tie' (1973: 1361).

4 When ego and alter do not agree and the statistic being assessed cannot address reciprocity, researchers make different assumptions including only counting ties when there is agreement or taking the average value of ego and alter estimates for tie strength.

5 One could also reference the average frequency across alters with whom there is a discussion relationship (Wasserman and Faust, 1994), although this may not be as theoretically meaningful in most cases related to political discussion.

6 Keep in mind that in Figure 19.1 many nodes are visually suppressed because they do not talk politics with anyone in the group.

REFERENCES

Barabási, A. L. (2003) *Linked: How Everything is Connected to Everything Else and What it Means for Business, Science, and Everyday Life*. New York: Plume.

Beck, P. A., Dalton, R. J., Greene, S. and Huckfeldt, R. (2002) 'The Social Calculus of Voting: Interpersonal, Media, and Organizational Influences on Presidential Choices', *American Political Science Review*, 96(1): 57–73.

Chambers, S. (2003) 'Deliberative Democratic Theory', *Annual Review of Political Science*, 6: 307–26.

Cho, J., Shah, D. V., McLeod, J. M., McLeod, D. M., School, R. M. and Goitlieb, M. R. (2009) 'Campaigns, Reflection, and Deliberation: Advancing an O-S-O-R Model of Communication Effects', *Communication Theory*, 19(1): 66–88.

Delli Carpini, M. X. and Keeter, S. (1996) *What Americans Know About Politics and Why it Matters*. New Haven, CT: Yale University Press.

Eulau, H. and Siegel, J. W. (1981) 'Social Network Analysis and Political Behavior: A Feasibility Study', *Western Political Quarterly*, 34(4): 499–509.

Eveland, W. P., Jr (2004) 'The Effect of Political Discussion in Producing Informed Citizens: The Roles of Information, Motivation, and Elaboration', *Political Communication*, 21(2): 177–93.

Eveland, W. P., Jr and Thomson, T. (2006) 'Is it Talking, Thinking, or Both? A Lagged Dependent Variable Model of Discussion Effects on Political Knowledge', *Journal of Communication*, 56(3): 523–42.

Eveland, W. P., Jr and Hively, M. H. (2009) 'Political Discussion Frequency, Network Size and "Heterogeneity" of Discussion as Predictors of Political Knowledge and Participation', *Journal of Communication*, 59(2): 205–24.

Eveland, W. P., Jr, Hively, M. H. and Morey, A. C. (2009) 'Discussing Measures of Political Discussion: An Evaluation of the Measurement of Network Size, Agreement, and Disagreement and Implications for Inferences', paper presented at the annual meeting of the International Communication Association. Chicago, IL.

Eveland, W. P., Jr, Hayes, A. F., Shah, D. V. and Kwak, N. (2005) 'Understanding the Relationship Between Communication and Political Knowledge: A Model-Comparison Approach Using Panel Data', *Political Communication*, 22(4): 423–46.

Granovetter, M. S. (1973) 'The Strength of Weak Ties', *American Journal of Sociology*, 78(6): 1360–80.

Holbert, R. L., Benoit, W. L., Hansen, G. J. and Wen, W. C. (2002) 'The Role of Communication in the Formation of an Issue-Based Citizenry', *Communication Monographs*, 69(4): 296–310.

Huckfeldt, R. and Sprague, J. (1995) *Citizens, Politics, and Social Communication: Information and Influence in an Election Campaign*. New York: Cambridge University Press.

Huckfeldt, R., Johnson, P. E. and Sprague, J. (2004) *Political Disagreement: The Survival of Diverse Opinions Within Communication Networks*. New York: Cambridge University Press.

Johnson, J. C. and Orbach, M. K. (2002) 'Perceiving the Political Landscape: Ego Biases in Cognitive Political Networks', *Social Networks*, 24(3): 291–310.

Katz, E. and Lazarsfeld, P. F. (1955) *Personal Influence: The Part Played by People in the Flow of Mass Communications*. Glencoe, IL: Free Press.

Knoke, D. (1990) *Political Networks: The Structural Perspective*. New York: Cambridge University Press.

Kwak, N., Williams, A. E., Wang, X. and Lee, H. (2005) 'Talking Politics and Engaging Politics: An Examination of the Interactive Relationships Between Structural Features of Political Talk and Discussion Engagement', *Communication Research*, 32(1): 87–111.

Lazarsfeld, P. F., Berelson, B. and Gaudet, H. (1944) *The People's Choice: How the Voter Makes Up His Mind in a Presidential Campaign*. New York: Columbia University Press.

Marsden, P. V. (2002) 'Egocentric and Sociocentric Measures of Network Centrality', *Social Networks*, 24(4): 407–22.

Marsden, P. V. (2003) 'Interviewer Effects in Measuring Network Size Using a Single Name Generator', *Social Networks*, 25(1): 1–16.

Marsden, P. V. (2005) 'Recent Developments in Network Measurement', in P. J. Carrington, J. Scott and S. Wasserman (eds.), *Models and Methods in Social Network Analysis*. New York: Cambridge University Press. pp. 8–30.

McClurg, S. D. (2006) 'The Electoral Relevance of Political Talk: Examining Disagreement and Expertise Effects in Social Networks on Political Participation', *American Journal of Political Science*, 50(3): 737–54.

Moy, P. and Gastil, J. (2006) 'Predicting Deliberative Conversation: The Impact of Discussion Networks, Media Use, and Political Cognitions', *Political Communication*, 23(4): 443–60.

Mutz, D. C. (2002) 'Cross-Cutting Social Networks: Testing Democratic Theory in Practice', *American Political Science Review*, 96(1): 111–26.

Mutz, D. C. (2006) *Hearing the Other Side: Deliberative Versus Participatory Democracy*. New York: Cambridge University Press.

Mutz, D. C. and Mondak, J. J. (2006) 'The Workplace as a Context for Cross-Cutting Political Discourse', *Journal of Politics*, 68(1): 140–55.

Nir, L. (2005) 'Ambivalent Social Networks and Their Consequences for Participation', *International Journal of Public Opinion Research*, 17(4): 422–42.

Pingree, R. J. (2007) 'How Messages Affect Their Senders: A More General Model of Message Effects and Implications for Deliberation', *Communication Theory*, 17(4): 439–61.

Putnam, R. D. (2000) *Bowling Alone: The Collapse and Revival of American Community*. New York: Simon & Schuster.

Reagans, R. and McEvily, B. (2003) 'Network Structure and Knowledge Transfer: The Effects of Cohesion and Range', *Administrative Science Quarterly*, 48(2): 240–67.

Richardson, B. and Beck, P. A. (2007). 'The Flow of Political Information: Personal Discussants, the Media, and Partisans', in R. Gunther, J. R. Montero and H. J. Puhle (eds.), *Democracy, Intermediation, and Voting on Four Continents*. New York: Oxford University Press. pp. 183–207.

Richey, S. (2009) 'Hierarchy in Political Discussion', *Political Communication*, 26(2): 137–52.

Roch, C. H., Scholz, J. T. and McGraw, K. M. (2000) 'Social Networks and Citizen Response to Legal Change', *American Journal of Political Science*, 44(4): 777–91.

Sandström, A. and Carlsson, L. (2008) 'The Performance of Policy Networks: The Relation Between Network Structure and Network Performance', *The Policy Studies Journal*, 36(4): 497–524.

Scheufele, D. A., Nisbet, M. C., Brossard, D. and Nisbet, E. C. (2004) 'Social Structure and Citizenship: Examining the Impacts of Social Setting, Network Heterogeneity, and Informational Variables on Political Participation', *Political Communication*, 21(3): 315–38.

Straits, B. C. (1991) 'Bringing Strong Ties Back in: Interpersonal Gateways to Political Information and Influence', *Public Opinion Quarterly*, 55(3): 432–48.

Wasserman, S. and Faust, K. (1994) *Social Network Analysis: Methods and Applications*. New York: Cambridge University Press.

Weatherford, M. S. (1982) 'Interpersonal Networks and Political Behavior', *American Journal of Political Science*, 26(1): 117–43.

Weimann, G. (1982) 'On the Importance of Marginality: One More Step into the Two-Step Flow of Communication', *American Sociological Review*, 47(6): 764–73.

Zuckerman, A. S. (2005) 'Returning to the Social Logic of Politics', in A. S. Zuckerman (ed.), *The Social Logic of Politics: Personal Networks as Contexts for Political Behavior*. Philadelphia, PA: Temple University Press. pp. 3–20.

20

Understanding the Content of News Media

Stephen D. Reese and Jae Kook Lee

This chapter reviews the major approaches to media content as a critical variable in its own right within political communication research. By 'content' we mean the complete range of visual and verbal information carried in the media, primarily the traditional mainstream professional media, but also increasingly by smaller more interactive and targeted channels. Content is no longer relatively easy to isolate within a select group of clearly defined publications and broadcast programs. The continuous online news stream, further amplified and dissected by the various tiers of blogs and social media, make fixing a sample of news content more difficult than in the pre-digital era.

Attempting to understand something as broad and amorphous as 'content' makes it necessary to specify more clearly what we are talking about. Many studies include news content as a variable, examining, for example, how people process specific stories or their elements, but we consider specifically how news content is explored as a symbolic environment, with its own internal coherence as a system of representation, from which a range of theoretical inferences in turn can be made about the forces shaping it and the resulting effects and societal implications.

CLASSIFYING CONTENT BY FUNCTION AND EFFECT

To understand news content, we can first consider the ways in which media content may be categorized. It may be categorized, for example, by audience appeal (highbrow/lowbrow), the medium itself (television, magazine, newspaper), some presumed effects (anti or pro-social) and by its format, genre or style. Another predominant approach is to move beyond this focus on content features to consider what basic societal functions the content is intended to serve; this helps distinguish news from other content. Functionalism has a long tradition in the field, exemplified by the work of Lasswell (1948) who identified three crucial functions of communication: (1) surveillance of the environment; (2) correlation of parts of society and (3) transmission of social heritage. To these, Wright (1986) added 'entertainment'. For a time, amid postwar confidence in society and institutions, these functions served to distinguish among surveillance-based news content, correlation-intended editorial and persuasive messages, the longer-term educational and socialization work of 'transmission' and 'entertainment' provided by-definition by the entertainment industries. A functional approach to content renders these societal needs as self-evidently true, and the meeting of those needs by media an accomplished fact.

These functions, however, no longer provide the mutually exclusive categories they once did. News has traditionally been differentiated from entertainment, but increasingly they are becoming blurred into 'infotainment' (Delli Carpini and Williams, 2001). Media content has become a much more fluid hybrid of forms. Once relatively easily differentiated, news, politics, entertainment and marketing have undergone 'discursive integration' (Baym, 2005). Content categories cannot easily now isolate substance from style.

Given this hybridized environment for news, it is helpful to take a less segmented view on where news is to be found, abandoning the idea that news functions are self-evidently provided. A more modern perspective on what media do is, as Castells says, to provide the 'social space where power is decided' (2007: 238). News content, in particular, provides that space. The study of media content, in turn, provides indicators as to the winners and losers; those who are privileged and underprivileged by the logic of media practices. Thus, we are interested in the content that has political consequences. Hence, in news content, we are concerned with that part of the symbolic environment that lays claim to connecting citizens to the political world and providing deliberative space for political voices. Most often, of course, this has been found in the work of the mainstream news media, which arguably continues to have the most impact on the political process. Thus, the increasing importance of the Internet notwithstanding, the focus here is on news in mainstream media, and reflects our own expertise on the US media.

HISTORICAL CONTEXT: TAKING CONTENT SERIOUSLY

Lippmann's (1922/1997) warning, that we act not on the 'world outside' but the 'pictures in our heads', has become a basic truism of communication research. When discussing content, there is a tendency to ask (guided by Lippmann) how 'objectively' media content reflects reality, expecting that it may distort but still have some correspondence with social reality. This possibility is often vigorously defended in attempts by news professionals to argue the accuracy of their work, in holding up a 'mirror to society'. In a subtler version of the mirror idea, a pluralist view holds that media objectivity emerges from the self-regulating and balancing compromises between those who sell information to the media and those who buy it. In either case, repudiating the mirror notion has been the project of countless media critiques and led to a broader area of political communication research. The popular conception of 'bias' used in critiques of press performance suggests that media deviate in some measurable way from a desirable standard, which can be independently known. Of course, the very idea of a 'reality' out there with which to

compare media is problematic. On a practical level, however, we often find it useful to compare 'media reality' with 'social reality' – that view of the world that is socially derived, what society knows about itself. Even if one were to accept the possibility of objectively portraying a 'world out there', the numerous studies over the years of media distortion compared to other social indicators of reality show that it is not a practical possibility. The media portray certain people, events and ideas, in ways that differ systematically from their occurrence in the 'real world' (see below).

Media 'mediate'; they stand between us and the social world, such that we can no longer think about our connection to the political world without media (Livingstone, 2009). In a pioneering study of mediation, Lang and Lang (1971) compared television coverage of the 1951 MacArthur Day parade in Chicago to the experience of those at the event. They found that television made the event more exciting and gave an inflated sense to viewers of the general's public support. The event provided an analytical benchmark to assess coverage. In the grander, more historical concept of 'mediatization', the world outside has adapted to that mediation, becoming more interdependent and absorbing, as a result, 'media logic'. Thus, now, of course, planners organize political events to maximize publicity and ensure a positive image with media coverage uppermost in mind. Institutional strategies have developed that make the political world 'part of the total media culture' (Altheide and Snow, 1979), and this dynamic has made it all the more appealing to look within news content as the manifest carrier and crucial terrain of that media logic. However, the question remains as to the proper benchmarks against which to compare news content. We still want to know how media logic refracts some wider political reality while still recognizing that the political and the media worlds have become inextricably interdependent and more difficult to separate analytically.

A rigorous examination of news content, whether a television newscast, newsmagazine, newspaper or online blog, opens up a host of normatively charged questions, which can be examined empirically using a number of performance criteria. These include the range of voices that are given access, the quality of that content in equipping citizens to act politically and the relative fairness of that representation to competing political interests. This includes the relative balance struck between political voices and those of journalists themselves, the extent to which political actors are allowed to speak without being 'filtered' via journalistic interpretation.

Framing News Content

Two major divisions in news content research lie in the effects tradition and the interpretive approach. The effects tradition, with a stimulus-response philosophical underpinning, relies on quantitative measures of systematic emphasis and relative frequency of elements in content. In a long tradition of content analysis, researchers have tried to find generalizable portraits of news content (Krippendorff, 2004). The interpretive approach, allowing a more critical and often qualitative perspective on content, examines the discourse and deeper narratives of news content with the goal of saying something about the broader culture in which media and publics participate. Lule (2001), for example, approaches news as a form of storytelling, analyzing the basic social myths, the archetypical stories on which news stories are based and rely for their structure. These myths include the hero, the victim, the good mother and the trickster, and they are examined for how they re-enact a cultural repertoire that sustains social order. News content in this context is tied to the ritual function of communication (Carey, 1989) rather than the transmission perspective of the effects tradition. Qualitative methods are particularly marked in critical analyses of underlying power relations, although of course it is entirely possible to combine qualitative and quantitative methodology. Thus, for example, the numerous case studies from the Glasgow Media Group (1976, 1980) use both quantitative and qualitative measures to critique the performance of organizations, such as the BBC, for coverage of labor relations, war and other controversies.

Both approaches to content are encompassed within the *framing* perspective, which has become a major thread in political communication research. The notion of media framing has become a widely adopted and multi-perspective research concept. Framing provides a way to tie news content to larger structures and develops new ways of capturing the power of media to define issues visually and verbally, thereby shaping audience perceptions (for example, Reese, 2001a). A widely accepted definition of news framing explains it as the communication of issues 'in such a way as to promote a particular problem definition, causal interpretation, moral evaluation, and/or treatment recommendation' (Entman, 1993: 52). The implication of cause and effect is inherent in this definition. An alternative definition leaves the issue of effects open – it states that frames are 'organizing principles that are socially shared and persistent over time, that work symbolically to meaningfully structure the social world' (Reese, 2001a: 11). Thus, framing connects visual and verbal,

quantitative and qualitative approaches to content, because they can all be seen as helping articulate some underlying organizing principle (Reese, 2007, 2009).

Framing, although often regarded as a close neighbor of the older 'agenda setting' tradition of research, is conceptually distinct. The agenda setting approach assesses content for its prioritization of various issues; but news content is of theoretical interest only to the extent that it influences public opinion priorities (Dearing and Rogers, 1996). This way of conceptualizing news content as 'topics' provides advantages in the analysis of public opinion, but it is less valuable for understanding content (Kosicki, 1993). Framing, by contrast, offers, in its 'organizing principle', a way to think about how news content itself is structured. The significance of frames, as contrasted to agenda-setting, becomes most noticeable when they take on broad over-arching properties. The War on Terror is a prime example, crucially providing the frame for mainstream news about the invasion of Iraq (Reese and Lewis, 2009).

Frames provide the basis for effects and cognitive research, the 'how' of framing. That is, how do frames, in manipulating certain treatments of issues and associated values, promote preference for a particular policy outcome? The more descriptive 'what' of framing looks more closely at the internal structure of news content and its connection with the surrounding culture. This approach can include examining latent aspects of content – linguistic structures and reasoning devices that signify underlying cultural meaning (Gamson and Modigliani, 1989). In this way, framing provides an empirically focused approach to questions of ideology, or meaning in the service of interests.

A more holistic, content-based approach to framing is advocated by Hertog and McLeod, who regard frames as 'structures of meaning made up of a number of concepts and the relations among those concepts' (2001: 140). Master narratives are among the devices that structure these concepts, providing rules for processing new content. When contrasted with the agenda/topic view, this gives frames a dynamic quality as they operate over time to assimilate and reconstitute new facts and concepts. Using a textual analysis of the US newspaper articles during the Gulf War, Hackett and Zhao (1994) documented that interpretative news frames used in covering antiwar protest were all broadly related to a master war narrative. The narrative describes a reluctant USA, with moral responsibility to restore order, forced by enemies to go to war and defeat villains (Hackett and Zhao, 1994). More recently, a content analysis of visual images from the US mainstream media revealed historic continuity in the master narrative of war reporting; a government-promoted patriotic perspective found in news content since the Civil War (Schwalbe et al., 2008).

NEWS CONTENT PATTERNS

Relationship Between News and the State

News content indirectly expresses political power, indicating among other things the important institutional relationship between press and state. Indeed, the patterns of content, although varying across media outlets, can be seen from a broader perspective to present a largely convergent institutional voice (Lawrence, 2006). Major national media are indeed similar in the way they cover major stories. Generally speaking, homogeneity of news content (for example, similar approach to issues and use of news sources) indicates support for an 'institutionalist' view of news production, in that content similarities point to its being produced by a single institution (Entman, 2006). This new institutionalist theoretical view of the press provides further impetus for examining news content per se within a broader theoretical context. Lawrence advocates linking news frames to their institutional context, by studying the product itself, 'where the rubber hits the road' (2006: 228). This perspective also supports our consideration of general patterns of news content (below), rather than highlighting differences among media.

Regarding the press as an institution leads to consideration of how it relates to the state, using news content as evidence of that relationship. Rojecki (2008), for example, examines *The Washington Post* and *The New York Times* editorials, as elite voices, finding that they largely supported the George W. Bush administration within a framework of American exceptionalism. In their content analysis of the US Patriot Act news coverage, Domke et al. (2006) found that the press largely echoed the administration. Main themes emphasized by the Bush administration about the Patriot Act were found to be widely present in the press, and further, that the coverage was highly favorable toward the administration. In a more general context, media coverage is said to 'index', be limited to, the range of views expressed in mainstream political debates about a given topic (Bennett, 1990). More controversially, and more forcefully, Herman and Chomsky (1988) applied a form of content analysis to coverage of the US foreign policy to support their famous 'propaganda model' of press–state relations, in which media, embedded in politico-economic power structures, effectively serves to manufacture public consent.

News Content Bias

Much attention has been directed at the question of the media's partisan bias. D'Alessio and Allen (2000), in a seminal meta-analysis review of research, gauge the extent to which media favor one side of a political campaign. Indicators included space (for print media) and time (broadcast) but failed to show a systematic partisan bias. Other content analyses of specific coverage have considered 'tone' in candidate treatment (Aday et al., 2005; Dalton et al., 1998). Positive or negative valence has been evaluated based on the proximity in texts of candidate names to key terms (Domke et al., 1999). This approach has found no evidence of the perennial claim to 'liberal media' bias (Watts et al., 1999), and in this respect confirms previous studies that failed to find systematic press bias (Hofstetter, 1978; Hofstetter and Buss, 1978; Robinson and Sheehan, 1983).

Conceptually, 'bias' brings its own standard for evaluation, assuming that content can be examined for deviation from some fixed standard (Hackett, 1984). Given the US two-party system, this standard often centers on whether content is balanced 50:50. However, because political fortunes are not always so equally balanced, other research has taken the view that bias claims require the examination of equivalent political behavior. Niven's (2003) study, for example, compared media coverage of party switchers. No differences were found in the tone of stories dealing with Republican compared to Democrat figures switching from one to the other. In campaign coverage of the 1996 presidential race, newspaper photograph selection did not suggest liberal bias but rather a strategic bias in favor of the front-runner (Waldman and Devitt, 1998). Groseclose and Milyo (2005) adopted a more sophisticated measure of bias outside of the election context by measuring news content against the institutional distribution of political leanings within Congress.

The numerous watchdog interest groups that monitor media content would regard as absurd the findings of a non-biased media. Media slant, particularly an alleged leftward bias, has become an article of faith for many groups. However, their methods used should be treated with caution, often selectively using content to support their view. This selectivity is not unknown in scholarly studies. In perhaps the most hotly charged international issue, the Israeli–Palestinian conflict, Wolfsfeld (2006) takes issue with Philo (Philo and Berry, 2004) for selectively including examples to support the claim that the British media unfairly support Israel, a view disputed by pro-Israel advocates. The term 'gunman' Philo regards as having a connotation favoring Israel, while the Israelis have regarded it as more positive than their preferred 'terrorist'. Thus, when it comes to content, a precise and careful analytical framework is essential. Although studies of the US media find no overt partisan bias, a wider (and less simplistic) pattern of structural biases is invariably built into news content.

Covering the Political Process

News content reveals important tendencies in how media approach the political process itself. News of elections typically focuses on the horserace aspects of the campaigns, partly to attract audience attention but also to avoid accusations of bias, to which issue-oriented coverage is prone (Patterson, 1993). This tendency is true of both print media and local television, where a national sample of stories found 9 in 10 stories effectively turned politics into a sport (Belt and Just, 2008). An analysis of local television political coverage found that even in a city known for civic involvement and news use (Minneapolis), campaign coverage was strategy-oriented with little issue-depth and opportunity for candidates to speak directly (Stevens et al., 2006).

Research on the shrinking 'sound bite' finds that the voices of political leaders have diminished in television news since the 1960s (Hallin, 1992, 1994; Lichter, 2001). A content analysis of television news coverage of elections showed that the average length of sound bite has decreased from 43 in 1968 to 9 seconds in the 1980s (Hallin, 1992). The trend continued through the 1990s (Lichter, 2001). Some studies suggest that the decline bottomed out during mid-1990s (Lowry and Shidler, 1998), but findings generally indicated shrinking sound bites (Barnhurst, 2003; Bucy and Grabe, 2007; Lichter, 2001). In his content analysis of National Public Radio shows, Barnhurst (2003) showed that the sound bites of expert sources in general, as well as political, news have shrunk by almost half from 1980 to 2000. Further, the average length of sound bites on the US television was shorter than that of European counterparts (Esser, 2008). Overall, the findings of sound bite research suggest that American journalism has become more interventionist in political news (Schudson, 1999). Patterson (1993) documents a long-term trend of news becoming more interpretive, with journalists themselves, rather than newsmakers, increasingly the source of that interpretation.

The horserace or 'strategic' framing of news appears to be particularly prevalent in the USA compared to Europe and Latin America. Strömbäck and Kaid's (2008) handbook of election coverage in 22 countries confirmed previous internationally comparative research (Esser and D'Angelo, 2006; Strömbäck and Dimitrova, 2006) that found that the metaframe of 'politics as a strategic game' was stronger in the US than elsewhere. This emphasis on strategy carries over into news of military conflict. Griffin and Lee (1995), for example, find that the major US news magazines covering the 1991 Gulf War included a narrow range of images that emphasized military weaponry and technology and served to promote government policy. Steele (1995) noted a similar tendency in Gulf War coverage as seen in the experts (predominantly military figures) selected to interpret military action.

News Sources and Topics

News content is built on news-makers. News is about self-perpetuating 'knowns', as observed early on by Gans (1979) in his fieldwork at the major US television networks and news magazines. People appear in news who have already been there, whether presidents, candidates, leading officials or well-known others. 'Unknowns' must break into the news arena somehow, often sensationally: as protestors, rioters, strikers, victims, violators or participants in unusual activities. One of the most robust findings of content studies then is that news favors officials who appear in routine ways through official channels (Cook, 1998; Gans, 1979; Sigal, 1973; Tuchman, 1978), while others must get there in ways that serve to underscore their deviance. The dominance of official sources results in a tight interlocking pattern of news-makers, who define the boundaries of political discourse (Reese et al., 1994).

In similar vein, alternative voices in social movements often have been treated as deviant and covered negatively in the news. Many studies have documented that protests are framed as negative and threatening to stability (Bennett et al., 2004). In his oft-cited study of the news media coverage of the New Left in Vietnam War era, Gitlin (1980) showed how mainstream media damaged the legitimacy of war protestors, by focusing on extreme elements. He identified framing devices such as trivialization, polarization and marginalization and argued that the framing devices worked as 'deprecatory' themes (Gitlin, 1980: 27). Continuing the theme, McLeod and Hertog (1998) noted a frequent story narrative of violent crime, leading reporters to describe protests as a 'scene of battle' between protesters and police.

News Quality Issues

News is commonly accused of sensationalism; stories designed to attract attention are often assumed to divert attention from serious, substantive public affairs. This tendency is closely related to the phenomenon of 'tabloidization', defined now largely by preference for the amusing, tititillating and entertaining (compared to more socially uplifting content). This is true for television news, particularly at the local level where dramatic coverage is assumed necessary to attract audiences. With its emphasis on crime, conflict, disaster and exciting video, as documented in a host of television content analyses (Bennett, 2001), sensationalism from a political standpoint works against the kind of news quality thought to encourage well-informed citizens. Television news, a particular target of research on these themes, has become more sensational over time both in the USA (Slattery et al., 2001) and Europe (Vettehen et al., 2005).

Closely related to sensationalism is the tendency of news to humanize or personalize its stories. Iyengar (1991) distinguishes between two kinds of news framings: an 'episodic' treatment of a single concrete event illustrating a broader issue versus a 'thematic' treatment including more general, often abstract evidence. Many stories, of course, include both kinds of information, but the more commonly found episodic news includes the anecdotal, humanized style of presentation, which is less likely to link events to broader policy. However, while episodic framing is criticized for its superficial treatment of social issues, a trend of analysis-centered journalism has been investigated as an important factor in making news tedious. In their extensive content analysis of newspapers from 1894 to 1994, Barnhurst and Mutz (1997) documented that stories, over the past 100 years have become longer, included more analysis, given less importance to individuals and more attention to groups. Thus, news is being stretched; at one and the same time we see more sensational news at one end of the spectrum and more lengthy analysis at the other. Barnhurst and Mutz's evidence lends support to the new 'long journalism' hypothesis. Historically, American journalism is moving from event-focus to analysis (Patterson, 1993; Schudson, 1978, 1982); news becomes longer and more analytical.

Quality of Representation of the Mediated World

Patterns of representation give us a sense of what is valued within news content, particularly in how news patterns differ from indicators of social reality. Indeed, newsworthiness means emphasizing those stories that have 'news value', that are significantly precisely because they are unusual.

Shoemaker and colleagues regard newsworthiness as a kind of 'deviance'. On this basis news, it is argued, serves as a signaling process deeply embedded in human nature and consistent across a variety of national contexts (Shoemaker and Cohen, 2006). Even if we do not expect the media map to line up with its real-life analog, the comparisons provide valuable clues for understanding systematic content tendencies and the shape of the overall logic. Below are some areas of research that have been the most commonly examined such patterns.

Behaviors

Media violence has attracted substantial research across the spectrum of content, including news. Research has long demonstrated misrepresentation of violent crimes in news stories in numbers and kinds of crimes. News emphasizes violent crimes (Antunes and Hurley, 1977; Windhauser et al., 1990) and crimes against people (Ammons et al., 1982; Fedler and Jordan, 1982) compared to non-violent or property crimes. A content analysis of *Time* magazine crime stories in five select years from 1953 to 1982 found that 73% of the sample were about violent crimes whereas 10% of crimes reported to the police involve violence (Barlow et al., 1995). The overrepresentation of violent crimes in news reports, particularly on television (Tunnell, 1998), is at expense of other crimes. From their content analysis of the *Los Angeles Times*, Rodgers and Thorson (2001) found that violent crimes such as homicide and domestic violence (25% of 416 sample crime stories) were much more likely to become news than property crimes (6%).

Demographic

Demographic patterns provide other unambiguous standards against which to assess news content. Coverage undercounts certain groups and is prone to reproduce cultural stereotypes. Women, for example, are underrepresented in news (Gans, 1979; Gersh, 1992; Len-Rios et al., 2005; Rodgers et al., 2000). Female candidates for the Senate have been shown to receive less coverage than their male opponents, and that coverage was often about their viability rather than issues (Kahn and Goldenberg, 1991). Other coverage of women often underscored their unequal power position by seizing on stories that suggested women's frailties, such as difficulty in finding mates after a certain age and genetic deficits in math (Corbett, 2001; Rivers, 1993; Ross, 2002). News media has been criticized for its disproportionate representation of minority groups, particularly in relation to crime stories. On local television newscasts, African Americans were overrepresented as law-breakers whereas whites and Latinos were under-represented, compared to recorded crime rates (Dixon and Linz, 2000). The same study also found that whites were overrepresented as law defenders, such as police officers, while Latinos were underrepresented. Network television showed slightly different patterns of racial repre-sentation in reports. Both African Americans and whites were represented as lawbreakers consist-ently with official crime reports, but African Americans were underrepresented as victims of violent crime while whites were overrepresented (Dixon et al., 2003).

Entman and Rojecki (2001) have done exten-sive content analysis of television and local news-paper coverage of minority communities, finding a number of ways in which minorities are given more negative treatment. Compared to black defendants, for example, whites charged with similar crimes are more often named, depicted as well-dressed and less often in the physical control of the police. These features are said to humanize whites more than their minority counterparts, who are also disadvantaged with fewer pro-defense sound bites (Entman, 1990, 1992). In his ethno-graphic study, Heider (2000) found that local tel-evision, even in communities with majority minority populations, restricted ethnic minority coverage to news of festivals and crime.

Geographic

News patterns can be compared against actual spatial benchmarks. Earlier studies of network news coverage found it skewed to overrepresent the Pacific Coast and Northeast (Dominick, 1977; Graber, 1989), with California, New York and Texas receiving a greater proportion of coverage than their electoral votes would indicate. News follows power, but in cases like this it exacerbates it. Many news organizations have been accused of having an 'inside the beltway' focus on official Washington, DC (Ryan, 1993). This television emphasis has changed somewhat, but the pattern remains rooted in cities of power, whether eco-nomic (New York), political (Washington) or cul-tural (Los Angeles). Replicating the Dominick (1977) study, Whitney et al. (1989) found similar geographical bias in news coverage on television. The top four states of New York, California, Illinois and Texas accounted for 50.6% of domes-tic news reports, while their population is about 30% of the US total. In the more recent satellite news era, the US media were found more likely to cover remote areas (Livingston and Van Belle, 2005). However, a content analysis of television

news from 1982 to 2004 documented that news patterns found in previous research still existed, despite advances in newsgathering technologies (Jones, 2008).

Patterns of international news content have been closely scrutinized, given the larger political debate over the imbalance of global information flows. Although globalization has brought greater potential access by the world to the world, inter-national news coverage continues to be vulnera-ble, especially given the cuts in overseas news bureaus. The first world receives disproportion-ately more US television news coverage than the rest, except in the tradition of 'coups and earth-quakes' reporting, when natural disaster or other sensational events occur (Larson, 1983). Generally speaking, news tracks relationships of political alliances, predominantly featuring the allies of the USA and her enemies (Shoemaker et al., 1991). However, recent studies have identified two other key indicators of media attention: trade volume and the presence of international news agencies (Wu, 2000). Golan (2008) also found that the low level of trade with the USA partially explained the meager coverage of the African continent by the US television news, despite newsworthy events.

FUTURE DIRECTIONS AND DEVELOPMENTS

Digital technologies have provided new opportu-nities for research. The Internet, in particular, has made possible a vast amount of news content that researchers can obtain readily and efficiently. Digitization rapidly increases the volume of con-tents online, making accessible once unreachable materials (Weare and Lin, 2000). Another benefit is lowered cost in collecting samples, with online archives and databases, such as LexisNexis, pro-viding easy data collection. Computerized coding procedure is another significant contribution to research. Digitization of contents made possible computerization of coding and increased reliabil-ity of studies, though it also has limitations. The enormous amount of information and ephemeral, ever-changing nature of online contents has made scientific random sampling more complicated as it does (McMillan, 2000). Search engines, often used in sampling, are not completely reliable because none of the engines covers the entire Internet population (Lawrence and Giles, 1999). The hyperlink, a unique feature of the Internet, has brought a sea change in ways of reading mate-rials and has complicated content analysis (Weare and Lin, 2000). In particular, hyperlinks have forced researchers to spend more time in defining the unit of analysis and how to set boundaries on the network to be examined (for example, Reese et al., 2007). Automatic coding of vast amounts of electronic text has allowed researchers to explore new content features, whether through cluster analyses of key vocabularies or trends in the news cycle (even from hour to hour) (Leskovec et al., 2009). Consistent with the network structure of the Internet, studies are mapping news patterns through their linking strategies, including the global blogosphere. Although most studies reviewed here have been confined to the professional news media, increasingly these sources of content are interlinked with the burgeoning social media. A key methodological question during the transition from offline to online media analysis is whether Internet content is different from offline content for the same news media. Hoffman (2006) examined online and offline versions of the same newspaper and found no difference between versions in terms of mobilizing information. Research must adapt to our rapidly changing environment to adequately evaluate the significant sites where news content is distributed, and how on- and offline worlds are interconnected.

CONCLUSION

News content provides a valuable site for examining the symbolic environment, and – having established significant patterns and regularities – inferences can be made about the hierarchy of influences shaping that environment (Reese, 2001b) or the way citizens are expected to be affected. The content of news media is potentially as diverse as life itself, making it important to understand the various ways we can narrow the key features of interest. We have not included many examples from the more interpretive and qualitative approaches to content, favoring here external validity with those studies making broader generalizations about content using more systematic methods.

Taken as a whole, news content provides a power map for the larger political system. We do not expect news to represent society as a quasi-'census', providing an exact analog to the way people, places, and roles are distributed in the society. Given the importance of news in the political process, we clearly have certain expectations for press performance involving quality, fairness and representation against which we can gauge our measures of content. News both reflects power and provides a site where power is worked out. We should not be surprised then to find disparities in gender, racial, class and geographical representation, since it reflects the present

distribution of privilege within the system. We do, however, expect that news as a social space will not work to exclude newcomers, marginalize important voices or degrade the political process with excessive sensationalism. These are all areas of press performance for which an understanding of news content provides important clues.

REFERENCES

Aday, S., Livingston, S. and Hebert, M. (2005) 'Embedding the Truth: A Cross-Cultural Analysis of Objectivity and Television of the Iraq War', *Harvard International Journal of Press/Politics*, 10(1): 3–21.

Altheide, D. and Snow, D. (1979) *Media Logic*. Beverly Hills, CA: Sage.

Ammons, L., Dimmick, J. and Pilotta, J. J. (1982) 'Crime News Reporting in a Black Weekly', *Journalism Quarterly*, 59(2): 310–13.

Antunes, G. E. and Hurley, P. A. (1977) 'The Representation of Criminal Events in Houston's Two Daily Newspapers', *Journalism Quarterly*, 54(4): 756–60.

Barlow, M. H., Barlow, D. E. and Chiricos, T. G. (1995) 'Economic Conditions and Ideologies of Crime in the Media: A Content Analysis of Crime News', *Crime and Delinquency*, 41(1): 3–19.

Barnhurst, K. G. (2003) 'The Makers of Meaning: National Public Radio and the New Long Journalism, 1980–2000', *Political Communication*, 20(1): 1–22.

Barnhurst, K. G. and Mutz, D. (1997) 'American Journalism and the Decline in Event Centered Reporting', *Journal of Communication*, 47(4): 27–53.

Baym, G. (2005) 'The Daily Show: Discursive Integration and the Reinvention of Political Journalism', *Political Communication*, 22(3): 259–76.

Belt, T. L. and Just, M. R. (2008) 'The Local News Story: Is Quality a Choice?', *Political Communication*, 25(2): 194–215.

Bennett, W. L. (1990) 'Toward a Theory of Press-State Relations in the United States', *Journal of Communication*, 40(2): 103–27.

Bennett, W. L. (2001) *News: The Politics of Illusion*. 4th edn. New York: Addison Wesley Longman. [1st edn, 1983.]

Bennett, W. L., Pickard, V. W., Lozzi, D. P., Schroeder, C. L., Lagos, T. and Caswell, C. E. (2004) 'Managing the Public Sphere: Journalistic Construction of the Great Globalization Debate', *Journal of Communication*, 54(3): 437–55.

Bucy, E. P. and Grabe, M. E. (2007) 'Taking Television Seriously: A Sound and Image Bite Analysis of Presidential Campaign Coverage, 1992–2004', *Journal of Communication*, 57(4): 652–75.

Carey, J. W. (1989) *Communication as Culture: Essays on Media and Society*. Boston, MA: Unwin Hyman.

Castells, M. (2007) 'Communication, Power and Counter-Power in the Network Society', *International Journal of Communication*, 1: 238–66.

Cook, T. E. (1998) *Governing With the News: The News Media as a Political Institution*. Chicago, IL: University of Chicago Press.

Corbett, J. B. (2001) 'Women, Scientists, Agitators: Magazine Portrayal of Rachel Carson and Theo Colborn', *Journal of Communication*, 51(4): 720–49.

D'Alessio, D. and Allen, M. (2000) 'Media Bias in Presidential Elections: A Meta-Analysis', *Journal of Communication*, 50(4): 133–56.

Dalton, R. J., Beck, P. A. and Huckfeldt, R. (1998) 'Partisan Cues and the Media: Information Flows in the 1992 Presidential Election', *American Political Science Review*, 92(1): 111–26.

Dearing, J. W. and Rogers, E. M. (1996) *Agenda-setting*. Thousand Oaks, CA: Sage.

Delli Carpini, M. X. and Williams, B. (2001) 'Let us Infotain You: Politics in the New Media Environment', in W. L. Bennett and R. M. Entman (eds.), *Mediated Politics: Communication in the Future of Democracy*. New York: Cambridge University. pp. 160–81.

Dixon, T. L., Azocar, C. L. and Casas, M. (2003) 'The Portrayal of Race and Crime on Television Network News', *Journal of Broadcasting and Electronic Media*, 47(4): 498–523.

Dixon, T. L. and Linz, D. (2000) 'Overrepresentation and Underrepresentation of African Americans and Latinos as Lawbreakers on Television News', *Journal of Communication*, 50(2): 131–54.

Dominick, J. R. (1977) 'Geographic Bias in National TV News', *Journal of Communication*, 27(4): 94–9.

Domke, D., Graham, E., Coe, K., Lockett John, S. and Coopman, T. (2006) 'Going Public as Political Strategy: The Bush Administration, an Echoing Press, and Passage of the Patriot Act', *Political Communication*, 23(3): 291–312.

Domke, D., Watts, M. D., Shah, D. V. and Fan, D. P. (1999) 'The Politics of Conservative Elites and the "Liberal Media" Argument', *Journal of Communication*, 49(4): 35–58.

Entman, R. M. (1990) 'Modern Racism and the Images of Blacks in Local Television News', *Critical Studies in Mass Communication*, 7(4): 332–45.

Entman, R. M. (1992) 'Blacks in the News: Television, Modern Racism and Cultural Change', *Journalism Quarterly*, 69(2): 341–61.

Entman, R. M. (1993) 'Framing: Toward Clarification of a Fractured Paradigm', *Journal of Communication*, 43(4): 51–8.

Entman, R. M. (2006) 'Punctuating the Homogeneity of Institutionalized News: Abusing Prisoners at Abu Graib Versus Killing Civilians at Fallujah', *Political Communication*, 23(2): 215–24.

Entman, R. M. and Rojecki, A. (2001) *The Black Image in the White Mind: Media and Race in America*. Chicago, IL: University of Chicago Press.

Esser, F. (2008) 'Dimensions of Political News Cultures: Sound Bite and Image Bite News in France, Germany, Great Britain, and the United States', *Harvard International Journal of Press/Politics*, 13(4): 401–28.

Esser, F. and D'Angelo, P. (2006) 'Framing the Press and Publicity Process in the US, British, and German General Election Campaigns: A Comparative Study of Meta-coverage', *Harvard International Journal of Press/Politics*, 11(3): 44–66.

Fedler, F. and Jordan, D. (1982) 'How Emphasis on People Affects Coverage of Crime' *Journalism Quarterly*, 59(3): 461–68.

Gamson, W. A. and Modigliani, A. (1989) 'Media Discourse and Public Opinion on Nuclear Power: A Constructionist Approach', *American Journal of Sociology*, 95(1): 1–37.

Gans, H. J. (1979) *Deciding What's News: A Study of CBS Evening News, NBC Nightly News, Newsweek, and Time*. New York: Pantheon Books.

Gersh, D. (1992) 'Promulgating Polarization Study Finds Media Coverage of Women, Minorities Tends to be Oversimplistic, which Exacerbates Social Strains', *Editor and Publisher*, 10 October: 30–1.

Gitlin, T. (1980) *The Whole World is Watching: Mass Media in the Making and Unmaking of the New Left*. Berkeley, CA: University of California Press.

Glasgow Media Group (1976) *Bad News*. London: Routledge.

Glasgow Media Group (1980) *More Bad News*. London: Routledge.

Golan, G. J. (2008) 'Where in the World is Africa? Predicting Coverage of Africa by US Television Networks', *International Communication Gazette*, 70(1): 41–57.

Graber, D. A. (1989) 'Flashlight Coverage: State News on National Broadcasts', *American Politics Research*, 17(3): 277–90.

Griffin, M. and Lee, J. (1995) 'Picturing the Gulf War: Constructing an Image of War in Time, Newsweek, and US News and World Report', *Journalism and Mass Communication Quarterly*, 72(4): 813–25.

Groseclose, T. and Milyo, J. (2005) 'A Measure of Media Bias', *Quarterly Journal of Economics*, 120(4): 1191–237.

Hackett, R. A. (1984) 'Decline of a Paradigm? Bias and Objectivity in News Media studies', *Critical Studies in Mass Communication*, 1(3): 229–59.

Hackett, R. A. and Zhao, Y. (1994) 'Challenging a Master Narrative: Peace Protest and Opinion/Editorial Discourse in the US Press During the Gulf War', *Discourse Society*, 5(4): 509–41.

Hallin, D. C. (1992) 'Sound Bite News: Television Coverage of Elections, 1968–1988', *Journal of Communication*, 42(2): 5–24.

Hallin, D. C. (1994) *We Keep America on Top of the World: Television Journalism and the Public Sphere*. London: Routledge.

Heider, D. (2000) *White News: Why Local News Programs Don't Cover People of Color*. Mahwah, NJ: Lawrence Erlbaum Associates.

Herman, E. S. and Chomsky, N. (1988) *Manufacturing Consent: the Political Economy of the Mass Media*. New York: Pantheon Books.

Hertog, J. K. and McLeod, D. M. (2001) 'A Multiperspectival Approach to Framing Analysis: A Field Guide', in S. D. Reese, O. H. Gandy Jr. and A. E. Grant (eds.), *Framing Public Life*. Mahwah, NJ: Lawrence Erlbaum Associates. pp. 139–61.

Hoffman, L. H. (2006) 'Is Internet Content Different After All? A Content Analysis of Mobilizing Information in Online and

Print Newspapers', *Journalism and Mass Communication Quarterly*, 83(1): 58–76.

Hofstetter, C. R. (1978) 'News Bias in the 1972 Campaign: A Cross-Media Comparison', *Journalism Monographs*, 58.

Hofstetter, C. R. and Buss, T. (1978) 'Bias in Television News Coverage of Political Events: A Methodological Analysis', *Journal of Broadcasting*, 22(4): 517–30.

Iyengar, S. (1991) *Is Anyone Responsible? How Televisions Frames Political Issues*. Chicago, IL: University of Chicago Press.

Jones, S. (2008) 'Television News: Geographic and Source Biases, 1982–2004', *International Journal of Communication*, 2: 223–52.

Kahn, K. F. and Goldenberg, E. N. (1991) 'Women Candidates in the News: An Examination of Gender Differences in US Senate Campaign Coverage', *Public Opinion Quarterly*, 55(2): 180–99.

Kosicki, G. M. (1993) 'Problems and Opportunities in Agenda-Setting Research', *Journal of Communication*, 43(2): 100–27.

Krippendorff, K. H. (2004) *Content Analysis: An Introduction to its Methodology*. Thousand Oaks, CA: Sage.

Lang, K. and Lang, G. E. (1971) 'The Unique Perspective of Television and its Effects: A Pilot Study', in W. Schramm and D. F. Roberts (eds.), *The Process and Effects of Mass Communication*. Urbana, IL: University of Illinois Press. pp. 169–88.

Larson, J. F. (1983) *Television's Window on the World: International Affairs Coverage on the US Networks*. Norwood, NJ: Ablex.

Lasswell, H. D. (1948) 'The Structure and Function of Communication in Society', in B. Lymon (ed.), *The Communication of Ideas*. New York: Institute for Religious and Social Studies. pp. 37–51.

Lawrence, R. (2006) 'Seeing the Whole Board: New Institutional Analysis of News Content', *Political Communication*, 23(2): 225–30.

Lawrence, S. and Giles, C. L. (1999) 'Accessibility of Information on the Web', *Nature*, 400(6740): 107–9.

Len-Rios, M. E., Rodgers, S., Thorson, E. and Doyle, Y. (2005) 'Representation of Women in News and Photos: Comparing Content to Perceptions', *Journal of Communication*, 55(1): 152–68.

Leskovec, J., Backstrom, L. and Kleinberg, J. (2009) 'Meme-Tracking and the Dynamics of the News Cycle', paper presented at the 15th ACM SIGKDD Conference on Knowledge Discovery and Data Mining. Paris, France.

Lichter, S. R. (2001) 'A Plague on Both Parties: Substance and Fairness in TV Election News', *Harvard International Journal of Press/Politics*, 6(3): 8–30.

Lippmann, W. (1922/ 1997) *Public Opinion*. New York: Free Press.

Livingston, S. and Van Belle, D. A. (2005) 'The Effects of Satellite Technology on Newsgathering from Remote Locations', *Political Communication*, 22(1): 45–62.

Livingstone, S. (2009) 'On the Mediation of Everything: ICA Presidential Address 2008', *Journal of Communication*, 59(1): 1–18.

Lowry, D. T. and Shidler, J. A. (1998) 'The Sound Bites, the Bitters, and the Bitten: A Two-Campaign Test of the Anti-Incumbent Bias Hypothesis in Network TV news', *Journalism and Mass Communication Quarterly*, 75(4): 719–29.

Lule, J. (2001) *Daily News, Eternal Stories: The Mythological Role of Journalism*. New York: Guilford Press.

McLeod, D. M. and Hertog, J. K. (1998) 'Social Control and the Mass Media's Role in the Regulation of Protest Groups: The Communicative Acts Perspective', in D. P. Demers and K. Viswanath (eds.), *Mass Media, Social Control and Social Change*. Ames, IA: Iowa State University Press. pp. 305–30.

McMillan, S. J. (2000) 'The Microscope and the Moving Target: The Challenge of Applying Content Analysis to the World Wide Web', *Journalism and Mass Communication Quarterly*, 77(1): 80–98.

Niven, D. (2003) 'Objective Evidence on Media Bias: Newspaper Coverage of Congressional Party Switchers', *Journalism and Mass Communication Quarterly*, 80(2): 311–26.

Patterson, T. E. (1993) *Out of Order*. New York: Alfred A. Knopf.

Philo, G. and Berry, M. (2004) *Bad News From Israel*. London: Pluto Press.

Reese, S. D. (2001a) 'Framing Public Life: A Bridging Model for Media Research', in S. D. Reese, O. H. Gandy Jr and A. E. Grant (eds.), *Framing Public Life*. Mahwah, NJ: Lawrence Erlbaum Associates. pp. 7–31.

Reese, S. D. (2001b) 'Understanding the Global Journalist: A Hierarchy-of-Influences Approach', *Journalism Studies*, 2(2): 173–87.

Reese, S. D. (2007) 'The Framing Project: A Bridging Model for Media Research Revisited', *Journal of Communication*, 57(1): 148–54.

Reese, S. D. (2009) 'Finding Frames in a Web of Culture: The Case of the War on Terror', in P. D'Angelo and J. Kuypers (eds.), *Doing News Framing Analysis: Empirical, Theoretical, and Normative Perspectives*. New York: Routledge.

Reese, S. D., Grant, A. E. and Danielian, L. H. (1994) 'The Structure of News Sources on Television: A Network Analysis of "CBS News," "Nightline," "MacNeil/Lehrer," and "This Week with David Brinkley"', *Journal of Communication*, 44(2), 84–107.

Reese, S. D. and Lewis, S. (2009) 'Framing the War on Terror: Internalization of Policy by the US Press', *Journalism: Theory, Practice, Criticism*, 10(6): 777–97.

Reese, S. D., Rutigliano, L., Hyun, K. and Jeong, J. (2007) 'Mapping the Blogosphere: Citizen-Based Media in the Global News Arena', *Journalism: Theory, Practice, Criticism*, 8(3): 235–62.

Rivers, C. (1993) 'Bandwagons, Women and Cultural Mythology', *Media Studies Journal*, 7(1–2): 1–17.

Robinson, M. J. and Sheehan, M. A. (1983) *Over the Wire and on TV: CBS and UPI in Campaign 80*. New York: Russell Sage Foundation.

Rodgers, S. and Thorson, E. (2001) 'The Reporting of Crime and Violence in the Los Angeles Times: Is There a Public Health Perspective?', *Journal of Health Communication*, 6(2): 169–82.

Rodgers, S., Thorson, E. and Antecol, M. (2000) '"Reality" in the St. Louis Post-Dispatch', *Newspaper Research Journal*, 21(3): 51–68.

Rojecki, A. (2008) 'Rhetorical Alchemy: American Exceptionalism and the War on Terror', *Political Communication*, 25(1): 67–88.

Ross, K. (2002) *Women, Politics, Media: Uneasy Relations in Comparative Perspective.* Cresskill, NJ: Hampton Press.

Ryan, C. (1993) 'A Study of National Public Radio', *EXTRA!,* April/May: 18–21.

Schudson, M. (1978) *Discovering the News: A Social History of American Newspapers.* New York: Basic Books.

Schudson, M. (1982) 'The Politics of Narrative Form: The Emergence of News Conventions in Print and Television', *Daedalus*, 111(4): 97–112.

Schudson, M. (1999) 'Social Origins of Press Cynicism in Portraying Politics', *American Behavioral Scientist*, 42(6): 998–1008.

Schwalbe, C. B., Silcock, B. W. and Keith, S. (2008) 'Visual Framing of the Early Weeks of the US-led Invasion of Iraq: Applying the Master War Narrative to Electronic and Print Images', *Journal of Broadcasting and Electronic Media*, 52(3): 448–65.

Shoemaker, P. J. and Cohen, A. A. (2006) *News around the World: Content, Practitioners and the Public.* London: Routledge.

Shoemaker, P. J., Danielian, L. H. and Brendlinger, N. (1991) 'Deviant Acts, Risky Business, and US Interests: The Newsworthiness of World Events', *Journalism Quarterly*, 68(4): 781–95.

Sigal, L. (1973) *Reporters and Officials.* Lexington, MA: D. C. Heath.

Slattery, K. L., Doremus, M. and Marcus, L. (2001) 'Shifts in Public Affairs Reporting on the Network Evening News: A Move Toward the Sensational', *Journal of Broadcasting and Electronic Media*, 45(2): 290–302.

Steele, J. (1995) 'Experts and the Operational Bias of Television News: The Case of the Persian Gulf War', *Journalism and Mass Communication Quarterly*, 72(4): 799–812.

Stevens, D., Alger, D., Allen, B. and Sullivan, J. L. (2006) 'Local News Coverage in a Social Capital: Election 2000 on Minnesota's Local News Stations', *Political Communication*, 23(1): 61–83.

Strömbäck, J. and Dimitrova, D. (2006) 'Political and Media Systems Matter: A Comparison of Election News in Sweden and the United States', *Harvard International Journal of Press/Politics*, 11(4): 131–47.

Strömbäck, J. and Kaid, L. L. (eds.) (2008) *The Handbook of Election News Coverage around the World.* New York: Routledge.

Tuchman, G. (1978) *Making News: A Study in the Construction of Reality.* New York: Free Press.

Tunnell, K. (1998) 'Reflections on Crime, Criminals, and Control in Newsmagazine Television Programs', in F. Y. Bailey and D. C. Hale (eds.), *Popular Culture, Crime, and Justice.* Belmont, CA: West/Wadsworth. pp. 111–22.

Vettehen, P. H., Nuitjen, K. and Beentjes, J. (2005) 'News in an Age of Competition: The Case of Sensationalism in Dutch Television news', *Journal of Broadcasting and Electronic Media*, 49(3): 282–95.

Waldman, P. and Devitt, J. (1998) 'Newspaper Photographs and the 1996 Presidential Election: The Question of Bias', *Journalism and Mass Communication Quarterly*, 75(2): 302–11.

Watts, M. D., Domke, D., Shah, D. V. and Fan, D. P. (1999) 'Elite Cues and Media Bias in Presidential Campaigns: Explaining Public Perceptions of a Liberal Press', *Communication Research*, 26(2): 144–75.

Weare, C. and Lin, W. Y. (2000) 'Content Analysis of the World Wide Web: Opportunities and challenges', *Social Science Computer Review*, 18(3): 272–92.

Whitney, D. C., Fritzler, M., Jones, S., Mazzarella, S. R. and Rakow, L. F. (1989) 'Geographic and Source Bias in Network Television News, 1982–1984', *Journal of Broadcasting and Electronic Media*, 33(2): 159–74.

Windhauser, J. W., Seiter, J. and Winfree, L. T. (1990) 'Crime News in the Louisiana Press, 1980 vs. 1985', *Journalism Quarterly*, 67(1): 72–8.

Wolfsfeld, G. (2006) 'A Review of: Bad News from Israel, by Greg Philo and Mike Berry', *Political Communication*, 23(4): 475–76.

Wright, C. R. (1986) *Mass Communication: A Sociological Perspective.* New York: Random House.

Wu, H. D. (2000) 'Systemic Determinants of International News Coverage: A Comparison of 38 Countries', *Journal of Communication*, 50(2): 110–31.

21

Ethnography as Theory and Method in the Study of Political Communication

Debra Spitulnik Vidali and Mark Allen Peterson

This chapter provides an introduction to both the theory and method of ethnography, as it reviews existing research and charts out new directions for future research, particularly around the topics of citizenship, modernity, globalization, national publics and new media. It considers both the ethnography of media production and the ethnography of media reception, as well as the ethnography of political discourse more broadly conceived. With the exception of the path-breaking newsroom studies by sociologists such as Gans (1980), Gitlin (1983) and Tuchman (1978), the qualitative method of ethnography, understood as participant-observation in everyday settings, has been largely under-utilized in the field of political communication. Recent advances in the new field of media anthropology, as well as in the more long-standing ethnography of communication tradition, provide a rich source of both theoretical and methodological models for deepening and expanding the study of political communication in contemporary contexts. We argue that ethnographic research is more important than ever as a way of grounding globalization in concrete locales, and as a check on assumptions generalized from anecdotal evidence. We also argue for ethnography as a method for enriching the understanding of media effects and influence, as well as for capturing not only the everyday workings of political communication, but the deeply human experience of political communication on both the production and reception ends.

ETHNOGRAPHY AS METHOD, LENS AND STYLE

Our starting point in this chapter is a threefold definition of ethnography: as a fieldwork method; as an analytical lens and as a style of writing and re-presentation. Derived from the Greek *ethnos* (folk/people) + *graphein* (writing), the term 'ethnography' means 'writing about a people or a culture'. In this chapter, we argue that ethnography is much more than a method of open-ended qualitative research that involves talking to people and spending time with them as they go about their daily lives. Doing ethnography is also a way of attending both theoretically and methodologically to three distinct realms of investigation, namely: (1) the complex interconnections across phenomena; (2) the systems of meaning that motivate and result from human action and (3) the ways that communication itself constitutes meanings and relationships. Ethnography is relevant for the study of political communication as a pilot methodology, as an organizing frame for a full-length study, and as one method within a mixed-methods project. In this chapter we discuss the connections between political communication research and the ethnography of media production, the ethnography of media reception, and the ethnography of political discourse.

The long-standing traditions of ethnographic research in anthropology and sociology are traced back to social anthropologist Bronislaw Malinowski (1922/1961) in the UK, cultural anthropologist Franz Boas (1989) in the USA and the urban sociologists of the Chicago School (Park and Burgess, 1921; Warner, 1941; Whyte, 1943). In the 1960s and 1970s, ethnography was introduced into communication studies primarily through ethnography of speaking traditions (see below) and into media and cultural studies through the work of David Morley (1980), Janice Radway (1988) and others (see Machin, 2002). In recent years, the field of media anthropology has grown exponentially (Askew and Wilk, 2002; Ginsburg et al., 2002; Peterson, 2003b; Rotherbuhler and Coman, 2005; Spitulnik, 1993), but its early history dates back to Hortense Powdermaker's (1950) pioneering ethnography of a Hollywood production studio and William Lloyd Warner's (1959) study of media's roles in a pre-World War II New England town.

While ethnography has a very strong and significant documentary function, as well as a distinctive methodological approach of intensive long-term fieldwork in the natural contexts of people's ongoing practices, we argue here that ethnography also embodies several kinds of theory, including a particular analytical perspective on the nature of culture and human experience, a theory of how to distill cultural meanings from documentary data and a theory of how the long-term participant-observer fieldworker is ideally transformed by fieldwork and thus better able to see and report on a culture or way of life from the inside. Before turning directly to the theoretical dimensions of ethnography and its applications for political communication studies, we discuss the practical dimensions of ethnography, including the formulation of ethnographic questions.

Formulating Ethnographic Questions

The core aim of ethnography is to develop a deep familiarity with – and an understanding of – a culture, a community or a group of individuals from an inside perspective, often referred to as 'the native's point of view' or 'emic' perspective. Typically ethnographers approach people(s) and their cultures as a distinctive way of being-in-the-world. The ethnographer's aim is thus not only to document practices as sets of behaviors, but to understand how these practices embody a unique 'worldview' or perspective on reality (Emerson et al., 1995, Geertz, 1973).

A range of qualitative methods are used in ethnographic work, including participant-observation, informal interviews, group conversations, genealogies, life-histories and case study methods

(Bernard, 1998, 2005b; Denzin and Lincoln, 2005). Ethnographers may also employ quantitative methods such as surveys, censuses and mapping, but always do so within the context of broader, in depth fieldwork. The overarching questions framing an ethnographic approach are: What are the habitual practices of the people in this setting? How are activities sequenced? What kinds of social roles do people occupy? What unspoken norms guide action? How do people know what normative behavior is? What kinds of cultural meanings are signaled by behaviors? What meanings do people attribute to their actions?

People's orientations to space, time and the circulation of goods and commodities are key areas of ethnographic research, as are the micro-rituals and rhythms of everyday routines. Within the ethnography of journalism, for example, the everyday routine practices of news gathering, editing and locating sources are central topics of investigation (Gans, 1980; Pedelty, 1995; Peterson, 2001; Tuchman, 1978; Van Hout and Jacobs, 2008). Documenting non-ordinary practices and peak events also falls within the purview of ethnography, particularly when such practices and events have great value for the community or when they reveal what is typically off-limits or sacred to the community. In many cases, peak events are occasions where many of a society's or subculture's core values are activated or even debated in a heightened way. For example, a presidential press conference (and the lead up to it) provides a fertile setting for examining the status hierarchy and political relations between news outlets, as well as the in-play cultivation of client relations with presidents and presidential handlers (see Goffman, 1981).

Ethnographers pay close attention to the ways that visual and verbal communications, as well as material artifacts, have symbolic and functional value within communities. For example, a newsroom ethnographer might document the placement of desks, the location and size of offices, wall decorations, noise level, the types of personal items placed on desks, office attire and types of technologies issued to different employees to gain a rich understanding of the culture of the newsroom workplace and how status, power and professional identity are constructed in this workplace environment. Other topics commonly explored in ethnographies of media production include how institutional ideologies are conveyed through everyday talk, mission statements, decision-making practices, product labels and choice of linguistic registers (Born, 2005; Fairclough, 2009; Rutherford, 2008; Spitulnik, 1998, 2010a).

Concepts of the person, including class, race, gender, caste and age-appropriate behaviors, are also central for ethnographic research. Lindquist's (2002) ethnographic study of communication in a working class bar in Chicago, for example, illustrates how personal identity is shaped around the consumption and display of political news knowledge, and how this is specifically inflected by gender and class dynamics. Many ethnographies of the reception of political communication track how this is a dynamic process of identity construction, one in which consumers imagine relations with media producers (Abu-Lughod, 2005; Mankekar, 1999).

Increasingly, communications researchers and anthropologists alike are conducting multisited ethnography, as well as various forms of global ethnography (Hannerz, 2003, 2004; Kosnick, 2007; Larkin, 2008; Marcus, 1995). For example, some studies are designed to track both the production and reception ends of a communication process or form (for example, Schroder and Phillips, 2007); others delve into either cultures of reception or cultures of production, but situate the work in multiple locations simultaneously.

No matter how an ethnographic project is framed, it is usually holistic in the sense that the ethnographer operates with an understanding that the specific project at hand is almost infinitely connected to myriad domains of life and fields of value (Ang, 1991; Spitulnik, 2010b). Of course, any given project is necessarily bounded by a choice of specific fieldwork contexts, the research timeframe and the choice of topics. At the same time, it is important to note that ethnography in the ideal sense involves more than a person-centered focus or an immersion into daily rhythms and routines: it operates as an open-ended qualitative method, one which is responsive to research opportunities and issues as they present themselves, in an effort to discover the cultural logics and 'member's meanings' behind observed behavior (Emerson et al., 1995; Janesick, 2000).

Practical Dimensions of Ethnography

In conducting fieldwork, a researcher often takes on many different roles, and may operate as either an 'insider ethnographer' or an 'outsider ethnographer'. Insider ethnographers typically have a pre-existing connection to the community or subculture under study and are active members in it. By contrast, outsider ethnographers are relatively new to the community or subculture and they may or may not take on a recognized role within the group once research is underway. Each approach has its advantages and challenges. Insider ethnographers have the advantage of immediate rapport, as well as a strong familiarity with the socio-cultural context. They already know the language, dialect or

appropriate registers for communication within chosen community or subculture. Most already possess what could be called the insider's (or native's) point of view and knowledge. But because of these advantages, insider ethnographers are often faced with the challenge of myopia: they may not see the unspoken cultural patterns and norms as vividly as an outsider might. Insider ethnographers thus employ various techniques to distance themselves from what they already know and expect, by adopting a stance which 'makes the familiar strange' and thus suspends knowledge about what 'normal' habits are or what meanings behaviors have for the participants being observed. By contrast, outsider ethnographers have the challenges of needing to establish rapport and figuring out how to move around and communicate in a new context, but they are at least initially better equipped to see culturally specific practices and beliefs with fresh eyes. Being new to a context, and attempting to fit into it in true participant-observer fashion, the outsider ethnographer often learns about norms and expectations by making mistakes, especially as he or she is resocialized into the community's or subculture's ways of interacting.

In the field of political communication, examples of insider ethnographies include Jennifer Hasty's (2005) study of Ghanaian practices of journalism and newsmaking while she worked as a journalist at several different newspapers in Accra, and David Graeber's (2009) study of North American activist movements, while engaged himself as an activist in street actions, planning meetings and informal coffee shop conversations. Examples of outsider ethnographies are more abundant. Vivid illustrations of researchers' social identities being negotiated and transformed over the course of research can be found in Alessandro Duranti's (1994) study of political discourse in a Samoan village, Lila Abu-Lughod's (2005) study of Egyptian women's responses to state television and Terence Turner's (1992, 1995, 2002) work with indigenous filmmakers in Brazil, just to name a few.

Regardless of 'insider' or 'outsider' status, good ethnographic fieldwork includes two essential techniques: (1) a close attention to context, form and the relations between them and (2) an open-ended process of questioning and discovery, one which involves a substantial amount of trial and error, as well as distilling and sifting through research data as research is underway. There is both an art and a science to taking and managing fieldnotes in ethnographic research (Bernard, 2005a; Emerson et al., 1995). In most cases, because of the open-ended nature of fieldwork, coding is built into the post-fieldwork part of an ethnographic study rather than in the research design, as is common with most quantitative studies. Research ethics are paramount in ethnographic fieldwork, and include principles of informed consent, confidentiality and risk minimization. The field of anthropology has had a particularly long history of explicit engagement with issues of research ethics and the American Anthropological Association's (1998) statement on ethics is an excellent resource for a wide range of disciplines.

Theoretical Dimensions of Ethnography

The practice of ethnography embodies several kinds of theories and assumptions about the nature of cultural meanings and cultural processes, as well as the avenues for uncovering them. Here we highlight three fundamental dimensions of ethnography as analytical lens. First, most ethnographers assume that cultures, communities and ways of life are organized systematically by implicit cultural logics. The discovery of these implicit logics (or indigenous meaning systems) and the ways in which they both motivate and create filters for human experience is one of the prime goals of ethnographic work. In this regard, the ethnographic aim of representing communities and subcultures from the 'native's point of view' entails more than documenting people's viewpoints, understood in a literal sense as their explicitly stated beliefs or opinions. Rather, 'point of view' is better understood as vantage point – or orientation – in (and to) the world, as well as the larger organizing system that lends meaning and motive to worlds in the first place.

The second dimension of ethnography as an analytical lens is directly linked to the first dimension. It involves the transformative nature of participant-observer fieldwork. More than just a method of interacting with people in their everyday contexts, participant-observation research can be a vehicle through which the ethnographer himself or herself ideally learns how to act, think and be like 'a native'. With stress on the 'participant' end of the participant-observation role, fieldworkers (particularly outsider ethnographers) become resocialized into the everyday routines, norms and expectations of the community or subculture that they are studying. To the degree that they are able to be conscious and reflective on their own resocialization, ethnographers are able to directly see and report on a culture or way of life from the inside.

In most cases, ethnography's analytical lens holds such actor-oriented (or emic or indigenous) perspectives in tension with observer-oriented (or etic or external) perspectives. This is the third sense in which a particular theoretical orientation is fundamental in ethnographic research. The implications of holding internal and external perspectives in tension is more than a matter of balancing interpretivism with positivism. Much like grounded theory approaches (Denzin and Lincoln, 2005), the idea is that theory can arise from engagement with data and the discovery process itself, rather being completely outside and prior to the particular inquiry at hand (Peterson, 2010a; Spitulnik, 1999, 2010b). One significant dimension of this concerns the investigation of the role of metaculture, understood as the recurring themes and frames that people use to account for their own cultural actions (Peterson, 2010a; Urban, 2001). While the tendency in ethnographic analysis is to stress the implicit or unconscious aspects of people's cultural frameworks, there is a growing realization that cultural frameworks (or elements of them) are often tangible and explicitly recognized by people in some form or another. Thus, 'the natives', wherever they live and wherever they produce and consume political communication – be it in newsrooms, boardrooms, public squares, living rooms, bars, public transportation or community gardens – often have very well-articulated vocabularies for commenting and theorizing about their own practices. Paying attention to these native theories and vocabularies is part of the hermeneutic work of ethnography, and it informs the development of both universal and local theories of how society and culture work.

Ethnographic Writing

Written ethnographies are particular genres of writing with their own unique textual conventions (Emerson et al., 1995; Katz, 2001, 2002; van Maanen, 1998). In many senses, the ethnographer is not only a documentarian but also a particular kind of translator – of lived realities, of unique ways of being-in-the-world and of complex behavioral milieus. Ethnographers use a host of stylistic and typographic conventions, ranging from 'realist' to 'confessional' to 'impressionist' (van Maanen, 1998). Many employ vignettes of scenes and interactions, as well as long quotations, to develop a sense of being alongside action as it is unfolding and being intimately part of a particular person's world. In this respect, ethnographic writing shares some common features with novelistic and travelogue writing. A kind of 'you are there' vivid ethnographic texture is built up through the use of the present tense and individualized third-person descriptions that include real actions and real voices. It would be misleading to conclude, however, that ethnographic writing remains exclusively at a kind of case study documentary reporting level. Thick descriptions of actual people and scenes are placed alongside of generalizations about typical types of people and events, and are used as highly condensed exemplars of cultural logics at work, ethnographic puzzles to unravel and the exceptional as well as normative dimensions of human predicaments.

ETHNOGRAPHY AND POLITICAL COMMUNICATION

The appeal of ethnography as a social science research method in recent decades has seen it expand from anthropology and sociology to many other areas of scholarly interest, including education, organizational studies, nursing and social work and marketing. Although ethnography has been employed by communications scholars since the 1960s, and is gaining vogue among some political scientists, it is almost entirely absent from professional publications in political communication. Roudakova's (2009) account of the changing agency of journalists in post-Soviet Russia is one of the very first ethnographically based research articles to be published in a political communication journal.

There are several reasons for the relative absence of ethnographic methods in political communication studies. McNabb (2004) suggest that ethnographic studies require more time than most political scientists want to commit, and do not easily lend themselves to immediate policy outcomes. In contrast, McNabb proposes that the intimate, comprehensive description associated with ethnography can provide fuller details about how institutions operate and how political decisions are made, as well as 'deep background information for long-term, strategic public policy forming' (2004: 398). Most importantly, ethnography has the capacity to produce new, unanticipated empirical information about political communication from which questions for subsequent quantitative research can be generated.

Ethnography of Political Discourse and the Micropolitics of Everyday Speech

Ethnographic studies of communication by anthropologists generally share with political communication two significant elements: first, a pragmatic orientation to the ways humans use language and other media to achieve particular ends, and second, an attention to the dimensions of power that are at play in all communicative acts. These two elements were central in the development of linguistic anthropology and sociolinguistics in the 1960s and 1970s, and in the break with mainstream linguistics from a number of academic corners during that time. As mainstream US linguistics followed the Chomskian revolution, studying language as an indicator of inner cognitive operations, anthropologists and sociolinguists, like rhetoricians, increasingly stressed the importance of investigating language in use, particularly within the full complexity of its political, economic, social and cultural contexts. Central in such work is a perspective on the power of language and communication in constituting – and not simply reflecting – social and political realities.

The break with mainstream linguistics was orchestrated in part by Dell Hymes (1974) who advised fieldworkers to forget 'language' as an object in favor of studying speech communities as they engage in particular kinds of speech events using many different kinds of codes, channels, and registers to produce particular kinds of outcomes. Hymes introduced an influential mnemonic device to help fieldworkers attend to the various components of speech events, the acronym SPEAKING which stands for: Setting (the physical situation and the cultural definition of the event); Participants (those physically present, as well as absent audiences and people on whose behalf someone else may be speaking); Ends (goals and outcomes); Acts (the sequence of activities through which the event unfolds); Keys (tone, mood or spirit of particular acts); Instrumentalities (the medium of communication, including language variety, style, register and channel (for example, voice, print, face-to-face, television or Internet); Norms and Genres. Detailed attention to these components as well as their interactions and correlations with each other allows the ethnographer to develop an account of both the cultural particularities and universalities of communication in particular contexts, as well as an account of the specific cultural knowledge about communication that is required for normative functioning in the society.

Much of the early work in this 'ethnography of speaking' pays attention to the micropolitics of everyday communicative activity. For example, Charles Frake's (1964) classic 'How to Ask for a Drink in Subanun' shows how elaborate rule-governed acts of collective drinking in a Philippine village serve as the basis for building political relationships among members of particular age cohorts. These political relationships become increasingly important as men age and take on greater responsibilities in their community; thus the precise verbal formulas they use to 'ask for a drink' have political consequences both for the specific interactional moments of collective drinking and well beyond.

A second trend in the ethnography of speaking tradition directly concerns formal political communications, structures and institutions. For example, many studies of political oratory in small-scale societies demonstrate the extent to which the speech of institutionally sanctioned political actors is shaped by genre conventions that circumscribe what can and cannot be said, and how things must be said, in public discourse (Bloch, 1975; Duranti, 1994). Successful political orators are those who can tweak these conventions just enough to create a rhetorical effect without risking their own status (Keenan, 1974). Similar processes are also examined in Warner's (1959) early study of the role of media in amplifying a political actor's rhetorical impact. Warner describes how a small US city politician's anti-city hall tactics attracted the attention of national newspapers, thus increasing his political capital. After his election as mayor, however, the tactics that brought him success as an opposition candidate were represented in the media as childish and his political capital diminished rapidly. Other studies examine everyday political conversations and the ways in which they circulate in and out of institutional settings (Passes, 2004); some have also looked at the role of media in this process (Spitulnik, 2002a).

Attention to the micropolitics of everyday speech and more specific forms of political communication are often interwoven in ethnographic studies. Peterson (2001, 2003a), for example, focuses on how the everyday verbal negotiations between reporters, multiple sources and editors produce particular types of political news accounts. In many instances, a published story produces reactions from sources that lead to further stories on the same topic. Similarly, William O. Beeman's (1986) classic ethnographic account of Iranian verbal interactions illustrates how the construction of hierarchical and in-group/out-group social relations occurs through multiple levels of language use, at micro (pronoun choice), median (theatrical performance) and macro (national political rhetoric) levels. In subsequent work, Beeman (2008) uses this analysis to argue that differences in culturally patterned modes of communication have consistently led both Iran and the USA to misinterpret, mischaracterize and misunderstand one another, with disastrous policy results on both sides.

Ethnography of Political Media

In shifting from interpersonal communication to more complexly mediated forms of political communication, the 'instrumentalities' component of Hymes' (1974) SPEAKING mnemonic deserves particular attention. It encompasses all senses of mass, alternative, old, new and small media, ranging from radio and television to fax machines, cell phone videos and YouTube (Spitulnik, 2002a). Much recent work in both media anthropology and media studies centers on how such media and technologies are integrated into everyday life and how the uses of objects intersect with the interpretation of content (Larkin, 2008; Silverstone, 1994; Spitulnik, 1999, 2002b). These accounts may prove useful to scholars in political communication seeking to 'test' the cross-cultural validity of their perspectives or imagine new possibilities for media technologies in different settings. Unexpected consequences often result from the adoption of new media, usually because of differences in communicative landscapes and sociopolitical contexts. For example, while the introduction of cassette player-recorder technologies in the 1970s transformed the music industries in many countries, including the USA and India (Manuel, 1993), in Iran it became an important political tool that could evade central control and rapidly disseminate political and religious messages from leaders abroad (Beeman, 1984; Sreberny-Mohammadi and Mohammadi, 1994).

Until recently, those ethnographic studies used by political communication scholars tended to focus on only on cultures of news production (Altheide, 1976; Bantz et al., 1980; Epstein, 1973; Fishman, 1980; Gans, 1980; Gitlin, 1983; Golding and Elliott, 1979; Schlesinger, 1978; Soloski, 1989; Tuchman, 1978; Warner, 1971). The underlying assumption of nearly all these studies is that news consumption is about the transfer of information from the newspaper to its readers and that news media can be understood as 'factories' or 'machines' that 'made', 'constructed' or 'manufactured' political messages.

While the importance of these studies in advancing our understanding of newsmaking is evident, they are insufficient for an adequate understanding of newsmaking in the 21st century for at least three reasons. First, the assumption that the professional cultures described in studies of American and British news media can be applied generally to practices of journalism worldwide is deeply problematic and may lead to a tendency to construct differences between Western and non-Western journalism practices as failures of development (Srivastava, 1998). Second, the classic ethnographies of newsmaking fail to attend to practices of news consumption, assuming relatively uncritical audiences passively consuming news. Finally, these studies, established in the 1970s and 1980s, no longer adequately describe the dramatic changes in news production and consumption that have occurred over the last two decades, including digital technologies, satellite and cable delivery systems, simultaneous production by multimedia news outlets, new corporate media players, new work practices and a growing demand for international 'multiskilled' journalists employed on short-term contracts and adopting 'flexible' work practices that allow them to 'package' different kinds of news according to a variety of news frames and formulas (Boyd-Barrett and Rantanen, 1998; Cottle, 2000; Thussu, 1999).

Fortunately, a new wave of ethnographic studies of media communication is emerging that promises to illuminate our understandings of the quotidian aspects of political communication around the world in the 21st century. Some of these studies focus specifically on newsmaking and have dramatically opened up the range of models and analytical tropes for understanding how news is created (Baisnée and Marchetti, 2006; Bird, 2000, 2010; Born, 2005; Hannerz, 2004; Machin and Niblock, 2006; Peterson, 2001, 2003a; Rao, 2010; Ståhlberg, 2002; Wolfe, 2005). This new generation of scholars continues to focus on microsocial activities, but no longer aims to discover overarching systems that 'manufacture' the news. Rather, cultures of media production are taken as dynamic sets of forces and intentions that may not be completely consistent or synchronized. Thus for example, whether looking at Palestinian journalists in the occupied territories (Bishara, 2006), Ghanaian news reporters during a period of liberalization and democratic consolidation (Hasty, 2005), East German journalists during reunification (Boyer, 2005), Russian newsmakers after the collapse of the Soviet empire (Roudakova, 2009) or even the US reporters during the contraction of the American newspaper business (Manzella, 2002), ethnographers are discovering the complex and often contradictory forces at work as journalists strive to develop authoritative systems of representation and reporting under conditions of rapid social and political change. Similarly, ethnographic work on cultures of media reception is informed by ever more complex models of what constitutes and what occurs during reception (Abu-Lughod, 2005; Askew, 2002; Bird, 2003; Dickey, 1993a; Mankekar, 1999; Postill, 2006; Spitulnik, 2002b). This point is discussed in more detail below.

FURTHER INSIGHTS FROM ETHNOGRAPHY

Just as political communication scholars once relied on ethnographies of media production for insights into how political news was shaped by institutional structures, attention to contemporary ethnographies of media can help the study of political communication by: (1) deepening and widening researchers' understanding of context as it bears on a research problem; (2) bringing into political communication the micropolitical details of everyday engagements with media production and consumption; (3) extending the media research agenda from its traditional North Atlantic heartland to remote parts of the world and (4) deepening and broadening the ways theories of political communication engage with media and globalization.

Media Textures and Entanglements

Dominated by quantitative methods and rational choice theories, contemporary works of political communication continue to be far more influenced by traditional sender-message-receiver-response models of communication than other contemporary communication and media theories. The challenge faced by political actors seeking to disseminate particular views and to persuade citizens to adopt them – 'how can we use this medium to further our political goals' – strongly influences much of the theory underpinning political communication. While this is often appropriate for particular kinds of research questions, it also might lead scholars to misrecognize the extent to which media's entanglements in peoples' everyday lives, social practices and political actions complicates models of linear causality and passive media consumption. The picture is further complexified as the technologies of media consumption are increasingly also technologies of production and distribution. Political messages circulate through complex media ecologies, undergoing many transformations beyond the intents of their initiators. Extended, open-ended fieldwork explores media practices as but one part of the broader social worlds of the people studied, and hence produces rich descriptions of the multiple ways media participate in human lives.

The Micropolitics of the Everyday

Starting with few presumptions about how media works, ethnography often reveals links between media consumption and the broader web of social relations within which people are embedded. For example, political communication studies describing the successes of film stars in Indian state electoral politics have tended to assume a direct relationship between the characters actors play and the electoral choices made by the voting public (for example, Hardgrave, 2008). Sarah Dickey's ethnographic work reveals the crucial importance of film fan clubs in mobilizing poor and working class citizens to vote for particular actors-turned-politician; many of these fan clubs already have local political capital because of charity work in the film star's name (Dickey, 1993b, 2001).

Ethnography also offers insights into the complex ways that people's imaginations engage with the political ideologies embedded in seemingly nonpolitical texts, and that subsequently give rise to micropolitical concepts of citizenship and national belonging, as when citizens use soap operas or melodramas to articulate complex relations with and against the nation-state (Abu-Lughod, 2005; Mankekar, 1999; Rofel, 1994), or, alternatively, to express feelings of alterity and diasporic longing (Naficy, 1993). Even discussions of the news of the day may turn out to be less about the content of the news, or the political frames of newsmakers, than they are about simultaneously constructing particular positions of citizenship and local social relationships (Peterson, 2010b; Spitulnik, 2010a).

De-westernizing Media Studies

As these examples suggest, ethnographic studies also broaden the research agenda in political communication from its traditional focus on North America and Western Europe to the most distant parts of the world. In doing so, ethnography can uncover unpredictable things: media continuities between pre-revolutionary and post-revolutionary regimes (Beeman, 1984); the role of unexpected media like karaoke (Adams, 1996) and landline telephones (White, 1999) in political communication; exposing the transcultural complexities of political communications usually theorized in uniformly negative ways, such as censorship (Allison, 1996; Boyer, 2005) and corruption (Gupta, 1995; Hasty, 2005) or emphasizing the importance of transnational media circuits in non-Western societies (Larkin, 2008).

While ethnography, with its time-consuming methodology is often behind the curve on changes in current events from a political science perspective, it can reduce tendencies to privilege anecdotal accounts and to assume that what is happening in the West reflects models of what will occur in the rest of the world. For example, Rao (2010) reveals the extent to which newspapers function locally as significant parts of community public spheres. In her work in Lucknow, she documents how local political actors, from temple governing bodies to civic councils, issue press releases that are subsequently run verbatim in the local editions of national newspapers. In this case, ethnography discovers an intersection of processes – national newspapers in India thriving in spite of a global downturn in the medium, alongside the use of newspapers by local leadership to construct

authority – that might otherwise be missed with alternative methods.

Theorizing Globalization and Social Change

By exposing ways in which the relationships between media and politics can differ dramatically in different societies, ethnographic studies can deepen and broaden the ways theories of political communication engage with issues of media and globalization. On the one hand, ethnographic discoveries can be integrated into theoretical models of communication, globalization and social change. On the other hand, ethnographies can serve as correctives for overenthusiastic assumptions about the revolutionary nature of new media and intercultural transformations. Finally, ethnographic studies draw attention to the fact that the 'local' in global/local relations is not always the nation-state, but often involves much smaller polities.

Ethnography offers grounded accounts of the use of media for political purposes by non-state actors including ethnic (Bai, 2007), indigenous (Bell, 2008; Giago, 1994) communitarian (Blank, 2001; Fordred, 1997; Fordred-Green, 2000) and sexuality-based (Boellstorff, 2003) groups to promote local political agendas at regional, national and even global levels. Terence Turner (1992, 1995, 2002) in an exemplary series of studies, shows how the Kayapo people of the Amazonian rainforest use video technologies to document their ongoing relations and confrontations with the Brazilian government, as well as to record many traditional ceremonies and facilitate communication between villages. Even these latter uses are deeply political, Turner notes, since they serve to assert Kayapo identity in the face of institutions that might seek to abridge Kayapo sovereignty. Moreover, the act of adopting video technologies is itself a doubly political act: first, it emphasizes that Kayapo decisions to maintain traditional political, social and economic structures are matters of choice, not ignorance or incapacity, and second, it creates possibilities for Kayapo people to disseminate their messages worldwide through documentary video, and to thus gain allies in their negotiations with the Brazilian state.

New media – media in which the wall between consumers and producers is breached – have become symbols of the effects of globalization. Ethnography illuminates the workings of these new media forms in everyday life while still attending to their place in webs of power relations. At its best, ethnography can undermine both the cheerleading theories that assume evidence of the adoption of new media technologies means successful integration into a global network organized by egalitarian principles (Wellman, 2001, 2002) and the pessimists who bemoan the impact of alien (and alienating) media technologies on the shared values of local communities (Gurstein et al., 2003; Weiner, 1997). Postill's (2011) extensive fieldwork in the highly networked Indonesian suburb Subang Jaya provides a prime example of how new media technologies are being used for very local, and not global, concerns. The Subang Jaya suburb is structured by numerous social formations, including peer groups, associations, gangs, clans, sects, mosques, families, action committees, mailing lists, online forums and twitter lists. Postill argues that users of new media technologies endeavor to create a greater sense of community among these disparate co-residents and their social divisions, in order to better address such concerns as crime, morality and local governance, and *not* to reach out to wider national or transnational networks.

CONCLUSION

The applications of ethnography in the study of political communication are limitless. Ethnography is relevant for the study of political communication production, circulation and reception, as well as for the study of the micro and macro processes of both everyday and official political discourse production, circulation and reception. A growing literature in media anthropology as well as more long-standing traditions in media studies and the ethnography of speaking provide a rich set of examples of how to frame ethnographic questions, how to conduct ethnographies of political communication and political media and how culture and context matter in accounts of political communication. In conclusion, we wish to emphasize that ethnography is more than a fieldwork method or a perspective that places emphasis on people's voices and viewpoints. It is a way of approaching processes and practices in their fullest possible contexts, with an eye toward (1) the complex interconnections across phenomena, (2) the systems of meaning that motivate and result from human action and (3) the ways that communication itself constitutes meanings and relationships. Ethnography might be considered a theory-method hybrid, since these dimensions are typically engaged in a dialectical way during a research project, with an open-ended methodology shaping the researcher's analytical lens, and vice versa. For a variety of reasons, it may continue to be the case that ethnography remains more or less of an

outlier within political communication circles, possibly being viewed as 'unscientific' and 'lacking rigor' in an era where quantitative research on political communication accrues higher value (Spitulnik, 2010b). At the same time, we have endeavored to carve out a new path for ethnography in the study of political communication, one where ethnography is relevant not only for the full-scale ethnographer and where dimensions of ethnographic theory and practice can productively be adopted within mixed-methods projects.

REFERENCES

Abu-Lughod, L. (2005) *Dramas of Nationhood: The Politics of Television in Egypt.* Chicago, IL: University of Chicago Press.

Adams, V. (1996) 'Karaoke as Modern Lhasa, Tibet: Western Encounters with Cultural Politics', *Cultural Anthropology*, 11(4): 510–46.

Allison, A. (1996) *Permitted and Prohibited Desires: Mothers, Comics and Censorship in Japan.* Boulder, CO: Westview Press.

Altheide, D. L. (1976) *Creating Reality.* Beverly Hills, CA: Sage.

American Anthropological Association (1998) 'Code of Ethics of the American Anthropological Association', http://www.aaanet.org/committees/ethics/ethcode.htm (accessed 2 December 2011).

Ang, I. (1991) 'Ethnography and Radical Contextualism in Audience Studies', in L. Grossberg, J. Hay and E. Wartella (eds.), *The Audience and Its Landscape.* Boulder, CO: Westview. pp. 247–62.

Askew, K. M. (2002) *Performing the Nation: Swahili Musical Performance and the Production of Tanzanian National Culture.* Chicago, IL: University of Chicago Press.

Askew, K. M. and Wilk, R. R. (eds.) (2002) *The Anthropology of Media: A Reader.* Malden, MA and Oxford: Blackwell.

Bai, Z. (2007) 'The Camera in "Native" Hands: The Making of Ethnicity in a Temple Video', *The Asia Pacific Journal of Anthropology*, 8(4): 309–19.

Baisnée, O. and Marchetti, D. (2006) 'The Economy of Just-in-Time Television Newscasting: Journalistic Production and Professional Excellence at Euronews', *Ethnography*, 7(1): 99–123.

Bantz, C. R., McCorkle, S. and Baade, R. C. (1980) 'The News Factory', *Communication Research*, 7(1): 45–68.

Beeman, W. O. (1984) 'The Cultural Role of the Media in Iran', in A. Arno and W. Dissanayake (eds.), *The News Media in National and International Conflict.* Boulder, CO: Westview. pp. 147–64.

Beeman, W. O. (1986) *Language, Status and Power in Iran.* Bloomington, IN: University of Indiana Press.

Beeman, W. O. (2008) *The Great Satan vs. the Mad Mullahs: How the United States and Iran Demonize Each Other.* Chicago, IL: University of Chicago Press.

Bell, W. (2008) *A Remote Possibility: The Battle for Imparja Television.* Alice Springs: IAD Press.

Bernard, H. R. (ed.) (1998) *Handbook of Methods in Cultural Anthropology*. Lanham, MD: AltaMira Press.

Bernard, H. R. (2005a) 'Field Notes: How to Take Them, Code Them, Manage Them', in H. R. Bernard (ed.), *Research Methods in Anthropology: Qualitative and Quantitative Approaches*. 4th edn. Lanham, MD: AltaMira Press. pp. 387–412.

Bernard, H. R. (ed.) (2005b) *Research Methods in Anthropology: Qualitative and Quantitative Approaches*. 4th edn. Lanham, MD: AltaMira Press.

Bird, S. E. (2000) 'Facing the Distracted Audience: Journalism and Cultural Context', *Journalism: Theory, Practice and Criticism*, 1(1): 29–33.

Bird, S. E. (2003) *The Audience in Everyday Life: Living in a Media World*. New York: Routledge.

Bird, S. E. (ed.) (2010) *The Anthropology of News and Journalism: Global Perspectives*. Bloomington, IN: Indiana University Press.

Bishara, A. (2006) 'Local Hands, International News: Palestinian Journalists and the International Media', *Ethnography*, 7(1): 19–46

Blank, J. (2001) *Mullahs on the Mainframe: Islam and Modernity Among the Daudi Bohras*. Chicago, IL: University of Chicago Press.

Bloch, M. (ed.) (1975) *Political Oratory in Traditional Societies*. London: Academic Press.

Boas, F. (1989) *A Franz Boas Reader: The Shaping of American Anthropology, 1883–1911*. G. W. Stocking Jr (ed.). Chicago, IL: University of Chicago Press.

Boellstorff, T. (2003) 'Dubbing Culture: Indonesian Gay and Lesbi Subjectivities and Ethnography in an Already Globalized World', *American Ethnologist*, 30(2): 225–42.

Born, G. (2005) *Uncertain Vision: Birt, Dyke and the Reinvention of the BBC*. London: Vintage.

Boyd-Barrett, O. and Rantanen, T. (1998) *The Globalization of News*. London: Sage.

Boyer, D. C. (2005) *Spirit and System: Media, Intellectuals, and the Dialectic in Modern German Culture*. Chicago, IL: University of Chicago Press.

Cottle, S. (2000) 'New(s) Times: Toward a "Second Wave" of News Ethnography', *Communications*, 25(1): 19–42.

Denzin, N. K. and Lincoln, Y. S. (eds.) (2005) *The SAGE Handbook of Qualitative Research*. 3rd edn. London: Sage.

Dickey, S. (1993a) *Cinema and the Urban Poor in South India*. Cambridge: Cambridge University Press.

Dickey, S. (1993b) 'Politics of Adulation: Cinema and the Production of Politicians in South India', *Journal of Asian Studies*, 52(2): 340–72.

Dickey, S. (2001) 'Opposing Faces: Film Star, Fan Clubs and the Construction of Class Identities in South India', in R. Dwyer and C. Pinney (eds.), *Pleasure and the Nation: The History, Politics and Consumption of Popular Culture in India*. New Delhi: Oxford University Press. pp. 212–46.

Duranti, A. (1994) *From Grammar to Politics: Linguistic Anthropology in a Western Samoan Village*. Berkeley and Los Angeles: Berkeley, CA: University of California Press.

Emerson, R. M., Fretz, R. I. and Shaw, L. L. (1995) *Writing Ethnographic Fieldnotes*. Chicago, IL: University of Chicago Press.

Epstein, E. J. (1973) *News from Nowhere: Television and the News*. New York: Random House.

Fairclough, N. (2009) *Media Discourse*. London: Bloomsbury.

Fishman, M. (1980) *Manufacturing the News*. Austin, TX: University of Texas Press.

Fordred, L. (1997) 'Natural Cockroaches Fly: Khaba Mkhize and Communitarian Journalism in KwaZulu-Natal, South Africa', in G. E. Marcus (ed.), *Cultural Producers in Perilous States: Editing Events, Documenting Change*. Chicago, IL: University of Chicago Press. pp. 23–54.

Fordred-Green, L. (2000) 'Tokoloshe Tales: Reflections on the Cultural Politics of Journalism in South Africa', *Current Anthropology*, 41(5): 701–12.

Frake, C. (1964) 'How to Ask for a Drink in Subanun', *American Anthropologist*, 66(6): 127–30.

Gans, H. (1980) *Deciding What's News*. New York: Vintage.

Geertz, C. (1973) *The Interpretation of Cultures*. New York: Basic Books.

Giago, T. N. K. (1994) 'Native Journalists: Setting the Record Straight on Media Stereotypes', *Cultural Survival Quarterly*, 17(4): 21–23.

Ginsburg, F. D., Abu-Lughod, L. and Larkin, B. (eds.) (2002) *Media Worlds: Anthropology on New Terrain*. Berkeley, CA: University of California Press.

Gitlin, T. (1983) *Inside Prime Time*. New York: Pantheon.

Goffman, E. (1981) *Forms of Talk*. Philadelphia, PA: University of Pennsylvania Press.

Golding, P. and Elliott, P. R. C. (1979) *Making the News*. London: Longman.

Graeber, D. (2009) *Direct Action: An Ethnography*. Oakland, CA: AK Press.

Gupta, A. (1995) 'Blurred Boundaries: The Discourse of Corruption, the Culture of Politics and the Imagined State', *American Ethnologist*, 22(2): 375–402.

Gurstein, M., Menou, M. J. and Stafeev, S. (eds.) (2003) *Community Networking and Community Informatics*. St. Petersburg: Centre of Community Networking and Information Policy Studies.

Hannerz, U. (2003) 'Being There and There and There! Reflections on Multi-Sited Ethnography', *Ethnography*, 4(2): 201–16.

Hannerz, U. (2004) *Foreign News: Exploring the World of Foreign Correspondents*. Chicago, IL: University of Chicago Press.

Hardgrave, R. L., Jr. (2008) 'Politics and the Film in Tamil Nadu', in S. Velayutham (ed.), *Tamil Cinema: The Cultural Politics of India's Other Film Industry*. London: Routledge. pp. 59–76.

Hasty, J. (2005) *The Press and Political Culture in Ghana*. Bloomington, IN: Indiana University Press.

Hymes, D. (1974) *Foundations in Sociolinguistics: An Ethnographic Approach*. Philadelphia, PA: University of Pennsylvania Press.

Janesick, V. J. (2000) 'The Choreography of Qualitative Research Design', in N. K. Denzin and Y. S. Lincoln (eds.), *Handbook of Qualitative Research*. 2nd edn. Thousand Oaks, CA: Sage. pp. 379–99.

Katz, J. (2001) 'From How to Why: On Luminous Description and Causal Inference in Ethnography, Part 1', *Ethnography*, 2(4): 443–74.

Katz, J. (2002) 'From How to Why: On Luminous Description and Causal Inference in Ethnography, Part 2', *Ethnography*, 3(1): 63–90.

Keenan, E. (1974) 'Norm-Makers, Norm-Breakers: Uses of Speech by Men and Women in Malagasy Society', in R. Bauman and J. Sherzer (eds.), *Explorations in the Ethnography of Speaking*. Cambridge: Cambridge University Press. pp. 125–43.

Kosnick, K. (2007) *Migrant Media: Turkish Broadcasting and Multicultural Politics in Berlin*. Bloomington, IN: Indiana University Press.

Larkin, B. (2008) *Signal and Noise: Media, Infrastructure, and Urban Culture in Nigeria*. Durham, NC: Duke University Press.

Lindquist, J. (2002) *A Place to Stand: Politics and Persuasion in a Working-Class Bar*. Oxford: Oxford University Press.

Machin, D. (2002) *Ethnographic Research for Media Studies*. New York: Arnold; Oxford University Press.

Machin, D. and Niblock, S. (2006) *News Production: Theory and Practice*. New York and London: Routledge.

Malinowski, B. (1922/1961) *Argonauts of the Western Pacific*. New York: E.P. Dutton.

Mankekar, P. (1999) *Screening Culture, Viewing Politics: An Ethnography of Television, Womanhood, and Nation in Postcolonial India*. Durham, NC: Duke University Press.

Manuel, P. L. (1993) *Cassette Culture: Popular Music and Technology in North India*. Chicago, IL: University of Chicago Press.

Manzella, J. C. (2002) *The Struggle to Revitalize American Newspapers*. Lewiston, NY: Edward Mellen Press.

Marcus, G. E. (1995) 'Ethnography in/of the World System: The Emergence of Multi-Sited Ethnography', *Annual Review of Anthropology*, 24(1): 95–117.

McNabb, D. E. (2004) *Research Methods for Political Science: Quantitative and Qualitative Methods*. Armonk, NY: M.E. Sharpe.

Morley, D. (1980) *The Nationwide Audience: Structure and Decoding*. British Film Institute Television Monograph No. 11. London: British Film Institute.

Naficy, H. (1993) *The Making of Exile Cultures: Iranian Television in Los Angeles*. Minneapolis, MN: University of Minnesota Press.

Park, R. E. and Burgess, E. (1921) *Introduction to the Science of Sociology*. Chicago, IL: University of Chicago Press.

Passes, A. (2004) 'The Place of Politics: Powerful Speech and Women Speakers in Everyday Pa'ikwene (Palikur) Life', *Journal of the Royal Anthropological Institute*, 10(1): 1–18.

Pedelty, M. (1995) *War Stories: The Culture of Foreign Correspondents*. New York: Routledge.

Peterson, M. A. (2001) 'Getting to the Story: Off-the-Record Discourse and Interpretive Practice in American Journalism', *Anthropological Quarterly*, 74(4): 201–11.

Peterson, M. A. (2003a) 'American Warriors Speaking American: The Metapragmatics of Performance in the Nation State', in M N. Dedaic and D. N. Nelson (eds.), *At War with Words*. Berlin: Walter de Gruyter. pp. 421–48.

Peterson, M. A. (2003b) *Anthropology and Mass Communication: Media and Myth in the New Millennium*. New York: Berghahn Books.

Peterson, M. A. (2010a) 'But it is My Habit to Read The Times: Metaculture and Practice in the Reading of Indian Newspapers', in B. Bräuchler and J. Postill (eds.), *Theorizing Media and Practice*. New York: Berghahn. pp. 127–145.

Peterson, M. A. (2010b) 'Getting the News in New Delhi', in S. E. Bird (ed.), *The Anthropology of News and Journalism: Global Perspectives*. Bloomington, IN: Indiana University Press. pp. 267–88.

Postill, J. (2006) *Media and Nation Building: How the Iban Became Malaysian*. New York: Berghahn Books.

Postill, J. (2011) *Localizing the Internet: An Anthropological Account*. New York: Berghahn Books.

Powdermaker, H. (1950) *Hollywood, the Dream Factory*. Boston, MA: Little, Brown, and Co.

Radway, J. (1988) 'Reception Study: Ethnography and the Problems of Dispersed Audiences and Nomadic Subjects', *Cultural Studies*, 2(3): 359–76.

Rao, U. (2010) *News as Culture: Journalistic Practices and the Remaking of Indian Leadership Traditions*. Oxford: Berghahn Books.

Rofel, L. B. (1994) 'Yearnings: Televised Love and Melodramatic Politics in Contemporary China', *American Ethnologist*, 21(4): 700–22.

Rotherbuhler, E. W. and Coman, M. (eds.) (2005) *Media Anthropology*. Thousand Oaks, CA: Sage.

Roudakova, N. (2009) 'Journalism as 'Prostitution': Understanding Russia's Reactions to Anna Politkovskaya's Murder', *Political Communication*, 26(4): 412–29.

Rutherford, D. (2008) 'Why Papua Wants Freedom: The Third Person in Contemporary Nationalism', *Public Culture*, 20(2): 345–73.

Schlesinger, P. (1978) *Putting 'Reality' Together*. London: Methuen.

Schroder, K. C. and Phillips, L. (2007) 'Complexifying Media Power: a Study of the Interplay Between Media and Audience Discourses on Politics', *Media Culture Society*, 29(6): 890–915.

Silverstone, R. (1994) *Consuming Technologies*. London: Routledge.

Soloski, J. (1989) 'News Reporting and Professionalism: Some Constraints on the Reporting of News', *Media, Culture and Society*, 11(2): 207–28.

Spitulnik, D. (1993) 'Anthropology and Mass Media', *Annual Review of Anthropology*, 22(1): 293–315.

Spitulnik, D. (1998) 'Mediating Unity and Diversity: The Production of Language Ideologies in Zambian Broadcasting', in B. Schieffelin, K. Woolard and P. Kroskrity (eds.), *Language Ideologies: Practice and Theory*. Oxford: Oxford University Press. pp. 163–88.

Spitulnik, D. (1999) 'Mediated Modernities: Encounters with the Electronic in Zambia', *Visual Anthropology Review*, 14(2): 63–84.

Spitulnik, D. (2002a) 'Alternative Small Media and Communicative Spaces', in G. Hyden, M. Leslie and

F. F. Ogundimu (eds.), *Media and Democracy in Africa*. New Brunswick, NJ: Transaction. pp. 177–205.

Spitulnik, D. (2002b) 'Mobile Machines and Fluid Audiences: Rethinking Reception Through Zambian Radio Culture', in F. D. Ginsburg, et al. (eds.), *Media Worlds: Anthropology on New Terrain*. Berkeley, CA: University of California Press. pp. 337–54.

Spitulnik, D. (2010a) 'Personal News and the Price of Public Service: An Ethnographic Window into the Dynamics of Production and Reception in Zambian State Radio', in S. E. Bird (ed.), *The Anthropology of News and Journalism: Global Perspectives*. Bloomington, IN: Indiana University Press. pp. 182–98.

Spitulnik, D. (2010b) 'Thick Context, Deep Epistemology: A Meditation on Wide-Angle Lenses on Media, Knowledge Production, and the Concept of Culture', in B. Bräuchler and J. Postill (eds.), *Theorising Media and Practice*. New York and Oxford: Berghahn Books. pp. 105–26.

Sreberny-Mohammadi, A. and Mohammadi, A. (1994) *Small Media, Big Revolution: Communication, Change, and the Iranian Revolution*. Minneapolis, MN: University of Minnesota.

Srivastava, S. (1998) *Constructing Postcolonial India: National Character and the Doon School*. London: Routledge.

Ståhlberg, P. (2002) *Lucknow Daily: How a Hindi Newspaper Constructs Society*. Stockholm: Almqvist and Wiksell.

Thussu, D. K. (1999) 'Privatizing the Airwaves: The Impact of Globalization on Broadcasting in India', *Media, Culture & Society*, 21(1): 125–31.

Tuchman, G. (1978) *Making News: A Study in the Social Construction of Reality*. New York: Free Press.

Turner, T. (1992) 'Defiant Images: The Kayapo Appropriation of Video', *Anthropology Today*, 8(6): 5–16.

Turner, T. (1995) 'Representation, Collaboration and Mediation in Contemporary Ethnographic and Indigenous Media', *Visual Anthropology Review*, 11(2): 102–6.

Turner, T. (2002) 'Representation, Politics, and Cultural Imagination in Indigenous Video: General Points and Kayapo Examples', in F. D. Ginsburg, L. Abu-Lughod and B. Larkin (eds.), *Media Worlds: Anthropology on New Terrain*. Berkeley, CA: University of California Press. pp. 75–89.

Urban, G. (2001) *Metaculture: How Culture Moves through the World*. Minneapolis, MN: University of Minnesota Press.

Van Hout, T. and Jacobs, G. (2008) 'News Production Theory and Practice: Fieldwork Notes on Power, Interaction and Agency', *Pragmatics*, 18(1): 59–84.

van Maanen, J. (1988) *Tales of the Field: On Writing Ethnography*. Chicago, IL: University of Chicago Press.

Warner, M. (1971) 'Organisational Context and Control of Policy in the Television Newsroom: A Participant Observation Study', *British Journal of Sociology*, 22(3): 283–94.

Warner, W. L. (1941) *The Social Life of a Modern Community*. New Haven, CT: Yale University Press.

Warner, W. L. (1959) *The Living and the Dead: A Study of the Symbolic Life of Americans*. New Haven, CT: Yale University Press.

Weiner, J. (1997) 'Televisualist Anthropology: Representation, Aesthetics, Politics', *Current Anthropology*, 38(2): 197–235.

Wellman, B. (2001) 'Physical Place and Cyber Place: The Rise of Networked Individualism', *International Journal of Urban and Regional Research*, 25(2): 227–52.

Wellman, B. (2002) 'Little Boxes, Globalization and Networked Individualism', in M. Tanabe, P. Van den Besselaar and T. Ishida (eds.), *Digital Cities II: Computational and Sociological Approaches*. Berlin: Springer. pp. 10–25.

White, J. (1999) 'Amplifying Trust: Community and Communication in Turkey', in D. Eickelman and J. Anderson (eds.), *New Media in the Muslim World: The Emerging Public Sphere*. Bloomington, IN: Indiana University Press. pp. 162–79.

Whyte, W. F. (1943) *Street Corner Society: The Social Structure of an Italian Slum*. Chicago, IL: University of Chicago Press.

Wolfe, T. C. (2005) *Governing Soviet Journalism: The Press and the Socialist Person after Stalin*. Bloomington, IN: Indiana University Press.

22

Political Visions: Visual Studies in Political Communication

Kevin G. Barnhurst and Kelly Quinn

Political communication and visual studies may seem not to intersect, given their independent growth and institutional separation in departments of art and government. But as multimedia communication via television, film and the Internet spread, scholars should pay more attention to the intersection. A substantial body of work has grown around the visual in political communication scholarship, and a smaller body has emerged around the political in visual communication studies as well. But political communication studies tend to tackle visual topics without connecting with visual theory, and, with only a few exceptions, visual studies of icons, images, visual rhetoric and the like merely allude to the political impact on policymakers and the public. Studies that concentrate on the construction of identity and representation from the perspectives of cultural studies and critical theory rarely go beyond theory to address political action. Three previous literature reviews give a broad picture of the state of visual political studies.

A critique of the state of political communication notes that scholars have attended amply to 'creating and maintaining high quality, democratic governance' (Graber and Smith, 2005: 481), while other aspects have received meager attention. The research in flagship political and communication scholarly journals, which the study tracked from 2000 to 2003, followed three main trends: comparing the different media that transmit political messages and images, assessing political learning through mass media among the electorate, and critiquing media portrayals of politically disadvantaged groups. Despite advancing understanding of how humans process information, the research uses a narrow range of methods and little audiovisual coding, limiting scholarly insight into the visual side. Most citizens receive political information through audiovisual communication over the air, cable or computer networks, and so political communication should attend to visual elements more.

Michael Griffin's (2001) earlier essay on the state of visual communication studies examines lens-based media – photography, film and television – and identifies two trajectories, one realist and the other formative. Instead of looking directly at politics, visual studies research concentrates on how either media producers or viewing audiences use and interpret images. Visual realism has led to concepts of composition and juxtaposition, such as *mise en scène* (constructing the image), montage (sequencing images through editorial processes), visual syntax and narrative, which apply linguistic, semiotic and psychological theories. The formative trajectory has contributed to concepts of representation, interpretation and attribution, which take images as a whole, as patterned rhetorical expression or semantic capabilities within a socio-cultural context. Even where images intersect with words, politics is not necessarily the focus of research. Word-and-image studies instead pursue iconology, the subject-spectator or specific forms of visual media. Politics is implicit in the social worlds where interdependent words and images emerge. But even visual concepts that have political overtones, such as social distinction, cultural identity, collective memory, historical mythology and cultures of vision, place emphasis on how images express a cultural vision. Like his colleagues in political communication, Griffin decries the lack of sustained attention to the visual. Most political research that uses the term *image*, for example, refers to how the public interprets candidates conceptually rather than to visual aspects of their presentation.

A later survey uses a rhetoric–pragmatic–semantic rubric to classify visual research (Barnhurst et al., 2004). Studies in visual rhetoric, which dominate mass media and popular culture research, consider images persuasive occasions and seek to expose their ideological underpinnings. Visual pragmatics research considers vision a practice and examines the processes and qualities emerging from image production and the sense making that occurs upon reception. And visual semantics takes the visual as text, concentrating on the internal structures of images: the grammar, syntax or logic organizing their meaning. In areas such as the representation of gender, ethnicity and national identity; cultural memory; and media practice, visual research does intersect with political communication, although not through explicit reference to its theories. The work in visual rhetoric, for instance, instead suggests ways that visual imagery influences ideas, ways of living and pictures of the world, particularly for marginal populations. Here politics remains implicit, without referring to political action.

The surveys of visual and political literature have a common theme, that scholars need more knowledge of their counterparts' theories, concepts, methods and results. But the surveys treat the crossroads of visuals and politics in passing, and so this chapter updates the state of the literature at the intersection of visuals and politics. By showing the emerging trends, we bring together scholars' efforts where two areas overlap and list a few prospects for exploring a dynamic and emergent inter-field nexus.

Reviewing across Disciplines

We began our review of the literature by examining the main journals in three disciplines: communication, political science and visual studies. Following the lead of previous reviews, we also inspected publications from related disciplines including anthropology, sociology and technical communication, each of which ventures into visuals, politics or both. Sociology, for example, has organized scholarly groups and journals in political sociology, sociology of culture and visual sociology, all with relevant work.

Searches of electronic databases provided the bulk of the literature, but we also searched library catalogs. Analyzing citations in the initial set of articles yielded more sources. A team of graduate student volunteers conducted the searches and analyses over a six-month period, generating a body of 281 articles, books and book chapters on visual and political communication topics.

Visual communication studies reached maturity in the past two decades, with a recent surge of literature (Barnhurst et al., 2004). For political research, we found the visual studies proliferated after 2001, but ranged back to 1956. Political communication matured earlier, but studies related to visuals grew during and ranged across the same periods.

The analysis began by identifying political and visual communication keywords. For political communication, keywords came from lists the Political Communication Division of the International Communication Association (ICA) uses to classify annual conference paper submissions and match papers to reviewer expertise, which the Political Communication Section of the American Political Science Association (APSA) has also used for planning pre-conferences. For visual communication, keywords came from a previous study (Barnhurst et al., 2004), from entry listings in relevant areas of the 2008 Blackwell *International Encyclopedia of Communication,* and from correspondence with the ICA Visual Communication Studies Division.

For each article, we assembled the full citation and abstract into a web-based bibliographic management application (www.CiteULike.org), a tool for attaching tags to articles. The site allowed imports from other web and stand-alone bibliographic applications, accommodated multiple users to collaborate on entries, and flowed the material into word processors for writing. It also permitted analysis of the tag categories in the form of a tag cloud, a visual representation of the prominence of the tags.

Each entry in the database also contained a full abstract and, when available, an attached electronic copy of the entire article. Volunteers examined each entry and then applied the relevant tags. Tags included classifications for academic discipline, for theoretical concepts and key authors cited, for the research methods employed, for the media examined, for the topics addressed and for the geographic areas included in each study. Volunteers met biweekly with the investigators to discuss unclear cases and refine definitions for the tags by consensus. Finally, one of the investigators reviewed all entries and classifying tags for consistency, consulting with the other investigator to reach consensus on cases remaining in doubt.

The result assembled the studies relevant to communication, political science and visual studies and combined bibliographical data with a new-media visualization technique. Unlike traditional content coding, tagging captures multiple fields, theories, techniques, outlets, issues and locations a single scholarly work contains and makes them visible. The publication data also revealed the trends and patterns in the research we used to discover emerging areas of inquiry.

VISUALIZING TAG CLOUDS

An important initial outcome of tagging was the discovery, as expected (Barnhurst et al., 2004), of works that appeared to be relevant during bibliographic searches but turned out to have only a nominal connection to the intersection of political and visual studies. An article from political science, might use the word like *seeing* in the title but contain nothing visual of substance. Or a visual studies article might take on a political topic without doing work on politics in theory or practice. After removing the 86 nominal studies (30.6%), we generated tag clouds for the remaining 195 works of visual-political substance. The nominal studies point to a broad interest but reiterate the need for political scholars to become informed about the visual and vice versa. With the substantial works only, each tag cloud – an alphabetical array of tags with the type size varying according how often the tag repeats (and dropping the infrequent tags) – visually represents disciplines, concepts, theorists and authors cited, objects of study, research topics and geographic purview.

Discipline tags indicate what organized areas of research (those with journals, meetings and the like; see Barnhurst et al. [2004]) turned up in the literature. The tag cloud shows about a dozen major fields (Figure 22.1), communication areas being the most important (with 212 of 352 tags for 9 of 27 areas). Other social sciences played a

anthropology art_history cultural_studies
ethology filmstudies gender_studies
history journalism
political_communication
political_science political_sociology popular_culture
rhetoric sociology visual_anthropology
visual_communication
visual_culture

case_study comparative_study concept_explanation
content_analysis
critical/cultural_reading
discourse_analysis document_analysis ethnography
experiment interviews questionnaire survey
visual_analysis

Figure 22.1   Main fields producing political-visual research and the methods employed

smaller role (with 88 tags for 8 areas), and the arts and humanities an even smaller one (with 48 tags for 8 areas). Math and science areas were the least prominent. The visual areas of research (with 137 tags in 7 areas) – including art history (8 tags), film studies (7 tags) and the like – were more diverse, and the political areas more concentrated and productive (with 111 tags in 3 areas). Political (96 tags) and visual (67) communication were the most prominent. Political communication, as a crossover area, could as easily have counted as part of political science (12 tags). In other disciplines outside communication, the active visual studies organizations of anthropologists and sociologists accounted for more activity (14 tags apiece, including their parent disciplines). Visual culture (44 tags), a subfield of art history, takes critical-cultural approaches, unlike journalism (34 tags), a subfield of communication that tends to the social scientific. History (18 tags), gender studies (9 tags) and popular culture and rhetoric (4 tags apiece) also hosted some visual-political work.

The research methods ranged across the spectrum of social studies. The qualitative and humanistic approaches were common and diverse (with 133 of 233 tags in 15 of 23 techniques), and the quantitative social science approaches more focused (with 100 tags in 7 techniques), and of course some studies were multi-method. The bibliography included some theoretical essays and explanations of concepts. Methods tended to bridge disciplines and apply equally well to political and visual studies (but purely visual techniques did turn up, with 32 tags in 2 techniques).

To the work published within the disciplines, we applied conceptual tags (899 tags for 199 concepts), which group into four main areas: social sciences (409 for 89), visual studies (359 for 73), critical-cultural studies (324 for 68) and communication studies (230 for 46). The groups represent general approaches and orientations to objects of study but do share some concept tags. Taking the overlaps into consideration, we found that social science shared concepts extensively with the other perspectives, especially cultural studies (which uses, for instance, race and gender prominently) and communication (which shares theories such as framing). Less than one-third of social science concepts were unique (31.5% not shared). Visual studies had the fewest overlapping concepts (63.0% unique), but was not entirely self-sufficient: some tags from social science (such as political symbolism and visual stimuli) were more important than the largest tags exclusive to visual studies (such as iconology). Visual studies tags were also more diffuse, with a wider range of tags having fewer instances in the literature (30.3% of the tags unique to visual studies had a single

appearance in the literature). Critical-cultural studies and communication were somewhat tighter theoretically, with fewer singletons, and social science concepts were the most concentrated, with research clustering on fewer main concepts. Except for *form* (Barnhurst and Nerone, 2001), no other visual studies concepts were native to communication studies. The same was true for critical/cultural concepts, but communication did generate some social science concepts we found.

The most prominent theorists were Roland Barthes and Erving Goffman, followed by Walter Benjamin and Michel Foucault. Kenneth Burke, Karl Marx and Marshall McLuhan round out the list of main theorists (very senior or deceased authors cited for theory in the literature). We identified four groups of other theorists, from social science (such as Emile Durkheim and Benedict Anderson), critical-cultural theory (such as Jean Baudrillard, Jürgen Habermas, Gilles Deleuze, Jacques Derrida and Antonio Gramsci), philosophy (such as Hannah Arendt, Susan Sontag, Martin Heidegger and Charles Sanders Peirce), visual theory (such as John Berger and Umberto Eco) and communication (such as Walter Lippmann and James W. Carey). Social science theorists were the largest group (13 of 39 theorists with 35 of 106 tags), but critical-cultural theory was only somewhat smaller (10 theorists with 32 tags). Philosophers (7 with 13) and visual theorists (5 with 19) were the smallest groups. Critical-cultural theory and visual studies theory had more tags concentrated on fewer theorists, contrary to the other two groups. Among other visual and political authors currently active, citations of Doris Graber, of Gunther Kress and Theo van Leeuwen, and of Paul Messaris were notable, as well as those of John Fiske, Kathleen Hall Jamieson and W. J. T. Mitchell.

The topics of the research ranged across politics, history, social issues and media practices. Election campaigns, public opinion, candidates, presidents and policies account for the largest number of tags (9 of 72 total topics with 66 of 180 total tags), highly concentrated on elections (31 tags), which makes sense given the preponderance of studies from political communication. In the period we examined, other research not surprisingly focused broadly on war, terrorism and violence, along with crises and disasters (17 topics with 45 tags). A wide range of other political issues and movements (20 topics with 37 tags), including -isms such as nationalism, looked at groups like labor and consumers, and at minorities, especially African Americans and the visual politics of race, part of another theme: identity and representation. Of the research on media forms and practices (17 topics with 20 tags), the main theme was truth and authenticity, examined

agenda_setting appearance attitude_formation bias
candidate_image civic_engagement
collective_memory colonialism critical_theory
cultural_politics cultural_values decontextualization democracy
diaspora difference dissent emotional_effects
emotions emotive_injury encoding-decoding framing
gaze gender gestalt globalization hegemony
iconology icons
identity/representation ideology
image_juxtaposition image-text intercultural_comm
media_ecology media_effects media_events
media_logic metonymy mise-en-scene mnemony
multimodality myth perception/cognition
political_bias political_symbols political_identity
political_imagery power priming production-consumption
propaganda psychological_stimuli
public_sphere race racism schema
semiotics sequencing simulacra
social_responsibility spectacle symbolic_politics
technological_distortion the_other video-style violence
visual_cues visual_elements visual_framing
visual_grammar visual_literacy
visual_manipulation visual_metaphors
visual_narrative visual_representation
visual_rhetoric visual_structure visual_syntax
voter_behavior voter_perceptions

Figure 22.2   Main concepts political-visual research employed

through images from ad-watch journalism, censorship and the like. Other studies continued to focus on earlier periods (9 topics with 12 tags), especially imagery from the mid-20th century depression era, but also recent watershed events such as post-communism.

The research topics intersected with disciplinary concepts. War and forms of violence, for example, aligned with psychological concepts such as risk perception and visual studies concepts such as ocular aggression (24 categories with 56 tags). Topics related to truth and reality aligned with concepts such as propaganda and forms of bias (25 with 92). The largest crossover occurred between the representation and identity topics and concepts such as the other, racial cueing,

anderson arendt barnhurst barthes baudrillard
benjamin burke castells edelman fiske foucault
goffman graber griffin habermas iyengar
jamieson kress marx r_d_masters mcluhan
messaris meyrowitz mirzoeff mitchell paivio
perlmutter sontag tufte van_leeuwen

abu_ghraib ad-watch_journalism candidates
election_campaigns ethics gulf_war
international_relations iraq_war nationalism new_deal
politics_of_race presidents public_opinion
public_policy social_movements terroism war

art_history body caricature/cartooning
documentary_photography facial_expression film
illustrations magazines new_media
newspapers nonverbal_cues paintings
photography political_advertising
poster_art print_photos satire television_news
television/video websites

Figure 22.3   Main authors cited, topics and objects of study in political-visual research

identification and the like (21 with 137). A smaller but interesting intersection occurred for emotion (11 categories with 28 tags), which seemed to draw attention across disciplines.

The objects of study included media, persons and works of art and architecture. The smallest, studies of the person (4 of 44 objects of study with 25 of 317 tags), encompassed non-verbal communication and facial expression, although some work took the body as a whole or considered physiognomy. Among artworks (7 objects with 32 tags), paintings predominated, along with art posters, buildings and memorials. The media were the overwhelming choice for study (9 objects with 188 tags). Photography was first (62 tags), followed by television and video (50). Cartoons and caricatures were surprisingly important objects of study (22 tags), apart from their home medium. And as expected, new media (15) caught attention,

but newspapers and magazines received some too (12 and 8). Our analysis separated media from their forms and content (22 genres with 72 tags). The main genres were political advertising (25 tags) and television news (12), along with websites (8). For visual studies, textual media were much less central than television and photos, and only one study had a radio tag.

Besides the USA, the research looked at many other countries (46 with 74 tags), most prominently Germany (7 tags), UK (6), China (5), India (4) and France (3). Comparative studies included more than one country (in two cases a continent and former colonies), and so the tagging overstates international work in the literature. The emphasis fell on Europe (16 countries with 32 tags), of course, but also on Asia and the Middle East (15 with 25) and Africa (11 with 13). Latin America had little research (only 2 countries with 2 tags). The number of studies for each country declined similarly, with most countries appearing only once (28 tags).

The overview from the tag clouds guided our selection for further discussion, and the following sections report primarily on the two key areas, political and visual communication. We also look at the growing theme of identity and representation and detour into two sub-areas: one form of imagery, cartoons and caricatures, and one emerging area of research, emotion, which crosses disciplines, concepts, media and topics.

Politics Envisioned

Political communication studies contained a large body of work crossing between the two fields. Visual symbols have grown central to political communication since the advent of television. With the focus on language, systematic analyses of news images are rare (Domke et al., 2002). The main currents in political communication concern images in framing, priming and agenda setting. Following precedent for experiments using television to explore visual framing (Iyengar, 1991), one study exposed students to images of violent or peaceful protests to show the impact on viewer evaluations of contentious issues (Arpan et al., 2006). Research about visual framing on television news also takes on war and terror (Fahmy, 2005; Shaul, 2006; see also Ayish, 2002 for a framing study focused on Middle East national politics). The studies also show the political predispositions of media outlets through visual analyses, looking for bias.

Visual aspects of priming emerged in studies of television political debates, war coverage and racial attitudes in political advertising. Unspoken but visible racial cues in the US political ads heightened racial schemas and primed viewer attitudes on race, so that the visual altered candidate selection criteria (Valentino et al., 2002). Video news stories on the Vietnam conflict activated political attitudes and prompted judgments about newsworthiness more than text-only content did in a study of college students (Domke et al., 2002). And studies of how audiences perceived video versus audio versions of the 1960 Kennedy–Nixon debates (Druckman, 2003) and of photographs with racial cues accompanying newspaper stories (Abraham and Appiah, 2006) showed that images prime different perceptions of political topics.

Agenda-setting research has demonstrated the connection between images and issue salience for newspaper readers (Wanta, 1988), and recent work has looked at second-level effects. Viewers tended to adopt media portrayals of candidate character traits after seeing network news shots of

candidates displaying non-verbal cues of those traits during the two months leading up to the November 2000 presidential election in the USA (Coleman and Banning, 2006).

Despite the arrival of the Internet, political research has focused on text, not images, and studies have tended to count and classify online visuals and compare them against other media (Barnhurst, 2002; Cooke, 2005). The advent of video streaming and the low cost of web distribution suggest the need for more research on political visuals, especially online video.

Picturing Political Emotion

Visual explorations within political communication have focused attention on the display of emotion. Cognitive studies have made the role of emotion clearer in information processing (Graber and Smith, 2005). At first, political communication studies measured the effects of emotional display on viewers. Newscasters, for instance, show how they feel about political candidates through facial expressions, and viewing them regularly correlated with voting behavior (Mullen et al., 1986). Political leaders' non-verbal emotional displays also affected viewer attitudes (Masters and Sullivan, 1989; Masters et al., 1986). Experimental research with televised political advertisements connected visual information with viewers' emotion and recall (Lang, 1991). The early effects studies laid the groundwork but tended not to examine what triggered political action.

A new wave of research since 2000 took up psychological triggers and semiotic structures. One experiment showed that emotional imagery influenced most the individuals who had deep involvement in and knowledge about an issue (Huddy and Gunnthorsdottir, 2000). Through *passionate reason*, individuals could find a message persuasive and then act. Another experiment before a state primary election (Brader, 2006), showed adult participants messages about education, crime and drugs accompanied either by uplifting music, colorful images of children and a positive script or by discordant music, grainy black and white pictures of violence and a negative script, producing heightened motivation and vigilance or changed candidate preferences.

Other research has examined how the non-verbal cues from political leaders elicit emotional reactions. Viewers who encountered inappropriate displays of emotion experienced more intense negative reactions and evaluated the leader's character traits lower (Bucy, 2000; Bucy and Bradley, 2004). More intense news images affected the leader's ability to allay anxiety in response to a crisis, which led viewers to feel less in control

(Bucy, 2003). Non-verbal cues police public–private boundaries in the use of technology, especially in the case of reactions when mobile phone users flaunt their devices as expressions of identity and display private emotions that disturb the public sphere (Vincent and Fortunati, 2009).

Emotion also has the potential to influence the political agenda. The emotional reaction of respondents to the 11 September 2001 attacks influenced their recall of visual images (Fahmy et al., 2006). Social science research on audience responses and media coverage draws links among emotion, visual information and political communication, which matter as political leaders become more visible not just on television but in new media (Verser and Wicks, 2006), where non-verbal and emotional messages proliferate.

Rhetorical studies in the 2000s also turned to emotion. Iconic photography in public media reveals aspects of democratic life such as citizenship, a strongly emotional norm for public order. The image of a young woman screaming in response to the 1970 killing of Kent State University protesters triggers emotions that bind viewers into civic relationships of mutual support. The visual representation of dissent provides resources for citizen advocacy and change, but visual media can also work for institutions, generating political loyalty, illustrating relationships of control and managing expectations of citizens (Hariman and Lucaites, 2007).

Using a semiotic framework, two case studies explored how documentary photographs to encourage emotional engagement (Starrett, 2003). Opposing political groups used documentary photographs to mobilize sub-groups, and news photos displayed the emotions of crowds, leaders and individuals. Groups then ascribed meanings perhaps differing from what the photographer intended to portray, but the attributed meanings facilitated political action, as individuals molded their inner state to conform to social norms of expression they perceived.

Recent investigations of emotion represent a growing nexus of visual and political communication, promising because they enrich visual studies with political insight and deepen the understanding of politics as lived, feeling experience.

The Visible Made Political

Visual studies scatter across the disciplines: communication and rhetoric, art history, sociology, anthropology and others. The core of research takes place in visual communication, visual rhetoric and visual culture, but extends into mainline social sciences, particularly political communication. Even so, the preponderance of work approaches the visual through rhetoric, continuing a trend from a decade ago (Barnhurst et al., 2004).

Political issues as a subset of visual communication scholarship range widely, from racial identity (Stange, 2003) to war (Perlmutter, 1999). The studies argue that images dominate communication in industrial societies and that archives and collections of images, in whatever form (even in textbooks), reflect social values (Perlmutter, 1992). In a period of conflicts, war emerged as a political theme in visual communication research. It followed work that had demonstrated the narrow range of visual images during the Gulf War (Griffin and Lee, 1995), which reflected official policy, touting military superiority and downplaying the human costs of war. The research also attended to what war images do not show: political processes such as discussions in the United Nations or anti-war demonstrations. Recent work has turned attention on the visual representation of political dissent (Perlmutter and Wagner, 2004).

Other research looks at manipulated or distorted images, focusing on visual communication as medium (Messaris, 1992) and as practice. When political figures employ the *photo opportunity,* for example, they compose photography to include symbols (Squiers, 1990), to make themselves prominent, and to leave other perspectives outside the frame. Using technology to distort still and moving images, once the province of skilled technicians, is now a widespread activity. Computer users with no training altered images digitally for humorous effect and distributed them by email after the 11 September 2001 attacks in New York and Washington (Frank, 2004). The users produced a kind of folklore that voiced reactions the traditional news media do not circulate, such as vengeance and victimization, and, by challenging mainstream media portrayals of the public reaction, also extended the public sphere.

Visual communication studies looking at the relation of image to reality were a staple only a decade ago. For politics, they looked for biased media images during election campaigns in the USA (Moriarty and Popovich, 1991; Waldman and Devitt, 1998) and elsewhere (Grabe, 1996). Studies comparing images to reality seem to have declined in the face of critiques showing the inherent malleability of images, but the image–text relationship has not received the attention it deserves (Gibson and Zillmann, 2000), despite the difficulty in parsing the contribution of each (Müller, 2007).

Visual culture studies move in other directions, toward history and toward visible objects other than camera images. Research on the Walker Evans photographs from the mid-20th century illuminated a perennial issue, poverty (Schneck, 2003).

A study of propaganda from the era of Lenin expanded visual studies to include visible monuments (Kruk, 2008), and another study pointed to the dematerialization of political monuments (Grider, 2007). Favored topics for visual culture ranged across the fine arts (Makela, 2007), but also popular arts, such as murals in an ethnic neighborhood (Mazurana, 2002).

Visual communication scholars trained in critical-cultural studies have done similar work. A typical study explored visual composition in the 1860 photographs of Yosemite Valley (DeLuca and Demo, 2000) – images that build a context where political action takes place, fostering *habits of seeing* the American wilderness that led to the US wilderness legislation. Greenpeace climate change ephemera between 1994 and 2006 relied on the visible at the expense of latent political consequences that remain hidden from view (Doyle, 2007). Growing out of the speech tradition, the studies bridge between visual culture, with its emphasis on art and history, and media research focused on current images. The visuals peculiar to each medium can make arguments that influence public understanding.

Visual work in other social studies journals has shown similar influences, looking at the arts and history from a critical perspective (Jia, 2005). A special issue of *American Anthropologist* contemplated media forms as technologies for making public any claims for human rights (McLagan, 2006), the documentary images becoming a strain of advocacy. Elsewhere, anthropologists have examined how the 1919 silent film *Ravished Armenia,* by documenting brutalities the Armenians suffered under the Ottoman Empire, encouraged humanitarian activity (Torshin, 2006). The layout and design of *The Colonies in Pictures*, a 1953 publication of the British government (Bowden, 2004), reinforced a colonial worldview. Earlier scholarship from black studies analyzed the televised 1984 Democratic presidential campaign debates (Merritt, 1986) and, from sociology, examined media events on television that form political reality in society (Manning, 1996).

Rhetorical studies of visual communication focus especially on imagery. A study of Charles Booth's maps of poverty circa 1900 reveals graphic images with a rosy view of London (Kimball, 2006). But speech and rhetoric also range across visual forms: The Civil Rights Memorial is a monument that reproduces political tactics (Blair and Michel, 2000); Norman Rockwell paintings about civil rights convey the power to make visible the shared humanity of blacks and whites (Gallagher and Zagacki, 2005) and the 1963 Birmingham campaign of Dr Martin Luther King, Jr, becomes an image event in *Life* magazine (Johnson, 2007). The studies reveal persuasive

and symbolic dimensions of the visible, examined through visual artifacts and through cultural practices of seeing (Olson et al., 2008), as well as through the interplay of words and images. A hybrid audio-visual format, political entertainment television (Jones, 2005), is re-shaping political discourse and challenging assumptions about political rhetors. And political advertising produces a kind of pulp politics (Richardson, 2000).

Some political communication scholarship itself belongs firmly within visual communication. A pioneer who studied audience perceptions of political candidates on television news, Doris Graber investigated how visuals contributed to the way viewers perceived candidate traits (Graber, 1987), how visuals contributed to viewer learning (Graber, 1990) and how, compared to words alone, audiovisual material helped viewers recall and understand information better and become more emotionally involved in politics (Graber, 1996).

Television images reinforce or contradict the messages of political candidates. Besides examining how candidate images manipulate voters (Rosenberg et al., 1991), research has explored how visual images in political advertising can distort perceptions among individuals of varying literacy (Noggle and Kaid, 2000). Video style, the verbal and non-verbal techniques used to produce political advertising, gave political operatives more control over the US candidate images from the 1952 through 1996 elections and became a means of manipulating voter perceptions (Kaid and Johnston, 2001).

Some recent visual communication research by political scholars still focused on questions of truth and illusion, exploring how manipulative editing, special effects and computer altered images influence viewer perceptions (Kaid et al., 2005; Scheufele et al., 2007). Digital alterations of candidate photographs, morphed to contain almost half of the study participant's own facial features, affected college students' political judgment, for instance (Bailenson et al., 2006; and see Iyengar and Vavreck, this volume).

Visual content analyses have for some time considered political media content, such as *image bites* (Barnhurst and Steele, 1997). The work has documented an increase in image bites that lose detail and complexity while speeding the spread and repetition of information (Bucy and Grabe, 2007).

The Internet provides a new forum for visual research about politics. Interactivity and viewer control differentiated the Internet from television (Kaid, 2002), along with links to pursue more resources. But users of new technologies can also reshape politics by cultivating cyber-communities (Jenkins, 2006). At the intersection of politics and fandom, new media have the capacity to broadcast and narrowcast images and texts. Visual studies scholarship across all its disciplinary homes has only begun to explore the political implications of new technology.

Representing Cultural Identity

Studies of identity and representation have done visual and political work without needing to resort to the policymakers' or producers' agendas, to measure effects on audiences, or to analyze news content (all common in political and visual communication). The studies have instead tended to read social meaning from texts and theorize its consequences for the production of social difference, making the personal political.

Some studies have involved cross-national comparisons, such as elections in the USA and Israel (Griffin and Kagan, 1996), television crossing European borders (Chalaby, 2005), official websites of small developing countries (Mohammed, 2004) or a quarter century of Sino-American relations depicted in *Time* magazine (Perlmutter, 2007). Others have ventured elsewhere to look at presidential tele-politics in Argentina (Guano, 2002) – a rare study on Latin America – or at geopolitical images of the Darfur conflict (Campbell, 2007).

But examinations of *the other* center on the developed West. The anthology, *Looking for America* (Cameron, 2005), brought scholars from American studies, language (rhetoric) and cultural history together with social anthropologists studying topics such as photography of the 'American Negro', family snapshots, depictions of the 'good American' in *Life* magazine, labor movement images in Chicago, the 1943 Zoot-Suit Riots, perceptions of Jews and 1950s sitcom homemakers. The main theorists considered identity at the level of self and nation (Anderson, 1991; Goffman, 1959). By focusing on minute physical differences in bodies, modern societies create physiological typologies, confusing biological with social traits. Even after science discredited the types, political institutions and police departments reinforced distinctions of 'the American' from *the other.*

The identity studies also came from disparate academic homes: new media studies, geography and visual culture, to name a few, as well as communication. An example from the journal, *Tourist Studies,* can illustrate (Favero, 2007). Local governments promote tourism for economic reasons but assume that cross-cultural exchanges encourage unity and dialog. An ethnographic critique showed how tourism promotes seeing difference instead. Tourist events such as a festival of culture

or a reconstructed village represent local life but also reinforce its *otherness.* Tour arrangers and guides turned local difference and cultural diversity into commodities. Tourism industries use communication to act as brokers between locals and travelers – political communication that enacts their mutual power relations and visual communication that channels their imagining and then acting toward each other.

Identity work from visual culture but grounded in visual grammar (Kress and van Leeuwen, 2006), examined the color pink as a social marker of gender, femininity and sexuality identity (Koller, 2008). The research was visual in its theory and political in its results. A project from a film studies journal illustrated gender in the context of family life (Haralovich, 1989). The US television situation comedies in the 1950s used 'deep focus photography' (Haralovich, 1989: 64) to show details of the household: tidy housekeeping, kitchens for women, dens and garages for men and 'tasteful' furnishings. Media images promoted an ideal of American family life, made a gendered home appear natural, defined the role of homemaker and reinforced an ideology of class and gender identity.

Research on identity also explored earlier periods. A semiotic analysis showed how Renaissance medical manuals depicting surgery on the female genitalia represented the female as the *other* (Brasseur and Thompson, 1995). A critical analysis showed how the male nude in neoclassical art accompanied political transformations of the Dutch Republic – calls to restore male virtue and patriotism – and excluded women from politics (Dudink, 2001).

Similar themes emerged in larger, systematic studies. A visual analysis of photographs, illustrations and advertisements in Swedish dailies and weekly newsmagazines found that the ideal woman changed from a silent body in 1925 to an altruistic pleaser in 1955, both forms emphasizing consumption with a focus on beauty and appearance, before becoming a representative of the political system by 1987 (Hirdman, 1998). A study of 5400 photographs from introductory sociology textbooks published in the 1980s found that gender and race did not overlap: when the textbook producers balanced racial representations, they defined women of color to represent race but to be without gender (Ferree and Hall, 1990).

The focus on producer intentions and responsibility for social progress continued through the 1990s in visual political studies of identity and representation (for example, Kuiper et al., 1998). An anthropological analysis showed that iconic photographs of poverty in the 1930s engaged in a search for the perfect victim of the Great

Depression, ignoring how camera operators filter the world and collect an incomplete record (Levine, 1988).

Visual analyses in new media studies have shown the Internet providing a dislocated space for political movements and groups in diaspora. Online representations support virtual communities such as the Tamil Eelam rebel movement of Sri Lanka (Enteen, 2006), the Zapatista movement of Mexico (Russell, 2005) and expatriates from India residing in the Americas (Mallapragada, 2006).

Cartoons and Caricature

The study of editorial caricatures and cartoons has been an idiosyncratic domain. The initial call for more study, drawing on the work of Kenneth Burke and Walter Benjamin (Streicher, 1967), proposed a definition: distorted and exaggerated images, usually mass reproduced, which employ iconic types and visual synecdoche (the substitution of a whole image for a part, or vice versa) to affect power in society. As a rhetorical form, political caricatures and cartoons have attracted the attention of psychoanalysis, sociology and communication (Medhurst and DeSousa, 1981). The form relates to oral persuasion, its visual styles invites viewer response and it operates in political settings.

A rhetorical approach in mainstream communication research examined the graphic portrayal of Uncle Sam over time (Bivins, 1987), showing that figure size and body type carry political meanings that symbolize the body politic, from muscular youth of the 1830s to the wizened Lincoln-type a century later. An analysis during the French referendum on the European Constitution showed how editorial cartoons appearing in British and Spanish newspapers employed metaphor and metonymy to build meaning and criticize political entities using visual humor and textual cues (Marín-Arrese, 2008).

Other projects came from speech, politics and culture studies. They focused on prominent political figures, such as controversial US Secretary of the Interior James Watt during the Bush era (Bostdorff, 1987), or an ethnic or religious group, such as Arabs and Muslims after the 11 September 2001 attacks (Diamond, 2002), or on a content genre of the media, such as news (Greenberg, 2002). Other research examined the work of an individual, such as Steve Bell, the liberal British political cartoonist for the *Guardian* (Plumb, 2004); the output surrounding notorious events, such as Hurricane Katrina (Romano and Westgate, 2007) or, in rare cases, an issue surrounding the images themselves, such as the controversy over

the Danish caricatures of the Prophet Muhammad (Müller et al., 2009). A study of political cartoons during the US 2004 elections examined non-political imagery to see how much pop culture knowledge readers would require to understand the underlying political reference (Conners, 2005). At least one book-length study covered the history of American political cartoons lampooning leaders (Lordan, 2006).

Many of the studies centered on the USA and Europe. Examples from elsewhere included images of Taiwanese politics (Hsiao, 1996), African dissent (Eko, 2007), Japanese rejection of the US hegemony (Gerteis, 2007) and Palestinian refugee identity (Najjar, 2007). The work ranged across social science and cultural studies and also analyzed gender role representations, as did the US-centered research (for example, Templin, 1999).

Political cartoons and caricatures provide visual commentary on political culture, often grounded in theories of representation and identity, but only a few mainstream visual or political communication scholars have taken up the call for research. Perhaps because the category is unusual – not a separate medium or formal component of politics. Cartoons ally closely with art, and the research has centered on print. But viewed through visual semiotics, political cartoons are icons that viewers analyze in context to understand complex social issues (Abraham, 2009).

PERSPECTIVES AND PROSPECTS

In response to calls for political research to do more than refer to visuals and for visual research to make its political implications explicit, scholars have expanded the field at the intersection of the two. The nexus has emerged with many characteristics of the overlapping fields: political communication scholars still did framing, priming and agenda-setting projects. Lacking grounding in visual studies, they also fell into the mimetic fallacy, testing whether political images reflect reality. Research on media content and audiences was extensive at the visual-political intersection, despite projects that attended to the visual only nominally. The Internet, which began with text and moved into images and design, has presented an ongoing opportunity, largely missed, for political researchers to collaborate on understanding visual media and its relation to text.

The research on emotion seemed especially focused on visual analysis. Initial work measured how emotional displays affect recall, attitude and voting behavior, and recent research examined their persuasive influences on political perception, to gauge how the intensity of the viewer's reaction varies with political content. The visible markers when newscasters and politicians express feelings appeared to influence political participation among their viewers. And critical work has sought to understand how images shape the emotions around political ideas such as citizenship and dissent. The blend of critical-cultural, semiotic, rhetorical and behavioral approaches has made emotion a growing area of visual-political inquiry.

Research that treats visuals with substance has taken place across fields and disciplines, been rich in history and developed enough breadth to include monuments and even vanishing images. But the fragmentation of visual studies research has meant that scholars in peripheral fields still pursued hoary questions already laid to rest within visual communication, such as whether images constitute truth. Visual studies scholars predictably take up topics such as war and conflict, where images seem most shocking, but have been slow to sort out the complex politics in the relationship of images to words.

Studies of cultural identity and representation at the intersection of political and visual communication went from documenting the problem of under-representation in the 1980s and 1990s to making broader critiques in the past two decades. Drawing primarily on close readings of selected texts, they also expanded to include long-range and quantitative analyses. Researchers in the mainstream of political communication took up some terms, such as *hegemony* and *ideology*, doing visual studies without necessarily importing the critical perspective. Visual communication scholars pushed beyond Europe and North America to engage in comparative political research. The critiques from cultural studies, feminism, gender studies and area studies enriched the research, especially for political identity and visual representation.

Editorial cartoons and caricatures form a special category, receiving attention from rhetorical and semiotic perspectives, but somewhat isolated, especially from critical theory and cultural studies. An area for exploration in future research has also emerged: the television shows and Internet videos using similar distorted and exaggerated images of political figures and events to influence public opinion, politics and daily life in society.

One marker of interactive visual politics has been the appearance of tag clouds, which news and political groups use on their network sites to show users the prominence of topics and issues. By employing the same visualization technique, we attempted to explore its potential. Unlike quantitative content categories, tags are neither mutually exclusive nor exhaustive, and so we reported results in raw numbers, listing percentages only in the presence of a definable whole. Visual scholars know that size is a poor statistical indicator but a powerful visual one. Because the typeface grows in two dimensions as its point size increases, it overstates quantity while emphasizing a quality key to public life in media-saturated cultures: popularity, celebrity and image. At the same time, we found the tag clouds performed well at illustrating the patterns in the research.

The illustration that matters for what we found is, of course, the list of references that follows. It is much richer than any tag cloud, reaching into most corners of the globe (except for another direction for future research: Latin America). Consider a political poster exhibition traveling during 2005 and 2006 (Schnapp, 2005). Instead of conforming to the conventional catalog classifying schemes – chronology, artist or political ideology – the curator took an unusual step, categorizing the artwork by graphics, icons and themes relating to political crowds. The political poster as a communication medium depends on those forms, and the project represents a nuanced visual effort that matters in the politics of unstable nations and may come closer to the way voters with lower literacy view and experience politics visually.

REFERENCES

Abraham, L. (2009) 'Effectiveness of Cartoons as a Uniquely Visual Medium for Orienting Social Issues', *Journalism Communication Monographs,* 11(2): 119–65.

Abraham, L. and Appiah, O. (2006) 'Framing News Stories: The Role of Visual Imagery in Priming Racial Stereotypes', *Howard Journal of Communications,* 17(3): 183–203.

Anderson, B. (1991) *Imagined Communities: Reflections on the Origin and Spread of Nationalism,* Rev edn. London: Verso. [1st edn, 1983.]

Arpan, L. M., Baker, K., Lee, Y., Jung, T., Lorusso, L. and Smith, J. (2006) 'News Coverage of Social Protests and the Effects of Photographs and Prior Attitudes', *Mass Communication and Society,* 9(1): 1–20.

Ayish, M. I. (2002) 'Political Communication on Arab World Television: Evolving Patterns', *Political Communication,* 19(2): 137–54.

Bailenson, J. N., Garland, P., Iyengar, S. and Yee, N. (2006) 'Transformed Facial Similarity as a Political Cue: A Preliminary Investigation', *Political Psychology,* 27(3): 373–85.

Barnhurst, K. G. (2002) 'News Geography And Monopoly: The Form of Reports on US Newspaper Internet Sites', *Journalism Studies,* 3(4): 477–89.

Barnhurst, K. G. and Nerone, J. (2001) *The Form of News, a History.* New York: Guilford.

Barnhurst, K. G. and Steele, C. A. (1997) 'Image Bite News: The Coverage of Elections on US Television, 1968–1992', *Press/Politics,* 2(1): 40–58.

Barnhurst, K. G., Vari, M. and Rodriguez, I. (2004) 'Mapping Visual Studies in Communication', *Journal of Communication,* 54(4): 616–44.

Bivins, T. H. (1987) 'The Body Politic: The Changing Shape of Uncle Sam', *Journalism Quarterly,* 64(1): 13–20.

Blair, C. and Michel, N. (2000) 'Reproducing Civil Rights Tactics: The Rhetorical Performances of the Civil Rights Memorial', *Rhetoric Society Quarterly,* 30(2): 31–55.

Bostdorff, D. M. (1987) 'Making Light of James Watt: A Burkean Approach To the Form and Attitude of Political Cartoons', *Quarterly Journal of Speech,* 73(1): 43–59.

Bowden, G. (2004) 'Reconstructing Colonialism: Graphic Layout and Design, and the Construction of Ideology', *Canadian Review of Sociology and Anthropology,* 41(2): 217–40.

Brader, T. (2006) *Campaigning for Hearts and Minds: How Emotional Appeals in Political Ads Work.* Chicago, IL: University of Chicago Press.

Brasseur, L. E. and Thompson, T. L. (1995) 'Gendered Ideologies: Cultural and Social Contexts for Illustrated Medical Manuals in Renaissance England', *Transactions on Professional Communication,* 38(4): 204–15.

Bucy, E. P. (2000) 'Emotional and Evaluative Consequences of Inappropriate Leader Displays', *Communication Research,* 27(2): 194–226.

Bucy, E. P. (2003) 'Emotion, Presidential Communication, and Traumatic News: Processing the World Trade Center Attacks', *Press/Politics,* 8(4): 76–96.

Bucy, E. P. and Bradley, S. D. (2004) 'Presidential Expressions and Viewer Emotion: Counter-Empathic Responses to Televised Leader Displays', *Social Science Information,* 43(1): 59–94.

Bucy, E. P. and Grabe, M. E. (2007) 'Taking Television Seriously: A Sound and Image Bite Analysis of Presidential Campaign Coverage, 1992–2004', *Journal of Communication,* 57(4): 652–75.

Cameron, A. (ed.) (2005) *Looking for America: The Visual Production of Nation and People.* Malden, MA: Blackwell Publishing.

Campbell, D. (2007) 'Geopolitics and Visuality: Sighting the Darfur Conflict', *Political Geography,* 26(4): 357–82.

Chalaby, J. K. (2005) 'Deconstructing the Transnational: A Typology of Cross-Border Television Channels in Europe', *New Media and Society,* 7(2): 155–75.

Coleman, R. and Banning, S. (2006) 'Network TV News' Affective Framing of the Presidential Candidates: Evidence For a Second-Level Agenda-Setting Effect Through Visual Framing', *Journalism and Mass Communication Quarterly,* 83(2): 313–28.

Conners, J. L. (2005) 'Visual Representations of the 2004 Presidential Campaign: Political Cartoons and Popular Culture References', *American Behavioral Scientist,* 49(3): 479–87.

Cooke, L. (2005) 'A Visual Convergence of Print, Television, and the Internet: Charting 40 Years of Design Change in News Presentation', *New Media and Society,* 7(1), 22–46.

DeLuca, K. M. and Demo, A. T. (2000) 'Imaging Nature: Watkins, Yosemite, and the Birth of Environmentalism', *Critical Studies in Media Communication,* 17(3): 241–60.

Diamond, M. (2002) 'No Laughing Matter: Post–September 11 Political Cartoons in Arab/Muslim Newspapers', *Political Communication,* 19(2): 251–72.

Domke, D., Perlmutter, D. and Spratt, M. (2002) 'The Primes of our Times?: An Examination of the "Power" of Visual Images', *Journalism,* 3(2): 131–59.

Doyle, J. (2007) 'Picturing the Clima(c)tic: Greenpeace and the Representational Politics of Climate Change Communication', *Science as Culture,* 16(2): 128–50.

Druckman, J. N. (2003) 'The Power of Television Images: The First Kennedy-Nixon Debate Revisited', *Journal of Politics,* 65(2): 559–71.

Dudink, S. (2001) 'Cuts and Bruises and Democratic Contestation: Male Bodies, History and Politics', *European Journal of Cultural Studies,* 4(2): 153–70.

Eko, L. (2007) 'It's a Political Jungle Out There: How Four African Newspaper Cartoons Dehumanized and "Deterritorialized" African Political Leaders in the Post-Cold War Era', *Gazette,* 69(3): 219–38.

Enteen, J. (2006) 'Spatial Conceptions of Urls: Tamil Eelam Networks On the World Wide Web', *New Media and Society,* 8(2): 229–49.

Fahmy, S. (2005) 'Emerging Alternatives Or Traditional News Gates: Which News Sources Were Used to Picture the 9/11 Attack and the Afghan War?', *Gazette,* 67(5): 381–98.

Fahmy, S., Cho, S., Wanta, W. and Song, Y. (2006) 'Visual Agenda Setting After 9/11: Individual Emotion, Recall and Concern About Terrorism', *Visual Communication Quarterly,* 13(1): 4–15.

Favero, P. (2007) '"What a Wonderful World!": On the "Touristic Ways of Seeing", the Knowledge and the Politics of the "Culture Industries of Otherness"', *Tourist Studies,* 7(1): 51–81.

Ferree, M. M. and Hall, E. J. (1990) 'Visual Images of American Society: Gender and Race in Introductory Sociology Textbooks', *Gender and Society,* 4(4): 500–33.

Frank, R. (2004) 'When the Going Gets Tough, The Tough Go Photoshopping: September 11 And the Newslore of Vengeance and Victimization', *New Media and Society,* 6(6): 633–58.

Gallagher, V. and Zagacki, K. (2005) 'Visibility and Rhetoric: The Power of Visual Images in Norman Rockwell's Depictions of Civil Rights', *Quarterly Journal of Speech,* 91(2): 175–200.

Gerteis, C. (2007) 'The Erotic and the Vulgar: Visual Culture and Organized Labor's Critique of US Hegemony in Occupied Japan', *Critical Asian Studies,* 39(1): 3–34.

Gibson, R. and Zillmann, D. (2000) 'Reading Between the Photographs: The Influence of Incidental Pictorial Information on Issue Perception', *Journalism and Mass Communication Quarterly,* 77(2): 355–66.

Goffman, E. (1959) *The Presentation of Self in Everyday Life.* Garden City, NY: Doubleday/Anchor Books.

Grabe, M. E. (1996) 'The South African Broadcasting Corporation's Coverage of the 1987 And 1989 Elections: The Matter of Visual Bias', *Journal of Broadcasting and Electronic Media,* 40(2): 153–79.

Graber, D. (1987) 'Kind Pictures and Harsh Words: How Television Presents the Candidates', in K. L. Schlozman (ed.),

Elections in America. Boston, MA: Allen and Unwin. pp. 115–41.

Graber, D. (1990) 'Seeing Is Remembering: How Visuals Contribute to Learning from Television News', *Journal of Communication,* 40(3): 134–55.

Graber, D. (1996) 'Say It With Pictures', *Annals of the American Academy of Political and Social Science,* 546(1): 85–96.

Graber, D. and Smith, J. M. (2005) 'Political Communication Faces the 21st Century', *Journal of Communication,* 55(3): 479–507.

Greenberg, J. (2002) 'Framing and Temporality in Political Cartoons: A Critical Analysis of Visual News Discourse', *Canadian Review of Sociology and Anthropology,* 39(2): 181–98.

Grider, N. (2007) '"Faces of the Fallen" and the Dematerialization of US War Memorials', *Visual Communication,* 6(3): 265–79.

Griffin, M. (2001) 'Camera as Witness, Image as Sign: The Study of Visual Communication in Communication Research', *Communication Yearbook,* 24: 433–63.

Griffin, M. and Kagan, S. (1996) 'Picturing Culture in Political Spots: 1992 Campaigns in Israel And the United States', *Political Communication,* 13(1): 43–61.

Griffin, M. and Lee, J. (1995) 'Picturing the Gulf War: Constructing an Image of War in Time, Newsweek, and US News and World Report', *Journalism and Mass Communication Quarterly,* 72(4): 813–25.

Guano, E. (2002) 'Ruining the President's Spectacle: Theatricality and Telepolitics in the Buenos Aires Public Sphere', *Journal of Visual Culture,* 1(3): 303–23.

Haralovich, M. B. (1989) 'Sitcoms and Suburbs: Positioning the 1950s Homemaker', *Quarterly Review of Film and Video,* 11(1): 61–83.

Hariman, R. and Lucaites, J. L. (2007) *No Caption Needed: Iconic Photographs, Public Culture and Liberal Democracy.* Chicago, IL: University of Chicago Press.

Hirdman, A. (1998) 'Male Norms and Female Forms: The Visual Representation of Men and Women in Press Images in 1925, 1955, and 1987', *Nordicom Review,* 19(1): 225–54.

Hsiao, H. W. (1996) 'Releasing the Clamps: Taiwanese Cartoonists Speak Out', *Journal of Asian Pacific Communication,* 7(1/2): 77–86.

Huddy, L. and Gunnthorsdottir, A. H. (2000) 'The Persuasive Effects of Emotive Visual Imagery: Superficial Manipulation Or the Product of Passionate Reason?', *Political Psychology,* 21(4): 745–78.

Iyengar, S. (1991) *Is Anyone Responsible? How Television Frames Political Issues.* Chicago, IL: University of Chicago Press.

Jenkins, H. (2006) 'Photoshop for Democracy: The New Relationship Between Politics and Popular Culture', in H. Jenkins (ed.), *Convergence Culture.* New York: New York University Press. pp. 206–39.

Jia, J. (2005) 'The Reconstruction of a Political Icon: Shi Lu's Painting "Fighting in Northern Shaanxi"', *Qualitative Inquiry,* 11(4): 535–48.

Johnson, D. (2007) 'Martin Luther King Jr.'s 1963 Birmingham Campaign as Image Event', *Rhetoric and Public Affairs,* 10(1): 1–25.

Jones, J. P. (2005) *Entertaining Politics: New Political Television and Civic Culture.* Lanham, MD: Rowman and Littlefield.

Kaid, L. L. and Johnston, A. (2001) *Videostyle in Presidential Campaigns: Style and Content of Televised Political Advertising.* Westport, CT: Praeger.

Kaid, L. L. (2002) 'Political Advertising and Information Seeking: Comparing Exposure Via Traditional and Internet Channels', *Journal of Advertising,* 31(1): 27–35.

Kaid, L. L., Keener, B. and Chanslor, M. (2005) 'Visual Manipulations in Political Spot Ads in the 2000 Presidential Primaries: A Source of Voter Alienation?', in M. McKinney, L. L. Kaid, D. G. Bystrom and D. B. Carlin (eds.), *Communicating Politics: Engaging the Public in Democratic Life.* New York: Peter Lang. pp. 163–73.

Kimball, M. A. (2006) 'London Through Rose-Colored Graphics: Visual Rhetoric and Information Graphic Design in Charles Booth's Maps of London Poverty', *Journal of Technical Writing and Communication,* 36(4): 353–81.

Koller, V. (2008) '"Not Just a Colour": Pink as a Gender and Sexuality Marker in Visual Communication', *Visual Communication,* 8(2): 181–205.

Kress, G. and van Leeuwen, T. (2006) *Reading Images: The Grammar of Visual Design.* 2nd edn. London: Routledge. [1st edn, 1996.]

Kruk, S. (2008) 'Semiotics of Visual Iconicity in Leninist "Monumental" Propaganda', *Visual Communication,* 7(1): 27–56.

Kuiper, S., Booth, R. and Bodkin, C. D. (1998) 'The Visual Portrayal of Women in IBM's Think: A Longitudinal Analysis', *Journal of Business Communication,* 35(2): 246–63.

Lang, A. (1991) 'Emotion, Formal Features and Memory for Political Advertisments', in F. Biocca (ed.), *Television and Political Advertizing: Psychological Processes.* Vol. 1, Hillsdale, NJ: Lawrence Erlbaum Associates. pp. 221–44.

Levine, L. W. (1988) 'The Historian And the Icon: Photography And the History of the American People in the 1930s and 1940s', in C. Fleischhauer and B. W. Brannan (eds.), *Documenting America, 1935–1943.* Berkeley, CA: University of California Press. pp. 15–41.

Lordan, E. J. (2006) *Politics, Ink: How America's Cartoonists Skewer Politicians, from King George II to George Dubya.* Lanham, MD: Rowman and Littlefield.

Makela, M. (2007) 'Politicizing Painting: The Case of New Objectivity', in P. C. McBride, R. W. McCormick and M. Zagar (eds.), *Legacies of Modernism: Art and Politics in Northern Europe, 1890–1950.* New York: Palgrave Macmillan. pp. 133–47.

Mallapragada, M. (2006) 'Home, Homeland, Homepage: Belonging and the Indian-American Web', *New Media and Society,* 8(2): 207–27.

Manning, P. K. (1996) 'Dramaturgy, Politics and the Axial Media Event', *Sociological Quarterly,* 37(2), 261–78.

Marín-Arrese, J. (2008) 'Cognition and Culture in Political Cartoons', *Intercultural Pragmatics,* 5(1): 1–18.

Masters, R. D. and Sullivan, D. G. (1989) 'Nonverbal Displays and Political Leadership in France and the United States', *Political Behavior,* 11(2): 123–56.

Masters, R. D., Sullivan, D. G., Lanzetta, J. T. and McHugo, G. J. (1986) 'The Facial Displays of Leaders: Toward an Ethology of Human Politics', *Journal of Social and Biological Structures*, 9(4): 319–43.

Mazurana, D. (2002) 'Juana Alicia's Las Lechugueras/The Women Lettuce Workers', *Meridians: Feminism, Race Transnationalism*, 3(1): 54–81.

McLagan, M. (2006) 'Technologies of Witnessing: The Visual Culture of Human Rights; Introduction: Making Human Rights Claims Public', *American Anthropologist*, 108(1): 191–5.

Medhurst, M. J. and DeSousa, M. A. (1981) 'Political Cartoons as Rhetorical Form: A Taxonomy of Graphic Discourse', *Communication Monographs*, 48(3): 197–236.

Merritt, B. D. (1986) 'Jesse Jackson and Television: Black Image Presentation and Affect in the 1984 Democratic Campaign Debates', *Journal of Black Studies*, 16(4): 347–67.

Messaris, P. (1992) 'Visual Manipulation: Visual Means of Affecting Responses to Images', *Communication*, 13(3): 181–95.

Mohammed, S. N. (2004) 'Self-Presentation of Small Developing Countries On the World Wide Web: A Study of Official Websites', *New Media and Society*, 6(4): 469–86.

Moriarty, S. E. and Popovich, M. N. (1991) 'Newsmagazine Visuals And the 1988 Presidential Election', *Journalism Quarterly*, 68(3): 371–80.

Müller, M. G., Özcan, E. and Seizov, O. (2009) 'Dangerous Depictions. A Visual Case Study of Contemporary Cartoon Controversies', *Popular Communication*, 7(1): 28–39.

Müller, M. G. (2007) 'What is Visual Communication? Past and Future of an Emerging Field of Communication Research', *Studies in Communication Research*, 7(2): 7–34.

Mullen, B., Futrell, D., Stairs, D., Tice, D. M., Baumeister, R. F., Dawson, K. E., Riordan, C. A., Radloff, C. E., Goethasl, G. R., Kennedy, J. G. and Rosenfeld, P. (1986) 'Newscasters' Facial Expressions and Voting Behavior of Viewers: Can a Smile Elect a President?', *Journal of Personality and Social Psychology*, 51(2), 291–95.

Najjar, O. A. (2007) 'Cartoons as a Site for the Construction of Palestinian Refugee Identity', *Journal of Communication Inquiry*, 31(3): 255–85.

Noggle, G. and Kaid, L. L. (2000) 'The Effects of Visual Images in Political Ads: Experimental Testing of Distortions and Visual Literacy', *Social Science Quarterly*, 81(4): 913–27.

Olson, L. C., Finnegan, C. A. and Hope, D. S. (2008) 'Visual Rhetoric in Communication: Continuing Questions and Contemporary Issues', in L. C. Olson, C. A. Finnegan and D. S. Hope (eds.), *Visual Rhetoric*. Thousand Oaks, CA: Sage. pp. 1–14.

Perlmutter, D. (1992) 'The Vision of War in High School Social Science Textbooks', *Communication*, 13: 143–60.

Perlmutter, D. (1999) *Visions of War: Picturing Warfare from the Stone Age to the Cyber Age*. New York: St Martin's Press.

Perlmutter, D. (2007) *Picturing China in the American Press: The Visual Portrayal of Sino-American Relations in Time Magazine, 1949–1973*. Lanham, MD: Lexington Books.

Perlmutter, D. and Wagner, G. L. (2004) 'The Anatomy of a Photojournalistic Icon: Marginalization of Dissent in the Selection and Framing of "A Death in Genoa"', *Visual Communication*, 3(1): 91–108.

Plumb, S. (2004) 'Politicians as Superheroes: The Subversion of Political Authority Using a Pop Cultural Icon in the Cartoons of Steve Bell', *Media, Culture and Society*, 26(3): 432–39.

Richardson, G. W. (2000) 'Pulp Politics: Popular Culture and Political Advertising', *Rhetoric and Public Affairs*, 3(4): 603–26.

Romano, S. K. and Westgate, V. (2007) 'Drawing Disaster: The Crisis Cartoons of Hurricane Katrina', *Texas Speech Communication Journal*, 31(1): 1–15.

Rosenberg, S. W., Kahn, S., Tran, T. and Le, M. T. (1991) 'Creating a Political Image: Shaping Appearance and Manipulating the Vote', *Political Behavior*, 13(4): 345–67.

Russell, A. (2005) 'Myth And the Zapatista Movement: Exploring a Network Identity', *New Media and Society*, 7(4): 559–77.

Scheufele, D. A., Kim, E. and Brossard, D. (2007) 'My Friend's Enemy: How Split-Screen Debate Coverage Influences Evaluation of Presidential Debates', *Communication Research*, 34(1): 3–24.

Schnapp, J. T. (2005) *Revolutionary Tides: The Art of the Political Poster 1914–1989*. New York: Rizzoli.

Schneck, P. (2003) 'The Purity of Poverty: Walker Evans and Iconic Autonomy', in U. Haselstein, B. Ostendorf and P. Schneck (eds.), *Iconographies of Power: The Politics and Poetics of Visual Representation*. Heidelberg: Winter Verlag. pp. 131–71.

Shaul, B. N. (2006) *A Violent World: TV News Images of Middle Eastern Terror and War*. Lanham, MD: Rowman and Littlefield.

Squiers, C. (1990) 'Picturing Scandal: Iranscam, The Reagan White House, and the Photo Opportunity', in the *Critical Image: Essays on Contemporary Photography*. Seattle, WA: Bay Press. pp. 121–38.

Stange, M. (2003). 'Not What We Seem: Image and Text in 12 Million Black Voices', in U. Haselstein, B. Ostendorf and P. Schneck (eds.), *Iconographies of Power: The Politics and Poetics of Visual Representation*. Heidelberg: Winter Verlag. pp. 173–86.

Starrett, G. (2003) 'Violence and the Rhetoric of Images', *Cultural Anthropology*, 18(3): 398–428.

Streicher, L. H. (1967) 'On a Theory of Political Caricature', *Comparative Studies in Society and History*, 9(4): 427–45.

Templin, C. (1999) 'Hillary Clinton as Threat to Gender Norms: Cartoon Images of the First Lady', *Journal of Communication Inquiry*, 23(1): 20–36.

Torshin, L. (2006) 'Ravished Armenia: Visual Media, Humanitarian Advocacy, and the Formation of Witnessing Publics', *American Anthropologist*, 108(1): 214–20.

Valentino, N. A., Hutchings, V. L. and White, I. K. (2002) 'Cues That Matter: How Political Ads Prime Racial Attitudes During Campaigns', *American Political Science Review*, 96(1): 75–90.

Verser, R. and Wicks, R. H. (2006) 'Managing Voter Impressions: The Use of Images on Presidential Candidate Web Sites During the 2000 Campaign', *Journal of Communication,* 56(1): 178–97.

Vincent, J. and Fortunati, L. (2009) *Electronic Emotion: The Mediation of Emotion via Information and Communication Technologies.* Bern: Peter Lang.

Waldman, P. and Devitt, J. (1998) 'Newspaper Photographs and the 1996 Presidential Election: The Question of Bias', *Journalism and Mass Communication Quarterly,* 75(2): 302–11.

Wanta, W. (1988) 'The Effects of Dominant Photographs: An Agenda-Setting Experiment', *Journalism Quarterly,* 65(1): 107–11.

23

News Framing Research: An Overview and New Developments

Claes H. de Vreese and Sophie Lecheler

INTRODUCTION

By investigating news frames and news framing effects we are offered a way of explaining why '(often small) changes in the presentation of an issue or an event produce (sometimes larger) changes of opinion' or other outcome variables (Chong and Druckman, 2007a: 104). As a result, framing has become ubiquitous in political communication research, and is currently one of the most popular approaches for investigating both content and effects of the news media.

The notion of framing has gained momentum in political communication, and a number of notable scholars have signaled it as one of the most fertile and rewarding concepts of the discipline (for example, Graber and Smith, 2005; McLeod et al., 2002). A fast growing number of empirical articles in journals of both political and communication science indicate just how important framing has become today (for example, Berinsky and Kinder, 2006; Entman, 1991; Kolmer and Semetko, 2009; Chong and Druckman, 2010). Several landmark book publications underline this importance even further (for example, Callaghan and Schnell, 2005; D'Angelo and Kuypers, 2009; Reese et al., 2001). Moreover, based on Entman's (1993) famous claim for a more homogenous use of the framing concept within the communication disciplines, numerous scholars have attempted to integrate framing into a cadre of communication theories together with agenda-setting and priming

(for example, Chong and Druckman, 2007a; D'Angelo, 2002; D.A. Scheufele, 1999). Matthes (2009) presented a meta-analysis of 131 academic articles on frame analysis. He notes a number of conceptual and methodological ambiguities within the examined studies, such as a general lack of operationalizable frame definitions, or a great focus on descriptive frame analysis at the cost of a more hypothesis-driven approach.

This chapter provides a short overview of the conceptual and methodological characteristics of framing research. First, we describe a process model of framing, followed by a short overview on frame-building, the nature of frames in the news, and the consequences of news framing for citizens' understanding of politics. Then, we sum up a number of theoretical and methodological advances of framing research, and conclude with a research agenda for studies to come.

A PROCESS MODEL OF NEWS FRAMING

The potential of the framing concept lies in the focus on communicative *processes*. Communication is not static, but rather a dynamic process that involves frame-building (how frames emerge) and frame-setting (the interplay between media frames and audience predispositions). Entman (1993) noted that frames have several locations, including the communicator, the text, the receiver and the culture. These components are integral to a process of framing that consists of distinct stages: frame-building, frame-setting and individual and societal level consequences of framing (D'Angelo, 2002; de Vreese, 2002, 2005; D.A. Scheufele, 1999).

Frame-building refers to the factors that influence the structural qualities of news frames. Factors internal to journalism determine how journalists and news organizations frame issues (Shoemaker and Reese, 1996). Equally important, however, are factors external to journalism. The frame-building process takes place in a continuous interaction between journalists and elites (Gans, 1979; Hänggli and Kriesi, 2010; Tuchman, 1978) and social movements (for example, Snow and Benford, 1992). The outcomes of the frame-building process are the frames manifest in the text.

Frame-setting refers to the interaction between media frames and individuals' prior knowledge and predispositions. Frames in the news may affect learning, interpretation and evaluation of issues and events. This part of the framing process has been investigated most elaborately, often with the goal to explore the extent to which and under what circumstances audiences reflect and mirror frames made available to them in, for example, the news. The *consequences* of framing can be conceived on the individual and the societal level. An individual level consequence may be altered attitudes about an issue based on exposure to certain frames. On the societal level, frames may contribute to shaping social level processes such as political socialization, decision making and collective actions. In framing processes, frames can be both independent variables (IV) and dependent variables (DV). For example, media frames may be studied as the DV, as the outcome of the production process including organizational pressures, journalistic routines and elite discourse. Media frames may also be studied as IV, as the antecedents of audience interpretations, opinions and behavior.

Drawing on the integrated process model of framing (see Figure 23.1), future research would benefit from linking features of the production of news with the content (frame-building) and/or content with studies of uses and effects (frame-setting). A link between either production and/or effects is needed to prevent a proliferation of studies that investigate frames that may have considerable appeal given the 'layman' nature of the frame, but that do not provide any evidence or discussion of the use of the frame in actual news reports (see also Matthes, 2009). The pitfall of such studies is that we cannot infer whether the frames are in fact, in the words of Cappella and Jamieson, 'commonly observed in journalistic practice' (1997: 47).

HOW NEWS FRAMES EMERGE

The frame-building process takes place as a continuous interaction between journalists and elites (Druckman, 2001a; Gans, 1979; Snow and Benford, 1992; Tuchman, 1978). So far, there is only little systematic information available on this relationship, simply because researchers have mainly focused on investigating frames in the news rather than the frame-building process (D.A. Scheufele, 1999; for a recent exception, see Hänggli and Kriesi, 2010). However, there are some authors that have attempted to describe and classify the variables that determine news framing. These studies draw on the multitude of studies that describe how journalistic work is influenced by individual, social, organizational or structural factors that surround them (for example, Shoemaker and Reese, 1996).

For instance, de Vreese (2005) distinguishes between *internal* and *external* factors of frame-building within the news room. Internal factors are editorial policies and news values, which shape the day-to-day work of journalists. External factors

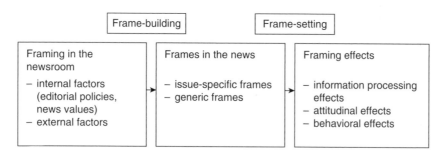

Figure 23.1   An integrated process model of framing

are elite influences and social movements, which play an equally important role for the frame-building process. Along these lines, D.A. Scheufele (1999: 115) also discusses some internal and external variables that inform the frame-building process. First, he lists so-called 'journalist-centered' influences, such as personal attitudes or opinions, and professional role conceptions. Second, news framing is informed by 'factors like the type or political orientation of the medium' a journalist is working for. For example, framing between a tabloid and a broadsheet differs substantially (see also Donsbach, 2004; B. Scheufele, 2006).

D.A. Scheufele (1999) also names external forces such as political elites or interest group as important for the framing process. Elite influence becomes apparent when journalists use parts of political speeches, or 'soundbites' to illustrate an issue. The author argues that journalists are most likely to adapt elite framing, when the issue at stake is 'relatively new' on the media agenda (D.A. Scheufele, 1999: 116). The idea of elite influence on the news framing process alludes to a widely discussed assumption in political research, namely that political attitudes and opinions in citizens are so volatile and susceptible to elite messages that subtle changes in the news media or political speech can lead to rather large effects on these attitudes and opinions (Zaller, 1992). Druckman (2001a,b, 2004) has repeatedly questioned this idea, and has presented multiple tests of the conditions under which elite framing does *not* take effect. The author takes empirical evidence on the limits of framing (for example, framing effects are limited by the credibility of sources) as an argument in favor of citizen competence when it comes to elite framing, and propagates a more nuanced look at elite influence on political attitudes.

FRAMES IN THE NEWS

There is a large variety of definitions of what a news frame is in both theoretical and empirical contributions. Conceptually, we define news frames as 'a central organizing idea or story line that provides meaning to an unfolding strip of events, weaving a connection among them. The frame suggests what the controversy is about, the essence of the issue' (Gamson and Modigliani, 1989: 143). In short, a news frame can affect an individual by stressing certain aspects of reality and pushing others into the background – it has a selective function. In this way, certain issue attributes, judgments and decisions are suggested (for example, Berinsky and Kinder, 2006; D.A. Scheufele, 2000).

Previous research on frames in the news shares little conceptual ground and most studies draw on tentative working definitions or operational definitions of frames designed for the purpose of the specific study. Therefore, there is little consensus as how to identify frames in the news. One approach is *inductive* in nature and refrains from analyzing news stories with *a priori* defined news frames in mind (for example, Gamson, 1992: Matthes and Kohring, 2008; Neuman et al., 1992). Frames emerge from the material during the course of analysis. Studies taking an inductive approach have been criticized for relying on too small a sample and for being difficult to replicate (Hertog and McLeod, 2001). A second approach is rather *deductive* in nature and investigates frames that are defined and operationalized prior to the investigation.

In any way, scholars have argued in favor of applying concise, *a priori* defined operationalizations of frames in content analyses. Cappella and Jamieson (1997) state that considering *any* production feature of verbal or visual texts as a candidate for news frames is a too broad view. They suggest four criteria that a frame must meet. First, a news frame must have identifiable conceptual and linguistic characteristics. Second, it should be commonly observed in journalistic practice. Third, it must be possible to distinguish the frame reliably from other frames. Fourth, a frame must have representational validity (that is be recognized by others) and not be merely a figment of a researcher's imagination (Cappella and Jamieson, 1997: 47, 89; see also de Vreese, 2002).

When working with a deductive approach, the relevant question is: *what* (which components) in a news story constitutes a frame? Entman suggested that frames in the news can be examined and identified by 'the presence or absence of certain keywords, stock phrases, stereotyped images, sources of information and sentences that provide thematically reinforcing clusters of facts or judgments' (1993: 52). Along these lines, Shah et al. refer to 'choices about language, quotations, and relevant information' (2002: 367). Gamson and Modigliani (1989) identify 'framing devices' that condense information and offer a 'media package' of an issue. They identify (1) metaphors, (2) exemplars, (3) catch-phrases, (4) depictions and (5) visual images as framing devices. The most comprehensive empirical approach is offered by Tankard (2001: 101), who suggests a list of 11 framing mechanism or focal points for identifying and measuring news frames, such as headlines, photos or quotes.

In sum, scholars within the empirical approach to measuring frames agree that frames are *specific textual and visual elements* or 'framing devices'. These elements are essentially different from the remaining news story, which may be considered *core news facts*. Price et al. operationalized a frame by varying 'introductory and concluding paragraphs to establish a unique journalistic frame' with information exclusive to the frame while the other paragraphs in the news articles were kept identical (1997: 488). In the same vein, Neuman et al. (1992: 126) in their content analysis divided news articles into sections containing 'frames' and sections containing 'facts'. The distinction between *core elements* and *frame-carrying elements* has effectively been applied in the operationalization of news frames in most studies of framing effects (for example, Cappella and Jamieson, 1997; de Vreese, 2004; Iyengar, 1991; Lecheler and de Vreese, 2011; Price et al., 1997; Valentino et al., 2001).

A TYPOLOGY OF NEWS FRAMES

While newsmakers may employ many different frames in their coverage of an issue, scholars agree that this abundance in choice in how to tell and construct stories can be captured in analyses as certain distinctive characteristics. In order to synthesize previous research and the different types of news frames that have been suggested, a more general typology or distinction with reference to the nature and content of the frame is suggested here. Certain frames are pertinent only to specific topics or events. Such frames may be labeled *issue-specific frames*. So far, studies of issue-specific news frames have looked at the framing of the EU Parliamentary elections (Williams and Kaid, 2006), the Internet (Roessler, 2001), labor disputes (Simon and Xenos, 2000) or biotechnology (Matthes and Kohring, 2008).

Other frames transcend thematic limitations and can be identified in relation to different topics, some even over time and in different cultural contexts. These frames can be labeled *generic frames* (de Vreese, 2002). This typology serves to organize past framing research focusing on differences that help explain the use of the catch-all 'framing' phrase. An issue-specific approach to the study of news frames allows for a profound level of specificity and details relevant to the event or issue under investigation. This advantage, however, is potentially an inherent disadvantage as well. The high-degree of issue-sensitivity makes analyses drawing on issue-specific frames difficult to generalize, compare and use as empirical evidence for theory building. The absence of comparability has led researchers to 'too easily finding evidence for what they are looking for' and to contribute to 'one of the most frustrating tendencies in the study of frames and framing [being] the tendency

for scholars to generate a unique set of frames for every study' (Hertog and McLeod, 2001: 150–1). Research on generic frames is mainly inspired by Semetko and Valkenburg (2000), who identified five generic news frames: 'conflict', 'human interest', 'attribution of responsibility', 'morality' and 'economic consequences'.

Framing studies typically employ either *equivalency* or *emphasis* frames (Chong and Druckman, 2007a). Equivalency frames refer to logically alike content, which is presented or phrased differently (for example, Kahneman and Tversky, 1984; O'Keefe and Jensen, 2006). Emphasis frames are closer to 'real' journalistic news coverage and present 'qualitatively different yet potentially relevant considerations' (Chong and Druckman, 2007a: 114). The concept of equivalency stems from the series of 'Asian disease'-studies by Kahneman and Tversky (for example, Kahneman and Tversky, 1984). Though their framing manipulation – altering the wording of a scenario outlining the consequences of a fatal illness – was appropriate to explore the psychological process, this definition of framing is rather narrow. Indeed simple question wording differences that reverse information are not easily compatible with more complex communicative situations and politics (Sniderman and Theriault, 2004).

Some theoretical arguments support the use of the narrow conceptualization in framing research (for example, D.A. Scheufele, 2000), but few empirical studies have investigated the 'reversed information' phenomenon. The vast majority of framing studies, more or less explicitly, apply an *emphasis* definition of frames. One strong argument for the use of emphasis frames is that most issues – political and social – cannot be meaningfully reduced to two identical scenarios. Political, economic and social events and issues are presented to citizens as alternative characterizations of a course of action (Sniderman and Theriault, 2004). When conceiving of, for example, oil drilling, citizens may be presented with frames such as economic costs of gas prices, unemployment, environment, or the US dependency on foreign energy sources (Zaller, 1992). Frames are parts of political arguments, journalistic norms and social movements' discourse. They are alternative ways of defining issues, endogenous to the political and social world.

It is, moreover, important to note that news frames used in empirical framing studies are characterized by a specific *valence*. In framing research, valence remains slightly underdiscussed, probably because the reference to 'positive' or 'negative' media messages touches on a different domain of media effects research, namely persuasion research (Bogdanova and Lecheler, 2009;

Levin et al., 1998). Yet, valence is central to the original study of framing in Kahneman and Tversky's (1984) Asian disease problem, where a cure is either described positively in terms of the lives that can be saved, or negatively on the number of deaths that can be expected (see also Druckman, 2011). Following this conceptualization, equivalency framing often displays valence openly, by stressing the positive or negative outcome of one set of considerations (for example, Levin et al., 1998). However, valence also pertains to one of the most fundamental characteristics of political discourse, namely that elites attempt to purposely affect support or rejection for an issue by connecting the positive or negative aspects of it with different sets of considerations, and can therefore also be applied to emphasis framing. For instance, political actors can frame altered privacy laws positively in terms of an increased need to fight criminal activity, or negatively in emphasizing that such altered legal standards could come at the cost of the privacy of innocent citizens.

Along these lines, de Vreese and Boomgaarden (2003) argue that only valenced news frames have the capacity to affect support for an issue, while neutral frames may only affect issue interpretation (see also Bizer and Petty, 2005). Other framing studies support this finding, and indicate that especially negative frames are very powerful in affecting peoples' opinion and attitudes (for example, Cappella and Jamieson, 1997, but see O'Keefe and Jensen, 2006).

FRAMING EFFECTS

News frames have been shown to affect citizens sense-making on a variety of political issues (for example, Berinsky and Kinder, 2006; Iyengar, 1991; Lecheler & de Vreese, 2011; Nelson et al., 1997). Studies have tested effects on a number of dependent variables, such as issue interpretation (for example, Valkenburg et al., 1999), cognitive complexity (Shah et al., 2004), public opinion and issue support (for example, Druckman and Nelson, 2003; Sniderman and Theriault, 2004) and voter mobilization (for example, Valentino et al., 2001). The variety of dependent variables in framing effects research covers all three dimensions of communications effect theory, cognitive, behavioral and affective variables (de Vreese, 2005; Iyengar and Simon, 2000).

Cognitive framing effects are at the center of current research literature, and political communication researchers focus mainly on the question of how frames in the news affect public opinion toward a specific issue or event (for example, Chong and Druckman, 2007a; Nelson et al., 1997).

However, some studies of framing argue that news frames are defined by their effect on information processing, that is on how citizens interpret and 'understand' a political issue (for example, Nabi, 2003; Price et al., 1997; Shen, 2004; Valkenburg et al., 1999). Some researchers have also investigated how frames affect mental models and cognitive complexity (for example, Baden and de Vreese, 2008; Shah et al., 2004). For instance, Shah et al. (2004) examine how individual or societal frames affected the complexity of individual thoughts on an urban growth issue. They find that societal frames resulted in more complex mental models than frames set in an individual context.

As mentioned, a majority of studies measure framing effects on attitudes or opinions toward a specific issue (for example, Chong and Druckman, 2007a). Nelson et al. (1997: 237) present a model of news framing effects on opinion, where the framing process is defined by the psychological processes that enable it. Frames affect attitudes and opinions in lending 'additional weight to an already accessible concept by influencing its perceived relevance or importance' (also D.A. Scheufele, 2000; but see Lecheler & de Vreese, 2012a; Slothuus, 2008). Beyond opinion, studies have also focused on other attitudinal variables, such as political cynicism (Cappella and Jamieson, 1997), knowledge (de Vreese and Boomgaarden, 2006) or trust (Valentino et al., 2001).

Behavioral framing effect studies have received a considerable amount of attention in the study of social movements, where scholars have studied how frames can enable mobilization and protest (for example, Entman and Rojecki, 1993; Snow and Benford, 1992; Snow et al., 1986). However, D.A. Scheufele notes that this data is 'of only limited use when examining the potential impact of individual frames on political participation or action', due to its 'aggregate-level' nature (1999: 113). On an individual level, behavioral framing effect studies focus on campaigns and the effects of news frames on voter mobilization or turnout (for example, de Vreese and Semetko, 2002; Elenbaas and de Vreese, 2008; Valentino et al., 2001). For example, Valentino et al. (2001) find that framing with a focus on strategy demobilizes less sophisticated citizens. However, in most cases, behavioral effects are measured by tapping 'behavioral intention' rather than actual behavior and the level of attitude-behavior consistency for framing effects is in need for further empirical investigation (D.A. Scheufele, 1999).

Lastly, the *emotional framing effect* deals with the effects of news framing on distinct emotions toward a political issue. There is, so far, only a limited number of studies that deals with emotions as outcome variables of news framing. An exception is presented by Gross and Brewer (2007), who investigate how conflict frames affect anger and disgust among citizens. The authors detect an effect of framing on emotion, depending on corresponding prior beliefs of the individual. We will discuss the role of emotion within framing research more thoroughly in a later section of this chapter.

In sum, we observe that framing effects studies have examined effects on numerous outcome variables. Based on the conjectural 'existence' of framing effects, the main goal of a number of other research projects is to accumulate knowledge about the mediators and moderators of framing. We will describe these in the following two sections.

Moderators of Framing Effects

Moderators are variables that have the potential to enhance, limit or even obliterate a framing effect. By exploring potential moderators, framing studies take into consideration the fact that the magnitude (as well as process) of framing must depend on individual as well as circumstantial characteristics of the respective framing scenario. Thus far, the literature presents a number of *individual-level* moderator variables such as knowledge (for example, Lecheler and de Vreese, 2010; Nelson et al., 1997) or values (for example, Shen and Edwards, 2005) as well as *contextual* moderators, attempting to bring the study of framing effect closer to 'real life', such as source characteristics (for example, Druckman, 2001a), interpersonal communication (for example, Druckman and Nelson, 2003) or competitive framing (for example, Chong and Druckman, 2007b; Sniderman and Theriault, 2004).

On an individual level, a number of studies deal with the question of how political knowledge influences the magnitude as well as the actual processing of a framing message. However, the evidence is divided and one group of scholars finds less knowledgeable individuals to be more susceptible to framing effects (for example, Kinder and Sanders, 1990; Schuck and de Vreese, 2006), whereas a second group argues the opposite (Krosnick and Brannon, 1993; Nelson et al., 1997). Druckman and Nelson (2003: 732) ascribe the opposing results to a general failure of measuring political knowledge. Accordingly, it may not be political knowledge *per se* that moderates framing effects, but the availability of relevant knowledge and the existence of prior opinions on that issue. The authors measure prior opinions by using the construct of 'need to evaluate', with

high need to evaluate individuals being less susceptible to framing effects.

Research aims, furthermore, at investigating framing effects in situations more akin to 'daily life'. This implies providing a frame within its natural *context* by offering different sources, other competing frames and social contacts (for example, Sniderman and Theriault, 2004). Druckman (2001a), for example, investigates the role of source characteristics on the framing process. Taking into account that hardly any political message comes without a specific messenger, he finds that framing effects are limited by the credibility of their source.

Beyond that, framing effects do also depend on the actual issue that is being framed. For example, Iyengar (1991) differentiates between episodic and thematic framing and finds that framing effects vary according to the particular issue at stake. However, he does not offer conclusive evidence on the conditions under which issue characteristics matter. Haider-Markel and Joslyn (2001) focus on a high salience issue, assuming that attitudes toward this issue and an issue frame are stronger as individuals attach high levels of importance to it. The impact of this importance on the framing process is examined by Lecheler et al. (2009), who report that a high-importance issue yields no effects, and that a low-importance issue large framing effects. This moderating function of issue importance depends on both personal importance assessments, and how important this issue is on the political and media agenda.

Mediators of Framing Effects

Political communication scholars increasingly focus on the intermediary psychological processes that are likely to underlie every framing effect and the conditions under which these pertain (for example, Chong and Druckman, 2007a; Matthes, 2007; Nelson et al., 1997; Slothuus, 2008).

Thus far, extant research has identified three basic processes that are likely to mediate framing effects: (1) accessibility change; (2) belief importance change and (3) belief content change (see Chong and Druckman, 2007a; Nelson et al., 1997; Slothuus, 2008). *Accessibility change* as an intermediary mechanism is hypothesized to function by making considerations in the individual's mind more salient and therefore more likely to be used when forming an opinion (for example, Iyengar, 1991; Nabi, 2003; Price and Tewksbury, 1997; B. Scheufele, 2004). D.A. Scheufele discards the notion of accessibility in framing theory, stating that 'framing influences how audiences think about issues, not by making aspects of the issue more salient, but by invoking interpretative schemas that influence the interpretation of incoming information' (2000: 309). Accessibility change, moreover, proves to be difficult to tap by empirical investigation (see Baden and de Vreese, 2008, but see Chong and Druckman, 2007a; Nabi, 2003).[1]

Belief importance change is thought to be the most significant mediator of framing effects (for example, Druckman, 2001a; Nelson et al., 1997; Nelson and Oxley, 1999). It refers to framing as 'altering the *weight* of particular considerations' in the individual's mind (Nelson et al., 1997: 236, italics in original). Thus, frames do not render certain frame-related beliefs more salient, but increase the weight that is assigned to those beliefs. As an intermediary, important considerations, in turn, are more likely to be incorporated into subsequent judgments (for example, Price and Tewksbury, 1997). Thus far, extant research has widely examined and supported models of belief importance change as a mediator of framing effects (for example, Druckman, 2001a; Druckman and Nelson, 2003; Nelson et al., 1997). Based on such findings, belief importance change is a theoretically as well as empirically plausible mediator of framing effects.

Recently, scholars have turned to a third complementary explanation for framing effects: *belief content change* (for example, de Vreese et al., 2010; Lecheler and de Vreese, 2012a; Lecheler et al., 2009; Shah et al., 2004; Slothuus, 2008). A belief content model refers to the addition of new beliefs to an individual's set and alludes to one of the most established mechanisms in media effects research – the persuasive effect (for example, Eagly and Chaiken, 1993; Petty and Cacioppo, 1986; Zaller, 1992). Yet, belief content change has been widely disregarded in framing effects, because it was argued that framing 'operate[s] by activating information *already at the recipients' disposal*, stored in long-term memory' (Nelson et al., 1997: 225, italics in original). However, political media frames often cover information that is remote and complex to the individual, and may therefore regularly convey importance change, *as well as* new information to the individual. Slothuus (2008: 7) proposes a 'dual-process' model of framing effects that combines belief importance and belief content change. Results of his experimental study show that frames do indeed affect opinion via both proposed mechanisms, with belief content change being more significant for individuals of low political knowledge (see also Lecheler and de Vreese, 2012a; Shah et al., 2004).

ADVANCES IN FRAMING RESEARCH

Theoretical Advances

Frame-Building

There is only little systematic information available on how news frames actually emerge, simply because researchers have often focused on investigating frames in the news rather than the frame-building process itself (see Gandy, 2001; D.A. Scheufele, 1999). Yet, the changing landscape of political communication is likely to greatly affect the interplay of political actors, the media and citizens in the frame-building process. We see the potential for future research in the following dimensions:

First, we expect the rise of social media and citizen-generated content to shift the power balance in the framing process, either toward external factors such as political interest groups, or toward a growing number of online citizen journalists (for example, Farrell and Drezner, 2008). How does, for example, the rise of citizen-generated content on news websites influence the journalistic 'filters' that information is normally processed by? Second, the professionalization of political PR, spindoctors and campaign management may lead to a stronger influence of 'professional framing' of political elites, and therefore to changes in how news frames emerge (for example, Negrine and Lilleker, 2002). This trend is illustrated by Lakoff's (2004) popular handbook *'Don't Think of an Elephant!'*, in which the author illustrates how political parties have used and can use framing to effectively communicate their image or campaign information. Third, more research is needed on the influences of social movements on political elites in the frame-building process and vice versa. Here, framing literature can take inspiration from recent research in agenda-setting (for example, Walgrave and Vliegenthart, Chapter 30 in this Handbook). Lastly, researchers must zoom in on the interplay between social or political actors and news media organizations in the framing process. So far, only little is known about how news frames are negotiated between these actors, and how differing framing mechanisms interact in this process (see Hänggli and Kriesi, 2010 for a recent example).

Framing and Emotion

In their account of framing theory, Chong and Druckman (2007a: 116) name a number of underdiscussed mediator and moderator variables in framing research, such as emotions, narratives and perceptions of public opinion. Among those, emotions emerge as a most interesting – and long neglected – category. Indeed, there are a number of recent studies of framing that recognize the importance of studying the role of emotion in news framing research (for example, Druckman and McDermott, 2008; Gross and Brewer, 2007; Gross and D'Ambrosio, 2004; Nabi, 2003; Schuck and de Vreese, 2009).

Among these, some take emotions as outcome variables: Gross and D'Ambrosio (2004: 21) provide a number of clues on the effect of framing on emotional response. The authors state that 'emotional reactions are conditioned by both predispositions and the information available in a given frame'. Gross and Brewer (2007) examine the impact of specific news frames on anger and disgust, and do also find only a conditional effect of framing on emotion, limited by the nature of personal beliefs connected to the framed issue. Yet, other studies presume that emotions must be an important mediator between frames in communication and their effects. Recently, Schuck and de Vreese (2009) posited risk perceptions to mediate a framing effect of political news on voter mobilization – conditioned by differing levels of political efficacy. Holm (2009) finds that individuals are more likely to be framed when feeling enthusiastic, while aversion reduces information processing.

All existing studies point out the lack of a systematic account of the role of emotions in framing research, be it as a dependent, a moderator or as a mediator variable. For example, Holm (2009: 24) argues that there is, thus far, no empirical investigation of 'when the cognitive route is likely to dominate the emotional route and vice versa' in the framing process, and whether the interplay between the two routes depends on situational factors, or on individual characteristics of the citizen. Gross and Brewer (2007) highlight the normative implications of integrating emotionality into the framing process, both regarding the actual benefits of evoking specific emotions by framing an issue, and the unanswered question of whether emotion facilitate or inhibit public deliberation. Beyond that, future research projects must investigate the role of emotion for specific issues of different political contexts, for political participation and action and disentangle the differences between discrete emotions that play a role in the framing process.

Framing and Persuasion

Several scholars have delimited framing from other theoretical approaches of political communications, such as agenda-setting and priming (for example, D.A. Scheufele, 2000; Scheufele and Tewksbury, 2007). However, only limited knowledge is available on the difference between framing and persuasion (for example, Smith and Petty, 1996). This distinction must be made, regarding both the antecedents as well as consequences of framed and persuasive messages. Moreover, a clear terminology must be found, especially because framing scholars have alluded to the 'persuasive power' of news framing (for example, Chong and Druckman, 2007a), and because the dependent variables of persuasion and framing seem rather similar.

One of the most important steps is the integration of recent findings that show that the mediational processes of framing and persuasion are very similar. Specifically, we refer to Slothuus (2008), who argues that persuasion's belief content change (see above in 'Mediators of Framing Effects'), is a determining mediator of framing effects also (see also de Vreese et al., 2010; Lecheler et al., 2009; Lecheler and de Vreese, 2012a). These results collide with one of the basic propositions of framing theory, namely that of the belief importance change model (Nelson et al., 1997). Given the new empirical evidence, an integrationist belief importance *and* content change mediation model requires researchers to re-think the boundaries of and overlaps between 'framing' and 'persuasion'.

D.A. Scheufele (1999) suggests that frames ought to be considered as an independent variable in the research process. Slothuus (2008: 22) did exactly that and suggests that a framing effect must be 'any effect of a frame in communication on a receiver's opinion'. Thus, while a *framing effect* may traditionally still be conceived as changing belief importance within an individual's mind, we support a more inclusive conceptualization, which enables a frame to cause an array of *different effects*. This may lead to the future conclusion that both persuasion and framing work by similar intermediary processes (Chong and Druckman, 2007a).

The Duration of Framing Effects

The greater part of extant framing effects studies emphasizes the relevance of their results for politics (see Druckman, 2004; Kahneman, 2000). However, such assumptions cannot be sustained without further theoretical and empirical investigation of the duration framing effects (Gaines et al., 2007). Only recently have framing scholars actually begun to include duration into their studies (for example, Chong and Druckman, Chapter 24, in this Handbook; de Vreese, 2004). With a small number of studies under way, knowledge and data regarding the rate of decay of framing effects after initial exposure and measurement is evolving slowly.

Tracing the effects of media messages over time is of course not a novel idea, and a consistent line of studies in learning, persuasion or agenda-setting effects research have included time as a significant variable in their designs (for example, Hovland and Weiss, 1951; Iyengar and Kinder, 1987; Mutz and Reeves, 2005; Wanta and Hu, 1994). Scholars of framing effects continue to be bashful when it comes to examining the over-time persistence of their effects. Studies that *do* consider durability arrive, moreover, at equivocal results, do only test one delayed time point, or fail to put full analytical focus on their over-time design.

Tewksbury et al. (2000) find a weaker, yet still significant, effect of advocate frames on issue interpretation three weeks after initial exposure. Vaguely, the authors conclude that 'exposure to a single news article … was sufficient to partially direct the comments made by subjects some time later' (2000: 818). Conversely, Druckman and Nelson (2003) report that their issue framing effect on opinion had dissipated 10 days after initial exposure to a news frame. de Vreese (2004) also suggests that framing effects perish quickly, after only two weeks. He indicates that the quick dilution of effects of a strategic frame on political cynicism may be ascribed to the almost total absence of access to related elite information in the interim period during data collection. Lecheler and de Vreese (2011) test the decay of framing effects across three delayed time points (after one day, one week and two weeks) and find significant effects up to one week after exposure. However, none of the extant studies does specifically discuss, why and when a framing effect would be persistent *enough* to be named 'lasting', 'transitory' or 'fleeting' (see Gaines et al., 2007). On a more general level, we also question the quality of any lasting or also non-lasting news framing effect, if this result only holds in the vacuum of single exposure. We thus see potential for a line of future research projects that aim at determining various rates of decay of news framing effects.

Whatever the rate of decay of framing effects over time may be, it is likely to vary from individual to individual. Thus far, a number of individual and contextual moderator variables of framing have already been identified (for a summary, see Chong and Druckman, 2007a). Research has yet to determine, which list of variables plays a role over time. However, Chong and Druckman (Chapter 24 in this Handbook) provide a theory of communication (and framing) effects over time, depending on whether on-line or memory-based processing takes place. Beyond that, we see potential for a number of other individual or contextual processing variables that can affect the decay process, such as political knowledge, issue importance or strength of related beliefs.

The Effects of Repetitive and Competitive Framing

Framing studies often take a rather microscopic view of the influence of news frames on how citizens make sense of politics, and have therefore measured the effects of only *one* frame at a time (for example, Nelson et al., 1997). However, in the political discourse, citizens are likely to be exposed to repetitive or competitive news messages over time, and the outcome of these two is likely to vary (Zaller, 1992, 1996). We thus also need to evaluate the 'meaning' of framing effects in a more realistic setting that adheres to the dynamics of day-to-day news use. In this respect, research has yet to deliver a satisfying theoretical account of the role of news framing *within* politics, where the dynamics of argumentation, dispute and consensus are the order of the day (Chong and Druckman, 2007b; Gaines et al., 2007; Sniderman and Theriault, 2004).

A number of political communication scholars simply argue that *repetitive news framing* leads to a higher and more constant level of accessibility, which in turn increases the applicability of a framed message (for example, Cappella and Jamieson, 1997; Iyengar, 1991; Nabi, 2003; Price and Tewksbury, 1996; but see Chong and Druckman, 2007b). So far, we cannot find a full account of the specific effects of repetitive framing, be it in terms of magnitude or process. There are studies that do expose participants to a number of repetitive news frames, but do not discuss how the framing effects of multiple frame exposures compare in magnitude and process to studies that had only used one news frame (for example, Berinsky and Kinder, 2006; Valkenburg et al., 1999).

Competitive news framing has received quite some attention in framing literature (for example, Chong and Druckman, 2007b; Hansen, 2007; Sniderman and Theriault, 2004). Most studies focus on the effects of competitive framing when two competing frames are presented at the same time. For instance, Sniderman and Theriault (2004) added another condition to their experimental design, and found that competitive framing increases the influence of personal beliefs in the process, and decreases the effects of news framing[2] (see also Chong and Druckman, 2007b). Increasingly, studies also test how competitive news frames affect opinion formation over time (for example, Chong and Druckman, Chapter 24 in this Handbook; Lecheler and de Vreese, 2012a). Yet, still, much research is needed to exactly determine, *how* conflicting messages in a dynamic communications flow affect opinion formation and other outcome variables (see also Chong and Druckman, in this volume).

Methodological Advances: The Evolution of the Framing Experiment

A large majority of available results on framing effects stems from experimental studies (Druckman, 2004; Kinder, 2007). This seems natural, given the fact that a well-designed experiment is the primary means of determining cause and effect, and for disentangling the complex processes that account for the effect (for example, Kinder and Palfrey, 1993; Lavine et al., 2002; McDermott, 2002).

However, the extensive use of framing experiments has left some researchers wondering to what extent 'realism' must play a larger role in future framing effects research (for example, Barabas and Jerit, 2008; Kinder, 2007). Kinder (2007), for instance, criticizes the use of experimental designs for future framing studies. He emphasizes that framing experiments may have exaggerated the power of the media, simply because they ensure that 'frames reach their intended audiences', instead of being deflected off a typically uninvolved media user. As a remedy, Kinder (2007) suggests the use of real-life events to generate natural experiments. However, he also acknowledges that doing so requires a 'decisive shift in the deployment of frames in some real-world setting' (2007: 157) – a condition very rarely fulfilled (see also Boomgaarden and de Vreese, 2007; Gerber et al., 2009).

How *can* researchers – in the absence of such events – keep track of realism in their framing effect studies, and still retain the qualities that a good experimental design offers? A number of recent studies suggest a greater focus on 'experimental realism' (McDermott, 2002: 333) in their design: Druckman (2004: 685), for instance, challenges the generalizability and persistence of many discovered framing effects. He suggests a greater focus on the experimental frame exposure scenario, the 'context of the study'. Along these lines, Chong and Druckman (2007b) present their participants with competing framing scenarios – yet still within an experiment. In doing so, the authors create a more realistic setting, as most media exposure on a particular issue is of course characterized not just by repetition of one specific, but a multitude of competing frames (see also Jerit, 2009; Sniderman and Theriault, 2004). Lecheler and de Vreese (2012a) expose participants to multiple repetitive as well as competitive news frames over time, and thus aim to mirror

Zaller's (1996) model of dynamic communication flows, where communication effects are determined by the amount and evaluative direction of a stream of media message that are perceived every day.

The contestability of existing framing effects research designs does not only depend on the exposure scenario itself, but also on the over-time persistence of the produced effect. All expressed criticism on the generalizability of framing effects alludes to the necessity of including the variable 'time' into future studies (Chong and Druckman, Chapter 24 in this Handbook). After all, only a time-persistent framing effect allows researchers to draw implications on the political and societal relevance of their results. If experimental framing effects prove to be short-lived, one must continue to question the applicability of purely experimental designs for framing effects studies. de Vreese argues that longitudinal experimental designs are a 'worthwhile path to pursue in the quest to disentangle the robustness and persistency of effects' (2004: 206). Gaines et al. (2007) strongly advocate the further use of survey experiments in social science research, but only if these are enriched with a focus on time and the duration of effects. The authors even suggest that 'determining the rates of decay of various treatment effects and deriving the political implications could be one of the most informative tasks that users of survey experiments undertake in the future' (Gaines et al., 2007: 6).

The development of the framing experiment hinges, furthermore, on the development of measurements used to tap effects. First, future studies must pay increased attention to the exact composition of the frame stimulus used in a study design. For instance, some researchers simply use multiple frame exposures, presumably to strengthen the 'power' of the news frame at stake. The results of these studies are compared to those only using *one* frame exposure, which leads us to argue that some sort of a standard must be found of how news frames are to be operationalized in framing effects studies. Beyond that, research must orient itself by other disciplines such as health communication, social psychology or even neurology, to improve current measurements. An interesting example is provided by De Martino et al., who investigate 'the neurobiological basis of the framing effect by means of functional magnetic resonance imaging' (2006: 684), that is, by measuring brain activity during exposure to a loss or a gain frame.

Future framing effects research should, thus, not move away from employing purely experimental designs, nor must it continue on producing 'simple' measurement results. By accompanying the participant from the laboratory to the outside world, and by incorporating improved measurements, realism and experimental standardization can be united.

CONCLUSION: A RESEARCH AGENDA

A rather large number of framing studies have stressed the pivotal role framing plays in contemporary political communication research. Framing allows researchers to examine the subtle nuances and sharp edges of news media coverage, and to determine how and to what extent exactly it affects citizens' understanding of politics. Yet, the versatility of the framing approach brings with it a great number of pitfalls, such as fuzzy definitions and inconsistent research designs. For instance, recently, some authors have come to question the quality of extant framing experiments, and have called out for a more sophisticated study of framing effects, based on natural experiments or the test of the real-life persistence of experimental effects (Gaines et al., 2007; Kinder, 2007). Others have analyzed the state of affairs from a more theoretical point of view, and have come to the conclusion that there are still numerous theoretical obscurities to tackle (Chong and Druckman, 2007a; Matthes, 2009; Scheufele and Tewksbury, 2007). We take these 'obscurities' as an inspiration for a future research agenda of framing research, and have presented a number of theoretical and methodological new avenues for studies to come. This research agenda should both enrich and update earlier accounts of a research agenda for framing (for example, Gandy, 2001). In this chapter, we focus on advances in framing effects research especially, and therefore complement authors that have put forward research plans for frame analysis (for example, Matthes, 2009; Matthes and Kohring, 2008).

We argue that framing theory should spend more time investigating the frame building process, and how different social, political, and journalistic forces interact in it. In doing so, we adapt claims by Gandy (2001), who highlighted the need for further research on frame-building, especially under consideration of the growing influence of computer-mediated communication flows (see also D.A. Scheufele, 1999). Moreover, research should pay increased attention to emotionality, which is a trend also visible in other communication and political disciplines (for example, De Martino et al., 2006; Marcus, 2000). We also ask for a more in-depth comparison of framing effects with persuasion. This comparison is especially important in regards to a media effects paradigm, be it that of large, medium or minimal media effects (for example, Bennett and

Iyengar, 2008). The 'real' importance of framing also depends on the further study of the duration and persistence of framing effects in a dynamic media use scenario. Along these lines, we strongly encourage future studies to include repetitive and competitive framing messages into their design. This brings us to a necessary methodological advancement of framing, namely the increased use of 'intelligent' framing experiments, where the effects of frames are tested under the consideration of multiple message exposure and tests for longevity of effects.

ACKNOWLEDGMENT

Parts of this chapter come from de Vreese (2005); de Vreese et al. (2010); Lecheler et al. (2009) and Lecheler and de Vreese (2011, 2012b).

NOTES

1   Baden and de Vreese (2008: 21) propose framing to be a two-step process, in which initially a form of 'smart accessibility' applies: Frames shift an individual's informational base by making specific beliefs more salient. However, this salience shift is not random, but follows the 'schematic relevance' of each belief (see also Price and Tewksbury, 1997).

2   These findings indicate a strong connection to the basic principles of motivated reasoning (Chong and Druckman, 2007a; Druckman and Bolsen, 2009), where the so-called 'disconfirmation bias' stands as a central mechanism which 'protect[s] or even bolster[s] … prior attitudes and beliefs in the face of discrepant evidence' (Taber et al., 2009: 138, see also Kunda, 1990; Taber and Lodge, 2006).

REFERENCES

Baden, C. and de Vreese, C. H. (2008) 'Semantic Association and Weighted Consideration: How Framing Shifts People's Information Bases in Opinion Formation', paper presented at the annual meeting of the International Communication Association. Montreal.

Barabas, J. and Jerit, J. (2008) 'Survey Experiments and the External Validity of Treatments', paper presented at the Conference on Experimentation in Political Science at the Annual Meetings of the Canadian Political Science Association. Vancouver, British Columbia.

Bennett, W. L. and Iyengar, S. (2008) 'A New Era of Minimal Effects? The Changing Foundations of Political Communication', *Journal of Communication*, 58(4): 707–31.

Berinsky, A. J. and Kinder, D. R. (2006) 'Making Sense of Issues Through Media Frames: Understanding the Kosovo Crisis', *The Journal of Politics*, 68(3): 640–56.

Bizer, G. Y. and Petty, R. E. (2005) 'How We Conceptualize Our Attitudes Matters: The Effects of Valence Framing on the Resistance of Political Attitudes', *Political Psychology*, 26(4): 553–68.

Bogdanova, P. and Lecheler, S. (2009) 'Valenced Strategy Framing and its Effects on Voters', unpublished manuscript.

Boomgaarden, H. G. and de Vreese, C. H. (2007) 'Dramatic Real-World Events and Public Opinion Dynamics: Media Coverage and its Impact on Public Reactions to an Assassination', *International Journal of Public Opinion Research*, 19(3): 354–66.

Callaghan, K. and Schnell, F. (2005) *Framing American Politics*. Pittsburgh, PA: University of Pittsburgh Press.

Cappella, J. N. and Jamieson, K. H. (1997) *Spiral of Cynicism: The Press and the Public Good*. New York: Oxford University Press.

Chong, D. and Druckman, J. N. (2007a) 'Framing Theory', *Annual Review of Political Science*, 10(1):103–26.

Chong, D. and Druckman, J. N. (2007b) 'A Theory of Framing and Opinion Formation in Competitive Elite Environments', *Journal of Communication*, 57(1): 99–118.

Chong, D. and Druckman, J. N. (2010) 'Dynamic Public Opinion: Communication Effects Over Time', *American Political Science Review*, 104(4): 663–80.

D'Angelo, P. (2002) 'News Framing as a Multiparadigmatic Research Program: A Response to Entman', *Journal of Communication*, 52(4): 870–88.

D'Angelo, P. and Kuypers, J. A. (eds.) (2009) *Doing News Framing Analysis: Empirical and Theoretical Perspectives*. New York: Routledge.

De Martino, B., Kumaran, D., Seymour, B. and Dolan, R. J. (2006) 'Frames, Biases, and Rational Decision-Making in the Human Brain', *Science*, 313(5787): 684–7.

de Vreese, C. H. (2002) *Framing Europe: Television News and European Integration*. Amsterdam: Aksant Academic Publishers.

de Vreese, C. H. (2004) 'The Effects of Strategic News on Political Cynicism, Issue Evaluations, and Policy Support: A Two-Wave Experiment', *Mass Communication and Society*, 7(2): 191–214.

de Vreese, C. H. (2005) 'News Framing: Theory and Typology', *Information Design Journal Document Design*, 13(1): 51–62.

de Vreese, C. H. and Boomgaarden, H. G. (2003) 'Valenced News Frames and Public Support for the EU: Linking Content Analysis and Experimental Data', *Communications. The European Journal of Communication*, 3(4): 261–81.

de Vreese, C. H. and Boomgaarden, H. G. (2006) 'News, Political Knowledge and Participation: The Differential Effects of News Media Exposure on Political Knowledge and Participation', *Acta Politica,* 41(4): 317–41.

de Vreese, C. H. and Semetko, H. A. (2002) 'Cynical and Engaged: Strategic Campaign Coverage, Public Opinion and Mobilization in a Referendum', *Communication Research*, 29(6): 615–41.

de Vreese, C. H., Boomgaarden, H. G. and Semetko, H. A. (2010). '(In)direct Framing Effects: The Effects of News Media Framing on Public Support for Turkish Membership in the European Union', *Communication Research*, 38(2): 179–205.

Donsbach, W. (2004) 'Psychology of News Decisions: Factors Behind Journalists' Professional Behavior', *Journalism*, 5(2): 131–57.

Druckman, J. N. (2001a) 'On the Limits of Framing Effects: Who Can Frame?', *Journal of Politics*, 63(4): 1041–66.

Druckman, J. N. (2001b) 'The Implications of Framing Effects for Citizen Competence', *Political Behavior*, 23(3): 225–56.

Druckman, J. N. (2004) 'Political Preference Formation: Competition, Deliberation, and the (Ir)relevance of Framing Effects', *American Political Science Review*, 98(4): 671–86.

Druckman, J. N. (2011) 'What's it All About? Framing in Political Science', in G. Keren (ed.), *Perspectives on Framing.*New York: Psychology Press Taylor & Francis Group. pp. 279–300.

Druckman, J. N. and Bolsen, T. (2009) 'Framing, Motivated Reasoning, and Opinions About Emergent Technologies', paper presented at the annual meeting of the Midwest Political Science Association 67th Annual National Conference. The Palmer House Hilton, Chicago.

Druckman, J. N. and Nelson, K. R. (2003) 'Framing and Deliberation: How Citizens Conversations Limit Elite Influence', *American Journal of Political Science*, 47(4): 729–45.

Druckman, J. N. and McDermott, R. (2008) 'Emotions and the Framing of Risky Choice', *Political Behavior*, 30(3): 297–321.

Eagly, A. H. and Chaiken, S. (1993) *The Psychology of Attitudes*. Fort Worth, TX: Harcourt Brace College Publishers.

Elenbaas, M. and de Vreese, C. H. (2008) 'The Effects of Strategic News on Political Cynicism and Vote Choice Among Young Voters', *Journal of Communication*, 58(3): 550–67.

Entman, R. M. (1991) 'Framing US Coverage of International News: Contrasts in Narratives of the KAL and Iran Air Incidents', *Journal of Communication*, 41(4): 6–27.

Entman, R. M. (1993) 'Framing: Toward Clarification of a Fractured Paradigm', *Journal of Communication*, 43(4): 51–8.

Entman, R. M. and Rojecki, A. (1993) 'Freezing Out the Public: Elite and Media Framing of the US Anti-Nuclear Movement', *Political Communication*, 10(2): 155–73.

Farrell, H. and Drezner, D. W. (2008) 'The Power and Politics of Blogs', *Public Choice*, 134(1–2): 15–30.

Gaines, B. J., Kuklinski, J. H. and Quirk, P. J. (2007) 'The Logic of the Survey Experiment Reexamined', *Political Analysis*, 15(1): 1–20.

Gamson, W. A. (1992) *Talking politics*. New York: Cambridge University Press.

Gamson, W. A. and Modigliani, A. (1989) 'Media Discourse and Public Opinion on Nuclear Power: A Constructionist Approach', *American Journal of Sociology*, 95(1): 1–37.

Gandy, O. H. (2001) 'Epilogue – Framing at the Horizon: Retrospective Assessment', in S. D. Reese, O. H. Gandy and A. E. Grant (eds.), *Framing Public Life*. Mahwah, NJ: Lawrence Erlbaum Associates. pp. 355–78.

Gans, H. J. (1979) *Deciding What's News*. New York: Pantheon Books.

Gerber, A. S., Karlan, D. and Bergan, D. (2009) 'Does the Media Matter? A Field Experiment Measuring the Effect of Newspapers on Voting Behavior and Political Opinions', *American Economic Journal: Applied Economics*, 1(2): 35–52.

Graber, D. A. and Smith, J. M. (2005) 'Political Communication Faces the 21st Century', *Journal of Communication*, 55(3): 479–507.

Gross, K. and Brewer, P. R. (2007) 'Sore Losers: News Frames, Policy Debates, and Emotions', *Harvard International Journal of Press/Politics*, 12(1): 122–33.

Gross, K. and D'Ambrosio, L. (2004) 'Framing Emotional Response', *Political Psychology*, 25(1): 1–29.

Haider-Markel, D. P. and Joslyn, M. R. (2001) 'Gun Policy, Opinion, Tragedy, and Blame Attribution: The Conditional Influence of Issue Frames', *The Journal of Politics*, 63(2): 520–43.

Hansen, K. M. (2007) 'The Sophisticated Public: The Effect of Competing Frames on Public Opinion', *Scandinavian Political Studies*, 30(3): 377–96.

Hänggli, R. and Kriesi, H. (2010). Political Framing Strategies and their Impact on Media Framing in a Swiss Direct-Democracy Campaign, *Political Communication*, 27(2): 141–157.

Hertog, J. K. and McLeod, D. M. (2001) 'A Multiperspectival Approach to Framing Analysis: A Field Guide', in S. D. Reese, O. H. Gandy and A. E. Grant (eds.), *Framing Public Life*. Mahwah, NJ: Lawrence Erlbaum Associates. pp. 139–62.

Holm, E. M. (2009) 'Do Emotions Affect the Effect of Issue Frames?', paper presented at the annual meeting of the ISPP 32nd Annual Scientific Meeting. Trinity College, Dublin, Ireland.

Hovland, C. I. and Weiss, W. (1951) 'The Influence of Source Credibility on Communication Effectiveness', *Public Opinion Quarterly*, 15(4): 635–50.

Iyengar, S. (1991) *Is Anyone Responsible? How Television Frames Political Issues*. Chicago, IL: University of Chicago Press.

Iyengar, S. and Kinder, D. R. (1987) *News that Matters: Television and American Opinion*. Chicago, IL: University of Chicago Press.

Iyengar, S. and Simon, A. F. (2000) 'New Perspectives and Evidence on Political Communication and Campaign Effects', *Annual Review of Psychology*, 51(1): 149–69.

Jerit, J. (2009) 'Issue Framing and Engagement: Rhetorical strategy in Public Policy Debates', *Political Behavior*, 30(1): 1–24.

Kahneman, D. (2000) 'Preface', in D. Kahneman and A. Tversky (eds.), *Choices Values and Frames*. Cambridge, UK: Cambridge University Press. pp. ix–xvii.

Kahneman, D. and Tversky, A. (1984) 'Choices, Values and Frames', *American Psychologist*, 39(4): 341–50.

Kinder, D. R. (2007) 'Curmudgeonly Advice', *Journal of Communication*, 57(1): 155–62.

Kinder, D. R. and Palfrey, T. R. (eds.) (1993) *Experimental Foundations of Political Science*. Ann Arbor, MI: University of Michigan Press.

Kinder, D. R. and Sanders, L. M. (1990) 'Mimicking Political Debate with Survey Questions: The Case of White Opinion on Affirmative Action for Black', *Social Cognition*, 8(1): 73–103.

Kolmer, C. and Semetko, H. A. (2009) 'Framing the Iraq War: Perspectives from American U.K., Czech, German, South African, and Al-Jazeera News', *American Behavioral Scientist*, 52(5): 643–56.

Krosnick, J. A. and Brannon, L. A. (1993) 'The Impact of the Gulf War on the Ingredients of Presidential Evaluations: Multidimensional Effects of Political Involvement', *American Political Science Review*, 87(4): 963–75.

Kunda, Z. (1990) 'The Case for Motivated Reasoning', *Psychological Bulletin*, 108(3): 480–98.

Lakoff, G. (2004) *Don't Think of an Elephant: Know Your Values and Frame the Debate*. White River Junction: Vermont: Chelsea Green Publishing.

Lavine, H., Lodge, M., Polichak, J. and Taber, C. (2002) 'Explicating the Black Box Through Experimentation: Studies of Authoritarianism and Threats', *Political Analysis*, 10(4): 343–61.

Lecheler, S. and de Vreese, C. H. (2011) 'Getting Real: The Duration of Framing Effects', *Journal of Communication*, 61: 959–983.

Lecheler, S. and de Vreese, C. H. (2012a) 'News Framing and Public Opinion: A Mediational Analysis', *Journalism & Mass Communication Quarterly*. In press.

Lecheler, S. and de Vreese, C. H. (2012b) 'What a Difference a Day Makes? Repetitive and Competitive Framing Over Time', *Communication Research*. In press.

Lecheler, S. and de Vreese, C. H. (2010) 'Framing Serbia: The Effects of News Framing on Public Support for EU enlargement', *European Political Science Review*, 2(1): 73–93.

Lecheler, S., de Vreese, C. H. and Slothuus, R. (2009) 'Issue Importance as a Moderator of Framing Effects', *Communication Research*, 36(3): 400–25.

Levin, I. P., Schneider, S. L. and Gaeth, G. J. (1998) 'All Frames are not Created Equal: A Typology and Critical Analysis of Framing Effects', *Organizational Behavior and Human Decision Processes*, 76(2): 149–88.

Marcus, G. E. (2000) 'Emotions in Politics', in N. W. Polsby (ed.), *Annual Review of Political Science*, Vol. 3. Palo Alto, CA: Annual Reviews. pp. 221–250.

Matthes, J. (2007) 'Beyond Accessibility? Toward an On-Line and Memory-Based Model of Framing Effects', *Communications*, 32(1): 51–78.

Matthes, J. (2009) 'What's in a Frame? A Content Analysis of Media-Framing Studies in the World's Leading Communication Journals 1990–2005', *Journalism and Mass Communication Quarterly*, 86(2): 349–67.

Matthes, J. and Kohring, M. (2008) 'The Content Analysis of Media Frames: Toward Improving Reliability and Validity', *Journal of Communication*, 58(2): 258–79.

McDermott, R. (2002) 'Experimental Methodology in Political Science', *Political Analysis*, 10(4): 325–42.

McLeod, D. M., Kosicki, G. M. and McLeod, J. M. (2002) 'Resurveying the Boundaries of Political Communication Effects', in J. Bryant and D. Zillmann (eds.), *Media Effects. Advances in Theory and Research*. Mahwah, NJ: Lawrence Erlbaum Associates. pp. 215–68.

Mutz, D. C. and Reeves, B. (2005) 'The New Videomalaise: Effects of Televised Incivility on Political Trust', *American Political Science Review*, 99(1): 1–15.

Nabi, R. L. (2003) 'Exploring the Framing Effects of Emotion: Do Discrete Emotions Differentially Influence Information Accessibility, Information Seeking, and Policy Preference?', *Communication Research*, 30(2): 224–47.

Negrine, R. and Lilleker, D. (2002) 'The Professionalization of Political Communication: Continuities and Change in Media Practices', *European Journal of Communication*, 17(3): 305–23.

Nelson, T. E. and Oxley, Z. M. (1999) 'Issue Framing Effects on Belief Importance and Opinion', *The Journal of Politics*, 61(4): 1040–67.

Nelson, T. E., Oxley, Z. M. and Clawson, R. A. (1997) 'Toward a Psychology of Framing Effects', *Political Behaviour*, 19(3): 221–46.

Neuman, W. R., Just, M. R. and Crigler, A. N. (1992) *Common Knowledge: News and the Construction of Political Meaning*. Chicago, IL: University of Chicago Press.

O'Keefe, D. J. and Jensen, J. D. (2006) 'The Advantages of Compliance or the Disadvantages of Noncompliance? A Meta-Analytic Review of the Relative Persuasive Effectiveness of Gain-Framed and Loss-Framed Messages', *Communication Yearbook*, 30: 1–43.

Petty, R. E. and Cacioppo, J. T. (1986) 'The Elaboration Likelihood Model of Persuasion', in L. Berkowitz (ed.), *Advances in Experimental Social Psychology*. New York: Academic Press. pp. 123–205.

Price, V. and Tewksbury, D. (1997) 'News Values and Public Opinion: A Theoretical Account of Media Priming and Framing', in G. Barnett and F. Boster (eds.), *Progress in Communication Sciences*. Norwood, NJ: Ablex. pp. 173–212.

Price, V., Tewksbury, D. and Powers, E. (1997) 'Switching Trains of Thought', *Communication Research*, 24(5): 481–506.

Reese, S. D., Gandy, O. and Grant, A. (eds.) (2001) *Framing Public Life: Perspectives on Media and our Understanding of the Social World*. Mahwah, NJ: Lawrence Erlbaum Associates.

Roessler, P. (2001) 'Between Online Heaven and Cyberhell: The Framing of the Internet by Traditional Media in Germany', *New Media and Society*, 3(1): 49–66.

Scheufele, B. (2004) 'Framing-Effects Approach: A Theoretical and Methodological Critique', *Communications*, 29(4): 401–428.

Scheufele, B. (2006) 'Frames, Schemata and News Reporting', *Communications*, 31(1): 65–83.

Scheufele, D. A. (1999) 'Framing as a Theory of Media Effects', *Journal of Communication*, 49(1): 103–22.

Scheufele, D. A. (2000) 'Agenda-Setting, Priming, and Framing Revisited: Another Look at Cognitive Effects of Political Communication', *Mass Communication and Society*, 3(2): 297–316.

Scheufele, D. A. and Tewksbury, D. (2007) 'Framing, Agenda-Setting, and Priming: The Evolution of Three Media Effects Models', *Journal of Communication*, 57(1): 9–20.

Schuck, A. R. T. and de Vreese, C. H. (2006) 'Between Risk and Opportunity: News Framing and its Effects on Public Support for EU Enlargement', *European Journal of Communication*, 21(1): 5–23.

Schuck, A. R. T. and de Vreese, C. H. (2009) 'When Good News is Bad News: Explicating the Underlying Moderated Mediation Dynamics Behind the Reversed Mobilization Effect', paper presented at the annual meeting of the International Communication Association. Chicago.

Shah, D. V., Watts, M. D., Domke, D. and Fan, D. P. (2002) 'News Framing and Cueing of Issue Regimes. Explaining Clinton's Public Approval in Spite of Scandal', *Public Opinion Quarterly*, 66(3): 339–70.

Shah, D. V., Kwak, N., Schmierbach, M. and Zubric, J. (2004) 'The Interplay of News Frames on Cognitive Complexity', *Human Communication Research*, 30(1): 102–20.

Shen, F. (2004) 'Chronic Accessibility and Individual Cognitions: Examining the Effects of Message Frames on Political Advertisements', *Journal of Communication*, 54(1): 123–37.

Shen, F. and Edwards, H. H. (2005) 'Economic Individualism, Humanitarianism, and Welfare Reform: A Value-Based Account of Framing Effects', *Journal of Communication*, 55(4): 795–809.

Shoemaker, P. and Reese, S. D. (1996) *Mediating the Message*. New York: Longman Publishers.

Semetko, H. A. and Valkenburg, P. M. (2000) 'Framing European Politics: A Content Analysis of Press and Television News', *Journal of Communication*, 50(2): 93–109.

Simon, A. and Xenos, M. (2000) 'Media Framing and Effective Public Deliberation', *Political Communication*, 17(4): 363–76.

Slothuus, R. (2008) 'More than Weighting Cognitive Importance: A Dual Process Model of Issue Framing Effects', *Political Psychology*, 29(1): 1–28.

Smith, S. M. and Petty, R. E. (1996) 'Message Framing and Persuasion: A Message Processing Analysis', *Personality and Social Psychology Bulletin*, 22(3): 257–68.

Sniderman, P. M. and Theriault, S. M. (2004) 'The Structure of Political Argument and the Logic of Issue Framing', in W. E. Saris and P. M. Sniderman (eds.), *Studies in Public Opinion*. Princeton, NJ: Princeton University Press. pp. 133–165.

Snow, D. A. and Benford, R. D. (1992) 'Master Frames and Cycles of Protest', in A. D. Morris and C. M. Mueller (eds.), *Frontiers in Social Movement Theory*. New Haven, CT: Yale University Press.

Snow, D. A., Rochford, Jr., E. B., Worden, S. K. and Benford, R. D. (1986) 'Frame Alignment Processes, Micromobilization, and Movement Participation', *American Sociological Association*, 51(4): 464–81.

Taber, C. S., Cann, D. and Kucsova, S. (2009) 'The Motivated Processing of Political Arguments', *Political Behavior*, 31(2): 137–55.

Taber, C. S. and Lodge, M. (2006) 'Motivated Skepticism in the Evaluation of Political Beliefs', *American Journal of Political Science*, 50(3): 755–69.

Tankard, J. W. (2001) 'The Empirical Approach to the Study of Media Framing', in S. D. Reese, O. H. Gandy and A. E. Grant (eds.), *Framing Public Life*. Mahwah, NJ: Lawrence Erlbaum Associates. pp. 95–106.

Tewksbury, D., Jones, J., Peske, M. W., Raymond, A. and Vig, W. (2000) 'The Interaction of News and Advocate Frames: Manipulating Audience Perceptions of a Local Public Policy Issue', *Journalism and Mass Communication Quarterly*, 77(4): 804–29.

Tuchman, G. (1978) *Making News. A Study in the Construction of Reality*. New York: Free Press.

Valentino, N. A., Beckmann, M. and Buhr, T. (2001) 'A Spiral of Cynicism for Some: The Contingent Effects of Campaign News Frames on Participation and Confidence in Government', *Political Communication*, 18(4): 347–67.

Valkenburg, P. M., Semetko, H. A. and de Vreese, C. H. (1999) 'The Effects of News Frames on Readers Thoughts and Recall', *Communication Research*, 26(5): 550–69.

Wanta, W. and Hu, Y.-W. (1994) 'Time-Lag Differences in the Agenda-Setting Process: An Examination of Five News Media', *International Journal of Public Opinion Research*, 6(3): 225–240.

Williams, A. P. and Kaid, L. L. (2006) 'Media Framing of the European Parliamentary Elections: A View from the United States', in M. Meier and J. Tenscher (eds.), *Campaigning in Europe – Campaigning for Europe: Political Parties, Campaigns' Mass Media, and the European Parliamentary Elections 2004*. Berlin: LIT Publishers. pp. 295–304.

Zaller, J. (1992) *The Nature and Origins of Mass Opinion*. Cambridge: Cambridge University Press.

Zaller, J. (1996) 'The Myth of Massive Media Impact Revived: New Support for a Discredited Idea', in D. Mutz, R. Brody and P. Sniderman (eds.), *Political Persuasion and Attitude Change*. Ann Arbor, MI: University of Michigan Press. pp. 17–79.

24

Dynamics in Mass Communication Effects Research

Dennis Chong and James N. Druckman

How do mass communications affect citizens' opinions? The answer to this question – perhaps the defining subject in the field of communication studies – has vacillated over several decades of research between minimal and maximal effects. Recent technological and social transformations may usher a new era of communications that requires updating of our observations and conclusions (Bennett and Iyengar, 2008). Our goal here is to take stock of our knowledge and, equally important in this period of transition, to offer a unifying framework for studying communications effects that will help to guide future research.[1]

THE TRANSFORMATION OF EFFECTS RESEARCH

By many accounts, McCombs and Shaw's (1972) agenda setting study constitutes the seminal contribution showing that mass communications have 'strong' or 'indirect', rather than minimal effects. McCombs and Shaw's (1972) study took place during the 1968 presidential campaign; they asked 100 undecided voters in Chapel Hill, North Carolina: 'What are you *most* concerned about these days? That is, regardless of what politicians say, what are the two or three *main* things which you think the government *should* concentrate on doing something about?' They then compared voter responses to the content of newspapers,

magazines and television broadcasts.[2] They found 'a very strong relationship between the emphasis placed on different campaign issues by the media … and the judgments of voters as to the salience and importance of various campaign topics' (1972: 181). McCombs and Shaw concluded that 'mass media set the agenda for each political campaign, influencing the salience of attitudes toward the political issues' (1972: 177).

This study spawned a research agenda on how political and media elites influence mass opinion. Much of this research compared the opinions of individuals who reported varying levels of exposure to mass communications (e.g., news broadcasts). Observed differences in opinion between these groups constituted evidence of a mass communication effect. Our confidence in these results depends on our ability to rule out several alternative explanations. One alternative hypothesis is that individuals who watch news are different from individuals who choose not to. News watchers are, for example, generally more interested in following politics. Not only do they watch more news, they are also more likely to talk politics with others and to participate at higher rates. Therefore, any differences between those who watch news and those who abstain might be the consequence of political discussion or attending political events and not exposure to mass communications.

Attempts to statistically control for variation in inter-personal discussion, participation and other factors can improve estimates of media effects but they cannot rule out the possibility the relationship between exposure to mass communication and opinion results from selection bias. Putnam explains, 'Without controlled experiments, we can't be certain which causes which. Virtually all non-experimental studies of the media find it hard to distinguish between "selection effects" (people with a certain trait seek out a particular medium) and "media effects" (people develop that trait by being exposed to that medium)' (2000: 218).

Another no less serious problem is that surveys that ask people to report the frequency with which they read or watch particular media tend to be extremely unreliable with people generally claiming higher levels of exposure than can be verified independently. This would not be a serious problem if biases were constant across demographic categories, but some groups (e.g., young people) over-report significantly more than others.

Experimental research addresses many of the methodological problems inherent in observational studies. The experimental design gives us confidence the observed effects result from the treatment and are not caused by selection bias or unobserved factors that are correlated with news exposure. Random assignment of individuals to treatment groups assures us that the groups are, on average, equal at the start of the experiment so that differences that emerge following exposure to the treatment can be attributed to the effect of the treatment. Moreover, the experimenter controls what individuals are exposed to, so there is no dependence on self-reports. For these reasons – the ability through randomization and control to resolve causal ambiguity and exposure problems – experimentation and the mass media were 'made for each other' (Nelson et al., 2011: 202).

No research study was more instrumental in popularizing the use of experimentation in media studies than Iyengar and Kinder's (1987) *News that Matters*. Their classic experiment on agenda setting randomly assigned individuals to watch alternative versions of a news broadcast that had been manipulated to emphasize one current issue or another (e.g., a story on energy or a story on defense policy). Following the treatment, participants were asked their opinion of the most important problems facing the country. Their answers depended on the content of the news broadcast they had watched; those who were exposed to a story about energy problems were more likely to give priority to the energy issue whereas those who had viewed a story on national defense were more likely to focus on defense. The experiment demonstrated the media's power to set the public agenda.

Iyengar and Kinder further extended media effects research by introducing the concept of priming.[3] 'By calling attention to some matters while ignoring others, television news influences the standards by which governments, presidents, policies, and candidates for public office are judged. Priming refers to changes in the standards that people use to make political evaluations' (Iyengar and Kinder, 1987: 63). For example, individuals exposed to news stories about defense policy tend to give greater weight to the president's actions on defense policy in their overall assessment of the president (or some other candidate). If they believe the president has done a good job protecting the country, they will express higher levels of overall approval. In contrast, individuals who have been primed by stories about energy policy will be more likely to base their overall presidential evaluations on his handling of energy policy.

Iyengar (1991) builds on work by Iyengar and Kinder (1987) by importing the concept of 'framing' to mass communication research. He focused on whether news stories that used either an episodic frame (e.g., a story of an individual on welfare) or a thematic frame (e.g., a story analyzing the distribution of benefits in the welfare system) affected viewers' attributions of responsibility for a problem (e.g., their explanation for why people are on welfare). Others apply framing to describe how an issue can be alternatively construed to influence public preferences; for example, one can frame a hate group rally as a free speech or public safety issue, or campaign finance as an issue of free speech or democratic corruption, with significant consequences for levels of public support.

McCombs and Shaw's (1972) study stimulated a large research agenda, which grew exponentially following the publication of Iyengar and Kinder's (1987) book – scholars began implementing laboratory, survey and field experiments on agenda setting, priming and framing across an enormous range of issues. A search of 13 prominent disciplinary journals, since 1994, reveals 308 articles that mention one or more of the concepts in the article's title and/or abstract.[4] Of these, about 43% focus on the effects of mass communications (e.g., as opposed to charting trends in media coverage), and approximately 61% of those employ experiments.[5]

Few contributions to the study of mass communication have been as important and impactful as Iyengar and Kinder (1987) and Iyengar (1991). Yet, from our perspective, the course of research since these works has been plagued by two fundamental problems.[6] First, the introduction of various supposedly distinct types of communication effects, including agenda setting, priming and framing, has been the source of substantial *conceptual ambiguity* contributing to a fragmented discipline where scholars become overly specialized on one particular type of effect (Iyengar, 2010).[7]

Second, scholars have worried appropriately about the generalizability of experimental conclusions. Of notable concern are laboratory experiments that rely on non-representative samples (often students) (Jacoby, 2000; Kinder, 2007).[8] Kam et al. (2007: 421) explain that many political scientists employ 'the simplistic heuristic of 'a student sample lacks external generalizability' (e.g., Gerber and Green, 2008: 358). Unfortunately, this focus has, inadvertently, led to a neglect of other aspects of generalizability, particularly when it comes to context and timing. In other words, external validity envelops multiple dimensions including the measures, stimuli, sample, context and timing. A growing body of evidence suggests that the dynamics – while depending on certain individual characteristics, such as prior opinion and knowledge – do not inherently differ between student and non-student samples (for general discussion see Druckman and Kam, 2011). We argue that a more important concern revolves around *context* and *time* – nearly all electoral and policy debates involve competition between sides, over time, yet extant work has only recently begun to consider the impact of competition and over-time processes.

In sum, we view three major areas in need of clarification: (1) the relationship between distinct concepts; (2) the impact of competitive contexts and (3) the impact of time. In what follows, we offer our perspectives on each of these topics, with the goal of providing a unified foundation on which other researchers can build.

COORDINATING ON A COMMON CONCEPTUAL LANGUAGE

We situate our discussion of how to define mass communication processes with what we see as the ultimate variable of interest: citizens' opinions. We represent an individual's opinion with a basic expectancy value model of an attitude (e.g., Ajzen and Fishbein, 1980; Nelson et al. 1997). In this model, an attitude toward an object consists of the weighted sum of a set of evaluative beliefs about that object. Specifically, $Attitude = \sum v_i * w_i$, where v_i is the evaluation of the object on attribute i and w_i is the salience weight ($\sum w_i = 1$) associated with that attribute. For example, one's overall attitude, A, toward a new housing development might consist of a mix of negative and positive evaluations, v_i, of the project on different dimensions i. An individual may believe that the project will *favor* economic growth by creating jobs ($i = 1$) but *harm* the environment by impinging on existing green spaces ($i = 2$). Assuming this individual places a positive value on both the economy and the environment, then v_1 is positive and v_2 is negative, and his attitude toward the project will depend on the relative magnitudes of v_1 and v_2 discounted by the relative weights (w_1 and w_2) assigned respectively to each attribute (Nelson and Oxley, 1999).

The following examples illustrate how this conceptualization of an attitude applies to any object of evaluation. First, a voter's preference between two candidates may vary according to whether the voter evaluates them on economic or foreign policy issues (Enelow and Hinich, 1984). In the 2008 US presidential election, a voter might have preferred John McCain to Barack Obama when evaluating them on their foreign policy positions, but preferred Obama to McCain when comparing their economic platforms. Second, an individual's attitude toward welfare recipients may depend on the extent he believes their plight is explained by their personal failures or by social and economic disadvantages (Iyengar, 1991). Third, one's tolerance for allowing a proposed hate group rally may hinge on the value one places on defending free speech versus maintaining public safety.[9] Ultimately, the attitude or preference in each of these situations depends on the valences and weights given to the competing considerations.

Individuals typically base their evaluations on a subset of dimensions, rather than on the universe of possible considerations. In the simplest case, they focus on a single dimension ($w_i = 1$) such as foreign policy or economic affairs in evaluating a candidate, free speech or public safety when considering a hate group rally request or lives saved or lives lost in assessing medical programs. Even when they incorporate more than one dimension, cognitive limitations and economies of thought may cause most individuals to rely on no more than a few considerations (e.g., Simon, 1955). The dimensions underlying one's attitude are *available* (i.e., an individual comprehends the meaning and significance of the dimension), *accessible* (i.e., the consideration *subconsciously* enters the individual's working memory) and *applicable* or appropriate (i.e., the individual *consciously* views the dimension as a relevant or important basis of opinion) (Althaus and Kim, 2006; Chong, 1996; Chong and Druckman, 2007a; Price and Tewksbury, 1997; Winter, 2008: 30).

Two points are relevant. First, accessibility increases with chronic use of a consideration over time *or* from temporary contextual cues – including repeated exposure to communications. Second, individuals assess the applicability of a dimension only when motivated by incentives (e.g., a desire to make the correct decision) or by contextual factors such as the presence of directly conflicting or competing information (that prompts applicability assessments) (Chong and Druckman, 2007a,b,c).

This model of attitude formation can be used to compare alternative conceptions of communication effects – framing, priming, agenda setting and persuasion. With framing, we might refer to the dimension or dimensions, the 'i's', that affect an individual's evaluation as an individual's *frame in thought*. For example, an individual who believes economic considerations trump all other concerns in making decisions about the proposed housing development has an 'economic' frame in thought on that issue. Or, if free speech dominates all other considerations in deciding a hate group's right to rally, the individual's frame would be free speech. Nothing (but economy of thinking) precludes an individual from employing a more complex frame in thought that mixes multiple frames, such as consideration of free speech, public safety and the community's image in contemplating whether a hate group should be allowed to hold a rally.[10]

The frames on which an individual bases his or her attitude have their origin in past experiences, ongoing world events, inter-personal discussions, and so on. Of particular relevance, given our focus, is the impact of communications from politicians and the media. Such elites employ a variety of approaches to purposefully influence the public's opinions. The most obvious strategy they employ is using rhetoric to influence how citizens construe political issues and events. A speaker emphasizes one interpretation of an issue to encourage the public to evaluate the issue along that dimension; for example, a news outlet states that a hate group's planned rally is 'a free speech issue', or a politician describes welfare in terms of its humanitarian effects rather than its impact on taxes. When such *frames in communication* influence an individual's frame in thought, it is called a *framing effect*. In many applications, frames are thought to involve alternative descriptions of an *issue* or an *event* (e.g., Entman, 2004: 5).

'Priming' also fits straightforwardly into our model. As explained, 'priming' in communication research refers to cases where mass communication emphasis on particular issues or images affect politician evaluations; that is, the object of evaluation is typically a *person*. The expectancy value model applies if we simply assume each consideration constitutes a separate issue or image dimension used to evaluate the politician (Druckman and Holmes, 2004). When a mass communication places attention on an issue, that issue will receive greater weight through increased accessibility and, possibly, applicability. In this case, then, priming is the same as framing and the two terms can be used interchangeably. Early mass communication work presumed that priming of candidate evaluations worked strictly via accessibility, whereas issue or event framing was often seen as working through more conscious applicability assessments. Yet, the evidence for this distinction is lacking (e.g., Miller and Krosnick, 2000), as is any evidence showing different processes at work in person as opposed to issue or event evaluations. Until such evidence can be produced, there is no reason to distinguish priming and framing in mass communication.

The model also encompasses agenda setting, which, as explained, occurs when a speaker's (e.g., a news outlet or politician) emphasis on an issue or problem leads its audience to view the issue or problem as relatively important (e.g., McCombs, 2004). For example, when a news outlet's campaign coverage focuses on the economy, viewers come to believe the economy is the most important campaign issue. In terms of the expectancy-value model – the focus (i.e., dependent variable) with agenda setting involves assessments of the salience component of the attitude (rather than the overall evaluation of the object). The previous example can be construed as the news outlet framing the campaign in terms of the economy, and the researcher simply gauging the specific salience weights (w_i) as the dependent variable.[11]

A final concept is persuasion. Nelson and Oxley (1999) define persuasion as involving a change in the evaluation component, v_i of an attitude in response to a communication (in contrast to the other concepts which involve the weight component, w_i [also see Johnston et al., 1992: 212]). For example, in assessing a new housing project, framing takes place if a communication causes economic considerations to become more important relative to environmental considerations. Persuasion occurs if the communication alters one's evaluation of the proposal on one of those dimensions (e.g., by modifying one's beliefs about the project's economic consequences). In practice, persuasion and framing/priming/agenda setting strategies often go hand in hand, as campaign communications for a candidate simultaneously steer voters to focus on certain issues in the campaign while also emphasizing the candidate's strong records on those issues.

In sum, we view framing, priming and agenda setting as equivalent processes that involve alterations of the weight component of an attitude through changes in availability, accessibility and/ or applicability. Our preference – and our practice in what follows – is to use the overarching term of 'framing', in part, because priming refers to a related but distinct procedure in psychology, and agenda setting is widely used in political science to refer to institutional agendas (e.g., in Congress; see Riker, 1986). We recognize that our argument about conceptual equivalency contrasts with common portrayals (e.g., Scheufele, 1999; McCombs, 2004). Yet, until definitive evidence reveals meditational or moderating differences, the concepts should be treated as the same, meaning research on each should be merged and redundancy avoided.[12]

INTRODUCING COMPETITION

While analysts have long recognized the potential importance of elite competition in affecting opinion formation (e.g., Entman, 1993: 55; Riker, 1996: 33; Schattschneider, 1960), only recently have they explicitly explored competitive mass communication effects. Sniderman and Theriault (2004) offered one of the first empirical forays, demonstrating, with two experimental surveys, that when competing frames are presented together (e.g., both free speech and public safety considerations are raised in regard to a hate group rally), they reduce the influence of one-sided frames. Competing frames make alternative positions equally accessible, which increases the likelihood people will be able to identify and choose the side that is consistent with their ideological values (also see Brewer and Gross, 2005; Hansen, 2007).

In some of our own work, we have built on Sniderman and Theriault (2004) by examining the variable impact of different types of competition. 'Competition' is most generally understood as the presence of frames aimed at promoting different sides of an issue, namely a 'pro' side and a 'con' side. Frames therefore have distinct positional *directions* (Chong and Druckman, 2007a,b,c). For example, the free speech frame promotes the right of individuals to organize a rally ('a pro frame') while the public safety frame provides a rationale for preventing the rally ('a con frame').

We further identify two dimensions of competition. One dimension concerns the *repetition* or *frequency* of each side's frame(s). Continuing with the example, the free speech frame (and/or other 'pro frames') may be presented once, twice, 10 times, etc., while the public safety frame (and/or other 'con frames') could be presented the same or any other number of times. Studies of communication effects can be classified by the relative frequency with which participants are exposed to each side's messages: (1) *asymmetric one-sided* studies in which individuals receive a frame (or multiple frames) representing only one side of the issue (e.g., the free speech frame one or

more times); (2) *dual* (or symmetric) studies in which individuals receive opposing frames from each side of the issue in equal quantity (e.g., the free speech and public safety frames once apiece) and (3) *asymmetric two-sided* studies in which individuals receive opposing frames in unequal quantities (e.g., the free speech frame twice and the public safety frame once). Asymmetric one-sided studies are therefore 'non-competitive' because individuals are exposed to only one side of a controversy, whereas dual and asymmetric two-sided designs model different 'competitive' environments.

The other dimension of competition is the *strength* of the frames – this gets at the likely effectiveness of the frame in actually influencing public opinion. In reference to our earlier psychological model (perceived), strength refers to the extent a frame emphasizes relatively available and applicable considerations. While strength presumably lies on a continuum, we simplify by referring to 'weak' frames that are typically seen as unpersuasive and 'strong' frames that are compelling. For example, most people likely regard 'maintaining public safety' as a stronger frame for prohibiting a hate group rally than 'preventing litter on the streets'. A study can employ strong frames exclusively, weak frames exclusively, or a mixture of strong and weak frames.

Table 24.1 crosses our dimensions of competition to create a typology of mass communication environments. (We will shortly discuss the cell entries.) Taken together, variations in the relative frequencies and strengths of frames combine to yield eight possible competitive contexts (a ninth cell is not applicable). The number of possible mixes of communications within each of these cells, in terms of frequency of repetition and relative strengths, is infinite (e.g., consider the asymmetric dual sided strong design can include 1 pro-2 con, 2 pro-3 con, 1 pro-18 con and so on). That said, in other published work, we explored 16 possible mixes – at least one that falls into each cell – in two laboratory experiments (one on the issue of urban growth and the other on a proposed hate group rally) (Chong and Druckman, 2007b). We find that, in competitive contexts, frame strength plays the most decisive role; a frame's relative strength matters more than its repetition (regardless of the side of the argument endorsed by the frame). Even when the weak frame is heard multiple times against a single exposure to the strong frame, the strong frame wins. Moreover, weak frames, when competing against opposing strong frames, sometimes backfire, pushing respondents in the direction that is opposite to its intended effect.

The importance of frame strength also emerges in Druckman's (2010) study of support for a

Table 24.1 Competitive communications

	Competitive situations		
	Asymmetric one-sided (exposure to just one message)	Dual (exposure to both messages in equal quantities)	Asymmetric two-sided (exposure to both messages in unequal quantities)
Strong messages	• Economic benefits • Social costs	• Economic benefits – social costs	• None in experiment. (*Example:* Economic benefits – social costs – economic benefits)
Weak messages	• Corruption • Corruption-morality	• Corruption-entertainment	• None in experiment. (*Example:* Corruption – morality – entertainment)
Strong and weak messages	• n/a	• Social costs-entertainment • Corruption – economic benefits	• Corruption – economic benefits – morality

publicly funded casino. Based on pre-test data that asked individuals to rate the effectiveness of distinct frames, Druckman identified two strong frames: a pro-economic benefits frame (revenue from the casino will support educational programs), and a con-social costs frame (casinos lead to addictive behavior). He also found three weak frames: a pro-entertainment frame, a con-corruption frame and a con-morality frame. He then exposed a distinct set of participants to nine combinations of these frames in the context of an election day exit poll in Illinois, at the conclusion of the 2006 Illinois gubernatorial campaign (on 7 November) ($N = 309$). The exact mixes, and where they fall in terms of our conceptual framework, appear in the cells of Table 24.1.

A summary of the results appears in Figure 24.1, which illustrates the shift in average opinion, by frame exposures, relative to a control group that received no frames. In every case, the strong frame moved opinion and the weak frame did not. For example, the final condition in Figure 24.1 shows that a single exposure to the strong economic benefits frame substantially moved opinion (by 41%) even in the face of two weak opposing frames. As in the urban growth and hate rally experiments, strength proved more important than repetition.

These results beg the question of what lies beyond a frame's strength. Why are some frames perceived as strong and others weak? Even the large persuasion literature offers little insight: 'Unhappily, this research evidence is not as illuminating as one might suppose … It is not yet known what it is about the "strong arguments" … that makes them persuasive' (O'Keefe, 2002: 147, 156). The little research thus far does not paint a particularly flattering portrayal of strength perceptions. For example, Arceneaux finds that 'individuals are more likely to be persuaded by political arguments that evoke cognitive biases' (2009: 1). Specifically, he reports that messages that highlight averting losses or out-group threats resonate to a greater extent than do other, ostensibly analogous arguments. Druckman and Bolsen (2011) report that adding factual information to messages does nothing to enhance their strength. They focus on opinions about new technologies, such as carbon nanotubes (CNTs). Druckman and Bolsen expose experimental participants to different mixes of frames in support of and opposed to the technology. For example, a supportive frame for CNTs states 'Most agree that the most important implication of CNTs concerns how they will affect energy cost and availability'. An example of an opposed frame is 'Most agree that the most important implication of CNTs concerns their unknown long-run implications for human health'. Druckman and Bolsen report that each of these two frames shifts opinions in the expected directions. More importantly, when factual information is added to one or both frames (in other conditions) – such as citing a specific study about energy costs (e.g., a study shows CNTS will double the efficiency of solar cells in the coming years), that information does nothing to add to the

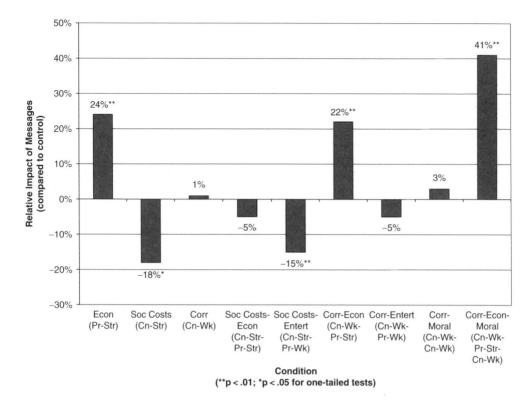

Figure 24.1   Likelihood of Casino support

power of the frame. In short, frames with specific factual evidence are no stronger (in their effects) than analogous frames that include no such evidence. This is troubling insofar as one believes scientific evidence should be accorded greater credibility.

Other work on frame strength suggests it increases in frames that highlight specific emotions (Petersen, 2007), include multiple, frequently appearing, arguments (Baumgartner et al., 2008) and/or have been used in the past (Edy, 2006). The initial studies on frame strength make clear that one should not confound 'strength' with 'normative desirability'. What exactly is normatively desirable lies outside the purview of this essay, but is a topic that demands careful consideration.

INTRODUCING TIME

As experimental designs become more realistic in taking account of political competition, they need also examine the role that time plays in modifying communication effects. Given the dynamic nature of political campaigns, it is surprising the vast majority of communications research are one-shot studies that examine how respondents react in the immediate aftermath of a treatment, such as exposure to a news editorial on a political issue. In reality, individuals are likely to be exposed to a stream of messages as competing sides make their case to the public, and the effect of a specific message is likely to depend on when it is received in the sequence of communications, and whether the effect is measured immediately or later in the campaign. Therefore, the results of an experiment should be interpreted within this longer-term temporal framework even if the experimental design is a one-shot study; otherwise, we risk misinterpreting the significance of the observed effects.

Participants do not come to experiments tabula rasa, nor are the effects of experiments likely to be permanent. When an experimental participant receives a message about a controversial political issue, the message is viewed through ideological and partisan predispositions and received against messages encountered previously (outside of the context of the experiment). Researchers routinely control for the respondent's prior values in examining the impact of the treatment, but they rarely have the ability to control for past exposure to information on the issue.

At the other end of the temporal continuum, researchers have rarely monitored the post-treatment trajectory of opinion. The limited available evidence of the longevity of communication effects suggests the opinion change induced by information, experiences or persuasive messages can be fleeting. In the few experimental studies of communication effects that retest opinions, the effects induced by the treatment vanished after several days (e.g., de Vreese, 2004; Druckman and Nelson, 2003; Mutz and Reeves, 2005; Tewksbury et al., 2000; cf. Iyengar and Kinder, 1987: 24–6).

These dynamics are consistent with several observational studies and field experiments showing that movements of public opinion in response to political events are often short lived as citizens give less weight to events as they recede into the past (e.g., Gerber et al., 2007; Hibbs, 2008). However, a more mixed picture of opinion change emerges in Shaw's (1999) comprehensive analysis of the effect of newsworthy campaign events on presidential candidate preferences. Shaw found variable rates of opinion change and decay over a brief 10-day interval following an event. Some events (e.g., retrospective and prospective messages) had minimal effects on public opinion while many other events (e.g., value appeals by the candidates, vice presidential debates, actions to increase party unity) had significant but temporary effects, with public opinion quickly spiking up and down in the days following the event. Only national conventions, presidential debates and scandals and blunders involving the candidates appeared to have a more sustained effect on preferences.

As the authors of these and other studies surmise, the rate of opinion decay likely varies across issues and individuals (also see Matthes, 2008; Albertson and Lawrence, 2009). In Shaw's study, transitory effects were more apparent on issues that tended to get limited rather than extended and

repeated coverage in the media. Minimal but enduring effects are consistent with what political psychologists refer to as 'online processing' of information while transitory but relatively large effects (spikes in opinion change) seem to reflect 'memory-based' opinion processes. We elaborate on these concepts below in discussing a dynamic theory of opinion change over time.

A Conceptual Scheme for Analyzing Communication Effects Over Time

In this section, we present a general conceptual framework that describes the dynamics of opinion change at any stage of a campaign in relation to the timing of experimental observations of opinion. If we define time t as the period in which we first expose the respondent to a treatment followed immediately by a measure of opinion, this allows us to divide the campaign at t to create a pre-t period and a post-t period. We further subdivide these periods according to whether additional communications (relevant to the topic of study) were received in the pre-t and post-t periods.

The four states in Table 24.2 represent all possible sequences of exposure to communications from the start of the campaign to time t, and from t to the end of the campaign (setting aside no exposure altogether). Individuals in cell 1 have not received any communications about the issue prior to t, whereas those in cell 2 have received information about the issue prior to the latest message at t. Individuals who receive no further communications on the issue in the post treatment period fall in cell 3, while those who are exposed to additional messages are in cell 4. Therefore, any individual's exposure to mass communications over the duration of the campaign can be represented by a combination of two cells drawn across the two periods. For example, an individual who received no message before t and multiple messages after t would fall in cells 1 (pre-t) and 4 (post-t). (Individuals who receive no messages throughout the course of the campaign are the

Table 24.2   Time and communication effects

		Exposure to messages	
		No messages	Mix of messages
Time	Before time t treatment	(1) Prior beliefs and values moderate effects.	(2) Pre-treatment exposure to messages moderates effects.
	After time t treatment	(3) Effects endure or decay over time.	(4) Post-treatment exposure to messages modifies effects.

residual group outside of this scheme; in an experiment, these individuals would be in the control group.)

Most studies of communication effects have been single treatment tests without regard for whether participants fall in cell 1 or cell 2. Individuals who begin the study in the state described by cell 1 are reasonably blank slates because they have learned nothing about the issue. Their reactions to the message, however, will still be affected by the values they hold, which is why researchers routinely control for values that are relevant to the issue when estimating the effect of the message (e.g., Brewer, 2001; Chong and Druckman, 2007a,b; Shen and Edwards, 2005).

Researchers however have generally ignored the potential impact of prior exposure to relevant messages (cell 2 in Table 24.2). Individuals in cell 2 who were exposed previously to discussions of the test issue might react differently to the treatment than those encountering the issue for the first time. In particular, their opinion on the issue at the start of the study may already reflect the influence of the argument being tested, thus making them immune to further persuasion by that message. However, this means only the argument was ineffective in the study, not in reality (Slothuus, 2008). As Gaines et al. explain, 'there is inevitably some possibility that respondents enter the experiment having already participated in a similar experiment, albeit one occurring in the real world' (2007: 13, 17).

Few studies have examined the opinion processes represented in cells 3 and 4. Cell 3 describes a post-treatment trajectory in which individuals do not receive any additional exposure to communications. In this case, we are interested in the durability of effects – to the end of the campaign or policy debate – in the absence of further stimulation. The original effects may vanish on their own or, alternatively, they may persist or become even stronger. In any event, these post-treatment updates may cause us to reassess the significance of the original findings. Most of the observational and experimental studies we cited earlier identify significant decay of effects of events and information over time.

Finally, cell 4 describes individuals who receive additional messages about the issue following treatment at time t. There has been mainly speculation, but little empirical work, on the effects of communication under different conditions of democratic competition.[13] In research on framing effects, for example, all work involving multiple frames has been conducted in a single period (e.g., Chong and Druckman, 2007b; Druckman, 2010; Hansen, 2007; Sniderman and Theriault, 2004), with participants encountering all frames in one session rather than over time. When a series of messages representing opposing positions is received over time, the effect of individual messages depends on rates of learning and decay of opinion under the pressure of competition.

Dynamic Theory of Opinion Change

To accommodate the dynamics of opinion change over time, we expand on the theory of competitive frames discussed in Chong and Druckman (2007a,b) to explain the magnitude of communication effects when individuals receive different mixes of messages in a single session. According to this theory, effects depend on the interaction of three factors: (1) the strength of the messages; (2) rates of exposure to (i.e., competition between) the arguments of opposing sides and (3) individual differences in attitudes, knowledge and motivation that affect how messages are processed.

Introducing time raises the general issue of whether messages have the same influence regardless of when they are received. For example, strong frames prevail over weak frames when they are received simultaneously (e.g., free speech trumps litter in the street), but will this pattern hold when they are received at different times? By the same token, dual frames of equal strength offset when received simultaneously, but will competition moderate opinion if the opposing messages are received sequentially over time? The answer to such questions depends on our assumptions about rates of learning and decay of opinion over time. If the effect of exposure to individual frames is independent of time – that is, there is no learning or decay of effects over time – then opinion depends only on the combination of messages received, not on their sequence or the interval between messages. However, if learning and decay of opinion vary systematically across individuals, then time may qualify conclusions drawn about the influence of strength and competition when messages are received simultaneously.

We expect significant individual differences in how people process the information they receive from a series of messages about an issue. The major distinction we hypothesize is between individuals who engage in either online or memory-based processing of information (Hastie and Park, 1986; for a review, see Druckman and Lupia, 2000).[14] As mentioned above, those who employ online processing of information routinely integrate considerations conveyed in a message about an object into an overall evaluation. This summary evaluation of the object is stored in memory, while the original considerations that contributed to this tally may be forgotten. When asked subsequently to reveal their attitudes toward the object, individuals do so by retrieving and reporting their online tally, as opposed to recalling the specific pieces of information that contributed to this summary evaluation (Wyer and Srull, 1989).

Memory-based information processors, by contrast, store considerations about the object in memory and draw upon those they can remember when asked their opinion about the object. Imperfect recollection of those considerations will lead to responses that are heavily dependent on the considerations that are available at the time of the survey. 'When a judgment is required, individuals retrieve as much of this information from memory as they can, evaluate the individual pieces of information, and then synthesize these "mini-assessments" into a global evaluation based on that retrieved information . . . [They are] dependent on recalled information' (Bizer et al., 2006: 646).

Processing mode creates variation in the opinions expressed at any moment (e.g., Lodge et al., 1989; McGraw and Dolan, 2007; McGraw et al., 1990), but less frequently noted is its effect on the durability of opinions. Attitudes formed online are stronger (Bizer et al., 2006), presumably making them more stable and influential (Bizer et al., 2006: 647; Krosnick and Petty, 1995; Tormala and Petty, 2001).

Those who engage in online processing of information therefore should respond differently to post-treatment events than those who use memory-based processing. First, individuals who process information online should exhibit more attitude stability than memory-based processors between time t and $t + 1$ if no additional messages are encountered in the post-treatment period. At $t + 1$, online processors will simply summon the online evaluation of the issue they formed and stored in memory at time t (we presume, here, the time t evaluation was affected by the messages at time 1). Memory-based processors, on the other hand, are unable to elicit an online tally, but instead have to draw upon their imperfect recollection of the messages they were exposed to earlier in forming an opinion on the spot (see Albertson and Lawrence, 2009; Matthes, 2008).

If additional messages are encountered in the post-treatment period, online processors will update the attitudes they formed at time t, but their evaluation of the latest messages will be colored by their prior attitudes (which, as noted, tend to be strong). The impact of the latest message received at time $t + 1$ will be inversely related to the strength of the attitude formed at time t. In general, online processors should be less likely to be influenced by communications at any point in time because they hold stronger attitudes than memory-based processors (see Druckman and Nelson, 2003; McGraw and Dolan, 2007; Tormala and Petty, 2001).

Moreover, online processors who are exposed to a sequence of messages over time should become increasingly resistant to effects because each exposure provides more information, stimulates further evaluation and strengthens attitudes toward the object. Memory-based processors, in contrast, rely on their recall, which favors information that was received recently.

Empirical Studies of Over-time Effects

One of the few explicit tests of a pre-treatment effect comes from a separate analysis of the data from Druckman's (2010) aforementioned casino study. Recall the study was implemented in the context of the Illinois gubernatorial campaign.[15] At the start of that campaign, the publicly funded casino and its budgetary impact had the potential to be a central issue. However, the emergence of major political corruption charges (on September 9) transformed the campaign, and ended up overwhelming all other issues. In Figure 24.2, we chart campaign coverage based on a content analysis of the *Chicago Tribune*.[16] The figure shows the coverage of the casino and the troubled budget dramatically shrank as corruption coverage grew to the point of receiving nearly half of all campaign coverage.

We expect this early coverage of the casino, with its focus on the casino's positive budgetary implications,[17] to affect the opinions of attentive online processors. These voters may have formed their casino initial opinions early in the campaign and then maintained/accessed these attitudes when later asked about the casino (in the exit poll). If this is the case, the economic frame in the survey experiment may *not* affect attentive online processors since their opinions have already been influenced by the frame (i.e., been pre-treated). They also might, on average, be more supportive of the casino since the economy frame is a strong-pro frame.

To test this, we define attentive voters in our sample as those who fall above the median in the amount they report reading the front page and/or metro section of a local paper, on average (see Druckman, 2004).[18] To distinguish online processors from memory-based processors, we use the well-established 'need to evaluate' (NE) individual difference measure (e.g., Jarvis and Petty, 1996; McGraw and Dolan, 2007: 311–2; Tormala and Petty, 2001). We labeled those who scored below the median as 'memory-based' processors and those above the median as 'online processors'. Attentive online processors were those voters above the median on both variables ($N = 98$).

Figure 24.3 displays the percentage shift in support for the casino, relative to the no-frame

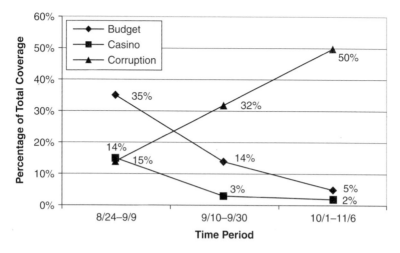

Figure 24.2   Issue emphasis

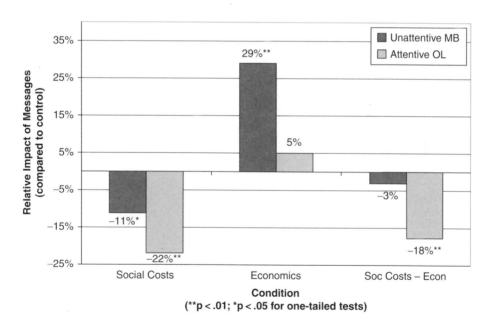

Figure 24.3   Likelihood of Casino support (pre-treatment effects)

control group, for the distinct groups of voters who were exposed to the social costs, economics and both social-costs and economic frames, respectively. We focus on these frame conditions since our interest lies in the impact of the strong-pro economic frame, which is the flip side of the strong-con social costs frame.[19] The results support our expectation that attentive online processors

experienced a pre-treatment effects – relative to the control, they were unaffected in the economic frame condition and significantly affected by the social costs frame when it was paired with the economic frame. This suggests that attentive online voters in the no frame control group were pre-exposed to and affected by the economic frame and thus, further exposure to that frame did not further move opinion (e.g., yet another exposure had no effect). In contrast, the experimental economic frame significantly influenced non-attentive and/or memory-based voters who were not pre-treated.[20] We also find the attentive online processors were, on average, more supportive of the publicly funded casino with 30% of them supporting the casino compared to 21% of others.[21]

These results point to the importance of considering time and processing mode when exploring opinion formation. The effect of early exposure sustains for online processors, but not memory-based processors. From a methodological perspective, the findings suggest that the failure to find an effect in an experiment does not necessarily indicate that the communication did not have an effect – in fact, it may be just the opposite.

The pre-treatment results imply that communication effects display greater inertia or longevity among online processors. Druckman et al. (2010) explore this in an experiment where participants watched a political debate involving two house candidates from a district different from their own. Experimental participants strongly preferred one of the candidates' issue positions (e.g., they agreed with his stance on Iraq), and the other on images (e.g., they viewed him more as a strong leader).[22] We refer to these candidates, respectively, as the 'issue candidate' and the 'image candidate'.

In the experiment, prior to watching the candidates' debate, the participants (randomly) received a news article about the campaign that emphasized *either* the importance of issues or images (i.e., an issue or image frame) (see Druckman et al., 2010, for design details). After viewing the debate, participants reported their likelihood of voting for the candidates on a seven-point scale with higher scores moving toward a preference for the 'issue' candidate. Participants then responded to this same question two-weeks later, thereby allowing for an examination of over-time communication effects. We differentiate online processors from memory-based processes by employing a median split of the aforementioned need to evaluate variable.

Figure 24.4 charts the average percentage increase in the likelihood of voting for the issue candidate for those exposed to the issue frame compared to those exposed to the image frame (i.e., on the 1–7 scale, we report the percentage difference in opinion between the two groups), for all respondents, memory-based processors and online processors, at the first session and the second session. The percentages can be seen as a measure of the substantive impact of receiving one (issue) frame instead of the other (image). The figure accentuates the dramatic differences at the two points in time. At the first session, respondents (both online and memory-based processors) exhibit a roughly statistically significant 15% difference in opinions due to the frame received. However, at the second session, the framing effect sustains for online processors (and increases to 21%), while nearly disappearing for memory-based processors (to 5%). These results are consistent with our theory that communication effects endure for those who engage in online processing but fade for memory-based processors (also see Chong and Druckman, 2010). They also provide an important qualification to previous studies suggesting constant rates of decline across the population.

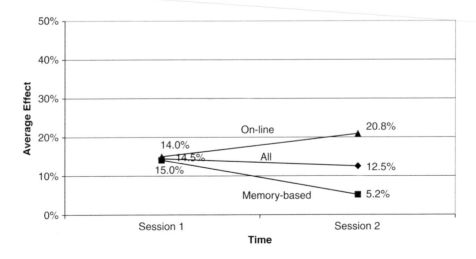

Figure 24.4   Communication effects over time

The results from the two experiments we presented are a preliminary indication of the importance of studying over-time processes. There are of course many avenues for future research including studying the flow of communications over-time (with multiple exposures), and pinpointing the role of motivated reasoning in over-time processes.

CONCLUSION: MAKING CONNECTIONS

Micro–Macro Relationships

Experimental results at the individual level demonstrate significant communication effects followed by rapid decay. The volatility of opinion exhibited in micro communications research appears to contrast with the general stability of aggregate public opinion on political issues. Although numerous factors may contribute to the ostensible micro–macro discrepancy, we suspect variation in opinion stability across studies can be traced to systematic differences in the issues examined and the types of information processing engendered by these issues. Aggregate studies focus on opinion stability and change on long-term issues (e.g., Gallup's most important problem surveys) that, by definition, have been salient for an extended duration. Wood and Vedlitz observe that: 'systemwide definitions of most issues remain relatively constant through time' (2007: 553), the implication being the prominence and understanding of such issues rarely changes (see Baumgartner et al., 2009: 175–8). It also may be characteristic of such issues, owing to their enduring salience, that they elicit more online processing of communications. As a result, individuals tend to maintain their opinions over-time. They discount new information and are less susceptible to framing effects (Lecheler et al., 2009), because online processors are more likely to engage in motivated reasoning or biased processing of new information (e.g., Druckman and Bolsen, 2011).

Many of the individual studies that report decay, in contrast, focus on attitudes toward relatively novel and specific issues that enjoy heightened salience for a short time period such as attitudes about a particular ballot proposition (Albertson and Lawrence, 2009), a competitive election involving a new candidate (e.g., Gerber et al., 2007) or regulation of hog farms (Tewksbury et al., 2000). Prior opinions are more likely to be weak or non-existent on such questions and, therefore, more amenable to influence by persuasive communications. Significant short-term effects have also been observed on more abstract and impersonal subjects, such as people's trust in

institutions (e.g., de Vreese, 2004; Mutz and Reeves, 2005), that may be more likely to induce memory-based processing (see McGraw and Dolan, 2007). In short, we speculate that varying levels of stability in macro- and micro-level studies of opinion may stem, in part, from differences in the issues explored and accompanying differences in how people process information about those issues.

Normative Implications of Communications Effects

Finally, what are the normative implications of elite influence, particularly the ability of opinion leaders to influence public opinion through framing strategies? Early research on elite influence suggested political elites can arbitrarily manipulate popular preferences to serve their own interests. It is this perspective, with all the negative connotations it entails for democratic processes, that led researchers to search for mechanisms that constrain influence (e.g., source credibility, deliberation, competition) and provide individuals with defenses against framing. More recently, researchers have come to recognize that framing and related communication effects are intrinsic to the formation of attitudes. Public opinion formation *always* involves the selective acceptance and rejection of competing frames containing information about candidates and issues. Discussion and debate over the appropriate frames for conceptualizing an issue leads to common (albeit often competing) perceptions and judgments about the consequences of a policy (Chong, 1996). Whether the public opinion that emerges from this process is an independent force in the democratic process is a question separate from whether framing has occurred, because surely it has.

Framing effects are a liability if individuals never acquire a basis for discriminating among frames and remain constantly vulnerable to changing representations of issues. Alternatively, individuals who reject other perspectives out of hand suffer from closedmindedness. Opinion stability also can stem from motivated reasoning where individuals oppose information that is inconsistent with their prior opinions even if using that information might improve the quality of their opinions (e.g., by making their opinions more consistent with their values) (e.g., Druckman and Bolsen, 2011). In short, at one problematic extreme we have citizens without sufficiently strong attitudes and cognitive defenses to resist elite manipulation, while at the other we have citizens whose attitudes are held so rigidly that they seek only to reinforce their existing views.

It is not apparent which portrait of the public is less desirable.

This suggests that, in the ideal, we desire citizens who are selective in following arguments that lead them to base their opinions on 'desirable' criteria. The problem is that no consensus has been reached about what this ideal should be and, in fact, little attention has been given to this issue (a notable attempt to define it is Lau and Redlawsk [2006]; for detailed discussion see Druckman et al. [2009]). Moreover, attempts that are made sometimes contradict one another; for example, for some, information short-cuts are treated as improvements in the quality of decisions (e.g., compared to opinions based on minimal information [Popkin, 1994]) and thus desirable, while others view reliance on cues as leading to poor decisions by most normative standards (e.g., Kinder [1998]; also, compare Iyengar and Kinder [1987] and Lenz [2009] on priming).

These reflections on framing and priming lead us to conclude that normative assessments of communication effects must evaluate details of process and substance in specific instances as opposed to making wholesale judgments. In terms of process, it is important to be realistic in one's normative standards for the public. It seems desirable that we expect citizens to fall somewhere between conscious selection of information in forming opinions and engaging in fully rational consideration of all conceivable considerations. At the same time, citizens are presumably best off if they engage in minimal motivated reasoning which can render conscious selection highly biased. Meeting these processing goals will depend, likely to a greater extent than citizens' abilities, on whether the political context stimulates suitable motivation and opportunity (e.g., by ensuring sufficient competition). Deliberative processes can be engineered to ensure exposure to balanced information and arguments and to create a context that is conducive to evaluating arguments representing competing positions.

In terms of substance, identifying the basis on which citizens should form their preferences is challenging, lest theorists end up making unrealistic, ill-defined and elitist demands on citizens. As Lupia explains, 'those who write about voter competence might recognize the differences between their interests and the interest of the people whom they study. Measures of competence that correspond more closely to the kinds of decisions voters actually face can yield social benefit' (2006: 219).

Our perspective leads us to focus on the nature of the frames on which individuals base their opinions. We introduced the distinction between strong and weak frames, with the exclusive focus being on the citizens' perceptions of strength. One could apply an analogous distinction between normatively desirable and undesirable frames. Desirable frames presumably have some logical basis and are correlated with an objective reality – for example, to return to the example of the proposed housing development we began with, those who frame their support in terms of future economic benefits should be willing to alter their judgments if no valid studies can support claims that the project will have an impact on local employment.

ACKNOWLEDGMENTS

Parts of this essay come from Chong and Druckman (2007c, 2011a,b) and Druckman (2010, 2011).

NOTES

1   We focus exclusively on the *effects* of mass communications and not on the construction of those communications such as agenda-building of framing-building (Scheufele, 1999; also see Chong and Druckman, 2011a,b).

2   They included measures of content from four local papers, *The New York Times*, *Time*, *Newsweek* and evening news broadcasts from NBC and CBS.

3   Iyengar and Kinder were drawing on priming work in social cognition, which is likely a distinct psychological process (see Druckman et al., 2009).

4   For a list of the journals included, contact the authors.

5   There also have been numerous review articles that detail the evolution of this work (e.g., Tai, 2009).

6   Neither problem is attributable to Iyengar and Kinder (1987) or Iyengar (1991), but rather reflect whatever dynamics drove the development of the subsequent research trajectory.

7   We could expand the list of related (and possibly identical) concepts to include 'learning', 'scripts', 'schemas', 'heresthetics' and so on.

8   Iyengar and Kinder (1987) largely use nonstudent participants, however, and also compliment their experiments with observational survey evidence.

9   Without loss of generality, i can be thought of as a dimension (Riker, 1996), a consideration (Zaller, 1992), a value (Sniderman, 1993) or a belief (Ajzen and Fishbein, 1980).

10   We focus exclusively on what scholars call 'emphasis' frames, 'issue' frames or 'value' frames, rather than equivalency frames (for discussion, see Druckman, 2011).

11   Many other agenda setting studies explore the effect of coverage on individuals' perceptions of the most important problems facing the country (rather than during a campaign). In this case, the news outlet can be construed as framing the country's problems.

12   Along similar lines, the extent to which persuasion and the other concepts differ remains unclear.

13   One partial exception is Mitchell and Mondak's (2007) paper on candidate evaluation.

14   See Redlawsk (2001) for a hybrid model.

15   Also see Slothuus (2008).

16   Details on the content analysis and other analysis details are available from the authors.

17   The vast majority of discussions of the casino emphasized its positive budgetary implications (i.e., it used an economy frame).

18   It turns out those above the median read a paper at least five days a week.

19   We were concerned that all respondents may have been pre-treated by the corruption frame, given the immense focus on the campaign on corruption (see Figure 24.2). For this reasons, we merged the control group with the corruption only frame group, and the economic only frame group with the economic-corruption frame group.

20   It is not clear why the social costs frame alone had a notably large impact on attentive online processors.

21   We characterized anyone as reporting a score of 5, 6 or 7 as being 'supportive' and we generated the percentages from a regression controlling for other variables. The difference in support is significant.

22   This was confirmed in both pre-tests and in the data from the experiment.

REFERENCES

Ajzen, I. and Fishbein, M. (1980) *Understanding Attitudes and Predicting Social Behavior.* Englewood Cliffs, NJ: Prentice-Hall.

Albertson, B. and Lawrence, A. (2009) 'After the Credits Roll', *American Politics Research,* 37: 275–300.

Althaus, S. L. and Kim, Y. M. (2006) 'Priming Effects in Complex Environments', *Journal of Politics,* 68(November): 960–76.

Arceneaux, K. (2009) 'Cognitive Biases and the Strength of Political Arguments', unpublished paper. Temple University.

Baumgartner, F. R., Berry, J. M., Hojnaacki, M., Kimball, D. C. and Leech, B. L. (2009) *Lobbying and Policy Change: Who Wins, Who Loses, and Why.* Chicago, IL: University of Chicago Press.

Baumgartner, F. R., De Boef, S. L. and Boydstun, A. E. (2008) *The Decline of the Death Penalty and the Discovery of Innocence.* New York: Cambridge University Press.

Bennett, W. L. and Iyengar, S. (2008) 'A New Era of Minimal Effects?', *Journal of Communication,* 58: 707–31.

Bizer, G. Y., Tormala, Z. L., Rucker, D. D. and Petty, R. E. (2006) 'Memory-Based Versus Online Processing', *Journal of Experimental Social Psychology,* 42: 646–53.

Brewer, P. R. (2001) 'Value Words and Lizard Brains', *Political Psychology,* 22: 45–64.

Brewer, P. R. and Gross, K. (2005) 'Values, Framing, and Citizens Thoughts about Policy Issues: Effects on Content and Quantity', *Political Psychology,* 26(6): 929–48.

Chong, D. (1996) 'Creating Common Frames of Reference on Political Issues', in D. Mutz, R. Brody and P. Sniderman (eds.), *Political Persuasion and Attitude Change.* Ann Arbor, MI: University of Michigan Press. pp. 195–224.

Chong, D. and Druckman, J. N. (2007a) 'A Theory of Framing and Opinion Formation in Competitive Elite Environments', *Journal of Communication,* 57(1): 99–118.

Chong, D. and Druckman, J. N. (2007b) 'Framing Public Opinion in Competitive Democracies', *American Political Science Review,* 101(4): 637–55.

Chong, D. and Druckman, J. N. (2007c) 'Framing Theory', *Annual Review of Political Science,* 10(1): 103–26.

Chong, D. and Druckman, J. N. (2010) 'Dynamic Public Opinion: Communication Effects Over Time', *American Political Science Review,* 104: 663–80.

Chong, D. and Druckman, J. N. (2011a) 'Identifying Frames in Political News', in E. P. Bucy and R. L. Holbert (eds.), *Sourcebook for Political Communication Research.* New York: Routledge. pp. 238–67.

Chong, D. and Druckman, J. N. (2011b) 'Public-Elite Interactions', in R. Y. Shapiro and L. R. Jacobs (eds.), *The Oxford Handbook of the American Public Opinion and the Media.* Oxford: Oxford University Press. pp. 170–88.

de Vreese, C. H. (2004) 'Primed by the Euro', *Scandinavian Political Studies,* 27(1): 45–65.

Druckman, J. N. (2004) 'Priming the Vote', *Political Psychology,* 25: 577–94.

Druckman, J. N. (2010) 'Competing Frames in a Political Campaign', in B. F. Schaffner and P. J. Sellers (eds.), *Winning with Words.* New York: Routledge. pp. 101–20.

Druckman, J. N. (2011) 'What's It All About?', in G. Keren (ed.), *Perspectives on Framing.* New York: Psychology Press/ Taylor & Francis. pp. 279–302.

Druckman, J. N. and Bolsen, T. (2011) 'Framing, Motivated Reasoning, and Opinions about Emergent Technologies', *Journal of Communication,* 61: 659–88.

Druckman, J. N., Hennessy, C. L., St. Charles, K. and Weber, J. (2010) 'Competing Rhetoric Over Time', *The Journal of Politics,* 72: 136–48.

Druckman, J. N. and Holmes, J. W. (2004) 'Does Presidential Rhetoric Matter?', *Presidential Studies Quarterly,* 34: 755–78.

Druckman, J. N. and Kam, C. D. (2011) 'Students as Experimental Participants', in J. N. Druckman, D. P. Green, J. H. Kuklinski and A. Lupia (eds.), *Handbook of Experimental Political Science.* New York: Cambridge University Press. pp. 41–57.

Druckman, J. N., Kuklinski, J. H. and Sigelman, L. (2009) 'The Unmet Potential of Interdisciplinary Research', *Political Behavior*, 31: 485–510.

Druckman, J. N. and Lupia, A. (2000) 'Preference Formation', *Annual Review of Political Science*, 3: 1–24.

Druckman, J. N. and Nelson, K. R. (2003) 'Framing and Deliberation', *American Journal of Political Science*, 47(October): 728–44.

Edy, J. A. (2006) *Troubled Pasts*. Philadelphia, PA: Temple University Press.

Enelow, J. M. and Hinich, M. J. (1984) *The Spatial Theory of Voting*. Boston, MA: Cambridge University Press.

Entman, R. M. (1993) 'Framing', *Journal of Communication*, 43(4): 51–8.

Entman, R. M. (2004) *Projects of Power: Framing News, Public Opinion, and US Foreign Policy*. Chicago, IL: University of Chicago Press.

Gaines, B. J., Kuklinski, J. H. and Quirk, P. J. (2007) 'The Logic of the Survey Experiment Reexamined', *Political Analysis*, 15: 1–20.

Gerber, A., Gimpel, J. G., Green, D. P. and Shaw, D. R. (2007) 'The Influence of Television and Radio Advertising on Candidate Evaluations', unpublished paper. Yale University.

Gerber, A. S. and Green, D. P. (2008) 'Field Experiments and Natural Experiments', in J. M. Box-Steffensmeier, H. E. Brady and D. Collier (eds.), *The Oxford Handbook of Political Methodology*. Oxford: Oxford University Press. pp. 357–81.

Hansen, K. M. (2007) 'The Sophisticated Public', *Scandinavian Political Studies*, 30(3): 377–96.

Hastie, R. and Park, B. (1986) 'The Relationship Between Memory and Judgment Depends on Whether the Judgment Task is Memory-Based or Online', *Psychological Review*, 93: 258–68.

Hibbs, D. A., Jr (2008) 'Implications of the "Bread and Peace" Model for the 2008 Presidential Election', *Public Choice*, 137: 1–10.

Iyengar, S. (1991) *Is Anyone Responsible?* Chicago, IL: University of Chicago Press.

Iyengar, S. (2010) 'Framing Research', in B. F. Schaffner and P. J. Sellers (eds.), *Winning with Words*. New York: Routledge. pp. 185–91.

Iyengar, S. and Kinder, D. R. (1987) *News That Matters*. Chicago, IL: University of Chicago Press.

Jacoby, W. G. (2000) 'Issue Framing and Public Opinion on Government Spending', *American Journal of Political Science*, 44: 750–67.

Jarvis, W. B. and Petty, R. E. (1996) 'The Need to Evaluate', *Journal of Personality and Social Psychology*, 70(1): 172–94.

Johnston, R., Blais, A., Brady, H. E. and Crete, J. (1992) *Letting the People Decide*. Stanford, CA: Stanford University Press.

Kam, C. D., Wilking, J. R. and Zechmeister, E. J. (2007) 'Beyond the "Narrow Data Base"', *Political Behavior*, 29(4): 415–40.

Kinder, D. R. (1998) 'Communication and Opinion', *Annual Review of Political Science*, 1: 167–97.

Kinder, D. R. (2007) 'Curmudgeonly Advice', *Journal of Communication*, 57(1): 155–62.

Krosnick, J. A. and Petty, R. E. (1995) 'Attitude Strength', in R. E. Petty and J. A. Krosnick (eds.), *Attitude Strength*. Mahwah, NJ: Lawrence Erlbaum Associates. pp. 1–24.

Lau, R. R. and Redlawsk, D. P. (2006) *How Voters Decide*. New York: Cambridge University Press.

Lecheler, S., de Vreese, C. H. and Slothuus, R. (2009) 'Issue Importance as a Moderator of Framing Effects', *Communication Research*, 36(3): 400–25.

Lenz, G. (2009) 'Learning and Opinion Change, Not Priming', *American Journal of Political Science*, 53(4): 821–37.

Lodge, M., McGraw, K. M. and Stroh, P. (1989) 'An Impression-driven Model of Candidate Evaluation', *American Political Science Review*, 83: 399–419.

Lupia, A. (2006) 'How Elitism Undermines the Study of Voter Competence', *Critical Review*, 18: 217–32.

Matthes, J. (2008) 'Media Frames and Public Opinion', *Studies in Communication Studies*, 8: 101–28.

McCombs, M. (2004) *Setting the Agenda*. Malden, MA: Blackwell.

McCombs, M. E. and Shaw, D. L. (1972) 'The Agenda-Setting Function of Mass Media', *Public Opinion Quarterly*, 36: 176–87.

McGraw, K. M. and Dolan, T. M. (2007) 'Personifying the State', *Political Psychology*, 28(3): 299–327.

McGraw, K. M., Lodge, M. and Stroh P. (1990) 'On-line Processing in Candidate Evaluation: The Effects of Issue Order, Issue Salience and Sophistication', *Political Behavior*, 12: 41–58.

Miller, J. M. and Krosnick, J. A. (2000) 'News Media Impact on the Ingredients of Presidential Evaluations', *American Journal of Political Science*, 44(2): 295–309.

Mitchell, D. G. and Mondak, J. J. (2007) 'The Dynamic Formation of Candidate Evaluation', paper presented at the Annual Meeting of the Midwest Political Science Association. Chicago, 12–15 April.

Mutz, D. C. and Reeves, B. (2005) 'The New Videomalaise', *American Political Science Review*, 99(1): 1–15.

Nelson, T. E., Bryner, S. M. and Carnahan, D. M. (2011) 'Media and Politics', in J. N. Druckman, D. P. Green, J. H. Kuklinski and A. Lupia (eds.), *Handbook of Experimental Political Science*. New York: Cambridge University Press. pp. 201–13.

Nelson, T. E. and Oxley, Z. M. (1999) 'Issue Framing Effects and Belief Importance and Opinion', *Journal of Politics*, 61: 1040–67.

Nelson, T. E., Oxley, Z. M. and Clawson, R. A. (1997) 'Toward a Psychology of Framing Effects', *Political Behavior*, 19(3): 221–46.

O'Keefe, D. J. (2002) *Persuasion*. 2nd edn. Thousand Oaks, CA: Sage.

Petersen, M. B. (2007) 'Causes of Political Affect', unpublished paper. Aarhus University.

Popkin, S. L. (1994) *The Reasoning Voter*. Chicago, IL: Chicago University Press.

Price, V. and Tewksbury, D. (1997) 'News Values and Public Opinion', in G. A. Barnett and F. J. Boster (eds.), *Progress in Communication Sciences*, Vol. 13. Greenwich, CT: Ablex Publishing Corporation.

Putnam, R. D. (2000) *Bowling Alone*. New York: Simon & Schuster.

Redlawsk, D. (2001) 'You Must Remember This', *The Journal of Politics*, 63: 29–58.

Riker, W. H. (1986) *The Art of Political Manipulation*. New Haven, CT: Yale University Press.

Riker, W. H. (1996) *The Strategy of Rhetoric*. New Haven, CT: Yale University Press.

Schattschneider, E. E. (1960) *The Semisovereign People*. New York: Holt, Rinehart, and Winston.

Scheufele, D. A. (1999) 'Framing as a Theory of Media Effects', *Journal of Communication*, 49: 103–22.

Sears, D. O. (1986) 'College Sophomores in the Laboratory', *Journal of Personality and Social Psychology*, 51(3): 515–30.

Shaw, D. R. (1999) 'The Methods Behind the Madness: Presidential Electoral College Strategies, 1988–1996', *The Journal of Politics*, 61(4): 893–913.

Shen, F. and Edwards, H. H. (2005) 'Economic Individualism, Humanitarianism, and Welfare Reform', *Journal of Communication*, 55: 795–809.

Simon, H. A. (1955) 'A Behavioral Model of Rational Choice', *Quarterly Journal of Economics*, 69: 99–118.

Slothuus, R. (2008) 'Parties Matter', unpublished paper. University of Aarhus.

Sniderman, P. M. (1993) 'The New Look in Public Opinion Research', in A. Finifter (ed.), *Political Science: The State of the Discipline*. Washington, DC: American Political Science Association. pp. 219–45.

Sniderman, P. M. and Theriault, S. M. (2004) 'The Structure of Political Argument and the Logic of Issue Framing', in W. E. Saris and P. M. Sniderman (eds.), *Studies in Public Opinion*. Princeton, NJ: Princeton University Press. pp. 133–65.

Tai, Z. (2009) 'The Structure of Knowledge and Dynamics of Scholarly Communication in Agenda Setting Research, 1996–2005', *Journal of Communication*, 59(3): 481–513.

Tewksbury, D., Jones, J., Peske, M. W., Raymond, A. and Vig, W. (2000) 'The Interaction of News and Advocate Frames', *Journalism and Mass Communication Quarterly*, 77(4): 804–29.

Tormala, Z. L. and Petty R. E. (2001) 'Online Versus Memory-Based Processing', *Personality and Social Psychology Bulletin*, 27(12): 1599–612.

Winter, N. J. G. (2008) *Dangerous Frames*. Chicago, IL: University of Chicago Press.

Wood, B. D. and Vedlitz, A. (2007) 'Issue Definition, Information Processing, and the Politics of Global Warming', *American Journal of Political Science*, 51(3): 552–68.

Wyer Jr, R. S. and Srull, T. K. (1989) *Memory and Cognition in its Social Context*. Hillsdale, NJ: Lawrence Erlbaum Associates.

Zaller, J. (1992) *The Nature and Origins of Mass Opinion*. New York: Cambridge University Press.

PART IV

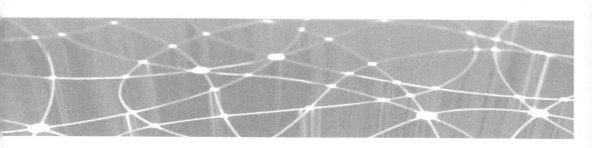

25

Media, Power and US Foreign Policy

Sean Aday, Robert M. Entman
and Steven Livingston

This review and synthesis of the literature explores the influence of media in the making of the US foreign policy. It emphasizes the nature of influence exerted by elites and the role of media and the public in the American government's decisions regarding war and peace. Although we fully recognize that war is far from the only important foreign policy decision, we concentrate on military interventions because they are the most costly, consequential and publicized policies. Wars also affect almost all other policy options and decisions, directly or indirectly, for years afterward. Lastly, our review considers the profound shift that has occurred in the last two decades concerning the nature of the international system, the declining resources and capability of the traditional news media and the concomitant expansion of digital information and communication technology.

STATE–MEDIA RELATIONS

Professional norms and practices guiding news production often short-circuit the public's ability to make meaningful connections between policies, policy outcomes and political leaders. This is not entirely the media's fault. On most matters of social and political significance, including war, ordinary citizens are not well informed.[1] Nor do the normal circumstances of their lives encourage or permit them to become so.[2] In part, this is because the media, especially in the USA,[3] only sporadically offer content that connects policies and outcomes in meaningful ways. Lacking the background to construct their own sophisticated analyses, most citizens remain dependent on news and infotainment (Baum, 2003) media[4] and the cues they offer for making sense of war and other aspects of foreign policy.

If citizens remain dependent on news infotainment, traditional news organizations remain dependent on officials in reporting the news. From Vietnam through the Iraq and Afghanistan wars, the main finding of scholars looking at war and foreign policy coverage is that the news tends to privilege official sources, especially those from the White House, and act as an intervening variable between elites and public opinion (Chanley, 1999). Most notably, Bennett (1990, 1994) has shown that news coverage of war and foreign policy is indexed to the limited range of elite opinions. Criticism and policy critiques rise and fall according to variations in the critical assertiveness of official sources. When leaders of both major political parties agree with the president's policy (or silently assent), mediated communication tends to be dominated by the White House's line. When dissent arises, media content becomes more diverse, though the extent and coherence of the challenge to the president's views tends to be limited to what the leaders in opposition are willing to say publicly – and how skillfully and energetically they say it. If opponents' attacks are restricted to criticizing means rather than ends, or are otherwise timid and scattered, so, too, will be the oppositional content in the media. Among many military interventions, this pattern of uncritical coverage that echoes rather than fundamentally challenges official (especially White House) views has been found in news about the US involvement in the Nicaraguan civil war under Reagan (Bennett, 1990), the US invasion of Panama (Dickson, 1995), the Persian Gulf War (Entman and Page, 1994; Mermin, 1999) as well as the Iraq War (Bennett et al., 2007).

Entman's (2003, 2004) theory of cascading network activation builds on the indexing hypothesis with an analytical framework depicting how mediated communication influences the flow of power over foreign policy. It posits a hierarchy of influence starting with the White House and continuing through other elites, journalists and the public, with feedback loops along the way that offer means for frame adjustment and contestation, though usually within strict boundaries. Thus, cascading activation allows for other actors and institutions ranging from Congress to media to the public, and perhaps global advocacy networks, to shape issue definitions and other aspects of policy discourse. But as the waterfall metaphor implies, these secondary players are themselves often responding to the initial frame promoted by the White House.

Notwithstanding the rare newsworthy violations of expectations such as Abu Ghraib (and the My Lai massacre 40 years earlier, during Vietnam), the media exercised their habitual deference to White House officials during the run-up and early months or years of the four major military interventions since television entered political life: Vietnam and Indochina; the 1990–91 Persian Gulf War; the Afghanistan War in 2001–02; and the Iraq War in 2002–05. Experience with those interventions suggests that presidential frames remain dominant for long periods, irrespective of conditions on the ground and regardless of the ready availability of non-official yet highly expert dissenting voices (see Aday et al., 2005a; Bennett et al., 2007; Entman, 2004; Hallin, 1986; Mermin, 1999; Zaller and Chiu, 1996). Beyond this core inference, we believe the existing literature supports the following conclusions on the general patterns in mainstream US media responses to foreign policy. The major national media outlets exhibit:

- a tendency toward coverage that is fragmented rather than coherent, particularly when it comes to 'connecting the dots' linking policies to outcomes, outcomes to officials, and tactics to strategies (Bennett, 2008; Entman et al., 2009);
- a propensity to gauge policy success or failure in short-run tactical terms, downplaying issues of military and geo-political strategy (Livingston and Bennett, 2003; Livingston and Van Belle, 2005);

- a bias against graphic and repeated reporting of casualties (Aday, 2005; Aday et al., 2005b; Entman et al., 2009; Hallin, 1986);
- a willingness to allow White House and Defense Department officials to change the definition of success at key moments of potential accountability (for example, Galbraith, 2008);
- a pattern of marginalizing and undermining the legitimacy of dissent from outside the Washington foreign policy establishment, including domestic protest and international opinion (Bennett, 1990; Entman, 2004; Gitlin, 1980);
- and a tendency to under-report 'peripheral' costs and measures of failure, such as in the Iraq War high numbers of seriously wounded soldiers, Iraqi civilian suffering, fatalities among 'shadow' soldiers for hire, the plight of war veterans when they return from the front and the true long-term financial costs from all of this (Bilmes and Stiglitz, 2006).

These characteristic traits of media content have predictable, problematic and self-reinforcing impacts on the incentives of American policymakers, encouraging them to:

- avoid energetic, vocal support of non-military solutions for fear of seeming 'weak on defense' (Entman and Page, 1994; cf. Mueller, 2006);
- inflate the strength of military threats against the US, often by imputing the false analogies of Hitler and Munich (Dorman and Livingston, 1994; Entman, 2004; Mueller, 2006);
- minimize in deed if not word diplomacy and international coalitions as alternatives to war (Entman et al., 2009; Wolfsfeld, 2004);
- mythologize public consent for war and militarism, despite surveys often showing majorities or large minorities in favor of other paths to resolution of crisis and conflict (for example, Entman, 2004; Page with Bouton, 2006; cf. Wolfsfeld, 2004).

Like a partner in an abusive relationship, the press simply fails to un-tether itself from official sources (especially in the White House and Congress) and their candied promises of access, flattery, a steady stream of stories and cocktail party soirees (for example, Bennett et al., 2007). Furthermore, according to entrenched news norms, anchoring stories to official sources facilitates explicit and implicit claims to objectivity, factuality and truth-claims without the burden of independent verification. Despite the professional lore of an adversarial press, research over the years has demonstrated a deep and abiding symbiotic relationship between the press and government (Dorman and Farhang, 1988; Schudson, 1981; Sigal, 1973).

One revealing example came in an online commentary from *The Atlantic Magazine*'s Marc Ambinder, who was explaining why journalists repeatedly accept top officials' assurances about foreign and defense policy even when the officials have a record of deception: 'Information asymmetry is always going to exist, and, living as we do in a democratic system, most journalists are going to give the government the benefit of some doubt, even having learned lessons about giving the government that benefit'.[5] He was explaining why journalists disregarded voluminous evidence that the Bush administration manipulated the color-coded terror alert process for political gain (for example, raising the alert level to distract from the Democratic National Convention's nomination of John Kerry), an interpretation confirmed by then-Homeland Security Secretary Tom Ridge[6] (Baker, 2009).

The dominance of official sources becomes crucial in constructing theoretical understandings of power and communication in foreign policymaking. We highlight the centrality of narrative framing in determining political outcomes and public understanding. What is the connection between who tells a story, how it is told and understood, and outcomes? That is what we turn to next.

MEDIA FRAMING AND FOREIGN POLICYMAKING

We emphasize the concept of framing as a mechanism for understanding media, public opinion and power in foreign policymaking. Framing in communication texts arises in the first instance from networks of officials whose duties make them professional communicators – national security advisors, secretaries of state and defense, the president and vice president and their spin-managers. All engage in strategic framing. Later, we will expand the list of possible networks of strategic communicators. By framing, we mean that they select some aspects of a perceived reality and construct messages that highlight cognitive and linguistic connections among them in ways that promote an interpretation favorable to their political interests and policies (Entman, 2004). 'Framing' (or 'to frame') is the verb form of the concept, as distinct from the noun form defined below. Communicators who engage in framing strategically seek to exert power over outcomes by inducing target audiences to accept interpretations that favor their interests or goals and include not just politicians and high-ranking officials, but bloggers, political satirists, advocacy networks,

editorial writers and pundits. Other communicators, most importantly reporters and news editors in mainstream national news media who adhere to norms of fairness and balance, normally engage in framing without strategically calculating their communications to push a particular policy or political goal (Entman, 2010). And most members of the public respond to the frames constructed by communicators in unself-conscious, non-strategic ways that can nonetheless feed back to significantly influence politics and policy.

Framing is distinguished from other communication by its diachronic nature and its cultural resonance. Successful frames call to mind currently congruent elements of *schemas* that were stored in the past. Schemas fit new perceptions to an existing organization of knowledge. Fiske and Taylor define schemas as 'cognitive structures that represent knowledge about a concept or type of stimulus, including its attributes and the relations among attributes' (1991: 131). Information is thus stored in an abstract form. People's prior knowledge allows them to decide (consciously or not) what information is relevant to a given schema so that they may make sense of specific new encounters (see Castells, 2009: Ch. 3 for a summary; cf. Lakoff, 2008; Westen, 2007). Many scholars have stressed the importance of schemas in information-processing routines as guides that allow people to simplify reality and function in a social world of otherwise overpowering complexity (Lupia et al., 2000).

Repeating frames over time in multiple texts gives a politically significant proportion of the citizenry a chance to notice, understand, store and recall the mental association for future application. Framing is thus diachronic in the sense that exposure during a given period is presumed to increase probabilities of particular responses during a future period, while diminishing the probability of thinking about other potentially relevant objects or traits. Once a frame has appeared enough to be widely stored in the audience's schema systems, it no longer needs to be repeated in concentrated bursts, nor must it be fully elaborated; citizens can summon the stored associations years later in response to a single vivid component ('9/11' or 'Berlin Wall').

Culture is the stock of schemas commonly found in the minds of a society's individuals, and the set of frames present in the system's communications, including literature, entertainment, news, conversations and other political discourse. By definition, these common schemas are the ones that form the basis for most individuals' reactions to framing communications. Elites do not have unlimited autonomy in framing events; they are constrained to choosing from a cultural stock, which records the traces of *past* framing. So any larger theory of framing in foreign policymaking must take into account prior time periods (Time -1), the current period (Time 1) and the future (Time 2,...,n) – it must be diachronic.

This is the perspective taken by the cascade model. If time is considered on the horizontal dimension in Figures 25.1 and 25.2, the vertical dimension taps the five levels in the hierarchy of networks through which mental associations spread, with the presidency at the top. The president's preferred frame may or may not engender opposition among elites. Where elites agree with each other in favoring the president's frame, it will activate and spread unimpeded through to most media personnel. They in turn will construct communications that prominently repeat words and visual images supporting the preferred frame. Finally, exposed almost entirely to the single framing, indicators of public opinion readily available to elites will likely support the president's policy. This at least constitutes an uncontested frame as it cascades from the White House to the public. But it is also important to keep in mind that oppositional frames may arise, forcing the White House and other elites to adapt to an oppositional feedback loop. Oppositional framing in the cascade may become more likely in a globally networked international system where challengers can exploit the digital micro-electronics revolution.

What differentiates a 'frame' in a communication from a persuasive message or a simple assertion? A frame repeatedly invokes the same objects and traits, using identical or synonymous words and symbols in a series of similar communications that are concentrated in time. These frames function to promote an interpretation of a problematic situation or actor and (implicit or explicit) support of a desirable response, often along with a moral judgment that provides an emotional charge (this definition and the rest of the discussion in this section is based on Entman et al. [2009]). If a communication does not exhibit repeated words and symbols that connect with the cultural associations of many citizens, then by these standards, it is not a frame. This is not to suggest that we can ignore aspects of foreign policy discourse not possessing such traits. But because of the cultural resonance and emotional potency of patriotism, war, enemies, threats, security, casualties and other common subjects in communication about foreign affairs (Edelman, 1988), framed communication as just discussed offers an especially illuminating lens through which to view media, public opinion and foreign policy. We illustrate this point below with an exploration of casualty framing in war.

Looking across time, Figure 25.1 suggests how the framing process moves from a hypothetical new event at Time 1, to reactions during Time 2, to framing responses at Time 3 based on anticipations of the future. The figure also suggests how cultural expectations inculcated at Time -1 shape succeeding communications. Figure 25.2 extends Figure 25.1 in time, further illustrating the diachronic nature of the framing cycle and indicating the many junctures at which framing occurs and might be investigated. It highlights the possibility – though in the US foreign policymaking, not the likelihood – that by Time 4 a competition over framing will break out among elites, diversifying media content and yielding important potential impacts on politics and policy. Importantly, this model also suggests that surveys or lab experiments, with their essentially synchronic structures and focus on members of the mass public, may tap only a restricted range of real world framing effects, as we now discuss in more detail.

Framing Effects: Elite and Mass Levels

Chong and Druckman (2007b) found that after a strong frame has diffused and increased the accessibility of a consideration, it more or less automatically applies to future communication about the framed object, working through low-effort 'peripheral' processing rather than more cognitively demanding central processing (Petty and Cacciopo, 1986). This diffusion of a strong frame, they say, leads to 'diminished framing effects' on the mass public's opinions, but it appears just as reasonable to infer that the measured effects of framing at Time 2 are lower because prior framing, say at Time 1 or Time -1, succeeded (Chong and Druckman, 2007b: 110). In other words, if strong existing opinions diminish framing effects on citizens at the time they are measured, this tells us little about framing effects in general because those prior attitudes may themselves have arisen from exposure to an earlier frame (Chong and Druckman, 2007a: 107; see also Matthes, 2007).

In addition, *omission* of information that could challenge the dominant frame and help activate and spread an alternative interpretation can be crucial to public attitudes, particularly when the dominant culture supplies potentially competing schematic interpretations (Sniderman and Theriault, 2004). In the case of Iraq, the absence of a fully developed oppositional frame from the popular American media was highly consequential. The dominance of a single frame, the one promoted by the White House, empowered the administration while discouraging potential opponents, at least in domestic networks. Regardless of any effects on individual citizens' actual opinions, by shaping *elite* perceptions of current majorities and anticipations of a future public that would

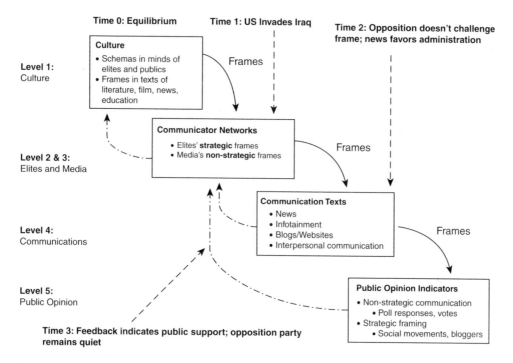

Figure 25.1   Cascading network activation and uncontested framing in the Year 1 framing of Iraq War (2003–04)

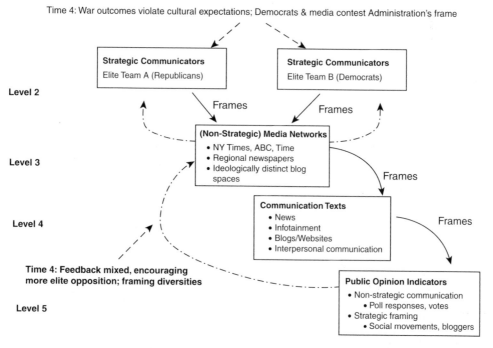

Figure 25.2   Contested framing of Iraq War (2006–07) as Levels 2 and 3 Differentiate

not have stored a schema justifying withdrawal from Iraq, it seems possible that the framing void discouraged cautious members of Congress – even after the 2006 election gave Democrats opposed to the war control of the legislative branch – from using the power of the purse to defund the war. That same fear would also repress Democrats' desires to mount an organized counter-framing campaign, and in a self-reinforcing circle, the vacuum of effective oppositional rhetoric would dissipate most leaders' inclination to openly opposing the administration.

Achieving this result helps explain, for instance, why George W. Bush and his subordinates went to great lengths to control the framing of Iraq (see for example, Bennett et al., 2007; Castells, 2009; Isikoff and Corn, 2006). They undertook such extraordinary measures as authorizing torture[7] of prisoners to compel them to provide evidence of a connection between Saddam Hussein and al Qaeda (Landay, 2009) and publicizing the identity of a high-level CIA agent, Valerie Plame Wilson, whose portfolio included preventing the proliferation of weapons of mass destruction (see Entman 2012: Chapter 8).

Elite competition, then, is not merely designed to influence individual citizens' issue and candidate opinions, but equally or perhaps more importantly, to influence aggregate indicators of public opinion embodied in what can be called polling opinion (majority responses to widely publicized surveys) and to affect elites' perceptions and anticipations of public opinion (Entman, 2004). The influence of media frames on public opinion in this larger sense works along at least three different paths: through effects on citizens' responses to pollsters' questions about the matter (data not necessarily equivalent to citizens' actual attitudes); through elites using news frames directly to draw inferences about the current and likely future state of public opinion and through elite assessments of how competing elites will react to all of this. For instance, regardless of actual public opinion, if elites at Time 2 believe that one frame will continue to dominate the media, they may anticipate significant Time 3 effects on the public opinion that is perceived by their competitors in the elite class and will inhibit them from promoting an alternative frame incongruent with perceived likely opinion (Entman, 2004).

Frame contestation is thus quite a complicated chess game, offering much grist for future research. Scholars need to broaden the study of framing effects, while connecting them to larger questions of democratic theory. Research should focus as much on frame quality and elite quality as citizen quality, devoting more attention to whose frames are most available, under which conditions and how framing both guides elites'

responses to indicators of public opinion and helps elites shape those manifestations. Such research would illuminate the production and circulation of frames and the feedback loops that trace the flow of political power among competing media, competing elites and mass publics. As Figures 25.1 and 25.2 indicate, framing occurs at multiple levels of the policymaking process, not just in the shaping of public opinion. And as we suggest below, global information flows and advocacy networks may be redrawing the conceptual boundaries of our models, including who might be considered elite (Bimber, 2003), the nature of institutional resources (Aday and Livingston, 2009), and the speed and complexity of frame competition. To make the prior discussion more concrete, and to connect it to some of the major concerns in the political science research literature, we now turn to the roles of media coverage of, and public responses to, military casualties in affecting government decisions on armed intervention.

FOCUS: MEDIA, CASUALTIES AND EMOTION IN PUBLIC OPINION

Elites' belief that media coverage suppresses support for military interventions by emphasizing the loss of American lives seems to have an important impact on policymakers, especially in leading decision makers to avoid committing ground troops (Blechman and Wittes, 1999). The assumption also has been shown to influence the military and political strategies of the USA's enemies, including Osama bin Laden. In the words of Somali warlord Mohamed Farah Aideed, 'We have studied Vietnam and Lebanon and know how to get rid of Americans, by killing them so that public opinion will put an end to things' (Blechman and Wittes, 1999: 5). However, political scientists have focused less on media framing than on the impact of casualties per se on public opinion (Burk, 1999; Eichenberg, 2005; Feaver and Gelpi, 2004; Gelpi et al., 2009; Jentleson, 1992; Kull and Ramsay, 2001; Larson, 1996; Larson and Savych, 2005; Mueller, 1973, 1994, 2005).

Between Vietnam and the Iraq War, the main finding of media scholars has been that the news tends be largely favorable, elite-driven, consensus-oriented and patriotic, especially during times of international conflict and war. A key ingredient of helpful coverage is the sanitizing of casualty reports, which occurred in all four major wars starting with Vietnam, as well as the smaller ones (Aday, 2005; Aday et al., 2005a,b; Center for Media and Public Affairs, 2003; Hallin, 1991;

Kellner, 1992). For instance, research on the Iraq War showed that, despite the easing of Reagan-era restrictions on press access to the battlefield, in the early years, American media still showed viewers a bloodless war, one almost entirely devoid of death (Aday, 2005). This extended to violence off the battlefield: Bennett et al. (2007) revealed that the US media largely avoided the word 'torture' in depicting interrogation techniques – despite photographs documenting actions defined by international law as torture. Even in Vietnam (Hallin, 1986; cf. Paletz and Entman, 1981) after media support wavered in the wake of the Tet Offensive, which seemed to contradict repeated official claims that victory was in sight, the media's reluctance to provide audiences with graphic illustrations of American casualties or with other gruesome images of war persisted (Bailey and Lichty [1972] on the execution of a suspected Vietcong soldier in front of an NBC cameraman during the 1968 Tet Offensive).

MEDIA, MILITARY INTERVENTION AND PUBLIC OPINION

A careful reading of the literature suggests that context determines if and when the media influence foreign policymaking generally and particularly in times of war and conflict. The most likely direction of that influence, however, is often not in the one most policymakers think. Rather than being responsible for depressing public support for intervention because of their putative obsession with casualties, media tend to matter most when they are *buttressing* elite consensus around use of force, as occurs during rally periods (Mueller, 1973, 2006). Typically, this is the consequence of showing engaging and casualty-free battle images and features about soldiers. Baker and Oneal (2001) argue that the occurrence and magnitude of rally effects are dependent in large part on how crises are framed in the press. And Oneal and Bryan (1995) found that front-page coverage in *The New York Times* played an important role in creating rallies.

Elite consensus favoring war policy spurs uncritical news coverage, which is more likely to focus on soldiers and exciting but bloodless battle images than casualty visuals (perhaps because editors are swept up in patriotic fervor, perhaps because they assume that's what audiences want). Such circumstances suppress partisanship (often by heightening positive emotions such as pride and nationalism) and exert a positive effect on the following attitudes: support for intervention, belief that it is justified and perception that it will succeed.

Media thus influence pre-war public opinion by contributing to building support for elite's framing of foreign policy objectives even before events have created their own inescapable narratives (Aday, 2010b).

Conversely, in times of elite dissensus, media effects will be subsumed by partisanship to the extent that the emotional reactions themselves depend largely on the political predispositions citizens bring to mediated communications more than on the images themselves. For an example from the Iraq War, Republicans would see the image of American soldiers fighting and feel pride, while Democrats would feel anger or even disgust (Aday, 2010b). In times of elite consensus, however, both groups would feel proud. In part, this is because in a consensus moment, partisans of all stripes are receiving the same, pro-war cue; but at the same time there is an additive effect of media exposure, often working through pride and stimulated by soldier/battle images, that bolsters support. Most administrations are fully if perhaps intuitively cognizant of this process and attempt through communication campaigns to bolster it.

This is consistent with the long-established finding that the public is most easily influenced by both media and elites when they act in concert, when they are mutually reinforcing or being uncritical of cultural, social and political norms (Gitlin, 1978; Lazarsfeld and Merton, 1948; Zaller, 1992). In addition, research in social psychology shows that a 'consensus breed correctness' heuristic cue makes messages like these particularly persuasive, especially with those less involved in an issue (Aday, 2007; Eagly and Chaiken, 1993). This is the case during consensus periods, such as in the rally phase leading up to and immediately after the start of a war, and in conflicts that remain popular or largely off the media radar. Importantly, however, in these cases the media are no mere epiphenomena. They exert a unique and significant effect of their own by not only transmitting the consensus cue but legitimizing it, what Lazarsfeld and Merton (1948) referred to as status conferral (also see Gitlin, 1980), and often buttressing it with pride-producing soldier/battle stories.

CASUALTY AVERSION HYPOTHESES AND THE CNN EFFECT

The belief that casualties and casualty coverage depresses American popular support for use of force has become the dominant view among politicians and pundits, and is based on two related theories. First, many policymakers accept the premise of the casualty aversion hypothesis, the notion that Americans will not support military action that results in high and increasing numbers of dead US soldiers (Lacquement, 2004). Second, there is a corresponding belief among elites in what scholars refer to as the so-called CNN effect, which comes in two versions. One, which Livingston calls the 'impediment' version, posits that vivid news coverage of casualties and 'bad news', especially on television, negatively affects public support (Livingston, 1997, 2000; Robinson, 2002) and causes policymakers to hesitate to intervene. Despite the research just discussed, most of the popular focus is on this perceived negative influence of media on public support for armed intervention. The other variant holds quite the opposite, arguing that images of humanitarian disaster can lead policymakers to perceive a public clamor for action, impelling them to undertake ill-considered interventions, as in Somalia and Bosnia during the 1990s. These arise from elites' anticipation of negative public opinion at Time 3, based on Time 1 and 2 coverage on CNN and elsewhere.

Scholars disagree about the validity of the casualty aversion hypothesis. Despite Mueller's (1973, 1994, 2005) work on casualty sensitivity, empirical tests using a variety of methodologies have found little support for the most deterministic interpretations of that theory (Burk, 1999; Eichenberg, 2005; Gartner and Segura, 1998; Klarevas, 2002). Rather, research tends to show that the influence of casualties on public opinion is contextual and varies across time and geography, with implications for public opinion and politics (Gartner and Segura, 2000; Gartner et al., 2004). Gartner (2004) found that local media in areas that lost servicemen in the bombing of the USS Cole devoted much more coverage to the event than media in less affected areas, and posited that this differential attention may help explain geographic variances in the relationship between opinion about international affairs and domestic politics. This body of research suggests the relevance of the cascade model, with its focus on hierarchical networks through which ideas activate and spread. For instance, Boettcher and Cobb (2006) showed experimentally that how the Pentagon frames casualties in the media – specifically whether they use casualty-ratios or just report either enemy or the US casualties – influences public perceptions of a battle's success, a key variable in the Gelpi et al. (2005/2006) model of casualties and public support.

A second cause for scholarly skepticism stems from studies of the CNN effect. This line of research has shown that media influence public attitudes about use of force far less than policymakers believe. Kull and Destler (1999), for instance, argue that public support for the US involvement in Somalia in 1993 did not wane because 18 American troops died in the 'Black Hawk Down' incident, but rather because policymaking elites turned against the intervention and the Clinton administration did not attempt a more full-throttled justification for it. Similarly, Livingston and Eachus (1995) argue that media content did not trigger America's intervention in Somalia, and Robinson (1999) found little evidence of media influence over humanitarian intervention policy generally. Conversely, in a demonstration of the media's impact on perceived and anticipated public opinion as suggested by the cascade model, Livingston (1997) argued that media can act as an inhibitor to elites' pursuit of policy goals, less because of media impacts on public opinion itself than on leaders' expectations that media coverage of casualties will dampen public support for intervention (see also Sobel [2001] on the constraining role of public opinion).

In summarizing the large body of research casting doubt on the presence of a CNN effect, Gilboa (2005) points scholars to the more subtle and important question of *when* media might have such effects and what they might be. Livingston (1997) has already addressed this to some extent in the policy arena by suggesting that, depending on the relevance of the conflict to domestic political and cultural interests and other forces, media may either promote or impede interventionist policy. The question remains, however, what if any role media coverage might play in shaping public opinion about such a policy, and, more importantly, when if ever such an effect might be evident to policymakers themselves.

Unanswered Questions and Unexplored Assumptions

Although the core claims of state-media theory developed over the last half of the 20th century appear to be as strongly supported as any in political communication, many empirical issues remain underexplored and assumptions challenged by changes in the media and political spheres. There are several key points to be considered here.

First, researchers tend to hold constant White House media management skills, assuming that presidents and administrations possess equal ability and inclination to manage news. The literature tends to generalize about presidents in undifferentiated fashion, depicting their influence as if all have the same capacity to dominate framing of foreign policy throughout their time in office. Yet the record contradicts such an assumption. Bill Clinton and Jimmy Carter lost control of foreign policy frames regularly (Entman, 2004), and although all the data aren't in, it may be that the George W. Bush administration failed to dominate Iraq and Afghanistan framing in their waning years, as the Johnson and Nixon administrations did at times during Vietnam (Hallin, 1986). There is variation between administrations and within them.

Second, the literature offers little guidance on whether media process all foreign policy events and issues similarly. It seems worth considering whether some developments and policy conflicts are more likely to stimulate not only the all-important open elite disputes, but also whether some variants offer the media more potential for autonomous contributions to oppositional framing than others. Events such as the 9/11 terrorist attacks offer little or no leeway for journalists to aggressively seek or voice critiques of the president's frame. Anything that smacked remotely of even explaining the heinous, traumatic attack could generate dissonance for audiences and for journalists themselves – not to mention energetic condemnation from the White House. A similar dynamic may explain the nature of at least the initial stages of war coverage.

A third, closely related concern might involve possible case selection bias. Although the broad area of research is media and foreign policy, the cases selected for analysis are often wars. This of course is what we have done in our overview. As noted earlier, wars are important, but they are not the sum total of concerns found under the heading of foreign affairs. Global environmental concerns, including global warming, deforestation, depletion of fish stocks and desertification transcend national borders, involve complex negotiations among international actors and are of profound significance. Similarly, human rights, trade policies, population growth policies and programs and other similar issues that can be broadly labeled as north–south relations are also properly understood as foreign relations. Yet we know of few case studies that explore this aspect of foreign affairs and media. By focusing on war as foreign affairs, we may inadvertently capture the nation-state and its institutions – especially the military – at its strongest moment, and in the process skew our understanding of state–media relations. This is especially true when studying the American military, one of the most powerful institutions in the world. The military has a preponderance of control over the battlefield, and therefore to the information most germane to war reporting: casualties, progress (or the lack thereof) in the war and nearly all of the other data-points found in war reporting. When at war, nation-states are typically in their strongest position to control the *in situ* story.

This is less true in other areas of deep international concern, however. Indeed, in non-military domains, the nation-state is thought by some scholars to be in crisis (Paul et al., 2003). A new power system in global affairs – a power system with the revolution in microelectronics at its core – is characterized by a plurality of sources of authority, with the nation-state just one, albeit still predominant. Nation-states share space with networks of capital, non-governmental organizations, communication, transnational religious identities, social movements and criminal organizations. 'Nation-states may retain decision-making capacity, but, having become part of a network of powers and counterpowers, they are dependent on a broader system of enacting authority and influence from multiple sources' (Castells, 2000: 356; see also Castells, 2009).

Fourth, the framing research literature tends to treat the media and information environment as a constant. At least two trends point to problems in doing so. In the first instance, the mainstream press faces competition from new media, changing media consumption habits of younger persons,[8] and the shrinking of traditional advertising revenue streams. Overseas bureaus have closed and thousands of journalists have been laid-off in just a handful of crisis years. In 2008 alone the US newspapers lost 15,974 jobs, followed by another 10,000 in the first six months of 2009. As writer Michael Massing observes, 'That's 26,000 fewer reporters, editors, photographers, and columnists to cover the world, analyze political and economic affairs, root out corruption and abuse, and write about culture, entertainment, and sports' (Massing, 2009).

The second trend concerns assumptions made in the political communication literature regarding the nature and capabilities of political elites. In failing to differentiate among elites outside the administration, much of the literature assumes that all potential opponents enjoy equal capability to effectively challenge White House frames (but see Entman, 2004). This raises an important though neglected question: assuming that conflict in elite preferences is the core requirement for contestation of the White House perspective, why do some elites decide to support and others to oppose the president? Lacking such opposition, we know the media will usually be dominated by the president's framing of at least many foreign policy issues. Determining which circumstances are conducive to elite opposition and which favor elite quiescence would seem a critical issue for scholars.

Finally, existing research tends to lump together media content in broad and sometimes vague categories, basically supporting or opposing a president's policy. It also frequently treats opposition that appears on page 16 of *The New York Times* pretty much the same as an identical story appearing on page 1, or on page 18 of another paper. Yet there is reason to assume that appearing anywhere in *The New York Times* carries more political weight than appearing on page one of a less influential newspaper. Content analyses generally do not emerge from a theory that differentiates media content and outlets, instead implying that all media and all statements of opposition and support have equal political import (Entman, 2010).

Besides these concerns and questions we want to draw attention to further systemic issues that should affect future research concerning media and foreign affairs. They involve the organization of the international system and resulting changes in issue dynamics.

NEW DIRECTIONS: RETHINKING FRAMING IN A GLOBALIZED MEDIA AND INFORMATION TECHNOLOGY ENVIRONMENT

Although we do not have space to develop this argument, we want to discuss changes in the political significance and roles of framing in power over foreign policy, as we move from a relatively homogeneous, nation-centered mass media environment to a more heterogeneous, fragmented, specialized yet globalized digital media world. There is a pressing need to take into consideration trends toward fragmentation and hyper-localization, while at the same time recognizing the global nature of contemporary debate in international affairs. James Rosenau (2003) has called these seemly contradictory but conceptually reconcilable trends 'distant proximities'.

First, we can assume that the broadcast and cable news networks servicing mostly American audiences (aside from Fox – see Aday, 2010a; Aday et al., 2005b), as well as major US newspapers and newsmagazines, will continue to carry essentially the same frames of major events (for example, Entman, 1991), allowing us to infer substantial political effects. But as the legacy media's market share shrinks, and online media outlets proliferate into ever more refined ideological niches, frames available to citizens become more diverse and more attuned to specific tastes (Bennett and Iyengar, 2008; Robinson et al., 2009). The cacophony of voices heard in a multiplicity of media outlets, from television news channels to bloggers, means that framing processes and impacts may take on new, largely unexplored dimensions.

For media corporations – as opposed to government leaders – frames serve as audience maintenance mechanisms used to define audiences according to niche markets. Bill O'Reilly, Glen Beck and other personalities offer a product line in a brand – Fox News – that is intent on attracting a politically definable demographic to advertisers (for demographic profiles of cable viewers in the USA, see Pew, 2009). In this way, the frames emphasized by newer media such as blogs, interest group websites, online magazines and infotainment like Comedy Central's *The Daily Show* with Jon Stewart serve to reinforce the brands for politically defined niche markets.

The political upshot of framing understood in this way is the creation of tribes in dialog mainly with themselves (Hindman, 2008). The ultimate consequences remain unclear. On the one hand, fragmentation of groups into isolated communities of interpretation could well undermine the empathy and trust needed to form broad oppositional coalitions across lines of difference. On the other, communication technologies might well be harnessed to help overcome longstanding barriers to collective action (Bimber et al., 2005). Although the future as always remains unpredictable, at this writing, we have little evidence that the burgeoning *availability* of views that challenge presidential policies have actually been *used* by sufficient numbers of citizens to flatten the traditionally steep power hierarchy governing the US foreign policy.

For instance, despite the many thoughtful, accurate and sophisticated rebuttals to George W. Bush's rationales and predictions for the Iraq War available to almost everyone through the Internet and cable channels such as MSNBC and the Comedy Channel, he defeated John Kerry in the 2004 election. This occurred more than 18 months after those justifications had been thoroughly disproved by events on the ground. Though Bush framed Iraq as the central front in the war on terror and his policies there were manifestly failing (see for example Ricks, 2006), polls showed large majorities approving his handling of terrorism.[9]

As this outcome suggests, and considerable evidence reinforces, the greater availability of information has served largely to exacerbate the knowledge gap that has long existed between the most interested and informed and the disconnected majority of citizens (Prior, 2007). Furthermore, even when the electorate seemingly delivered an anti-war message by voting the Democrats into control of the House and Senate in 2006, the Bush administration chose to escalate the Iraq war (the 'surge') and the new Congress went along. At least when it came to Iraq, the first major war to occur after the Internet became pervasive, there was little indication that the US elites were becoming more responsive to a more independent (albeit perhaps fragmented) public opinion.

Hence, future research must reconsider the *scale* of framing contests. To date, framing research assumes a geographically delimited domestic political arena and information space; one rooted in what Benedict Anderson calls the imagined community of the nation-state (Anderson, 2006). But as Manuel Castells (2000) tells us communities are now imagined – or constructed – through networks made possible by the *global* microelectronics revolution. 'Our society is constructed around flows: flows of capital, flows of information, flows of technology, flows of organizational interaction, flows of images, sounds and symbols. Flows are not just one element of social organization: they are the expression of the processes *dominating* our economic, political, and symbolic life' (Castells, 2000: 442, emphasis in original). Flows exist in networks about the globe without regard to time and space (Castells, 2000, especially chapters 6 and 7). Under the logic of global networks, local determination is the product of forces found at the core of global networks themselves. Networks in short redefine the arena of politics, even in the USA. What impact does a redefinition of the political arena have on framing and foreign affairs? Limited space allows us to hint at only a few.

Earlier, we said that existing literature sometimes fails to distinguish among domestic elites and their possibly uneven abilities to engage the White House in framing contests. Networked information challenges us to consider an expanded scale of elite engagement, one not necessarily delimited by national borders. New information technology has created new elites by empowering social movements and NGOs with new methods for creating and distributing truth-claims (Aday and Livingston, 2008, 2009). To understand how requires brief mention of technologies other than the Internet.

The microelectronics revolution transcends the Internet, and carries a more complex array of effects that at this writing have only begun to receive systematic scholarly attention. For example, an estimated 6.1 billion multifunctional mobile phones are distributed around the globe (O'Brien, 2012). Understood as nodes in an adaptable network of event surveillance, cellular telephony distributes framing capacity – though often oriented around discrete events – to a wider array of individuals throughout the world (Livingston, 2007). The growing list of examples of this network's potential impact (see, for example, Bailard, 2009) includes a striking camera-phone video showing the 2009 shooting of a young Iranian woman named Neda Agha Soltan during anti-government protests that followed the disputed presidential election. Video sharing and viewing has exploded as witnessed by upward of 1,000,000 viewings on YouTube.

From pockets to space, high resolution commercial imagery satellites now offer detailed geo-spatial analyses (more than just pictures) to NGOs, universities, news media and governments without the means to launch and maintain space-based surveillance systems (Aday and Livingston, 2009; Livingston, 2001). These technical and scientific developments open up new framing options for advocacy networks involved in issues of environmental change, deforestation and arms proliferation, among other issues. As these diverse groups communicate, share information and services, circulate personnel and exchange funds, they work together to influence policy and affect political outcomes. Transnational networks seem most likely to emerge at precisely those moments when domestic groups are marginalized within a domestic political domain (Keck and Sikkink, 1998).

Put another way, reductions in information costs have opened up political competition to what previously would have been, at best, marginal groups and interests. Bruce Bimber and other social movement theorists argue that information technology has introduced a new 'information regime', one characterized by near zero-information costs and highly fluid group coalition formations and scalability of focus (Bimber, 2003).

Scalability is a defining element of network politics. Information systems are *global*, networking all media and political systems, including the US media and politics. Network politics are distantly proximate, as Rosenau (2003) defines it. Framing contests may well reach and be affected by forces beyond the US Congress and White House and domestic elites. 'In the international arena, new trans-border social movements, rising to defend women's causes, human rights, environmental preservation, and political democracy, are making the Internet an essential tool for disseminating information, organizing, and mobilizing' (Castells, 2000: 392; Keck and Sikkink, 1998).

CONCLUSION

We have reviewed many key findings in scholarship on media and foreign affairs, identified the assumptions and unanswered questions found in the research literature, and drew attention to a few ramifications of changes in the information environment. Yet, even if the structures of political communication had not been undergoing such rapid transformation, scholars would not be able to provide a well-integrated theoretical framework or to advance confident inferences. We believe such a paradigm could be developed, and should be. It will likely apply existing insights about framing, and an extension of frameworks (such as the cascade model) that focus on spreading activation in domestic and, increasingly, international networks linking individuals, groups and governments across the globe.

NOTES

1   Steven Kull, 'Misperceptions, the Media and the Iraq War', The PIPA/Knowledge Network Poll, 2 October, 2003. http://www.worldpublicopinion. org/pipa/pdf/oct03/IraqMedia_Oct03_rpt.pdf

2   See Michael X. Delli Carpini and Scott Keeter, *What Americans Know About Politics and Why It Matters* (New Haven: Yale University Press, 1996); John Zaller, *The Nature and Origins of Mass Opinion* (New York: Cambridge University Press, 1992); Daniel Kahneman and Amos Tversky, 'Choice, Values, and Frames', *American Psychologist* 39: 341–350; Michael X. Delli Carpini and Scott Keeter, What Americans Know and Why it Matters (New Haven: Yale University Press, 1998).

3   See Hallin and Mancini (2004) on variations in media systems that likely make more diverse and informative news about foreign policy available to citizens of many Western European systems; see Scheafer and Wolfsfeld (2007) comparing the diversity in Israeli media coverage of foreign policy to the relative homogeneity of the US media depictions.

4   At this stage of our analysis, by 'media' or 'mediated communications' we refer to the content of the major national news outlets: a handful of leading newspapers including *The New York Times* and *The Washington Post*, *Newsweek* and *Time* newsmagazines; the nightly news reports and news talk shows broadcast by the big three networks (ABC, CBS, NBC) and by cable news channels (CNN, MSNBC, Fox); the infotainment outlets particularly influential among younger adults (such as *The Daily Show* on Comedy Central) and the websites and blogs run by these outlets, which garner the greatest share of online news consumption (Hindman, 2008). Toward the end of our analysis, we will loosen this definition to accommodate our consideration of the larger information environment.

5   Marc Ambinder, 'Don't Cry for Tom Ridge'. http://politics.theatlantic.com/2009/08/dont_cry_for_tom_ridge.php

6   Glenn Greenwald, 'Fringe Leftist Losers: Wrong Even When they are Right'. http://www.salon.com/opinion/greenwald/2009/08/20/ambinder/index.html

7   Supporters of torture in the White House and elsewhere employed 'enhanced interrogation techniques' to frame an array of physically and psychologically abusive behaviors, including sleep deprivation and water-boarding.

8   Internet users in the USA watched 21.4 billion videos in July 2009, up 88% from the year. Google's YouTube streamed 9 billion of these videos, followed by video sites from Viacom and Microsoft (Lardinois, 28 August, 2009).

9   For example, a CBS News poll in early September 2004 found 62% approved of Bush's handling of the 'campaign against terrorism' versus just 31% disapproving (www.pollingreport.com/terror.htm). A Time magazine poll later that month found 57% approved and 39% disapproved of Bush's handling of the 'war on terrorism' (http://www.pollingreport.com/terror2.htm).

REFERENCES

Aday, S. (2005) 'The Real War Will Never Get on Television: An Analysis of Casuimagery in American Television Coverage of the Iraq War', in P. Seib (ed.), *Media and Conflict in the 21st Century*. United Kingdom: Palgrave Macmillan. pp. 141–56.

Aday, S. (2007) 'The Framesetting Effects of News: An Experimental Test of Advocacy versus Objectivist Frames', *Journalism and Mass Communication Quarterly*, 83(4): 767–84.

Aday, S. (2010a) 'Chasing the Bad News: An Analysis of 2005 Iraq and Afghanistan War Coverage on NBC and Fox News Channel', *Journal of Communication*, 60(1): 144–64.

Aday, S. (2010b) 'Leading the Charge: Media, Elite Cues, and Emotion in Public Support for War', *Journal of Communication*, 60(3): 440–65.

Aday, S. and Livingston, S. (2008) 'Taking the State Out of State-Media Relations Theory: How Transnational Advocacy Networks are Rewriting (Some) of the Rules about What We Think We Know about News and Politics', *Media, War, and Conflict*, 1(1): 99–107.

Aday, S. and Livingston, S. (2009) 'NGOs as Intelligence Agencies: The Empowerment of Transnational Advocacy Networks and the Media by Commercial Remote Sensing', *Geoforum*, 40(4): 514–22.

Aday, S., Cluverius, J. and Livingston, S. (2005a) 'As Goes the Statue, So Goes the War: The Emergence of the Victory Frame in Television Coverage of the Iraq War', *Journal of Broadcasting and Electronic Media*, 49(3): 314–31.

Aday S., Livingston, S. and Hebert, M. (2005b) 'Embedding the Truth: A Cross-Cultural Analysis of Objectivity and Television Coverage of the Iraq War', *Harvard International Journal of Press/Politics*, 10(1): 3–21.

Anderson, B. (2006) *Imagined Communities*. London: Verso.

Bailard, C. (2009) 'Mobile Phone Diffusion and Corruption in Africa', *Political Communication*, 26(3): 333–53.

Bailey, G. and Lichty, L. (1972) 'Rough Justice on a Saigon Street: A Gatekeeper Study of NBC's Tet Execution Film', *Journalism Quarterly*, 49: 221–29, 238.

Baker, P. (2009) 'Bush Official, in Book, Tells of Pressures on '04 Vote', *The New York Times*, 20 August, http://www.nytimes.com/2009/08/21/us/21ridge.html?_r=1

Baker, W. D. and Oneal, J. R. (2001) 'Patriotism or Opinion Leadership? The Nature and Origins of the 'Rally "Round the Flag' Effect", *Journal of Conflict Resolution*, 45(5): 661–87.

Baum, M. (2003) *Infotainment Wars: Public Opinion and Foreign Policy in the New Media Age.* Princeton, NJ: Princeton University Press.

Bennett, W. L. (1990) 'Toward a Theory of Press-State Relations', *Journal of Communication*, 40(2): 103–25.

Bennett, W. L. (1994) 'The News about Foreign Policy', in W. L. Bennett and D. L. Paletz (eds.), *Taken by Storm: The Media, Public Opinion, and US Foreign Policy in the Gulf War.* Chicago, IL: The University of Chicago Press. pp. 12–42.

Bennett, W. L. (2008) *News: The Politics of Illusion.* 8th edn. New York: Longman Publishing.

Bennett, W. L., Lawrence, R. and Livingston, S. (2007) *When the Press Fails: Political Power and the News Media from Iraq to Katrina.* Chicago, IL: University of Chicago Press.

Bennett, W. L. and Iyengar, S. (2008) 'A New Era of Minimal Effects? The Changing Foundations of Political Communication', *Journal of Communication*, 58(4): 707–31.

Bilmes, L. and Stiglitz, J. (2006) 'The Economic Costs of the Iraq War: An Appraisal Three Years After the Beginning of the Conflict', *NBER Working Paper Series #12054*, http://www.nber.org/papers/w12054

Bimber, B. A. (2003) *Information and American Democracy: Technology in the Evolution of Political Power.* Cambridge: Cambridge University Press.

Bimber, B., Flanagin, A. J. and Stohl, C. (2005) 'Reconceptualizing Collective Action in the Contemporary Media Environment', *Communication Theory*, 15(4): 365–88.

Blechman, B. M. and Wittes, T. L. (1999) 'Defining Moment: The Threat and Use of Force in American Foreign Policy', *Political Science Quarterly*, 114(1): 1–30.

Boettcher, W. and Cobb, M. (2006) 'Echoes of Vietnam?: Casualty Framing and Public Perceptions of Success and Failure in Iraq', *Journal of Conflict Resolution*, 50(6): 831–54.

Burk, J. (1999) 'Public Support for Peacekeeping in Lebanon and Somalia: Assessing the Casualties Hypothesis', *Political Science Quarterly*, 114(1): 53–78.

Castells, M. (2000) *The Rise of the Network Society.* Malden, MA: Wiley Blackwell.

Castells, M. (2009) *Communication Power.* New York: Oxford University Press.

Center for International Media Assistance (2008) 'The Role of Cell Phones in Carrying News and Information', http://cima.ned.org/reports/cell-phone-report-2.html

Center for Media and Public Affairs (2003) 'The Media Go to War: TV News Coverage of the War in Iraq', *Media Monitor*, 17(2), http://www.cmpa.com/files/media_monitor/03julaug.pdf

Chanley, V. A. (1999) 'US Public Views of International Involvement from 1964–1993: Time Series Analyzes of General and Militant Internationalism', *Journal of Conflict Resolution*, 43(1): 23–44.

Chong, D. and Druckman, J. N. (2007a) 'A Theory of Framing and Opinion Formation in Competitive Elite Environments', *Journal of Communication*, 57(1): 99–118.

Chong, D. and Druckman, J. N. (2007b) 'Framing Theory', *Annual Review of Political Science*, 10: 103–26.

Dickson, S. H. (1995) 'Understanding Media Bias: The Press and the US Invasion of Panama', *Journalism Quarterly*, 71(4): 809–19.

Dorman, W. and Farhang, M. (1988) *The US Press and Iran: Foreign Policy and Journalism of Deference.* Berkeley, CA: University of California Press.

Dorman, W. A. and Livingston, S. (1994) 'News and Historical Context: The Establishment Phase of the Persian Gulf Policy Debate', in W. L. Bennett and D. L. Paletz (eds.), *Taken by Storm: The Media, Public Opinion, and US foreign Policy in the Gulf War.* Chicago, IL: University of Chicago Press. pp. 63–81.

Eagly, A. H. and Chaiken, S. (1993) *The Psychology of Attitudes.* Fort Worth, TX: Harcourt Brace Jovanovich.

Edelman, M. (1988) *Constructing the Political Spectacle.* Chicago, IL: University of Chicago Press.

Eichenberg, R. C. (2005) 'Victory has Many Friends: US Public Opinion and the Use of Military Force, 1981–2005', *International Security*, 30(1): 140–77.

Entman, R. M. (1991) 'Television Access and Political Power: The Networks, the Presidency, and the "Loyal Opposition"', *American Political Science Review*, 85(3): 1022.

Entman, R. M. (2003) 'Cascading Activation: Contesting the White House's Frame after 9/11', *Political Communication*, 20(4): 415–23.

Entman, R. M. (2004) *Projections of Power: Framing News, Public Opinion, and US Foreign Policy.* Chicago, IL: University of Chicago Press.

Entman, R. M. (2010) *Scandals of Media and Politics.* Boston, MA: Polity Press.

Entman, R. M. and Page, B. I. (1994) 'The News Before the Storm: The Iraq War Debate and the Limits to Media Independence', in W. L. Bennett and D. L. Paletz (eds.), *Taken by Storm: The Media, Public Opinion, and US Foreign Policy in the Gulf War.* Chicago, IL: University of Chicago Press. pp. 82–104.

Entman, R. M., Matthes, J. and Pellicano, L. (2009) 'The Nature, Sources and Effects of News Framing', in K. Wahl-Jorgensen and T. Hanitzsch (eds.), *Handbook of Journalism Studies.* New York: Routledge. pp. 175–90.

Entman, R. M., Livingston, S. and Kim, J. (2009) 'Doomed to Repeat: Iraq News, 2002 2007', *American Behavioral Scientist*, 52(5): 689–708.

Entman, R. M. (2012). *Scandal and Silence.* Cambridge, UK: Polity Press.

Feaver P. D. and Gelpi, C. (2004) *Choosing Your Battles: American Civil-Military Relations and the Use of Force.* Princeton, NJ: Princeton University Press.

Fiske, S. T. and Taylor, S. E. (1991) *Social Cognition.* 2nd edn. New York: McGraw Hill.

Galbraith, P. W. (2008) *Unintended Consequences: How War in Iraq Strengthened America's Enemies.* New York: Simon & Schuster.

Gartner, S. S. (2004) 'Making the International Local: The Terrorist Attack on the USS Cole, Local Casualties, and Media Coverage', *Political Communication,* 21(2): 139–59.

Gartner, S. S. and Segura, G. M. (1998) 'War, Casualties, and Public Opinion', *Journal of Conflict Resolution,* 42(3): 278–300.

Gartner, S. S. and Segura, G. M. (2000) 'Race, Opinion, and Casualties in the Vietnam War', *The Journal of Politics,* 62(1): 115–46.

Gartner, S. S., Segura, G. M. and Barratt, B. (2004) 'Casualties, Positions, and Senate Elections in the Vietnam War', *Political Research Quarterly,* 53(3): 467–77.

Gelpi, C., Feaver, P. and Reifler, J. (2005/2006) 'Success Matters: Casualty Sensitivity and the War in Iraq', *International Security,* 30(3): 7–46.

Gelpi, C, Feaver, P. D. and Reifler, J. (2009) *Paying the Human Costs of War: American Public Opinion and Causalities in Military Conflicts.* Princeton, NJ: Princeton University Press.

Gilboa, E. (2005) 'Global Television News and Foreign Policy: Debating the CNN Effect', *International Studies Perspectives,* 6(3): 325–41.

Gitlin, T. (1978) 'Media Sociology: The Dominant Paradigm', *Theory and Society,* 6(2): 205–53.

Gitlin, T. (1980) *The Whole World is Watching.* Los Angeles: University of California Press.

Hallin, D. C. (1986) *The 'Uncensored' War.* New York: Oxford University Press.

Hallin, D. C. (1991) 'Images of the Vietnam and the Persian Gulf Wars in US Television', in Rabinovitz and S. Jeffords, (eds.), *Seeing Through the Media: The Persian Gulf War.* New Brunswick, NJ: Rutgers, pp. 45–58.

Hallin, D. C. and Mancini, P. (2004) *Comparing Media Systems: Three Models of Media and Politics.* New York: Cambridge University Press.

Hindman, M. (2008) *The Myth of Digital Democracy.* Princeton, NJ: Princeton University Press.

Isikoff, M. and Corn, D. (2006) *Hubris: The Inside Story of Spin, Scandal, and the Selling of the Iraq War.* New York: Crown Publishers.

Jentleson, B. W. (1992) 'The Pretty Prudent Public: Post-Vietnam American Opinion on the Use of Military Force', *International Studies Quarterly,* 36(1): 49–74.

Keck, M. and Sikkink, K. (1998) *Activists Beyond Borders: Advocacy Networks in International Politics.* Ithaca and London: Cornell University Press.

Kellner, D. (1992) *The Persian Gulf TV War.* Boulder, CO: Westview Press.

Klarevas, L. (2002) 'The "Essential Domino" of Military Operations: American Public Opinion and the Use of Force', *International Studies Perspectives,* 3(4): 417–37.

Kull, S. (2003) 'Misperceptions, the Media and the Iraq War', The PIPA/Knowledge Network Poll', 2 October. http://www.worldpublicopinion.org/pipa/pdf/oct03/Iraqmedia_Oct03_rpt.pdf

Kull, S. and Destler, I. M. (1999) *Misreading the Public: The Myth of a New Isolationism.* Washington, DC: Brookings Institution Press.

Kull, S. and Ramsay, C. (2001) 'The Myth of the Reactive Public: American Public Attitudes on Military Fatalities in the Post-Cold War Period', in P. Everts and P. Isernia (eds.), *Public Opinion and the International Use of Force.* Oxford: Routledge Press. pp. 205–28.

Lacquement, R. A. (2004) 'The Casualty-Aversion Myth', *Naval War College Review,* LVII(1): 38–57.

Lakoff, G. (2008) *The Political Mind.* New York: Penguin Group.

Landay, J. (2009) 'Report: Abusive Tactics Used to Seek Iraq-al Qaida Link', *McClatchy,* 21 April, http://www.mcclatchydc.com/227/story/66622.html

Larson, E. (1996) *Casualties and Consensus: The Historical Role of Casualties in Domestic Support for US Military Operations.* Santa Monica, CA: Rand.

Larson, E. and Savych, B. (2005) *American Public Support for US Military Operations from Mogadishu to Baghdad.* Santa Monica, CA: Rand.

Lazarsfeld, P. and Merton, R. (1948) 'Mass Communication, Popular Taste, and Organized Social Action', in W. Schramm (ed.), *Mass Communication.* Urbana: University of Illinois Press. pp. 492–503.

Livingston, S. (1997) *Clarifying the CNN effect: An Examination of Media Effects According to Type of Military Intervention.* Cambridge, MA: Joan Shorenstein Center on the Press Politics and Public Policy John F. Kennedy School of Government Harvard University.

Livingston, S. (2000) 'Media Coverage of the War: An Empirical Assessment', in A. Schabnel (ed.), *Kosovo and the Challenge of Humanitarian Intervention: Selective Indignation, Collective Action, and Individual Citizenship.* New York: United Nations University Press. pp. 360–84.

Livingston, S. (2001) 'Remote Sensing Technology and the News Media', in J. Baker, K. O'Connell and R. Williamson (eds.), *Commercial Observation Satellites: At the Leading Edge of Global Transparency.* Rand Corporation and the American Society for Photogrammetry and Remote Sensing. pp. 485–502.

Livingston, S. (2007) 'On Bullshit, by Harry G. Frankfurt. On Truth, by Harry G. Frankfurt', *Political Communication,* 24(4): 476–81.

Livingston, S. and Eachus, T. (1995) 'Humanitarian Crises and US Foreign Policy: Somalia and the CNN Effect Reconsidered', *Political Communication,* 12(4): 413–29.

Livingston, S. and Bennett, W. L. (2003) 'Gatekeeping, Indexing, and Live-event News: Is Technology Altering the Construction of News?', *Political Communication,* 20(4): 363–80.

Livingston, S. and Van Belle, D. (2005) 'The Effects of Satellite Technology on Newsgathering from Remote Locations', *Political Communication,* 22(1): 45–62.

Lupia, A., McCubbins, M. D. and Popkin, S. L. (2000) *Elements of Reason: Cognition, Choice, and the Bounds of Rationality.* New York: Cambridge University Press.

Massing, M. (2009) 'A New Horizon for the News', *The New York Review of Books,* 14 September, http://www.nybooks.com/articles/23050

Matthes, J. (2007) 'Beyond Accessibility? Toward an On-Line and Memory-Based Model of Framing Effects', *Communications: The European Journal of Communication Research*, 32(1): 51–78.

Mermin, J. (1999) *Debating War and peace: Media Coverage of US Intervention in the Post-Vietnam Era*. Princeton, NJ: Princeton University Press.

Mueller, J. (1973) *War, Presidents, and Public Opinion*. New York: John Wiley and Sons.

Mueller, J. (1994) *Policy and Opinion in the Gulf War*. Chicago, IL: University of Chicago Press.

Mueller, J. (2005) 'The Iraq Syndrome', *Foreign Affairs*, November/December: 44–54.

Mueller, J. (2006) *Overblown: How Politicians and the Terrorism Industry Inflate National Security Threats, and Why We Believe Them*. New York: Free Press.

O'Brien, K.J. (2012). "Top 1% of Mobile Users Consume Half of World's Bandwidth, and Gap is Growing." New York Times, January 5, 2012: http://www.nytimes.com/2012/01/06/technology/top-1-of-mobile-users-use-half-of-worlds-wireless-bandwidth.html?_r=1&ref=technology

Oneal, J. R. and Bryan, A. L. (1995) 'The Rally 'Round the Flag Effect in US Foreign Policy Crises, 1950–1985', *Political Behavior*, 17(4): 379–401.

Page, B. I. with Bouton, M. (2006) *The Foreign Policy Disconnect: What Americans Want from our Leaders but Don't Get*. Chicago, IL: University of Chicago Press.

Paletz, D. L. and Entman, R. M. (1981) *Media Power Politics*. New York; London: Free Press; Collier Macmillan.

Paul, T. V., Ikenberry, G. J. and Hall, J. A. (eds.) (2003) *The Nation-State in Question*. Princeton, NJ: Princeton University Press.

Petty, R. E. and Cacciopo, J. T. (1986) *Communication and Persuasion: Central and Peripheral Routes to Attitude Change*. New York: Springer-Verlag.

Pew Research Center's Project for Excellence in Journalism. (2009) *The State of the News Media*. Washington, DC: Pew Research Center.

Prior, M. (2007) *Post-Broadcast Democracy: How Media Choice Increases Inequality in Political Involvement and Polarizes Elections*. Cambridge: Cambridge University Press.

Ricks, T. (2006) *Fiasco: The American Military Adventure in Iraq*. New York: Penguin.

Robinson, P. (1999) 'The CNN Effect: Can the News Media Drive Foreign Policy?', *Political Communication*, 25(2): 301–9.

Robinson, P. (2002) *The CNN Effect: The Myth of News, Foreign Policy, and Intervention*. Oxford: Routledge Press.

Robinson, P., Goddard, P., Parry, K. and Murray, C. (2009) 'Testing Models of Media Performance in Wartime: U.K. TV News and the 2003 Invasion of Iraq', *Journal of Communication*, 59(3): 534–63.

Rosenau, J. (2003) *Distant Proximities: Dynamics Beyond Globalization*. Princeton, NJ: Princeton University Press.

Scheafer, T. and Wolfsfeld, G. (2007) 'Competing Actors: The Construction of Political News and the Contest Over Waves in Israel', *Political Communication*, 23(3): 333–54.

Schudson, M. (1981) *Discovering the News: A Social History of American Newspapers*. New York: Basic Books.

Sigal, L. (1973) *Reporters and Officials: The Organization and Politics of Newsmaking*. Lexington, MA: D.C. Heath.

Sniderman, P. and Theriault, S. (2004) 'The Structure of Political Argument and the Logic of Issue Framing', in P. M. Sniderman and W. W. Sarris (eds.), *Studies in Public Opinion: Gauging Attitudes, Nonattitudes, Measurement Error, and Change*. Princeton, NJ: Princeton University Press. pp. 133–65.

Sobel, R. (2001) *The Impact of Public Opinion on US Foreign Policy since Vietnam: Constraining the Colossus*. New York: Oxford University Press.

Westen, D. (2007) *The Political Brain*. New York: Public Affairs.

Wolfsfeld, G. (2004) *Media and the Path to Peace*. Cambridge: Cambridge University Press.

Zaller, J. (1992) *The Nature and Origins of Mass Opinion*. Cambridge: Cambridge University Press.

Zaller, J. and Chiu, D. (1996) 'Government's Little Helper: US Press Coverage of Foreign Policy Crises, 1945–1991', *Political Communication*, 13(4): 385–405.

26

News Media and War

Piers Robinson

Today, the study of the relationship between news media and violent conflict forms a major strand of research, straddling the fields of cultural studies, communication studies and political science. This is of no surprise, given the unprecedented developments in communications technology witnessed over the course of the 20th century and the proliferation of violent conflict, which made that century the most violent in human history. The launch in 2008 of the first journal dedicated to the field, *Media, War, Conflict*[1] symbolizes how important this research strand has now become. In general terms, research in this area has focused on three distinct issues and, as I shall argue, largely ignored a fourth. First, descriptive research has sought to identify how news media cover conflicts and crisis analyzing in particular the content and form of media representation of war. Second, description has often been used as a route to theorizing and attempting to explain why wartime coverage takes the form that it does. Third, the influence of news media upon both public attitudes as well as the behavior of governments has received scholarly scrutiny. The poor relation to these three research foci has been the normative question of how news media *should* behave in wartime. Underlying most of this research is the perennial political communication concern with the extent to which news media maintain independence, scrutinize the actions of governments and the military, and accurately convey the realities of war and crisis. However, before outlining the structure of this chapter and how it aims to introduce the reader to these aspects of research into news media and war, the historical and normative backdrop to this research agenda is worth outlining.

As key defining moments of the early 20th century, World War I and World War II marked the start of contemporary warfare, involving the whole scale mobilization of nations onto a war footing, extensive targeting of civilians as part of strategic war aims and the mechanization of warfare, all conducted in the context of newly emerging forms of mass communication. With the arrival of wireless radio, newsreels shown in cinemas and mass circulation newspapers, the importance and power of media was fully recognized. From the deployment of Nazi propaganda, masterminded by Goebbels, through to the creation of the Ministry of Information in the UK, tasked with the 'maintenance of morale', media became to a large extent part of national war efforts (Carruthers, 2000: 54–107). In conditions of total war, where national survival was at times threatened, the normative expectation that media should become part of the war effort and a 'munition of the mind' was largely accepted by governments, media and publics. As Hallin describes, wartime media state relations were characterized by a 'relationship between the state and civil society [including media] which involved not primarily the suppression of civil society by the state, but co-operation, co-optation and blurring of the lines' (1997: 209). In short, the idea of an impartial and independent wartime media was largely irrelevant in the context of total war. The history of news media and war since the two world wars, however, has not necessarily implied a significant shift toward greater 'objectivity' and independence. Even in the context of limited wars in which national survival was not directly at stake, as was the case with so-called proxy wars fought during the Cold War, most scholars agree that news media have usually served 'their' state rather well (Carruthers, 2000; Knightley, 2003; Taylor, 1997). The prevalence of the realist mindset among governments and military, which is instinctively wary of allowing too great a role for public opinion and news media in foreign policy formulation (Holsti, 1992; Lippman, 1955), and the patriotic commitment of journalists to 'their' nation (Zandberg and Neiger, 2005), both provide a powerful normative under-pinning for news media deference in times of war. At the same time, from the Vietnam War onward, an increasing body of scholarship has analyzed the extent to which news media can play a more independent and influential role during war. Indeed, it was the US military defeat during the Vietnam conflict, and the associated allegation that an oppositional media helped erode public support for that war, which gave birth to the belief that news media and public opinion were capable of determining the course of a war, the so-called Vietnam Syndrome. Regardless of the empirical validity of the Vietnam Syndrome, subsequent events have bolstered the quantity of scholarly literature exploring the news media as an inde-pendent force during war and crisis. In particular, the CNN effect debate during the post-Cold War 1990s revolved around the ability of news media to cause armed intervention during humanitarian crises in countries such as Somalia (1992–93) and Bosnia (1995) (Robinson, 2002); post-9/11, in addition to the burgeoning literature on terrorism and its relationship to news media, scholarly analysis has paid attention to the allegedly trans-formative effect of new communication technolo-gies that appear to fundamentally challenge the ability of governments and military to influence news media, even in times of war and crisis. In contrast to the realist perspective, liberal concep-tualizations concerning the value of a free and independent media, capable of holding govern-ments to account even in matters of high foreign policy such as war, have provided normative sup-port for this mode of news media performance (see Holsti, 1992; Robinson, 2008).

The structure of this chapter reflects this his-torical trajectory and the continuing debate over the extent to which the relationship between news media and war has changed from that witnessed during the two World Wars. At the outset, I should make clear that the focus of this chapter is largely on social scientific research, and to a lesser extent historical studies, and pays less attention to the plethora of cultural studies accounts which focus on the style and form of media representation of war. Also, the discussion here is primarily con-cerned with news media and does not, in a detailed way, engage with the related literature on public opinion and foreign policy. In the closing pages however, the need for more research which attempts to examine the interrelationship between news media and public opinion will be discussed. The first section of this chapter discusses the aca-demic orthodoxy, highlighting the subservient role news media play in relation to governments

during war. From Hallin's (1986) seminal study of the US media and the Vietnam War, through to the Glasgow University Media Group (GUMG) (1985) critique of British coverage of the 1982 Falklands Conflict, this section outlines the descriptions, explanations and theoretical concep-tualizations offered by this literature. Section two deals with the contemporary challenges to the orthodox position, including the CNN effect debate of the 1990s and current post-9/11 analyses of both the 'war on terror' and the major conflict in Iraq. Theoretical developments, including the work of Entman (2004) and Wolfsfeld (1997), all of which have attempted to offer a more pluralized and nuanced understanding of news media and foreign policy, are the focus of concern here. The chapter concludes by assessing the current state of knowledge and highlighting, in particular, the need for greater attention to comparative research across time and national contexts and the need to grapple with how to explain and justify patterns of war-time news media coverage.

THE ORTHODOX VIEW: NEWS MEDIA AS 'FAITHFUL SERVANT'[2]

The orthodox view on wartime news media-state relations can be traced directly to the American experience during the Vietnam War. This conflict ran hand in hand with the establishment of televi-sion news as the principle source of trusted news information. In tandem with mass circulation newspapers, this form of communication remained unrivaled throughout the latter half of the 20th century. The conflict resulted in millions of deaths in South East Asia while dividing the US society; it also triggered a heated debated over the impact of news media and public opinion upon the ability of the US to fight and win. In his memoirs, Richard Nixon declared:

> The Vietnam War was complicated by factors that never before occurred in America's conduct of war ... More than ever before, television showed the terrible human suffering and sacrifice of war. Whatever the intention behind such relentless and literal reporting of war, the result was a serious demoralization of the home front, raising the question whether America would ever again be able to fight an enemy abroad with unity and strength of purpose at home. (1978: 350)

While the idea that the US news media adopted an oppositional stance during the Vietnam War, the 'oppositional media thesis' (Hallin, 1984), received a degree of scholarly support, much of the driving force for this debate can be related to a broader conservative critique emerging in the 1970s. This critique argued that declining American public confidence toward the US political institutions was being furthered by a cantankerous and oppositional news media. As such, much of this early debate needs to be understood as part of a broader political and ideological debate that emerged in the US during the 1970s. At the same time, the specific claim that news media (and public opinion) had led to the US military failure has been advocated by a variety of scholars, military officials and politicians, some of whom were involved in the war (for example, Braestrup, 1994; Hammond, 1989; Westmoreland, 1979). The outcome of this debate was the birth of the *Vietnam Syndrome* described earlier.

Daniel Hallin's (1986) seminal study, *The Uncensored War* has been largely successful, however, in debunking the oppositional media thesis. Based upon a systematic content analysis of 779 television broadcasts from between 1965 and 1973, as well as *The New York Times* coverage of the war, he argues that the US news media coverage of the war was broadly supportive of it until 1968. During this phase, the US news media operated within a 'sphere of consensus', which had been defined by political agreement over the course of the war. During this period, coverage reflected well upon the US forces. In 1968, however, communist forces launched the Tet Offensive, which involved an uprising throughout South Vietnam. At this point, according to Hallin, critical reporting did start to emerge in the mainstream US news media, but this was only because elements within the Johnson administration itself had started to argue publicly over the course of the war: the scope of reporting had extended to embrace a 'sphere of legitimate controversy', involving *procedural criticism* pertaining to whether or not the US was winning the war in South East Asia. Importantly, however, the US news media coverage never moved beyond this point into a 'sphere of deviance' whereby *substantive criticisms* of the legitimacy of the US action in Vietnam were made. In short, whatever claims have been made with regard to the Vietnam War, the Vietnam Syndrome and the oppositional media thesis, Hallin's influential study paints a picture of a relatively docile and compliant wartime news media.

The impact of Hallin's work has been extensive. On the one hand, through debunking the idea of an oppositional media in this easy, or paradigm, case, his work casts doubt upon the idea that news media can ever maintain the independence necessary to challenge a government in wartime. Put another way, given the controversial and long running nature of the Vietnam War, one might reasonably expect to find a good deal of critical and oppositional journalism: failure to find this means that we are even less likely to find evidence for media independence when examining less controversial conflicts. Indeed, and in line with Hallin's analysis, the case for news media deference in wartime has been repeatedly reaffirmed across a series of academic studies. In the UK context, the GUMG (1985) analyzed and critiqued the UK news media coverage of the 1982 Falklands Conflict, highlighting the willing complicity of broadcasters to provide 'a nightly offering of interesting, positive and heart-warming stories of achievement and collaboration born out of a sense of national purpose' (1985: 173–4). With respect to the Israeli context, Tamar Liebes (1997) details how hegemony has shaped and limited journalists covering conflict in the Middle East while, with respect to the US news media and the 1991 Gulf War, the widely cited *Taken by Storm*, edited by Bennett and Paletz (1994), provides further empirical evidence of news media deference to government. Throughout this literature is the assumption, rarely addressed explicitly, that journalists and news media *should* be doing more to maintain independence and autonomy in wartime and which, conversely, challenges ideas that news media should, through loyalty and duty, support their side during war.

News Media Representation of War

In terms of the empirical question of what deferential wartime coverage looks like, based upon detailed and systematic content and framing analysis of news media coverage, a reasonably consistent picture emerges from this critical literature. At its most deferential, such coverage adopts a jingoistic and overtly patriotic stance, highlighting the heroic actions of 'our boys'. Perhaps the most notorious example of such coverage occurred when the British tabloid newspaper, *The Sun*, reported the sinking of the Argentine cruiser *General Belgrano* during the 1982 Falklands Conflict with the headline 'Gotcha'. More often, such coverage is dominated both by the voices of 'our side' and the subject of how well the military campaign is proceeding. In particular, for example, news media coverage of the 1991 Gulf War provided a textbook example of how dramatic visuals of guided missiles and offensive military action, communicated via large set piece coalition news media briefings, came to dominate much of the media reporting of that war. Another important characteristic of such coverage is the propensity of media reports to avoid substantive level issues (relating to the fundamental objectives and justifications for official policy) and covering instead only procedural level criticisms (relating to the conduct of policy): Journalists might criticize how a war is being fought and whether the tactics will lead to victory, but are unlikely to question either the fundamental justification for a war or the legitimacy and good intentions of 'their own side'. Of course, what matters also is the news that is not covered. The difficulty with which non-official or alternative voices struggle to be heard is a consistent criticism of wartime media: from the opinions of antiwar activists through to aid agencies and international organizations such as the United Nations, as well as the perspectives of those civilians caught in the midst of a conflict. As a result, relatively little serious and sustained attention is paid to humanitarian issues, political and diplomatic processes, and the death and injury of civilians. Just as the critical literature tends not to address its implicit normative stance, that norms of independence and impartiality *should* be maintained under the conditions of war, it is also left unclear as to precisely what kind of coverage would constitute impartial or balanced representation of war. The broader question of how news media should cover war, will be returned to in the concluding section.

Explaining Wartime News media Performance

While the literature provides a reasonably consistent critique of the inadequacies of wartime news media coverage, there is less consistency with regard to explaining this failure of news media to maintain autonomy and independence from government. On the one hand, an array of what can be described as *elite driven theories* have sought to explain both wartime and non-wartime media deference through reference to various factors that conjoin to ensure the dominance of official and/or elite viewpoints in the news. The leading and most widely cited account is provided by Bennett's (1990) indexing hypothesis which postulates that journalists instinctively index the news to the range of official debate in Washington: if politicians are in agreement on an issue, journalists will rarely question that consensus; when politicians are debating an issue, journalists will report both sides of the argument. The indexing hypothesis is similar to Hallin's own explanation for his observations of the US news media and the Vietnam War. Indeed, his finding that the contours of news media coverage of that war followed elite consensus and dissensus is explained partly through reference to the routine of objective journalism, whereby objectivity is operationalized as the reporting of the range of viewpoints across

the US executive and legislative. Other scholars have also placed considerable importance on the relationship between journalists and official sources (for example, Schlesinger and Tumber, 1994) while Wolfsfeld's *Political Contest Model* describes wartime news media as an ideal type example of 'media as faithful servant' to the state whereby the conditions of privileged access and control of information creates a power imbalance firmly in favor of the military and political officials. He draws upon the 1982 Falklands War to illustrate this point, showing how journalists traveling the 8000 miles to the war zone with the British Royal Navy were almost entirely reliant on British officials and military both for information and the capacity to communicate reports back to the UK. Of course, recent approaches to news media management, involving the embedding of journalists with military units, further strengthens the link between journalists and official sources. The logical implication of these accounts is that news media output is largely shaped and determined by official sources with journalists serving as passive receptacles for official perspectives.

Other elite driven accounts, however, identify broader power structures that act to shape the behavior of journalists during both war and peace. Hallin (1986) as well as Herman and Chomsky (1988) note the importance of ideology during the Cold War period which ensured that journalists shared the same interpretation of crises around the world as policymakers. Taking, for example, the case of the Vietnam War, Cold War ideology ensured that journalists and policymakers shared the belief that the war could only be perceived as a righteous struggle to save the Vietnamese from the 'evil' of communism. Alternative explanations for the war – presenting it, for example, as an ongoing struggle by a large section of the Vietnamese population (North and South) against the intervention of first France and then the US – fell so far outside the anti-communism frame that most journalists probably never entertained such an interpretation. Herman and Chomsky's (1988) *propaganda model* highlights also the significance of economic power structures: because news media outlets are owned by major conglomerates, there exists a limit to news media independence which is determined, ultimately, by the economic interests of big business. With respect to foreign affairs and war, the charge that Herman and Chomsky level against the US media industry is that successive US governments have pursued foreign policy endeavors, including war, that reflect the economic interests of big business. Finally, patriotism also forms the basis for explaining wartime news media deference (Bennett and Paletz, 1994; GUMG, 1985; Liebes, 1997). To the extent that patriotism can be understood as an ideological process, its effects upon news media output occurs through a variety of processes. On the one hand, some of the elite driven accounts emphasize how the appeal to patriotism is a powerful rhetorical tool employed by policymakers in order to silence dissent. At the same time, as Mueller's (1973) *rally round the flag* thesis describes, populations tend to instinctively support their leadership at times of national crisis; and, as Bennett and Paletz (1994: 284) argue, commercial news media are vulnerable to the concern that patriotic publics will not welcome critical coverage during war. In addition, the patriotic sentiments of journalists themselves might naturally incline them to support 'their' side during a war (Liebes, 1997). Of course, the realist mindset noted earlier expects, and indeed demands, such behavior. As such the normative stance of these critical accounts is at odds with the realist one, implying as it does that impartiality, not patriotism, should prevail among journalists covering war.

To summarize, the elite driven models, and claims that news media are deferential to governments and military during conditions of war, draw upon a range of causal factors in order to explain this pattern of performance. Reliance upon official sources, ideology, economic imperatives and patriotism are all understood to play a role in shaping news coverage. At the same time, the relative explanatory weighting accorded to each factor remains under-determined. Most accounts tend to emphasize the importance of official sources (the indexing hypothesis), while others attach greater importance to patriotism and ideology. In fact, it is entirely plausible that, under conditions of war, patriotism becomes the overriding factor that shapes coverage. If this is the case, elite driven accounts, such as the indexing hypothesis (Bennett, 1990), might well be overplaying the importance of political elites and ignoring what is actually a bottom-up process, whereby wartime coverage is much more a consequence of a national mood dominated by patriotism. Making sense of the causal mechanisms variously proposed by elite driven models is further complicated by their analytical focus: Most of them have been articulated as relevant to media–state relations generally (not just for cases of news media and war), even though they have often been tested against cases of news media and war. On the one hand, this means that these models have been inattentive to the specific dynamics of media-state relations during war, including factors such as patriotism, which might be more relevant during conditions of war than during periods of peace. As a consequence, there is plenty of uncertainty vis-à-vis the explanatory weighting to be attached to the various causal mechanisms. On the other

hand, cases of news media and war are arguably easy ones in which to find evidence of news media deference: testing general theories of media–state relations in these contexts is likely to produce a distortion of the evidence in favor of the elite driven accounts. The task of resolving these issues is one that will be returned to at the end of this chapter. In addition to this theoretical/explanatory uncertainty, Althaus (2003) has also raised serious questions with regard to the accuracy with which studies have analyzed the empirical content of wartime news reporting. Specifically, he argues that many studies, both of media and war, and media state relations more generally, have actually tended to undermeasure press criticism by ignoring critical contributions raised by journalists, failing to distinguish adequately between procedural and substantive types of criticism, and by relying upon proxy data rather than analyzing actual news content. The problem identified by Althaus (2003) is that large-scale content analyses can often fail to capture the nuances of news coverage. This was a point also made by historian David Culbert (1998) in response to Hallin's claims on Vietnam. Culbert argues that the broadness of Hallin's study, which involves analysis through systematic quantification, fails to capture the impact of precise moments when particular news stories have a major political impact. By way of example, he focuses upon the notorious footage of General Loan executing an alleged communist fighter during the Tet uprising. He argues that this imagery, broadcast on the US network news, was a powerful influence both on the US public opinion and upon the US President Johnson himself. The provocative and challenging conclusion reached by Althaus is that, due to methodological limitations, scholars might well have been measuring the news inaccurately for some time:

> the bottom line arising from all this confusion is that we simply don't know how independent news discourse might be from the parameters of official debate ... like blind men sizing up the elephant, none has yet fitted these pieces into a picture of the whole. (2003: 388)

Finally, as noted at several points thus far, the orthodox critical literature assumes a commitment to liberal notions of independence and impartiality, a position at odds with realist arguments vis-à-vis the need for loyalty and support during war. Connected with this is the continuing lack of clarity over what *good* or *independent* wartime coverage would look like. These areas of uncertainty will be returned to in the conclusion.

Beyond the limitations internal to the orthodox position there are also a broader set of debates, that emerged from the late 1980s onward, concerning developments in communication technology and the passing of the Cold War which have brought in to question the continued relevance of the orthodox position. It is to these debates, and the associated neopluralist turn, that we now turn.

THE CNN EFFECT DEBATE AND THE NEOPLURALIST TURN

During the 1990s, for a number of reasons, it became increasingly tempting to understand foreign policy and media–state relations as having undergone some kind of transformation characterized by a pluralization of power. Indeed, it was the apparent relationship between news media reporting of conflicts (for example, Bosnia 1992–95), and foreign policy decisions to deploy armed forces in support of humanitarian operations, which signaled to many that a new era of media power had emerged. The groundbreaking decision to create safe havens in Northern Iraq following the 1991 Gulf War, the deployment of 28,000 US troops in to Somalia in order to defend aid deliveries and the increasingly forceful responses to human rights violations in the Bosnian war of 1992–95, all were drawn upon to demonstrate the validity of what became known as *the CNN Effect:* the idea that news media coverage of humanitarian crises influenced policymakers to undertake a new form of military action, namely humanitarian intervention. As such, the 1990s appeared to herald the arrival of a new form of warfare, humanitarian intervention, in which news media played a different role from that played in previous 'non-humanitarian' conflicts: here, news media representation focused upon the plight of suffering people in 'other peoples' (Carruthers, 2000) wars, rather than representing the progress of 'our boys' in battle; at the same time, news media were an active force in causing policymakers to engage in humanitarian warfare, as opposed to simply deferring to the state as was the case in traditional wars of national interest. The recent intervention in Libya (2011), involving extensive media coverage and an initial humanitarian authorization under the Responsibility to Protect doctrine, appears to raise similar issues. More generally, with the turn of the millennium, the issue of global terrorism and the associated wars in Afghanistan and Iraq created further developments in our conceptualization and understanding of wartime media–state relations. Before addressing these, however, our focus turns to the CNN effect debate, which generated considerable theoretical and empirical scholarly analysis.

The CNN Effect Debate

In addition to the empirical verification apparently provided by interventions in Northern Iraq, Somalia and Bosnia, two explanations emerged to explain the newly discovered power of news media to 'move and shake' (Cohen, 1994: 9) governments. First, many commentators argued that the passing of the Cold War had freed journalists to become more independent of their respective governments. The ideological bond of the anti-communism consensus, identified in some of the critical orthodox literature discussed earlier, was no longer a feature of the relationship between journalists and policymakers. The result, journalists were freer to criticize their own government even in the realm of high foreign policy. Indeed, in addition to the CNN effect debate of the 1990s, scholars have regularly drawn upon the Cold War/ Post Cold War transition in order to provide an explanatory grounding for a more pluralist understanding of media state relations. For example, Entman argued that:

> [J]ournalistic motivations embodied in independent, watch-dog self-images and ideals, often encourage a move toward questioning government authority more than was the habit during the Cold War. Indeed, even during popular and seemingly successful wars, the news media now pounce upon any signs of failure or 'quagmire' and in doing so apply their own evaluative criteria as much as indexing elite opposition. (2003: 423)

In tandem with the loosening of Cold War ideological bonds, technological developments were also understood as determinants of the CNN effect. First and foremost, the emergence of 24-hour news channels, predicated on live coverage of international events, was understood to have created increased transparency of hitherto underreported conflicts from around the world, while the ability to report in *real-time* enabled news organizations to bypass official channels and report directly from a conflict zone. In addition, the emerging importance of the Internet was heralded by some as a new source of empowerment for non-elite groups. For example, analyzing the 'David and Goliath' struggle between the indigenous Chiapas guerrilla army and the Mexican state, Douglas Kellner claims that: 'From the beginning, the peasants and guerrilla armies struggling in Chiapas, Mexico used computer data bases, guerrilla radio, and other forms of media to circulate news of their struggles and idea' (1998: 182). The net result of these developments was that news media had become less dependent upon government information sources in covering events and in defining the news agenda, more likely to include alternative and critical viewpoints and, therefore, weakened the control of governments over the information environment.

Empirical verification of the CNN effect was, in fact, limited, although not entirely absent. Initial research conducted by Gowing (1994), based upon interviews with policymakers, suggested that the influence was far more limited than suggested by many advocates of the CNN effect. Indeed, Gowing concluded that influence was limited to moments of uncertainty, when policymakers had failed to develop a clear policy in relation to a crisis. And, even then, the most likely scope of influence was on tactical decisions (not strategic) or the creation of cosmetic policy responses. For example, Gowing (1994) argued that news media occasionally triggered limited tactical air strikes during the 1992–95 war in Bosnia and superficial acts such as the airlifting of a small number of injured children out of the war zone. In their study of the intervention in Somalia 1992, Livingston and Eachus (1995) concluded that news media, in fact, were following the indexing norm with the US government officials drawing the attention of journalists to Somalia, not the other way round. Later research, based upon detailed case study analysis, found that news media impact upon policy was likely to have played a role in causing policymakers to deploy air power, but not ground troops, in pursuit of humanitarian goals (Babak, 2007; Robinson, 2002).

Overall, initial claims regarding the CNN effect, some of which went so far as to suggest that control of the policy making process had been lost to the news media, were almost undoubtedly inaccurate and exaggerated. On the one hand, explaining military interventions during humanitarian crises through reference to news media pressure tended to obscure the range of factors that conjoined to determine when and where intervention occurred. At best, news media was one factor among many. Another problem confronting analysis of the CNN effect lay in the inherent difficulty of trying to explore the thought processes by which policymakers came to particular decisions. And yet, as outlined above, some evidence did surface to suggest that that there was news media influence on government, at least in the context of 'other peoples' wars and the issue of humanitarian intervention. At the very least, the CNN effect debate highlighted the possibility that the media–state relationship was not always one of straightforward subservience. Running alongside the CNN effect debate, although not necessarily directly connected to it, were a series of attempts to theorize a more pluralist, nuanced and two-way understanding of the influence between news media and state, both in conditions of war and foreign policy more generally.

Neopluralist Accounts

None of the major theoretical developments over the last 15 years have sought to completely overturn the elite driven theories, but rather have attempted to understand circumstances where news media play a more, rather than less, independent role. For example, a complex model, *the political context model*, was developed by Wolfsfeld (1997) which, while acknowledging the usual dominance of authorities over news media, postulated the conditions under which non-elite groups come to set the news media agenda. At the core of his conceptual framework was the idea that, when non-elite groups were able to initiate events, control the information environment and gain the support of at least parts of a political elite, they can be tremendously successful at influencing news media. By way of example, he analyzes the first Palestinian Intifada (1987–1993) when Palestinians were able to *initiate* the uprising, limit the *control* that Israel had over the movement of journalists in the occupied territories and mobilize *elite* support from the Israeli political left. As a result, news media coverage, according to Wolfsfeld, was framed in a way that promoted the cause of the Palestinians. The *policy-media interaction model* (Robinson, 2002) theorizes the CNN effect as the outcome of a breakdown in elite consensus which, in turn, provides news media the opportunity with which to challenge government officials and to influence them; Finally, Entman's (2004) *cascading activation model* theorizes independent and oppositional news media as occurring when (1) dissensus exists among officials at the top level of government, (2) mid-level officials promote challenges to existing policy and (3) events occur that are culturally ambiguous and open to contestation.

Themes common to all these theoretical developments are the importance of levels of elite agreement/disagreement in determining when greater levels of news media independence might occur and the role of 'events' that occur beyond the control of authorities. The latter factor has formed the basis of what has become known as the *event driven news thesis*. In *The Politics of Force*, Lawrence (2000) argues that unexpected, dramatic and disturbing occurrences can 'provide legitimizing pegs to support relatively independent and critical news narratives. A useful example of this idea, drawn from wartime coverage, is provided by Wolfsfeld (1997: 180–91): He describes how the allied bombing of the Amiriya air raid shelter during the 1991 Gulf War, with the loss of many civilian lives, generated an event beyond the control of the US officials:

This is a story that could only partially be controlled by the US military; it was one that got away.

The President's 'spin patrol' (McDaniel and Fireman, 1992) was dealing with damage control, and while they seem to have done an admirable job, important limits were being set by the images and information of civilian victims ... However few and brief, these windows of opportunities did provide Iraq with some moments of international sympathy for their claims against their powerful enemies.

Of course, by their nature, many events in wartime – including civilian casualties and 'friendly fire' incidents – are beyond the control of governments and can, potentially, weaken their influence over media. Moreover, linking in with the debate outlined earlier regarding new communication technologies, the proliferation of advanced news-gathering equipment, 24-hour news channels including non-Western-based outlets such as Al Jazeera, and the Internet have all potentially increased the occurrence of event-driven news by making journalists less dependent upon official sources.

Summing up, debates over the CNN effect, the passing of the Cold War and the proliferation of new communication technology provided an environment in which a more variable understanding of the media state relationship flourished. But the neopluralist turn, at least with respect to the topic of news media and war, needs to be understood also in the context of the humanitarian wars of the 1990s (to which can possibly be added the 2011 intervention in Libya which was initially authorized as a humanitarian intervention). In all these cases news media covered, and sometimes empathized with, the suffering of 'other people', and on occasions military force was deployed to protect civilians. Perhaps these types of cases provide greater potential for more independent news media, as opposed to more traditional wars experienced during the Cold War? Or perhaps the passing of the Cold War and the arrival of new communication technology did indeed pluralize media state relations? Whatever the answer to these questions, the events of 9/11 have ushered in a distinctly new and complex phase. And it is to two topics that have dominated the political scene, and political communication scholarship, ever since the 2001 attacks on America that we now turn.

CURRENT DEBATES: TERRORISM AND THE 2003–10 CONFLICT IN IRAQ

Terrorism and News media

The events of 9/11, and the subsequent declaration of a 'war on terror', transformed the geopolitical landscape and initiated two major wars, both of which have dominated the first 10 years of the new millennium. Indeed, from the perspective of political communication scholars, it is difficult to separate the material consequences of 9/11 from the visual representation and real-time communication of the attacks. The attacks sought to both kill and to communicate a message to a global audience. Put simply, news media attention to terrorism matters and terrorist acts are often themselves principally a form of communication. Accordingly, significant quantities of political communication scholarship have addressed terrorism, and its relationship to news media.

Broadly speaking, scholarship focused on news media and terrorism has divided along what Cox (1981) described as the 'problem solving theory' versus 'critical theory' divide. Problem-solving approaches treat the prevailing political and economic structures as unproblematic, and focus upon issues that pertain to the 'correct' functioning of these existing orders. In contrast, work informed by critical theory calls into question existing political and economic orders (paraphrased from Corner and Robinson, 2006: 39). Applied to research on terrorism and news media, problem-solving approaches have tended to tackle the issue from the perspective of states and political authority. Working in tandem with the agenda of much of the field of terrorism research, considerable scholarship has been devoted to critiquing news media for providing, as British Prime Minister Margaret Thatcher once described, the 'oxygen of publicity' to groups employing violence for political ends. For example, Brigitte Nacos (2002) in *Mass Mediated Terrorism* provides a compelling analysis of how news media can, inadvertently, end up serving the goals of terrorists: she notes how, following the 9/11 attacks, Osama Bin Laden appeared on the US television more often than the US President Bush. Of course, in the era of 'global media' these concerns have shifted to the issue of non-Western media, such as Al Jazeera, and criticism over their decision to air recordings made by Osama Bin Laden. More recently, and in the context of the Internet era, increasing attention has been paid to the ways in which terrorist groups utilize new communication technology in order to mobilize, organize and to carry out terrorist related activities. Indeed, it is precisely the diverse and non-hierarchical networks that characterize contemporary terrorism which appear to meld with the equivalent networking facilitated by the Internet. Recently, scholarly attention has been paid to the consequences of today's 'new media ecology' (Cottle, 2006; Hoskins and O'Loughlin, 2010), dominated by the Internet, digital recording technology and multiple news outlets, and how this shapes the radicalization of terrorists and influences public perceptions (Hoskins and O'Loughlin 2009: 81).

More critically, an increasingly wide range of scholarship has adopted a far more questioning stance on the entire issue of terrorism and news media. This literature, in terms of its normative and theoretical orientation, forms part of the critical orthodox war and media literature discussed earlier. For example, attention has been given to the ways in which the issue of terrorism can become a political tool for powerful interests, how mainstream discourses shape perceptions of terrorism in a way that precludes deeper understanding of this phenomenon and how Western involvement in terrorism has been marginalized within mainstream political and news media debate. For example, the public opinion scholar John Mueller (2006) argues in *Overblown* that the terrorism threat following 9/11 has been grossly exaggerated, ultimately to the advantage of some US politicians who have preyed on public fears. Similarly, in *Terrorism and the Politics of Fear*, David Altheide (2006) has analyzed the linkage of terrorism, victimization, crime and social control, arguing that a new mass-mediated 'politics of fear' has enabled public acceptance of increased surveillance and social control. Most critically, some scholarship has highlighted how news media can become complicit in the support of Western governments engaged in both human rights abuses and activities that can be plausibly described as terrorist. For example, Bennett et al. (2006) have carefully documented how mainstream US news media were complicit with White House objectives in describing events at the Abu Ghraib prison in Iraq as 'abuse' rather than 'torture', despite credible evidence in support of the latter interpretation.

However, while this is now a key area of research and debate, and as much as terrorism and the proclaimed 'war on terror' have shaped broader scholarly and political debates, it is the return to the more familiar territory of traditional armed conflict that has occupied just as much time and attention from the academy. In the following final section, we turn to the ongoing situation in Iraq and how political communication scholarship has sought to understand this conflict.

The Iraq War; 2003–10

The 2003 invasion of Iraq, the buildup to it, and the ensuing low intensity conflict which followed the invasion, have become deeply controversial. Not surprisingly, the Iraq War has become the focus of a significant proportion of scholarship. Afghanistan, while remaining somewhat out of view for sometime, has in recent years risen up the political agenda and is now receiving evermore attention from scholars. Given the ongoing nature of events, and the time that it takes for authoritative scholarship to emerge, the following discussion will attempt to summarize current understanding that has emerged from some of the leading studies that have focused on the Iraq conflict.

Before assessing recent scholarship in this area, it is relevant to note that, to a large extent, the questions asked of the Iraq War case are familiar ones. To what extent has news media been able to maintain its autonomy in the face of government and military influence? Has the new media environment pluralized the information environment leading to more adversarial coverage and a more enlightened public? To what extent have new ideological imperatives shaped news reporting? How much about wartime media state relations can be observed to have changed, how much has remained the same? At the heart of attempts to address such questions remains detailed content and framing analysis of news media reports. In this vein, a series of studies have analyzed in depth news media coverage of the invasion phase of the Iraq War. Some aspects of these studies suggest the existence of greater variability in levels of news media independence than claimed by the critical orthodox position. Other aspects suggest important continuities. I shall examine each in turn.

Certainly, employing a sophisticated array of content and framing analysis methodologies, recent studies paint a complex picture of wartime media performance in the case of Iraq. Tumber and Palmer's (2004) early study of British news media coverage of the war highlights both the levels of prewar debate and dissent in British newspapers and finds more critical than supportive coverage of the actual military campaign. Aday et al.'s (2005) comparison of the US network news, Fox News and Al Jazeera established a good deal of objective reporting with Fox News being the news outlet likely to deviate most from objective reporting. Recent in-depth studies of British television news and newspaper coverage demonstrate significant variation across both news media outlets and subject areas: for example, a small proportion of the British press and one television news channel produced significant levels of independent and oppositional reporting, while news stories concerning civilians and military casualties and humanitarian operations were notably critical of the coalition (Goddard et al., 2008; Robinson et al., 2009a,b). At the same time, many studies have indicated continuing patterns of wartime news media deference. Lewis et al. (2006), in their analysis of British television news coverage of the invasion, established the dominance of officials sources and a subtle but pervasive prowar bias with broadcasters more likely than not to accept official claims regarding weapons of mass destruction (WMD) existing in Iraq. Similarly, Robinson et al. (2009, 2010) identify the prevalence of pro-military coverage of battle and the largely uncritical acceptance of official narratives surrounding WMD and the humanitarian nature of the war. In their analysis of the US, British, Czech, German, South African and Al Jazeera news, Kolmer and Semetko find that 'reporting of the war was conditioned by the national contexts in which it was produced ... [raising] ... serious questions about the credibility and impartiality of TV news in the reporting of war' (2009: 654). Finally, assessing the US news media coverage of Iraq in the post-invasion phase and up to 2007, Entman et al. (2009) argue that an accountability gap has emerged in which the rising costs of the war are not mirrored in the US news media reporting. This, they suggest, is a product of news media deference to the White House, coupled with the declining newsworthiness of casualties. The result has been that 'official good news frames tended to dominate news narratives' (Entman et al., 2009: 689).

For some scholars, a factor that is further complicating our understanding of national level news media performance is the rise of global news media, the omnipresence of the Internet, and the evolution of sophisticated perception management strategies employed by states. Global news media, in particular the rise to prominence of non-Western outlets such as Al Jazeera, are potentially an alternative source of information for Western news media and a source of critical and oppositional coverage. For example, during the Iraq War the US and British governments regularly criticized the network for showing images of killed and injured soldiers and reports about the suffering of civilians, some of which filtered back to Western news media outlets. In addition, given the strategic imperative of winning hearts and minds in the Middle East in the context of invading an Arab country, Western governments have struggled to penetrate the emerging Arab public sphere created by these new outlets. In short, the Iraq war has been fought in a truly global sense and in an environment where Western news media do not dominate in any meaningful sense, as argued at length by Seib (2008) in the *Al Jazeera Effect*. For some scholars, this means that research needs to be focused away from the national level and on to the global information environment. At the same time, the Internet has created a transparency and ease of information flow which appears to have created a fundamentally new media environment, or a 'new media ecology' (Cottle, 2006) in which

the broadcast era, whereby a limited number of news media outlets communicated news to the masses, has been overtaken by a radically pluralized information space created by the Internet (among other new communication technologies). The images from Abu Ghraib, and their global circulation, are an example of this phenomenon: once the images had been captured (through the use of personal digital cameras) they could then be circulated instantaneously throughout the world with little being done to stop this. Fighting wars and winning 'control of the information environment' (Wolfsfeld, 1997) would appear to be more challenging than ever for governments. At the same time, as much as new communication technologies might have increased the potential power of news media over the state, increasingly professional government news media management techniques have emerged. For example, Western military operations in Kosovo, Afghanistan and the 2003 Iraq War have been accompanied by sustained and highly organized attempts to influence news media agendas (Cioppa, 2009; Robinson et al., 2009a). In the Iraq War, these approaches to perception management included the remarkably successful promotion of the existence of WMD in Iraq, the exaggerated story of the retrieval of Jessica Lynch and, of course, the strategy of embedding journalists alongside military units. So, as much as new technology has a pluralizing effect, governments have not been slow to devise new approaches to influence the information environment.

THE STATE OF THE FIELD

To date, the complexity of findings that have emerged from current study of events post-9/11, principally the war in Iraq and the global 'war on terror', suggest that, at the very least, the neopluralist frameworks that surfaced after the end of the Cold War, remain both relevant and worthy of further development. Certainly, the critical orthodox theoretical frames, however relevant to the Cold War era, require modification if they are to help in understanding the variations that occur in media–state relations. At the same time, before getting carried away with the more hyperbolic claims regarding new communication technology and the passing of old ideological struggles, it is important to recognize the continued relevance of many of the insights provided by the critical orthodox literature: Patriotism continues to shape much of wartime coverage while ever more sophisticated media-management operations help to maintain the influence of official sources. Overall, it seems reasonable to conclude that there exist significant variations in levels of media independence/dependence, even under the conditions of war: As Bennett and Livingston describe, '[t] here is no inherent contradiction in the idea that press-government relations are characterized by potentially extreme variations from independence to dependence. Rather than continuing to debate the extremes of [media] autonomy or dependence, it makes sense to explore the uneasy and often disjointed combinations of the two' (2003: 360–1).

However, if knowledge is to progress in this area, and to understand better the variability suggested in this chapter, several issues stand out as being in need of attention. First and foremost, there needs to be greater precision in terms of what we mean and understand by war. Much of the literature has a tendency to conflate a variety of different types of conflict and crisis, in a way that does not help our understanding of what are actually distinct phenomena. Traditional wars of national interest, such as Vietnam and perhaps the 2003 invasion of Iraq, suggest a different set of dynamics than 'other peoples' wars and cases of so-called humanitarian intervention or humanitarian warfare. At the very least, patriotism is likely to be of less relevance in shaping coverage of humanitarian crises than when troops are fighting to defend their own country.

There also needs to be greater differentiation between wars involving major combat operations (for example, the invasion of Iraq in, 2003) and 'low intensity' conflicts such as the current conflict in Afghanistan or Iraq post invasion. Patriotism and news media management might reach peaks during brief and intense fighting, but dissipate as wars become less intense and more drawn out. At the same time, there also needs to be greater precision in terms of the application of various theoretical frames. As noted throughout the chapter, many elite driven and neo-pluralist theories are presented as relevant to the complete domain of foreign policy (and media state relations in general), not just war, while often they are tested against cases of war and news media. As a result, our ability to understand and explain the specific dynamics of news media and war is compromised through failure to attend, in theoretical terms, to the specific characteristics of wartime media. At the same time, biasing case selection toward cases of war might lead to overconfirmation of some theories (in this case the elite-driven accounts).

Once these important distinctions are understood, perhaps the most fruitful avenue for future work lies in the development of a comparative research agenda. Much of the major work to date on news media and war has focused upon single case studies that offer sometimes limited insight into the causal processes at work. Comparative analysis should explore variations across the phases of conflict (as described in the preceding paragraph), the different types of conflict and different news media outlets. Here, our explanatory understanding can be deepened by measuring how news media performance varies across time and circumstance. For example, measuring levels of news media autonomy across phases of both major combat operations and low intensity conflict, when levels of media-management tend to vary, would help determine the extent to which media management influences news media performance. Again, comparing levels of news media autonomy across patriotic/national interest wars and humanitarian conflicts can be useful for evaluating the impact of patriotism on journalism. Finally, comparing news media performance across different media outlets and measuring variations in levels of dependence on official sources might yield evidence vis-à-vis the impact of official sources on coverage. Overall, the goal here should be greater clarity with regard to our explanatory understanding of the media state relationship and resolution of current uncertainties about, for example, the relative influence of official sources versus patriotism noted earlier in the chapter.

More broadly, and perhaps the most challenging to realize, comparative research across time would yield valuable insights into the 'big debates' over changing geopolitical circumstances and the emergence of new communication technology that so often dominate debate over news media and war. Comparison between Cold War and post-Cold War conflicts would help measure whether variations in the ideological landscape have led to a weakening of media deference, while comparing levels of media technology across conflicts would facilitate testing of the claim that new communication technology has changed levels of news media independence. Also, so much of the research into news media and war has revolved around Anglo-American cases. More by way of comparative research across different national contexts might reveal further variability and nuance. Certainly, the idea that the elite driven and neo-pluralist frameworks discussed in this chapter, which were developed mainly in the US context, can be readily applied outside that national context requires systematic testing. Of course, comparative research might also yield insights into continuities between different media systems, as indicated by Kolmer and Semetko (2009) discussed earlier: but such research might also indicate the greater openness of some media systems to autonomy and dissent in time of war (for example, Goddard et al., 2008).

In addition, although immensely challenging, more work needs to be done in terms of integrating analysis of public opinion, news media and foreign policy. Our focus in this chapter has been on news media and its relationship to the state during war and we have not engaged in a detailed manner with the large literature on public opinion and foreign policy. In fact, a major limitation of the public opinion – foreign policy literature is its tendency to ignore the importance of news media as a crucial intervening variable. It is only recently that more concerted and systematic attempts have appeared that try to trace the interactions between foreign policy, news media and public opinion. Here, in particular, work by Baum and Groeling (2010), Baum and Potter (2008) and Entman et al. (2009), provide useful elaborations of this relationship, as well as a starting point for a future media-public opinion-foreign policy research agenda.

While the research agenda outlined above would go some considerable way in terms of both progressing our theoretical/explanatory purchase on matters of news media and war, as well as developing Bennett and Livingston's (2003: 360–1) call for a better understanding of the 'extreme variations from dependence to independence', there also needs to be greater attention paid to the normative question of how news media *should* report war. Description and explanation are necessary steps and must remain a focus of work. But there seems to be enough evidence accumulated to date, albeit insufficiently precise and nuanced, of news media function in wartime to warrant detailed exploration of normative questions. As noted at points in this chapter, much of the research output in this field works with under-discussed assumptions about how news media should cover war: largely, critical scholarship works with the assumption that news media could and should be doing more to maintain independence from government. And yet, as noted at the start of this chapter, many in the military and government (the realist perspective) expect and often demand loyalty from journalists when a country goes to war. So, the question of what news media should be doing remains poorly explored and an avenue for further enquiry and debate. Principally, more focused thinking is required regarding the problems inherent to both news media remaining deferential to the state (as advocated by realist thinking) and news media remaining independent or impartial (as advocated by liberal thinking). The ultimate goal of such an agenda for scholarship would be to provide a more informed and coherent picture of what standards journalists and editors might aspire to when confronting the difficult task of covering armed conflict.

ACKNOWLEDGMENTS

Thanks to Stefanie Haueis, Peter Goddard and Holli Semetko for feedback on the first draft of this chapter.

NOTES

1 *Media, War, Conflict*, Editors Andrew Hoskins, Philip Seib and Barry Richards (Sage).
2 The phrase 'faithful servant' is borrowed from Wolfsfeld (2007).

REFERENCES

Aday, S., Livingston, S. and Hebert, M. (2005) 'Embedding the Truth: A Cross-Cultural Analysis of Objectivity and Television Coverage of the Iraq War', *Harvard International Journal of Press/Politics*, 10(1): 3–21.

Althaus, S. L. (2003) 'When News Norms Collide, Follow the Lead: New Evidence for Press Independence', *Political Communication*, 20(3): 381–414.

Altheide, D. L. (2006) *Terrorism and the Politics of Fear*. Lanham, MD: AltaMira.

Babak, B. (2007) *The CNN Effect in Action: How the News Media Pushed the West Toward War in Kosovo*. Basingstoke: Palgrave Macmillan.

Baum, M. and Groeling, T. (2010) *War Stories: The Causes and Consequences of Public Views of War*. Princeton, NJ: Princeton University Press.

Baum, M. and Potter, P. (2008) 'The Relationship Between Mass Media, Public Opinion and Foreign Policy: Toward a Theoretical Synthesis', *Annual Review of Political Science*, 11: 39–66.

Bennett, W. L. (1990) 'Toward a Theory of Press-State Relations in the United States', *Journal of Communication*, 40(2): 103–27.

Bennett, W. L. and Livingston, S. (2003) 'Editors Introduction: A Semi-Independent Press: Government Control and Journalistic Autonomy in the Political Construction of News', *Political Communication*, 20(4): 359–62.

Bennett, W. L., Lawrence, R. and Livingston, S. (2006) 'None Dare Call it Torture: Indexing and the Limits of Press Independence in the Abu Ghraib Scandal', *Journal of Communication*, 56(3): 467–85.

Bennett, W. L. and Paletz, D. L. (eds.) (1994) *Taken by Storm: The Media, Public Opinion, and US Foreign Policy in the Gulf War*. Chicago, IL: University of Chicago Press.

Braestrup, P. (1994) *Big Story: How the American Press and Television Reported and Interpreted the Crisis of Tet 1968 in Vietnam and Washington*. Novato, CA: Presidio.

Carruthers, S. L. (2000) *The Media at War: Communication and Conflict in the Twentieth Century*. Basingstoke: Palgrave Macmillan.

Cioppa, T. M. (2009) 'Operation Iraqi Freedom Strategic Communication Analysis and Assessment', *Media, War and Conflict*, 2(1): 25–45.

Cohen, B. (1994) 'A View from the Academy', in W. L. Bennett and D. L. Paletz (eds.), *Taken By Storm: The Media, Public Opinion, and US Foreign Policy in the Gulf War*. Chicago, IL: University of Chicago Press. pp. 9–10.

Corner, J. and Robinson, P. (2006) 'Politics and Mass Media: A Response to John Street', *Political Studies Review*, 1(3): 36–41.

Cottle, S. (2006) *Mediatized Conflict: Developments in Media and Conflict Studies*. Maidenhead: Open University Press.

Cox, R. W. (1981) 'Social Forces, States and World Orders: Beyond International Relations Theory', *Millennium Journal of International Studies*, 10(2): 126–55.

Culbert, D. (1998) 'Television's Visual Impact on Decision-Making in the USA, 1968: The Tet Offensive and Chicago's Democratic National Convention', *Journal of Contemporary History*, 33(3): 419–49.

Entman, R. M. (2003) 'Cascading Activation: Contesting the White House's Frame After 9/11', *Political Communication*, 20: 415–23.

Entman, R. M. (2004) *Projections of Power: Framing News, Public Opinion and US Foreign Policy*. Chicago, IL: University of Chicago Press.

Entman, R. M., Livingston, S. and Kim, J. (2009) 'Doomed to Repeat: Iraq News 2002–2007', *American Behavioral Scientist*, 52(5): 689–708.

Glasgow University Media Group (GUMG) (1985) *War and Peace News*. Milton Keynes: Open University Press.

Goddard, P., Robinson, P. and Parry, K. (2008) 'Patriotism Meets Plurality: Reporting the 2003 Iraq War in the British Press', *Media, War and Conflict*, 1(1): 7–27.

Gowing, N. (1994) 'Real Time Television Coverage of Armed Conflicts and Diplomatic Crises: Does it Pressure or Distort Foreign Policy Decisions', The Joan Shorenstein Center on the Press, Politics and Public Policy at Harvard University, Working Paper Series.

Hallin, D. C. (1984) 'The Media, the War in Vietnam and Political Support: A Critique of the Thesis of an Oppositional Media', *The Journal of Politics*, 46(1): 2–24.

Hallin, D. C. (1986) *The Uncensored War: The Media and Vietnam*. Berkeley, CA: University of California Press.

Hallin, D. C. (1997) 'The Media and War', in J. Corner, P. Schlesinger and R. Silverstone (eds.), *International Media Research*. London: Routledge. pp. 206–31.

Hammond, W. (1989) 'The Press in Vietnam as an Agent of Defeat: A Critical Examination', *Reviews in American History*, 17(2): 312–23.

Herman, E. and Chomsky, N. (1988) *Manufacturing Consent: The Political Economy of the Mass Media*. New York: Pantheon.

Holsti, O. (1992) 'Public Opinion and Foreign Policy: Challenges to the Almond-Lippmann Consensus Mershon Series: Research Programs and Debates', *International Studies Quarterly*, 36(4): 439–66.

Hoskins, A. and O'Loughlin, B. (2009) 'Pre-Mediating Guilt: Radicalization and Mediality in British News', *Critical Studies on Terrorism*, 2(1): 81–93.

Hoskins, A. and O'Loughlin, B. (2010) *War and Media: The Emergence of Diffused War*. Cambridge: Polity Press.

Kellner, D. (1998) 'Intellectuals, the New Public Spheres, and Techno-Politics', in C. Toulouse and T. W. Luke (eds.), *The Politics of Cyberspace: A New Political Science Reader*. New York and London: Routledge. pp. 167–86.

Kolmer, C. and Semetko, H. A. (2009) 'Framing the Iraq War: Perspectives from American, UK, Czech, German, South African, and Al-Jazeera News', *American Behavioural Scientist*, 52(5): 643–56.

Knightley, P. (2003) *The First Casualty: The War Correspondent as Hero, Propagandist and Myth-Maker from the Crimea to Iraq*. London: André Deutsch.

Lawrence, R. G. (2000) *The Politics of Force: Media and the Construction of Police Brutality*. Berkeley, CA: University of California Press.

Lewis, J., Brooks, R., Mosdell, N. and Threadgold, T. (2006) *Shoot First and Ask Questions Later: Media Coverage of the 2003 Iraq War*. New York: Peter Lang.

Liebes, T. (1997) *Reporting the Arab-Israeli Conflict: How Hegemony Works*. London: Routledge.

Lippman, W. (1955) *Essays in the Public Philosophy*. Boston, MA: Little, Brown.

Livingston, S. and Eachus, T. (1995–1996) 'Humanitarian Crizes and US Foreign Policy: Somalia and the CNN Effect Reconsidered', *Political Communication*, 12(14): 413–29.

McDaniel, A. and Fireman, H. (1992) 'The President's "Spin" Patrol', in H. Smith (ed.), *The Media and the Gulf War*. Washington, DC: Seven Locks Press.

Mueller, J. (1973) *War, Presidents and Public Opinion*. New York: Wiley.

Mueller, J. (2006) *Overblown: How Politicians and the Terrorism Industry Inflate National Security Threats and Why We Believe Them*. New York. Free Press.

Nacos, B. L. (2002) *Mass Mediated Terrorism: The Central Role of the Media in Terrorism and Counterterrorism*. Lanham, MD: Rowman and Littlefield.

Nixon, R. M. (1978) *Memoirs*. New York: Grossett and Dunlap.

Robinson, P., Goddard, P., Parry, K., Murray, C. and Taylor, P. (2010) *Pockets of Resistance: British News Media, War and Theory in the 2003 Invasion of Iraq*. Manchester: Manchester University Press.

Robinson, P., Goddard, P., Parry, K. and Murray, C. (2009a) 'Testing Models of Media Performance in War: UK TV News and the 2003 Invasion of Iraq', *Journal of Communication*, 59(3): 534–63.

Robinson, P., Goddard, P. and Parry, K. (2009b) 'UK Media and Media Management During the 2003 Invasion of Iraq', *American Behavioural Scientist*, 52(5): 678–88.

Robinson, P. (2002) *The CNN Effect: The Myth of News, Foreign Policy and Intervention*. London and New York: Routledge.

Robinson, P. (2008) 'The Role of Media and Public Opinion', in S. Smith, A. Hadfield and T. Dunne (eds.), *Foreign Policy: Theories, Actors, Cases*. Oxford: University of Oxford Press. pp. 137–54.

Schlesinger, P. and Tumber, H. (1994) *Reporting Crime: The Media Politics of Criminal Justice*. Oxford: Oxford University Press.

Seib, P. (2008) *The Al Jazeera Effect: How the New Global Media Are Reshaping World Politics*. Dulles, VA: Potomac Books.

Taylor, P. M. (1997) *Global Communications, International Affairs and the Media Since 1945*. London: Routledge.

Tumber, H. and Palmer, J. (2004) *Media at War: The Iraq Crisis*. London: Sage.

Westmoreland, W. (1979) 'Vietnam in Perspective', *Military Review*, 59(1): 34–43.

Wolfsfeld, G. (1997) *The Media and Political Conflict: News from the Middle East*. Cambridge and New York: Cambridge University Press.

Zandberg, E. and Neiger, M. (2005) 'Between the Nation and the Profession: Journalists as Members of Contradicting Communities', *Media, Culture and Society*, 27(1): 131–41.

27

The Power of Rhetoric: Understanding Political Oratory

Vanessa B. Beasley

In Plato's dialog *Gorgias* (c. 386 BCE), Socrates asks Gorgias 'what in the world the power of rhetoric can be' (as cited in Bizzell and Herzberg, 2001: 93). Gorgias was a good person for Socrates to ask. He was a Sophist, an itinerant teacher of rhetoric, whose extraordinary skills were in high demand throughout ancient Greece. Socrates, suspicious of this fame and the oratorical prowess that won it, spends much of the dialog questioning Gorgias about the exact nature of his art. Not surprisingly, Plato has Gorgias fumble through many of his answers; although Plato was also deeply suspicious of rhetoric, he seems to have mastered it well enough in his own writings. Interestingly, though, Plato also has Gorgias repeatedly answer such hostile questions by referencing the indisputable impact of oratory on democratic politics in ancient Greece.

For example, when Socrates asks what Gorgias calls his craft, Gorgias responds, 'I call it the ability to persuade with speeches either judges in the law courts or statesmen in the council chamber or the commons in the Assembly or an audience at any other meeting that may be held on public affairs' (as cited in Bizzell and Herzberg, 2001: 91). Likewise, because it takes political leaders, not craftsmen, to build 'these great arsenals and walls of Athens, and the construction of your harbors', Gorgias argues a bit later, 'whenever there is an election of such persons … you see it is the orators who give the advice and get resolutions carried in these matters' (as cited in Bizzell and Herzberg, 2001: 93). Finally, later in the dialog, and even after conceding to Socrates that 'so great, so strange is the power of this art', Gorgias again locates that power within the

political realm: 'the orator is able, indeed, to speak against every one and on every question in such a way as to win over the votes of the multitude, practically in any matter he may choose to take up' (as cited in Bizzell and Herzberg, 2001: 93).

This last possibility was exactly what worried Socrates and Plato, of course. What was it about oratory that made it so compelling and potentially so powerful? As Plato would analogize elsewhere in the *Gorgias*, how was it possible that human speech could sometimes have almost the same effect as a drug, intoxicating its listeners to the point of passive consent? Similar questions about spoken rhetoric and its potential impact on democratic politics are still asked, as I will discuss shortly, even if today the rhetorical landscape seems increasingly crowded and unkempt. At a time when Twitter posts, blog comments, fake news shows and pseudo-personalized e-mails from political actors have ostensibly replaced the ancient Greek Assembly as central locations for political communication designed to 'win over the votes of the multitude', it can still be difficult to know how to understand the power or even the place of oratory.

I use terms such as *speech*, *spoken rhetoric* and *oratory* purposefully here in order to distinguish this form of persuasive discourse from many others, including written, visual or otherwise mass-mediated rhetoric. The other chapters in this Handbook serve as strong evidence that the study of political communication is increasingly concerned with an ever-expanding range of suasory messages intended to change attitudes or behavior(s), created and distributed through an astonishingly wide variety of old and new technologies, and for assumed consumption by multiple and diverse audiences. This expanding focus is surely a good thing. Yet my topic in this chapter is on the power of oral rhetoric – human speech, if you will, particularly as manifest as individual instances of public speaking within explicitly political contexts – and how this power has been understood within democratic politics in the USA. Aware that such an Americanist focus is a limitation of this chapter, I conclude by suggesting that the US case may be viewed as heuristic, or at least as a prompt, for more comparative discussions of our understanding of the power of rhetoric within other democracies. In the USA at least, political oratory may be more worthy of scholarly attention now than ever, especially if we reconceptualize the nature of its power as an enduring, if protean, technology for democracy.

To develop this argument, this chapter proceeds in three parts. First, I probe the place of the notion of fear of rhetoric as a guiding force within political communication research, broadly defined. Fear of both rhetoric and popular responses to it has been generative within communication scholarship on oratory in particular. Second, I offer a brief historical overview of the idea that oratory – especially when conceived as 'public speaking' – was once not feared but in fact was perceived a basic skill for democratic citizenship in the USA. This section suggests that, within the USA at least, there was once a popular belief in oratory as a, if not *the*, chief instrument of democratic engagement for citizens and leaders alike. Within more recent scholarship on how to assess the functions and impact of oratory within the US politics, however, there has been far less agreement. The final section references two representative and related debates on (1) how the power of oratory can best be understood, that is, at the case level or more conceptually across cases and (2) if the power of a particular kind of political oratory can (or should) be measured quantitatively. These debates raise important questions about if, how, and why oratory can be understood as having impact while also demonstrating the dangers of taking only one position on such matters. To illustrate the benefits of conceptual pluralism within scholarly assessments, I identify some alternative approaches to understanding the power of political rhetoric by referencing three examples from the 2008 US presidential election. In concluding the essay, I restate the argument that the power of rhetoric must be both understood from multiple scholarly perspectives and that such research might also be conducted in comparative and transnational contexts.

At the outset, though, it is worth returning to the previously mentioned classical fears of the power of oratory to make an introductory point

about their centrality to the academic study of political speech. Such fears are not silly; indeed, one needs to look no further than demagogic rhetoric of individuals such as Huey Long in the US case or Adolph Hitler within an international context to understand why they are warranted. In addition, these fears are productive in the sense that they have motivated scholars to study oratory with the goal of discovering its nature and limits.

Consider, for instance, that most fears about political speech seem to manifest in one if not both of two directions. First, people may fear oratory because it can seem mesmerizing, at least if it is perceived to be capable of dulling listeners' critical or otherwise intellectual faculties. Spoken rhetoric in particular is sometimes thought to keep people from truth by seducing their souls, to return to more Socratic language, making the unreal appear real and vice versa (Reale, 1986: 239). Within contemporary discussions of political communication, this fear can drive ethical judgments, including the pejorative use of the term 'rhetoric' to refer to public instances of pandering or outright lying. Examples are plentiful across time, party and nation; even if the specific lies themselves manifest differently based on ideology, one person's 'public option' within a healthcare program can be another person's 'death panel', for example.

This same fear also factors into aesthetic judgments, in which politicians, à la Bill Clinton or Tony Blair, or political surrogates are accused of being 'slick' or eloquent enough to influence political behavior while simultaneously diverting voters' attention away from their actual goals. As these examples suggest, the power of oratory in this paradigm is typically assumed to emanate from an individual speaker who possesses extraordinary rhetorical skills, much like Gorgias himself did. This fear is therefore not necessarily a fear of rhetoric per se, but instead an interest in studying the choices of people who appear to use it well. Accordingly, some scholars have been most interested in analyzing 'touchstones', specific texts that demonstrate a rhetor's exceptional use of oratory on a specific occasion (Leff and Mohrmann, 1974; Lucas, 1973; Zarefsky, 1988). As I have argued elsewhere, humanists are far more likely than social scientists to engage in this sort of research (Beasley, 2009a).

A second and related fear also concerns the potential power of rhetoric to divert 'the people's' attention away from reality, but here the fear centers on 'the people' themselves and, more specifically, the potential for their poor judgment as a collective. Again, this fear is as old as the practice of rhetoric itself. Just as Socrates worried in the *Gorgias* that audiences and thus society could be harmed by a skillful orator, he also warned in the *Crito* against heeding public opinion because the public typically has no expertise (or frequently even any understanding) of the things it judges. If the first fear aligns with concerns about oratory being magical, this second one suggests that this form of discourse, once unleashed, is ubiquitous and uncontainable. Once a particular rhetoric gains traction among the public, there might be little one can do to stop or restrain it as it spreads and changes to facilitate multiple meanings among and within different audiences.

Consider as an example the circulation of Internet images and inaccurate characterizations during the 2008 US presidential campaign of then-candidate Barack Obama as a Muslim. Many observers worried then that a particular rhetoric was being activated to make xenophobia seem patriotic, and also that 'the people' might not be smart enough to question such messages. (Socrates would not have been surprised.) For this reason, some scholars have been more likely to engage in a more audience-driven model of research, in which questions of reception, attitude change and effects drive the methodology. Again, and as I have noted elsewhere, social scientists are more likely than humanists to operate within this paradigm (Beasley, 2009a).

I mention these two particular fears – one of a too-powerful speaker and one of a *demos* unable or unwilling to exercise its power(s) critically – to return to the idea that, as enduring as such fears have been throughout the history of the practice of rhetoric, they have also been productive to the study of the power and impact of oratory. Whether scholars have sought to appreciate or dissect political messages, a healthy fear of rhetoric has motivated experts from multiple disciplines and methodologies to create a growing literature on public discourse and its functions within electoral politics especially. Humanists and social scientists have approached this task in vastly different ways, as I have suggested. Yet for the most part, they have been united in a foundational assumption about the need for something akin to Paul Ricoeur's (1970) hermeneutics of suspicion. That is, they typically begin from a critical posture that never takes political discourse at face value, but instead examines words and symbols with the aim of unmasking their meanings, motives and possible impact. Fear and politics, it would seem, go hand in hand.

If that is true, then there is arguably no subfield of the study of human communication that places more value on suspicion as a critical epistemology than political communication. From this standpoint, even the classical Greeks' writings on rhetoric could be considered as studies in political communication, broadly defined, because these efforts originated in tandem with the development of early democratic practices in ancient Greece during the 5th and 4th centuries BCE. An increase in literacy among elite Greeks at this time facilitated the codification of laws as well as the need for technical guides for disputation related to legal argument and persuasive techniques for use in the assembly (see Havelock, 1981). These developments suggest that there was a growing interest in oral rhetoric as *praxis* within both law and politics as citizens sought to protect their interests within a new social system.

Not surprisingly, questions of ethics came up immediately. What if the best argument or candidate, and not necessarily the more truthful one, won? What if oratorical style was more persuasive than argumentative substance? It was within this historical context that the Platonic dialogs on rhetoric, most notably the *Gorgias* and the *Phaedrus*, were written. Similar discussions would lead Aristotle to his study of the modes of communicative interaction within civil society, a study he systematically divided into three interrelated components: *The Politics*, *The Rhetoric* and the *Poetics*. Importantly, Aristotle also suggested that ethics were located in human decisions about how to engage with each other within each mode, and therefore not intrinsically subsumed within each of these arenas themselves In addition, it is from Aristotle that we get the notion that rhetoric is best understood as both an art and a science, as both *techne* and *episteme*. It would be this Aristotelian view of rhetoric, in combination with a Ciceronian notion of the role of speech within a republic, which would eventually influence much of the academic study and teaching of oratory within the USA. In the next section, I offer a truncated review of why, how, and to whom public speaking was assumed to be powerful as a technology for democracy in the USA.

PRACTICING ORATORY WITHIN THE USA: FOUNDATIONS IN POLITICS AND EDUCATION

It was not a fear of the power of speech but instead fear of tyranny that motivated the founders of the USA to embrace oral rhetoric as one of the new nation's most important democratic tools. The country's founders intentionally privileged speech, according to William Keith (2007: 2–3), and viewed 'governance through talk' as the clearly preferable alternative to the 'organized use of force' to form the basis of the state's stability. To this end, they were heavily influenced by an understanding of Ciceronian civic republicanism. 'Cicero's account of republican civil society affirms that the power of speech both constitutes and enables social and political life', Keith (2007: 2–3) explains. 'Discord and the triumph of force are natural to the human condition, and the discovery of speech or rhetoric, as a sort of technology, funds the possibility of civic and civil life'.

If speech was viewed as technology for democracy – here invoking Aristotelian pragmatism in service of Ciceronian political philosophy – then it is not a surprise that public speaking was considered an essential part of the basic curriculum at the first universities in the USA. '[T]he educational demands of citizenship were framed in terms of both knowledge and action', writes Keith (2007: 11). 'One had to *know* enough to be able to *speak* on the important issues of the day' (emphasis in original). To wit, in 1806 Senator John Quincy Adams began teaching at Harvard University as its first Boyslton Professor of Rhetoric and Oratory. His purpose was to teach 'as a man of the world preparing others to be men in the world', and he promised to instruct students in 'reason, clothed with speech' (as cited in Heinrichs, 1995). Oratorical skills were of paramount importance 'under governments purely republican', Adams noted, '… where government itself has no arms but those of persuasion' (as cited in Keith, 2007: 51). This opinion was not just Adams' alone. During the late 18th and early 19th centuries, 'oratory became identified with an idealized understanding of the American political process' (Keith, 2007: 31). The power of rhetoric, in other words, was thus then associated with an individual citizen's exercise of democratic power through advocacy, deliberation, and public address designed to persuade other citizens.

Throughout the 19th century, this vision would be somewhat challenged within the US secondary and higher education. Following British trends, most notably the Elocutionary Movement, as well as the influential writings of Scottish philosopher Hugh Blair and the *belles lettres* movement, many US educators were encouraged to view speech pedagogy as a stylistic enterprise with great emphasis on delivery and performance (Keith, 2007: 24). This change resulted from a variety of festering philosophical and pragmatic tensions within a developing system of higher education within the USA, and Keith (2007) has identified five larger social and political factors interacting during this time that reinforced a change in views about how, why and to whom oratory should be taught. Whatever the causes, the overall results were a shift in emphasis 'to aesthetics from civics' within the teaching of speech (Keith, 2007: 24). Oratory was not viewed primarily as a political instrument intended for use by citizens but instead as the manifestation of an aesthetic sensibility to be cultivated among the well-educated, like a love of poetry or art might be. As Lee Cerling has written, it seemed that 'American oratory could not continue to be, throughout the 19th century, both refined and democratic, both a classical and a popular art' (as cited in Keith, 2007: 32).

By 1915, however, there were signs of a potential revival of the notion of oratory as a more egalitarian means of democratic and even personal empowerment. According to Keith (2007: 33), one key development was the 1914 creation of the 'National Association of Academic Teachers of Public Speaking' (NAATPS), formed by 10 instructors who taught public speaking classes within English departments, as would have been the standard academic home for such instruction then. These teachers sought to create national standards for public speaking instruction, and their purpose was clear: '"Public speaking" was designed to make it clear that attention was to be focused on direct, communicative public address rather than on the half-horse-half-alligator antics of the elocutionists' (Weaver, 1959: 196). James A. Winans, one of their leaders, made the argument that such instruction was necessary to ensure social mobility in the USA, claiming that '[e]ngineers, architects, and agriculturalists are awakening to the fact that if they are to take the executive positions that they aspire to, they must be able to think and talk on their feet. We must meet these technical and other students on their own ground … and … give them what they need' (as cited in Keith, 2008: 250). Around the same time that the NAATPS was gaining members and gathering momentum, academic departments of 'speech' or 'speech communication' to house such instruction separate and apart from English departments were being created.

Keith (2007) and Gehrke (2009) have recently published excellent histories of why, how and where the creation of these departments occurred, enabling 'speech' and 'communication' to be increasingly viewed as legitimate academic disciplines in their own right (as opposed to branches of English, History or even Political Science, for example). For my purposes here, there are two important points about the creation of these departments. First, both the professional motives and intellectual rationale behind their creation resuscitated the notion that oratorical training was key to prepare citizens for the performance of democratic engagement. Importantly, to speak of 'performance' in this context was not derogatory or even suspect the way it was for Plato and Socrates when they fretted about the individual speaker who might use his (sic) performative skills to bamboozle 'the people'. By contrast, in this model 'the people' are themselves deserving of oratorical training in order to maximize their potential for agency; a functioning and fair democracy demands their rhetorical performance. As Medhurst has written, 'from the outset, public address as an academic subject was understood primarily in terms of performance – learning how to give a speech' (1993: xii). These skills mattered for fundamentally democratic reasons: '[t]o be able to articulate a point of view, defend a proposition, attack an evil, or celebrate a set of common values' Medhurst (1993: xi) explained, 'was seen as one of the central ways in which people retained their freedoms and shaped their society'.

Second, in teaching how to give a speech, these instructors also began to create a canon of their own, one that was distinct from, say, what would have been taught in the English departments from whence most of these first instructors hailed. Students of oratory, for example, would have also been encouraged to participate in the classical practice of *imitatio*: 'the study and emulation of the great orators of the past' (see Medhurst, 1993: xii). Within the Americanist tradition, such instruction complimented the study of the history of the nation, as works by speakers such as John Winthrop, Jonathan Edwards, George Washington, Daniel Webster, Abraham Lincoln and so on were presented to students as exemplars not only of style for its own sake, but also as great speakers who used oratory to rise to the occasion in moments of historic consequence to the colonists and, later, citizens of a young republic.

This idea – that a 'great speech' could be a consequential instrument for political action – would signal a subtle but important addition to the way its power was understood: oratory was not only a tool for citizens' actions, but also both a technology for and characteristic of great leadership within a democracy. Assuming that both the leader and the led had these skills, the assumption was that democratic decision making would be facilitated by public argument. An elected leader could make his or her case to Congress or popular audiences of voters, for instance, and members of the audience would have the critical thinking skills as well as the knowledge of oratory to respond wisely. Because they would know the previous speeches used at such moments – when a US president tried to make the case for war, for example, or when the US senators tried to advocate for compromises that they taught would help avoid it – the audience would be familiar with the arguments that had been used before as well as their consequences. In theory, then, the study of oratorical public address, as the study of great speeches was sometimes known, also encouraged the development of a particular kind of cultural literacy, familiarizing students with both the US history and the words that made a difference in its outcomes. Indeed, today this model of instruction is still operating within the US education in grammar and secondary schools as well as within higher education, when we teach Abraham Lincoln's 'Gettysburg Address' during units on the Civil War, for example, or Martin Luther King, Jr's 'I Have a Dream Speech' while discussing the Civil Rights Movement of the 1960s.

In addition to the cultural literacy component, this model also suggests that oratory is powerful to the extent that it has measurable 'real world' electoral and otherwise materially political consequences. Yet it is these consequences, of course, that so frequently raise fears about rhetoric, taking us right back to the Platonic dialogs. How, then, have contemporary scholars responded to the question of oratory's power as understood through its consequence(s)? Put differently, as the scholarly study of rhetoric matured as a distinct academic discipline during the 20th century, how was the impact of oratory been understood?

TWENTIETH-CENTURY SCHOLARLY DEBATES: CAN ORATORY'S POWER BE THEORIZED OR MEASURED?

Acknowledging that there are many different ways to answer such questions, here I will review only two related scholarly debates (and even here, of course, I will only be able to provide a truncated review of influential moments within these literatures). The first debate, older and longer-running than the second, concerns whether or not the power of oratory can be theorized: that is, whether or not rhetorical scholars would or even could move past critical insights taken from their study of single or even multiple speech texts in order to engage in theory-building. This debate is relevant to this chapter because it speaks directly to how the power of rhetoric can be understood and presumes that there are two basic possibilities: either in terms of conclusions drawn from specific cases (and thus specific texts) or in terms of larger principles and/or conceptual laws associated with human persuasion. The second debate echoes important parts of the first but concerns a particular kind of the US rhetoric to ask a more specific set of questions within the context of contemporary US democracy: Does presidential rhetoric matter? If so, how can its power be understood? This debate has frequently led interdisciplinary audiences to squabble because it implicates obvious methodological differences around standards of measurement. If presidential rhetoric is powerful, says one camp, we should be able to measure its impact quantitatively, while the other 'side' maintains that doing so is myopic and can draw attention away from rhetoric's most enduring functions.

As mentioned, the first debate revolves around questions of whether the power of oratory can or should be theorized. To provide some context, I must briefly indulge again in some disciplinary history. For most of the 20th century, the dominant paradigm used to analyze instances of spoken rhetoric was known as rhetorical criticism. Herbert Wichelns (1925) defined this line of inquiry as 'necessarily analytic' and proposed a neo-Aristotelian categorization of topics for the critics to address. From Wichelns, then, came the idea that oratory could and should be analyzed systematically, and the resulting scholarship was largely descriptive. Thonssen and Baird (1948) added an important component to the traditional paradigm of rhetorical criticism by describing this line of inquiry as the 'intellectual effort … to reveal the significant role of speechmaking in the historical process'. These authors emphasized the notion that because the consequence(s) of oratory mattered, as discussed above, oratory itself mattered too; the texts most worthy of scholarly attention were necessarily those that had an arguably 'significant role' on social and political outcomes. Not surprisingly, according to Lucas, 'to be a rhetorical critic in those days usually meant that one was also a student of British or American public address' because these two nations' political histories would have been presumably the most familiar to the US scholars (1993: 180).

Edwin Black (1965) challenged this paradigm with his book *Rhetorical Criticism: A Study in Method*. Seeking to 'stimulate and expand the dialog on rhetorical criticism', Black defined it as 'the criticism of rhetorical discourses' (1965: 11, 39). Of note here is that it is the rhetorical nature of the object of analysis rather than a specific methodology that defined rhetorical criticism for Black. As he acknowledged, the question of exactly what was 'rhetorical' and what was not was an open one; in 1965, as remains the case today, there were scholars who sought to move the 'rhetorical' out of the realm of the purely 'oratorical', noting that pamphlets and other mediated texts designed to be read rather than simply heard were surely rhetorical to the extent that they were meant to be persuasive. Black agreed. For our purposes here, however, the most important contribution of Black's book was its thesis that a piece of rhetoric, oratorical or otherwise, did not have to have an effect in order to be worthy of study; in other words, oratory did not have to result in a specific social or political consequence to be meaningful. It could have intrinsic qualities within the text that explained or otherwise contributed to its power, broadly defined. Thus, Black argued against the predominant practices of neo-Aristotelian criticism to suggest that a text could be worthy of study purely for its internal qualities

in, on, and for whatever terms the critic argued were appropriate to his/her analysis.

It is an understatement to say that Black's book was influential. As Medhurst has written, it changed the field by moving scholarship 'from a predominant emphasis on style and delivery to a primary focus on strategy (or movement from a focus on the text or speaker to a focus on the critic and his or her interpretive powers)' (2008: 11). This change led to rise in the publication of 'textual criticism' (Medhurst, 2008: 11). 'While scholars of rhetoric had always claimed to be interested in speeches, the plan fact was that whether examining presidential rhetoric or any other kind of discourse, speech scholars had been wholly remiss in taking seriously the rhetorical dynamics within the speech text' (Medhurst, 2008: 11). After Black, however, there was 'consistent experimentation in how best to study discourse rhetorically' (Medhurst, 2008: 12) as well as 'a growing interest in close analysis of rhetorical texts' (Lucas, 1993: 186).

Not everyone was satisfied with the move to textual criticism, however, or at least not of the ways in which it was being conducted during this period. Roderick Hart's (1976) essay 'Theory-Building and Rhetorical Criticism: An Informal Statement of Opinion' lamented an 'academic provincialism' within textual analysis and more specifically its tendency toward 'documentarianism' to analyze the 'persuasive event in question' without regard for the task of 'collecting and structuring their insights in ways that would lead to the development of refined, probative theories of rhetoric and persuasion' (Hart, 1976: 70). For Hart, then, the power of oratory was not necessarily limited to the text itself, whether its immediate impact was arguably consequential or not, but something else entirely: in terms of what analyses of texts could reveal regarding 'synthetic, inclusive, and predictive theoretical statements about human persuasion' (Hart, 1976: 70). He urged 'rhetorical critics to describe suasory messages extensively enough so that intelligent hypotheses would emerge, eventually lend themselves to experimental verification or rejection, and, later to theoretical enlargement' (Hart, 1976: 77). Ten years later, Hart made his case even more breathlessly in the essay, 'Contemporary Scholarship in Public Address: A Research Editorial'. There he wrote:

I believe that our studies in this sub-field can no longer be motivated by an attempt to 'complete the historical record.' I believe that we must be concerned insistently and exclusively with the conceptual record because that is the only record that will outlive us (if it is wisely developed), because it is that record and that record alone that will insure the continued intellectual vitality of this field of inquiry, and because only a rich and detailed conceptual record can replace the often antiquarian musings of some brands of traditional research in the area. (1986: 284)

Not surprisingly, Hart's critique created a stir. It was rejected most famously by James Darsey (1994) in the essay 'Must We All be Rhetorical Theorists? An Anti-democratic Inquiry'. Darsey (1994: 168) argued that Hart's rebuke was merely 'the social scientist speaking' with the view that 'an individual datum is ... important only insofar as it can be representative of some larger group'. To accept Hart's assumptions, according to Darsey, would be to accept the 'ease with which scientific analyses eclipses the voice of humanistic criticism' (1994: 169). This latter voice characteristically champions the exceptional rather than the representative ('Is Michelangelo's ceiling in the Sistine Chapel only to be valued for what it can tell us about the principles of painting?' [Darsey, 1994: 171]) while also urging scholars to wade into the typically normative realm of ethics and aesthetics ('What should be? What is of value?' [Darsey, 1994: 178]). To speak well to these matters, Darsey argues, the rhetorical critic has a clear obligation to 'focus on the detail of the specific case' via the 'remarkably inductive tradition in its emphasis on individual texts and taste' (1994: 178). The power of oratory is to be found therein, promises Darsey, through the humanistic attention to 'a full harmonious perfection' in the artistry of the language itself á la Matthew Arnold (as cited in Darsey, 1994: 178).

The tensions between Darsey's and Hart's positions have not been resolved across the discipline of rhetorical studies, nor should they be. Indeed, this debate has been remarkably productive to the extent that now rhetorical critics typically exercise some degree of self-reflexivity in choosing and justifying their commitments to text or theory or a mixture of both (Murphy, 2009) as well as to the terms through which they choose to offer a rationale for their analyses (for example, consequences or not). Nevertheless, the open struggle between humanistic and social scientific impulses seems to animate one sub-field of public address scholarship more than any others: presidential rhetoric, the intellectual home of the second debate under review here.

Within communication studies, the study of presidential rhetoric grew out of the more traditional interest in public address within the US electoral politics via disciplinary developments I have already referenced (see Medhurst, 2008: 4–19). The study of presidential rhetoric as a type of public address does not, therefore, share disciplinary or even philosophical roots with the study of the presidency as traditionally conducted by political scientists in the USA. If there was ever any doubt about how much these different lineages mattered, George C. Edwards' (2003) *On Deaf Ears: The Limits of the Bully Pulpit* provides hearty evidence. In fact, the book itself is the byproduct of Edwards' exposure to the scholarship of rhetoric scholars as presented at the Conference on Presidential Rhetoric sponsored annually by the Program in Presidential Rhetoric at Texas A&M University from 1995 through 2004. There, to use Edwards' words, scholars gathered to discuss 'some aspect of how presidents articulate their views' on particular topics (for example, the environment, civil rights, immigration, etc.) (2003: x).

To Edwards' mind, what was missing from many of those conversations (as well as within other analytical quarters interested in the contemporary US presidency) is 'an understanding of the linkage between what the president says and does and the public's response' (2003: xi). He writes:

[S]cholars are commentators routinely refer to the White House as a 'bully pulpit' and assume that a skilled president can employ it to move the public and create political capital for himself. The fact that such efforts almost always fail seems to have no effect on the belief in the power of public leadership. (Edwards, 2003: xi)

Throughout the book, Edwards presents evidence drawn almost exclusively from public opinion polls to support his basic argument that there is no quantitative support for this power. If presidential rhetoric was effective at moving public opinion, his reasoning goes, there would be opinion change that we could measure and otherwise correlate to particular messages. Finding none, Edwards casts doubt on the notion that presidential oratory has much power at all.

Yet even casual observers of recent presidential politics in the USA might find Edwards' thesis difficult to accept, as the importance of oratory seems to be growing with direct proportion to the rise of mass media (see Jamieson, 1988) and now social networking media. My own view is not that Edwards' analysis is incorrect, but instead that his definition of the power and/or impact of rhetoric is too narrow. It may be, instead, that presidential rhetoric is simply powerful in ways that are difficult, if not impossible, to measure via public opinion polling. For example, multiple scholars (Beasley, 2004; Dorsey, 2007; Stuckey, 2004) have suggested that the power of presidential rhetoric is in its constitutive force – that is, in its ability to provide articulate a compelling discursive idiom for national identity, both in the abstract and with regard to specific policy decisions. This constitutive function of telling the American people who they are and what they have in common also results in rhetorical patterns that constitute the notion of who (and what) their enemies might be, a tendency that has been observed repeatedly within presidential rhetoric on foreign policy (Bostdorff, 1994; Hasian, 2008; Ivie, 1996). Others (Murphy, 2003, 2004; Zarefsky, 2005) have suggested that the power of presidential rhetoric can be best understood as an instrumental force on public opinion, just as Edwards' model would suggest, but one that moves incrementally (via evoking particular framing metaphors, for instance) in ways that cannot be easily captured by methods such as those used by Edwards. Similarly, others (Beasley, 2009b; Condit, 2009; Jasinski and Murphy, 2009) have argued that presidential rhetoric can impact the collective moral imagination of its audiences for both good and ill. From this perspective, presidential oratory 'crafts' public morality (Parry-Giles and Parry-Giles, 2009: ii) in complex ways that do not easily lend themselves to statistical analysis.

As we have seen, then, scholars who are explicitly interested in the US political oratory, especially presidential rhetoric, have differing views on how to conceptualize, measure or even identify this power, resulting in a lack of conceptual consensus within scholarly literature. But such questions are not merely academic, as it were. Indeed, there was plentiful evidence from the recent 2008 US presidential elections that, once again, oratory mattered because it was perceived to be both powerful and mysterious.

Indeed, during the 2008 campaign season, it seemed as if every observer had an answer to Socrates' question about 'what in the world the power of rhetoric [could] be'. Writing in both mass and new media outlets, for example, the US journalists certainly paid attention to the role of public address in the campaign, at times even detailing for their audiences the specific requirements necessary for a text to be sufficiently powerful to meet its goals. In these cases, some commentators sounded like the humanists eager to understand the particulars of the texts that would emerge from such a historic context. At other times, they sounded much like Edwards, reading to conduct pre- and post-testing on public opinion before and after a big speech. To wit, some of the most recurring questions of the campaign season concerned single, specific instances of public oratory, perhaps upholding the humanistic perspective that particular rhetorical events were especially worthy of close textual analysis while also suggesting that speeches serve functions that can have important consequences indeed.

Consider, first, Mitt Romney's 7 December 2007, speech in College Station, Texas, in which he explained how his religion would not interfere with his ability to be president. Coverage of this text inevitably featured comparisons to John F. Kennedy's 1960 speech to the Houston Ministerial Association, suggesting that reporters at least had a sense of the history of the US political public address that enabled them to make such a comparison. 'Is this Romney's Kennedy moment?' asked Michael Duffy (2007) in *Time* magazine. Michael Luo (2007), writing for *The New York Times,* seemed to reply to this question in the negative with his assessment of the speech by noting that, '[w]hen John F. Kennedy addressed the issue of his Roman Catholic religion in a similar speech when he was running for president in 1960, he took hostile questions hurled at him by ministers. Mr. Romney's was a friendly crowd that included, in the front row, four of his five sons and his wife, Ann, as well as many affiliated with the campaign'. This latter comment especially suggests a familiarity not only with Kennedy's speech as a familiar touchstone for comparison, but also with the notion that democratic engagement, as a communicative process, requires rhetoric delivered successfully before a hostile audience.

To wit, and for the second example, consider the speech given on 18 March 2008, in Philadelphia, Pennsylvania, as candidate Barak Obama responded to increased media attention to his 'Rev. Wright problem'. This speech was widely regarded as without precedent in terms of the precipitating events. And how could it have been? No African-American man had ever run for president as the presumptive nominee of a major party in the USA before, and no presidential candidate had experienced an exigence quite like this before. Clearly, knowledge of the same rhetorical history and analog triggered in the Romney case was not helpful here. What could be said? Without a clear comparison point, and owing to the eloquence of the speech itself, the media could declare this text as itself a touchstone, just hours after it was delivered. To wit, *ABC News* (Tapper et al., 2008) noted that New Mexico governor and long-time Clinton friend Bill Richardson identified the speech itself as the key ingredient he needed to make up his own mind about who to support. 'Obama is a once in a lifetime leader', Governor Richardson said. His evidence? 'I think what kind of clinched it for me, although I made a decision a week ago, was Sen. Obama's speech on race', he told reporters (Tapper et al., 2008). This speech was not heralded for its artistic merits – recall here, perhaps, Darsey's reference to the Sistine Chapel – but it was thus also presumed to be effective in the most pragmatic way possible within electoral politics, recalling both Edwards' more recent standard (without public opinion polls as the measure, though) and the neo-Aristotelian paradigm in the speech communication discipline in the mid-20th century.

As a third example, consider the attention given to Hillary Clinton's speech on 7 June 2008, in Washington, DC. On this occasion, Clinton spoke before a packed audience at the National Building Museum and announced that her presidential campaign had concluded and that she would support Barack Obama. The *Los Angeles Times* (2008) was one of the first newspapers to label the speech a success, calling Clinton's delivery 'centered and gracious and impossible to lampoon'. The next day, *The Washington Post* columnist Dana Milbank (2008) offered his own rhetorical criticism by stating that the speech was more of a 'thank you note to 18 million voters' than a concession speech. Milbank (2008) also offered an explicitly aesthetic evaluation of, again, Clinton's delivery: 'There can be little doubt that her last speech of the campaign was also her best'.

Some observers might say that these examples do not suggest anything at all about the power of oratory within contemporary US politics. They might say, instead, that the presidential candidates of 2008 were simply blessed with an unusually high degree of oratorical talent. Nevertheless, I offer these examples at the end of the section on scholarly debates on how to best understand the power and impact of oratory in order to argue for the value of analytic pluralism. As my comments within each example illustrate, it is possible that no one 'side' of the debates I have referenced has sufficient explanatory force to explain how and why oratory can come to matter within any given political context. Is it via comparative judgments (for example, Romney), singular linguistic artistry (for example, Obama) or appropriate delivery (for example, Clinton?) that orality gets its power to move listeners and/or voters. It is my opinion that we need a multiplicity of approaches, drawn from humanistic and social science traditions, in order to understand both the situated and the larger foundational lessons here about the power of rhetoric. We need scholars from both methodological traditions to put rhetoric under their microscopes, so to speak, to see what makes it work and also to argue about what even that assessment means.

We also need to know more about how oratory functions in other democracies around the world. Within the public address literature I have referenced here, there has historically been a tendency to focus primarily on the US cases – a tendency Danisch (2007) suggests may have roots in an Americanist philosophical tradition linking rhetoric, democracy and pragmatism in particular ways.

Yet other people and other nations have their own historical orientations and cultural frameworks relative to orality. Whereas stirring political oratory may be viewed as a positive sign of the livelihood of democracy in the USA, this is not necessarily the case in Germany, for example, where patently emotional rhetoric designed to influence the masses can understandably be viewed with some suspicion post-Hitler. This single contrast, with its differing assumptions about the core (and even the moral) relationship between public speaking and democracy, is instructive. It is foolish to assume that there are not many other assumptions about orality at work within other democracies, both old and young. Rather than impose an Americanist paradigm on other cultures, we might identify its historic ambivalences to oratory – in both 'real world' and scholarly realms' – and then stand them in contrast to other paradigms from other parts of the world. Research that asks questions about the power of rhetoric across culture and nation will presumably become increasingly important within a global political context in which images, information and, yes, even speeches travel quickly and uncontrollably to and among diverse audiences.

REFERENCES

Beasley, V. B. (2004) *You, the People: American National Identity in Presidential Rhetoric.* College Station, TX: Texas A&M University Press.

Beasley, V. B. (2009a) 'Between Touchstones and Touch Screens: What Counts as Contemporary Political Rhetoric?', in A. A. Lunsford (ed.), *The Sage Handbook of Rhetorical Studies.* Thousand Oaks, CA: Sage pp. 587–603.

Beasley, V. B. (2009b) 'George H. W. Bush and the Strange Disappearance of Groups from Civil Rights Talk', in S. J. Parry-Giles and T. Parry-Giles (eds.), *Public Address and Moral Judgment: Critical Studies in Ethical Tensions.* East Lansing, MI: Michigan State University Press. pp. 31–60.

Black, E. (1965) *Rhetorical Criticism: A Study in Method.* New York: Macmillan.

Bostdorff, D. (1994) *The Presidency and the Rhetoric of Foreign Crisis.* Columbia, SC: University of South Carolina Press.

Bizzell, P. and Herzberg, B. (2001) *The Rhetorical Tradition: Readings from Classical Times to the Present.* Boston, MA: Bedford/St. Martin's.

Condit, C. M. (2009) 'Where is Public Address? George W. Bush, Abu Ghraib, and Contemporary Moral Discourse', in S. J. Parry-Giles and T. Parry-Giles (eds.), *Public Address and Moral Judgment: Critical Studies in Ethical Tensions.* East Lansing, MI: Michigan State University Press. pp. 1–30.

Danisch, R. (2007) *Pragmatism, Democracy, and the Necessity of Rhetoric*. Columbia, SC: University of South Carolina Press.

Darsey, J. (1994) 'Must We all be Rhetorical Theorists? An Anti-Democratic Inquiry', *Western Journal of Communication*, 58(3): 164–81.

Dorsey, L. G. (2007) *We Are all Americans, Pure and Simple: Theodore Roosevelt and the Myth of Americanism*. Tuscaloosa, AL: University of Alabama Press.

Duffy, M. (2007) 'Is this Romney's Kennedy Moment?', 5 December, http://www.time.com/time/politics/article/0,8599,1691319,00.html

Gehrke, P. J. (2009) *The Ethics and Politics of Speech: Communication and Rhetoric in the Twentieth Century*. Carbondale, IL: Southern Illinois University Press.

Edwards, III, G. C. (2003) *On Deaf Ears: The Limits of the Bully Pulpit*. New Haven, CT: Yale University Press.

Hart, R. P. (1976) 'Theory-Building and Rhetorical Criticism: An Informal Statement of Opinion', *The Central States Speech Journal*, 27(1): 70–7.

Hart, R. P. (1986) 'Contemporary Scholarship in Public Address: A Research Editorial', *Western Journal of Speech Communication*, 50(3): 283–95.

Hasian, Jr., M. (2008) 'The Return to the Imperial Presidency', in J. A. Aune and M. J. Medhurst (eds.), *The Prospect of Presidential Rhetoric*. College Station, TX: Texas A&M University Press. pp. 69–98.

Havelock, E. A. (1981) *The Greek Concept of Justice*. Princeton, NJ: Princeton University Press.

Heinrichs, J. (1995) 'How Harvard Destroyed Rhetoric', *Harvard Magazine*, July/August: 37–42.

Ivie, R. (1996) 'Tragic Fear and the Rhetorical Presidency: Combating Evil in the Persian Gulf', in M. J. Medhurst (ed.), *Beyond the Rhetorical Presidency*. College Station, TX: Texas A&M University Press. pp. 153–78.

Jamieson, K. H. (1988) *Eloquence in an Electronic Age: The Transformation of Political Speechmaking*. New York: Oxford University Press.

Jasinski, J. and Murphy, J. M. (2009) 'Time, Space, and Generic Reconstitution: Martin Luther King, Jr.'s "A Time to Break Silence" as Radical Jeremiad', in S. J. Parry-Giles and T. Parry-Giles (eds.), *Public Address and Moral Judgment: Critical Studies in Ethical Tensions*. East Lansing, MI: Michigan State University Press. pp. 97–126.

Keith, W. M. (2007) *Democracy as Discussion: Civic Education and the American Forum Movement*. Lanham, MA: Rowman and Littlefield.

Keith, W. M. (2008) 'On the Origins of Speech as a Discipline: James A. Winans and Public Speaking as Practical Democracy', *Rhetoric Society Quarterly*, 38(3): 239–58.

Leff, M. C. and Mohrmann, G. P. (1974) 'Lincoln at Cooper Union: A Rhetorical Analysis of the Text', *Quarterly Journal of Speech*, 60(3): 346–58.

Los Angeles Times. (2008) 'Critic's Notebook: Hillary Clinton's Concession Speech', 7 June, http://latimesblogs.latimes.com/showtracker/2008/06/critics-noteboo.html

Lucas, S. E. (1973) 'Theodore Roosevelt's "The Man with the Muck Rake": A Reinterpretation', *Quarterly Journal of Speech*, 59(4): 452–62.

Lucas, S. E. (1993) 'The Schism in Rhetorical Scholarship', in M. J. Medhurst (ed.), *Landmark Essays on American Public Address*. Davis, CA: Hermagoras Press. pp. 139–62.

Luo, M. (2007) 'Romney, Eye on Evangelicals, Defends His Faith', *The New York* Times, 7 December, http://www.nytimes.com/2007/12/07/us/politics/07romney.html?pagewanted=1&_r=1

Medhurst, M. J. (1993) 'The Academic Study of Public Address: A Tradition in Transition', in M. J. Medhurst (ed.), *Landmark Essays on American Public Address*. Davis, CA: Hermagoras Press. pp. ix – xliii.

Medhurst, M. J. (2008) 'From Retrospect to Prospect: The Study of Presidential Rhetoric, 1915–2005', in J. A. Aune and M. J. Medhurst (eds.), *The Prospect of Presidential Rhetoric*. College Station, TX: Texas A&M University Press. pp. 3–27.

Milbank, D. (2008) 'A Thank-You for 18 Million Cracks in the Glass Ceiling', *The Washington* Post, 8 June, http://www.washingtonpost.com/wpdyn/content/article/2008/06/07/AR2008060701879.html

Murphy, J. M. (2003) '"Our Mission and our Moment": George W. Bush and September 11th', *Rhetoric and Public Affairs*, 6(4): 607–32.

Murphy, J. M. (2004) 'The Language of the Liberal Consensus: John F. Kennedy, Technical Reason, and the "New Economics" at Yale University', *Quarterly Journal of Speech*, 90(2): 133–62.

Murphy, J. M. (2009) 'Stability and Change in Public Address Research', paper presented at the National Communication Association's 95th Annual Meeting. Chicago, IL.

Parry-Giles, S. J. and Parry-Giles, T. (2009) *Public Address and Moral Argument: Critical Studies in Ethical Tensions*. Lansing, MI: Michigan State University Press.

Reale, G. (1986) *A History of Ancient Philosophy: From the Origins to Socrates*. Binghamton, NY: SUNY Press.

Ricoeur, P. (1970) *Freud and Philosophy: An Essay in Interpretation*. Trans. Denis Savage. New Haven, CT: Yale University Press.

Stuckey, M. E. (2004) *Defining Americans: The Presidency and National Identity*. Lawrence, KS: University Press of Kansas.

Tapper, J., Miller, S. and Song, J. H. (2008) 'Richardson Backs Obama, Rebuffs Clinton', 21 March, http://abcnews.go.com/Politics/Vote2008/story?id=4497694&page=1

Thonssen, L. and Baird, A. C. (1948) *Speech Criticism: The Development of Standards for Rhetorical Appraisal*. New York: The Ronald Press Company.

Weaver, A. T. (1959) 'Seventeen Who Made History–The Founders of the Association', *Quarterly Journal of Speech*, 45(2): 195–99.

Wichelns, H. (1925) 'The Literary Criticism of Oratory', in A. G. Drummond (ed.), *Studies in Rhetoric and Public Speaking in Honor of James Albert Winans*. New York: Century Publishing. pp. 198–209.

Zarefsky, D. (1988) 'Approaching Lincoln's Second Inaugural Address', *Communication Reports*, 1(1): 9–13.

Zarefsky, D. (2005) *President Johnson's War on Poverty: Rhetoric and History*. Tuscaloosa, AL: University of Alabama Press.

28

The Power of Everyday Conversations: Mediating the Effects of Media Use on Policy Understanding

Jisuk Woo, Min Gyu Kim and Joohan Kim

INTRODUCTION

Deliberative democracy depends on the presence of an engaged and informed citizenry (Barber, 1984; Fishkin, 1991). Although citizenship has many attributes, scholars have highlighted characteristics such as active participation in political and civic activities (Delli Carpini and Keeter, 1996), having consistent and concrete opinions about policy issues (Zaller, 1992) and having adequate knowledge and refined opinions about issues and participating in rational-critical debates and conversations (Moy and Gastil, 2006). Some scholars have recently contended that the terms of participatory democracy are inconsistent with those of deliberative democracy (Mutz, 2006). Ardent participation does not equal or always bring about informed decisions or an informed citizenry. While enthusiastically participating citizens are eager to convey their opinions and persuade others, they tend to make this effort with like-minded people and avoid talking to people with opposing views (Mutz, 2006). Such polarization has also been found on the Internet, sometimes to a greater degree (Adamic and Glance, 2005; Sunstein, 2007). Mutz (2006) argued that a deliberative environment requires its citizens to learn from an early age to hear the other side in private conversations and everyday discussions.

Park (2000) also regarded two-way communication, through listening to others' views as well as speaking, as the most fundamental element of deliberation.

In this way, recent discussions on democracy have emphasized not only ascertaining one's opinions and actively participating in discussions and decision making, but also one's understanding of others and of the outside world. However, most empirical studies on deliberative democracy have focused on citizens' 'quality of opinions' rather than their 'quality of understanding'. Numerous studies have examined the quality of opinions, especially factors that constitute sophistication of opinions such as internal consistency and incorporation, opinion differentiation and stability (Kim, 2001). Yet the depth or level of understanding of relevant issues, as a factor of the quality of understanding, has not been much studied.

Therefore, it is important to examine knowledge or understanding of public policies among different citizens and possible factors that might enhance that understanding. Some empirical evidence and theoretical reasoning supports the expectation that understanding public policy issues is related to the use of news media as well as to discussions or conversations with other people. Media use and political conversations were found to influence the formation of sophisticated opinions (Kim et al., 1999). The effects of interpersonal communication on enhancing knowledge of relevant issues have been widely studied, since the two-step flow theory of communication posited that media effects occur when people talk to others around them after reading newspapers (Katz and Lazarsfeld, 1955). Online and offline communication may also play different roles. In theory, the interactive nature of the Internet permits sharing of perspectives and concerns with others, but empirical analyses of the contents of online political discussions have shown otherwise (Mutz, 2006; Sunstein, 2007), suggesting that participation in online discussions and offline conversations should be examined separately. Thus, we probed the structural relationships between level of policy understanding, news media use and participation in online and offline discussions and conversations. Our particular focus was on a comparison of older and younger respondents in terms of the effects of media use on policy understanding and how those effects were mediated by online discussions and everyday political conversations.

THEORETICAL CONSIDERATIONS

Media Use and Knowledge About Policy and Politics

The need for a rational debate based on a thorough understanding of public issues is a critical component in the theory of deliberative democracy (Habermas, 1989). The development of cafés and coffee houses that functioned as the public sphere in Habermas's analysis was connected with the emergence of political newspapers. In other words, discussions of social issues require the participants to have acquired information, mostly through the media, prior to forming opinions (Habermas, 1989). Thus, the breadth and depth of citizens' knowledge about public issues is largely connected to information-acquiring activities, and the information is mainly derived from the mass media (Zaller, 1992). Research that examines the relationship between media use and policy understanding is scarce, although somewhat relevant studies in journalism and political science have focused on the effects of media use on political knowledge in the context of elections. In these studies, media use was found to generally enhance political knowledge, and many empirical studies have indicated that, among the media, newspapers contribute the most significantly in supplying political knowledge (Eveland and Scheufele, 2000; Patterson, 1980; Robinson and Davis, 1990).

However, other scholars have argued that in reality newspapers contain less and less mobilizing information that helps readers comprehend the issues (Schudson, 1995), and that other media such as television, which offers both auditory and visual commentary, may be more effective in helping citizens acquire political information (Graber, 2001). Thus, there seem to be conflicting notions regarding the effects of news media use on the acquisition of political knowledge. This chapter investigates how each medium – newspapers, television and the Internet – was associated with policy understanding.

Studies of the effects of the Internet on knowledge enhancement have found that the participation in online discussions is less clearly related to participants' understanding or knowledge of relevant issues than to their participation in political activities. Scholars who conducted deliberative polling found that both online and offline discussions about policy issues influenced political knowledge (Fishkin, 1991; Fishkin and Luskin, 1999). In contrast, a study of online participation in discussion forums showed that the participants were more likely to strengthen their pre-existing opinions after reading and posting comments than to change their opinions or acquire newly formed opinions (Han, 2005). That is, even when participants in online discussions encounter others' opinions, their opinions are not likely to change because of that encounter. If this lack of change applies to knowledge and understanding as it does to opinions, then online discussions may only help participants to confirm their pre-existing knowledge, and may not help them to acquire new information or enhance their level of understanding. Previous studies have achieved mixed results when considering whether, and how much, participation in online discussions can enhance participants' knowledge of current issues. Thus, this study sought to examine how the level of participation in online discussions actually relates to the level of policy understanding.

The Importance of Everyday Talk in Deliberation

The theories of deliberative democracy also posit that free and equal participation by the public in talking about public issues enhances the quality of their opinions and of the decision-making processes. American scholars have empirically examined the effects of collective discussions in the public-issues forums formed in local communities. They found that participation in collective discussions, which took place in somewhat formal settings, enhanced political knowledge (Fishkin and Luskin, 1999), resulted in more differentiated and synthesized opinion formation and made opinions more stable (Gastil and Dillard, 1999). But scholars differ on the subject of which type of conversation is most meaningful for deliberation or has greater democratic values. Schudson (1997) argued that there are two types of political conversations – social conversation for the sake of conversation, and 'rule governed' and 'problem solving' conversations – and that only the latter contribute significantly to democracy and can be tools for executing public and democratic principles. Based on this argument, some scholars have focused their studies on problem-solving conversations rather than on social conversations (Moy and Gastil, 2006). Mutz (2006) also argued that because most informal conversations fall short of deliberative ideals, ordinary citizens should be provided with rules for deliberation before they engage in conversations.

Other scholars have criticized this instrumental view of political communication and have questioned the existence of the rational citizen who already knows everything needed for sound judgment, which is a premise of the instrumental view (Kim, 2005; Wyatt et al., 2000). According to these scholars, what is important is that self, the precondition for rational communication, can be formed through conversations. Thus, informal everyday talk is a prerequisite to purposive and rational deliberations (Kim and Kim, 2008). Habermas's theory of communication also indicates that through everyday political talk, a citizen produces communicative reasons and achieves mutual understanding of the self and others (Habermas, 1984). In the same vein, Tarde (1899) emphasized the role of daily conversations, arguing that interchanges of stories without specific purpose and endlessly repeated exchanges of words are the invisible sources of public opinion.

Empirical findings generally suggest that talking about an issue with friends and family in an informal setting helps people to formulate coherent and consistent opinions about an issue. Although everyday talk may not be rigorously deliberative, it has been found to help people work out their preferences and learn justifications for them (Conover and Searing, 2005). In addition, everyday political discussion has been found to enhance political knowledge that operates as a basis for informed opinion (Eveland, 2004).

Where and with whom do people have everyday talk? Many studies have indicated that people talk about politics and personal matters with friends and family at home and work, and in civic organizations, restaurants, bars, shopping malls and other places (McLeod et al., 1999; Mutz and Mondak, 2006; Wyatt et al., 2000). Eliasoph (1998) even found that American people talk

freely about politics only in the private sphere: his ethnographical study with suburban volunteers and activists found that people silenced their opinions in official settings but freely talked about political issues during intimate, late night conversations. These findings led us to conjecture that formal discussions in online forums and everyday political conversations with family, friends and colleagues would affect the level of policy understanding in different ways, and that became a primary focus of our study.

Generational Difference

We also posit that generational differences play a role in the relations between media use, online discussion and everyday political conversation, and policy understanding. Members of the older generation are believed to read newspapers more and to have a higher level of political knowledge, while they watch television less and use the Internet less frequently and less skillfully (Cho et al., 2009; Jung, 2008; Shah et al., 2007b). But whether these differences actually exist, and if so, how they interrelate to influence the level of political understanding, have not been the subject of systematic study.

In previous studies, age, along with other socio-demographic variables such as gender, education and income, and personal variables such as interest and motivation, was often associated with the information divide and knowledge gap (Eveland and Schuefele, 2000; Kolondinsky et al., 2002; Korupp and Szydlik, 2005). Members of the 'parent' generation, especially those who are more than 40-years-old, have less self-efficacy regarding Internet use, which often results in an Internet divide (Park and Park, 2009). Shah et al. (2001) analyzed the relationship between Internet use and the individual-level production of social capital in three generations and found that each generational group had a distinctive medium that most significantly accounted for its reserves of social capital. But they also found that the use of the Internet for information exchange (that is, searching for information and exchanging email) had a universally positive impact on the production of social capital across all three generations. Therefore, different generations seem to use each medium differently, but more research is needed to draw a clear conclusion regarding the role of the Internet in political understanding and civic life among older people. This study examined how the older generation differed from the younger generation in their use of different media and their policy understanding, and how the influence of media use on each generation's policy understanding was mediated by communication with others.

HYPOTHETICAL MODEL

The purpose of this study was to examine the structural relationships between four components of deliberative democracy: news media use, everyday political conversations, online discussions and level of policy understanding. We examined how news media use was related to the level of policy understanding and to the rate of online discussions and everyday political conversations; how participation in online discussions and everyday political conversations was related to level of policy understanding and how the structural relationships between news media use, online discussions, everyday political conversations and level of policy understanding differed across generations. The hypothetical model is presented in Figure 28.1.

METHOD

Data Source and Sample

The data for this study were drawn from the 2008 Citizen Perception Survey (CPS) conducted by the Knowledge Center for Public Administration and Policy at Seoul National University and Gallup Korea, a nationwide sample of enfranchised South Korean citizens. The data on a

variety of demographic, social and familial variables, perceptions about society and government and media use and conversation variables were obtained by face-to-face interviews as well as self-completed questionnaires. The 2008 CPS sample consists of 913 citizens – 451 female (49.4%) and 462 male (50.6%), with a mean age of 40.94 and a standard deviation of 13.35.

Measures

News Media Use
News media use is measured by newspaper reading, television news watching and Internet news searching. Respondents were asked about frequency of newspaper reading, viewing of television news programs and Internet news searching. All responses were measured on a scale ranging from 1 (never) to 4 (almost daily). These three measures were not combined into one, because we expected newspaper, television news and Internet to be quite different in their effects.

Participation in Online Discussions
This study defined participation in online discussions as reading other peoples' opinions as well as posting one's own opinions on online message boards devoted to political and public issues. Respondents were asked how often they participated

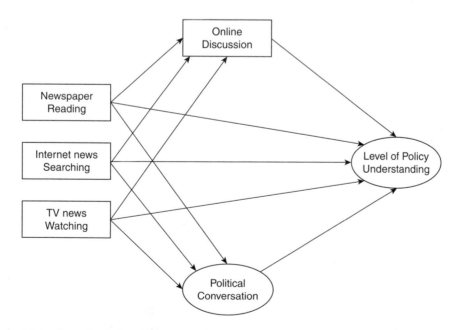

Figure 28.1 Hypothetical model

in such discussions; responses were measured on a scale ranging from 1 (never) to 4 (almost daily).

Participation in Everyday Political Conversations

Political conversations typically take place among people who know each other, such as family members, friends and colleagues. To measure participation in everyday political conversations, respondents were asked how often they talked about two types of issues – matters relating to the government (including the administration, president, Congress and courts), and social and local issues – with other people including family members, friends and colleagues. All responses were measured on a scale ranging from 1 (never) to 4 (often). The reliability of the two items was adequate ($r = 0.673$).

Level of Policy Understanding

The survey asked respondents how well they understood the following public policy issues: economy, education, culture and arts, environment, foreign and national security and reunification, labor, health and medicine, real estate, social welfare, science and technology, and taxes. Responses were measured on a scale ranging from 1 (not at all) to 5 (thoroughly). Following Kishton and Widaman (1994), this study randomly created three parcels, using averages of those eleven items in each parcel as the indicators of the latent variable: three items for one parcel and four items for the other two parcels. The reliability of the items was adequate (Chronbach's $\alpha = 0.899$).

Control Variables

The study controlled for the respondents' political inclination and trust of the government as well as a variety of demographic variables, including age, gender, income and years of education. Political inclination was measured on a scale ranging from 1 (very liberal) to 5 (very conservative). An index for trust of the government was created by taking the sum of each respondent's answers to questions on how much they trust the central government, the prosecutory authorities, the national tax service, the police bureau and the legislature. All responses were measured on a scale ranging from 1 (not at all) to 5 (entirely).

Missing Data

The data for this study did not have many missing cases, but each indicator had one or two. Because listwise-deletion and pairwise-deletion can result in biased parameter estimates due to non-random attrition (Arbuckle, 1996), this study employed the full-information maximum-likelihood (FIML) estimation, which has been found to be very efficient for incomplete data (Enders and Bandalos, 2001; Schafer and Olsen, 1998), especially in structural equation modeling analysis (Arbuckle, 2007). With regard to the normality assumptions of the FIML, we investigated the normality of each variable in terms of its kurtosis and skewness. According to the guideline of normality (skewness < 2, kurtosis < 4) proposed by West, Finch, and Curran (1995), results may be distorted when the assumption of normality is severely violated. The normality assumption, however, was well met for all the variables used in our model. Descriptive statistics of indicators are presented in Table 28.1.

Table 28.1 Overall descriptive statistics

	Younger (n = 448)				Older (n = 465)			
	Mean	SD	Skew	Kurtosis	Mean	SD	Skew	Kurtosis
Newspaper reading	1.462	0.818	1.746	2.116	1.501	0.804	1.480	1.243
Internet news searching	2.460	1.181	0.055	−1.494	1.529	0.947	1.529	1.086
Television news watching	2.455	1.167	−0.049	−1.482	2.936	1.071	−0.590	−0.944
Online discussion	2.159	0.613	1.246	2.593	1.658	0.758	1.079	0.898
Political conversation 1	1.891	0.720	0.419	−0.194	1.981	0.714	0.384	0.010
Political conversation 2	2.049	0.700	0.208	−0.235	2.161	0.718	0.348	0.102
Policy understanding 1	2.686	0.821	−0.138	−0.323	2.793	0.742	−0.033	−0.071
Policy understanding 2	2.591	0.823	−0.060	−0.385	2.692	0.725	0.083	−0.190
Policy understanding 3	2.474	0.824	0.014	−0.287	2.567	0.753	0.023	−0.133

Statistical Analysis

Analyses were done through structural equation modeling. First, a full structural model was developed as a hypothetical model in which news media use influenced the level of policy understanding through online discussions and everyday political conversations. Second, we used the residualized covariance matrix as input in the hypothetical model to regulate control variables (Cho et al., 2009). Shah and his colleagues (2007a) suggested that residualized covariance matrices help manage control variables. The residualization process, in addition, may suggest that 'any variance accounted for by the hypothetical model should be interpreted as one being above and beyond the variance already explained by the set of control variables' (Shah et al., 2007a: 689). Third, with the hypothetical model, the effects of news media use, participation in online discussions and everyday political conversations on the level of policy understanding were compared across younger (40 years old or less) and older (41 years old or more) generations. To perform a multi-group analysis, metric invariance of the hypothetical model across the samples must be confirmed (Hong et al., 2003; Levesque et al., 2004). The test of metric invariance can be conducted by constraining the factor pattern coefficients to be equal across waves, because the pattern of the coefficients carries the information about the relationship between the latent scores and the observed scores.

RESULTS

Before analyzing the structural relationships between the main variables (that is, newspaper reading, television news watching, Internet news searching, online discussions, everyday political conversations and the level of policy understanding), statistical differences in results for the younger and older groups were compared. To assess the between-group differences, a one-way ANOVA was conducted. The results showed that there were statistically significant differences for five of the six variables, including television news watching (F [1, 911] = 41.989, $p < 0.001$), Internet news searching (F [1, 911] = 157.661, $p < 0.001$), online discussions (F [1, 911] = 119.832, $p < 0.001$), everyday political conversations (F [1, 911] = 5.490, $p < 0.05$) and level of policy understanding (F [1, 911] = 4.504, $p < 0.05$). In contrast, no significant differences were found in newspaper reading (F [1, 911] = 0.651, $p = 0.420$). The effect sizes (η^2) between the younger group and the older group were as follows: 0.027 for

newspaper reading, 0.210 for television news watching, 0.384 for Internet news searching, 0.341 for online discussions, 0.077 for everyday political conversations and 0.070 for level of policy understanding. Younger respondents carried out Internet news searching and online discussion substantially more often than older respondents; in addition, the effect size was strong for both Internet news searching and online discussion. Older respondents watched television more often, took part in informal conversations with other people more often and had greater understanding of government policies.

The study investigated how statistical differences between the main variables were influenced by differences in the structural relationships of the younger and older groups. The structural relationships among the constructs between the younger group and the older group were compared through a multi-group analysis. That comparison was expected to indicate whether different types of news media use had different impacts on the level of policy understanding for both the younger and the older groups.

Test of the Hypothetical Model Using Explicit Covariance

In the hypothetical model (that is, the explicit covariance hypothetical model, Model A), three independent variables (newspaper reading, television news watching and Internet news searching) influenced one dependent variable (level of policy understanding) through two mediating variables (participation in online discussions and everyday political conversations). The fit of the hypothetical model was good: χ^2 (16, $N = 913$) = 14.486, $p = 0.563$, TLI = 1.001, RMSEA = 0.000. All news media use variables were associated with online discussion. Only newspaper reading, however, had a significant influence on everyday political conversations. Further, newspaper reading, television news watching and everyday political conversations had a statistically significant and positive association with the level of policy understanding. The results are presented in Table 28.2.

Mediation was assessed using the Sobel test (MacKinnon et al., 1995; Sobel, 1982) and the bootstrapping procedure (Arbuckle, 2007). The Sobel test provides an estimate of the indirect effect of the independent variable on the dependent variable through the mediator. This study first examined whether online discussion mediated the effect of news media use on the level of policy understanding. It was found that newspaper reading, Internet news searching and television news

Table 28.2   Standardized path coefficients of hypothetical model

	Parameters	Model A	Model B
Paths	Newspaper reading → online discussion	0.117***	0.128***
	Newspaper reading → political conversation	0.225***	0.174***
	Newspaper reading → policy understanding	0.098**	0.074*
	Internet news searching → online discussion	0.456***	0.315***
	Internet news searching → political conversation	0.025	0.043
	Internet news searching → policy understanding	−0.015	−0.048
	Television news watching → online discussion	−0.146***	−0.083**
	Television news watching → political conversation	0.066	0.044
	Television news watching → policy understanding	0.070*	0.060
	Online discussion → policy understanding	0.060	0.035
	Political conversation → policy understanding	0.206***	0.213***

Notes: Numbers in the two columns are standardized regressions. Model A is the explicit covariance hypothetical model. Model B is the partial covariance hypothetical model controlling for age, gender, income, years of education, political inclination and trust of the government. $N = 913$. $^*p < 0.05$; $^{**}p < 0.01$; $^{***}p < 0.001$.

watching had no indirect effects on the level of policy understanding through online discussion. The study also examined whether everyday political conversation mediated the effect of news media use on the level of policy understanding. It was found that only newspaper reading had an indirect effect through everyday political conversation on the level of policy understanding ($\beta = 0.046$, $p < 0.05$, $z = 1.874$).

Test of the Hypothetical Model Using Residualized Covariance

As a preparatory step, this study created a residualized (partial) covariance matrix to control for age, gender, education, income, political inclination and trust of the government by regressing all measures on these variables. The control variables account for a substantial amount of the variance (from 4.4% to 25.5%), as indicated in Table 28.3.

The fit of this hypothetical model (that is, the partial covariance hypothetical model, Model B) was still good: χ^2 (16, $N = 913$) $= 18.922$, $p = 0.273$, TLI $= 0.997$, RMSEA $= 0.014$. The results confirmed that using the residualized covariance matrix as an input in the hypothetical model can manage control variables. All news media use variables were associated with online discussion ($\beta = 0.128$, $p < 0.001$ for newspaper reading; $\beta = -0.083$, $p < 0.01$ for television news watching; $\beta = 0.315$, $p < 0.001$ for Internet news searching). Also, only newspaper reading influenced everyday political conversations ($\beta = 0.174$,

$p < 0.001$). Unlike the hypothetical model's prediction, however, television news watching did not influence the level of policy understanding, which was only influenced by newspaper reading ($\beta = 0.074$, $p < 0.05$) and everyday political conversations ($\beta = 0.213$, $p < 0.001$). The results are presented in Table 28.2. The result of the indirect effects in the partial covariance hypothetical model (Model B) was similar to the result of the indirect effects in the explicit covariance hypothetical model (Model A). The path of newspaper reading through everyday political conversations to level of policy understanding was statistically significant ($\beta = 0.031$, $p < 0.05$, $z = 1.675$).

The results of the hypothetical model using the residualized covariance matrix showed that all news media use enhanced online discussion, but online discussion did not enhance policy understanding. Among different types of news media use, only newspaper reading enhanced the level of policy understanding. Furthermore, newspaper reading enhanced the frequency of everyday political conversations, which then enhanced the level of policy understanding.

Test of the Structural Model Invariance Across the Samples

To perform a multi-group analysis, this study first estimated a baseline model in which measurement parameters (factor loadings) were simultaneously and freely estimated. The baseline model, simultaneous testing of the hypothetical model to the two

Table 28.3 Regression analyses for residualization

	Newspaper reading	Internet news searching	Television news watching	Online discussion	Political conversation	Policy understanding
Age	0.112**	−0.339***	0.261***	−0.323***	0.146***	0.087*
Education	0.205***	0.202***	−0.051	0.257***	0.148***	0.152***
Income	0.006	−0.028	0.005	0.019	0.067*	0.015
Gender (male = 1)	−0.186***	−0.139***	−0.055	−0.077**	−0.087**	−0.118***
Political ideology	−0.051	−0.001	−0.057	−0.050	−0.015	−0.067*
Trust of government	−0.022	0.038	0.029	−0.012	−0.047	0.241***
R^2	8.5%	23%	8.1%	25.5%	4.4%	10.1%

Notes: Numbers are standardized regression coefficients. $^*p < 0.05$; $^{**}p < 0.01$; $^{***}p < 0.001$.

samples, showed that the model fit was adequate: χ^2 (32, $N = 913$) = 32.371, $p = 0.448$, TLI = 1.000, RMSEA = 0.004. In the metric invariance model, all of the factor loadings were constrained to be equal for both the younger and older groups. This model assessed metric variance, or between-group differences in the strength of association between measured variables and the latent construct. The fit of the metric invariance model was still good: χ^2 (35, $N = 913$) = 36.119, $p = 0.416$, TLI = 0.999, RMSEA = 0.006. The chi-square difference was statistically significant, but differences in fit were minimal: $\Delta\chi^2$ (3, $N = 913$) = 3.748, $p = 0.290$, ΔTLI = −0.001, ΔRMSEA = 0.002. These results mean that all the constructs were similarly understood by the younger group and the older group.

Comparisons of the hypothetical models revealed that measurement parameters were generally invariant across the samples. To determine whether structural relationships among independent and dependent variables were also invariant across the samples, this study tested the equivalence of structural links among the latent constructs. When all eleven paths were constrained to be equal across the samples, the fit of the path coefficients invariance model was still good: χ^2 (46, $N = 913$) = 93.942, $p < 0.001$, TLI = 0.969, RMSEA = 0.034. However, the chi-square difference was statistically significant: $\Delta\chi^2$ (11, $N = 913$) = 57.823, $p < 0.001$; and model fit change was substantial: ΔTLI = −0.030, ΔRMSEA = 0.028. To identify paths of equality constraints, which increase the chi-square values significantly, each of the eleven paths was individually constrained and compared with the metric invarianced model. One of the 11 paths was revealed as statistically different across the groups. The results are presented in Table 28.4. Figure 28.2 presents the model that was found to be the best fit to the data across the samples.

The findings show that there was a generational difference in how news media use influenced

online discussion. The path from Internet news searching to online discussion was much stronger among older respondents than among younger respondents, and this difference was statistically significant. Thus, although older respondents were involved with Internet use less often than younger respondents, when they did use the Internet for news searching, they tended to participate in online discussions more actively.

CONCLUSION

Our study found that policy understanding was enhanced by newspaper reading but not by television watching or Internet use. This result was consistent with previous research indicating that newspapers help readers acquire information and accumulate knowledge, and with theoretical considerations that cognitive involvement tends to be encouraged more by print media than visual media. Yet the key finding of this study was that everyday political conversations had an effect on policy understanding, while online discussions did not. Those who participated in public online discussions more frequently did not gain a higher level of policy understanding, but those who frequently talked with family, friends and colleagues about governmental issues or social and local issues showed enhanced levels of policy understanding. This result illustrates that the effects of interpersonal communications are manifested not only in the dimension of opinion formation or sophistication, but also in the dimension of policy understanding. It signifies the importance of informal, private, interpersonal communications in the policymaking process.

The reasons that everyday political conversations, rather than online discussions, enhance policy understanding may be manifold. One reason may be the formality of online discussions, which to varying degrees may be comparable with

Table 28.4 Standardized path coefficients and chi-square value differences with invariance constraints

	Parameters	Younger	Older	$\Delta\chi^2$ (df = 1)	ΔTLI	ΔRMSEA
Paths	Newspaper reading → online discussion	0.142**	0.111**	0.063	−0.001	−0.004
	Newspaper reading → political conversation	0.216***	0.130**	1.120	0.000	3740.000
	Newspaper reading → policy understanding	0.013	0.138**	2.553	0.001	0.003
	Internet news searching → online discussion	0.176***	0.487***	46.563***	0.037	0.032
	Internet news searching → political conversation	0.036	0.044	0.064	−0.001	−0.004
	Internet news searching → policy understanding	−0.020	−0.079	0.681	0.000	−0.001
	Television news watching → online discussion	−0.066*	−0.089*	0.345	−0.001	−0.002
	Television news watching → political conversation	0.075	0.014	0.625	0.000	−0.001
	Television news watching → policy understanding	0.083	0.027	0.783	0.000	−0.001
	Online discussion → policy understanding	0.035	0.036	0.010	−0.001	0.004
	Political conversation → policy understanding	0.241***	0.184***	1.248	0.000	0.000

Notes: Younger = 40 years old or less; older = 41 years old or more. Numbers in these two columns are standardized regression coefficients in the metric invariance model. $\Delta\chi^2$ indicates the increased chi-square values when each of the paths was constrained to be equal across the samples. ΔTLI indicates the increased TLI values when each of the paths was constrained to be equal across the samples. ΔRMSEA indicates the increased RMSEA values when each of the paths was constrained to be equal across the samples. *$p < 0.05$; **$p < 0.01$; ***$p < 0.001$.

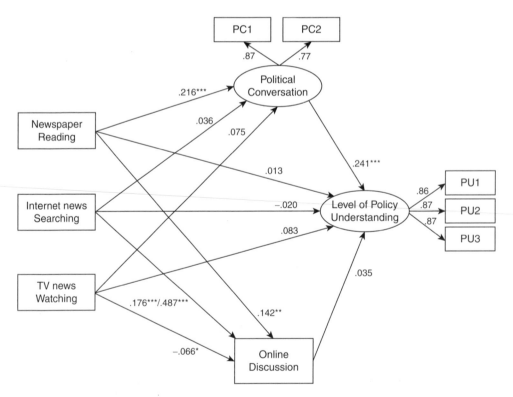

Figure 28.2 Structural model with all paths constrained across the sample
Notes: For the equivalent regression paths across the samples, the standard regression coefficients are presented for the younger group. For the non-equivalent regression path (from Internet news searching to online discussion), the coefficients for both groups are presented (younger/older). *$p < 0.05$; ** $p < 0.01$; *** $p < 0.001$.

the 'rule governed' and 'problem solving' discussions that Schudson (1997) argued to be necessary in a democracy. Although non-purposive and intimate conversations do take place in online discussion groups sometimes, online debates tend to be made in more public settings, cover more limited issues and be governed by more specific rules. But with family, friends and colleagues, people are less likely to talk about predetermined topics in a predetermined time and space. Our findings seem to suggest that people may learn more about public issues from naturally occurring communication with people they know than from formal and public communication.

The bidirectional nature of communication in a private setting should also be considered. Online discussions can be both bidirectional and unidirectional. But in forums based on posting comments rather than on real-time discussions, participants tend to focus on expressing their own opinions. Also, those who read the postings can skim through them and easily avoid uncomfortable comments. Conversely, face-to-face conversations are not likely to be unidirectional, because it is relatively harder to carry on one-sided conversations or to evade conversations without damaging personal relationships. If everyday conversations with family, friends and colleagues involve more two-way communication, they are more likely to increase participants' opportunities to acquire new knowledge.

The participants' different motives for engaging in communication should also be noted. In a study of everyday political talk in six American and British communities, Conover et al. (2002: 51) found that the motives of expressing preferences and persuading others were regarded as among the least important by all participants, whereas 'gaining information' was the most frequently mentioned motive. Social and personal motives such as learning about the lives of others and seeking common ground also turned out to be important in the participants' minds (Conover et al., 2002). In other words, people strive for reciprocity in everyday political talk, which makes their communication less one-sided and more accepting of others' views and new information. Therefore, future research should focus on the motives and elaboration processes of those who participate in everyday political conversations. Eveland (2004) has used the notions of anticipatory elaboration and discussion-generated elaboration to explain the ways in which political discussion translates into increased political knowledge. Drawing on these notions, it will be interesting to study whether there are differences in the elaboration processes when participating in online discussions and engaging in everyday political conversations.

The possibility of reciprocal communication, especially that open to opposing views, has always been a subject of interest in theories of deliberative democracy. Delli Carpini et al. (2004) suggested that among various types of political talk, talk that involves exchange of dissimilar perspectives is especially beneficial to individuals and society at large. This has significant implications for the role of online discussions, if the Internet primarily enables interactions with like-minded people (Sunstein, 2001). An empirical study analyzing chat room and message board users has showed that most online exchanges occur with people who agree rather than disagree, and this is true regardless of the kind of chat room or message board considered (Wojcieszak and Mutz, 2009). In contrast, political discussions that occur within non-political online groups frequently involve participants who disagree with each other, exposing them to dissimilar perspectives and suggesting a promising way for casual political talk online to contribute to policy understanding (Wojcieszak and Mutz, 2009). Our finding that political conversations with family, friends and colleagues enhanced policy understanding can also be explained by the possibility that those engaged in everyday political conversations were exposed more frequently to new perspectives or dissimilar opinions, which resulted in a higher level of policy understanding. Therefore, it seems to be important to revisit the observation made by Mutz (2006) that identified two-way communication and talking to people with oppositional views as a fundamental condition of deliberation. Presumably, in order to make informed decisions or to become informed citizens, we need to enhance our understanding of others or of the outside world more than we need to refine or solidify our own opinions.

Our analysis of generational differences also suggests the need to further study the role of Internet use and online discussions in deliberative democracy. Although the structural relationships between news media use, online discussions, everyday political conversations, and policy understanding were found to be similar between younger and older people in most paths, the difference in the effect of Internet news searching on the participation in online discussions was significant between the young and the old. Although older respondents used the Internet less often and participated in online discussions less frequently than younger respondents, those who did use the Internet for news searching participated much more actively in online discussions than their younger counterparts. This finding indicates that the Internet may be more widely used by the young, but that its impact on older people who choose to use it may be significantly larger.

There are several limitations to this study. It relied on respondents' self-reports to measure the level of policy understanding. Future studies may benefit from measuring policy-related knowledge in a more objective way by questioning respondents about the contents of a certain policy. We also did not distinguish, in measuring participation in online discussions, between actively voicing opinions by posting comments and simply reading others' comments. Previous studies have found some differences in how these two activities changed participants' opinions. Thus, in analyzing the relationship between communication and policy understanding in the future, it will be useful to distinguish between these two activities.

Despite these limitations, this study confirmed that the significance of informal, non-purposive conversation in private settings, which has previously been emphasized in relation to civic and political participation, is also sustained in the area of understanding public policies.

REFERENCES

Adamic, L. A. and Glance, N. (2005) 'The Political Blogosphere and the 2004 US Election: Divided They Blog', paper presented at the annual workshop on the Webloging Ecosystem, WWW2005. Chiba, Japan.

Arbuckle, J. L. (1996) 'Full Information Estimation in the Presence of Incomplete Data', in G. A. Marcoulides and R. E. Schumacker (eds.), *Advanced Structural Equation Modeling: Issues and Techniques*. Mahwah, NJ: Lawrence Erlbaum Associates. pp. 243–78.

Arbuckle, J. L. (2007) *AMOS User's Guide*. Chicago, IL: SPSS, Inc.

Barber, B. R. (1984) *Strong Democracy*. Berkeley, CA: University of California Press.

Cho, J., Shah, D. V., McLeod, J. M., McLeod, D. M., Scholl, R. M. and Gotlieb, M. R. (2009) 'Campaigns, Reflection, and Deliberation: Advancing an O-S-R-O-R Model of Communication Effects', *Communication Theory*, 19(1): 66–88.

Conover, P. J. and Searing, D. D. (2005) 'Everyday Political Talk', *Acta Politica*, 40(3): 269–83.

Conover, P. J., Searing, D. D. and Crewe, I. M. (2002) 'The Deliberative Potential of Political Discussion', *British Journal of Political Science*, 32(1): 21–62.

Delli Carpini, M. X., Cook, F. L. and Jacobs, L. R. (2004) 'Public Deliberation, Discursive Participation, and Citizen Engagement: A Review of the Empirical Literature', *Annual Review of Political Science*, 7: 315–44.

Delli Carpini, M. X. and Keeter, S. (1996) *What Americans Know About Politics and Why it Matters*. New Haven, CT: Yale University Press.

Delli Carpini, M. X. and Williams, B. (1994) 'Methods, Metaphors, and Media Messages: The Uses of Television in Political Conversation', *Communication Research*, 21(6): 782–812.

Eliasoph, N. (1998) *Avoiding Politics: How Americans Produce Apathy in Everyday Life*. Cambridge: Cambridge University Press.

Enders, C. K. and Bandalos, D. L. (2001) 'The Relative Performance of Full Information Maximum Estimation for Missing Data in Structural Equation Models', *Structural Equation Modeling*, 8(3): 430–57.

Eveland, W. P. (2004) 'The Effect of Political Discussion in Producing Informed Citizens: The Roles of Information, Motivation, and Elaboration', *Political Communication*, 21(2): 177–93.

Eveland, W. P. and Scheufele, D. (2000) 'Connecting News Media Use With Gaps in Knowledge and Participation', *Political Communication*, 17(3): 215–37.

Fishkin, J. S. (1991) *Democracy and Deliberation: New Directions For Democratic Reform*. New Haven: CT: Yale University Press.

Fishkin, J. S. and Luskin, R. C. (1999) 'Bringing Deliberation to the Democratic Dialogue', in M. McCombs and A. Reynolds (eds.), *A Poll With a Human Face: The National Issues Convention Experiment in Political Communication*. Mahwah, NJ: Lawrence Erlbaum Associates. pp. 3–38.

Gastil, J. and Dillard, J. P. (1999) 'Increasing Political Sophistication Through Public Deliberation', *Political Communication*, 16(1): 3–23.

Graber, D. A. (2001) *Processing Politics: Learning From Television in the Internet age*. Chicago, IL: University of Chicago Press.

Habermas, J. (1984) *The Theory of Communicative Action: Reason and the Rationalization of Society, Vol. 1*. T. McCarthy (trans.). Boston, MA: Beacon Press.

Habermas, J. (1989). *The Structural Transformation of the Public Sphere: An Inquiry into a Category of Bourgeois Society*. T. Burger (trans.). Cambridge, MA: MIT Press.

Han, H. K. (2005) '"Internet users" Civic Virtues and Experiences of Public Deliberation in Cyberspace', *Journal of Broadcasting and Telecommunication*, 19: 604–43.

Hong, S., Malik, M. L. and Lee, M. K. (2003) 'Testing Configural, Metric, Scalar, and Latent Mean Invariance Across Genders in Sociotropy and Autonomy Using Non-Western Sample', *Educational and Psychological Measurement*, 63(4): 636–54.

Jung, K. H. (2008) 'An Empirical Analysis of the Policy Literacy Function: A Focus on Civic Activities', *Korea Journal of Public Administration*, 46: 73–104.

Katz, E. and Lazarsfeld, P. F. (1995) *Personal Influence: The Part Played by People in the Flow of Mass Communications*. Glencoe, IL: Free Press.

Kim, J. (2001) 'On the Roles of News Media Use and Political Conversation in the Political Process', *Korean Journal of Journalism and Communication Studies*, 45: 86–116.

Kim, J. (2005) 'Primacy of Conversation in Democracy: Political Conversation as a Communicative Action in the Public Sphere', *Media and Society*, 13: 75–99.

Kim, J. and Kim, E. J. (2008) 'Theorizing Dialogic Deliberation: Everyday Political Talks as Communicative Action and Dialogue', *Communication Theory*, 18(1): 51–70.

Kim, J., Wyatt, R. O. and Katz, E. (1999) 'News, Talk, Opinion, Participation: The Part Played by Conversation in

Deliberative Democracy', *Political Communication,* 16(4): 361–85.

Kishton, J. M. and Widaman, K. F. (1994) 'Uni-dimensional Versus Domain Representative Parceling of Questionnaire Items: An Empirical example', *Educational and Psychological Measurement,* 54(3): 757–65.

Kolodinsky, J., Cranwell, M. and Rowe, E. (2002) 'Bridging the Generation Gap Across the Digital Divide: Teens Teaching Internet Skills to Senior Citizens', *Journal of Extension,* 40, http://www.joe.org/joe/2002june/rb2.php.

Korupp, S. and Szydlik, M. (2005) 'Causes and Trends of the Digital Divide', *European Sociological Review,* 21(4): 409–22.

Levesque, C., Zuehlke, A. N., Stanek, L. R. and Ryan, R. M. (2004) 'Autonomy and Competence in German and American University Students: A Comparative Study Based on Self-determination Theory', *Journal of Educational Psychology,* 96(1): 68–84.

MacKinnon, D. P., Warsi, G. and Dwyer, J. H. (1995) 'A Simulation Study of Mediated Effect Measures', *Multivariate Behavioral Research,* 30(1): 41–62.

McLeod, J. M. and Scheufele, D. A. and Moy, P. (1999) 'Community, Communication, and Participation: The Role of Mass Media and Interpersonal Discussion in Local Political Participation', *Political Communication,* 16(3): 315–36.

Moy, P. and Gastil, J. (2006) 'Predicting Deliberative Conversation: The Impact of Discussion Networks, Media Use, and Political Cognitions', *Political Communication,* 23(4): 443–60.

Mutz, D. (2006) *Hearing the Other Side: Deliberative Versus Participatory Democracy.* New York: Cambridge University Press.

Mutz, D. and Mondak, J. J. (2006) 'The Workplace as a Context for Cross-cutting Political Discourse', *The Journal of Politics,* 68(1): 140–55.

Park, S. G. (2000) 'The Significance of Civility in Deliberative Democracy', *Korean Journal of Journalism and Communication Studies,* 45: 162–94.

Park, W. K. and Park, Y. J. (2009) 'The Relationship Between Internet Self-efficacy and Internet Digital Divide: Focused on Parents-children', *Korean Journal of Journalism and Communication Studies,* 53: 395–417.

Patterson, T. E. (1980) *The Mass Media Election: How Americans Choose Their President.* New York: Praeger.

Robinson, J. P. and Davis, D. K. (1990) 'Television News and the Informed Public: An Information-processing Approach', *Journal of Communication,* 40(3): 106–19.

Schafer, J. and Olsen, M. (1998) 'Multiple Imputation for Multivariate Missing-data Problems: A Data Analyst's Perspective', *Multivariate Behavioral Research,* 33(4): 545–71.

Schudson, M. (1995) *The Power of the News.* Cambridge: Cambridge University Press.

Schudson, M. (1997) 'Why Conversation is not the Soul of Democracy', *Critical Studies in Mass Communication,* 14(4): 297–309.

Shah, D. V., Kwak, N. and Holbert, R. L. (2001) '"Connecting" and "Disconnecting" With Civic Life: Patterns of Internet Use and the Production of Social Capital', *Political Communication,* 18(2): 141–62.

Shah, D. V., Cho, J., Nah, S., Gotlieb, M. R., Hwang, H., Lee, N.-J., et al. (2007a) 'Campaign Ads, Online Messaging, and Participation: Extending the Communication Mediation Model', *Journal of Communication,* 57(4): 676–703.

Shah, D. V., McLeod, D. M., Cho, J., Scholl, R. and Gotlieb, M. R. (2007b) '*Political Ads, Communication Mediation, and Participation: Modeling Campaign Effects Across Generational Groups',* paper presented at the annual meeting of the International Communication Association. San Francisco, CA.

Sobel, M. E. (1982) 'Asymptotic Confidence Intervals for Indirect Effects in Structural Equation Models', in S. Leinhart (ed.), *Sociological methodology.* San Francisco, CA: Jossey-Bass. pp. 290–312.

Sunstein, C. R. (2001) *Republic.com.* Princeton, NJ: Princeton University Press.

Sunstein, C. R. (2007) *Republic.com 2.0.* Princeton, NJ: Princeton University Press.

Tarde, G. (1989) *Opinion and Conversation.* J. Ruth (trans.), unpublished translation of 'L'opinion et la conversation' [Opinion and conversation] in G. Tarde, *L'opinion et la foule* [Mass opinion]. Paris: Presses Universitaires de France. (Original work published 1899).

Wyatt, R., Katz, E. and Kim, J. (2000) 'How Feeling Free to Talk Affects Ordinary Political Conversation, Purposeful Argumentation, and Civic Participation', *Journalism and Mass Communication Quarterly,* 77(1): 99–114.

West, S. G., Finch, J. F. and Curran, P. J. (1995) 'Structural Equation Models With Non-normal Variables: Problems and Remedies', in R. Hoyle (ed.), *Structural Equation Modeling: Concepts, Issues and Applications.* Newbury Park, CA: Sage. pp. 56–75.

Wojcieszak, M. E. and Mutz, D. (2009) 'Online Groups and Political Discourse: Do Online Discussion Spaces Facilitate Exposure to Political Disagreement?', *Journal of Communication,* 59(1): 40–56.

Zaller, J. (1992) *The Nature and Origins of Mass Opinion.* New York: Cambridge University Press.

29

Leaders on the Campaign Trail: The Impact of Television News on Perceptions of Party Leaders in British General Elections

Holli A. Semetko, Margaret Scammell
and Andrew Kerner

Scholars in democracies and societies with elections continue to debate the effects of media coverage in election campaigns on political attitudes and voting behavior. The conceptualization of campaign effects on the vote as a reinforcement effect dates back to the work of Paul Lazarsfeld (1948) in some of the early postwar US presidential elections. The idea that campaigns matter for more than just reinforcing partisan predispositions is evident in a number of more recent studies in democracies that point to the direct effects of information on issue salience, candidate evaluations and mobilization (see Curtice and Semetko [1994], Norris and Wlezien [2005], Norris et al. [1999], Scammell [1995, 1999] for examples from the UK, Johnston et al. [1992] and Nadeau et al. [2008] on Canada and Johnston et al. [2004] as well as Holbrook [1996] for recent US examples).

Television has long been citizens' most preferred source of information about politics and election campaigns. In the context of the UK in the 1960s, for example, reliance on television for campaign information meant that citizens could learn more about parties that were not as often in the routine news about political affairs outside of the election campaign period (Blumler and McQuail, 1968). In light of more recent research on the role of visuals on how the brain processes political information (Graber, 2001), television is arguably the most likely place from which citizens can learn and best retain information about the leaders, the parties and the issues at stake in a campaign. In this chapter, we discuss the influence of television news on perceptions of political party leaders in the UK. We identify whether television news reporting on the parties and their leaders had any influence on perceptions of the party leaders during the 2005 general election campaign for which we have data.

The contemporary debate over campaign effects in recent elections in the UK continues to be shaped in large part by how these effects are measured. Sanders et al. (2003: 24) argue that the campaigns of the main political parties 'significantly influenced electoral choice' but they operationalize campaign influence as the direct role of local party contacts (see Sanders et al., 2004), and they ignore the way that the political parties prioritize communicating to voters during election campaigns via daily television news. This may be the reason why the 2005 British Election Study (BES) failed to ask respondents a single question about attention or exposure to television news during the campaign in the more than 1600 items on the pre- and post-campaign waves.

Despite the missing questions in the 2005 BES, other BES questions reveal that the public was interested in the campaign and local party contacts were even less common than watching party election broadcasts (PEBs), the often boring free television time slots allocated to parties during the campaign. The 2005 BES data show that 97.2% paid at least some attention to politics and 94.9% paid at least some attention to the campaign. A full 43% of BES respondents claimed to be 'very interested' in the campaign. Despite the manifest interest in politics among BES respondents, only 12% had a canvasser come to their door while 54.3% reported having seen a PEB on television. MORI surveys showed that 89% of the electorate turned to the news media for information about the campaign (Worcester et al., 2005), and surveys suggest that for those who went online, television news websites were the most preferred destination for information during the campaign (see Tables 29.1 and 29.2). We therefore suspect that even if some reportedly interested BES respondents were merely providing a socially desirable response, many of those who expressed interest were probably turning to television news for campaign-related information.

BBC and Independent Television News (ITN) are the nation's most widely watched news programs. They reach broad cross-sections of the electorate, including those who are not committed to any particular political party and whose interest in politics may be marginal. Television news in the UK's public service broadcasting system is perceived as a more credible source of information than newspapers whose journalists and owners are often expressing political opinions. MORI's Veracity Index puts 'television news readers' 10 places above 'journalists' (the last on the list), 9 places above 'politicians generally' and 8 places above 'government ministers' in terms of the proportion of the public who say they trust them to tell the truth (Worcester et al., 2005: 277). The MORI Veracity Index shows remarkable consistency in the rank order over more than a decade. Above television news readers on the 2005 MORI Veracity Index, from first place to sixth place were: doctors 91%, teachers 88%, professors 77%, judges 76%, clergy/priests 73%, scientists 70%, with television news readers on 63%. They were followed by the police 58%, the ordinary man/woman on the street 56%, pollsters 50%, civil servants 44%, trade union officials 37%, business leaders 24%, government ministers 20%, politicians generally 20%, journalists 16% (Worcester et al., 2005: 277).

From 5 April to 4 May 2005, the main political parties operated their daily campaigns just as they had in previous British general elections. Mornings began with press conferences in London, followed by leaders' activities on the campaign trail across the country, and evening rallies designed to make it into the local and national evening news. Research on the battle over the campaign news agenda in previous elections showed that this

Table 29.1   Public sources of news during the 2001 and 2005 general elections

	2001[a] (%)	2005[b] (%)
Watched election coverage on TV	89	89[c]
Read national newspaper	n/a	43
Heard election news on the radio	39	50
Used the Internet for election information	2	7[c]

Source: Electoral Commission (2005).
Notes: [a]MORI survey June 2001; [b]ICM survey June 2005; [c]MORI post-election poll 5–10 May 2005.

Table 29.2   Website destinations: UK general election, 2005

Websites used for election news	%[a]
BBC news	22.2
Google/MSN/Yahoo	10
Guardian.co.uk	4.0
Any party site	3.5
Any blog	0.5
None	74

Source: BBC/MORI Citizenship Survey May 2005.
Note: [a]Percentages reflect multiple use of sites and hence add up to more than 100%.

traditional and structured approach to campaigning gives British politicians a leg up in getting their message out, as British television news gives a prominent place to these structured highlights in their daily campaign reporting (Semetko, 2000). Traditional notions of 'balance' in election television news at one time led news organizations to actually 'stopwatch' the amount of time they devoted to the political parties to a 5:5:4 ratio – for every five minutes devoted to the Conservatives, there was five minutes devoted to Labour and four to the Liberal Democrats. Although this practice was officially abandoned many elections before 2005, our content analysis data suggest a remarkable coincidence. Taking the total amount of time on BBC and ITN devoted to soundbites from the three main party leaders in the main evening news during the 2005 general election campaign, the ratio was 36% for Labour leader Tony Blair, 36% for Conservative leader Michael Howard and 28% for Liberal Democrat leader Charles Kennedy, or 1765, 1747 and 1362 seconds, respectively.

Previous research shows that the three main political parties move onto a more equal footing on television news during campaigns because of Britain's PSB model which emphasizes fair and impartial reporting of politics and never more so than at election time (Blumler and McQuail, 1968; Semetko, 1992). During non-campaign periods the main opposition party, Conservative or Labour, has numerous opportunities in the House of Commons to raise questions and debate issues that bring the leader's and the party's viewpoints into the news. The main opposition party receives a boost onto largely equal footing in terms of visibility in television news once the election campaign begins. The earlier incarnations of the Liberal Democrats, known as the Liberal-Social Democrat Alliance in the British general elections in the 1980s, and as the Liberal Party prior to that, were much more often in the news during campaigns than in other periods.

BBC and ITV devoted approximately 60% of their flagship evening news programs during the 2005 general election campaign to political news. We are interested in determining whether television news reporting on the parties and their leaders had any influence on perceptions of the party leaders during the 2005 general election. Given the extent to which television news broadcasts play a role in informing the public about the campaign, it seems reasonable that the tone of television news coverage should influence public perceptions of candidates and party leaders in particular. We might further expect that the tone of television news coverage would have an unequal effect across candidates and party leaders. By 2005, Tony Blair and, perhaps to a lesser extent, Michael Howard were very much 'known quantities' about whom the British public had pre-established feelings, at least relative to the third-party leader, Charles Kennedy. This is borne out in BES polling. When asked prior to the campaign to assess their feelings toward the three major party leaders on a 0 (strongly dislike) to 10 (strongly like) scale, 44.9% of respondents rated Charles Kennedy a relatively neutral 4, 5 or 6, compared to 33.9% for Michael Howard and 27.8% for Tony Blair. Because the BES survey did not ask how familiar respondents were with the various candidates, it is impossible to know whether respondents' relative neutrality toward Kennedy was the result of a lack of familiarity or the product of a well-informed sense of neutrality, though we suspect the former possibility played a strong role. It stands to reason, then, that the tone of television coverage should be most important for Charles Kennedy.

To address the role of television news coverage in the 2005 campaign on influencing the perceptions of party leaders, we draw upon our content analysis of television news coverage of the campaign which captures both the visibility of the parties and leaders as political actors in the news and the tone of the news stories toward the political parties and their leaders. From these data we construct a simple statistical test of whether the favorability of the previous night's news coverage impacted assessments of candidates during the BES' rolling campaign survey.

Dependent Variable

Our dependent variables are questions 41, 42 and 43 from the 2005 BES rolling survey.[1] These questions are standard 'feeling thermometers' for each of the three major party leaders in the 2005 British general election. Full descriptive statistics for these and the other variables used in our statistical model can be found in Appendix 1. Question 41 from the survey, which is the feeling thermometer for Tony Blair, is reproduced in Figure 29.1.

Independent Variables

The primary independent variables measure the tone of television coverage from the preceding day's evening news. In the original content dataset, every television news story featured on the evening broadcast of either BBC or ITV was coded to register the relative prominence of the main actors in the story and the tone of the story toward each of these actors. To create the variables we use here, we included stories that featured the leader in question as one of the two most prominent actors. We used the tone of the story

Now, thinking about party leaders for a moment. Using a scale that runs from 0 to 10, where
0 means strongly dislike and 10 means strongly like, how do you feel about Tony Blair?

0 – Strongly dislike

1

2

3

4

5

6

7

8

9

10 – Strongly like

Don't know

**Figure 29.1   Measuring public attitudes towards UK party leaders: Question wording for the
11 point feeling thermometer**

toward the leader as another variable and discarded those that were neutral. Having isolated
those stories that featured a party leader prominently, and in a non-neutral tone, we took the
daily average of these measures to arrive at our
variables. For example, if there were a day in
which there was only one story featuring Tony
Blair in a non-neutral tone and that story had a
tone of 1, the day would be coded as 1 for Tony
Blair. If there were two stories featuring Tony
Blair in a non-neutral tone on a certain day and
these stories carried tones of 4 and 6 on the
7-point scale, where 1 is very unfavorable and 7 is
very favorable, that day would be coded as 5, and
so on for all days during the campaign and for all
three party leaders.

Control Variables

We use a battery of control variables to ensure that
the statistical relationships between party leader
assessments and the previous evening's news coverage are not spurious. Most notably, we control
for the responses given by the respondents to feeling thermometers of the party leaders before the
campaign began. By controlling for the respondent's attitude before the campaign began, we are
confident that our model is measuring shifts in
attitude toward the candidates that are plausibly
linked to the tone of television stories on the evening
news. We also include demographic controls for the
age of the respondent as well as dichotomous indicators coded as 1 if the respondent owns a home,
attended a university, is a minority or is female.

Statistical Model

We use an ordered probit specification to study
the relationship between the tone of news and
attitudes toward party leaders. Our dependent
variable is measured on a 10-point ordinal scale,
so our model could reasonably be estimated with
a linear regression model. In practice, the results
do not change in any significant way if a linear
regression model is used. Given that the variable
is not, strictly speaking, continuous, we prefer the
non-linear specification. We report estimates using
robust standard errors to guard against unspecified
forms of heteroskadasticity.

RESULTS

The results of the main models can be seen in
Table 29.3. Model 1 assesses the relationship
between the tone of the previous nights' television
coverage toward Charles Kennedy and respondent
attitudes toward Charles Kennedy in that day's
rolling BES survey. Models 2 and 3 repeat this
exercise for Tony Blair and Michael Howard,
respectively. Interestingly, and somewhat intuitively, given his lower profile and the lower profile
of his party in the news in the months leading up
to the election campaign, the tone of coverage in
the preceding day's evening news has a statistically significant effect on public evaluations of
Liberal Democrat leader Charles Kennedy only.
Public evaluations of Conservative leader Michael
Howard display a weakly significant *negative*

Table 29.3   Television news influences on attitudes toward the party leaders.

Variable	Coefficient (Std. Err.)	Coefficient (Std. Err.)	Coefficient (Std. Err.)
Dependent Variable: Likability of ...	Kennedy	Blair	Howard
pre-campaign attitudes toward candidate	0.492**	0.589**	0.555**
	(0.014)	(0.017)	(0.016)
favorability of coverage to Kennedy	0.090*	0.039	0.000
	(0.035)	(0.036)	(0.037)
favorability of coverage to Blair	0.010	−0.024	−0.040
	(0.028)	(0.030)	(0.031)
favorability of coverage to Howard	0.034	0.013	−0.060†
	(0.030)	(0.032)	(0.031)
age	−0.004**	−0.004**	0.000
	(0.002)	(0.002)	(0.002)
homeowner	−0.068	−0.027	0.065
	(0.053)	(0.052)	(0.056)
university	0.034	−0.094†	0.023
	(0.049)	(0.050)	(0.050)
minority	0.013	−0.044	−0.054
	(0.126)	(0.127)	(0.125)
gender	0.186**	0.070	0.012
	(0.044)	(0.045)	(0.046)
N	2209	2367	2249
Log-likelihood	−4006.191	−3628.436	−3614.269
$\chi^2_{(9)}$	1096.443	1322.737	1286.225

Significance levels: † : 10%; * : 5%; **: 1%

association with the tone of television coverage, though without a stronger level of statistical significance, we refrain from elaborating possible interpretations of this finding.[2] Opinions of incumbent Prime Minister and Labour leader Tony Blair appear to be completely impervious to the tone of television coverage.

Table 29.4 takes a closer look at the relationship between television coverage and support for Charles Kennedy. To do so, we split the sample into four groups according to their view of Charles Kennedy prior to the election. One sample includes respondents who reported a strongly negative view of Charles Kennedy prior to the campaign (feeling thermometer score of 2 or lower), respondents who reported a moderately negative view of Charles Kennedy prior to the election (feeling thermometer score between 3 and 5), respondents who reported a moderately positive view of Charles Kennedy before the election (feeling thermometer score between 6 and 7) and respondents with strongly positive view of Charles Kennedy prior to election (feeling thermometer score greater than 8). If, as we surmise, the large and statistically significant effect of television cover-

age on perceptions of Charles Kennedy is due to his being relatively unknown prior to the campaign, we would expect that this effect should be particularly pronounced among those who lacked strong opinions of Charles Kennedy prior to the campaign. Conversely, respondents who reported strong positive or negative feelings toward Charles Kennedy prior to the campaign should be relatively unmoved by news coverage.

The results of re-estimating model 1 using these restricted samples are noted in Table 29.4. In keeping with our expectations, news coverage has the largest and most statistically significant effect on perceptions of Charles Kennedy among those who claimed to be in the middle range of the 10-point scale or neutral toward Charles Kennedy prior to the election and in particular those who began the campaign with moderately positive views of Charles Kennedy. Notably, the much larger coefficients in models 5 and 6 suggest the increased statistical significance in these models is not simply an artifact of the larger sample size.[3]

While we believe the foregoing analysis is thought provoking, it is important to note some of

Table 29.4   Impact of the tone of television news on attitudes toward the Liberal Democrat Party leader, controlling for pre-campaign attitudes

Model #	Model 4		Model 5		Model 6		Model 7	
Attitude prior to elections	Negative		Moderately negative		Moderately positive		Positive	
Variable	Coefficient	SE	Coefficient	SE	Coefficient	SE	Coefficient	SE
Pre-campaign attitude toward Kennedy	0.510	0.081**	0.456	0.050**	0.352	0.084**	0.607	0.066**
Favorability of coverage toward Kennedy	0.005	0.120	0.102	0.056+	0.178	0.063**	0.052	0.078
Favorability of coverage toward Blair	0.012	0.072	0.012	0.046	−0.066	0.056	0.075	0.064
Favorability of coverage toward Howard	0.072	0.082	0.077	0.050	−0.056	0.052	0.096	0.068
Age	0.003	0.005	−0.007	0.003*	−0.006	0.003*	−0.002	0.004
Homeowner	−0.130	0.151	−0.047	0.085	−0.021	0.107	−0.076	0.111
University	0.122	0.163	0.044	0.084	0.084	0.088	−0.083	0.100
Minority	−0.022	0.291	−0.236	0.218	0.119	0.286	0.294	0.195
Female	0.349	0.128**	0.091	0.072	0.151	0.083	0.338	0.096**
N	290		819		621		479	
Log-likelihood	−517.711		−1514.786		−1109.355		−808.424	
Wald $\chi^2(9)$	56.500		96.550		34.770		120.340	

Significance levels: + 0.1%; * 0.05%; ** 0.01%

its limitations. First, we were not able to control for other forms of media coverage that respondents may have been exposed to. To the (likely) extent that there are significant correlations between the tone of coverage in the previous nights news broadcasts and the following mornings newspapers, for example, it is possible that effects that we are attributing to television news coverage may in fact be the joint product of television news and other media sources, or (less likely, we believe), the sole effect of other forms of media. Another limitation is that it is impossible to disentangle the subjective, or editorial, tone of the television news broadcast from the objective tone of the story being covered. For example, a scandal involving a party leader would, almost by necessity, take on a negative tone, though the negativity of the story would to some degree by influenced by presentational decisions made by ITV or BBC. Our measures conflate these two aspects of tone by necessity. As such, these results should not necessarily be interpreted as attributing a causal effect to television newsreaders themselves, separate from the stories they are covering.

However, our core findings of interest, that the tone of television news coverage correlates with perceptions of party leaders *only* for Charles Kennedy and, even then, *only* among respondents with previously neutral stances toward Charles Kennedy are unaffected by these limitations.

CONCLUSION

The idea that party leaders influence support for political parties is hardly new. Previous research on the British case suggests that leader images can indeed be important to vote choice. Bean and Mughan (1989: 1169–95) argue, for example, that the major party leaders had an electoral impact independent of party identification in the 1983 British and 1987 Australian general elections. Stewart and Clarke demonstrate that in the 1987 British general election campaign, perceived competence and responsiveness of the party leaders, particularly leaders of opposition parties, were important and they conclude that 'leader images had strong effects on party choice' (1992: 447). Mughan points out the conditionality of the effects of party leaders on vote choice: 'At one extreme, they may have no independent effects in, say, a highly polarized election where the partisan lines are clearly and uncompromisingly drawn. At the other extreme, however, leaders may be the difference between victory and defeat for their party when an election is closely fought' (2005: 1). Bartle and Crewe (2002) argue that the evidence for leadership effects on the vote nevertheless remains weak.

Our study shows that television news coverage did have an important and significant effect on perceptions of the third-party leader in 2005, especially among those who did not have strong feelings about him prior to the campaign. Might this have translated into support for the party at the polls? Given the Liberal Democrats' tactical voting campaign in 2005 and what was subsequently described as the party's 'counterproductive 'decapitation' strategy' (Worcester, 2005: 264–5), coupled with the sample design of the BES, it was not possible for us to address the question about whether liking the third-party leader support translated into a vote for the party.

Five years later, in an historic campaign, Labour Prime Minister Gordon Brown was defeated and the Liberal Democrats were ushered into a coalition government with the Conservatives after a campaign in which the third party was best placed to benefit from the main evening news coverage on the flagship programs. Television's most memorable moments in 2010, however, were found in the historic live party leader debates and in the

news coverage that followed. In each of the live television debates (one each on ITV, BBC and Sky), Liberal Democrat leader Nick Clegg was physically positioned center stage between Conservative Party leader David Cameron and incumbent Labour Party leader and Prime Minister Gordon Brown. In the much anticipated first debate with more than 10 million viewers, Clegg took every opportunity to present himself as the voice of "fairness" and viewers, as well as the media, quickly named him the winner: 'Election debate: Nick Clegg emerges victorious' (Wardrop, 2010). The physical set up of the debates likely reinforced Liberal Democrat leader Nick Clegg's strong rhetorical position in the debates against the establishment or the old two-party system.

The 2010 party leader debates served to magnify the favorable reporting of the Liberal Democrat leader, beyond what was found in our study of 2005 reporting of television news. Our findings from the 2005 general election campaign on the influence of television news on attitudes toward the third-party leader suggest a potentially powerful role for Britain's television news in future elections. As the UK general elections become more closely fought, and election outcomes are more likely to be coalitions rather that one-party governments, the potential for party leaders to influence outcomes may be, as Mughan (2005) suggested, the difference between victory and defeat.

Appendix 1: Descriptives

Variable	Mean	Standard deviation	Obs.
Likability of Blair	4.054	3.253	5916
Likability of Kennedy	5.434	2.471	5688
Likability of Howard	3.529	2.979	5726
Pre-survey likability of Blair	3.997	3.207	7548
Pre-survey likability of Kennedy	5.404	2.48	7036
Pre-survey likability of Howard	3.75	2.889	7190
Favorability of coverage toward Blair	3.639	0.672	3951
Favorability of coverage toward Kennedy	4.609	0.663	2687
Favorability of coverage toward Howard	3.714	0.743	3621
Gender	1.496	0.500	6068
Age	45.427	14.714	7782
Homeowner	0.724	0.446	7793
University	0.261	0.439	7794
Minority	0.041	0.199	7794
Partisanship	10.733	0.735	3481

NOTES

1   It is important to note that not every respondent answered all three of these questions, which leads to slightly different sample sizes for each dependent variable.

2   Were we to interpret this finding, we would draw upon research that shows that partisans' responses to political information about their preferred candidate are based on emotion rather than reason (Westen, 2007). This finding is based on experiments utilizing a functional MRI, which enables the researcher to see what parts of the brain are active (reason versus emotion) when processing political information. This experimental research supports what Beck et al. (2002: 62) described in survey and content based research on the influence of the press in the 1992 US presidential election as the 'hostile media phenomenon' which was found among Republicans in 1992 and 'produced systematic misperceptions of bias where it did not, based on our content analysis, actually exist.

3   In unreported tests, we estimated models of support for Blair and Howard using samples disaggregated according to pre-campaign feeling thermometers for both candidates. We found no evidence that television coverage impacts support for either candidate at any level of pre-campaign support.

REFERENCES

Aarts, K. and Semetko, H. A. (2003) 'The Divided Electorate: Effects of Media Use on Political Involvement', *The Journal of Politics*, 65(3): 759–84.

Bartle, J. and Crewe, I. (2002) 'The Impact of Party Leaders in Britain: Strong Assumptions, Weak Evidence', in A. King (ed.), *Leaders' Personalities and the Outcomes of Democratic Elections*. Oxford: Oxford University Press. pp. 70–95.

Bean, C. and Mughan, A. (1989) 'Leadership Effects in Parliamentary Elections: Australia and Britain', *American Political Science Review*, 83(2): 165–79.

Beck, P. A., Dalton, R. J., Greene, S. and Huckfeldt, R. (2002) 'The Social Calculus of Voting: Interpersonal, Media, and Organizational Influences on Presidential Choices', *American Political Science Review*, 96(1): 57–73.

Blumler, J. G. and McQuail, D. (1968) *Television in Politics: Its Uses and Influence*. London: Faber and Faber.

Clarke, H., Sanders, D., Stewart, M. and Whiteley, P.F. (2005) *British Election Study, 2005: Comparative Study of Electoral Systems* [computer file]. Colchester, Essex: UK Data Archive [distributor], November 2006. SN: 5495, http://dx.doi.org/10.5255/UKDA-SN-5495-1.

Clarke, H. D., Sanders, D., Stewart, M. C. and Whiteley, P. (2004) *Party Choice in Britain*. Oxford: Oxford University Press.

Curtice, J. and Semetko, H. A. (1994) 'Does it Matter What the Papers Say?', in A. Heath, R. Jowell and J. Curtice (eds.), *Labour's Last Chance? The 1992 Election and Beyond*. Aldershot: Dartmouth. pp. 43–64.

Electoral Commission (2005) 'Election 2005: Engaging the Public in Great Britain', http://www.electoralcommission.org.uk/files/dms/Engaging_19456-14157__E__S__W__.pdf

Graber, D. A. (2001). *Processing Politics: Learning from Television in the Internet Age*. Chicago, IL: University of Chicago Press.

Holbrook, T. (1996) *Do Campaigns Matter?* London: Sage.

Johnston, R., Blais, A., Brady, H. E. and Crete, J. (1992) *Letting the People Decide: Dynamics of a Canadian Election*. Montreal: McGill-Queen's Press.

Johnston, R., Hagen, M. G., Jamieson, K. H. (2004) *The 2000 Presidential Election and the Foundations of Party Politics*. New York: Cambridge University Press.

Lasarsfeld, P. F. Berelson, B. R. and Gaudet, H. (1948) *The People's Choice*. New York: Columbia University Press.

Mughan, A. (2005) 'On the Conditionality of Leader Effects', paper presented at the 2005 EPOP meeting. University of Essex, 9–11 September.

Mughan, A. (2001) *Media and the Presidentialization of Parliamentary Elections*. London: Macmillan.

Nadeau, R., Nadeau, N., Blais, A. and Gidengil, E. (2008) 'Election Campaigns as Information Campaigns: Who Learns What and Does It Matter', *Political Communication*, 25(3): 229–48.

Norris, P. and Wlezien, C. (eds.) (2005) *Britain Votes*. Oxford: Oxford University Press.

Norris, P., Curtice, J., Sanders, D., Scammell, M. and Semetko, H. A. (1999) *On Message: Communicating the Campaign*. London: Sage.

Sanders, D., Clarke, H., Steward, M. and Whiteley, P. (2003) 'The Electoral Impact of the 2001 UK General Election Campaign', paper presented at the Societa Italiana di Studi Elettorali, VIII Convegno Internazionale, Le campagne elettorali. Venice International University, 18–20 December.

Sanders, D., Clarke, H., Steward, M. and Whiteley, P. (2004) *Party Choice in Britain*. Oxford: Oxford University Press.

Scammell, M. (1995) *Designer Politics*. London: Macmillan.

Scammell, M. (1999) 'Political Marketing: Lessons for Political Science', *Political Studies*, 47(4): 718–39.

Semetko, H. A. (1989) 'Television News and the "Third Force" in British Politics: A Case Study of Election Communication', *European Journal of Communication*, 4(4): 453–81.

Semetko, H. A. (1992) 'Broadcasting and Election Communication in Britain', in F. J. Fletcher (ed.), *Media, Elections and Democracy*, Vol. 19 of the research studies of the Canadian Royal Commission on Electoral Reform and Party Financing. Toronto: RCERPF and Dundurn. pp. 25–62.

Semetko, H. A. (2000) 'Great Britain: The End of the News at Ten and the Changing News Environment', in R. Gunther and A. Mughan (eds.), *Democracy and the Media: A Comparative Perspective*. Cambridge: Cambridge University Press. pp. 343–74.

Semetko, H. A., Van der Brug, W. and Valkenburg, P. (2003) 'The Influence of Political Events on Attitudes towards the EU', *British Journal of Political Science*, 33(4): 621–34.

Stewart, M. C. and Clarke, H. D. (1992) 'The (Un)Importance of Party Leaders: Leader Images and Party Choice in the 1987 British Election', *The Journal of Politics*, 54(2): 447–70.

Wardrop, M. (2010) 'Election Debate: Nick Clegg Emerges Victorious', *Daily Telegraph*, http://www.telegraph.co.uk/ news/election-2010/7596176/Election-debate-Nick-Clegg-emerges-victorious.html (accessed 10 May 2010).

Westen, D. (2007) *The Political Brain: The Role of Emotion in Deciding the Fate of the Nation*. New York: Public Affairs Books.

Worcester, R., Mortimore, R. and Baines, P. (2005) *Explaining Labour's Landslip: The 2005 General Election*. London: Methuen.

30

The Interdependency of Mass Media and Social Movements

Rens Vliegenthart and Stefaan Walgrave

This chapter provides an overview of the large literature on social movements and the mass media. While mass media are of course an important player all kinds of other communication channels – especially new media and the internet – are relevant for social movements as well. They are discussed in other chapters in this Handbook (Bimber, Chapter 9, and Bennett et al., Chapter 10, in this Handbook). There is a large amount of theoretical and empirical work on the relationship and interaction between social movements and the mass media. Remarkably enough, one does not find many of those publications in the journals and book volumes scholars interested in political communication turn to. Research about social movements is mainly generated by sociologists and much of the research on movements and media is found in sociological journals and books. Maybe as a consequence, there is little knowledge in the field of political communication about the relevant work movement scholars conduct, apart from maybe some of the work by people such as Bill Gamson and Todd Gitlin. The lack of integration of both fields is especially striking, since a lot of the questions that are addressed in the specialized social movement literature are very similar. Movement scholars are interested in media selection processes to understand when, why and how social movements and their protest events make it into the news. They conduct large-scale content analyses to map and describe the coverage of movements, their issues and their actions. And increasingly, they look at movement outcomes

and investigate how media content might affect their successes in terms of mobilization and the achievement of political goals. At least partly, students of social movements use a similar terminology as political communication scholars. For example, *framing* is one of the key concepts in the research relating to movements and their communication techniques. It has the same roots as framing in political communication and it is used by social movements scholars in ways that are comparable to its use in political communication.

The main difference between the two realms is that the object of study differs. While political communication scholars are mostly interested in the institutional, organized and 'routine' side of politics and their focus is on political parties, politicians and elections, movement scholars focus on the non-institutional, the non-organized and contentious side of politics. This has important implications in terms of the power balance between the media and the political actors that are studied. Because of the fact that politicians have a clear institutional power base – due to representation in parliament, participation in government and other democratic institutions – they almost automatically carry a certain relevance for journalists. In contrast, social movements, almost by definition, do *not* have an institutional power base and, consequently, have to struggle harder for attention for their events, issues and claims. They have to 'demonstrate' in different ways – by staging events, mobilizing publics and public opinion or by making valid claims – that they are newsworthy.

We will show that social movements have less access to the mass media than institutional political actors but that they, at the same time, are more dependent on the mass media to get their message across. Despite this important difference between the political communication of social movements and of, for example, political parties, we believe that research into the interaction between movements and media is highly relevant for political communication in general; many of the dynamics described in this chapter have their equivalents in the research into relations between media and institutional political actors.

We begin by discussing the relation between movements and media and why this relationship can be seen as one of mutual dependency. After that, we look into detail to the research that has been done on various elements of this relationship. We adopt a classic political communication process approach and discuss *causes* of media coverage of social movements and the protest they stage, the *content* of media coverage of movements/protest and the various *consequences* of media coverage for social movements/protest.

WHY SOCIAL MOVEMENTS NEED MASS MEDIA (AND VICE VERSA)

One of the first scholars to analyze the importance of the mass media for social movements was Todd Gitlin. In his seminal book *The Whole World is Watching* (1980), he describes the interaction between mass media and the US New Left movement in the sixties. Gitlin documents how the media and their framing of the movement initially helped it to gain broader support. However, the requirements for movement events to have characteristics that make them newsworthy – such as drama, conflict and personalization – made the movements' main leaders increasingly focus on media strategies. Intensive coverage of internal struggles and anomalies within the movement ultimately resulted in erosion of its public support. Gitlin's study clearly demonstrates the problematic nature of the relationship between movements and media: on the one hand, movements need media more than other political actors to mobilize potential supporters, gain public support for their claims and, ultimately, political change ('send my message'). On the other hand, mass media need movements since they stage newsworthy events, they 'make news' ('make my news'). But the interests of movement actors and journalists most often do not coincide. As movements are interested in getting their message out their aim is to direct the media's (and the public's) attention to

an issue, journalists often do not focus on the problem or issue the movement is signaling, but rather consider other things newsworthy. They are, for example, more interested in covering the violent characteristics of contentious confrontations, the internal conflicts in the movement, or personal details about movement leaders. In many ways, the interaction between movements and media resemble that between politicians and journalists.

However, due to the non-institutional position of social movements the relationship between movements and the media is inherently more asymmetrical than the interaction between politicians and the media. News media prefer to rely on sources with a political power base – these sources provide the 'official' story – and will usually take these political elite views as the starting point of their coverage (Bennett, 1990; Gamson, 1992; Gamson and Modigliani, 1989; Gamson et al., 1992; Gans, 1980). Movements have to fight to get attention and when they get covered, it is far from certain that the news takes over their frame or interpretation of the issue (Smith et al., 2001). While the movements' position vis-à-vis the media is disadvantageous and getting favorable coverage is in many instances an uphill struggle, it is of crucial importance. Compared to political parties movements very often have a weak membership base and little other communication means – though it can be argued that the latter has changed due to the rise of new media and the Internet (see Bimber, Chapter 9, in this Handbook). Hence, in order to target their audiences movements need the mass media more than any other political actor. Moreover, the only real means of influencing policies most social movements have – apart from those movements that have become political 'insiders' or that have the power to disrupt social and political life – is playing on public opinion. Movements essentially mobilize the public, or at least their constituents, to show to the power holders that large numbers of people do not agree and want change (or no change). Without public support social movements are powerless and their actions toothless. It is, among other means, via the mass media that movements can reach out to both potential protest participants and to the public at large (Gamson, 2004). Institutional political actors such as political parties do not need the media so much as they can enact policies even without public support.

Some even argue that the entire interaction between social movements and political authorities takes place not as real-life encounters, but rather through claims made in the mass media. Rather than in real-life encounters, social movements interact with the authorities via the media: authorities learn about the movements and their protest via the media while the movements learn about political opportunities through media coverage of the actions (or absence thereof) of targeted political elites (Koopmans, 2004).

Since media coverage is so crucial for social movements, students of social movements have studied quite extensively what strategies movements employ to get into the media. Dieter Rucht, for example, describes the media strategies of social movements since the 1960s and distinguishes four different strategies: abstention (no attempts to get in the media), attack (critique on mass media), adaptation (exploitation of mass media rules) and alternatives (create own movement media) (Rucht, 2004). This chapter mainly deals with adaptation strategies, which can be argued to be for many movements the most important ones.

The extensive literature on movements and the media documents that movement scholars deal with very similar questions as political communication scholars dealing with parties, parliaments and governments do. First, they focus on the direct movement–media interaction and look at the strategies movements and their leaders use to obtain media coverage and get into the news. Second, they look at the content of movements' claims and especially of the protest events they stage and how these are covered in the mass media. And third, they look at the possible consequences of media coverage – on support for the movement (mobilization), on politicians and policy makers and on public opinion (Gamson and Wolfsfeld, 1993).

GETTING INTO THE NEWS

Scholars in political communication need little introduction to the mechanisms that determine why certain events or actors get coverage while others do not. News values, the gatekeeping function of the mass media, and fierce competition over the limited available space in the media (Hilgartner and Bosk, 1988) are a daily reality for social movements. Every day, hundreds of messages are send by all kind of movements in the hope that they will be picked up by journalists and editors (Koopmans, 2004). What then, determines the successful penetration of movement messages in the media?

One of the most often employed tools for movements is the organization of protest activities. Considerable research has dealt with determining the characteristics of protest events that result in media coverage. Studies have focused on the possible selection bias of media coverage of protest events – looking at the question what determines whether or not an issue makes it into

the news – and on the potential description bias – what information about the event is (erroneously) reported.

Research into *selection* bias has identified four factors that explain why some events are covered and others not (Earl et al., 2004; Oliver and Maney, 2000). These factors are *event* characteristics, *news agency* characteristics, *issue* characteristics and *time* characteristics. Regarding the first, scholars find that events that are staged in proximity of a news outlet's main office are likely to receive more attention in that outlet (McCarthy et al., 1996; Mueller, 1997). Furthermore, also the size of the event is of importance: higher protest turnout results in more coverage (Oliver and Myers, 1999). Additionally, intensity, violence, the presence of police, counter-demonstrations and the social movement organization that organizes the event are all factors that affect the quantity of coverage (Barranco and Wisler, 1999; Myers and Caniglia, 2004; Oliver and Maney, 2000). Second, news agency characteristics, such as news routines in both the production process (Gamson, 1992) and among reporters (Oliver and Myers, 1999) affect the likelihood that the event is covered. For example, events that are planned in such a way that journalists can write about it before the newspaper's daily deadline, that are not staged simultaneously with other events and that are communicated well in advance to journalists are more likely to receive coverage (Oliver and Myers, 1999; Ryan, 1991). Third, issue type matters: events on issues that receive more media attention in general and are higher on the issue attention cycle (Downs, 1972) are more likely to be covered (McCarthy et al., 1996). Also events that deal with issues that are simultaneously discussed by politicians and legislators are more likely to be covered (Oliver and Maney, 2000). Rucht and Verhulst (2010), for example, show that the anti-war protests in 2003 were comparatively more covered in countries in which the government officially opposed war (German and Belgium) compared to countries where the government supported war (the UK, USA, Spain, Italy). Finally, time matters as well: the day on which the event is staged affects the likelihood of coverage: Monday events are more likely to be covered (Myers and Caniglia, 2004; Oliver and Maney, 2000) and, in the USA, protest is less likely to be covered when the legislator is in session (Oliver and Maney, 2000).

Description bias received way less scholarly attention than selection bias. Smith and et al. (2001) established that media outlets make quite some mistakes in reporting about the 'hard' facts of demonstrations – though newspapers are more accurate than television broadcasts – and focus mainly on the disruptive strategies movements use instead of on their claims.

Remarkably, many students of social movements see the selection and description bias not as phenomena that have to be studied in their own right but rather as data problems. Instead of taking the variation in coverage as an starting point to theorize about the relationships between protest and mass media, the main question that drives most investigations is how useful media data, especially newspaper data, are to serve as an 'objective' measure for the occurrence and characteristics of protest events (see, among others, the discussions in Earl et al., 2004; McCarthy et al., 2008; Ortiz et al., 2005; Strawn, 2008). Large-scale content analyses, mainly of newspaper coverage, are regularly carried out (early examples include Tarrow, 1989; Tilly, 1978; more recent ones are Rucht et al., 1999; Rucht and Verhulst, 2010; Soule and Earl, 2005). Methodological discussions relating to protest events analysis resolve around the earlier mentioned selection and description bias, as well as sampling of newspapers and days to get a representative picture of movement activity (Koopmans and Rucht, 2002). The resulting data on protest have been used in many groundbreaking studies, especially those that focus on political opportunity structures, one of the classical theories in the study of social movements (some of the most well-known examples include Kriesi et al., 1995; McAdam, 1982). The result of this predominant focus on media as source of information on protest events is fairly little theorizing about the mechanisms that affect the biased selection and description of protest events. Noteworthy exceptions in this respect are the studies of Oliver and Maney (2000) and Oliver and Myers (1999), who relate their findings to existing theories with regard to news holes, journalistic practices and selection mechanisms referring elaborately to the journalism and political communication literature.

Only a few studies look beyond the coverage of protest events and discuss the coverage of social movement *organizations* and their issues. An interesting example is the study by Amenta et al. (2009) who content analyzed a century of *The New York Times* coverage of the US social movements and try to explain why social movement organizations receive attention. The authors find that disruptive strategies and resource mobilization contribute to frequent appearance. Also when there have been recent policy changes that favor a social movement's constituency, the result is more media attention for the movement.

In sum, many of the findings relating to the question when movements and their activities receive media coverage are entirely in line with theories that discuss the gatekeeping function of journalists, news values and news routines. Movements and their events have a hard time

getting passed the news gates (many events do not get any coverage at all), they need to score high on the news values to get coverage (for example, disruptiveness, numbers, violence) and they need to tap into the news routines of the newsmakers (for example, easy access, close to media headquarter, announced beforehand) to increase the chance of being covered. These rules of the 'media game' are clearly important for social movements, probably even more so than for political actors with an institutional power base and with better access to the public. Additionally, movements' opportunities to get into the media are often constrained and sometimes facilitated by the external political and institutional context in which the movement operates. Even when a movement follows the exact 'recipe' to get media coverage by staging a 'mediagenic' event, external political circumstances still affects its chances of being successful (for example, political attention cycle, legislator in session, counter-mobilization). Hence, movements must not only take into account the rules of the media game as such, but also the larger political context and the potential reactions of adversaries.

SOCIAL MOVEMENTS IN THE NEWS

Fewer studies than the ones tackling movements' access to the mass media focus on *how* social movements, their protests and the issues they put forward are covered in the mass media. In general, ideas and research regarding *framing* are well established in this area. Students rely considerably on to the earlier mentioned work by Gitlin (1980) and Gamson (1992), as well as on David Snow and Robert Benford (1988), whose work on framing tasks and frame alignment (Snow et al., 1986) has been very influential. Their itemization of frames in a diagnostic (what is the problem and who is responsible?), prognostic (what is the solution and who needs to take care of it?) and motivational (a call for collective action) aspect has been widely considered as a useful starting point to analyze media coverage (for example, Rohlinger, 2002, 2006; Snow et al., 2007).

When investigating media framing of social movements and their issues, studies have looked at strategies employed by movements to receive coverage in line with their frames and at the political context that contributes to this. Rohlinger (2002), for example, looks at several pro-life and pro-choice organizations in the US abortion debate. She finds that media strategies of movement organization, such as the use of frames that resonate with wider societal debates, as well as establishing an organizational structure that fosters an efficient interaction with journalists, contribute to media framing that is in line with the framing of the organization. Furthermore, she finds that movement organizations adjust their media strategies depending upon the political context: in a favorable political context where access to the political elite exists, organizations choose deliberately to stay silent in order not to start any public discussions and thus maximize political gains. In less favorable times when they are denied access to politics, organizations seek the media and choose to work with allies (Rohlinger, 2006).

Another example of a study looking into the impact of social movements on media's issue framing is the research by Terkildsen et al. (1998). Based on a content analysis of, again, the abortion debate coverage in the major US media outlets during the 1960s and 1970s, they show that media coverage often takes over frames that had been initiated by the pro- and anti-abortion groups; most media frames could be traced back to at least one interest group within the larger pro- or anti-abortion movement. The authors claim that the media may sometimes 'invent' frames but that most of the time the terms of the debate are set by organizations that strategically produce issue frames. The study, however, also stresses the autonomous role of the media by selectively and repetitively opening its gates for specific groups. Also, as the conflict and the issue matures, the media start playing a gradually more active role and are more reluctant to embrace movement frames.

An example of work that addresses a similar question, but focuses specifically at protest events is the study of Smith and colleagues on the coverage of protest events in Washington, DC, in 1982 and 1991. They conclude that when movements get attention because of their protest events '... the reports represent the protest events in ways that neutralize or even undermine social movement agendas' (Smith et al. 2001: 1398). They find that protest event coverage tends to focus on the drama of the event and the details of the event itself (for example, violence, arrests) and movements seem to fail to draw attention to the issue they mobilize for. In political communication terms: mass media tend to frame protest 'episodically' while movements' aims would be most served by a 'thematic' framing (Iyengar and Kinder, 1987). This work supports earlier work by McLeod and Hertog (1992) that shows that protest is often subtly described by reporters as being deviant highlighting the divide between protesters and the public.

In contrast, Rucht and Verhulst's (2010) case study of how the demonstrations against the war on Iraq on 15 February 2003 were covered in eight countries points out that movements do not always have to complain about the media coverage they get. They write: 'The February 15 demonstrations received a newspaper coverage of which most organizers only can dream of: protests were said not only to be the largest ever seen, but in addition, attracted ordinary people from all parts of the country and all layers of society' (Rucht and Verhulst 2010: 255). The newspapers gave ample of attention to the slogans, claims and frames of the protesters and highlighted their arguments against war on Iraq.

In line with the earlier mentioned study of Gitlin, Liesbet van Zoonen's (1992) study of the relation between the Dutch women movement and the media demonstrates that news media tend to exaggerate differences and conflicts within the movement and focus on the feminist side of the movement, which does not work in its advantage. However, she argues that even in a situation where the dominant media frame differs considerable from the movement frame, social movements have opportunities to express their ideas and opinions in the mass media.

Other authors have made similar arguments that, even when media framing may not be directly supportive for the movement, getting in the news creates in any case occasions to express a movement's views and fosters responses by other political actors. Theoretically and methodologically, this idea has been elaborated by Koopmans and Statham (1999) who developed a method of media content analysis, which they labeled 'political claims analysis', examining the claims that social movements and other political actors make through violent acts, protest, public statements, etc. In later work, Koopmans (2004) theoretically develops the idea of 'discursive opportunities' for groups that put forward claims and challenge political elites. Through these discursive opportunities – essentially windows of increased media coverage for movements, their issues and claims – movements get access to the news. Such a temporary opening of the media gates is related to the legitimacy of the movement's claim (the extent to which other actors respond supportive to the message) and its resonance (the number of responses of other actors).

The study of media coverage of social movements resembles in many ways the classic political communication studies of, for example, election campaign coverage. There is an interest in visibility of actors and their issues and in the frames they manage (or not) to get across in the media. The available research emphasizes the role of movements' own activities in getting the message across (agency), as well as the political context (structure) that influences the way movements and their issues are presented in the news.

Movements can be successful in gaining favorable coverage, they can generate frames of the contentious issue that are picked up in the media, but the media do tend to be tough to convince as journalists are often more interested in the personal and conflictual peculiarities of the movement than in its message. Movements must take advantage of discursive opportunities that are not in their own hands but depend on the way other actors react to their claims generating a temporary cycle of news attention.

CONSEQUENCES OF NEWS

Following the influential article by Gamson and Wolfsfeld (1993), consequences of media coverage of social movements and protest can be roughly classified in three categories. First, media can have an impact on the direct sympathizers and exert an influence on a wide variety of actual forms of participation of these people – ranging from joining protest activities to making financial donations. This can be labeled the *mobilizing* function of the mass media. Second, media coverage legitimizes the existence of the movement and its claims, making it a relevant actor for those holding political power. In that way, media coverage is a requirement for movements to affect politicians, policymakers and the political agenda and decision-making processes. Gamson and Wolfsfeld label this the *validation* function of the media. The third purpose for which movements need media coverage is *scope enlargement*. If the movement is successful in getting its claims and demands in the media, it draws attention to the conflict from actors that were not previously involved and can function as an ally. The main relevant actor might well be the general public (Gamson, 2004). A favorable opinion from an involved public is one of the key legitimizing sources for the movements' claims and a powerful tool to exert political influence. In this section, we will consecutively deal with mass media's role in movements' *mobilization*, with how mass media can be instrumental for movements to help them reach their *political* goals, and with how mass media coverage can create a favorable *public* opinion toward movements and/or their issues.

Mass Media and Mobilization

The mobilizing function mass media have been demonstrated in several studies, looking at a wide range of coverage characteristics and protest activities. In their study of the spread of anti-immigrant violence in Germany, Koopmans and Olzak (2004) demonstrate that the previously mentioned discursive opportunity structure matters: visibility of claims by radical-right actors and anti-immigrant claims by other actors foster violent behavior against asylum seekers and other immigrants, while anti-radical right statements decrease the occurrence of violent events. In a similar vein, Vliegenthart et al. (2005) demonstrate that the visibility of Dutch environmental organizations in newspapers contribute to increases in their membership figures. Smith (1999) found that more than one-fourth of the members of Friends of the Earth became member after viewing media coverage of this environmental movement organization.

Several recent studies have conceptualized the mobilizing role of media within a *diffusion* framework (Soule, 2004): by considering the mass media an indirect tie between sender and receiver, the coverage of (successes of) certain protest tactics might result in an adoption of those tactics by groups elsewhere, which is called a diffusion process. Myers (2000), for example, focuses on the distribution of media outlets across the US cities in the period 1964–71. He demonstrates that riots that take place in cities that have their own network affiliated television station are more likely to diffuse than riots that take place in cities that do not have such a television channel. Very similarly but in a different context, Braun and Vliegenthart (2009) show that media attention for fan violence in the four weeks preceding a soccer match in the Dutch competition increases the chance that fan sides will get involved in collective violent behavior (see also Braun and Vliegenthart, 2008). Andrews and Biggs (2006), finally, focus on the spread of the 'sit-in' as a protest tactic among the US equal rights movement in the 1960s. Using circulation figures of newspapers, they demonstrate that also in this case, media can be considered as an important transmitter of information about protest events taking place at different locations.

Another perspective on the potential mobilizing role of the mass media focuses on the idea of 'collective identity' and how mass media may contribute to establishing such an identity. In fact, social movement scholars agree that for people to take action together they must have a kind of 'we'-feeling, a distinct feeling of belonging together (often opposed to a 'them'). Such a collective identity can be constructed. Studies have investigated to what extent and how mass media coverage may contribute to creating such a 'collective identity frame' (Gamson, 1995). An example of such a study is the work by Roscigno and Danaher (2001), who investigated the textile workers' insurgency in the South of the US in 1929–34. Internet nor television existing, and with hardly any organizations in the form of unions, the textile workers collective identity that led to strikes was co-produced by the advent of local radio stations that played songs about working in the textile mills featuring textile workers.

Also when it comes to investigating the mobilizing role of media coverage, scholars of social movements have relied on the framing theory. The theoretical argument has been made by Gamson (1995) who states that all three 'collective action frames' – sets of beliefs that inspire and nurture collective action – are strongly affected by media coverage. Media coverage can nurture the feeling of injustice and fuel the preparedness of taking action by, for example, dramatizing and personalizing responsibility for the grievance. Media can spur the feeling of agency by, sometimes, depicting citizens that can alter the conditions and terms of their daily lives. Media can contribute to feelings of collective identity by describing the aggrieved groups as unitary and by defining clear adversaries.

Cooper (2002) investigated peace protest in Germany and compared several waves of peace protest. She finds that the size of these protest waves is associated with the interpretative frames of the issue in the German media: when mass media and movements concur in their framing of the (peace) issue, mobilization is facilitated and the protest wave is larger. But media framing can not only contribute but also thwart a movement's mobilization efforts. Entman and Rojecki (1993) investigated the media framing of the US anti-nuclear movement in the 1980s. They show that *The New York Times* and *Time* magazine provided unfavorable coverage of the nuclear freeze movement (focusing on the emotionality of its appeals, the absence of expertise, the non-political nature of its demands, the impotency of its actions, the disunity in the movement, etc.). As a consequence, although supported by the majority of citizens, mobilization remained limited. What the media did according to Entman and Rojecki, was not eroding the support for the issue of the movement – support remained fairly stable over time – but rather discouraging people from participating in the movement by creating the impression that they adhered to a minority point of view and that their potential efforts would be in vain.

Most studies deal with how mass media, through their 'normal' and non-partisan coverage, unintentionally contribute to the turnout social movements can realize. Increased mobilization is considered as a side-product of routine coverage. Yet, sometimes, under specific circumstances, mass media seem to willingly mobilize in support of a (weakly organized) movement. Walgrave and Manssens (2005) analyze the case of the White March in Belgium, the biggest collective action

event ever happening in that country, and show how the newspapers not only amplified the triggering events that sparked the mobilization (child kidnappings and murders) but that they also, and apparently deliberately, mobilized people to participate in the march. They referred extensively to the White March as a 'solution' to their anger, they stressed that there would be no violence, they printed posters that announced the march and they stated beforehand that the march would be a big success. Arguably, such an active mobilizing role of the media is exceptional and remains confined to instances where there are no strong movement organizations that can mobilize themselves, where there is no countermovement, and where the issue is a valence issue. These circumstances are not that exceptional, however. Research on the Million Mom March in the USA, the marches of the Movement Against Senseless Violence in the Netherlands and the Anti-Gun movement in the UK – all mobilizations in reaction to random violence – has lead to similar observations of active media mobilization (Walgrave and Verhulst, 2006).

Although the media do most of the time not act as directly mobilizing agencies, they are often indirectly instrumental in spreading the information that a protest event is planned. Mobilization is often described as the link between supply and demand of protest. Aggrieved people search for a way to let their voices be heard (demand), movement organizations stage protest events (supply) (Klandermans, 2004). Bringing demand and supply together requires communication and information. Depending on the context, many potential participants receive the mobilizing word via the mass media. Several studies based on protest surveys, direct surveys with people demonstrating, have shown that many of the participants got informed about the upcoming event via the mass media (Walgrave and Klandermans, 2010; Walgrave and Verhulst, 2009).

Mass Media and Political Elites

Mass media coverage may not only be advantageous (or disadvantageous) for mobilization but it may also have a direct impact on political elites and on how they respond to the protest. In terms of political elites' direct reaction to the protest itself, Giugni and Wisier (1999) examined protest policing and media coverage of protest events in Switzerland. Their results suggest that mass media coverage works against repression. When protest gets a lot of media attention – it is 'under the spotlights' – authorities are less willing to resort to repression against the events as violence may create adversarial attitudes among the population (and further reinforce the movement's support).

In a broader perspective, these results can be connected to a larger theme in the social movements literature regarding the action repertoire of social movements. Especially, the work by Charles Tilly has proved to be very influential in this regard. In one of his last books, Tilly (2006) elaborates the notion of so-called 'WUNC'-displays. WUNC is an acronym referring to the typical traits of collective action by social movements: collective action should display 'Worthiness', 'Unity', 'Numbers' and 'Commitment'. Implicitly, Tilly suggests that the more WUNC a collective action is, the more it will impress the power holders and the larger the chance that it will result in political change (or in preserving the status quo). It is clear that political elites, most of the time, do not directly observe collective action; but learn about it primarily via mass media coverage. This implies that the more a collective action event is described by journalists as consisting of many worthy, united and committed participants, the more the event will impress power holders and the larger the chance that they will act accordingly. In this sense, the picture sketched by the mass media of the protest has potentially large effects for their effectiveness. It is no coincidence, then, that movement spokespersons, journalists and police, after an event, often engage in verbal battles about the numbers of people that showed up (McPhail and McCarthy, 2004).

There are few studies that try to measure directly to what extent media coverage of movements, their issues and their protest events affect political elites and the policies they enact. An exception is a recent study by Walgrave and Vliegenthart (2012) who show that mass media act as an intermediary actor. In a study in Belgium 1993–2000, they assess the agenda-setting power of protest: when people demonstrate, does the issue they turn to the streets for receive more attention in parliament and government in the subsequent period? Their results support the idea that media coverage matters for protest effectiveness. Protest has a direct effect on the political agenda but the media largely act as an intermediary: protest is often picked up by the media leading to an increase of attention to the issue; this, in turn, leads to substantial effects on the parliamentary and governmental agendas. Earlier work by Costain and Majstorovic (1994) pointed in a similar direction. They argue that the movement's rights movement legislative successes were the consequence of a congruent effect of movement activities and media coverage (and public opinion).

Mass Media and Public Opinion

Can social movements, via the mass media, impact public opinion? Many studies in the broad realm of political communication have claimed that media frames have an effect on the audience and may change what people think about particular issues (Scheufele and Tewksbury, 2007). The same most likely applies to the frames social movements want to communicate to the public. When movements manage to get their frames in the news, it is likely that (parts of) the public will develop attitudes that are favorable to the movement's issue. In a previous section, we showed that movements sometimes are successful and can inject new ideas and frames into the public debate and the media. So, one can assume that movements may sometimes reach and affect the public via the media. But studies directly investigating this triadic relationship are rare.

An exception is a study by Terkildsen and Schnell (1997). They examined how mass media outlets in the USA from the 1960s onward framed the feminist struggle. The five frames they discerned in real media coverage where then embedded in an experiment to see whether these 'real' frames had an impact on the public. They found that these frames indeed had a substantial impact on the subjects. Most frames generated a significant negative or positive impact on the saliency and direction of subjects' attitudes regarding women's rights. The study thus shows that when movements' issues are framed in a certain way in the media, that this framing affects public opinion in favor or against the movement.

Specifically related to protest coverage, McLeod (1995) found that how protest is covered affects how people perceive protest. Experimental subjects were shown two slightly different television stories of the same protest event. These differences in framing and focus of coverage led to significant differences in subjects' perceptions of the protesters and their legitimacy. In a follow-up study, McLeod and Detenber (1999) set up a similar experiment on news coverage of anarchist protests. They suggest that differences in coverage not only lead to differences in identification with the protesters, but more generally to more/less support for the right of people to protest and to different levels of support for the issue at stake. In short, framing of protest in the media leads to more or less support for the status quo.

From a much more general perspective, Gamson (1995) has convincingly argued that movements need mass media discourse in order to be able to connect with public opinion. Gamson not only states that movements can reach the audience *via* the mass media but that a shared understanding created by the media is a precondition to reach, via the media or not via the media, the audience. Media coverage, not specifically on social movements but in general, creates a kind of common understanding and knowledge that can be used by social movements to mobilize. Media provide the common background and make sure the public and movements speak the same language and refer to the same events. In short, social movements draw on available media discourse to create 'collective action frames' that are a necessary precondition to turn parts of the public into participants.

Wrapping up the section on the consequences of media coverage for social movements, we can state that research is well developed especially when it comes to mobilization. Ample research has convincingly shown that media coverage has a positive effect on mobilization for protest and recruitment in movement organizations. The mechanisms are diverse and range from diffusion processes over information dissemination to direct and deliberate mobilization by the media. Far fewer studies have investigated the direct effects of movement or protest coverage on political elites and their policies. The available studies suggest that media coverage also affects the political outcomes of social movements: media act as an intermediary conveying the protest to political elites who perceive movements only in their mediatized form. Finally, a few experimental studies established that the way protests are covered in the news has considerable effects on the perception of the staging movement, on its legitimacy and on the support for the movement's issue.

CONCLUSION

We begun this chapter by contending that mass media are of crucial importance for social movements. Even more than any other political actor, movements are highly dependent on media coverage to reach their constituency, to turn bystanders into potential participants and to convey their message to the protest targets. After reviewing the research literature, it is obvious that our initial claim is warranted by the facts; media are key for movements. One could even state that it is difficult to imagine that social movements would exist without the mass media (we would in any case not be aware of their existence).

A second observation is that social movement scholars are dealing extensively with the mass media. The research field is vast and quickly expanding. We could only review a part of this exhaustive literature here. The largest stream in the movements and media literature, deals with mass media as a source of information about movements and their events. Apart from that, by far most work has been focusing on how and under what circumstances social movements get access to the news. We know quite well why some movements get coverage while the public remains oblivious concerning others. That work is entirely in line with mainstream communication research on news values and news routines. Another substantial body of studies examines the effects of media coverage on mobilization. Some fields of research have developed to a much lesser extent. Concurring with the relatively poor performance of social movement scholarship when it comes to assessing the political impact social movements have, we know relatively little whether and how coverage of social movements affects their political outcomes. We have every reason to expect that media are an important interface relaying protest with political elites but we hardly have studies that scrutinize this relationship empirically. This probably is where movement and media studies can still make most progress.

Finally, the most remarkable conclusion is the 'splendid isolation' of students of social movements dealing with media on the one hand and the mainstream political communication scholarship on the other. Both communities deal with largely similar questions – how do political actors get into news, how are they covered and with what effect? – they do so relying on similar theoretical approaches – framing, gatekeeping, diffusion – and they even draw on identical methods – content analyses, case studies, experimental designs – but they do not seem to be really on speaking terms. We hope this chapter increases the awareness among students of political communication that there is an entire community of like-minded scholars tackling very similar questions that may be worthwhile to turn to.

REFERENCES

Amenta, E., Caren, N., Olasky, S. J. and Stobaugh, J. E. (2009) 'All the Movements Fit to Print: Who, What, When, Where, and Why SMO Families Appeared in the New York Times in the Twentieth Century', *American Sociological Review*, 74(4): 636–56.

Andrews, K. T. and Biggs, M. (2006) 'The Dynamics of Protest Diffusion: Movement Organizations, Social Networks, and News Media in the 1960 Sit-Ins', *American Sociological Review*, 71(5): 752–77.

Barranco, J. and Wisler, D. (1999) 'Validity and Systematicity of Newspaper Data in Event Analysis', *European Sociological Review*, 15(3): 301–22.

Bennett, L. (1990) 'Toward a Theory of Press-State Relations', *Journal of Communication*, 2(40): 103–25.

Braun, R. and Vliegenthart, R. (2008) 'The Contentious Fans: The Impact of Repression, Media Coverage, Grievances and Aggressive Play on Supporters Violence', *International Sociology*, 23(6): 796–818.

Braun, R. and Vliegenthart, R. (2009) 'Violent Fan Fluctuations: A Diffusion Perspective to Explain Supporters Violence', *Mobilization: An International Quarterly*, 14(1): 23–44.

Cooper, A. H. (2002) 'Media Framing and Social Movement Mobilization: German Peace Protest against INF Missiles, the Gulf War, and NATO Peace Enforcement in Bosnia', *European Journal of Political Research*, 41(1): 37–80.

Costain, A. and Majstorovic, S. (1994) 'Congress, Social Movements and Public Opinion: Multiple Origins of Women's Rights Legislation', *Political Research Quarterly*, 47(1): 111–35.

Downs, A. (1972) 'Up and Down with Ecology – The Issue Attention Cycle', *Public Interest*, 28(1): 38–50.

Earl, J., Martin, A., McCarthy, J. D. and Soule, S. A. (2004) 'The Use of Newspaper Data in the Study of Collective Action', *Annual Review of Sociology*, 30: 65–80.

Entman, R. and Rojecki, A. (1993) 'Freezing out the Public: Elite and Media Framing of the US Anti-Nuclear Movement', *Political Communication*, 10(2): 155–73.

Gamson, W. A. (1992) *Talking Politics*. Cambridge: Cambridge University Press.

Gamson, W. A. (1995) 'Constructing Social Protest', in H. Johnston and B. Klandermans (eds.), *Social Movements and Culture*. London: UCL Press. pp. 85–106.

Gamson, W. A. (2004) 'Bystanders, Public Opinion, and the Media', in D. A. Snow, S. A. Soule and H. Kriesi (eds.), *The Blackwell Companion to Social Movements*. Malden: Blackwell Publishing. pp. 242–61.

Gamson, W. A. and Modigliani, A. (1989) 'Media Discourse and Public Opinion on Nuclear Power: A Constructionist Approach', *American Journal of Sociology*, 95(1): 1–37.

Gamson, W. A. and Wolfsfeld, G. (1993) 'Movements and Media as Interacting Systems', *Annals of the AAPSS*, 28(5): 114–25.

Gamson, W. A., Croteau, D., Hoynes, W. and Sasson, T. (1992) 'Media Images and the Social Construction of Reality', *Annual Review of Sociology*, 18: 373–93.

Gans, H. (1980) *Deciding What's News*. New York: Vintage Books.

Gitlin, T. (1980) *The Whole World Is Watching: Mass Media in the Making and Unmaking of the New Left*. Berkeley, CA: University of California Press.

Giugni, M. and Wisier, D. (1999) 'Under the Spotlight: The Impact of Media Attention on Protest Policing', *Mobilization*, 4(2): 171–87.

Hilgartner, S. and Bosk, C. L. (1988) 'The Rise and Fall of Social Problems: A Public Arenas Model', *American Journal of Sociology*, 94(1): 53–78.

Iyengar, S. and Kinder, D. R. (1987) *News That Matters: Television and American Opinion*. Chicago, IL: University of Chicago Press.

Klandermans, B. (2004) 'The Demand and Supply of Participation: Social Psychological Correlates of Participation in Social Movements', in D. A. Snow, S. A. Soule and H. Kriesi (eds.), *The Blackwell Companion to Social Movements*. Maulden: Blackwell. pp. 360–79.

Koopmans, R. (2004) 'Movements and Media: Selection Processes and Evolutionary Dynamic in the Public Sphere', *Theory and Society*, 33(3): 367–93.

Koopmans, R. and Olzak, S. (2004) 'Discursive Opportunities and the Evolution of Right-Wing Violence in Germany', *American Journal of Sociology*, 110(1): 198–230.

Koopmans, R. and Rucht, D. (2002) 'Protest Event Analysis', in B. Klandermans and S. Staggenborg (eds.), *Methods of Social Movement Research*. Minneapolis,MN: University of Minnesota Press. pp. 231–59.

Koopmans, R. and Statham, P. (1999) 'Political Claims Analysis: Integrating Protest Event Data and Political Discourse Approaches', *Mobilization*, 4(1): 203–21.

Kriesi, H., Koopmans, R., Dyvendak, J. W. and Giugni, M. G. (eds.) (1995) *New Social Movements in Western Europe: A Comparative Analysis*. Minneapolis, MN: University of Minnesota Press.

McAdam, D. (1982) *Political Process and the Development of Black Insurgency, 1930–1970*. Chicago, IL: University of Chicago Press.

McCarthy, J. D., McPhail, C. and Smith, J. (1996) 'Images of Protest: Dimensions of Selection Bias in Media Coverage of Washington Demonstrations, 1982 and 1991', *American Sociological Review*, 61(3): 478–99.

McCarthy, J. D., Titarenko, L., McPhail, C., Rafail, P. S. and Boguslaw, A. (2008) 'Assessing Stability in the Patterns of Selection Bias in Newspaper Coverage of Protest During the Transition from Communism in Belarus', *Mobilization: An International Quarterly*, 13(2): 127–46.

McLeod, D. M. (1995) 'Communicating Deviance: The Effects of Television News Coverage of Social Protest', *Journal of Broadcasting and Electronic Media*, 39(1): 4–19.

McLeod, D. M. and Detenber, B. H. (1999) 'Framing Effects of Television News Coverage of Social Protest', *Journal of Communication*, 49(3): 3–23.

McLeod, D. M. and Hertog, J. K. (1992) 'The Manufacture of "Public Opinion" by Reporters: Informal Cues for Public Perceptions of Protest Groups', *Discourse Society*, 3(3): 259–75.

McPhail, C. and McCarthy, J. (2004) 'Who Counts and How: Estimating the Size of Protests', *Context*, 3(3): 12–18.

Mueller, C. (1997) 'International Press Coverage of East German Protest Events, 1989', *American Sociological Review*, 62(5): 820–32.

Myers, D. J. (2000) 'The Diffusion of Collective Violence: Infectiousness, Susceptibility and Mass Media Networks', *American Journal of Sociology*, 106(1): 173–208.

Myers, D. J. and Caniglia, B. S. (2004) 'All the Rioting That's Fit to Print: Selection Effects in National Newspaper Coverage of Civil Disorders, 1968–1969', *American Sociological Review*, 69(4): 519–43.

Oliver, P. E. and Maney, G. M. (2000) 'Political Processes and Local Newspaper Coverage of Protest Events: From Selection Bias to Triadic Interactions', *American Journal of Sociology*, 106(2): 463–505.

Oliver, P. E. and Myers, D. J. (1999) 'How Events Enter the Public Sphere: Conflict, Location, and Sponsorship in Local Newspaper Coverage of Public Events', *The American Journal of Sociology*, 105(1): 38–87.

Ortiz, D. G., et al. (2005) 'Where Do We Stand with Newspaper Data?', *Mobilization: An International Quarterly*, 10(3): 397–419.

Rohlinger, D. A. (2002) 'Framing the Abortion Debate: Organizational Resources, Media Strategies, and Movement-Countermovement Dynamics', *Sociological Quarterly*, 43(4): 479–507.

Rohlinger, D. A. (2006) 'Friends and Foes: Media, Politics, and Tactics in the Abortion War', *Social Problems*, 53(4): 537–61.

Roscigno, V. J. and Danaher, W. F. (2001) 'Media and Mobilization: The Case of Radio and Southern Textile Worker Insurgency, 1929 to 1934', *American Sociological Review*, 66(1): 21–48.

Rucht, D. (2004) 'The Quadruple "a": Media Strategies of Protest Movements since the 1960s', in W. Van de Donk et al. (eds.), *Cyberprotest. New Media, Citizens and Social Movements*. London/New York: Routledge. pp. 29–56.

Rucht, D., Koopmans, R. and Neidhardt, F. (1999) *Acts of Dissent: New Developments in the Study of Protest*. Lanham, MD: Rowman and Littlefield Pub Inc.

Rucht, D. and Verhulst, J. (2010) 'The Framing of Opposition to the War on Iraq', in S. Walgrave and D. Rucht (eds.), *Protest Politics: Demonstrations against the War on Iraq in the Us and Western Europe*. Minneapolis, MN: University of Minnesota Press. pp. 239–60.

Ryan, C. (1991) *Prime Time Activism: Media Strategies for Grassroots Organizing*. Boston, MA: South End Press.

Scheufele, D. A. and Tewksbury, D. (2007) 'Framing, Agenda Setting, and Priming: The Evolution of Three Media Effects Models', *Journal of Communication*, 57(1): 9–20.

Smith, J., McCarthy, J. D., McPhail, C. and Augustyn, B. (2001) 'From Protest to Agenda Building: Description Bias in Media Coverage of Protest Events in Washington, DC', *Social Forces*, 79(4): 1397–423.

Smith, P. (1999) 'Political Communication in the UK: A Study of Pressure Group Behaviour', *Politics*, 19(1): 21–7.

Snow, D. A. and Benford, R. D. (1988) 'Ideology, Frame Resonance and Participants Mobilization', *International Social Movement Research*, 1: 197–219.

Snow, D. A., Rochford, E. B., Worden, S. K. and Benford, R. D. (1986) 'Frame Alignment Processes, Micromobilization, and Movement Participation', *American Sociological Review*, 51(4): 464–81.

Snow, D. A., Vliegenthart, R. and Corrigall-Brown, C. (2007) 'Framing the French "Riots": A Comparative Study of Frame Variation', *Social Forces*, 86(2): 385–415.

Soule, S. A. (2004) 'Diffusion Processes Within and Across Movements', in D. A. Snow, S. A. Soule and H. Kriesi (eds.), *The Blackwell Companion to Social Movements*. Maulden: Blackwell. pp. 294–310.

Soule, S. A. and Earl, J. (2005) 'A Movement Society Evaluated: Collective Protest in the United States, 1960–1986', *Mobilization: An International Quarterly*, 10(3): 345–64.

Strawn, K. D. (2008) 'Validity and Media-Derived Protest Event Data: Examining Relative Coverage Tendencies in Mexican News Media', *Mobilization: An International Quarterly*, 13(2): 147–64.

Tarrow, S. G. (1989) *Democracy and Disorder: Protest and Politics in Italy, 1965–1975*. Oxford: Oxford University Press.

Terkildsen, N. and Schnell, F. (1997) 'How Media Frames Move Public Opinion: An Analysis of the Women's Movement', *Political Research Quarterly*, 50(4): 879–900.

Terkildsen, N., Schnell, F. and Ling, N. (1998) 'Interest Groups, the Media, and Policy Debate Formation: An Analysis of Message Structure, Rhetoric, and Source Cues', *Political Communication*, 15(1): 45–61.

Tilly, C. (1978) *From Mobilization to Revolution*. Reading, MA: Addison-Wesley.

Tilly, C. (2006) *Regimes and Repertoires*. Chicago, IL: Chicago University Press.

Van Zoonen, E. A. (1992) 'The Women's Movement and the Media: Constructing a Public Identity', *European Journal of Communication*, 7(4): 453–76.

Vliegenthart, R., Oegema, D. and Klandermans, B. (2005) 'Media Coverage and Organizational Support in the Dutch Environmental Movement', *Mobilization: An International Quarterly*, 10(3): 365–81.

Walgrave, S. and Klandermans, B. (2010) 'Patterns of Mobilization', in S. Walgrave and D. Rucht (eds.), *Protest Politics: Antiwar Mobilization in Advanced Industrial Democracies*.

Walgrave, S. and Manssens, J. (2005) 'Mobilizing the White March: Media Frames as Alternatives to Movement Organizations', in H. Johnston and J. H. Noakes (eds.), *Frames of Protest: Social Movements and the Framing Perspective*. Lanham, MD: Rowmann and Littlefield. pp. 113–42.

Walgrave, S. and Verhulst, J. (2006) 'Towards "New Emotional Movements"? A Comparative Exploration into a Specific Movement Type', *Social Movement Studies*, 5(3): 275–304.

Walgrave, S. and Verhulst, J. (2009) 'Government Stance and Internal Diversity of Protest. A Comparative Study of Protest against the War in Iraq in Eight Countries', *Social Forces*, 87(3): 1355–87.

Walgrave, S. and Vliegenthart, R. (2012) 'The Agenda-Setting Power of Protest. Demonstrations, Media, Parliament, Government, and Legislation in Belgium, 1993–2000', Forthcoming in *Mobilization*.

PART V

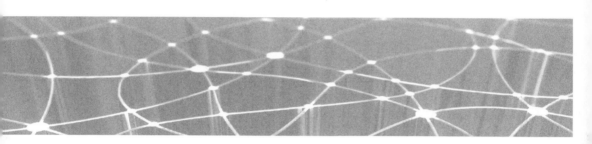

31

Media Consolidation, Fragmentation and Selective Exposure in the USA

Diana Owen

The media system has been undergoing a significant transformation for a quarter century. Digital technologies have given rise to a vast array of new media options that complement, challenge and enhance traditional mass media. The number and variety of platforms hosting political content have expanded exponentially. While established media continue to form the backbone of the media system, they are adapting to the shifting environment, as traditional formats give way to current innovations. Tracking the evolution of the media system is like shooting at a moving target, as innovation is constant and established platforms morph or die slowly.

The audiences for political media in the current era must navigate a complex and ever-changing labyrinth of choices. Many people continue to rely on traditional media for political news and information, even as the audiences for print newspapers and television network news have declined. Television news, with its general interest focus, is still the main source of information for the majority of the American public, and more than half the population still reads a print newspaper daily (Pew Research Center, 2008a). Still, with the proliferation of new media channels and formats, people increasingly are turning to specialized outlets for political information and abandoning tradition media. Young people, in particular, have come to rely heavily on online sources of political information to the exclusion of established media options (Owen, 2006). Further, a growing audience segment gets political news from a combination of traditional and online media sources. New media are not a supplement to or a substitute for traditional media, but instead are an integrated component of their media use (Pew Research Center, 2008a).

The proliferation of sources of political news and information raises issues of what this means for democracy. Some scholars argue that for a democratic society to function there must be a shared understanding of issues and concerns as well as appropriate forums for discourse surrounding these issues. They fear that the proliferation of sources can lead to people to selective exposure to specialized media, closing off the possibility for meaningful national dialog. Others refute this contention, arguing that most people get their information from a limited number of high profile media sources.

This chapter provides an overview of the nature and scope of the current media environment which features both consolidation of media organizations and fragmentation of media sources. It begins by providing an overview of the media environment in the digital era, and discusses the implications of a media system that is both converging and splintering at the same time. While the opportunity for audience members to access and create specialized content has increased, many media are controlled by a small number of professional conglomerates that disseminate largely redundant messages. Most audience members get their political information from a small number of dominant sources even as the number of options has grown markedly. The discussion then turns to an examination of the shift from a system based on mass media to one that incorporates micro media that enhance individuals' ability to control the flow of information as well as middle or hybrid media forms. We next examine the audiences for particular political media, noting the shifts in orientation that have occurred in the era of digital media. Selective exposure to political media is explored in light of the transition from mass to new media and the proliferation of sources. Finally, the debate over the consequences of selective exposure for a democratic polity is laid out.

THE MEDIA ENVIRONMENT IN THE DIGITAL ERA

Media Fragmentation and Consolidation

The media environment in the current era is characterized by both fragmentation and consolidation. The traditional broadcast model of communication, whereby messages of general interest to society at large are widely disseminated to a mass audience, now coexists with a narrowcasting model in which specialized messages are aimed at particular individuals or groups. While these trends may appear contradictory in some ways, they are intrinsic to a system that is in the midst of an ongoing transition.

The media have become increasingly fragmented as the number of available political media options offering both general interest and specialized content has grown. Individuals have greater capacity to narrow the focus of their information consumption to conform to their personal tastes, interests and needs. They are able to tailor their preference both in terms of the content to which they are exposed and the platform through which it is disseminated (Chaffee and Metzger, 2001; Tewksbury, 2005). Audience members are able to play an active role in the creation of content, widening the number of perspectives in the communication marketplace. Citizen journalists, acting without formal training or credentials, are contributing an expanding amount of content in areas of politics and government that have received scant attention from the mainstream media.

While new media technologies have brought about significant, even radical, shifts in the nature and dissemination of political news, elements of the traditional media system remain strongly apparent. In the new media era, large media institutions have become heavily consolidated, as a small number of large media corporations have expanded their holdings. Media ownership has been consolidating through mergers and buyouts since the 1980s. Whereas 80% of American newspapers were independently owned in 1945, more than 80% were owned by publicly traded chains in 2000 (Klinenberg, 2005). Fewer than 10 mega media conglomerates own the sources through which most people get their news and information today (McChesney, 1999). In 2008, some of the largest included Disney (which owns ABC News and ESPN in addition to its massive entertainment holdings), Time Warner (which owns AOL and CNN) and Viacom (which owns MTV and BET). Consolidation is nothing new, as the financial barriers to entry and the finite broadcast spectrum for radio and television historically have limited the number of players in the market (Baker, 2002).

Business consolidation influences the content of communication. Commercial concerns shape the production and substance of political information and have contributed to a shift away from serious news in favor of an infotainment agenda that is redundant across channels. Audience members encounter similar story lines regardless of the corporate media product they are consuming (Baker, 2002; Chester, 2007; Hamilton, 2004; McChesney, 2004). As news organizations seek to cut costs in a period of economic downturn and declining advertising revenues, they have sharply reduced their reporting and editorial staffs, and limited the amount of investigative reporting. They have come to rely heavily on wire service stories, especially from the Associated Press (AP). Media corporations are partnering to cut costs and are sharing resources, which has resulted in further consolidation of content (Kiss, 2009). Some newspapers have entered into agreements to combine material in order to broaden their coverage. On 1 January 2008, *The Washington Post* and *The Baltimore Sun*, owned by the Tribune Corporation, began sharing national and international news stories, features, sports coverage, photos and their propriety wire service reports (Rosenwald, 2008). There is an emerging problem of news organizations aggregating and repurposing content from their competitors without their consent (Sanders, 2009). These trends contribute to globalization, as people around the world are exposed to a limited number of similar media messages (Katz, 1996).

Mass Media, Micro Media and Hybrid Media

Mass media long have constituted the foundation of the media system. They consist of the set of media organizations and institutions having the capacity to disseminate information to a large, geographically dispersed audience through various channels instantaneously (Schramm, 1954). Mass communication is characterized by the unidirectional flow of information from a source to an undifferentiated audience (Chaffee and Metzger, 2001). Messages considered to be of general interest to society broadly construed are disseminated through these channels. Mass media present large audiences with 'the task of drawing personal uses and gratifications from centrally produced, common inputs' (Bennett, 2005: 111). In other words, individual audience members with a variety of motivations for media use, such as seeking information, reinforcing personal views, social interaction and integration and entertainment, attend to mass media that may or may not satisfy their needs (Blumler et al., 1985; McQuail and Windahl, 1981). Traditional mass media channels include print newspapers, television, radio, magazines, books and film.

The late 1980s signaled the start of a new era in political media. Established mass media with primarily non-political origins took on political roles. While maintaining entertainment as a priority, radio and television talk programs, television news magazines, celebrity television shows and magazines, print and television tabloids, music television and comedy programs increasingly crossed into the political realm. These so-called 'new media' broadened audience access to political information by reaching those who typically did not tune in to news programming. The new media appealed to audience segments that preferred their information packaged in the fast-paced, encapsulated, comedy-and-drama-laced style of popular media (Davis and Owen, 1998). At the same times, technological innovations made possible the development of entirely new outlets and content delivery systems. Computer networks allowed people to communicate interactively through email and electronic discussion boards, while websites and online publications, such as *Slate*, provided new spaces for political news and commentary (Owen, 2005).

The 1992 presidential campaign was a watershed for these new political media as candidates sought to expand their outreach to voters by circumventing traditional news media gatekeepers. Reform Party candidate Ross Perot declared his candidacy on *Larry King Live*. Democratic nominee Bill Clinton famously played his saxophone on *The Arsenio Hall Show* and became a fixture on the talk radio circuit. The new media's role in presidential elections evolved with each passing campaign. It was well-established in 2008, as the campaigns courted the entertainment media. Barack Obama and John McCain each appeared with their families on the cover of the celebrity gossip magazine *People Weekly*, with its ubiquitous newsstand visibility and readership of 43.6 million adults (Johnson-Greene, 2009). These appearances generated more publicity for the candidates than the 25 *Time* and *Newsweek* covers featuring Obama and the 10 picturing McCain.

Domination by the mass media has given way to a convoluted system which encompasses a wide spectrum of channels and platforms. Established and emerging technologies, including the Internet, personal computers, cell phones, pagers and personal digital appliances (PDAs), have opened the possibility for an almost limitless number of communication channels. The current media environment is comprised of a highly diverse assortment of platforms that can accommodate political content, including websites, online newspapers, television and radio sites, discussion boards, blogs, vlogs (video blogs), microblogs, social networking sites, video sharing sites, podcasts, email, Twitter and instant messages. These digital media forms have altered the relationship between communicators and audience members fundamentally by providing the opportunity for unprecedented interactivity, feedback and networking. Individuals and groups unrelated to the established media industry can produce and distribute political content readily on their own, acting as reporters, informers, fact-checkers and analysts.

The Internet, which currently hosts the majority of digital era political media applications, is a multifaceted medium that combines elements of mass media and interpersonal communication (Chaffee and Mutz, 1988; Morris and Ogan, 1996). It is substantially different from existing communications technologies (Havick, 2000). Some applications, such as major web news aggregators like *The Drudge Report*, serve similar functions as traditional mass media, and primarily disseminate information from one to many. Other outlets constitute what Bennett has labeled micro media, personalized digital media channels that 'blur the distinction between producers and consumers of information' (2005: 11). Micro media, which include email, instant messages, personal blogs, Twitter feeds and podcasts, are highly adaptable, and offer users the capacity to create and circulate information from one-to-one, one-to-few or one-to-many. Their evolution has been hastened further by the development of portable, individualized technological devices, such as the Blackberry, iPhone and very small, lightweight, inexpensive personal computers. Because micro media enable multi-path interactivity, they afford new mechanisms for managing information, contributing content, tailoring uses and gratifications, and encouraging participation (Bennett, 2005). Middle or mixed media, such as many news websites, community blogs, online advocacy organization sites and webzines, combine elements of mass and micro media. These hybrid forms are designed to reach a mass audience with a general message and at the same time provide opportunities for individuals with particular interests to engage. Campaign websites fall into this category, as they promote candidates' mass-based appeals, provide an information pipeline for journalists and offer partisan supporters a platform for involvement.

Some scholars have gone so far as to predict that traditional mass media may be facing extinction as micro media technologies and applications proliferate. Bennett contends that fundamental differences in the producer/consumer relationship and the ability to personalize content that micro media offer are reshaping what people consider to be news and public information. Audiences will no longer accept hierarchical, one-way political media. Content producers will be able to microtarget their messages to users with ease (Chaffee and Metzger, 2001; Howard, 2006). Advertisers, who are able to reach less than a third of the audiences that they had previously contacted through traditional media, are turning increasingly to micro media to reach consumers (Rubinson, 2008). In addition, some traditional mass media have been facing economic hardships which threaten established ways of doing business. Newspaper revenues have declined precipitously, forcing organizations to fire journalists or shutter completely. During the 2008 presidential election, few professional journalists filed stories directly from the campaign trail, relying instead on video feed and secondhand accounts (Steinberg, 2008). Citizen reporters, acting without formal credentials or pedigrees, used micro media to fill in the gaps in on-the-spot coverage. Personal blog accounts of rallies and cell phone videos of candidates interacting with voters have become a part of the repertoire of campaign coverage (Owen, 2009).

Rather than face extinction, however, traditional media have been moving in the direction of middle media, and have been creating hybrid forms that appeal to changing audience orientations. As Chaffee and Metzger argue, '... media institutions are changing such that mass production is less mass' (2001: 369). Major news organizations have established websites that incorporate sophisticated interactive platforms, video, networking capabilities and other features. By 2008, 95% of the top 100 US newspapers had incorporated journalists' blogs into their online products (Technorati, 2008). Papers have integrated personalized media into their product, such as amateur eyewitness reports from audience members, RSS (real simple syndication) feeds that customize and distribute news, podcasts to narrowly targeted groups and individualized digital dashboards. Faced with

closing down, the *Baltimore Sun* established a division that oversees 'audience engagement', the use of social networking sites, blogs and mobile applications to bring in new readers (Serpick, 2009). These hybrid communication forms allow established media organizations to shore up their interests by offering audience members one-stop-shopping for their general and personalized news needs. They can capitalize on their brand name recognition that distinguishes them as reliable sources of information subject to editorial scrutiny, something that is not guaranteed by personalized micro media (Lawrence, 1993).

Politico: A Digital Era Media Organization

Politico exemplifies a news organization which has originated and thrived within the parameters of the digital-era media environment. It is an example of middle media, as it combines elements of mass and micro media. It is backed by an established media corporation, yet it is not tethered to conventional practices. The organization takes a diversified approach to disseminating content while providing detailed coverage of a specialized topic area – Washington, DC politics. *Politico* targets a select inside-the-beltway audience for whom politics and government is a fixation, if not a profession. Its content producers operate under, and have helped to create, the fluid, non-hierarchical, personalized conventions of a journalism that aims to meet particularized audience needs. At the same time, its coverage of topics of interest to the general population, such as healthcare and economic recovery, sets the agenda for other news outlets.

John F. Harris, Jim VandeHei and Mike Allen, three political reporters with experience at top-level national newspapers, founded *Politico* in January 2007. The initiative was financed by Allbritton Communications, whose holdings include local television and radio stations. The goal of *Politico* is to provide dedicated, in-depth coverage of Congress, lobbying and advocacy organizations, and election campaigns 'with enterprize, style and impact'. *Politico* recruited experienced print journalists as well as print and video bloggers to create content that is disseminated via Web site, print newspaper, television, radio and Twitter feed. Political celebrity gossip items are reported prominently alongside serious news coverage of issues and events, analysis, insider takes on the workings of government and campaigns, partisan commentary, fact-checking and full texts of speeches.

Politico seeks to be 'a one-stop source for Washington news' (Wolff, 2009: 76). The organization's web site, politico.com, is the centerpiece of the operation. The site, which is populated with fresh content every 20 minutes, is a hub of late-breaking information, including real time chats with newsmakers and officials and on-the-spot photos and video. Audience members can be kept in the loop with email news alerts and RSS feeds. Content produced for the site is repurposed for a tabloid-sized print newspaper version of *Politico* that is distributed gratis through Washington, DC, area newsstands and in Capitol Hill offices. *Politico* writers and editors disseminate their media product further by doing several hundred cable television and radio interviews per week, frequently on stations owned by Allbritton. In November of 2011, *Politico* published its first eBook, *The Right Fights Back* by columnists Mike Allen and Evan Thomas, which focuses on the 2012 elections.

Politico caters to an audience of government leaders, Capitol Hill staffers, politicians and political junkies. During the final year of the 2008 presidential campaign, *Politico's* Web audience increased from 4 million unique visitors per month to over 11 million, an increase 360% (Lipsman, 2008). Following an anticipated post-election drop-off, its online audience averaged 6.7 million unique visitors per month in 2009. *Politico* expanded publication of its tabloid-sized print newspaper from three to four days a week after the campaign as the subscriber base rose from 25,000 to 32,000 (Arango, 2009). The print newspaper is responsible for more than half of the company's revenues, and is one of the only print editions in the digital era to become more profitable over time. In November 2011, *Politico* reached 11.3 million people through its various holdings according to Quantcast.

Politico's influence on politics, government and the journalistic establishment is significant, especially as its reporters have access to top decision makers and can set the agenda for political deliberation. In 2009, *Politico* had eight journalists at the White House, representing the largest cohort in the presidential press corps. Bloggers for the web site remain in contact with high ranking sources through Instant Messenger, which allows them to break stories before the competition (Wolff, 2009). The *Politico* 'Playbook', a digest of top stories and insider insights which is posted on the site and arrives in subscribers' email boxes early each morning, routinely is consulted by politicians and journalists.

POLITICAL MEDIA AUDIENCES

There are significant differences in the basic characteristics of the audiences for traditional mass media and that for digital communication. The television audience represents a 'diverse, heterogeneous cross-section of society that encompasses all classes and types of people' (Havick, 2000: 275). The US Census Bureau reports that 98.2% of American households have a television set. The skills required to watch television are minimal, as the technology is not literacy-based. Television is conducive to transmitting political messages, such as presidential speeches, instantaneously and simultaneously to societal audiences with little effort on the part viewers. The same is true for other broadcast media.

While the number of Internet users has expanded rapidly, it still does not approach the size of the television audience. According to the Pew Internet and American Life Project, 78% of Americans have accessed the Internet as of May 2011. However, only 61% have been exposed to information about politics and government. Online political experiences require greater effort and skill than is the case for television (Havick, 2000). Experiences also differ greatly across individuals, as some people treat digital applications as simply the electronic versions of mass media, while others make heavy use of their unique interactive features.

In the early days of the Internet and digital communication platforms, audience shifts away from traditional media to new media were limited. The new media generally supplemented, rather than supplanted, traditional news sources. People would get their political news primarily from newspapers and television, turning to online platforms for further information (Davis and Owen, 1998). More recently these patterns have been changing, as media audience orientations have become far more complex. The majority of the population maintains at least some form of traditional mass communication as part of their media diet, especially television (Pew Research Center, 2008a). There also remains a distinct audience for print publications representing an elite readership of individuals in higher socioeconomic status groups who are willing to pay a premium for publications with in-depth, quality content (Project for Excellence in Journalism, 2009). Some audience members, however, are gravitating away from established mass media in favor of online political sources. The preference for digital political media is especially pronounced among particular segments of the population, especially young people, which some observers contend is creating a generational media divide (Wattenberg, 2008; Winograd and Hais, 2008). However, use of digital political media for politics has been increasing among older people, who read and post to blogs more frequently than younger people. Further, there is evidence that a critical mass is developing a sophisticated, assimilated approach to their political media consumption. A 2008 Pew Research Center study found that 23% of the public displays patterns of integrated news consumption, gathering general interest and specialized information from a variety of traditional and online media.

The 2008 presidential election brought these evolving trends in political media use to light. Interest in the campaign was high, and public exposure to news media swelled. Audience preferences for campaign media were notably different than just four years earlier, as Internet sources began to replace or reinforce traditional media for a substantial percentage of voters. Television remained the primary source of election news for a majority of people, but the percentage dropped from 76% in 2004 to 68%. There was a similar drop in the percentage of people reading campaign news in print newspapers from 40% to 31%. A record number of people followed the tremendous amount of campaign coverage that appeared online. Nearly 60% of voters used the Internet to engage with the campaign in some way. Online news was a main source of election information for 36% of the public, which represents a 15 percentage point increase over 2004, when 21% of the audience regularly consulted online media (Pew Research Center for the People and the Press, 2008b; Owen, 2009).

The following section describes trends in the public's use of television, print, radio and online media. The data presented collectively illustrate the fact that general interest media use is prevalent, and that while specialization exists, it is far less widespread. Audience members are drawn heavily to a small number of sources associated with consolidated media organizations. Similarly, regular users of digital age online media are drawn to the same few sources. The online audience overwhelmingly gets its news from a handful of sites associated with major news organizations, and the vast majority of blog readers flock to a handful of high profile sites despite the fact that they have thousands of options from which to choose (Graf, 2006; Hindman, 2009).

Television

Americans still habitually rely on television news for their information about politics. Even as the Internet and new media platforms offered alternatives beginning in the late 1980s, the appeal of television news remained fairly constant. Throughout the 1990s, Pew Research data reveal that 80% or more of the public regularly tuned into some form of television news programming. The percentage dipped slightly in the new

millennium from 80% in 1998 to 75% in 2008 (see Table 31.1). While reliance on television news generally has not dropped tremendously in the digital era, there have been shifts in the audience's television news programming preferences. The most momentous change has been in the audience for nightly news programming. In 1987, 71% of the public watched the three major networks – ABC, CBS and NBC. The percentage had dropped to 44% by 2008, with the three networks splitting a diminished share of the market. Local news programs also have witnessed a significant decline in audience. In 1993, 73% of the public regularly watched local news, dropping to 64% in 1998 and 52% a decade later. These trends are a result of the fixed time slots for network and local news programs making them less convenient for consumers, competition from cable news sources and failure to find successful formulas for distinguishing their news product in a crowded marketplace. Other network television news programming has maintained a more stable audience base. As Table 31.1 shows, there has been little fluctuation in the percentage of people who regularly watch morning television news shows, Sunday morning shows and late night programs across the past decade. The popularity of television news magazines, a staple in the early phases of the new media era, has declined notably. These programs still populate the airwaves, as they are less expensive than other types of programs to produce, but the percentage of regular watchers has dropped from 37% in 1998 to 18% in 2008.

Cable news has been providing 24-hour television coverage of events since the founding of CNN in 1980. Today, approximately 40% of the public relies regularly on cable news (see Table 31.1). The audience for cable news is driven, to some extent, by major events, including the first Gulf War, the undecided presidential election of 2000, and the terrorist attacks of 11 September 2001. In 2008, the presidential election helped to drive up cable news viewership, and there was evidence that the major cable news providers, CNN, MSNBC and Fox News Cable Channel, retained some of that increased audience in 2009 (Project for Excellence in Journalism, 2009). In addition to the convenience offered by round-the-clock coverage, cable news benefits from a web presence that is more firmly established and better integrated into the news product than is the case for network news. MSNBC.com and CNN.com are among the top news destinations on the Web (Langeveld, 2009). These brands epitomize the digital era notion of platform agnosticism, whereby the same content is conveyed through multiple related venues allowing the user to seamlessly follow story lines from different points of access.

Table 31.1   Americans who watch television media

Television	1998 (%)	2004 (%)	2008 (%)
Television news	80	79	75
Network££	59	52	44
Nightly network news	38	34	29
CBS Evening News	–	16	8
ABC World News Tonight	–	16	14
NBC Nightly News	–	17	13
The NewsHour	4	5	5
Local television news	64	59	52
Morning television news shows	23	22	22
Sunday morning news shows	–	12	12
Television news magazines	37	22	18
Late night television shows	8	10	9
Entertainment television shows	8	10	9
The Daily Show with Jon Stewart	–	4	5
The Colbert Report	–	–	5
Cable television news	–	38	39
CNN	23	22	24
Fox News Cable Channel	17	25	23
MSNBC	8	15	15
CNBC	12	10	12
BBC	–	–	5
C-SPAN	6	5	5
Larry King Live	4	5	6
Countdown with Keith Olbermann	–	–	3
Hannity & Colmes	–	–	7
Lou Dobbs Tonight	–	–	4
The O'Reilly Factor	–	8	10

Entertainment news programs that incorporate political news have developed a steady audience since the 1990s. As Table 31.1 indicates, around 10% of the population regularly watches this type of programming. 'Fake news' shows, especially *The Daily Show with Jon Stewart* and *The Colbert Report*, are especially popular with young people. Watching these programs has been shown to influence the attitudes of people who are less interested and engaged in politics, including opinions of presidential candidates (Baum, 2005; Baumgartner and Morris, 2006; Morris, 2009). In addition, viewing political comedy programs can act as a gateway to serious news consumption by leading audience members to seek additional real news sources (Xenos and Becker, 2009). However, comedy programs may be less effective than hard news programs in providing factual information (Kim and Vishak, 2008).

Print Media

There has been a precipitous decline in the audience for traditional print newspapers over the past decade. As Table 31.2 demonstrates, the percentage of regular newspaper readers dropped 16 percentage points from 70% in 1998 to 54% in 2008. The decline in daily and local newspaper readership has been less abrupt, as the audiences for these products are more educated, have higher incomes, and work in white collar professions. The decline in daily newspaper readership between 2004 and 2008 can be partly explained by readers accessing the online version of print papers. The small regular audience for tabloid newspapers has remained relatively stable over time.

Traffic to newspaper web sites has climbed as print readership has fallen off. Papers raised prices for their print editions in the wake of declining

Table 31.2 Americans who read print media regularly

Print media	1998 (%)	2004 (%)	2008 (%)
Newspaper	70	60	54
Daily newspaper	52	54	46
Local community newspaper	–	36	33
Tabloid newspapers	3	4	2
News magazines	15	13	12
Political magazines/*Time, Newsweek*	–	2	2
Business magazines	5	4	5
Atlantic, Harpers, New Yorker	2	2	2
Personality magazines/*People*	8	7	8
Technology magazines/*Wired*	–	–	4

Source: Pew Research Center Biennial News Consumption Survey, August, 2008.

advertising revenues and the global economic recession, further encouraging the shift to the web. Print circulation dropped by almost 5% in 2008 from the previous year, and fell and additional seven percent in 2009. All but one of the top 25 newspapers experienced a drop in circulation, with *The New York Post* losing 20.6% of its hard copy audience (Arango, 2009; Project for Excellence in Journalism, 2009). At the same time, online newspaper readership during the first quarter of 2009 increased markedly, as the audience grew by 10.5%; 43.6% of all Internet users has accessed the online version of a print paper. Over 73.3 million unique visitors viewed more than 3.5 billion pages of digital newsprint during that time period. The audience for *The New York Times* online grew by 7% in 2009, while Tribune web newspapers experienced a 16% increase in readership (Nielsen Online, 2009). Still, print newspapers maintain a core readership among those with higher levels of education and income, many of whom consume news in both print and online formats. Almost 90% of Americans who hold a post-graduate degree read a daily print or online newspaper compared to 34% who go online exclusively. Similarly, 83% of those with a household income of $100,000 read a newspaper in either format, compared to 28% who read only the online version (Newspaper Association of America, 2009). While online newspaper readership is growing at the expense of its print counterpart, other web news destinations are outpacing them. The top three news destinations on the Web in 2009 – MSNBC, CNN and Yahoo! News – each individually drew more unique visitors and had more page views than the entire online newspaper industry (Langeveld, 2009).

Similarly, print magazines have been experiencing a decline in sales, as newsstand circulation fell 12.4% for the first half of 2009. As Table 31.2 indicates, news magazine readership has trended downward over the past 10 years. As a result, magazines have been adapting their business model to meet the times by moving an increasing amount of their content to the Web. *US News and World Report* effectively transitioned its reporting operation online, replacing its weekly print magazine with a monthly news guide. *Newsweek* and *Vanity Fair* have scaled down the hard copy of their magazine, and direct readers to their online versions for additional content. Magazine readership is highly fragmented. As Table 31.2 reveals, audiences for particular types of magazines are compact, with even the most popular variety – entertainment magazines – attracting only 8% of the public as regular readers. In the current era, magazines are becoming even more of a niche medium. High end consumers desirous of substantial content are willing to pay for it, as magazines like *The Economist*, *The New Yorker* and *The Atlantic*, have gained readers (Project for Excellence in Journalism, 2009).

Radio

Audiences in the digital era have a growing number of radio options, including Internet-based radio such as *Pandora*, satellite radio and podcasts downloaded onto PDAs. The general audience for traditional AM/FM radio has declined slightly, although it remains the primary way for people to listen to news (Project for Excellence in Journalism, 2009). As Table 31.3 demonstrates, the percentage of people who regularly listen to radio news dropped from 52% in 1998 to 46% 10 years later. The specialized audience for National Public Radio has experienced a notable decline from 15% regular listeners in 1998 to 10% in 2008.

Talk radio was among the most prominent of the early new media that employed established technology. The format took off in the late 1980s,

Table 31.3   Americans who listen to radio regularly

Radio	1998 (%)	2004 (%)	2008 (%)
Radio news	52	49	46
NPR	15	16	10
Talk radio	23	17	17
Rush Limbaugh's Radio Show	5	6	5

Source: Pew Research Center Biennial News Consumption Survey, August, 2008.

as baby boomers' preference for music waned and radio stations sought ways to revitalize their AM programming. The first Gulf War and several high profile criminal trials, most notably the O.J. Simpson case, established talk radio as a place where callers could participate in open discussion (Davis and Owen, 1998). Talk show personalities attracted audiences with provocative, often highly partisan, banter. The audience for political talk radio has leveled off somewhat since the early years, but remains stable. In 1998, 23% of the public regularly listened to talk radio. This figure dropped to around 17% after 2000 and has remained at roughly that level since. Talk radio attracts a committed group of listeners who share the opinions of the hosts, who are often highly conservative (Barker, 2002; Jamieson and Cappella, 2008). As Table 31.3 shows, Rush Limbaugh's regular audience has remained relatively stable across time, averaging around 5% of the population.

Online Media

The scope of the online political media audience has become difficult, if not impossible, to determine comprehensively, especially as the amount and location of content on the Internet is unbounded (Chaffee and Metzger, 2001). The number of Internet users worldwide reached 2 billion in 2011 according to the United Nations telecommunications agency. American Internet users in 2011 numbered 270 million people. In 2009, Americans spent an average of 61 hours, 11 minutes and 56 seconds online per month. They averaged 386 billion page views per month, with only a miniscule fraction of those visits – approximately 1.2% – going to news sites (Nielsen Online, 2009). However, it is difficult to determine the length of the 'long tail' of Internet communication (Anderson, 2006), and to measure precisely the extent to which people are seeking and producing highly specialized political content that is shared among only a handful of users. Thus, current estimates may understate the scope of the online political media audience.

The audience for online news sites has increased dramatically in recent years. As Table 31.4 indicates, the percentage of people who regularly visit web news sites increased from 27% to 37% between 2006 and 2008. While there are countless sites for political news online, only a handful attract sizable audiences – Yahoo! News, MSN, CNN, Google News and MSNBC. Fewer than 10 news websites are visited regularly by more than 8% of the population. Beyond these sites, the online news audience is divided among a wide range of offerings, including the online counterparts of print papers, web-only newspapers, like *Scoop44* and news aggregators, such as *The Drudge Report*.

Blogs, or weblogs, are websites where individuals post entries consisting of news, commentary, jottings, photos and videos. They range in form from rudimentary personal journals to professional quality platforms that resemble online newspapers, such as *Talking Points Memo* and *Huffington Post*. Many blogs make use of the interactive features of the Internet, and invite comments from readers, provide links to additional content and run online polls. It is difficult to gauge the exact extent of the blogosphere, the collective community of all blogs, as thousands of blogs are started each day while many others have been abandoned. Estimates place the number of blogs of all types created between 2002 and 2008 at 133 million (Technorati, 2008). Fewer than 10% of American adults have created a political blog (Graf, 2006; Smith, 2008).

Although the blogosphere is vast, political blogs represent a very small percentage of the overall number of sites. Only 0.12% of web traffic goes to political sites (Hindman, 2009). The daily audience for political blogs is small (Graf, 2006), but it increases in response to significant political events. In early 2008, as the presidential election was unfolding, about one-quarter of adults reported reading a political blog regularly. Contrary to expectations, senior citizens are more likely to read political blogs regularly than younger people. As Table 31.5 indicates, 26% of people over age 63 who are online are frequent blog users compared to 19% of 18- to 31-year-olds.

Table 31.4   Americans who regularly visit web news sites

Web news sites	2006 (%)	2008 (%)
News online	27	37
Yahoo! News	23	28
MSN	31	19
CNN	23	17
Google	9	11
MSNBC	–	10
AOL	8	8
Fox	8	7
New York Times	5	4
Local News Website	–	4
BBC	2	2
ABC	4	2
Drudge Report	3	2
CNBC	–	2
Wall Street Journal	1	2
USA Today	1	2
Washington Post	2	2
CBS	1	1

Source: Pew Research Center Biennial News Consumption Survey, August, 2008.

Table 31.5   Americans online who regularly read political blogs, by age

Age	2008 (%)
18–31	19
32–43	17
44–62	23
63+	26

Source: Harris Interactive, *The Harris Poll #25*, March 2008.

Social networking and video sharing websites have become platforms for political communication. These Web 2.0 applications employ digital technology to enhance information sharing and collaboration through the development and management of online communities. There has been a massive growth in the number of people who use social networking sites. In 2009, there were over 300 million active Facebook users worldwide (54.5 million US users) and 125 million MySpace users (76 million US users) (Arrington, 2009).

The 2008 presidential campaign witnessed a surge in the use of social media for political purposes. In addition to sharing information about candidates and hosting discussions, social networking sites were used to organize events, recruit volunteers and raise funds, especially by young people. The distinct generational divide in the use of social media for political communication has persisted after the campaign. Young adults are far more likely to use social networking sites to share political content than are older cohorts. As Table 31.5 indicates, 29% of 18- to 24-year-olds use social networks for political purposes versus 5% or less of people age 35 and older. Similarly, 30% of 18- to 24-year-olds have posted political content online to a Facebook wall or other location compared to 7% of 45- to 64-year-olds and 3% of those 65 and older.

SELECTIVE EXPOSURE TO MEDIA

The abundance of available political media choices presents challenges to audience members who are bombarded with a relentless onslaught of messages (Gitlin, 2002; Prior, 2007). As the foregoing discussion illustrates, political information is dispersed across a dizzying array of platforms,

Table 31.6   Americans who use social network sites for political purposes and who post political content online, by age

	18–24	25–34	35–44	45–54	55–64	65+
Social network sites (%)	29	15	5	3	3	1
Post political content online (%)	30	17	11	7	7	3

Source: Pew Internet and American Life Project, *The Internet and Civic Engagement*, 2009.

forcing consumers to make sense of the communication marketplace. Some people are able to navigate the media environment by integrating information in sophisticated ways. An increasing number have formed communities within the digital culture to share and make sense of the barrage of messages. Many more, however, seek ways of simplifying their exposure to political media.

Individuals may consciously engage in selective exposure by monitoring particular media and ignoring others. Selective exposure is defined generally as 'behavior that is deliberately performed to attain and sustain perceptual control of particular stimulus events' (Zillmann and Bryant, 1985: 2). It can occur when people choose to attend to information that matches their preexisting beliefs, opinions and interests and 'to avoid unsympathetic material' (Klapper, 1960: 19). Jamieson and Cappella (2008) have evoked the notion of an 'echo chamber' to describe a media environment that is conducive to selective exposure. The echo chamber is defined as 'bounded, enclosed media space that has the potential to both magnify messages delivered within it and insulate them from rebuttal' (Jamieson and Cappella, 2008: 76). They identify a conservative media establishment consisting of Fox News, Rush Limbaugh's talk radio program, and the opinion pages of the *Wall Street Journal* representing a 'self-protected enclave' that isolates audience members from exposure to alternative perspectives.

There are a number of explanations for selective exposure to media. People may seek information that conforms to their partisan and ideological identifications, or they may be guided by their interest in particular issues or political actors. They may seek relief from cognitive dissonance, the discomfort that results from being confronted with information with which they disagree (Jamieson and Cappella, 2008; Sears and Freedman, 1967). Selective exposure can be related to individuals' motivations for attending to media, as well as the gratifications that they expect to receive from the experience. People may selectively engage political media to find useful information, to learn, to reinforce their

beliefs, to be entertained, to be able to participate in conversations with others and to gain acceptance. Selective exposure also may be unrelated to motivations, and may be linked to the availability of information. Finally, some people's deliberate media consumption is aimed at avoiding politics completely, as their preferences tend toward sports, celebrity gossip or the weather (Prior, 2007).

The notion that individuals will focus their media consumption on particular sources in line with their political predispositions came into vogue around the 1960s, as evidence of strong, direct hypodermic effects of mass media was lacking. However, empirical support for selective exposure in the mass media era was mixed, especially as the number of outlets with clear political leanings was limited (Sears and Freedman, 1967). A raft of studies found a correlation between people's beliefs and their exposure to political media, although the causal relationship was difficult to establish. Other research casts doubt on the extent to which individuals actively seek out sources based on predispositions (see Stroud, 2008). Most individuals have neither the motivation nor the energy to engage habitually in rigidly directed media consumption (Kinder, 2003). Still another perspective contends that people may be inclined to expose themselves to a variety of opinions, rather than isolating themselves by limiting their knowledge of issues (Stromer-Galley, 2003). New media, in particular, provide enhanced opportunities for exposure to diverse views.

The digital age media environment, with its wealth of sources representing discrete perspectives, has reinvigorated the debate over selective exposure. The Internet, in particular, gives users greater control over their content choices. The interactive features of digital media allow people the opportunity for a more engaged communication experience and to more readily share their opinions with others. It may be the case that people who regularly use more interactive formats have a greater tendency toward selective exposure. There is evidence that the relatively small regular audience for political blogs goes to these sources because they are disenchanted with mainstream media, and feel that their perspectives are not entirely represented. Regular blog users are politically interested and active, inclined to place themselves at the far end of the political spectrum and willing to take strong positions on social issues. They tend to engage in activities online that allow them to express their opinions, such as signing online petitions, participating in online polls and emailing politicians (Graf, 2006). Further evidence suggests that blog users visit sites that promote discussion in line with their own opinions with the goal of reinforcing their views and expressing themselves within a supportive context. However, blog users do not actively avert challenging opinions (Garrett, 2009).

Consequences of Media Fragmentation and Selective Exposure

The belief that participatory democracy requires a central space where all citizens can be informed about the key issues and events of the day is widespread. Such a space provides individuals with the ability to make enlightened decisions and to engage in meaningful debate. The mass media are the most practical mechanism for providing that space for national integration. Media allow citizens to unite en masse around shared mediated political experiences, such as national nominating conventions and major presidential addresses, and to come together as a nation. Newspapers, radio and television historically have made it possible to convey information of common interest to a general audience (Katz, 1996). In the current era, Internet communication is increasing fulfilling this role.

Some scholars, however, have expressed concerns that digital era communication has been leading to increased societal atomization, as media messages are tailored to appeal to individual consumers. The more choice individual media consumers have, the more likely they are to exclude opinions with which they disagree (Mutz and Martin, 2001; Chalif, 2011; Stroud, 2011). As the preceding discussion of selective exposure suggests, excessive customization of information enables people to attend to only certain content or to avoid consumption of news and political information altogether (Sunstein, 2001; Tewksbury, 2005). This type of behavior may lead people to develop highly polarized views on issues. 'Different patterns of news exposure may lead people to develop different impressions of what is happening in the world around them' (Stroud, 2008: 366). Further, avoidance of political information and debate may be more prevalent among those who have the least in society. The result may

be to further concentrate influence over the political process more firmly in the hands of elites and particular segments of society whose stakes are already strong established (Prior, 2007).

The concern over the increased specialization of information in message silos attended to selectively by audiences is matched by a concern over the tendency toward globalization, where everyone will receive the same limited messages (Katz, 1996). That there are numerous outlets where ideological content is prevalent does not necessarily mean that people will engage in selective exposure. The increased consolidation of media ownership and the tendency to produce similar content that is disseminated and widely consumed worldwide provides some support for the globalization hypothesis.

CONCLUSION

The current political media landscape is filled with contradictions. The offerings are vast and growing, yet the content is constrained and repetitious. The audience has never had more platform choices, but individuals gravitate toward a small number of highly visible options. While there are significant opportunities for people to tailor their media use to conform to their political predispositions, evidence of selective exposure is mixed at best.

As the political media system grows in complexity and scope, it is becoming increasingly difficult to study and evaluate. As Jenkins observes, 'We are in an age of media transition, one marked by tactical decisions and unintended consequences, mixed signals and competing interests, and most of all, unclear directions and unpredictable outcomes' (2006: 11). Identifying the audiences for political communication has become challenging, especially as the online environment defies traditionally boundaries. Assessing the effects of the abundant varieties of media on audiences and society has become an especially complicated undertaking. Evaluations of the implications of the media system for democratic societies no doubt will become even further contested. It is likely that the evolution, reach and consequences of a media system which is both consolidating and fragmenting will remain the subject of much scholarly research and debate for decades to come.

REFERENCES

Anderson, C. (2006) *The Long Tail.* New York: Hyperion.

Arango, T. (2009) 'Fall in Newspaper Sales Accelerates to Pass 7%', 27 April, http://www.nytimes.com/2009/04/28/business/media/28paper.html?_r=1 (accessed 2 August 2009).

Arrington, M. (2009) 'Facebook Now Nearly Twice the Size of MySpace Worldwide', 22 January, http://www.techcrunch.com/2009/01/22/facebook-now-nearly twice-the-size-of-myspace-worldwide/ (accessed 14 August 2009).

Baker, C. E. (2002) *Media, Markets, and Democracy*. New York: Cambridge University Press.

Barker, D. C. (2002) *Rushed to Judgment*. New York: Columbia University Press.

Baum, M. A. (2005) 'Talking the Vote: Why Presidential Candidates Hit the Talk Show Circuit', *American Journal of Political Science*, 49(2): 213–34.

Baumgartner, J. and Morris, J. S. (2006) 'The Daily Show Effect', *American Politics Research*, 34(3): 341–67.

Bennett, W. L. (2005) 'The Twilight of Mass Media News', in T. E. Cook (ed.), *Freeing the Presses*. Baton Rouge, LS: Louisiana State University Press.

Blumler, J. G., Gurevitch, M. and Katz, E. (1985) 'Reaching Out: A Future for Gratifications Research', in K. E. Rosengren, L. A. Wenner and P. Palmgreen (eds.), *Media Gratifications Research: Current Perspectives*. Beverly Hills, CA: Sage. pp. 255–73.

Chaffee, S. H. and Mutz, D. C. (1988) 'Comparing Mediated and Interpersonal Communication Data', in R. P. Hawkins, J. M. Wiemann and S. Pingree (eds.), *Advancing Communication Science*. Newbury Park, CA: Sage. pp. 19–43.

Chaffee, S. H. and Metzger, M. J. (2001) 'The End of Mass Communication', *Mass Communication and Society*, 4(4): 365–79.

Chalif, R. (2011) 'Political Media Fragmentation: Echo Chambers in Cable News', *Electroni Media and Politics*, 1(3): 46–65.

Chester, J. (2007) *Digital Destiny*. New York: The New Press.

Davis, R. and Owen, D. (1998) *New Media and American Politics*. New York: Oxford University Press.

Garrett, R. K. (2009) 'Echo Chambers Online?: Politically Motivated Selective Exposure Among Internet News Users', *Journal of Computer-Mediated Communication*, 14(2): 265–85.

Gitlin, T. (2002) *Media Unlimited*. New York: Henry Holt and Company.

Graf, J. (2006) 'The Audience for Political Bogs: New Research on Blog Readership', research report. Washington, DC: Institute for Politics, Democracy and the Internet, George Washington University.

Hamilton, J. T. (2004) *All the News That's Fit to Sell*. Princeton, NJ: Princeton University Press.

Havick, J. (2000) 'The Impact of the Internet on a Television-based Society', *Technology and Society*, 22(2): 273–87.

Hindman, M. (2009) *The Myth of Digital Democracy*. Princeton, NJ: Princeton University Press.

Howard, P. N. (2006) *New Media Campaigns and the Managed Citizen*. New York: Cambridge University Press.

Jamieson, K. H. and Cappella, J. N. (2008) *Echo Chamber*. New York: Oxford University Press.

Jenkins, H. (2006) *Convergence Culture*. New York: New York University Press.

Johnson-Greene, C. (2009) 'AARP Shows Largest Growth in Readership', 18 May, http://www.foliomag.com/2009/aarp-shows-largest-readership-growth-people-largest-audience (accessed 20 August 2009).

Katz, E. (1996) 'And Deliver Us from Segmentation', *Annals of the American Academy of Political and Social Science*, 546: 22–33.

Kim, Y. M. and Vishak, J. (2008) 'Just Laugh! You Don't Need to Remember: The Effects of Entertainment Media on Political Information Acquisition and Information Processing in Political Judgment', *Communication*, 58(2): 338–60.

Kinder, D. R. (2003) 'Communication and Politics in the Age of Information', in D. O. Sears, L. L. Huddie and R. Jervis (eds.), *Oxford Handbook of Political Psychology*. New York: Oxford University Press. pp. 357–93.

Kiss, J. (2009) 'What's Yours and Mine Is Ours', *The Guardian*, 5 January, http://www.guardian.co.uk/media/2009/jan/05/digital-media-downturn (accessed 12 August 2009).

Klapper, J. T. (1960) *The Effects of Mass Communication*. Glencoe, IL: The Free Press.

Klinenberg, E. (2005) 'Convergence: News Production in a Digital Age', *Annals of the American Academy of Political and Social Science*, 597(1): 48–64.

Langeveld, M. (2009) 'Online Newspaper Audience Growth: Good News? Not Really', 26 April, http://www.niemanlab.org/2009/04/online-newspaper-audience-growth-good-news-not-really/ (accessed 17 August 2009).

Lawrence, Jr, D. (1993) 'Why Future Is Promising for Newspaper Industry', *Newspaper Research Journal*, 14(2): 11–7.

Lipsman, A. (2008) 'Huffington Post and Politico Lead Wave of Explosive Growth at Independent Political Blogs and News Sites this Election', 22 October, http://www.comscore.com/press/release.asp?press=2525 (accessed 22 November 2008).

McChesney, R. W. (1999) *Rich Media, Poor Democracy*. New York: The New Press.

McChesney, R. W. (2004) *The Problem of the Media*. New York: Monthly Review Press.

McQuail, D. and Windahl, S. (1981) *Communication Models for the Study of Mass Communication*. New York: Longman.

Morris, J. (2009) 'The Daily Show with Jon Stewart and Audience Attitude Change During the 2004 Party Conventions', *Political Behavior*, 31(1): 79–102.

Morris, M. and Ogan, C. (1996) 'The Internet as Mass Medium', *Journal of Communication*, 46(1): 21–32.

Mutz, D. C. and Martin, P. S. (2001) 'Facilitating Communication Across Lines of Political Difference: The Role of Mass Media', *American Political Science Review*, 95(1): 97–114.

Newspaper Association of America (2009) 'Newspaper Web Site Audience Increases More Than Ten Percent in First Quarter to 73.3 Million Visitors', 23 April, http://www.naa.org/PressCenter/SearchPressReleases/2009/News

paper-Web-Site-Audience-Increases-More-Than-Ten-Percent.aspx (accessed 17 August 2009).

Nielsen Online (2009) 'MSNBC, CNN Top Global NEws Sites in March, NY Times Top Paper', 21 April, http://blog.nielsen.com/nielsenwire/online_mobile/msnbc-and-cnn-top-global-news-sites-in-march/ (accessed 17 August 2009).

Owen, D. (2005) '"New Media" and Contemporary Interpretations of Freedom of the Press', in T. E. Cook (ed.), *Freeing the Presses*. Baton Rouge, LS: Louisiana State University Press. pp. 139–62.

Owen, D. (2006) 'The Internet and Youth Civic Engagement in the United States', in S. Oates, D. Owen and R. K. Gibson (eds.), *The Internet and Politics*. New York: Routledge. pp. 20–38.

Owen, D. (2009) 'The Campaign and the Media', in J. M. Box-Steffensmeier and S. E. Schier (eds.), *The American Elections of 2008*. New York: Rowman & Littlefield. pp. 9–32.

Pew Research Center for the People and the Press (2008a) 'Audience Segments in a Changing News Environment', research report. Washington, DC: Pew Research Center for the People and the Press.

Pew Research Center for the People and the Press (2008b) 'Few will Miss Campaign News', 12 November, http://people-press.org/report/470/favorite-campaign-journalists (accessed 19 November 2008).

Prior, M. (2007) *Post-Broadcast Democracy*. Princeton, NJ: Princeton University Press.

Project for Excellence in Journalism (2009) 'The State of the News Media 2009', research report. Washington, DC: Project for Excellence in Journalism.

Rosenthal, P. (2008) 'New Newspaper Paid-circulation Figures Out', 27 October, http://newsblogs.chicagotribune.com/towerticker/2008/10/new-newspaper-p.html (accessed 20 November 2008).

Rosenwald, M. (2008) 'Washington Post, Balitmore Sun to Begin Sharing Some News Content', 24 December, http://www.washingtonpost.com/wpdyn/content/article/2008/12/23/AR2008122301161.html

Rubinson, J. (2008) 'Marketing in the Era of Long-Tail Media', *Journal of Advertizing Research*, 48(3): 301–2.

Sanders, K. (2009) *Communicating Politics in the Twenty-first Century*. New York: Palgrave Macmillan.

Schramm, W. (1954) *Process and Effects of Mass Communication*. New York: Basic Books.

Sears, D. O. and Freedman, J. L. (1967) 'Selective Exposure to Information: A Critical Review', *Public Opinion Quarterly*, 31(2): 194–213.

Serpick, E. (2009) 'Stop the Presses', *Baltimore Magazine*, September: 86–93, 134.

Smith, A. (2008) 'New Numbers for Blogging and Blog Readership', 22 July, http://www.pewinternet.org/Commentary/2008/July/New-numbers-for-blogging-and-blog-readership.aspx (accessed 3 August 2009).

Smith, A., Schlozman, K. L., Verba, S. and Brady, H. (2009) 'The Internet and Civic Engagement', research report. Washington, DC: Pew Internet and American Life Project.

Steinberg, J. (2008) 'The Buzz on the Bus: Pinched, Press Steps Off', 26 March, http://www.nytimes.com/2008/03/26/us/politics/26bus.html?hp (accessed 1 November 2008).

Stromer-Galley, J. (2003) 'Diversity of Political Conversation on the Internet: User's Perspective', *Journal of Computer-Mediated Communication*, 8(3).

Stroud, N. J. (2008) 'Media Use and Political Predispositions: Revisiting the Concept of Selective Exposure', *Political Behavior*, 30(3): 341–66.

Stroud, N. J. (2011) *Niche News: The Politics of News Choice*. New York: Oxford University Press.

Sunstein, C. (2001) *Republic.com*. Princeton, NJ: Princeton University Press.

Technorati (2008) 'State of the Blogosphere/2008', http://technorati.com/blogging/state-of-the-blogosphere/ (accessed 14 August 2009).

Tewksbury, D. (2005) 'The Seeds of Audience Fragmentation: Specialization in the Use of Online Media', *Journal of Broadcasting and Electronic Media*, 49(3): 332–48.

Wattenberg, M. P. (2008) *Is Voting for Young People?* New York: Pearson/Longman.

Winograd, M. and Hais, M. D. (2008). *Millennial Makeover*. New Brunswick, NJ: Rutgers University Press.

Wolff, M. (2009) 'Politico's Washington Coup', *Vanity Fair*, August: 74–7.

Xenos, M. A. and Becker, A. B. (2009) 'Moments of Zen: Effects of The Daily Show on Information Seeking and Political Learning', *Political Communication*, 26(3): 317–32.

Zillmann, D. and Bryant, J. (1985) 'Selective-Exposure Phenomena', in D. Zillmann and J. Bryant (eds.), *Selective Exposure to Communication*. Hillsdale, NJ: Lawrence Erlbaum Associates. pp. 1–10.

32

Democratization and the Changing Media Environment in South Korea

June Woong Rhee and Eun-mee Kim

HOW DO MEDIA CONTRIBUTE TO DEMOCRATIZATION?

Media scholars have long wondered whether media serve as an agent of change or stability in the democratization of developing countries (Ette, 2000; Gross, 2002, 2008; Hughes and Lawson, 2005; Ojo, 2007; Porto, 2007; Yang, 2000). The ebbs and flows of democracy coupled with the dual role of the media as a conveyer of democratic values and as an instrument of authoritarian rule defy any easy generalization. While it sounds utterly cliché to say that the role of media may vary depending on factors such as their relation to political power, the extent and ways of state control, development of civil society and size of media market, the interaction between the media and political system needs further elaboration.

What would be the consequences of a newly founded democracy's liberalizing media policy? Does the expansion of media market contribute to media independence and journalistic professionalization? How do the new media affect traditional print and broadcasting industry? Does distrust and cynicism about existing media lead to popularization of alternative news media? How do the Internet media stimulate a new form of public engagement in politics? These questions were repeatedly asked and answered, only to pile up particular cases from massively dissimilar contexts.

We believe the experiences of South Korea (hereafter, Korea) provide a vantage point from which to observe and theorize the role of the media in a rapidly changing society. The reasons are twofold. First, the case of Korean democratization makes it possible to examine the complex interactions among state power, civil society and the media in the process of democratization. Korea, rapidly transformed into a developing economic power under bureaucratic authoritarian regimes from 1961 to 1987, passed the threshold of democratic transition when people's movement of June 1987 forced the authoritarian regime to amend the constitution for direct presidential election and to accept liberalizing reform policies. The current sixth Republic of Korea, having secured five consecutive peaceful turnovers of political power under the current constitution, is taking firm steps toward democratic consolidation. In the process, the mass media, both traditional and new, and the Internet have played significant roles.

Second, a strong academic tradition of media and communication studies in Korea has produced data and interpretations in the field of political communication, which makes it possible to assess the role of the media in democratization. Two major academic societies, Korean Society for Journalism and Communication Studies (KSJCS) and Korean Association for Broadcasting and Telecommunication Studies (KABS), boast a union set of more than 500 scholars and professionals. Celebrating the 50th anniversary of KSJCS, Choi (2009) reviewed research articles in the field of political communication published in the flagship journal, *Korean Journal of Journalism and Communication Studies*. During the period of democratic consolidation (1988–2008), a total of 202 articles were published in the journal. Among them, 65 studies (33%) were election studies, 136 studies (67%) employed empirical research methods. That is, the Korean case is not only an interesting illustration but also comes with extensively annotated collections of data.

This chapter consists of two parts. The first focuses on the relationship between the political system and the media. We look at Korean political system in democratic transition and consolidation and then present three interrelated changes on the part of the media in relation to the transition: changes in media market; changing media representations of politics and new experiences of media users. These changes had consequences for how individuals reflect upon the political climate, how they trust or distrust the media and how they see themselves as citizens. Being closely intertwined with political actors – such as governments, political parties and civil society movements – the media contributed to political changes such as intensifying political parallelism, stimulating political engagement and enhancing democratic values and practices.

The second part examines the effects of increased use of the Internet on democratic citizenship. Although we emphasize the differing roles of print media, public service broadcasters and the Internet media in enhancing democratic citizenship, our primary focus will be on increased use of the Internet as a news provider and a discussion space. In Korea, the Internet has been considered the most important medium for democratization. Indeed, the potential it has for building up a public sphere seemed to actualize a renewed expectation of discursive democracy. However, what should be considered is that the increased use of Internet news, popularization of Internet discussion and its ability to bring people out on the street occurred within the context of an existing media and political system in a transitional democracy.

ROLE OF THE MEDIA IN DEMOCRATIC TRANSITION AND CONSOLIDATION IN KOREA

A Democratic Transitional Model of Political System

Inspired by Hallin and Mancini's (2004) suggestion that the comparative systematic approach be applicable to media systems outside of Western Europe and North America, Rhee et al. (2010) proposed a democratic transitional model, the Korean case. The model was built up to examine the relationship between the Korean media and political system during the democratic transition in 1987–92 and subsequent consolidation in 1993–2009 (see Table 32.1). The model incorporated the same four dimensions of a media system that Hallin and Mancini proposed: the development of mass circulation press; political parallelism; journalistic professionalism and state intervention in the media system. However, the authors argued the political system variables discussed in Hallin and Mancini's had to be substantial revised and extended to capture the transitional nature of the Korean political system.

Rhee et al. (2010) summed up the nature of the Korean political system by underlining (1) a contrast between strong bureaucratic state power and week political power of governments, (2) declining political party system, (3) fragmented civil society and self-regarding social movement organizations, (4) strong presidential system and majoritarian political culture and (5) a lack of rational-legal authority and strong clientelism. Characterized in this way, the Korean political system looks similar to the Mediterranean or polarized pluralist model. But the ambiguity of state power, weak political parties and strong majoritarianism based on a presidential system set it apart. Among the five variables, the last two are equivalent to the two of Hallin and Manici's: majoritarian government and rational-legal authority. However, the first three need further elaboration.

Weakening Political Power of Democratic Governments

During the democratization, state power was divided into two separate entities of strong bureaucratic institutions and weak governments (Choi, 2005). State power, strengthened by brute force and ideologies, such as aggressive anti-Communism and industrial developmentalism under the authoritarian regimes from 1961 to 1987, was considered the most important power institution in Korea. The so-called 'condensed modernization' in the authoritarian era was achieved by the state-controlled mobilization of both industrial and social resources (Han, 1995; Im and Chung, 1999). During the five consecutive peaceful turnovers of political power after the democratic transition 1987–97, however, the separation between the bureaucratic power of administrative institutions and political power of the government got widened. The former remained strong, while the latter fluctuated to such an extent that the governments were not able to build what Rhee et al. (2010) referred to as 'democratic hegemony'.

Administrative institutions dominated all policy areas including industry, finance, education, culture and media. For example, since 1988, the media regulators Korean Broadcasting and Telecommunication Commission and Korean Broadcasting and Telecommunication Standard Commission, having started as an independent civic commissions, then turned into governmental bodies that wielded strong regulatory powers over broadcasters with programming regulations, quality evaluation and content standard reinforcement.

However, the democratic governments could not command respect from political oppositions, civil society groups and the media. The governments after Kim Young Sam's have been exposed to severe criticisms by major newspapers without having any effectual measure of defense. At the first phase of democratic consolidation 1993–97 (see Table 32.1), the conservative Kim Young Sam government started with a relatively high level of popular support as well as support from the conservative base. By contrast, at the successive phase of democratic consolidation, the reformative Kim Dae-Jung and Roh Moo-Hyun governments and the conservative Lee Myung-Bak government managed to garner support only from their own supporters (Rhee et al., 2010). The governments in this period have been routinely attacked and thus swayed by hostile print media and opposing civil society groups as well as the opposition parties. The democratization of state institutions did not go with substantial representativeness of political parties and consolidation of civil society. A fragmented civil society and weak party system were curious companions of democracy in Korea.

Fragmented Civil Society and Weak Party System

During the transitional period, civil society groups and social movement organizations tested out political candidates, monitored political representatives and set citizen-generated agenda. After the democratic transition, however, the civil society became fragmented. Conflicts were transformed from 'civil society versus the state' into 'civil society versus civil society' (Choi, 2005). Social movement became self-regarding without creating a common ground for public interests. Traditional political conflicts among provincial regions and ideological camps were superseded by societal ones among generations, solidarities, religions and ecological positions (Kim, 2000).

Major political parties in Korea, conservative or liberal, have long suffered from divisionism rooted in regionalism and dependence on leader popularity. Under the authoritarian regimes, when civil society was underdeveloped, political parties and social movement groups were the only institutions representing and organizing people's interests and demands. During the democratic transition 1987–92, political parties contributed to political pact-making so as to smooth the transition. However, as Choi (2005) persuasively argued, when the democratic transition was made and people raised their voices to demand better lives, political parties failed to represent the people's interests and to practice accountability. In particular, owing to the fact that the political ideologies of the major political parties were confined within a limited range of the political spectrum, people in the middle and the end-sides of the political spectrum came to feel unrepresented. Accordingly, the people who perceived themselves to be unrepresented by major political parties and traditional media became deeply dissatisfied with politics-as-usual and turned to new forms of political engagement in Internet activities (Rhee, 2005). The fragmentation of civil society exacerbated the lack of representativeness of political parties.

Korean Media System in Democratization

A media system, even when underdeveloped, interacts with other sub-systems of a society. It contributes to differentiation and integration of the total system by mediating communication among sub-systems. In a rapidly changing society, such as Korea, its role becomes even greater. Existing media might play critical role in shaping political institutions. Newly established media might make for a space in which actors in political institutions and civil society become engaged with one another, which in turn creates a new media milieu.

In what follows, we examine three interrelated changes in the Korean media system: changes in media market; the changing role of government in intervention of the media and intensified political parallelism. We do this in terms of the four dimensions of media system in Hallin and Mancini (2004) in order to highlight the similarities and differences of the Korean system to those of Western Europe and North America. Another reason is to demonstrate that the Korean case does not quite 'fit' with any ideal type of the developed models that Hallin and Mancini proposed, implying that it will develop into a new kind of democratic model.

Table 32.1 Governments and the media in Korean democratic transition and consolidation

President	Park Chung-Hee Chun Doo-Hwan (1961–87)	Roh Tae-Woo (1988–92)	Kim Young Sam (1993–97)	Kim Dae-Jung (1998–2002)	Roh Moo-Hyun (2003–07)	Lee Myung-Bak (2008–)
Government ideology Democratization	Authoritarian –	Conservative Transitional	Reformative conservative Consolidation (1st phase)	Liberal	Reformative liberal Consolidation (2nd phase)	Conservative
State power	Oppressive	Weak democratic hegemony	Strong democratic hegemony (1st half)		Weakening democratic hegemony	
Media policy	Oppressive regulation	Regulated liberalization	1st de-regulation	Regulation of newspaper market	Failed press regulation	2nd deregulation
Media industry	Controlled market	Expansion of market			Increasingly competitive market	
Major events	Oppressive media consolidation (80); Color television broadcasting (80)	Journalist unions (87); Korean Broadcasting Commission (88); Reformative paper *Hankyoreh* launched (88); Commercial broadcaster SBS launched (90); 1st political TV ads (92)	KBS 1 going ad-free (94); 1st TV debates (95); Licensing CATVs (95); Severe newspaper competition (95); Abolishing newspaper directives (98)	New broadcasting act (00); *Ohmynews* lunched (00); Reviving newspaper directives (01); Growing popularity of Internet portals' news service (02)	Presidential impeachment (04); Amendment to public official election act(05); Closing news rooms in the government (07)	Citizen protests against import of the US beefs (08); Amendments to the broadcasting act and the newspaper act (09)

Source: Rhee et al. (2010).

Expansion and Fluctuation of Media Market

The 'controlled regulation' of the media market during the Roh Tae-Woo government, 1988–92, and the aggressive deregulation in the Kim Young Sam government, 1993–97, led to a rapid expansion of the media market (Cho, 2003). Examples of this expansion include: a reformative newspaper *The Hankyoreh* launched into the already competitive newspaper market in 1988; licensing of a commercial broadcaster, SBS, which effectively broke up the duopoly of public service broadcasting in 1990; the introduction of cable television in 1995 brought new business for program providers and system operators. The media market expanded as the advertising industry grew at a phenomenal rate.

It has to be emphasized that the expansion of the media market in democratic Korea was achieved on top of a significant development of the mass circulation press. Hallin and Mancini (2004) considered the development of the mass circulation press a crucial yardstick in characterizing a media system. One indicator is newspaper sales per adult population, in which the countries in the North European Model score highest, those in the North Atlantic Model score modestly and those in the Mediterranean Model score rather low (Hallin and Mancini, 2004: 23). The available statistic for Korea in *World Press Trends 2006* (World Association of Newspapers, 2006) showed Korea ranking sixth among about 200 countries. Its rank was right next to Sweden and Switzerland and above the UK and Germany. Considering the newspaper sales have been plummeting during the 2000s mainly because of increasing online news users and public perception of 'unfairness' (Rhee and Choi, 2005), the indicator might be even higher in the 1990s. The almost perfect literacy rate, excessively high level of higher education, fast developing economy and relatively low subscription fee may contribute to the high development of mass circulation dailies in Korea (Rhee et al., 2010), which would put Korea in a unique position in the group of the democratic transitional countries.

During the second phase of democratic consolidation, 1998–2009, however, the expanded media market fluctuated due to two economic predicaments, the 1998 foreign exchange crisis and the 2008 financial crisis, as well as to the rise of Internet media. National newspapers, having invested heavily in printing infrastructure to cope with increasing competition in early 1990s, had to endure shrinking subscription and advertising revenues in late 1990s onward. With the introduction of new media such as cable, satellite, digital multimedia broadcasting for mobile devices (DMB) and internet protocol-based TV (IPTV) to the market, the total revenue of the broadcasting industry steadily increased. Among the electronic media, the revenue share of terrestrial broadcasting has been decreasing. In terms of the amount of time spent on media, the declining ratings of terrestrial broadcasters were caused by increasing Internet use (Lee, 2005; Rhee et al., 2006). The equivalent negative correlation between newspaper circulation and Internet media was not substantiated. Internet service providers, including portals, social networking and game service providers, have themselves grown at a phenomenal rate, infiltrating the print and broadcasting market.

Government Intervention of the Media

The Korean government traditionally regarded licensing new media and driving media policies as an opportunity to create professional jobs and to stimulate the cultural industry. At the same time, the government put in place effective measures to control public service broadcasters and other licensed media companies. For example, under the newly amended Broadcasting Act 2000, state intervention on public service broadcasting was so strong that, as the shift in political power from conservative to liberal occurred, the political orientation of the major public service broadcaster changed over time in a way to align its orientation with that of the government in power.

When it comes to print media, however, state intervention through government advertisement, tax reduction and legal control seemed ineffectual. The major reason is that the Korean press itself became a political power after the democratic transition (Kang, 2004a; Park and Chang, 2000). Youm (1996) observed that the Korean media turned themselves from a 'voluntary servant' into an 'equal contender' of the state. When the democratic government political power weakened in the later phase of democratic consolidation, lacking 'democratic hegemony' over conflicting political parities and fragmented civil society, the media took their chance to attack the ideologically opposite governments. For example, the conservative newspapers routinely editorialized against reformist policies, such as the 'engagement' policy toward North Korea, the progressive real estate holding tax and the education reform policy. They also fiercely resisted the reformative governmental initiatives for media reform including 'media tax audit' and 'newspaper directives', condemning them as 'an attempt to tame critical newspapers' (Yang, 2005: 30). Equally, liberal newspapers, such as *The Hankyoreh* and *Kyung Hyang*, attacked the conservative governments by editorializing against them.

Under the governmental support for 'information industry', Korean Internet business grew faster than anyone's expectations. From 1997 to 2002, the Internet media were established as a major journalistic institution in Korea (Choi, 2006). Web versions of major newspapers and broadcasters were available early in 1997. By the time of the 2002 presidential election, which was recognized as 'the first election with extensive Internet campaigns', Internet portals emerged as a dominant news provider. They placed news at the center of front pages and allowed search engines to access all the news from existing news media, news agencies and mushrooming online news providers. Since the government had regarded Internet business as an object of industrial promotion, Internet service providers, including major portals and online news providers, enjoyed full support. After the conservative party returned to power in 2007, the government found the Internet media to be a threat to conservative political ideology as well as a uncontrollable medium in which privacy, personal reputation and copyrights are routinely violated.

of factual information. Asked how much they influence public opinion, the average answer of Korean journalists was 7.5 on a scale of 0 to 10 (Korea Press Foundation, 2007). This result contrasted with their self-evaluations of 'fairness' and 'professionalism': only 35% and 24% of the journalists thought of themselves on the side of 'fair' and 'professional', respectively.

Citizens' trust in the print and the broadcasting media declined with some fluctuations (Rhee, 2005). A recent audience survey revealed that 69% of 5000 respondents considered print journalists 'political biased' and 62% 'the failure to distinguish between facts and opinions'. Regarding broadcast journalists, the percentages of the respondents for the same questions were 63% and 51%, respectively (Korea Press Foundation, 2008). Declining trust in the news media was reflected in journalists' perception of their trustworthiness. The Korean journalists perceived the general public's evaluation of the trustworthiness of the press and the broadcasting's trustworthiness as 6.2 and 6.6, respectively, on the scales of 0 to 10 (Korea Press Foundation, 2007).

Journalistic Professionalism and Citizens' Distrust of the Media

Reviewing professional assessments of major events related to the violation of journalistic ethics and survey results conducted by the Korean Press Foundation, Rhee et al. (2010) assessed that journalistic professionalism was not substantially practiced in Korea. The strong ideological orientations of major newspapers and the weak defense of the public service broadcaster against governmental interventions were the recurring major themes. Higher ranking journalists shared political ideologies with elite politicians and often left the profession to join in the politics (Chang, 2006). The increasingly competitive nature of the media market led journalists to concentrate only on job security (Lee and Kim, 2006). A 2007 survey of journalists confirmed the lack of professionalism: only 52% of 907 responding journalists considered themselves 'very free' or 'somewhat free' in their journalistic practices although this was an improvement when compared to 47% in 2003. They particularly found advertisers (61% of the respondents), their publisher (40%) and the government (34%) to be threats to their freedom (Korea Press Foundation, 2007).

In general, Korean journalists consider themselves to 'influence public opinion' and find this a journalistically important function. That is, their role orientation seems to be geared toward to 'publicist' or 'advocate' rather than to a provider

Intensified Political Parallelism and Changing Media Milieu

As democracy consolidated in Korea, the role of the news media in politics has grown. One area of research showing this tendency is election studies. During the authoritarian regimes and the democratic transitional period, the determining factors of voting were found to be voters' regionalism. However, numerous election studies conducted during the second phase of the democratic consolidation revealed that voters' perception of candidate images, attitudes toward candidates, emotions toward candidates and issue proximities influenced voting in addition to the independent effects of regionalism, age group and political ideology (for a review, see Choi, 2009). Importantly, the images, attitudes, emotions and issue positions of candidates were conveyed, interpreted and reinforced by the coverage of election campaigns, television debates and election poll reports.

Korean news media became a powerful political institution in terms not only of influencing citizens' perception and attitude but also of functioning as ideological agents. Major newspapers decided to take sides with major political parties, while the public service broadcaster oscillated depending on who was in power (Cho, 2003; Yang, 2000). For example, Yoon (2001) found major national newspapers' editorials about the government policy of North Korea had significantly changed in such a way that the content of conservative and the liberal dailies were ideologically differentiated over time. It was concluded that the press–party parallelism measured by ideological orientation of news content had intensified between the Kim Young Sam government (1993–97) and the Kim Dae-Jung government (1998–2002).

Rhee et al. (2010) even argued that the mainstream press was the determining actor reinforcing political parallelism during the democratic transition and consolidation. The press became politically stronger by proposing initiatives for the ideological agenda and by wielding political power even over political parties.

The Internet news media had a significant effect in the shaping of the social–political agenda and even in changing the direction of election campaigns since the 2002 presidential election (Choi, 2006). By 2006, news consumption on the Internet was comparable to those of the print and broadcasting. A comprehensive survey of news users conducted by Korean Advertiser Association (2006) showed that 44% of 10,000 adult respondents were regularly exposed to Internet news on a weekly base as compared to 61% and 98% to the press and broadcasting, respectively. Users, on average, spent 26 minutes accessing news per day, while 30 and 42 minutes were spent on the print and broadcasting, respectively.

A multitude of ideologically oriented news providers mushroomed on the Internet, representing political extremes and social minorities. Some online news providers experimented with 'citizen journalism' with the help of voluntary reporting by citizens as in *Ohmynews*. Internet portals emerged as the biggest news provider offering additional services such as editable news boxes, search engines and related bulletin boards. In addition to this, Internet news media as a whole provided a new mode of news consumption. First, Internet news users could access different sources and channels of news so that they could compare a diverse range of perspectives represented in different news media (Han, 2003; Park, 2001). Second, they could access other users' comments and interpretations in the attached replies and express their opinions and comments (Na and Rhee, 2008). And finally, they could even mobilize popular support by initiating collective actions on- or offline (Park, 2001).

USING INTERNET MEDIA AND ITS IMPACT ON DEMOCRATIC CITIZENSHIP

As early as the late 1990s, media scholars and commentators in Korea pointed to the possibility that the changes Internet uses brought about would have political consequences by widening civic participation, increasing political information production and dissemination and heightening citizens' political engagement (Whang, 1996; Yoon, 1998). Although it may be still early to predict whether the Internet will renew the public sphere in the sense of the enlargement of open and equal discursive participation in the end, some of the changes concomitant with the spread of Internet use in Korea show signs of being a step in the direction of building a discursive and participatory democracy. This section focuses on the Internet, especially Internet news provision and political discussions, in relation to the democratic citizenship of Korean people.

Internet News and Political Awareness

The Internet was hailed as an alternative news source in Korea. Although established newspapers were quick to test the opportunity of a new medium in late 1990s, it was an alternative news service, such as *Ohmynews*, exclusive to the Internet, which initially revolutionized the way Korean Internet users consumed news. In a exercise of tracking how a news story diffused on the Internet, Im et al. (2008) were able to record the complex and dynamic process of diffusion, addition of facts and opinions, displacement, reuse and decline of a news story. In a similar vein, Kim and Lee (2006) proposed the concept of 'reverse agenda-setting' by showing a process in which a news story initiated by individual Internet users became carried by diverse channels on the Internet news providers and finally taken up by mainstream news media.

With increasing access to the Internet, the sheer number of news providers increased sharply. In particular, as portals functioned as an integrated gateway to access a broad range of news channels and sources, more people began to rely on the portals to compare news from diverse news channels and sources and to consult comments and replies attached to the news. Big portals in Korea successfully provide a one-stop service including not only news and news replies boards but also discussion forums, search engine, online community services, shopping, blogs, email and messaging.

Although there is no denying that the amount and diversity of news provided on the Internet increased, some research pointed out that the consumption of news, if it is limited to 'political' news, did not really increase that much and was the preserve of a particular subsets of Internet population, mostly college-educated males (Park, 2004). Regarding news consumption and the posting of comments on the Internet, Kim and Rhee (2006) emphasized that the major political consequences of Internet use came from the users' activity of 'reading'. Here 'reading' refers not only to reading news and commentaries of professional news providers but also to reading comments and replies of fellow citizens. The effect of reading activity was evident in increasing tolerance of divergent opinion from one's own, increasing intention to participate in political actions and an increasing belief that online discussion should hold up to a certain normative standard, while the effect of writing was only found in the intention to participate.

Both readers and writers are more likely to be male, aged and of a high education level (Kim and Rhee, 2006; Park 2004). The profile was contrary to the common belief in Korea that those who discussed politics online were rather the less-educated and inexperienced young who did not know much about politics. An interesting finding was that the strength of ideological orientation of either direction was significantly related to reading activity but not to the posting (Kim and Rhee, 2006). Internet reading was closely related to political knowledge and newspaper reading. However, comparable findings were not made for Internet writing. It seems that those who sought information to gain political knowledge and to consult others' interpretations read more on the Internet but they did not necessarily engage in expressing their voice in writing.

Hwang (2001) underlined that the types of information rather than the amount of information that people consumed mattered for political participation. Categorizing the political information available on the Internet, as of 2000, into political news, mobilization and entertainments, he found that those who were traditionally active in participation were more likely to seek political news on the Internet. In addition, it was found that among the three types of political information, only the use of political organization websites affected political participation while others and the amount of general Internet use did not.

The empirical results reported above implied that, in terms of Internet use for political information, we need to differentiate the type of users, the type of information and the type of activities. The increased access to news of diverse channels and sources combined with political discussion, especially reading others' opinions, not only helped citizens to gain political knowledge but also allowed them to express their own opinions through news consumption. In summary, using Internet as a news media involves the interactive process whereby news is consumed, appropriated and reused by users who relay, add or put in comments. It seems that Korean users' active involvement in 'using' Internet news encourages discursive participation and in the process subverts the established relationship between the media, audiences and information gain. As the line between news consumption and discursive participation gets thinner, it becomes harder to tell which side of the relation between media and users adds value of information.

Discursive Participation

Avid political discussion and civic journalism activities by citizen journalists can be attributed to the profound distrust in mainstream journalism (Park, 2001; Rhee, 2005). Korean citizens' interest and participation on online discussion forums pre-dated the wide diffusion of broadband. Pre-Internet computer network users' activity in political discussions left a legacy on how general people in Korea perceived and expected the potential of this emerging medium (Park, 2001). Student activists who have been one of the key citizen groups that drove democratization movements used networked computers in the early and mid-1990s to release information which could not have been distributed through the established media outlets and to discuss such information among themselves.

However, Yoon (1998) showed that discussion of political issues, even by the most elitist group of college students, did not quite qualify as deliberative discussion. He pointed out that there was no sign of openness, prudence, tolerance of those with divergent opinion or respect of others but only criticisms and attacks and concluded that Internet discussion sites provided a new kind of public sphere for expressing the resistance and identifying differences rather than for reaching understanding and building consensus.

In Rhee and Kim (2004), key social characteristics of Internet discussion participants were surprisingly similar to those of other traditional political activity participants, such as voting or news reading. Writers in Internet political discussion boards were more likely to be male, aged in their late 30s and educated. In addition the writers are more likely to have higher political knowledge and be active news users. Rhee et al. (2005b) analyzed profiles of political discussion participants including communication competence, technical aptitude and ideological orientation to examine the way they related to quality and quantity of political talks. They showed that individual online communication competence, not technical aptitude, affected the participation of online political discussion. Those who were responsive, controlling and relevant in Internet interaction showed better performance in deliberation. Internet user efficacy also contributed to quality of deliberation. In terms of ideological orientation, liberals were more likely to read and write online. However, it was notable that the strength of ideological orientation was only related to reading but not to writing online. The result was the same with the relation to political knowledge and to newspaper consumption. In seems that those who sought information to gain knowledge read more but they did not necessarily engage in writing. However, once they did participate in the online discussion, the quality of deliberation varied by the factors of age, liberalism, Internet communication competency and political involvement.

Rhee et al. (2007) identified online opinion leaders in terms of their ability to gain popular attention and positive reactions from other participants in a portal-based political discussion site. The evidence for popular attention and positive reaction were gathered by compiling the data of the number of hits and the numbers of 'like' or 'dislike' responses regarding each of the comments and replies on the political discussion site. Using this operational definition, they estimated that online opinion leaders made up only 11% of those who participated in the discussion forum studied. The analysis of a sample of 6542 online discussants showed that online opinion leaders are predominantly male, educated, communicatively competent, politically knowledgeable and participatory when compared to the general online public. The picture emerging from these findings was not terribly different from the opinion leaders identified and characterized in the traditional studies of opinion leadership (Katz, 1957, 1980; Rogers and Shoemaker, 1971; Shah and Scheufele, 2006; Weimann, 1991). In addition, informational use of print and broadcasting news were significantly associated with online opinion leadership. That is, the online opinion leaders were more likely to be active users of newspapers and television news.

Korean scholars have raised questions on the quality of online discussion (Kim, 2002; Yoon 1998). However, it seems that concern for quality hinges upon how one defines it. Kim and Rhee (2007), by analyzing the argumentative qualities and narrative structure of the postings on a political discussion site, criticized the conventional concept of deliberation focused too narrowly upon rationality and critical reasoning. They found that most of the postings that elicited engagement, support and replies, by other participants, were based on personal stories and the expression of personal feelings, which was far from the so-called 'rational' discussion. It resonated with earlier research involving newspaper and television news (Kim 2001) that found the effect of private conversation muddled with small talk and affec-

tive exchanges, in addition to news media use, in political opinion formation and participation.

In response to the polarized views on the potential of Internet for renewing the public sphere, Rhee et al. (2005b) argued that not all discussion is the same on the Internet and that the quality and quantity of Internet deliberation might depend on structural and regulative conditions of communication offered by webpage designs and applied discursive rules. Since quality and quantity of deliberation should matter for political knowledge, opinion and civic virtues, structural and regulative conditions might indirectly affect the consequences of online deliberation. The structural and regulative conditions they focused on in a field experiment were exposure of social identity cues, the intervention of moderators in deliberation, and the presence of a mechanism that shows one's level of participation as a graphical device. For example, whether the social identity cues of discussants were shown on the Internet was believed to be linked to the level of social presence. Social identity cues initially seemed to function as a facilitator of quality deliberation. However, this particular effect disappeared when the covariates such as liberalism, Internet user efficacy, Internet communication competency and political involvement were taken into account. It was also found that lack of social identity cues resulted in increased engagement. In summary, the results confirmed that it is worthwhile exploring the conditions of online deliberation that affect how discussion is carried out and how the participants perceive the deliberation and themselves.

Internet Use and Development of Civic Virtues

Efforts have been made to test whether the online activities actually produce civic virtue. There were some evidence suggesting a positive relationship between Internet use and political efficacy and tolerance. Rhee and Kim (2006) revealed that when social identity cues, such as gender and age, were not shown and there was a graphical device showing one's level of participation, online political discussion did have an impact on the political discussion efficacy of participants.

Internet political discussions were empirically examined in relation tolerance. Song et al. (2006) revealed that exposure to divergent opinions on the Internet enhanced cognitive elaboration of others' opinion, which in turn had positive consequences for political tolerance. This study provided strong evidence that exposure to diverse points of view while participating in Internet discussion can affect civic attitude, for example, promoting political tolerance through the mediation of cognitive elaboration. The effect of having conversation with people on tolerance and trust was also studied by Na (2007). Na first differentiated the levels whereby Internet users perceived diversity of viewpoints: the individual level and the collective level. It was found that individual attitudes, such as trust and tolerance, were affected only by the diversity perceived on a collective level, not individual level. However, diversity perceived both individual and collective level was found to increase participation.

Noting that the Internet is a medium for engaging in social connections, there has been a surge of research on the social capital, trust and civic engagement in relation to Internet use. Rhee et al. (2005a) explored such effects and, reflecting the previous research on the uniqueness of 'social trust' in Korea, they explored how Internet use built up institutional trust and interpersonal trust. It was found that both information and entertainment uses of the Internet were build up institutional and interpersonal trust. However, only information use was positively related to social participation while entertainment use was negatively related. Min and Joo (2007) found through an online survey that the amount of time spent on the Internet decreased social capital while the amount of time spent on participating in political discussion increased it. Kang (2004b) also reported that the amount of time spent on the Internet had negative influences on organizational activities and civic voluntary activities. By contrast, Han (2005) found a positive effect of participation in online discussion on tolerance, sense of autonomy and sense of community. In addition, it was confirmed that those with raised sense of autonomy and tolerance were more likely to seek opinions and comments on the Internet but less likely to express their own.

SUMMARY AND IMPLICATIONS

In this chapter, we have tried to present how the transitional Korean political system and the media system formed to make a base to allow the Internet to play a role in terms of the medium of democratization. It is emphasized that the social and political milieu provided a fertile ground for such active use of the Internet as a medium for political information and discussion, which eventually had concomitant consequences for democratic citizenship. The Internet provided citizens with different channels and sources of information, and interpretations so that they could compare a diverse range of news and opinions. The Internet also functioned as a public sphere in which citizens could

seek the opinions of others and express their own. Finally, the Internet could be a mobilizing stimulus to increase civic and political participation.

Of course, the Internet was not solely responsible for the positive roles, but only under specific conditions of the existing media and political system. It should also be noted that political democratization was by no means always triumphant in Korea just like in any other countries. It was plagued by transitional characteristics specific to the Korea political system, such as the contrast between the strong bureaucratic state power and week political power of governments, declining political party system, fragmented civil society and self-regarding social movement organizations. In addition, traditional news media ideologically differentiated. Political parallelism between political parties and the media became intensified. The mainstream media suffered from declining public trust.

The main argument of this chapter can be summarized as follows. As democracy consolidated, political actors and civil society groups were fragmented and accordingly the need for political discussion and social integration increased. The media, traditional and new, played differing roles in democratization. The ideologically differentiated press contributed to intensifying political parallelism by mobilizing political supports. Public service broadcasters tended to be a battleground of political conflicts. Internet media opened up a space for new forms of political engagement. Each medium played a differentiated role. The case of Korea indicates that the increases of communication channels and diversification themselves elicited changes in political communication.

What is taking place in Korea highlights that social communication is one of the central forces that influences democratic transition and consolidation. It is the interaction process among the many facets that make up a society and that bring about changes, whichever direction they take. For example, discursive citizen participation in Korean may provide a detailed case of what Bennett (2008) termed as actualizing citizenship as opposed to dutiful citizenship, that is, an emerging new citizenship. Ultimately, the key driving force behind any social change should be the actors in the system.

When it comes to democratization, according to a theory of democratic transition (Rustow, 1970), it may be worth focusing on the actual process rather than the external conditions of what constitute democracy. Increased and diversified consumption of news and political discussion on the Internet has contributed to the emergence of a new form of citizenship, which in turn contributed to successful consolidation of democracy in Korea. Here, seemingly not-so-rational talks and emotionally charged discussions, if they are widely and consistently practiced, can instigate positive changes, such as increased political efficacy and participatory actions among citizens. It is our conclusion that an integrated theory of media and democratization can be developed by examining specific communication conditions under which a new form of actualizing citizenship emerges out of media use and political discussions.

REFERENCES

Bennett, W. L. (2008) *Civic Life Online: Learning How Digital Can Engage Youth.* Cambridge, MA: MIT Press.

Chang, H. Y. (2006) 'A Study of the Korean Journalists External Networks as a Social Capital: Analysis of Impact Factors and Structural Equivalence', *Korean Journal of Journalism and Communication Studies,* 50(2): 243–66 (in Korean).

Cho, H. (2003) *Democratization and Media Power in Korea.* Seoul: Hanul Academy (in Korean).

Choi, J. G. (2005) *Democracy After Democratization: The Conservative origin of Korean Democracy.* Seoul: Hamanitas (in Korean).

Choi, M. J. (2006) *The Agenda-setting Function of Portal Media.* Seoul: Korea Press Foundation (in Korean).

Choi, S. Y. (2009) 'Fifty Years in Political Communication Studies', in the 50th anniversary committee of KAJCS (ed.), *The History of Fifty Years of Korean Association of Journalism and Communication Studies.* Seoul: KAJCS. pp. 717–82 (in Korean).

Ette, M. (2000) 'Agent of Change of Stability? The Nigerian Press Undermines Democracy', *The Harvard International Journal of Press/Politics,* 5(3): 67–86.

Gross, P. (2002) *Entangled Evolutions: Media and Democratization in Eastern Europe.* Baltimore, MD: The Johns Hopkins University Press.

Gross, P. (2008) 'Forward to the Past: The Intractable Problems of Romania's Media system', *The Harvard International Journal of Press/Politics,* 13(2): 141–52.

Hallin, D. and Mancini, P. (2004) *Comparing Media Systems: Three Models of Media and Politics.* Cambridge: Cambridge University Press.

Han, H. K. (2003) 'The Perception of Public Opinion in Internet: The Comparative Analysis of Tendency to Perceive a False Consensus Between Digital Chosun Visitors and Ohmynews Visitors', *Korean Journal of Journalism and Communication Studies,* 47(4): 5–33 (in Korean).

Han, H. K. (2005) 'Internet Users Civic Virtues and Experiences of Public Deliberation in Cyberspace', *Korean Journal of Broadcasting and Telecommunication Studies,* 19(4): 604–43 (in Korean).

Han, S. J. (1995) 'Korean Society Fifty Years After the Liberation', *Thought Quarterly,* Summer: 140–70 (in Korean).

Hughes, S. and Lawson, C. (2005) 'The Barriers to Media Opening in Latin America', *Political Communication,* 22(1): 9–25.

Hwang Y. S. (2001) 'A Exploratory Study of the Relationship Between Internet Use and Political Participation', *Korean Journal of Journalism and Communication Studies,* 45(3): 421–56 (in Korean).

Im, H. J. and Chung, I. J. (1999) 'Developmental Experiences and Reflexive Modernization in Korea', *Economy and Society,* 41: 123–51 (in Korean).

Im, Y. H., Kim, E., Kim, K. and Kim, Y. (2008) 'News Perceptions and Uses Among Online-news Users', *Korean Journal of Journalism and Communication Studies,* 52(4): 179–204 (in Korean).

Kang, M. K. (2004a) 'Media War and the Crisis of Journalism Practices', *Korean Journal of Journalism and Communication Studies,* 48(5): 319–48 (in Korean).

Kang, N. W. (2004b) 'Effect of Internet and Mass Media Uses on Citizens Participation: Generational Differences', *Korean Journal of Journalism and Communication Studies,* 48(3): 116–43 (in Korean).

Katz, E. (1957) 'The Two-step Flow of Communication: An Up-to-Date Report on an Hypothesis', *Public Opinion Quarterly,* 21(1): 61–78.

Katz, E. (1980) 'On Conceptualizing Media Effects', *Studies in Communication,* 1: 119–41.

Kim, H. K. (2000) 'The Structure and Change of Civil Society, 1987–2000', *Korean Society,* 12: 63–87 (in Korean).

Kim, E. and Rhee, J.W. (2006) 'Rethinking 'Reading' Online: The Effects of Online Communication', *Korean Journal of Journalism and Communication Studies,* 50(4): 65–95 (in Korean).

Kim, H. S. and Rhee, J. W. (2007) 'Telling Stories About Politics: Exploring the Narrative Structure of the Internet Political Discussions', *Korean Journal of Journalism and Communication Studies,* 51(5): 168–96 (in Korean).

Kim, J. (2001) 'On the Roles of News Media Use and Political Conversation in the Political Process', *Korean Journal of Journalism and Communication Studies,* 45(2): 86–116 (in Korean).

Kim, S. T. and Lee, Y. H. (2006) 'New Functions of Internet Mediated Agenda-setting: Agenda-rippling and Reversed Agenda-setting', *Korean Journal of Journalism and Communication Studies,* 50(3): 175–204 (in Korean).

Kim, Y. K. (2002) 'Deliberative Democracy and Political Discussion in Cyberspace', *Media & Society,* 10(1): 74–113 (in Korean).

Korean Advertiser Association (2006) *Media Use Survey.* Seoul: ICR-SNU (in Korean).

Korea Press Foundation (2007) *Korean Journalist Survey.* Seoul: FPF (in Korean).

Korea Press Foundation (2008) *Media User Survey.* Seoul: KPF (in Korean).

Lee, J. H. (2005) 'Internet, Traditional Media and Time-use Pattern: A Proposal of a Time Re-allocation Hypothesis', *Korean Journal of Journalism and Communication Studies,* 49(2): 224–54 (in Korean).

Lee, J. H. and Kim, K. (2006) 'The Historical Formation of Professional Identity Among Korean Journalists', *Korean*

Journal of Journalism and Communication Studies, 50(6): 59–88 (in Korean).

Min, Y. and Joo, I. H. (2007) 'Social Capital and its Democratic Consequences: Effects of Media Uses and Social Capital on Political Interest, Trust, and Participation', *Korean Journal of Journalism and Communication Studies*, 51(6): 190–217 (in Korean).

Na, E. K. (2007) 'Democracy Based on Difference: Multi-faceted Relationship Between Diversity and Civic Attitudes Depending on the Different Level of Perceived Online Social Network Heterogeneity', *Korean Journal of Journalism and Communication Studies*, 51(6): 163–89 (in Korean).

Na, E. K. and Rhee, J. W. (2008) *A Study of Internet Culture of Replies: Internet News Uses and Discursive Publics*. Seoul: Korea Press Foundation (in Korean).

Ojo, T. (2007) 'The Nigerian Media and the Process of Democratization', *Journalism*, 8(5): 545–50.

Park, S. G. and Chang, K. S. (2000) 'Political Transition and Changes in the State-Media Relationship in Korea', *Korean Journal of Broadcasting and Telecommunication Studies*, 14(3): 81–113 (in Korean).

Park, S. H. (2001) 'The Possibilities of On-line Media as an Alternative Communication Channel', *Studies of Communication Science*, 2(3): 153–84 (in Korean).

Park, S. H. (2004) 'Political News Use on Internet: Use Patterns and Users Characteristics', *Korean Journal of Journalism and Communication Studies*, 48(3): 436–83 (in Korean).

Porto, M. (2007) 'TV News and Political Change in Brazil: The Impact of Democratization on TV Globo's Journalism', *Journalism*, 8(4): 363–84.

Rhee, J. W. (2005) 'The Emergence of Critical Discursive Publics and Their Demand For Fairness in Journalism', *Studies of Broadcasting Culture*, 17(2): 139–72 (in Korean).

Rhee, J. W. and Choi, Y. J. (2005) 'The Crisis in Korean Newspapers: Functional Displacement, Provision of Lower Value, and Trust Crisis', *Korean Journal of Journalism and Communication Studies*, 49(5): 5–35 (in Korean).

Rhee, J. W. and Kim, E. (2004) *DAUM Deliberative Democracy Project*. Seoul: ICR-SNU (in Korean).

Rhee, J. W. and Kim, E. (2006) 'Effects of Online Deliberation on Political Discussion Efficacy', *Korean Journal of Journalism and Communication Studies*, 50(3): 393–424 (in Korean).

Rhee, J. W., Kim, E. and Kim, H. S. (2007) 'Exploring Online Opinion Leadership', *Journal of Journalism and Communication Studies*, 51(3): 358–84 (in Korean).

Rhee, J. W., Kim, E. and Moon, T. J. (2005a) 'Communicative Foundations of Social Capital in Korea: Impacts of Media Uses on Trust, Civic Engagement, and Socio-political Participation', *Korean Journal of Journalism and Communication Studies*, 49(3): 234–62 (in Korean).

Rhee, J. W., Kim, E. and Moon, T. J. (2005b) 'The Impacts of Structural and Regulative Dimensions of Communication on the Quantity and Quality of Internet Discussion: A Field Experiment Within the Context of the 17th General Election', *Korean Journal of Journalism and Communication Studies*, 49(1): 29–56 (in Korean).

Rhee, J. W., Kim, E. and Shim, M. S. (2006) 'Exploring Dispositional Media Use Motives: An Extension of the Uses and Gratification Theory in a Multimedia Environment', *Korean Journal of Journalism and Communication Studies*, 50(1): 252–85 (in Korean).

Rhee, J. W., Cho, H., Song, H. J. and Jung, J. H. (2010) 'A Comparative Systematic Approach to Media System: The Korean Case', *Communication Theories*, 6(1): 82–125 (in Korean).

Rogers, E. M. and Shoemaker, F. F. (1971) *Communication of Innovations*. New York: Free Press.

Rustow, D. A. (1970) 'Transitions to Democracy: Toward a Dynamic Model', *Comparative Politics*, 2(3): 337–63.

Shah, D. V. and Scheufele, D. A. (2006) 'Explicating Opinion Leadership: Nonpolitical Dispositions, Information Consumption, and Civic Participation', *Political Communication*, 23(1): 1–22.

Song, H. J., Shin, S. M. and Park, S. G. (2006) 'Reading Dissonant Opinions on the Internet and its Effects on Argument Repertoire and Tolerance', *Korean Journal of Journalism and Communication Studies*, 50(5): 160–83.

Yang, S. (2000) 'Political Democratization and the News Media', in L. Diamond and D. C. Shin (eds.), *Institutional Reform and Democratic Consolidation in Korea*. Stanford, CA: Hoover Institution Press. pp. 149–70.

Yang, S. (2005) 'Democratization and Media Reform: The Case of South Korea', in C. Schafferer (ed.), *Understanding Modern East Asian Politics*. New York: Nova Science. pp. 21–44.

Yoon, Y. C. (1998) 'PC Communication as Alternative Media: An Analysis of Computer Bulletin Board Service on Hanchongrean's Activities', *Korean Journal of Journalism and Communication Studies*, 43(1): 184–218 (in Korean).

Yoon, Y. C. (2001) *Democracy and Media in Korea*. Seoul: Yumin Cultural Foundation. (in Korean).

Youm, K. H. (1996) *Press Law in South Korea*. Ames, IA: Iowa State University Press.

Weimann, G. (1991) 'The Influentials: Back to the Concept of Opinion Leaders?', *Public Opinion Quarterly*, 55(2): 267–79.

Whang, S. J. (1996) 'A Feasibility and Limitation of Cyberspace as a Sphere for Democratic Communication', *Korean Journal of Journalism and Communication Studies*, 38(3): 43–86 (in Korean).

World Association of Newspapers (2006) *World Press Trend 2006*. Paris: ZenithOptimedia.

33

The Changing Landscape of Political Communications in China

Xian Zhou

INTRODUCTION

In light of the rapid growth of the Chinese economy and the current economic crisis in western developed countries, China is advancing on the world stage as a major force among developing nations. Predictions and observations about China's influence and how it will meet its responsibilities as a major world power can be seen in the headlines of various media. From reports on the G20 to the BRIC thesis, and even the so-called G2, China's rise has attracted world interest in the future development of this ancient country. Without a doubt, China's economic reform policies have been a main contributing factor to this fiscal progress. In 2008, China's GDP exceeded $3 trillion (US dollars), ranking third in the world, and according to some documents, it surpassed Japan's in 2010, which would place it second. These economic reforms, however, have also brought about a dramatic change in Chinese social culture. As Huang points out:

As China is seen to rise as a major power in the global economy and politics, there has been growing academic interest in the country's changing media landscape. It is, however, never an easy task to read media systems in a post-Communist market authoritarian society like China. Students of Chinese media studies are often excited by the rapid growth and commercialization of the media industry, on the one hand, and puzzled and frustrated by its lack of press freedom and professionalism, on the other hand. (2007: 402)

This chapter will examine the developing trends of Chinese political communication over the past decade, emphasizing the mutual relationship between political communication and social development in China. In other words, this article focuses on the interactive process of political communication concerning the Communist Party of China (CPC), the media and the public by examining four key issues: (1) the commercialization of the media and political communication; (2) the limited freedom and transparency of information; (3) the rise of grassroots media and (4) the development of media professionalism.

THE COMMERCIALIZATION OF THE MEDIA AND POLITICAL COMMUNICATION

It is widely known that China is a socialist country, and that its basic system of government is based on a socialist model. Ever since China initiated economic reforms in 1978, its economic system changed from a planned economy to a market economy; however, China still insists that it maintains a socialist political system. On the surface, it might appear that a market economy conflicts with a socialist political system. Some observers and political theorists contend that the development of a market economy will bring about inevitable change in China's political system, as they propose that a free market economy will demand a democratic government. However, as embodied in the unique Chinese term 'socialist market economy', these two 'contradictory' systems have merged to form a socialist political system that coexists with a market economic model.

Following the process of China's economic reform, state-run government media organizations have also begun such a transition. Before 1978, all Chinese media functioned as propaganda organs of the CPC, but economic reform brought with it new possibilities in the media industry. Ever since the implementation of these market-based reforms, the mass media has been governed by two forces: the supervision of the existing political system, which makes the media a propaganda tool for the CPC's policy, and the lure of the market economy, especially the success of cultural industry in western developed countries, in which the mass media not only reduces the government's economic burden, but also turns propaganda into entertainment. As such, integrating the mass media with the market economy gradually became part of the CPC agenda. From 1992 onward, the Central Committee of the CPC has established policies promoting the reform of the cultural system (Jiang, 1992). In 1996, the CPC announced that such reforms should strengthen the positive role of the market system (Central Committee of the CPC, 1996). The pivotal point of this reform came in 2000, when the Fifth Plenary Session of the Fifteenth Central Committee of the Party expressly stated that it intended to improve cultural industry policy, strengthen the construction and administration of the cultural market, and put forward the development of the cultural industry (Central Committee of the CPC, 2000).

The marketization of the mass media in China is reflected in several aspects of the reform process. First, administrative budget control was adopted to reform the budget system. Once this reform was enacted, China Central Television Station's (CCTV) revenue grew from 120 million yuan in 1990 to 5.75 billion yuan in 2000, the number of channels increased from three in 1991 to nine in 2000 and the average broadcasting time rose from 31 hours a day in 1991 to 156 hours a day in 2000. During this period, CCTV spent approximately 1.2 billion yuan on global broadcasting, and by 2000, CCTV broadcast signals covered 98% of the world.

Second, group integration of the mass media was implemented in response to new developments in China after entering the WTO. Since 2001, group integration and reconstruction have begun in journalism, publishing, broadcasting, film and television and performance industries in China, aiming to enhance the competitiveness of cultural enterprises. By 2002, 72 such groups had

been formed, including 38 newspaper groups, 10 publishing groups, 5 distribution groups, 12 broadcasting and television groups and 5 film groups. By the end of 2008, a total of 13 enterprises in China's cultural industry were listed on the stock market, showing marked progress in financial operation.

As China rises to economic prominence, Chinese leaders have realized that developing cultural industries can be used as a strategic tool to increase the nation's 'soft power'. As State Councillor Liu Yandong has asserted, China must develop an advanced culture consistent with its economic prowess that will become the source of its influence as a modernized nation, as well as a spiritual underpinning on which Chinese nation will stand among the nations of the world (Liu, 2009). In facing the current global economic crisis, the Chinese government outlined 'The National Plan to Develop Cultural Industry' in 2009, which essentially promoted making social impact a top priority, and striving to ensure the unity of social and economic aims. Its specific goal is to complete the institutional transformation of operational cultural enterprises (State Council of PRC, 2009). 'Institutional transformation' refers to the process of transferring government projects to private industries, from state-run agencies to market-oriented enterprises.

Many western observers favor the commercialization of the mass media in China. Some claim that a commercial mass media would challenge the current system and change the norms of communication, which could lead to changes in the Chinese political system. Others believe that there is no relationship between commercialization and political changes. As Huang summarizes:

> While the liberal-optimistic approach believes that a mature capitalist development of the Chinese economy in general and the media sector in particular would positively contribute to an 'eventual' political transition to democracy in China, the liberal-pessimistic approach doubts any necessary or logical relationship between economic liberalization and political-media democratization of the Chinese media industry and a profound democratic change of Chinese politics, pessimistic liberal critics argue, media commercialization alone has little power to challenge government's control of the media. (2007:402)

In my view, however, both of the above opinions are inaccurate.

At first glance, commercial media and socialist propaganda might appear to be different and conflicting forms of media. The former is market-oriented, and directed by the entertainment industry; the latter is ideology-oriented, focused on disseminating the CPC's views and government policy. Media commercialization would primarily result in a clear separation of the two. In major forms of Chinese media such as newspapers, radio broadcasting, television and publishing, there is usually a space reserved for political propaganda, through which CPC policies are transmitted to the public. Examples include television news and other programs that relate current events, such as CCTV, as well as the front pages of CPC or local newspapers. Regardless of how market-based or commercial the mass media becomes, this reserved space will continue to exist, controlled by the government's propaganda department. Aside from this, however, the remainder of the media is filled with entertainment meant to attract markets and viewers, from celebrity news and gossip stories to foreign happenings and cultural or sports news.

Third, commercialization of the media operates under the principle of free market competition. Profit in business is only achieved through constant innovation and adaptation; political propaganda, however, continues to surface at all levels of media. This has caused Chinese political communications to develop a distinctive character – whereas the entertainment industry is full of innovation and change, where companies are forced to compete for audiences and ratings, and are often driven to copy each other in the process, the propaganda sector of the media has neither competition nor any kind of pressure that would spur it to innovation.

Fourth, although there are two different sectors, political propaganda and the entertainment industry, government control over the media has never relaxed. If marketization is an economic issue, then the marketization of the Chinese media is restricted to some extent. In the market-based media, the government controls media by different means. One is by periodically holding a 'National Conference on Ideological Propaganda', comprising participants who are the leaders of provincial or municipal propaganda. The other is by establishing various levels of CPC organizations in media enterprises, through which instructions from the CPC Central Committee are delivered and executed. In this way, the gatekeeper need not appear, and the marketization of the mass media can still be prevented from bringing about any substantive changes to contemporary political communication in China.

As for the content of political communication, two distinct categories have appeared in contemporary Chinese media: propaganda discourse and entertainment discourse. Political propaganda has its own fixed expressions and characteristic rhetoric, such as: 'coordinated development of

socialist material civilization, political civilization and spiritual civilization', 'three representatives', 'insistence on prioritizing social effects' and 'highlighting the themes of the times while encouraging diversity'. Conversely, entertainment discourse occupies a great deal of space in various forms of media, and has become highly competitive and market-oriented. Entertainment programs have become part of mainstream radio as well as television, including CCTV and local television stations, and entertainment columns have become mainstream in various newspapers, especially local evening newspapers and tabloids.

Messages sent through the two channels of political and entertainment discourse have different positions and target audiences, a situation that differs from mass media in western developed countries, where entertainment, news and politics all mix together. This combination of public culture and political communications has caused the emergence of infotainment, which seeks to reach audiences with political discourse through popular entertainment (Edelman, 1995). Although it is traditional practice to deliver propaganda in an entertaining manner, as current media continues the commercialization process, separating political and entertainment discourse is a viable option to ensure the image of legitimacy in propaganda. It is also a strategy to support the cultural industry.

The influence that this separation of the two has on audiences and on communication as a whole is complicated. First, after the separation of political discourse and entertainment in cultural industry, political reporting still maintains its original characteristics, while entertainment opens a broad venue for public expression. The diversity and richness of entertainment relieves, to some extent, public attention to politics and the impulse to participate, providing an alternative form of psychological satisfaction. Second, the separation of politics and entertainment has two main consequences, the first of which being public political apathy. This happens because it is difficult for the political discourse of government media to become a platform for the public to participate in and express their ideas. Another reason is that the high-entertainment media has provided alternate channels to satisfy the public, which causes the people to focus on entertainment and reduces their enthusiasm for politics. The other consequence is opposite: a long-term apathy that results in the phenomenon of intermittent 'hysteria'. Although entertainment has to a great extent satisfied the audience's need for cultural participation, the public's political impulse still exists and will instantly manifest when a sudden serious incident occurs. This hysterical outburst has two main characteristics: one is the appearance of unprecedented emotional discussions among the populace, especially when dealing with issues of nationalism; the other is that this burst of political enthusiasm and the impetus to participation will disappear and fall back into apathy shortly thereafter, where it will wait for the next intermittent burst. Such behavior from the citizenry constitutes an abnormal psychological reaction to political matters.

TRANSPARENCY AND LIMITED FREEDOM OF COMMUNICATION

Over the last 10 years, owing to developments in communications and information technology, changes in the methods of message transmission and the implementation of an open-door policy, the circulation of information is less restricted than before the period of reform. There are several factors to consider that have contributed to this extension of limited freedoms, and have also promoted government transparency in contemporary Chinese political discourse.

The first factor was the government's reaction to certain incidents and emergencies in China's recent history. Restricting information about these incidents to the public gave the government a negative image and caused difficulties in keeping social order. The SARS epidemic of 2003 is a fitting example of this. From November 2002, when the first SARS case was identified in Foshan, Guangdong, to mid-February 2003, the spread of SARS and censorship of the press frightened Guangdong citizens. People began to panic, purchasing large amounts of supplies and medicine, and rumors began to spread unchecked in the streets. On 10 February, *Nanfang City News* first reported the outbreak, followed soon after by *Guangzhou Daily* and *Nanfang Weekend*, and after these reports appeared, the wave of panicked buying gradually subsided. With the rapid outbreak of SARS throughout China, the government issued 'The Proposal on Reporting the Prevention and Treatment of SARS'. From 17 February onward, CCTV began reporting on SARS, promoting the coverage of the epidemic through the entirety of the media and contributing to the control of SARS and China's eventual return to stability. The way that the situation changed after the restrictions on reporting were lifted paved the way for a shift in Chinese media reporting, revealing the relationship between freedom of communication and social stability as well as abandoning the traditional idea of resolving internal issues behind closed doors. In addition, the reporting of SARS also began a new era of disaster reporting in Chinese media, in which reports included specific

data to reflect developments in the incident, such as a daily report on the number infected by a disease and the number of patients cured or discharged. This was a complete change from the standard practice of 'not reporting on specific details such as areas affected, casualties, and economic loss' (Jiang, 2003). In subsequent reports of other major emergencies such as the Wenchuan Earthquake, official journalists no longer withheld information, but made detailed, transparent reports, which became general practice in the years following. Some scholars believe that the SARS reporting caused an information climax, and accelerated the lifting of government restrictions on news reporting, thus bringing about unprecedented opportunities and challenges to journalists in China (Yang, 2003).

The second factor leading to the extension of limited freedom of communications in China was the emergence of alternate information sources, caused by developments in information technology. This allowed the access and transmission of information through other channels outside of mainstream, heavily regulated media. For example, the rapid popularization of mobile phones in China has changed the public's traditional means of communication. According to a statistic cited in 2009 by the Bureau of Operation, Monitoring, and Coordinating in the Ministry of Industry and Information Technology, the number of mobile phone subscribers had reached 641.23 million in mainland China by July 2008 with an average monthly increase of 8.7 million new users (Ministry of Industry and Information Technology, 2008). Among this vast community of mobile phone users, text messaging has become a cheap and convenient channel for information exchange. As soon as a significant event occurs, witnesses can inform friends and relatives via text messaging, spreading information about the event within seconds and causing a snowball effect, passing the word across the nation. The Internet is another channel for transmitting information that has not only changed the methods people use to communicate, but also their lifestyle and the concept of communication. One statistic from the China Internet Network Information Center (CNNIC) shows that by 30 June 2009, the number of Internet users in China had reached 338 million, covering 25.5% of the population (CNNIC, 2009a). These Internet users produce a massive amount of information, while at the same time also exchanging and receiving information. According to CNNIC's 'Research on the Influence of Internet Media on Societal Events', the Internet has played an important role in social crises. For example, information on the 2008 Wenchuan Earthquake in Sichuan was first reported and spread via the Internet. CNNIC's findings state that during the Wenchuan Earthquake, 87.4% of Internet users chose to obtain information regarding the earthquake online, relying more on the Internet than television or any other source of information in learning about the incident. The relative freedom of information on the Internet has made it an important channel for the public to obtain information about current events and crises. CNNIC's study also revealed that among users who said they paid attention to societal happenings via the Internet in 2008, 52.1% of them stated that the Internet was their preferred method for learning news. In addition, they found that the average time Internet users spend browsing news stories is approximately 55.9 minutes per day, and that the Internet's users are becoming increasingly diverse (CNNIC, 2009b).

A third possible factor is the growth of satellite television (SATV), as major metropolitan areas in China are seeing an increase in the prevalence of satellite reception equipment. Although the government has enacted regulations to restrict satellite signals, there are still many channels that viewers have access to. Television stations in the Chinese language, especially Phoenix, SUNTV and Taiwan's TVBS, are attractive to the mainland Chinese audience, and the cultural proximity of their programs makes them particularly suitable to mainland viewers. As such, the aforementioned satellite stations also supply viewers with world news reports, including reports about China from an international perspective that would not appear on official news stations.

The final factor in the extension of limited freedom of communication is the government itself. With China's emphasis on rapid globalization, its increasingly important role on the world stage and increased scrutiny from other countries, the Chinese government has become more concerned about the image it projects to the world. Research demonstrates that China is frequently demonized in the western media, which might be closely related to the differences in political communication between China and western countries. Therefore, establishing a positive image in other countries has become a critical issue for Chinese leaders (Shen, 2001). Although China had appointed a government press spokesperson as early as 1983, it was not until after the SARS epidemic that this office was effectively implemented. This was an action taken by the CPC and the government in order to 'make "party" and "government" affairs public'. As Guo Weiming, Press Secretary of the Information Bureau of the State Council's Information Office, stated in an interview:

We feel that the image of a country is much like the image of a person. What kind of person do others hold in high regard? One that is honest and responsible, one that responds appropriately to the praise, criticism, and discredit given him by others, and one that is credible, the type of person that communicates and deals well with others. On an international scale, a country should project a similar image. To maintain an image of responsibility, an influential country should keep its actions transparent to the public, and when issues arise, it should release accurate information in a timely fashion to prove its honesty. It should also quickly respond to any discrediting accusations and unfold the truth of the matter to reduce their negative impact. When an international dilemma arises, or a politically sensitive event takes place, the Information Bureau plays an important role in releasing timely information and providing explanations and guidelines for proper reporting. (Yu and Lei, 2007: 19)

On 28 December 2004, the Information Office also announced the list of spokesmen from the various departments of the State Council and their contact information. A three-stage press release system was then established that flowed from central to provincial to county government, in which 62 departments of the State Council and 20 provinces and cities have set up a system with a press spokesperson. On 5 April 2007, a document entitled 'Regulations on Information Openness in the PRC' was issued, which specified that 'the administrative departments should actively distribute government information to the public via government announcements, official websites, and press conferences, as well as newspaper, radio broadcasts, and television'. In 2008, the CPC and the State Council held 521 press conferences while provincial government information offices (as well as those of autonomous regional and municipalities) organized 983 press conferences. There were a total of 1587 press conferences organized in this fashion, from the Information Office of the State Council and the various departments of the central government to the provincial, autonomous and municipal governments (this number excludes the 300 press conferences held by the Beijing Olympic Games Press Center and the Beijing International Press Center during the Beijing Olympic Games). Some observers have noted, however, that although the press spokesperson system has made party and government affairs public to some degree, many fundamental problems still obstruct public view of government activity, including information monopoly, rejection of interviews, evasive answers to questions, avoidance of public scrutiny, concealing of government mistakes and a lack of professional qualifications among spokespersons. This proves that the complete openness and transparency of information has yet to be achieved in Chinese political discourse, and that the circulation of information has still only attained limited public freedom (Txxx9.com, 2009; Wu, 2005).

THE RISE OF GRASSROOTS MEDIA

There is, to a certain extent, à dualistic media structure in contemporary China, in which each side is defined by different content and discourse as well as different production processes and audiences. One of the most important developments in present political communications in China is the rise of grassroots media.

'Grassroots media', also called 'private media' or 'self-media', refers to non-government individuals and organizations that voluntarily provide information on video or forum websites. These types of media are spread to people at various locations, with the Internet as their primary channel of communication. As mentioned above, there were over 338 million Internet users in China, meaning a vast number of potential media contributors. The historical process of the development of the Internet in China could be divided into two periods based on whether or not name registration was required. From the emergence of the Internet in China until around 2003, real-name registration was not required for users on websites. Then, between 2003 and 2005, a series of laws and regulations regarding the Internet were implemented that began a real-name registration system, and since then, any users who wish to express opinions or share information or media must log on using their real names. In this way, Internet users can be monitored with their identities bare to censors, which serves to both restrict users from spreading rumors that could confuse or mislead others, as well as severely limit freedom of speech on the Internet.

The dualism between government and non-government political communication is obvious when considering the distinctions between grassroots media and official media, as grassroots media more accurately reflect the public's ideals and opinions. Grassroots media have to some extent changed the character of official media propaganda, as they bring about discussion, negotiation and dialog among the public like never before. Min Dahong gives this description of grassroots media:

The meaning of grassroots media is the idea that by utilizing simple transmission tools, common people can build their own communication forums, discuss issues they have dealt with, share viewpoints, express their opinions, and even unite a group to take action. It is a kind of medium that the public can participate in through the use of simple technology. At present, the most accessible method is the application of Internet technology. The rise of grassroots media is overthrowing the traditional mass media, breaking down the boundaries between the 'communicator' and the 'audience,' and completely changing the position of the audience in media discourse. The establishment of grassroots media, the efforts of grassroots journalists, and the growing diversity of grassroots journalism have brought news transmission into a totally new era. Grassroots media have manifested a high level of inclusiveness, equality, and participation among its users. (2008: 9)

Forms of grassroots media include electronic bulletin boards, weblogs, podcasts, text messages, email and websites, such as tianya.cn, youku.com, tudou.com, blogchina.com and antiwave.net, that are among the most popular outlets of grassroots media in China. The rise of grassroots media is closely connected to developments in information technology. It has been observed that the progress of information technology has contributed significantly to political communications in China, notably in the wide-scale application of Web 2.0, which provides opportunities for the growth of various grassroots media (Zhou and Shen, 2009). Technology is a 'two-sided coin', which can both bring new vigor to the diversity of the political communications, but also be used to enforce stricter media control by censors. At the initial stage of applying new forms of technology, it is common to hear overwhelmingly optimistic reports about it; however, when government censorship and other controls become involved, this attitude can turn pessimistic. As Lagerkvist points out:

Interesting in China nowadays is that since government censorship and regulatory practices effectively control the traditional media, the internet serves as an alternative means of agenda setting, as is seldom the case in less authoritarian countries. More critical, sensitive, controversial or political news are first set in internet news forums. When a significantly large critical mass of upset chat room posting makes something an issue for everybody to take seriously, it enters the traditional media as well. (2005: 127)

In terms of grassroots media production, the development of information technology has indeed brought about a greater degree of public participation. Grassroots media has reached a level of 'one person, one medium', where 'everyone sends messages to everyone' (Min, 2008: 9). There are many young people in China who are well educated and in comfortable economic situations who know how to operate modern Internet technology and actively exchange information and participate in discussions via grassroots media. As such, online communities have formed: virtual communities characterized by the release, circulation and acceptance of individual information, or, in Anderson's (1983) words, 'imagined communities'. Grassroots media are beneficial to the development of journalism as well, in both public and private spheres. Tianya.cn illustrates this point. The website was established in March of 1999, and attracted the attention and participation of Internet users. The following year, it collaborated with *Tianya* magazine, focusing on humanist issues and becoming one of the more symbolic public websites. A series of important events (such as the Chinese–US air crash incident in 2001) and topics (such as intellectuals, the liberal left and right-wing politics in China) drew out animated discussions on the website, which formed a virtual public forum for debate. The Community Management Commission of Tianya.cn, the operation of the website, the appointment and rights of moderators, the censorship of comments and the procedures of discussion and coordination all retain characteristics of a public forum (Baike.baidu.com, 2008). This has to some extent manifested Chinese citizens' social awareness and political participation, and has helped to cultivate their political consciousness and introduce them to procedures of reasoned debate. It has also begun to facilitate the growth of democratic participation in Chinese society.

The content of grassroots media is a topic worthy of detailed analysis. Bakhtin (1984) once noted that an analysis of the differences between folk culture and official culture will reveal a series of contrasts between the two. Grassroots media and official media can be likewise compared, and analyzing the content of grassroots media will reveal its importance and unique contribution to China's current state of political communications.

First, we must summarize the various types of content that appear in grassroots media by separating them according to agenda and examining the significance of each category. Grassroots media could theoretically include everything, but there are four areas that cover the subject of political communications. (1) A report of a public event, such as an earthquake, fire or other socially significant incident, especially reports that focus on marginalized groups, such as 'the stubbornest householder in history' or 'the illegal brick kiln incident in Shanxi Province'. In the process of reporting on events like these, grassroots media has played an important role in protecting the interests of the weaker parties, sometimes even

pressuring local governments to revise the policies surrounding the issue. (2) Track, report and discuss corruption among officials in various government departments. In this regard, grassroots media have provided a means of discovering, tracking and exposing corrupt officials through what is known in China as a 'cyberspace manhunt'. Owing to the wide-scale participation of Internet users, corrupt officials are often quickly discovered so they can be prosecuted. One of the most theatrical of these cases involved Zhou Jiugeng, former director of the Jiangning House Bureau in Nanjing. After he gave a speech regarding the sensitive issue of real estate purchases, a number of enraged Internet users began searching for information about Zhou that they could use against him. They eventually found evidence from photographs and other sources that the cigarettes Zhou smoked were extremely expensive – costing 150 yuan per pack – and that his younger brother was a real estate developer. Exposure of this information online drew the attention of the local authorities, and after four months, Zhou was placed under investigation. One year later, he was found guilty of taking bribes of up to 1 million yuan and was sentenced to 11 years in prison. (3) Discussions on political issues, such as public intellectuals in China. Discussing these issues is seldom allowed in official media, if not forbidden outright. (4) Discussion and criticism of policies made by the central and local governments. Topics of discussion include education, environmental protection, healthcare reform, Internet censorship, real estate, high-speed railways and local officials' pork barrel projects. Some of these discussions draw the government's attention, and may even contribute to policy decisions.

In grassroots media, most agenda setting seeks to achieve different purposes than those of the official media, showing the opinions and viewpoints of the people as an alternative to official propaganda. Conversely, grassroots media does at times influence public policy, and may pressure the official media into changing its reporting strategies to bring out some of the people's views.

Some Chinese scholars claim that the impact of grassroots media has been to exert pressure through public opinion, as well as providing tools for organization and mobilization (Min, 2008). Others believe that grassroots media have formed their own special sphere of public influence in modern China (Zhou and Shen, 2009). Some overseas scholars have begun to wonder if the rise of grassroots media has formed a kind of citizen media or citizen journalism in China. In one scholar's opinion, '[g]rassroots media have played an essential role in decentralizing "citizenship"'. Active audience participation in online discussions, petitions and protests can influence public opinion, check the authority and even challenge the political agendas of the government (Yu, 2006: 303). Also, according to Lagerkvist, '[i]n general, internet opinion is gaining a certain influence over how Chinese leaders can act and present themselves in the international arena' (2005: 126).

In my opinion, the rise of grassroots media has had an overall positive influence on current political communications in China. First, it has changed the centralized communication structure of the official media and defined the two cultural spheres, official and public, to which Bakhtin referred. Second, grassroots media have provided the public a channel through which to express their opinions. Although freedom of expression is still limited, grassroots media have begun to impact government decisions on various levels, forcing officials to take the voice of the masses into consideration when making or revising policies. Finally, the tension with grassroots media has resulted in an interesting development among official media, as reporters have begun to learn strategies and reporting methods from those popular with grassroots media users. In short, grassroots media have exerted a liberalizing influence on the government, society and the public under the current political system but their influence is still limited, as all expressions of the public will happen only at the consent and within the control of the government.

THE DEVELOPMENT OF MEDIA PROFESSIONALISM

Since the 1990s, the idea of media professionalism has been introduced from the west (primarily the USA) into China's media industry. With developments in the media industry and growing competition with grassroots media, a trend of professionalism has emerged among the official media. While media professionalism has naturally come as a result of western influence, it is also a product of the unique environment of Chinese political communications.

The concept of media professionalism was first introduced into Chinese research in 1999 (Chen, 2008). Among media researchers, professionalism is defined as having the following five characteristics:

1 The media is a tool of public communication, and serves the public benefit, not only that of certain political or interest groups.
2 News reporters are social observers and reporters of truth, not mouthpieces for interest group propaganda.

3 They are gatekeepers of information circulation, not the participants in or agitators of political or interest conflicts.
4 They judge the authenticity of their facts by rational standards of empirical science and make truthful reporting their first priority, never submitting to any outside political power or economic force.
5 They are bound by professional standards based on the above principles and accept the internal rules of their profession, never allowing outside authority or powers to control them (Lu and Pan, 2006: 20).

Professionalism applies to official media rather than grassroots media, as grassroots media reflect the voice of the people, while the official media's role in reporting on internal matters makes professionalism more of an issue. As such, there is a complicated relationship between professionalism and political propaganda in China. Professionalism focuses on two goals, autonomy and objectivity. Interestingly enough, strategies to promote professionalism in China are developed within the framework of party propaganda, rather than western strategies of professionalism, which directly oppose and conflict with propaganda. As a result, we have seen a series of various political communications that exhibit a Chinese style of professionalism, where they seek for limited expressions of professionalism within the boundaries of party propaganda. Some scholars present the function of communication media in China as a combination of contradictions: (1) the right to information and the right of communication are citizens' rights, protected by the Constitution, and as such, communication media should respect those rights; (2) communication media are mouthpieces not only of the party and the government, but also of the people; (3) communication media not only provide the country's ideological machine, but also have the management intelligence of an industry or a business (Tong, 2003: 18–9). This paradoxical dual definition demonstrates how professionalism seeks to achieve its goals under the present circumstances without conflicting with party ideology. Through applying Constitutional principles and affirming the media's function as a public mouthpiece and a valid industry, this approach legitimizes professionalism in communications, which can be seen as a uniquely Chinese revision on the idea of professionalism.

Professionalism has two prominent expressions in modern Chinese political communications. The first is that it uses important public news stories to reflect social issues that have arisen since the beginning of China's reform period. CCTV's 'Topics in Focus' (Jiaodian Fangtan) is an example of what professionalism struggles to achieve, as its stated aim is to report 'central, breaking and difficult' issues. Some of its programs criticize policies implemented by local governments, and expose public hardships brought about through industrial and commercial development, even dealing at times with politically sensitive topics. As Liang Jianzeng, producer of the program, has summarized, there were three 'firsts' when 'Topics in Focus' began, two of which were that it was the first program to focus on expressing public opinion, and that it was the first program to deal with sensitive topics (Liang, 2004: 5–6). However, the only reason that such a news program can reveal current social issues and internal problems in China without repercussions is due to its adherence to a few strategic principles: 'to observe society and analyze problems from the correct standpoint', and 'not to avoid the contradictions and issues encountered ... [but] to keep the overall tone positive, calling for constructive rather than destructive solutions' (Shi, 2003: 99). Put another way, it aims to 'assist rather than trouble' the government's work (Chen, 2004: C17). Operating under the premise of leaving party propaganda unchallenged, 'Topics in Focus' has been able to achieve a measure of professionalism despite government limitations.

Another example of professionalism in the Chinese media is *Nanfang Weekend*, a local Guangzhou newspaper. One significant instance that illustrates this point is a report on the investigation of AIDS in the Shangluo District of Shaanxi Province. The report uncovered the local health department's various policy blunders and administrative failures, pointing out that the AIDS virus was spread due to the department buying blood from the local peasantry. The publication of this report was a shock to the public, and incited several high officials in Shaanxi Province to investigate the reporting, after which they accused four local journalists of 'disclosure of secrecy' and delivered them to local law enforcement. This news drew the attention of state leaders, and instructions were soon given to clear up the matter (Zhao, 2004). The significance of the case is that it paved the way for public supervision by non-local sources, which has become an effective strategy to promote media professionalism. Four levels of government exist in China's current political system – central, provincial, municipal and county – and each level has its own official media. This kind of vertical administrative system provides the possibility of mutual supervision among the different provinces. Local newspapers, for example, will not directly criticize policy decisions made by local party and government leadership, but they may criticize leaders or expose problems in other provinces. As *Nanfang Weekend* is not under the control of Shaanxi Province, it could bring these news items to light without fear of censorship by local authorities, thus incorporating aspects of media professionalism into China's particular political scene. Over the last few years, supervision by non-local public opinion has helped to form a unique landscape of political communications in China.

Due to their dexterous use of the limited options available in China's current political situation, journalists have explored new strategies for implementing professionalism in the gradually maturing official media. In my opinion, those attempting to practice professionalism are primarily public intellectuals among official media organizations who both understand the methods of party propaganda as well as commercial marketing strategies. Despite pressure from propaganda demands and commercial interests, they insist on maintaining the social and moral responsibilities of proper news reporting. As such, they project a different voice among the propaganda of the official media, demonstrating the relative flexibility of current political communications despite government controls.

CONCLUSION

Over the past decade, political communications in China have changed considerably. In light of increasing globalization, China's rise on the international stage is greatly influencing world politics, while at the same time the outside world is changing China. This chapter draws four conclusions about modern China. First, the field of political communications is becoming more diverse than ever before, as technological developments have opened new channels and methods of communication, allowing for limited public participation. Whether the media involved are official or grassroots media, they are no longer as easy for the government to control as the traditional media of 20 years ago. Second, each new advancement soon brings new forms of scrutiny. As advancements in technology provide greater possibilities for political communication, more effective methods of control and censorship are invented along with them. As an old saying goes, 'when the priest climbs a post, the Devil climbs ten'. While the current situation of Chinese political communications is more relaxed than it was 10 years ago, a trend of appearing relaxed on the outside but being restricted inside still exists to some extent. Third, and because of this, there are still many limitations to freedom in political communication, such as limited availability and openness of information, censorship of grassroots media and restrictions that impede developments in media professionalism. Fourth, according to recent trends, some claim that political communications in China are shifting from a state of control to one of negotiation. In my opinion, however, this only shows a change in forms, as the core issue that remains is whether or not it is possible for China to change from a hard authoritarian system to a soft authoritarian one.

REFERENCES

Anderson, B. (1983) *Imagined Communities: Reflection on the Origin and Spread of Nationalism*. London: Verso.

Baike.baidu.com (2008) 'Tianya Community', http://baike.baidu.com/view/5437.htm?fr=ala0_1_1

Bakhtin, M. M. (1984) *Rabelais and His World*. Bloomington, IN: Indiana University Press.

Central Committee of the CPC (1996) 'The Communique of the Sixth Plenary Session of the Fourteenth Central Committee of the Party', http://cpc.people.com.cn/GB/64162/64168/64567/65398/4441784.html

Central Committee of the CPC (2000) 'On Making the 10th Five-year Plan of National Economic and Social Development in the Central Committee of the CPC', http://www.china.com.cn/ch-15/plan2.htm

Chen, Y. (2004) 'Topics in Focus: A Review of the Past 10 Years', *Nanfang Weekend*, 6 May.

Chen, Y. (2008) 'The Comparison of the Two Forms of Media Professionalism in Contemporary China', *International Journalism*, 8: 65–9.

CNNIC (2009a) 'The 24th Survey on China's Internet Network Development', http://research.cnnic.cn/html/1247710466d1051.html

CNNIC (2009b) 'Research on Socially Important Events and the Influence of Network Media', http://research.cnnic.cn/html/1261558815d1700.html

Edelman, M. (1995) *From Art to Politics*. Chicago, IL: University of Chicago Press.

Huang, C. (2007) 'From Control to Negotiation: Chinese Media in the 2000s', *The International Communication Gazette*, 69(5): 402–12.

Jiang, X. Z. (2003) 'The Differences in Reporting Emergencies Between Chinese and Western Media', *International Journalism*, 5: 14–18.

Jiang, Z. (1992) 'Report at the 14th Plenary Session of the CPC', http://cpc.people.com.cn/GB/64162/64168/64567/65446/4526312.html

Lagerkvist, J. (2005) 'The Rise of Online Public Opinion Forums in the People's Republic of China', *China: An International Journal*, 3(1): 119–30.

Liang, J. (2004) 'The 3 Firsts in the Initial Period of 'Topics in Focus', *Journalist*, 7: 5–8.

Liu, Y. (2009) 'Liu Yandong: Cultivate Strong Soft Power of Culture to Provide Powerful Support for Constructing a Rich, Strong, and Harmonious Modern Country', http://www.mcprc.gov.cn/xxfb/xwzx/whxw/200911/t20091125_75064.html

Lu, Y. and Pan, Z. (2006) 'Imaginations of Being Famous: Media Practitioners' Construction of Professionalism through Discourse in the Social Transformation Process', *Mass Communications Research*, 71: 17–59.

Ministry of Industry and Information Technology (2008) 'The Communique of Communication Industry', http://yxj.miit.gov.cn/n11293472/n11295057/n11298508/11979497.html

Min, D. (2008) 'Grassroots Media: The New Power in the Structure of Communications', *Youth Journalist*, 5: 9–11.

Shen, J. (2001) 'Media Communication and China's International Image', *International Politics Quarterly*, 2: 130–4.

Shi, A. (2003) 'The Change of Media Ecology and Re-construction of Media Professionalism in Contemporary China', *Journalism and Communication Review*, 1: 95–100.

State Council of PRC (2009) 'The National Plan to Develop Cultural Industry', http://www.china.com.cn/policy/txt/2009–09/27/content_18607771.htm

Tong, B. (2003) 'Political Civilization: The New Issues of Media Communication Research', *Journalism and Communication*, 3: 13–20.

Txxx9.com (2009) 'Main Problems in the Current Press Spokesperson System in China', http://www.txxx9.com/view_xx.aspx?ID=21850

Wu, X. 'The Contemporary Press Spokesperson System in China', http://news.sina.com.cn/c/2005–01–10/14564775639s.shtml

Yang, M. (2003) 'Direction, Time, and Depth', *Academic Journal of Chinese Radio & TV*, 7: 6–10.

Yu, H. (2006) 'From Active Audiences to Media Citizenship', *Social Semiotics*, 16(2): 303–24.

Yu, M. and Lei, X. (2007) 'New Year, New Beginning–Re-interview with Guo Weimin, Director of the Information Bureau of the Information Office of the State Council', *International Communications*, 1: 17–9.

Zhao, S. (2004) *Investigating China–Stories Behind the Journalism*. Beijing: Fangzheng Press.

Zhou, R. and Shen, Z. (2009) 'The Formation of Grassroots Media over the web2.0 Period', *News World*, 9: 145–6.

34

Political Communication in Latin America

Silvio Waisbord

The purpose of this chapter is to identify and discuss key issues in political communication research on Latin America. The premise of the analysis is that the study of media and political processes in Latin America illustrates the contributions of 'areas studies' to the field at large.[1]

First, Latin American scholarship expands the scope of inquiry by considering research questions and findings that have not been closely considered in the West. The literature has largely reflected academic concerns and debates in the USA and, to a lesser degree, in a handful of European countries. The combination of the 'third wave' of democracy, the global impact of market principles across media systems and the spread of digital technologies offers tremendous opportunities to enlarge the analytical range in the field of political communication.

Second, the development of Latin American scholarship suggests that 'area studies' in political communication research need to go beyond region-specific issues, and engage with broad conceptual and analytical debates in the field. The 'de-Westernization' (Curran and Park, 2000) should not only widen the range of cases and analytical perspectives. It also needs to contribute to theoretical development by bringing up cases and findings from across the world. Unfortunately, such bifocal approach on particular regional issues and broad theoretical questions is rare. 'Area studies' research tends to make findings and conclusions mainly relevant to regional specialists.

The growth of cross-national and comparative research (Esser and Pfetsch, 2004) is certainly an auspicious development. It purposefully sets out to bridge this gap by using country and regional cases to refine conceptual thinking and conclusions. To avoid the compartmentalization and marginalization of 'areas studies', country and regional research should contribute to a common body of knowledge defined by theoretical and analytical questions. Even if studies are not formulated as comparative projects, they should keep "comparative" perspective in mind.

Approaching 'regions/areas' as units of analysis is not problem-free. Regions are typically defined on the basis of shared characteristics such as political history, language, geography, media systems, culture and so on. Yet, as comparative politics scholars (Mainwaring and Perez Liñan, 2005) have argued, regions are not homogeneous entities. They comprise significant similarities and differences that need to be considered not only descriptively, but analytically, too.

Taken as a political-communication unit of analysis, Latin America is heterogeneous. On the one hand, it features three basic commonalities. First, most countries have a similar political history. With different degree of continuity and intensity, all have experienced political authoritarianism for much of the 20th century. Since the 1980s, however, no country has experienced a serious reversal of democracy. Second, all media systems have been historically organized similar principles: market principles, frequent and discretionary government intervention and almost non-existent public broadcasting. Third, contemporary democracies are characterized by similar negative and positive trends. Whereas they are beleaguered by strong anti-party sentiments and the low legitimacy of democratic institutions, citizens' mobilization and the existence of innovative participatory mechanisms (for example, referenda, participatory budget) suggest the vitality of participation (Seele and Peruzzotti, 2009).

On the other hand, the region offers heterogeneous political and media developments. The index of democratic performance is wide ranging: the quality of democratic politics in Chile, Costa Rica and Uruguay stands in sharp contrast with the chronic weakness and tumultuous politics of most countries in the region. Drug-trafficking, guerilla movements and armed gangs threaten state authority in Colombia, El Salvador, Guatemala and Mexico. While traditional parties continue to take turns in power in some countries, historic parties have been in dire straits elsewhere. Also, differences in media systems are significant. Whereas few families control media companies in Central America and the Caribbean, media ownership is more diversified in countries with bigger economies (Lugo, 2008; Rockwell and Janus, 2002a). Whereas the professional culture of journalism has found better ground in metropolitan news organizations, it is notoriously weaker in the provinces. Whereas governments are the largest media advertisers in the interior, media revenues are more diversified in urban areas. Whereas newspaper readership remains low, both radio and television have high penetration and large audiences (Bisbal, 2006; Fox and Waisbord, 2002).

With this context in mind, this chapter is organized around three issues that have been at the center of research agenda in the region: the mediatization of politics, the challenges for media democracy, and the linkages between media, civic participation and political conflict.

THE MEDIATIZATION OF POLITICS

Similar to other regions, the mediatization of politics in Latin America has attracted a great deal of academic attention during the past decades. The focus has been on the causes and the consequences of the mediatization of politics. Mediatization refers to the process by which political actors and dynamics are increasingly oriented around the media (Mazzoleni and Schulz, 1999). It includes four dimensions: the role of the media as the main source of political information; the independence of the media from political institutions; the prevalence of the media logic and the influence of the

media logic on political process (Stromback, 2008). Much of the literature on Latin America, however, has been primarily concerned with the last question: how political actors use and follow the 'media logic' to achieve and maintain power.

Interest in this dimension of mediatization is present in several lines of research in recent scholarship. Studies have examined how presidential communication has utilized the media for 'going public' (Kernell, 1997). Such dynamics are not entirely new. The political science and communication literature extensively discussed this issue in relation to the media strategies of populist leadership in the 1950s, and the propaganda tactics of military dictatorships in the 1960s and 1970s (Fox, 1988). More recently, the focus has been on presidential strategies intended to set the news agenda and build popular support. In order to achieve these goals, administrations have produced weekly radio and television programs, and presidents frequently give nationally broadcast speeches (Gómez et al., 2006, Rincón, 2008). The literature has critically assessed such tactics as shrewd attempts to set the news agenda bypassing the intermediary role of the press, and strengthen the 'personal' ties between citizens and charismatic leaders. Such goals are also evident in the absence of regular press conferences by heads of state, or refusing to be interviewed by oppositional media. Whereas strategies for 'going public' in the US politics are typically intended to drum up popular support for presidential agendas, Latin American presidents have used it to bypass the adversarial press.

The recurrent utilization of such tactics put in evidence the consolidation of the 'permanent campaign' (Conaghan and de la Torre, 2008) and 'media Cesarism' (Rincón, 2008) in the region. They are not designed to promote dialog between elites and citizens, or to hold presidents accountable. Rather, they are calculated strategies to promote personalistic leaderships and reinforce plebiscitary politics. In a region with a pronounced deficit of democratic accountability, such strategies further deepen old problems of transparency and representation.

Another manifestation of the mediatization of politics has been the transformations of election campaigning. The focus has been on the professionalization of election communication namely, the central role of the media in campaign strategy, the strategic management of candidates' media appearances, the extensive use of opinion polling and segmented campaigning (Skidmore, 1992; Waisbord, 1994). Across the region, political parties and candidates have widely embraced technological and managerial innovations in election campaigns. The personal attributes of candidates have overshadowed partisan ideologies.

While political marketing was a novelty during the first elections held in the early 1980s, political consultancy and 'spin doctors' have become ubiquitous in past campaigns (Plasser, 2000). Also, television advertising has become central to campaign strategies. Although the frequency and funding of television ads vary according to national electoral laws, paid advertising is common and attracts the lion's share of campaign investments. The astronomical growth of campaign expenditures is attributed to the incorporation of professional techniques, particularly the intensive use of television advertising (Lozano, 2006).

Within this context, the media have taken over the 'mediation' between political parties and citizens. The rise of candidate-centered, capital-intensive, 'modern' campaigns is inseparable from the crisis of traditional forms of representation. Although campaigns often bear a resemblance to the US campaigns, they are hardly the outgrowth of external and global trends. Rather, they are the product of indigenous political and media developments (Waisbord, 1996).

The mediatization of politics has also been studied around the blurring of the boundaries between politics and entertainment. In a region historically dominated by entertainment media, there has never been a stark distinction between the realms of politics and mediated entertainment. Entertainment programming often brings in political news, and political elites frequently reach out to entertainment media to go public. Television programming regularly addresses political issues, and producers find inspiration in political headlines for plots and characters. *Telenovelas*, the melodramas that have historically been the most popular television genre, often address contemporary politics (Palaversich, 2006; Porto, 2005). Newsweeklies and entertainment magazines frequently cover politicians like entertainment celebrities (Landi, 1992). Likewise, game shows, reality shows and comedies make frequent references to political news. Politicians' media appearances are tailored to appeal to tabloid and entertainment templates. Taking advantage of name recognition and popularity, dozens of show-biz celebrities (for example, singers, actors, filmmakers) have jumped into politics throughout the region. Just as political news provides material for a range of media content, entertainment media provide larger audiences for political communication (Martin-Barbero and Rey, 1999).

Studies have attributed the consolidation of mediated politics to the crisis of political representation. Mediatization is not seen simply as another manifestation of the dominant role of the media in contemporary societies. Instead, there are specific political reasons that have spawned new media politics. The conventional argument is that the crisis of representation has pushed the media into centerstage (Bisbal, 2004). In several countries (for example, Argentina, Bolivia, Venezuela), the traditional party system collapsed. Political parties became fragmented, and new electoral forces emerged. Party identities have become weaker. The secularization of political identities happened even in countries (for example, Chile, Colombia, Uruguay) where traditional parties have remained in control of electoral politics. Also, anti-party sentiments have become dominant, and paved the way for the rise of new political forces (for example, Bolivia, Brazil, Uruguay, Venezuela). The incapacity to maintain autonomous communication channels is part of the broad institutional difficulties of traditional and new political parties.

The consequences for democratic governance of the mediatization of political communication have generated much discussion. The tone of the conclusions has been generally pessimistic. Informed by familiar condemnations of 'video-politics' (Bourdieu, 1999; Sartori, 1998), scholars have offered bleak assessments about the current situation. The notion that televised politics fosters 'personalism' (instead of institutions), de-politicized 'spectators' and 'consumers' (instead of active citizens) and emotions (instead of rational debates) are common in the literature (Catalán and Sunkel, 1989; Martin-Barbero and Rey, 1999; Rey, 1998; Rincón, 2008; Rincón et al., 2003; Silva, 2004). Likewise, the arguments that entertainment media cultivate political cynicism and passivity, and democracy is hamstrung by commercial television are ubiquitous (Landi, 1988; Schmucler and Mata, 1992).

Regrettably, such assessments have not been sufficiently nuanced or consistently grounded in evidence to effectively determine the corrosive effects of mediated politics on democracy. They reflect a tendency in Latin American communication scholarship to make sweeping assessments that are neither properly supported in evidence nor disaggregated into 'middle-level' research questions. Because they are formulated at a high level ('the power of the media'), they fail to distinguish the impact of various media on political attitudes and behaviors across different populations and political systems in the region.

Although they did set out to challenge pessimistic conclusions, recent studies suggest that the media do not necessarily cultivate political malaise. The news media have contributed to civic mobilization during elections, referendums, coup attempts and political crisis (Calderón et al., 2008; Hughes and Lawson, 2004; Kaiser, 2002; Subite and Gutierrez, 2006; Torrico and Sandoval, 2007). These studies throw into question whether the media necessarily reinforce cynicism and apathy in Latin American democracies. Given the complexity of the news–consumption–participation nexus among various groups, and the scarcity of evidence-based conclusions in the region, further research is required.

THE IMPACT OF COMMERCIALIZATION

Latin American scholarship has paid considerable attention to the structural challenges to media democracy by studying the linkages between media, economics and politics. The mediatization of democratic politics has renewed long-standing interest about the obstacles for media democracy in the region. Here media democracy is understood in terms of systems that promote critical and diversified information as well as leveled opportunities for a range of issues and perspectives to be expressed in the public sphere. Media democracy requires a system that prioritizes pluralism and expectations from both liberal theories (for example, oversight of political power, fair and quality information, presence of diverse opinions) and communitarian approaches (for example, the media as institutions that promote civic representation and participation, and the expression of minority voices).

Studies have identified a range of obstacles for media democracy (Hughes and Lawson, 2005). Obstacles can be clustered in two fundamental set of problems: the runaway commercialization of the media, and the persistence of media patrimonialism.

Commercial principles became dominant in the print press during the first half of the 20th century. Although the modern press was born in the late 19th century as partisan platforms for elite politics, a market-oriented press subsequently developed linked to the emergence of urban markets and commercial advertising. Many newspapers that were born amidst aristocratic politics (for example, Argentina's *La Nación*, Brazil's *Estado de São Paulo*, Chile's *El Mercurio*, Peru's *El Comercio*) became market-oriented, and have remained dominant. Furthermore, political turmoil and authoritarianism made the existence of the partisan press impossible. Even in countries with longer periods of stable democracy (for example, Chile, Colombia, Venezuela), where a 'party-press parallelism' survived longer than in the rest of the region, the growth of commercial newspapers overshadowed partisan media.

The rise and consolidation of market-oriented press did not bring about a radical shift in journalistic ideals. Although newspapers gradually shed off partisan linkages, they did not embrace the ideals of professional objectivity commonly identified

with the US press.[2] Despite the growing influence of the US journalism in the region, particularly after World War II, the principle of political neutrality never took firm roots. Instead, newspapers generally mixed editorial and reporting, and openly revealed ideological and partisan preferences. Although newspapers basically operated according to commercial principles, the European model of 'journalism of opinion' remained influential.

Market principles also dominated the historical evolution of broadcasting systems. A strong tradition of public broadcasting never took root in the region. In some countries, there have been attempts to develop 'public' television and radio by assigning a small number of licenses to governments and universities. These initiatives, however, never became true alternatives to private broadcasting. The lack of independent management, chronic under-funding (which pushed stations to rely on advertising just like private media) and the tendency of governments to see 'public' broadcasting as personal communication fiefdoms, undermined the prospects for strong public media institutions.

The early consolidation of market interests accounts for why contemporary Latin American media systems feature dominant multimedia corporations (which are mostly privately owned), and are intertwined with a range of industrial interests (Fox and Waisbord, 2002; Lugo, 2008). Brazil's Globo, Mexico's Televisa and Venezuela's Venevisión have ranked among the largest media companies worldwide (Sinclair, 1999). In most cases, they originally were family-owned newspaper and radio companies that subsequently expanded into other media sectors (over-the-air, cable and satellite television, telephony, Internet) during the second half of the 20th century.

Despite the domination of market principles, the news media did not severe its ties with the political sphere. The press and the political sphere remained intertwined. There was neither a 'full market revolution' nor major political shifts that could have dislodged media business from the state. News organizations have been generally aligned with competing political factions at both national and provincial levels. Particularly in the provinces, political elites have directly or indirectly owned the main media outlets, a pattern that remains dominant until today. During authoritarian periods, military dictators tightly controlled the press through censorship and persecution, and thus maintained close ties between the news media and the political sphere.

A mix of economic and political reasons explains why the news media never gained full autonomy vis-à-vis the state. Despite economic growth and the expansion of national advertising markets, the state remained one of the largest advertisers, particularly in the provinces and countries with smaller economies. This situation put government officials in a powerful position in media economics. They held power over key decisions affecting the interests of press owners, such as official advertising, government contracts, tax breaks, importation permits, loans from government-owned banks and media policies. Discretionary management of decisions affecting media business gave officials tremendous power vis-à-vis press companies. In turn, the ability to cultivate close relations with governments gave media owners significant business advantages.

Also, ideological and political reasons underlie the close proximity between private media and governments. Conservative media owners openly supported right-wing administrations. The ideological alliance between leading news organizations and military dictatorships has been extensively documented (Fox and Waisbord, 2002). Media barons unabashedly defended official policies and aligned their companies with the government. By the same token, publishers with liberal and populist positions openly supported like-minded governments. Just like the conservative media did, the values of press criticism and independence were eschewed when sympathetic administrations were in power.

The combination of commercial media and cozy relations between the press and governments has informed pessimistic conclusions about media democracy in the region. The dominating presence of private companies and profit-making principles stifled the possibilities for non-commercial, minority and civic media. Market interests distort the priorities of the news media. Given the influence of advertisers, the news media have cautiously approached or simply ignored business issues with direct political implications. Because support for official policies brought favorable economic deals, major news organizations sacrificed the value of independence and critical reporting in covering governments. Quality journalism has suffered from business decisions to prioritize cost-cutting, and produce news on shoestring budgets. Horizontal integration leads to the homogenization of news content. Media companies are reluctant to scrutinize the same governments that they need to advance business goals. Conceived as tools of broad political and business interests, the news media largely function as communication platforms for political and economic elites rather than horizontal mechanisms for the expression and participation of citizens. In summary, commercialization meant the triumph of business interests over the public mission of the press.

For several scholars, the consolidation of democracy has not altered the basic market orientation of the press (Mastrini and Becerra, 2006; Sunkel and Geoffroy, 2001). The fundamental pillars of market-based media system have been left intact even as democracy settled throughout the region. The affirmation of political democracy has not resulted in media democracy. Furthermore, the adoption of liberalization and deregulation policies by civilian governments has greatly contributed to the expansion of leading news companies into old and new media sectors. Across the region, leading news organizations are units of multimedia corporations and/or diversified industrial conglomerates with interests in key economic sectors (for example, banking, food, retail, agriculture and mining). Given the fact that press, political and economic interests are tightly intertwined, they argue, it is impossible for news organizations to meet effectively democratic expectations of critical and diverse reporting. Market logic is anathema to the needs of democratic governance.

Despite its merits, this line of argument is insufficient to explain the complexity of contemporary media politics in the region. As an explanation of the fundamental structures of media systems, it correctly points out at the importance of the collusion between political and economic actors. Commercial principles, indeed, remain unchallenged and government policies (particularly during the 1990s) helped to cement the dominant role of few corporations. As an analysis of political communication processes, however, the 'commercialization' argument misses important aspects. The news media in the region are more diversified than what those approaches typically recognize. Although leading news organizations largely espouse conservative economics and politics, 'the press' is splintered into a myriad of market-based yet ideologically diverse news organizations. These divisions underlie the changing relations between news media and presidents.

Also, important significant differences across administrations contribute to shaping news and perspectives that are more diverse than what economicistic approaches typically recognize. For the past three decades, Latin American democracies have been governed by administrations with contrasting ideological and political positions. At one time or another, national and state governments have promoted free-market and Keynesian economics, conservative and populist politics and a range of policies on crime, environmental protection, human rights, indigenous rights, unions, abortion rights and foreign investment. Because governments wield significant power in newsmaking (Miralles, 2003; Montenegro, 2007; Muraro, 1997; Waisbord, 2000), political differences across administrations offer changing opportunities for covering a range of issues and perspectives.

The combination of news organizations and ruling administrations with diverse ideologies and politics has produced conflictive and dynamics relations between 'the press' and 'the state'. Relations cannot be neatly described based on ownership patterns, or the dominant presence of commercialization. Nor can we say that there have been static relations between news organizations and governing elites. The ideological fractures inside the press as well as the substantial differences among and inside governments have rendered news with plenty of conflict and disagreement. Just as conservative media and populist administrations have done it, progressive news organizations and neo-conservative governments have battled out their differences in the news. Differences have been particularly salient during times of political polarization and crisis, which are not unusual in the region.

One can certainly argue whether such confrontations have undermined journalistic autonomy, fairness and neutrality. The fact that media owners frequently drag newsrooms into pro- or anti-government camps has deepened the historical weakness of journalistic neutrality and fairness (Monsivais and Scherer, 2003). Yet the confrontations between the press and government suggest that commercialization does not fully explain the dynamics of political communication. The interaction between politics and media actors and processes are crisscrossed by the rowdy nature of the region's politics.

MEDIA PATRIMONIALISM AND MEDIA DEMOCRACY

The literature has also extensively discussed the problems for media democracy associated with, what I call, 'media patrimonialism'. Following Max Weber's classic typology of political rule, patrimonialism is defined by the domination of particularistic politics and the weak rule of law. Government officials exercise discretionary power. Rules and impersonal procedures are either absent or ineffective in binding personal behavior. Power is used for the benefit of rulers and personal dependents. Patronage, that is, exchange relations between rulers and followers, is dominant. This order is antithetical to the effective functioning of the rule of law found in rational-legal, bureaucratic, modern political systems.

Patrimonialism has been central to the modern development of political-media systems in Latin America. It actively shaped the historical evolution and the functioning of media markets. As many studies have documented, the personal hand

of government officials was often directly responsible for shaping market structures including ownership, funding and legal framework. Heads of state have typically approached the media as a prolongation of their personal power. They have exercised discretion in decisions affecting news business. In countries with a notorious deficit of accountability mechanisms, secrecy and personalism have often dictated key decisions. Such practices allowed government officials to keep the media on a short leash, achieve political and economic benefits and reward cronies. In turn, media patrimonialism has been critical to the formation of large media business. The rise and consolidation of media corporations throughout the region is intertwined with the domination of patrimonialist politics.

Why is media patrimonialism detrimental to media democracy? By favoring the pursuit of particular benefits, patrimonialism runs contrary to the promotion of wide, public interests. By opposing any system of rules, it is contrary to media systems based on notions of transparency and accountability. Because it is driven by personal ties between officials and business, it is incompatible with public regulation, fair competition and social responsibility. By approaching public communication resources such as broadcasting licenses and official funds as personal property, it has deepened the weakness of the rule of law.

Media patrimonialism has continued despite the affirmation of democratic rule in the region. The continuation of civilian administrations during the past three decades is, no doubt, a historical landmark given the region's troubled political history. This is particularly remarkable considering that, during that period, democracies were rocked by sharp economic downturns, coup attempts, presidential impeachments and resignations and armed insurgency. The abolition of state-sponsored censorship and systematic persecution of dissident substantially changed the overall conditions for political communication. Democratic rule, however, has been insufficient to roll back the legacy of media patrimonialism. Not only administrations have been reluctant to undo that legacy. They have also perpetuated old practices to further their own goals. Old practices, such as no-bid assignments of official advertising, government contracts and broadcasting licenses to cronies, have continued (Kodrich, 2008; Rockwell and Janus, 2002b).

Scholars have concluded that the media policies of conservative administrations directly benefited large news companies, such as the decision of the Menem administration to privatize two television stations in Argentina in 1989, and the media law sponsored by the Fox government in Mexico in 2005 (Mastrini and Becerra, 2006;

Sanchez Ruiz, 2007). The Fujimori government, which ruled throughout the 1990s in Peru, infamously stands out as the embodiment of the worst excesses of media patrimonialism (Conaghan, 2005). Besides conventional patronage methods, it resorted to persecution, coercion and bribes to secure a sycophantic press.

During the past decade, much of the analysis on media patrimonialism has focused on neo-populist governments. Since former lieutenant colonel Hugo Chavez was elected president in Venezuela in 1999, a wave of populist administrations has swept the region.[3] Neo-populism patently illustrates the problems of media patrimonialism. Studies have shown the persistence of patronage in decisions affecting media economics, discretionary use of public resources and advertising, and cronyism in the relations between governments and the media. Critics have charged that populist governments have tried to control the media and benefit cronies. Such conclusions were based on various developments, such as the Chavez administration's decision not to renew the license of a leading television network and 2006 'social responsibility' press law, the Morales government control of a network of local radio stations in Bolivia, and the decision by the Correa government to expropriate two television networks in Ecuador (Cañizales and Correa, 2003; Grebe, 2007; Rincón, 2008). Furthermore, populist administrations have done little to address the weakness of transparency and accountability mechanisms through. Actions such as sponsoring and enforcing 'freedom of information' law, transferring control of official advertising to independent bodies, and overhauling 'gag' laws are necessary to strengthen media independence.

Amid these conflicts, the literature has raised attention to civic efforts that promote media pluralism and curb the power of both markets and governments.

One set of initiatives is aimed at promoting diversity and government accountability through pushing for media reforms. Civic groups have spearheaded public debates and conducted advocacy with policymakers to promote legal changes on freedom of information, broadcasting, press rights and community media. Experiences from Mexico to Uruguay show not only that media democratization has become a demand for citizens, but also that organized publics opened up spaces for deliberation and built alliances to spearhead changes (Gill and Hughes, 2005; Pinto, 2009; Waisbord, 2009). The impact of such actions has been significant. In some countries, they provided the impetus for landmark legislation that allows public access to government information, and recognizes community media. Likewise, citizens' media observatories have become important

references for media criticism and policy debates (Alfaro, 2005; Rey, 2003).

A second set of efforts was intended to expand grassroots media spaces for deliberation outside the mainstream media that are organized around public, rather than market or state, principles. They have been focused on carving out autonomous communication, citizen-centered platforms (Rodriguez, 2001). Such efforts are rooted in the strong tradition of community media activism in the region. Since the 1950s, there have been numerous experiences of civic mobilization that were envisioned to provide alternatives to media dominated by elite interests (Gumucio, 2001). Examples include community radio, 'alternative' press, and video and television cooperatives (Salazar and Cordova, 2008). This tradition of 'participatory media' had played important roles during both authoritarian regimes and contemporary democracies. Because many had been linked to peasant and workers' unions and social movements, their development has been closely linked to the political evolution of specific organizations.

Studies on the politics of media reform and community media offer a picture that diverges from the bleak assessments about the consequences of 'video-politics' and media-centered politics. Although they recognize the lopsided distribution of communication resources, they find promising signs of media democratization in contemporary democracies. Citizens' initiatives may be incipient and small scale to overcome entrenched hurdles posed by unregulated markets and patronage politics, yet they represent important innovations and trends in the mediated politics of the region.

MEDIA, CIVIC SOCIETY AND POLITICAL CONFLICT

In line with this modestly optimistic view, other studies have called attention to instances showing that the news media effectively meets democratic expectations. Several examples show that the press has scrutinized power, fairly covered citizens' demands and offered reasonably accessible platforms for civic debates. Certainly, unregulated commercialization and patrimonialism limit opportunities for democratic debate given that they shape the media ecology of the region. They do not suppress, however, changing relations among media institutions, political elites and civic actors. Because neither one is a unified bloc nor do they maintain static relations, the analysis needs to sharpen the focus in search of nuances and conflicts.

The turbulence of mediated politics in the region yields processes that are significant for the quality of democracy. Consider the case of watchdog journalism and scandal politics. From Mexico to Argentina, scores of press denunciations have been published in the past decades (Hughes, 2006; Matos, 2008; Waisbord, 2000). They have uncovered government wrongdoing, human rights abuses and business malfeasance. The publication of exposes was indicative of novel developments in a region where the press has been historically subjected to pressures and censorship.

First, they suggested the intention of a limited yet influential number of news organizations and journalists to break stories despite persecution and intimidation. The rise of 'institutional entrepreneurs' and maverick journalists, and the adoption of 'professional values' in newsrooms shook up old cozy relations the press and political power (Alves, 2005; Hughes, 2003; Lawson, 2002 Waisbord, 2000; Wallis, 2004). Ideological and economic rivalries between specific news media and administrations underlie press exposes. Whereas leftist and liberal news media delved into corrupt practices of conservative administrations, the traditional press exposed wrongdoing during populist governments. Second, watchdog journalism offered opportunities for powerful sources to wage conflict 'by other means'. Infighting among government officials, whistle-blowing politics and intra-elite battles frequently provided the original impetus for exposes. Studies have shown that many high-profile denunciations were the result not only of the perseverance of enterprising reporters, but also the actions of self-interested sources who leaked information to the press to battle their rivals (Waisbord, 2000).

Several press denunciations spawned political scandals. The combination of congressional and judicial investigations on crimes originally reported in the news, and steady media attention on wrongdoing and cover-ups fueled scandals. Virtually all democracies in the region have been rocked by scandals during the past decades. They revealed abuses of power such as cash-for-votes schemes, cozy relations between politicians and criminals, bribes and kickbacks and human rights violations. As a consequence of scandals, several presidents were impeached or resigned, and dozens of cabinet secretaries, governors and members of Congress stepped down.

The politics of watchdog journalism and scandals have significant implications for democratic governance. They suggest new forms of social accountability by which the media shame public officials, and activate accountability mechanisms (Peruzzotti and Smulovitz, 2006). Commercialization and patrimonialism may limit but they do not completely suppress opportunities for public scrutiny of political and economic power. Furthermore, they show that the media play a key role in channeling political conflict. Both the interests of specific news media and elite competition foster changing political communication dynamics.

Similar dynamics are also evident in news coverage of civic mobilization. Several studies have argued that the media fail to provide quality and sustained coverage of a range of civic and social issues (Gonzalez Bombal, 1996; Larrain and Valenzuela, 2004). News coverage of issues linked to 'social development' such as environment, health and education, has many shortcomings. It is focused on individual events rather than long-term processes. It is focused on political and economic elites, and ignores citizens' voices (Alfaro, 2008). The provision of basic health and educational services, poverty and appalling sanitation and water conditions get sporadic attention from the media. Central environmental problems such as rural degradation caused by the expansion of the agricultural exploitation and mining rarely get the attention they deserve. The volume of environmental news has modestly grown, but coverage remains superficial and intermittent (Carabaza et al., 2007; Luft, 2005). Public safety, an issue that has become a top priority in public opinion and elections recent years, is frequently covered as waves of individual crimes committed against private property as it affects middle- and upper-class neighborhoods (Cerbino, 2005; Luchessi, 2007; Rey, 2005).

These shortcomings are explained by two reasons. First, given the market-driven structure of the media, news organizations generally cover issues that attract audiences and do not offend advertisers. Because the mainstream news media are geared toward urban and well-off populations, they typically ignore issues that affect poor, indigenous and rural communities. Second, the strong orientation toward political elites in the professional culture of journalism explains why the press gives scant attention to ordinary citizens. Unlike political elites, average citizens lack power to make news.

Although such conclusions correctly assess basic problems, they are analytically too blunt to capture the complex interaction between the news media, civic groups and political conflict. Studies have shown that news coverage does not necessarily offer either a warped view of mobilized publics or consistently positive views of political elites (Bisbal, 2004; Bonilla and Garcia, 1995; Maia, 2009).

This conclusion is found in several recent studies. Bonner (2009) has convincingly argued that national news about police violence against protesters in a southwestern province in Argentina prominently featured citizens' voices, and offered sympathetic views of the protesters. By criticizing the governor who firmly defended police officers accused of killing protesters in cold blood, the coverage pushed for holding political authorities accountable. Waisbord and Peruzzotti (2009) have shown that the Argentine press offered a positive coverage of citizens' protests against the building of paper mill plants on the Uruguayan side of the Rio Uruguay (which serves as the natural border with Argentina). Concerned about the environmental impact of pulp production, citizens from the Argentine cities directly across the sites mobilized to stop the building of the plants. During several years, they kept intermittent blockades of roads and bridges between both countries. As long as national and state officials supported the movement's goals, national and local news coverage was also supportive. As the situation spiraled into an international conflict, and Argentine officials took distance from the movement's intransigent positions, media coverage of the movement became less positive. Another example is offered by Kowalchuk (2009) in her study of Salvadoran newspaper coverage about civic opposition to the privatization of the healthcare system. She demonstrates that the main press not only offered a sympathetic portrayal of citizens who resorted to both protest and legislative strategies, but it also criticized the government plan.

These studies raise two key points. First, news coverage offers complex and changing perspectives of protest actions and social movements. Leading news media neither necessarily distort citizens' demands nor portray them negatively. Second, elite positions about civic protests as well as intra-elite competition play a significant role in shaping news coverage. Given the news-making power of key political officials, elite support for popular protests and disagreements among elites produce mixed frames about public demands and social movements.

To be clear, these studies do not argue that the findings are representative of all news about citizens' movements or applicable across all possible cases. Such conclusions would be impossible given the endless number of cases. Nor do they intend to demonstrate that political and economic structures are irrelevant. Rather, they suggest the need for nuanced analyses of the factors that shape news coverage of social and political conflict. The news media are not a homogeneous bloc with predictable, clear-cut, unwavering positions vis-à-vis civic mobilization, social problems and political conflict. Divergent editorial positions and reporters' views, elite competition and the media strategies of civic groups influence press coverage (Waisbord, 2009). The fact that media systems are subjected to the influence of commercialization and patrimonialism should not lead to rule out *ex ante* that the relations between various news organizations and political actors may spawn different coverage of civic issues and social demands.

CONCLUSION

This chapter reviewed and discussed key issues in contemporary political communication research in Latin America.

Specific regional developments as well as academic traditions have informed research priorities. Consider the study of mediatization. Notably absent in the region is research on the impact of the news media on public opinion and policy, or on the effects of press frames on political attitudes and behavior, issues that have attracted a great deal of attention in the recent US and European literature. A few exceptions are worth mentioning. Studies have shown that, although media-centered campaigns in Mexico fail to bridge the 'knowledge gap' between voters from different socioeconomic backgrounds (McCann and Lawson, 2006), they do not necessarily contribute to political demobilization and disenchantment (Hughes and Guerrero, 2009). Also, research has shown that frames of news and political ads affect public perception of problems in Brazil (Porto, 2007), and that the availability of multiple frames promotes reasoned debates and multiple perspectives (Maia, 2009).

Attention has been largely put on understanding whether mediatization exacerbates the crisis of political representation in the region, and whether populism further weakens the roles of oversight and accountability of the news media. In both cases, the conclusions are affirmative. The centrality of the media has sharpened the problems of political representation. Media populism aggravates the problems of accountability through news management practices and media policies to circumvent critical news media. Interest on the institutional impact of mediatization and media politics issues dovetails with broad concerns about the persistent troubles of party systems, strong executives and weak parliaments and the tenuous linkages between public opinion and the legislative process in the region (Morgenstern and Nacif, 2002).

Likewise, regional developments explain why the literature has focused on the challenges and opportunities for media democracy. The persistent 'double whammy' of runaway commercialization and patrimonialism on media systems in the region explains why these issues remain at the center of the research agenda. By the same token, the literature remains focused on the study of community broadcasting, media reform movements and civic media advocacy as important, citizen-led developments aimed at shaking up traditional patterns in the relationship between media and political actors.

Research priorities also reflect scholarly traditions, namely, structuralist and institutionalist theories as well as qualitative methodologies in both communication studies and political science. Other set of theoretical questions and methodological approaches (for example, media effects, the dynamics between media and public opinion, quantitative research), which have been dominant in the US and European political communication research, never found a strong grounding in the region. In fact, the exceptions previously mentioned were produced by scholars based in the USA and/or who were trained outside Latin America.

The review also provides ideas for lines of research to contribute to a theoretically ambitious, global research agenda. 'Area studies' in political communication have often been balkanized in separate set of countries and regions. This is understandable given that, as mentioned earlier, local developments largely drive research priorities. Yet, it is important not to lose sight of the need to tackle broad theoretical questions that can be informed by findings from regional studies.

Two sets of questions coming out of Latin American research need further global and comparative attention. One set of questions address whether citizens' mobilization and new information technologies effectively transform the core of media systems. Does civic engagement around a range of social, political and media issues effectively change the way the news media cover social problems? Do social media and other Internet-based platforms improve opportunities for public expression in media systems limited by commercial and government interests? How do global forms of participation contribute to fostering more plural and egalitarian media at the national level? Another set of questions is related to the linkages between media, elites and political conflict. What are the consequences of intra-elite confrontations and stridently ideological news media for mediated politics? Do they suppress or foster a diversity of views? Do they contribute to addressing problems of accountability and transparency in new democracies? Do internal divisions within governments and the press as well as between both institutions open opportunities for critical and diverse news coverage?

The review shows not only the contributions of Latin American political communication scholarship to understanding the dimensions of mediatization, the challenges for media democracy and the linkages between media and political conflict in the region. They also suggest a wealth of experiences and arguments that helps to diversify the pool of evidence, research questions and conceptual frameworks in the field.

NOTES

1   Although the role of 'area studies' has been extensively argued in comparative politics and sociology (Bates, 1997; Hall and Tarrow, 1998), it remains notoriously under-discussed not only in political communication but also in the field of communication. This gap is particularly remarkable, considering the large number of studies on 'international' issues, and the towering presence of the 'globalization debate' in the field of communication during the past two decades.

2   The glaring exception is Brazil, where particularly the leading newspapers based in the Rio-Sao Paulo have embraced central tenets of the model of objectivity since the process of the 'modernization' of the press in the 1950s (de Abreu, 2002).

3   Whereas some scholars have dubbed this trend a 'left turn' in the region (Beasley-Murray et al., 2009), others have argued that the ideological complexity of these administrations falls outside conventional left/right categories (de la Torre, 2009). Despite a substantial literature, populism remains an equivocal concept. Unlike European contexts, Latin American populism does not refer to right-wing, xenophobic political parties. Instead, it is identified with governments that promote certain economic policies (Keynesianism, distributionism), political ideology (anti-liberalism, anti-party), style of political leadership (hierarchical, charismatic) and rhetoric (appeals to 'the people' and 'the nation', and discursive opposition against imperialism and oligarchy).

REFERENCES

Alfaro, R. M. (2005) *Hacia Nuevas Rutas Éticas en Nuestros Medios. Memoria Dela Campaña Ciudadana Sobre la Ley de Radio y Televisión*. Lima: Veeduría Ciudadana de la Comunicación Social.

Alfaro, R. M. (ed.) (2008) *¿Desarrollo? Encuentros y Desencuentros Entre Medios y Ciudadanía*. Lima: Asociación de Comunicadores Calandria.

Alves, R. (2005) 'From Lapdog to Watchdog: The Role of the Press in Latin America's Democratization', in H. de Burgh (ed.), *Making Journalists*. London: Routledge. pp. 181–204.

Bates, R. H. (1997) 'Area Studies and the Discipline: A Useful Controversy?', *PS: Political Science and Politics*, 30(2): 166–9.

Beasley-Murray, J., Maxwell, C. and Herschberg, E. (2009) 'Latin America's Left Turn: An Introduction', *Third World Quarterly* 30(2): 319–30.

Bisbal, M. (2004) 'Medios, Ciudadanía y Esfera Pública en la Venezuela de Hoy', *Quorum Académico*, 1(1).

Bisbal, M. (2006) 'Redescubrir el Valor del Periodismo en la Venezuela del Presente', *Contratexto* 14: 52–78.

Bonilla, J. I. and García, M. E. (1995) 'Nuevas Dinámicas de Representación Política: Espacio Público, Movimientos Sociales y Redes de Comunicación', *Diálogos de la Comunicación*, 42: 5–17.

Bonner, M. (2009) 'State Discourses, Police Violence and Democratisation in Argentina', *Bulletin of Latin American Research*, 28(2): 227–45.

Bourdieu, P. (1999) *On Television*. New York: New Press.

Calderón, C. A., Cañizález, A. and Moret, J. (2008) 'Los Medios Como Proyección de las Preocupaciones Ciudadanas', *Comunicación*, 142: 80–93.

Cañizales, A. and Correa, C. (2003) *Venezuela: Situación del Derecho a la Libertad de Expresión e Información*. Caracas. Espacio Público.

Carabaza, J., Lozano, J.C., González, J., Pasco, L., Reyes, L., Berumen, A. and Alvarez, P. (2007) 'Cobertura del Medio Ambiente en la Televisión Mexicana', *Comunicación y Sociedad* 7.

Catalán, C. and Sunkel, G. (1989) *La Política en Pantalla*. Santiago: ILET.

Cerbino, M. (ed.) (2005) *Violencia en Los Medios de Comunicación, Generación Noticiosa y Percepción Ciudadana*. Quito: FLACSO. http://redalyc.uaemex.mx/redalyc/pdf/726/72620204.pdf

Conaghan, C. (2005) *Fujimori's Peru: Deception in the Public Sphere*. Pittsburgh, PA: University of Pittsburgh Press.

Conaghan, C. and de la Torre, C. (2008) 'The Permanent Campaign of Rafael Correa: Making Ecuador's Plebiscitary Presidency', *International Journal of Press/Politics*, 13(3): 267–84.

Curran, J. and Park, M. J. (eds.) (2000) *De-Westernizing Media Studies*. London: Arnold.

de Abreu, A. (2002) *A Modernização da Imprensa (1970–2000)*. Rio de Janeiro: Jorge Zahar Editor.

De la Torre, C. (2009) 'Populismo Radical y Democracia en los Andes', *Journal of Democracy*, 1: 24–37.

Esser, F. and Pfetsch, B. (eds.) (2004) *Comparing Political Communication: Theories, Cases, and Challenges*. Cambridge: Cambridge University Press.

Fox, E. (ed.) (1988) *Media and Politics in Latin America: The Struggle for Democracy*. Thousand Oaks, CA: Sage.

Fox, E. and Waisbord, S. (eds.) (2002) *Latin Politics, Global Media*. Austin, TX: University of Texas Press.

Gill, J. and Hughes, S. (2005) 'Bureaucratic Compliance with Mexico's New Access to Information Law', *Critical Studies in Mass Communication*, 22(2): 121–37.

Gómez, J. C. (2005) 'Del Régimen de Comunicación Política del Presidente de Colombia Álvaro Uribe Vélez', *Palabra Clave*, 13: 1–27.

Gómez, J. C., Pacheco, A., Turbay, J. and Matiz, W. (2006) 'La Personalización en la Política, Una Práctica a Prueba de Reformas', *Palabra Clave*, 9(2): 53–65.

González Bombal, I. (1996) *La Visibilidad Pública de las Asociaciones Civiles*. Buenos Aires: CEDES.

Gumucio, A. (2001) *Making Waves: Participatory Communication for Social Change*. New York: Rockefeller Foundation.

Grebe, R. (2007) 'Evo Morales y los Medios', *Chasqui*, 98: 10–15.

Hall, P. A. and Tarrow, S. (1998) 'Globalization and Area. Studies: When Is Too Broad Too Narrow?', *Chronicle of Higher Education*, 44: B4–B5.

Hughes, S. (2003) 'How Institutional Entrepreneurs Transformed Mexican Journalism', *Harvard International Journal of Press/Politics*, 8(3): 87–118.

Hughes, S. (2006) *Newsrooms in Conflict: Journalism and the Democratization of Mexico*. Pittsburgh, PA: University of Pittsburgh Press.

Hughes, S. and Guerrero, M. (2009) 'The Disenchanted Voter: Emotional Attachment, Social Stratification, and Mediated Politics in Mexico's 2006 Presidential Election', *The International Journal of Press/Politics*, 14(3): 353–75.

Hughes, S. and Lawson, C. (2004) 'Propaganda and Crony Capitalism: Partisan Bias in Mexican Television News', *Latin American Research Review*, 39(3): 81–105.

Hughes, S. and Lawson, C. (2005) 'The Barriers to Media Opening in Latin America', *Political Communication*, 22(1): 9–25.

Kaiser, S. (2002) 'Escraches: Demonstrations, Communication and Political Memory in Post-Dictatorial Argentina', *Media, Culture & Society*, 24(4): 499–516.

Kernell, S. (1997) *Going Public: New Strategies of Presidential Leadership*. Washington, DC: CQ Press.

Kodrich, K. (2008) 'The Role of State Advertising in Latin American Newspapers: Was the Demise of Nicaragua's Barricada Newspaper Political Sabotage?', *Bulletin of Latin American Research*, 27(1): 61–82.

Kowalchuk, L. (2009) 'Can Movement Tactics Influence Media Coverage? Health-Care Struggle in the Salvadoran News', *Latin American Research Review*, 44(2): 109–35.

Landi, O. (1992) *Devórame Otra Vez*. Buenos Aires: Planeta.

Larrain, S. and Valenzuela, A. (2004) *Televisión y Ciudadanía*. Santiago: Fucatel.

Lawson, C. (2002) *Building the Fourth Estate: Democratization and the Rise of a Free Press in Mexico*. Berkeley, CA: University of California Press.

Lozano, J. C. (2006) 'Political Advertising in Mexico', in L. L. Kaid and C. Holtz-Bacha (eds.), *The SAGE Handbook of Political Advertising*. Thousand Oaks, CA: Sage. pp. 259–67.

Luchessi, L. (2007) 'Narraciones del Delito: Pánico y Control Social', *Diálogos de la Comunicación*, 75: 1–8.

Luft, S. (2005) *Jornalismo, Medio Ambiente e Amazonia: Os Desmatamentos nos Jornais*. São Paulo: Annablume.

Lugo, J. (2008) *The Media in Latin America*. Milton Keynes: Open University Press.

Maia, R. (2009) 'Mediated Deliberation: The 2005 Referendum for Banning Firearm Sales in Brazil', *International Journal of Press/Politics*, 14(3): 313.

Mainwaring, S. and Perez-Linan, A. (2005) 'Why Regions of the World are Important: Regional Specificities and Region-Wide Diffusion of Democracy', http://kellogg.nd.edu/publications/workingpapers/WPS/322.pdf

Martin-Barbero, J. and Rey, G. (1999) *Los ejercicios del ver*. Barcelona: Gedisa.

Mastrini, G. and Becerra, M. (eds.) (2006) *Periodistas y Magnates: Estructura y Concentración de las Industrias Culturales en América Latina*. Buenos Aires: Prometeo.

Matos, C. (2008) *Journalism and Political Democracy in Brazil*. Lanham, MD: Lexington.

Mazzoleni, G. and Schulz, W. (1999) "Mediatization" of Politics: A Challenge for Democracy?', *Political Communication*, 16(3): 247–61.

McCann, J. and Lawson, C. (2006) 'Presidential Campaigns and the Knowledge Gap in Three Transitional Democracies', *Political Research Quarterly*, 59(1): 13–22.

Miralles, A. M. (2003) *Periodismo, Opinión Pública y Agenda Ciudadana*. Bogotá: Norma.

Monsiváis, C. and Scherer, J. (2003) *Tiempo de Saber. Prensa y Poder en México*. Mexico: Editorial Nuevo Siglo.

Montenegro, S. (2007) *Los Medios de Comunicación como Actores Políticos en Nicaragua*. Managua: Centro de Investigación de la Comunicación.

Morgenstern, S. and Nacif, B. (eds.) (2002) *Legislative Politics in Latin America*. Cambridge: Cambridge University Press.

Muraro, H. (1997) *Políticos, Periodistas, y Ciudadanos*. Buenos Aires: Fondo de Cultura Económica.

Palaversich, D. (2006) The Politics of Drug Trafficking in Mexican and Mexico-Related Narconovelas, *Aztlan*, 31(2): 85–110.

Peruzzotti, E. and Smulovitz, C. (eds.) (2006) *Enforcing the Rule of Law: Social Accountability in the New Latin American Democracies*. Pittsburgh, PA: University of Pittsburgh Press.

Pinto, J. (2009) 'Transparency Policy Initiatives in Latin America: Understanding Policy Outcomes from an Institutional Perspective', *Communication Law & Policy*, 14(1): 41–71.

Plasser, F. (2000) 'American Campaign Techniques Worldwide', *Harvard International Journal of Press/Politics*, 5(4): 33–55.

Porto, M. (2005) 'Political Controversies in Brazilian TV Fiction: Viewers Interpretations of the Telenovela Terra Nostra', *Television & New Media*, 6(4): 342–59.

Porto, M. (2007) 'Framing Controversies: Television and the 2002 Presidential Election in Brazil', *Political Communication*, 24(1): 19–36.

Rey, G. (1998) *Balsas y Medusas: Visibilidad Comunicativa y Narrativas Políticas*. Bogota: CEREC Fundación Social.

Rey, G. (2003) *Ver Desde la Ciudadanía. Observatorios y Veedurías de Medios de Comunicación en América Latina*. www.veeduria.org.pe/articulos/rey.htm

Rey, G. (2005) *El Cuerpo del Delito*. Bogotá: Centro de Competencia en Comunicación para América Latina.

Rincón, O. (2008) *Los Tele-Presidentes: Cerca del Pueblo, Lejos de la Democracia*. Bogota: Centro de Competencia en Comunicación para América Latina.

Rincón, O., Bonilla, J., García, S. and Londoño, A. (2003) *Campañas Políticas Presidenciales y Medios de Comunicación en Colombia 2001–2002*. Bogota: FESCOL-Universidad Javeriana.

Rockwell, R. and Janus, N. (2002a) *Media Power in Central America*. Urbana, IL: University of Illinois Press.

Rockwell, R. and Janus, N. (2002b) 'The Politics of Coercion: Advertising, Media, and State Power in Central America', *Journalism*, 3(3): 331–54.

Rodríguez, C. (2001) *Fissures in the Mediascape. An International Study of Citizens' Media*. Cresskill, NJ: Hampton Press.

Salazar, J. F. and Cordova, A. (2008) 'Imperfect Media and the Poetics of Indigenous Video in Latin America', in P. Wilson and M. Stewart (eds.), *Global Indigenous Media: Cultures, Poetics, and Politics*, 39–57. Durham, NC: Duke University Press.

Sánchez Ruiz, E. E. (2007) *¿Concentración Mediática o Gobernabilidad Democrática? Gobernabilidad Democrática, Cultura Política y Medios de Comunicación en México*.

Sartori, G. (1998) *Homo Videns: La Sociedad Teledirigida*. Mexico: Taurus.

Schmucler, H. and Mata, M. C. (eds.) (1992) *Política y Comunicación: Hay un Lugar para la Política en la Cultura Mediática?* Córdoba: Universidad de Córdoba.

Seele, A. and Peruzzotti, E. (eds.) (2009) *Participatory Innovations and Representative Democracy in Latin America*. Washington, DC: Woodrow Wilson Press/John Hopkins University Press.

Silva, P. (2004) 'Doing Politics in a Depoliticized Society: Social Change and Political Deactivation in Chile', *Bulletin of Latin American Research*, 23(1): 63–78.

Sinclair, J. (1999) *Latin American Television: A Global View*. Oxford: Oxford University Press.

Skidmore, T. (ed.) (1992) *Television, Politics, and the Transition to Democracy in Latin America*. Washington, DC: Woodrow Wilson Center.

Stromback, J. (2008) 'Four Phases of Mediatization: An Analysis of the Mediatization of Politics', *International Journal of Press/Politics*, 13(3): 228–46.

Subite, E. and Gutierrez, M. (2006) *Espacios de Intermediación en Tiempos de Conflicto: Medios de Comunicación en Bolivia*. La Paz: CIPCA CRS.

Sunkel, G. and Geoffroy, E. (eds.) (2001) *Concentración Económica de los Medios de Comunicación*. Santiago: Lom.

Torrico, E. and Sandoval, V. (2007) *Un Año de la Constituyente en la Prensa*. La Paz: Observatorio Nacional de Medios y PNUD.

Waisbord, S. (1994) 'Television and Election Campaigns in Argentina', *Journal of Communication*, 44(2): 125–35.

Waisbord, S. (1996) 'Secular Politics: The Modernization of Argentine Electioneering', in D. Swanson and P. Mancini (eds.), *Politics, Media, and Modern Democracy.* Westport, CT: Praeger. pp. 207–26.

Waisbord, S. (2000) *Watchdog Journalism in South America.* New York: Columbia University Press.

Waisbord, S. (2009) 'Advocacy Journalism in a Global Context: The "Journalist" and the "Civic" Model', in K. Wahl-Jorgensen and T. Hanitzsch (eds.), *Handbook of Journalism Studies.* New York: Routledge. pp. 371–85.

Waisbord, S. and Peruzzotti, E. (2009) 'The Environmental Story that Wasn't: Advocacy, Journalism, and the Ambientalismo Movement in Argentina', *Media, Culture & Society,* 31(5): 691–709.

Wallis, D. (2004) 'The Media and Democratic Change in Mexico', *Parliamentary Affairs,* 57(1): 118–30.

35

Political Communication and Media Effects in the Context of New Democracies of East-Central Europe

Hubert Tworzecki

New democracies offer political communication researchers a unique opportunity to study media effects in a setting where they ought to be at their strongest. It is reasonable to expect that in new political systems the complex interconnections between social-structural variables, group loyalties, values, organizations and patterns of behavior that characterize state–society relations in older democracies have not yet matured, and the citizenry does not yet have the benefit of a lifetime of personal experience with a political system's key actors, institutions and policy outputs. This chapter focuses on countries of East-Central Europe – Poland, Hungary and the Czech Republic – where highly competitive and technologically sophisticated media systems exist today in the context of a brevity of democratic experience and relative underdevelopment of political parties and civic associations. While it is true that, on balance, the multiple transformations that took place in these countries after 1989 – from authoritarian to liberal-democratic politics, from state-controlled to market-based economics and from isolation behind the barbed wire of the Iron Curtain to full membership in the European Union – have been remarkably successful, in recent years these countries have been showing signs of 'democratic malaise', that is, of growing public cynicism and disenchantment with politics (Tworzecki, 2008),

arguably fueled at least in part by a steady diet of revelations of incompetence, corruption and cronyism on the part of elected officials, served up by fiercely competitive and scandal-hungry news media. In short, the combination of short democratic history, weak parties and increasingly 'tabloidized' politics would seem an ideal environment for media outlets to play an outsized role in the electoral process, and so in what follows we look at how the current state of affairs came about and examine the media's role in these new democracies today.

POLITICAL COMMUNICATION UNDER COMMUNIST RULE

The decade of the 1980s marked a slow, but ultimately irreversible decline of communist regimes of East-Central Europe, culminating in their domino-like collapse during the summer and fall of 1989. One aspect of this complex and multifaceted process was the regimes' gradual but inexorable loss of control over the media and, more broadly, over political communication in general. Indeed, for all the massive changes in the media system brought about by the post-1989 transitions to markets and democracy – including liberalization of content, deregulation and commercialization of media markets, and a vast expansion of the number of outlets – it is important not to lose sight of the fact at least some of these processes began much earlier, long before anyone imagined that communist regimes were on they way to the 'rubbish heap' of history. Furthermore, far from the caricatured view of communist-era media content as, in *The Economist's* words, a 'steady diet of propaganda and "Swan Lake"',[1] there was in fact no single model of political communication shared by all members of the Eastern Bloc either in the 1980s or in earlier decades. While there were some common elements (the regimes outlawed private competition to the state-run press, radio and television and imposed political censorship on the content of media messages), both the extent and the effectiveness of these policies, as well as the availability of uncensored alternatives to the state-run media, varied considerably from country to country and from one time period to another (Sparks, 2000). Likewise, it would be too simplistic to claim that the advent of democracy brought an instant end to the domination of media markets by state-owned behemoths, or halted attempts at political meddling in the management of media companies and in the content of media messages. In short, it will be argued that as far as East-Central Europe was concerned, the transitions of 1989 were just one step along a lengthy path rather than a sharp, clear line separating one era of political communication from another.

In Poland, for example, the decomposition of the totalitarian model, with its Orwellian manipulations of language and control over all public discourse, began quite early in the communist regime's history. Following the 1956 protests in favor of political liberalization, the regime sought to improve its legitimacy in the eyes of the population by reaching a *modus vivendi* with the Catholic Church. The arrangement included provisions enabling the church to reach the faithful not only through the pulpit but also through a few titles of officially sanctioned Catholic press (for example, *Tygodnik Powszechny*) which, while still subject to censorship, was nonetheless able to spread the message of Christianity, rather than the supposedly ruling Marxist–Leninist ideology. This post-1956 compromise (which also included other aspects, such as an end to the forced collectivization of agriculture) essentially amounted to the regime giving up on its one-time ambition of indoctrinating Polish society into Soviet-style communism. Once this model of 'national-consensus communism' (Kitschelt, 1995) was in effect (defined by a tacit agreement between the rulers and the ruled along the lines of 'don't question our legitimacy and we won't try to turn Poland into another Soviet Union'), the path was open to further liberalization of media content. And so while censorship as such was not abolished (indeed, a handbook of its myriad of Byzantine rules was smuggled out to the West in the 1970s and subsequently published as the *Black Book of Polish Censorship* (Curry, 1984), the regime tried to ingratiate itself with the population further by giving it a window on the western world in the form of movies and television. Consequently, within a few years the Polish regime began to source large amounts of media content from the USA and Western Europe, treating movie and television audiences to everything from the latest Hollywood blockbusters, to British television miniseries (*I, Claudius, The Forsyte Saga*), French historical documentaries and popular American television programs such as *Kojak, Columbo* and even *Charlie's Angels*.

Similar to Poland, in Hungary the model of 'goulash communism' that eventually came in the wake of the crushed revolution of 1956 signified the regime's abandonment of its early, totalitarian ambitions of remaking society in the Soviet mold. As television sets became more widely available, the Hungarian regime resigned itself to the fact that about a third of the population was able to watch programming from Austria, eventually even printing Austrian television listings in some state-run newspapers and, as in Poland, featuring increasing amounts of western content on domestic television channels (Jakubowicz, 1994). Hungary was also the first country in the region to experiment with cable television, with over 40 municipality-run cable systems in operation in the late 1980s. Remarkably for an era when residents of some neighboring countries (Ceausescu's Romania, pre-Gorbachev Soviet Union) were still straining to hear the crackling short-wave broadcasts of Radio Free Europe for a few snippets of uncensored news, some of these Hungarian cable systems actually carried western satellite channels such as Britain's Sky and France's TV5 (Noam, 1991: 287).

In the late 1980s, individual satellite dishes were also beginning to make their way into the Eastern Bloc, brought in by people who traveled to the West as tourists, suitcase-traders or guest-workers, as many Poles, Hungarians and Yugoslavs (but not Czechoslovaks or East Germans) were able to do in the final years of communist rule. The dishes were used exclusively to receive signals from western stations, since domestic satellite television did not as yet exist. Along with VCRs, which despite their high price (about US$500 in the late 1980s, or about US$850 in today's prices) were also becoming more common, these devices added to the variety of media content available to audiences in at least some countries of the Eastern Bloc.

While we will never know for sure what contribution, if any, this mass, sustained exposure to western movies and television made to the eventual demise of communism, one may hypothesize that at the very least it made people aware of the growing gap in living standards between the East and the West. According to a famous anecdote, in the 1940s Stalin banned the film *The Grapes of Wrath* from Soviet cinemas because of its central image of supposedly destitute Americans in the depths of the Depression traveling in search of a better life *in their own vehicle* – a consumer good which at the time was completely beyond the reach of Soviet citizens. It is possible, in other words, that the economically underperforming Eastern Bloc regimes which allowed their populations to be exposed to images of western living standards were doing themselves a major disservice. It is also tempting to hypothesize that people who routinely watched Hollywood crime dramas, where the ending often involved the suspect being advised of his rights – 'you have the right to remain silent', 'you have the right to an attorney', etc. – were inspired by revelations about the legal protections available to individuals confronted by state power in democratic societies. Such conjectures, however, remain in the realm of speculation.

In contrast to Poland and Hungary, with the exception of a brief period of liberalization in 1968 known as the 'Prague Spring', the Czechoslovak regime remained consistently hardline, both in overall political terms and in the extent of control it was able to exercise over media content. Indeed, as late as 1989 the state-run Czechoslovak television featured virtually no western-sourced materials (Jakubowicz, 2007: 332), but it did devote an entire channel to the rebroadcasting of Russian-language programming from the Soviet Union for the benefit of Soviet troops stationed in the country since the 1968 invasion. Even so, the Czechoslovak regime's hold over political communication was far from total, given the fact that people in southern parts of the country were able to receive Austrian television and given that, following Mikhail Gorbachev's *glasnost* campaign of 1987, the Russian-language channel became *the* place to see free-wheeling political discussions of the sort unimaginable in Czechoslovak media (Culik, 2004).

In addition, regardless of the domestic political and media situation, the people of communist East-Central Europe had the ability to tune into foreign radio stations such as the BBC World Service, Voice of America and Radio Free Europe, which offered programming in most of the region's languages and which, despite jamming, attracted a considerable audience, especially in places too far east to receive western television signals.[2]

Some portion of the population was also able to receive information from the *samizdat* news bulletins printed (or recorded on cassette tapes) clandestinely by opposition groups and passed around from one person to the next. As with everything else, there were differences between countries and time periods in the scope and reach of samizdat publishing. Around the time of the Solidarity crisis of 1980, Poland probably had the largest circulation of such literature, with some underground news bulletins reaching 100,000-copy daily print runs (Skilling, 1989). Last but not least, political communication under communism also included informal channels such as private conversation, gossip, rumors, political jokes and so forth, which played a significant role in the flow of information and over which the authorities had essentially no control (Jakubowicz, 2007: 130).

All in all, it is safe to say that by the 1980s the communist regimes of East-Central Europe were unable to genuinely enforce control over the content of political communication. Between the foreign radio and television stations, the *samizdat*, the churches, and the Western-sourced content on domestic television, any hopes those regimes might once have had of using the media to keep their populations securely in the grip of communist ideology must have been long gone. In any case, by that time the ideology had very few true believers, even within the regimes themselves (Malia, 1993).

Finally, a few words about 'bottom-up' political communication during the communist era. In democracies, the most important mechanism through which the general public can communicate its approval or disapproval of the authorities' actions involves free and fair elections. Elections in the communist world were neither; nonetheless, they did contain some elements of choice in that the citizenry could cross out (that is, vote against) either individual candidates or entire lists (the details varied across time and across countries) as an expression of no-confidence in the regime. Citizens could also cast a spoiled ballot or simply stay at home in defiance of compulsory voting laws. Again, the costs of such non-compliance varied depending on the time (they could be quite severe during the Stalinist era but comparatively minor in later years) and the place (negligible in 1980s Hungary or Poland, but still significant in Czechoslovakia). In fact, in Poland during the 1980s electoral abstention was such a mass phenomenon that political scientists routinely used turnout data as a proxy measure of popular support for the regime, detecting consistent patterns of non-participation in some regions of the country (more rural, more religious, with a more settled population) but not in others (urban, industrial, with more migratory populations).

Most interestingly, these regional variations in turnout would later carry over into democratic elections in the post-1989 period as patterns of support for the communist successor party (Jasiewicz, 1991; Tworzecki, 1996).

In addition to electoral turnout, communist regimes received feedback by a variety of other means. All of them subjected their populations to some level of covert surveillance carried out by networks of agents and informants, while other expressions of 'public opinion', such as letters sent to newspaper editors or reports from workplace meetings with employees, were also gathered and carefully analyzed, although their representativeness was always open to question. What is less well known is that scientifically designed opinion surveys actually has a long history in several countries of the former Eastern Bloc. Public opinion research institutes were established immediately after the end of World War II in both Hungary and Czechoslovakia, and conducted survey work as early as 1945 (Henn, 1998). Their operations were curtailed during the Stalinist era and their methods condemned as 'bourgeois pseudo-science', but Stalin's death opened up new possibilities, especially in the relatively liberal climate of post-1956 Poland, where mass opinion research was soon being done by both government institutes and by individual academics (CBOS, 1994). Surprisingly, the Polish public proved willing to tackle even the most politically sensitive questions, such as confidence in the communist regime. Its answers consistently showed that it was quite divided on this matter, with about one-quarter of respondents answering in the affirmative, another quarter expressing lack of confidence, the third quarter placing itself in the neither/nor category and the remainder describing themselves as uninterested in politics (Jasiewicz, 1991). In Hungary, mass opinion research was made possible by Kádár's 'thaw' in the mid-1960s, and in Czechoslovakia (for a brief time) by the spirit of openness and debate accompanying the Prague Spring reforms of 1968 (Piekalkiewicz, 1972; Tőkés, 1997).

In the event, even when the authorities allowed opinion research to be conducted, its results remained confidential. Public opinion data was rarely, if ever, released to the media by the regime's censors, and the circulation of academic works featuring such information was severely restricted (Mink, 1981). Still, as the 1980s drew to a close, the regimes in Poland and Hungary had at their disposal a substantial body of survey research, and there is some evidence that these data played a role in the process of democratic transition. Awareness of rapidly falling approval ratings may well have prompted the Polish and Hungarian regimes to conclude negotiations with the opposition sooner rather than later – in the belief that their position would only worsen with time and any chance for gaining a measure of popular legitimacy through the electoral process would be lost (Tőkés, 1997).

MEDIA SYSTEM TRANSFORMATION AFTER THE 1989 DEMOCRATIC TRANSITIONS

The transition to democracy and market-based economics that followed the collapse of communism had a powerful impact on media landscapes and on political communication across East-Central Europe. Most fundamentally, it brought about the end of state monopoly in print and broadcasting, and opened up domestic media markets to competition from private enterprise. But managing this process was not an easy task for the region's new democracies. Apart from the legal, technical and logistical issues, not to mention political resistance to transforming the old state-run outlets into genuinely 'public' services, there was the complex task of drafting the appropriate legislation needed to provide a legal framework for the operation of their new, commercial competitors. In retrospect, much of what transpired was very haphazard, with a 'make it up as you go along' quality, but it is worth recalling that in the late 1980s commercial television broadcasting was still a relatively new phenomenon even in Western Europe (West Germany, for example, saw its first privately owned television channel go on the air only in 1984), so the post-communist democracies were essentially learning how to commercialize their media markets along with everyone else in Europe, with only scant guidance from the European Union and its directives which, as prospective members of the EU, they were increasingly obliged to follow.[3]

In developing media policy, one of the first tasks facing the new democracies was to provide the nascent political parties and civic organization with a means of communicating with the wider society for both electoral campaigning and, more broadly, for the purpose of restoring pluralism of opinion in public discourse. In the print realm, this was largely achieved by breaking up the giant, state-owned media enterprises, such as Poland's 'RSW', which in the final years of communist rule published 244 different press titles and employed close to 100,000 people, including almost 60% of all Polish journalists. As part of the transformation process about 60 of these titles were handed over to political parties and various civil society organizations and the remainder were put up for sale to the highest bidder, including some foreign investors such as the French *Groupe Hersant* (Dobek-Ostrowska, 1998: 40).

In the electronic realm, there was a complicating technical factor having to do with the scarcity of available broadcasting frequencies and the consequent need for an appropriate regulatory framework. In the Polish case, would-be radio and television entrepreneurs chose not to wait for politicians and policy makers, and so the first years of the new era were characterized by a dizzying proliferation of new media outlets, at first mostly local radio stations operating from low-power transmitters in something of a 'pirate' fashion. Some of these stations lacked sufficient financial resources and ultimately did not survive the rigors of the marketplace, but others, such as *Radio Małopolska Fun* (operating since January 1990 and today called RMF-FM), eventually evolved into major commercial broadcasters with a national reach. Owing to higher startup costs there were initially fewer players on the television side, but the overall pattern was much the same as with radio, with a number of small, unlicensed stations appearing on the air starting in 1990.[4] This dynamic growth of new media outlets soon attracted the attention of both foreign and domestic investors. Perhaps the most widely known, not to mention the most flamboyant of these early entrepreneurs was Nicola Grauso, an associate of Silvio Berlusconi, who by 1993 acquired a controlling stake in 13 Polish television stations and integrated them into a quasi-national network featuring rather unambitious programming (20-year-old American television shows, Latin American soap operas, erotic movies) sent in by way of Berlusconi's *Reteitalia* network, prompting Britain's *Guardian* to call him the 'pirate king of Polish television'.[5] Grauso's brazen tactics did not win him many friends among Poland's politicians and regulators, and so when the first allocations of broadcasting frequencies took place in 1993 and 1994, he failed to win a license and was eventually forced off the air and onto satellite. Instead, the state-owned television (TVP) acquired competition from the domestically owned Polsat, which in 1994 won the first commercial terrestrial television license in Poland, and which in 1997 was joined by another privately owned broadcaster, TVN.

In contrast to Poland's free-for-all, the commercialization of electronic media systems in Hungary and Czechoslovakia was more sedate, which in part was due to prolonged legislative wrangling over the allocation of frequencies, and in part reflected the hesitation on the part of potential investors concerned about the relatively small size of their media markets (each of these two countries has a population of about

10 million, compared to Poland's 38). In Hungary's case, in 1989 the government declared a moratorium on the allocation of broadcasting frequencies, effectively freezing the growth of commercial electronic media outlets for much of the 1990s (Szekfu, 1994). Consequently, Hungary did not see its first privately owned television channels, TV2 and RTL-Klub, go on the air until 1997. In Czechoslovakia, the post-communist restructuring of the media system was complicated further by political wrangling over the future of the federal state itself, which in due course led to its division (in 1993) into the Czech Republic and Slovakia. Prior to that point, of the three television channels of the state-owned broadcaster (CST), the first one was a 'federal' channel transmitted throughout the country, the second one a 'national' channel that broadcast in Czech in Czech lands and in Slovak in Slovakia, and the third one transmitted Soviet programming in Russian (Noam, 1991: 281). After the dissolution of Czechoslovakia, the Czech state broadcaster (CT) retained two of the frequencies and the third one was allocated in 1994, amid much controversy and accusations of favoritism, to a private channel called TV Nova, later joined by another privately owned channel, Prima.

From today's perspective, these early 1990s battles over the allocation terrestrial broadcasting frequencies seem almost quaint, since the individuals and companies involved in them failed to anticipate the extremely strong growth of cable and satellite systems with their ability to offer hundreds of channels of simultaneous programming. By the early 2000s, the penetration of cable and satellite television, fueled by rapidly falling cost of consumer electronics, reached almost 70% of households in Hungary and around 40% of households in Poland and the Czech Republic (Jakubowicz, 2007: 333). And with the price of satellite 'receiver + antenna + 6 month free subscription' packages dropping to as little as the equivalent of US$100,[6] this new technology became available to virtually all demographic groups, including lower-income residents of rural areas, who hitherto were forced to rely exclusively on over-the-air broadcasts.

This technological change, with its proliferation of outlets and consequent fragmentation of the audience, was also not anticipated by the region's politicians. Having spent much of their own lives under the shadow of communist media monopolies, they seemingly internalized the belief that control of the media – especially television – is one of the attributes of political power.[7] Consequently, post-1989 attempts to transform state-run media outlets into genuinely independent, public broadcasters with a mission to provide the kind of programming that commercial outlets were unwilling or unable to produce, have time and again clashed with political resistance, leading to an almost two-decade long pattern of so-called 'media wars' waged in all countries of East-Central Europe.

Although the details varied, the conflicts had a number of common elements. One was the formation of national broadcasting councils, whose aim was to provide oversight over the public media. In theory, their members were to be independent individuals appointed by national parliaments, but in practice control over them fell to political parties, which enthusiastically packed the councils with their own appointees, exploiting the public media as vehicles for both political patronage and electoral self-promotion (Mungiu-Pippidi, 2003). And then there was ideology. In Hungary and Poland, the ideological roots of conflict over the public media lay in the 'pacted' nature of the 1989 political transition, which allowed the former communist parties not only to survive as powerful organizational entities, but also to rebrand themselves into democracy-and-market friendly social democrats. This transformation was never accepted as genuine by the ideological right, which was also outraged by the former rulers' apparent success in avoiding retribution or even accountability for their time in power. As a consequence, the political scene in Hungary and Poland became structured by the conflict between a glibly pragmatic post-communist left (Hungarian Socialist Party [MSZP], Poland's Democratic Left Alliance [SLD]) – interested in glossing over the past) – and a stern, moralizing anti-communist right (Hungarian Democratic Forum [MDF], Young Democrats [Fidesz], Poland's Solidarity Electoral Action [AWS], Law and Justice [PiS]) fixated on settling accounts with history. Caught in the middle were social-liberal parties – Poland's Democratic Union/Freedom Union (UD/UW), Hungary's Alliance of Free Democrats (SZDSZ) – despised by the right for their 'let bygones be bygones' attitude to the past and their refusal to join in the anti-communist crusade.

It was this fundamental ideological conflict, not disputes over the specifics of economic or foreign policies, which have dominated and continue to dominate electoral competition in both countries, and in many respects the infamous 'media wars' were simply one of its aspects. With their righteous zeal and a sense of historic mission, the right in both countries was infuriated by what it saw as the prevalence of left-liberal voices in both print and broadcast media, and sought to correct this imbalance by appointing right-thinking (so to speak) individuals to key journalistic and management positions. An advisor to Hungary's Prime Minister, Viktor Orban (Fidesz) once explained this philosophy thus:

In decades prior to the political transformation, the various colors of the communist, socialist worldview had a quasi-monopoly in Hungary's print press and broadcast media ... The so-called spontaneous privatization at the end of the previous decade was controlled by the elite of journalists and former party functionaries ... Positive discrimination promoting the representation of right values in the press is morally justified by the suppression of these values under socialism as well as their [negative] discrimination in the transformation years. (Quoted in Bajomi-Lazar, 2003: 102)

In Poland, one of the vice-chairman of the public radio network appointed in 2006 by the Kaczyński brothers' PiS party was even more blunt, reportedly telling one employee that she was being dismissed as part of his mission to cleanse the radio of 'communist dregs'.[8] Of course the left, for its part, was hardly blameless, in that, following their electoral wins in Poland (1993, 2001) and Hungary (1994, 2002, 2006), the communist successor parties in both countries showed little hesitation in using public radio and television for shameless self-promotion, though perhaps without the holier-than-thou moralizing characteristic of the right.

Lastly, in the Czech case the nature of the conflict was somewhat different owing to that country's mode of transition from an authoritarian to a democratic regime (that is, through collapse, not negotiation). With an unrepentant and unreformed Communist Party largely confined to the margins of the political scene, the public Czech Television (CT) became caught in the clash between a more idealistic, participatory model of democracy favored by the dissident-playwright-turned-president Vaclav Havel and a more structured, party-driven model favored, naturally enough, by leaders of the largest political parties keen to divide up the spoils of power – including control of the public media – among themselves. The conflict reached a climax in the fall of 2000, when employees of public television went on strike in protest against partisan meddling in the media, aided by mass public demonstrations in the streets of Prague and encouraging words from President Havel. The events prompted Vaclav Klaus, leader of the right-of-center Civic Democrats (ODS), to utter the much-quoted phrase that the crisis would end either in 'victory for normalized democracy' or in the 'triumph of Havlocracy', which he saw as a kind of mob rule.[9]

Why were the region's politicians so intent on retaining control of the public radio and television channels? For starters, for much of the 1990s the public media were by far the dominant players in their respective markets, with audiences that dwarfed those of the just-emerging privately owned stations. Audience fragmentation came only gradually as cable and satellite gained more subscribers and as operators of these services began to feature ever-increasing variety of specialized, thematic channels. But even after these developments public television news programs were still able to command large audiences: for example, Polish data from mid-2005 show that the main public channel (TVP1) registered a daily average of 3.2 million viewers for its flagship 7.30 pm news broadcast and additional 2.7 million and 2.6 million for the 5.00 pm and 10.00 pm editions, respectively. By comparison, the privately owned TVN claimed about 2 million viewers for its 7:00 pm news program while another private station, POLSAT, had about 1.4 million viewers for its 6.45 pm program.[10] Given those large audiences, and given that television news remains the dominant source of election-related information for citizens of Hungary and the Czech Republic (in Poland it is second only to political advertising, see Table 35.1[11]), the politicians' motives become easier to understand.

Second, it is worth recalling that at the beginning of the post-1989 transition process most of East-Central Europe's new political parties were quite small, with few members and limited organizational structures, making them heavily dependent financially on state subsidies, and electorally dependent on the media for contact with potential voters. The sources of this problem lie in the fact that, compared to Western Europe, the region's party membership figures as percentage of the total electorate were (and still remain) quite low: around 2.8%, compared to a west European average of 5.5% in 1999 (Kopecky, 2006; Walecki, 2003). With few dues-paying members, the parties depend on state subventions ranging from direct funding (whose amount is based on the proportion of seats won in the last election), to various indirect subsides, including free media time (for example, during parliamentary election campaigns Czech political parties receive 14 hours on

public television, divided equally among them) (Walecki, 2003). In practice, however, this free media time has proved to be of limited value because the programs – each only a few minutes long – tended to be lumped together into 15–20 minute blocs, making them a bit tedious for even the most civic-minded of viewers. Plus, at the beginning of the 1990s the quality of some these party programs was embarrassingly low, and consequently some people watched them more for their comedic value than for any informational content. As time went on the quality of this programming improved, but nonetheless there was always the temptation to go beyond it and secure favorable coverage in news programs by either pressuring or coopting journalists and their managers. Of course it takes two to tango, and indeed from the journalistic side there was also at times the temptation to improve one's career prospects by serving the powers that be, with sometimes deleterious impact on the quality of journalism and on professional ethics. As a consequence, the history of the past two decades offers a veritable smorgasbord of cases of political pressure being applied to news programming in the public media, with some of the more blatant cases drawing critical attention from the OSCE in its election monitoring reports from Hungary (OSCE, 2002) and Poland (OSCE, 2008).

But was this political meddling worth it in the sense of producing electoral outcomes favorable to incumbents? The available evidence suggests that it was not. In one of the best-documented early cases – that of intensely propagandistic, pro-government turn in the Hungarian public media in 1990–94 – the data suggest that the effort actually backfired, contributing to the government's defeat in the 1994 parliamentary elections (Popescu and Toka, 2002). Much the same situation occurred in Poland during 2005–07, when blatant pressure from the government on both public and private media contributed to the sense that democratic freedoms were at stake, resulting in a surge of

Table 35.1   Sources of election-related information (respondents reporting frequent or occasional reliance on...)

	Poland 2005 (%)	Hungary 2006 (%)	Czech Rep. 2006 (%)
Television news	86	91	75
Printed press	57	71	71
Party or candidate advertising	91	53	70
Talking with friends	74	80	73
Political meetings or rallies	5	13	21
Internet sites	10	9	16

Table 35.2 Party mentions on TVP1, TVP2 and TVP Info, 4 May–5 June 2009 (hours:minutes)

PO	PiS	SLD	PSL	Libertas
37:41	24:01	13:07	9:17	13:00

support for the opposition that ousted the incumbents in the 2007 elections. But perhaps the most brazen and the most spectacularly futile attempt to use the public media for political self-promotion occurred in Poland during the 2009 European elections. The story involved the euroskeptic Libertas party (founded by the Irish businessman Declan Ganley and fielding candidates in a number of EU states) which, despite a massive promotional campaign waged on its behalf by sympathizers ensconced in key management positions in Poland's public television (TVP), won only an embarrassing 1% of the vote and no seats in the European Parliament. Indeed, content data (Table 35.2[12]) would later confirm that during the campaign Libertas received a share of television airtime out of all proportion to its near-zero standing in the pre-election opinion polls, but in the end this effort paid no dividends and a few weeks later Libertas completely disappeared from the Polish political scene.

CONCLUSION: MEDIA EFFECTS IN NEW DEMOCRACIES

Over the past several decades, the political communications literature has been structured by two fundamental questions having to do with the strength and the direction of media effects in the context of proliferation of new outlets, audience fragmentation and the rise of 24-hour news channels in advanced industrial democracies. On the question of strength, opinion has been divided between scholars who saw political competition evolving in recent years into a media-driven 'audience democracy' (Manin, 1997) and, on the other side, those who expected to see a diminution of the media's role as a consequence of the fragmentation of what as once a mass, 'inadvertent' audience into a plethora of discrete, ideologically self-selected groups (Bennett and Iyengar, 2008). The question of direction has been addressed in the so-called 'malaise versus mobilization' debate, where some studies have linked media exposure, especially exposure to television, to various symptoms of the former, including erosion of social capital, growing levels of public cynicism,

disenchantment with democracy and disengagement from the public sphere, as evidenced by declining election turnouts and diminishing involvement in civic activities (Brehm and Rahn, 1998; Cappella and Jamieson, 1997; Putnam, 1995). Conversely, scholars have reported evidence for a 'virtuous circle' of influence between media exposure and political engagement (Norris, 2000).

All in all, however, in surveying the results of recent research, it is difficult to escape the conclusion that in established democracies media effects are, in Newton's words, a 'comparatively weak force, whose effects can be deflected, diluted and diffused by stronger forces [... including ...] bedrocks political values associated with class, religion, age, gender and education, as well as social networks and discussions, distrust of the mass media, and personal knowledge and experience' (2006: 209). This is why the study of new democracies offers political communication researchers a unique opportunity to study media effects in a setting where they ought to be at their strongest, simply because in new democracies the various forces mentioned by Newton would have had less time to form, and the citizenry would not have the benefit of a lifetime of personal political experience that would make it less susceptible to being swayed by media messages.

Does this expectation hold up in the light of available evidence? Quantitative studies of media effects in the new democracies of East-Central Europe are still in their infancy, but there is some data from Hungary and Poland showing that certain kinds of media exposure – specifically, exposure to 'quality' press and to television news – has a positive impact on political knowledge, support for democratic values and certain kinds of participation (Schmitt-Beck and Voltmer, 2007; Tworzecki and Semetko, 2010). There are also several well-known examples of 'malaise' effects prompted by media-hyped political scandals that had deleterious impact on public confidence in elected officials and on approval of democracy itself. In Poland's case, the most notorious was the 2003 'Rywin-gate' scandal, which involved the proposition of a bribe in exchange for regulatory approval for a merger of two private media companies. The scandal eventually led to the formation of a parliamentary commission of inquiry whose televised hearings gripped the nation for much of 2003. The commission's revelations of deep-seated government corruption had a dramatic impact on citizens' trust in political institutions and in the political system as whole: as the hearings progressed, answers to survey questions about satisfaction with the way democracy functioned in Poland fell to an unprecedented 20% of respondents, with 70% expressing dissatisfaction.[13] And the impact was not limited only to opinion polls: in the next elections (held in 2005), far-right parties questioning the achievements of the post-1989 democratic transformation were able to come to power, only to be defeated two years later after their authoritarian ambitions became a source of concern to many voters. Hungary experienced a similar moment in 2006, when Prime Minister Ferenc Gyurcsany (MSZP) was caught on tape admitting that his government had been 'lying morning, noon and night' and was aided and abetted by the media in doing so. The release of the recording led to a crash of public confidence in the government and several days of riots in the streets of Budapest (Schopflin, 2006), which itself was ironic given that Gyurcsany simply dared to voice a deep political truth left unspoken even in Western democracies.

So much for malaise, but what about mobilization? One outstanding example of the latter is the phenomenon of Poland's Radio Maryja (Radio Virgin Mary). Founded in 1991, Radio Maryja is now part of a major media conglomerate whose outlets also include a daily newspaper (*Nasz Dziennik*), a television channel (TV Trwam) and even a mobile telephony operator. It is sometimes argued that Radio Maryja, under the leadership of its founder, Father Rydzyk, has acquired some characteristics of a religious cult, with only a tenuous link to mainstream Catholicism, although it does enjoy support among a significant segment of the Polish clergy. Its programming consists of a mixture of religious services, call-in shows and nationalist, xenophobic political commentary inundating listeners with conspiracy theories in which freemasons, Jews, international bankers, foreign companies, the European Union, liberals, progressive Catholics and assorted free-thinkers are identified as threats to the nation and its traditional values. Although its reach is comparatively small (about 2% share, or 1 million regular listeners[14]), Radio Maryja's overwhelmingly rural, elderly (70% are over 60 years old) listeners have acquired a reputation for following the station's political endorsements[15] and, even more importantly, for actually showing up at the polls at election time. Against the backdrop of low turnouts and high voter volatility, this group of voters became a prize keenly sought after by right-wing politicians, giving the radio considerable influence on the Polish political scene during the election campaigns of 2005 and 2007 (Jasiewicz, 2008). Furthermore, there is some evidence suggesting that regular listening to Radio Maryja leads to other forms of social and political mobilization, such as participation in rallies, individualized contacting of politicians, joining of grassroots organizational structures (the so-called 'families of Radio Maryja') and so forth (Burdziej, 2008).

Given that Polish society is characterized by generally low levels of social capital,[16] the Radio Maryja phenomenon is truly exceptional; however, it must be borne in mind that it mobilizes people to action mainly through negative emotions, namely fear and hostility toward outsiders, making the interpersonal capital it generates rather more 'unsocial' than 'social' (Levi, 1996).

In conclusion, the story of political communication in post-1989 East-Central Europe is one of a truly remarkable transformation, whereby in the span of 20 years strict political control and a relative paucity of choice has given way to unprecedented freedoms and an exuberant variety of programming. Along the way, this transformation was accompanied by rapid technological change and the emergence of new types of media and media delivery methods, starting with cable and satellite television in the 1990s and extending, most recently, to the rise of blogs and social networking web sites that are increasingly important as carriers of information. Last but not least, this change has unfolded in parallel and likely dynamically linked with the development of democratic institutions and democratic cultural norms from what was largely a blank slate 20 years ago. All these factors make East-Central Europe an ideal laboratory for the study of media effects and will continue to do so in the future as the region is posed on the cusp of another informational revolution (that is, the rapid spread of broadband connectivity) that will further erode the audiences of traditional media.

The implications of these developments for the future course of democratic transformation are difficult to predict. On the one hand, the new technologies may enhance the levels of civic engagement by making it possible for individuals to participate in the life of their community – for example, through electronic social networking – with unprecedented ease and immediacy. On the other hand, they may foster social fragmentation by making it even easier for individuals to cluster in ideologically like-minded groups, speaking exclusively among themselves and losing sight of broader societal concerns. In new democracies, where the shared 'symbolic space', that is, a widely understood framework for talking about the political world has barely begun to coalesce, such fragmentation may have a number of negative consequences, such as erosion of trust in the institutions of government that can eventually lead to a serious crisis of legitimacy (Siedentop, 2003). The region of East-Central Europe offers many such quandaries, and while most of them cannot be resolved just yet, they do make for an exceptionally rich research agenda for future scholarship.

NOTES

1 'Central European Television: Off-beam', *The Economist*, 28 December 1994, p. 69.

2 At its height the Radio Free Europe/Radio Liberty network produced regular radio broadcasts in over 20 languages of the Eastern Bloc. Audience figures for most countries are difficult to estimate, but we know from opinion surveys that in Poland the regular audience of RFE and other Western radio stations rose from about 20% of the adult population in 1976, to 31% in 1979, to 48–53% at the height of the Solidarity crisis of 1980–81 (Hoover Institution, 2004).

3 The most important of these was the 1989 Council directive 'Television without Frontiers' (89/552/EEC), which set out the framework for establishing a common market in broadcasting.

4 By the end of 1992, at the height of the 'pirate era' in Polish broadcasting, 24 privately owned radio and 10 television stations operated throughout the country (Dobek-Ostrowska 1998).

5 Julian Borger, 'On the Profit Frequency', *Guardian*, 6 December 1993, p. 19.

6 Offer listed on page www.polsat.pl, accessed on 19 December 2006.

7 Unfortunately, they would have reached much the same conclusion if they looked for guidance to contemporary Western Europe. In 1980s Italy, for example, the public channels were allocated among the major political parties – Raiuno was controlled by the Christian Democrats, Raidue by the Socialists, Raitre by the Communist Party – and this arrangement was hardly unique at the time (Noam, 1991: 150–1).

8 Agnieszka Kublik, 'Wokół widzę same stare kobiety!', *Gazeta Wyborcza*, 13 April 2007.

9 'Constitutional Watch', *East European Constitutional Review*, Winter 2001.

10 Source: http://www.mediarun.pl/news/id/11165, accessed on 11 January 2006.

11 Polish data are from the 2005 Polish General Election Survey (PGSW). Czech and Hungarian data come from national random sample surveys commissioned commercially by the present author during those countries' parliamentary elections of 2006.

12 Source: http://www.krrit.gov.pl/bip/Wiadomosci/WYBORYDOPARLAMENTUEUROPEJSKIEGO/tabid/390/Default.aspx, accessed on 12 August 2009.

13 CBOS report 'Polacy o demokracji' (BS/141/2003).

14 As per audience research figures by Millward Brown SMG/KRC reported on http://www.radiomaryja.pl.eu.org , accessed on 4 November 2009.

15 Whether this reputation is justified is another matter. As Grabowska points out, survey data show that in elections of 2001 and 2005 only about 40% of Radio Maryja's listeners followed the station's endorsements (Grabowska, 2008).

16 For more information on social capital in Poland see, for example, research reports from the Social Diagnosis series of surveys: http://www.diagnoza.com/index-en.html.

REFERENCES

Bajomi-Lázár, P. (2003) 'Press Freedom in Hungary, 1998–2001', in M. Sukosd and P. Bajomi-Lazar (eds.), *Reinventing Media: Media Policy Reform in East-Central Europe*. Budapest: Central European University Press. pp. 85–114.

Bennett, W. L. and Iyengar, S. (2008) 'A New Era of Minimal Effects? The Changing Foundations of Political Communication', *Journal of Communication*, 58(4): 707–31.

Brehm, J. and Rahn, W. M. (1998) 'Individual-Level Evidence for the Causes and Consequences of Social Capital', *American Journal of Political Science*, 41(3): 999–1023.

Burdziej, S. (2008) 'Voice of the Disinherited? Religious Media after the 2005 Presidential and Parliamentary Elections in Poland', *East European Quarterly*, 42(2): 207–26.

Cappella, J. N. and Jamieson, K. H. (1997) *Spiral of Cynicism: The Press and The Public Good*. New York: Oxford University Press.

CBOS (1994) *Społeczeństwo i władza lat osiemdziesiątych w badaniach CBOS*. Warsaw: CBOS.

Culik, J. (2004) 'Czech Republic, Slovakia', in H. Newcomb (ed.), *Encyclopedia of Television*. New York: Fitzroy Dearborn. pp. 640–3.

Curry, J. L. (ed.) (1984) *The Black Book of Polish Censorship*. New York: Random House.

Dobek-Ostrowska, B. (1998) 'Przemiana Systemu Medialnego w Polsce po 1989r. Tło Procesów Transformacyjnych', in S. Dabrowski and B. Rogowska (eds.), *Z badań nad przemianami politycznymi w Polsce po 1989 roku*. Wrocław: Wydawnictwo Uniwersytetu Wrocławskiego. pp. 37–50.

Grabowska, M. (2008) 'Radio Maryja–Polska Prawica Religijna', *Znak*, 640: 11–16.

Henn, M. (1998) 'Opinion Polling in Central and Eastern Europe under Communism', *Journal of Contemporary History*, 33(2): 229–40.

Hoover Institution (2004) Cold War Broadcasting Impact: Report on a Conference Organized by the Hoover Institution and the Cold War International History Project of the Woodrow Wilson International Center for Scholars. Stanford University.

Jakubowicz, K. (1994) 'Internationalization of Television in Central and Eastern Europe', in K. Jakubowicz (ed.), *Central and Eastern Europe: Audiovisual Landscape and Copyright Legislation*. Antwerp: Maklu. pp. 65–74.

Jakubowicz, K. (2007) *Rude Awakening: Social and Media Change in Central and Eastern Europe*. Cresskill, NJ: Hampton Press.

Jasiewicz, K. (1991) 'Polski Wyborca–w Dziesięć lat po Sierpniu', *Krytyka*, 36: 23–47.

Jasiewicz, K. (2008) 'The New Populism in Poland: The Usual Suspects?', *Problems of Post-Communism*, 55(3): 7–25.

Kitschelt, H. (1995) 'Formation of Party Cleavages in Post-Communist Democracies: Theoretical Propositions', *Party Politics*, 1(4): 447–72.

Kopecky, P. (2006) 'Political Parties and the State in Post-communist Europe: The Nature of Symbiosis', *Journal of Communist Studies & Transition Politics*, 22(3): 251–73.

Levi, M. (1996) 'Social and Unsocial Capital: A Review Essay of Robert Putnam's Making Democracy Work', *Politics and Society*, 24(1): 45–56.

Malia, M. (1993) 'Leninist Endgame', in S. R. Graubard (ed.), *Exit From Communism*. New Brunswick, NJ: Transaction Press. pp. 57–76.

Manin, B. (1997) *The Principles of Representative Government, Themes in the Social Sciences*. Cambridge: Cambridge University Press.

Mink, G. (1981) 'Polls, Pollsters, Public Opinion and Political Power in Poland in the Late 1970s', *Telos*, 47: 125–32.

Mungiu-Pippidi, A. (2003) 'From State to Public Service: The Failed Reform of State Television in Central Eastern Europe', in M. Sukosd and P. Bajomi-Lazar (eds.), *Reinventing Media: Media Policy Reform in East-Central Europe*. Budapest: Central European University Press. pp. 31–62.

Newton, K. (2006) 'May the Weak Force be with You: The Power of the Mass Media in Modern Politics', *European Journal of Political Research*, 45(2): 209–34.

Noam, E. M. (1991) *Television in Europe*. New York: Oxford University Press.

Norris, P. (2000) *A Virtuous Circle: Political Communications in Postindustrial Societies, Communication, Society, and Politics*. Cambridge: Cambridge University Press.

OSCE Office for Democratic Institutions and Human Rights (2002) 'Republic of Hungary: Parliamentary Elections of 7 and 21 April, 2002', election observation report. Warsaw.

OSCE Office for Democratic Institutions and Human Rights (2008) 'Republic of Poland: Pre-term Parliamentary Elections, 21 October 2007', OSCE/ODHIR election assessment mission final report. Warsaw.

Piekalkiewicz, J. A. (1972) *Public Opinion Polling in Czechoslovakia, 1968–69: Results and Analysis of Surveys Conducted During the Dubcek Era*. New York: Praeger.

Popescu, M. and Toka, G. (2002) 'Campaign Effects and Media Monopoly: The 1994 and 1998 Parliamentary Elections in Hungary', in D. M. Farrell and R. Schmitt-Beck (eds.), *Do Political Campaigns Matter? Campaign Effects in Elections and Referendums*. London: Routledge. pp. 58–77.

Putnam, R. D. (1995) 'Tuning In, Tuning Out: The Strange Disappearance of Social Capital in America', *PS: Political Science and Politics*, 28(4): 664–83.

Schmitt-Beck, R. and Voltmer, K. (2007) 'The Mass Media in Third-Wave Democracies: Gravediggers or Seedsmen of Democratic Consolidation', in R. Gunther, J. R. Montero and H. J. Puhle (eds.), *Democracy, Intermediation, and Voting on Four Continents*. Oxford: Oxford University Press. pp. 75–134.

Schopflin, G. (2006) 'Hungary's Cold Civil War', http://www.opendemocracy.net/democracy-protest/hungary_civil_4093.jsp

Siedentop, L. (2003) 'We, the People, do not Understand', *Financial Times*, 4 June.

Skilling, H. G. (1989) *Samizdat and Independent Society in Central and Eastern Europe*. Columbus, OH: Ohio State University Press.

Sparks, C. (2000) 'Media Theory after the Fall of European Communism: Why the Old Models from the East and the West Won't Do Any More', in J. Curran and M.-J. Park (eds.), *De-Westernizing Media Studies*. New York: Routledge. pp. 35–49.

Szekfu, A. (1994) 'Hungarian Audiovisual Media: From Boom to Bust to Ö ?', in K. Jakubowicz (ed.), *Central and Eastern Europe: Audiovisual Landscape and Copyright Legislation*. Antwerp: Maklu. pp. 40–8.

Tőkés, R. L. (1997) 'Murmur and Whispers: Public Opinion and Legitimacy Crisis in Hungary 1972–1989', the Carl Beck papers in Russian and East European Studies (1206).

Tworzecki, H. (1996) *Parties and Politics in Post-1989 Poland*. Boulder, CO: Westview Press.

Tworzecki, H. (2008) 'A Disaffected New Democracy? Identities, Institutions and Civic Engagement in Post-Communist Poland', *Communist & Post-Communist Studies*, 41(1): 47–62.

Tworzecki, H. and Semetko, H. A. (2010) 'Media Uses and Effects in New Democracies: The Case of Poland's 2005 Parliamentary and Presidential Elections', *International Journal of Press/Politics*, 15(2): 155–74.

Walecki, M. (2003) 'Money and Politics in Central and Eastern Europe', in R. Austin and M. Tjernstrom (eds.), *Funding of Political Parties and Election Campaigns*. Stockholm: International IDEA. pp. 71–94.

36

Post-Soviet Political Communication

Sarah Oates

This chapter examines the historical effect of the Soviet communist system on the media in the post-Soviet region. While the discussion focuses on the Russian Federation as the largest successor state to the Soviet Union, it also reflects on the differential development of media systems from the monolithic Soviet era into a contemporary range of independent states. At the heart of this inquiry is the extent to which media systems are products of their past as opposed to how effectively they can embrace democratic systems after decades of control. This is an analytical approach that challenges the assumption that media naturally work as a force for democracy and openness in society. Rather, the post-Soviet experience presents compelling evidence that media often work more in the service of the state than as servants of the public. This suggests that regime types and state governance of media can provide more powerful explanations of the nature of media systems within countries than transnational, normative models of media. This chapter also will analyze the degree to which post-Soviet media resemble their Communist counterparts of the past – or whether media in this region of the world are less 'neo-Soviet' and better understood by highlighting the ways in which they may resemble or differ from Western systems.

At first glance, there is a vast difference between the relatively staid, controlled Soviet media and the vibrant post-Soviet media sphere. There is a broad range of television programs, newspapers, magazines, and radio broadcasts throughout most of the 15 successor states to the Soviet Union. The Internet is not systematically blocked in most of the region and is often available to anyone who can visit an Internet café, not to mention to the more affluent citizens who now have home and work Internet connections. However, on closer inspection it is clear that the most influential and popular mass media – in particular the largest television outlets – remain well-controlled by the twin powers of state oversight and self-censorship. Thus, while there are far more channels on television, a greater variety on the newsstands, and online connections in much of the region, media in many post-Soviet states do not regularly function as either watchdogs on political power or as challengers to the established authorities. While there are some notable exceptions to this, particularly in the Orange Revolution in Ukraine, they would appear to be isolated incidents. At the same time, there is scant evidence of the potential for cyber-democracy in the region.

Why would post-Soviet media mirror Western format but remain more authoritarian in their function in society? There are several key factors, but it is important first to address the general role of the Soviet legacy in modern post-Soviet society. The Soviet Union was a monolithic state, allegedly ruled on behalf of the working class by the Communist Party of the Soviet Union after the 1917 Russian revolution. In practice, the Soviet Union was an oligarchy, in which a handful of party elites set key economic, military, and social policies without reference to public opinion. Censorship and repression, including the internment of political dissidents in prison camps and mental hospitals, were hallmarks of the

Soviet regime. Although the subjugation of citizens reached a peak under the rule of dictator Josef Stalin, even in more tolerant periods the Soviet Union remained an authoritarian state in which dissidence was not tolerated. All media were owned by the state and viewed as central instruments in inculcating the masses with Communist ideology. No foreign media that criticized the Soviet state were allowed, and radio signals from pro-Western stations such as Voice of America and Radio Liberty were routinely jammed.

The Soviet state managed to both control the monolithic media well as create an attentive and dutiful media audience. In addition to the millions in daily circulation of central newspapers such as *Pravda* (*Truth*) and *Izvestiya* (*Faith*), Soviet television was popular and well-distributed. While only about 5% of the Soviet population could watch television in 1960, at least one channel was available to about 99% of the 280 million Soviet citizens spread across 11 time zones by the 1990s (while 60% of homes still lacked a phone and 13% lacked even running water).[1] The spread of state-controlled information – particularly via the influential and authoritative television Channels 1 and 2 – was viewed as a state priority and the audience responded with high levels of attention (Mickiewicz, 1988). Within the constraints of the Soviet system, entertainment and high professional standards of cinema still could flourish, as Soviet citizens enjoyed classic films, games shows, sports, and professional news productions that were careful to showcase the best aspects of the Soviet system.

Ironically, although this chapter will argue that post-Soviet media play little role in political engagement today, media in the late Soviet era were central to the collapse of the Communist state (McNair, 1991; Mickiewicz, 1999). When Soviet leader Mikhail Gorbachev introduced a policy of glasnost in the mid-1980s, he intended this policy of greater media transparency to lead to a more energetic, informed debate on the nature of Communist Party rule. However, once media outlets realized that they could criticize the state and publish a far broader range of information than ever before – including the results of public opinion surveys that showed little support for the Communist Party – Soviet media spearheaded a revolt against Party rule. Just a few years after the introduction of glasnost, the Communist Party was thrown out of power and banned, as Boris Yeltsin took over as the first Russian president in 1991. The failed coup by the Communist Party in a last bid for control of the nation was followed live on television by hundreds of millions both in the Soviet Union and around the world. Soviet television defied the Communist Party to show soldiers refusing to shoot fellow citizens and massive crowds flooding the streets of the country to call for a new government.

The role of media in the collapse of the Soviet Union might have predictably led to a greater respect for the power of journalism to effect popular change. Actually, post-Soviet leaders appeared to learn a different, albeit understandable, lesson from the experience. Mass media, particularly television, were shown to be immensely powerful political tools. In particular, it demonstrated to post-Soviet leaders that television needs to be harnessed and channeled in a way that avoids further popular revolt. Thus, while the form of post-Soviet media is different from that of Soviet media, arguably there are key parallels in way in which media work in service of the state.

Throughout much of the post-Soviet region there is a mix of state and commercial media ownership. There is a distinction between the former Communist sphere, which included military and political control of much of Eastern Europe, and the former Soviet Union itself. In Eastern Europe, Soviet rule was generally seen as an occupying force. As such, national political and media systems were quicker to reject continuities with the Soviet past, even though communist parties have continued to enjoy some success in parts of Eastern Europe (Lewis, 2001). While there were varying levels of resistance of the 'Sovietization' in the 14 post-Soviet republics outside of the Russian Federation, the vast range of cultures and historic experiences across the former Soviet Union make it difficult to generalize. However, the post-Soviet experience has made some trends clear. First, the Baltic states of Estonia, Latvia, and Lithuania, occupied by Soviet forces since World War II, maintained a stronger Western identity than much of the rest of the Soviet Union. Their media systems are deemed relatively free by international observers, including Freedom House (2008).

Two other distinctive regions of the former Soviet Union are Central Asia (Kazakhstan, Kyrgyzstan, Tajikistan, Turkmenistan, and Uzbekistan) and the Caucuses (Armenia, Azerbaijan, and Georgia). The Central Asian countries have been marked by a trend toward authoritarian leadership, although the extent has varied from a relatively populist leader in the more peaceful state of Kazakhstan to extremely repressive measures in Turkmenistan. This is reflected in Freedom House reports on media in the regime, which are discussed below. In the Caucasian states, Georgia is particularly noted for its lack of assimilation into the Soviet system. Georgia and Russia have a strained relationship over disputed territory, which culminated with a brief incursion by Russian troops into Georgia in 2008. This led to the first major 'cyber' war in the region, in which Russia apparently attacked and took over major websites in Georgia, according to media reports in the West.[2] Of the remaining successor states, Ukraine is the largest and shows evidence of a more robust civil society, as noted below. Belarus is an authoritarian regime, with a Soviet-style system while Moldova struggles with economic and political issues.

What has been the fate of media freedom in these diverse post-Soviet regions? Freedom House rates the level of democracy and freedom of the media worldwide in annual reports (for a full description of their methodology and reports, see www.freedomhouse.org). Overall, the organization found 37% of 195 countries worldwide rated to have free media, 30% to have partly free media and the remaining 33% not to have free media. In its 2008 report, Freedom House estimated that more than half of the citizens (56%) across the former communist region in Central Europe, Eastern Europe and the former Soviet Union live in countries without free media. In addition, the average freedom score for the media in the region dropped farther than in any other area worldwide. Freedom House found that countries in the former Soviet Union had significantly less media freedom than in the former Soviet satellite states: 'While the region shares a common history of communist oppression, the trajectory of countries in the former Soviet Union has diverged significantly from that of Central and Eastern Europe in terms of respect for fundamental political rights and civil liberties'. All of the Central European countries and the three Baltic countries were assessed as having free media. However, 10 of the remaining 12 former Soviet countries were assessed as not free, although there was even significant variation within this category (see Table 36.1). Even more worryingly, three of the countries judged as having the worst media liberty in world were found in the former Soviet Union – Belarus, Uzbekistan, and Turkmenistan.

Freedom House highlighted several problems in the post-Soviet countries. Although the media and political environment had shown signs of liberalization in Kyrgyzstan, 2007 saw an increase in attacks on journalists and the confiscation of print runs of some newspapers (Freedom House, 2008). Georgia's score for media oppression increased due to the forced closure of the television station that opposed the government, as well as the closure of all broadcast media during a state of emergency. Armenia showed evidence of rising government pressure on the media before elections. Both Azerbaijan and Kazakhstan closed media outlets for political reasons. Even Belarus, already an abysmal performer in terms of media freedom, managed to drop still further in the international media freedom rankings by harassing

Table 36.1 Freedom House 2008 scores of media freedom in the former Soviet Union

Country	Status	World ranking (out of 195)
Estonia	Free	16
Lithuania	Free	25
Latvia	Free	40
Ukraine	Partly free	110
Georgia	Partly free	128
Armenia	Not free	144 (tie)
Moldova	Not free	144 (tie)
Kyrgyzstan	Not free	156
Azerbaijan	Not free	168 (tie)
Tajikistan	Not free	168 (tie)
Russia	Not free	170 (tie)
Kazakhstan	Not free	170 (tie)
Belarus	Not free	188
Uzbekistan	Not free	189
Turkmenistan	Not free	193

Source: Freedom House (2008).

media outlets as well as by increasing restrictions on the Internet. While Russia is by no means the worst performer in media freedom in the region or worldwide, Freedom House notes that Russia is particularly important as it 'serves as a model and sponsor for a number of neighboring countries'. Russia has seen continuing declines in its Freedom House score, in particular when it dropped from 'partly free' to 'not free' in the 2003 ratings. In addition to the high level of personal security problems for journalists and state influence over media outlets, Russia's worsening score was linked to 'a significant deterioration in the legal and political environment for the media' including 'hundreds of journalists facing criminal or civil cases and at least two taken into temporary psychiatric detention after criticizing local authorities' (Freedom House, 2008). The question remains of why the promise of the 1991 Russian revolt against the Communist Party and the role of media in political change failed to develop into a permanent feature in most post-Soviet countries and, most notably, in Russia.

If the problems endemic to the former Soviet states are correlated, several possible factors in a 'neo-Soviet' model of the media emerge (Oates, 2007).

A Lack of a Law-based State

Although Russian governance is based on a liberal constitution adopted in 1993, in practice there is little transparency or equality in law in Russia. Laws are used routinely to consolidate the power of the elites rather than guarantee the rights of the masses in Russia. In this context, it is very difficult for media outlets or journalists to rely on legal protection if they anger politicians, bureaucrats or powerful business people (and these groups overlap to a large degree in Russia).

Selective Use of the Law to Suppress Media Freedom and Criticism of the Government

For example, when Russian commercial television NTV continued to criticize some Kremlin policies in 2001, including the progress of the war in Chechnya, financial laws were selectively used to force a change in ownership at the station. Since then, NTV has been markedly less critical of the Kremlin.

Violence Against Journalists

According to international groups such as Reporters Without Borders, Russia is one of the deadliest countries in the world for journalists. Although part of this is due to the ongoing civil war in Chechnya, it is even more worrying that Russian journalists are routinely being murdered for their professions far away from the war zone. The most high-profile case is the murder of journalist Anna Politkovskaya, who wrote in depth on the Chechen war and other issues for the liberal *Novaya Gazeta* newspaper in Moscow. No one has been convicted of the 2006 slaying. The Committee to Protect Journalists has estimated that 29 journalists were killed in a decade in post-Soviet Russia.

Self-censorship

Given the legal and personal threat facing journalists who challenge powerful people in Russia, it is unsurprising that many Russian journalists choose to self-censor to both keep their jobs and possibly even stay alive. Aside from a handful of small media outlets such as *Novaya Gazeta*, the news is relatively sanitized and a limited range of political viewpoints is tolerated. It is important to note that lack of objectivity and balance is widely accepted by Russian journalists, who tend to view their duty to report information in ways that support, rather than challenge, the political viewpoint or patron of their media outlet (Pasti, 2007; Voltmer, 2000).

Audience Acceptance of Bias

Studies of the Russian audience suggest that it understands and even supports the notion of bias (Oates, 2006; Oates et al., 2010). The Soviet-defined role of mass media as central to the stability of society is still an important part of the Russian public view of media. Openness or freedom of speech is often equated with the severe economic and social disruption of the late Soviet and early Russian period under President Boris Yeltsin. Many people in Russia feel that media should guide the populace rather than reflect the factions and disagreements found in the public sphere. As such, many Russians accept that media, particularly influential news programs on state-run television, will reflect the needs of the state rather than the wishes of the people.

It would be logical to assume that two new elements in Russia – commercial media and the Internet – would fundamentally challenge the notion of neo-Soviet media. In particular, Russians have significantly more choice in terms of television, as commercial stations have proliferated and state-run stations have expanded their offerings from Soviet times. In fact, the Russian television audience has a relatively wide and growing selection of broadcast offerings (Kachkaeva et al., 2006). This includes programming on the two main state-run channels, which attract the largest audience: Channel 1 (also known as The First Channel) that is 51% owned by the Russian state and *Rossiya (Russia)* on Channel 2 that is fully owned by the state. Both channels have a prime-time news show, entertainment and analytical programs, although they have become progressively narrower in political diversity over time (Oates, 2006). Commercial television, especially the national NTV network, also is relatively well watched. According to Fossato (2007), regional television in Russia remains popular even with the large national television challenges for audience, as local television has been more likely to cover domestic health and social issues. However, Fossato's research also found evidence that the Russian government is attempting to control large regional networks by concentrating new broadcast licenses in the hands of a few owners.

As in Western countries, access to a wealth of media offerings also comes at a price. Although Russia rapidly developed a relatively affluent middle class in many urban centers during the recent economic boom, much of Russia's population is poor by Western standards. This means that they cannot afford satellite television and, in many cases, do not have regular access to the Internet. Thus, much of the Russian audience is badly served for information needs in the post-Soviet state. While there are state television channels, they have no commitment to providing information in a disinterested way to inculcate the public with useful political knowledge and engagement. Rather, the state uses television (particular

Channels 1 and 2) to present information in a limited and biased fashion in order to generate support for the Kremlin elite (Oates, 2006). In particular, this involves replacing news with what is essentially state propaganda during Russian elections for parliament and president by failing to provide information on alternative parties, creating distorted news reports about the Kremlin's opponents as well as by providing excessive promotion to those already in power (European Institute for the Media, 1994, 1996a,b, 2000a,b; Oates, 2006; OSCE/ODHIR, 2004a,b). In 1996, this included collusion between state and commercial television broadcasters to hide the fact that Yeltsin had suffered a heart attack, as it was feared this would make him more vulnerable to challenge from the Communist Party contender for president (Mickiewicz, 1999).

If commercial media, especially television, have offered little to counter state control of information, it would be reasonable to assume that the Internet could provide some balance. After all, the Internet offers a very low-cost ability to disseminate information without censorship and even to aggregate political interests across vast physical distances (Chadwick, 2006). It would appear that these two attributes of the Internet would be particularly useful in Russia. Internet use has exploded in the country, rising from a relatively low base given the country's economic development (Cooper, 2008) to an internet penetration rate of 43% by 31 March 2011 (according to World Internet Stats, see http://www.internetworldstats. com/stats.htm). From 2000 to 2010, Russia experienced the largest online growth of any major European country over the course of the decade, according to the measurement by World Internet Stats. The organization estimated that Russia had 59.7 million Internet users out of a population of 138.7 million. In fact, Russians made up the second-largest online population in Europe by mid-2010, trailing only Germany, and were on track to become the largest online population in the region. The Russian government itself predicted almost total penetration (99%) of the internet for those under 40 by 2016 (Russian Federal Agency on the Press and Mass Communication, 2010.)

At the same time there has been a massive growth in internet use, there is little evidence that the internet is providing impetus for political diversity in Russia (Fossato et al., 2008). Indeed, there is more evidence that the internet is being effectively used by the state as another channel for its own information distribution and control (Fossato et al., 2008; Oates, 2008; Deibert and Rohozinski, 2010). Perhaps the most interesting aspect to post-Soviet communication is the nature of the relationship among the state, the Internet and the public in Russia. Unlike in China, which employs an elaborate regime of Internet monitoring and control, it would appear that Russia's approach to information control on line is more about co-optation than control (Fossato et al., 2008). In a study of three prominent Russian political blogs during the 2007 Russian parliamentary elections, Fossato et al. found that blogs on alternative political movements had little audience or attention in Russia. In the case of one blog on motorists' rights that did attract a reasonably large following, the researchers found that the blogger himself was co-opted by authorities to drop challenges to the state about the unfair arrest of motorists. This led the researchers to the conclusions that the Russian Internet reflects, rather than challenges, the controlled Russian political communication sphere. While Freedom House has found that the Russian Internet is still 'partly free' while they have labeled the Russian media itself 'not free', by mid-2011 the Russian public had not used the communication and organizational power of the Internet to organize any political resistance to the virtual political monopoly held by the Kremlin, the United Russia party, and Russian leader Vladimir Putin.

The study of elections throughout the former Soviet sphere has attracted a considerable amount of attention from governments, non-governmental organizations, policy analysts, and scholars (for example, see Colton, 2000; Hutcheson, 2003; Löwenhardt, 1998; Moser, 2001; Rose and Munro, 2002; Smyth, 2006; White et al., 1997; Wyman et al., 1998). There were high expectations that the successful mounting of elections and transfer of power would confirm the arrival of democracy to the region. In the end, however, elections only effected the arrival of democracy in part of the post-Soviet sphere. As noted above, democratic development has been uneven across the post-Soviet region. There have been many elections in post-Soviet states, but they usually have not resulted in transparent and fair democratic governance. Electoral rules about fairness and transparency have not always been followed. There have been well-founded accusations of vote return falsification, as well as convincing evidence of media bias and political bullying. It was difficult, if not impossible, for most post-Soviet political parties and candidates to formulate meaningful policies, much less communicate them effectively to the voters via biased media systems.

As the media performance at elections came under particular scrutiny in the former Soviet Union, it is useful to reflect on the different results of 'free' elections in the central case studies of Russia and Ukraine. Both countries have broadly similar elections rules, including free television spots for parties and candidates; the requirement of fair coverage and equal time for parties and candidates in the media; and the ability to buy advertising time on television. While language, culture and attachment to the former Soviet regime differ markedly between the two countries, both new states inherited the same Soviet structure and the same aging Soviet industrial base. In Russia, there has been a steady erosion of the ability of voters to have reasonable choice in elections. The first parliamentary elections of 1993 offered perhaps the greatest choice, with a surprising victory for an extremist nationalist party (the Liberal Democratic Party of the Russian Federation) and a relatively poor showing for a pro-Western, pro-Kremlin party called Russia's Choice. By 1995, the revived Communist Party took the largest percentage of the party-list vote, provoking a reaction by both state and commercial media to collude in unfair coverage of the Communists in the 1996 presidential elections. By the 2003 elections, the Kremlin managed to craft both a reasonable state party of power called Unity and a relentless media campaign that combined lack of coverage with a smear campaign against the communists. Voters have had increasingly little access to information about alternative political movements and leaders to the Kremlin elites via the traditional mass media. This has created a cyclical effect, in that as communist parties and other opposition parties lost votes, they were unable to maintain critical mass in the parliament. The Kremlin also amended the electoral law to limit the ability to challenge large, state-funded parties (which are technically illegal). As noted above, the Internet offers little ability for networking for social capital in Russia, and arguably it is difficult to create social movements completely on line in most societies.

If Russia is an example of the slow attrition of political freedom via poor media performance at elections, Ukraine is a far more volatile case of the potential for social unrest in new democracies. Electoral fraud and media manipulation were important factors in the Orange Revolution of 2004–05 that led to the rejection of rigged voting results in the presidential election. The November 2004 Ukrainian election was a contest between Viktor Yanukovych who was supported by the pro-Russian incumbent president and Viktor Yushchenko, more pro-Western and less friendly with the Kremlin. The two men mirrored an ongoing cleavage in Ukrainian politics, in which the eastern half of the country is dominated by the Russian language and culture and the western half by allegiance to Ukrainian nationalism. Thus, Ukrainian politics offered two central power bases, unlike in Russia in which there is little challenge to the Kremlin elite in Moscow. Ukrainian media, particularly during elections, had been marked by similar bias and distortion to that found

in the Russian media since the collapse of the Soviet Union (European Institute for the Media, August 2002). However, it should be noted that the Internet had played a significant political role in Ukraine, particularly in a scandal in which the Ukrainian president was implicated in the assassination of the founder of the first online newspaper in the country (Krasnoboka and Semetko, 2006). Yanukovych was declared the winner of the runoff, which sparked massive protests and street demonstrations. Yushchenko suffered considerable harassment during the campaign and was even poisoned by dioxin – which left him disfigured. In the wake of national and international protests, a new election was held and Yushchenko was declared the new president of Ukraine. Political observers, however, are quick to point out that there has been little fundamental difference in Ukrainian politics and media since the Orange Revolution, in which there remain problems with transparency and fairness. In particular, the arrest and imprisonment in 2011 of former Ukrainian Prime Minister Yulia Tymoshenko (on charges of abuse of office while brokering a gas deal with Russia) suggest that Soviet-style manipulation of the court system and the asymmetric application of the law are still prevalent in Ukrainian political life. However, Ukraine scores higher in international assessments of democracy and media performance than most other non-Baltic Soviet successor states. The different experience of Russia and Ukraine demonstrates that the post-Soviet environment does not necessarily dictate a neo-Soviet media environment.

If the study is widened from the performance of the media in specific countries to the former Soviet region in general, some clear trends emerge from an examination of reports from the European Institute for the Media in 18 elections in Russia, Ukraine, Belarus, Moldova, and Armenia from 1993 to 2001 (Oates, 2004). The following elements appeared in the study: media bias, particularly on state-run television channels: self-censorship; state influence on election coverage; bias in commercial media outlets; a lack of journalistic professionalism; inadequate laws to protect media; funding problems for the media outlets that often made them dependent on state handouts and goodwill and media harassment. The study also found varying levels of bribery; 'news' reports that were really paid advertising for candidates or parties as well as significant amounts of crime and violence against journalists. The study also highlighted a problem endemic in much post-Soviet election coverage, the appearance of compromising material against candidates (sometimes loosely based on fact but often simply fabricated rumors) that is known as *kompromat* (an abbreviation of the Russian for 'compromising material').

Ukraine exhibited the worst media bias in elections from 1993 to 2001, although bias was strong in all five countries (see Table 36.2). Belarus had the highest amount of state censorship, while Ukraine had the strongest evidence of undue government influence. Belarus also exhibited more problems with legal issues, a lack of media funding, harassment of journalists, violation of electoral rights, self-censorship, and crime against journalists. This is not surprising, in that as studies by Freedom House and others have shown, Belarus is one of the most authoritarian of the Soviet successor states. However, other problems were more pervasive in countries aside from Belarus, suggesting that challenges to post-Soviet media democracy can take many forms. For example, Russia showed a pervasive problem with bribery of journalists and smear campaigns with *kompromat*. Although Ukraine was arguably more democratic than Belarus during this time period, it scored just as high as Belarus in violation of rights. In addition, journalists had less to fear for their physical safety in Belarus than Ukraine, according to evidence offered in these reports.

What do the overall findings from this cross-national analysis of media performance at elections suggest? One of the most significant conclusions is a strong correlation between harassment of the mass media and four important flaws in a media system: (1) censorship; (2) violation of electoral rights; (3) crime against journalists and (4) violence against journalists. Yet, in addition to showing a consolidation of trends of harassment and violence, the analysis also suggests that an atmosphere of media harassment can possibly lead to this more extreme behavior, especially crime and violence against journalists. As media harassment is so often led by government officials via unreasonable registration restrictions or the sudden removal of favorable leases in government offices for recalcitrant state media, this finding suggests that a more tolerant and democratic attitude on the part of the government could in fact 'trickle down' and create a better atmosphere for journalists in general. If it is clear that if the government has a lack of respect for journalists and the difficulty with which they carry out their jobs, it makes the media easier prey for

Table 36.2 Variations in media performance in five post-Soviet states, 1993–2001

	Armenia	Belarus	Moldova	Russia	Ukraine	Average
Bias	3.00	3.75	3.75	3.20	4.00	3.54
Censorship	1.00	3.00	1.50	1.00	1.00	1.50
Commercial influence	0.00	0.00	2.00	2.20	2.50	1.34
Government influence	2.67	3.75	2.75	3.20	4.00	3.27
Lack of professionalism	1.67	3.00	2.25	2.60	2.50	2.40
Legal problems	1.00	3.50	2.25	1.80	1.50	2.01
Lack of funding	1.67	3.00	2.25	2.60	2.50	2.40
Harassment	1.33	2.75	1.25	1.00	2.00	1.67
Violation of rights	1.67	3.00	2.50	2.60	3.00	2.55
Bribes	0.00	0.00	0.25	2.20	1.50	0.79
Hidden ads	0.33	0.00	1.75	3.00	2.50	1.52
Kompromat	0.00	1.25	0.25	2.20	1.00	0.94
Self-censorship	1.00	3.00	1.50	1.00	1.00	1.50
Crime against journalists	1.67	2.00	0.50	0.00	1.00	1.03
Violence against journalists	1.00	1.25	0.50	0.20	2.50	1.09

Source: Analysis by author of the reports from the European Institute for the Media (now defunct, but the reports are archived at www.media-politics.com): Armenia 1999 parliamentary, Armenia 1998 presidential, Armenia 1995 parliamentary and referendum, Belarus 1996 referendum, Belarus 2001 presidential, Belarus 1994 presidential, Belarus 1995 parliamentary, Moldova 1998 parliamentary, Moldova 1996 presidential, Moldova 2001 parliamentary; Russia 2000 presidential, Russia parliamentary 1999, Russia 1996 presidential, Russia 1995 parliamentary, Russia 1993 parliamentary and referendum, Ukraine parliamentary 2002, Ukraine parliamentary 1998.

An analysis of 18 elections in Russia, Ukraine, Belarus, Moldova and Armenia from 1993 to 2001 highlights that the central problem lies in the lack of professionalism on the part of the journalists. In order to better provide a better longitudinal and cross-national analysis, each country was scored on a scale of 0–4 under 11 categories and sub-categories. Each election element was given a score of '1' for some evidence of the problem, '2' for between some and much evidence, '3' for much evidence and '4' for such strong evidence that suggested that no part of the mass media was free from this particular problem. If there was no evidence of the problem, a score of '0' was given. For full details of coding of the reports, see Oates 2004.

others that want to silence them. Nor is censorship operating in a relatively benign vacuum, above the uglier elements at work against journalists in post-Soviet society. The analysis showed that censorship is strongly linked with media harassment as well as with crime; it is less strongly correlated with the violation of electoral fights and self-censorship (Oates, 2004). In turn, self-censorship is correlated with bias, commercial influence on the media, the lack of journalistic professionalism, and the violation of electoral rights. What is worrying about self-censorship is that it both digs its roots far deeper into journalistic culture and, by its very nature, is far harder to identify, control, or stop. Once journalists have ceased to perceive themselves as willing or able to report freely, the quality of information will suffer. In turn, trust and reliance on the mass media should suffer as well.

Were there trends over time in this study of the media performance in five post-Soviet countries from 1993 to 2001? There is no pervasive evidence that, over all, media performance in elections in these five countries worsened over time. However, there were clear trends *within* countries over the time period. Media performance in Armenian elections appears to have become more free and fair from 1995 to 1999. Ukraine's score also improved slightly from 1998 to 2001. However, for Russia, Moldova, and Belarus there was a clear downward spiral, as media performance scores deteriorated with each election. A more detailed knowledge of the elections, that is not reflected well in this analysis, is that different problems in media performance disappear in some elections, but are often replaced by others. For example, overt governmental control tends to cut down on crime, but as governmental control dwindles, criminal elements may become more apparent. In addition, this type of analysis does not really explain the Orange Revolution in Ukraine, which is better understood against an historic understanding of the tension between pro-Russian and pro-Western cleavages within the country. The analysis is, however, useful in elucidating that challenges to media freedom can take many forms, both in the post-Soviet context in particular and in a range of political situations in general.

CONCLUSION

This chapter has presented ideas about comparative media models, the attempt to understand the relationship among the state, the media and the public in a general way that could be employed usefully in different countries. It is a difficult topic, because often there is not agreement on how this relationship works within a specific country – such as the argument in the USA over to what degree special interests and corporations dictate the direction of news coverage – which makes construction of a cross-national model particularly challenging. At the same time, it is important to consider the relationship between media and politics in an abstract way that frees one from specific details to theorize about how the relationship *should* work. Seminal work in this area includes Siebert et al. (1963), who identified four models of the media: the libertarian (commercial), socially responsible, Soviet communist, and authoritarian types of the press. Siebert et al. demonstrate that media in both democrat and non-democratic societies can take different forms. While these models in some senses described particular countries at the time – the USA as libertarian, the British broadcast media as socially responsible, the USSR as communist, etc. – it was also a useful study in the relationship between the state and the media sector. In a more contemporary study, Hallin and Mancini (2004) classified media systems in North America and Western Europe as liberal with a smaller role of the state and the prevalence of commercial media (for example, the UK, the USA, Canada); democratic corporatist with commercial media and media tied to organized social and political groups (as in northern Europe); and polarized pluralist, where media are integrated into party politics with a weaker commercial media and a strong presence of the state in the media sphere (such as in Italy). Although the scholars take different approaches, all are using evidence from the relationship among the state, the media and the public to generalize about this relationship. As Hallin and Mancini highlight, it is very difficult at times to separate aspects of media that are specific to a certain country from elements in media that can be measured and evaluated across a range of countries.

This raises the question of how to assess the effect of the Soviet experience on the post-Soviet media. It is clear from the experience in countries such as Poland, the Czech Republic, Latvia, Lithuania and Estonia that a Soviet legacy does not preclude the growth of a democratic mass media. At issue is whether the nature of the post-Soviet media in countries such as Russia is better understood as a reflection of the Soviet past or via another type of media 'model'. As is clear from Table 36.3, there are some compelling similarities between the Soviet and the Russian media systems. Bias, censorship, and governmental influence remain. At the same time, new problems have arisen in the post-Soviet sphere, including commercial pressures on the media, harassment of media outlets as well as widespread threats against journalists themselves. As is evident from the

Table 36.3 Comparing elements in the Soviet and Russian media

	Soviet media	Russian media
Bias	Virtually monolithic control of information flow	Strong bias in material that is supposed to be news
Censorship	Large censorship bureaucracy and enforcement, with strong norm of self-censorship	Broad-based voluntary censorship developed through punishment of reporters/media outlets that challenge Kremlin on key points
Governmental influences	The media were formally designated as part of the state apparatus	Formal for state-run media such as television Channels 1 and 2; informal yet powerful for commercial media through selective application of financial laws, etc.
Commercial influences	Not relevant	Accepted for commercial media that outlets should serve political interests of owners
Media in service of the public interest	Not applicable, public interest was not permitted	Has not developed.
Mass media law	Media were propaganda outlets	Exists, but does not provide adequate protection for journalists or media outlets against powerful political and/or financial interests
Protection for free speech	In theory but never in practice	In theory by limited by constraints listed above and below
Funding problems	Subsidized completely by state	Inadequate state subsidies so many outlets also need advertising or corporate sponsors
Media harassment	Not an issue as all media controlled by the state except for very small-circulation dissident media (including foreign radio)	Severe issues, including closures of media outlets by uneven application of array of laws
Violence against journalists	Not an issue. Although dissidents were imprisoned and even killed in labor camps, there was a distinction between Soviet journalists who worked for the state and Soviet dissidents	Violence (including murder) against journalists common
Audience	Subjects who embraced the Soviet world view	Subjects who embrace the Russian world view

table, one of the most intriguing factors is the apparent lack of significant change in attitudes by the post-Soviet media audience in Russia.

The study of audiences in comparative perspective is a relatively neglected field in comparative political communication. However, it is important to acknowledge that just as media systems have distinctive features within country borders – such as different forms of ownership, regulation, and distribution – media audiences are also culturally specific. There are virtually no reports on the public opinions of the Soviet media audience, although it is clear from the emphasis that the Soviet state put on the mass media that it was

recognized as a vital part of the political sphere. There have been a wealth of studies of attitudes toward information and democracy in the post-Soviet era. While social scientists were initially surprised by lingering affection for elements of the Soviet system, it has since been recognized that much of the Russian state identification is intertwined with Soviet pride as well. The reconciliation of two apparently incompatible issues – affection for the Soviet state and acceptance of democratic institutions – became apparent through a series of 34 focus groups conducted with Russian citizens in 2000 and 2004 (Oates, 2006; Oates et al., 2010). In these focus groups,

Russians often spoke of the need for a media that promoted order over chaos, even at the expense of withholding some information from the public. The frenzied events of the late Soviet era and early Russian period – in which many citizens lost their life savings, their jobs, and even their homes to rampant capitalistic speculation – are understandably viewed in a negative light by many Russians. This chaos was reflected in media coverage, much of it in the more sensationalist commercial outlets, and many of the focus-group members found this distressing rather than informative. Indeed, they found that media sometimes 'smacked their lips' over distressing images of terrorism or other upsetting issues. While accepting that media outlets tend to have a bias toward their political and financial patrons, the Russian focus-group participants rejected the idea that media could effectively work in the service of society. Rather, it is necessary for the audience to 'glean' news from a range of outlets, piecing together different sides of a story. While it is understandable both how the Russian audience would reject sensationalist news in a relatively fragile society as well as how they would fail to embrace the notion of objectivity, this means that Russians do not much challenge the bias, censorship, or harassment of media endemic to their system. By accepting these elements, the Russian audience faces growing limitations on the type of information that is available to them on state or commercial media.

NOTES

1   The figures on availability of telephones and running water are from the State Committee of the Russian Federation on Statistics, 1996, *Uroven' Zhizni Naseleniya Rossii,* Moscow, Goskomstat, p. 165.

2   For example, see Georgia: Russia 'conducting cyber war': Russia has been accused of attacking Georgian government websites in a cyber war to accompany their military bombardment, by Jon Swaine, in the (London) *Independent* newspaper, 11 August 2008, retrieved 12 September 2009, from http://www.telegraph.co.uk/news/worldnews/euro pe/georgia/2539157/Georgia-Russia-conducting-cyber-war.html

REFERENCES

Chadwick, A. (2006) *Internet Politics: States, Citizens, and New Communication Technologies.* Oxford: Oxford University Press.

Colton, T. (2000) *Transitional Citizens: Voters and What Influences Them in the New Russia.* Cambridge: Harvard University Press.

Cooper, J. (2008) 'The Internet in Russia – Development, Trends and Research Possibilities', presentation at the CEELBAS Post-Soviet Media Research Methodology Workshop. University of Birmingham, 28 March.

Deibert, R. and Rohozinski, R. (2010) 'Beyond Denial: Introducing Next-Generation Information Access Controls', in R. J. Deibert, M. Haraszti, J. G. Palfrey, R. Rohozinski and J. Zittrain (eds.), *Access Controlled: The Shaping of Power, Rights, and Rule in Cyberspace.* Cambridge, MA: MIT Press. http://mitpress.mit.edu/catalog/item/default. asp?ttype=2&tid=12187&mode=toc

European Institute for the Media (1994) 'The Russian Parliamentary Elections: Monitoring of the Election Coverage of the Russian Mass Media', Düsseldorf: European Institute for the Media, http://www.media-politics.com/ eimreports.htm

European Institute for the Media (1996a) 'Monitoring the Media Coverage of the 1995 Russian Parliamentary Elections', Düsseldorf, The European Institute for the Media, February, http://www.media-politics.com/eimre ports.htm

European Institute for the Media (1996b) 'Monitoring the Media Coverage of the 1996 Russian Presidential Elections', Düsseldorf, The European Institute for the Media, September, http://www.media-politics.com/eimreports.htm

European Institute for the Media (2000a) 'Monitoring the Media Coverage of the December 1999 Parliamentary Elections in Russia: Final Report', Düsseldorf, European Institute for the Media, March, http://www.media-politics. com/eimreports.htm

European Institute for the Media (2000b) 'Monitoring the Media Coverage of the March 2000 Presidential Elections in Russia (Final Report)', Düsseldorf, European Institute for the Media, August, http://www.media-politics.com/eimre ports.htm

European Institute for the Media (2002) 'Monitoring the Media Coverage of the March 2002 Parliamentary Elections in Ukraine (Final Report)', Düsseldorf, European Institute for the Media, August, http://www.media-politics.com/ eimreports.htm

Fossato, F. (2007) 'Television and National Identity in the Russian Regions (1999/2005)', MPhil dissertation. University College London School of Slavonic and East European Studies.

Fossato, F., Lloyd, J. and Verkhovsky, A. (2008) *The Web That Failed: How Opposition Politics and Independent Initiatives Are Failing on the Internet in Russia.* Oxford: Reuters Institute for the Study of Journalism, Oxford University. http://reutersinstitute.politics.ox.ac.uk/fileadmin/docu ments/Publications/The_Web_that_Failed.pdf

Freedom House (2008) *Freedom of the Press 2008.* Washington, DC: Freedom House. http://www.freedom-house.org/template.cfm?page=16

Hallin, D. C. and Mancini, P. (2004) *Comparing Media Systems: Three Models of Media and Politics.* New York: Cambridge University Press.

Hutcheson, D. (2003) *Political Parties in the Russian Regions.* London: Routledge.

Kachkaeva, A., Kiriya, I. and Libergal, G. (March 2006) 'Television in the Russian Federation: Organizational Structure, Programme Production and Audience', a report prepared by Internews Russia for the European Audiovisual Observatory. Moscow, Educated Media.

Krasnoboka, N. and Semetko, H. A. (2006) 'Murder, Journalism and the Web: How the Gongadze Case Launched the Internet News Era in Ukraine', in S. Oates, R. K. Gibson and D. Owen (eds.), *The Internet and Politics: Citizens, Activists and Voters.* London: Routledge. pp. 183–206.

Lewis, P. (2001) *Party Development and Democratic Change in Post-Communist Europe.* London: Routledge.

Löwenhardt, J. (1998) *Party Politics in Post-Communist Russia.* London: Frank Cass.

McNair, B. (1991) *Glasnost, Perestroika and the Soviet Media.* London: Routledge.

Mickiewicz, E. (1988) *Split Signals: Television and Politics in the Soviet Union.* New York: Oxford University Press.

Mickiewicz, E. (1999) *Changing Channels: Television and the Struggle for Power in Russia.* 2nd edn. Durham, NC: Duke University Press.

Moser, R. G. (2001) *Unexpected Outcomes: Electoral Systems, Political Parties, and Representation.* Pittsburgh, PA: University of Pittsburgh Press.

Oates, S. (2004) 'From the Archives of the European Institute for the Media: Analysing the Results of a Decade of Monitoring of Post-Soviet Elections', paper prepared for the British Association for Slavonic and East European Studies Conference. Fitzwilliam College, Cambridge, England.

Oates, S. (2006) *Television, Democracy and Elections in Russia.* London: Routledge.

Oates, S. (2007) 'The Neo-Soviet Model of the Media', *Europe-Asia Studies,* 59(8): 1279–97.

Oates, S. (2008) 'Comrades Online?:How the Russian Case Challenges the Democratizing Potential of the Internet', paper presented at Politics: Web 2.0: An International Conference, New Political Communication Unit, Department of Politics and International Relations, Royal Holloway. University of London, London.

Oates, S., Kaid, L. L. and Berry, M. (2010) *Television, Elections, and Terrorism.* New York: Palgrave Macmillan.

Organisation for Security and Co-operation in Europe/Office for Democratic Institutions and Human Rights (OSCE/ODIHR) (2004a) 'Russian Federation Presidential Election 14 March 2004 OSCE/ODIHR Election Observation Mission Report', Warsaw: Office for Democratic Institutions and Human Rights, 2 June, http://www.osce.org/odihr-elections/14520.html

Organisation for Security and Co-operation in Europe/Office for Democratic Institutions and Human Rights (OSCE/ODIHR) (2004b) 'Russian Federation Elections to the State Duma 7 December 2003 OSCE/ODIHR Election Observation Mission Report', Warsaw: Office for Democratic Institutions and Human Rights, 27 January, http://www.osce.org/item/8051.html

Pasti, S. (2007) *The Changing Profession of a Journalist in Russia.* Tampere: Tampere University Press.

Rose, R. and Munro, N. (2002) *Elections Without Order: Russia's Challenge to Vladimir Putin.* New York: Cambridge University Press.

Siebert, F. S., Peterson, T. and Schramm, W. (1963) *Four Theories of the Press: The Authoritarian, Libertarian, Social Responsibility and Soviet Communist Concepts of What the Press Should Be and Do.* Chicago, IL: University of Illinois Press.

Smyth, R. (2006) *Candidate Strategies and Electoral Competition in the Russian Federation: Democracy without Foundation.* New York: Cambridge University Press.

Voltmer, K. (2000) 'Constructing Political Reality in Russia: Izvestiya – Between Old and New Journalistic Practices', *European Journal of Communication,* 15(4): 469–500.

White, S., Rose, R. and McAllister, I. (1997) *How Russia Votes.* Chatham, NJ: Chatham House Publishers.

Wyman, M., White, S. and Oates, S. (eds.) (1998) *Elections and Voters in Post-Communist Russia.* London: Edward Elgar.

37

Al-Jazeera Arabic, Transnational Identity and Influence

Sam Cherribi

REIMAGINING THE SUCCESS OF AL-JAZEERA

In the Qatari capitol of Doha, in a stately, quiet residential area, the headquarters of Al-Jazeera stand out in a markedly Western way. The building could easily blend into an upscale business park in the USA. Its lines are clean and boxy; it is white, and it is surrounded, as is everything in Qatar, by palm trees. Its lobby might well 1be any lobby in any corporate headquarters in the world except for one overwhelming element: a huge poster that reads in stark letters without any artistic feature: 'The world watches CNN, and CNN watches Al-Jazeera'. The irony of this is amplified by the fact that the building is probably less than one-quarter of the size of CNN's Atlanta head-quarters. Some years ago, its small boxy shape caught the eye of visiting former Egyptian president Hosni Mubarak, who reportedly commented, 'All these problems are from this Match box' (Zaidi, 2003: 6).

His sentiment has been echoed numerous times in the Arab halls of government. They think of Al-Jazeera as a matchbox in a gunpowder depot. The depot is the Arab world with its problems of illiteracy, unemployment and religious extremism compounded by the new problem of transitioning to emancipation and democracy. Like CNN, Al-Jazeera thrives in times of crisis, but its style of reporting on crises has made it far more controversial internationally than CNN.

Al-Jazeera is loved by the Arab street but hated by entrenched governing authorities from Rabat to Gaza,[1] authorities who have at times banned the network or closed down some its offices. In 2002, the Gulf Cooperation Council advocated a boycott of Al-Jazeera at their meeting in Muscat.[2] In 2004, Iraq closed the offices of Al-Jazeera in Baghdad which prompted Al-Jazeera to claim 'The closure by the interim Iraqi government is due to pressure from the USA'.[3] Some western governments, such as America's Bush administration, as well as the governments of France, the UK and Israel, also have been irritated by Al-Jazeera's way of reporting, an understandable irritation give that Al-Jazeera made its early fame by broadcasting videotapes of Osama Bin Laden along with extensive and exclusive reporting on Al Qaeda. Israel accused Al-Jazeera of inciting Palestinians resistance in addition to offering an unbalanced picture of the recent war in the Gaza Strip.[4] In an attempt to contain Israeli anger, Al-Jazeera conceded that one of their programs seriously violated ethical norms in a statement released in 2008.[5]

In a way, the creation of Al-Jazeera in 1996 by the Emir of Qatar, Sheikh Hamad bin Khalifa, was the most transformative development in the Arab world since the ascendance of Gamal Abdel Nasser (1918–70). It was Nasser who inspired Arab Nationalism from the Arabic Gulf to Morocco on the Atlantic Ocean. It was Al-Jazeera that revolutionized and modernized the passive and domesticated landscape by rattling governments and redefining the standard for Arab media (El-Nawawy and Iskandar, 2003; El Qadiri Issa, 2007; Miles, 2005). A recent poll by the Knowledge World Center for Polls' office in Jordan asked Arab political science and media professors in 19 countries their opinions of Al-Jazeera's professionalism. The polls shows the professors overwhelmingly prefer viewing Al-Jazeera to most other news sources. They also rate the network's professionalism very highly.

Significantly, the poll results show that 47% of respondents believe Al-Jazeera gave programs on Nasser's era more attention than it gave to programs on religious trends and political Islam.[6] However, it is worth noting that most Arab academics do not watch the more religiously themed programs, so their perception may not be accurate. Nonetheless, the idea that Al-Jazeera should give more attention to Nasser's era is generally met with approval among Arab academics.

In his book *La Pensée Arabe*, Algerian-French intellectual and philosopher Mohammed Arkoun explains the crucial period of 'the Arab socialist revolution' in the 1950s and 1960s. The crucial period of 'the Arab socialist revolution' started with Nasser, Ba'ath parties in Syria and Iraq. In the freshly independent Algeria, President Boumedienne, like the other leaders of the Arab nationalist movement, gained power with a coup d'état. Boumedienne is responsible for creating a powerful ideological machine: the State-Nation-Party; this party raised many hopes in the Arab world (Arkoun, 1981). Decades of political improvisation and ideological control by the State-Nation-Party included demographic expansion, uprooting of rural population and deterioration of the cities. A century before the emergence of Socialist Arab Nationalism, Arkoun argued that Rifa'a al-Tahtawi wrote the first reformist manual showing the dynamism of the Arabic Renaissance in *Takhlis al-Ibriz fi Talkhis Bariza* where he discussed signs of the weakness, retreat and regression of the Arabic language in the governing elites. The book reveals, in the words of Arkoun, the ills, defects, delays and needs of Egyptian society, which gives birth to Pan-Arabic nationalism. Arkoun, similarly to Morocco's Al Jabiri, Syria's Tizini, Egypt's Hanafi and Lebanon's Makdis agreed that the psychological process is repeated regularly in all Arabs and Muslims who discover the Western environment for the first time. Arkoun talks about his own experience where he finds Arab intellectuals in quest of space, freedom and liberty. He discusses, however, that space of liberty one can only find outside of Arab regimes comes with a stigma attached. That stigma of Westernization leads to marginalization and rejection in the Arab world (Arkoun, 1981).

The Arab intellectuals of the Nahda (Arab Renaissance), according to Arkoun, as well as those of the 21st century are trying to diagnose Arab malaise and economic underdevelopment and find a remedy to cure the feeling of inferiority and inequality via-a-vis the West. The generalized feeling of inequality and inadequacy was amplified by European colonization, which arrived after the decomposition of the oppressive Ottoman empire. The feeling of inadequacy, in the words of Arkoun, became greater and more complicated after the birth of the state of Israel.

The 1979 Ayatollah Khomeini-led Islamic revolution in Iran inspired and awoke the latent Islam of Arab countries, an awakening nudged along by the official Islamization of Arab states in the late 1960s after the decline of Arab Nationalism and the repression of Islamic groups such as The Muslim Brotherhood in the 1950s. Under Nasser's secular Arab Nationalism, most Muslim religious leaders who had become politically active had been killed, persecuted or, like Al-Jazeera's preacher Al Qaradawi, fled their home countries – in Al Qaradawi's case, Egypt, where the Socialist-Arab-Nationalism did not tolerate a militant version of Islam.

The failure of secular Pan-Arab-Nationalism and the resulting disillusion, opened the doors to Pan-Islamism, which uses Arabic as a means of expression and Islam as the only legal social structure. Understanding this series of developments that led to Al-Jazeera 's ideological choices and the feeling of Arab inferiority that defined the past two centuries of Middle Eastern history, is important in order to comprehend the primary focus of Arab intellectuals: the quest to determine from whence this inferiority complex sprang.

Al-Jazeera became the instrument of choice in dissecting and exploiting that inferiority complex and its possible sources. As Arab governments witnessed the political usefulness of such an instrument, a fierce competition between them emerged. They rushed their own state owned television channels into satellite broadcasting or developed their own satellite channels. Hundreds of new Arab satellite stations were launched and are still being birthed with money from the Gulf countries. Lebanese media researcher El Qadiri Issa compares this overwhelming media rush to the discovery of new oil wells. This rush for Arab audiences is worldwide: the USA created Al Hurra and radio Sawa; the French fostered France 24; the Russians developed Russia Al Yawm and the Chinese and many others are interested in launching Arabic speaking channels (Lewis, 2002; Lynch 2006; Mellor 2007; Rugh 1987).

Meanwhile, Al-Jazeera has built a huge media empire: Al-Jazeera Arabic (1996), Al-Jazeera Documentary, Al-Jazeera Kids, Al-Jazeera Sport and Al-Jazeera International (in English) all launched on the 10th anniversary of

Table 37.1 The table shows the number of Arab countries that ratified the Arab charter limiting press freedom and their ranking in Freedomhouse.org. (Israel, USA and Iran have been included for comparison purposes)

Rank 2008	Country	Ranking	Status	Arab media code (*)	Limited reporting (**)
2	Kuwait	54	Partly free	Yes	Yes
3	Lebanon	55	Partly free	Yes	
4	Egypt	59	Partly free	Yes	Yes
5	Algeria	62	Not free	Yes	Yes
6	Jordan	63	Not free	Yes	Yes
7	Morocco	64	Not free	Yes	Yes
9	United Arab Emirates	68	Not free	Yes	
10	Iraq	69	Not free	Yes	Yes
11	Bahrain	71	Not free	Yes	
13	Yemen	78	Not free	Yes	Yes
14	Saudi Arabia	81	Not free	Yes	Yes
16	Syria	83	Not free	Yes	
17	A.A & W.B (***)	84	Not free	Yes	Yes
19	Libya	94	Not free	Yes	
20	Comoros	54	Partly free	Yes	
22	Mauritania	56	Partly free	Yes	
35	Djibouti	72	Not free	Yes	
41	Sudan	78	Not free	Yes	Yes
	Qatar	64	Not free	No	
	Oman	71	Not free	Yes	
	Tunisia	81	Not free	Yes	Yes
	Somalia	84	Not free	Yes	Yes
1	Israel	28	Free		
	United States	17	Free		
18	Iran	85	Not free		Yes

*22 Arab countries, except Qatar, adopted the Arab media Code or Charter to curb media freedom (2008); **Countries that shut down for a short a longer period the offices of Al-Jazeera, or limited the freedom of its reporters; ***Palestinian Authorities and West Bank

Source: 2008 Data from http://www.freedomhouse.org/

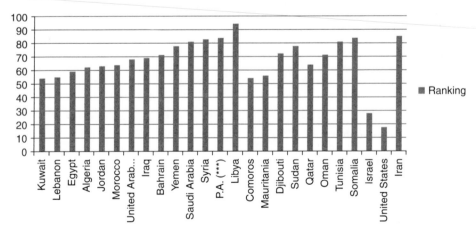

Figure 37.1
Note: Media freedom ranking in Arab countries. The height of the bar corresponds to greater restrictions and lack of freedoms.
Source: Lamloum, 2004, 7.

Al-Jazeera Arabic. In addition to all these television expressions of Al-Jazeera, the Al-Jazeera Center of Study established in Qatar with the mission of reflecting critically on the work of Al-Jazeera has been in operation since 2008. Table and Figure 37.1 provide a snapshot of the constraints on freedom of the press in the region based on information gathered by Freedom House.

Al-Jazeera has expanded beyond satellite broadcast into the fertile field of online news. Al-Jazeera.net was designed to be the first major Internet news site in Arabic. Its daily viewership has exceeded a million since its inception in 2004. According to Al-Jazeera, it 'soon reached the summit of Arab sites and entered the competition at the top of the world famous sites'.[7] The Arabic version of Al-Jazeera is aiming to build an integrated network of all Al-Jazeera sites on the Internet and provides web surfers four sources of knowledge: (1) comprehensive news coverage around the clock; (2) in-depth knowledge-based analysis and scientific research and studies; (3) a database of up-to-date, full records of Al-Jazeera programs and products; (4) a tool for marketing Al-Jazeera's services and products. Al-Jazeera tries in particular to reach decision makers, diplomats and intellectuals, media and researchers, students and young people.[8]

Neither CNN nor the BBC have the comprehensiveness of Al-Jazeera.net, with its audio, video and full text transcripts of every news report including correspondents work being searchable by text, section, the state, subject and date within 36 hours of the broadcast.

More than 129,000 individuals log into the Forum site and more than 70,000 participate directly in the programs of the channel live.[9] More than half a million members are registered on the site. The Al-Jazeera presence on social networking sites on the Internet and YouTube is ubiquitous.

In 2007, Arabic-language Al-Jazeera celebrated its 10th anniversary by festively advertising its plethora of daily shows, which reach more than 50 million viewers around the world. This chapter addresses two general questions: (1) How does Al-Jazeera evaluate its place and contribution to more objective journalism in the Arab world during the decade since its launch? (2) Is Al-Jazeera self-critical in looking back on that decade of reporting? In addressing these questions, I explore the ways in which Al-Jazeera portrays itself after more than 10 years of seniority in the global media landscape.

AL-JAZEERA AS ALTERNATIVE PRESS

Research shows that Al-Jazeera often displays its expertise, diversity and independence as the only Arab channel that can compete with, and even beat, Western news media in the game of influence and dedicated viewership (Cherribi, 2006). Al-Jazeera considers itself an alternative to the 'commercially biased and "hegemonic" Western media' on key issues and causes for the Arab 'Umma', which traditionally refers to the Islamic community as a whole.[10] Al-Jazeera focuses on what it calls the 'Arab nation', a transnational Islamic and Arab community. Al-Jazeera's special anniversary programming ran for several months beginning in 2006 and continuing into 2007.

During that time period, Al-Jazeera's four flagship current affairs programs – *The Opposite Direction, Sharia and Life, From Washington* and *For Women Only* – each contained segments devoted to the 10th anniversary. These popular weekly hour-long programs are rebroadcast several times over several days. Using the Arabic-language website to compare the transcribed versions of the programs online with the televised audio content for veracity, and then producing a qualitative interpretive analysis of how Al-Jazeera presents itself, frames history and contributes to television journalism in the Arab world over its 10 years of existence, it becomes clear that Al-Jazeera believes its ethical standards are higher than those of Western media – its program hosts say so.

Earlier research (Cherribi, 2006) regarding Al-Jazeera's reporting on the veil, especially on the popular weekly program on religious matters hosted by Al-Qaradawi called *Sharia and Life*, and, in particular, his views on the French debate over the veil, reveals his constant religious message. The same Muslim underpinnings are evident in the network's other programming, as well as in the many exclusive stories about the veil in Al-Jazeera's daily news programming. An overview shows more similarities than differences across these current affairs programs during the channel's first decade of reporting. Additionally, the reporting and discussion related to the anniversary lacked a critical perspective. Al-Jazeera is essentially a religious channel, the kind that would attract only the elderly or the uneducated in the West, yet it is seen as a viable, credible news source in the Arab world. Why is that?

In their book, *The Culture of Al-Jazeera: Inside An Arab Media Giant,* Mohamed Zayani and Sofiane Sahraoui say 'Al-Jazeera's success can hardly be reduced to a stroke of luck. In fact, if one can venture a set of key factors which contributed to the success of Al-Jazeera, chief among these are wealth of talent, the structure of freedom available to the network' (2007: 35). These factors, talent, discipline, an enabling organizational structure and a margin of freedom are the basic ingredients in the success of any serious news organization. Three factors of eminent importance while examining the history of Al-Jazeera are as follows: first, the Islamic niche market; second, the anti-Arab establishment's or anti-Arab government's message and the corresponding anti-Western, anti-Israel message; third, the pan-Arabic ideology. Let us begin with the first.

The Islamic Niche

A meticulous look at the programs of Al-Jazeera show how it uses Islam as a marketing vehicle for itself much as insurance companies and car manufactures in the USA rely on rock songs of the 1970s to help them reach the enormous financial assets of America's largest demographic, the baby boomer generation. So, too, does Al-Jazeera rely upon religious touchstones, including the Quran, to reach one of the largest and fastest growing demographics in the world. The cement of the fragmented Arab audience is Islam. Within that audience is a wealth of disparate cultures. For example, an Arab growing up in Yemen is influenced more by Egypt than by France whereas an Algerian is influence more by France than by Egypt. Or, consider the contrasting cultures of Tunisia and Saudi Arabia. In Tunisia, the veil is seldom seen – there are open bars that serve alcohol, and women can drive cars and are socially mobile. In Saudi Arabia, women are veiled – one can barely see their faces and they are, at least in the lower classes, socially restricted. Culturally, Arab countries are different from one another. Camel races are popular in the Gulf but not in the Maghreb, where different kinds of leisure prevail. However, these Arab countries have something very significant in common: men still hear the call to prayer. Ramadan, in all Arab countries separated even by culture and distance, is a common denominator.

Now, Arabs also have Al-Jazeera in common, even outside the traditional geographical boundaries of the Arab world. One will find it wherever there are Muslims, however minor their presence might be. In India, Malaysia, Europe and the USA, one will find televisions tuned to *Sharia and Life*, which is rerun on Al-Jazeera just as CNN's *HeadLine News* reruns top news stories, that is to say, over and over again. This particular program is of critical importance in understanding how Al-Jazeera has managed to tap into its worldwide market and its role in uniting the Arab world across linguistic and cultural borders. Moreover, it is this program that provides us with the sharpest lens through which to view the Islamization of the Arab world.

Far from being the CNN of the Arab world – a comparison that is often made among critics of media – Al-Jazeera is more like the Christian Broadcast Network, a network that promotes a particular set of beliefs in order to focus its marketing efforts and grow its target audience. Although it casts itself as a way of seeing the world 'through Arab eyes', its most consistent feature is the dominant voice of Islamic clerics. Even shows that purport to represent secular and Westernized Arabs, talk shows that invite entertainers and scholars of an un-Muslim cast, always include, as if it is haute de rigueur, an Islamic personality who almost always gets to pronounce the judgment of Islam upon the content in what amounts to a summarizing statement. In effect, Al Jazeera might say, 'Here is rock music, even practiced by an Arab, and here is what the Quran has to say about that'. By featuring the Islamic opinion in such a prominent fashion, it is clear that the Arab eyes through which Al-Jazeera views the world are the eyes of Muslim clerics.

The bigger question (and one that is not limited to Al-Jazeera) is, 'What explains the rush to attract famous clerics to serve the growing audiences of Arab satellite channels?' Radio and television start and end the day with a recitation from the Quran, and there are programs where a mufti, an imam or preacher, explains religious matters. Even on the street, wherever you go in the Arab world – at the souk and in many cyber cafes – you hear Quran recitations. Recitations of the famous Egyptian sheikhs like Al Hussari and Abdel Bassit abd Assamad are dominant on Arab television and radio, and the words of Egyptian religious scholars like Al Sharaoui and other celebrities of Al Azhar University in Cairo are prevalent as well. The market for religious goods on television, radio and on cassettes, the sermons of mobile preachers and marabous, was very important in creating a predisposition for a religious habitus in Arab publics beyond the mosque. An excellent example of the continuous competition among Arab states to escape the dominance of one country's television evangelists is the success of the new M6 radio – the 24-hour Quran radio channel broadcast from Morocco and created by King Mohammed VI. Every Islamic country wants to create its own iconic television preachers who guide the Arab publics into their own version of Islam. From the 1960s through 1990, exiled Syrian radio and television preacher Sheikh Ali Tantawi, broadcasting from Saudi Arabia, was very popular in the Gulf region and was the voice of the Saudis par excellence. He set the boundaries between the hallal and the harem – the licit and the illicit in Islam (Lamloum, 2004: 63).

When Al-Jazeera was launched, it was necessary to find an alternative to the dominance of the Saudis and the Egyptians by finding a credible, populist and erudite voice. This competition was not only regional but reached pan-Islamic dimensions. Al Qaradawi graduated from Al Azhar in Cairo and joined with Hassan Al Bana, the founder of the Muslim Brotherhood in Egypt. Then, after the coup d'état led by Gamal Abd Nasser and his Free Officers movement in Egypt in 1952, Al Qaradawi fled to Qatar and became a Qatari citizen. More than 40 years later, Al-Jazeera found Al Qaradawi and used him as an antidote to Saudi and Egyptian influences.

Today, a decisive element in the construction of the dominant narrative on Al-Jazeera is the channel's religious voice as represented by Al Qaradawi (Cherribi, 2006). Together, the reruns of his weekly television program and the content on his website form a rich source for evidence of how Al-Jazeera is focused on Islamizing pan-Arabism. His program *Sharia and Life* addresses a broad range of issues from politics, society and international affairs. On the 10th anniversary of *Sharia and Life*, Al Qaradawi summed up the purpose of the program as followed 'In the name of God the Merciful ... First I would like to give special congratulations to Qatar and the viewers generally. This satellite channel [Al-Jazeera], which originates in beloved Qatar, expresses our hopes and our values and our orthodoxy, and by it we seek something that is good, we appeal to Allah for it, and seek a beacon of guidance and a tool for building something new ...'. While a 10-year younger Al Qaradawi's picture appeared on the screen a thankful and serene Al Qaradawi said:

In the name of God the Merciful God, prayer and peace on the Prophet of Allah. This picture [his picture as shown on Al-Jazeera during its first year] sends me back 10 years ago and as the days have passed as quickly as a play of light on a spectrum or a summer cloud, as they say, I have cherished these memories in the first phase of this feast of programming. May God bless the Almighty that makes the good and the guidance and light for our nation. Throughout all of this, even in the first program, it does not say it's a religious program, but an Islamic program via a news satellite channel ... This was something new and has been copied by other satellite channels. God is caring for this channel [Al-Jazeera] and this particular program, which was the first to reflect the Sharia.[11]

His condoning of suicide bombings in Israel caused him problems when he visited London in 2005; however, he did condemn the terrorist attacks of 9/11. Regarding Iraq, two incidents are worth mentioning: a call to kill the US civilians and a call to support the Iraqi constitution (because its basis is Islamic). First, at least 431 blogs as of 3 June 2006 talked about a fatwa or religious opinion issued by Al Qaradawi that triggered worldwide controversy: the killing of American contractors in Iraq as an Islamic duty. The contro-

versial statement – which could be construed as a fatwa – were, according to Islam Online (9 September 2004), later denied by Al Qaradawi, who confirmed what is oft repeated on Al-Jazeera: that Islam forbids the killing of civilians. Second, Al Qaradawi's views on the Iraqi constitution illustrate the pro-Islamic stance: 'The first constitution was made in Medina by the prophet, prayers be upon him, in order to regulate relations in the civil society. What was the civil society? A society of Muslims, Jews ...' (Islam Online, 9 September 2004).

Al Qaradawi states that the Quran is 'above the constitution', because the constitution can change and 'many things change in our life, but the Quran doesn't change'. Al Qaradawi says the Umma is ready to fight for the Quran but not for the constitution. This explains why the Islamic resistance to occupation is successful. The constitution must mean, according to Al Qaradawi, 'under the *Shades of Islam* (a book by Said Qutb of the Muslim Brotherhood) ... (*if*) Islamic principles are put in the constitution, this spirit that governs us is the reference, in this case the constitution has its sacredness and it becomes an Islamic constitution ... Islam doesn't forbid us to copy other peoples' laws ...'.

In answering the question of boycotting participation in the referendum on the Iraq constitution on his call-in program *Sharia and Life*, Al Qaradawi said:

No. Iraq is a different situation. The Sunnis ask for the boycott because Iraq is still under occupation. The occupiers still decide and have a specific position. In a normal situation, we ask Muslims to participate in elections. Sometimes people think the elections are a comedy and have no impact. What the government decides happens. In our countries we still have three nines: 99.9. Some people are tired of that.' (Meaning that the outcome of elections in Arab countries are a joke where the incumbents get 99.9% of the vote. In fact there is a joke in the Arab world that goes like this: an aid of Syria's president Assad said to the president 'Congratulations, you won the election with 99.9% of the vote,' to which the president answered angrily 'Get me the name of the one who didn't vote for me.')

Al Qaradawi also acknowledged:

Iraq is a special case. That makes people disagree about the articles of the constitution. I believe that, prayers to God, as I saw the draft of the constitution sent to me by brother Dr. Ali Al Qura Daghi, the draft is, in general, good except for some simple things. They said Islam is the official religion of the state and the source of legislation and this is very good language ... it is not allowed to make a law that is against the constants of the law of Islam. It's not allowed to make a law against the principles of democracy. It's not allowed to create a law in contradiction with the basic rights and freedoms that are in the constitution … It means that the constitution guarantees the protection of the Islamic identity of the majority of the Iraqi people as it guarantees the complete rights for all individuals as the freedom of religious practice for Christians.

It is interesting to note that the participation of the Sunnis in the referendum was actually stimulated by Al-Jazeera's predictions that Sunnis would be marginalized. A number of programs on Al-Jazeera were dedicated to the future religious makeup of Iraq. The fear of a possible dominance of Shii groups over the Sunnis was clear, even though Shiis were invited to the programs to state their views. The voice of Al Qaradawi gives legitimacy and credibility not only to Al-Jazeera but also to Qatar as the most powerful media state in the Arab world.

THE AL-JAZEERAN VIEW OF DEMOCRACY

A senior editor of Al-Jazeera, M'hamed Krichen, explained in the newspaper *Al Qods Al Arabi*, that 'Al-Jazeera is the political party, the most popular in the Arab world'.[12] This shows that Al-Jazeera is also a political project – one that uses the Al Qaradawi approach to framing a number of issues of democracy in the Arab world. Take for example the Algerian civil war. It has been analyzed on many programs in the manner exemplified by Al Qaradawi, who frames the violence in Algeria as a reaction to the injustice done to the Islamic Front of Salvation (FIS) and as a consequence of trying to marginalize the FIS in the democratic process. Many programs such as *More than One Opinion* and *Without Borders*, in the sense that they present violence as a response to being shut out of the political process, have done the same (Lamloum, 2004).[13]

Just as it did in the Algerian case, Al-Jazeera has also consistently taken the side of Hezbollah's leader Hassan Nasrallah in the ongoing disputes with Israel. It has even taken its advocacy a step further, promoting Nasrallah as the torch-bearer for pan-Arabism, a sort of heir to the legacy of Nasser with a democratic flair. As such, they tout him as the key to democracy in the Middle East. Hassan Nasrallah is portrayed as a hero not only in the 2006 war with Israel but since May 2000 when Hezbollah declared the end of the Israeli presence in southern Lebanon. Unlike the Western media which presents Hezbollah as

the foreign legion of Iran, Al-Jazeera accords Hezbollah a sovereign status, one that shows the group as made up of native Lebanese liberators. In so doing, Al-Jazeera grants Nasrallah a more powerful and more independent status than he is granted in the West. He was interviewed in 1999, 2000, 2004, 2005 and 2006. He was filmed as a genuine leader who let his son fight and die in the struggle against Israel and who buried him with his own hands. Olfa Lamloum explains that Nasrallah is seen as a leader whose example must be followed by other movements in the Arab world to counter Israel and the USA (Lamloum, 2004).

Another element that amplifies the dominant narrative in Al-Jazeera's reporting on Iraq is the constant link between Islamic resistance to the Americans in Iraq and the Palestinian resistance to the state of Israel. The extensive reporting on the Sunni resistance in Fallujah also became a model of religious courage and challenge to the US power. The killing of the nearly blind 'frail quadriplegic' Sheikh Ahmad Yassin, the spiritual leader and founder of Hamas, in a missile strike on 22 March 2004 in Gaza was the kind of event that created a tremendous amount of momentum for Arab solidarity to the extent that people were glued to Al-Jazeera's reporting on the death of this important man.

Sheikh Ahmad, who studied at the world-renowned Al-Azhar University in Cairo, spent some time in Israeli jails and had already become an Islamic icon. He was uncompromising on peace with Israel. His organization, Hamas, which means 'zeal' in Arabic, won the Palestinian election in 2006. Al-Jazeera's take on this was that even when the USA gets the change it wants toward democracy in the Arab world, the USA wants 'only the outcomes that suit her, otherwise how do you explain the rejection of Hamas as a democratically elected party? And what happens if most Islamic parties win other elections in other Arab countries? The answer is the US will not like it'.[14]

In addition to the overwhelming power of the images of victims, violence, armed marines, Humvees, and tanks, the constant linking by Al-Jazeera between the Islamic resistance against the USA and Israel, presents a unified front to the Arab world that is not necessarily an altogether accurate depiction.

In the terminology of Roland Barthes (1977), the 'visual substance' of Al-Jazeera's reporting is reinforced by its 'linguistic message'. The Arabic language has high dramatic qualities (think of the Arab poet Adonis whose social and political commentary makes a strong emotional appeal in works like his book *The Constant and the Mobile*), and shapes an 'iconic message' of resistance that caters to a 'desperate' Arab public looking for meaning in an increasingly complex reality.

The American Direction and the Opposite Direction

Finally, I want to mention an important voice in the edification of the dominant narrative of Al-Jazeera, the voice of Faisal Al Kassim, the presenter of the most popular political discussion program *The Opposite Direction*. His real position is always articulated at the beginning of his show even though it appears that he is sometimes giving room to the other opinion. When one reads his columns online, or his independent blogs, one can see that he almost always turns his first stated opinion from the show into a column. For the rest of the program, mainly in an interactive Q&A format, his positions on Iraq are crystal clear. For example, Kassim silenced one pro-American guest when he said, 'Aren't you lying to yourself … Condoleezza said we committed thousands of mistakes. Fukuyama who planned for the invasion of Iraq is against it now …' There are also many personal attacks on his program that are significant. Here is one example of an Egyptian attacking another guest:

I thought you are Sudanese, but the American administration put you there. You are defending this American democracy that is bombing medicine factories in Sudan? Why was nobody in Sahat Al Firdaaws (the place where the statute of Saddam Hussein was toppled), nobody could go there, even the American soldiers who put the American flag there? Nobody celebrated or could celebrate the anniversary of the independence because of fear. We sing Washington now as they sang Moscow in the past.

Al Kassim recollects almost with nostalgia the time of Saddam Hussein as way of contrasting the current situation in Iraq. He equates Islamic resistance in Iraq with Palestinian resistance in the Middle East. He gives authority and credibility to these views on Al-Jazeera and in his columns printed in various media.

The Place of Arab Women

Even programs like *For Women Only* (which airs every Monday with a rerun on Wednesday) promote an Islamic agenda, if only a moderate one. *For Women Only* defends women's rights and attacks the hardliners in Islam. Muslim feminists are invited to speak and criticize the austerity of dogmatic Islam. Even leaders of feminist Islamic movements such as Nadia Yacine, the daughter of Sheikh Yacine in Morocco, have been invited. Nahawand Al Qadiri from the University of Bayreuth made the groundbreaking observation that the name of the program itself is controversial for many reasons. The program functions in a judgmental way and navigates between repressed speech and suppressed speech (El Qadiri, 2006). The hostess of the show, Leila Shelbi, acts as the arbiter of all that is hallal. Her authoritative presence exudes an image of the strong, free Arab woman and yet her insights are often only those that are acceptable to the male Arab community.

In a previous paper, I spoke about how Al-Jazeera is successful in creating identification frames that explain its own success in the Arab media market. The Al-Jazeera identification frame functions as magnet for those who identify themselves with the underdog position. It is one in which Arabs and Muslims are 'trapped' within the feeling of war that has afflicted pain on Arab-Islamic nations. There is no doubt among those at Al-Jazeera that Al-Jazeera is representing the underdog and has acted as the voice of the Arabs and Muslims in the war in Iraq. With this being the case, Al-Jazeera has framed the war as one that threatened to become a war against Muslims and Arabs worldwide. Al-Jazeera clearly positions itself as representing the eyes and ears of the majority of Arab public – a captive audience that represents a market of 270 million people.

AL-JAZEERA PROPELS ARABIC TO NEW HEIGHTS

Colonization by the Turks and then the Europeans pushed Arabic into the lower classes of North Africa and the Middle East. The educated classes, those with influence and government connections, identified themselves by speaking French or English. Only the most entrenched Arabs clung to Arabic, refusing to use foreign languages. Consequently, in the halls of power, despite the Arabization policies of post-colonialism, Arabic was dead. Generations of the upper class had grown up speaking French or English as the languages of social mobility. The Arabic language has been revived as a tongue of power through Al-Jazeera. Since decolonization Arab linguists experts have been struggling with how to Arabize Western words. Many scholars have spoken about the inability of Arabic to adapt to modernity. The growing competition in the media industry has put pressure on Al-Jazeera to become the translation factory of the Arab world.

Thirty years ago, my own teachers in Morocco liked to tell the story of how Arabic scholars spent months figuring out how to translate the word 'sandwich', for example, in a way that the Arabization policies would countenance. Now, however, there is no time for semantic, linguistic and ontological quibbling. Instead, Al-Jazeera quickly slams the Western idea into an Arabic construction, assigning an Arabic word to the idea. It is a yeoman's translation and it works for Al-Jazeera's audience. The French influence in the Maghreb and the English influence in the Middle East have been un-shuttered to reveal new linguistic horizons in Arabic, and Al-Jazeera's website has played a crucial role in this new Arabic. Thanks to Al-Jazeera's dynamism, Arabic is not only recovering, but thriving.

In his program devoted to the Arabic language, Al Qaradawi explains that God chose to send his book, the Quran, in Arabic, and therefore Arabic is the language of God. Al Qaradawi reiterates that the decline of the Arabic language is the result of children being raised outside their mother tongue by nannies and domestic servants from India, the Philippines and Indonesia who do not speak Arabic as natives.[15]

THE HOME FIELD ADVANTAGE

Arab pundits, journalists and commentators on Al-Jazeera stress the power and the cutting edge of its reporting. It is not only the expertise and the mastery of journalistic métier but also the affinity for Iraqi fieldwork and the possession of the cultural and linguistic capital necessary to exist in that field that Arabs and Muslims have in the first place. Western journalists, according to Al-Jazeera, need translators, have different problems to adjust to in Muslim society and, in the case of Iraq, were embedded in Baghdad's 'Green Zone'. Al-Jazeera has seen itself as dominating the field of genuine reporting from the real-life experience of poor Iraqis. Al-Jazeera contends that the contradictions of the Western media – for example, bias against Muslims while promoting the sovereignty of an Islamic nation, Iraq, built on an Islamic constitution; a stated desire for democracy while ignoring election results that favored Hamas – are obvious. Al-Jazeera also calls attention to those instances in which Western media outlets were obliged to cite the genuine and leading work of Al-Jazeera in their reporting on such topics as the killing of civilians or the capture of the US or British soldiers. President Bush and Prime Minister Blair criticized Al-Jazeera for showing prisoners of war, but such attacks, even if they are attacks by Arab governments or personalities, work in Al-Jazeera's favor by drawing attention to the channel's influence.

Al-Jazeera acquired the capital of symbolic power that thrives on the motto 'the opinion and the other opinion' and provides an Arab voice that is utterly dependent upon an Islamic perspective. By symbolic power I mean 'the capacity to intervene in the course of events, to influence the actions of others and indeed to create events, by means of the production and transmission of symbolic forms' (Thompson, 1995: 17). This approach forces us to acknowledge that the field of media – the game of media, if you will – has specific ground rules and certain stakes.

I use the terminology of sociologist Pierre Bourdieu (1988, 1990) to understand how the field is structured around positions and has a specific logic. The field is also a space of competition and struggle between actors of agents in those positions. At stake is the appropriation of the legitimate capital, which can be cultural, political, economic, etc. Not everyone is fortunate enough to have legitimate forms of capital, not everyone has a share, for example, in the economic capital and the unequal distribution of capital makes some dominant and others dominated. This brings us to the power relation in a field. Influencing public opinion is the goal of the media, and all sorts of reporting on different capital are used toward that end. It is the journalistic capital, itself a cultural capital, and the ability to convince that comes with it that Bourdieu (1990) calls meaningful symbolic capital. The field is a configuration of objective relations between different sorts of capital and positions. A field of any kind is defined by its measurable effects (Entman, 2004; Hallin and Mancini, 2004; Livingston and Bennett, 2003; Schudson, 1995; Wolfsveld, 1997).

Al-Jazeera has produced measurable effects that were specific to its own goals, thereby creating its own field – no longer is Al-Jazeera a player in the field of media or journalism, it, like CNN, has created its own field upon which others are players as well. An example of this is when Al-Jazeera or CNN does something, or reports on something that has not been reported on by others which produces a response from other media or from governments. This means that they are capable of making the news as much as they are capable of reporting it.

CONCLUSION

The ambiguity of Al-Jazeera remains enormous when it comes to Israel, the US and Qatar itself. Its motto 'The opinion and the other opinion' is superficial. First, Al-Jazeera is the first Arab channel that shows and interviews on a regular basis Israeli politicians, scholars and military personnel.

The Israeli flag accompanies the news items on Israel. This visual message contributes to the acceptance of visuals from Israel in the Arab world, visuals that were previously unheard of in the Arab media. But this opening at the level of the visual does not herald less hostile reporting or less inflammatory rhetoric toward Israel. The same is also true of its coverage of issues related to the USA. Both Israel and the USA are very often linked in conspiracy theories involving Palestine and Iraq that are discussed on Al-Jazeera. Qatar, as the main financier of Al-Jazeera is reviewed favorably, despite the glaring fact that it is, both, home to the regional central command outpost for the US military and does not have a democratic government, two things that would otherwise provide Al-Jazeera with an incentive to skewer and roast Qatar.

Al-Jazeera's religious and political lenses help shape a bipolar agenda: pan-Arabism, after all, relied on a secular ideology that even excluded the Muslim Brotherhood, yet Al-Jazeera tries to combine pan-Arabism with an Islamic view that originates in al-Qaradawi's experiences with the Muslim Brotherhood. Essentially, pan-Arabism has failed and left in its place an aspiration toward a cohesive Arab culture whose adherents seem to be throwing up their hands and saying 'Forget secular pan-Arabism, we can't do it without Allah'. Islam and pan-Arab nationalism fuel the 'emotional engine' of Al-Jazeera, which has succeeded in showing the diversity in the discourse of radical Muslims and to make distinctions between the different ideological goals of each stream or group. Most radical Muslims, both typical and verboten, have found a podium on Al-Jazeera: the Muslim Brotherhood, Hassan Al Turabi of Sudan, Rachid Al Ghanoushi of Tunisia, Abassi Madani (the leader of the Islamic Front of Algeria), Mullah Kreakar of Ansar Al Islam, Nadia Yacine (the daughter of the leader of the Moroccan fundamentalist movement), Hassan Nassrallah of Hezbollah and the many leaders of Hamas. This diversity has contributed to widening the circle of understanding of the radical agenda of Islamic movements. Their faces and voices are becoming more accessible to larger audiences, and this accessibility gives legitimacy to radicalism in Islam but also contributes to its banalization (Lamloum, 2004: 69). We need only consult the chat exchanges from all over the world on www. Al-Jazeera.net to witness the overwhelming acceptance of these radical groups and support from the viewers.

Al-Jazeera is the place of confrontation between secular and non-secular Muslims, but the outcome is that in the Arab world, Islam is impossible to treat as a merely religious presence in a secular society.

Even Turkey's democratic version of Islamic governance is more democratic than Islamic, an imbalance that is key in preserving Turkey's secularism. The focus on Turkey was big before, during, and after the election of Prime Minister Rejeb Erdogan – who has introduced an Islamic resurgence. In terms of its reporting on Turkey, Al-Jazeera is creating a regime of identification frames that are at the same time interpretative, giving meaning to events and offering an explicit reading to their publics. It uses Turkey as a model of democratic Islamic possibility.

Can Al-Jazeera criticize Al-Jazeera? (The title of one of Pierre Bourdieu's studies was *Can TV criticize TV?*) Al-Jazeera has devoted a number of programs to illuminating its contributions to the world of media and journalism. Al-Jazeera has quoted many studies, such as the one by Hugh Miles, who went to Egypt, Palestine, America, Switzerland and France to see how Arab publics watch Al-Jazeera and was very positive about an Al-Jazeera seen as a form of media resistance to the Western model. Al-Jazeera clearly constructs itself not only as an Arab media outlet but also as the Arab media representative that contrasts with American and Western media. To illustrate that Al-Jazeera is unable to look at itself in the mirror and to be reflexive of its past, present and future reporting, consider the interview of Waddah Khanfar, the general manager of Al-Jazeera with the host of *Open Dialogue:*

> Ghassan Ben Jeddou [Al-Jazeera host of *Open Dialogue*]: Perhaps the question brought before you as general manager of Al-Jazeera network, Waddah Khanfar, is, naturally, we can now hold ourselves accountable and we can save ourselves by being able to criticize ourselves, but Al-Jazeera's coverage has had in some way supporters and opponents. If there is another war, is Al-Jazeera going to cover it in the same spirit?
>
> Waddah Khanfar network: This is no doubt, my brother Ghassan, the truth. Allow me first to greet all colleagues and say I believe that the success in covering the war was thanks to the determination and courage of our correspondents, a cadre that distinguished itself over the past years by reporting from the battle fields with courage and high professional ethics. No doubt that Al-Jazeera's methodological endeavor over the past decade formed our spirit and the spirit of viewers: a contract of contracts between us and the audience is a commitment to the highest professional commitment and taking sides in fact in favor of the human right to knowledge ... [Al-Jazeera] tries to offer our viewers something without bias towards a specific or party or creed or religion or ideology ... [Al-Jazeera] faced pressure too often during the coverage of wars and also faced pressure from

powerful states and governments worldwide in different stages by it. [Al-Jazeera] stood up, was patient ... the truth is that the pressure has not stopped. [Consider] the battles throughout the years since the war began in Afghanistan.[16]

According to Al-Jazeera, its journalists make poignant what Americans do not allow or are not capable of accurately reporting because the Arab media is in its own territory and continues to excel at reporting from it. Nourredine Miladi, the then host of the show *From Washington*, has said:

> The situation in Iraq and its coverage by Arab and Western media have put the Western policy to a very dangerous test: being objective in times of wars and controversies and during the coverage of the event. The distinction of Al-Jazeera, for example, in the war on Afghanistan was totally opposite in its coverage to what we were used to seeing during the first Gulf war ... The western media was partial in its coverage of the war on Iraq. What we saw in the coverage of Iraq shows the extreme failure of American coverage.

Al-Jazeera often poses the question of the failure of Arabs to become major players on the global scene and relates it to a future question: What can we do to return to the Arab golden age? It is the Arab-Islamic civilization, not simply the Arab civilization, to which Al-Jazeera refers. Al-Jazeera connects the stories of the American invasion in Iraq and the Palestinian problem in Israel to the decline of Arab and Islamic unity over the course of the 20th century and the inability of Arab leaders to act and to solve their own problems. Al-Jazeera suggests that a renaissance is needed to resuscitate Arab-Islamic civilization and transnational identity. More than simply covering and marginally influencing that renaissance, Al-Jazeera has been its chief architect. After all, the growth of its audience relies upon such a renaissance.

FUTURE RESEARCH

Here are some points that future research on Al-Jazeera should focus on. First, the nature and size of the Al-Jazeera's Arabic audiences per country. If Al-Jazeera International succeeded to measure its own audiences worldwide using a special site called: I want Al-Jazeera English.[17] Al-Jazeera Arabic, despite of its Center of Studies, does not have a single location in its entire Aljazeera.net website that shows statistics about its audience. The site describes their targeted audiences (students, intellectuals and policymakers)

without displaying any numbers. Is Al-Jazeera English more accountable than Al-Jazeera Arabic? Is it more problematic to show the audiences per country or region that put Al-Jazeera's unifying pan-Arab message at stake? According to an interesting but questionable source, http://www.allied-media.com, statistics are available. Many methodological questions about the reliability of the Allied Media? exist. A big uncertainty is how to measure who watches Al-Jazeera in the Arab world. With a low penetration of registered satellite dishes and uncontrolled use of the improvised devices such as couscous pans on a normal antenna as is the case in Morocco, Algeria and Tunisia illustrate an obvious issue (Miles, 2005). Let assume, however, that these statistics are reliable. A closer look raises a number of questions. How is possible that 8 million people in Morocco, with a population of 30 million, are watching Al-Jazeera versus 4 million in Egypt, with a population of 80 million? What is the significance of a bigger audience at the periphery of Arab nationalism, Morocco, but not in the heart and the birth place of pan-Arabism, Egypt?

Also, there is no survey data about the 22 Arab countries, however, many results that are available come from a survey that is conducted semi-regularly in six Arab countries by the Anwar Sadat Chair for Peace and Development Department of Government and Politics at the University of Maryland. More results and the actual micro-data from these surveys are available for download: http://sadat.umd.edu/surveys/index.htm. There are also reports and aggregated results from international Gallup polls via Gallup's site itself: http://www.gallup.com/home.aspx. The Birzeit University also conducts opinion polls which can be found by searching for "Al-Jazeera".

Second, Al-Jazeera Arabic is a totally different beast from Al-Jazeera English. My own comparisons and the ones of Media Tenor show that Al-Jazeera English meet the highest standards of the Western media. Al-Jazeera English, however, has an interesting disclaimer on their special site: I want Al-Jazeera English. It displays famous journalists from *The New York Times*, the *Boston Globe*, the *Jerusalem Post* and *Haaretz*. In a section entitled Hits and Myths, Al-Jazeera English attempts to answers a 'number of misperceptions and myths' about Al-Jazeera and Al-Jazeera English in North America. These 'myths and misperceptions' are formulated in the form of seven questions that include: Does Al-Jazeera supports terrorism? Is Al-Jazeera Anti-Semitic? Is Al-Jazeera Anti-American? Does Al-Jazeera show beheadings? Is Al-Jazeera English a translation of the Arabic Channel? Has Al-Jazeera a specific agenda? Is Al-Jazeera English the diplomatic portal of Al-Jazeera empire? Is it the smooth western diplomatic mission at the service of an Islamized Pan-Arabism?

Third, What was the role of Al Jazeera in paving the way for the "Arab Spring" uprisings? How did the network's involvement change during their coverage of the revolutions? How do Al Jazeera's unconventional origins fit into its conception of pan-Arabism, its motivations, and its power as the strongest media voice in and of the Arab World?

NOTES

1   http://www.aljazeera.net/NR/exeres/8325827E-C57C-437C-A8FC-501EA6549145

2   http://www.aawsat.com/details.asp?section=4andissueno=11188andarticle=527742andsearch=قناةالجزيرة20%andstate=true

3   http://www.aljazeera.net/News/archive/archive?ArchiveId=40652

4   http://www.aljazeera.net/channel/archive/archive?ArchiveId=98011

5   http://www.aljazeera.net/NR/exeres/04659523-C953–41FF-AD11–34FE17CEAEC4.htm

6   http://www.aawsat.com/details.asp?section=1andissueno=10846andarticle=481941andsearch=قناةالجزيرة20%andstate=true

7   www.kwcpolls.net

8   http://aljazeera.net/NR/exeres/4BCD5157–145B-417E-9334-BF9E966B9144.htm

9   Ibid.

10   Ibid.

11   www.aljazeera.net

12   http://www.aljazeera.net/channel/archive/archive?ArchiveId=1031426

13   M'hamed Krichen, *Al Qods Al Arabi*, London, 1 October 2002 in Lamloum (2004): 17.

14   See also http://www.aljazeera.net/programs/shareea/articles/2000/11/11–30.htm

15   http://www.aljazeera.net/NR/exeres/E3EFFCDB-5D94–4BC7-B1F7–35F7E78FF62A.htm

16   http://www.aljazeera.net/NR/exeres/62BBBEAA-21AE-4492-A967-BB09F3BEFC60.htm

17   http://www.aljazeera.net/NR/exeres/F6F0-8EB3-A1DA-4121–979D-5E02BFA1AB83.htm

18   http://www.iwantaje.net/

REFERENCES

Arkoun, M. (1981) *La pensée arabe*. 4th edn. Paris: PUF.

Barthes, R. (1977) *Elements of Semiology*. New York: Hill and Wang.

Bourdieu, P. (1988) *On Television and Journalism*. London: Pluto.

Bourdieu, P. (1990) *On Language and Symbolic Power*. Cambridge: Polity.

Cherribi, S. (2006) 'From Baghdad to Paris: Al-Jazeera and the Veil', *The Harvard International Journal of Press/Politics*, 11(2): 121–38.

El-Nawawy, M. and Iskandar, A. (2003) *Al-Jazeera: The Story of the Network that is Rattling Governments and Redefining Modern Journalism*. New York: Westview Press.

El Qadiri Issa, N. (2006) 'For Women Only: From the Repressed to the Suppressed', unpublished study emailed to me by the author in June 2006.

El Qadiri Issa, N. (2007) *Qira'a fi thaqafat al fada'yat al arabiya: al wuquf ala thukhum atafkik*. Beirut: The Center of the Arab Unity Studies.

Entman, R. M. (2004) *Projections of Power: Framing News, Public Opinion, and U.S. Foreign Policy*. Chicago, IL: University of Chicago Press.

Hallin, D. C. and Mancini, P. (2004) *Comparing Media Systems: Three Models of Media and Politics*. New York: Cambridge.

Lamloum, O. (2004) *Al-jazira, miroir rebelle et ambigu du monde arabe*. Paris. La découverte.

Livingston, S. and Bennett, W. L. (2003) 'Gate-keeping, Indexing and Live Event News: Is Technology Altering the Construction of News?', *Political Communication*, 20(4): 363–80.

Lewis, B. (2002) *What Went Wrong? Western Impact and Middle East Response*. Oxford and New York: Oxford University Press.

Lynch, M. (2006) *Voices of the New Arab Public: Iraq, al-Jazeera, and Middle East Politics Today*. New York: Columbia University Press.

Mellor, N. (2007) *Modern Arab Journalism: Problems and Prospects*. Edinburgh: Edinburgh University Press.

Miles, H. (2005) *Al-Jazeera: How Arab TV News Challenges America*. New York: Grove Press.

Rugh, W. (1987) *The Arab Press: News Media and Political Process in the Arab World*. Syracuse: University of Syracuse Press.

Schudson, M. (1995) *The Power of the News*. Cambridge, MA: Harvard University Press.

Thompson, J. (1995) *The Media and Modernity: A Social Theory of the Media*. Stanford, CA: Stanford University Press.

Wolsfeld, G. (1997) *Media and Political Conflict: News from the Middle East*. New York: Cambridge University Press.

Zaidi, M. (2003) *Al-Jazeera*. Beirut, Lebanon: Dar al Talia.

Zayani, M. and Sahraoui, S. (2007) *The Culture of Al-Jazeera: inside an Arab Media Giant*. Jefferson, NC: McFarland and Company, Inc., Publishers.

38

Grassroots Political Communication in India: Women's Movements, Vernacular Rhetoric and Street Play Performance

Christine Garlough

Unknown to most, Indian street theater originated as a folk art form that explored the feelings of common people through traditional motifs, tropes and narratives. More recently, it has manifested as 'theater of the oppressed' where day-to-day life problems are confronted (Indianetzone, 2008)

Performance often provides a means to imagine new forms of social relationships. Consequently, I believe in theater's potential as a place to reflect upon the ways peace, equality, and a more participatory democracy might be possible. In addition, theater may provide a space in which to connect to emotionally and spiritually with other people. Performance requires that we listen attentively to the speech of others, feel their humanity, and its connection to our own.

Performance creates ever-new publics, groups of spectators who come together for a moment and then disperse out across a wide social field, sometime (hopefully) sharing the knowledge they have gained, the emotions and the insights they experienced at the theater. (Dolan, 2005: 91)

Given this perspective, in what ways might we understand grassroots street play performance as a form of political communication? How might theatre be conceptualized as a potentially radical site for protest? What happens when audiences are approached as 'citizen actors' and the stage is recognized as an important facet of the public sphere that encourages deliberation and debate over the exigencies that face local and global communities?

As Jill Dolan suggests above, performance might then be understood as a form of civic relationality that contributes to democratic ethos and practices. Dolan's astute reflections upon the potential of performance as political activism have intrigued me for quite some time. Perhaps this is because they so closely echo the sentiments of the South Asian feminists I have been working with for more than a decade in Gujarat, India. Through street theater practices, these feminist activists seek to model civic engagement and deliberation in democratic contexts. Indeed, they argue that the very act of creating or participating in street theater is a type of grassroots civic engagement that effectively engages in political discourse.

Much recent scholarship on grassroots political communication has focused upon local and global efforts toward democratizations, with a good deal of emphasis on the development of grassroots movements in non-Western countries. Yet, there have been relatively few analyses of grassroots feminist movements in India that focus upon the wide variety of political communication strategies they employ, particularly the ways performance sometimes serves political purposes. This chapter hopes to fill this gap. In doing so, it demonstrates the wide swath of political discourse I consider important for communication scholars to address, from platform speeches, to protest songs, to street play performances. As such, the orientation I bring to this exploration of grassroots political communication is decidedly interdisciplinary, bringing together the fields of rhetoric, folklore, women's studies and performance studies.

To begin, this chapter provides an historical review of South Asian women's groups and feminist political communication in India providing a broad look at grassroots activism, political communication strategies and issues frequently addressed. Next, I explore the potential of conceptualizing performance as political communication. Finally, drawing upon a decade of fieldwork with feminist groups in Gujarat, I explore the ways contemporary feminist groups in India use street performances to carve out a public space for women, enabling them to make their presence and desires known. Focusing upon grassroots advocacy concerns, I consider the ways these aesthetic texts and performances contribute to broader political goals, providing a platform to articulate pressing concerns about issues such as gender equity in the workplace, rape, dowry death inheritance laws or educational opportunities.

INDIAN DEMOCRACY AND GRASSROOTS SOCIAL ACTIVISM

The population of India is more than a billion people, the second highest population in the world after China and nearly one-sixth of the planet's total population. As such, India is the world's largest democracy, with 23 official languages and more than 1000 dialects spoken. Within the nation's 28 states, there exists a rich variety of regional and tribal cultures, in addition to a wide array of religious affiliations including Buddhism, Christianity, Hinduism, Jainism, Judaism, Islam, Sikhism and Zoroastrianism, to name but a few. To be sure, it is a democratic context characterized by deep diversity.

In its ideal form, such a democracy could be conceived of as both a political system and a creative culture that provides ordinary people a voice in responding to the exigencies that characterize their lives, whether that be at the international, national, local community or interpersonal level. In reality, like any democracy, there exists deep disparity among those who are able to tap and harness this creative political and cultural potential. Throughout history, a large majority of Indians have lived in poverty. In recent years, however, the rise of India's new middle class has received much media attention. This category of citizen, close to 200 million people, is not simply financially advantaged. They also are often socially and culturally identifiable due to their knowledge of English and education levels. New research from organizations such as the McKinsey Global Institute suggests that spending patterns are changing significantly as discretionary purchasing becomes a larger portion of consumer practices. India's shift to a consumer society has important implications for a variety of democratic institutions. For example, the growing number of press outlets and broadcast channels are experiencing exciting levels of growth and are seeking to provide documentaries and educational programming that will reaching the new middle class and above.

While outlets such as community radio continue to provide a forum for civil society organizations and community groups, a good deal of the media programming, aimed at the growing middle class, is missed by those in less fortunate economic positions. A focus upon English medium programming, lack of access to the Internet, or the dearth of local media outlets (to name but a few) make it difficult for the disenfranchised to engage with equal potential. Indeed, as Bystydzienski and Sekhon note,

At a time when democracy is supposedly spreading around the world, great disparities between rich and poor people, and between wealthy and impoverished countries, challenge the notion of popular control of governance. Marginalized groups within nation states struggle to make their needs and desires known. Centralization of power in the hands of corporations and regional and world bodies outside existing states has reduced citizen input in decisions that profoundly affect people's lives. And many women, the poor, as well as ethnic, religious, and other groups in numerous countries continue to be excluded from meaningful political participation. (1999: 2)

One important way in which women deprived of power and resources have found to engage in the political contexts that shape their lives is through involvement in grassroots women's movements (Kalpagam, 2004: 339). Through these community-based initiatives, women work at the local level to develop their communities and respond to economic inequalities related to: gender, caste, class, cultural oppression, state centralization, capitalist economic development and environmental degradation. As such, while not every grassroots organizations could be considered progressive, many have played an important role in efforts to create spaces for democratic deliberation, consciousness raising, promoting group solidarity and individual self-development.

CONTEMPORARY INDIAN WOMEN'S MOVEMENT

Over the years, the Indian women's movement has encompassed a range of organizations, from institutional to grassroots, urban to rural and radical to reformist. In the early years, these women's groups developed within an historical context of political instability and protest – often in combination nationalist movements or struggles against authoritarianism (Ray, 1999: 12). For example, during the 19th and early 20th centuries, when India was under British colonial rule, several social reform movements began to political campaigns to address issues of religious reform, child marriage, as well as the status of women, the lower castes, peasants and tribal groups. Consequently, the first all-India women's organizations were formed in the early 20th century, such as the women's India Association (WIA), the National Council of Indian Women (NCIW) and the All India Women's Conference (AIWC) (Omvedt, 2004: 189). Many of these movements involved mobilization of people at the grassroots level and ultimately, 'with increasing resistance to policies of the colonial administration, many of the movements for reform and resistance were incorporated into the nationalist struggles against British imperialism' (Kothari, 1989: 26). After India gained Independence in 1947, the Congress Party government attempted in limited ways to fulfill the promises it had made to women. For example, the constitution asserted the equality of men and women, a limited number of administrative bodies were instituted to create social opportunities for women, and a handful female politicians made their way into the government positions. Consequently, in the 1950s there was a lull in feminist campaigning.

However, by the mid-1960s it became clear that parliamentary government in India had been unable to serve the people in various ways: poverty in urban and rural areas was widespread; unemployment was prevalent; ecological degradation was unchecked and droughts plagued the country. As Omvedt notes, 'In this situation, a new ferment of political activity began in the country. People organized in order to protest against the situation under many banners and around many issues' (2004: 180). As such, the beginnings of the contemporary women's movement are usually traced to the early 1970s. During this time period, women were especially active in radical protests against the Indian state. As Ray contends, this included women from Maoist movements (Progressive Organization of Women) and (Purogami Stree Sanghatana and Stree Mukti Sanghatana), along with movements like the anti-price rise agitations in Maharashtra, the Self-employed Women's Movement (SEWA) and Nav Nirman (New Light) in Gujarat (Ray, 1999: 4). Another excellent example, as Kumar illustrates, is the Shahada movement:

> The Shahada movement, in Dhulia district of Maharashtra, was a Bhil tribal landless laborers' movement against the exploitive practices of non-tribal local landowners. Drought and famine in Maharashtra during this period exacerbated the poverty already created by invidious rates of sharecropping, land alienation, and extortionate money lending charges, and these conditions contributed to rising militancy among the Bhils. The Shahada movement began as a folk protest (through radical devotional song clubs) in the late 1960s. It took on a more militant campaigning thrust when the New Left joined the movement in the early 1970s and helped the Bhils form an organization, the Sharmik Sangathana (Toiler's Organization) in 1972. Accounts of the Shahada movement say that women were more active than men and that as their militancy grew , they began to take direct action on issues specific to them as women, such as the physical violence associated with alcoholism … (Kumar, 1995: 61)

In addition, the 1970s also began the emergence of the 'autonomous' women's movement within which many educated women took to radical politics, and simultaneously promoted an analysis of women's issues. These women's issues were later given national legitimacy by a report on the status of women published in 1974 as well as by the United Nations Declaration of 1975 as International Women's Year (Ray, 1999: 4). As part of this effort, in 1977, a group of women in Delhi started a journal about women and society called *Manushi*. This journal was successful and has become an important site that chronicles the various aspects of the women's movement in India. In addition, during the late 1970s and 1980s, 'A number of magazines and journals devoted to promoting women's equality came into being, many of them in regional languages. These included *Feminist Network* (English: Bombay), *Baiza* (Marathi: Pune), *Ahalya, Sabala Sachetana*, and *Pratibadi Chetana* (Bengali: Calcutta), *Women's Voice* (English: Bangalore), and *Stree Sangharsh* (Hindi: Patna). The city-based groups also played an important role in mobilizing public opinion and press coverage ...' (Sen, 2004: 197). Fervent protests by the poor, landless agriculturalists, tribal groups, lower castes and women culminated in Prime Minister Indira Gandhi's declaration of a state emergency and suspension of constitutional rights in 1975. During this time, thousands of activists were arrested and many had to suspend their political activities and find refuge underground, including those involved in women's organizations. The emergency was lifted in 1977 and resistive political activity resumed publicly.

In recent years, the Indian women's movement has been taken up by groups representing a diverse range of ideologies and worked vigorously on issues of personal law, dowry, rape, the rights of Dalit women, alcohol abuse by husbands, domestic abuse, sexual assault, forced prostitution of children, communal violence and the portrayal of women in the media. Through speeches, political protests, political advertising, web sites and political pamphlets, these women's groups aid in efforts to unionize domestic workers and demand equal wages, employment, maternity leave, working women's hostels and legal reforms. They also continue to engage in heated debates over core questions such as: What are the roots of women's oppression? Should women's organizations remain autonomous or connect with larger institutional agencies? How might feminists best ally themselves with other women's organizations? What are the most effective forms of political communication for women's organizations to use in particular contexts; platform speeches, political pamphlets, demonstrations? Or perhaps street plays?

INDIAN STREET THEATER AND POLITICAL PARTICIPATION

Street theater's heritage grows from a long tradition of folk performance in India. Similar to other theatre genres, it not only provides the audience with entertainment but also an opportunity for shared understanding and a chance to reflect upon the meanings of one's personal identity or one's membership in different communities. However, in contrast to other dramatic forms, modern street theater is primarily characterized by political, often militant, overtones providing an opportunity to deliberate exigencies that characterize people's everyday lives. Such street theater, in its modern form, began to be used most widely in the 1940s, particularly by IPTA (India People's Theater Association), a Bengali group affiliated with the Communist Party of India. This organization spent decades writing and performing street theater pieces, such as *Aaj Ka Sawaal* (The Problems of Today), *Charge Sheet, Bhook Ki Jwaala* (The Flames of Hunger) and *Swathantra Sangram* (Independence Struggle) to be used as a tool to engage the masses in social activism against colonial forces (Garlough, 2007). These performances were characteristically experimental, linking the traditional and the modern and utilizing content drawn from contemporary reality. In particular, organizations and actors strategically appropriated folk culture in order to create a cultural forum in which disenfranchised people might communicate. This interventionist theater hoped, and still hopes, to affect the social order. It is not a movement imposed from above; rather it is decidedly grassroots in its orientation with roots deep in the cultural awakenings of the masses of India. Indeed, the People's Theater, which still plays a community role in Calcutta, continues to be a political idea, the core of which is experimentation and cultural change.

Today, theater in the streets in India is often still an artistic expression of left wing politics. Born out of the need for social change it is still essentially a people's theater embracing the daily life of the common man (Garlough, 2007). These performances are strategically designed to raise consciousness about issues of social relevance, provide social critiques and involve people at a grassroots level to effect change. Indeed, a variety of groups use street theater to communicate complex issues in a simple, engaging, often idiomatic fashion. Indeed, religious reformers, mainstream politicians, citizen groups, factory workers, students and others all have used this form in the hopes of gaining support for their agenda. However, the largest group of practitioners continues to be middle-class urban activists who believe that as privileged, educated people they bear a responsibility to educate the masses on important social issues.

Although the government has occasionally attempted to shut down these performances, taking punitive measures against authors and artists, these performances continue to be produced for audiences that range from handfuls to hundreds. Interestingly, the success of street theater as an artful form of political engagement has attracted the attention of Indian government officials for more self-interested reasons. Indeed, those who work for the Song and Drama Division, hoping to generate support for mainstream political policies, have hired actors for street performances that advance the agendas of the controlling party and its leaders. In this way, street theater, a creation of revolutionary spirit and critical consciousness, has been occasionally itself been appropriated (Garlough, 2008).

Women's organizations across India use street theater; these efforts not only critique prevailing social and cultural issues and norms, but also voice alternative visions of the future. Their representations reflect a multiplicity of perspectives that often highlight gender inequalities in kinship, caste, class and community relationships. Re-imagining and re-representing emerging identities, these performances create a space for Indian women to portray themselves in their own terms rather than those of mainstream society. Beyond this, live performances provide a place where these identities can be enacted. These performances have had a profound and long-term effect upon a broad range of citizens, from the educated and elite to the illiterate and impoverished. Activist performers re-imagined public streets as vital forums for a disenfranchised people, playing with a rich heritage of folk theater forms, figures and practices and infusing them with elements of popular culture and political discourse – an experimental mix of the traditional, popular and political. Such performances, which continue to erupt on public sidewalks and in communal courtyards, are part of a broader pragmatic aesthetic movement, focusing on direct engagement with 'the people' and the goal of socio-cultural transformation. These events provide a platform from which to respond to actions and discourses of both contemporary and historical import, a means by which to raise consciousness and constitute identities (Garlough, 2007).

Groups continually experiment with revolutionary techniques and concepts. Often, scripts evolve through group discussion, beginning with the selection of a topic where social action is desired. Common themes include the caste system, communalism, healthcare, political corruption, terrorism, current economic trends, alcoholism, sexism and police brutality. Sometimes, authors reference real-life cases in the scripts; indeed, many activists feel that contextualizing issues through current events is the key to engaging the audience and successfully communicating their agendas. Popular film tunes, folk songs and dances, as well as characters from popular literature or media are also frequently included in the scripts, not only to provide entertainment but also to serve as touchstones or familiar comparison points. Interestingly, these folk elements also are often appropriated to resist and critique

mainstream practices and discourses. Typically, the language in these performances is colloquial, using appropriate regional dialect. Militant and provocative in character, this discourse bears a metaphoric resemblance to graffiti.

Ultimately, while the structure of street theater resembles other literary dramatic pieces, in comparison to many other genres, its form is experimental and flexible (Garlough, 2008). Moreover, the performances often possess a dynamic, interactive and emergent nature. For example, during the play the audience might respond to the discourse, prompting further unscripted remarks from the actors. This opportunity for both actors and audience members to contribute to a political discussion in a public space allows for a unique exchange that is not often available to many citizens. Indeed, because street theater is essentially a mobile medium, actors can go out in search of an audience. This mobility means that often no stage exists and props are kept to a minimum. Costumes, particularly masks sometimes provide a bit of illusion; however, emphasis is placed most heavily upon the performance of the actors.

Indeed, I would argue that these street plays hold the potential to create a public forum in which audiences, who choose to come together for a moment in time, may come to feel allied with one another and find a place to scrutinize public meanings important to the community (Farrell, 1993). In some cases, they also demonstrate how to be active citizens to audiences who might not regularly see themselves as agents in their own lives or political systems (Dolan, 2005). As such, they are not simply epideictic spectacles but demonstrate a 'radical performance pedagogy' that create profoundly deliberative occasions and model the ways one might engage in a participatory democracy through attentive listening and dialogic reciprocity.

Viewed as an intervention and embodied struggle, these performances are meant to broaden consciousness. In doing so, they are not necessarily interested in providing information or answers for audiences, although they sometimes do. Instead, they also are concerned with asking questions or performing a request for acknowledgment that enacts an approach toward a desired audience. These performances are also intensely reflective. They make available mirrors for individuals and communities to probe as they enact narratives that may reanimate social solidarity or provide a place for social critique that widens community borders and may make public what has been veiled (Hamera and Conquergood, 2006: 421). Of course, there is no guarantee that this will work. As Pollock notes:

> As oriented as performance may be toward change, performance does not work instrumentally.

In the symbolic field of representation, effects are unpredictable, even uncontrollable. They may be fleeting or burrow deeply, only to emerge in an unexpected place, at another time. They may unfurl slowly, even invisibly, on affective currents that may compete with what we think a given performance is or should be doing. Or they may refuse to come out altogether, preferring instead to rest in the discourses of 'mere' entertainment or passing pleasure. (2005: 2)

Yet, the potential exists. In performing a desire for recognition and acknowledgment, and by making claims of vulnerability, a petition for future relations and a stake in one's own being is made. These performances keep trauma visible, testify to the suffering of others and engage in the rhetorical work of speaking, listening, deliberating and 'knowing together'. They offer an opening for talk (or meaningful silence) − a creation of space and time that is personal, interpersonal and significantly political. The stage is a place where new cultural possibilities are explored, performed and suggested with the hope of utopian impact.

Perhaps this seems an obvious point to make in the wake of the well-known and regarded scholarship of Roger Abrahams (1968), Dwight Conquergood (1992, 2006), Jill Dolan (2005), Judith Hamera (2002, 2006, 2007), Hauser (1999) and Della Pollock (1998, 2005). For more than four decades, this interdisciplinary body of work has demonstrated that performance is a fundamental and inherent part of political communication and the public sphere. Cultural performance is more than simple entertainment. It can be a powerful rhetorical practice. This is in keeping with the movement toward 'big rhetoric' that began in the 1960s, or what Edward Schiappa (2001) describes as a conception of rhetorical studies no longer bound to the traditional paradigm of public address.

For those interested in critical and postcolonial theory, this has been a crucial turn, allowing for better consideration of marginalized voices in non-Western or diasporic contexts. As Raka Shome, one of the few scholars to theorize the connection between postcolonial and rhetorical theory states:

Public address has been a realm where imperial voices were primarily heard and imperial policies were articulated. The colonized did not always have access to a public realm, or if they did, their speeches were not always recorded in mainstream documents, since the means of production rested with the imperial subject. All this means that we have built a lot of our understanding of rhetoric by focusing on (and often celebrating) imperial voices. (1996: 74)

To some, expanding the scope of rhetorical discourse to include everyday cultural forms threatened a necessary disciplinary separation put at risk by the 'rhetorical turn' in anthropology, English and folklore departments (Bitzer and Black, 1971). In contrast, I believe, along with many others, that 'what is significant about the rhetorical turn is not that "everything is rhetoric" but that a rhetorical perspective and vocabulary can be used to understand and describe a wide range of phenomenon' (Schiappa, 2001: 268). Indeed, putting 'rhetoric' into dialog with other core communication concepts such as 'performance' has resulted in a great deal of important research related to political communication in the past four decades. In particular, the work of Bauman (1977, 1986, 1992a,b, 1993), Bauman and Briggs (1990), Kapchan (1996), Kirshenblatt-Gimblett (1983), Mieder (1987), Radner and Lanser (1993) and Zipes (1983), among others, all speak to the ways individuals use performance forms to communicate marginalized or potentially threatening social perspectives. As Della Pollock astutely notes:

Performance − whether we are talking about the everyday act of telling a story or the staged reiterations of stories − is an especially charged, contingent, reflexive space of encountering the complex web of our respective histories. It may consequently engage participants in new and renewed understandings of the past. It may introduce alternative voices into public debate. It may help to identify systemic problems and to engage a sense of need, hope, and vision. As live representation, performance may in effect bring imagined worlds into being and becoming, moving performers and audiences alike into palpable recognition of possibilities for change. (2005: 1)

Indeed, in recent years scholars from both rhetorical studies and performance studies have begun to understand just how much common ground they share with regard to concerns for testimony, witnessing, oral history, community building and social transformation. From many disciplinary corners, there is a growing appreciation of the ways that people can construct and participate in 'public' life through personal narratives embedded within cultural performances. This perspective is reflected in my work on grassroots feminist groups in Gujarat, India, in which I explore the ways traditional women's folk forms have been critically appropriated and, through the process of rhetorical invention, used in feminist performances to create social change (Garlough, 2007, 2008).

THE MONKEY SHOW

For the last decade, I have had the privilege of working with a group of women in the state of Gujarat who are affiliated with the grassroots feminist group called *Sahiya*r. This fledgling Gujatati feminist group is, surprisingly, the first of its kind in the modern city of Baroda (located 112 km south of Ahmedabad and 419 km north of Bombay). Contrasting itself against more conventional women's organizations, *Sahiya*r's approach to activism is decidedly radical. Rather than focusing upon trade skills or literacy, their fundamental goal is to promote critical awareness of women's social oppression. Their work addresses the immediate needs of the women in their community, due to the rise of rape, domestic violence, communal violence, dowry harassment and the use of sex-determination tests in recent years.

A relatively small organization, its staff includes only a small number of part-time volunteers and a staff director, all of whom are women. While the size of *Sahiyar* does limit the types of activities they can sponsor, they often receive support by maintaining connections with other local groups such as *Manthan* (Youth Organization), *Parivartan* (Cultural Organization), *Manav Ekta Manch* (Anti-Communal Front) and *Swashray* (Organization of Women Workers), as well as the Women's Studies Department at Maharaja Sayaji University of Baroda. *Sahiyar* also obtains funding from individual donations and a small grant from the India Development Service.

This group's activities include organizing demonstrations, outreach to poverty stricken communities, counseling for 'family affairs' and 'personal problems', work with Dalit and Muslim women to battle communalism and casteism, and the publication of a feminist magazine called *Narimukti*, which is produced in collaboration with other feminist organizations in Gujarat. In addition, the group has organized a workshop to study Maharatra's pioneering Anti-Sex Determination Act, with the goal of having a similar law passed in Gujarat. *Sahiyar* also has provided an 'Awareness Program' for school-aged children that focuses upon critiquing traditional gender stereotypes and providing a forum for imagining gender roles. Of course, they also engage in cultural performance, such as street plays. For example, during my fieldwork with grassroots feminist groups in Baroda, Gujarat, I came to know of a street play titled *The Monkey Show*. The play, written in colloquial Gujarati and performed in local courtyards, alleyways and community centers, explores the violence associated with gender inequalities, domestic abuse and dowry death through the marriage of two unlikely protagonists – monkey newlyweds.

The play begins with the Narrator, a 'Monkey Man', addressing and offering respectful greetings to an audience possessing an assumed diversity. He beckons, 'To all the kind, appreciated, respected people – My pranam (bow down) to the Hindus, a salute to the Muslims, and sasriyakaal to all the Sikhs'. In doing so, he not only extends an invitation for hospitality but implicates everyone (regardless of cultural or religious orientation) in the exigencies being discussed. He then speaks to his colleagues: Ballu, The Monkey Man, and Banno, The Monkey Woman. He asks, 'So what show are you presenting today – Romeo and Juliet, Shiri Farhaad, or that of Salim and Anaarkali?' The Chorus (represented as a crowd) responds with a resounding 'No!' because all these tragic love stories (from disparate cultures) are old. Rather, they want to see some thing new – something that represents contemporary relationships in India.

The monkeys agree to this request. The play then begins with a hero wooing a young girl. At first, she is unsure of her feelings but later is convinced that this boy is the love of her life. As the romance unfolds within the performance, colloquialisms, metaphors, similes and informal grammatical structures abound. For instance, the Monkey Narrator states, 'Alrighty! These two are in love now. Since they are in love, we'll have to get them hitched. But a wedding is not child's play. We need the advice of their respected elders in that'. Meanwhile, the chorus sings, 'Silver bicycle, golden seat. Let's go darling! We'll go double seat'. Indeed, the script draws upon a wide range of aesthetic traditions, including *naksha*, a satirical folk performance form and folk language that includes proverbs, nursery rhymes and idiomatic turns of phrase that engage the audience. Rather than striving for aesthetic purity or transcendence, its form is eclectic serving the ends of a critical agenda.

However, as is typical for the street play genre, while the language is poetic, the arguments advanced are not subtle; instead the claims and ideological orientations are offered in a direct fashion. Specifically, this play focuses upon four key issues effecting women in India: (1) work and gender equity; (2) domestic abuse; (3) bride burning and dowry death and (4) the lack of social response to these issues. These issues are initially addressed by the Monkey Narrator who invites the audience to peek into the couple's domestic life after marriage,

Alright! Ballu and Banno are married now. Let's see what's going on in their house. Banno cooks the food, Ballu eats the food. Banno washes the clothes, Ballu wears the clothes. Banno stays at home, Ballu goes to work.

And as the plot develops, the potential for inequity and violence within the institution of marriage is further explored. At this point, the initial exigence shifts slightly to focus more directly upon the suffering faced by young women as a result of incessant demands for dowry. The Narrator asks:

Oh!!! Why is Ballo upset today? What has happened? Listen! He says his business went in loss. He needs some money. Where will he get it? Ö What is the big deal after all? There is always one solution. Go and tell your wife to get some money from her parents.

Upon being asked, the female money declines. The narrator responds, 'She says no? What kind of a man are you? You could not even convince your wife to do such a small thing? Go and tell her again. And if she doesn't agree then give her two or three slaps. Then she will definitely agree'.

Despite the beatings, however, the wife does not. Exasperated, the narrator yells, 'Now what happened? What kind of hero are you? Ö Go get some kerosene oil from the store and burn her. Then marry some other girl. You'll get a lot of dowry.' At this point in the play, drawing upon Marxist-feminist perspectives, the actors and audiences explore the possibility that Indian women have been conceptualized as a piece of capital in an economic exchange. Understood as a possession of the natal family, she is theirs to be acted upon – to be given away or destroyed at will. Symbolically infused with commercial value, 'the bride' is reduced to the level of a sign communicating information about class status and familial prestige. On the other end of this transaction the bride's worth is calculated by her husband and in-laws in terms after assessing her beauty, domestic skills, education level, as well as the dowry she will bring. Exposing the rationality supporting dowry and broader kinship traditions, this line of reasoning reveals a social contract that justifies the limitation of women to private family life and institutionalizes a position of objectivity supported by discourses of subordination.

When the Ballo the monkey husband hesitates to resort to 'bride burning' the Monkey Narrator chastises him saying,

Hey! Why are you afraid? Nothing will happen. Don't you read the newspapers daily? 'Burnt.' 'Killed.' Is anyone ever punished? Are you afraid of society? People will forget in two or three days. Rather, even her sister will agree to marry you.

After a pregnant pause, Ballu and Banno whisper to each other and then whisper into the Money Narrator's ear. Soon afterward, the Monkey Narrator addresses the audience and says, 'Do you know what this monkey and his wife tell me? They said that this awful and disgusting job of burning and killing wives – we monkeys cannot even do it in a play. Only human can do that.'

With this turn, the four previous explored issues (work and gender equity, domestic abuse, bride burning/dowry death and the lack of social response to these issues) are cleverly subsumed under the broader banner of human rights discourse. The ethical question at stake, they argue, is 'What makes us human?' Humanity, in this way, is understood as a value that can be interrogated. That is, the play shows what is unharmonizable between what we characterize as 'human' and the inhuman behavior that manifests in the four issues addressed. This critical play between human and animal opens space to invite questions of a hermeneutical nature, calling forth new perspectives that provide the opportunity for a reinterpretation of prior events and texts. The aporia reflected upon here revolves around questions of ethics and relationality and a recognition of bare life that results from situations where humans do not act with humanity toward one another. As such, the play issues a call of conscience.

FINAL THOUGHTS

Most generally, it is my hope that this chapter calls attention to the ways street plays function as rhetorical sites of ideological conflict, the ways people use vernacular resources to counter oppression and the ways people struggle over the subjects they are called to become. More specifically, I believe this rhetorical analysis advances our understanding of South Asian rhetoric in substantial ways. The rhetorical work created by social reformers and activists in groups like *Sahiyar* testifies to the liberating possibilities of strategically taking from a cultural heritage what we regard as positive and framing it in innovative ways, possibly by combining it with elements that seem foreign or, at times, antithetical. This also alludes to the fact that rhetoric is often produced at the intersection of cultures.

In addition, this analysis further calls attention to the necessity of examining folk and popular culture when exploring the political communication practices of grassroots groups. Taking this into consideration, it seems important to spend more time focusing upon the pragmatic, everyday ways in which culture is used for rhetorical purposes, exploring the mosaic of culture, folk and popular as well as official and authorized texts, and considering texts not traditionally identified as political, but that have political implications.

Grassroots groups, such as *Sahiyar*, use folk forms as a moralizing force to craft new identities among those who feel their latent power. For such grassroots groups, creating a rhetorical folk form is a creative process that requires mapping and referencing a common history and mythology that best suit the purpose of the persuasive effort. Shared folk forms, strategically selected and transformed, contain the potential to engender a progressive sense of identity, while continuing to acknowledge deeply held customs and conventions. This active and purposeful transformation of folklore promotes ideas about identity by asking audiences to re-imagine their selves and communities in relation to nation and culture. When it is performed, it becomes a framed event, in contrast with everyday life, that promotes reflexive awareness. Street theater, used in cites across India to increase the public's awareness of social and political issues and mobilize action, likely has more persuasive sway over the audiences most Indian feminist organizations wish to reach than formal speeches. Flexible, collective, participatory, familiar and entertaining, this folk form has great potential, not only for intervention and social change, but also for a reassertion of progressive values with each performance.

REFERENCES

Abrahams, R. (1968) 'Introductory Remarks to a Rhetorical Theory of Folklore', *Journal of American Folklore*, 81(320): 144–58.

Bauman, R. (1977) *Verbal Art as Performance*. Prospect Heights, CA: Waveland Press, Inc.

Bauman, R. (1986) *Story, Performance, and Event: Contextual Studies of Oral Narrative*. Bloomington, IN: Cambridge University Press.

Bauman, R. (1992a) 'Contextualization, Tradition and the Dialogue of Genres: Icelandic Legends of the Kraftaskald', in A. Duranti and C. Goodwin (eds.), *Rethinking Context*. Cambridge: Cambridge University Press. pp. 125–46.

Bauman, R. (1992b) *Folklore, Cultural Performances and Popular Entertainments: A Communication-centered Handbook*. Oxford: Oxford University Press.

Bauman, R. (1993) *Folklore and Culture on the Texas-Mexican Border*. Austin, TX: CMAS Books.

Bauman, R. and Briggs, C. L. (1990) 'Poetics and Performance as Critical Perspectives on Language and Social Life', *Annual Review of Anthropology*, 19: 59–88.

Bitzer, L. and Black, E. (eds.) (1971) *The Prospect of Rhetoric: Report of the National Development Project*. Englewood Cliffs, NJ: Prentice-Hall.

Bystydzienski, J. M. and Sekhon, J. (eds.) (1999) *Democratization and Women's Grassroots Movements*. Bloomington, IN: Indiana University Press.

Conquergood, D. (1992) 'Ethnography, Rhetoric, and Performance', *Quarterly Journal of Speech*, 78(1): 80–123.

Conquergood, D. (2006) 'Rethinking Ethnography: Towards a Critical Cultural Politics', in D. S. Madison and J. Hamera (eds.), *The SAGE Handbook of Performance Studies*. London: Sage. pp. 351–65.

Dolan, J. (2005) *Utopia in Performance: Finding Hope at the Theater*. Ann Arbor, MI: University of Michigan Press.

Farrell, T. B. (1993) *Norms of Rhetorical Culture*. New Haven, CT: Yale University Press.

Garlough, C. (2007) 'Transfiguring Criminality: Eclectic Representations of a Female Bandit in Indian Nationalist and Feminist Rhetoric', *Quarterly Journal of Speech*, 93(3): 253–78.

Garlough, C. (2008) 'On the Political Uses of Folklore: Performance and Grassroots Feminist Activism in India', *Journal of American Folklore*, 121(480): 167–91.

Hamera, J. (2002) 'An Answerability of Memory: "Saving" Khmer Classical Dance', *The Drama Review*, 46(4): 65–85.

Hamera, J. (2006) 'Performance, Performativity, and Cultural Poiesis in Practices of Everyday Life', in D. S. Madison and J. Hamera (eds.), *The SAGE Handbook of Performance Studies*. London: Sage. pp. 46–64.

Hamera, J. (2007) *Dancing Communities: Performance, Difference, and Connection in the Global City*. New York: Palgrave Macmillan.

Hamera, J. and Conquergood, D. (2006) 'Performance and Politics: Themes and Arguments', in D. S. Madison and J. Hamera (eds.), *The SAGE Handbook of Performance Studies*. London: Sage. pp. 419–26.

Hauser, G. (1999) *Vernacular Voices: The Rhetoric of Publics and Public Spheres*. Columbia, SC: The University of South Carolina Press.

Indianetzone (2008) 'Indian Street Theatre', http://www.indianetzone.com/5/indian_street_theatre.htm

Kalpagam, U. (2004) 'Perspectives for a Grassroots Feminist Theory', in M. Chaudhuri (ed.), *Feminism in India*. New Delhi: Kali for Women.

Kapchan, D. (1996) *Gender on the Market: Moroccan Women and the Revoicing of Tradition*. Philadelphia, PA: University of Pennsylvania Press.

Kirshenblatt-Gimblett, B. (1983) 'Studying Immigrant and Ethnic Folklore', in R. M. Dorson (ed.), *Handbook of American Folklore*. Bloomington, IN: Indiana University Press. pp. 39–47.

Kothari, S. (1989) *State Against Democracy: In Search of Humane Governance*. Delhi: Ajanta Publications.

Kumar, R. (1995) 'From Chipko to Sati: The Contemporary Women's Movement', in A. Basu (ed.), *The Challenge of Local Feminisms: Women's Movements in Global Perspective*. Oxford: Westview Press. pp. 58–86.

Mieder, W. (1987) *Tradition and Innovation in Folk Literature*. London: University Press of New England.

Omvedt, G. (2004) 'New movements and New Theories in India', in M. Chaudhuri (ed.), *Feminism in India*. New Delhi: Kali for Women.

Pollock, D. (ed.) (1998) *Exceptional Spaces: Essays in Performance and History*. Chapel Hill, NC: The University of North Carolina Press.

Pollock, D. (ed.) (2005) *Remembering: Oral History Performance*. New York: Palgrave Macmillan.

Radner, J. and Lanser, S. (1993) 'Strategies of Coding in Women's Culture', in J. Radner (ed.), *Feminist Messages: Coding in Women's Folk Culture*. Chicago, IL: University of Illinois. pp. 1–30.

Ray, R. (1999) *Fields of Protest: Women's Movements in India*. New Delhi: Kali for Women.

Schiappa, E. (2001) 'Second Thoughts on the Critiques of Big Rhetoric', *Philosophy and Rhetoric*, 34(3): 260–74.

Sen, I. (2004) 'Women's Politics in India', in M. Chaudhuri (ed.), *Feminism in India*. New Delhi: Kali for Women. pp. 187–210.

Shome, R. (1996) 'Postcolonial Interventions in the Rhetorical Canon: An "Other" View', *Communication Theory*, 6(1): 40–59.

Zipes, J. (1983) *Fairy Tales and the Art of Subversion: The Classical Genre for Children and the Process of Civilization*. New York: Routledge.

39

Political Communication in Post-apartheid South Africa

Ian Glenn and Robert Mattes

INTRODUCTION

Any politically interested foreigner visiting South Africa from the developed world would see and hear much in the country's mass communications infrastructure that would appear familiar. Much of this is due to the country's colonial legacy, which shaped both the country's media and political models. The oldest newspaper, for example, the *Cape Times*, as well as the state broadcaster, the South African Broadcasting Corporation (SABC) overtly modeled themselves (the latter following input from Lord Reith, head of the BBC) on British originals. In the post-*apartheid* era, the tabloid *The Daily Sun* pays tribute, in name if not in substance, to the UK's leading tabloid.

South Africa has four local national free-to-air television channels as well as subscription satellite television services carrying around a dozen international news channels. Each major city and many smaller ones have newspapers, often several. Large subscription papers are either in English or in Afrikaans, but many local newspapers publish in African languages. The country's papers carry extensive political coverage with robust commentary and debate, as well as sharp political satire in the form of cartoons or even satiric comic strips. More recently, tabloid newspapers have entered the market reaching new audiences and portraying new concerns. Much international material makes its way into local political news reporting, and many international publications such as the *Financial Times, Time* or

Newsweek are printed and distributed locally. There is also a robust culture of political discussion on talk radio and a growing, lively culture of Internet debate and political blogging and even a satiric Internet-based news parody show, *Z-news*, on the lines of *Spitting Image*.

Yet this sense of familiarity risks missing many of the features that make South Africa – as a developing society with a racially diverse population and massive enduring social inequities – such an intriguing study of 'mixed' political communications. Because it combines features of pre-modern, modern and post-modern political communication, the influence of a local chief or union steward, broadcast political news and new media forms such as blogging and Facebook all matter. For many black South Africans, the media landscape may seem characteristically modern, with access limited to broadcast television or news provided in indigenous languages by a public broadcaster, or to widely read populist tabloid newspapers. For many wealthier South Africans, particularly whites, the media landscape now has all the characteristics of post-modernity: it is characterized by fragmentation, almost unlimited choice, and a diminishing sense of national conversation or shared political destiny.

We attempt to describe political communication in South Africa by looking, in turn, at (1) citizens, (2) media organizations and professionals and (3) politicians and political parties, using survey data or other rigorous evidence wherever possible. The focus will be on how these actors communicate with one another, primarily through formal media but more broadly through the larger political system, as well.

This approach represents something of a departure from previous scholarly work, which has scarcely tried to bring the three actors into the same focus in any systematic way. In this previous work, we can distinguish five broad trends. The first tradition is that of studies taking the political economy of the media approach, with much of the work since the end of apartheid concerned with complex issues such as the effect of new patterns of media ownership, the role of the state broadcaster in a political economy system or of ways in which the press have been seen to support a neoliberal consensus around issues of government privatization (Berger, 2004; Duncan, 2001; Mayher and McDonald, 2007; Peet, 2001; Teer-Tomaselli, 2004; Tomaselli, 2004).

A second major body of work has analyzed political communication during elections, either from the point of view of analysts or consultants or indeed politicians (Greenberg, 2009; Hofmeyr and Rice, 2000; Leon, 2008; Mattes, 1995; Piombo and Nijzink, 2005; Stromback and Kaid, 2008; Southall and Daniel, 2009).

A third body of work which may remain largely invisible but has probably been far more influential than most academic analysis has come from professional bodies or analysts such as the Media Monitoring Project or Media Tenor South Africa, who often act as consultants to government or opposition parties or have been called on to analyze media coverage at contentious points such as during the Human Rights Commission's hearings into racism in the media.

A fourth influential body of work has come from commentators on the South African Truth and Reconciliation Commission and its work in South Africa but this work has in general dealt with issues of discourse or the findings or mechanisms of the commission rather than with the question of how many South Africans actually followed or were affected by the work of the commission (Doxtader et al., 2007; Krabill, 2001; Krog, 1998; McEachern, 2002; Posel and Simpson, 2002; Sanders, 2007).

Fifth, there is a body of work that works more closely with issues of textual analysis, drawing on disciplines such as literary or rhetorical analysis. The most famous or infamous example of this kind of analysis was probably an analysis produced for the Human Rights Commission by Claudia Braude on racism in the media that drew on notions of subliminal racism and a methodology of deep reading that exasperated many media professionals and academics (Berger, 2001; Glaser, 2000). While Braude's work may have drawn justifiable suspicion, there has been work that has looked at political rhetoric, in particular that of Mandela, Tutu and Mbeki, with more convincing results (Salazar, 2002).

There are many other important scholarly and institutional analyses to which such a short summary cannot do justice, such as Adrian Hadland's attempt to apply the Hallin-Mancini model of political-media systems to South Africa, or Jane Duncan's analysis of the ANC's changing media policy, or work by Rob Horwitz and others on media policy and the forces shaping it (Duncan, 2009; Duncan and Glenn, 2009; Hadland, 2007; Horwitz, 2001).

CITIZENS

Introduction

The world's image of South Africa was shaped by years of print news reports and photographs, and television footage of sustained mass resistance to the apartheid regime, culminating in the country's first democratic election and massive voter turnout captured in memorable images of long snakelike lines of voters patiently waiting to cast their ballots. The clear image is one of a politically conscious, highly engaged citizenry. The reality, however, is very different and has clear implications for the potential development of news media and political communication in the country.

First of all, South Africans have consistently displayed low levels of what political scientists call *cognitive engagement* (a combination of political discussion and political interest) (Dalton, 2009). Since 1995, no more than one-fifth of citizens have ever told interviewers they 'follow' politics always or most of the time, or that they 'frequently' discussed politics with friends or family. Measured in another way, no more than 30% has ever claimed to be 'very interested' in politics.[1]

Some of this may reflect a 'post-transition exhaustion' with politics, though the lack of pre-1994 national data prevents a firm conclusion. However, we do know that newspaper sales dropped dramatically after the 1994 election (Hadland, 2007). Survey evidence shows that South African's *virtual engagement* with the political system via the news media plunged dramatically after the country's first democratic election. For example, the percentage of citizens who reported listening to radio news every day or a few days a week declined from 86 to 73%. But unlike cognitive engagement, self-reported rates of radio news listenership recovered quickly, and television news viewership more slowly (87% now listen to radio news broadcasts on a regular basis, and 85% watch television news).

Newspaper readership of the broadsheets, however, still has yet to return to the levels recorded in 1994 (67% regularly read newspapers in 1994, compared to 54% today). Many newspaper readers have abandoned the traditional broadsheets, which carried at least a modicum of government and political affairs coverage in favor of a swath of new, far less politically oriented tabloid newspapers aimed at working-class black readers. The single most widely used newspaper during the 2009 election was *The Daily Sun* (read by 16% of all eligible voters).

Radio remains the most frequently used source of news in South Africa, though television has almost caught up. Yet regardless of which is ahead, most South Africans get their news about politics from the South African Broadcasting Corporation (SABC) particularly as it dominates news in indigenous languages. And while South Africa has a very high rate of mobile telephone penetration, access to the Internet remains the preserve of a very small minority: just 2% told interviewers in a 2009 post-election survey that they had used the Internet to follow news on the recent election campaign. Thus, South Africans' 'virtual engagement' with the political system remains one dominated by more passive forms of viewership and listenership (rather than the more active form of reading), and one dominated by news generated by state, rather than private news organizations.

Finally, South Africans' *physical engagement* with their political system has plummeted dramatically since 1994, though the most recent election saw a slight recovery. The easiest form of participation, voting, plunged 29 percentage points from 86% in 1994 to 57% in 2004, recovering slightly to 60% in 2009 (measured as a percentage of all eligible voters). The same trend characterizes attendance at campaign rallies (falling from 44% in 1994 to 23% in 2004, rebounding to 31% in 2009). But doing work for a political party, or donating campaign funds has continued to fall to microscopic levels (now at 4% and 1%, respectively).

While the trend appears more recent, it appears that the frequency with which South Africans contact their elected leaders or government representatives is increasing, though from very low levels (increasing from 16% in 2002 to 27% in 2008). Yet regardless of this trend, South Africans display some of the lowest levels of physical engagement with the political system in sub-Saharan Africa (at least among the 20 countries surveyed by Afrobarometer in 2008) (see Mattes, 2010, for a fuller discussion). Just 13 and 12% reported contact with national government officials or MPs, respectively. Yet these low levels of engagement should not be attributed to a lack of capacity: South Africans have the highest levels of

formal education and news media use across these countries. The real culprit is the country's almost pure form of party list proportional representation which provides party leaders with almost total leverage over elected officials and gives ordinary voters almost none, and thus offers few incentives (and many disincentives) for elected officials to go out of their way to find out ordinary people's problems, or for ordinary people to seek out their representatives to communicate their problems to them.

If South Africans believed that their complaints would receive attention, they would almost certainly communicate more often. When President Zuma opened a Presidential Hotline for complaints from the public, the line was overwhelmed with callers, some 27,000 on the first day of operation. Soon the hotline, touted as an example of accountability and a new ethos, was failing to answer most of its calls.

One area in which South Africans *are* on top of the log is in protest, much of it often violent. In 2008, one out of five respondents told surveyors that they had taken part in a protest or demonstration, and 6% said they had used force or violence. The Minister of Police, for example, reported that almost 6000 protest actions took place countrywide during the financial year 2004–05, of which 881 were illegal. Typically, complaints, mostly from the poorest places in the country, centered on 'service delivery', meaning the slow or flawed construction of cheap, subsidized housing, and sanitation, water and electricity grids. Protests usually involve petitions and marches, but when they turn violent also involve erecting barricades with objects like burning tires to close streets or even main roads or national highways and destroying municipal property. In related events, labor strikes have turned violent more frequently, with the most dramatic example being a 2006 nationwide strike by private security guards that led to the killing of some 69 people, either because they were suspected of not joining the strike or of being hired to replace the strikers, yet without any arrest of any of the murderers (Gordin and Momberg, 2007). In one sense, it is possible to interpret this as a simple return to the more familiar form of political expression learnt during the struggle against apartheid. However, whatever frustrations people may have about the scope and speed of welfare and infrastructural development, they are exacerbated by what people experience as marginalization at the hands of an indifferent, if not hostile set of elected representatives.

The spasm of violence directed against foreigners in May 2008 brought the issues of urban township discontent to national and international prominence. During a three-week period of xenophobic violence, some 100,000 foreigners (many of them asylum seekers, many without legal papers, but many legally in the country) and many locals were driven from their homes, 62 killed and the country's image shaken. While some media analysts attacked local tabloids for stereotyping foreigners as criminals, media coverage seemed, in the inquest afterward, to have played a relatively minor role in what happened and there is certainly evidence that the quality broadsheets and state media had neglected growing unrest among poorer South Africans about the pressures created by a large and growing number of foreigners in the country. Some evidence suggests that local instigators of violence, often alleged to be community leaders, were able to use modern communication forms, such as SMS messaging on cell phones, to mobilize informal networks. There is also some evidence from a government inquiry after the event that something of a copy-cat result was in evidence, where the broadcast of xenophobic violence in some areas helped set it off elsewhere (Glenn, 2008b).

Racial Difference and Political Communication

Given the history of apartheid and its enduring social and economic legacies, one could be excused for asking whether the trends described above adequately describe all South Africans. Table 39.1 displays the percentage differences across apartheid race categories. While there are some racial differences in the levels of cognitive engagement, the more important point is that they are relatively low across all groups. Conversely, virtual engagement, at least in terms of radio and television news, is very high across all groups, though there might be more important differences in the type of television that are masked by these numbers. Many whites, and to a lesser extent Indian and the 'colored' (mixed race in South African apartheid categories) people have shifted away from the SABC to digital satellite television – a move that could be attributed both to a dislike or distrust of the news they were and were not seeing and to a growing trend of opting out of local news for international entertainment and a typical post-modern fragmentation of television viewing.

The only real, major difference can be seen with respect to newspaper readership. Reflecting their economic and educational advantages, and their largely urban residence, rates of newspaper readership among whites (82%) and Indians (86%) almost double those of black (48%) and colored (57%) South Africans.

There are much larger differences in levels of physical engagement, especially in terms of

activities that involve collective action. Africans are three times more likely to have attended an election rally, and almost twice as likely to have gone to a community meeting or joined together with others to raise an issue as other South Africans. At first glance, it might seem that Africans violate this pattern with their higher rates of contacting elected leaders and government officials, but responses to follow-up questions show that Africans are far more likely to contact formal leaders as part of a group (rather by themselves) than other citizens are. Finally, the figures in Table 39.1 reveal that the waves of protest sweeping the country have been centered largely in the African community.

Yet the African electorate has also experience profound changes since 1994. Largely as a result of affirmative action in government hiring or black economic empowerment in the marketplace, the black middle class has grown exponentially; in relative terms moving from 1% of all blacks in 1990 to over 10%; in absolute terms, it is now as large as the white middle class. The rise of this new black elite, now labeled by the marketing industry as 'Black Diamonds', has been accompanied by a change in media style, ownership and concerns. The flagship English-medium broadcasting channels such as SABC 3 news and SAFM radio have catered increasingly to the black middle class while SABC 1 and SABC 2, carrying African language programming, have concentrated on the emergent urban working class.

Yet it is not always clear that the new black elite has any strong impulse to found new forms of political communication or media that would reflect that. Attempts to start new media aimed directly at the black male middle class have tended to founder. For example, *Bl!nk*, a magazine aimed at black men, influenced by African-American concerns about black manhood, lasted only a few issues, and other media oriented toward a black elite have faced similar problems. It seems that wealthier black South Africans follow mainstream western entertainment and advertising. The major success story of black media has been the tabloids and the growth of African language newspapers such as *Isolezwe*, but there are as yet no studies of their political importance.

At the same time, while the top one-fifth of the African population have made real progress, and the extension of welfare networks and a lengthy period of economic growth under the new ANC government has led to a reduction in some of the worst forms of poverty and brought millions into higher economic categories, other observers argue that the bottom two-fifths have moved backward in real terms (Leibbrandt et al., 2001). It is among this segment that political protest and violence

Table 39.1 Racial differences in political communication

	Black	White	Colored	Indian	Racial Differences
Cognitive engagement					
Interest in politics	**24**	(15)	17	20	9
Discusses politics	20	(15)	21	**23**	8
Interested in 2009 campaign	**22**	10	(8)	(8)	14
Virtual engagement					
Radio news	88	89	(80)	**93**	13
Television news	(82)	95	93	**97**	15
Newspaper	(48)	82	57	**86**	38
Physical engagement					
Voting					
Reported voting in 2004 last election	66	(50)	58	**73**	23
Campaign activity					
Attend campaign rally	**38**	10	11	(2)	36
Work for candidate/party	**4**	1	3	(0)	4
Contribute money	1	0	1	0	1
Communing					
Attend community meeting	**59**	(18)	34	39	41
Join with others to raise issue	**44**	(17)	24	20	27
Contacting					
Local councillor	**32**	(10)	18	12	22
MP	**14**	5	4	(1)	13
Government official	**16**	6	8	(3)	13
Religious leader	**27**	(14)	34	23	20
Traditional leader	**17**	(1)	(1)	4	16
Other local influential	**15**	10	13	(9)	6
Unconventional activity					
Protest	**22**	6	15	(3)	19
Use force/violence	**9**	2	2	(0)	9

Source: Round 4 Afrobarometer, South Africa survey 2008; South Africa National Election Study/ Comparative National Elections Project, 2009

have become a favored medium through which to communicated increasing frustration with the state of public services and the quality of political representation.

On the other end of the spectrum, white South Africans are characterized by the politics of withdrawal. By some estimates, over 800,000 whites, or some 20% of the pre-1990 population, have left the country, driven by concerns about crime and reduced life chances, and fearful about the future stability of the country (Johnson, 2009). For many whites, events in Zimbabwe – especially arbitrary land seizures – seemed an ominous warning about their own futures. Those who remain display high levels of news media use, but their rates of voting, campaign activity, community activity and contacting political parties are far lower than either Africans or colored citizens. It should also be noted that many whites living in South Africa are either foreign nationals or have dual citizenship, increasing the likelihood that many whites in the country will live in a sense as inner émigrés.

Colored and Indian South Africans were historically middle groups in the apartheid social rankings. But patterns of political engagement among the economically better-off Indian community tend to resemble those of whites. The colored community, on the other hand, seems to occupy a truly unique space between the high rates of community-centered participation of Africans and the levels of political withdrawal of whites and Indians. One often hears the complaint that while they were seen by whites as 'too black' under apartheid, colored people are now seen by the majority African population as 'not black enough'. While many of the ANC's leading figures came from both these communities, tensions have surfaced over time, particularly between African and colored voters or factions in the Western Cape Province. The ANC's loss of the city of Cape Town in 2005 and the larger province in the 2009 elections has to be seen primarily as the result of the disillusionment of working-class colored voters in the Western Cape, where this group represents a majority of all voters.

The medium that represented this disillusionment most powerfully was the *Daily Voice*, a new tabloid aimed at colored voters (Glenn and Knaggs, 2008). While the paper eschewed any overt political role, at one point fairly typically treating all the local political figures as Smurfs, its toughest criticisms were aimed at the ANC Mayor of Cape Town mayor, Nomaindia Mfeketo and her controversial advisor, Blackman Ngoro, who had written on his website in 2005 that Africans were 'culturally superior' to coloreds, who would 'die a drunken death' if they did not undergo ideological transformation. Ngoro was suspended and eventually fired, partly a result of the *Daily Voice's* aggressive campaign against him. The Irish editor of the paper, Karl Brophy, recalls that the journalists of his paper received a heroes' welcome in a local night club in Cape Town, when the DJ introduced them, suggesting that at least in this case the aggressive stance of the tabloid in favor of its community was strongly appreciated.

Though South Africans may have turned violently against the government in power, evidence suggests that South Africans have come to accept a political system and peaceful change of government through the ballot box. This may be, to some extent, because it might be difficult to determine what exactly the major electoral ideological differences between political parties are in terms of economic and political policy, so that much of the

debate in recent elections has focused on questions of moral fitness to govern, the character of opposing political leaders and the dangers of one party dominance.

In 1994, it is widely argued that the final election results in Kwa-Zulu Natal were not an accurate reflection of the votes cast, but a political compromise based on the intransigence of Inkatha Freedom Party leader Buthelezi. In 2009, the IFP lost the election to the ANC in Kwa-Zulu Natal, while the ANC lost the Western Cape to the Democratic Alliance, and COPE, a new party arising out of a split in the ANC moved to becoming the official opposition in five provinces. All of these results were accepted without major complaints or outbreaks of violence and this is, given South Africa's previous history and many gloomy predictions of the likelihood of ongoing sectarian violence, a significant achievement.

It does seem that the inclusive style of government practiced by Nelson Mandela during his administration did manage to reduce the political tension in the country more generally, but it may also be that some media programs, such as Asikhulume, aimed explicitly at encouraging debate, have helped. In any event, it is worth recording that while citizens have turned violently against the state and party officials in power, they have been less likely to turn on political opponents.

THE ROLE OF THE MEDIA

Broadcast News

Partly because of the need to broadcast in 11 official languages in radio and on television, the South African Broadcasting Corporation (SABC), with an estimated staff of close to 1000 in its news divisions, is one of the world's largest news-gathering organizations. Because there have been few real news alternatives for African language speakers, the SABC plays a huge role in forming the political perceptions of around four out of every five South Africans. Not surprisingly, the SABC has been at the center of passionate partisan and ideological clashes, and experienced intense internal conflict over the past two decades.

Because the SABC had been so blatantly a tool of state propaganda during apartheid, a strong coalition of domestic and international media experts worked to bring best modern practice to bear, especially regarding political coverage during elections, to ensure that it did not turn into a mouthpiece for the new government (Horwitz, 2001). Two of the positive outcomes were the appointment of an ostensibly independent SABC Board to control the SABC and of an Independent

Broadcasting Authority (IBA) that started operation in 1994 to ensure that broadcasting did not become a fief of the political party in control. (In 2000, the IBA was merged into the Independent Communications Authority of South Africa [ICASA] with the new body assuming control of broadcasting and telecommunications.)

For a time, the new SABC appeared to approach the ideals of an independent public broadcaster but political interference from the president's office in the selection of later SABC boards and a series of incidents and high profile resignations have dented the SABC's credibility as an independent news source. For much of the Mbeki presidency it was widely seen by most independent analysts to exude a strong pro-ANC bias, especially since the news department came under the control of former ANC propagandist Snuki Zikalala. Several incidents drew particular condemnation: the non-coverage of the booing of Deputy President Phumzile Mlambo-Ngcuka at a rally (Mofokeng, 2005); the 'blacklisting' of political commentators who took a line contrary to the SABC's preferences (FXI, 2006) and the lengthy coverage of the ANC's election manifesto launch in January 2009, which escaped the restrictions of election coverage rulings by occurring before the election campaign had officially started.

In spite of the arguments about the manifesto coverage in 2009, the rift within the ANC caused by the unprecedented, successful 2008 challenge of President Thabo Mbeki by Jacob Zuma for party leadership (after Mbeki had fired Zuma for corruption in 2005) arguably led to more balanced news coverage of the 2009 general election by the SABC. The new party COPE received fairly extensive coverage, with the ANC complaining at points that it was receiving far more coverage from the SABC than was warranted and some in the ANC calling for the removal of Zikalala, seen as a pro-Mbeki figure secretly favoring COPE.

The SABC has also come under fire for its manipulation of the news agenda and ignoring social, economic and political problems embarrassing to the ruling party. For instance, some argue that the emphasis on corporate profitability and on supporting the government's privatization campaigns have led it to ignore certain audiences and under-report the extent and legitimacy of anti-privatization campaigns and service delivery protests (Duncan, 2005). The SABC has also been seen to soft-pedal crime coverage in South Africa, especially murder or rape. In a country with 50 murders a day, the SABC 3 evening news, according to Media Tenor figures for 2006, covered murder on average once a week.

A major problem for the SABC in terms of revenue and, arguably, ideology was that it lost its monopoly on domestic television broadcast news. While the private subscription channel M-Net, launched in 1986 carried a minimum of news, its one-hour weekly investigative news show *Carte Blanche*, based on the American *60 Minutes*, remained influential, yet scarcely dented nightly news viewing. But in 1998, a broadcasting license was granted to e-tv, a new, privately owned television channel. E-tv news began to win over many viewers, particularly whites who were dissatisfied at the SABC's failure to cover the disputed Zimbabwean elections in 2000 and the seizures of white farmers' land as thoroughly as e-tv was doing.

Broadcasting policy decisions may have changed the political communication significantly, particularly in the decision to leave the state broadcaster largely reliant on advertising revenue and to opt for national rather than local independent television stations, leaving South Africa without local television networks or news services (Duncan and Glenn, 2009). This has reinforced a sense of politics as an elite national discourse and weakened the importance of local and provincial government at the expense of national government (Simeon and Murray, 2001). Had there been provincially based television news services, local political figures and local and regional politics and investigations might have had different importance and weight. In reality, the ANC goes into elections without even indicating who the provincial premier will be after the election – the equivalent of the Democrats or Republicans asking voters in California or New York to vote for them without indicating who their candidate for governor will be.

If local television news tends, as a host of American academic studies suggests, to emphasize violent crime and imaginary dangers (Gerbner and Gross, 1976; Gross and Aday, 2003; Kang, 2005), then South Africa, with a violent crime rate some 8 to 10 times greater than that in the USA, might well have found local news making crime a hot political issue faster than happened in South Africa, where the national broadcaster has certainly shown great restraint. Violent local protests against service delivery would probably also have received more attention and had more effect on local news stations.

While the new SABC is nominally a national broadcaster with government funding, it has become more reliant on advertising for the major part of its revenue, and thus also has to attempt to meet commercial imperatives. In such an environment, there is a tension between meeting the pressures (real or perceived) from political masters, on the one hand, and providing news that is seen as ideologically hostile and drives away lucrative audiences, on the other. Thus, armed with increasingly sophisticated market research, news organizations may unconsciously or consciously try and to please or meet the expectations of a particular viewer group, particularly as advertisers are also basing their choice of channels on the same market research and place their advertisements where wealthier consumers might see them.

One important consequence of the increased competition from e-tv, which aired its evening television news an hour earlier than the SABC, was that the SABC moved its flagship SABC3 news broadcast to the same time slot, but also hired e-tv's news producer Jimi Matthews. Ironically, while the old SABC television news programs had been structured along racial lines, apartheid political concerns ensured that all South Africans were given the *same* version of the news as a form of censorship. And during the early days of the new SABC and under the leadership of Allister Sparks, conscious steps were taken to ensure a common approach to news. Under Matthews, however, the SABC moved to a balkanized or federalized approach where news agendas are differentiated along language and even commercial grounds. Studies have found, for example, significant differences between English and Nguni service coverage of developments in Zimbabwe, or English and Zulu coverage of Jacob Zuma during his 2007 rape trial. English-language television broadcasts on the SABC, in line with English print media and international media, framed Zimbabwe and, by implication, Africa more generally, as a realm or zone of disorder, while the SABC Zulu and Xhosa broadcasts took it for granted that Zimbabwe and, by extension, Africa more generally, was a realm of order threatened by neo-colonial interventions such as the attempted coup planned for Equatorial Guinea (Glenn, 2005). Thus, it is less likely now than under apartheid that citizens of different races or language groups watch or share the same news. Elihu Katz (1996) has warned, drawing on the example of Israel, of the dangers for citizenship of having a segmented fragmented news media landscape, particularly for television news. In South Africa the evidence suggests that white and black South Africans get very different pictures of, say, Robert Mugabe, Zimbabwean President, and his role in and effect on his country. Given how strongly the resonances of Zimbabwean experience are felt in South Africa, the SABC, by segregating views according to the channels watched, failed to try to forge a common understanding on, or even debate about, Zimbabwe.

Political broadcasts are much more scrupulously monitored and political coverage is probably fairer during election campaigns than at other times as it is based on the number of candidates fielded. During elections, the ANC thus receives a smaller share of coverage from the SABC than its share of the actual vote. During the 2004 campaign, e-tv went a step beyond the public broadcaster by providing free airtime to all political parties with parliamentary representation to present their election manifestos.

There have been very few studies of the SABC's African language radio stations, though they attract far more viewers than most commercial radio stations. More interest has been given to talk radio because while talk radio in the USA is seen largely as a right-wing phenomenon, in the last days of the apartheid regime, and in the early 1990s, talk radio on private radio stations such as Radio 702 and on the SABC's SAFM became a space for inter-racial discussion and questioning of the status quo. The private talk stations have increasingly become spaces for anti-government voices to be heard though they are far from being univocal right-wing or whites-only spaces.

The SABC has, for most of the period, while increasing its footprint and attracting new black viewers, lost former viewers, esteem and money and become an institution that seems to be in permanent crisis. Yet regardless of this, or elite criticism of the SABC, public opinion data tells a rather different story about how broadcast journalism is seen by ordinary people. Since the relevant questions have been asked, the SABC has been the most trusted national institution in South Africa (with levels of trust above 60% between 2000 and 2009), followed closely by e-tv (with e-tv overtaking SABC in the most recent 2009 survey – 67% to 63% for SABC – which suggests that the criticisms of the SABC have had some effect). Both consistently score higher than newspapers, as well as other institutions such as the courts, policy and army.

Print

Before the end of apartheid, South African news print media were divided into sharply opposing camps. On the one hand, most of the Afrikaans-medium press (along with the SABC) sought to justify, for an internal white audience in particular, the apartheid system. Most of the white, liberal English-medium press, usually linked to business interests, and some private radio stations such as Radio 702 opposed the apartheid regime and the National Party government, though they may have been uncertain as to what alternatives they supported. The third important grouping was a group of black-owned papers which strongly and vociferously opposed apartheid, ranging from *The Sowetan* to an alternative, radical press usually funded by foreign donors. These latter two groups, however, were often subjected to heavy censorship and draconian media restrictions, even closure, designed by the National Party government to prevent alternative, critical debates and news from reaching either white or black South Africans.

Two important trends mark the change from the old to new South Africa in print media. First, the commercial, formerly white English and Afrikaans print media have appeared to move closer to each other ideologically, providing increasingly critical assessments of the performance of the ANC government. Second, the old apartheid-era, left-wing alternative papers such as *South, New Nation, Grassroots, Vrye Weekblad* (along with the more commercial *Weekly Mail,* now *Mail and Guardian*) which had been voices of anti-government, investigative journalism had operated largely on the basis of foreign funding (Opatrny, 2006; Switzer and Adhikari, 2000). Once a new democratically elected government took power, foreign donors withdrew from this area of funding support and these publications failed to cope. From one perspective, the editors of these papers failed to read the mood and interests of their readers and build a strong basis for survival. Others, however, argue that they fell victims to what Robert Horwitz called the 'commercial juggernaut' of a well-established commercial press, with sophisticated marketing and distribution networks, that has taken a strong stance to inhibit any profound project of social transformation.

Have the print media changed significantly since liberation? At various points, ANC leaders from Mandela on have railed against what they characterized as unreformed white media, and the Human Rights Commission, in its hearings into media complicity in racist practices, followed this line of argument. The later careers of journalists who worked in these alternative publications gives support for arguing both that the alternative press represented radical views out of touch with general citizens or that they were politically restrained by commercial pressures. Ryland Fisher, a former journalist on *Grassroots*, rose to become editor of the country's oldest newspaper, the *Cape Times* but was moved out after a few years during which the paper's circulation plummeted – in part, critics alleged, because Fisher was pushing a political line that many of the paper's traditional readers disliked. From the point of view of Fisher and his supporters, it was his refusal to follow the commercial logic of the Independent Group and their marketing strategies that led to his removal. The *Mail and Guardian* survived, but as a paper highly critical of the new government, though scarcely a paper supporting the official opposition, the white-dominated Democratic Alliance.

As a result of the convergence of the former white English and Afrikaans media and the disappearance of a radical left-wing press, there is, in effect, no daily newspaper that regularly conveys and supports government policies. While the ANC toyed with ideas of starting its own newspaper, it eventually opted for an online news site, *ANC Today,* which became a favorite vehicle for Mandela's successor, Thabo Mbeki to disseminate party positions as well as his own personal, often highly idiosyncratic views on topics such as HIV/AIDS. South Africa must be one of the few countries in the past decades where an acting president took such an active part in writing large parts of the party's weekly political communication.

The fairly strong critiques of the ANC in most of the print media have remained in spite of ownership of many print media houses passing from white into black control, with many of the latter prominent ANC members. The broadsheets produced by them have also become dependant on increasingly large numbers of black readers. This might seem to destroy the credibility of any analysis that argues that ownership controls media content, but the political economy school has found ways of trying to salvage some coherence by arguing for class and economic interests of the owners as key determinants (Berger, 2002; Berger, 2004; Tomaselli, 2004). These arguments tend, however, to neglect crucial differences in coverage and political stance between newspapers in the same group produced for different audiences.

A paradigm example of the difficulty of assigning political allegiance or content to the role of the owners can be seen in the role and importance of the political cartoonist Zapiro (Jonathan Shapiro). A former struggle activist with strong ANC sympathies, Zapiro's work has consistently excoriated the governing party on matters ranging from scandal and corruption to President Thabo Mbeki's theories and policies on HIV/AIDS. He is currently being sued by current President Jacob Zuma for defamation after the publication of hostile cartoons about Zuma during the latter's rape trial. He has been named Journalist of the Year in South Africa because of his influence and is arguably the most important single media producer in the post-apartheid period. He publishes his work in the *Sowetan, Mail and Guardian* and *Sunday Times,* three of the country's most influential papers, but all belonging to different media groups, which suggests that his political sensibilities are shared quite widely across the political spectrum, whatever the ownership or racial grouping of readers.

A third major trend in print media in the post-apartheid era has been the rise of the tabloid press, which has now outstripped older papers in terms of sales and readership. The most significant of these is the *Daily Sun,* started by a veteran white Afrikaner journalist, Deon du Plessis in collaboration with the former pro-apartheid media group Naspers. Many politically progressive critics have seen the *Sun* and other tabloids as a retrograde development (Glenn and Knaggs, 2008), but this misses the ways in which Du Plessis and his team drew on the experience of tabloids in other developing countries, particularly India, to find ways of reaching new readers for whom they became an indispensable guide to living in and coping with the new South Africa (Jones et al., 2008; Wasserman and du Bois, 2006). While these papers have not, for the most part, involved themselves directly with party political or electoral issues, their potential influence should not be underestimated because they seem to enjoy the trust and interest of their readers.

New Media

Given the extent of the digital divide and the importance of English on new media forms such as the Internet, the obvious conclusion is that new media have predominantly been a space for a privileged minority to engage in political debates and discussions. For many whites, writing in English or Afrikaans, the Internet provided a space where they were able to escape public media spaces and indulge either in nostalgia for an old South Africa, or rail against the new. President Mbeki on several occasions made public the contents of emails circulating among white South Africans to complain about resistance to change and the evidence of lingering racism.

Yet it may be that the two most interesting uses of new media for political communication have not been by white South Africans but by the ANC in official guise (ANC Today – http://www.anc.org.za/) or the Friends of Jacob Zuma website (http://www.friendsofjz.co.za/) set up by Zuma supporters to raise money for him and rally support after his removal from the office of deputy president. The former site acted as the ANC's attempt to set the agenda for political coverage but also reacted against what it saw as unfair coverage from mainstream media. The latter became a virtual rallying point for Zuma supporters and may have played an important role in helping an anti-Mbeki coalition to form within the ANC, particularly during Zuma's rape trial when the site carried substantive reports that were often at odds with what mainstream media were reporting.

Conclusion

How well, then, have the media performed in the new South Africa, and what role will they come to play? While Mandela and other railed against an unreconstructed white press, those opposed to the ANC, like former DA leader Tony Leon, argue, with some force, that many reporters in South Africa, fearful of appearing racist or questioning any aspects of the new democracy, abandoned a proper Fourth Estate role as skeptical interrogators of government and turned themselves into 'praise-singers' of the new government and overlooked major flaws and problems in the Mandela presidency in particular (Leon, 2008). Others argue that this trend already started during the struggle, where the liberal press began to ignore human rights violations by the ANC, or justify them as defensive reactions to provocations by apartheid security forces or allied organizations such as the Inkatha Freedom Party (Wentzel, 1995; Jeffery, 2009)

There is no doubt some truth in all these claims and perceptions. The media have by turns probably been too servile and too critical. Yet there have been moments where the print media and particularly the independent media, have performed very well. Before and during the Polokwane conference that led to the rise of Jacob Zuma to the presidency of the ANC and the supplanting of Thabo Mbeki, the media played a strong and robust role in reflecting the debates and arguments from both camps.

Media Organizations

Our brief, descriptive tour of the importance of South African media in political communication would be incomplete without at least some mention of the fact that the country is characterized by a relatively dense web of civil society organizations, many of which are actively involved in debate about press freedom and partisan balance, and a few are exclusively devoted to these issues, such as the Institute for the Advancement of Journalism and the Freedom of Expression Institute.

While the South African constitution protects the freedom of speech and media, the new government has not been above trying to rein in what it saw as an overly hostile, irresponsible press. It has introduced various pieces of legislation or other regulations governing publication, and other legislation attempting to define and outlaw hate speech in overly broad terms. These attempts have usually been successfully countered by South Africa's vigilant civil society, including organizations such as the South African Freedom of Expression Institute (Duncan, 2008), usually through warnings of court challenges to their constitutionality. The most recent and serious attempt to control the media, the Protection of Information Bill, met strong media and civil society opposition and is likely to face a Constitutional Court challenge.

Foreign Media in South Africa

Finally, an important feature of the South African media landscape is its sensitivity to international news media. The National Party's attempts to manipulate news media coverage of apartheid were not only limited to South Africa. The 'Information Scandal' of the mid 1970s revealed that it had tried to buy a number of newspapers around the world, including the *The Washington Times,* in order to increase favorable international coverage. This attempt may have failed but it revealed an ongoing trend: the extent to which elite domestic debates were increasingly mediated by sensitivity to international opinion of South Africa. Thus, South African media coverage of major domestic events often includes coverage of how the rest of the world has covered those very same events, or what we might call 'media triangulation'.

While this sensitivity might be unsurprising for a country that depends heavily on foreign investment, it also has deeper psychological roots. While the ANC enjoyed favorable coverage from the liberal or left-wing international media during the last years of its struggle against apartheid as well as during the Mandela government, Thabo Mbeki's AIDS denialism did much to change that (Power, 2003). One of the key developments in the post-apartheid period has been the way in which international media have treated Africa and South Africa more harshly (Schraeder and Endless, 1998). After Rwanda and Darfur, and the more recent violence in Zimbabwe and Kenya, international Afro-pessimism has revived and in many journalistic accounts, the question about South Africa is whether it can be an exception to the rule, or misrule (Guest, 2004).

The ANC certainly has showed itself more sensitive, on many occasions, to international news stories about the country than to internal criticisms. Thus, when the BBC reported on the high rates of crime in the country, or André Brink wrote about the 'tsunami of crime' in *Le Monde,* the government felt compelled to respond at length, while the internal criticisms tended to be ignored. Currently, international media attention tends to focus on the high crime rate in South Africa and the dangers this poses for foreign teams and tourists, showing that this has become the dominant image of South Africa in foreign media perceptions.

POLITICAL PARTIES

Political parties are an essential part of political communications process, recruiting the country's future leaders, aggregating voter preferences, articulating interests, presenting alternative ideas of how the country should be governed and mobilizing mass political participation. Since 1990, South Africa's parties, particularly opposition parties, have revealed their deficiencies both in terms of resources as well as skills and imagination. These problems have been exacerbated, however, by a regulatory framework that has implicitly created a 'home field advantage' for the governing party.

Any analysis of the country's party system must proceed from the fact that just two parties that functioned under the apartheid political system remain in the current democratic system: the official opposition Democratic Alliance (which can be directly traced back to the liberal Democratic Party, and before that the Progressive Federal Party) and the Inkatha Freedom Party, which governed the old KwaZulu homeland. Three current parties have their origins in the anti-apartheid struggle: the governing African National Congress, the Pan Africanist Congress and the Azanian People's Organization. All other parties have been formed since 1994.

Thus, virtually all of the country's political parties have been on various learning curves attempting to master the arts of democratic communication and organization. The former liberation organizations have also faced the task of having to *un*learn many of the habits of secrecy, the cult of the leader, strict discipline, intolerance of dissent and loyalty to comrades developed during their years in exile (Glenn, 2008a).

Based largely on the credit in earned by leading the struggle to overthrow apartheid, as well as an innovative and forward looking campaign, the ANC won the founding 1994 election with a resounding 62% of the vote. And based at least partly on considerable public satisfaction with its delivery of infrastructure and development, it steadily increased its proportion of the popular vote over the next two elections to 66% in 1999, and 69% in 2004, with a slight regression in 2009 to just under 66%. Yet as we have already seen, the increasing ANC vote totals between 1994 and 2004 occurred alongside a simultaneous counter trend of rapidly declining voter turnout. One of the main reasons behind declining participation and increasing ANC dominance has been that the country's political parties – particularly the opposition parties, have failed to develop into effective vote-gathering machines.

In terms of voter identification with political parties, the ANC has indeed maintained a decisive advantage over the opposition parties in terms of partisan identification. However, the absolute level of voter identification with the ANC has never been overwhelming. Indeed there has been at any given time a substantial share of the electorate with no strong ties to any political party. But while there is no evidence of any secular increase in identification with the ANC, there seems to have been – with some fluctuation – a steady decrease over time in identification with opposition parties. This suggests that as voters moved away from opposition parties such as the NP, they move into the independent column rather than to the ANC.

Previous statistical analyses of the factors affecting South Africans' voting choices have consistently identified the crucial role of voters' images of whether a given party is inclusive, representing all South Africans, or exclusive, representing one group to the exclusion of others (Ferree, 2010; Schulz-Herzenberg, 2009; Mattes, 1995; Mattes and Piombo, 2001). In contrast to the usual expectations advanced by analysts of elections in divided societies (for example, Horowitz, 1986), few voters are attracted to a party because they see it as representing their group to the exclusion of others. On the contrary, most voters are repelled away from parties with such an image.

This is not good news for South Africa's opposition parties, because no opposition party has ever been able to convince a majority, or even substantial minority of voters that they are inclusive, representing the interests of all. Opposition parties enjoy low levels of voter trust. Opposition parties have failed to create the crucial image of inclusiveness. Perhaps most telling is the fact that opposition parties enjoy low levels of voter visibility. Only small minorities tell survey researchers that that any opposition party represents the 'interests of one group only'. The most frequent answer is for people to say they 'haven't heard enough' to know who an opposition party represents.

Few opposition parties give evidence of a well-thought out strategy to court voters on a continuous basis by using their parliamentary platform or other events as opportunities to generate free media publicity between elections. Most wait and mount their campaign in the six to eight weeks leading up to the election, at which point it is far too late to shape or reshape your public image in any significant way.

Such asymmetries occur not only in how parties present themselves to the voters, but are also manifest in terms of their abilities to reach voters. During the 2009 election, the ANC was able to attract 25% of the electorate to one of its campaign rallies, eight times as many as its nearest competitors the DA and COPE. The governing party contacted one out every five eligible voters (20%), three-quarters of these in person, compared to 9% and 8%, respectively for the DA and COPE. But overall, just 25% of all voters were

contacted by any political party. When compared to other post-election surveys carried out by the Comparative National Elections Project, this puts South Africa slightly above recent campaigns in places like Mexico (18%), Indonesia (15%) or Bulgaria (12%), but far lower than Mozambique (36%), Taiwan (41%), Hungary (61%) or the USA (72%). These data also reveal that party activities remain firmly within the ambit of traditional face-to-face politics. Mass direct mailing and telephone canvassing, let alone more technologically intensive methods such as SMS or email, are almost completely absent from the repertoire of South Africa's political parties.

Much of this is a function of ill-considered strategy and lack of imagination. But much of it is also due to a series of rules that systematically work against the interests of opposition parties. First, television advertising is one of the quickest ways that an opposition party, particularly a new one, could build an image in the public mind. Yet because many media advisors had warned against American-style television-based electoral campaigning out of a fear that this would mean domination of politics by moneyed interests, television election advertising was not allowed in South Africa between 1994 and 2008 (with the exception of short 'public election broadcasts', which were allocated based on existing legislative representation and the number of candidates standing). The broadcast regulatory body, ICASA, surprisingly reversed itself ahead of the 2009 campaign, promulgating new regulations that gave all parties free television space to broadcast their own advertisements, and distributed that space not according to legislative seats but on the basis of the number of candidates fielded. Both of these seemed (to anybody suspiciously minded) as though they may have been tailored to assist COPE, the new breakaway party from the ANC. However, because these new rules came into effect very late in the day, and because the actual free time was allocated to parties even later, many smaller parties were never in a position to produce the advertisements and take advantage of this new opportunity.

Second, radio and newsprint advertising is relatively expensive, and few opposition parties have the financial means to run sustained advertising campaigns. Third, while public funding has been available to political parties since 1997, the lion's share of this money (90%) is allocated to parties based on their national and provincial legislative representation. Ten percent of the fund is divided among the provincial legislatures, depending on their size, and then given equally to each party represented in that assembly. All of this means that the ruling ANC receives the great proportion of these public funds.

Public funds, moreover, cover only a small share of all campaign expenses. In 1999, for example, parties spent an estimated R300 to R500 million during the campaign, with only R53 million coming from the public purse. Political parties are not required to disclose any funds donated by private sources, but it is widely believed that the ANC (due to its control over public policy and state contracts) and the DA (due to its historical links with the business community) receive far more private donations than any other political party. Certainly, only the ANC and to a lesser extent DA are able to employ professional, permanent staff for things like fundraising, market research, policy development or publicity. And in the 2004 campaign, these two parties dominated the rest across all forms of advertising media, with the ANC outpacing the DA in spending on paid outdoor advertising (such as billboards, murals and ads on taxis) by R12 million to just R200,000, and in print advertising by R3.8 million to R800,000. Yet the DA actually purchased more radio time than the ANC by R5.9 million to R4.8 million. Other opposition parties were largely restricted to a heavy reliance on streetside posters that could contain only very simple messages and captions.

Thus, while the country now has competent, effective and largely autonomous electoral machinery, the institutionalization of South Africa's elections will remain incomplete until voters are presented with at least two or more effective party organizations that are able to provide voters with a visible and credible choice and reason to vote.

CONCLUSION

These impressions might lead one to conclude that South Africa is on the path of what Hallin and Mancini characterize as the 'liberal' drift toward an apolitical press and media, driven by professional standards, focused on issues rather than any deep-seated and ideological rivalries (Hallin and Mancini, 2004). One could adduce in support of this that there have been decreasing rates of electoral participation and of party membership during the period to argue that much of the heat has gone out of political partisanship in post-apartheid South Africa. This is part of the truth about political communication in the new South Africa, but it is only part of the truth. In fact, Adrian Hadland, in the most significant attempt to apply the Hallin-Mancini model in an examination of South African print media post-1994, concluded that South Africa was closer to the Polarized Pluralist model than the Liberal or Democratic Corporatist model,

while sharing significant features with the latter two (Hadland, 2007). It may be safest to conclude that South Africa in its mix of forms of political communication makes any imported model an imperfect fit.

NOTE

1 The data reported here on citizen engagement, trust and participation is available upon request from the authors.

REFERENCES

Berger, G. (2001) 'Problematising Race for Journalists: Critical Reflections on the South African Human Rights Commission Inquiry into Media Racism', *Critical Arts: A South-North Journal of Cultural and Media Studies*, 15(1–2): 69–96.

Berger, G. (2002) 'Theorizing the Media-Democracy Relationship in Southern Africa', *Gazette*, 64(1): 21–45.

Berger, G. (2004) 'More Media for Southern Africa? The Place of Politics, Economics and Convergence in Developing Media Density', *Critical Arts: A South-North Journal of Cultural and Media Studies*, 18(1): 42–75.

Dalton, R. (2009) *Citizen Politics: Public Opinion and Political Parties in Advanced Industrial Democracies*. 5th edn. Washington, DC: Sage.

Doxtader, E., Salazar, P. J. and Institute For Justice and Reconciliation (South Africa) (2007) *Truth and Reconciliation in South Africa: The Fundamental Documents*. Claremont, South Africa: New Africa Books.

Duncan, J. (2001) *Broadcasting and the National Question: South African Broadcast Media in an Age of Neo-Liberalism*. Johannesburg: Freedom of Expression Institute.

Duncan, J. (2005) 'Beyond State and First Economy', *Rhodes Journalism Review*, 25: 40–1.

Duncan, J. (2008) 'Executive Overstretch: South African Broadcasting Independence and Accountability Under Thabo Mbeki', *Communicatio: South African Journal for Communication Theory and Research*, 34(1): 21–52.

Duncan, J. (2009) 'The Uses and Abuses of Political Economy: The ANC's Media Policy', *Transformation: Critical Perspectives on Southern Africa*, 70: 1–30.

Duncan, J. and Glenn, I. (2009) 'Television Policy and Practice in South Africa Since 1990', in D. Moyo, and W. Chuma (eds.), *Media Policy in a Changing Southern Africa: Critical Reflections on Media Reforms in the Global Age*. Pretoria: Unisa Press. pp. 51–90.

Ferree, K. (2010) *Framing the Race in South Africa: The Political Origins of Racial Census Elections*. Cambridge: Cambridge University Press.

FXI (2006) 'SABC 'Blacklisting' Report'.

Gerbner, G. and Gross, L. (1976) 'Living with Television: The Violence Profile', *Journal of Communication*, 26(2): 172–94.

Glaser, D. (2000) 'The Media Inquiry Reports of the South African Human Rights Commission: A Critique', *African Affairs (London)*, 99(396): 373–93.

Glenn, I. (2005) 'Racial News? How Did SABC 1 Nguni News and SABC3 English News Cover Zimbabwe in 2004?', in D. P. Conradie (ed.), *Communication Science in South Africa: Contemporary Issues. Proceedings of the 2005 Annual Conference of the South African Communication Association.* Cape Town: Juta. pp. 136–49.

Glenn, I. (2008a) 'Cryptic Rhetoric: The ANC and Anti-Americanization', *Safundi*, 9(1): 69–79.

Glenn, I. (2008b) 'The Watchdog That Never Barked', *Rhodes Journalism Review*, 28: 18–20.

Glenn, I. and Knaggs, A. (2008) 'Field Theory and Tabloids', in A. Hadland, E. Louw, S. Sesanti and H. Wasserman (eds.), *At the End of the Rainbow: Power, Politics and Identity in Post-Apartheid South African Media.* Cape Town: HSRC Press. pp. 104–23.

Gordin, J. and Momberg, E. (2007) 'Security Guards Died Like Dogs. So Who Cares?', *Sunday Independent*, 3 June: p. 1.

Greenberg, S. B. (2009) *Dispatches From the War Room : In the Trenches With Five Extraordinary Leaders.* New York: Thomas Dunne Books/St. Martin's Press.

Gross, K. and Aday, S. (2003) 'The Scary World in Your Living Room and on Your Neighborhood: Using Local Broadcast News, Neighborhood Crime Rates, and Personal Experience to Test Agenda Setting and Cultivation Hypotheses', *Journal of Communication*, 53(3): 411–26.

Guest, R. (2004) *The Shackled Continent: Africa's Past, Present and Future.* London: Macmillan.

Hadland, A. (2007) 'The South African Print Media, 1994–2004: An Application and Critique of Comparative Media Systems Theory', Ph.D dissertation, Centre For Film and Media Studies. University of Cape Town.

Hallin, D. C. and Mancini, P. (2004) *Comparing Media Systems: Three Models of Media and Politics.* Cambridge: Cambridge University Press.

Hofmeyr, J. and Rice, B. (2000) *Commitment-Led Marketing.* New York: Wiley.

Horwitz, R. B. (2001) *Communication and Democratic Reform in South Africa.* Cambridge: Cambridge University Press.

Horowitz, D. (1986) *Ethnic Groups in Conflict.* Berkeley, CA: University of California Press.

Jeffery, A. (2009) *People's War: New Light On the Struggle for South Africa.* Johannesburg: Jonathan Ball Publishers.

Johnson, S. (2009) 'Fleeing from South Africa', *Newsweek*, 14 February.

Jones, N., Vanderhaegen, Y. and Viney, D. (2008) 'The Daily Sun and Post-Apartheid Identity', in A. Hadland, E. Louw, S. Sesanti and H. Wasserman (eds.), *Power, Politics and Identity in South African Media.* Johannesburg: HSRC Press. pp. 167–83.

Kang, J. (2005) 'Trojan Horses of Race', *Harvard Law Review*, 118(5): 1489–593.

Katz, E. (1996) 'And Deliver us from Segmentation', *The Annals of the American Academy of Political and Social Science*, 546(1): 22–33.

Krabill, R. (2001) 'Symbiosis: Mass Media and the Truth and Reconciliation Commission of South Africa', *Media Culture and Society*, 23(5): 567–85.

Krog, A. (1998) *Country of my Skull.* Johannesburg: Random House.

Leibbrandt, M., Poswell, L., Naidoo, P., Welch, M. and Woolard, I. (2001) 'Measuring Recent Changes in South African Inequality and Poverty Using 1996 and 2001 Census Data', Center for Social Science Research, University of Capetown Working Paper No. 84.

Leon, T. (2008) *On the Contrary.* Johannesburg: Jonathan Ball.

Mattes, R. B. (1995) *The Election Book: Judgement and Choice in South Africa's 1994 Election.* Capetown: IDASA.

Mattes, R. B. (2010) 'Overview: Controlling Power–Africans Views on Governance, Citizenship and Accountability', in M. Claasen and C. Alpin-Lardies (eds.), *Social Accountability in Africa: Practitioners' Experiences and Lessons.* Johannesburg: Affiliated Network for Social Accountability. pp. 14–30.

Mattes, R. and Piombo, J. (2001) 'Opposition Parties and the Voters in South Africa's General Election of 1999', *Democratization*, 8(3): 101–28.

Mayher, A. and Mcdonald, D. A. (2007) 'The Print Media in South Africa: Paving the Way For "Privatization"', *Review of African Political Economy*, 34(113): 443–60.

Mceachern, C. (2002) *Narratives of Nation Media, Memory and Representation in the Making of the New South Africa.* New York: Nova Science Publishers, Inc.

Mofokeng, M. (2005) 'How a Lone Cameraman 'Dented' SABC's Credibility', *Mail and Guardian Online*, 19 August, http://www.mg.co.za/article/2005–08–19-how-a-lone-cameraman-dented-sabcs-credibility

Opatrny, L. (2006) 'The Post-1990 Demize of The Alternative Press', *Centre For Film and Media Studies.* MA dissertation. University of Cape Town.

Peet, R. (2001) 'Ideology, Discourse and the Geography of Hegemony: From Socialist to Neoliberal Development in South Africa', *Antipode*, 34(1): 54–84.

Piombo, J. and Nijzink, L. (2005) *Electoral Politics in South Africa: Assessing the First Democratic Decade.* New York: Palgrave Macmillan.

Posel, D. and Simpson, G. (2002) *Commissioning the Past: Understanding South Africa's Truth and Reconciliation Commission.* Johannesburg: Witwatersrand University Press.

Power, S. (2003) 'The Aids Rebel', *The New Yorker*, 19 May.

Salazar, P. J. (2002) *An African Athens: Rhetoric and the Shaping of Democracy in South Africa.* Mahwah, NJ: Lawrence Erlbaum Associates.

Sanders, M. (2007) *Ambiguities of Witnessing: Law and Literature in the Time of a Truth Commission.* Stanford, CA: Stanford University Press.

Schraeder, P. J. and Endless, B. (1998) 'The Media and Africa: The Portrayal of Africa in the New York Times (1955–1995)', *Issue,* 26(2): 29–35.

Schulz-Herzenberg, C. (2009) 'A Silent Revolution? Partisanship in South Africa, 1994–2006', Ph.D dissertation. University of Cape Town.

Simeon, R. and Murray, C. (2001) 'Multi-Sphere Governance in South Africa: An Interim Assessment', *Publius*, 31(4): 65–92.

Southall, R. and Daniel, J. (2009) *Zunami!: The South African Elections of 2009.* Auckland Park, South Africa Dunkeld, South Africa, Jacana Media: Konrad Adenauer Foundation.

Stromback, J. and Kaid, L. L. (2008) *The Handbook of Election News Coverage Around the World.* New York: Routledge.

Switzer, L. and Adhikari, M. (2000) *South Africa's Resistance Press: Alternative Voices in the Last Generation Under Apartheid.* Athens, OH: Ohio University Press.

Teer-Tomaselli, R. (2004) 'Transforming State Owned Enterprises in the Global Age: Lessons From Broadcasting and Telecommunications in South Africa', *Critical Arts: A South-North Journal of Cultural and Media Studies*, 18: 7–41.

Tomaselli, K. G. (2004) 'Transformation of the South African Media', *Critical Arts: A South-North Journal of Cultural and Media Studies*, 18: 1–6.

Wasserman, H. and Du Bois, M. L. (2006) 'New Kids on the Block: Tabloids Entrance Into the Print Media Market', in A. Olorunnisola (ed.), *Media in South Africa: A Cross-Media Assessment.* Lewiston, NY: The Edwin Mellen Press. pp. 171–86.

Wentzel, J. (1995) *The Liberal Slideaway.* Johannesburg: South African Institute of Race Relations.

40

Some Caveats about Comparative Research in Media Studies

Paolo Mancini and Daniel C. Hallin

In 2004, Michael Gurevitch and Jay Blumler commented that comparative research in political communication was finally, after years of neglect and drift, 'poised for maturity'. They noted the large amount of new research that had been published in the few years before that date, and observed that comparative research seemed very suddenly to have become 'fashionable'. Nicely they remembered how, through the years, they changed their opinion about comparative research in media studies and how their judgment about its improvement had become more and more positive. Similar observations on the dramatic increase in comparative media research have been made by many other scholars (Esser and Pfetsch, 2004; Hanitzsch, 2009; Livingstone, 2003). This rapid development was, not surprisingly, accompanied by many problems and ambiguities about goals and methodologies, so much so that we could fairly call this a period of 'tumultuous' development. These practical and methodological issues will be the focus of our discussion here; we will leave aside, for the most part, more specific discussions of the concepts, theories and research questions that are emerging in this growing field.

DEVELOPMENT OF THE FIELD

Despite this recent progress there is no doubt that, compared with neighbor social sciences such as sociology or political science, comparative research in political communication and in media studies in general has developed late and shows clear signs of the absence of real tradition and experience. The tumultuous development of these very recent years arrived after years of silence. Consider this: the first edition of *The Civic Culture* by Almond and Verba came out in 1963. This book may be seen as the first truly comparative study in modern political science, representing also an inspiring monument for sociology and empirical methods in sociology. But, before this book, Almond had already published 'Comparative Political Systems' (1956) while Macridis wrote his *The Study of Comparative Government* in 1955. In 1967, Lipset and Rokkan published another seminal work in comparative politics, *Party Systems and Voter Alignments*. These publications, together with many others and with their personal involvement in the project 'International Studies of Values in Politics' persuaded Adam Przeworski and Henry Teune to write in 1970 *The Logic of Comparative Social Inquiry* that can be considered the first attempt to critically consider the improvement of comparative research in social sciences and that represents even today a seminal work in this area.

The field of political science in particular developed a comprehensive approach that gave birth to a coherent discipline that in many countries received the name of 'comparative politics' with specific courses and, in some cases, departments too. Many social issues (for example, development, social stratification, health systems) were addressed in a comparative manner so that sociology too had enough material to reflect on its own development and direction. In 1966, Richard Merrit and Stein Rokkan edited a book *Comparing Nations: The Use of Quantitative Data in Cross-National Research* that sought to discuss the state of the art in this field. Many other attempts followed this one.

In those years media studies seem to follow a completely different path, putting very little interest in comparative studies. In a chapter on comparative research, written in 1975 for a handbook of political communication, Gurevitch and Blumler wrote that 'nobody could claim to be able to paint an assured portrait of the field of investigation to be described in this essay. It is not merely that few political communication studies have been mounted with a comparative focus. More to the point, there is neither a settled view of what such studies should be concerned with, nor even a firmly crystallized set of alternative options for research between which scholars of different philosophic persuasions could choose' (Blumler and Gurevitch, 1975: 325). The lag in the development of comparative research does not apply only to political communication but to the more general field of media studies and certainly to journalism studies. Indeed, after *Four Theories of the Press*, published in 1956 and representing the first attempt in comparative journalism studies – albeit one that, in contrast to the work in political science and sociology of that time, was not supported by any empirical data – for many years no other theoretical study or empirical research followed. This vacuum was due to several factors: media scholars in the USA and in other parts of the world focused on media effects at the individual level, while in Europe the debate on critical theory was not at all interested in comparative research or, in many countries, more generally in empirical research. Moreover, for many years a large number of media scholars have been involved with professional education, and this focus has moved the interest of these scholars away from basic research. The publication of textbooks and manuals was more important than looking at media practice in other systems.

In these same years, while communication scholars were silent in the area of comparative research, scholars of comparative politics and political sociology were silent on the media. Karl Deutsch advanced what was essentially a communication theory of politics, but it never gave rise to any research on the media; modernization theorists such as Daniel Lerner saw media as central to the modernization process, but again no real research tradition developed in this area. There have been other comparative research projects carried out within the frameworks of international

organizations, such as UNESCO, IAMCR, EBU and ISA (Cohen et al., 1990; Sreberny et al., 1980; Stevenson and Shaw, 1984), which were focused mainly on content analysis of news media in different countries, but these studies did not establish any valuable interpretive framework that could be used beyond the specific research occasion. This was no doubt in part a response to the 'limited effects' hypothesis that dominated media studies starting in the 1950s. It was probably also due in part to the absence of empirical data, and the difficulties of comparative data in media studies, the reasons of which we will explore in greater detail as we go along. Elections produce large amounts of comparable data on party systems; producing data on media content that would be comparable across systems is much more difficult.

In 1989, when Jay Blumler, who held a strong personal interest in the topic, was its President, the International Communication Association adopted 'Comparatively Speaking' as the theme of its annual conference. It is reasonable to say that since that date there has been an abundance of studies in a way that, as already reported, Jay Blumler himself together with Michael Gurevitch recently talked of a state of maturity. Swanson (1992) made an interesting list of the studies that followed or were contemporary to that conference. From his list we understand that most of these studies focused on content analysis and on the interactions between media professionals and politicians. Comparative research, or cross-national research, as it was called, was back at the core of media scholars' interest, at least of those working on political communication. After these initial studies many others have followed so that there has been some sort of 'deluge' of comparative research that has become even more relevant in the very recent years.

What were the motives of such a sudden development? First of all there is no doubt that globalization, in the most general meaning of the word, has had a primary role in expanding this kind of research. Research questions linked to the increasingly globalized circulation of cultural products were the first push toward comparative studies, but the increased internationalization of the scholarly community has played an important role too. Conferences, seminars, journals and translations of books have been important occasions to start comparative projects. Another important incentive has been represented by funding: starting with the different agencies linked to European Union, recent years have seen the birth and growth of many organizations interested in promoting international collaboration and joint scientific projects. Political and policy goals of the possible funders have connected with the interests of a community of scholars that was becoming more and more internationalized and used to frequent meetings and discussions. The fall of Berlin wall and the enlargement of EU toward East Europe has increased enormously the interest in that area even relative to the Western world.

PRACTICAL PROBLEMS

After a period of silence that followed the publication of *Four Theories of the Press* comparative research in media studies and particularly in political communication suddenly has erupted. In particular, journalism has become a main subject of comparative study: today the number of such studies is too large to list all the possible references.[1] Besides journalism, election campaigns, media economics, media regulation and other topics have been investigated in a comparative perspective. Often a small number of cases (two or three) are investigated, but more and more there is a trend toward comparing large number of cases in different parts of the world with a limited level of similarity and proximity among them. Some of these studies rely on primary sources, that is, they are based on empirical research, both through content analysis and survey research, while others examine and discuss secondary sources in connection to structures and relationships among systems.

Of course, all these studies may represent an important improvement for theory and research in our field. But they reveal problems too: minor and major problems. First of all, there is a problem of data availability in the case of empirical research. This may appear a trivial problem but in the end it can produce important bias in the result of the study. One of the most common areas for comparative research has to do with journalists' professional values and role-perceptions, and most of these studies are carried on through survey research. One very important problem is simply the fact that journalists in many countries seem to be increasingly reluctant to be interviewed. In many countries, perhaps – including Italy – they were never very keen on being interviewed, but the problem seems to be increasing. Journalists are busy people always struggling with time; they have never had, particularly in some countries, confidence in academic research particularly when academy looks at them. In their view, scholars lack the everyday and practical experience that is necessary to understand the job of the reporters. In many cases, journalism has been under a critical investigation that has stressed, rightly in my view, all the problematic and negative features and practices of newsgathering and news processing.

In the end, this has produced a sort of prejudice on the part of reporters toward the scholarly community.

Moreover, and not just because of the development of comparative research, journalists have been flooded with a large number of interview requests that they are not able to manage anymore. Increasingly it takes time, it takes a lot of phone calls and even if at the end one succeeds in having the reporter interviewed, often he is still reluctant, is not sincere and does not have all the time that the questionnaire would require. The answers are superficial, very often are not sincere and most of the times just guided by common sense and social and professional expectations. Of course this is not what the scholar is looking for. Even worse is when the survey is an e-survey. As everyone is experiencing today, all of us are forced to select among an enormous number of emails we get everyday. Of course, we cannot pay any serious attention to what is going on on the web nowadays aside from what interests us. Most of the time after the reply to the first e-survey, the second one ends in the e-garbage. These problems are not peculiar to comparative research, but they can be even more dramatic when they involve, as frequently happens, scholars coming from other countries who are not familiar with the habits and attitudes existing among journalists in a different country.

And this, of course, is a practical problem in a form of research that is popular in part because it is easier to carry out, particularly with teams from different countries, than other forms of research, ethnographic observation, for example, or content analysis. Ultimately, however, the latter are necessary, because ultimately we are interested not just in what journalists – or other actors involved in political communication – say about themselves, but in what they actually do and the messages they produce.

It is not by chance that Sonia Livingstone (2003), discussing the challenges of comparative studies, defines as 'exhausting', 'a nightmare', 'frustrating' the experiences of those who have been involved in such studies. We shall see later on, how it is not just an organizational problem (traveling, setting meetings, being on schedule, etc.) but here we deal with problems arising from different 'philosophies' (Blumler and Gurevitch, 1975) and from different cultural and methodological aspects that combine together also with the difficulty to get the necessary data. Indeed, Livingstone points out how the difficulty of comparative research lies essentially in the confusion between methodological and personal problems that, at the end, generates experiences that may be 'exciting' at best, frustrating and methodologically problematic at worst.

THE 'WHY COMPARATIVE' QUESTION

The list of problems and questions that are linked to comparative studies can be enormously long. We will try to shorten this list by bringing back all the existing questions (at least those we are aware of) to two main points: (1) the 'why am I going comparative' question; (2) the question of decontextualization. These two points are closely bound, of course.

The discussion that follows focuses on comparative research in political communication and more exactly in journalism studies. Of course, there are some specificities of these fields, but many of the points we will raise may apply to other scientific fields as well, in particular to sociology and political science. Indeed, as these two last fields have more experience with comparative research than media studies, many of the suggestions we present here come precisely from the political science and sociology literature. In the long run, it may be that media studies can make important contributions of its own to the methodology of comparative analysis, particularly where issues of culture are involved. It is easy to bracket questions of meaning and culture when one is dealing with voting data or industrial production; much harder when one is dealing with media partisanship or ideological diversity in the press.

In our view, many comparative studies miss one main point: they do not start with the fundamental question: why are we going comparative? Much of the methodological literature that has developed in the fields where comparative analysis has a long history stresses vigorously this point: it is necessary to define what is the goal of the comparative research. Why do we want to carry out research on this particular question in a comparative manner? Is comparison really necessary? And what do we want to compare? Roles? Interactions among systems? Contents? But how do contents relate to different professional actors, traditions, routines, etc.? What kind of explanation are we looking for? And, most important, within what body of theory shall we place our results? With the recent relative abundance of sources of financing, funders are not so much interested in theoretical questions but rather in policy solutions that only rarely meet the necessity of a sufficient theoretical framework.

The sociologist Scheuch, in his contribution to the collection put together by Else Oyen, asks exactly this same question in a section, not by chance, titled 'The Central Problem Is not Technical but Theoretical': 'why does one need to be comparative? What do different settings stand for?' (1990: 27). Beyond the personal and organizational problems Sonia Livingstone was talking about, here the main question is theoretical: in many cases scholars who start a comparative project are not enough aware of the reason of their enterprise. They do not ask the necessary starting question: what is our goal? What do we want to accomplish with our comparative study? There is not a clear interpretive framework within which to place the data that are collected, and which will be 'tested', if not in the narrow sense of confirming or disconfirming its predictions, then in the broader sense of assessing its usefulness as a research program. Within what theoretical framework, for instance, shall I place the possible differences I find through content analysis? The content of the news, like the self-perception of journalists is a 'predictor' or 'indicator' of something else (Przeworski and Teune, 1970: 8) something which has to be conceptualized before I start my project. Before going comparative, I need to have some ideas on the possible connections between predictors or indicators and the general theory that may explain differences and similarities or establish their conceptual significance. As we wrote in *Comparing Media Systems*, comparative research in social theory 'can be understood in terms of two basic functions: its role in concept formation and clarification and its role in causal inference. It is valuable, in the first place, because it sensitizes us to variation and to similarity, and this can contribute powerfully to the refinement of our conceptual apparatus ... the second reason comparison is important in social investigation is that it may allow us to test hypotheses about the interrelationships among social phenomena' (Hallin and Mancini, 2004: 2–4). To make this possible we need to have some clear ideas on where (within which theory) to place the indicators we are using.

In large collaborative projects this theory very frequently is not sufficiently developed, articulated and shared by all the scholars involved so that it may constitute the direction toward which the research is directed. Often this lack of clarification makes harder the integration of the scholars who may come from very different cultural and theoretical experiences: not being directed by a unique and clear goal they continue to be directed by their own background, missing the possibility to work within a common framework. The comparative project ends in the frustrating experience Sonia Livingstone was talking about. Indeed, the necessity of the integration among scholars who come from different countries and cultural background is one of the major problems outlined in almost all the literature on the topic (Hanitzsch, 2009; Livingtsone, 2003; Swanson, 1992, 2004).

At the best, in these cases, what Swanson (1992: 27) calls the 'pre-theoretical strategy' is implicitly adopted by the research team – that is among the scholars involved in the project there is just 'a general orientation to the subject' and not a general and formalized theoretical view that combines together all those who are involved in that project.[2] Even if there is not any formal decision about this, scholars, because of many reasons (few occasions to meet, lack of leadership in the group, too deep theoretical differences among them, etc.) do not place their study within 'a theory', that is a formalized schema that directs their methodological choices and within which to place and evaluate the research results. The most obvious result of this lack of clarification on the goals of the comparative project is research that is in the end is merely descriptive: most of the times comparative studies which fail to answer the question 'why are we going comparative' are limited to a description, more or less accurate, of the object they study (Wirth and Kolb, 2004). This object is not placed within any theoretical framework able to illustrate and to explain its relations with the society at large. Scholars describe what has been observed but are unable 'to explain and predict why certain events occur when and where they do', which, as Przeworski and Teune continue, 'is the goal of science' (1970: 18).

Indeed, the opposition between interpretation and description seems to be a standard dilemma in comparative studies: most of the times it derives from the absence or weak clarification of 'why are we going comparative?' Missing any sort of common interpretive framework, scholars cannot do anything other than describe what they observed in their own country. Many projects result in books each chapter of which describes the situation in a single country without pointing out similarities and differences with other realities and without shedding light on the recurrent relationships between the variables that are placed under observations in different realities, which should be principal goal of comparative research.

THE PROBLEM OF DE-CONTEXTUALIZATION

Comparative research is essentially about context; at the same time, context or 'de-contextualization' is a central methodological problem in comparative research. De-contextualization has many faces that we shall try to outline in this section but, first of all, let us start with defining what we are talking about. De-contextualization indicates that the observations that are carried out and the results that derive from them are placed outside of their original context.

Communication implies culture, as James Carey (1992) has demonstrated in a very convincing way; and therefore all studies dealing with communication have to do with the cultural context within which they originate and develop. This is particularly true for journalism studies, and it does not have to do just with discourse procedures, ideology, etc. but also with politics, with the system of rules, both implicit and explicit, that direct the behavior of journalists and other social actors. A particular journalistic behavior that the research seems to point out or a particular set of data that emerge from content analysis, may assume different meanings in connection with the specific professional routines of that country, with the traditional habit of media coverage in that particular context, with the way in which people interact each other in that particular country. Most of the time the researcher is not able to give the exact meaning to the data he possesses because, as Przeworksi and Teune state: 'social phenomena are not only diverse but always occur in mutually interdependent and interacting structures, possessing a spatiotemporal location … specific observations must be interpreted within the context of specific systems' (Przeworksi and Teune, 1970: 12ff.). De-contextualization means that the instruments used for the research and the data coming out of that research are not placed within the right cultural contexts that are made up by interactions among systems and actors, by cultural habits and by historical evolution. History, in particular plays an important role in understanding how communication works, how it directs the performance of the actors involved in the process and what kind of effects it can produce (Kohn, 1989). Stevenson (2004), for example, in an essay devoted to the role of culture in comparative research in communication, observes that history has made Europeans more interested in the external world than Americans. This, he argues, is a powerful enough influence that it dwarfs the effects of most other variables on public knowledge of world affairs, whether these variables have do with individual-level characteristics or media systems.

The importance of culture, however, reinforces the practical difficulties of comparative research. How much knowledge does an individual researcher need to have in order to make generalizations across different cultural contexts? In many cases, cultural contextualization of findings requires insider knowledge (Livingstone, 2003), and this is why comparative studies in communication so often are collaborative, with native scholars taking responsibility for each particular country. This solution of course takes us back to the problem we explored in the previous section. If there is not a strong and clear interpretive framework that is shared by all the scholars involved in the research, comparison among the different realities observed is very difficult if not impossible: each scholar places the outcomes of the research within the cultural context and also the theoretical schema he or she is more used to. Similarities and differences are not easy to be pointed out: stable connections between the variables that have been studied are not investigated and stressed. As Przeworksi and Teune argue, it is difficult 'to state the conditions under which it always or usually takes place, that is, to cite general statements (laws) from which other statements concerning properties of specific events can be inferred with some reasonable certainty (1970: 19)', or, if the research is more interpretive than causal in its aims, difficult to know whether or not the phenomena we are looking at really belong to the same category. Very often this lack of comparability brings us right back to the already-discussed 'descriptive approach': each scholar, usually a 'native scholar', describes what he observed, puts it within the history of his country, relates the findings to the culture of the country but the comparative dimension, that is the possibility to point out 'the conditions under which a social phenomenon takes place or not' is missing.

The alternative solution is that a single scholar takes care of all the cases that are analyzed and puts these cases under a common theoretical and interpretive framework but, at this point, the risk is that of de-contextualization. Does this scholar possess all the knowledge that is needed to connect the emerging data to the culture of the different countries under observation?

The problem of de-contextualization works also at the level of the instruments that are used for the research. Here it is useful to recount two cases that come from our personal experience. In a cross-national study of the self-perception of journalists in different countries (Donsbach and Klett, 1993; Donsbach and Patterson, 1992), there was the need to translate the same questionnaire in different languages. The Italian team had difficulty translating the following question 'What is in your view a good news reporting?' It was essentially impossible to translate this question into Italian because it was based on the assumption that that there is a distinction between news *reporting*, as a specific journalistic function, and journalism more generally; it assumes a distinction, in particular, between reporting and commentary. But this distinction is not clearly drawn in Italian journalistic practice; in Italy, the figure of reporter distinguished from that of journalist/commentator does not exist, or only exists in the sense that a very few distinguished journalists are free at the end of their careers simply to present their opinions and not to produce the usual mix of reporting and commentary.

Another case is the 'unitizing' involved in content analysis of news. Usually in these kinds of studies, the unit of analysis is intended to be the single news 'story'. But this does not take in account that news items can be organized in very different ways in different parts of the world: in Italy, for instance, a single news item is organized around the statements released by the different political actors. This is very different from the 'package' that dominates American coverage, which is unified by the role of the correspondent who weaves material into a single story. Other studies may use the paragraph as a reference, or the source citation. But this again varies in different systems; French newspapers have much longer paragraphs than American ones, for example, and journalists do not always signal explicitly for the reader when they are citing a source (Benson and Hallin, 2007). We forget that news items are culturally and professionally rooted in different cultural and political realities and we assume one way of telling the story to be the universal model when it is not. Anyone who has been involved in comparative research can furnish hundreds of these examples, each of which poses a difficult though sometime instructive challenges for developing comparable indicators across systems.

These kinds of examples of course underscore the significance of the 'western bias' in comparative media research (Hanitzsch, 2009). Indeed, even more specifically than a 'western' bias, it has been very common to build both concepts and methods around what Chalaby (1996) calls the 'Anglo-American' model of journalism (a concept we try to de-construct, to a degree, in *Comparing Media Systems*, by emphasizing the many differences between American and British journalism). As Hanitzsch continues: 'Most studies compare other nations to their own countries by evaluating other cultures through the lens of their own cultural value-systems' (2009: 422), or, to extend him a bit, by comparing other cultures to those most fully theorized in media studies, which means western and particularly the Anglo-American liberal systems. At least in many studies, different realities are analyzed and judged on the basis of what is supposed to be the 'professional' model or the 'narrative model' for news reporting without taking in account that the communication culture of the different countries that are studied may propose different models for acting in journalism and for reporting, and without really trying to theorize that culture on its own terms.

This very last discussion brings to the fore the opposition between 'the most similar cases design', in which cases are selected that will have many characteristics in common, and 'the most different cases design', in which we maximize rather than minimize variations in context. It is very possible that the risks of de-contextualization may be much more frequent and dramatic in 'a most different cases strategy' where, of course, cultural diversity is deeper and may affect both the way in which reality is observed – and the kinds of methods and indicators we use in research – and the interpretation of the results. A most different cases strategy is appealing in many ways, and is adopted in part out of the desire to avoid the usual 'Western bias' by bringing into what usually starts out as a western-centered study a wider range of systems. Most different cases designs certainly also have can have important intellectual advantages if used in the right way. To go back to our earlier discussion of the uses of comparative analysis, most-different systems designs can open the door to particularly interesting interrogations of dominant concepts in the field, and also tests of causal hypotheses, as when we look to see whether a certain media system characteristic, usually assumed to result from a particular context, might also exist in a radically different context, where none of the usual explanatory factors may be present. In *Comparing Media Systems*, which was based on a most similar systems design, we departed briefly from that strategy in a couple of places in order to clarify some of the conceptual issues we wanted to raise. One of our key variables in that book, for example, is professionalization of journalism. In order to use that concept in comparative analysis, however, we believed it was important to subject it to some degree of critical scrutiny. The concept of journalistic professionalization, it seemed to us, as it had been developed in the media studies literature, was strongly tied to the American case, and we believed it was important to break down its components, and to raise the possibility that they might not all occur in the same pattern in which they had in the USA. We tried to show that a different form of professionalization had developed in Northern Europe, one that was not based in the same way as the American on the 'objectivity norm', or the idea that journalism should be politically neutral. We also made use of the research of Curry (1990) on Polish journalism in the Communist era, which was intriguing to us because Curry argued that despite the radically different nature of the Polish media system – state control of most media and a culture in which journalists were explicitly seen as political agitators and organizers – many of the characteristics we normally associate with professionalism did exist in Polish journalism. It seems to us self-evident, however, that the risks of de-contextualization are much greater with a most different systems design; risks of misinterpreting phenomena in one system because they are being interpreted though the lens of concepts appropriate for another, risks of employing a least-common denominator theoretical framework so impoverished that it

does not really advance comparative analysis, and the closely related risk of avoiding common concepts in an effort to be culturally sensitive, and ending up with work that is essentially descriptive.

For these reasons, we tend to be skeptical of grand global studies that purport to cover the world as a whole. *Four Theories of the Press* was of course an extreme version of exactly that approach, and we believe the fact that its universalizing framework became so dominant is in part what killed off comparative analysis in communication in the second half of the 20th century. The 'three models of media and politics' we propose in our own book, *Comparing Media Systems*, the Liberal, Democratic Corporatist and Polarized Pluralist models, are intended as ideal types that represent concrete historical patterns of development of the media in Western Europe and North America. These are concrete social formations that arose in particular times and places, not universal categories that can be applied to any media system in any context. Other aspects of our analysis, including the four dimensions we use for comparing media systems (structure of media markets, role of the state, political parallelism and journalistic professionalization) may be more generalizable, though their particular conceptualization in our book and their importance relative to their possible dimensions of comparison is again context-dependent. We see this as a strength of our analysis, and not as a weakness, even though, or really precisely because, it underscores the limited applicability of much of our conceptual framework. It is a strength, we would argue, because it gives researchers a way to think through what it would mean to compare other realities with the ones we analyzed.

It is important to emphasize here that although we talk about context as the root cause of many of the difficulties that beset comparative research, we certainly do not want to pose a dichotomy between comparative theory and sensitivity to context. It is precisely the importance of context that makes comparative analysis valuable; theorizing the role of context is precisely what comparative analysis is about. Comparative analysis can be extremely valuable to a scholar trying to understand the specificity of his or her own system. This is in part how the two of us started out on this path: doing a comparison of the US and Italian television news, we were amazed about how much we learned about the conventions of our own television news by comparing it with another model (Hallin and Mancini, 1984). And at the same time, good theory should be clear about the scope of its application, about the contexts within which its concepts and generalizations apply.

CONCLUSION

This discussion has focused on problems in the conduct of comparative analysis. In quoting Blumler and Gurevitch's statement that comparative analysis in communication is 'poised for maturity', we would perhaps stress their qualification more than anything else, and argue that it is 'poised' to advance rather than to claim that it is really a mature field of study. That does not mean we want to sound a discouraging note, either to deny the important progress the field has made in recent years or to cast doubt on the promise of comparative research. We think the 'deluge' of comparative research is incredibly exciting, and offers dramatic possibilities to give the media studies far more powerful tools for developing social theory.

We have focused in this chapter to a large extent on large-scale, cross-national comparative studies, because these are often seen as the gold standard in comparative analysis, and as signs that the field is becoming 'mature'. We have pointed out a lot of problems that can arise in these kinds of study, though of course they can also be extremely valuable if carried out in the right way. It is important to keep in mind, however, that in a truly mature field knowledge develops from the decentralized collaboration of many scholars, working independently but engaging with one another's work and orienting around common concepts and research problems. As it has often been noted in the literature on comparative method, studies of one or two cases can contribute to comparative analysis if they follow the method of 'structured, focused comparison', analyzing particular cases through the use of concepts developed in other research and addressing questions raised in a wider literature.[3] This is only possible, of course, once there is a wider literature within which scholars can begin to situate their work, and we are just reaching that point now. Some of the best comparative studies produced to date are two-country studies (for example, Feree et al., 2002; Semetko et al., 1991), in which issues of context can be theorized much more carefully (even if the theorization of these studies might have been stronger had there been more comparative research at the time to serve as a context). These studies, like many of the multi-country studies, involved large research teams. But smaller-scale studies, including single case studies, can contribute substantially to comparative research, if they are rooted in the existing comparative literature. They are important, for one thing, to pave the way for later, more synthetic multi-case analysis. This is important to stress, because graduate students and other younger scholars as well as scholars in parts of the world where state funding for research is limited often do not have access to the kind of funding that is necessary for large multi-case studies. But expanding the field urgently requires the participation of exactly these scholars.

NOTES

1   A few of the projects we are aware of include, the project 'Foreign News Around the World' directed by Akiba Cohen, the follow up of the investigation of Patterson – Donsbach on self-perception of journalists, the project 'Political Communication Cultures in Western Europe – A Comparative Study' directed by Barbara Pfetsch, the project on 'European Journalism' at the University of Oxford conducted by Henrik Ornebring, the Cost A30 Action on 'East of the West – Setting a New Central and Eastern European Media Research Agenda', the project on 'Media and Democracy in Central and Eastern Europe: Qualities of democracy, Qualities of the Media' directed by Jan Zielonka at the University of Oxford the project 'Worlds of Journalisms' at the University of Zurich' coordinated by Thomas Hanitzsch, the project on Europeanization of Public Sphere at The Jacobs University of Bremen.

2   Swanson distinguishes among three possible strategies to deal with the theoretical diversity of the scholars involved in comparative studies: (1) the avoidance strategy: scholars involved in the project already share a common theoretical approach; (2) the pretheoretical strategy: there is a general common orientation toward the subject to be observed; (3) the metatheoretical strategy: there is a very general interpretive framework within which different approaches can be accommodated (Swanson, 1992).

3   The classic statement of this approach is George and McKeown (1985).

REFERENCES

Almond, G. (1956) 'Comparative Political Systems', *Journal of Politics*, 18(3): 391–405.

Almond, G. and Verba, S. (1963) *The Civic Culture: Political Attitudes and Democracy in Five Nations.* Princeton, NJ: Princeton University Press.

Benson, R. and Hallin, D. C. (2007) 'How States, Markets and Globalization Shape the News: The French and U.S. National Press, 1965–1997', *European Journal of Communication*, 22(1): 27–48.

Blumler, J. G. and Gurevitch, M. (1975) 'Towards a Comparative Framework for Political Communication Research', in S. Chaffee (ed.), *Political communication: Issues and Strategies for Research.* Beverly Hills, CA: Sage. pp. 165–93.

Carey, J. G. (1992) *Communication as Culture: Essays on Media and Society.* New York: Routledge.

Chalaby, J. (1996) 'Journalism as an Anglo-American Invention: A Comparison of the Development of French and Anglo-American Journalism, 1830–1920s', *European Journal of Communication*, 11(3): 303–26.

Cohen, A., Adoni, A. and Bantz, R. (1990) *Social Conflict and Television News*. Newbury Park, CA: Sage.

Curry, J. L. (1990) *Poland's Journalists: Professionalization and Politics*. Cambridge: Cambridge University Press.

Donsbach, W. and Klett, B. (1993) 'Subjective Objectivity: How Journalists in Four Countries Define a Key Term of Their Profession', *Gazette*, 51(1): 53–83.

Donsbach, W. and Patterson, T. (1992) 'Journalists' Roles and Newsroom Practices: A Cross National Comparison', paper presented at 42nd conference of the International Communication Association.

Esser, F. and Pfetsch, B. (2004) (eds.) *Comparing Political Communication*. Cambridge: Cambridge University Press.

Feree, M. M., Gamson, W. A., Gerhards, J. and Rucht, D. (2002) *Shaping Abortion Discourse: Democracy and the Public Sphere in Germany and the United States*. Cambridge: Cambridge University Press.

George, A. L. and McKeown, T. J. (1985) 'Case Studies and Theories of Organizational Decision Making', in R. Coulman and R. Smith (eds.), *Advances in Information Processing in Organizations*. Greenwich, CT: JAI Press. pp. 21–58.

Gurevitch, M. and Blumler, J. G. (2004) 'State of Art of Comparative Political Communication Research', in F. Esser and B. Pfetsch (eds.), *Comparing Political Communication*. Cambridge: Cambridge University Press.

Hallin, D. C. and Mancini, P. (1984) 'Speaking of the President: Political Structure and Representational Form in U.S. and Italian TV News', *Theory and Society*, 13(6): 829–50.

Hallin, D. C. and Mancini, P. (2004) *Comparing Media Systems: Three Models of Media and Politics*. Cambridge: Cambridge University Press.

Hanitzsch, T. (2009) 'Comparative Journalism Studies', in K. Wahl-Jorgensen and T. Hanitzsch (eds.), *The Handbook of Journalism Studies*. New York: Routledge. pp. 413–27.

Kohn, M. (1989) 'Cross National Research as an Analytical Strategy', in M. Kohn (ed.), *Cross National Research in Sociology*. Newbury Park, CA: Sage. pp. 77–100.

Livingstone, S. (2003) 'On the Challenges of Cross-National Comparative Research', *European Journal of Communication*, 18(1): 477–501.

Lipset, S. and Rokkan, S. (1967) *Party Systems and Voter Alignments*. New York: The Free Press.

Macridis, R. C. (1955) *The Study of Comparative Government*. New York: Doubleday.

Merrit, R. and Rokkan, S. (1966) (eds.) *Comparing Nations: The Use of Quantitative Data in Cross-National Research*. New Haven, CT: Yale University Press.

Przeworski, A. and Teune, H. (1970) *The Logic of Comparative Social Inquiry*. New York: Wiley Interscience.

Scheuch, E. (1990) 'The Development of Comparative Research: Towards Causal Explanations', in E. Oyen (ed.), *Comparative Methodology: Theory and Practice in International Social Research*. Newbury Park, CA: Sage. pp. 19–36.

Semetko, H. A., Blumler, J. G., Gurevitch, M. and Weaver, D. H. (1991) *The Formation of Campaign Agendas: A Comparative Analysis of Party and Media Roles in Recent American and British Elections*. Hillside, NJ: Lawrence Erlbaum Associates.

Siebert, F., Peterson, T. and Schramm, W. (1956) *Four Theories of the Press*. Urbana, IL: University of Illinois Press.

Sreberny, A., Nordestreng, K., Stevenson, R. and Ugboajah, F. (1980) 'The World of News–The News of the World', a draft report of the 'Foreign Images' project undertaken by IAMCR for UNESCO. Caracas.

Stevenson, R. (2004) 'Problems of Comparative Political Communication Research: Culture as a Key Variable', in F. Esser and B. Pfetsch (eds.), *Comparing Political Communication: Theories, Cases, and Challenges*. Cambridge: Cambridge University Press. pp. 367–383.

Stevenson, R. and Shaw, D. (1984) *Foreign News and the New World Information Order*. Ames, IA: The Iowa State University Press.

Swanson, D. (1992) 'Managing Theoretical Diversity in Cross-National Studies of Political Communication', in J. G. Blumler, J. McLeod and K. Rosengren (eds.), *Comparatively Speaking: Communication and Culture Across Space and Time*. Newbury Park, CA: Sage. pp. 19–34.

Swanson, D. (2004) 'Transnational Trends in Political Communication: Conventional Views and New Realities', in F. Esser and B. Pfetsch (eds.), *Comparing Political Communication*. Cambridge: Cambridge University Press. pp. 45–65.

Wirth, W. and Kolb, S. (2004) 'Designs and Methods of Comparative Political Communication Research', in F. Esser and B. Pfetsch (eds.), *Comparing Political Communication: Theories, Cases, and Challenges*. Cambridge: Cambridge University Press. pp. 87–114.

41

Never Waste a Good Crisis: The British Phone Hacking Scandal and its Implications for Politics and the Press

Richard Tait

It is hard to think of any political and media scandal in the UK in recent years which comes near to the events of the 2011 phone hacking scandal in scale and intensity. In the course of four weeks in July, the chief executive of the UK's most influential newspaper group resigned, followed by the country's most senior policeman; the prime minister's former head of communications was arrested and Rupert Murdoch, the most powerful media magnate in the world, saw the resignation of the chief executives of two of his key companies, Dow Jones and News International, together with the collapse of a takeover deal that would have given him unprecedented dominance of the UK media and secured his family's long-term control of the global media company he founded, News Corp. British politicians have been challenged as never before over their relationship with media power; British journalists face a fundamental review of their ethics, practices and professional standards; the balance of the law between the right to freedom of expression and the right to privacy is in question.

However dramatic and apparently unexpected the course of events in July 2011 appeared to be, the roots of the crisis lay in some fundamental characteristics of the British system of political communications, in successive governments' media policies, in the attitude of journalists, police

and judges to privacy and in the very limited extent to which these issues were understood or discussed in public life. The narrative of events in the summer of 2011 is only the starting point for investigation and analysis of the causes of the crisis and potential remedies – a view the government has now accepted with the appointment of a senior judge, Lord Justice Leveson, with the brief to inquire in to the wider political, journalistic and legal implications. The Leveson inquiry has the potential to change the culture of British politics – its responsibilities include making recommendations for 'the future conduct of relations between politicians and the press' (Number 10, 2011). What is certain is that the relationships between media power and political power in the UK will be examined – and exposed – as never before.

Anatomy of a Scandal: Milly Dowler

Ironically, but for some reassuringly, the scandal was revealed by a piece of dogged investigative journalism. Monday 4 July the *Guardian* newspaper, revealed that its front page lead the next morning would be a story by Nick Davies that the *News of The World*, the best selling Sunday tabloid newspaper in Britain, had hacked into the mobile phone of Milly Dowler, a schoolgirl who had gone missing in 2002, and had (although this was later disputed and is now not believed to have been the case) deleted messages from her mailbox, leading her family to hope that she was still alive. In fact, Milly Dowler had been murdered and the trial of her killer had just come to an end with a huge wave of public sympathy for the Dowler family who had been attacked in court by the killer's defence counsel (Davies, 2011).

On the course of the week it also emerged that relatives of those killed in the 7 July 2005 terrorist attacks in London, widows of British service personnel killed in Afghanistan and the families of Holly Wells and Jessica Chapman – another high profile child murder case – had also been targeted by private investigators working for the *News of the World*. But Milly Dowler and her family became the symbol of media abuse (BBC, 2011; Davies 2011; *The New York Times*, 2011a).

This was not the first time the public and politicians had heard of phone hacking by the media. In January 2007 the *News of The World* royal editor, Clive Goodman, and a private investigator, Glenn Mulcaire, had been jailed for four months and six months, respectively, for hacking into the phones of aides to Prince William. News International, the owners of the *News of the World*, argued at the time that this was an isolated case of a 'rogue reporter' and that although the editor of the *News of the World*, Andy Coulson, had resigned, neither he nor anyone in senior management had known about it. Clive Goodman was fired and the paper and its owners sought to draw a line under the affair. However, as a number of civil cases brought by celebrity hacking victims against the *News of the World* began to work their way through the courts, often settled by large payouts from News International in return for confidentiality, the 'rogue reporter' line seemed increasingly hard to believe.

In July 2009, the *Guardian* newspaper, a long standing critic of Rupert Murdoch's role in British media and politics, had published a series of articles alleging that hacking had been much more widespread. *The New York Times* had also vigorously pursued the story, unlike most of the rest of the UK and US press (*The New York Times*, 2011a). Despite that, News International maintained its position that this had been an isolated incident and that rigorous internal investigations had confirmed this. News International executives gave evidence to that effect at a parliamentary inquiry in 2009 and were supported by the Metropolitan Police who also gave evidence to parliament that the hacking had only involved a handful of cases (Davies, 2011; *The New York Times*, 2011a).

The police re-opened their investigations in January 2011 and within days revealed that the former Deputy Prime Minister, John Prescott, was among the potential victims. A number of arrests were made and it emerged that the names and details of about 4000 potential targets had been found in the papers of Glenn Mulcaire at the time of the original 2006 investigation. However, the story was still largely confined to the pages of the *Guardian, The New York Times* and the columns of *Hansard*.

The *Guardian* revelations in July 2011 of the targeting of Milly Dowler's phone transformed the situation in terms of public and political opinion. The story dominated the news agenda. News International apologized profusely and announced the closure of the *News of the World*. The last edition was on 10 July. News International also let it be known it had now found evidence of more widespread hacking and of paying police for information.

Anatomy of a Scandal: Denials and Resignations

Five days later Rebekah Brooks, chief executive of News International and editor of the *News of the World* at the time of Milly Dowler's disappearance, resigned, denying any knowledge of phone hacking. Les Hinton, chief executive of Dow Jones, publishers of the *Wall Street Journal*, and one of Rupert Murdoch's closest colleagues, resigned on the same say, again denying all knowledge of phone hacking at News International when he had been executive chairman from 1995 to 2007. Two days later, Rebekah Brooks was arrested by police (BBC, 2011; Davies, 2011; *The New York Times*, 2011a).

However, the Metropolitan Police itself was facing mounting criticism for their previous assurances that the 2007 case had been an isolated incident. The Metropolitan Police Commissioner, Sir Paul Stephenson, resigned on 17 July, followed the next day by his head of counter-terrorism, Assistant Commissioner John Yates, the officer who had assured parliament in 2009 there was nothing further to investigate.

When the scandal broke, News Corp was on the verge of being given government approval to take over BSkyB, the enormously profitable UK satellite broadcaster of which it already owned 39%. The government position had been that any issues at News International were irrelevant to whether the takeover should be allowed. The scandal changed all that. On 13 July News Corp withdrew its proposals, pre-empting a debate in the UK parliament on an opposition motion asking it do so. On 19 July Rupert Murdoch, executive chairman of News Corp and his son James, chairman and chief executive of News International appeared before a parliamentary committee.

They apologized for what had happened – Rupert Murdoch saying 'this is the most humble moment of my life' – but they denied that either of them had any knowledge of what had been happening. In particular, James Murdoch denied that he had been shown in 2009 a crucial email which did suggest the practice had been much more widespread (BBC, 2011; Davies, 2011; *The New York Times*, 2011a).

The British government was under particular pressure as the Prime Minister, David Cameron, had appointed the former *News of the World* editor, Andy Coulson, as his media chief in opposition and then after the election made him director of communications at 10 Downing Street. Coulson, who has always denied all knowledge of phone hacking, had resigned from the government in January 2011. On 8 July, he was arrested and questioned by police. The leader of the opposition, Ed Miliband, took the initiative in demanding a judge-led investigation and on 13 July the government appointed a senior judge, Lord Justice Leveson, to head an inquiry into the culture of the media, its relations with the public, police and politicians and the future of press regulation. He was to be assisted by a panel of experts from the fields of law, journalism and civil liberties.

The scandal continued to claim high profile victims with the announcement on 29 July that Baroness Buscombe, the chair of the Press Complaints Commission (PCC), was stepping down after government and public criticisms of its failure to investigate phone hacking. And further revelations from the criminal investigation continued to put pressure on News International. At the end of July it emerged that one of the best known victims of crime of the last decade, Sara Payne, whose young daughter Sarah had been murdered in 2000, was on a list of *News of The World* potential hacking targets. The *News of The World* under Rebekah Brooks had campaigned with Sara Payne for a 'Sarah's Law' on similar lines to 'Megan's Law' in the USA and she had put her name to an article in the final edition of the paper thanking them for their help. And the scandal began to move beyond just one media company with legal actions being announced against other newspapers and beyond phone hacking with the police broadening their investigations to include allegations of computer hacking by journalists (BBC, 2011; Davies, 2011; *The New York Times*, 2011a).

British Politics and Rupert Murdoch – A Secret History

Although the crisis was at first driven solely by public anger at tabloid tactics, some wider themes soon emerged. The 2011 phone hacking scandal revealed some fundamental issues in British political communications, the political system and the practice and regulation of journalism.

The first and most striking victim of the scandal was the influence of Rupert Murdoch on British politics. For more than 30 years conventional political wisdom had held that the support of Murdoch's British newspapers was a key factor in winning general elections. Murdoch had supported Margaret Thatcher's Conservatives and after her resignation helped John Major win a close election in 1992 – *The Sun*, the best selling newspaper in Britain, attacked the then Labour leader Neil Kinnock in the most personal terms, with an election day front page showing his face in a light bulb with the headline 'If Kinnock Wins Today will the Last Person to Leave Britain Please Turn the Lights Out'. Kinnock duly lost and *The Sun* then claimed credit for the Tory win with the headline 'It Was The Sun Wot Won It' (McKie, 1995).

In July 1995 Tony Blair, the Labour Leader, travelled half way round the world to address the News Corporation conference on Hayman Island in Australia, as part of his campaign to win the endorsement of the same newspaper that claimed to have destroyed his predecessor (Blair, 2010). On 18 March 1997 in the run up to the next general election, *The Sun* announced it was backing Blair and continued to support Labour till September 2009 when it changed sides again, announcing 'Labour's Lost It'.

Although most research into the influence of newspapers suggests that politicians (and journalists) have greatly exaggerated the real effect of these endorsements (Curtice and Semetko, 1994; Mckie, 1998), British politicians continued to operate on the basis that Murdoch was, as Tony Blair thought, 'immensely powerful' or as his Australian counterpart Paul Keating put it 'He thought Rupert a bastard but one you could deal with' (Blair, 2010).

The detailed history of Murdoch's relations with successive British prime ministers remains to be written (Wolff, 2008). Murdoch and his newspapers have been consistently Eurosceptic, in favour of free market policies and hostile to the BBC for three decades. How far he and they directly influenced British government policy needs further detailed investigation. What is already clear is that his business empire clearly and consistently benefited from political decisions by both Conservative and Labour governments.

The Conservative Thatcher government nodded through both his purchase of Times Newspapers in 1981 which gave him a dominant position in the UK newspaper market and the merger with British Satellite Broadcasting in 1990, creating in British

Sky Broadcasting (BSkyB) a monopoly satellite broadcaster, which he effectively controlled with a 39% stake. Neither deal was referred to the regulatory authorities. Although one of Tony Blair's closest media advisers, Barry Cox, did suggest in a 2003 lecture that BSkyB might need to be broken up (Cox, 2011), his proposal fell on deaf ears as BSkyB became the dominant commercial broadcaster. The Labour government's 2003 Communications bill even suggested BSkyB should be also allowed to buy one of the terrestrial broadcasters, Channel Five, and this was only thwarted by a parliamentary committee led by David Putnam insisting, despite Downing Street's apparent disapproval, on the introduction of a media plurality clause (Dyke, 2004).

By 2010, when Murdoch was poised to take full control of BSkyB, now by far the most powerful and profitable commercial broadcaster in the UK, with 10 million subscribers, a respected industry analyst, Claire Enders, could talk of the UK's 'Berlusconi moment' – comparing the potential outcome as a market and political influence akin to that wielded by the Italian prime minister in his country (Enders, 2010). Enders made her remarks in a memorandum to the Coalition Government's Trade Secretary, Vince Cable, a Liberal Democrat, who had the power to block the takeover. But within a couple of months, Cable had lost responsibility for media regulation after a couple of undercover reporters from the *Daily Telegraph* taped him boasting that he had 'declared war' on Rupert Murdoch. Responsibility for approving the takeover went to the culture secretary, Jeremy Hunt, a Conservative, who was on the verge of approving the deal when the *Guardian* story about Milly Dowler's phone changed the political context.

Both main political parties were forced to reveal their contacts with Rupert Murdoch and his senior managers. The government was particularly vulnerable because of David Cameron's decision to appoint Andy Coulson as his communications chief both in opposition and in government. The government released figures showing Cameron had met News International and News Corp executives 26 times since becoming prime minister; that James Murdoch, Rebekah Brooks and Andy Coulson had all been guests at his weekend residence, Chequers, and that figures for the rest of the government showed that ministers were meeting representatives of the Murdoch media empire on average once every three days. Ed Miliband followed suit, revealing that he had met News International and News Corp executives on 11 occasions since becoming leader of the Labour Party (Labour Party, 2011).

The sense that this was a crisis of confidence in the political system as a whole rather than just the government of the day was strengthened by Rupert Murdoch's own evidence to the parliamentary committee on 19 July which revealed that both David Cameron and his Labour predecessor Gordon Brown had invited him to a number of meetings at 10 Downing Street but he had always been asked to enter by the back door, apparently to avoid photographers. Murdoch denied imposing any preconditions on political leaders as the price of his support, but the image of back door influence was a damaging one.

The reputation of British politicians had not yet recovered from the expenses scandal of 2009 (Bell, 2009). In the Commons the next day, David Cameron argued that fundamental change was now necessary in the relations between politicians and media power:

> The point I would make is that we have all got to be open about the fact that both Front Benches spent a lot of time courting Rupert Murdoch, courting News International, courting the Russian who owns *The Independent*—and the *Daily Mail*, and the BBC while we are at it. *[Interruption.]* Everybody has done it. And we have got to admit that this sort of relationship needs to be changed and put on a more healthy basis. Now we are prepared to admit it, but basically, if you like, the clock has stopped on my watch, and I am determined to sort it out. (House of Commons, 2011)

The Conservatives' proposed remedy was to rely on greater transparency in publishing all meetings between politicians and media representatives and to refer the rules of engagement to Lord Justice Leveson's enquiry. The other main political parties went further and focused on the particular role which Murdoch and his companies had played. The Deputy Leader of the Liberal Democrats, the junior partners in the coalition government, asked Ofcom, the media regulator, to investigate whether News Corp would pass the 'fit and proper person' test to enable it to hold a broadcast licence (Liberal Democrats, 2011).

Labour went further still with the first front bench challenge in 30 years to the media and political influence of the Murdoch empire. Under Blair and Brown, his approval had been courted and the government had been content to watch the emergence of BSkyB as the dominant commercial broadcaster. Ed Miliband had initially been advised to be cautious about linking the hacking scandal to the BSkyB takeover. But on 10 July, he said that the deal should not be allowed to go through while police investigations into hacking were underway and called for a Commons debate unless News Corp withdrew their bid. A week later he called for the break up of the Murdoch media empire in the UK, arguing that he had 'too much power over British public life' (*Guardian*, 2011a).

An Opportunity for Parliament: A Challenge for the Murdochs

The crisis also had a reinvigorating impact on the work of parliamentary committees. In February 2010, the Culture Media and Sport Committee's second report on press standards, privacy and libel had contained a devastating indictment of the behaviour of the management of News International:

> In seeking to discover precisely who knew what among the staff of the *News of the World* we have questioned a number of present and former executives of News International. Throughout we have repeatedly encountered an unwillingness to provide the detailed information that we sought, claims of ignorance or lack of recall, and deliberate obfuscation. We strongly condemn this behaviour which reinforces the widely held impression that the press generally regard themselves as unaccountable and that News International in particular has sought to conceal the truth about what really occurred. (Culture Media and Sport Committee, 2010)

Although that report was effectively ignored by the government at the time, the committee was well placed to investigate the developing scandal in July 2011 – its session with Rupert and James Murdoch was carried live on BBC 2 with a 1.2 million television audience; a further 1.5 million watched a video stream on their computers. Its hearings and those of the home affairs select committee, which interrogated the police and pursued the issue of how much News International executives knew and when, became the events which pushed the story on (Home Affairs Committee, 2011). As the phone hacking scandal developed, MPs and lawyers who had criticized the Murdoch empire had began to allege previous threats and intimidation from News International (*Independent*, 2011b). A number of well-informed back-bench MPs, such as Chris Bryant and Tom Watson, pursued the key questions through the committees, in print and on television.

The longer-term impact of the phone hacking on scandal on News Corp would depend on what more emerged at News International – in particular the issue of what senior management knew about hacking. The crucial element of James Murdoch's account to the parliamentary committee was immediately challenged by former colleagues, Colin Myler the former editor of the *News of the World*, and Tom Crone, the paper's former legal manager (Davies, 2011; *The New York Times*, 2011a).

Ominously for the Murdoch case that illegal activities were restricted to a small group of journalists and that senior executives knew nothing, the House of Commons Culture Committee released on 17 August a document that some critics of the Murdoch empire dubbed 'the smoking gun'. It was a letter of March 2007 from Clive Goodman, the *News of The World*'s royal editor, who had been gaoled in the original hacking case. He was appealing against the paper's decision to sack him and wrote to News International's director of human resources. In the letter he alleged that other staff were carrying out the same illegal procedures and that 'This practice was widely discussed in the daily editorial conference until explicit reference to it was banned by the editor'. The letter had been copied to both the managing editor of the *News of the World* and Les Hinton, the executive chairman of News International (*Independent*, 2011a).

What already seemed clear was that a model of political and media influence which had worked with great success largely below the radar of public awareness had been exposed and would never work so successfully again. With the prospect of years of police investigations into phone hacking and a judge-led inquiry into the wider issues, there seems little or no possibility of News Corp being permitted to buy the rest of BSkyB in the foreseeable future.

The BSkyB takeover would not only have given Rupert Murdoch an unprecedented degree of media power and political influence in the UK – it would have brought 100% share of a hugely profitable subsidiary with the potential to transform News Corp's balance sheet. The acquisition would also have strengthened James Murdoch's claim to succeed his father at some stage as the head of News Corp. The future of News Corp will be decided by its US shareholders who are likely to determine the future direction and management of the company by the strictly commercial terms of what is best for them. For the first time, there were questions raised over the future of the group's UK newspapers, which included *The Times* and *The Sunday Times* as well as *The Sun*, and even of the long-term dominance of the Murdoch family in News Corp's management (*Guardian*, 2011c; *The New York Times*, 2011b).

Press Self-regulation Under Pressure

A second major casualty of the scandal was the British system of press and media regulation. This had relied on self-regulation through the Press Complaints Commission (PCC) and on the criminal and civil law to maintain and police ethical standards in journalistic practice. Both the regulator and the law were seen to have failed to protect the public and the Leveson inquiry was tasked to investigate why and recommend remedies.

The PCC is a voluntary body, financed and supported by most (though not all) major newspaper groups, with the brief to deal with complaints from the public about newspapers and magazines, offering both pre-publication advice and in some cases mediation together with a complaints process after publication with the ability to require the publication of apologies and/or corrections (PCC, 2011a). However, it lacks many of the attributes of a regulator – investigative powers with the right to summon executives and see papers and emails, and sanctions such as fines and disciplinary action. Its performance over the phone hacking scandal put its long-term future in serious doubt.

Not only did the PCC fail to take the allegations of phone hacking beyond the few cases in 2006 seriously, it found itself in the uncomfortable position of defending The *News of the World*'s initial position and attacking those people who, it turned out correctly, had challenged News International. A PCC Report in November 2009 dismissed investigations in the *Guardian* that suggested hacking had been more widespread, arguing:

> there did not seem to be anything concrete to support the implication that there had been a hitherto concealed criminal conspiracy at the *News of the World* to intrude into people's privacy. (PCC, 2009)

The PCC was forced to withdraw this report on 6 July 2011. Equally embarrassingly, in November 2010, the PCC and its chair, Lady Buscombe, were forced to apologize and pay damages to settle a libel action brought by Mark Lewis, a media lawyer who represented a number of victims of hacking, who had given evidence to a parliamentary committee that phone hacking had been much more common than News International had admitted. Lady Buscombe had wrongly cast doubt on his evidence in a speech to the UK Society of Editors the previous year (PCC Watch, 2011).

The leaders of the three main political parties were unanimous that as an institution the PCC had failed and one of the Leveson inquiry's first tasks was to recommend a new structure of press regulation. The challenge will be to find a regulatory framework that combines effective regulation of media standards and rigorous investigation of complaints with preserving freedom of expression. There has been a growing debate within the media industry in recent years with a division of opinion largely, but not exclusively, between tabloid and 'broadsheet' newspapers. British popular journalism has sometimes seemed to take ethical issues less seriously than other journalistic cultures – Kelvin Mackenzie, a highly successful editor of *The Sun* in the 1980s, once remarked 'ethics is a place to the East of London where the men wear white socks' (Hargreaves, 2003).

Since 2009, the Media Standards Trust has been campaigning for a more effective system of regulation (Media Standards Trust, 2009), with the broad support of leading editors such as Lionel Barber of *The Financial Times* and Alan Rusbridger of the *Guardian*, arguing that the public interest cannot justify the current level of intrusion into the lives of celebrities and private individuals (Barber, 2011; Rusbridger, 2010). Others, such as Paul Dacre, editor of the most successful mid-market newspaper in Britain, the *Daily Mail*, have been unconvinced and much more concerned that any extension of the law on privacy will inhibit legitimate journalistic investigation (Dacre, 2008).

A Casual Attitude to Privacy

The scandal also revealed a casual attitude to the protection of private information on the part of the police and the courts. In 2006, the head of the UK Information Commission Office (ICO), Richard Thomas, published two reports into the unlawful trade in private information. His focus was on 'blagging' – private investigators obtaining confidential information by subterfuge. Many of their clients were newspapers (ICO, 2006a).

There is a public interest defence for blagging (unlike phone hacking). But the commissioner was so concerned by the scale of the practice that he published the names of the national newspapers – the list included almost all the national titles, both tabloid and broadsheet. In all, 305 journalists were involved. He argued that the courts were not taking the offence sufficiently seriously, only imposing small fines. A major investigation, which included cases of police corruption, ended in conditional discharges for those found guilty. Thomas argued that the law needed to be changed to bring the maximum penalty up to that for phone hacking – two years imprisonment. He also referred to the phone hacking case involving the *News of the World* (ICO, 2006b).

Despite this, little action was taken. The PCC refused the Information Commissioner's request to change its Code to underline that it was unacceptable to use bribery or subterfuge to obtain confidential information unless it was in the public interest; the Labour government brought forward legislation in 2008 to increase the maximum penalty for blagging to two years' imprisonment but the current Information Commissioner, Christopher Graham, complained that it was never implemented, after protests from media organizations.

The relatively small penalties and the courts' apparent reluctance to take such cases seriously may help explain the attitude of the police. The former Metropolitan Police Commissioner Ian Blair told a parliamentary committee that phone hacking was 'not a major issue' during his term, from 2005 to 2008. In 2009, the Metropolitan Police were asked to review the evidence of phone hacking at the *News of the World* in view of evidence emerging from civil cases that it was more widespread than a single 'rogue reporter'. John Yates, the senior officer in charge of the review, reported back after a cursory look at the file that there was no new evidence to justify re-opening the police investigation. This decision cost him his career two years later and he accepted that with hindsight that he had made a mistake – he was the country's leading anti-terrorism officer and had had other priorities.

But as well as operational mistakes, the police found their relations with News International and other journalists under scrutiny. It emerged that News International had passed evidence on to the police both that phone hacking had been much more extensive than previously admitted and that some journalists on the *News of the World* had made payments to the police for information. And the senior management of the police were accused of too close a relationship with News International and its executives. The Metropolitan Police Commissioner Sir Paul Stephenson resigned after criticism of the Metropolitan Police's decision to hire Neil Wallis, a former executive editor of the *News of the World*, as a public relations consultant. Neil Wallis was arrested by police investigating phone hacking on 14 July – the Commissioner resigned three days later.

Ironically, at the same time as the regulatory and legal framework was proving inadequate to deal with hacking, the courts were causing concern to journalists, politicians and the public with a series of injunctions banning publication of embarrassing facts about celebrities and companies. The controversy over what was called 'super-injunctions' a few months previously had focused on the extent to which the law was permitting rich individuals and corporations to gag the media. In a number of cases, the injunctions were then broken by social media sites and Twitter feeds.

terrorism and war on the other reflected the dilemma facing politicians and journalists in trying to agree a new settlement both on their relationship and on press regulation. The central ethical dilemma in British journalism and media law is how to reconcile the competing rights in the European Convention on Human Rights – Article 8 of which guarantees the right to privacy and Article 10 of which guarantees the right to freedom of expression (Council of Europe, 1996).

The answer has been to rely on the concept of public interest to justify media intrusion. Public interest is defined in the various press and media codes as the exposure of crime and corruption. The editorial codes under which British journalists work (Editors' Code of Practice, Ofcom Programme Code, BBC Editorial Guidelines) also state there is a public interest in freedom of expression itself, but it is debatable whether that justifies subterfuge in exposing an adulterous footballer or actor as opposed to using these methods to investigate a drug smuggler or a corrupt politician. Over the last decade, the cult of celebrity and the ferocious commercial competition in the popular newspaper market has encouraged a growth in stories which may well be 'of interest to the public' but may not be 'in the public interest' (BBC, 2010; Ofcom, 2011; PCC, 2011b).

In the absence of a formal privacy law in the UK, much has depended on the judgements of individual cases and the attitudes of the regulators. In the UK, there is a clear distinction between broadcast and press regulation. While broadcast regulation is on a statutory basis, with a public body, Ofcom, with investigative powers and the right to fine offending companies, the press has always relied on self-regulation and resisted any form of state intervention. Lord Justice Leveson's panel of expert advisers (which includes two distinguished former political editors, Elinor Goodman of Channel 4 News and George Jones of the *Telegraph*) would have the difficult job of steering a course between two opposing and strongly held views – that the failures of self-regulation were the price society had to pay for having a free press (Beckett, 2011) and the alternative argument that self-regulation had failed and that newspaper journalists would have to accept a measure of external regulation (Tambini, 2011).

Conflicting Human Rights: Privacy versus Freedom of Expression

The confusion in the public mind about heavy handed injunctions on behalf of the wealthy and powerful on one side and the hacking of the mobile phones of the families of victims of crime,

Conclusion: A Once in a Generation Opportunity

How well Leveson succeeds in finding a compromise that reins in editorial abuses without undermining the freedom of the press will have a major role in the long task of restoring public confidence in journalists and politicians. In June 2011, before the scandal broke, politicians and journalists were already languishing at the bottom of MORI's veracity index as the professions least likely to be trusted by the British public to tell the truth, even below bankers (Ipsos MORI, 2011).

The consequences of a dramatic four weeks in July 2011 are likely to be working their way through the British political system and British political communications for many years to come. The largely secret influence of newspapers and their proprietors on policies and politicians and the largely unreported trade-offs between political support and regulatory relief have been a different sort of scandal from the criminal hacking of voicemails. The Leveson inquiry offers a once in a generation opportunity to reveal what has happened in the past and to propose reforms for the future. However, British political inquiries and investigations into scandals have a tendency to take so long to conclude that by the time they report much of the impetus for reform or change has been lost. As an added complexity in this case, the final findings of Lord Justice Leveson and his team may have to wait on the conclusion of the police inquiries and any criminal proceedings.

But although it would be wrong to be over-optimistic about the eventual outcome, the phone hacking scandal of 2011 has at least ensured that these important issues will be debated with a degree of seriousness and transparency that has been absent in the past. The role of the media in British political communications, the flaws in the current systems of media regulation, the ethical challenges facing British journalists have all been exposed to the public as never before and it is hard to believe that British democracy will not be the healthier for it. This crisis is undoubtedly too good to waste.

REFERENCES

Barber, L. (2011) 'Lionel Barber's Hugh Cudlipp Lecture: The Full Text', http://www.guardian.co.uk/media/2011/jan/31/lionel-barber-hugh-cudlipp-lecture (accessed 1 August 2011).

BBC (2010) 'Editorial Guideline', http://www.bbc.co.uk/editorialguidelines/

BBC (2011) 'BBC NEWS Phone-hacking Scandal: Timeline', http://bbc/news/uk-14124020 (accessed 1 August 2011).

Beckett, C. (2011) 'Phonehacking and Press Reforms: Beware Dangerous Dogs', htpp://blogs.lse.ac.uk/polis/2011/07/17/phonehacking-and-press-reforms-beware-dangerous-dogs/ (accessed 1 August 2011).

Bell, M. (2009) *A Very British Revolution: The Expenses Scandal and How to Save Our Democracy.* London: Icon.

Blair, T. (2010) *A Journey.* London: Hutchinson.

Cox, B. (2003) 'Paying the Piper but not Calling the Tune', http://www.guardian.co.uk/media/2003/feb/11/broadcasting.comment (accessed 1 August 2011).

Council of Europe (1996) 'European Convention on Human Rights and its Five Protocols', htpp://www.hri.org/docs/ECHR50.html (accessed 1 August 2011).

Culture, Media and Sport Committee (2010) 'Press Standards, Privacy and Libel', http://www.publications.parliament.uk/pa/cm200910/cmselect/cmcumeds/362/36202.htm (accessed 1 August 2011).

Curtice, J. and Semetko, H. A. (1994) 'Does It Matter What the Papers Say?', in A. Heath, R. Jowell and J. Curtice (eds.), *Labour's Last Chance: The 1992 General Election and Beyond.* Aldershot: Dartmouth Publishing Company, pp. 43–64.

Dacre, P. (2008) 'Paul Dacre's Speech in Full', http:www.dailymail.co.uk/news/article-1084453/Paul-Dacres-speech-in-full.html (accessed 1 August 2011).

Davies, N. (2011) 'Journalism and Books', http ://www.nick-davies.net/category/phone-hacking-scandal/ (accessed 1 August 2011).

Dyke, G. (2004) *Inside Story.* London: Harper Collins.

Enders, C. (2010) 'Memo for Vincent Cable', http://www.beehivecity.com/wp-content/uploads2010/09/For-Vincent-Cable.pdf (accessed 1 August 2011).

Guardian (2011a) 'Rupert Murdoch's Empire must be Dismantled – Ed Miliband', http://www.guardian.co.uk/politics/2011/jul/16/rupert-murdoch-ed-miliband-phone-hacking (accessed 1 August 2011).

Guardian (2011b) 'Phone Hacking: Tom Crone and Colin Myler Raise the Stakes', http://www.guardian.co.uk/media/2011/jul/21/tom_crone_colin_myler_analaysis (accessed 1 August 2011).

Guardian (2011c) 'Murdoch Considers the Nuclear Option – Selling off Wapping', http://www.guardian.co.uk/media/greenslade/2011/jul/13/rupert-murdoch-newsinternational (accessed 1 August 2011).

Hargreaves, I. (2003) *Journalism: Truth or Dare?* Oxford: Oxford University Press.

Home Affairs Committee (2011) 'Unauthorized Hacking into or Tapping of Mobile Communications', http;//www.parliament.co.uk/documents/commons-committees/home-affairs/CRCFinalReportEmbargoed.pdf (accessed 1 August 2011).

House of Commons (2011) 'House of Commons Debate', 20 July 2011, column 940. htttp://www.publications.parliament.uk (accessed 1 August 2011).

ICO (2006a) *What Price Privacy?* London: Stationery Office.

ICO (2006b) *What Price Privacy Now?* London: Stationery Office.

Independent (2011a) 'Phone-Hacking: The Smoking Gun', http://www.independent.co.uk/news/uk/crime/phonehacking-the-smoking-gun-2338855.html (accessed 1 August 2011).

Independent (2011b) 'Murdoch Ally "Warned MP not to Pursue Hacking Scandal"', http://www.independent.co.uk/news/politics/murdoch-ally warned-mp-not-to-pursue-hacking-scandal-2238673.html (accessed 1 August 2011).

Ipsos MORI (2011) 'Veracity Index', http;//www. Ipsos-mori. com/Assets/Docs/Polls/Veracity2011.pdf (accessed 1 August 2011).

Labour Party (2011) 'Meeting with Proprietors, Editors and Senior Media Executives – Ed Miliband', http://www. labour.org.uk/meeting-with-proprietors-editors-and-senior-media-executives (accessed 1 August 2011).

Liberal Democrats (2011) 'Simon Hughes: Ofcom Must Investigate Whether BSkyB Is "Fit and Proper"', http://www.libdems.org. uk/press_releases_detail.aspx?title=Simon_Hughes%3A_ Ofcom_must-investigate_whether_BSkybB_ is%E2%80%98fit_and_proper% (accessed 1 August 2011).

Media Standards Trust (2009) *A More Accountable Press?* London: Media Standards Trust.

McKie, D. (1995) 'Fact Is Free but Comment Is Sacred', in I. Crewe and B. Gosschalk (eds.), *Political Communications, The General Elections Campaign of 1992.* Cambridge: Cambridge University Press. pp. 121–36.

McKie, D. (1998) 'Swingers, Clingers, Waverers, Quaverers: The Tabloid Press in the 1997 General Election', in I. Crewe, B. Gosschalk and J. Bartle (eds.), *Political Communications: Why Labour Won the 1997 General Election.* London: Frank Cass. pp. 115–30.

Number 10 (2011) 'PM Announces Panel for Judge-led Inquiry and Publishes Terms of Reference', http://www.number10. gov.uk/news/leveson-inquiry-panel-terms-of-reference/

Ofcom (2011) 'The Ofcom Broadcasting Code', http://stake-holders.ofcom.org.uk/broadcasting/broadcast-codes/ (accessed 1 August 2011).

PCC (2009) 'PCC Report on Phone Message Tapping Allegations', http://pcc.org.uk/news/index.html?article= NjAyOA== (accessed 1 August 2011).

PCC (2011a) 'Making a Complaint', http://www.pcc.org.uk/ complaints /makingacomplaint.html (accessed 1 August 2011).

PCC (2011b) 'Editors' Code of Practice', http://www.pcc.org. uk/cop/practice.html (accessed 1 August 2011).

PCC Watch (2011) 'Libel, Buscombe and the PCC: What's Going On?', http://www.pccwatch.co.uk/libel-buscombe-and-the-pcc-whats-going-on/ (accessed 1 August 2011).

Rusbridger, A. (2010) 'Weak Press Self-regulation Threatens Decent Journalism', http://journalism.co.uk/editors/2010 /03/02/alan-rusbridger-weak-press-self-regulation-threatens-decent-journalism/ (accessed 1 August 2011).

Tambini, D. (2011) 'Phonehacking and Press Reforms: Beware Dangerous Blogs', htpp://blogs.lse.ac.uk/mediapolicy-project/2011/07/25/phonehacking-and-press-reforms/ (accessed 1 August 2011).

Telegraph (2011) 'BSkyB: Profits Jump as it Hands Back £1 Billion to Shareholders', http://www.telegraph.co.uk/ finance/newsbyzector/mediatechnologyandtelecoms/ 8670654/BSkyB-profits-jump-as-it-hands-1bn-to-share holders.html (accessed 1 August 2011).

The New York Times (2011a) 'Times Topics: British Phone Hacking Scandal (News of The World)', http://topics. nytimes.com/top/reference/timestopics/organizations/n/ news_of_the_world/index/html (accessed 1 August 2011).

The New York Times (2011b) 'Scandal Splinters a Family Business', http://www.nytimes.com/2011/07/25/business/ media/scandal-splinters-the-murdoch-family business. html?_r=18ref=newsoftheworld (accessed 1 August 2011).

Wolff, M. (2008) *Murdoch: The Man Who Owns the News.* London: The Bodley Head.

Name Index

Subject Index